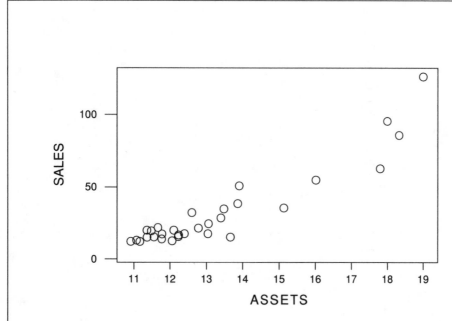

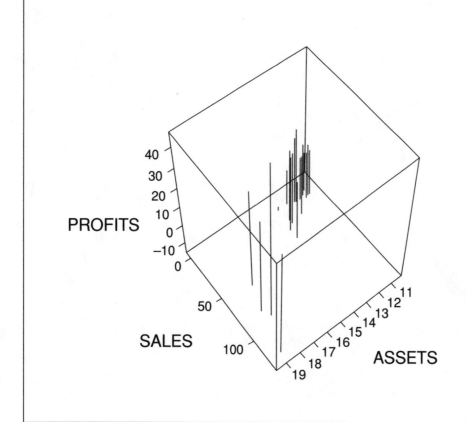

Statistical Thinking and Data Analysis Methods for Managers

Wynn Anthony Abranovic
University of Massachusetts at Amherst

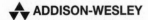 **ADDISON-WESLEY**

An imprint of Addison Wesley Longman, Inc.

Reading, Massachusetts • Menlo Park, California • New York • Harlow, England
Don Mills, Ontario • Sydney • Mexico City • Madrid • Amsterdam

Sponsoring Editor: Michael Roche
Developmental Editor: Maxine Effenson Chuck
Project Coordination: Elm Street Publishing Services, Inc.
Art Development Editor: Vita Jay
Design Administrator: Jess Schaal
Text and Cover Design: Jeanne Calabrese
Cover Illustration: Kevin Irby
Production Administrator: Randee Wire
Compositor: Interactive Composition Corporation
Printer and Binder: R. R. Donnelley & Sons Company
Cover Printer: Phoenix Color Corp.

Statistical Thinking and Data Analysis Methods for Managers

Library of Congress Cataloging-in-Publication Data

Abranovic, Wynn Anthony.
    Statistical thinking and data analysis methods for managers / Wynn
Anthony Abranovic. -- 1st ed.
        p.   cm.
    Includes index.
    ISBN 0-673-99296-9
    1. Industrial management--Statistical methods.   2. Industrial
management--Statistical methods--Data processing.   3. Minitab for
Windows.   I. Title.
HD30.215.A27   1997
519.5--dc20   96-7505

1 2 3 4 5 6 7 8 9 10—DOC—00 99 98 97 96

Dedicated to the Curious Student

CONTENTS

Chapter 5
The Normal Distribution   207

Chapter 6
A Mix of Tools for Business and Economic Data   248

Chapter 7
Sampling Distributions, Single Sample Confidence Intervals, and Hypothesis Tests   293

Chapter 8
Exploring Relationships Between Pairs of Variables   348

Chapter 9

Classical Methods for Summarizing Relationships Between Pairs of Variables   410

Chapter 10

The Analysis of Categorical (Qualitative) Variables and Tests of Goodness of Fit and Independence   458

Chapter 11

Simple Regression Analysis and the Analysis of Variance   507

# PREFACE

To The Reader

In this book you will be introduced to statistical knowhow that will help you grapple with interesting problems. For example, when Toyota, General Motors, Ford, or Chrysler aspires to produce automobiles of world-class quality, those of you who have had your car repaired recently or who are considering a purchase might be interested in company quality reputations. You might be interested in survey results about owner satisfaction by J.D. Power and Associates. You might be interested in how experiments are used to improve product designs. Quality improvements in product designs, manufacturing processes, and final inspections frequently depend on companywide understanding and application of statistical methods. Other types of examples where statistical methods play an important role are numerous and apparent from simply reading the daily newspaper.

By reading this book, you will learn how to use statistical methods in a variety of applications. Statistical skills will help you to quickly gain experience in unfamiliar work environments and to survive in today's competitive workplace. You will learn why statistical methods work and what their limitations are.

What Is Statistics, and Why Is It Challenging?

Statistics is the art and science of interpreting numerical observations. The analysis of numerical information helps us think about answering interesting questions, such as those on product quality.

The challenge is that statistics, like tennis, basketball, golf, baseball, medicine, economics, and management, can't be learned in a day. You have to take the time to understand the components of the statistics game, the art of putting the components together, and how to keep your game in tune through practice.

Modern statistics books are likely to be weighty because they include so many methods. Yet, they contain considerable and valuable knowledge. The sheer multitude of statistical methods makes the subject both difficult and interesting for the novice as well as the expert.

Nevertheless, most students of management, economics, the social sciences, and other disciplines are expected to learn the fundamentals of statistics in one or two semesters. What is expected of the novice is often, simply, too much. Such a stiuation can create anxiety for both student and teacher. Improving this situation is the reason for this book.

Modern Textbook Design Themes

While few claim to have found all the solutions to the teaching and learning problems in introductory statistics, many have tried, as evidenced by the proliferation of introductory textbooks. The variety of texts alone suggests that teachers work hard at delivering a unique, high-quality classroom experience for the student. Several common features that support the efforts of teachers and students have emerged in textbook designs. This textbook was written with all the following features in mind:

1.   Applications and methodology are integrated to give students reasons to learn the basic methodology. Applications that students already know something about are used, such as the popcorn experiment in Chapter 1, where brand and amount are related to yield.

2.   The text was written for the nonmathematician. It drains the technical swamp where busy students can get bogged down and discouraged, without sacrificing statistically rigorous thinking. For example, in regression analysis, statistical software can be used to ease the formula-based computational burden.

3.   Examples and exercises are relevant and plentiful, using mostly real data and no less than realistic data. Data sets on diskettes are included for convenient computer access. For example, for students of management, such diverse fields as personnel, quality control, economics, marketing, accounting, operations management, and finance are drawn on.

4.   Some case studies are provided, usually as examples or exercises, to frame the role that the analysis plays in the big picture as well as to motivate and provide a discussion platform. For example, one case is about a company that machines mold cavities out of steel for injection molding of plastic parts. The company was seesawing from profit to loss and needed to know why it was losing so much money on some jobs and how to cut costs. The data analysis results led to managing large jobs differently from small ones. The profit picture improved and operations ran smoother.

5.   Computer output is shown as well as chapter appendixes of MINITAB commands. Therefore, students can walk through the chapter examples actively on their own. Those who prefer other software, such as SAS, SPSS, or BMDP, can adapt easily. The option to use the computer is available in 18 chapters, with little investment needed by the instructor. The software encourages self-study and reduces the teaching time allocated to computational formulas. More time can be spent on conceptual interpretation rather than computation. Nevertheless, standard computational formulas can be demonstrated when there is a need to look under the hood at the engine.

6.   Recognizing modern statistical practice, we introduce exploratory data analysis (EDA) tools such as stem-and-leaf diagrams and boxplots. However, they do not overshadow tradtional methods. Traditional foundations of statistical inference are integrated with data analysis ideas and take advantage of the visual (graphical) flavor of EDA.

7.   Quality control concepts are included because global industrial competition requires it. Furthermore, quality control's high corporate profile offers proof that students must have statistics in their portfolio of skills.

8.   To simplify and reveal the connecting thread that runs through statistics, a kernel of building block concepts is provided for organizing the textbook, thus smoothing the transition from simple ideas to complex ones. Where possible, graphical displays are used to build visual representations of methodology, letting each of the data speak for itself. For example, a pair of side-by-side boxplots can test, informally, for two equal population medians, ideawise leading to tests for population means. Several side-by-side boxplots can illustrate regression analysis concepts.

9.   This textbook is user friendly and very flexible. It accommodates different teaching styles, variations in course content, and a variety of learning styles. For example, an instructor who uses a computer lab intensively (where students work through chapter appendixes) can cover two semesters of statistics with few lectures. On the other hand, a lecture-intensive course can be supplemented with a few computer lab sessions.

10.   The writing style kindles student interest and makes teaching easy and effective. The reader relates to the subject matter because it covers a broad range of real-life scenarios, including managerial issues, social events, business decisions, sports, economics, and other topics familiar to the reader.

How Does This Textbook Stand Out from the Crowd?

Many statistics books draw on at least some of the features listed above, but they often try to be all things to all people, thus losing their identity and becoming clone-like in appearance. This textbook preserves its identity with the following pedagogical features:

1. *Writing Style.*   Students tell me this book is fun to read because it's written in a way that is clear, down to earth, easy to understand, and motivating. For example, Chapter 1 begins with an observation on a December day that raises the question, Why are there still ducks on the campus pond? To answer the query, we suggest that it might help to collect data on where ducks winter and see what the analysis reveals.

The chapters begin with short motivational scenarios that give students a reason to read on. Chapter 3 introduces a statistical model in which the mean is a typical value and an observation's deviation from the mean is an error. Because these concepts can be important in executive decision making, Chapter 3 begins like this:

> Stories about major executive decisions and costly gambles are plentiful. Consider Barnaby Feder's account of General Electric's high-stakes locomotive wager.
>
> GE embarked on a $500 million modernization plan that got derailed as diesel orders slumped. For GE, the sales forecasts were wrong. Typically, domestic railroads buy 1,700 locomotives a year, but only 300 new locomotives were bought in the year that the modern facilities were available. This forecasting error reflected management's failure to understand how much the actual demand might deviate from the typical demand. This error cost GE a lot of money.

2. *Concept Linking.*   Seldom is a concept presented and not used shortly thereafter. Many concepts are tied to graphical building blocks such as histograms, scatterplots, stem-and-leaf diagrams, boxplots, dotplots, and the like. As an example, when introducing hypothesis tests for the difference between two means, side-by-side boxplots may lead to tentative, graphically based conclusions, which are confirmed by more formal tests that follow. Such visual, intuitive lead-ins to formal methods, common in this text, help students learn new ideas by fitting them into a familiar context and provide concept repetition by reusing what was learned earlier.

3. *Concept Distribution.*   New concepts are presented in bite-size chunks. Thus, high concept density is avoided when introducing complex ideas. Students are not intimidated by new methods, techniques, or displays.

4. *Flexibility.*   Primarily, this text is designed for a one- or two-semester introductory course without prerequisites. The instructor can vary the speed of coverage and, with the addition of computer lab sessions and exercises, use the text at the undergraduate or graduate levels, with MBAs in mind at the graduate level.

5. *Artful Use of Simulation.*   A major use of modern computers is for "what if" simulations. Many examples and exercises offer students and instructors the opportunity to actively experiment on the computer and summarize the results statistically. The simulation approach augments the multitude of real-data examples and exercises in the text.

6. *Examples.*   To give you a flavor of the examples, below are some listed in sequence for Chapter 1.

Chapter 1   *The Kaleidoscopic World of Applied Statistics:* The Scurvy Experiment; Box and Hunter's Popcorn Experiment; The Strawberry and Williams Observational Study (Baseball); Automobile Inspection Observational Study; The Gypsy Moth Population; Prediction—Maine Lobster Outlook: Down; Key Variables As Early Warning Signals for the Economy; Why Aren't People Buying American Cars; Tom Martin Creek.

7. *Optional Computer Use for Addtional Flexibility.* Where statistical software is used in examples, a chapter appendix is provided of MINITAB commands so the student can do each example as well as similar exercises. Each appendix listing of MINITAB commands includes line-by-line commentary, explaining what the commands do. The students can, in effect, go to the computer lab and work through examples in the entire text on his or her own, roughly completing a chapter a week.

Such guided, walk-through-the-examples type of activity produces the usual, barren computer output. MINITAB prints or creates a file of this output. The file can be retrieved by a word processor. This document can be edited and integrated into a formal report, in which the student adds commentary. The comments, which parrot the textbook discussion, assure the instructor that the students are reading and mastering the key ideas. Extra exercises can be assigned and done without such structured guidance. Often, deliverable products from these activities can be substituted for examinations as the students engage in active learning.

Alternatively, the file of MINITAB results can be printed in its original barren form and the students can add commentary by hand. This reduces lab time because the word processor is not needed and comments can be written at home.

In addition to data sets on diskettes, the MINITAB appendixes are available in the form of chapter macros. A macro command produces output for a whole chapter of examples. Therefore, what the students do, say, for an hour-and-a-half, one command at a time, can be done in a minute by a macro. Under instructor control, the macro feature can be useful when the instructor feels the students have gained enough command familiarity, proceeding one command at a time. Also, the output from these macros can be projected on a screen for lecture purposes. Macros can speed up the course, they relieve tedium at the right time, they can be used by teaching assistants, and they can form a basis for team projects, exams, and presentations by students.

Of course, all this works best if you are using the latest version of MINITAB in a lab of networked personal computers. However, the chapter appendixes are detailed enough so that one experienced in SAS, SPSS, BMDP, or some other software system can substitute appropriate commands.

Although this text can be used in a regular class situation without computer laboratory work, I find it easy and effective to conduct most of my classes in a computer lab. Typically, I give a few start-up lectures and then move the class to the computer lab, fitting in occasional review lectures when necessary. After the start-up phase, I sit back and let the course run by itself.

Students refer to this phase of the course as "being on cruise control." Avoiding the lecture format, I find it quite pleasant to get paid for the less strenuous task of being a helper, a coach, and having fun teaching. Students become gladiators rather than spectators.

One Course or Two?

Our texbook design is flexible to accommodate the wide variety of feasible course designs needed for meeting local teaching requirements. Depending on the depth and speed of coverage, the first 12 chapters form a sound basis for a one- or two-semester introductory statistics course. The remaining chapters provide additional topics for higher-level courses, particularly when the students are exposed to two full semesters of statistics.

You will notice that the chapter sequencing is similar to what has become the traditional pattern. However, as in the practice of applied statistics, exploratory data analysis takes on a more important role than in the past, and EDA is used as a lead-in to traditional topics with emphasis on its graphical portrayal of concepts. The instructor has the option of emphasizing the classical analysis, the exploratory analysis, or a balanced blend of the two approaches.

As the experienced instructor might expect, fitting the first 12 chapters into a single semester is a squeeze play, possibly with something thrown out. Yet, in two semesters, it looks like a walk.

Some of This Textbook's Design Differences

This text is designed to be a little different from certain chapters in other texts. The following items alert you to some of these differences.

1.   After a lively and broad introduction in Chapter 1, Chapter 2 concentrates on descriptive exploratory methods for actively getting familiar with data sets. Such methods require few assumptions about the data. It is not until Chapter 3 that the classical measures of central tendency and variability are introduced. Chapter 4 on probability theory and Chapter 5 on the normal distribution follow to enrich the framework for thinking about observed data.

2.   Chapter 6 is integrative and makes use of methods from the preceding chapters to make data sets, such as the gross domestic product (GDP), more meaningful to students and managers. The, new material on sampling distributions, confidence intervals, and hypothesis testing is presented in Chapter 7.

3.   Exploratory ways of comparing and relating two variables are covered in Chapter 8. The front end of Chapter 9 discusses planning and designing experiments prior to the simplest kind of an experiment that formally compares sample means. Furthermore, it is shown that sample means can be compared using the usual t tests. However, similar results are obtained from simple regression analysis. Thus, these methods are introduced and related in the same context. More advanced applications of these methods that come later are easier to understand because of this presentation.

Many introductory texts don't say much about planning experiments. If they do, it is delayed until more complicated designs are presented in an analysis of variance chapter.

4.   Chapter 10 consolidates methods for categorical variables. For example, yes or no responses on questionnaires lead to confidence intervals and hypothesis tests on proportions and differences in proportions. Other texts discuss these intervals and tests in parts of different chapters. Thus, the methods appear scattered about in many books. The remainder of Chapter 10 is traditional. Some instructors may prefer to cover Chapter 10 later, perhaps after Chapter 12.

5.   A careful development of the simple regression model and theory occurs in the beginning of Chapter 11. Some instructors may give this beginning section less emphasis than others. When less emphasis is given, the instructor can concentrate on the applications that follow the theory.

Chapter 11 presents the pooled t test, simple regression, and one-way analysis of variance as alternative ways of doing the same analysis. Most texts discuss the pooled t test earlier and, unfortunately, never relate it to these other methods.

6.   Because the theory for multiple regression analysis is formidable, Chapter 12 begins multiple regression analysis by example and as an extension of simple regression. This is followed by a technical reference section on the theory. Thus, instructors can use a very applied approach or one that is more theoretical. This makes Chapter 12 long, but most instructors will not find it necessary to cover it all.

Some data sets are not listed in the exercises at the end of Chapter 12. Rather, they are available as files on a data disk.

7.   Many chapters beyond Chapter 12 include special topics that can be used to enrich earlier chapters. For example, Chapter 13 covers special probability distributions. It extends the probability theory of Chapter 4 and goes well beyond the normal distribution in Chapter 5. Even less common distributions are mentioned. Cumulative distribution functions and their inverses are covered thoroughly.

Instructors who want their students to have a larger dose of probability theory would cover much of Chapter 13 and perhaps, include Chapter 14. Chapter 14, on statistical quality control, demonstrates important uses of the distribution theory from Chapters 4, 5, and 13.

In Chapter 18, the nonparametric methods are rough and ready and easy to compute. As a result, these methods are versatile and good for taking a first look at a data set. Therefore, with these methods some instructors may supplement subject matter in Chapters 2, 7, 9, and 15.

As you can see, the special topics chapters are organized and located in proximity to related chapters where possible. Furthermore, the topical coverage exceeds what most instructors need, providing options and flexibility.

Chapter Pedagogy

All chapters have a similar architecture. Some common chapter pedagogical features are

Objectives   A short list of key objectives is presented.

Prelude   A broad overview of the chapter is given in a few short paragraphs.

Introductory Discussion   An interesting, attention-getting, real-life example or situation is used to expand upon the chapter objectives, getting more specific than the prelude.

Sections   Sections break the chapters into manageable chunks. Some sections are independent of others and may be treated as optional, giving the instructor some flexibility within a chapter. Sections develop specific topics. For example, Chapter 2 presents a number of exploratory tools and has the following section topics: The Stem-and-Leaf Diagram; Computer Results; A Primitive Plot; Summary Statistics, Medians, Quartiles and Extremes; Summary Statistics, Computer Results; Checking for Randomness to See If the Summary Statistics Are Valid; Boxplots; Stem-and-Leaf Diagram Variations; Exploring Several Variables, One at a Time; A Population, a Sample, Different Samples with Different Summary Values.

To illustrate teaching flexibility, an instructor wishing to deemphasize computer use and exploratory methods could easily omit section topics on computer results and stem-and-leaf diagram variations. The scope of sections is limited to fundamental tools and concepts. This avoids clutter and does not overwhelm the student with too many new ideas at one time.

Each section contains interesting, real-world examples with plenty of exercises at the end of the chapter. There are MINITAB commands in the appendix for most examples. These commands (also in the form of macros)

can be used as guides to work through the chapter examples for assignments or for computer laboratory sessions that substitute for some lectures.

Statistical Highlights   After detailed procedures or after a sequence of new terms and ideas, what to know summaries are provided within sections to help the student consolidate and review what was learned.

Key Terms   Key terms are set in bold within the chapters for emphasis and listed at the end of the chapter.

Numerous Exhibits   The emphasis on learning from visual graphics is brought out in the many exhibits.

Chapter Summaries   These are brief reviews of key concepts.

Exercises   Exercises are numerous and varied. Some are long enough to integrate several chapter sections.

Ancillaries

Many will find this textbook self-contained, however, an *Instructor's Manual* and *Test Bank* are also available. Additionally, data sets and macros are provided on diskettes.

Wynn A. Abranovic

Acknowledgments

My students motivated me to write this book. It seemed that I had searched for a decade for a course design that had both the old and the new ideas, enough conceptual rigor, and, perhaps most of all, the ability to capture the interest of students with or without a technical background. Therefore, students who left my course saying "I never knew that statistics and data analysis could be so interesting" gave me the incentive to go on when there were many better things to do, like ski, play tennis, or fly fish for trout.

Here's to you Elias Halamandaris, Chris Stefanou, Carol Savoy, Two Hugs, and the like. Former students seem to make more of an impression on me than I do on them. Elias still sees that I get a beautiful calendar each year from the Bank of Greece, even though it has been decades since we had dinner in a Greek taverna. Chris has such a thirst for knowledge and adventure that he simply puts his whole family on a Greek freighter and takes an odyssey covering the wide waters that connect three continents, all in the spirit of exploration. Simply talking to Carol for a couple of hours makes a university's homecoming weekend seem too short, and it is nice to hear that my data analysis course was a favorite. And, to be sure that there is a little California sunshine in this book, thanks Angie for your individuality and for being such an inquisitive student. Incidentally, Two Hugs squeeze a big university into something smaller and certainly warmer.

Many others influenced me. Some, though I know only through their writing, shaped my thinking tremendously: those such as John Tukey, Frederick Mosteller, and Harry Roberts. Also, John Wilkinson and Richard Carter taught some great courses that got me interested in probability and statistics when studying clashed with Saratoga Performing Arts concerts. Richard Carter's foundation of probability problems remains unrivaled. A few simplified adaptations of his problems appear as exercises.

Special thanks to Barbara Dixon and Steve Archer at Willamette University. Barbara worked on the book's first draft, which formed the basis for the monster that has emerged. Steve stressed the need for motivational material that gives the student a reason to read. It took me a long time to figure out how to accomplish what he said was needed.

Mike Royer, Richard Lindgren, Chad Johnson, and The Great Ganguli encouraged me to play good tennis and to try to write a great book. Doug Tucker encouraged me, too, and also demonstrated perfect skiing turns. Thanks to old friends Dede, Jean, and Patty, who are long ago and far away, and Peggy who is not. My parents, brothers, and sister made it possible to persist and to write this book in an interesting style that combines text and graphics. In the early stages, Louis Wigdor did some first-rate editorial work for me. Vesta Powers made her usual extra effort to get me quality first-draft copies that could be tested in class. Thanks to my brother Tony who treated me to a fly fishing trip in Vermont in June—a break I needed after writing the first six chapters. Thanks to Barbara and Willard Weeks.

I am also grateful for the advice, feedback, and suggestions of the many reviewers which, undoubtedly, made this a better book. The reviewers were:

Mary S. Alguire, *University of Arkansas*
Wallace R. Blishke, *University of Southern California*
Michael Broida, *Miami University*
Roger Champagne, *Hudson Valley Community College*
Sangit Chatterjee, *Northeastern University*
David A. Cohen, *Northern Arizona University*
Eugene A. Enneking, *Portland State University*
Rob Godby, *Laurentian University*
Anil Gulati, *Western New England College*
Ramadan Hemaida, *University of Southern Indiana*
Rodney G. Hurley, *Hillsborough Community College*
Carla Inclan, *Georgetown University*
George A. Johnson, *Idaho State University*

Dae S. Lee, *Kentucky State University*
Douglas A. Lind, *The University of Toledo*
Jerrold H. May, *University of Pittsburgh*
Charles E. McClean, *Old Dominion University*
Joe D. Megeath, *Metro State University*
Ruth K. Meyer, *St. Cloud State University*
Daniel Mihalko, *Western Michigan University*
R. Ramesh, *State University of New York at Buffalo*
Charlene Robert, *Louisiana State University*
Alan Roshwalb, *Georgetown University*
Patrick Thompson, *University of Florida*

All the folks associated with Addison-Wesley Publishers were wonderfully helpful. They include Michael Roche, Melissa Rosati, Arthur Pomponio, Maxine Effenson Chuck, developmental editor at B. Czar Productions Inc., the reviewers, and others who helped place this book in the hands and minds of students and teachers are much appreciated. Maxine was relentlessly excellent in shaping my seemingly crude early work. Similar praise goes to Julie Webber, Nancy Moudry, and other professionals at Elm Street Publishing Services.

We all hope that students will want to keep this book.

W. A. A.

CHAPTER 1

The Kaleidoscopic World of Applied Statistics

OBJECTIVES

- ◆ Introduce terminology
- ◆ Describe data collection circumstances
- ◆ Explain the scientific learning process
- ◆ Build an appreciation of the applications cornucopia

PRELUDE

This chapter is designed like a kaleidoscope. With every turn of a page you will see a different picture of where data analysis has made an inroad. With each excursion, you will begin to see that numerics are an integral part of the stories we tell about the world around us.

Data analysis permeates your life. It occurs when your doctor prescribes four pills a day, when your dentist fills two teeth, when you drive miles to work, and when you walk to school or carry your lunch. Numerics capture where you have been, where you are, where you are going, and whom you talk to on the telephone. ◆

OBSERVING PHENOMENA

Statistics is the art and science of making sense of numerical observations.

Observations Making Us Wonder

Late in December in New England, Joseph McCormack, a college student, was expecting blizzards, but the campus pond was not frozen yet. The ice-free pond was full of ducks. Joseph puzzled over the unusually warm winter weather, asked some questions, proposed some answers, and recorded his thoughts as follows:

> Why are there still ducks on the campus pond? The first fact about nature that children learn is that ducks fly south for the winter. It is winter. Santa is already feeding Rudolph high-octane carrots . . .
>
> Do they enjoy winter sports? Are they taking classes over intersession? . . . waterfowl guides suggest that duck behavior does not include skiing, education, or slam dancing. No, the answer is rooted in the evils of the welfare state.
>
> Somebody is feeding those ducks. The mallards are simply too lazy to fly south and rely on the goodwill of the community for handouts. Judging from the amount of noise they make, there is nothing wrong with them. If they stay around let them find work. A job as a Peking duck pays quite handsomely . . .[1]

Like Joseph McCormack wondering about the ducks, we all wonder about nature's mysteries. Observed phenomena precipitate thoughts that may lead to inferences, decisions, actions, and conclusions. Exploratory questions often trigger thinking. Then theories emerge. The confirmation or denial of a theory might result. Simply, we learn from experience. As the subject we study becomes more complex, the learning process becomes more scientific and dependent on the methods of statistics as a guide.

BASIC TERMINOLOGY

This section defines basic terminology indigenous to the field of statistics and used throughout this text.

The ducks on the pond are not the whole universe, or **population,** of ducks; those on the pond are referred to by statisticians as a **frame** of ducks, **elementary units** relevant to a particular study. A frame may or may not be representative of the population; ideally a frame is representative. When frames consist of a large number of units, we tend to be economical and observe a smaller group, a **sample,** selected from the frame. We prefer to obtain a representative sample and make **inferences** (educated guesses from sample information) about the characteristics of the population as a whole, such as the average weight of all the ducks in the universe, a population **parameter.**

When we observe a sample member, or **subject,** a particular duck here, we might determine and list a duck's **attributes,** such as weight, feather count, gender, and so forth. Statisticians refer to these attributes as **variables.** The values of the variables are referred to as **data values,** or simply **data,** such as:

Duck #1   2.6 lb, 1.23 million feathers, female (hen)

Usually there is more than one duck on the pond and in the sample, so we end up with a row of data for each duck, which is called a **data set.** The data set below consists of a sample of five ducks described by three attribute variables:

Duck #1   2.6 lb, 1.23 million feathers, hen
Duck #2   2.8 lb, 1.30 million feathers, drake
Duck #3   2.4 lb, 1.22 million feathers, hen
Duck #4   2.9 lb, 1.28 million feathers, hen
Duck #5   3.1 lb, 1.33 million feathers, drake

The numbers are rounded to make them easy on the reader's eye and mind. Avoid presenting the reader with numbers that contain too many digits; however, all the digits can be handled by computers without rounding them.

The weight variable is an **amount,** the number of feathers is an integer value, a discrete **count,** and the gender is a **category.**

Because ducks can't tell us these things, we must collect the weight, feather count, and gender data. If ducks could write or fill out forms, perhaps we could **survey** them to collect this data, having them respond to a **questionnaire** about weight, feather count, and gender. A survey of all the ducks in the population is called a **census.**

Common use of the term *statistics* means data or fact. Often statisticians refer to a **statistic** as a summary value computed from data. You will learn how to compute and use various statistics to help you in the process of making decisions. The subject of statistics encompasses data collection, analysis, and interpretation.

STATISTICS AS A GUIDE TO LEARNING FROM EXPERIENCE

Statistical methods for data analysis are proven, time-tested ways of learning from experience.

Observations Leading to Questions

Peter Stoler thought about the great fights in the career of a world heavyweight champion. His thoughts were precipitated by the report that the former champion checked into the Columbia-Presbyterian Medical Center. Peter Stoler expressed himself as follows:

> He could float like a butterfly, sting like a bee. The young Muhammad Ali dazzled all who saw him perform in the ring, where his dancer's footwork and lightning-fast combinations enabled him to win the world heavyweight championship three times. And out of the ring, his nonstop chatter, his doggerel verse and his insistence that he was the greatest won him worldwide affection.
>
> But the Ali who checked into the Neurological Institute at New York City's Columbia-Presbyterian Medical Center evoked a much different emotion. For at least two years, journalists and associates had noticed that Ali appeared to have aged beyond his years: his hand-eye coordination seemed to be impaired, and his speech was frequently unintelligible. The question was asked, aloud and in print: Could Ali . . . be suffering from some kind of brain disorder? . . . The doctors' report raised the inevitable questions about whether Ali's problems were a product of his profession, and triggered anew debate over whether boxing should be banned.[2]

We observe and wonder about Ali. After exploring the symptoms similar to those of Parkinson's disease, a disease that often affects the elderly and causes shaking and other symptoms, some theorized that Ali was suffering from dementia pugilistica, a medical term for punch-drunk. Doctors denied that he was punch-drunk and that he had Parkinson's disease.

We question and learn through observation, which often includes numerical measurements. Sometimes what we think, see, hear, or feel generates a theory. The confirmation or denial of a theory is based on the analysis of observations.

Statistics and data analysis help us learn from experience by providing numerical interpretations of events and situations. When doctors examine the brains of former fighters, they learn about brain damage. When wildlife biologists study the migration patterns of ducks, they may learn why there are mallards on a New England campus pond in December.

In many applications, statistics is a guide to the unknown. Statistical tools are learning devices, keys for unlocking the secrets of nature. Those curious and serious about expanding their knowledge become very dependent on statistical methods. Researchers use data analysis tools to help test theories, summarize large amounts of data, confirm relationships, discover new relationships, and interpret numbers.[3]

Data Sources   If one collects data for a specific research need and these data are not already published, the data are called **primary data.** Many researchers use published data, such as that found in government and industry publications, which is referred to as **secondary data.** Making use of secondary data requires that it be consistent, accurate, and applicable.

EXPERIMENTS

A **planned experiment** is a planned set of actions that produces observable outcomes that are not perfectly predictable. An example of a planned experiment in making popcorn is presented later in Example 2. The planned set of actions includes testing two brands, ordinary and gourmet, with two amounts of kernels, $\frac{1}{3}$ and $\frac{2}{3}$ cups. The observable outcome is the yield in cups of popcorn, which is not perfectly predictable. Part of the plan is to obtain yields from an unpatterned, **random** sequence of the various brand and amount pairings to avoid order-induced biases.

The ideal is to design an experiment that holds everything constant except the variables of interest. In the popcorn experiment, the variables of interest are brand, amount, and yield; brand and amount are changed to see what happens to yield. We can hold the heat source constant by always using the same electric stove burner at one setting. By holding nuisance variables constant, such as the heat source, we **control** them. Such control enables us to get a clear, unclouded view of the variables of interest. Thus, it is less likely that we will be fooled by what we observe. True observations tend to yield good answers to the questions posed by the experimenter. Our theories can be put to a fair test, confronting data and fact.

As you progress through this book, you will learn to expand your knowledge through the analysis of data collected from planned and unplanned experiments.

EXAMPLE 1

THE SCURVY EXPERIMENT[4]

Problem Statement   A mysterious, life-threatening disease called scurvy was prevalent among seamen during long sea voyages in 1747.

Problem Solution   Fortunately for the seamen of that time, a Scottish doctor named James Lind conducted a planned experiment. From a total of 12 British Royal Navy seamen with scurvy, 2 were fed citrus fruits while the remaining 10, a control group, were not given the fruit. The 2 seamen in treatment and on the citrus fruit diet recovered completely while the 10 seamen in the control group, who were not fed the fruit, remained ill.

Problem Discussion   In such clinical trials, the principle is that two groups are compared but only one is actually treated. The subjects in the control group did not receive the treatment in order to hold everything constant. In a controlled experiment, the investigator determines which subjects will be in control and which in treatment. Individuals are randomly assigned to each group; a coin can be tossed and an outcome of "heads" assigns an individual to one group while an outcome of "tails" assigns an individual to the other group. The two groups are much the same except for the variables of interest. In this way, background variables are controlled, and we can focus on the variables of interest and see that the citrus fruit diet cured the scurvy. The curative agent was vitamin C, but that was not known until 1932.

EXAMPLE 2

BOX AND HUNTER'S POPCORN EXPERIMENT

Problem Statement   In making popcorn, does the yield in cups depend on the brand and the amount?

Problem Solution   Box, Hunter, and Hunter designed an experiment you can try to replicate.[5] The yield of popcorn in cups resulting from four of their experimental runs is shown below; each experimental run had a specific brand (gourmet or ordinary) and amount ($\frac{1}{3}$ or $\frac{2}{3}$ cups of kernels).

Yield (cups)	Brand	Amount (cups)
6.25	Ordinary	1/3
8.00	Gourmet	1/3
9.00	Ordinary	2/3
17.00	Gourmet	2/3

There are three variables (columns) in the above data set. Yield and amount are quantitative because they consist of numerical measurements. Brand is qualitative because it is categorical.

There are four rows of data, runs of the experiment; in the context of an earlier example, ducks on the pond, here each row is like a duck, Duck #1, Duck #2, Duck #3, and Duck #4. Therefore, each row consists of observed values on variables for a particular entity.

A plot, or graph, of the data reveals that yield tends to be higher when brand is gourmet (G) rather than ordinary (O) at both levels of amount. From an inspection of the plot, an informal conclusion is that yield does depend on brand and amount.

Problem Discussion   Each row of data [for example (6.25 ordinary $\frac{1}{3}$)] records the results of an experimental run; for example, a 6.25 cup yield resulted when brand was ordinary and amount was $\frac{1}{3}$ cup. Typically, experimental runs are conducted in a random order; for example, to randomize, on four separate pieces of paper you would (1) write each BRAND and AMOUNT pairing [(a) ordinary $\frac{1}{3}$, (b) gourmet $\frac{1}{3}$, (c) ordinary $\frac{2}{3}$, (d) gourmet $\frac{2}{3}$]; (2) place the four pieces of paper in a hat; and (3) draw the experimental run sequence at random. Randomization provides some insurance that unknown background factors will not lead you to erroneous conclusions about the effect of brand and amount on yield.

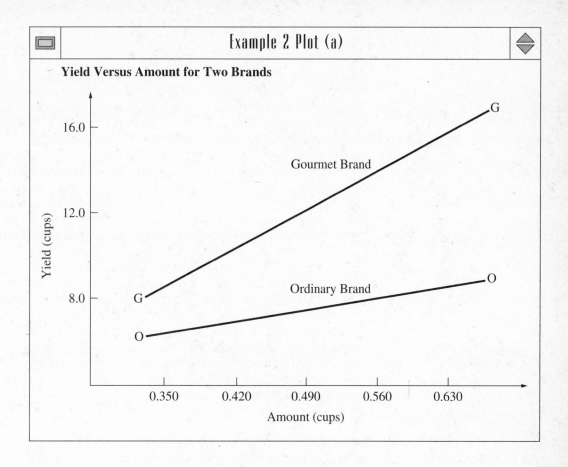

Example 2 Plot (a)

Yield Versus Amount for Two Brands

Statistics to Describe, Predict, or Control

Statistical methods can be used to describe, predict, or control phenomena. A simple look at the popcorn data set describes the results of the experiment, letting the data speak for itself. You will learn about various tools of **descriptive statistics,** such as the plot of yield versus amount in the previous example.

In addition to descriptive statistics, you will learn about **inferential statistics.** For example, in the popcorn experiment inferential statistics will help us predict or control yield based on our statistical estimate of the relationship between yield, brand, and amount; knowing or setting brand and amount in the popcorn production process can be used to predict or control the process yield. Experiments like the popcorn experiment are important in industry. There are many examples where the blend of ingredients is examined to determine the relationship to yield or the quality of a product.

OBSERVATIONAL STUDIES

An **unplanned experiment** is called an **observational study.** An unplanned set of actions produces observable outcomes that are not perfectly predictable. For example, the unplanned activity of the national economy produces observable, gross domestic product (GDP) figures that are not perfectly predictable. Intentional randomization, like that done by an experimenter, is seldom possible.

Therefore, Example 3, a comparison of baseball players Darryl Strawberry and Ted Williams, is an observational study. Producing definitive conclusions by studying the baseball statistics is difficult because the two individuals played in different eras. Thus, it is impossible to hold constant background factors such as pitching that might invalidate the comparison.

To see this lack of control in another setting, take, for example, a study of the effects of cigarette smoking on health. The investigator cannot select one group of subjects and have them smoke for a number of years and have another group not smoke. In a sense, the investigator has no control because whether or not the subjects smoke is predetermined.

An observational study is a departure from the more desirable planned experiment. And, because observational studies are unplanned, one becomes less certain of the conclusions, which sometimes have a high chance of being wrong. Nevertheless, something might be learned by studying the data from observational studies.

EXAMPLE 3

THE STRAWBERRY AND WILLIAMS OBSERVATIONAL STUDY

Problem Statement   From baseball statistics over their first four years of play, compare Darryl Strawberry and Ted Williams.

Problem Solution   In the *New York Times,* according to Dave Anderson, when Darryl Strawberry played for the Mets, he had been touted as "the black Ted Williams."[6] This was quite a burden for Strawberry, but how did he compare to Williams? The legendary Ted Williams is well established in all the record books while Strawberry, in his early years, had only considerable promise in the big leagues. Over their respective first four seasons, the statistics are:

	Williams	Strawberry
Homers	127	108
Runs batted in	515	343
Strikeouts	196	495
Bases on balls	493	267
Hits	749	471
Average	.356	.260

In every category except homers, Strawberry was not even close to Williams. But, is the comparison valid? How would Williams do against today's pitchers? What do you think?

Problem Discussion   If all other factors were the same, the statistics show Williams as a much better rookie. But all other factors were not the same. They played in different ballparks, with different pitchers, and had 44 years between their rookie seasons. Nevertheless, it is interesting to speculate as to whom the better player might be.

Notice that, in contrast to some data sets shown earlier, the data set rows are the variables (homers, strikeouts, and so forth) and the columns (the two players) are the entities, the elementary units, individuals, or subjects studied. You will see data sets presented in different ways, so be alert and distinguish between the individual subjects and the variables.

EXAMPLE 4

AUTOMOBILE INSPECTION OBSERVATIONAL STUDY

Problem Statement   Do automobile safety inspections save lives?

Problem Solution   While at Princeton University, Edward Tufte addressed this problem.[7] He compared automobile accident death rates in states with and without inspections. This is an observational study because the investigator cannot control which states mandate or do not mandate inspections.

The comparison revealed that automobile accident death rates tended to be lower than expected in states that inspect compared to those that do not inspect. This led to the conclusion that inspections lower death rates, provided that other factors are equal (controlled).

But other factors may not be equal in observational studies. For example, Tufte noted that inspections may be just a part of a larger safety effort that might include better roads, different speed limits, strong checks on drunken driving, and so on. The reader is encouraged to examine Tufte's thorough analysis that demonstrates the value of data analysis in high-level policy decisions.

Tufte's analysis resulted in the assertion that states with lower death rates than expected are generally states that have inspections.

Problem Discussion   Why conduct an observational study rather than an experiment? An observational study was a more practical approach than a designed experiment. As Tufte pointed out, suppose our question on inspection was being studied in a carefully designed experiment. Two randomly chosen groups of cars could be selected. The treatment group would be inspected and their accident history followed. The control group would not be inspected but their accident history would be followed. Because fatal automobile accidents are a relatively rare event, the group sizes would have to be enormous in order to compile an accident history. There are also other difficulties that make a planned experiment impractical.

SCIENCE AND STATISTICS

You have seen that observed phenomena lead to questions or problems. Frequently, planned experiments or observational studies are undertaken to collect numerical data that shed light on the questions. Then, statistical analysis of the data guides the thinker to numerically based opinions. The data comprise a factual basis for testing ideas.

From the early examples it might seem that a single experiment or observational study provides the answer; however, that seldom happens in practice. The reality of scientific study is an ongoing learning process comprised of a sequence of studies. To emphasize this approach, we will describe the *scientific learning process*, or *scientific method*.

The Out-of-Control Gypsy Moth Population

On a summer night while lying in bed, you can hear them chomping. In the park woods on a sunny day, it sounds like rain. Later in the summer the woods are brown and leafless as if it were late autumn. The gypsy moth population has exploded out of control. The **time series** data in Exhibit 1 highlight the population rises and falls.[8]

We can't count all the moths, therefore, numbers of moths are not plotted over time. Rather, a **surrogate variable,** acres defoliated, is used in place of the number of moths. A surrogate variable is commonly used when measuring the real variable is too difficult or expensive. Note that a surrogate variable can be a problem as well as a solution. The problem in practice is that surrogate variables can mistakenly lead us to the wrong conclusions about other variables. For example, we may think that the defoliation is due to the gypsy moth, yet in some parts of the forest the defoliation may be due to diseased trees. Watch out for variables lurking in the background.[9]

The types of question spawned by our observation of tree-leaf destruction may include: Why do gypsy moth invasions terminate so abruptly? Why don't the moths, after several years of defoliating trees, kill the trees? How do trees respond to these attacks? For example, some contend that gypsy moth populations die because they eat themselves out of their food supply. Others contend that the real reason for the dramatic population downturns is that

EXHIBIT 1 Defoliation by Gypsy Moths in Massachusetts

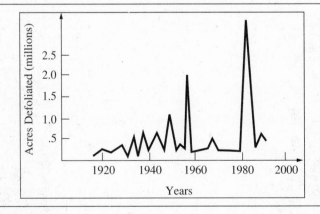

the second-growth leaves have new chemical structures the moths can't thrive on.

As you can see, science loves a mystery, and statistical tools are helpful in the unraveling process. The **scientific method** or **scientific learning process,** involves (1) **observation** (gypsy moth populations die off rapidly), (2) expressing provisional conjecture as **hypotheses** (they eat themselves out of their food supply), (3) **hypothesis testing** (statistical analysis shows that populations die even when second-growth leaves are available as food), (4) if necessary, **revising hypotheses** (second-growth leaves have new chemical structures the moths can't thrive on), and (5) cycling through this process as much as necessary to establish theory, which is the entrenched explanation accounting for known facts or phenomena. This time-tested approach together with a statistical toolbox is known as **process improvement** in quality control circles.

George Box emphasized special aspects of this scientific learning process, which is depicted in Exhibit 2.[10] The first is **iteration** (repeated interaction) between conjecture (idea) and fact (data). Iteration between conjecture and fact is shown by the upward and downward arrows in Exhibit 2. As time progresses from left to right in the exhibit, theory, models, and ideas at the representation level are tested against data from the actual, real-world fact level. In this way, ideas are refined.

Idea refinement depends on both induction and deduction. Recall that **deduction** involves reasoning from the general to the particular—like "dogs have four legs"; "cows have four legs"; therefore, "cows must be dogs." Obviously, it is worth checking a deductive idea or theory with real-world facts. Recall that **induction** is the process of drawing general conclusions from particular facts. Through data collection, analysis, and presentation, we learn that cows are bigger than dogs and that cows give milk and have bells. Induction requires us to revise our initial idea that cows are dogs. We might agree that both are animals but not the same kind of animals.

George Box emphasized other aspects of the scientific learning process. They include (1) flexibility of tentative theory and approach, (2) economical description of natural phenomena (parsimony, keeping things simple), (3) appropriate concern and focus on the relevant factors, and (4) the artful employment of mathematics. You will acquire these skills in the chapters ahead.

EXHIBIT 2 Deduction-Induction Diagram

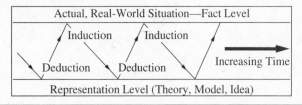

Source: George Box, *Journal of the American Statistical Association,* Dec. 1976, vol. 71, no. 356.

Identifying Key Variables and Thinking about How They Might Be Related

From the beginning of a scientific study, the investigator must identify key variables and think about how the variables might be related.

Prediction—Maine Lobster Outlook: Down   Maine's 4,000 full-time lob-sterpersons have been concerned because some scientists believe that after another good catch the trend will reverse itself and continue downward until the end of the century. The lobster catch is predicted to drop about 50% because of a cooling trend in the water.

There has been a strong **correlation,** or relationship, between water temperature and catch totals. The catch has declined steadily from a record 11,068 metric tons in 1957, when the temperature level was 10.5°C, an ideal temperature. The catch has decreased as the temperature has dipped to 7.5°C.

Water temperature seems to be the key, as indicated by a strong, positive correlation between temperature and catch. A strong, positive correlation signals that high water temperatures are associated with a large catch and low water temperatures are associated with a small catch. Other factors considered include fishing pressure, which is measured by the number of lobster traps. The number of traps has doubled in ten years, but the catch does not reflect a corresponding change. As a result, the number of traps, almost 2 million, shows little correlation with the catch. Perhaps the lobsters will move south to warmer water, but it is unlikely that Maine lobsters will thrive in the sandy-bottom habitats of more southerly water.[11]

S T A T I S T I C A L   H I G H L I G H T S

When working with pairs of variables, we are interested in the direction and the strength of the relationship between the pairs. A correlation is a summary (not perfect) of a simple plot of a pair of variables.

Although correlation does not necessarily imply cause and effect, observed association spurs us to trace the logical basis for a possible cause-and-effect relationship.

Correlation coefficients have signs, positive or negative, that tell direction. When the correlation is positive, both variables move in the same direction, increasing or decreasing together. When the correlation is negative, the variables move in opposite directions, with one increasing and the other decreasing.

Correlations have magnitude to tell the strength of the association—near zero for weak relationships and near an absolute value of one for strong relationships.

Key Variables as Early Warning Signals for the Economy   In monitoring economic activity, executives watch key economic variables and think about how they might be related to their company's sales. Because economic activity is cyclical, the executives like to know where the economy has been, where it is, and where it is going. Such information is so important for business decisions that the National Bureau of Economic Research (NBER) publishes statistics on *lagging, coincident,* and *leading economic indicators.* These indicators are correlated with aggregate economic activity.

Leading economic indicators warn of economic downturns or upturns. Variables that tend to lead are new orders for durable goods, construction contracts, formation of new business enterprises, hiring rates, and the average length of the workweek.

Coincident economic indicators coincide with aggregate economic activity. Gross domestic product (GDP), industrial production, personal income, employment, unemployment, wholesale prices, and retail sales are current measures of economic performance.

Lagging economic indicators tell us where the economy has been. The movement of labor cost per unit output, long-term unemployment, and yield on mortgage loans follow (lag) aggregate economic activity.

These and other related indicators are published monthly in *Business Conditions Digest*. Such timely information is important to managers and other decision makers in business, government, labor, and academia. The economic pulse of the country is an important guide to policy making. Tanur et al. give more details about warning signals for the economy.[12]

STATISTICS FOR QUALITY CONTROL

Statistical methods have become an important component in efforts to improve the quality of products and services. **Quality control** is a term used for the collection of quality improvement activities. Applications of statistics in quality control are numerous. For example, the output of a manufacturing process might be monitored by measuring, say, the diameter of pistons being produced. A sequence of observational studies amounts to continuous monitoring of production processes.

Why People Weren't Buying American Cars

It's fall. School starts, bathing suits are put away. Sensible season. In October the odometer on your Chevrolet tops 90,000 and the rear end goes; the shop wants $600 to fix it.

You go to the new-car dealer for the first time in years, and you're hit by a feeling you'd almost forgotten, like your first romance: the love of the new. You see your face in the finish. You sit inside and the newness surrounds you: not a speck of dirt, fresh-smelling upholstery, classy instrumentation. The door thunks shut; you start the engine and hardly hear it. You accelerate, smooth and steady; you turn corners without a lurch.

Then you look at the sticker and you are hit by another feeling, something like nausea.[13]

As a result of high sticker prices and market factors such as foreign competition, the American car industry suffered its worst sales slump in two decades during the early 1980s. It questioned why people weren't buying American cars. Finding the answer was critical, because Japanese cars were selling and their market share was steadily increasing. A major reason for their success was high quality at competitive prices.

The Japanese learned much about quality control from W. Edwards Deming, a well-known American statistical expert in quality control. Deming taught the Japanese that most quality problems come from flaws in the system rather than workers' mistakes or isolated equipment failures and that flaws become evident only by keeping detailed statistical records. So important was Deming's work that the Japanese annually award the Deming Prize to a company honored for gains in product quality. By adopting Deming's methods, Detroit has narrowed Japan's lead in quality.

Modern communication and transportation systems have moved what once was local industrial competition into the global arena. To survive, many industries have had to become world-class competitors. Manufacturing and service firms have streamlined production processes. Statistical methods have become recognized as essential tools needed by organizations to become world-class competitors. Because of statistical methods, products and processes can be better designed and their quality characteristics better monitored.

Automobiles and many other products are assembled from many components. The proper functioning of the product depends on the proper functioning of the components. Defective components degrade product quality and may result in product failure. As a result, manufacturers statistically monitor quality characteristics of components as well as the end product.

Process-related Statistics   As mentioned previously, an example of monitoring a manufacturing process is a production worker measuring the diameter of pistons being produced. Pistons cannot be produced with exactly the same diameters. There will be **variability** in the diameter measurements from one piston to another.

Defective pistons can be spotted by using a simple statistical tool called a **control chart** (see Exhibit 3). A control chart is a plot of individual measurements, or statistics such as averages, in production order; additionally, an **upper control limit (UCL)** and a **lower control limit (LCL)** are drawn on the plot.

As long as the variability is small enough so that the diameter measurements are within reasonable control limits, the pistons can function properly in an engine. In Exhibit 3 the first 30 pistons produced had diameters inside the control limits shown on the plot. Some **chance variability** within the limits is expected because its cause cannot be found and eliminated. If piston diameter is too large or too small, outside the control limits, the piston won't fit properly into a cylinder. As can be seen in Exhibit 3, there are production problems after piston 30 is produced; pistons 31, 33, and 35 are far above the upper control limit (diameters too large) and piston 37 is far below the lower control limit (diameter too small).

A measurement that strays beyond the control limits constitutes an alarm signal; this condition is no longer simply due to chance variability but to some systematic cause. Thus **systematic variability,** like that due to machine-tool wear, can be identified and corrected. Pistons that have diameters larger or smaller than the control limits may be replaced or machined to the proper size. When used with other quality control activities, statistical process controls have been documented to improve product quality.

S T A T I S T I C A L   H I G H L I G H T S

Expect variability in what you observe but learn to distinguish between chance variability and systematic variability.

EXHIBIT 3 Control Chart for Individual Piston Diameters

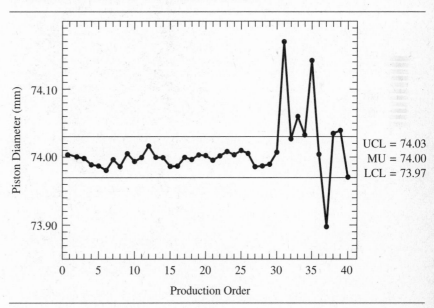

EXPLORATORY AND CONFIRMATORY ACTIVITIES IN THE SCIENTIFIC LEARNING PROCESS

As the scientific learning process progresses, two phases become apparent, the **exploratory phase** and the **confirmatory phase.** Numerous questions tend to be generated and discoveries made in the exploratory phase. By the time the confirmatory stage has been reached, the questions have been framed as hypotheses that are tested.

Exploratory and Confirmatory Statistical Methods

Many statistical methods are designed to probe data sets, to expose unusual observations, and to generate questions and ideas; these are **exploratory methods.** Other statistical methods tend to be better at testing ideas expressed as hypotheses; these are the classical **confirmatory methods.**

In theory, classical statistical methods are dependent on certain assumptions. But in practice the classical statistical tools withstand moderate violations of these assumptions.

Exploratory methods have been designed to withstand major assaults on the assumptions that buttress the classical methods. Because of their relative freedom from restrictive assumptions, exploratory tools are said to be **robust.** They resist being unduly influenced by a few unusual data values.

For exploratory work, we like robust and resistant tools. For confirmatory work, we like more efficient and tailored tools that are not robust and resistant. The distinction between confirmatory and exploratory statistical tools will be brought into sharper focus as you progress through this text.

S T A T I S T I C A L   H I G H L I G H T S

When you drive the family car to town, you might assume that there is enough gas in the tank to get there. That assumption might even be validated by looking at the fuel guage. Similarly, when you use classical statistical methods, you would generally depend on certain conditions (assumptions) being true. If the assumptions are not valid, you might not get all the way to town or reach sound conclusions in a research project.

The Exploratory Mentality

Tom Martin Creek   Richard Brautigan sampled the trout fishing at the mouth of Tom Martin Creek. He caught one good-looking trout that danced all over the top of the pool. His initial exploratory probe made him curious. Here is how Richard Brautigan described the experience:

> I walked down one morning from Steelhead, following the Klamath River that was high and murky and had the intelligence of a dinosaur. Tom Martin Creek was a small creek with cold, clear water and poured out of a canyon and through a culvert under the highway and then into the Klamath.

I dropped a fly in a small pool just below where the creek flowed out of the culvert and took a nine-inch trout. It was a good-looking fish and fought all over the top of the pool.

Even though the creek was very small and poured out of a steep brushy canyon filled with poison oak, I decided to follow the creek up a ways because I liked the feel and motion of the creek.

I liked the name too.

Tom Martin Creek.

It's good to name creeks after people and then later to follow them for awhile seeing what they have to offer, what they know and have made of themselves.

But that creek turned out to be a real [expletive deleted]. I had to fight it all the . . . way: brush, poison oak and hardly any good places to fish, and sometimes the canyon was so narrow the creek poured out like water from a faucet. Sometimes it was so bad that it just left me standing there, not knowing which way to jump.

You had to be a plumber to fish that creek.

After that first trout I was alone there. But I didn't know that until later.[14]

Investigate Unusual Observations   One 9-in. trout caught at the mouth of the creek was not a good indicator of fishing success upstream; however, it was an influential occurrence, or data point. Exploration ensued. More information was collected before it was confirmed that the fishing was not good.

Let Each of the Data Speak for Itself   In the early days of statistics before the development of many methods of analysis, each of the data was simply presented so that it could speak for itself, like fishing a pool at the mouth of the creek and letting Tom Martin Creek speak for itself in terms of one trout dancing all over the top of the pool.

A Model Confronting Data   As the methods of statistics developed, statisticians found that they could do better than just letting each of the data speak for itself. The more contemporary model-building approach to statistics emerged.

The idea of a conceptual model is evident in the Tom Martin Creek episode. After his initial success, the fly fisherman probably thought that Tom Martin Creek, with its cold, clear water, was going to be a dream. The model for the creek was a small, little-fished stream full of trout. Perhaps the creek was thought to be like one that proved good in the distant past, or maybe it was thought to be a fisherman's Shangri-la. The model was then tested with more data that were collected. The model did not fit in the end, for "You had to be a plumber to fish that creek." After catching the first trout, the fisherman was alone, even though he didn't know it until later.

People Working Together Solve Organizational Problems   When you participate in or manage a statistical study, remember that many statistical studies involve groups of people working together. Such interaction is essential. The serious user of statistics should not end up alone like the fly fisherman on Tom Martin Creek.

SCALES OF MEASUREMENT

The procedure of assigning numbers to an elementary unit's attribute variables is referred to as **measurement.** A measure of duck weight is 2.6 lb. A measure of a duck's gender is, say, 1 for a male and 0 for a female. The weight and gender variables have different rules for assigning numbers. Weight can be an integer or noninteger value (continuous). The rules require that gender be an integer value, either 0 or 1. A set of rules defines a **scale.** The procedure of assigning numbers to an elementary unit's attribute variables defined by a set of rules constitutes a **measurement scale.**

You will encounter different measurement scales. For example, duck weight is measured on a *ratio scale* while duck gender is measured on a *nominal scale.* These and other scales will be defined later. Recognition of the measurement scale helps you analyze the data and interpret the results meaningfully.

Even though you would not think of gender, a category, as being associated with a numerical measurement, it can be assigned arbitrary, numerical values. For example, in a data set males could be denoted by 1 and females by 0 (1s or 2s would be just as appropriate).

A number assigned to a category is arbitrary and simply a way to record the category in a data set or to partition the data set in the analysis phase. It would not be meaningful to try to interpret a statistic, such as an average, based on such an arbitrary form of measurement, say, 1s for males and 0s for females. We don't know what an average equal to, say, .60 would represent for a gender variable. When measurements consist of numbers or symbols that represent classes or categories, the magnitude of the numbers may not convey much meaning because of the arbitrary assignment of numbers to categories. Computing certain statistical summary values may be meaningless. Thus, a numerical-valued category is a **weak measurement form** because of the arbitrary numbers assigned to the categories. In contrast, duck weight would be a **strong measurement form.**

Traditional Measurement Scales

Many statisticians rely on the following traditional *scales of measurement* developed by Stevens: *nominal, ordinal, interval,* and *ratio.*[15]

The **nominal scale** classifies or categorizes observations. Qualitative variables or factors, at two or more distinct levels, are nominally scaled. For example, individuals may be classified by gender and designated as male or female; production data may come from different machines; production shifts might be the first shift, the second, or the third; sales may vary by the day of the week, the season, or the month; financial figures may come from different corporate divisions.

Nominal data may be identified by a name, letter code, arbitrary symbol, or number; for example, Monday—M, Tuesday—T, and Wednesday—W using symbols or Monday—1, Tuesday—2, Wednesday—3, using numbers. Numerical designations are generally preferred when preparing data for computer analysis, but they are merely identification tags and provide the barest information.

The nominal scale enables us to tell when entities are the same or not the same with respect to a specific property. For example, Monday (1) is not the same as Wednesday (3). Often it is meaningless to add, subtract, multiply, or use any arithmetic operation on nominally scaled variables. For nominal data, certain traditional statistics, such as the average, are not meaningful summary measures. Nevertheless, the knowledge gained by accounting for qualitative variables is valuable, and some statistics are applicable.

The **ordinal scale** not only assigns numbers to categories like the nominal scale but also rank orders the categories according to some property. Thus the ordinal scale is a stronger form of measurement than the nominal scale. Numerical indicators represent both category and rank. For example, the categories Good, Better, Best may be coded 1, 2, 3. The ordinal scale does not assume equal intervals between the numerical indicators, nor does it show if some individual observation is void of the property being measured.

If the order is preserved, transformations are appropriate on this scale, such as adding or multiplying by a constant. For example, a transformation by multiplication—2 times 1, 2, and 3 (for Good, Better, Best)—preserves the order and meaning, yielding 2, 4, and 6.

As with the nominal scale, some statistical summary measures, such as the average, may not be meaningful with ordinal data. On the other hand, the mode, the most frequently occurring data value, is an appropriate statistic. Usually, we employ statistics called **order statistics,** which have been specially developed for ordinal data.

The **interval scale** categorizes and orders like the ordinal scale but it requires that numerically equal distances on the scale represent equal changes in the property being measured.

A classic illustration of the interval scale is temperature measurements, which display all the interval scale properties. For example, temperatures in degrees of 30, 35, 40, 45, and 50 categorize, order, and have equal distances that represent equal temperature changes. A temperature change from 30° to 45° (a 15° change) is the same as the change from 45° to 60°. Because of the arbitrary zero point, we cannot say that 60° is twice as warm as 30°.

Transformations, such as multiplying interval measurements by a constant and adding another constant, preserve the measured properties; therefore, we can, for example, use either Celsius or Fahrenheit equally well to measure temperature.

Powerful statistical methods can be employed with data on the interval scale. The reason for this is that arithmetic operations of addition and subtraction produce meaningful results. In computing an average, for example, data values are added and divided by the total number of values; therefore, a statistic such as average temperature is meaningful. Integer (discrete) or continuous measurements are possible on the interval scale, improving on the discrete character of the nominal and ordinal scales.

The **ratio scale** includes all the features of the other three scales; it also includes the concept of an absolute zero point or origin. An absolute zero point permits multiplication and division. Remember that on the interval scale we could not consider 60° twice as warm as 30°. In contrast, on the ratio scale six yards is twice as long as three yards.

Most statistical methods discussed in this book apply to ratio and interval scale measurements, whereas some methods in this book may not apply to the data measured on the other scales, especially the nominal and ordinal scales. Sometimes ratio data will be referred to as amounts or counts.

According to Stevens, it is vital to recognize that not all statistical methods are meaningful nor valid when data are measured on certain scales, particularly on nominal and ordinal scales. The data analyst must recognize the measurement scale and choose the statistical methods appropriate for that scale. Most methods in this text are applicable to interval and ratio scale data.

Contemporary Measurement Scales

Velleman and Wilkinson point out that using nominal, ordinal, interval, and ratio scales for data can be misleading and may be an oversimplification.[16] As a result, other measurement scales have been suggested as competitive alternatives, even though some scale similarities are apparent. Mosteller and Tukey promote the following scales of measurement: *names* and *grades, ranks, counted fraction, counts, amounts,* and *balances.*[17]

For **names** such as robin, blackbird, and sparrow, it is not meaningful to associate the names with numbers unless the numbers simply substitute for the names. Nevertheless, we use such numbers in data sets as name substitutes so that the computer, saving us work, can count the number of robins, blackbirds, and sparrows in a data set. For example, if 12 of 100 birds are sparrows, $\frac{12}{100} = .12$ is a **counted fraction,** constrained between 0 and 1. **Grades,** such as A, B, and C differ from names in that it makes sense to associate numbers with them, say, A(4.0), B(3.0), and C(2.0). Grades are ordered labels; the numbers associated with grades don't have to be integer values. Clearly, **ranks** are ordinal discrete values. **Amounts** and **counts** are nonnegative real numbers and integers, respectively. **Balances** are unbounded positive or negative values.

Modern data analysis philosophies and methods require us to go beyond the rigidness of the nominal, ordinal, interval, and ratio scales. Some modern statistical tools are formulated in such a way that they resemble chameleons, changing themselves enough to transcend the traditional measurement scales.

Regardless of the choice of measurement scale, always look at the data with an attitude of discovery and query. Choose any statistical method or data transformation that is meaningful in answering the questions at hand or that exposes anomalies in the data that lead to new discoveries or questions. Of course, the meaningfulness of the statistical tool may depend to some extent on the measurement scale, but this should not be your main concern. Be open-minded. Don't be overly restrictive in your approach or method. Accept new information as valid evidence that leads to discovery or supports your answers.

CHAPTER SUMMARY

This chapter was designed to stimulate the reader's imagination and to build an appreciation of the applications cornucopia. We introduced statistical terminology and data collection circumstances and differentiated planned and unplanned experiments. We emphasized that statistical methods help guide us in unknown worlds via the scientific learning process. The methods of statistics are vital to research in many disciplines. Additional applications are found in the literature of all fields of study. Some interesting collections are found in Tanur, Fairley and Mosteller, and Tufte.[18]

Most important, perhaps, is that statistics has an impact on the way we think. I am reminded of a Fulbright orientation lecture I heard in Athens, Greece, a long time ago. A number of us were surprised to hear that the ultimate in Byzantine chanting was to just barely miss the beat. Based on the our past experience, we believed that the ultimate was to be on the beat. The revelation that in some Greek music one should just miss the beat changed the way we thought about music. Statistical knowledge changes the way we think too.

KEY TERMS

amount, 3
amounts, 20
attributes, 3
balances, 20
category, 3
census, 3
chance variability, 15
coincident economic indicators, 13
confirmatory phase, 16
confirmatory methods, 16
control, 5
control chart, 14
correlation, 12
count, 3
counted fraction, 20
counts, 20
data, 3
data set, 3
data values, 3
deduction, 11
descriptive statistics, 7
elementary units, 2
exploratory methods, 16
exploratory phase, 16
frame, 2

grades, 20
hypotheses, 11
hypothesis testing, 11
induction, 11
inferences, 2
inferential statistics, 7
interval scale, 19
iteration, 11
lagging economic indicators, 13
leading economic indicators, 13
lower control limit (LCL), 14
measurement, 18
measurement scale, 18
names, 20
nominal scale, 18
observation, 11
observational study, 8
order statistics, 19
ordinal scale, 19
parameter, 3
planned experiment, 5
population, 2
primary data, 4
process improvement, 11
quality control, 13

questionnaire, 3
random, 5
ranks, 20
ratio scale, 20
revising hypotheses, 11
robust, 16
sample, 2
scale, 18
scales of measurement, 18
scientific learning process, 11
scientific method, 11
secondary data, 4
statistic, 3
statistics, 3
strong measurement form, 18
subject, 3
surrogate variable, 10
survey, 3
systematic variability, 15
time series, 10
unplanned experiment, 8
upper control limit (UCL), 14
variability, 14
variables, 3
weak measurement form, 18

EXERCISES

General Exercises

1. If a theory is a proposed but unverified explanation, what data-based approaches might be used to test the following theories my students proposed? The students' last names are used to identify the theories.

Risk Theory: Virgos are hard to get along with if you happen to be a Leo or a Saggitarius.

McCormack Theory: Mice know when you are looking at them and when you are not.

Nazarian Theory: (1) Aspirin does not really help the sick get well; it is all in the mind. (2) A person is more likely to cough after hearing someone else cough than before.

Span Theory: (1) If you are waiting for a friend to pick you up and he is late, he will come while you are in the bathroom. (2) You can study better in a room full of people studying than in the same room alone.

Hines Theory: People eat more and feel better about their meal if the food is colorful.

Jarowski Theory: Raccoons are more likely to tip over the garbage cans of pizza lovers than of nonpizza lovers.

Timmons Theory: (1) The harder one tries to find a relationship with a member of the opposite sex, the less the chance of that relationship occurring. (2) If someone is sick, the longer he or she dwells on being sick, the longer it takes to get better.

Forte Theory: People don't sleep as well as they normally do when there is a full moon.

2. Write two theories of your own and state how you might test them.

3. Record some theories you think your mother or father have had. Have you been involved in testing any of them?

4. Describe your best friend to a stranger. Record statistics you might use.

5. Suppose you are driving along a road that is heavily patrolled and where speed traps are in place. In order to control your speed, you frequently check your speedometer. How do you process the speed data, and what actions do you take?

6. Discuss some statistics of interest you have found in a newspaper or magazine.

7. Suppose you are a teacher and have a number of scores available on each student for examinations, homework, class participation, and so on. How would you use this data to determine grades?

8. Find a world sports record. List the specifics. Because new world records usually break old world records, study and report on the length of time records have stood. Do recently set records seem to last as long as those set in the distant past?

9. Suppose you lived near the well-known 4,000-megawatt nuclear power plant at Chernobyl, 80 miles north of Kiev in the Ukraine. If you were at the Chernobyl accident, April 1986, what statistics would you like to know?

10. If you were hired by Wendy's to perform a $1 million study to find the best hamburger, how might you proceed? Wendy's expects you to run taste tests in six cities over a nine-month period. It would like you to try out 9 buns, 40 sauces, 3 types of lettuce, 4 package design boxes, and several names.

11. Dr. T. Theodore Fujita developed a method for classifying the severity of tornadoes by the damage they do. His F scale ranges from F1 to the most severe, F5. An F5 storm has winds up to 318 mph and can blow entire houses through the air, tear the bark off trees, and kill nearly every living thing in its path. An F4 storm whips winds to 260 mph, levels frame houses, and blows cars through the air. An F3 tornado has 206 mph winds, rips off roofs, and snaps off trees. An F2 has 113 mph winds, demolishes trailer houses, pushes over railroad boxcars, and blows cars off roads. An F1 storm is the weakest and has winds of 72 mph, wrecks sign boards, and blows over dog pens. With an average of 700 tornadoes and 114 deaths a year in the United States, tornadoes are one of nature's most destructive storms.[19] If you were managing a Severe Storms Forecast Center, how would you alert people to a potentially severe storm on a particular day?

12. Discuss some statistics that might reflect your health. Suppose you are not feeling well and think you might have the flu. You decide to see a doctor. How might a doctor use statistics to assess your condition, monitor the treatment process, and decide when you will be well again?

13. Form a committee consisting of yourself and four other members you select. The committee's charge is to plan a public health experiment. A new vaccine has been developed for a serious disease; large-scale testing of the vaccine has not been done. What expertise would you want on the committee? What are the critical elements of the plan to test the vaccine on a large scale?[20]

14. Much of the surgery done in hospitals requires the use of anesthetics. Some anesthetics have side effects such as producing fevers or liver damage and may even cause death. If a surgical operation is to be performed on you, what statistics would you like to know about the anesthetic? What would you think about this information?[21]

15. A pharmaceutical company is searching for an effective drug in treating cancer. A particular compound, one blend of ingredients of many possible blends, is thought to reduce tumor weight, a positive sign in fighting a cancer. The following tumor weights (in grams) were observed in three animals treated with the compound and six untreated control animals:

Treated: 0.95   1.57   1.13
Controls: 1.31   1.59   2.26   1.35   1.78   2.23

Do you think that the particular compound has any merit? Why?[22]

16. You are planning your first big party of the year. A simple but good punch you intend to serve blends ginger ale and cranberry juice. The right mixture is mixed up in your mind; the right blend will make your guests happy with the taste. After thoughtful consideration, you and three friends decide to test the following four blends (ounces of ginger ale to ounces of cranberry juice): (a) 7 to 1; (b) 5 to 3; (c) 3 to 5; (d) 1 to 7. Which of the following behavioral descriptions do you think were observed to be associated with the taste of the above blends: (1) unhappy; (2) slightly unhappy; (3) slightly happy; (4) happy? What amount of ginger ale would you decide on for the punch? Can you think of other, more practical situations where the right mixture is important to us? What are they?[23]

17. The majority of health experts believe that smoking is bad for your health. "Bad for your health" can be thought of as the percentage of individuals surviving to a certain age. If we consider three tobacco usage classes, nonsmokers, moderate smokers, and heavy smokers, and if we are given three percentages (percent surviving to 60) 45%, 65%, and 70%, which percentage is associated with which smoker class? Do the same for the percentages surviving to 70, 50%, 28%, and 40%. Plot these points on a graph of the percentage surviving versus age; using three separate lines, connect the two points for nonsmokers, the two points for moderate smokers, and the two points for heavy smokers. Through

extrapolation, extend these lines to include other possible ages.[24]

18. It has been suggested that some people postpone their death in order to witness their birthday. If true, for a selected group of individuals, the number of deaths in the five months before the birthday month should be less than the number of deaths in the five months after the birthday month. See if this is true for a group of notable Americans.[25]

19. Is Jack highly intelligent (1) because of his early training in the right environment or (2) because his parents are both intelligent? More generally, is intelligence largely due to environmental or genetic factors? If the root of intelligence is in the environment, can we place Jill in the right environment to improve her intelligence? How might these questions be studied? What if Jack has an identical twin who grew up separated from Jack in another environment in another family? Why are identical twins useful in the study of questions of this sort?[26]

20. As of Sunday, June 27, 1987, major league baseball players had hit 2,122 homers, 22% more than the 1,746 at this point last year. Is this due to lively balls, deadly pitchers, or dead-armed pitchers?[27] How do you explain and think about unusual events of this sort?

21. Some species of plants and animals are in danger of becoming extinct. "Save the Whales" bumper stickers are an example of public concern. Suppose you are a member of a study group formed to gather data and to suggest ways of analysis that answer questions about the plight of the whales. Some reasonable questions include: How many whales of particular types are there? How many young are born each year? How many whales die from natural and man-made causes each year? How are the birth and death rates of whales affected by variables that man controls?

Counting whales is more difficult than counting ducks on a pond, so some counting methods are suggested for your thinking. The marking method involves attaching visible tags to some of the whales in the herd; later, when the whales are killed commercially, use the proportion of tagged to untagged dead whales to get an estimate of the whale population. In the catch-per-day method, divide the number of whales killed in a season by the change in the catch rate to estimate the whale population. The age method examines age specific capture rates from year to year.[28]

22. Youth Consultation Services (YCS), a social agency, provided a counseling service that was thought to reduce juvenile delinquency among teenage girls. If we were able to predict which girls in a large group were likely to have problem behaviors, how could we test the effectiveness of the YCS social program?[29]

Exercises to Illustrate Management Uses of Statistics

23. In the practice of management, managers blend and apply the concepts of planning, standard setting, and control. After plans are made or standards set, managers compare what actually happens to what ought to happen (according to plans or standards). When what ought to happen is out of line with what is happening, control action is taken to correct the discrepancy between actual and desired events.

As a manager, discuss the data you might need, how you might collect it, and how you might use that data in the following project planning situations:

(a) Locating a new manufacturing plant while considering the source of raw materials, the location of the market, transportation, labor supply, wage rates, cost of living, climate, tax rates, and so on.

(b) Forecasting sales based on the sales history of the firm and the history's relationship to economic time series that tend to lead sales.

(c) Changing the mix of your advertising media.

(d) Changing the blend of financing for a new business venture, where you might consider raising the money using a blend of debt (bonds) and equity (stocks).

(e) Creating an operating budget based on anticipated sales. Be sure to consider inventory requirements and how inventory is related to the manufacturing program. Estimate receipts, expenditures, and other items that relate to income statements and balance sheets.

(f) Preparing subsidiary budgets for specialized departments such as personnel, purchasing, advertising, and so on.

(g) Planning inventory levels to meet sales needs while maintaining smooth production operations.

As a manager, discuss the data you might need, how you might collect it, and how you might use that data in the following cases that involve setting standards:

(h) A beverage product has characteristics that include syrup to water ratio, syrup age, water purity, water chemistry, water taste, odor, and so on. The product is bottled in bottles that have requirements such as finish, capacity, weight, color, and so on.

(i) A clothing manufacturer sets requirements on fabrics that include length, width, durability, shrink resistance, bursting strength, texture, and so on.

(j) A manufacturer of copiers and duplicators establishes standards of excellence to maintain leadership in this business field in the face of increased foreign competition. Benchmarks are product quality, cost, and delivery targets.

(k) A large manufacturer examines lost time in production operations caused by machine breakdown and repair, cleaning and maintenance, power interruptions, lack of manpower, and so on.

Discuss the control actions that might be necessary for the situations listed above. Discuss the data you might need, how you might collect it, and how you might use that data in the situations listed above.

24. For a common product such as bread or milk, discuss the data and the analysis that might be needed for inventory planning and control. Management is concerned about the coordination of production, sales, and inventories. One strategy is to use inventories to cope with fluctuations in sales while keeping the production rate fairly uniform. Another strategy is to improve sales forecasting and design a production system flexible enough to vary the production rate as needed.

25. What data and analysis do you anticipate needing as a retailer dealing with the problem of stocking different sizes of pants, shirts, socks, shoes, hats, suits, and so on. You might consider the same problem from the point of view of the manufacturer.

26. Industry is concerned about quality control. Quality standards are established and maintained for products; statistical process control (SPC) activities help maintain high quality standards during the manufacturing process and the shipment or receipts of product lots are inspected to protect the producers or the consumers. Discuss the role of data analysis in quality control.

27. Making plans, setting standards, and achieving control apply to managerial activity as a whole but these activities also take place in functional areas such as marketing, production, personnel, finance, and accounting. As a manager with functional responsibility in one of these areas, what anticipated role would facts and figures play in the conduct of your job? Assume that you are dealing with a particular product and a particular company.

28. Outline the essential features of a process for preparing a sales budget. The marketing function should provide some key inputs such as sales estimates from salespersons and branch managers. To improve the quality of these estimates, salespersons and branch managers should be supplied with historical sales records and information on expected changes in the product line, advertising, prices, and so on. Although salespeople are in direct contact with the market, they may not be able to consider all relevant factors; therefore, marketing forecasts may have to be adjusted for economic, industry, demographic, and geographic considerations. Market characteristics such as income, climate, urbanization, population, age, race, and education are important.

29. New products and product changes often occur in response to changes in consumer preferences. An important area of marketing research involves monitoring consumer preferences. Select some evolving product that you use and design a short questionnaire aimed at evaluating consumer preferences for a cross section of prospective customers.

30. A key marketing decision is the price of a product. Two broad pricing strategies are common. A skimming strategy is often used for a new product where a company has a technological competitive advantage. The product is priced high at first then gradually lowered, skimming substantial profits from those who will pay the price. When a new product can be cloned easily, a penetration pricing strategy is often effective. The company selects a low price that captures a large market quickly and establishes a brand name. Suppose you are a manager about to make a pricing decision. What information would you have your staff provide to help you make the decision?

31. List two different advertising or selling methods. Design a way to compare the two methods.

32. For a number of products you use, list some magazines (rank by probable circulation size) that reach the type of people who buy your products. Do the same for television programs. How might you appraise the effectiveness of alternative advertising media?

33. Sources of new product ideas, ranked in importance, are: marketing, research and development, top management, new-product department, management, and others. As a manager, would you be happy with this simple ranking or would you want more specific figures, such as the percentage of ideas from each area?

34. When there are many new product ideas, alternative ideas can be rated, screening the "good" from the "bad." Typically, a product rating is a weighted combination of factors such as sales potential, competition, patent protection, technical competitive advantage, raw material availability, value added, and similarity to existing products. Assign what you think are appropriate weights (that sum to 1) to

the above factors. After evaluating alternative ideas, how would you use this data to select ideas for development?

35. Suppose you are a distributor of beer and soft drinks. You have a fleet of delivery trucks. What data should you keep about the fleet to plan for the replacement of trucks in the future?

36. Suppose you have four factories that supply four distribution centers. You are beginning to think about how much product to ship from each factory to each distribution center. You suspect that there must be some optimal shipping plan that minimizes transportation costs. To investigate this problem further, what data would you collect?

37. Create a list of productive systems, listing the type of company and the production capacity measurement. Examples are airlines, seats per day per route; hospitals, number of beds; and machine shops, machine hours.

38. In assembly-line balancing, each workstation carries out a set of tasks; a unit of product is assembled as it passes through all the workstations. The idea of balancing is to allocate the right number of tasks to each workstation so that the product being assembled spends about the same amount of time at each workstation; hence, work stations have very little idle time (the work load is balanced). For a simple product such as a paper plane or a wagon, list the assembly task steps and estimate the time required for each task.

39. Waiting-line theory, or queuing theory, involves times between customer arrivals and service times at a service facility. If you were managing a large market, what data would you use to make staffing decisions at checkout counters?

40. In personnel administration, what kinds of personnel interest or aptitude tests might be given for matching people to jobs?

41. In preparation for management and labor union contract negotiations, what data would you want to study in addition to the Consumer's Price Index (constructed by the Bureau of Labor Statistics)?

42. Financial managers eye financial ratios to assess and monitor a firm's financial condition and operating efficiency. There are four basic types of financial ratios that measure liquidity, leverage, activity, and profitability. Current assets divided by current liabilities (current ratio) measures liquidity. Total debt to total assets (debt ratio) measures leverage. Sales to inventory (inventory turnover ratio) measures activity. Net profit after taxes to sales (profit margin) and net profit after taxes to total assets (return on total assets) measure profitability. As a manager, what would be the format and timing of reports you would like to receive that include financial ratios?

43. Sales forecasting is important to the financial manager who plans for the future financial needs of the firm. Forecasted sales revenue is the basis for estimating future levels of related balance sheet accounts, such as accounts receivable, inventories cash, accounts payable, and so on. Sales revenues and related balance sheet accounts, expressed as a percentage of sales, are projected into the future and projected (pro forma) balance sheets are constructed. When a firm is growing, the pro forma balance sheet is out of balance by the amount of funds needed to finance the expansion. Discuss the data requirements and the effect of underestimating financing needs; when the amount of long-term financing is underestimated, more expensive short-term financing results.

44. Accounting data are used for reports to stockholders, banks, the Internal Revenue Service, and others; these data also help in the management of the firm. Statistical methods are most useful in the internal management functions of the firm. One such function is auditing. In auditing, a small number of accounts, a sample, are examined in detail to check them for accuracy; inferences are then made about the accuracy of the remaining unchecked accounts. Explain what data and analysis might be needed to audit customer charge accounts.

45. Customers do not always pay their bills in full at the time of purchase. The sum of all such amounts of money outstanding, accounts receivable, are monitored by management. Receivables are aged; reports are produced that show the number of days outstanding amounts are past due. A percentage of those amounts are considered uncollectible. How might you present such data in a report?

46. If you were to start your own insurance company, discuss some ideas for determining premium amounts.

47. Because you should not put all your eggs in one basket, discuss how you might allocate and monitor your investment portfolio among stocks, bonds, savings, and so on.

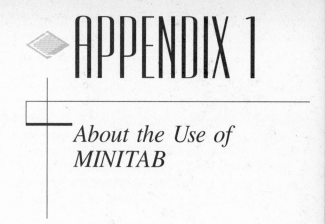

APPENDIX 1

About the Use of MINITAB

This appendix makes some suggestions to novice and more advanced users about utilizing this textbook in conjuction with MINITAB statistical software. Because computer users have access to other statistical packages and other software products, we suggest that you use these other products to improve your analysis and polish your presentation and communication of results and conclusions.

USING MINITAB WITH THIS TEXTBOOK

The following 17 chapters each have appendixes that list MINITAB statistical software commands for doing most examples in each chapter. You can do the examples and similar exercises using these commands. Line-by-line commentary explains what the commands do. By working the chapter examples, you can learn on your own, which means that your instructor can spend more time teaching you the *why* rather than the *how* of statistical methodology.

If you have access to other statistical software packages such as SAS, SPSS, or BMDP, you can easily adapt the command structure of MINITAB to that of another product.

The diskette on the inside back cover of this book contains all data sets and MINITAB macros needed to solve the examples and related exercises in this book.

To take advantage of MINITAB's full capability, use Release 10 Xtra or 11 for Windows and Macintosh. You may have MINITAB installed on a stand-alone machine or networked in a lab environment on campus. The commands given in this book are compatible with MINITAB Release 10 Xtra for Windows and Macintosh, but they will also work with earlier and future releases of MINITAB or with student versions. For information on ordering MINITAB, call 800-448-3555 (United States and Canada) or 814-238-3280. For documentation, the *MINITAB User's Guide* provides information about installation, the windows operating environment, and step-by-step sample sessions. For a comprehensive reference, use the *MINITAB Reference Manual*.

Starting and Driving MINITAB

After MINITAB is installed in a Windows or Macintosh operating system environment, start by using a mouse to double-click the MINITAB icon. A window will appear briefly to announce the startup; then a *Session* window and a *Data* window will appear simultaneously. Nothing further happens until you act.

For operational simplicity, I recommend that you first type all chapter appendix MINITAB commands in the session window. In the corner of this window to the right of its name, *Session,* there is an upward-pointing arrowhead. Click this arrowhead to enlarge the session window. Then, after the prompt (MTB >) appears, type GSTD and press the *Enter* key. GSTD makes standard graphics available and displays all of the output in the session window. Thus, your complete analysis, resulting from several commands, can be reviewed by scrolling through this window with the vertical scroll bar on the right side of the window. Also, the session window can be printed by selecting the *Print window* from the *File* drop-down menu list.

By working entirely within the session window (henceforth called the *Session window command approach*), you avoid the potentially confusing hodgepodge of windows produced by the *full-feature approach,* which involves professional graphics (MTB > GPRO) in conjunction with the drop-down menu lists and dialog boxes. When I began writing and class testing earlier versions of this manuscript, I experimented with examples that illustrated the drop-down menu lists, dialog boxes, and full use of the features provided by professional graphics. With the full-feature approach, I found that my writing became very procedural and that many students became bogged down in the procedural minutiae and were not grasping the statistical concepts I was trying to convey. Because, the session window command approach simplified my teaching and student learning, I decided to use the session window command approach. By using this approach, examples involving several analysis steps can be presented succinctly and many more examples can be covered.

In the following example of the session window command approach, a MINITAB data set is retrieved, information is obtained about the data set, and bear age versus weight is plotted. (MTB > is a MINITAB prompt.)

```
MTB > GSTD
MTB > RETRIEVE 'BEARS'
MTB > INFO

Information on the Worksheet

     Column   Name        Count   Missing
     C1       ID          143     0
     C2       Age         143     0
     C3       Month       143     0
     C4       Sex         143     0
     C5       Head.L      143     0
     C6       Head.W      143     0
     C7       Neck.G      143     0
     C8       Length      143     0
     C9       Chest.G     143     0
     C10      Weight      143     0
     C11      Obs.No      143     0
  A  C12      Name        143     2

MTB > PLOT 'AGE' 'WEIGHT' # ALSO PLOT C2 C10
```

EXHIBIT 4

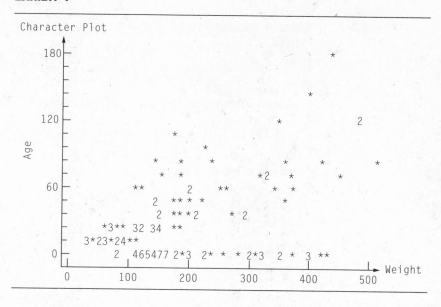

Character Plot

Those experienced in both the Windows environment and MINITAB may use this book's MINITAB command lists to guide them through the drop-down menus and dialog boxes. However, for a mix of students at various computer skill levels, I recommend the session window command approach. A first statistics course can be intimidating enough without including statistical software. Therefore, all MINITAB commands in this book are presented in a manner consistent with the session window command approach.

After your preliminary analysis of a particular problem is completed in the session window, use the drop-down menus lists and the dialog boxes for professional graphics for report writing. Each MINITAB command in a chapter appendix can be used to select an item from a drop-down menu list.

The example of the full-feature professional graphics approach on the following page parallels the session window command approach shown above. First, in the File menu, Open Worksheet is selected.

EXHIBIT 5

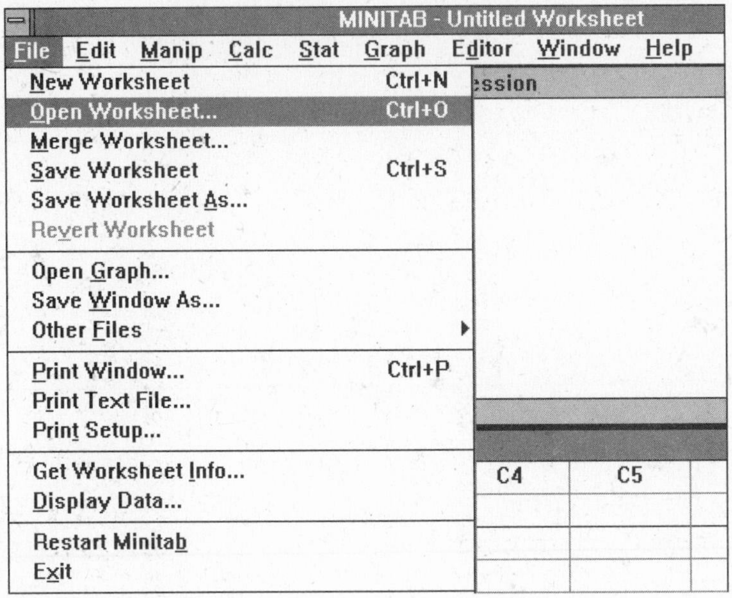

Next, an Open Worksheet dialog box appears on the monitor. The worksheet, bears.mtw, is selected and opened by double-clicking (or by clicking bears.mtw to select and then clicking the OK button.)

EXHIBIT 6

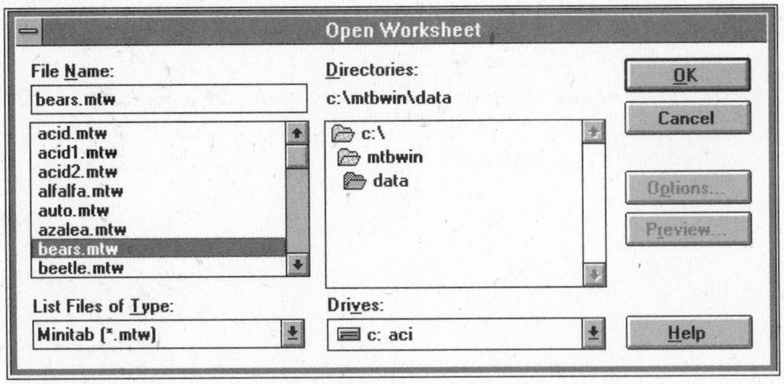

Next, the Graph drop-down menu list is used to select Plot.

EXHIBIT 7

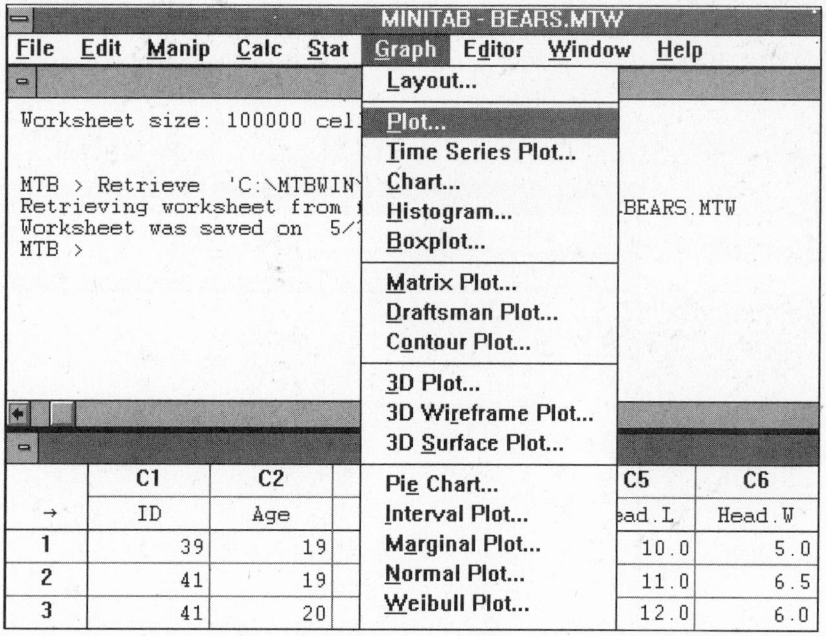

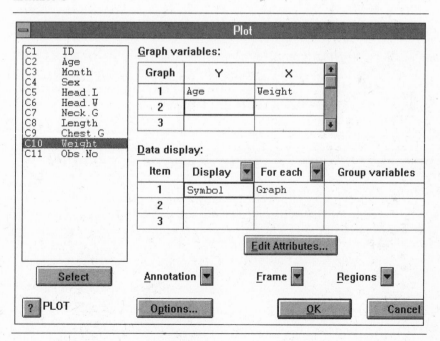

		C1	C2			C5	C6
→		ID	Age		ead.L	Head.W	
1		39	19			10.0	5.0
2		41	19			11.0	6.5
3		41	20			12.0	6.0

This selection produces a dialog box that lists the data variable names on the left. Double-click the age data variable name, do the same for weight, and click on the OK button. (Other dialog box options might be selected by more experienced users.)

EXHIBIT 8

These actions produce the following plot in a window; the plot can be copied from MINITAB and pasted into a word-processing document.

EXHIBIT 9

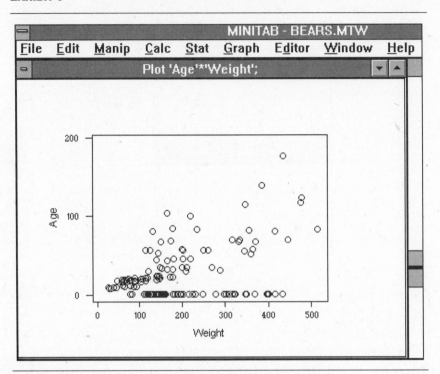

MINITAB produces a variety of graphs (see Appendix 1 Exhibit 7) in addition to the one shown in Appendix 1 Exhibit 9. These can be explored by the MINITAB user with help available in the Help drop-down menu list. Also, a menu-map of Release 10 Xtra is provided on the inside back cover of this textbook.

THE PRESENTATION OF IDEAS AND STATISTICAL RESULTS

In addition to statistical software, computer users have access to many other powerful software products. These other products should be used advantageously in the presentation of ideas and statistical results. Output from statistical software can be exported to word processors and Lotus-style worksheets and vice versa. Graphical presentation can be improved by using products such as PowerPoint and Harvard Graphics to better communicate results and conclusions.

Much of the mathematical basis for sophisticated statistical routines is pushed into the background and captured within the statistical software. Thus, while the science of statistics relies heavily on mathematical principles, the art of interpreting and using statistical results by the practitioner draws on many disciplines. Language makes the words work to convey the essence of the meaning hidden in the data. For example, many advertising campaigns rely on data analysis that points to the superiority of a product; however, the sterile presentation of the analysis results convinces few to purchase the product. Thus, the effective user of analysis results relies on insights of the behavioral, cultural, political, and sociological characteristics that shape both the data and its interpretation.

The graphics used in the data analysis process tends to be informal while that used to persuade or sell tends to be more formal or dressed up. Polished graphical displays appear daily in newspapers, magazines, company annual reports, and sales presentations. In these publications the basic textbook statistics you learn is used to persuade others to accept a view or to sell an idea or product. Often a series of graphs is used to emphasize "before and after" information. Some computer software can combine a series of graphics to form animations. These are movielike and give a visual account of the data.

In presenting you ideas and results, keep in mind your audience and your message. Construct the information in a manner that meets your needs and your audience's needs and that conforms to ethical and moral standards.

CHAPTER 2

Exploring the Features of a Single Variable

- Learn to explore data like a detective does
- Describe data using stem-and-leaf diagrams, boxplots, histograms, plots, polygons, and pie charts
- Compute exploratory summary statistics
- Distinguish between random and nonrandom data
- Understand that a sample is part of a population

PRELUDE

Exploratory data analysis is more an approach to discovery than a collection of methods. This chapter concentrates on a few basic methods that will be used to help develop this approach. In this chapter we focus on a single variable; for example, the daily retail sales of eggs. What you will learn about a single variable will form a foundation for the study of many variables. In this chapter you will learn to build a few simple but effective data displays, such as stem-and-leaf diagrams, boxplots, and histograms.

The goal of this chapter is to help you understand the data by means of a divide-and-conquer strategy. On one hand, you will see the main features of a data set through a statistic such as the median, which is a typical data value. On the other hand, outlying data points will draw your attention to the unusual features of a data set. Both the main and the unusual features of the data help build a more comprehensive understanding of the numbers a manager might have to consider in preparing to make a managerial decision. ◇

It was love at first sight.

The first time Yossarian saw the chaplain he fell madly in love with him.

Yossarian was in the hospital with a pain in his liver that fell just short of being jaundice. The doctors were puzzled by the fact that it wasn't quite jaundice. If it became jaundice they could treat it. If it didn't become jaundice and went away they could discharge him. But this just short of jaundice all the time confused them.[1]

THE DATA EXPLORATION MENTALITY

In exploratory work we look for clues. Like detectives, we seek to uncover "who done it." In the above quotation, for example, the doctors seek to uncover the source of Yossarian's pain. General features of the data are sought out, just as the doctors might characterize the general features of jaundice and Yossarian's condition. Unusual features of the data are exposed and scrutinized, like the doctors puzzling over a pain just short of being jaundice. Often, it is just as puzzling for an executive to ponder the behavior of sales figures in preparing to make an important marketing or financing decision.

During this scrutinizing process, we might snoop for variables that lurk behind the scenes and then expose them. Yossarian, for example, was faking the pain because he did not want to fly combat missions anymore. The executive might look behind a recent growth spurt in sales and see that it was due to a one-time special promotional effort rather than a lasting new trend in sales.

Sometimes the initial set of observations answers few questions. When the initial observations provide only meager explanatory clues, there might be a need for better planning and additional data collection. New data can create fresh views and different perspectives. When data send ambiguous messages, it is acceptable to try to clear up the confusion by using unorthodox and unplanned methods. The exploratory attitude frees you from the confines of a predetermined set of tools. Flexibility and open-mindedness are the watchwords for the explorer.

Although the exploratory attitude is the essential ingredient, there are a number of helpful exploratory tools. In this chapter, you will learn about *stem-and-leaf diagrams,* which, broadly speaking, summarize the main features of the data and expose the unusual. You will also learn about similar displays such as *histograms.* Another helpful exploratory tool is the *boxplot,* which summarizes stem-and-leaf displays. Boxplots are easy to look at and do some things better than stem-and-leaf displays; for example, several boxplots reveal patterns. They focus attention on both the main and the unusual features of a data set.

Summary statistics, such as a *median,* are obtained easily from stem-and-leaf diagrams. Usually some summary statistics are displayed on a boxplot, making it rich in information about the data set. Medians locate the focal points of the main features. A summary value, such as a median, subtracted from an individual data value produces a **residual.** Residuals magnify the unusual and help us spot outlying data points. Example 1 illustrates the way different theories develop from the interplay between the main and the unusual features of what is observed.

EXAMPLE 1

THE GREAT SIBERIAN METEOR[2]

Problem Statement   What smashed into the earth on the morning of June 30, 1908?

Problem Solution   The flash of light was seen 400 miles away. From the nearest village there were reports of a huge fireball; one farmer said that his shirt was nearly burned off his back. Yet puzzled investigators found no hole. A circular pattern of devastation extended 50 miles across; nearly every tree was uprooted or laid flat, pointing away from the epicenter. In addition to these main features, it seemed unusual that many trees were standing upright near the epicenter. Many thought that this ruckus was caused by a meteor.

The absence of a huge hole or crater cast doubt on the meteor theory. Competing theories emerged. An astronomer said that it was probably a comet, a loose conglomeration of dust and ice that vaporized before it touched the treetops. Two American physicists proposed that it was a black hole as small as an atom with the mass of a large asteroid. A black hole would shoot right through the earth and, perhaps, create a massive geyser in the ocean on the other side of the earth. It was suggested that additional data might be sought through the inspection of maritime records; hopefully, the new data might show an outlandish oceanic disturbance that morning, on the other side of the earth, where the black hole would emerge. Other physicists theorized that a piece of antimatter might have hit a piece of matter in the air above the devastated area of Siberian real estate.

Still others believed that the so-called meteor was really a nuclear explosion resulting from the malfunction of an extraterrestrial spaceship engine.

Problem Discussion   This example relates to what you will learn in this chapter in various ways. For example, the main and unusual features of the devastation from the "Siberian meteor" stimulated thinking and produced different theories. As you observe numerical data, you will learn how to describe and summarize it with stem-and-leaf diagrams, boxplots, histograms, and other statistical tools that accentuate the main and unusual features of data sets. This descriptive view of data sets stimulates thoughts and generates theories about the phenomena being studied.

An Example in a Management Context

When managers have problems to solve, such as the quality control problem in Example 2, they need to examine data and entertain a wide range of theories during their journey from the symptoms of the problem to the solution. The investigation of competing theories usually involves planning, data collection, data analysis, and reporting the results.

EXAMPLE 2

THE GREAT QUALITY CONTROL PROBLEM

J. M. Juran, a quality control expert, has developed an approach for managing quality control problems. The discussion that follows incorporates some of his views.[3]

Problem Statement   The so-called "Great Quality Control Problem" came to light in the United States in 1989. Far too many companies produced products and parts that didn't work properly. Poor production quality resulted in too much scrap. Some companies that collected data on scrap found that as much as 20% to 30% of the work effort was on rework, fixing someone else's mistakes. Juran said that a single factory was like two factories, one produced good products and the second produced scrap. As a result of the high cost of poor quality, improvement in product quality has begun to receive the managerial attention needed for American firms to compete in the global marketplace.

Problem Solution   In the typical factory, the number of defective units produced is monitored, plotted on a graph over time. This time series plot displays the health of the production process. Often the number of defective units is converted to percent defective; in a particular plant, let's say that the percent defective is typically 10%. Percent defective does not always hold steady at exactly 10%; it varies around 10%. Suppose 99% of the time percent defective is between 8% and 12%, $10 \pm 2\%$ 99% of the time. Wisely, Juran warned us that this 10% level of defectives can be viewed as acceptable when breakthrough reductions in percent defective is achieved.

Next, suppose the percent defective suddenly jumps to an unacceptable level, say, 18% defective. This jump sets off alarms because management recognizes this level as unusually high; percent defective has gone far beyond the normal region. This is a symptom that something is wrong; to recognize that there is something wrong, management must understand the numbers, both percent defective and the related costs. The symptom, 18% defective, triggers management to search for a cause and then a remedy.

When there is a jump to an unusually high percentage of defectives, the problem is not always simple to solve. Complex problems require careful management organization and planning in preparation for the journey from symptom to remedy.

First, a problem to be solved is identified as a project, and management assembles a project team. After the project team lists the symptom or symptoms, segregating the important from the trivial it tries to obtain an exhaustive list of theories about what is causing the problem. Sorting through and testing the alternative theories is difficult and time consuming. Theory testing requires designing a plan for data collection and analysis. Next, the data must be collected and analyzed. Finally, when a solution to the problem is found, the results of the study must be summarized and presented and a remedy implemented.

Statistical Tools Help Solve Management Problems

Elementary data analysis tools and ideas are presented in this chapter to help you solve problems. These are universal tools and ideas that provide the understanding managers need to conceptualize and solve many problems. More sophisticated but related tools are discussed in other chapters.

The descriptive tools discussed in this chapter tend to work well in a wide variety of situations. As a result, they might be used by an executive and a worker on the shop floor. They are useful because they quickly help you make sense of a data set. Sometimes they make a more detailed analysis unnecessary.

THE STEM-AND-LEAF DIAGRAM

A good way to take a first look at a data set and get a feel for a variable's numerical values is to construct a **stem-and-leaf diagram.** A stem-and-leaf diagram is a descriptive display of data values; it organizes numbers by ordering them and by grouping them into classes to show how the numbers are distributed across the classes. A stem-and-leaf diagram is a good tool for a rough-and-ready look at a batch of data values.

EXAMPLE 3

A STEM-AND-LEAF DIAGRAM OF EGG'S EGG SALES

Problem Statement   Egg, the eggman, has been in the egg business for several years. Egg is a young, prosperous businessman. Everyone in town seems to know him. People smile when they see Egg. They are always asking, "How do you do it, Egg? What is your secret to success?"

Problem Solution   Egg's response is that he keeps a close watch on sales like any smart businessman. Using recent sales figures, a pencil, and a piece of paper, Egg showed his friend, Molly, how to construct a stem-and-leaf diagram. Molly owns the bakery and is interested in ways to display sales data. Egg had the following, unorganized sales figures scribbled on a piece of paper:

50, 95, 25, 23, 48, 18, 33, 43, 15, 28, 26, 34, 59

Each value is the number of dozens of eggs sold on a particular day. Thirteen days of sales is a day short of two weeks because Egg had shut down operations for a day to go skiing. This set of values was chosen to illustrate construction features of a stem-and-leaf diagram.

From the initial crude list of values, the data are organized as shown in Exhibit 1. From left to right in the exhibit, the numbers are sorted into convenient classes, frequency counts (the number of values in each class) are recorded for each class, and a stem-and-leaf diagram is shown on the far right.

EXHIBIT 1 The Organization of Egg's Sales Data

	Data Sorted into Classes	Frequency Count	Stem-and-Leaf Display	
Nineties	95	1	9	5
Eighties	—	0	8	
Seventies	—	0	7	
Sixties	—	0	6	
Fifties	59, 50	2	5	0, 9
Forties	48, 43	2	4	3, 8
Thirties	33, 34	2	3	3, 4
Twenties	23, 28, 25, 26	4	2	3, 5, 6, 8
Teens	15, 18	2	1	5, 8

Structural Details of a Stem-and-Leaf Diagram

The stem-and-leaf display shows all the original data values in a simple, compact way. In Exhibit 1, the stem-and-leaf display has leading digits of each class to the left of a vertical line. These leading digits form the **stems.** To the right of the vertical line are the trailing digits of the data values in each class, separated by commas. These trailing digits are the **leaves.** The stem-and-leaf display has a number of stems corresponding to the classes, and the leaves correspond to the data values within each class. The interested reader should consult John Tukey's definitive book on exploratory data analysis for variations and more details.[4]

Construction Steps for a Stem-and-Leaf Diagram   The steps in constructing a stem-and-leaf diagram are Step (1) pick a number of classes; Step (2) construct an initial stem-and-leaf, without attempting to order the leaves (digits) within each stem (simply, get the numbers into classes); and Step (3) reconstruct the stem-and-leaf diagram, but arrange the leaves on each stem in order of increasing magnitude.

Step (1):   Here the appropriate classes are formed by the tens digits of the data values; they form the stems. Writing down the stems for a stem-and-leaf diagram is the first step, as shown in Exhibit 2.

EXHIBIT 2 Step (1): Writing Down the Stems

Nineties	9	
Eighties	8	
Seventies	7	
Sixties	6	
Fifties	5	
Forties	4	
Thirties	3	
Twenties	2	
Teens	1	

In general, two-digit numbers are a luxury. When there are more than two digits, you might round the numbers or make adjustments such as using two- or three-digit leaves. Some ideas become clear in the examples that follow.

Feel free to personalize the exploratory methods. View what is presented as a rough starting point, and then tailor these methods to suit the situation.

Step (2): An initial stem-and-leaf display is constructed without attempting to order the leaves on each stem. Record the leaves according to the natural sequence in which the data values were observed. Whereas the stems are formed by the leading digits of the data values, the leaves are formed by the trailing digits. See Exhibit 3. Sometimes the leaves are separated by commas.

EXHIBIT 3 Step (2): Stems with Unordered Leaves

```
9 | 5
8 |
7 |
6 |
5 | 9, 0
4 | 8, 3
3 | 3, 4
2 | 3, 8, 5, 6
1 | 5, 8
```

Step (3): Next the leaves on each stem are arranged in order of increasing magnitude.

Some leaves may not require re-arrangement if they are already ordered naturally. In larger data sets, however, this is unusual. You can see that the leaves on the stems for fifties, forties, and twenties are ordered in Exhibit 4, but they were not ordered initially in Exhibit 3.

EXHIBIT 4 Step (3): Stems with Ordered Leaves (completed display)

```
9 | 5
8 |
7 |
6 |
5 | 0, 9
4 | 3, 8
3 | 3, 4
2 | 3, 5, 6, 8
1 | 5, 8
```

STATISTICAL HIGHLIGHTS

To construct a stem-and-leaf diagram, pick the classes and form the stems, build an initial display without regard for the order of the leaves on each stem, and order the leaves on each stem by building a new and final display.

GETTING HELP FROM THE COMPUTER

Personal computers and statistical software are tremendously helpful in the data analysis process. An example of this software is MINITAB statistical software, which is used worldwide. MINITAB is a registered trademark of Minitab Inc. Because of MINITAB's functionality and Minitab Inc.'s author assistance program, the software is used throughout this book.

Using the Minitab Statistical Package

Although it is recommended that some exploratory work be done by hand for small data sets, modern computer packages for data analysis, such as MINITAB, include exploratory tools. A MINITAB-produced stem-and-leaf diagram is shown in the next example. The MINITAB commands needed to produce this result, along with commentary, appear in the second Appendix; likewise, MINITAB commands for most examples in this text appear in chapter appendixes. If you have access to the MINITAB statistical package, execute the command sequences shown in the appendixes for each example.

EXAMPLE 4

A STEM-AND-LEAF DIAGRAM OF EGG SALES DATA USING MINITAB

Problem Statement   Because it is difficult to analyze large data sets by hand, some experience in obtaining computer-produced stem-and-leaf diagrams is essential. Use MINITAB to duplicate the stem-and-leaf diagram constructed by hand earlier.

Problem Solution   The MINITAB-produced stem-and-leaf diagram is:

```
STEM-AND-LEAF DISPLAY OF SALES
  LEAF DIGIT UNIT =   1.0000

1   58     REPRESENTS 15 AND 18
2   3568   REPRESENTS 23, 25, 26, AND 28

    Depths         Stem-and-Leaf
      2              1| 58
      6              2| 3568
     (2)             3| 34
      5              4| 38
      3              5| 09
      1              6|
      1              7|
      1              8|
      1              9| 5
```

Problem Discussion   To understand the MINITAB printout, some items need to be explained because MINITAB's output format is not exactly the same as that used in constructing a stem-and-leaf diagram by hand. MINITAB flips the diagram, putting small data values at the top and large values at the bottom. As you read from the top to the bottom of the diagram, data values increase in magnitude.

MINITAB prints a column labeled depths that contains the values 2 6 (2) 5 1 1 1 1. These depth values are cumulative counts of the leaves down to the stem marked (2) or up to the stem marked (2). The (2) in the third position down the depth column is the leaf count on the stem that contains the *median* (the middle data value—33 here—with 50% of the remaining values above and 50% below). If the median had fallen between two stems, the (2) would not have been printed. MINITAB's depth column is particularly useful when there are many observations because summary values can be located quickly.

A Histogram

Like a stem-and-leaf diagram, a **histogram** is a descriptive display of data values; however, once the numbers are grouped into classes, symbols replace the numbers (leaves) to show the distribution across the classes. In MINITAB, asterisks replace the leaves.

EXAMPLE 5

A HISTOGRAM FOR EGG SALES DATA

Problem Statement   Construct a histogram for the egg sales data. Group the data into classes and pick class widths that result in a histogram that resembles the stem-and-leaf diagram in Example 4.

Problem Solution   Classes of width 10 replace stems; the class width is specified in the MINITAB command. These classes start at 10 and run through the 90s; class midpoints are at 15, 25, 35, . . . , 95. The count of the number of data values in a class is equal to the number of asterisks shown for that class; in effect, the stars replace the leaves of the stem-and-leaf diagram.

Histogram of dozens of eggs sold, (C1), over a 13-day period. N = 13 (total number of observations).

```
Midpoint    Count

   15.0        2       **
   25.0        4       ****
   35.0        2       **
   45.0        2       **
   55.0        2       **
   65.0        0
   75.0        0
   85.0        0
   95.0        1        *
```

What to Look for in Stem-and-Leaf Diagrams and Histograms

Both stem-and-leaf diagrams and histograms show (1) the range of numerical values from the smallest to the largest data value; (2) how the data are distributed across classes, including where the data are concentrated; (3) whether the distribution of data is nonsymmetrical, tailing off more on one side than the other, or symmetrical; and (4) gaps in the data, single stray values, or clusters of strays. Because these features of the data are influenced by the number and size of the classes, we will discuss this issue next.

More Formal Grouping of Data into Classes

For the exploratory analysis of small data sets, we can be informal and group data into, say, five to twenty classes. In the previous example, there were nine classes—teens, twenties, . . . , nineties. As data sets increase in size, the informal stem-and-leaf diagram tends to be replaced by particular types of histograms and other displays; furthermore, formal terminology is introduced to deal with class groupings of data in more detail.

Statistical packages automatically choose class intervals and midpoints. The usual approach is to simply say, "Show me the computer-produced displays with intervals, midpoints, and so forth selected by the computer." If the computer-software-based decisions don't suit you, override them with decisions of your own regarding class size, number, midpoints, starting points, and so forth. In MINITAB, this is accomplished with SUBCOMMANDS.

For the egg sales data, the software selected nine classes. The number of classes is arbitrary because it depends on the width of the class interval. If we choose a class interval of width ten, then to span the data the approximate number of classes needed is:

(maximum value − minimum value)/class interval width
(95   −   15   )/   10 = 8

Eight is the approximate number of classes needed. MINITAB added a half a class on each end, beginning at 10 and ending at 100; this yielded $8 + 1 = 9$ classes.

All the classes and midpoints are shown in Exhibit 5. As you can see, there are nine classes—(starting point) 10 to 20 (not including 20), 20 to 30, 30 to 40, . . . , 90 to 100. The class midpoints are 15, 25, . . . , 95; the midpoints have a half a class interval on each side.

The midpoints can be used as typical data values for the class group: think of two repetitions of the first class midpoint, 15 and 15 (two 15s), as representative of the two actual values in the first class, 15 and 18; four 25s as representative of the four actual values in the second class, 23, 25, 26 and 28, and so forth.

EXHIBIT 5 Frequency Counts and Relative Frequencies

Class Intervals	Class Midpoints	Frequency Counts	Relative Frequencies
10 to 20	15.0	2 **	2/13
20 to 30	25.0 (mode)	4 ****	4/13
30 to 40	35.0	2 **	2/13
40 to 50	45.0	2 **	2/13
50 to 60	55.0	2 **	2/13
60 to 70	65.0	0	0/13
70 to 80	75.0	0	0/13
80 to 90	85.0	0	0/13
90 to 100	95.0	1 *	1/13
TOTALS		13	13/13 = 1

Frequencies and Relative Frequencies for the Classes

A **frequency count** is the number of data values in a class, represented by asterisks in Exhibit 5. The **relative frequency** equals the ratio (frequency count/total frequency count). For the class intervals, frequency counts and relative frequencies are computed and listed in Exhibit 5.

When the total frequency count exceeds 100, stem-and-leaf diagrams become cumbersome. Therefore, when the data set is large, it is recommended that you explore small subsets of the large data set or take advantage of the grouping nature of histograms. This will be discussed in more detail later in the chapter.

The Mode

For **grouped data,** the **mode** is the midpoint of the class interval with the largest frequency count; for the egg sales data shown in Exhibit 5, the mode is 25 for the 20 to 30 class interval with a frequency count of 4. When half of the remaining frequency counts are above the modal class and half below, the mode represents the middle, otherwise the mode simply identifies the class interval with the most observations.

For **ungrouped data,** the mode is the data value that appears most often. You can think of this as a situation where the class intervals have shrunk to the point where each interval contains, at most, a data value and clones of that data value. For example, if you roll a die seven times and get the following faces that have been ordered

1, 1, 2, 3, 3, 3, 5,

the mode is 3 because it appears most often.

A Percentile

A **percentile** is 100 times the proportion of the data values less than or equal to a specific value. For example, using the data given above, we place the data in ascending order and write an index below each data value.

Data values   1,   1,   2,   3,   3,   3,   5,
Index i =   1   2   3   4   5   6   7(n)

A percentile is simply i/n times 100; for example, $\frac{3}{7}$ or 43% of the data values are equal to two or less; $\frac{6}{7}$ or 86% of the data values are equal to three or less. When data values repeat themselves, use the largest index associated with the repeats.

COMPUTING SUMMARY STATISTICS BY HAND

After data is organized and displayed with a stem-and-leaf diagram, a condensed summary of the variable being studied can be expressed by a few numbers.

Medians, Quartiles (Hinges), and Extremes

To summarize sales data, for example, a number representing the typical sales level tells us the location of the center (middle) of the stem-and-leaf diagram. Half the time sales are above the middle and half the time sales are below; this middle value is called the **median.** In our example, the typical sales level is 33 dozen eggs per day, the median. Median sales help us answer queries about how sales are behaving.

A **typical data value** is quite useful. If egg sales are typically 33 dozen eggs per day, for ten typical days total unit sales can be estimated easily, $10 \times 33 = 330$ dozen. With estimates like this, managers can make projections of items on financial statements such as total dollar sales and total costs.

Median sales, however, do not tell us anything about the highs and the lows. When a banker asks probing questions, it might be necessary to tell her the best and the worst sales figures; the difference between the **extreme high** and the **extreme low** tells her the **range** in sales. The larger the range, the more **variability** in the data. But the range between the best and the worst is an inflated measure of the variability. The best and the worst consist of only two observations.

A more representative way to characterize the variation in sales is desirable. For example, if we find a sales level such that a quarter of the time sales are above this level, we can call this number an **upper quartile.** If we find a sales level such that a quarter of the time sales are below this number, we can call this a **lower quartile.** One-half or 50% of the data values lie between the upper and lower quartiles. The larger the **quartile spread,** the distance between the quartiles, the more the variability in the data.

The quartiles are easy to find. Because the median splits the stem-and-leaf diagram in half, with half the data values above and below the median, the quartiles simply split the upper and lower halves of the stem-and-leaf diagram.

What we just described is like getting four quarters for a dollar. The dollar represents 100% of the data points on a stem-and-leaf diagram. The first quartile (also percentile) marks the lower 25% of the data values with 75% above. The median has 50% of the data above and below. The upper quartile has 25% of the data values above it and 75% below. Some authors refer to quartiles as **hinges;** the terms are interchangeable.

It is not practical to remember or to always show the whole stem-and-leaf diagram; therefore, summary values, at the extremes and at the 25%, 50%, and 75% points, characterize the data's general disposition. Summary values are few in number, making them excellent for communication purposes and easy to remember.

The sales figures from our example stem-and-leaf diagram are plotted on an elementary graph in Exhibit 6. A plot is a convenient structure for locating summary values visually. Exhibit 6 shows the commonly used summary values—the extreme points, the hinges (quartiles), and the median (which is in the middle). Usually when working with a larger sample of data points, the

EXHIBIT 6 Summary Values—Extremes, Hinges, and the Median Shown Graphically on a Plot

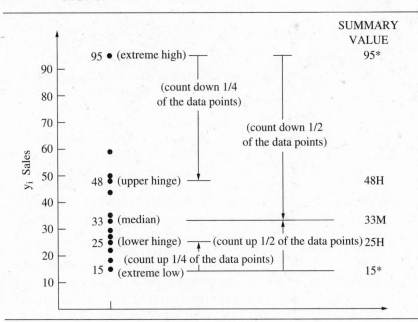

graph becomes too cluttered; then we work directly with the stem-and-leaf diagram. Here the graphics make the visual location of the summary statistics easy.

Depth Definitions for Locating Summary Statistics

Depth   The term **depth** is a count of data points to determine the location of a summary value. Counting from the top of Exhibit 7, we find that the highest sales figure or the upper extreme has a depth of one. If we continue to count from the top to the bottom extreme, the lowest sales figure, the lower extreme is at depth n = 13, the total number of observations. You can begin counting from the top or from the bottom of the plot of a stem-and-leaf diagram. As a result, depth is measured as a count from a reference point at the top or bottom of a stem-and-leaf diagram.

Definition 1—Extreme Depth   Extreme depth locates the maximum and minimum data values; therefore, for ordered data values the first and last data values are the extremes. Depth of an extreme is 1 or n (where n is the total number of observations). In Exhibit 7, the depth will be 1 at the top when counting down and n = 13 at the bottom. When counting up, the depth will be 1 at the bottom and n = 13 at the top.

EXHIBIT 7 Summary Values and Their Depths, Extremes, Hinges, and Medians

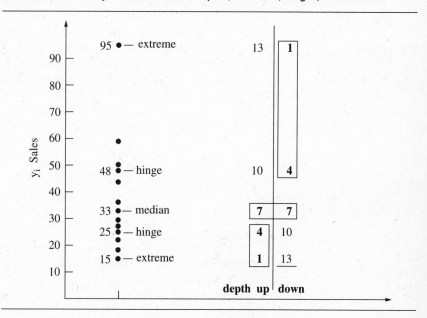

Definition 2—Median Depth   Median depth locates the middle data value of an ordered data set when the number of observations (n) is an **odd number.** When n is an **even number,** the median depth falls between two data values, which are averaged to obtain the median value. The *d*epth, d, of the *M*edian, M, is written d(M), notationally, and

$$depth\ (Median) = d(M)$$

$$= \frac{n + 1}{2} = \frac{total\ \#\ of\ observations\ plus\ 1}{2}$$

EXAMPLE 6

USING DEPTH TO LOCATE THE MEDIAN

Problem Statement   Compute the depth of the median and locate the median of the 13 observations in Exhibit 7.

Problem Solution

$$depth(Median) = d(M) = \frac{13 + 1}{2} = 7$$

Thus, the location of this median is at depth 7 in the plot or on the stem-and-leaf diagram. The value of the median is 33. Exhibit 7 shows the depth and the corresponding median located by counting up or counting down.

Definition 3—Hinge Depth   Because the hinge splits each half of the stem-and-leaf diagram to form quarters, the hinge depth is computed from the median depth, d(M). In the notation, where a star or asterisk is used to indicate that rounding must be done, let d* (M) equal (d(M) with any fraction dropped); then the *d*epth, d, of the *H*inge, H, is written d(H).

$$depth(Hinge) = d(H) = \frac{d*\ (M) + 1}{2}$$

If the hinge depth falls between two data values, the two data values are averaged to obtain the hinge value.

EXAMPLE 7

LOCATING THE HINGES (QUARTILES)

Problem Statement   Compute the depth of the hinges and locate the hinges (quartiles) of the 13 observations in Exhibit 7.

Problem Solution

$$depth(Hinge) = d(H) = \frac{d*\ (M) + 1}{2} = \frac{7 + 1}{2} = 4$$

The location of the hinges is at depth 4 as shown on both Exhibits 6 and 7. Exhibit 7 shows depth counted up from the bottom or down from the top. The value of the upper hinge is 48 and the value of the lower hinge is 25.

Problem Discussion   In this example, there was no fraction to be dropped because d(M) = 7 hence d(M) = d∗ (M). If d(M) were equal to some other number with a fraction, say, 7.50, then d(M) would not equal d∗ (M). If d(M) = 7.50, then, with the fraction dropped, d∗ (M) = 7.

Definition 4—Other Letter-Value Depths   Medians and hinges have been identified by using the letters M and H. The letter values of the medians and the hinges in the example above were M = 33, H (upper) = 48, and H (lower) = 25. The median splits an ordered batch of data values in half, the hinge splits a half in half to get a quarter, an eighth splits a quarter in half, producing an eighth, and so on. Many new letter values are possible and could be defined by other letters, such as D, C, B, A, Z, Y, X, and W. These other letter values are not used frequently, so they are given little attention here. The formula to obtain the depths of other letter values is a generalization of

$$d(H) = \frac{d∗ (M) + 1}{2}, \text{ where}$$

$$d(\text{next letter value}) = \frac{d∗ (\text{previous letter value}) + 1}{2}$$

Again, the star or asterisk signals us to drop any fraction.

Locating Summary Statistics on a Stem-and-Leaf Diagram

Locating summary values at specific depths is easy in a plot of a small number of data values. For large numbers of data values, the plotted points tend to overlap; then it is advisable to use the stem-and-leaf diagram to locate summary values. Beginners should count carefully. The direction of increasing magnitudes on each stem is from left to right across the leaves. The direction of decreasing magnitudes on each stem is from right to left across the leaves. For practice, you may wish to look back at Exhibit 4 and find the median on the stem-and-leaf diagram by counting a depth of seven in from the top and from the bottom; then examine Exhibit 6, where the graphical display clearly orders the data points so there can be no confusion about the location of the median.

S T A T I S T I C A L   H I G H L I G H T S

The extremes are the top and bottom data values in a stem-and-leaf diagram. The hinges are one-quarter of the way up from the bottom and one-quarter of the way down from the top of the stem-and-leaf diagram. The median is halfway from the top or the bottom. Depth in from the top or the bottom marks the location of each of these summary values.

COMPUTER-PRODUCED SUMMARY STATISTICS

Often the first look at a data set involves constructing a stem-and-leaf diagram by hand without using the computer. Then computer can be used to speed up your investigation.

MINITAB Examples of Various Summary Values

Rather than determine summary values one at a time, MINITAB finds all the important summary values you need and presents them in a single table. The most frequently used summary values are the median, two hinges, and two extremes; these statistics comprise what is called a **five-number summary** of the data.

EXAMPLE 8

SUMMARY VALUES FOR THE EGG SALES DATA

Problem Statement   For the egg sales data, show an example of computer-produced letter values (medians, hinges, and so forth) from the MINITAB commands in Appendix 2.

Problem Solution   N = 13 (total observations).

LETTER	DEPTH	LOWER		UPPER
M	7		33 *(Median)*	
H	4	25		48 *(Hinges)*
	1	15 *(Extreme low)*		95 *(Extreme high)*

Problem Discussion   The output format is MINITAB's, and it is edited to show only depths, the median, hinges, and extremes. The median, two hinges, and two extremes comprise a five-number summary of the data; the standard format for the five-number summary positions the median above and between the hinges and extremes.

A PLOT OF DATA IN THE SEQUENCE OBSERVED

Stem-and-leaf diagrams, histograms, and summary values can help us understand a variable, such as sales, in terms of level (median), variability (difference between the hinges), and distribution. Another view of the level and variability is through a plot of the data in the sequence observed. When the data are observed over a time sequence, the plot is a **time series plot.** Sometimes a horizontal line at the level of the median, called a **center line (CL),** is added to the time series plot.

EXAMPLE 9

A PLOT OF SALES DATA VERSUS TIME

Problem Statement   For the egg sales data, construct a time series plot, connect the plotting points, and add a center line to the plot.

Problem Solution   Using the MINITAB command, TSPLOT, sales is plotted; the label C1 is a MINITAB data column label. The plotting point symbols are the integers, 1, 2, . . . , 9, for the first nine values. For the next four values, 10, 11, 12, 13, the second digits, 0, 1, 2, 3, are used as plotting point symbols. Lines are drawn on the plot to connect these plotting points, and a center line is added to the plot. Recall that median sales, the center line, is 33 dozen. Also notice that the next-to-last observation, 34, is above the median, but the scale compression masks this fact.

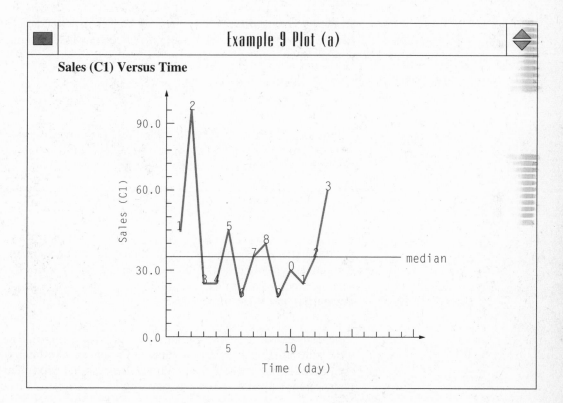

Example 9 Plot (a)

Sales (C1) Versus Time

CHECKING FOR RANDOMNESS IN THE DATA, VALIDATING SUMMARY STATISTICS

Stem-and-leaf displays, histograms, and summary values work best when the sequence of data values has no pattern. A series of data values without a pattern is said to be **random.**

Conversely, when there is a pattern to the data sequence, the series is **nonrandom.** Often a nonrandom series produces worthless or misleading stem-and-leaf displays, histograms, and summary values.

A plot of the data values in the sequence they were observed can be examined to see if there is an obvious pattern or not. Thus, visual inspection is an informal way to check for randomness and to validate summary statistics (valid when the data are random). Because some patterns are difficult to spot, the following approximate test for randomness is given.

An Approximate Test for Randomness

In the previous example on the time series plot, lines connecting adjacent data points trace the evolving data sequence and show up and down movements of the series. Up and down movements can be seen in better detail in a list of the data, where the letters U or D between two data values designate an up or a down.

$$50 \quad 95 \quad 25 \quad 23 \quad 48 \quad 18 \quad 33 \quad 43 \quad 15 \quad 28 \quad 26 \quad 34 \quad 59$$
$$U \quad D \quad D \quad U \quad D \quad U \quad U \quad D \quad U \quad D \quad U \quad U$$

A sequence of U's or D's (one or more) is called a **run;** a **runs count** of the runs up and down can be used in a rough test for randomness of the series. Here the runs count is nine as shown below.

$$U \quad DD \quad U \quad D \quad UU \quad D \quad U \quad D \quad UU$$
$$1 \quad 2 \quad 3 \quad 4 \quad 5 \quad 6 \quad 7 \quad 8 \quad 9$$

A Randomness Test Interval   A rough test for randomness is based on the theoretical behavior of the number of observed runs. The observed number of runs is either within or outside the following **test interval,** where N is the number of data values in the series.

$$(.6 \times N - 3) \quad \text{to} \quad (.75 \times N + 2.5)$$

Test Rule: If the observed total number of runs falls within the interval, we are confident that the series is random. Otherwise, conclude that the series is nonrandom.

EXAMPLE 10

TESTING THE EGG SALES DATA FOR RANDOMNESS

Problem Statement   Find a test interval for the nine runs in the egg sales data set (13 observations) and decide if the series is random or nonrandom. Would you conclude that the stem-and-leaf diagram, histogram, and summary statistics are valid?

Problem Solution   The number of observations, N, equals 13, and the test interval is from $[(.6 \times 13 - 3) = 4.8]$ to $[(.75 \times 13 + 2.5) = 12.25]$. This interval includes the observed runs count, which is nine. Conclude that the egg sales series is random and that the stem-and-leaf diagram, histogram, and summary statistics are valid.

Discussion of Randomness and Its Implications

A random series has no predictable pattern of change from one observation to the next. Egg's egg sales are random; each sales figure has a **deviation** from the median that is unpredictable within the bounds of the variation. Observations of past sales provide no clues about future sales behavior other than the typical sales level and the typical level of variability. As Roberts pointed out, no amount of study or pondering will reveal secrets about what the next value will be in a random sequence.[5] Therefore, the sequence of Egg's egg sales is said to be in a **state of statistical control** because of its randomness; a constant median and a constant level of variability is maintained. Without an upward or downward trend or other types of patterned movements, median sales will remain at a constant level.

If the future is like the recent past, a reasonable forecast of the typical sales level for a future day, say, day 14, is the median, 33 dozen. In this simple forecasting situation, the centerline of the time series plot is extended into the future. Of course, actual sales will deviate from the forecast. From an examination of past data, we learned that the typical deviation from median sales remained constant over a short period of time.

Fortunately for most organizations, sales patterns tend to be nonrandom, especially when they are viewed over longer time periods. As a result, some systematic components of sales patterns tend to be predictable. Predictable sales is like predictable weather; they give managers a basis for planning what to do next.

A Circumstance That Makes Our Previous Summary of Sales Misleading

When sales are nonrandom, they have some pattern over time. You will see that patterned data can produce misleading stem-and-leaf diagrams, histograms, and summary statistics.

EXAMPLE 11

WHAT IF SALES IS A NONRANDOM SERIES?

Problem Statement (a)   Suppose the sales figures had occurred in a different sequence; the new sequence is

Day	1	2	3	4	5	6	7	8	9	10	11	12	13
Sales	15	18	23	25	26	28	33	34	43	48	50	59	95

Does a time series plot of these data show a pattern? If so, what are the implications when interpreting a stem-and-leaf diagram, a histogram, and summary statistics?

Problem Solution (a)   The time series plot shows a nonrandom sales pattern trending upward to the right. Although the stem-and-leaf diagram, histogram, and summary statistics remain the same as before, they are useless and misleading because they don't expose the nonrandom pattern in the data.

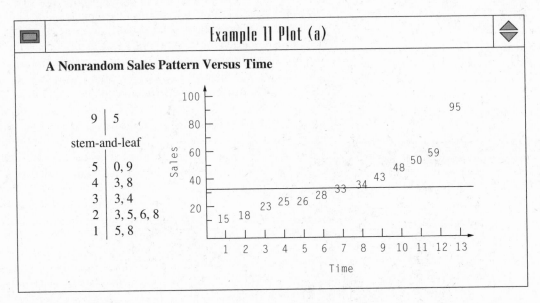

Example 11 Plot (a)

A Nonrandom Sales Pattern Versus Time

Problem Statement (b)   Although the nonrandomness is obvious and dramatic, perform a randomness test.

Problem Solution (b)   There is a total of one run, all ups (UUUUUUUUUUUU); the total number of runs falls outside the randomness test interval. The interval is:

$$(.6 \times N - 3) \quad \text{to} \quad (.75 \times N + 2.5)$$

$$(.6 \times 13 - 3) = 4.8 \quad \text{to} \quad (.75 \times 13 + 2.5) = 12.25$$

Conclude that this sales series is nonrandom.

Problem Discussion   Growing from a sales level of 15 dozen eggs, sales reach the median of 33 dozen on day 7 and finally reach a maximum of 95 dozen eggs on day 13. The stem-and-leaf diagram, shown on page 54, is exploded over time to form the time series plot that can be constructed by hand too; the digits are written directly on the plot as they were observed.

If sales continue to grow in the future as in the recent past, a sales forecast of 33 dozen (using the median) seems absurd. Previously, with a random series, a sales forecast based on the median, 33 dozen, was reasonable; however, using the median to forecast sales is likely to underestimate the future sales level if the growth trend continues into the future.

When Changes in a Nonrandom Series Are Random, Stem-and-Leaf Diagrams, Histograms, and Summary Values Are Valid for Changes

When the tools we know don't work on the data in a new situation, what should we do?

One alternative is to learn about new tools or create them. This alternative, however, is expensive. The efficient manager is going to resist an expensive retraining program; he or she may not have the time to wait for the discovery of new tools to fit a certain situation. A second and popular alternative is to see if there is any way to **transform** the data so that familiar statistical tools can be used.

In Example 12, adjacent data values are subtracted from one another to obtain **changes** or **differences.** Also, changes can be expressed as **percent changes,** the difference of adjacent values as a percentage of the first value. If we find that changes in sales are random, the median change in sales is a valid summary. Therefore, the median change in sales can help us forecast.

EXAMPLE 12

CHANGES IN THE NONRANDOM SALES SERIES

Problem Statement (a)   Recall that the original sequence of sales figures was random; therefore, median sales were a reasonable predictor of future sales. Next, to introduce some new ideas, we considered a particular nonrandom sequence, a trend of increasing sales. Here median sales would tend to underestimate future sales if the trend continued. Thus, the median is a misleading summary of a nonrandom series. The problem is to transform nonrandom sales into changes in sales; then use the familiar summary tools when the changes are random. First find changes in sales.

Problem Solution (a)   A change is a difference and is written as $y_i - y_{i-1}$; for example, the difference between the first two sales figures is $y_2 - y_{2-1} = y_2 - y_1 = 18 - 15 = 3$. The computation of changes transforms the original data. If changes are random, we can summarize the changes in sales with familiar statistical tools, stem-and-leaf diagrams, histograms, medians and so forth. Because the median of random changes is a valid summary statistic, it can be used in forecasting sales.

Changes in sales are calculated as follows and shown below: (1) list the sales sequence (C1); (2) lag sales one period by creating C2 (C2 is column C1 pushed down one row); and (3) subtract C2 from C1 getting C3, changes in sales.

Symbolically, let y_i represent a sales figure in column C1 and row i. Let y_{i-1} represent a sales figure in column C2, which is from column C1 and row $(i - 1)$; C2 is C1 lagged one period. Changes in sales C1 − C2 = C3 can be written as $y_i - y_{i-1}$; for example, in row two, $y_2 - y_{2-1} = y_2 - y_1 = 18 - 15 = 3$.

```
ROW   C1   C2   C3
 1    15    *    *         Asterisks or stars indicate no data values here;
 2    18   15    3         no data prior to row one.
 3    23   18    5
 4    25   23    2         NOTE: C2 is C1 lagged by one row
 5    26   25    1               C3 = C1 - C2
 6    28   26    2               C3 = changes in sales
 7    33   28    5
 8    34   33    1
 9    43   34    9
10    48   43    5
11    50   48    2
12    59   50    9
13    95   59   36
```

Problem Statement (b)   Plot both sales and changes in sales over time and comment on the pattern or lack thereof.

Problem Solution (b)   A time series plot of sales (C1) verifies the nonrandom or patterned behavior over time.

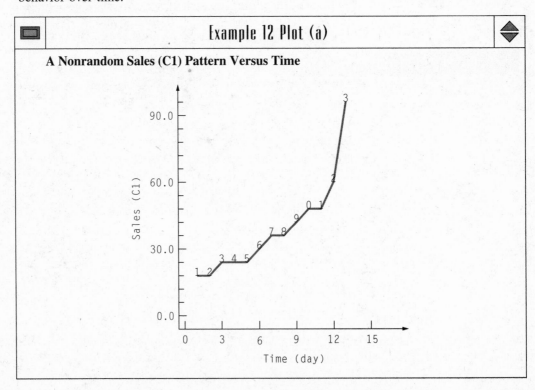

Example 12 Plot (a)

A Nonrandom Sales (C1) Pattern Versus Time

Below, changes in sales (C3) appear to be more nearly random compared to the earlier plot of sales. Excluding the one unusually large change of 36 dozen on day 13 the remaining changes in sales look random.

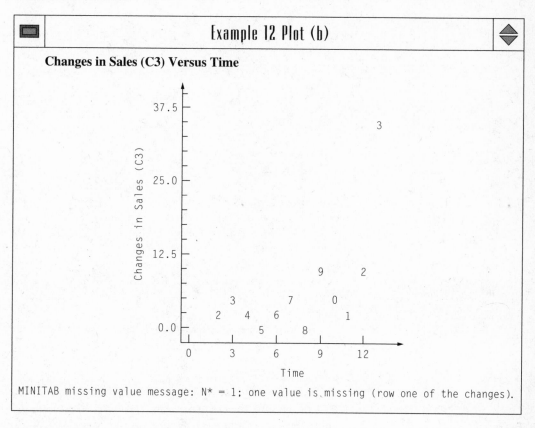

Example 12 Plot (b)

Changes in Sales (C3) Versus Time

MINITAB missing value message: N* = 1; one value is missing (row one of the changes).

Problem Statement (c)   Summarize changes in sales.

Problem Solution (c)   Excluding the one unusually large change of 36 dozen on day 13, the typical change in sales is nearly constant, with no dramatic patterns in the changes. The variability of the changes in sales is nearly constant; however, a small increase in variability occurs after day 7. Because of these facts, a rather simple summary is possible. Summary statistics for changes in sales, C3, are:

	DEPTH	LOWER	UPPER	SPREAD
N =	12			
M	6.5		4 (median)	
H	3.5	2	7	5 (hinge spread)
	1	1	36	35 (range)

The median of changes in sales is four dozen. Fifty percent of the time changes in sales are between 2 and 7 dozen; $7 - 2 = 5$ is the hinge spread, a measure of variability and uncertainty.

Using the median of 4 and column C3, you can count the runs above and below the median and show that changes in sales are random. Our summary statistics work well when the series is random.

```
Stem-and-leaf of C3        N = 12
Leaf Unit = 1.0

Depths    Stem-and-Leaf
   6      0|112223
   6      0|55599
   1      1|
   1      1|
   1      2|
   1      2|
   1      3|
   1      3|6
```

Some Thoughts on Forecasting Sales   How might we forecast future sales based on our summary of how past sales have changed? Watching sales grow over time from a low of 15 to a high of 95 is like going up a staircase consisting of random changes in step sizes. Think of the ground floor at a sales level of 15 and the first step at a sales level of 18; (18 − 15) is a change of +3. The second step is from 18 to 23; (23 − 18) is a change of +5. These changes, +3 +5 +2 +1 +2 +5 . . . . . , are listed in columns C3 shown above.

Because the series of changes in sales is random, the typical change, the median = 4, is a particularly useful summary. If on day 12 (sales = 59), we wish to predict sales on day 13, 59 plus the typical change of 4 yields a forecast of 59 + 4 = 63.

Twenty-five percent of the time the changes in sales were 2 or less and 25% of the time the changes were 7 or more. Therefore, in addition to using the typical change in sales to forecast, 59 + 4 = 63, we might express our uncertainty in the forecast by using 59 + 2 = 61 and 59 + 7 = 66 as approximate 50% bounds on forecasted sales.

Actual sales on day 13 turned out to be 95, far from what we predicted based on the trend analysis. Perhaps some factor outside the historical data set came into play. Maybe day 13 was the day before Easter and that would explain the jump in sales. Maybe 95 was a mistake in recording the data. Maybe there was a special, favorable story in a newspaper about newly discovered health benefits of eggs, and so on. It is very likely that management would investigate the circumstance surrounding the unusual jump in sales. The analysis, and especially the plots, helps us know and understand what is typical and what is atypical behavior in the sales pattern. The analysis raises questions, makes us think, and helps us better understand sales and the consequences of managerial action.

Suppose the unusually high sales figure of 95 on day 13 can be considered a one-time happening and that the historical trend is expected to continue. To forecast sales for day 14, we might ignore day 13 and start with sales on day 12 and add typical changes. So, a forecast of sales for day 14 is $59 + 4 + 4 = 67$. Note that this forecast came about because sales in this example is a nonrandom trending pattern; the nonrandomness led us to work with changes, which are random.

Our original summary of these same sales figures yielded median sales $= 33$; that median was a useful summary when sales were random over time and did not follow a trend. Had we not noticed the trend, our forecast of sales for day 14 would be 33 rather than 67. For these reasons, it is important that you check on the randomness of a series of observations before you go ahead and use summary statistics with reckless abandon.

Notice that the typical change in sales, 4, becomes a smaller percentage of sales as time goes on. For example, 4 divided by 15, sales on day 1, is 27%; 4 divided by 59, sales on day 12, is 7%. A manager should notice this and realize that a linear trend in sales does not paint a rosy picture. When the scales on plots are arithmetic, a linear trend means, for example, that sales are increasing at a decreasing rate.

We will not always be so lucky with business or economic data as we have been in this example. Sometimes both the original data series and changes in that series are nonrandom. Changes often show dramatic increases in variability. Under such circumstances, it will be necessary to rely on a more sophisticated analysis. Frequently we find it necessary to work with changes of logarithms of the time series variable.

EXAMPLE 13

YEARLY SALES, CUMMINS ENGINE COMPANY, A CASE STUDY

Problem Statement (a)   Illustrate the need to work with changes when examining sales of a large corporation. Extend the notion of changes to percent changes. Plot and interpret sales, changes, and percent changes.

Problem Solution (a)   Net sales in billions of dollars for the Cummins Engine Company are examined over a 14-year period.[6] The sales sequence in column C1 is lagged 1 year and placed in column C2. By subtracting and dividing whole columns, year-to-year changes in sales, $C3 = C1 - C2$, is divided by C2, where C2 is sales at the beginning of each year. Thus

$$\text{percent changes} = 100 \text{ times } \frac{C1 - C2}{C2}$$

produces the percent sales change per year, which is rounded for convenience in C5.

ROW	C1	C2	C3	C4	C5
1	0.80	*	*	*	*
2	0.76	0.80	-0.04	-5.00	-5
3	1.03	0.76	0.27	35.52	36
4	1.26	1.03	0.23	22.33	22
5	1.52	1.26	0.26	20.63	21
6	1.77	1.52	0.25	16.44	16
7	1.67	1.77	-0.10	-5.64	-6
8	1.96	1.67	0.29	17.36	17
9	1.59	1.96	-0.37	-18.87	-19
10	1.60	1.59	0.01	0.62	1
11	2.33	1.60	0.73	45.62	46
12	2.15	2.33	-0.18	-7.72	-8
13	2.30	2.15	0.15	6.97	7
14	2.77	2.30	0.47	20.43	20

A plot of sales (C1) is nonrandom and trending upward to the right.

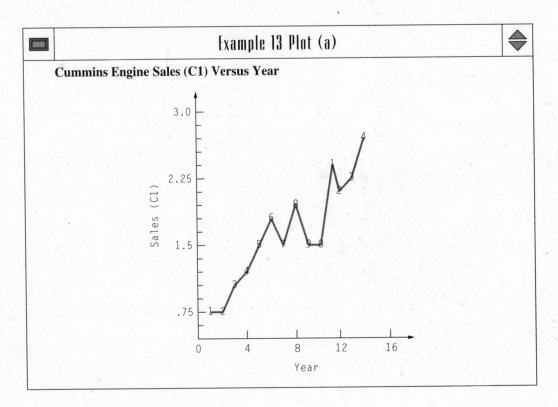

Example 13 Plot (a)

Cummins Engine Sales (C1) Versus Year

Changes in sales C3 are plotted over time. Computing changes removes the trend that was apparent in the previous plot.

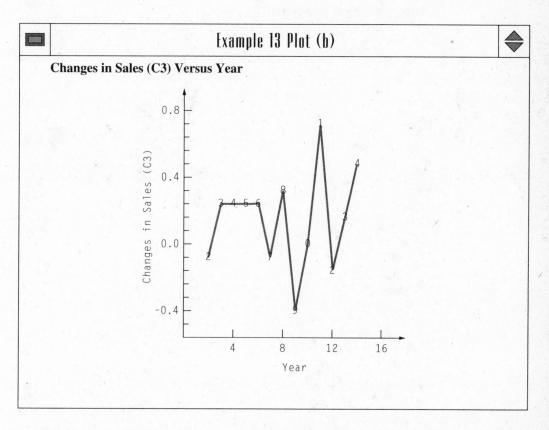

Example 13 Plot (b)

Changes in Sales (C3) Versus Year

Roughly, from the plot, you can see that the typical change in sales is about one-quarter of a billion dollars, that is, $250,000,000. Changes have a random appearance except for the variability increase over time; the variability increase suggests that a more sophisticated analysis should be considered. The minimum and maximum changes are −$370 and $730 million. For planning purposes, the executives would use these figures to begin to frame their thinking.

Percent changes in sales C4 are plotted over time. Roughly, the median percent change in sales is 16. Using 16, a runs count above and below the median (see rounded percents in C5 that are listed earlier), we can confirm our visual impression that this series is random. A runs test does not identify the variability increase.

Example 13 Plot (c)

Percent Changes in Sales (C4) Versus Year

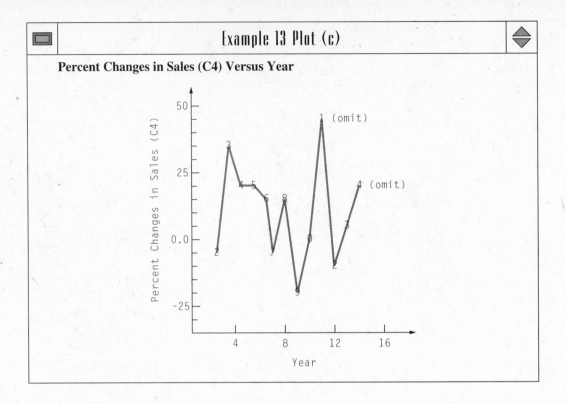

Problem Statement (b)   Connect what you see in the data to the management situation in which the company finds itself.

Problem Solution (b)   In the plot of percent changes, after excluding the two data points for years 11 and 14 (marked omit), the remaining plotting points tend to decrease with time. This suggests that Cummins Engine Company's sales have been increasing at a decreasing rate. Although sales have been increasing by a nearly constant amount of one-quarter of a billion a year, this amount is a decreasing proportion of total sales. Perhaps you would not be surprised to learn that the latter part of this time period was a bad time financially for Cummins. The management of Cummins should have foreseen problems, particularly if the economy softened. Management should have attempted to improve the sales growth rate through mergers, acquisitions, new products and so forth.

Problem Statement (c)   Summarize changes and percent changes in sales with a stem-and-leaf diagram, obtain medians, hinges, extremes, and measures of spread (variability).

Problem Solution (c)   The stem-and-leaf diagram of C5 (rounded percent changes in sales) is:

```
N=13, number of differences; there is one asterisk (N* = 1) indicating a missing
value because fourteen figures were differenced.

Leaf Unit = 1.0
     1    -1|8
     4    -0|755
     6     0|06
    (2)    1|67
     5     2|002
     2     3|5
     1     4|5
```

A summary of C3 is expressed as changes in sales in billions of dollars.

```
      DEPTH     LOWER      UPPER     SPREAD
N=    13
M    7.0              0.230
H    4.0    -0.040     0.270     0.310
      1     -0.370     0.730     1.100 (range)
```

A summary of C5 is expressed as rounded percent changes in sales.

```
      DEPTH     LOWER      UPPER     SPREAD
N=    13
M    7.0               16
H    4.0       -5         21        26
      1       -19         46        65
```

Problem Discussion   The summary information presented above gives managers a remarkably good view of percent changes in sales; this is like taking the pulse of the company. In addition to the summary statistics, the plots are absolutely necessary because the summary statistics alone do not adequately show the decreasing trend in the rate of growth in sales. The summary statistics alone might be somewhat misleading.

Although the changes and percent changes are random (using all the data points), one might encounter nonrandomness over a longer time span because of the relationship between sales and general economic activity.

Business organizations are designed and managed such that they not only survive in bad times but prosper in good times. They must quickly respond to the level and the variability of the percent change in sales. Our analysis provided an insightful view. The manager can see the firm's history of sales changes and then reflect on the strengths and weaknesses of how these situations were managed in the past.

The yearly data of Cummins Engine Company provides a longer-term perspective; therefore, it contrasts with the short-term view of Egg's daily egg sales. What is impressive is that the same core of analysis tools are effective in summarizing both situations.

If we had been working with ending year (or month) prices of a stock instead of sales, the percent change would be referred to as a return on the stock, excluding stock splits and dividends. Thus, this conversion of a change to a percent change becomes important to us in the study of other problems.

Other Companies During the Same Time Period

For comparative purposes, percent changes in sales over the same period is shown for two other companies, H. J. Heinz Company and General Electric Company.[7] Notice the blocks of time in which sales growth rates are low and high in variability; these subgroups of data points can be summarized separately. Periods of high variability present management with considerable uncertainty as to what will happen next. As a result, management will have to maintain inventory levels and production capabilities to cope with the circumstances.

EXAMPLE 14

PERCENT CHANGES IN SALES, H. J. HEINZ COMPANY

Problem Statement   Compute, plot, and interpret percent changes in sales for H. J. Heinz Company.

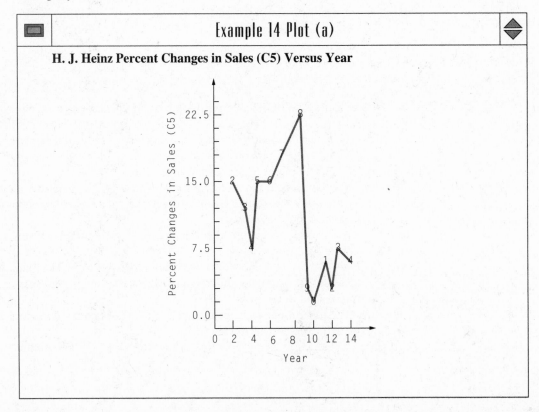

Problem Solution Notice two major clusters of data points, a high 15% growth rate in the early years and a 4% rate over the last six years.

EXAMPLE 15

PERCENT CHANGES IN SALES, GENERAL ELECTRIC COMPANY

Problem Statement Compute, plot, and interpret percent changes in sales for General Electric Company.

Problem Solution Note the stability in sales growth of about 12% in the early years; later growth rates tend to be lower with more volatility. The volatility makes the manager's job more difficult.

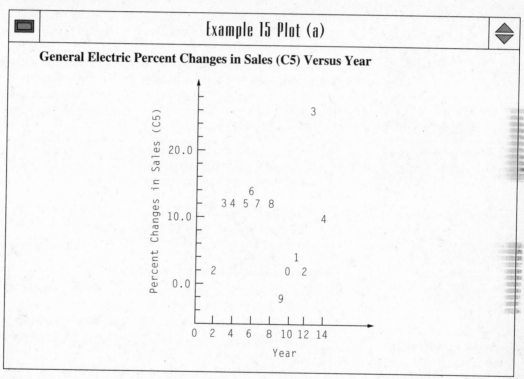

Example 15 Plot (a)

General Electric Percent Changes in Sales (C5) Versus Year

FOCUSING ON THE DATA'S MAIN AND UNUSUAL FEATURES WITH BOXPLOTS

A **boxplot** is an accessory to a stem-and-leaf diagram (see Exhibit 10). It consists of a rectangular box drawn to connect the hinges and to cover the middle 50% of the data values. A line in the box marks the location of the median. On each side of the box, two lines, called "whiskers," extend across the remaining 50% of the data values, when there are no unusual data points. When unusually large or small data points exist, they are identified as potential **outliers** and are not covered by the whiskers. Outliers are labeled to make them stand out and be investigated.

A boxplot's unique structure provides focus on both the main and the unusual features of the data. Boxplots, short for **box-and-whisker plots,** display both the bulk of the data and the observations standing apart from the bulk of the data. Typically, the construction of a stem-and-leaf diagram is followed by the construction of a boxplot.

Outliers, Unusual Features of the Data

Beckman and Cook stated that in the opinion of the investigator, observations standing apart from the bulk of the data have been called "outliers," "discordant observations," "rogue values," "contaminants," "surprising values," "mavericks," and "dirty data."[8] These unusual observations were of interest and documented as early as 1777.

The following scenario provides an example of what is meant by an outlier as a surprising data value standing apart from the bulk of the data. Imagine how much Mr. Hadlum was surprised about the circumstances surrounding Mrs. Hadlum's pregnancy. Barnett used this legal case of Hadlum vs. Hadlum as an example:[9]

> 349 days after Mr. Hadlum departed for military service abroad, Mrs. Hadlum gave birth; Mr. Hadlum judged the observation of 349 days to be discordant when compared with the average gestation time of 280 days and therefore petitioned for divorce. In this case, the issue is not whether the discordant observation should be discarded or downweighted in estimation, but is how to judge the weight of evidence against the hypothesis that the discrepant observation is a valid (albeit extreme) realization from the distribution of gestation times.

Boxplot Features and Construction

Exhibit 8 frames some construction features of a boxplot. The distance between the hinges is called the **box length.** The box length is the spread between the hinges, a measure of the variability in the data. The box length is also the distance between the quartiles, the **interquartile distance** or **interquartile range.**

The **outlier cutoffs** are one-and-a-half box lengths beyond the box ends. Outlier cutoffs mark outer boundaries; data values beyond these boundaries are marked as outliers and scheduled for further study.

The construction steps for Exhibit 8 and Exhibit 9 are:

Step (1):   A box is drawn from hinge to hinge.

Step (2):   Outlier cutoff marks are made at a distance of one-and-a-half box lengths beyond each hinge. These mark crude outlier cutoff locations; hardly any observations stray this far from the rest of the data unless they are unusual.

EXHIBIT 8 The Skeletal Framework for a Boxplot

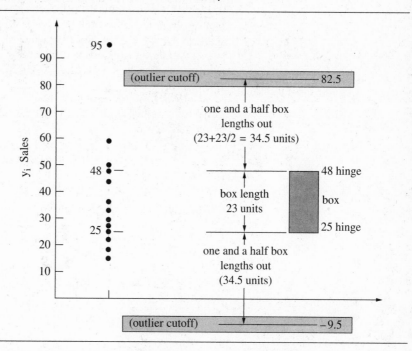

EXHIBIT 9 Finishing Touches to a Boxplot

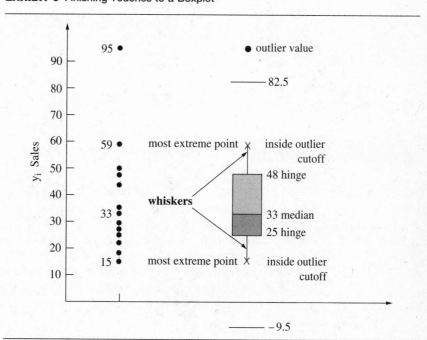

Step (3): "Whiskers" are the lines emerging from the top and the bottom of the box (see Exhibit 9). On each side of the box, a whisker extends to the *outermost data value* that is *on or inside* the outlier cutoff location. When there are a very large number of observations, the whiskers are likely to extend out to the outlier cutoff locations. For small samples, it is unlikely that the whiskers extend as far out as the outlier cutoffs.

Exhibit 9 shows a finished boxplot. The boxplot is on the right side of the graph. The data points to the left are not part of the boxplot; they are shown as reference only.

Exhibit 10 displays a stem-and-leaf diagram and a boxplot as they might appear in actual use, unencumbered with the graphics and descriptive material.

EXHIBIT 10 Stem-and-Leaf and Boxplot Unencumbered

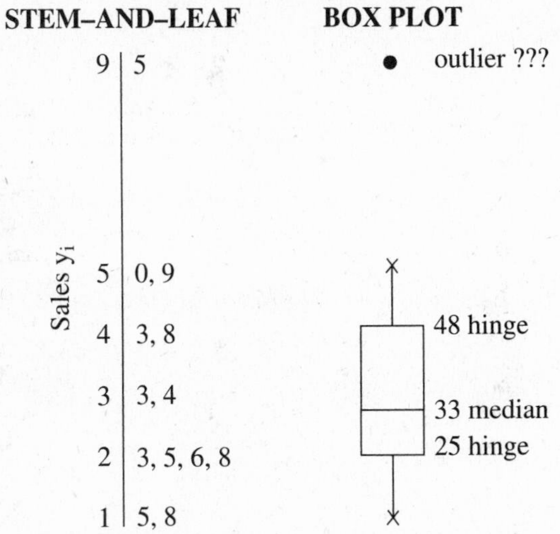

STEM–AND–LEAF	BOX PLOT
9 | 5	● outlier ???
5 | 0, 9	✗
4 | 3, 8	48 hinge
3 | 3, 4	33 median
2 | 3, 5, 6, 8	25 hinge
1 | 5, 8	✗

Sales y_i

EXAMPLE 16

MINITAB-PRODUCED BOXPLOT

Problem Statement   Construct a boxplot for the egg sales data using MINITAB.

Problem Solution   Compared to the boxplot exhibits you have seen, the computer-produced boxplot is flipped on its side, saving paper if printed.

On the scale below the boxplot, MINITAB labels the mark above the number 20, FIRST TICK, and goes on to print FIRST TICK AT 20. Also, spacing information is provided in the output by ONE HORIZONTAL SPACE = .20E + 01 = $.2 \times 10^1$ = 2. The horizontal

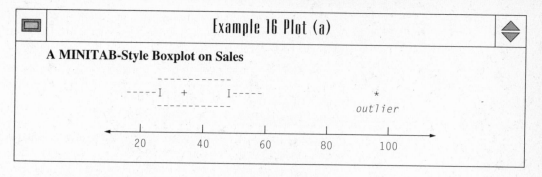

spacing and the first tick value are provided so that the axis underneath the boxplot can be labeled and read.

Discussion of the Boxplot Tool

The box covers about 50% of the data values; the whiskers extend over nearly all of the remaining 50% of the data values, roughly 25% on each side. The box and the whiskers focus our view on the bulk of the data.

Outlying data values are beyond the whiskers ends and beyond the outlier cutoffs. Outliers are labeled in some way to draw attention to them or to explain why, if possible, they are so unusually far from the rest of the data points. Try to understand the circumstances surrounding their origin. What conditions might have given rise to such unusual values? In this way, new insights and discoveries are made about the phenomenon being studied.

Although we are not always sure, we suspect that outliers don't belong to the batch of data for some reason. For example, Mrs. Hadlum's unusually long gestation time led Mr. Hadlum to believe that the child did not belong to him. Also, Egg might tell you that the unusually large sales figure in Exhibit 9 of 95 dozen eggs occurred on the last shopping day before Easter.

In addition to highlighting the outliers, the boxplot displays summary information about typical values, spread or variation, and the general disposition of the data values. The central tendency or level is captured by the median, which is marked on the box. The box length is a measure of the variation or spread in the distribution of the data.

If the median is in the middle of the box and the whiskers are about equal in length, the data (excluding outliers) are distributed *symmetrically*. **Symmetry** of the data distribution is a necessary characteristic for using the well-developed framework of classical statistics.

We prefer symmetrical distributions of data. When initial boxplots show **asymmetry,** data transformations are employed in an attempt to obtain symmetry. Common transformations include differences, square roots, logarithms, and reciprocals of the original data values. After the transformations, new stem-and-leaf diagrams and boxplots are constructed.

The data analyst might build many of these displays in the course of an investigation. It is common to modify the data set in a variety of ways such as trimming data values, working with subgroups of data, and making transformations. Once the data set is changed, stem-and-leaf diagrams and boxplots are reconstructed. New learning about the data set at hand might occur at any stage of the analysis.

> ### S T A T I S T I C A L   H I G H L I G H T S
>
> For a boxplot, a box is drawn from hinge to hinge. Outlier cutoff locations are one-and-a-half box lengths beyond each hinge. From each side of the box, whisker lines extend to the outermost data value that is on or inside the outlier cutoff location. Outliers are beyond the whiskers; they should be clearly labeled on the boxplot to draw attention to them. The circumstances surrounding the origin of outliers should be investigated.

STEM-AND-LEAF DIAGRAM VARIATIONS AND EXTENSIONS

Basic stem-and-leaf diagrams can be augmented by including additional information. For example, we have used daily egg sales amounts as leaves on stem-and-leaf diagrams; letter codes that identify the days of the week can be added to the diagrams. The codes reveal any sales pattern such as high Saturday sales. Tukey may be consulted for additional ideas on coding stem-and-leaf diagrams; however, use your imagination and create.[10] Improvisation is encouraged.

E X A M P L E   17

ADDING CODES TO STEM-AND-LEAF DIAGRAMS

Problem Statement   Capture-day-of-the-week sales information on a stem-and-leaf diagram by adding letter codes. A new sequence of sales is used here to illustrate these new ideas.

Problem Solution   A day letter code appears beside each data value listed below. The days of the week are coded as follows: M—Monday, T—Tuesday, W—Wednesday, Th—Thursday, F—Friday, and S—Saturday with no sales on Sunday. Data values with codes are:

23M, 15T, 33W, 26Th, 43F, 48S, 25M, 18T, 59W, 28Th, 50F, 95S, 34M

Stem-and-leaf diagrams are augmented with these letter codes as shown below. Several variations are presented. The sales data and the day codes may be mixed in with the leaves or separated from the leaves with a colon. Also, the day codes and the sales figures may be placed back to back, with letter codes on one side and the data values on the other.

THIS		OR THIS		OR THIS		
9	5S	9	5:S	S	9	5
8		8			8	
7		7			7	
6		6			6	
5	0F, 9W	5	0, 9:FW	WF	5	0, 9
4	3F, 8S	4	3, 8:FS	SF	4	3, 8
3	3W, 4M	3	3, 4:WM	MW	3	3, 4
2	3M, 5M, 6Th, 8Th	2	3, 5, 6, 8:MMThTh	ThThMM	2	3
1	5T, 8T	1	5, 8:TT	TT	1	5, 8

Problem Discussion From the displays above, it appears that sales on Fridays, Wednesdays, and Saturdays tend to be greater than on the other days of the week. Sales tend to be lower on Mondays, Tuesdays, and Thursdays. The median sales figure is 33 dozen, a typical sales level. Fifty percent of the time sales are between the hinges of 25 and 48 dozen.

We suspect there is something unusual about the value 95; it is beyond the outlier cutoff on a boxplot. Unusually large sales of eggs might occur right before Easter; perhaps that is the reason for the jump in sales. As managers, we should try to determine why the unusually large sales figure of 95 dozen occurred.

EXAMPLE 18

DAY AND WEEK CODES

Problem Statement Suppose the 13 days of Egg's egg sales preceded an Easter holiday. Let an E code represent daily sales the week preceding Easter. Let an N code represent the week before that, a more normal week.

Problem Solution The new stem-and-leaf diagrams are:

	WITH EXTRA CODE			E-CODED DATA DELETED SELECTIVE TRIMMING		
S	9	5 :E			9	
	8				8	
	7				7	
	6				6	
WF	5	0, 9:NE		F	5	0
SF	4	3, 8:NN		SF	4	3, 8
MW	3	3, 4:EE			3	
ThThMM	2	3, 5, 6, 8:NENN		ThThM	2	2, 6, 8
TT	1	5, 8:NE		T	1	5

Problem Discussion   It appears that there might be an increase in Egg's sales just before Easter. A plot of sales over time might be used to follow up this impression.

The study of these displays has practical consequences. Information on the behavior of sales might be essential in planning inventory levels or staffing. Of course, these are tentative conclusions that resulted from exploratory work. It is evident that we seem to have a better understanding of these data than we had at the start when a simple list of data values was presented.

Although color coding is not shown, the leaves on stem-and-leaf diagrams can be color coded.

Modifying Stem-and-Leaf Diagrams with Few Stems

A little experience constructing stem-and-leaf diagrams reveals the problem of too few stems. Such diagrams appear crowded with too many leaves on a stem. The opposite situation, too many stems, can also occur. Thus the right number of stems requires some thought and construction decisions.

If there tends to be too many leaves on a stem, split the stems; the following long stems are split. Thus

```
9 | 001225667889

8 | 0001115558889
```

becomes

```
9.  | 5667889

9*  | 00122

8.  | 5558889

8*  | 000111
```

The asterisks (in 9* and 8*) and the periods (in 9. and 8.) are reminders that the original stems were each split in two. For even less crowding, the above stems can be split further, resulting in two digits on each stem.

```
9.  | 889          .    for digits eight and nine

9s  | 667          s    for digits six and seven

9f  | 5            f    for digits four and five

9t  | 22           t    for digits two and three

9*  | 001          *    for zero and one

8.  | 889               and so forth

8s  |

8f  | 555

8t  |

8*  | 000111
```

A Rule for the Right Number of Stems

With a little practice, one gets an intuitive feel for the appropriate number of categories. Sometimes intuition can be combined with simple rules to guide the construction process. Hoaglin, Mosteller, and Tukey suggested some rules for organizing stem-and-leaf diagrams.[11] Roughly, for the number of observations n $\leq$ 50, the approximate number of stems needed is

$$2 \times n^{1/2}$$

FREQUENCY, RELATIVE FREQUENCY, AND DENSITY HISTOGRAMS

As data sets increase in size to the point where the total frequency count exceeds 100, stem-and-leaf diagrams become cumbersome and are replaced by histograms. Histograms have considerable flexibility in grouping data into classes. To illustrate the mechanics of constructing histograms and to show that histograms are extensions of stem-and-leaf diagrams, we continue to work with egg sales data, a small data set. You will see that a stem-and-leaf diagram is similar to a **frequency histogram,** which is a display of frequency counts of data values in class intervals.

A frequency histogram of dozens of eggs sold per day for 13 days is shown in Exhibit 11. In MINITAB the asterisks represent frequency counts. Frequency histograms can be portrayed also by bars or rectangles (see Exhibit 12); MINITAB draws either rectangular-bar or asterisk-style histograms.

Exhibit 11 is a copy of Exhibit 5 with one additional column added. The last column shows **density,** defined as

$$\text{density} = \frac{\text{relative frequency}}{\text{class interval length}}$$

EXHIBIT 11 Frequency Histogram, Relative Frequencies, and Density

Class Intervals	Class Midpoints	Frequency Counts	Relative Frequencies	Density
10 to 20	15.0	2 **	2/13	2/130
20 to 30	25.0 (mode)	4 ****	4/13	4/130
30 to 40	35.0	2 **	2/13	2/130
40 to 50	45.0	2 **	2/13	2/130
50 to 60	55.0	2 **	2/13	2/130
60 to 70	65.0	0	0/13	0/130
70 to 80	75.0	0	0/13	0/130
80 to 90	85.0	0	0/13	0/130
90 to 100	95.0	1 *	1/13	1/130
TOTALS		13	13/13 = 1	

EXHIBIT 12 Relating Stem-and-Leaf Diagrams to Frequency, Relative Frequency, and Density Histograms

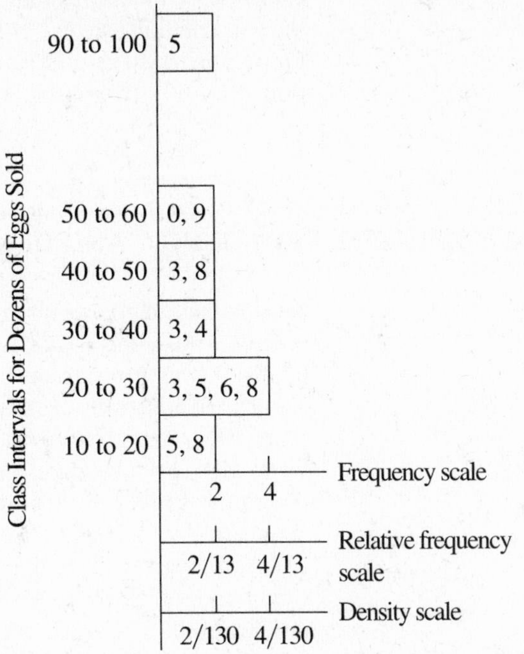

Class Intervals for Dozens of Eggs Sold	
90 to 100	5
50 to 60	0, 9
40 to 50	3, 8
30 to 40	3, 4
20 to 30	3, 5, 6, 8
10 to 20	5, 8

Frequency scale — 2   4

Relative frequency scale — 2/13   4/13

Density scale — 2/130 4/130

In this tabulation, the length of each class interval is ten, 10 to 20, 20 to 30, and so on. Density is relative frequency per unit of interval length.

The tabulated frequency counts, relative frequencies, and densities are shown on separate scales at the bottom of the stem-and-leaf diagram in Exhibit 12. The scales refer to bar lengths for the particular histogram they define, **frequency, relative frequency,** or **density histograms.** Because relative frequency equals the density times the class interval length, relative frequency is equal also to the area of density histogram bars when reading the density scale in Exhibit 12.

By showing three different scales in Exhibit 12, three related but different displays are presented simultaneously. This is a powerful way to show how these histograms are related. In actual practice, one scale at a time is used because the different histograms are for the following different purposes:

1. Frequency histograms are useful in comparing data distributions for a moderate number of observations in samples of the same size.

When comparing raw materials from different suppliers, we might weigh 100 bags of potato chips made from Maine potatoes and compare that frequency histogram to another based on 100 bags of chips made from Idaho potatoes.

2. Relative frequency histograms are useful, for example, in comparing data distributions for moderate or large numbers of observations in samples of different sizes. When comparing the distributions of daily production rates (units produced per day) for the first six months of the year compared to the last six months, relative frequency histograms adjust for the fact that there are different numbers of workdays in these periods.

3. Although more complex, density histograms can substitute for frequency or relative frequency histograms. Density histograms have advantages over its two competitors in comparing data distributions for large numbers of observations in samples of different sizes, where the number of observations within class intervals differs greatly from sample to sample. For example, density histograms would work well when comparing personal income distributions of college graduates compared to noncollege graduates across many income classes.

Note that interval sizes, starting points, and so forth are arbitrary in constructing histograms; therefore, the same data set can produce histograms that have different appearances.

Polygons, Pie Charts, and Ogives

A **polygon** is a smoother representation of a histogram in which bars are replaced by connected line segments. In Exhibit 13 the midpoints of bar ends are connected by line segments to form a polygon. Although the bars still show in Exhibit 13, in practice a polygon would be a substitute for the histogram.

Exhibit 14 displays a **pie chart** for the relative frequencies of egg sales data. A pie chart is an easy-to-read alternative to the histogram. For classes 10 to 20, 20 to 30, . . . , and 90 to 100, recall that the relative frequencies are

$$\frac{2}{13}, \frac{4}{13}, \frac{2}{13}, \frac{2}{13}, \frac{2}{13}, \frac{0}{13}, \frac{0}{13}, \frac{0}{13}, \frac{1}{13}.$$

A pie shape is a 360° circle, so we can use wedge-shaped pie pieces as basic units that cut out $\frac{360}{13} = 27.6°$.

EXHIBIT 13 A Polygon,
a Smoother Histogram
Representation

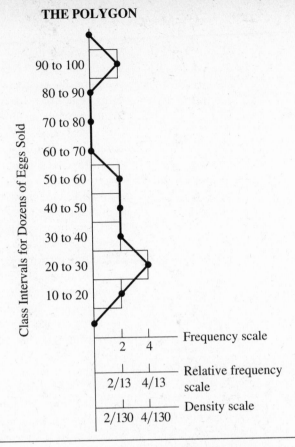

THE POLYGON

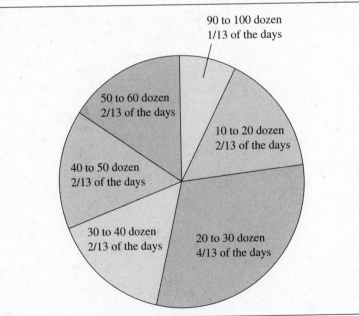

Using Spreadsheet Programs for Data Displays

Although popular spreadsheet programs like Excel or Lotus do not have the capability of full-blown statistical packages, they can display data. In spreadsheet programs, the term **chart** refers to all pictorial representation of information. The pie chart in Exhibit 15 was produced by Excel with the click of a mouse button. In Excel, the relative frequencies are converted to percentages, and the pie chart is constructed from these percentages.

The chart was constructed by selecting the data, clicking the pie chart button (with a mouse) at the bottom of the spreadsheet, and dragging over an area of the spreadsheet (with the mouse) where the chart is to appear. Excel does the rest. As you can see from the variety of buttons, many common statistical displays are available as charts in spreadsheet programs.

An **ogive** is a plot of class intervals versus cumulative relative frequencies or cumulative frequencies. Exhibit 16 shows a column of cumulative relative

EXHIBIT 15 A Spreadsheet-Produced Pie Chart

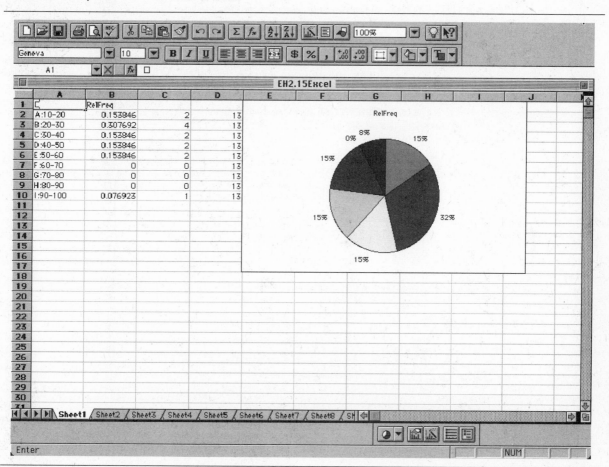

EXHIBIT 16 Cumulative Relative Frequency Calculations

Class Intervals	Class Midpoints	Frequency Counts	Relative Frequencies	Cumulative Relative Frequencies
10 to 20	15.0	2 **	2/13	2/13
20 to 30	25.0 (mode)	4 ****	4/13	6/13
30 to 40	35.0	2 **	2/13	8/13
40 to 50	45.0	2 **	2/13	10/13
50 to 60	55.0	2 **	2/13	12/13
60 to 70	65.0	0	0/13	12/13
70 to 80	75.0	0	0/13	12/13
80 to 90	85.0	0	0/13	12/13
90 to 100	95.0	1 *	1/13	13/13
TOTALS		13	13/13 = 1	

frequencies (the last column), which are sums of relative frequencies for all classes less than or equal to a particular class.

The ogive in Exhibit 17 is a plot of the classes versus the cumulative relative frequencies. The ogive is read by first picking a class or value on the vertical axis, moving horizontally to intersect the smooth ogive curve, and dropping to the horizontal axis to read off the cumulative relative frequency.

EXHIBIT 17 An Ogive for Cumulative Relative Frequencies

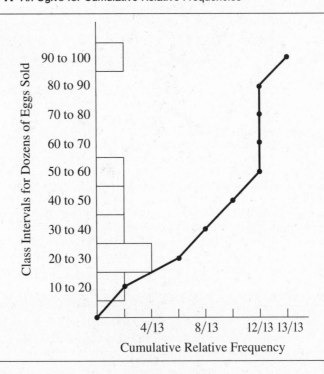

The cumulative frequency times 100 is the percentage of the data values within or less than the chosen class, a *percentile.*

Relative frequency bars are shown in Exhibit 17 for reference purposes. The bars can be stacked on top of one another cumulatively, moving upward to higher classes, thus constructing the ogive visually.

EXPLORING SEVERAL VARIABLES ONE AT A TIME

In many businesses, it takes years for managers to gain the experience to be of great value to an organization. When an experienced manager leaves an organization, it is difficult to replace that resource. When an organization suffers a recent loss of experience, it wants to recover as soon as possible. Statistical knowhow is a time compressor; it enables one to learn, and it can accelerate the process of gaining experience.

Traces of experience are often found in the data. For example, an experienced manager in the lumber business knows trees. Because we sometimes walk in the woods, we know something about trees too. However, a manager in this business probably thinks of the raw material in terms of tree height, diameter, volume, and other attributes. Seldom does a single variable describe something completely.

Often, we are forced to characterize several variables to describe something more completely. A data analyst may look at several variables, one at a time, to become familiar with each. The following example uses this approach to help us become more familiar with black cherry trees.

Example 19 uses the MINITAB 'TREES' data set. Not only do you have many powerful statistical tools at your fingertips in MINITAB, but MINITAB has many different and interesting data sets available that can be retrieved. Thus, you can explore these data sets and gain valuable experience using statistical tools.

EXAMPLE 19

GETTING TO KNOW BLACK CHERRY TREES BETTER THROUGH THE VARIABLES, DIAMETER, HEIGHT, AND VOLUME

Problem Statement   Thirty-one black cherry trees were cut and measurements were taken on diameter, height and volume. (These data are listed below.) For each variable, find a stem-and-leaf diagram, the median, hinges, extremes, box length, and range. Comment on each set of results after the output is examined.

Forest industry people are interested in knowing what these trees are like. What are the characteristics of a typical black cherry tree in this section of the forest? How do the remaining trees differ from the typical tree? Data analysis will be helpful in answering these questions.

The reader may carry out additional work such as plotting the variables in the order they were observed and checking for randomness. To economize on space, an exhaustive analysis is not performed here.

DIAMETER IN COLUMN C1 (INCHES)

8.3	8.6	8.8	10.5	10.7	10.8	11.0	11.0	11.1	11.2	11.3
11.4	11.4	11.7	12.0	12.9	12.9	13.3	13.7	13.8	14.0	14.2
14.5	16.0	16.3	17.3	17.5	17.9	18.0	18.0	20.6		

HEIGHT IN COLUMN C2 (FEET)

70	65	63	72	81	83	66	75	80	75	79	76	76	69	75	74
85	86	71	64	78	80	74	72	77	81	82	80	80	80	87	

VOLUME IN COLUMN C3 (CUBIC FEET)

10.3	10.3	10.2	16.4	18.8	19.7	15.6	18.2	22.6	19.9	24.2
21.0	21.4	21.3	19.1	22.2	33.8	27.4	25.7	24.9	34.5	31.7
36.3	38.3	42.6	55.4	55.7	58.3	51.5	51.0	77.0		

Problem Solution   MINITAB results are followed by commentary.

```
STEM-AND-LEAF DISPLAY OF DIAMETER
LEAF DIGIT UNIT = .1000
 8 (as a stem) and 3 (as a leaf) represent 8.3 inches in diameter.

depth           stem-and-leaf

   3             8 | 368
   3             9 |
   6            10 | 578
  14            11 | 00123447
  (3)           12 | 099
  14            13 | 378
  11            14 | 025
   8            15 |
   8            16 | 03
   6            17 | 359
   3            18 | 00
   1            19 |
   1            20 | 6
```

The smallest tree is 8.3 inches in diameter and the largest is 20.6 inches in diameter. Most are between 10.5 and 14.5 inches in diameter. The data analyst may wonder about the gaps and clusters in this display. Most likely, we would try to find the exact location in the forest where the trees that stand out or form clusters were cut. We may learn something about the topography, soil fertility, moisture and sunlight conditions. Notice that the distribution of diameters is more spread out or skewed in the direction of larger diameters. A typical black cherry tree in this section of the forest has a diameter of about one foot. Additional summary statistics for tree diameters are presented in MINITAB's format with the median above and between the hinges.

```
        DEPTH    LOWER    UPPER    SPREAD

N =    31
M      16             12.90 median
H     8.5     11.05    15.25     4.20 box length
       1       8.30    20.60    12.30 range
```

These letter values hone our impressions that were obtained from the stem-and-leaf diagram. The typical tree has a median diameter of M = 12.9 inches. Fifty percent of the trees have diameters between 11.05 and 15.25 inches. The box length is 4.2 inches. With the outlier cutoffs at one-and-one-half box lengths beyond the hinges, the upper outlier cutoff is 15.25 + (1.5 times 4.2) = 21.55 and the lower one is at 4.75. Thus, the extreme observations, 8.3 and 20.6, are not outliers. Nevertheless, we might gather more information about these trees and their largest and smallest diameters. In addition, we might try to learn more about the clusters. The reader should now construct a boxplot to the right of the stem-and-leaf diagram shown above.

```
STEM-AND-LEAF DISPLAY OF HEIGHT
LEAF DIGIT UNIT = 1.0000
6 (as a stem) and 3 (as a leaf) represents 63 feet in height.
```

The following stems are split—otherwise there would be too many leaves on a stem. Recall that in 6t, 6f, 6s, 6. and 7*, the t, f, s, . and * represent leaf digits that consist of twos and threes, fours and fives, sixes and sevens, eights and nines, zeros and ones.

```
depth              stem-and-leaf
  1                  6T 3
  3                  6F 45
  4                  6S 6
  5                  6. 9
  7                  7* 01
  9                  7T 22
 14                  7F 44555
 (3)                 7S 667
 14                  7. 89
 12                  8* 0000011
  5                  8T 23
  3                  8F 5
  2                  8S 67
```

We are now beginning to know our trees better. A typical black cherry tree in this section of the forest is 12.9 inches in diameter and 76 feet tall. Height is more evenly distributed and changes more uniformly than diameter, which is more clustered in distribution. The stem-and-leaf diagram is more lopsided or skewed in the direction of the shorter trees. Other things being equal, tall trees seem to have tall trees for neighbors. However, we would have to inspect the section of the forest that was cut to be sure. Additional summary statistics for tree heights are:

```
      DEPTH     LOWER     UPPER     SPREAD
N =    31
M      16                  76
H     8.5        72         80        8
       1         63         87       24
```

The box length relative to the median is $\frac{4.2}{12.9}$ for diameters and $\frac{8}{76}$ for heights, about one-third for diameters and one-tenth for heights. Thus, we are likely to look at these trees as all being fairly tall without much variation. The difference in diameters, however, is likely to be more obvious to us with some noticeably skinny trees and some noticeably fat ones.

```
STEM-AND-LEAF DISPLAY OF VOLUME
LEAF DIGIT UNIT = 1.0000
1 (as a stem) and 5 (as a leaf) represents 15 cubic feet in volume.

depth            stem-and-leaf
  3               1* | 000
 10               1. | 5688999
 (7)              2* | 1112244
 14               2. | 57
 12               3* | 134
  9               3. | 68
  7               4* | 2
  6               4. |
  6               5* | 11
  4               5. | 558
```

A trimmed value of volume is labeled HI77.

One tree had an unusually high volume figure of 77 cubic feet. Notice that this high value was trimmed from the stem-and-leaf diagram and listed as HI77. A typical black cherry tree in this data set is about 12.9 inches in diameter, 76 feet tall, and has a volume of about 24 cubic feet.

Additional summary statistics for tree volumes are:

	DEPTH	LOWER	UPPER	SPREAD
N =	3			
M	16		24.2	
H	8.5	19.40	37.30	17.90
	1	10.20	77.00	66.80

MINITAB did some rounding to construct the stem-and-leaf diagram. However, exact figures were used in calculating the summary statistics. Note that the upper outlier cutoff is about 64 cubic feet. The largest tree either appears to be a monster in terms of volume, or the volume of 77 cubic feet is a mistake.

A POPULATION, A SAMPLE, DIFFERENT SAMPLES WITH DIFFERENT MEDIANS, AND OTHER SUMMARY VALUES

Recall that an **elementary unit** is a subject or individual in a statistical study. A **population** is the totality of elementary units. A **sample** is any part of the population. Usually, it is less expensive to sample than to examine the complete population. Why incur the cost burden of observing (if possible) a population of data values when a sample can provide a representative view of the big picture? A very small, inexpensive sample may not shed enough light on the unknown characteristics of the population and, a very large, expensive sample may not be worth its size. Thus costwise, we seek the optimal sample size.

Choosing a sample is accomplished by accessing the population through a **frame.** Ideally, a frame is a numbered list of all the elementary units in a population. The population and the frame are then the same. Realistically, some elements of the population might be inaccessible. When this occurs, a frame becomes a numbered list of accessible elementary units relevant to the study. A frame should be representative of the population.

Simple Random Samples

Numbering the elementary units in a frame is useful in choosing a sample. Suppose that the elementary units are numbered **1** to **N.** Instead of the usual six-sided die, imagine having an **N**-sided die to roll. Each roll of the die gives each number (face) an **equal chance** of occurring on top. **n** rolls can be used to choose a **simple random sample** of elementary units. Practically, the **n** random numbers can be computer generated or chosen from a table of random numbers.

Sampling **with replacement** allows a sampling unit to appear in the sample more than once. **Without replacement** means that you ignore rolls of the **N**-sided die when a particular face occurs more than once, and you roll the die again.

Simple random samples are attractive because of the objective, unbiased way of selecting elementary units. Simple random samples lead to nice theoretical results that permit statements about how different the sample characteristics might be from those of the population.

Random (Probability) Samples

When the word "simple" is dropped from simple random sampling, **random** or **probability sampling** is the result. Think of the **N**-sided die as a loaded one in which the chances of rolling a particular face are known but not necessarily equal.

Systematic Random Samples   In a frame numbered 1 to N, a **systematic random sample** can be taken by counting, for example, by fives and selecting elementary units numbered 5, 10, 15, and so forth. You can count by any number $\mathbf{k} = \frac{N}{n}$. If the list of elementary units is not patterned in any way that biases the systematic sample, it can be as effective as a simple random sample.

Stratified Random Samples   Sometimes the frame can be stratified by some variable. For example, individuals can be stratified by gender. From each strata, simple random or systematic samples can be taken. This is called **stratified random sampling.**

Clustered Random Samples   Sometimes the elementary units in a frame are clustered physically, such as by geographical accessibility. Homes can be clustered as suburban or urban, for example. From each cluster, simple random, systematic, or stratified samples can be taken.

Nonrandom Samples

In some situations, **nonrandom samples** are chosen because of their economy and convenience. Nonrandom samples tend to be less objective than random samples and are subject to various sorts of bias. A **convenience sample** is chosen because of its expediency. A **judgment sample** is slightly more sophisticated since its selection relies on experienced judgment.

Data from Random or Nonrandom Sampling Schemes

Whether the sampling scheme is random or nonrandom, it provides no guarantee that the data collected are random. The randomness or non-randomness of the data itself must be tested on its own regardless of the sampling scheme.

Different Samples Yielding Different Summary Statistics

Egg Sales Revisited   If Egg the eggman were in business for only 13 days, the 13 sales figures used in earlier examples would have been the universe, population, totality, or complete picture of sales figures. If Egg were in business for more than 13 days, the 13 sales figures would be a sample. It is unlikely that such a sample would not be very representative of sales over a long span of time.

Let us assume that Egg was in business for more than 13 days. Therefore, these sales figures constitute a sample or part of the population of sales figures.

With a sample, you see part of the picture and make **inferences** about what the complete picture might be. The practice of making inferences is not new to you. For instance, many inferences are needed for the successful assembly of a jigsaw puzzle.

The complete sales picture, the population of Egg's egg sales, was not available. Therefore, the median we obtained was not the population median or the median over the long haul. Our convenience sample consisted of 13 days of sales. What we have been calling simply, the median, should be more properly dubbed the **sample median.** Sample median sales turned out to be 33 dozen for Egg's egg data. The sample median is an estimator of the unknown population median.

All the summary values we obtain from a sample are estimators of their population counterparts. Sample estimators (**statistics**) are used to make educated guesses, or inferences, about their population counterparts (**parameters**).

The sample median of 33 (egg sales data) arose from the analysis of sales for 13 days. What would the median be if we picked another set of 13 days? An answer to such a question builds a better understanding of the typical sales level because we are likely to see a different sample median with each different sample. We can't answer this question until we analyze at least another 13 days of sales.

CHAPTER SUMMARY

This chapter introduced exploratory data analysis for one variable at a time. Exploratory data analysis is an attitude and an approach as well as a collection of methods. Nevertheless, some tools such as stem-and-leaf diagrams, box-plots, and computers can help the investigator make sense out of the numbers. General characteristics of a batch of data received our attention as well as unusual features.

The early parts of this chapter were concerned with building stem-and-leaf displays. Usually, two stem-and-leaf diagrams are built in sequence. First, the leaves are written without regard to data value order. Second, the leaves are ordered on the stems. Ordering the data values simplifies the location of summary values such as medians and hinges. Hinges or quartiles are a quarter of the way from the extremes. The median is half-way from the extremes.

As long as the data sets are random, these statistics are valid and help summarize the data. Some data, time series in particular, tend to exhibit nonrandom patterns in plots. Often, transforming the data to changes or percent changes results in random sequences that can be summarized nicely.

Boxplots summarize stem-and-leaf diagrams. In a boxplot, a box is drawn from hinge to hinge and whiskers extend from both sides of the box. Outliers, if they exist, are marked distinctively and conditions that underly their birth are studied.

Statistics such as the median were found to be particularly useful for exploratory work because they resist being influenced by outliers.

Many other descriptive displays are also useful. Close relatives of the stem-and-leaf display such as frequency, relative frequency, and density histograms were also discussed. Polygons, pie charts, and ogives were presented, too.

KEY TERMS

asymmetry, 69
box length, 66
boxplot, 65
box-and-whisker plots, 66
center line (CL), 51
changes, 55
chart, 77
clustered random sample, 83
convenience sample, 83
density, 73
density histogram, 74
depth, 47
deviation, 53
differences, 55
elementary unit, 82
equal chance, 83
even number, 48
extreme high, 45
extreme low, 45
five-number summary, 50
frame, 82
frequency, 44
frequency count, 44
frequency histogram, 73, 74
grouped data, 44
hinge, 46

histogram, 42
inferences, 84
interquartile distance, 66
interquartile range, 66
judgment sample, 83
leaves, 39
lower quartile, 45
median, 45
mode, 44
nonrandom, 52
nonrandom sample, 83
odd number, 48
ogive, 77
outlier, 66
outlier cutoffs, 66
parameters, 84
percent changes, 55
percentile, 45, 79
pie chart, 75
polygon, 75
population, 82
probability sample, 83
quartile spread, 45
random, 52
random sample, 83
range, 45

relative frequency, 44
relative frequency histogram, 74
residual, 36
run, 52
runs count, 52
sample, 82
sample median, 84
simple random sample, 83
state of statistical control, 53
statistics, 84
stem-and-leaf diagram, 38
stems, 39
stratified random sample, 83
summary statistics, 49
symmetry, 69
systematic random sample, 83
test interval, 52
time series plot, 51
transform, 55
typical data value, 45
ungrouped data, 44
upper quartile, 45
variability, 45
with replacement, 83
without replacement, 83

EXERCISES

General Exercises

1. If you don't have a campus pond for this exercise, substitute something such as the number of cars at a light or in a parking lot. For the next class period, obtain a count of the number of ducks on or around the campus pond. Also, based on a 24-hour clock, record the hour number (rounded to the nearest hour) in which you made the count. You will record two numbers:

Duck Count _____ Hour Number _____

Bring this data to class to share with others. We will pool these individual observations to form a larger data set for analysis. We want to know about how many ducks party at the campus pond. We need to think about the space reserved for them, how much popcorn to order, etc. The analysis should indicate how many ducks the pond supports at a certain time of the year. Additionally, we have been learning ways of expressing our impressions about what the data set reflects. Complete the following and be prepared to discuss each item:

(a) Outline some difficulties and problems that might have occurred in the data collection process. For example, ducks taking off and landing, some students faking counts, etc.

(b) By hand, produce a stem-and-leaf diagram, median, box length and boxplot for duck count.

(c) In a convenient way, include the hour number information on the stem-and-leaf diagram for duck count.

(d) Use MINITAB or another statistical package to generate computer printouts that verify your work in (a). Hand these in.

(e) Be prepared to explain the printouts.

2. Variations of the previous exercise might include data sets such as the number of cars in a parking lot, the number of people walking past a certain spot during a specific time interval, the number of cars driving past a particular place during a specific time interval, the number of cars waiting at a certain red light, the number of people waiting in line at the Bursar's office or at the supermarket, the number of students in another class, the number of students playing basketball in the gym, the number of hours of studying completed in a week's time, the pulse rates of the students in the class, etc.

You might also consider analyzing data found in the newspaper such as stock prices, daily temperatures in different cities across the country, house prices, automobile prices, monthly apartment rents, and scores or other sports statistics. Consider using data from almanacs and other similar sources.

By using individuals or teams of students to collect data, repeat the analysis specified in the previous exercise.

3. The following data are student examination scores in a statistics course. About the time of the examination, a scientific journal reported that males (coded M) tend to perform better than females (coded F) in mathematics. Because a statistics course depends on some mathematics, the professor, who gave the exam, wondered if his male students did better than females on the examination. As a result, the exam scores were coded M or F to denote the gender of the student. Additionally, some students didn't do (coded DD) a homework set, one student didn't do two (coded DDT) homework sets, and some students did a poor job (coded DPJ) on at least one homework set. The coded exam scores from high to low are:

97F, 95M,92M, 92F, 91F, 89F, 89M, 87M, 84M, 84F, 83F, 82F, 82M,
81M, 81M, 80M, 78F, 77F, 77M, 76F, 76F, 76F, 76F, 74M, 74M, 73F,
73M, 73F, 72F, 72M, 72F, 72M, 70F, 69M, 68F, 68M, 68M, 68F, 68F,
67F, 67F, 66F, 66F, 66F, 66M, 64M, 63F, 62M, 62F DD, 62M DD, 61M DD,
61F DD, 61M, 61M, 60M, 60M, 59M, 59F DD, 58M DPJ, 58F, 58F,
57F, 56F, 55M, 53M, 53M, 53F DD, 51M, 50F, 49M DD, 49M DD, 49F DPJ,
45F, 42M, 41M DPJ, 38M DD, 37F DD, 23M DDT

(a) Obtain a stem-and-leaf diagram, boxplot, and appropriate summary values for these exam scores.

(b) Incorporate the codes on the stem-and-leaf diagram. The M's and F's might be grouped opposite each stem, for example FFF;MMMMM |8| 0,1,1,2,2,3,4,4. Although the grouping may destroy the letter and score correspondence, you gain a better visual comparison of males and females. Because too many letters get confusing, in place of DPJ's you can simply circle the appropriate leaves. In place of DD's you can draw squares around the appropriate leaves. For DDT's you can draw two concentric squares. If you wish, you can use your imagination and do it your own way.

(c) Roughly, did males seem to outperform females as the scientific report might have suggested?

(d) How did students with a history of low quality homework fare on the exam? Were there any unusually high or low scores?

(e) If you were the professor, how would you present a summary of the performance to the class?

(f) Acting again as the professor, make some decisions about grades. These scores convert to what grades? Who gets A's, B's, C's etc.? Why? Defend your decisions.

4. The following data set consists of player weights and position codes for a professional football team.[12] The weights are in pounds. Some position codes are DE (defensive end), RB (running back), WR (wide receiver), LB (line backer), QB (quarter back), etc. If you don't know the other codes, ask around. Questioning is an important part of data analysis!

263DE, 200RB, 188WR, 260DE, 235LB, 260(OC), 184WR/KR, 178WR,
260DE, 195DB, 212RB, 189P, 200QB, 186RB, 198PK, 258DE,
190CB, 220TE, 236LB, 202RB, 185DB, 255DE, 195DB, 260DE,
265(OG), 230RB, 235TE, 185WR, 165P, 185PK, 185DB, 178DB,
250TE, 270(OL), 194RB, 260(OG), 220(OLB), 240ILB, 275NT,
208QB, 279(OT), 265(OG), 245TE, 232(OLB), 195CB, 275DT,
200RB, 273(OT), 230LB, 189CB, 204RB, 184WR/KR, 185RB, 260(OT),
190QB, 230(OLB), 225P/PK, 192DB, 196FS, 235(OLB), 250DE,
231(OLB), 270NT, 180WR, 166WR, 255(OC), 230ILB, 194QB, 252DT,
210QB, 180WR, 180DB, 206QB, 192DB, 279DE, 185K, 174CB, 192DB,
229RB, 260(OG), 175WR/KR, 231LB, 195WR, 197RB, 217RB, 218LB,
185WR, 255(OT), 230TE, 272NT, 257(OG), 235TE, 232ILB

(a) Create a stem-and-leaf diagram, boxplot, and summary values.

(b) Discuss the relationships between clusters of weights and the performance characteristics needed for players at specific positions. Because players get injured, it is important to have players who can play more than one position. Can you see from the distribution of weights which positions have more depth than others?

(c) Use MINITAB, RETRIEVE 'B:PATSCAMP' This is not the same data set as the one shown above. Use INFO and PRINT to look at the data. Perform a similar analysis to (a) above for height, weight, and experience. Comment as necessary, noting any relationship to the position played.

5. The MINITAB statistical package includes many interesting data sets as well as commands for analyzing the data. Check your computer facility and a MINITAB manual for what is available.

Typically, you can access one of these data sets quite easily. For example,

```
MTB > RETRIEVE 'TREES'
MTB > INFO
MTB > PRINT C1
```

In order to leave MINITAB, get into DOS, list all the MINITAB data set file names, return to MINITAB, and do the following:

```
MTB > SYSTEM
DIR / P
EXIT
MTB > RETRIEVE 'anyMinitabFileName'
MTB > INFO
```

With these data sets available, students are able to concentrate on the analysis rather than on the typing.

When using the student version of MINITAB rather than the network version, these data sets are placed on a separate diskette. While in DOS (A> prompt showing on the screen), place the data set diskette in drive B, type (after A>) B: You will get the prompt B>. Then type DIR/P. The DIRectory command produces a list of all data set names. You may wish to print a hardcopy list of these data set names by depressing the SHIFT and PRT SCREEN keys.

To retrieve a data set from a diskette, get MINITAB up and running (MTB> prompt showing). With the data set diskette in drive B, type the MINITAB command RETRIEVE 'B:dataSetFilenameHere'. Use the INFORMATION command to find out more about the data set. The MINITAB manual as well as other books that utilize MINITAB, usually have appendices that provide additional details about these data sets.

A few of MINITAB's data sets are:

(1) Students participated in a simple experiment that involved taking resting and running pulse rates (variables named PULSE1 and PULSE2): (MINITAB student version) RETRIEVE 'B:PULSE'; (network version) RETRIEVE 'PULSE'. Use INFO for information. The following commands obtain summary information on various variables: STEM 'PULSE1'; LVALS 'PULSE1'; BOXPLOT 'PULSE1' (Note: Each command should be placed on a separate line).

How does your resting pulse rate compare to those in the data set? What if you stand up and run in place? How does your pulse change relative to the typical resting pulse rate? Because height and weight are also in this data set, find the height, weight, and pulse rate of a typical person in the data set and compare those observations to yours.

(2) Some anthropologists have studied environmental change and blood pressure. Peruvian Indians migrated from a very primitive environment at a high altitude to a modern, urban environment at a much lower altitude. It has been suggested that the migration might increase blood pressure.

There are ten variables in the data set. You might wish to examine each of these singly to get a feel for the typical values, for the spread of the distributions and for unusual data values. To access this data set use (MINITAB student version), RETRIEVE 'B:PERU' (network version), and RETRIEVE 'PERU'. Use the INFO command to obtain information about the variables. What are the main features of each variable? Are there any unusual features?

6. In his first year, Tony Armas played baseball for Pittsburgh. During the next six years, he played for Oakland. Afterwards, he was traded to Boston. His batting averages were:[13]

.333   .240   .213   .248   .279   .261   .233   .218   .268   .265   .264

(a) Obtain a stem-and-leaf diagram, boxplot, and summary values.

(b) Plot the data over time, comment on whether or not the data are random and its implication in regard to your interpretation of the summary statistics found in part (a).

(c) Using the median as a reference point (perhaps as a horizontal line on a time series plot), verbally characterize his batting performance in three career stages: early, middle, and late periods.

7. Fred Lynn started playing baseball for Boston where he stayed for seven years. Then, he was traded to California and stayed for four years. His last two years were with Baltimore. Fred Lynn had the following batting averages during that time:[14]

.419   .331   .314   .260   .298   .333   .301   .219   .299   .272   .271   .263   .287

(a) Obtain a stem-and-leaf diagram, boxplot, and summary values.

(b) Using the median as a reference point on a time series plot, verbally characterize his batting performance in two career stages: before and after his trade to California.

(c) Using hindsight, look at Lynn's batting performance alone. Assume that during his last season with Boston, management expected his future batting to be below par. Was management correct?

(d) Observe the time series plot and comment on whether or not the data appear to be random. What is the effect of randomness or the lack thereof on your interpretation of the summary statistics?

8. The *World Almanac* lists accidental deaths by month due to drowning in one year as:[15]

JAN.											DEC.
200	260	300	420	750	980	1,310	950	533	270	200	180

(a) What is the median?

(b) Would you expect the number of drownings in particular months to be above or below the median consistently from year to year? Why?

(c) What are the extremes? Can you think of some reasons for the high and the low in particular months?

(d) Plot the data over time. Comment on whether the data are random and on the effect of randomness, or the lack thereof, on your interpretation of the summary statistics.

(e) Perform the same type of analysis on deaths due to falls.

JAN.   DEC.

1058	985	1034	933	961	944	989	993	1006	1011	997	1113

9. Past records indicate that the leading rushers in football compiled the following average yards per carry:[16]

> Walter Payton 4.4; Eric Dickerson 4.4; Tony Dorsett 4.3; Jim Brown 5.2; Franco Harris 4.1; John Riggins 3.9; O. J. Simpson 4.7; Otis Anderson 4.0; Earl Campbell 4.3; Marcus Allen 4.1; Jim Taylor 4.4; Joe Perry 4.8; Gerald Riggs 4.1; Larry Csonka 4.3; Freeman McNeil 5.4; Roger Craig 4.1; James Brooks 4.7; Thurman Thomas 4.4; Herschel Walker 4.2; Mike Pruitt 4.0; Leroy Kelley 4.2; John Henry Johnson 4.3; Wilbert Montgomery 4.4; Chuck Muncie 4.3; Mark van Eeghen 4.0; Lawrence McCutcheon 4.3; Lydell Mitchell 3.9; and Floyd Little 3.8.

(a) Using a boxplot, pick out the top and bottom quarter of these leading rushers in terms of the available statistics.

(b) Suppose you have a friend who personally knows one of the top draft choices this year. Your friend is willing to bet a considerable sum of money that this rookie rusher will average 4.9 yards per carry in his first season. Would you take an even bet on this? Discuss your answer in light of the the data on leading lifetime rushers.

(c) Do you think that these average yards per carry figures, because they are over a lifetime, have less variability than season-by-season figures (not available here) might have? If so, how would you factor this variability factor into your thinking about the bet? If you don't like this bet, come up with a counter proposal.

10. An example in this chapter analyzes the diameter, height, and volume of 31 black cherry trees. Once in MINITAB then enter (MINITAB student version): RE-TRIEVE 'B:TREES' or, (network version): RETRIEVE 'TREES'. Using the information from this data set, make any additional calculations that might be necessary to answer the questions posed in this problem.

Suppose that the total volume (TV) of black cherry wood on order makes it necessary for you to calculate the typical number of trees needed (TN) to be cut to meet the demand of the order.

(a) Your manager wants you to study the data and produce a rule that makes the calculation of TN simple.

(b) Because of the variability in the data, management is not comfortable with just one number for TN. So, decide on and explain some reasonable bounds of the form

$$TN \ \pm \ (some \ quantity)$$

(c) Prepare a short (10 minute) oral and written presentation to management that addresses the specific questions above and provides a general overview of the analysis with any additional recommendations that you might have.

11. Summarize the following data set on the number of home runs hit by home run leaders starting in 1924 in the National League.[17]

27	39	21	30	31	43	56	31	38	28	35	34	33	31	36	28	43	34
30	29	33	28	23	51	40	54	47	42	37	47	49	51	43	44	47	46
41	46	49	44	47	52	44	39	36	45	45	48	40	44	36	38	38	52
40	48	48	31	37	40	36	37	37	49	39	47	40	38	35	46	43	

12. Many textbooks provide data sets on diskettes. For example, *Data Analysis for Managers,* by Harry Roberts,[18] is an excellent reference and comes with a valuable collection of business related data sets. When the data sets are stored as standard text files (ASCII, American Standard Code for Information Interchange), they can be retrieved by MINITAB. For your information, most modern personal computer software packages (Lotus 123, Excel, BASIC, MINITAB, word processing, etc.) have the capability to produce ASCII files.

As an example, the files on the Roberts data diskette are all stored in ASCII. Sometimes it is necessary to use filenames with an extension. Roberts uses the extension .ASC that looks a lot like ASCII. The full filename includes the extension—filename.ASC. Some examples of getting the data into MINITAB from the Roberts data diskette are:

```
MTB> SET 'B:GRANT1.ASC' INTO C1
MTB> SET 'B:DJ.ASC' INTO C1
MTB> READ 'B:IBM.ASC' INTO C1-C2
```

And away you go! Explore!!!

13. Often you will have access to data sets created by word processors (saved as text files, ASCII files) or files created by spreadsheet programs such as EXCEL or LOTUS. These programs can create ASCII files. They may produce filenames with the .DAT extension or another extension that you specify. Again, these are easily brought into MINITAB. For example, showing the .DAT extension, we have

```
MTB> SET (or READ) 'B:theFilename.DAT' INTO C1 (or C1 C2 etc.)
```

In WINDOWS, the data may be copied from a word processing document and pasted directly into MINITAB.

14. Many interesting and relevant data sources are available to supplement the few data sets shown here. Most good university libraries are excellent sources of data. You can learn a lot from projects that encourage you to explore the data sets available at your local library and through the library system.

Some useful data sources are: *World Almanac, Information Please Almanac, Statistical Abstract of the United States, Standard and Poor's Industry Surveys, Federal Reserve Bulletin, Monthly Labor Review, Survey of Current Business, Moody's Investors Service, A User's Guide to Bureau of Economic Analysis* (U.S. Department of Commerce/BEA has publications, computer tapes, diskettes and other information services).

Visit your library and find five additional sources of data.

15. In MINITAB, RETRIEVE 'B:QUAKES', use INFO and PRINT to look at the data. Then summarize the earthquake data.[19] To order the data in time, use the following command(s) and subcommand:

```
SORT C1 C2 C3, PUT C1 C2 C3;
BY C1.
PRINT C1 C2 C3
TSPLOT C3
```

Exercises to Illustrate Management Uses of Statistics

In planning activities, managers, whether in the public or private sector, must look ahead. The Transportation Research Board and the National Research Council in Washington, D.C. produced special report #220: *A Look Ahead, Year 2020.*[20] This report formed a planning basis for the nation's highway and public transit systems. Statistics from that report are used in the following block of exercises because these statistics are relevant to business planning in general.

16. A long-term outlook for the U.S. economy is captured by the percent of average annual growth of key economic indicators, projected through year 2011. Baseline figures are shown.

Inflation	4.3
Productivity (total)	1.4
Productivity (mfg.)	3.4
Imported oil	5.6
Employment	1.2
Real disposable income	2.3
Real GNP	2.6
Consumption	2.3
Investment (nonresidential)	3.6
Investment (residential)	1.2
Government expenditures	1.8
Exports	4.4
Imports	2.3

(a) Summarize the growth rates by hand and with MINITAB. Include a stem-and-leaf diagram, boxplot, and summary values. Record your observations, including comments on typical growth rates, the distributional pattern, the unusually high and low values, and the upper and lower quartiles.

(b) If imported oil grows at a rate of 6.6 percent instead of 5.6, most other growth rates will likely be reduced. Discuss.

17. The year 2020 will bring changes in demographics and life-style. Statistical methods help characterize past, present, and future population and employment change. Computer readable files from the *Current Population Survey and Census of Population and Housing* show regional migration of people moving out of the Northeast and Midwest and to the South and West, with the number migrating South nearly three times that of the West. The projected percent changes (over a 23-year period) in state populations (alphabetically) are:

13(Alabama)   41   55   10   36(Cal.)   24   10   23   8(Dist. of Columbia)   46   45
44(Hawaii)   7   −1   −2   −16   4   −1   1   10   25   7   −1   8   15(Miss.)   8   −3
−4   50   38   17   48   2   27   −9   3   7   10   −6(Penn.)   10   23   2   31(Texas)
28   11   26   17   −15   −2   −3.8(Wyoming)

(a) Summarize these projected changes in state populations using the exploratory methods learned in this chapter.

(b) For you future real estate tycoons, projected percent population increases for large metropolitan areas are: (only the five largest are shown)

West Palm Beach	60
Las Vegas	54
Orlando	53
Phoenix	47
Tucson	44

18. Projected percent employment changes by region and industry are (over a 32-year period to the year 2015):

	Northeast	**Midwest**	**South**	**West**
TOTAL	29	25	40	56
Agric.	23	−5	5	29
Mining	20	40	30	59
Const.	40	40	40	75
Manuf.	13	17	34	50
TPUC	34	27	50	60
W/R Trade	33	28	52'	62
Fire	43	43	62	73
Services	49	49	65	82
Gov't	−1	−1	10	16

(a) Summarize rows and columns (excluding the Total Row) separately, obtaining, at minimum, row and column medians.

(b) Should you move West young person?

(c) What industry has the highest median projected percent employment change?

(d) For those of you planning to open branch offices for your employment agencies, projected percent employment changes for large metropolitan areas for the same period are: (only the five largest are shown)

Nashville	82
Tucson	79
Austin	78
Phoenix	69
Fresno	67

19. The American Iron and Steel Institute[21] tabulates shipments of steel products by market classification. Percent changes in shipments are shown below. For the different years, construct side-by-side (or back-to-back) stem-and-leaf diagrams and include letter codes for the market types. Are there any particularly unusual changes that might require some pondering?

Market	% Chg. yr1	% Chg. yr2
Appliances	0.3	−1.0
Automotive	10.7	−4.4
Construction	9.8	3.0
Containers	1.1	1.0
Converting & proc.	18.0	−6.0
Electrical equip.	3.6	−3.0
Machinery	22.9	−4.0
Oil & Gas	−0.8	−25.0
Svc centers & dist.	6.0	−7.0
Domestic & comm'l equip.	4.4	−1.0
Other	25.0	−5.0
Nonclassified	1.6	4.0
Exports	140.0	38.0

20. Summarize the capacities (millions of tons) below of integrated United States steel companies.[22] What is the capacity of a typical mill? Fifty percent of the mills fall between what capacity limits? You can work with names (alpha data) as well as numbers (numeric data) in MINITAB. Set each name in a column separately, using the following commands:

```
SET C1;        # FIRST ENTER ALPHA DATA, NAMES, ONE PER LINE
FORMAT (A10).  # (A10) RESERVES 10 CHARACTERS FOR NAMES
# NOW ENTER THE NAMES ONE LINE AT A TIME
SET C2         # ENTER THE NUMERIC DATA
```

USX 26.2   LTV 19.1   BETHLEHEM 18.0   INLAND 9.3   ARMCO 6.8
NATIONAL 5.6   WEELING 4.5   WEIRTON 4.0   FORD 3.6   CALIFORNIA 2.1
MCLOUTH 2.0   CF&I 2.0   INTERLAKE 1.4   SHARON 1.0

21. For the marketing areas, letter coded A, B, . . . I, a marketing research study indicated potential beer sales volumes, in terms of shipping container weight (thousands), as:

11   6   66   30   45   12   90   6   10

(a) Divide the potentials into quartiles so you can assign your better sales people to the most promising marketing areas.

22. An inventory policy that many companies adopt is to stock high volume items at retail outlets, medium volume items only at warehouses, and low volume items at centralized distribution/warehouse centers. Because only a few of the products account for most of the sales, it is economical to concentrate resources on the high volume items. A common rule, the "20-80" rule, focuses attention on the 20% of the products that generate 80% of total sales. Suppose your company found it appropriate to modify the rule to "25-75". Using a stem-and-leaf diagram and a boxplot, identify the products that the "25-75" rule would focus upon. A list of products (P1 . . . P14) and monthly sales in thousands of dollars are presented below.

P1 145   P2 199   P3 5120   P4 720   P5 185   P6 1150   P7 385   P8 165
P9 3820   P10 450   P11 195   P12 167   P13 214   P14 936

23. Managers who worry about the characteristics of their service facilities often sample queue lengths, recording the number of customers waiting to be served at different times.

(a) Summarize the following sample of queue lengths.

QUEUE LENGTHS (# OF CUSTOMERS WAITING FOR SERVICE)
4   7   3   8   2   2   5   6   12   9   7   6   6   9   13   11

(b) Astute managers realize that queue length is related to the time it takes to service a customer (service time) as well as the time between consecutive arrivals (interarrival time). Queue lengths tend to increase (longer waiting lines) when the ratio of the typical service time to the typical interarrival time is increased. So, in addition to queue lengths, service times and interarrival times are often sampled, giving us a more complete view of the problem at hand. Summarize the following figures.

SERVICE TIMES (MINUTES)
3.4   3.3   3.7   4.9   3.2   4.5   4.0   4.1   3.4   4.0   3.7   4.1

INTERARRIVAL TIME (MINUTES)
7.6   5.7   8.8   3.2   4.1   3.2   4.3   3.4   7.6   3.7   1.9   6.4   5.3
3.6   5.4   4.8   4.4   6.5   2.1   2.5   1.4   7.5   3.3   4.5   7.2   5.6
4.4   6.7   4.2   7.7   3.3   2.4   7.8   6.2   5.0   4.2   5.1   6.0   8.9

(c) From a summary of these data, find the ratio of the typical service time to the typical interarrival time. This is the fraction of time the server is busy.

24. The following are yearly percent changes in the consumer price index:[23]

5.8   6.5   7.7   11.3   13.5   10.4   6.1   3.2   4.3   3.6   1.9   3.6
4.1   4.8   5.4   4.2   3.0   3.0

(a) Is this sequence of observations random or nonrandom? Show how you tested for randomness.
(b) Do you see any problems of interpretation for summary statistics?

25. Accounts receivable amounts of balance in hundreds of dollars for a sample of GMO company debtors are:

21   22   28   65   78   61   30   38   33   48   49   56   41   55   54   9   12
23   40   45   49   54   37   35   30   51   33   37   42   49   41   50

(a) What does the typical debtor owe GMO company?

(b) If this sample is representative and if GMO has a total of 1,500 debtors, estimate the total accounts receivable amount.

26. A wholesale magazine distributor generates invoices for customers twice a week since there are two deliveries per week to each retail outlet. An invoice contains a listing of all books, magazines, and newspapers available for distribution to the retailer. Usually, a particular retailer receives a subset of the items available.

In the wholesaler's warehouse, the invoices are the basis for packaging retailer deliveries. Because the packaging is manual and there are many items and retailers, some packaging errors are inevitable. Therefore, some retailers may receive more or less items than the amounts stated on their invoices. Usually, a retailer requests a credit for shortages. The percentage of retailers receiving shortage credits is computed weekly as a control mechanism. When the shortage claims do not occur at random, retailers who make repeated claims are suspected of lying and their deliveries are double checked at the warehouse.

Present the following data in such a way that an employee without statistical training can use the results to monitor future percentages and to provide feedback (about packaging errors) to those employees doing the packaging.

WEEKLY PERCENTAGES OF RETAILERS RECEIVING SHORTAGE CREDIT

```
1.5  6.4  .5  5.5  2.5  3.5  4.5  3.0  12.2  9.0  4.5  2.5  3.5
 .8  6.6  1.5  5.7  3.4  2.0  .5  6.0  3.0  2.0  2.2
```

27. The number of businesses within industries that discharge toxic pollutants into U.S. rivers, lakes, oceans, and waterways are listed alphabetically.[24]

Coal	2
Food processing	3
Inorganic chemicals	13
Iron and steel	17
Leather tanning	5
Metal finishing	135
Natural gas	55
Organic chemicals	22
Ore mining	12
Other	102
Petrol. refining	21
Pharmaceuticals	1
Plastics, synthetics	5
Pulp and paper	94
Rubber	7
Steam/electric	11
Super fund sites	7
Textile mills	16

(a) Reorder these figures according to the number of businesses. This reordering puts the focus on the industries with the largest number of offenders.

(b) If the government has a limited budget for regulating these industries, suppose it is necessary to focus on the top quarter of the industry polluters. Identify the top quarter.

(c) Convert the above figures to the percent of the total number of businesses and use the ordered percents to construct a histogram. In the quality control terms, this histogram is called a Pareto diagram. It enables one to identify and work on the *biggest* leaks in the roof, *first*.

28. Current assets divided by current liabilities is known as the current ratio. The current ratio is a liquidity ratio—the higher it is the more the cash and near-cash assets are available to cover current liabilities if necessary. When too high, you have excess current assets that are idle (not invested) and, therefore, not earning a return. When it is too low, you might not be able to meet current liabilities such as payroll. When possible, a company has a target value for this ratio and

attempts to reduce the variability of the ratio. Keep in mind that in actual practice no ratio is examined in isolation.

The typical current ratio for a company depends upon custom, risk posture, economic conditions, industry, etc. A good source for this information is Dun & Bradstreet's *Industry Norms & Key Business Ratios.* They provide personal computer access by phone or diskette. Their services allow you to compare your financial statements against industry data, create pro forma statements and project a company's performance, define your own ratios along with 14 key ratios, graph your ratio's against industry ratios, and model financial statements.

For a manufacturing example of the use of statistics and the amount of detail, consider the current ratio for establishments indexed by Standard Industrial Classification (SIC) codes. For SIC 0252 (Chicken Eggs, 54 establishments), the lower, median, and upper quartiles are 1.0 1.8 3.6. For SIC 0213 (Hogs, 59 establishments), the lower, median, and upper quartiles are 1.8 4.6 12. For SIC 5181 (Beer and Ale, 472 establishments) the lower, median, and upper quartiles are 1.7 2.8 5.7.

Broader based statistics are available in the *Statistical Abstracts of the United States.* Current ratios for nonfinancial corporations[25] over an eleven-year period are:

1.69 1.69 1.65 1.55 1.48 1.46 1.49 1.46 1.46 1.46 1.44

(a) Are these random? What did you expect? Examine percent changes. Be sure to show appropriate plots.

(b) *Moody's Industrial Manual* contains information for individual companies. For example, seven years of current ratios for Anheuser-Bush and Gillette companies are:[26]

| A-Bush | 1.09 | 1.24 | 1.10 | 1.13 | 1.00 | 1.07 | 1.01 |
| Gillette | 2.01 | 2.02 | 1.89 | 1.70 | 1.65 | 1.64 | 1.80 |

Plot these ratios: compute percent changes; plot percent changes and residuals (deviations from median percent changes). Comment on the plots. Does each plot seem to provide a different emphasis?

Sometimes when examining a ratio, it is smart to look at the components of the ratio separately. In this case, look at current assets and current liabilities. Often, changes in a ratio over time are influenced primarily by changes in one of these components.

29. Over a 21-year period, the per capita personal income as reported by the Department of Commerce, Bureau of Economic Analysis[27] was (in thousands of dollars, rounded):

4.4   4.8   5.2   5.6   6.2   6.8   7.6   8.7   9.7   10.1   10.7
11.6   12.3   12.9   13.5   14.5   15.3   16.2   16.7   17.6   18.2

(a) Thinking of per capita personal income as the price paid for a stock called labor, find the returns (percent changes per capita personal income) and summarize them.

30. Summarize the following starting salaries of college graduates (in thousands of dollars):

32, 41, 33, 31, 39, 37, 38, 38, 42, 33,
35, 38, 32, 32, 34, 40, 33, 30, 31, 35

(a) Are these random?

(b) What is the typical starting salary?

(c) Which salary figures are in the top quarter?

31. The Motor Vehicle Manufacturers Association tracks total motor vehicle sales. Over several years in the U.S., total car sales figures (in millions) were:[28]

9   8.5   8   9.1   10.3   11   11.5   10.3   10.5   9.8   9.3   8.2   8.2   8.5

(a) Compute percent changes and find what is typical.

32. For a Super Bowl football game between the Buffalo Bills and the Dallas Cowboys, a number of TV advertisements were rated. Advertisement names and ratings (higher is better) are available to you as a MINITAB worksheet, RETRIEVE 'B:SBADS'. After retrieving the data set, INFO will give you column and name references. PRINT the columns for examination.

(a) Obtain a stem-and-leaf diagram, histogram, boxplot, and summary values (LVALS) for the ratings in column C6.

(b) Plot the ratings in the order they were observed. Are they random?

(c) In MINITAB, use the following command(s) and subcommand:

```
SORT C5 C6, PUT C1 C2;
BY C6.
PRINT C1 C2
TSPLOT C2
```

Note that the ordering shows up on the plot. However, the resulting nonrandomness is imposed by the data analyst. Therefore, the summary statistics remain valid. That are the top and bottom three advertisements and what are their ratings?

(d) What is the difference between the extremes (the rating range)? What is the box length? Recall that the box length is an exploratory measure of spread.

33. In a small manufacturing operation, parts arrive at the first work station for assembly, the assemblies are painted different colors at one of the next two work stations, and the painted assemblies are packaged at a fourth work station. Finally, packages are moved to a storage area. The time from part arrival to package storage is recorded as a flow time through the manufacturing system. When flow time increases for each unit produced, this is an indication of a bottleneck in the system that might be in need of additional resources. In MINITAB, RETRIEVE 'B:MFGTIME'. Use INFO, PRINT, LVALS and TSPLOT commands. Is there a bottleneck in this manufacturing system? Explain.

34. Vibration tests are performed on 20 guidance systems. The response (roll resonant frequency) is thought to be related to five predictor variables, roll transmissibility, pitch resonant frequency, pitch transmissibility, yaw resonant frequency, and yaw transmissibility (RETRIEVE 'B:GDANCE'). Perform a preliminary examination of these variables and summarize them individually in preparation for a more complex analysis to be performed later.

35. A total of 21 wards in England (comparable to a census tract in the United States) were examined in terms of four social condition variables and rates of incidence of three diseases (RETRIEVE 'B:MGOLD'). The social condition variables measured overcrowding, poor toilet facilities, no car and the number of low skilled workers. The first three variables are expressed as rates per thousand households while the fourth variable is the number per thousand involved in low skilled work. The diseases were infectious jaundice, measles, and scabies in rates per hundred thousand people. Perform a preliminary examination of these variables and summarize them individually in preparation for a more complex analysis to be performed later.

36. A sample of professional golfers with low and high earnings is provided (RETRIEVE 'B:GOLF').[29] Perform a preliminary examination of age, height, weight, experience (years on the tour), average score, and earnings in preparation for a more complex analysis to be performed later.

37. This problem considers the proportions of light FCC, alkylate, butane, and reformate in the prediction of gasoline octane number.[30] The ability to select a blend that increases the octane number by as little as one point means millions in profits to oil companies. RETRIEVE 'B:GAS' and use INFO and PRINT C1-C5 to get started. Perform a preliminary examination of these variables and summarize them individually in preparation for a more complex analysis to be performed later.

38. The variables in this data set characterize 28 molds built for plastic injection molding machines. The mold cavities are machined out of steel. Two blocks of steel (for example, each 20 inches long, 12 inches wide and 5 inches thick) are machined so that, when the blocks are sandwiched together, a cavity (in the shape of a plastic part or parts) exists in the middle of the sandwich. Separate channels for molten plastic and coolant are also machined out. The variables are financial in nature.

To examine these data in MINITAB, RETRIEVE 'B:TOG1' then request information with INFO and PRINT C1-C9. The variable names are TNUM (a mold number for identification), PRICE (revenue, the bid price of the mold), BGTHRS (hours budgeted to make the mold), ACTHRS (actual hours to make the mold without corrective work on errors), CORHRS (corrective work hours), TOTHRS (=ACTHRS+CORHRS), ESTNP (estimated net profit), SUBCON (subcontracting cost) and REDGR (an artificial variable that is used to plot an R, called Reds, for those molds that the company lost a lot of money on, a G, called Greens, for those molds that the company made a lot of money on, and an A for all other molds). Perform a preliminary examination of these variables and summarize them individually in preparation for a more complex analysis to be performed later.

APPENDIX 1

General Overview of MINITAB

(Readers familiar with MINITAB and its start up procedure should skip ahead in this appendix to APPENDIX 2 MINITAB EXAMPLES)

MINITAB is a registered trademark of Minitab Incorporated whose cooperation has been appreciated by the author. Any reference in this book to MINITAB implies MINITAB Statistical Software. MINITAB Statistical Software is easy to set up and run on personal and mainframe computers. For product information, contact Minitab Inc., 3081 Enterprise Drive, State College, PA 16801-3008, phone 814-238-3280, fax 814-238-4383.

In order to get MINITAB up and running, you will have to acquaint yourself with your particular personal computer's start up procedure and commands. Different computers may have slightly different system commands to call up MINITAB, but MINITAB is easy and fun to run regardless of the computer of choice.

First, boot up your computer and monitor. Next, for a WINDOWS style operating system, double click the MINITAB application icon. Once MINITAB is up and running, you will see the MINITAB prompt MTB>. Certain commands (SET or READ) and command line endings (;) produce a few other prompts such as DATA> and SUBC>. A semicolon (;) produces a SUBC> prompt; a period must be typed to get back to a MTB> prompt.

Since specific MINITAB commands remain the same from one computer to another, MINITAB commands like SET, PRINT, and STEM will stay the same regardless of your computer.

MINITAB speaks, at most, four letter words. In longer command words, letters after the fourth are ignored. Also, words not in MINITAB's vocabulary will be ignored. This means that one can be verbose when typing commands, leaving a clear trail of your actions and your thinking. Or, the experienced MINITAB user might prefer the shorthand and use four letter command words.

For command line documentation of your work history, the # sign on a command line designates the beginning of a comment. Comments are provided throughout the text to help explain commands. Comments are located to the right of the MINITAB commands. For example,

```
MTB > SET DATA INTO C1         # C1 IS A COLUMN NAME FOR THE
                               # DATA
 DATA> 50 95 25 23 48 18 33    # EGG'S SALES DATA IN DOZENS
 DATA> 43,15,28,26,84,59       # SEPARATE WITH BLANKS OR
 DATA> END                     # COMMAS
MTB > NAME C1 'SALES'          # THE NAME INCLUDES THE QUOTES
```

Generally, the MINITAB command language is worth examining, even if you don't plan to use the computer in a course of study or if you plan to use a different statistical package. The emphasis is not on teaching you MINITAB but, rather, on the flavor and feel for computer assisted data analysis. Regardless of what statistical package you use, you will find many conceptual similarities between what is shown here and what you can do in any statistical package.

USING MINITAB IN A UNIVERSITY PERSONAL COMPUTER (PC) LABORATORY

Each MINITAB example in this text is designed to run in any PC laboratory that has the MINITAB statistical package available. The laboratory described here uses a network version of MINITAB.

STARTING UP

From a display menu of available software, select MINITAB by keying in the letter corresponding to the MINITAB selection or use the arrow keys to move the selection highlighter to MINITAB, then press ENTER. Or, in a WINDOWS style operating system, double click the MINITAB application icon.

First, MINITAB displays a logo and may ask you to depress a key to continue. Next, a prompt (MTB>) lets you know that MINITAB is ready to accept the commands shown in each example. STOP gets you out and back to the main system menu.

USERS OF THE STUDENT VERSION OF MINITAB

The student edition of MINITAB includes detailed instructions and diskettes. In addition to these disks, it is assumed that you have an additional formatted diskette for saving data sets and copies of your work. The student edition of MINITAB is a limited version of MINITAB. It will run most but not all of the commands shown in this textbook.

APPENDIX 2

MINITAB Examples

In the First MINITAB Session that follows, you are shown how to enter data values, correct or edit data values, have MINITAB plot data, construct a stem-and-leaf diagram, create a histogram and compute summary statistics.

THE FIRST MINITAB SESSION

EXAMPLE

EGG'S EGG SALES ANALYSIS USING MINITAB

MINITAB produces the same results that were presented throughout the chapter. Verification can be done by hand if necessary.

Operational Comment For simplicity, avoid using dialog boxes and do all work in the **Session Window** by typing commands line-by-line as shown below. When MINITAB is ready, it responds with a few informational messages and prompts, MTB> or DATA> or SUBC>. Each prompt, shown below, is followed by commands that you are expected to type.

```
Commands you type.              Extra comments so you know what and
                                why things are done.

MTB > SET DATA INTO C1      # C1 IS A COLUMN NAME FOR THE
                            #  DATA
DATA> 50 95 25 23 48 18 33  # EGG'S SALES DATA IN DOZENS
DATA> 43,15,28,26,84,59     # SEPARATE WITH BLANKS OR
DATA> END                   # COMMAS
MTB > NAME C1 'SALES'       # THE NAME INCLUDES THE QUOTES

MTB > PRINT 'SALES'         # TO CHECK FOR INPUT ERRORS

SALES

    50   95   25   23   48   18   33   43   15   28   26   84   59
```

Comment   The next to last, the 12-th data value, was typed incorrectly. You learn how to correct an errant data value.

```
MTB > LET 'SALES'(12) = 34   # CORRECT AN ERROR--CHANGE
                             # 84 TO 34
                             # THE 12-TH, 'SALES'(12),VALUE
                             # IS CHANGED
MTB > PRINT 'SALES'          # TO VERIFY THE CORRECTION

  SALES
50   95   25   23   48   18   33   43   15   28   26   34   59
```

Comment   For the SAVE command that follows, be sure to have a formatted diskette to receive the data in drive B: Alternatively, drive A: can be used. However, student version users would need drive A: for the MINITAB disks.

   Network users may prefer to use drive A: If so, all references to drive B: should be changed to A: in what follows, throughout the text.

```
MTB > SAVE  'B:EGGDATA'      # SO WE CAN RETRIEVE DATA
                            # WITHOUT RE-ENTERING IT
MTB > GSTD  # FOR STANDARD GRAPHICS IN THE SESSION WINDOW
MTB > TSPLOT 'SALES'
MTB > DESCRIBE 'SALES'
MTB > STEM-AND-LEAF 'SALES'; # THE SEMICOLON (;) INDICATES
                            # A SUBCOMMAND WILL FOLLOW
SUBC> TRIM.      # THE PERIOD (.) ENDS THE SUBCOMMAND
```

Comment   With the TRIM subcommand, unusually large or small data values are automatically trimmed from the stem-and-leaf diagram.

```
MTB > STEM 'SALES'       # SHORT COMMAND, NO TRIMMING
MTB > HIST C1 15 10      # AN ALTERNATIVE DISPLAY

GO ON TO ANOTHER EXAMPLE OR IF FINISHED, MTB >STOP
```

Comment   STOP ends a MINITAB session. You can now remove all the diskettes from the computer and turn it off.

SECOND MINITAB SESSION

Data that you saved in the first MINITAB session is retrieved (or re-entered) and the analysis is continued.

Operational Comment   At first for simplicity, avoid using dialog boxes and do all work in the Session Window by typing commands line-by-line as shown below. When MINITAB is ready it responds with a few informational messages and prompts, MTB> or DATA> or SUBC>.

The prompt is followed by commands that you are to type:

```
Commands you type,    Extra comments so you know what
                      and why things are done.
```

Be sure to have the disk that you saved the EGGDATA data on in drive B; if not, re-enter the sales data as shown below.

Network users may prefer to use drive A: If so, all references to drive B: should be changed to A: in what follows, throughout the text.

```
MTB > RETRIEVE 'B:EGGDATA' # SO WE CAN RETRIEVE THE DATA
                           # WITHOUT RE-ENTERING IT
```

Operational Comment Type INFO at this point if you need INFORMATION on the file that you just retrieved. Type PRINT C1 to see the data values.

If RETRIEVE was successful skip over the next SET command and DATA entry values. Data re-entry is necessary only if the retrieve failed.

```
MTB > SET DATA INTO C1     # C1 IS A COLUMN NAME FOR
                           # THE DATA
DATA> 50 95 25 23 48 18 33 # EGG'S SALES DATA IN DOZENS
DATA> 43,15,28,26,34,59    # SEPARATE WITH BLANKS OR
DATA> END                  # COMMAS

START HERE IF RETRIEVE WAS SUCCESSFUL
MTB > PRINT 'SALES'        # TO CHECK FOR INPUT ERRORS

 SALES
 50  95  25  23  48  18  33  43  15  28  26  34  59
```

THIS CHAPTER SHOWS OUTPUT FROM A COMMAND THAT IS NOT IN
THE PRESENT STUDENT VERSION OF MINITAB, MTB > **LVALS 'SALES'**
YOU MAY HAVE TO SUBSTITUTE, MTB > **DESCRIBE 'SALES'**

Comment DESCRIBE computes the median and the first (Q1) and third (Q3) quartiles. These are either the same or close (due to slight computational differences) to the LVALS results.

Complete MINITAB output from the LVALS command is shown below. MINITAB obtains letter values (the median, the hinges, the extremes) and a few other items of interest. The MID is the average of two letter values. Here, for the hinges, the MID is 36.5 and, for the extremes, the MID is 55. These two MID values are considerably different from each other and the median. When midsummaries (MIDs) are considerably different from the median or when midsummary values in the MID column change radically, there is a lack of symmetry in the distribution of the data.

SPREAD refers to the differences between letter values: the larger the spread the more spread out is the distribution of data values. The difference between the hinges is called the boxlength, showing the span of 50% of the data values. The difference between the extremes is called the range, showing the span of all the data values. More complete output from the LVALS command is shown below.

```
    DEPTH      LOWER      UPPER     MID     SPREAD
N = 13(total observations)
M    7                  33(Median)
H    4          25          48     36.5    23(box length)
     1          15          95     55      80(range)
```

MINITAB prints some additional rows (labeled E, D, C, and B) between the row for the hinges (H) and the last row for the extremes. I have edited out these rows (E, D, C, and B) because we don't need this level of detail at the present time.

```
GO ON TO ANOTHER EXAMPLE OR IF FINISHED, MTB>STOP
```

EXAMPLE

A TIME SERIES PLOT (TSPLOT) OF SALES

If no pattern is evident in the plot below, the series is said to be random. Then, the summary statistics shown above are valid.

DON'T RETRIEVE IF YOU ARE CONTINUING ON FROM THE PREVIOUS EXAMPLE WITHOUT STOPPING

```
MTB > RETRIEVE 'B:EGGDATA'
MTB > GSTD  # FOR STANDARD GRAPHICS IN THE SESSION WINDOW
MTB > TSPLOT 'SALES'
GO ON TO ANOTHER EXAMPLE OR IF FINISHED, MTB> STOP
```

CREATING A FILE OF MINITAB OUTPUT FOR IMPORT INTO A WORD PROCESSOR

Operational Comment   Make sure you have the formatted diskette that contains the EGG-DATA.MTW data set in drive B. The OUTFILE command shown below creates a file of MINITAB output (that you see on the screen) with the file name, EGGOUT.LIS. MINITAB adds the extension .LIS to EGGOUT and the extension .MTW to EGGDATA. While running MINITAB you therefore don't have to be concerned with the extensions.

```
MTB > OUTFILE 'B:EGGOUT.LIS'
MTB > RETRIEVE 'B:EGGDATA'
MTB > GSTD  # FOR STANDARD GRAPHICS IN THE SESSION WINDOW
MTB > TSPLOT 'SALES'
MTB > DESCRIBE 'SALES'
MTB > STEM-AND-LEAF 'SALES';  # THE SEMICOLON (;) INDICATES
                              # A SUBCOMMAND WILL FOLLOW
 SUBC> TRIM.   # THE PERIOD (.) ENDS THE SUBCOMMAND
MTB > STEM 'SALES'      # SHORT COMMAND, NO TRIMMING
MTB > HIST C1 15 10    # AN ALTERNATIVE DISPLAY
MTB > NOOUTFILE        # NOT REQUIRED--CLOSES THE OUTFILE
MTB > STOP
```

Now, get into your word processor and import EGGOUT.LIS. Add text of your own to produce a report on your analysis. When in a word processor and importing EGGOUT.LIS, you must use the extension. In WordPerfect, you retrieve this file by entering in response to a retrieve prompt: B:EGGOUT.LIS.

When in your word processor, set margins to $\frac{1}{2}$ inch on each side so MINITAB plots don't wrap around (some may have to use a 10 point font size and a non-proportional font such as Courier). Also, select and delete MINITAB's pagebreaks which are not needed in addition to those supplied by your word processor.

If you save your word-processing document under a new name (not using a .LIS extension) and return to MINITAB, you can begin your next session with the same outfile name, OUTFILE 'B:EGGOUT.LIS'. MINITAB appends the new output to the old. Often, you will choose a new outfile name because there will be no need to append.

Note   In WINDOWS, you can cut and paste to and from MINITAB and a word processor.

For Those Working with a Single Disk Drive

Sometimes files such as EGGDATA.MTW and EGGOUT.LIS are on different diskettes and you are using a single disk drive and must swap diskettes in and out of that drive. Before removing the diskette containing EGGOUT.LIS, you must use the MINITAB command NOOUTFILE. Also, after re-inserting the EGGOUT.LIS diskette, you must repeat the MINITAB command, OUTFILE 'B:EGGOUT.LIS'. The following commands illustrate disk swapping, NOOUTFILE and OUTFILE command sequences.

Have the diskette with the EGGOUT.LIS file in drive B.

```
MTB > OUTFILE   'B:EGGOUT.LIS'
MTB > SET IN C1      # SUPPOSE YOU ARE DOING SOME OTHER WORK
DATA > 3 44 66 5 88 19
DATA > END
MTB > DESCRIBE C1
MTB > NOOUTFILE        # YOU DECIDE TO GET EGGDATA FROM
                       # ANOTHER DISK

# SWAP DISKETTES IN DRIVE B:

MTB > RETRIEVE 'B:EGGDATA'    # EGGDATA DISK IN THE DRIVE

# SWAP DISKETTES IN DRIVE B:

MTB > OUTFILE   'B:EGGOUT.LIS' # EGGOUT DISK IN THE DRIVE
MTB > GSTD  # FOR STANDARD GRAPHICS IN THE SESSION WINDOW
MTB > TSPLOT 'SALES'   # SOME ADDITIONAL ANALYSIS
MTB > DESCRIBE 'SALES' # APPENDED TO EGGOUT.LIS
MTB > NOOUTFILE
GO ON TO ANOTHER EXAMPLE OR IF FINISHED, MTB> STOP
```

In the session above, replace B: with A: if working with drive A. Also, disk swapping can be avoided if you are using both drives A: and B: or a hard drive, say, C:.

Outfile Users in General

If you would like to create a file of your work from here on, place a formatted disk in drive A: and open an OUTFILE with the following command:

```
MTB > OUTFILE   'A:CH2.LIS'
```

If you retrieve most data sets from the network file server via the command RETRIEVE 'SomeFileName', your outfile can be on either drive A: or B: as you specify.

    If you use the textbook's data disk in drive B: and retrieve most data sets from B:, then it is most convenient to use drive A: for the outfile.

    If you are running the student version of MINITAB out of drive A: then you will probably use drive B: for the textbook's data disk and a separate disk for an outfile. This requires disk swapping in drive B: and is the least desirable mode of operation.

EXAMPLE

CHANGES IN THE NONRANDOM SALES SERIES

(If you have the textbook's data diskette, **RETRIEVE 'B:NRSEGG'** and omit the data entry using SET below.)

(If you are on a network and have the textbook's data stored in subdirectory DATA under the directory MINITAB, **RETRIEVE 'NRSEGG'** and omit the data entry using SET below.)

```
DON'T SET DATA IN C1 IF RETRIEVE WAS SUCCESSFUL
      MTB > SET DATA IN C1 # NEW SALES SEQUENCE IN C1
                          # A TREND OF INCREASING SALES
      DATA> 15 18 23 25 26 28 33 34 43 48 50 59 95
      DATA> END

START HERE IF RETRIEVE WAS SUCCESSFUL
MTB > LAG 1 C1 C2    # EACH ROW OF C2 CONTAINS SALES
                     # FROM THE PREVIOUS ROW OF C1

MTB > LET C3 = C1 - C2 # DIFFERENCES, TODAY'S SALES MINUS
                       # YESTERDAY'S SALES FOR ALL DAYS
                       # C3 = CHANGES IN SALES

MTB > DIFF 1 C1 C4    # EASIER WAY TO GET C3, C3 = C4
                      # C4 IS ALSO CHANGES IN SALES
```

C4 was obtained directly using the MINITAB command, DIFF 1 C1 C4. This command places the differences (changes) of adjacent values of sales (C1) into C4. C3 is the same as C4, but, by using LAG 1 C1 C2 and LET C3 = C1 - C2, the reader can see exactly how the changes were obtained.

```
MTB > PRINT C1 C2 C3 C4
MTB > GSTD  # FOR STANDARD GRAPHICS IN THE SESSION WINDOW
MTB > TSPLOT C1    # SALES PLOTTED OVER TIME
MTB > TSPLOT C3    # CHANGES IN SALES OVER TIME

MTB > DELETE ROW 1 OF C3  #LVALS COMMAND CAN'T HANDLE
                          #MISSING VALUES

# THE FOLLOWING COMMAND IS NOT IN THE PRESENT STUDENT
# VERSION OF MINITAB,
MTB > LVALS C3
# YOU MAY HAVE TO SUBSTITUTE
MTB > DESCRIBE C3

MTB > STEM C3
GO ON TO ANOTHER EXAMPLE OR IF FINISHED, MTB> STOP
```

EXAMPLE

YEARLY SALES, CUMMINS ENGINE COMPANY

(If you have the textbook's data diskette, **RETRIEVE 'B:CUMMINS'** and omit the data entry using SET.)

(If you are on a network and have the data stored in subdirectory DATA under the directory MINITAB, **RETRIEVE 'CUMMINS'** and omit the data entry using SET below.)

```
DON'T SET IF RETRIEVE WAS SUCCESSFUL
    MTB > SET DATA IN C1     # SALES IN BILLIONS OF DOLLARS
                            # CUMMINS ENGINE COMPANY
    DATA> .8 .76 1.03 1.26 1.52 1.77 1.67
    DATA> 1.96 1.59 1.60 2.33 2.15 2.30 2.77
    DATA> END

START HERE IF RETRIEVE WAS SUCCESSFUL
MTB > LAG 1 C1 C2       # C2 CONTAINS SALES ONE PERIOD BACK
MTB > LET C3 = C1 - C2  # CHANGES IN SALES

MTB > LET C4 = (C3/C2)*100   # YEARLY PERCENT CHANGES
MTB > ROUND C4 PUT IN C5     # ROUNDED

MTB > PRINT C1 C2 C3 C4 C5
MTB > GSTD  # FOR STANDARD GRAPHICS IN THE SESSION WINDOW
MTB > TSPLOT C1    # SALES IN BILLIONS OF DOLLARS
MTB > TSPLOT C3    # CHANGES IN SALES
                   # THAT SEEM TO BE INCREASING
MTB > TSPLOT C4    # PERCENT CHANGES IN SALES
                   # OMIT TWO POINTS, COVER WITH YOUR
                   # HAND, IN YEARS 11 AND 14
MTB > STEM C4
MTB > DELETE ROW 1 COLUMNS C2 C3 C5
           # LVALS COMMAND WON'T HANDLE THE MISSING
           # VALUE IN ROW ONE THAT RESULTS FROM WORKING
           # WITH CHANGES RATHER THAN SALES
```

```
# OUTPUT IS SHOWN FROM A COMMAND THAT IS NOT IN THE PRESENT
# STUDENT VERSION OF MINITAB,  MTB > LVALS C3
# THIS PROVIDES SUMMARY STATS ON CHANGES IN SALES

# YOU MAY HAVE TO SUBSTITUTE   MTB > DESCRIBE C3
```

Comment   DESCRIBE computes the median and the first (Q1) and third (Q3) quartiles. These are either the same or close (due to slight computational differences) to the LVALS results.

```
MTB > LVALS C5   # ROUNDED, PERCENT CHANGES IN SALES
GO ON TO ANOTHER EXAMPLE OR IF FINISHED, MTB> STOP
```

E X A M P L E

MINITAB PRODUCED BOXPLOT

(If you have the textbook's data diskette, **RETRIEVE 'B:EGGDATA'.**)
(If you are on a network and have the data stored in subdirectory DATA under the directory **MINITAB, RETRIEVE 'EGGDATA'.**)

```
MTB > INFO
MTB > BOXPLOT C1  # YOU CAN USE EITHER NAME C1
                  # OR 'SALES'
GO ON TO ANOTHER EXAMPLE OR IF FINISHED, MTB> STOP
```

E X A M P L E

GETTING TO KNOW BLACK CHERRY TREES BETTER THROUGH THE VARIABLES DIAMETER, HEIGHT, AND VOLUME

(Assuming you have the textbook's data diskette, **RETRIEVE 'B:TREES';** otherwise, SET the data in columns. The data are listed in the chapter.)
(If you are on a network and have the data stored in subdirectory DATA under the directory **MINITAB, RETRIEVE 'TREES';** otherwise, SET the data in columns. The data are listed in the chapter.)

```
MTB > INFO       # IN CASE YOU WANT MORE DETAILS
                 # ABOUT THE SAVED DATA FILE
MTB > STEM  'DIAMETER'
MTB > LVALS 'DIAMETER'   # OR USE, DESCRIBE 'DIAMETER'
MTB > STEM  'HEIGHT'
MTB > LVALS 'HEIGHT'  # OR USE DESCRIBE
MTB > STEM  'VOLUME'
MTB > LVALS 'VOLUME'  # OR USE DESCRIBE

MTB > PRINT 'DIAMETER'
MTB > PRINT 'HEIGHT'
MTB > PRINT 'VOLUME'

GO ON TO ANOTHER EXAMPLE OR IF FINISHED, MTB > STOP
```

CHAPTER 3

Classical Methods of Summarizing a Single Variable

OBJECTIVES

◆ Introduce classical methods of summarizing a single variable

◆ Estimate a distribution's center with a sample mean

◆ Remove the mean from data values to get residuals

◆ Estimate variability with a sample standard deviation

◆ Understand how sample means and standard deviations work together

◆ Become familiar with the shape of the normal distribution of data

PRELUDE

Because of their pictorial nature and ease of use, exploratory methods for summarizing data have much appeal, especially to the beginner. Exploratory tools help you become familiar with a data set for the first time without having to worry about background conditions. If you discover that a stem-and-leaf display has a familiar form, that of the normal (also called Gaussian) distribution, you can use classical statistical tools advantageously because they are better under these circumstances.

A thorough analysis often means that you have examined the data from both exploratory and classical views. If the same results come from either view, then the summary of the data is unambiguous. When the exploratory tools paint a different picture than do the classical ones, you must find the reasons for the differences. In so doing, you will become more familiar with the nuances of the data set and their practical implications.

This chapter covers in classical terms what the previous chapter did in exploratory terms for a single variable. It provides the manager with a more complete set of tools and a more complete framework for summarizing a single variable. ◆

INTRODUCTION

Stories about major executive decisions and costly gambles are plentiful. Consider the following account of General Electric's high-stakes locomotive wager.[1]

A typical locomotive sells for about one million dollars. Therefore, it is not surprising that the two main competitors are large and established companies: General Motors and General Electric. While in second place, GE embarked on a $500 million modernization plan in response to favorable sales forecasts. As it turned out, the new facilities were ready at the wrong time because diesel locomotive orders slumped. Unfortunately, the anticipated large profits did not materialize because the modern, cost-effective manufacturing capacity was out of phase with the demand.

Typically, domestic railroads purchased 1,700 locomotives a year, but only 300 new locomotives were bought in the year that the modern facilities were available. Contributing to the precipitous drop in sales were (1) falling oil prices that decreased the need for new fuel-efficient locomotives; (2) an elimination of peripheral routes due to deregulation; and (3) more efficient deployment of the existing fleet.

GE executives failed in the risky business of forecasting. This forecasting error reflected management's failure to understand how much the actual demand (300 locomotives) might deviate from the typical demand (1,700 locomotives). The new high-capacity facilities were amortized as an expense on the income statement while low demand depressed revenues. This error cost GE a lot of money.

Fundamental Characteristics of the Data Relate to Decisions

Typical values, such as sales of 1,700 locomotives a year at a price of $1 million each, are crucial numbers for decision making. Multiplying these figures, one obtains $1.7 billion in revenues. If General Electric and General Motors divide this revenue pie equally, GE's half is $850 million. Thus, the decision to modernize GE's facilities at a cost of $500 million seems reasonable, particularly if the plant has at least a 5-year life.

If actual demand is 300 locomotives a year, GE's share of the revenue falls to $150 million. Now the $500 million modernization plan does not look so good and may warrant a different decision. Thus, it is not only important to understand typical demand but also how much actual demand might deviate from typical demand. As this chapter develops, you will gain a better understanding of typical values. As a consequence, deviations of individual data values from what is typical are made clearer too. This discussion should put you one step ahead of the GE executives who erred in forecasting locomotive sales.

THE SAMPLE MEAN, RESIDUALS, AND STANDARD DEVIATION

In the previous chapter you were introduced to the sample median as a typical value representing the central tendency of a data set. This chapter introduces an alternative typical value, the *sample mean.*

The sample median rather than the sample mean is recommended in exploratory work because at first we don't know much about the data values and their distribution. In particular, we take advantage of the sample median's insensitivity to outliers and distributional shapes. The median provides some insurance that problematic data does not distort the typical value.

If we learn from exploratory work that the data distribution is reasonably symmetrical and without outliers, then the sample mean is preferred as a typical value measure. Furthermore, when stem-and-leaf diagrams or histograms have a **normal distribution** of a "bell-shaped" pattern, we can take advantage of useful theory associated with the sample mean.

The same thinking applies to measures of variability that indicate the spread of the data distribution. In exploratory work, variability is expressed in terms of the box length. When the data distribution is normal and without outliers, the **sample standard deviation** is the preferred measure of variability. For large samples from normal distributions, the sample standard deviation is about three-fourths of the box length. This rule of thumb provides a convenient link between the exploratory and classical measures of variation.

The standard deviation computation depends on the deviation of a data value from the sample mean. This deviation is defined as a classical **residual.** We introduce residuals in this chapter because of their fundamental focus on variation. Unusually large residuals might be outliers that expose unusual data features. Also, the distribution of the residuals reflects the distribution of the data values.

If random observations are drawn from normal distributions, a rich body of well-developed theory can be applied to practical data analysis problems. Even when the data distributions are nonnormal, sometimes the data can be transformed to produce normal distributions. The assumptions of normality and randomness are indigenous to many formal classical statistical methods. In general, assumptions tend to restrict applicability; nevertheless, the classical methods are widely used and work well when the assumptions are valid.

A mathematical model called a *naive regression model* integrates and structures many of the ideas in this chapter. The naive regression model, sample mean, and standard deviation enable managers to augment their exploratory view of the data, thus giving them a better picture of what the data tells them about pending decisions.

One Variable at a Time, the Classical Approach

Like the exploratory tools, classical methods enable us to characterize the data structure in terms of the main and the unusual features. Classical methods go a step further and make possible the formal confirmation or denial of hypotheses that might have been generated in early stages of the analysis. Such extensions are possible because of the definitions and relationships associated with the naive regression model.

Naming the Data Values   More formal notation is introduced to take advantage of the power and flexibility of mathematical models. The i-th data value is named y_i; the subscript "i" $= 1, 2, \ldots, 13$ designates particular data values in the egg sales data set. In general, the largest subscript value is the total number of data values "n," the sample size. Thus, y_i is indexed i $= 1, 2, \ldots, n$.

The symbols and subscripts simplify and clarify the discussion. The symbols are names for particular data values as shown below. The names are necessary to identify particular data values. For example, instead of data value names such as Mary, Tony, and John, we use y_1, y_2, and y_3. Like a family name, the y part of the name is the same for all individual observations, indicating a single variable, y. The subscripts "i" $= 1, 2, \ldots, 13$, are distinct and identify each data value. For the egg sales data, the names are shown with the data value that the name identifies written below it:

$$y_1, \; y_2, \; y_3, \; y_4, \; y_5, \; y_6, \; y_7, \; y_8, \; y_9, \; y_{10}, y_{11}, y_{12}, y_{13}$$
$$50, \; 95, \; 25, \; 23, \; 48, \; 18, \; 33, \; 43, \; 15, \; 28, \; 26, \; 34, \; 59$$

In the exhibits that follow, four data values and their corresponding names are displayed.

$$y_i = y_2 \quad y_4 \quad y_9 \quad y_{13}$$
$$\text{Data values} = 95 \quad 23 \quad 15 \quad 59$$

Plotting the Data Values   Egg sales data from Chapter 2 are shown in Exhibit 1. In this elementary graph, y_i is plotted on the vertical axis, and because no other variable is considered, an arbitrary point locates the data values on the horizontal scale. This plot becomes a cornerstone for a naive regression model.

The term **regression** has roots that are more historical than logical. In studies of inheritance, Galton noticed that tall fathers tended to have tall sons and short fathers tended to have short sons. But on average the sons were not quite as tall as taller-than-average fathers nor quite as short as shorter-than-average fathers. Thus, heights of sons on average moved toward or "regressed" toward the average height of the male population. This phenomenon is referred to as regression toward the mean.

The naive regression model has two component parts, an **exact value** and an **individual chance error.**

An individual measurement is broken into two parts to carry out a divide and conquer strategy for understanding the data value. Thinking about the exact value and the individual chance error separately simplifies things. For example, to understand your pulse measurement, you might want to know (1) the median pulse for a large population of individuals (an exact value), and

EXHIBIT 1 The Genesis of Observed Data Based on a Naive Regression Model

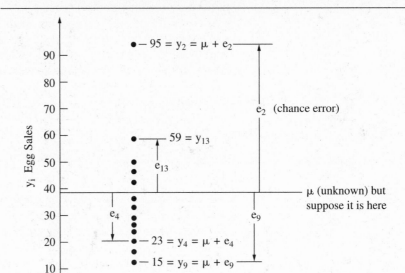

(2) how much different your pulse is from the median (an individual chance error).

An Exact Value   An exact value locates the center of a population of observations; it is a typical value for a population. In exploratory work, we think of an exact value as the population median, informally, the median of a very large number of observations. In classical statistics, the exact value is the population mean, μ.

For a population of size N, the **population mean** is defined as

$$\mu = \frac{\Sigma\, y_i}{N}$$

where the summation includes all individuals in the population. Although this formula is provided as a definition, it is rarely used because seldom are all population members accessible.

Often the exact value is a conceptual reference because it is unknown. For example, the median or mean pulse of thousands of individuals may not be available. Therefore, the exact value might be estimated from a relatively small quantity of data available in a sample.

For a sample of size n, the **sample mean** is defined as

$$\bar{y} = \frac{\Sigma\, y_i}{n}$$

where the summation includes all individuals in the sample. Applications of this formula will be presented later in the chapter.

An Individual Chance Error   An individual chance error is the deviation of an individual data value from the exact value. Thus, the individual chance error is computed by subtracting the exact value from an individual measurement:

(individual measurement − exact value) = individual chance error

A Naive Regression Model

In practice, the relationship between an individual measurement, exact value, and individual chance error is expressed with symbols in a mathematical equation. Each individual observation, y_i, consists of two additive components; together they form an **additive model.** The additive components are

1. the unknown population mean, μ, an exact value
2. the unknown individual chance error, e_i

The sum of these two terms creates the following **naive regression model:**

individual measurement = exact value + individual chance error

$$y_i \quad = \quad \mu \quad + \quad e_i$$

Exhibit 1 demonstrates the genesis of observed data based on this simple model structure. To construct the exhibit, it was necessary to choose a value for μ as if this exact value were known.

Usually, μ is unknown and estimated from data; however, there are occasions when it is regarded as known. For example, in statistical process control of a manufacturing process, a quality control engineer might have enough historical data on a product's size or weight that the population mean size or weight is considered known. Or a financial planner might ask, "If the population mean level of sales is 50,000 units, then what profit is likely?" To evaluate the profitability of this sales scenario, mean sales is regarded as known.

To illustrate the naive regression model graphically, 4 of 13 egg sales figures are highlighted in Exhibit 1. The exhibit emphasizes the relationship between an individual measurement (data point), exact value (μ), and individual chance error (arrow length) for these 4 data points. In equation form, four instances of the naive regression model can be written, one for each highlighted data point in the exhibit.

$$95 = y_2 = \mu + e_2$$
$$23 = y_4 = \mu + e_4$$
$$15 = y_9 = \mu + e_9$$
$$59 = y_{13} = \mu + e_{13}$$

The naive regression model splits the individual measurement into two parts, an exact value and an individual chance error. The exact value represents an unknown typical value while the chance error represents each measurement's unknown deviation from the typical value. The deviations reflect variability.

Exhibit 2 extends Exhibit 1 to emphasize that the 13 sales figures comprise a sample from a population of sales figures. The sample members are the plotted data points on the left side of Exhibit 2; on the right side, the bell-shaped normal (Gaussian) population is sketched. The 13 sample points are drawn from the population with a mean, μ.

You can think of the population's bell shape as a smoothed polygon fitted to a density histogram for a very large number of data values. In theory, this population consists of an infinite number of data values. Exhibit 2 allows us to think beyond the sample data values to the population where the data values originated.

Sample data can and does arise from nonnormal distributions too. Thus the distribution on the right side of Exhibit 2 can have many other shapes. However, the discussion in this chapter focuses on the normal shape to simplify things in the beginning. Additionally, when the population is normal, a large body of statistical theory can be drawn on and put to use.

EXHIBIT 2 An Observed Sample of Data Values from a Normal Distribution

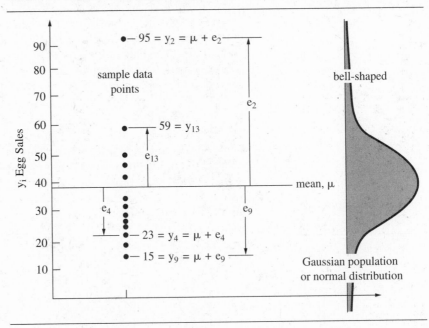

Because of the normal distribution's theoretical role, the distributional shape of the sample data is examined routinely in the data analysis process. Stem-and-leaf diagrams or histograms of sample data and residuals that are normal validate the use of contingent statistical tools.

To verify the normality of sample data, other graphical displays are also used. A **dotplot** is like a stem-and-leaf display in which the data values are represented by dots. In Example 1, measurements are taken on weights of soap bars, and a dotplot reveals the general shape of the distribution of data values.

Expressing an individual measurement in a sample as

individual measurement = exact value + individual chance error

implies that the individual measurement and the individual chance error have the same distribution. Also note that the exact value is a constant and has no variation.

The exact value fixes the location of the normal distribution's center or mean, μ. Because the normal distribution is symmetrical, the mean is the same as the median and the mode; thus symmetry is of considerable value in simplifying things. The spread of the distribution is characterized by σ, the **population standard deviation,** which is about three-fourths of a box length.

Computer Simulation and Data Analysis

Using the computer to mimic an actual process is called **computer simulation.** Simulation has become a valuable tool for carrying out experiments on the computer; some evidence is in the success of spreadsheet software such as Lotus 1-2-3 or Excel. Simulation approximates a real system and can help managers validate new ideas quickly, diagnose potential problems, optimize the performance of complex systems, and learn about something complex. Managers find that a major purpose of personal computers is to perform simulations. The data resulting from simulations usually require statistical analysis.

The simulation examples in this chapter don't require that you perform the simulations to understand the results. But they give you the opportunity to experiment on your own and simulate data. To gain familiarity with the shape of the normal distribution, use the MINITAB commands for generating such data listed in Appendix 1. After examining the MINITAB commands, you may wish to try them.

EXAMPLE 1

A MANUFACTURER WEIGHING BARS OF SOAP

A manufacturer produces soap bars with mean weight $\mu = 100$ grams, nominally. To assess the weight aspect of product quality, the bar-molding process is monitored by an electronic device called Red Eye that weighs and records the weight, y_i, of each bar of soap.

Red Eye turns on a red light when the molding process starts producing soap bars that weigh too much and a yellow light when the bars weigh too little. Red Eye and the molding machines need occasional tuning to ensure proper operation; therefore, Red Eye creates a data file for analysis on a personal computer. In addition to bar weight, y_i, it was found that deviations, e_i, from the nominal of 100 grams provided the clearest signal for indicating when bars weigh too much or too little, because deviations are accompanied by plus signs (over-weight bars) and minus signs (underweight bars). A data set similar to what Red Eye produces is shown in the problem solution. The components of the naive regression model stand out clearly.

For simulating data from the normal distribution, you must supply the location of the center ($\mu = 100$ in this example and called MU in MINITAB) and the spread ($\sigma = .33$ in this example and called SIGMA in MINITAB). As a reminder and a reference, SIGMA is about three-fourths of a box length. Both μ and σ will be discussed more completely as we proceed.

Problem Statement (a) In order to monitor recent production, examine weights of soap bars. Represent the weight data in a regression model format and show that actual weight minus nominal weight produces individual chance errors.

Problem Solution (a) The regression model format is evident below and shows that actual weight minus nominal weight (μ) produces individual chance errors. If you try to replicate these results, your computer is likely to simulate different weight figures.

ROW	BARWT	NOMINAL	DEV
	y_i	$-$ μ	$=$ e_i
1	99.22	100	-0.78
2	99.26	100	-0.74
3	99.97	100	-0.03
4	100.01	100	+0.01
5	99.60	100	-0.40
6	100.21	100	+0.21
7	99.52	100	-0.48
8	100.03	100	+0.03
9	100.15	100	+0.15
10	100.03	100	+0.03
11	99.92	100	-0.08
12	100.31	100	+0.31
13	99.99	100	-0.01
14	100.31	100	+0.31
15	99.60	100	-0.40
16	99.83	100	-0.17
17	99.49	100	-0.51
18	99.43	100	-0.57
19	100.15	100	+0.15
20	100.13	100	+0.13

Problem Statement (b) Obtain and display (1) a distribution of weights for a small and large sample; and (2) for the large sample, also show a distribution of individual chance errors.

Problem Solution (b) For a small sample, the distribution of weights is shown first as a dotplot of the 20 observations on BARWT, the variable name in MINITAB. Although the 20 observations are generated from a normal distribution, such a small sample produces a dotplot that does not have the normal distribution's bell shape.

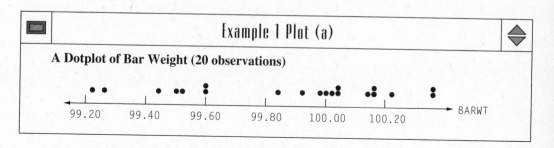

The two distributions that follow are for a large sample of weights (named BARWT) and individual chance errors (named DEV). When the number of simulated observations is increased from 20 to 100, both the BARWT and DEV distributions begin to take on the normal distribution's bell shape.

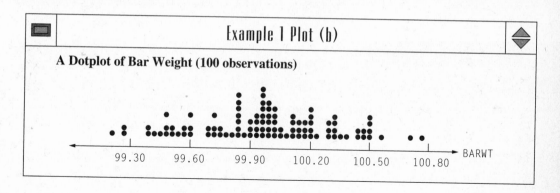

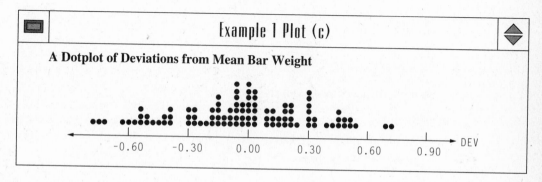

Estimating the Population Mean μ with the Sample Mean $\bar{y}$

Because μ, the population mean, is usually unknown, it is desirable to estimate μ from sample data. Under certain conditions, $\bar{y}$, the **arithmetic mean** or sample mean, is the preferred estimator of central tendency.

$$\bar{y} = \frac{\Sigma \, y_i}{n}$$

In the presence of competing exploratory estimators of central tendency that include the sample median and mode, which estimator do we use? The sample mean works well when the data distribution is normal and without outliers. Therefore, in the previous example, the bell-shaped dotplot with no outliers of 100 observations on BARWT would lead us to work with the sample mean. Also, even the symmetrical dotplot with no outliers of 20 observations on BARWT would lead us to work with the sample mean.

Under conditions of symmetry and without outliers, the sample median and mode may be close in value to the sample mean; however, the sample mean is the estimator of choice. Theoretically, without outliers the sample mean will vary less from sample to sample than competing estimators; therefore, it tends to be more on target. However, the sample mean is sensitive to outliers, which explains the preference for the sample median in exploratory analysis.

EXAMPLE 2

THE SAMPLE MEAN WEIGHT OF BARS OF SOAP

Problem Statement   Using the weights of 20 bars of soap in the previous example, compute the sample mean with and without MINITAB statistical software.

Problem Solution   The computational formula results in the following sample mean:

$$\bar{y} = \frac{\Sigma \, y_i}{n} = \frac{99.22 + 99.26 + \cdots + 100.13}{20} = 99.86$$

In MINITAB, the command, AVERAGE, followed by the name of the data column, 'BARWT', produces the same result.

Problem Discussion   The numerator in the computational formula for the sample mean is the sum of all the observations, $(\Sigma \, y_i) = (99.22 + 99.26 + \cdots + 100.13)$. If a data recording error were made with the first data value recorded as 9922 rather than 99.22, both the sum and the sample mean would be inflated. This is how outliers can inflate the sample mean. The median would be less sensitive to this data recording error because it does not depend on this sum and is simply the middle value in an ordered list of data values.

EXAMPLE 3

CASH FLOW FROM AN INVESTMENT

Managers gamble when they make an investment. Suppose an investment of $100,000 is necessary to produce freeze-dried beer. From sales of this new product, the managers expect a net cash flow of $25,000 at the end of each year. Think of the net cash flow roughly as the sales revenues less any operating expenses that occur during a year.

A net cash flow of $25,000 at the end of each year is not certain. In fact, the $25,000 could be viewed as a best guess of a population mean (μ = $25,000). Often little or no marketing research data are available to fully justify this figure.

The number of years it takes for the net cash flows to pay back the investment is called the payback period. An approximate payback period is computed by dividing the investment by the net cash flow, for example, $\frac{\$100,000}{\$25,000}$ = 4 years. The shorter the payback period the better. Many practitioners use the payback period as a rough guide in investment decisions.

Since a single value, like $25,000, does not capture the uncertainty of the situation, many managers prefer to think of a range of figures. For example, suppose 50% of the time the net cash flows are expected to be between $22,000 and $28,000. This interval, ($28,000 − $22,000) = $6,000, is a variability measure, a box length. Roughly, three-fourths of a box length ($4,500) is a standard deviation.

Problem Statement (a)   Simulate 1,000 potential cash flows from a normal distribution with a mean of $25,000 and a standard deviation of $4,500. Display these cash flows in a dotplot and note the distributional shape. Are any outliers present?

Problem Solution (a)   The following dotplot allows a manager to make a visual assessment of cash flow possibilities. The distribution is normal and without outliers. (Each dot represents four potential net cash flow values.)

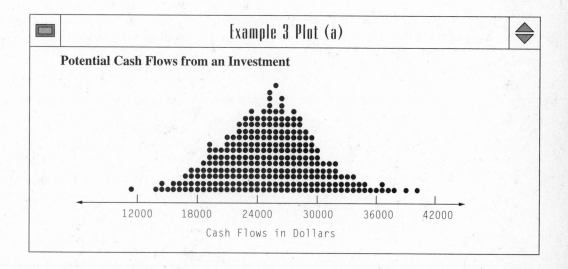

Problem Statement (b)   Obtain potential payback periods by dividing the investment amount, $100,000, by the simulated cash flows. Display these payback periods in a dotplot and note the distributional shape. Are any potential outliers present?

Problem Solution (b)   The following dotplot allows a manager to make a visual assessment of the payback period possibilities. The distribution is nonnormal with potential outliers in the right tail of the distribution. (Each dot represents five potential payback periods.)

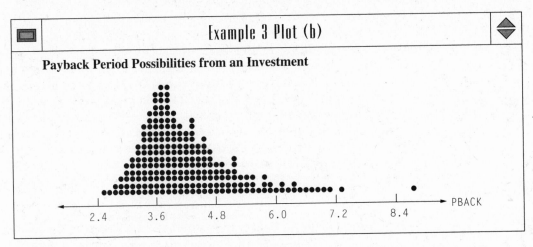

Problem Statement (c)   Because the net cash flow distribution is normal and without outliers, it can be summarized best by classical methods, using the sample mean and standard deviation. However, this is not the case for the payback period.

Although the payback period computation relies on normal net cash flow figures, the resulting payback period is nonnormal in distribution. The right tail of the distribution is longer than the left one; therefore, the distribution is skewed to the right. The observations in the right tail of the distribution will inflate the sample mean and the sample standard deviation. Exploratory summaries are designed to resist such inflation. Therefore, the median and the box length are recommended summaries of central tendency and variability for the payback period.

Find and discuss both the exploratory and classical summary statistics; note that the classical summaries are inflated.

Problem Solution (c)   The exploratory summary statistics for the potential payback periods are

```
     DEPTH      LOWER      UPPER     SPREAD

N=  1000
M    500.5             3.957 (median)
H    250.5     3.576     4.534     0.958 (box length)
       1       2.489     8.876     6.387 (range)
```

The classical summary statistics for the potential payback periods are

	N	MEAN	MEDIAN	STDEV
PBACK	1000	4.1307	3.9572	0.8054

	MIN	MAX	Q1(HINGE)	Q3(HINGE)
PBACK	2.4893	8.8764	3.575	4.534

Notice that the sample mean and sample standard deviation are inflated relative to their exploratory counterparts, the median and ($\frac{3}{4} \times$ box length).

Problem Discussion   Typically the investors get their money back in 3.96 years. One quarter of the time it takes more than 4.53 years for payback and one quarter of the time it takes less than 3.58 years. The manager must decide whether or not to pursue this investment opportunity. The decision may depend on available alternatives.

Origin of the Formula for the Sample Mean

A well-known and widely used method for deriving the formula for the sample mean is the **ordinary least squares method (OLS).** The term *least squares* means to find an estimator of μ that results in the minimum (least value) **sum of the errors squared.** The naive regression model

$$y_i = \mu + e_i$$

provides the structural ingredients for the OLS method because a squared error is

$$(y_i - \mu)^2 = e_i^2$$

An OLS estimator minimizes the sum of the errors squared, Q, where the summation is over all observations, i = 1, 2, . . . , n.

$$Q = \Sigma (y_i - \mu)^2 = \Sigma e_i^2$$

A value of Q larger than the minimum, Q_{min}, is undesirable because Q reflects the cumulative squared distance of the estimator from the data values. By choosing the sample mean

$$\bar{y} = \Sigma \frac{y_i}{n}$$

as an estimator of μ, Q is minimized.

Unfortunately, outliers can produce large errors that may have a dramatic influence on the sample mean and the sum of the errors squared. Thus, the sample mean and the OLS method tend to perform better when the data distribution is symmetrical and without outliers.

In contrast, Q will not be minimized by the sample median or mode; however, the median and mode are insensitive to outliers. Therefore, the decision to use a particular estimator depends on the data distribution.

A Prediction Equation

When y_i is random and distributed symmetrically about μ, the sample mean is a reasonable **predictor** of a future y_i value.

$$\text{predicted } y_i = \overline{y}$$

This simple equation is referred to as a **prediction equation.** Usually the term *predicted* in predicted y_i is dropped and implied by a caret mark on top of the letter.

$$\text{predicted } y_i = \hat{y}_i = \overline{y}$$

If no additional variables other than y are available to help in the prediction, this equation remains simple and relies on the sample mean.

Many decisions managers make depend on predicted outcomes. For example, managers might be interested in predicting a future net cash flow value, a future payback period, or a future value of sales.

EXAMPLE 4

PREDICTING EGG SALES

Problem Statement   Using the egg sales data from Chapter 2 that were random, find the typical sales level using the classical approach. Predict a future value of sales.

Problem Solution   The classical sample mean typifies these random sales figures and can be used to predict a future value of sales.

$$\overline{y} = \Sigma \frac{y_i}{n} = \text{predicted } y_i = \frac{497}{13} = 38.23 \text{ (dozen)}$$

Problem Discussion   Recall that the sample median and mode were found to be 33 and 25, respectively; both of these summary values are lower in numerical value than the sample mean. The sample mean was influenced by one large data value, $y_2 = 95$, while the sample median and mode were not influenced as much. Thus, either the sample median or mode would be a more representative typical value than the sample mean.

The Sample Mean for Grouped Data (Optional)

Statistics such as the sample mean are usually calculated from the individual data values. Sometimes data are available only in **grouped form,** or frequency distribution form; therefore, the **grouped sample mean** needs to be described.

For the egg sales data, class intervals, midpoints, frequency counts, and relative frequencies (frequency count/total frequency count) are in the first four columns of Exhibit 3. A fifth column is computed by multiplying class midpoints times relative frequencies; the sum of the fifth column is the grouped sample mean.

The total of the weighted midpoints in the last column, 495/13, equals 38.08, the grouped sample mean. Note that the ungrouped sample mean is 38.23 (from the previous example); clearly the grouped mean is an approximation because the class midpoints are surrogates for the actual data values.

The procedure for computing the group mean is summarized in the following formula.

Let

$$f_i = \text{frequency count for the i-th class}$$
$$\Sigma \, f_i = n, \text{ the sample size}$$
$$m_i = \text{the midpoint of the i-th class}$$

Then the grouped sample mean is

$$\overline{y}_g = \Sigma \, \frac{f_i}{n} \times m_i$$

where the summation is over all classes.

EXHIBIT 3 The Grouped Sample Mean Computations

Class Intervals	Class Midpoints	Frequency Counts	Relative Frequencies	Class Midpoints Multiplied by Relative Frequencies
10 to 20	15.0	2	2/13	$(15 * 2/13) = 30/13$
20 to 30	25.0	4	4/13	$(25 * 4/13) = 100/13$
30 to 40	35.0	2	2/13	$(35 * 2/13) = 70/13$
40 to 50	45.0	2	2/13	$(45 * 2/13) = 90/13$
50 to 60	55.0	2	2/13	$(55 * 2/13) = 110/13$
60 to 70	65.0	0	0/13	0
70 to 80	75.0	0	0/13	0
80 to 90	85.0	0	0/13	0
90 to 100	95.0	1	1/13	$(95 * 1/13) = 95/13$
TOTALS		13	1	
			Total and Grouped Sample Mean	495/13

Estimating an Error, e_i, with a Residual, $\hat{e}_i$

To obtain a better grasp of how each observation differs from what is typical, the typical value is taken away. The actual observation minus a summary value is called a residual. When the summary value in the prediction equation is the sample mean, the residual is an estimator of an unknown individual chance error. An equation for the residual is given in words and symbols below.

$$\text{(individual measurement } - \text{ exact value)} = \text{individual chance error}$$
$$\text{(estimator)} \qquad \text{(estimator)}$$
$$(y_i \qquad\qquad - \text{ predicted } y_i) = \qquad \hat{e}_i$$

EXAMPLE 5

CLASSICAL RESIDUALS FOR THE EGG SALES DATA

Problem Statement   For the egg sales data, the summary value in the prediction equation is the sample mean, 38.23. Find four residuals by subtracting the sample mean from observations y_4, y_9, y_2, and y_{13}.

Problem Solution

$$(y_4 - \text{predicted } y_4) = (23 - 38.23) = -15.23 = \hat{e}_4$$
$$(y_9 - \text{predicted } y_9) = (15 - 38.23) = -23.23 = \hat{e}_9$$
$$(y_2 - \text{predicted } y_2) = (95 - 38.23) = +56.77 = \hat{e}_2$$
$$(y_{13} - \text{predicted } y_{13}) = (59 - 38.23) = +20.77 = \hat{e}_{13}$$

Problem Discussion   These residuals estimate the unknown individual chance errors. Only 4 of the 13 residuals for the egg sales data are shown in Exhibit 4. You should also realize that these residuals estimate the unknown errors shown in Exhibit 1.

Residuals are generally more informative than the original data values. One reason is that they are signed; therefore, one can see easily which data values are above (+'s) or below (−'s) the sample mean. In addition, large residuals far from the sample mean draw attention and generate thoughtful questions about the unusual aspects of the data.

Residuals based on classical summary statistics such as the sample mean can be somewhat deceptive. For example, large data values are influential in determining the magnitude of the sample mean. Thus large data values draw the sample mean toward them, making the corresponding residuals smaller than residuals from an exploratory summary value such as the median. Thus residuals based on exploratory summary statistics may be more useful for spotting unusual data values.

EXHIBIT 4 Residuals that Estimate the Unknown Errors

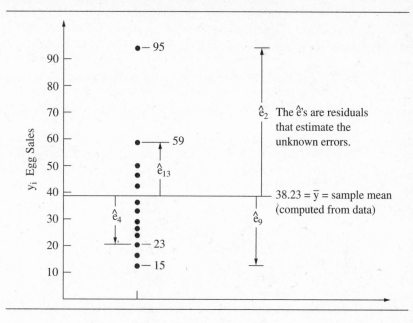

Because much of classical statistics assumes that the unknown errors are normal in distribution, the normal assumption can be validated by obtaining a stem-and-leaf diagram, a histogram, or a probability plot of the residuals.

> ## S T A T I S T I C A L   H I G H L I G H T S
>
> The exact value (a distribution's center) is estimated by the sample mean, but there are competitive alternatives such as the sample median or mode.
>
> The errors are estimated by residuals. However, there are alternatives to the residuals from the sample mean. Residuals from the sample median are likely to reveal unusual values that the residuals from the sample mean might lead us to overlook.

E X A M P L E 6

CLASSICAL RESIDUALS FOR A MANUFACTURER WEIGHING BARS OF SOAP (CONTINUED)

A manufacturer produces soap bars that weigh 100 grams, nominally. An electronic device called Red Eye monitors the weight, y_i, of each bar of soap. Red Eye turns on a red light when the molding process goes out of control and starts producing soap bars that weigh too much.

It turns on a yellow light when the bars weigh too little. For adjusting the molding machine, Red Eye creates a data file of weight information.

In addition to bar weight, y_i, it was found that deviations, e_i, from the nominal of 100 grams provided the clearest signal about bars weighing too much or too little, because deviations are accompanied by plus signs (overweight bars) and minus signs (underweight bars).

If the nominal value of 100 grams were not known, the sample mean could be used to estimate the nominal value. An unknown nominal value implies that the chance errors are not known either and residuals estimate the chance errors.

Problem Statement   Examine weights of bars of soap. Represent the weight data in a regression model format and show that actual weight minus nominal weight produces individual chance errors. Show that actual weight minus the sample mean weight produces the residuals.

Problem Solution   The MINITAB computations are shown below.

ROW	C1	C2		C3	C1	C4		C5
	y_i	μ	=	e_i	y_i	$\bar{y}$	=	$\hat{e}_i$
1	99.22	100		-0.78	99.22	99.858		-0.638
2	99.26	100		-0.74	99.26	99.858		-0.598
3	99.97	100		-0.03	99.97	99.858		0.112
4	100.01	100		0.01	100.01	99.858		0.152
5	99.60	100		-0.40	99.60	99.858		-0.258
6	100.21	100		0.21	100.21	99.858		0.352
7	99.52	100		-0.48	99.52	99.858		-0.338
8	100.03	100		0.03	100.03	99.858		0.172
9	100.15	100		0.15	100.15	99.858		0.292
10	100.03	100		0.03	100.03	99.858		0.172
11	99.92	100		-0.08	99.92	99.858		0.062
12	100.31	100		0.31	100.31	99.858		0.452
13	99.99	100		-0.01	99.99	99.858		0.132
14	100.31	100		0.31	100.31	99.858		0.452
15	99.60	100		-0.40	99.60	99.858		-0.258
16	99.83	100		-0.17	99.83	99.858		-0.028
17	99.49	100		-0.51	99.49	99.858		-0.368
18	99.43	100		-0.57	99.43	99.858		-0.428
19	100.15	100		0.15	100.15	99.858		0.292
20	100.13	100		0.13	100.13	99.858		0.272

THE SAMPLE STANDARD DEVIATION, A CLOSE LOOK

If the observations, y_i, are normal in distribution with a mean, μ, and a standard deviation, σ, the chance errors must also have a normal distribution with the same standard deviation. This is apparent in the following relationship because μ is a constant and it merely shifts the location of the distribution:

(individual measurement $-$ exact value) $=$ individual chance error
$$(y_i \qquad - \qquad \mu) \qquad = \qquad e_i$$

The usual estimator of the population standard deviation, σ, is the sample standard deviation, s_y. The subscript, y, will be dropped here because it is understood that we are working with a single variable, y.

Although you are likely to use a statistical package to obtain the sample standard deviation, the computational formula is described here. The **residual sum of squares,** which is in the numerator of the following expression, is divided by $(n - 1)$ to obtain the **sample variance.**

$$s^2 = \frac{\Sigma \, (y_i - \overline{y})^2}{n - 1}$$

The square root of the sample variance s^2 is s, the sample standard deviation.

Because $\overline{y} = $ (predicted y_i) and $(y_i - $ predicted $y_i) = \hat{e}_i$, a residual, the formula for the sample variance can be written in terms of the prediction equation or the residuals, as below.

$$s^2 = \frac{\Sigma \, (y_i - \text{predicted } y_i)^2}{n - 1} = \frac{\Sigma \, \hat{e}_i^2}{n - 1}$$

Like the box length in exploratory work, the sample standard deviation is a measure of how spread out the data values are; however, the sample standard deviation is not resistant to outliers. A single stray observation can inflate the sample standard deviation considerably, but, when the data are normal, the sample standard deviation is the best estimator of the spread.

The term *sample standard deviation*, as defined earlier, is commonplace; however, a more accurate name would simply be "an estimator of the population standard deviation," which would reflect the statistic's intended use. Technically, the proper divisor in a standard deviation computation is (n), not (n $-$ 1), but because we estimate the population standard deviation so frequently and (n $-$ 1) produces the better estimator, the colloquial use of sample standard deviation is common even though it is not strictly correct.

Although the (n $-$ 1) divisor is most popular in practice, using (n) as a divisor has a conceptual advantage. That is, if (n) is allowed to grow as large as the population size, say (N), and the population mean replaces the sample mean in the formula above, then the sample standard deviation becomes the population standard deviation. Hence, dividing by (n) produces a sample standard deviation consistent with the definition of the population standard deviation.

EXAMPLE 7

THE SAMPLE STANDARD DEVIATION FOR THE EGG SALES DATA

Problem Statement For the egg sales data set, find the sample variance and its square root, the sample standard deviation.

Problem Solution

$$s^2 = \frac{\Sigma \ (y_i - \bar{y})^2}{n - 1}$$

$$s^2 = \frac{5567.07}{12} = 463.92 \ \text{(sample variance)}$$

$$s = 21.54 \ \text{(sample standard deviation)}$$

Problem Discussion Recall that the box length was found to be 23 in Chapter 2. Three-fourths of a box length, $\frac{3}{4} \times 23 = 17.25$, is an approximate standard deviation. Comparatively, the actual standard deviation (21.54) is inflated by a single sales value of 95 dozen eggs. Generally the approximation improves with sample size if the data are normal in distribution.

The Sample Standard Deviation for Grouped Data (Optional)

Statistics such as the standard deviation are usually calculated from the individual data values. But sometimes data are available only in frequency distribution form (grouped); therefore, the **grouped sample standard deviation** is described here.

For grouped data, the standard deviation can be obtained with the following formula.

Let

$$f_i = \text{frequency count for the i-th class}$$

$$\sum f_i = n, \text{ the sample size}$$

$$m_i = \text{the midpoint of the i-th class}$$

$$\bar{y}_g = \sum \left(\frac{f_i}{n}\right) \times m_i, \text{ the grouped mean}$$

If the sample variance is defined with the divisor n,

$$s^2 = \frac{\Sigma \ (y_i - \bar{y})^2}{n}$$

the grouped data version of the sample variance is

$$s_g^2 = \sum \left(\frac{f_i}{n}\right) \times (m_i - \overline{y}_g)^2$$

A little algebra streamlines this formula to produce the following alternative formulation:

$$s_g^2 = \left(\sum \left(\frac{f_i}{n}\right) \times m_i^2\right) - \overline{y}_g^2$$

The computations in Exhibit 5 are based on the latter formula.
The $\overline{y}_g^2$ is subtracted from the sum of the last column in Exhibit 5 to obtain the grouped sample variance, s_g^2.

$$s_g^2 = \left(\sum \left(\frac{f_i}{n}\right) \times m_i^2\right) - \overline{y}_g^2 = 1886.54 - 1450.09 = 436.45$$

The s_g^2 used the divisor n for computational simplicity. The s_g^2 can be converted to a sample variance based on the $(n - 1)$ divisor by multiplying s_g^2 by $n/(n - 1)$. As a final step, multiply s_g^2 by $n/(n - 1) = 436.45 \times \frac{13}{12} = 472.82$; the square root is 21.74, the grouped standard deviation based on the $(n - 1)$ divisor. The grouped standard deviation, 21.74, approximates the ungrouped standard deviation of 21.54 that we found earlier in the chapter.

EXHIBIT 5 Computations for the Grouped Sample Variance

Class Intervals	Class Midpoints	Relative Frequencies	$\frac{f_i}{n} \times (m_i^2)$
10 to 20	15.0	2/13	$(2/13) \times 15^2 = 34.62$
20 to 30	25.0	4/13	$(4/13) \times 25^2 = 192.31$
30 to 40	35.0	2/13	$(2/13) \times 35^2 = 188.46$
40 to 50	45.0	2/13	$(2/13) \times 45^2 = 311.54$
50 to 60	55.0	2/13	$(2/13) \times 55^2 = 465.38$
60 to 70	65.0	0/13	0
70 to 80	75.0	0/13	0
80 to 90	85.0	0/13	0
90 to 100	95.0	1/13	$1/13 \times 95^2 = 694.23$
TOTALS		1	$(\sum f_i/n \times m_i^2) = 1886.54$

EXAMPLE 8

PROFIT PLANNING

In profit planning, managers make educated guesses about expected profits at anticipated sales levels. Profit depends on the number of units (quantity) sold of a product. However, the quantity that will be sold is an uncertain future event. To deal with a range of possible profit outcomes, managers ask "What if" questions about sales levels. Profit can be projected for each "What if" scenario and computed from the following relationship:

$$\text{profit} = \text{revenue} - (\text{total variable costs} + \text{total fixed costs})$$

Total fixed costs is an aggregation of depreciation on plant and equipment, rentals, interest charges on debt, executive salaries, and so on. Total fixed costs does not change within certain quantity ranges. In this example, total fixed costs equals $40,000.

Revenue and total variable costs depend on quantity. Suppose each unit of product is sold for $2.00; therefore, revenue equals $2.00 times the quantity of units sold. Variable cost per unit of product includes direct production costs, such as factory labor, raw materials, sales commissions, and so on. In this example, the variable costs per unit sold is $1.20; therefore, total variable costs equals $1.20 times the quantity of units sold. The uncertainty in quantity translates to uncertainty in revenue and total variable costs because they are quantity dependent.

Problem Statement (a)   Suppose the number of units sold (quantity) is a random amount from a normal distribution with a mean of 70,000 units and a standard deviation of 10,000 units. Simulate 100 sales scenarios. Examine and summarize potential profit figures using a dotplot, the sample mean, and standard deviation.

Problem Solution (a)   The dotplot of profits has a normal bell shape. When the quantity distribution mean is 70,000 units, only 3 of 100 scenarios result in a loss of money (negative profit); this is made evident by the 3 left-most points on the dotplot.

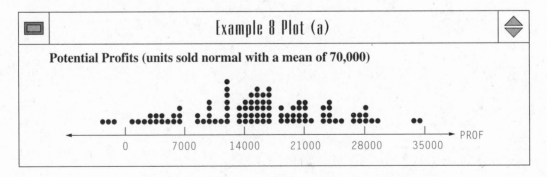

Example 8 Plot (a)

Potential Profits (units sold normal with a mean of 70,000)

PROF

0   7000   14000   21000   28000   35000

The sample mean (15377) and standard deviation (8013) summarize the profit dotplot's center and spread. Because the distribution of profit is normal and without outliers, the sample mean is about the same as the sample median, as shown below.

	N	MEAN	MEDIAN	STDEV
PROF	100	15377	15506	8013

	MIN	MAX	Q1	Q3
PROF	-2834	34421	10131	20752

Problem Statement (b)   Suppose the number of units sold (quantity) is a random amount from a normal distribution with a mean of 50,000 units and a standard deviation of 10,000 units. Simulate 100 sales scenarios. Examine and summarize potential profit figures using a dotplot, the sample mean, and standard deviation.

Problem Solution (b)   The dotplot of profits has a normal bell shape. When the quantity distribution mean is 50,000 units, about half the scenarios result in a loss of money (negative profit).

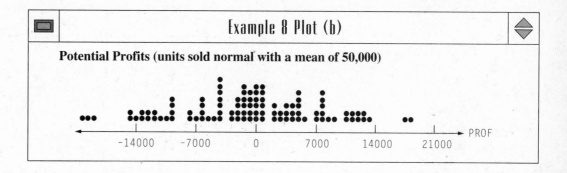

The sample mean (−623) and standard deviation (8013) give a concise summary of the profit dotplot. Because the distribution of profit is normal and without outliers, the sample mean is about the same as the sample median, as shown below.

	N	MEAN	MEDIAN	STDEV
PROF	100	-623	-494	8013

	MIN	MAX	Q1	Q3
PROF	-18834	18421	-5869	4752

Problem Statement (c)   List the values of important variables for the first 5 of the 100 scenarios.

Problem Solution (c)

ROW	Q	REV	VCOST	FCOST	PROF	TCOST
1	42780	85560	51336.0	40000	-5776.0	91336
2	35167	70334	42200.4	40000	-11866.4	82200
3	50357	100714	60428.4	40000	285.6	100428
4	44252	88504	53102.4	40000	-4598.4	93102
5	48666	97332	58399.2	40000	-1067.2	98399

Problem Statement (d)   Use scatterplots to reveal relationships between important variables; if necessary, plot variables simultaneously.

Problem Solution (d)   Revenue (REV, plotting symbol A) and total costs (TCOST, plotting symbol B) are both plotted and related to quantity. Several A's or B's at a single plotting location are printed as a number. Because the plotting points are represented by letters, relationships are approximated by straight lines through the plotting point locations. The two crossing straight lines represent revenue and total costs.

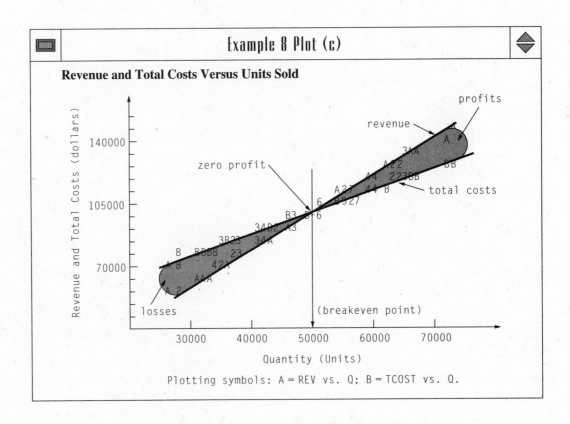

Example 8 Plot (c)

Revenue and Total Costs Versus Units Sold

Plotting symbols: A = REV vs. Q; B = TCOST vs. Q.

Problem Discussion   The revenue and total cost lines intersect at 50,000 units sold; the intersection point is breakeven, where the profit is zero. Quantities above breakeven result in profits and quantities below result in losses. The manager must decide whether or not to market this new product based on the analysis. If further analysis is necessary, the manager may simulate additional scenarios using other means and standard deviations for quantity sold.

THE COEFFICIENT OF VARIATION

The **coefficient of variation** is the ratio of the standard deviation to the mean; therefore, it is a relative measure of variability.

The Synergy of the Sample Mean ($\overline{y}$) and the Sample Standard Deviation (s) Working Together

The location (center) and variability of a population are specified in absolute terms by μ and σ, respectively. The corresponding estimators, $\overline{y}$ and s, are calculated from a random sample of data. Location and variability individually characterize important features of a distribution. Together in a ratio, σ/μ, these distributional characteristics form a powerful marriage for understanding a distribution in relative terms and comparing distributions.

The Coefficient of Variation

The coefficient of variation is a relative measure of variability; it is defined as the ratio of the standard deviation to the mean, σ/μ. From sample data, the estimator is $s/\overline{y}$.

By forming a ratio, the measurement units such as pounds, feet, inches, and ounces are the same in the numerator and denominator of the ratio. When the units are the same in the numerator and denominator, they cancel out in division. Thus, the ratio has no units. As a result, the coefficient of variation can be used to compare the relative variability of two different data sets that are measured in different units. In some comparisons, the measurement units of the data sets are the same but the orders of magnitude are different.

Consider Example 8 on profit planning. One distribution has a mean of 50,000 units sold and a standard deviation of 10,000 units sold. The second distribution has a mean of 70,000 units sold and a standard deviation of 10,000 units sold. The two coefficients of variation are $\frac{10,000}{50,000} = \frac{1}{5}$ and $\frac{10,000}{70,000} = \frac{1}{7}$. Relatively the variation is higher at the lower mean sales volume of 50,000 units. Thus, not only is the sales volume lower at 50,000 units, but relatively the variation is higher, making the lower level of sales even riskier.

The two profit distributions can be compared also. The sample coefficients of variability for profits at the two sales volumes are $\frac{8013}{623}$ and $\frac{8013}{15,377}$; the first ratio is higher and it reflects higher risk at the lower mean sales volume.

CHAPTER SUMMARY

This chapter completed the discussion of a single variable in classical terms and compared the classical and exploratory approaches. From the early exploratory work, robust estimators such as the median were obtained. At that time, little was assumed about the underlying data distribution. If it is found that the data distribution is symmetrical, like the normal, and without outliers, classical estimators such as the sample mean are preferred. Under such conditions, the standard deviation is preferred to the box length as a measure of variability.

A naive regression model was used to represent an observed data value. This representation partitioned each data value into two additive components: (1) an unknown parameter representing the population mean, and (2) an error term representing each observation's deviation from the population mean.

When the population mean is unknown, it can be estimated by the sample mean, $\bar{y}$. The sample mean is a least squares estimator.

The sample mean alone is not enough to characterize a distribution for it is mum on variability. As a result, sample standard deviation, s, was introduced as a measure of variability. For large samples from normal distributions, the sample standard deviation is about three-fourths of the box length.

To measure variability in relative terms, the standard deviation is divided by the mean and equals the coefficient of variation.

We suggested a simple data analysis strategy. First, display and summarize the data in exploratory terms. Second, if the data distribution is symmetrical and without outliers, summarize the data with classical statistics. If the results do not differ substantially, either set of results is adequate. If the classical and exploratory results differ substantially, try to find the reasons while depending on exploratory results for early guidance.

KEY TERMS

additive model, 113
arithmetic mean, 118
coefficient of variation, 133
computer simulation, 115
dotplot, 115
exact value, 111
grouped form, 122
grouped sample mean, 122
grouped sample standard
  deviation, 128

individual chance error, 111, 113
naive regression model, 110, 113
normal distribution, 110
ordinary least squares method
  (OLS), 121
population mean, 112
population standard deviation, 115
prediction equation, 122
predictor, 122

regression, 111
residual, 110
residual sum of squares, 127
sample mean, 112
sample standard deviation, 110, 127
sample variance, 127
σ, 126
sum of the errors squared, 121

EXERCISES

General Exercises

1. Which of the following sample measures of central tendency are not thrown off target much by stray data values (outliers): (a) median or (b) mean?

2. When the data values are normal in distribution, the best estimator of the population mean, μ, is _____ ; the best estimator of the population standard deviation, σ, is _____ . Why? Discuss.

3. For large samples from a normal distribution, the sample standard deviation, s, is about _____ box lengths; a box length is _____ sample standard deviations.

4. Are classical or exploratory methods more dependent on assumptions? Which tends to generate hypotheses and which tends to confirm or deny them?

5. Express a naive regression model verbally in terms of an individual chance error, an individual measurement, and an exact value. Discuss this model in reference to applications involving, say, measurements on weight, height, a stock price, the price of a house, a company's return on investment, and so on. In making a decision, say, to purchase a house, how can it be useful to think of the price in these terms?

6. Suppose we are interested in studying starting salaries of students graduating from a large university. Write out in symbolic form the linear statistical model that might be used; define y_i, μ, and the individual chance error. If the response, y_i, is normal in distribution, what is the distribution of the error term? How might we estimate μ? How might we estimate the chance errors? Compute these estimates from a sample of starting salaries (in thousands of dollars) that follow:

$$32, 41, 33, 31, 39, 37, 38, 38, 42, 33, 35, 38, 32, 32, 34, 40, 33, 30, 31, 35$$

What would be your prediction for the starting salary of the next student who gets an offer?

7. Compute the sample standard deviation of the starting salaries in the previous exercise.

8. Smith and Iglewicz suggested some effective classroom techniques for generating data sets.[2] They created experiments with known exact values in order to see how close different types of estimators got to the known exact values. Don't lose sight of the fact that in most practical problems the exact value is unknown. Their list of experiments and exact values (true values) is

Experiment	Exact Value
(a) Estimate the weight of a package given a 2-lb weight as a reference.	1.2 lb
(b) Estimate the weight of another package given a 2-lb weight as a reference.	4.6 lb
(c) Estimate when 60 seconds have passed (1st trial).	60 sec
(d) Estimate when 60 seconds have passed (2nd trial) given the first trial result.	60 sec
(e) Measure the diameter of a tennis ball with a ruler in millimeters.	7.41148 mm
(f) Measure the diameter of a basketball with a ruler in inches.	?
(g) Estimate the height of a mark on the wall given one foot as a reference.	6.845 ft
(h) Estimate the height on another mark on the wall given one foot as a reference.	7.3012 ft
(i) Estimate the number of words on a page given the number of words on a second page as a reference.	329 words
(j) Estimate the size of the angle between two flat sticks glued together.	42.5°

Conduct some of these experiments in class having 20 to 30 students record their estimates. For each data set, compute the sample mean and the sample standard deviation.

9. Pick any exercise in Chapter 2 and summarize the data using both exploratory and classical methods. If the data distribution is asymmetrical and if outliers are present, explain what effect, if any, this has on the summary statistics.

10. Using MINITAB, RETRIEVE 'B:PATSCAMP'. Use INFO and PRINT to look at the data. DESCRIBE height, weight, and experience; comment as necessary, noting any relationship to the position played.

11. In MINITAB, RETRIEVE 'B:QUAKES'. Use INFO and PRINT to look at the data, then summarize the earthquake data, comparing the classical summary information (DESCRIBE command) to the exploratory summary information (LVALS command). To order the data in time, you might use the following command(s) and subcommand:

```
SORT C1 C2 C3, PUT C1 C2 C3;
BY C1.
PRINT C1 C2 C3
TSPLOT C3
```

Exercises to Illustrate Management Uses of Statistics

12. Part of an assembly operation is done by hand. The nominal time to assemble one unit is 10.5 min. A sample of observed times follows.

8.5	12.2	10.0	9.6	10.4	10.8	9.5	9.6	12.0	11.3
10.9	10.5	13.5	14.2	8.4	11.0	9.1	10.1	8.0	13.1

(a) Compute the average and standard deviation of the assembly time. Using MINITAB or another statistical package, print three columns: observed assembly time, nominal time, and the deviation from the nominal. Find the mean and standard deviation of the deviations. Obtain a dotplot of the assembly times and the deviations.

(b) Using MINITAB or another statistical package, print three columns again: observed assembly time, average assembly time, and deviations from average assembly time (residuals). Compute the mean and standard deviation of these deviations. Discuss any similarities or differences between these results and those in part (a).

13. A company has developed a low-cost manufacturing method for a part used in televisions, and the managers are profit planning. The sales price per part is $1.00, and the variable cost per unit is $.60. The total fixed costs are $400,000. Analysis is needed before the part is put into production because of different demand estimates.

(a) Simulate profits for a set of 100 demand scenarios from a normal distribution with a mean of 1,100,000 units and a standard deviation of 120,000. Present a dotplot and summary statistics for profits. Plot revenue and total costs versus quantity sold.

(b) Repeat the analysis selecting different means and standard deviations for demand.

14. As part of the analysis for an investment decision (investing approximately $120,000), different cash inflow scenarios are considered. Suppose a manager expects the cash inflow to be normal with a mean of $22,000; two levels of risk, reflected in the standard deviations of $6,000 and $10,000, are to be considered. Using MINITAB or another statistical package, simulate 1,000 cash inflows for each of the risk levels and present dotplots and other summary statistics for the distributions of the payback periods.

15. Total factory overhead costs (supervision, insurance, depreciation, utilities, and so on) are budgeted for each month of the year. The factory produces a different number of units each month. A monthly overhead rate in dollars per unit produced is established by dividing budgeted overhead by the units produced in that month. Different overhead rates are not acceptable because they do not represent what are typical production conditions. For the following monthly (January through December) overhead rates, find the mean (what is typical) and standard deviation. Is the sequence of rates random? Discuss.

3.50	2.65	2.25	2.10	4.30	6.00	10.00	34.00	11.00	5.00	4.30	3.00

16. A machine shop performs operations such as milling, cleaning, grinding, and facing. Direct labor cost (hours times wage rate) is computed for each of these operations by job number and type. For a specific job type, the direct labor cost amounts (in dollars) for grinding were

42.46	43.60	65.05	66.19	53.80	72.23	51.31
66.87	70.63	66.80	63.51	75.54	65.84	75.32
53.81	60.90	50.39	48.74	70.47	70.08	77.74
53.33	80.23	60.89	80.79	67.18	71.52	67.12
75.19	130.50	75.63	65.67	57.24	71.71	72.27
76.43	73.25	49.81	66.97	56.65	81.37	81.54
66.85	59.38	63.90	69.01	79.45	82.58	61.16
98.00	62.80	71.57	69.60			

(a) Find the mean and standard deviation of the direct labor costs for grinding for this job type.

(b) In the cost analysis for a bid preparation, which involves 2,000 grinding operations of the above job type, what is the total direct labor cost for grinding that you regard as typical?

17. The following are annual percentage changes in the consumer price index:[3]

 5.8 6.5 7.7 11.3 13.5 10.4 6.1 3.2 4.3 3.6 1.9 3.6 4.1 4.8 5.4 4.2 3.0 3.0

What is the typical annual percentage change? Test for randomness and normality.

18. For the financial instruments listed below, over nearly 60 years the following items are tabulated: the average annual returns (unadjusted for inflation) and the standard deviations of returns (a risk measure).[4]

	Average Annual Returns	Standard Deviation of Returns
Treasury bills	3.5	3.4
Long-term government bonds	4.4	8.2
Corporate bonds	5.1	8.3
Common stock	12.0	21.2

Suppose you have a fixed number of dollars to invest. The MINITAB commands shown below allow you to experiment with different allocations, putting all your money in one instrument or dividing it into different instruments. These hypothetical portfolios are then projected ten years into the future to simulate their future values.

A dollar invested grows or contracts in value each period; $[(1 + \text{return for the period}) \times \text{the}$ dollar investment] compounds to a value at the end of a period. Therefore, on average for common stocks, a dollar invested in the beginning of a year is worth $(1 + .12)$ at the end of the year. At the end of the second year, the dollar is worth $(1 + .12)(1 + .12)$, and so on.

Compounding based on averages, however, gives one no feel for the variability in return, which can be substantial. Therefore, a few MINITAB commands are shown below that enable you to experiment with any of the instruments listed above. Ten years of returns are simulated 20 times for compounding a $1,000 investment in common stocks; you can make the necessary modifications to simulate portfolio values using other instruments or combinations of them.

```
STORE 'B:STKSIM'  # NOTE THAT THIS FORM OF A MACRO MAY REQUIRE
# MODIFICATION IN FUTURE VERSIONS OF MINITAB
NOECHO  # SUPPRESSES REPETITIOUS COMMAND LISTS
RANDOM 1 PUT INTO C1-C10;  # TEN YEARS
NORMAL MU=1.12 SIGMA=.212.  # MEAN, STD.DEV. FOR COMMON STOCK
STACK C1-C10 PUT INTO C11  # FOR TSPLOT TO DO LATER
LET C12(K1)=1000*C1*C2*C3*C4*C5*C6*C7*C8*C9*C10
LET K1=K1+1
ECHO
END

LET K1=1
EXEC 'B:STKSIM' 20 TIMES    # TO VIEW 20 POSSIBLE FUTURE VALUES
                            # OF YOUR $1000 INVESTMENT IN COMMON
DOTPLOT C12
DESCRIBE C12
PRINT C12
TSPLOT C11 # PLOT OF RETURNS 20TH TEN YEAR PERIOD SIMULATED
```

You can create simulations like this one for the other instruments and for investing different dollar amounts. Be sure to replace C12 with C13 then C14 then C15; this will enable you to aggregate the total of your portfolio value to work with.

If you want to value your future investment in real terms (adjusting for inflation), randomly generate ten years of inflation rates and subtract them from your returns before compounding.

19. A particularly bad type of a fall in skiing is a twisting one because a spiral fracture can occur in the lower leg. Ski bindings are designed to release before the twist torque in foot pounds gets to a critical level. The critical level of twist torque depends on skier weight. Tabulated figures are used to set twist torque (T) releases based on weight (W) in pounds. By hand (or use the DESCRIBE command in MINITAB), summarize each of these variables separately.

W	55	75	95	115	135	155	175	195	215	235
T	16	20	24	28	32	36	40	44	48	50

20. A random sample of professional golfers had the following one-year official earnings (in thousands of dollars several years ago) and scoring averages.[5] By hand (or use the DESCRIBE command in MINITAB), summarize each of these variables separately.

Averages

71.5   72.75   71.34   71.27   70.95   71.65   72.49   71.46   71.95   71.61   72.39

Earnings

71.6   55.8   147.8   117.4   112.3   82.7   22.8   58.8   60.5   55.4   43.6

21. A firm produces prefabricated houses by order only (a job-shop rather than an assembly-line production facility) because a large number of styles and options are available to customers. For pricing purposes, the managers used budgeted costs, because actual costs were not available until after the job was finished. However, a problem became apparent in recent cost figures for part of the prefabrication work; the higher the actual cost (AC), the larger the absolute deviation (DC) from budget. As a first step in preparation for a more complex analysis, by hand (or use the DESCRIBE command in MINITAB), summarize each of these variables separately.

AC	35640	35730	35740	36000	37760	38700	39930	41210	43560
DC	500	610	615	854	1640	1100	1875	2044	1123

22. Some manufacturing companies refer to true physical production cost for a period as gross product. For financial planning in manufacturing, it is necessary to summarize variables such as gross product and payroll costs. By hand (or use the DESCRIBE command in MINITAB), summarize each of these variables separately.

GP	69	210	156	166	120
PAY	66	143	115	122	117

23. A company maintains a fleet of automobiles. Management is interested in minimizing the total cost of ownership and operation. A portion of the total cost is for maintenance and operating costs (O&M dollars per mile); O&M costs tend to increase with vehicle age. As a first step in the analysis, by hand (or use the DESCRIBE command in MINITAB), summarize each of these variables separately.

O&M	.20	.28	.27	.316	.38	.42	.44
VA	1	2	3	4	5	6	7

24. In establishing labor forecasts for a shipping center, it was necessary to examine two variables, man-hours (MH) and shipping units (SU in hundreds of units). By hand (or use the DESCRIBE command in MINITAB), summarize each of these variables separately.

MH	3470	4650	5370	8320	5190	4180	3420	3890	3650	5410	4110	3740
SU	2178	3229	5530	6442	3767	2497	2229	3561	3791	4184	3246	2813

25. A manufacturing company found that the greater the capital investment (CI in hundreds of dollars) in automation, the fewer people employed (PE). By hand (or use the DESCRIBE command in MINITAB), find the sample means and sample standard deviations of each of these variables.

CI	985	715	585	500	412	198	190	146	56	14
PE	50	20	110	430	312	250	620	415	512	675

26. Flexible budgeting is needed in factories because production volume varies. Predicting cost behavior from past production experience is one supporting pillar of flexible budgeting. Although industrial engineering studies are used to determine how costs should vary with volume, statistical analysis is also used to summarize past cost-volume experience. Total mixed cost (TMC), a mixture of fixed and variable components, and production volume measures such as machine hours (MH) are important variables to examine. By hand (or use the DESCRIBE command in MINITAB), summarize each of these variables, TMC (in hundreds of dollars) and MH.

TMC	20	21	24	14	15	8	10	13	14
MH	22	27	23	19	18	14	13	10	12

27. Simulate 100 ROE (return on equity) figures and summarize your results. Assume the following relationship holds:

$$ROE = \frac{\text{assets} \times \text{profit rate} - \text{debt} \times \text{interest rate} - \text{taxes}}{\text{equity}}$$

Let assets = $2,000; profit rate is normal with a mean of .10 and a standard deviation of .01; debt = $1,600; interest rate = .08; taxes = 0.0; and equity = $400.

Think of this firm as small (figures as given) or large (all dollar figures in millions). As an option, you may wish to experiment with different tax levels, perhaps introducing a tax rate.

28. Suppose an individual is trying to assess his or her total wealth, which consists of savings, a house, stock, and an automobile. Savings is known for certain to be $15,000, but the other components of wealth have uncertain values. Suppose we assume normal distributions for the uncertain components of wealth; the means and standard deviations are the house ($150,000, $5,000), the stock ($100,000, $10,000) and the automobile ($20,000, $1,000). Using MINITAB or some other statistical package, simulate 100 total wealth scenarios. Present a dotplot and other summary statistics for total wealth.

29. Assume that the assessed values of homes in a particular area are normally distributed with a mean of $150,000 and a standard deviation of $30,000. If the tax rate is 2.5%, simulate tax collections on 700 homes, summarize collections, and find the total amount of taxes collected. (Hint: In MINITAB, SUM C1 PUT INTO K1 and PRINT K1 might be helpful.)

30. Cities and towns fund much of public education, safety, and local highway maintenance through tax revenues. The tax-revenue-raising capacity is a function of property valuation per household. Suppose property taxes are $2\frac{1}{2}$% of property value. Further suppose per household property value is normal with a mean of $50,000 and a standard deviation of $10,000, normal(50,000,10,000). Simulate property values for a small town of 2,000 households. Multiply property values by $2\frac{1}{2}$% and sum to estimate the total tax revenue collected from these households.

31. Imagine a state in an imaginary nation. The state has only two towns, each having the same population; the property values are [notationally, normal (mean, standard deviation)]: TownOne, normal($50,000, $10,000), and TownTwo, normal($30,000, $10,000). Because of the disparity in mean property values, TownOne collects more tax revenues than TownTwo and therefore has the capacity to finance the development of better schools, roads, and so on.

The state government runs a lottery and distributes the proceeds to the towns in a way that counterbalances the property value disparity. For distributing lottery proceeds, the following formula is being considered:

$$\text{TownTwo share} = \frac{50,000}{30,000 + 50,000} \times \text{lottery proceeds}$$

TownOne's share is the remaining amount. If monthly lottery proceeds are normal ($10,000, 2,000), simulate 12 months of dollar distributions to both towns and find the totals for the year.

32. A consulting company conducts quality control training programs. Trainees are charged $572 each, where T is the number of trainees. When T ranges from 10 through 59, two consultants are needed. When T ranges from 60 through 89, four consultants are needed. When T ranges from 90 through 120, six consultants are needed. Revenue is T × 572 and expenses are roughly $4,180 per consultant. Net profit = T × 572 − 4180 × (# of consultants). Suppose T is normal in distribution with a mean of 75 and a standard deviation of 1. Simulate 100 profit scenarios and summarize net profit.

33. For a super Bowl football game between the Buffalo Bills and the Dallas Cowboys, a number of TV advertisements were rated: Advertisement names and ratings (higher is better) are available to you as a MINTAB worksheet, RETRIEVE 'B:SBADS'. After retrieving the data set, INFO will give you column and name references; PRINT the columns for examination:

(a) Obtain classical descriptive statistics (DESCRIBE) for the ratings in column C6. Write down the sample mean, standard deviation, and quartiles.

(b) Plot the ratings (TSPLOT C6) in the order they were observed Are they random?

(c) In MINITAB, use the following command(s) and subcommand:

```
SORT C5 C6, PUT C1 C2;
BY C6.
PRINT C1 C2
TSPLOT C2
```

Note that the ordering shows up on the plot; however, the resulting nonrandomness is imposed by the data analyst. Therefore, the summary statistics remain valid. What are the three top and three bottom advertisements, and what are their ratings?

(d) From part (a) obtain the sample mean and subtract it from each rating, obtaining residuals (LET C8 = C2 − 6.2). PRINT C1 C2 C8 and notice how easy it is to see which ads are above or below the mean and by how much. Similarly, TSPLOT C8.

34. In a small manufacturing operation, parts arrive at the first workstation for assembly, the assemblies are painted different colors at one of the next two workstations, and the painted assemblies are packaged at a fourth workstation. Finally packages are moved to a storage area The time from part arrival to package storage is recorded as a flow time through the manufacturing system. When flow time increases for each unit produced, this is an indication of a bottleneck in the system that might be in need of additional resources. In MINITAB, RETRIEVE 'B:MFGTIME' use INFO, PRINT, DESCRIBE, and TSPLOT commands. Is there a bottleneck in this manufacturing system? Explain.

35. Vibration tests are performed on 20 guidance systems. The response, roll resonant frequency, is thought to be related to five predictor variables: roll transmissibility, pitch resonant frequency, pitch transmissibility, yaw resonant frequency, and yaw transmissibility (RETRIEVE 'B:GDANCE'). Find classical summary statistics for the individual variables in preparation for a more complex analysis to be performed later.

36. Cans of pizza sauce had the following weights in ounces (the data are sorted):

14.63	14.65	14.65	14.66	14.67	14.69	14.69	14.69
14.69	14.69	14.69	14.70	14.70	14.71	14.72	14.72
14.72	14.72	14.73	14.73	14.73	14.73	14.73	14.73
14.73	14.73	14.73	14.74	14.74	14.74	14.75	14.75

14.75	14.75	14.75	14.76	14.76	14.76	14.77	14.77
14.77	14.77	14.77	14.77	14.78	14.78	14.78	14.78
14.78	14.78	14.79	14.79	14.80	14.80	14.80	14.81
14.81	14.81	14.81	14.81	14.82	14.82	14.82	14.82
14.82	14.82	14.83	14.83	14.86			

These weights are available in file PIZZA.MTW.

(a) Find the coefficient of variation

(b) Find which data values fall outside an interval formed by the sample mean $\pm$ (two standard deviations). What percentage of the observations are outside this interval?

37. The time between arrivals of parts at an assembly operation had the following values in minutes (the data are sorted):

0.03	0.15	0.16	0.22	0.49	0.49	0.67	0.75
0.78	1.01	1.22	1.29	1.45	1.98	2.11	2.26
2.46	2.49	2.86	3.01	3.12	3.37	3.70	4.46
4.54	4.54	4.69	4.70	4.98	5.81	5.84	6.06
7.08	7.33	7.40	7.83	7.90	8.08	8.12	8.69
8.81	9.07	9.10	9.36	9.92	9.96	10.22	11.08
11.28	11.66	11.89	12.24	12.49	13.90	13.99	14.21
14.71	15.39	15.65	16.10	16.24	16.54	17.03	17.21
17.73	18.21	21.43	22.35	23.69	23.86	26.41	26.70
27.26	28.81	29.88	30.82	32.38	40.85	42.64	60.68

These times are available in file ARVT.MTW.

(a) Find the coefficient of variation.

(b) Find which data values fall inside an interval formed by the sample mean $\pm$ (two standard deviations) What percentage of the observations are inside this interval?

38. Find the sample mean and standard deviation of the weights of 87 burgers. On a dotplot, mark the location of the sample mean and an interval formed by the sample mean $\pm$ (two standard deviations). What is the general shape of the distribution of weights? These weights are available in file BURGER.MTW.

8.47	8.55	8.56	8.57	8.59	8.69	8.69	8.73	8.74	8.75	8.75
8.76	8.76	8.78	8.78	8.82	8.84	8.84	8.85	8.85	8.87	8.88
8.88	8.88	8.89	8.89	8.89	8.90	8.91	8.93	8.94	8.96	9.00
9.00	9.01	9.02	9.02	9.02	9.03	9.03	9.03	9.04	9.04	9.05
9.05	9.05	9.05	9.07	9.10	9.10	9.10	9.10	9.11	9.12	9.13
9.14	9.15	9.15	9.15	9.18	9.19	9.19	9.19	9.20	9.21	9.21
9.22	9.23	9.23	9.23	9.26	9.27	9.27	9.27	9.29	9.30	9.31
9.36	9.36	9.43	9.46	9.48	9.48	9.52	9.53	9.68	9.71	

APPENDIX 1

Minitab Examples

EXAMPLE

A MANUFACTURER WEIGHING BARS OF SOAP

(If you are using the WINDOWS version of MINITAB, you might issue the GSTD command first to use standard graphics in the session window. Also, if you want to save your output on a file, use the command OUTFILE 'A:CH3.LIS' to echo output to this file.)

```
MTB > RANDOM 20 OBSERVATIONS INTO C1;    # A SAMPLE OF
                                         # 20 FROM A
SUBC> NORMAL MU = 100 SIGMA = .33.       # POPULATION WITH
                                         # THESE PARAMETERS
MTB > LET C1 = C1 * 100       # PUTS 4 DIGITS TO THE LEFT
                             # OF THE DECIMAL POINT
MTB > ROUND C1 PUT IN C1     # KEEPS ONLY DIGITS LEFT
                             # THE OF THE DECIMAL
MTB > LET C1 = C1/100   # RESETS THE DECIMAL POINT
MTB > SET C2            # EXACT VALUES IN C2
DATA> 20(100)  # NO BLANKS ALLOWED IN THIS LINE

DATA> END      # PRODUCED A COLUMN OF NOMINAL VALUES

MTB > LET C3 = C1 - C2
                  # INDIVIDUAL CHANCE ERRORS, DEVIATIONS

MTB > NAME C1 'BARWT' C2 'NOMINAL' C3 'DEV'
MTB > SAVE 'B:SOAP'      # HAVE A DATA DISK IN DRIVE B
# OR, DESIGNATE DRIVE A: IF NECESSARY
MTB > PRINT 'BARWT' 'NOMINAL' 'DEV'  # BECAUSE THE DATA
    # ARE SIMULATED AT RANDOM, YOUR DATA IS LIKELY
    # TO BE DIFFERENT FROM MINE
MTB > STEM 'BARWT'  # OUTPUT NOT SHOWN, YOU MIGHT TRY THIS
```

```
MTB > STEM 'DEV'      # OUTPUT NOT SHOWN, TRY!
MTB > HIST 'BARWT'    # OUTPUT NOT SHOWN, BUT THE
                      # DOTPLOT COMMAND
                      # THAT FOLLOWS ALSO DISPLAYS THE SHAPE
                      # OF THE DISTRIBUTION
MTB > DOTPLOT 'BARWT' # NEW COMMAND, LIKE STEM-AND-LEAF
                      # OR A HISTOGRAM ROTATED 180 DEGREES
                      # COUNTER CLOCKWISE
MTB > AVERAGE 'BARWT' # AVERAGE OF 20 VALUES,
                      # ESTIMATE OF NOMINAL
MTB > STD DEV 'BARWT' # SAMPLE STANDARD DEVIATION
MTB > MEDIAN C1
```

Comment   The small sample of 20 observations, from a normal population, was not large enough for the sample distribution to look much like the parent. So, the sample size was increased to 100 to see if the sample distribution begins to look like the parent population in shape.

```
# REPEATING THE ABOVE PROCEDURE FOR 100 OBSERVATIONS
# MORE REPRESENTATIVE OF THE POPULATION

MTB > RANDOM 100 OBSERVATIONS INTO C1;
SUBC> NORMAL MU = 100 SIGMA = .33.

MTB > LET C1 = C1 * 100
MTB > ROUND C1 PUT IN C1
MTB > LET C1 = C1/100
MTB > SET IN C2
DATA> 100(100)   # NO BLANKS ALLOWED IN THIS LINE
DATA> END

MTB > LET C3 = C1 - C2
MTB > DOTPLOT 'BARWT'   # WITH 100 OBS. LOOKS MORE NORMAL
MTB > DOTPLOT 'DEV'     # SAME PATTERN AS BARWT EXCEPT
                       # FOR MINOR SCALING DIFFERENCES

GO ON TO ANOTHER EXAMPLE, OR IF FINISHED MTB > STOP
```

EXAMPLE

SAMPLE MEAN WEIGHT OF 20 BARS OF SOAP

```
MTB > RETRIEVE 'B:SOAP' # OR GENERATE IT AGAIN
MTB > AVERAGE  'BARWT'  # THE ARITHMETIC AVERAGE
                       # OF 20 VALUES
                       # USED TO ESTIMATE THE
                       # NOMINAL WHICH
                       # IS KNOWN TO BE 100 GRAMS HERE

#   SAMPLE MEAN = 99.858 = ȳ
GO ON TO ANOTHER EXAMPLE, OR IF FINISHED MTB>STOP
```

EXAMPLE

CASH FLOWS FROM AN INVESTMENT

```
MTB > INFO          # ERASE ALL OLD COLUMNS IN THE WORKSPACE
MTB > ERASE C1-C3   # A RETRIEVE DOES THIS AUTOMATICALLY
                    # BUT WE DON'T RETRIEVE HERE

MTB > RANDOM 1000 OBSERVATIONS INTO C1;
SUBC> NORMAL MU = 25000 SIGMA = 4500.

MTB > DOTPLOT C1       # C1 CONTAINS 1000 POSSIBLE
                      # CASH FLOWS
MTB > LET C2 = 100000/C1
                      # EACH CASH FLOW HAS A PAYBACK PERIOD
                      # THAT IS COMPUTED HERE
MTB > NAME C2 'PBACK'
MTB > DOTPLOT 'PBACK'  # DEPENDING ON THE PARTICULAR
   # RANDOM NUMBERS, YOUR OUTPUT MAY OR MAY NOT
   # RESEMBLE MINE

MTB > MEDIAN 'PBACK'    # AGAIN, YOUR NUMBERS MAY
                       # DIFFER FROM THESE
                       # DUE TO THE RANDOM NUMBER
                       # GENERATOR

SKIP THIS COMMAND IF IT REFUSES TO WORK BECAUSE OF A FULL
WORKSPACE            MTB> BOXPLOT 'PBACK'

SKIP THIS COMMAND IF USING A STUDENT EDITION OF MINITAB THAT DOES
NOT EXECUTE IT   MTB > LVALS 'PBACK'

MTB > DESCRIBE 'PBACK'  # THIS MINITAB COMMAND
                       # PRODUCES A MIX OF CLASSICAL
                       # AND EXPLORATORY SUMMARY
                       # INFORMATION
     # A TRIMMED MEAN AND STANDARD ERROR HAVE
     # BEEN EDITED OUT-- TO BE DISCUSSED LATER
GO ON TO ANOTHER EXAMPLE, OR IF FINISHED MTB>STOP
```

EXAMPLE

CLASSICAL RESIDUALS FOR A MANUFACTURER WEIGHING BARS OF SOAP (CONTINUED)

```
MTB > RETRIEVE 'B:SOAP' # OR SIMULATE THE DATA AGAIN

MTB > AVERAGE C1     # YOUR VALUES MAY DIFFER BECAUSE OF THE
                     # RANDOM NUMBER GENERATOR

     (SAMPLE) MEAN  =  99.858
```

```
MTB > SET IN C4        # THE SAMPLE MEAN IS USED HERE
DATA> 20(99.858)       # NO BLANKS ALLOWED IN THIS LINE
DATA> END

MTB > LET C5 = C1 - C4  # SOMETIMES THIS IS CALLED CENTERING
MTB > PRINT C1 C2 C3 C1 C4 C5

 # C1 C2 C3 SHOW THE REGRESSION
 # MODEL ASSUMING KNOWN PARAMETERS;
 # C1 C4 C5 SHOW THE ESTIMATED
 # MODEL USING THE SAMPLE MEAN AND THE RESIDUALS
```

The following manipulations show a variety of ways to obtain a sample standard deviation, via the algebraic formula and, later, directly.

```
MTB > LET C6 = C5 * C5  # SQUARES THE RESIDUALS
MTB > LET K1 = SUM(C6)  # SUM OF SQUARED RESIDUALS
MTB > PRINT K1
# K1        2.22452

MTB > LET K2 = SQRT(K1/19)   # SQUARE ROOT OF THE
 # SUM OF SQUARED RESIDUALS DIVIDED BY (THE NUMBER
 # OF OBSERVATIONS MINUS ONE)

MTB > PRINT K2
#                  K2   0.342170 (SAMPLE)ST.DEV.

MTB > STD DEV C5       # C5 CONTAINS THE RESIDUALS
#                  0.34217  (SAMPLE)ST.DEV.

MTB > STD DEV C1       # C1 CONTAINS SOAP BAR WEIGHTS
#                  0.34217  (SAMPLE)ST.DEV.
GO ON TO ANOTHER EXAMPLE, OR IF FINISHED MTB > STOP
```

EXAMPLE

PROFIT PLANNING

```
MTB > RANDOM 100 OBS INTO C1;
SUBC> NORMAL MU = 70000 SIGMA = 10000.
MTB > ROUND C1 PUT C1
MTB > NAME C1 'Q'                # QUANTITY OF UNITS SOLD
MTB > NAME C2 'REV'
MTB > LET 'REV'='Q' * 2.00       # REVENUE COMPUTATION

MTB > NAME C3 'VCOST'
MTB > LET 'VCOST'='Q' * 1.20     # VARIABLE COST COMPUTATION

MTB > NAME C4 'FCOST'
MTB > SET IN 'FCOST'
DATA> 100(40000)                 # NO BLANKS ALLOWED IN THIS LINE
DATA> END
```

```
MTB > NAME C5 'PROF'              # PROFIT COMPUTATION
MTB > LET 'PROF' = 'REV' - ( 'VCOST' + ('FCOST'))
MTB > DOTPLOT  'PROF'
MTB > DESCRIBE 'PROF'      # THESE STATISTICS ARE ALL ESTIMATORS
                          # OBTAINED FROM A SAMPLE
MTB > MPLOT 'REV' 'Q' 'PROF' 'Q'   # PLOTS REVENUE AND PROFIT
                                  # ON THE SAME GRAPH
```

Comment   Next, we replicate the above analysis, changing the mean level of sales from 70,000 to 50,000 units.

```
    # RE-EXAMINATION WITH A NEW MEAN SALES LEVEL

MTB > RANDOM 100 OBS INTO C1;
SUBC> NORMAL MU = 50000 SIGMA = 10000.
MTB > ROUND C1 PUT C1

MTB > LET 'REV' = 'Q' * 2.00
MTB > LET 'VCOST' = 'Q' * 1.20
MTB > LET 'PROF' = 'REV' - ('VCOST' + ('FCOST'))
MTB > DOTPLOT 'PROF'    # NOTICE YOU LOSE MONEY AT LEAST HALF
                # THE TIME, 50000 UNITS IS THE BREAKEVEN POINT
MTB > DESCRIBE 'PROF'

MTB > MPLOT 'REV' 'Q' 'PROF' 'Q'
MTB > NAME C6 'TCOST'
MTB > LET 'TCOST' = 'VCOST' + 'FCOST'

MTB > PRINT C1 C2 C3 C4 C5 C6     # TO CHECK COMPUTATIONS
MTB > MPLOT 'REV' 'Q' 'TCOST' 'Q' # THE BREAKEVEN POINT
 # SHOWS UP ON THIS PLOT AND IS WHERE
 # THE LINES CROSS AT ABOUT 50000 UNITS SOLD
GO ON TO ANOTHER EXAMPLE, OR IF FINISHED MTB > STOP
```

CHAPTER 4

Introduction to Probability

OBJECTIVES

- Introduce probability theory
- Describe probability distributions
- Accumulate probabilities in cumulative functions
- Define population means and variances
- Illustrate commonly encountered distributions

PRELUDE

"Show me the hobo who sleeps out in the rain. And I'll show you a young man with so many reasons why. And there but for Fortune go you or I. Show me the whiskey that stains on the floor. Show me the drunkard as he stumbles out the door. And I'll show you a young man with so many reasons why. And there but for Fortune go you or I..." (Phil Ochs)

Fortune is a blind god who influences individual and corporate lives, decisions, finances, and so on. In nearly everything we observe, Fortune deals some of the cards. For example, whether or not it will rain tomorrow or exactly what a company's profit or loss will be is seldom known for sure. Until now, very little has been said about the chance mechanisms that play a role in generating the data that we know how to analyze. The complete data analyst understands the theory that underpins the data. As a result, the multitude of data-generating conditions are put in perspective. For example, sometimes a farmer gets a good crop because of a new wheat variety that has been developed, but the yield might have been influenced by chance phenomena such as the weather, which is beyond anyone's control. To put our observations, analysis, and subsequent conclusions in the proper perspective, the concept of probability is critical to our thinking. Yet, probability makes for uncertain footing because it demarcates the slippery ground between ignorance and perfect knowledge. ◇

INTRODUCTION

The Misfortune Problem[1]   There is a person to whom all of the following things happened on the same day. First, his son totaled the family car and was seriously injured. Next, he was late for work and nearly got fired. In the afternoon he got food poisoning at a fast-food restaurant. In the evening he got word that his father had died.

How would you account for all these things happening to one person on the same day? Have you ever had something very unlikely happen to you or someone you know? How do you make sense of a day when everything seems to go wrong?

Clifford Konold's misfortune problem was presented to several people to see how they interpreted such an unusually bad day. When this bad day began, the things that were about to happen were uncertain. Therefore, Konold's more general interest was in the person's interpretation of uncertain situations and the thinking rationale used.

The way we think, live, and make decisions is influenced by both instincts and what is learned from observing the world around us. Often, chance plays an important role in generating observations. Because of our reliance on observation for decision making in day-to-day living, we are dependent on how chance phenomena are interpreted.

The purpose of this chapter is to (1) remind you that our observations often include an element of uncertainty; (2) map out the basics of probability theory, a structure that helps us think about uncertainty; (3) introduce simple discrete and continuous probability distributions; and (4) define means and variances of probability distributions.

Probability theory is a systematic method of treating uncertainty problems through mathematical reasoning and notation. Probability theory supplies the cosmic matter of ideas for building the statistical universe. For example, particular theoretical probability distributions have definite shapes; therefore, in practical problems, stem-and-leaf diagrams or histograms with a specific shape can be related to the background theory. If the data analysis reveals a normal data distribution, probability theory validates the use of particular statistical methods. Because probability theory describes the universe of data values, it encourages generalizations from the sample data at hand.

THE NATURE OF PROBABILITY THEORY

This section characterizes the uncertain consequences of a management decision and introduces some basic terminology used in probability theory.

Possible Results of an Experiment or Observation in Question

Probability theory develops from an idealized framework. Of first concern is an accepted agreement as to what constitutes the possible outcomes of an experiment or observation.

The Harvest Moon Bakery Experiment **Random experiments** produce observable outcomes that are not perfectly predictable. For example, suppose the Harvest Moon Bakery plans to conduct such an experiment that results from a management decision. The manager decides to bake 5 loaves of a new bread every day, a bread the bakery calls Moist Berry Wheat Bread. This type of a decision is made in any business situation when the demand is uncertain and the product must be available on demand.

On a particular morning, Harvest Moon displays 5 good-smelling loaves of bread for sale on a shelf. As the day's **events** unfold for Moist Berry Wheat Bread, 0 or 1 or 2 or 3 or 4 or 5 loaves will be sold. These are **simple events** because they cannot be constructed from anything simpler. Simple events and **outcomes** are synonymous. By the end of the day, one of these simple events will have occurred as an outcome of the experiment.

Because only one of these simple events can occur by day's end, these simple events are said to be **mutually exclusive;** for example, selling exactly 3 loaves precludes the possibility of selling any other number on that day. Also, the simple events are **exhaustive** because they include all possibilities. For example, Harvest Moon can't sell, say, 7 loaves, because they only baked 5 loaves.

Sometimes it is necessary to refer to a group of simple events, such as selling 2 loaves or fewer. The group, 2 loaves or fewer, includes 0, 1, and 2 loaves. Groups of simple events are **unions,** which are also called **compound events.**

IMPOSSIBLE, CERTAIN, AND RANDOM EVENTS

A list of simple events is a **set.** On a particular day for the Harvest Moon Bakery experiment, the set of outcomes consists of all possible numbers of loaves sold—0, 1, 2, 3, 4, 5. This set of simple events is written as

possible number of loaves sold set = [0, 1, 2, 3, 4, 5]

For reference purposes, the simple events are named $E_1 = 0$, $E_2 = 1$, . . . , $E_6 = 5$; therefore,

$$[0, 1, 2, 3, 4, 5] = [E_1, E_2, E_3, E_4, E_5, E_6]$$

In general, E_i refers to the i-th simple event.

As long as the manager's decision is to bake 5 loaves a day of Moist Berry Wheat Bread, each day's sales is a number (a data value) from this list of possibilities. A sample of sales consists of numbers from the list in the set. All the numbers in the set will not necessarily show up in the sample; however, the larger the sample, the more likely it is that this will happen. Suppose a sample of sales for ten days results in the following data set:

Day	1	2	3	4	5	6	7	8	9	10
Loaves sold	1	1	0	4	2	5	5	3	3	4

Perhaps because sample data, in a sense, is drawn from a set of possible outcomes (simple events), this set

$$\text{possible number of loaves sold set} = [0, 1, 2, 3, 4, 5]$$

is also called the **sample space** (discrete) for the experiment; the simple events, 0, 1, 2, 3, 4, 5, are called **sample points.**

Conceptually, a sample can be made large enough to become the whole population. Therefore, in a random experiment, a set of possible outcomes forms a numerical foundation for both samples and populations. If you can imagine a sample as large as a population, then a statistical tool, such as a frequency histogram, describes how often particular numbers in a set appear in a population. The proportion of the time that simple events occur in a population is their **probability.** Thus, probability involves the chance mechanisms responsible for generating the data.

Impossible Events

With respect to the specific set of conditions at the Harvest Moon for Moist Berry Wheat Bread, an **impossible event** is to sell more than 5 or less than 0 loaves. Impossible events have a zero probability of occurring.

$$P(\text{impossible event}) = 0$$

If the specific set of conditions changes, say Harvest Moon decides to bake 7 loaves a day, selling 6 or 7 loaves is no longer impossible. Therefore, impossibility is gauged with respect to a specific set of conditions associated with the experiment.

Certain Events

An event that is certain has a probability of 1. It is certain that 1 of the simple events in a set will occur. For example, we don't know ahead of time which number of loaves will be sold in a day, 0 or 1 or 2 or 3 or 4 or 5; nevertheless, we are certain 1 of those numbers will be an outcome.

$$P(\text{an event that is certain}) = 1$$

> ## S T A T I S T I C A L   H I G H L I G H T S
> The boundaries for probability are:
> $$0 \leq P(\text{any event}) \leq 1$$

When probabilities are near 0, events are rare, such as the probability of you being kicked by a horse. Probabilities near 1 indicate that events are practically certain. Interestingly, many people tend to conclude that, say, a .8 probability of rain tomorrow means certain rain; they tend to equate .8 to 1. Would a .8 probability of rain in a forecast force you to change your picnic plans? Midway between 0 and 1, a .5 probability of an event is like a coin flip; heads or tails are equally likely.

Random Events and Variables

On or within the boundaries of impossibility and certainty is the territory staked out by the concept of probability. Clifford Konold likes to say that "probability is the slick middle ground between belief and knowledge." Konold asserted that the uniquely troublesome aspect of probability is the territory it stakes out.

> Through probability, we attempt to demarcate the amorphous state somewhere between the imagined extremes of total ignorance and perfect knowledge. And, it is trying to keep one's footing in this nowhere land that is particularly disturbing. Like a frictionless surface, the conceptual landscape not only trips you up, but keeps you sliding once you're down.[2]

At the Harvest Moon Bakery, for each day's experimental trial (or run), a particular simple event may or may not occur; we don't know which number of loaves will be sold on a particular day, 0, 1, 2, 3, 4, or 5. Such events are said to be **random events;** formally, experiments that produce random events are random experiments. Random events are neither certain nor impossible.

Instead of writing all the possible numerical results of an experiment, such as 0, 1, 2, 3, 4, or 5, often it is convenient to let a variable, say, y represent the possible numerical results. Such a variable is called a **random variable.**

Knowing that an event is random locates us on the knowledge scale somewhere between ignorance and perfect knowledge. This knowledge is less than perfect because we don't know which of the possible outcomes will be observed. Yet, this knowledge is more than ignorance because we know which outcomes are possible.

Records of previous outcomes may or may not add to our limited knowledge that a variable is random. For example, it is well established that a history of past changes in the Dow Jones average is of little help in predicting tomorrow's change because there is no pattern to these changes. In contrast, patterns tend to appear in variables such as retail sales; such patterns are helpful in predicting future sales. For example, an experienced retailer would know the busier sales days. With the help of statistical tools, an inexperienced retailer can quickly learn to predict on which days high proportions of the week's sales tend to occur. Such proportions can be used to estimate probabilities. Therefore, in addition to knowing that an event is random, we become more knowledgeable by assigning probabilities to random events.

ASSIGNING PROBABILITIES TO RANDOM EVENTS FROM RANDOM EXPERIMENTS

Three common ways of assigning probabilities to random events are relative frequency, classical (equally likely outcomes), and subjective methods.

The Relative Frequency Method of Assigning Probabilities

Although we don't know which simple event will occur in a particular experimental trial or run, we can use past outcomes to compute the proportion of times an event has happened, the **relative frequency.** Relative frequencies estimate event probabilities. Because a history of past outcomes is essential to the relative frequency method of assigning probabilities, this method is empirical.

Suppose ten day's sales of Moist Berry Wheat Bread (loaves) at the Harvest Moon are

Day	1	2	3	4	5	6	7	8	9	10
Loaves sold (y)	1	1	0	4	2	5	5	3	3	4

The loaves sold figures are realizations of a random variable, y, and constitute a sample of ten data values.

These loaves sold figures arise from the set of possibilities, [0, 1, 2, 3, 4, 5]; these simple events are named $[E_1, E_2, E_3, E_4, E_5, E_6]$. In general, E_i refers to the i-th simple event, for i = 1, 2, . . . , 6, where i is an index for the set members.

$E_1 = 0$ and appears one time in the following sample data list.

Loaves sold (y)   1   1   0   4   2   5   5   3   3   4

The single occurrence of E_1 is recorded as a frequency count, $f_1 = 1$. $E_2 = 1$ and appears two times in the sample data list; it is recorded as a frequency count, $f_2 = 2$. $E_3 = 2$ and appears one time in the sample data list; it is recorded as a frequency count, $f_3 = 1$, and so on. In general, the frequency counts, f_i, for the i-th simple event in the loaves sold sample data list are

f_1	f_2	f_3	f_4	f_5	f_6
1	2	1	2	2	2

The total frequency (the sample size) is n = 10; therefore, the relative frequencies, $\frac{f_i}{n}$, of the events can be computed easily. They are

$\dfrac{f_1}{n}$	$\dfrac{f_2}{n}$	$\dfrac{f_3}{n}$	$\dfrac{f_4}{n}$	$\dfrac{f_5}{n}$	$\dfrac{f_6}{n}$
$\dfrac{1}{10}$	$\dfrac{2}{10}$	$\dfrac{1}{10}$	$\dfrac{2}{10}$	$\dfrac{2}{10}$	$\dfrac{2}{10}$

S T A T I S T I C A L   H I G H L I G H T S

Let

$$f_i = \text{frequency count for simple event } E_i$$
$$\Sigma f_i = n, \text{ the sample size}$$

Then the relative frequencies are

$$\frac{f_i}{n} = \text{the relative frequency for simple event } E_i$$

Because relative frequencies are based on sample data, they are likely to change from sample to sample. Therefore, relative frequencies are random. Sample-to-sample changes in relative frequencies are troublesome because relative frequencies are used to estimate simple event probabilities, which are unique, nonrandom numbers. Fortunately, when samples are large, the relative frequency of an event changes little from sample to sample and will be close to its probability. When there is a long history of past outcomes, consider relative frequencies equal to event probabilities.

$$P(E_i) = \frac{f_i}{n}$$

The assignment of relative frequencies to event probabilities is supported by an important statistical law, the **law of large numbers.** The law of large numbers states that, for large samples, the relative frequencies will be close to event probabilities.

The relative frequency method of assigning probabilities has much appeal because of its objectivity and because it does not depend on potentially biased observers; however, it does have some drawbacks. One drawback is that the method does not exploit other history beyond the sample data such as management experience. The relative frequency method has no way to incorporate into probability estimates management's product knowledge and business experience. Another drawback is that relative frequencies simply describe the sample data rather than arising from mathematical logic and reasoning.

The Classical Equally Likely Outcomes Method of Assigning Probabilities

On the first day at the Harvest Moon Bakery, before any of Moist Berry Wheat Bread loaves were sold, no history of past sales existed. Therefore, it would be impossible to calculate relative frequencies without sample data. In an attempt to predict potential sales, a manager might use sales data of another bread, say, Three Grain Black Bread. However, there is a danger in making predictions this way because these bread products may not be similar enough.

Suppose management has to confront the fact that no sample data are available to calculate relative frequencies. Even under these difficult circumstances, there is a way to assign probabilities to simple events. If the simple events can be thought of as **equally likely,** this would mean that every simple event has the same probability. If so, then selling 0 loaves of bread would be as likely as selling 1, 2, 3, 4, or 5 loaves. This situation is like rolling a die, which has six possible equally likely faces. In this case, the equally likely outcomes method assigns each simple event a probability of $\frac{1}{6}$. Therefore, on a particular day, 0, 1, 2, 3, 4, or 5 loaves will be sold, each with a simple event probability of $\frac{1}{6}$.

S T A T I S T I C A L   H I G H L I G H T S

For equally likely outcomes, assign probabilities to an event, which may be a collection of simple events, using the rule

$$P(E_i) = \frac{\text{number of outcomes in the event}}{\text{total number of outcomes}}$$

In general, if there are k equally likely simple events in total, the probability of a simple event is $\frac{1}{k}$. Equally likely outcomes refer to simple events, which are mutually exclusive.

The classical equally likely method is based entirely on logical reasoning that precedes data collection; hence, the classical method is also referred to as an a priori approach.

The equally likely method has some deficiencies. One deficiency is that it can fail to produce probabilities when conditions make equally likeliness unbelievable. For example, equally likeliness is believable when rolling a balanced die made from homogeneous plastic; however, a biased die, weighted in favor of certain faces, has probabilities that elude the equally likely method.

Another deficiency is that the assigned probability cannot be determined if k is infinite rather than finite. For example, if a company wants to find the probability of realizing a particular earnings-per-share figure, the equally likely method does not help because the earnings-per-share ratio has an infinite number of possibilities. Furthermore, finding the probability that earnings per share exceeds some value, such as zero, escapes determination via the equally likely method. The relative frequency method would be better suited for this type of problem; yet, neither method utilizes other information such as management's belief and intuition.

Subjective Method of Assigning Probabilities

The subjective method of assigning probabilities relies on intuition and belief. For example, suppose you look at the sky and see a gathering storm in the clouds. Suppose you believe that it is likely to rain in the afternoon. In fact, you might be willing to state that there is an 80% chance of rain. This subjective probability is uniquely personal because someone standing next to you might say that the chances of rain are only 60%. With the subjective method, probabilities are assigned that reflect a degree of belief in the outcomes. Care must be taken to stay within the boundaries of probability; probabilities of events must be between 0 and 1; the sum of all the assigned probabilities must be 1.

As another example, the manager at the Harvest Moon Bakery, who knows about bread sales, may want to rely on intuition and assign probabilities subjectively for the daily sales of Moist Berry Wheat Bread. The manager may examine past sales but would not rely on them exclusively as required by the relative frequency method. Seldom does the future behave exactly like the past; therefore, the relative frequency method of assigning probabilities might not be that useful. Even though objectivity is lacking, the subjective method of assigning probabilities may be the method of choice because it draws upon intuitive evaluations of the future sales environment.

At the Harvest Moon Bakery, the manager assigned the following probabilities subjectively; they reflect his optimistic belief that daily sales for Moist Berry Wheat Bread are more likely to be high than low.

Loaves sold	0	1	2	3	4	5
Subjective probabilities	.05	.10	.15	.20	.20	.30

COLLECTIONS OF SIMPLE EVENTS

Simple events can be collected like building blocks to construct more sophisticated events called compound events or unions. For example, selling 0 or 1 or 2 loaves of bread is a compound event constructed from three simple events.

Unions (Compound Events)

Suppose the Harvest Moon Bakery doesn't make a profit on the Moist Berry Wheat Bread product unless more than 2 loaves are sold per day. A manager who considers replacing unprofitable products needs to look beyond isolated simple events and outcomes; therefore, compound events are constructed.

What is the probability that this product won't make a profit, the probability that a day's sales are only 0 or 1 or 2 loaves? Working with the subjective probabilities, the probability of not making a profit is the probability of selling (0 or 1 or 2) loaves, the sum of the probabilities for three simple events,

$$P(0 \text{ or } 1 \text{ or } 2) = .05 + .10 + .15 = .30$$

Some of the simple events (outcomes) were collected to form a compound event or union of simple events (0 or 1 or 2). Because simple events are mutually exclusive, the probability of the union is simply the sum of the probabilities. Thus we find that there is a 30% chance that this product won't make a profit.

> ### S T A T I S T I C A L   H I G H L I G H T S
>
> A compound event is a collection of outcomes. Whereas the terms *simple events* and *outcomes* can be used interchangeably, compound events are not outcomes but collections of outcomes.

Using "Or" to Designate the Union of Events

The word **or** has been used to connect simple events and to designate a union. "Or" is often replaced by the symbol $\cup$, such as in (0 or 1 or 2) = ($0 \cup 1 \cup 2$) loaves of bread; therefore, a probability statement may be written either way.

$$P(0 \text{ or } 1 \text{ or } 2) = P(0 \cup 1 \cup 2) = .05 + .10 + .15 = .30$$

Because simple events are mutually exclusive, the probability of the union is the sum of simple event probabilities.

Using "Not" to Designate the Complement of an Event

The word **not** designates the **complement** of an event. For example, not making a profit is the complement of making a profit. In our example, the probability of making a profit is selling (3 or 4 or 5) loaves, also written ($3 \cup 4 \cup 5$). So the probability of this union is the sum of the following simple event probabilities:

$$P(3 \text{ or } 4 \text{ or } 5) = P(3 \cup 4 \cup 5) = .20 + .20 + .30 = .70$$

Notice that the probability of profit, .70, equals 1 minus the probability of not making a profit, $1 - .30 = .70$; thus the two complementary compound events are related in the following way:

$$P(\text{making a profit}) = 1 - P(\text{not making a profit})$$

The **odds** of an event is the ratio of complementary probabilities. The odds in favor of making a profit is defined as the ratio.

$$\frac{P(\text{making a profit})}{P(\text{not making a profit})} = \frac{.70}{.30}$$

The odds or relative chances can be written as $\frac{.70}{.30}$, $\frac{7}{3}$, or 7:3. The colon notation is often encountered although the division symbol states the calculation explicitly.

S T A T I S T I C A L   H I G H L I G H T S

In general, the probability of an event E_i is 1 minus the probability of its complement (not E_i),

$$P(E_i) = 1 - P(\text{not } E_i).$$

Using "And" to Designate the Intersection of Events

The word **and** designates the **intersection** of events. Consider conducting two experiments in sequence. For example, if a coin is flipped and then a die is rolled, let (H and 5) represent the occurrence of a head (H) on the coin and a five (5) on the die. "And" is often replaced by the symbol $\cap$, therefore $(\text{H and 5}) = (\text{H} \cap 5)$.

Consider a more sophisticated example in which two compound events intersect. First, the compound events are defined in terms of loss, break-even, and profit. If the Harvest Moon Bakery sells exactly 2 loaves of Moist Berry Wheat Bread per day, it breaks even on this product. Break-even means the bakery makes no profit and suffers no loss. Furthermore, it loses money if fewer than 2 loaves of this bread are sold per day. If more than 2 loaves of bread are sold, it makes a profit.

Let

$CE_1 =$ the compound event, lose money or break even

$CE_1 = (0 \cup 1 \cup 2)$ loaves sold

$CE_2 =$ the compound event, break even or make a profit

$CE_2 = (2 \cup 3 \cup 4 \cup 5)$ loaves sold

Then the probability of the compound events are

$$P(CE_1) = P(0 \cup 1 \cup 2) = .05 + .10 + .15 = .30$$
$$P(CE_2) = P(2 \cup 3 \cup 4 \cup 5) = .15 + .20 + .20 + .30 = .85$$

Notice that these two compound events overlap. The event that 2 loaves are sold (break even) is included in the definition of each compound event. This overlap is the intersection.

$$\text{an intersection} = (CE_1 \text{ and } CE_2) = (CE_1 \cap CE_2)$$
$$= (2 \text{ loaves sold})$$

A Warning about Unions of Intersecting Events and Related Probabilities
Case 1: Mutually exclusive events don't intersect. The probability of a union of mutually exclusive events is found by adding probabilities. For example, the union of two simple events has the following probability:

$$P(0 \cup 1) = .05 + .10 = .15$$

Case 2: Events that intersect are not mutually exclusive, then the addition of event probabilities requires an adjustment to reduce the sum because the intersection probability is counted twice. For example, the compound events CE_1 and CE_2 are not mutually exclusive because the 2 loaves sold outcome is included in both compound events and the following probabilities:

$$P(CE_1) = P(0 \cup 1 \cup 2) = .05 + .10 + .15 = .30$$
$$P(CE_2) = P(2 \cup 3 \cup 4 \cup 5) = .15 + .20 + .20 + .30 = .85$$

By adding $P(CE_1) + P(CE_2) = .30 + .85 = 1.15$, the intersection (.15) is counted twice. A probability greater than 1 is impossible. To adjust for this double counting, subtract .15 from the incorrect total of 1.15. Thus, the correct probability for this union of intersecting events is

$$P(CE_1 \cup CE_2) = P(CE_1) + P(CE_2) - P(CE_1 \cap CE_2)$$
$$= .30 + .85 - .15 = 1$$

Addition Law   The **addition law** is a rule for finding the probability of a union of events. This law accumulates probabilities and adjusts for the intersection of events. For example, the addition law states that the probability of $(CE_1 \cup CE_2)$ is

$$P(CE_1 \cup CE_2) = P(CE_1) + P(CE_2) - P(CE_1 \cap CE_2)$$
$$P(CE_1 \cup CE_2) = .30 \quad\quad + .85 \quad\quad - .15$$

The intersection, $(CE_1 \cap CE_2)$, has a nonzero probability; therefore, these compound events are not mutually exclusive. As a result, the probability of the union requires the subtraction of the intersection probability, $P(CE_1 \cap CE_2)$, from $P(CE_1) + P(CE_2)$. If it were true that $P(CE_1 \cap CE_2) = 0$, the events would be mutually exclusive.

This particular union, $(CE_1 \cup CE_2) = (0 \cup 1 \cup 2 \cup 3 \cup 4 \cup 5)$ loaves sold, is exhaustive and covers all possibilities, loss, break-even, or profit. Thus, $P(CE_1 \cup CE_2) = 1$.

In general, the addition law for any two simple or compound events, say, CE_i, CE_j is

$$P(CE_i \cup CE_j) = P(CE_i) + P(CE_j) - P(CE_i \cap CE_j)$$

If the two events don't intersect, $P(CE_i \cap CE_j) = 0$; therefore, nothing is lost by using this formulation for either case, unions of events with or without intersections.

Again, the boundaries for the union of compound events are 0 and 1.

$$0 \leq P(CE_i \cup CE_j) \leq 1$$

INTERSECTIONS OF INDEPENDENT AND DEPENDENT EVENTS

The probability of an intersection of events involves the multiplication of event probabilities as specified in the **multiplication law.** To choose the correct probabilities to multiply, you must know whether the events are **dependent** or **independent.** When events are dependent, the probability of one event is affected by the occurrence of the other event. When events are independent, the probability of one event is not affected by the occurrence of the other event.

Multiplication Law   The multiplication law is a rule for finding the probability of an intersection of events. For example, the multiplication law states that the probability of the intersection of two events, such as $P(E_i$ and $E_j) = P(E_i \cap E_j)$, is

$$P(E_i \cap E_j) = P(E_i)\, P(E_j \mid E_i)$$

The right-most part of the above expression is $P(E_j \mid E_i)$, the probability of E_j "given" E_i has already occurred. Therefore, $P(E_j \mid E_i)$ is a **conditional probability.** $P(E_j)$ is an **unconditional probability.**

The multiplication law states that

$$P(E_i \cap E_j) = P(E_i)\, P(E_j \mid E_i)$$

$P(E_j \mid E_i)$ = the probability of E_j "given" E_i has already occurred, a conditional probability.

Independent Events   Events are independent when the conditional and unconditional probabilities are equal, $P(E_j|E_i) = P(E_j)$. Therefore, there is no need to use conditional probabilities in the multiplication law, and

$$P(E_i \cap E_j) = P(E_i)\ P(E_j|E_i) = P(E_i)\ P(E_j)$$

When events are independent, simply multiply their unconditional probabilities for the probability of an intersection.

Consider conducting two experiments in sequence. For example, if you flip a coin and then roll a die, the coin and the die are independent of one another; therefore, so are the outcomes. Thus, the multiplication law produces the following result:

$$P(\text{flip heads and roll a five}) = \frac{1}{2} \times \frac{1}{6} = \frac{1}{12}$$

Consider another example. If you can assume that Harvest Moon's sales of Moist Berry Wheat Bread are independent from day to day, the probability of selling 2 loaves on one day and 5 loaves on the next day (2 and 5) is

$$P(2 \text{ and } 5) = P(2 \cap 5) = .15 \times .3 = .045$$

S T A T I S T I C A L   H I G H L I G H T S

For independent events, the probability of one event and another is simply the product of unconditional probabilities.

$$P(E_i \cap E_j) = P(E_i) \times P(E_j)$$

Dependent Events   Events are dependent when the conditional and unconditional probabilities are not equal, $P(E_j|E_i) \neq P(E_j)$. When applying the multiplication law to dependent events, you must consider the sequence of events and use an unconditional probability followed by a conditional probability, as specified in the multiplication law.

$$P(E_i \cap E_j) = P(E_i)\ P(E_j|E_i)$$

Consider the intersection of the two compound events defined earlier for the Harvest Moon Bakery experiment.

$$(CE_1) \cap (CE_2) = (\text{lose or break even}) \quad \text{and} \quad (\text{break even or profit})$$

The probability of the intersection is

$$P(CE_1 \cap CE_2) = P(CE_1)\ P(CE_2|CE_1)$$

In the above expression, $P(CE_1)$ is an unconditional probability.

$$P(CE_1) = P(0 \cup 1 \cup 2) = .05 + .10 + .15 = .30$$

P(0), P(1), and P(2) are probabilities associated with the first three simple events listed below:

Loaves sold	0	1	2	3	4	5
Subjective Probabilities	.05	.10	.15	.20	.20	.30

The unconditional probability, $P(CE_1) = .30$, is multiplied times the conditional probability, $P(CE_2|CE_1)$, for the probability of the intersection

$$P(CE_1 \cap CE_2) = .30 \times P(CE_2|CE_1)$$

To evaluate the above expression completely, we must find the conditional probability, $P(CE_2|CE_1)$. Because we are given that $(CE_1) = (0 \cup 1 \cup 2)$ has occurred, this rules out the possibility of having sold part of CE_2, which includes 3, 4, or 5 loaves. Recall that $(CE_2) = (2 \cup 3 \cup 4 \cup 5)$, and $P(CE_2)$ is the unconditional **prior probability** without any information given. Once we are given that $(CE_1) = (0 \cup 1 \cup 2)$ has occurred, the only part of $(CE_2) = (2 \cup 3 \cup 4 \cup 5)$ that could have occurred is 2 loaves; 2 loaves is the overlap of the two compound events. The fraction of the time the overlap occurs, given CE_1 has occurred, is the ratio of .15 to .05 + .10 + .15; therefore,

$$P(CE_2|CE_1) = \frac{.15}{.05 + .10 + .15}$$

$P(CE_2|CE_1)$ is a conditional **posterior probability;** in other words, $P(CE_2|CE_1)$ is made conditional by revising an unconditional *prior* probability, $P(CE_2)$.

Thus, the multiplication rule for the intersection of these two dependent events produces the following result:

$$P(CE_1 \cap CE_2) = .30 \times P(CE_2|CE_1) = .30 \times \frac{.15}{.30} = .15$$

Bayes' Theorem **Bayes' theorem** determines conditional posterior probabilities as follows:

$$P(CE_2|CE_1) = \frac{P(CE_1 \cap CE_2)}{P(CE_1)}$$

This equation is obtained by solving

$$P(CE_1 \cap CE_2) = P(CE_1)\, P(CE_2|CE_1)$$

for the conditional probability on the right side of the equation.

The substitution of numerical values in the following equation results in the same conditional probability that was found above.

$$P(CE_2 | CE_1) = \frac{P(CE_1 \cap CE_2)}{P(CE_1)}$$

$$P(CE_2 | CE_1) = \frac{.15}{.05 + .10 + .15}$$

This result is the fraction of the time the overlap ($CE_1 \cap CE_2$) occurs, given CE_1 has occurred. This is simply the ratio of .15 to (.05 + .10 + .15). Effectively, we have revised or updated the original $P(CE_2)$ using new information about CE_1.

ALL POSSIBLE EVENTS INCLUDING CERTAINTY AND IMPOSSIBILITY

A set of simple events lists possible outcomes of a random experiment. Unions of simple events form compound events. All possible events include simple events as well as those events constructed from simple events. In applying probability theory to practical problems, it is important to enumerate all possible events in order to assign probabilities to them. The probability numbers represent the relative likelihood of events in a random experiment. The probability numbers or measures are governed by **probability axioms.** All probability theory follows from the acceptance of three axioms.

The quality control problem described next is an illustration of all possible events.

Quality Control at the Harvest Moon Bakery

As a loaf of bread is taken out of the oven, its appearance is evaluated. Loaves that don't meet the appearance standard for Moist Berry Wheat Bread are deemed defective and sold as seconds. The letter D stands for the simple event of a defective loaf of bread. The letter G represents a loaf with a good appearance. Notice how pervasive probability concepts are and how easy it is to apply these concepts to different aspects of business. The enumeration of all possible events includes

	1. D	(defective)
	2. G	(good)
Certainty	3. G ∪ D	(good or defective)
Impossibility	4. ∅	(neither good nor defective)

The symbol ∅ indicates an empty set, or **null set.** The null set is equivalent to G ∩ D, the intersection of mutually exclusive simple events. Also, there is a complementary relationship between certainty and impossibility; therefore,

$P(G \cup D) = 1 - P(G \cap D)$. This relationship can also be expressed as $P(G \cup D) = 1 - P(\text{not } (G \cup D))$.

Certainty and impossibility are compound events constructed from simple events. The two simple events, D and G, produced $G \cup D$ and $\emptyset$. In all, there are four possible events. Because the four possible events are related, they are referred to collectively as a **family.** Each family member is defined by the inclusion or exclusion (two states) of the simple events; therefore, there are $2 \times 2 = 2^2 = 4$ family members.

Probability Axioms or Postulates An **axiom** (or **postulate**) is a recognized truth. Probability numbers or measures are governed by the three probability axioms described here. All possible events can be assigned probabilities. The family of all possible events arise from simple events E_i where $i = 1, 2, \ldots , n$; the family size is 2^n. Family member, event probability assignments are governed by the following three axioms:

Axiom 1. Each event in the family has a nonnegative probability measure associated with it.

Axiom 2. The union of all simple events has a probability of 1.

Axiom 3. The union of any two mutually exclusive events has a probability equal to the sum of each event's probability.

VISUAL REPRESENTATIONS OF EVENTS AND PROBABILITIES

Three important graphic displays of events and probabilities are *Venn diagrams, probability trees,* and *joint probability tables.* A **Venn diagram** is a pictorial display of a sample space and its simple events. On Venn diagrams, unions, intersections, and complements of events can be pictured, making these diagrams very useful. A **probability tree** displays events and probabilities for a sequence of experiments in a treelike diagram. Probability trees are particularly useful in decision analysis. An alternative to a probability tree for a sequence of two experiments is a **joint probability table.**

Venn Diagrams

A Quality Control Problem A Venn diagram will be constructed for the quality control problem at the Harvest Moon Bakery. Exhibit 1 shows the preliminary construction features of the Venn diagram, where the simple events are represented by squares. The square on the left represents the event that a loaf of Moist Berry Wheat Bread looks good and meets the appearance standard. The square on the right represents the event that a loaf does not meet the appearance standard and is deemed defective. The two squares sit side by side to form a rectangle representing $(G \cup D)$, a certain compound event. In order to show what is impossible, the null set, the rectangle is

EXHIBIT 1 Preliminary Construction Features of a Venn Diagram

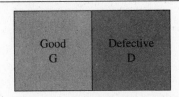

framed in Exhibit 2, completing the Venn diagram. Other geometric figures can be used for the simple events such as the circles in Exhibit 3.

The completed Venn diagram in Exhibit 2 pictures all possible events for the quality control problem at the Harvest Moon Bakery. The square on the left represents the event that a loaf of Moist Berry Wheat Bread looks good and meets the appearance standard. From the list of all possible events, this event is item two.

2. G   (good)

The square on the right represents the event that a loaf does not meet the appearance standard and is deemed defective. From the list of all possible events, this event is item one.

1. D   (defective)

Together the squares form a rectangle, and the rectangle represents certainty. From the list of all possible events, this event is item three.

Certainty   3. G ∪ D   (good or defective)

In order that all possible events are included in the Venn diagram, Exhibit 1 is enclosed in a frame, as shown in Exhibit 2. Between the inner rectangle and the outer, rounded-rectangular frame, the space represents the impossibility event, which is the empty or null set. From the list of all possible events, this event is item four.

Impossibility   4. ∅   (neither good nor defective)

EXHIBIT 2 A Venn Diagram for all Possible Events

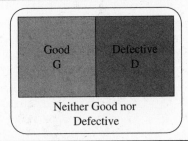

EXHIBIT 3 A Venn Diagram for Two Mutually Exclusive Events

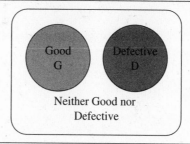

If you are distracted by the impossibility event (neither good nor defective), you can shrink-wrap the frame onto the inner rectangle.

Other geometric figures can represent simple events, such as the circles in Exhibit 3. Otherwise Exhibit 3 is the same as Exhibit 2. The nonintersecting circles emphasize that simple events are mutually exclusive.

Sales at the Harvest Moon Bakery Exhibit 4 shows a Venn diagram for the possible number of loaves sold of Moist Berry Wheat Bread when 5 loaves are baked per day. There are six squares, one for each of the simple events; the six squares form a rectangle that represents $(0 \cup 1 \cup 2 \cup 3 \cup 4 \cup 5)$, the union of all simple events. It is certain that one of the events in the union will occur. The region between the frame and the six elementary events represents the null or empty set.

Recall that

> CE_1 = the compound event, break even or lose money,
> $(0 \cup 1 \cup 2)$ loaves sold (the first three squares
> on the left, Exhibit 4)

> CE_2 = the compound event, break even or profit,
> $(2 \cup 3 \cup 4 \cup 5)$ loaves sold (the four squares
> on the right, Exhibit 4)

EXHIBIT 4 A Venn Diagram for Possible Sales Amounts

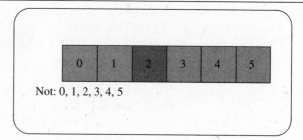

EXHIBIT 5 A Venn Diagram for Possible Sales Amounts

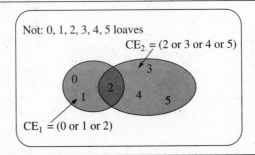

These two compound events overlap because break even (2 units sold) is included in both sets. This intersection is $CE_1 \cap CE_2$ and is emphasized with darker shading of the third square in Exhibit 4. Venn diagrams can emphasize intersections and draw your attention to the fact that the two compound events are not mutually exclusive.

Oval-shaped geometric figures can be used to represent events in Venn diagrams. As an example, an equivalent Venn diagram for Exhibit 4 is shown in Exhibit 5. Two intersecting egg shapes represent the compound events, CE_1 on the left and CE_2 on the right. The intersection, $CE_1 \cap CE_2$, has the darker shading.

Although the Venn diagrams above show only events, the corresponding probabilities can also be displayed on the diagrams.

Probability Trees

A Quality Control Problem   Before the Harvest Moon Bakery puts bread on sale, freshly baked loaves of bread are inspected to see if they meet appearance standards. Consider inspecting two loaves of bread in sequence. The first loaf is judged either good or defective in appearance, and then the second loaf is examined and another judgment is made. Based on past experience, the probability of baking a good (G) loaf is .9 and a defective (D) loaf is .1. Thus, the odds in favor of getting a good loaf are $\frac{.9}{.1} = \frac{9}{1}$, also written 9:1. Assume that (1) G and D are mutually exclusive (a loaf can't be judged defective and good simultaneously), and (2) the results of each inspection in a sequence are independent.

For this sequence of inspection experiments, events and probabilities can be displayed in a probability tree. In Exhibit 6, the probability tree branches display the events clearly and lay out all possible event sequences. The probability tree is constructed by connecting small circles (nodes) with lines to form branches. The connecting lines have the event labels G or D; the circles (nodes) contain the probabilities of reaching a node after starting from the root node on the far left of Exhibit 6.

EXHIBIT 6 A Probability Tree for a Sequence of Inspections

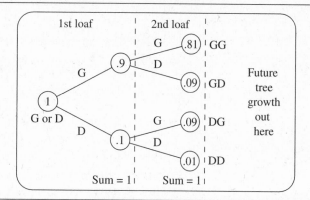

For example, the top-most branch of the tree displays a G for the first loaf (probability .9); continuing out that branch you find a G for the second loaf (probability .9). Both loaves in the top branch sequence have been good, producing GG, which is (G $\cap$ G) with a probability $.9 \times .9 = .81$. The four possible sequences and their probabilities are shown: GG, GD, DG, and DD. Running down the dashed lines in the exhibit covers all possible events and the probabilities must add to 1.

Sometimes probability trees can be used to visualize conditional probabilities as well. For example, suppose you are given information that one branch end, DD, did not occur. This information eliminates the bottom branch. Furthermore, suppose you want the probability of GG given DD did not occur. Then from the probability tree, P(GG|DD did not occur) is

$$P(GG\,|\,DD \text{ did not occur}) = \frac{.81}{.09 + .09 + .81}$$

Joint Probability Tables

For a sequence of two inspection experiments, the branch ends of the probability tree in Exhibit 6 can also be displayed as the joint probability table in Exhibit 7. Row and column sums are appended to the table and are called **marginal probabilities;** row and column marginal probabilities sum to 1.

EXHIBIT 7 A Probability Table for a Sequence
of Inspections

First Loaf	Second Loaf		
	Good	**Defective**	**Row Sums**
Good	GG(.81)	GD(.09)	.90
Defective	DG(.09)	DD(.01)	.10
Column Sums	.90	.10	1.00

COUNTING TECHNIQUES

Counting techniques are necessary for finding the number of outcomes in an event and the total number of outcomes. The ratio of these counts is a probability. Thus, counting techniques help in determining probabilities.

The equally likely method of assigning probabilities to an event depends on the following ratio of counts:

$$P(E_i) = \frac{\text{number of outcomes in the event}}{\text{total number of outcomes}}$$

Finding the components of the ratio can involve tedious counting when the number of outcomes is large. Counting techniques are designed to relieve this tedium. Although the term *counting* may lead you to expect that the addition operation will be used, these techniques all rely on multiplication.

The Multiplication Rule

If the first element of a sequence can occur in n_1 ways and the second element in n_2 ways, there are $(n_1 \times n_2)$ possible sequences of length two, and so on for longer sequences, $(n_1 \times n_2 \times n_3 \ldots)$.

For example, consider flipping a coin followed by rolling a die, where a head followed by a 5 is designated as the sequence H5. The first element of the sequence is heads or tails and $n_1 = 2$. The second element of the sequence is one of six faces and $n_2 = 6$. Thus, there are $2 \times 6 = 12$ possible sequences of length two, which is a count of all possible outcomes. The probability of H5 is $\frac{1}{12}$.

EXAMPLE 1

PART NUMBERS

In order to computerize a manufacturing system, parts are identified by a numbering system, much like cars having license plates. Long part numbers are not easy for manufacturing personnel to remember. If part numbers are too short, there might not be enough of them to identify all the parts uniquely. These are some considerations in designing a part numbering system.

Problem Statement If the part number of a manufactured item consists of a letter of the alphabet followed by a single digit (such as J8), how many part numbers are possible?

Problem Solution All letters in the alphabet are available; consequently, $n_1 = 26$. Ten digits are available, 0, 1, . . . , 9; therefore, $n_2 = 10$. The total part numbers possible is $(n_1 \times n_2) = 26 \times 10 = 260$.

Let's extend the previous example and consider part numbers consisting of two letters followed by a single digit (such as BJ8). Furthermore, suppose the letters are written on 26 pieces of paper and the digits on 10 other pieces of paper. The letters and numbers are placed in two separate hats from which they will be drawn to form part numbers. The letters will be drawn from the hat in two different ways, with and without replacement of the first letter drawn. How many part numbers are possible for each way of drawing letters from the hat?

With Replacement   When letters are drawn with replacement, the first letter is drawn and recorded. Then, the piece of paper is returned to the hat (replacement). Therefore, the first letter has a chance of being drawn again on the second draw. How many part numbers are possible?

For two letters followed by a digit such as BJ8, there are 26 possibilities for the first letter, 26 possibilities for the second letter (because of replacement) and 10 possibilities for the digit. In all, according to the multiplication rule, the total number of part numbers possible is

$$26 \times 26 \times 10 = 6,760$$

The generalization of what has been done is $(n_1 \times n_1 \times n_2)$.

Without Replacement   When letters are drawn without replacement, the first letter is drawn and not returned to the hat. Therefore, the first letter has no chance of being drawn again on the second draw. How many part numbers are possible?

For two letters followed by a digit such as BJ8, there are 26 possibilities for the first letter, $(26 - 1) = 25$ possibilities for the second letter (because of no replacement), and 10 possibilities for the digit. In all, according to the multiplication rule, the total number of part numbers possible is

$$26 \times 25 \times 10 = 6,500$$

The generalization of what has been done is $(n_1 \times (n_1 - 1) \times n_2)$.

Factorials   A **factorial product** is a special case of the multiplication rule. For this case, each element of the sequence beyond the first is a function of n_1. For example, $n_2 = (n_1 - 1)$; therefore, the subscript is dropped. If the first element of a sequence can occur in n ways and the second element in $(n - 1)$ ways, there are $(n \times (n - 1))$ possible sequences of length two, and so on for longer sequences, $(n \times (n - 1) \times (n - 2) \ldots)$.

When the sequence of product terms in

$$(n \times (n - 1) \times (n - 2) \times \cdots \times 1)$$

extends from n to 1, this product is called a **complete factorial.** For example, five factorial is $5 \times 4 \times 3 \times 2 \times 1 = 120$. A complete factorial product can be written with the multiplication signs implied, as in $n(n - 1) \ldots 1$, or as in n! where the exclamation point denotes the factorial product.

An **incomplete factorial** extends from n but stops before it gets to 1. Thus, 5×4 is an incomplete factorial and so is $5 \times 4 \times 3 \times 2$.

EXAMPLE 2

NAMING NEW PRODUCTS (FACTORIALS)

Problem Statement   A consulting company specializes in helping clients choose names for new products. First the consultant and the client agree on the number of letters from the alphabet and which letters are to be used. If each letter can be used only once and the required letters are E, L, S, U, and X, how many names are possible from these letters?

The consultant enters the required letters as input to a computer program. The program writes a file of all possible letter arrangements, which are potential product names. Another computer program reads each name and pronounces it aloud through a speaker. A consumer panel listens to the sound of each name and indicates the preferred names, which are later reviewed with the client. How many names does a panel member have to listen to?

Problem Solution   Given the required letters—E, L, S, U, and X—the first letter of a product name can be any one of 5 letters, the second any one of the 4 remaining letters, the third any one of 3, and so on. A panel member has to listen to 120 names, which is five factorial.

$$5 \times 4 \times 3 \times 2 \times 1 = 120$$

Notice that the automobile LEXUS is one of the names, and, if the letters are chosen at random, the probability of spelling LEXUS is $\frac{1}{120}$.

Permutations   A **permutation** is a discernible ordered arrangement of items drawn from a group of distinct items. For example, drawing from a group of friends with different names, suppose you list Bob, Mary, and Linda. This is a permutation. Another ordering of the same names is another permutation, such as Mary, Linda, and Bob. Other ordered lists of three from the group are also permutations, such as Tom, Sue, and Linda.

A count of all permutations is a special case of the multiplication rule and is an incomplete factorial. In general, if you list y friends from a group of n friends with different names, the total number of permutations, $_nP_y$, is

$$_nP_y = n \times (n - 1) \times \cdots \times (n - y + 1)$$
$$= n(n - 1) \ldots (n - y + 1)$$

Also, it can be shown that

$$_nP_y = \frac{n!}{(n - y)!}$$

For example, if you list y = 3 friends from a group of n = 10 friends with different names, the total number of permutations $_nP_y$ is

$$_{10}P_3 = n(n-1)(n-y+1) = 10(10-1)(10-3+1)$$
$$= 10(9)(8) = 720$$

Alternatively,

$$_{10}P_3 = \frac{10!}{(10-3)!} = \frac{10!}{7!} = 10(9)(8) = 720$$

When listing the names of three friends, there are 10 choices for the first name, 9 for the second, and 8 for the third.

E X A M P L E 3

NAMING NEW PRODUCTS (PERMUTATIONS)

Problem Statement   Suppose the previous example is modified as follows. Five letter names are chosen from six letters. Previously you were given the letters E, L, S, U, and X. Now you are given six letters from which to choose, A, E, L, S, U, and X. How many five-letter new product names are possible? The total number of permutations is needed because different orderings of the same letters produce new names.

Problem Solution   With six letters available for a five-letter product name, the first letter can be any one of 6, the second any one of 5 remaining, the third any one of 4, and so on. This gives you

$$6 \times 5 \times 4 \times 3 \times 2 = 720$$

possible product names.
    Also,

$$_6P_5 = \frac{6!}{(6-5)!} = \frac{6!}{1!} = 6(5)(4)(3)(2) = 720$$

Problem Discussion   The additional (sixth) letter vastly increases the possible number of five-letter product names. The automobile LEXUS is one of the names, and if the letters are chosen at random, the probability of spelling LEXUS is $\frac{1}{720}$.

> ***Derivation of*** $_nP_y = n!/(n-y)!$ ***(Optional)***   To make an incomplete factorial complete, continue the product, making each additional end term one less than the previous term. Therefore, the incomplete factorial for counting permutations, $n(n-1) \ldots (n-y+1)$, when completed becomes
>
> $$n(n-1) \cdots (n-y+1)(n-y+1-1)(n-y+1-2)$$
> $$(n-y+1-3) \cdots (1) = n!$$

The continuation beyond the number of permutations part (the first part in bold) of the expression is the factorial,

$$(n - y + 1 - 1)(n - y + 1 - 2)(n - y + 1 - 3) \cdots (1)$$
$$= (n - y)!$$

Thus, in general, the count of permutations for n things taken y at time is given by the expression

$$_nP_y = n(n - 1) \cdots (n - y + 1) = \frac{n!}{(n - y)!}$$

which is a ratio of two factorials. With this formulation, it is helpful to know that zero factorial is defined as one; if $y = n$, then $(n - y)! = (0)! = 1$.

Combinations   A **combination** is a discernible arrangement of items drawn from a group of distinct items without regard for order within the arrangement. Unlike permutations where distinct orders of the same items are distinct permutations, any order of the same items is a single combination. For example, drawing from a group of friends with different names, suppose you list Bob, Mary and Linda. This listing and all other listings of the same names, such as Mary, Linda, and Bob, are regarded as a single combination. Without regard to order, other lists of three names from the group are also combinations, such as Tom, Sue, and Linda.

A count of all combinations is related to the count of all permutations because permutations of the same distinct items count as one combination. Thus, by not counting different orders of the same items, the number of combinations can be found by dividing the number of permutations, $_nP_y$, by $y!$, the number of ways to reorder. If y distinct items are selected from a group of n distinct items without regard for order, the total number of combinations, $_nC_y$, is n things taken y at time.

$$_nC_y = \frac{_nP_y}{y!} = \frac{n!}{y! \, (n - y)!} = \binom{n}{y}$$

EXAMPLE 4

NAMING NEW PRODUCTS (COMBINATIONS)

Problem Statement   Suppose the previous example is modified as follows. Five-letter names are chosen from six letters, but the following restriction is imposed: once five distinct letters are used in a name, the same five letters can't be used for another name. From the six letters, A, E, L, S, U, and X, five are chosen. Without regard to order (combinations), how many five-letter new product names are possible?

Problem Solution   The result of the previous problem provides a starting point. Specifically, it was found that the number of permutations is $_6P_5 = 720$ where order matters. If order does not matter, a specific set of letters in any order is a combination; thus expect fewer combinations than permutations. Because order matters with permutations, the number of permutations is y! times larger than the number of combinations. Thus the number of combinations is found by dividing the number of permutations by y!.

$$_6C_5 = \frac{_6P_5}{5!} = \frac{720}{120} = 6 \text{ combinations}$$

Problem Discussion   LEXUS is the same combination as SUXEL, SUXLE, and so on. This distinct set of letters is one of the six combinations. Replacing the U with an A produces a second of these six combinations, any ordering of LEXAS. Therefore, first A was left out in LEXUS and then U was left out in LEXAS. Continuing in this fashion, we can leave each of the six available letters, yielding six combinations.

PROBABILITY DISTRIBUTIONS

Probability distributions relate random variables to probabilities. Probability distributions can be in the form of a graph, a table, or a formula. Because probability distributions specify all possible observations of a random variable, they characterize populations.

For **discrete distributions,** a discrete random variable, say, y, is directly related to the probability, P(y); in a graphical display, the probabilities are represented by lines (spikes) at each value of the random variable.

For **continuous distributions,** a continuous random variable, y, is indirectly related to the probability, because P(y) is zero at y. Therefore the **density,** f(y), is used at a particular value of y. Continuous probability distributions are referred to as **probability density functions** because the distribution directly relates y and the density, f(y). As a result, probability is with respect to y being between two constants, P(a < y < b). Probability, P(a < y < b), is the area under the density function between the constants. The probability that y equals any particular value (constant) is zero for continuous distributions.

In the next section, data are used to find relative frequencies. Then, based on the relative frequency method of assigning probabilities, the relative frequencies are treated as probabilities in a discrete distribution. Continuous distributions are also described.

Random Variables, Data, Relative Frequencies, and Probability Distributions

Random variables represent random numerical results of experiments. By observing experimental results and collecting data, probabilities can be estimated from relative frequencies.

EXAMPLE 5

NUMBER OF LOAVES SOLD

Problem Statement   A short, ten-day sales history of Moist Berry Wheat Bread (loaves) at the Harvest Moon Bakery produced the following data set:

Day	1	2	3	4	5	6	7	8	9	10
Loaves sold (y) =	1	1	0	4	2	5	5	3	3	4

The random variable y represents the numerical results of bread sales on a particular day. Because the baker bakes only 5 loaves of this bread per day, y is restricted to the discrete values 0, 1, 2, 3, 4, 5. For this sales history, find the relative frequencies for y and estimate the corresponding probabilities.

Problem Solution   For each value of y, the occurrence frequency is divided by the total number of observations to obtain the relative frequencies.

Random variable	y = 0	1	2	3	4	5
Relative frequencies	$= \dfrac{1}{10}$	$\dfrac{2}{10}$	$\dfrac{1}{10}$	$\dfrac{2}{10}$	$\dfrac{2}{10}$	$\dfrac{2}{10}$

The probabilities, $P(y)$, are unknown but can be estimated by these relative frequencies. Assuming the conditions of the random experiment stay fixed, the longer the history the better the relative frequencies are at estimating the probabilities.

Consider another example where the random variable y represents random results for a different set of observations.

EXAMPLE 6

SITTING ON THE DOCK OF A BAY COUNTING SHIPS

Problem Statement   Suppose you sit on a dock of a bay for eight clear days and record the number of ships that come into port on each of the eight days. The observed number of ships that arrive on each day are

Day	1	2	3	4	5	6	7	8
Number of ships (y)	1	0	3	2	2	1	2	3

For this arrival history, find the relative frequencies for y and estimate the corresponding probabilities.

Problem Solution   For each value of y, the occurrence frequency is divided by the total number of observations to obtain the relative frequencies.

Random variable	y = 0	1	2	3
Relative frequencies	$= \dfrac{1}{8}$	$\dfrac{2}{8}$	$\dfrac{3}{8}$	$\dfrac{2}{8}$

The probabilities, P(y), are unknown but can be estimated by these relative frequencies. Assuming the conditions of the random experiment stay fixed, the longer the history the better the relative frequencies are at estimating the probabilities.

Problem Discussion   Although here we are observing ships, there are many business situations where you might collect data on arrivals; for example, on parts arriving at an assembly area, customers arriving at a checkout counter, patients arriving at an emergency room, and trucks arriving at a loading dock.

Discrete and Continuous Probability Distributions

In reference to the previous example, the number of ships arriving each day are shown in Exhibit 8 in the familiar stem-and-leaf diagram, dot diagram, and histogram. Deliberately, the data set is kept small so that you can grasp all the essential details. The histogram is especially useful when there are many more data values. Therefore, the histogram is used to conceptually link the diagrams in Exhibit 8 to the probability distributions in Exhibit 9.

Because the values of the random variable y are integers, imagine collapsing the histogram's rectangular bars into lines (or spikes with lengths equal to relative frequencies) as shown on the left side of Exhibit 9. The resulting relative frequency distribution is a sample mimic of a discrete probability distribution. When the lengths of the spikes are actual probabilities, P(y), rather than relative frequencies, the left side of Exhibit 9 is a discrete probability distribution.

In many experiments, data values are not discrete; instead, continuous variables are measured such as weight, height, and earnings per share. When the data values are not integers, it no longer makes sense to represent probabilities graphically as spikes. Under such circumstances for continuous data values, a smooth curve is drawn through the midpoints of the histogram's bars as shown on the right side of Exhibit 9. The area under the smooth curve must equal 1, the total probability. When the data set is large, this smooth curve approximates the probability density of continuous probability distributions. Continuous distributions can be described economically by mathematical formulas that can take the place of pictures.

EXHIBIT 8 y = Number of Ships Arriving per Day

Stem-and-Leaf	Dot Diagram	Histogram

y 0 | 0
   1 | 1, 1
   2 | 2, 2, 2
   3 | 3, 3
	y 0 | ●
	   1 | ● ●
	   2 | ● ● ●
	   3 | ● ●
		y 0
		   1
		   2
		   3

EXHIBIT 9 Types of Probability Distributions

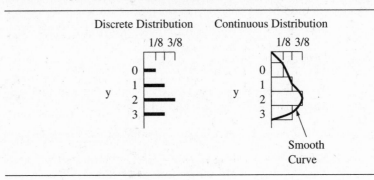

On the left side of Exhibit 9, the discrete distribution summarizes the results of observing and counting ships followed by computing relative frequencies. One of eight, or $\frac{1}{8}$, is the proportion of days that no ships came into port. For 1, 2, or 3 ships, the relative frequencies are $\frac{2}{8}, \frac{3}{8}$, and $\frac{2}{8}$, respectively. From a sample of eight observations, these relative frequencies estimate probabilities.

Although this small sample serves as a good illustration, larger samples would produce better estimates of the probabilities. For example, under the same set of conditions, if we could sit on a dock for an infinite number of days and count ships, then these relative frequencies would closely approximate the probabilities. Exhibit 10 is treated as if the discrete probabilities resulted from a long history of observations. In discrete probability distributions, all probabilities sum to one, $P(0) + P(1) + P(2) + P(3) = 1$, and none of the $P(y)$ values are negative.

EXHIBIT 10 A Probability Distribution for the Number of Arriving Ships

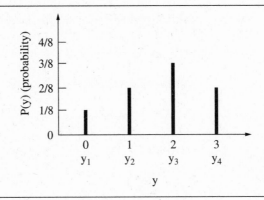

CUMULATIVE PROBABILITY FUNCTIONS

Cumulative probability functions relate random variables to cumulative probabilities. In particular, for y ≤ (a specific value of y) the cumulative probability function displays P(y ≤ (a specific value of y)). Cumulative probability distributions can be in the form of a graph, table, or formula.

For the discrete probability distribution in Exhibit 10, the related, staircaselike cumulative probability function is shown in Exhibit 11. The height of each step is equal to the corresponding probability spike in the discrete probability distribution. When y is a continuous random variable, the staircase is replaced by a smooth continuous function.

Exhibit 11 is a cumulative probability distribution for the number of ships arriving in a port per day. The cumulative probability function answers questions related to the probability that y ≤ (a specific value of y). For example, suppose we consider P(y ≤ 2), or what proportion of days did two or fewer ships arrive?

The answer to this question can be read directly from the vertical axis of the cumulative function in Exhibit 11. Start on the horizontal axis at y = 2, and proceed in the vertical direction (follow the vertical arrow) to the top of the step. From there, take a left to the second arrow pointing to the vertical axis where the cumulative probability is

$$P(y \leq 2) = \frac{6}{8}$$

EXHIBIT 11 A Cumulative Probability Function for the Number of Arriving Ships

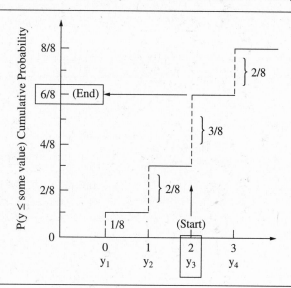

Two or fewer ships arrive per day $\frac{6}{8}$ or $\frac{3}{4}$ or 75% of the time.

Sometimes questions are posed so that the inverse of the cumulative probability is needed. For example, what value or less of y occurs a specified percentage of the time? Specifically, consider $P(y \leq$ what value?) $= \frac{6}{8}$. The above procedure for reading the cumulative probability is reversed. Start on the vertical axis at a probability of $\frac{6}{8}$ and proceed in the horizontal direction to the staircase. From there, drop down to the horizontal axis and read the value of y.

$$P(y \leq 2) = \frac{6}{8}$$

In this way, many practical probability questions can be answered using a cumulative probability function.

MEANS AND VARIANCES OF DISCRETE DISTRIBUTIONS

A probability distribution or population of observations can be characterized briefly in terms of where its center is located and how spread out it is. A measure of central tendency is the distribution's mean. A measure of spread (variation) is the standard deviation. Sometimes the squared standard deviation, the variance, is used as a spread measure.

Both of these concepts have been used earlier, but they have not been defined in terms of random variables and probabilities. For discrete distributions, the process of summing random variables or functions of random variables multiplied by probabilities is referred to as an **expected value procedure.** The next section defines population means, standard deviations, and variances in expected value terms.

The Mean Expressed As the Expected Value of y

From Exhibit 10, the discrete distribution of y, the number of ships coming into port, is used to illustrate the expected value procedure. The mean of this probability distribution is found, which is the typical number of ships coming into port daily. In expected value terms, the population mean, μ, is $E(y)$. For this distribution, it will be shown that $E(y)$ equals 1.75 ships per day, the mean. Look back at Exhibits 10 and 11 and locate 1.75 on the horizontal axes to get a feel for where the mean is located.

In the notation, $E(y)$, the operator, E, designates the procedural operations necessary to compute the mean, using y and $P(y)$. $E(y)$ is computed by taking each value of y times its corresponding probability and summing.

$$\text{expected value} = E(y) = y_1 P(y_1) + y_2 P(y_2) + \cdots + y_4 P(y_4)$$

$$E(y) = \sum_1^n y_i P(y_i) = 0 \times \frac{1}{8} + 1 \times \frac{2}{8} + 2 \times \frac{3}{8} + 3 \times \frac{2}{8}$$

$$E(y) = 1.75$$

S T A T I S T I C A L   H I G H L I G H T S

To obtain the population mean, $E(y)$, for discrete distributions, the expected value procedure is to multiply the values of the random variable, y, times the corresponding probabilities and sum.

The Sample Mean $\bar{y}$ As an Estimator of E(y)

Probabilities must be known in order to compute $E(y)$. In many situations, these probabilities are unknown and must be estimated by relative frequencies. Then $\bar{y}$ estimates $E(y)$. In the formula for $\bar{y}$, the term $\frac{1}{n}$ weights each observation equally and has the effect of estimating probabilities with relative frequencies.

$$\bar{y} = \sum_{1}^{n} \frac{y_i}{n} = \sum_{1}^{n} y_i\left(\frac{1}{n}\right)$$

Variance (Standard Deviation Squared) Expressed As an Expected Value

For the probability distribution in Exhibit 10, a crude measure of the variability in the number of ships that come into port is the **range**. The range is the difference between the maximum and the minimum of the random variable.

$$(y_{max} - y_{min}) = (3 - 0) = 3$$

The range is not the most effective measure of variability because $(y_{max} - y_{min})$ ignores the probabilities of these extreme values occurring. For example, a value of $y = 0$ has a $\frac{1}{8}$ chance of occurring; $y = 3$ has a $\frac{2}{8}$ chance. These probabilities do not enter into the range calculation. Furthermore, the range does not consider y values other than the minimum and the maximum. Nevertheless, when sample sizes are small, the range can be useful.

For larger sample sizes, the standard deviation is a better measure of variability than the range. The standard deviation is the square root of the variance. The expected value procedure is used to find the variance, $V(y)$, which is defined as

$$V(y) = E(y_i - E(y))^2$$

For the variance, the expected value procedure is carried out on a function of the random variable, $(y_i - E(y))^2$, which is a deviation from the mean squared. Again the operator, E, designates the procedural operations necessary to compute the variance, using $(y_i - E(y))^2$ and $P(y)$. $E(y_i - E(y))^2$ is computed by taking each value of $(y_i - E(y))^2$ times its corresponding probability and summing.

$$V(y) = \sum_{1}^{n} (y_i - E(y))^2 P(y_i)$$

Notice that the above expression can be written

$$V(y) = \sum_{1}^{n} (y_i - E(y))(y_i - E(y)) \, P(y_i)$$

The latter formulation is shown because of its structural similarity to the **covariance,** which is a variancelike measure for pairs of variables.

The discrete probability distribution in Exhibit 10 is used for a numerical example of the variance computation. Recall that in $E(y)$ the E simply denotes a procedure for computing the sum of the probabilities times the values of y. Similarly, for the variance, V denotes a procedure that takes the deviations $(y_i - E(y))$ squared times their corresponding probabilities and sums the results. As an illustration, note that $E(y) = 1.75 = \frac{7}{4}$, therefore

$$V(y) = \sum_{1}^{4} \left(y_i - \frac{7}{4}\right)\left(y_i - \frac{7}{4}\right)P(y_i)$$

$$V(y) = \sum_{1}^{4} \left(y_i - \frac{7}{4}\right)^2 P(y_i)$$

$$V(y) = \left(0 - \frac{7}{4}\right)^2\left(\frac{1}{8}\right) + \left(1 - \frac{7}{4}\right)^2\left(\frac{2}{8}\right)$$

$$+ \left(2 - \frac{7}{4}\right)^2\left(\frac{3}{8}\right) + \left(3 - \frac{7}{4}\right)^2\left(\frac{2}{8}\right)$$

$$= \frac{15}{16}$$

An Alternative Computational Method   By expanding and simplifying $E(y_i - E(y))^2$, an alternative formulation for the variance results.

$$V(y) = [E(y_i^2)] - (E(y))^2$$

The first term on the right of the equality is

$$[E(y_i^2)] = \left[0^2\left(\frac{1}{8}\right) + 1^2\left(\frac{2}{8}\right) + 2^2\left(\frac{3}{8}\right) + 3^2\left(\frac{2}{8}\right)\right] = \frac{64}{16}$$

and the second term is

$$(E(y))^2 = \left(\frac{7}{4}\right)^2 = \frac{49}{16}$$

Then

$$V(y) = [E(y_i^2)] - (E(y))^2 = \frac{64}{16} - \frac{49}{16} = \frac{15}{16}$$

General Notation and Usefulness of the Standard Deviation

The variance of y is written as

$$V(y) = \sigma^2$$

where the lowercase Greek letter sigma, σ, represents the standard deviation. The variance, unfortunately, is in units that are difficult to comprehend because of the squared terms in the definition. As a result, its square root, the standard deviation, is more useful

$$\text{standard deviation} = \sigma = (V(y))^{1/2}$$

As temperature reported in Fahrenheit is more meaningful to many of us than in Celsius, the standard deviation may have more meaning to many than the variance.

The Sample Variance s^2 As an Estimator of σ^2

Probabilities must be known in order to compute $V(y)$. In many situations, these probabilities are unknown and must be estimated by relative frequencies then s^2 estimates $V(y)$. In the formula for s^2, when using the divisor n rather than $(n - 1)$, $(\frac{1}{n})$ weights each squared deviation equally and has the effect of estimating probabilities with relative frequencies.

$$s^2 = \sum (y_i - \bar{y})^2 \left(\frac{1}{n}\right)$$

The Mean and Standard Deviation Working Together

Although additional parameters may exist, the essential features of many probability distributions can be characterized economically by just two parameters: the mean and the standard deviation. The mean and the standard deviation provide summary information that is easy to comprehend and remember. They summarize two fundamental features of the random variable y.

Continuing with our example, the typical number of ships coming into port is

$$\mu = E(y) = 1.75$$

The standard deviation is nearly one.

$$\sigma = \left(\frac{15}{16}\right)^{1/2} \approx 1$$

Working together, the mean plus and minus two standard deviations form an interval that spans this whole distribution.

$$E(y) \pm 2 \times \text{(standard deviations)}$$
$$E(y) \pm 2 \times (1) = 1.75 \pm 2 = -.25 \text{ to } +3.75$$

For the distribution in Exhibit 10, this interval spans all values of y, which are 0, 1, 2, and 3. Therefore, the mean plus and minus two standard deviations gives us a feel for the number of ships coming into port without dealing with the details of the probability distribution.

A two-standard deviation will not always span the whole distribution. For example, when the distribution is bell-shaped, or normal, the mean plus or minus two standard deviations spans 95% of the distribution. In any case, the two parameters, μ and σ, and the interval help us describe a distribution.

MEANS AND VARIANCES OF CONTINUOUS DISTRIBUTIONS (OPTIONAL, KNOWLEDGE OF CALCULUS REQUIRED)

For continuous distributions, the concepts of mean and variance remain the same as with discrete distributions, but the mechanics of the expected value process change. In the expected value procedure, the probability $P(y)$ is replaced by $f(y) \, dy$, the density $f(y)$ times the differential dy. Also, summations are replaced by integrals. Thus, $E(y)$ is defined as

$$E(y) = \int_{-\infty}^{+\infty} yf(y)dy$$

The variance is defined as

$$V(y) = \int_{-\infty}^{+\infty} (y - E(y))^2 f(y)dy$$

which can be written in an alternative form as

$$V(y) = \int_{-\infty}^{+\infty} (y)^2 f(y)dy - (E(y))^2$$

EXAMPLE 7

MEAN AND VARIANCE OF A TRIANGULAR DISTRIBUTION

Problem Statement (a)   Let the demand, y, for a petroleum product be described by a continuous probability density function, $f(y) = ky$, where k is an unknown constant and y ranges from 0 to 1. A graph of $f(y)$ versus y forms a distribution triangular in shape. Find the mean, $E(y)$.

Problem Solution (a)   First, the constant k is found. The density is $f(y)$. Probability is determined by finding the area under the density function. The total area must equal the total probability, which is 1. With a triangular density function, ky, ranging from y = 0 to 1, the area of the triangle is $\frac{1}{2}$ the base $(1 - 0) = 1$ times the height k and

$$\frac{1}{2}(1)(k) = 1$$

Solving for k results in k = 2. Substituting k = 2 in the density function produces f(y) = 2y.

When the density function is not a simple geometric shape, a more general way of determining k is necessary, therefore

$$\int_0^1 (ky)dy = k\frac{y^2}{2}\Big|_0^1 = 1$$

Evaluating this expression yields k = 2.

The mean is

$$E(y) = \int_0^1 y(2y)dy = 2\frac{y^3}{3}\Big|_0^1 = \frac{2}{3} = \mu$$

Problem Statement (b)   Find the variance, V(y).

Problem Solution (b)   First, the mean squared, $(E(y))^2 = (\frac{2}{3})^2 = \frac{4}{9}$, is found and substituted in the expression for the variance.

$$V(y) = \int_0^1 (y^2)f(y)dy - \left(\frac{2}{3}\right)^2$$

Next, f(y) = 2y is substituted in this expression.

$$V(y) = \int_0^1 (y)^2(2y)dy - \left(\frac{2}{3}\right)^2$$

$$V(y) = \int_0^1 2(y)^3dy - \left(\frac{2}{3}\right)^2$$

The integral is evaluated as

$$V(y) = \frac{2}{4}y^4\Big|_0^1 - \left(\frac{2}{3}\right)^2$$

Finally, the variance is

$$V(y) = \left(\frac{2}{4}\right) - \left(\frac{2}{3}\right)^2 = \left(\frac{18}{36}\right) - \left(\frac{16}{36}\right) = \frac{2}{36} = \sigma^2$$

THE BINOMIAL DISTRIBUTION (DISCRETE)

An important discrete distribution is the **binomial,** which is applicable in binary situations (two possibilities, say head or tail in a coin flip) where the probability of a specific outcome (say getting a head in a coin flip) is constant from trial to trial, and the trials are independent.

The binomial distribution is applicable to the bread quality inspection process at the Harvest Moon Bakery discussed earlier. Recall that a loaf of bread is taken out of the oven and examined for appearance. Loaves that don't meet the appearance standard are deemed defective and sold as seconds. Let the letter D stand for the simple event of an appearance problem. Let G stand for good appearance. For each loaf, there are two possible outcomes, D or G. For baking two loaves in sequence, the possible outcomes are:

GG
DD
GD
DG

If the production process is in a state of statistical control, the condition of one loaf is independent of the other loaf and the probabilities are constant, P(G) = .90 and P(D) = .10. Using the multiplication rule for independent events, the probabilities are

P(GG) = (.90)(.90) = .81
P(DD) = (.10)(.10) = .01
P(GD) = (.90)(.10) = .09
P(DG) = (.10)(.90) = .09

Although you are equipped already to find these probabilities, we demonstrate how you can take advantage of using a formula for obtaining the binomial probabilities. Notice that there is *one way* to get GG, *one way* to get DD, and *two ways* to get a single G and D; there are four combinations in all. Larger problems can involve tedious counting and long lists. To relieve the tedium, the combinations counting rule and the multiplication rule are used together in a formula for finding binomial probabilities.

Assuming constant and independent probabilities, if p is the probability of success (G, a good loaf) and (1 − p) is the complement (D, a defective loaf), the probability of y successes out of n trials can be expressed in the formula form of the binomial distribution as

$$P(y) = \binom{n}{y} p^y (1 - p)^{(n-y)}$$

Let (1 − p) = q; then the mean is E(y) = np and the variance is V(y) = npq = σ^2.

Substituting for n, y, p, and $(1 - p)$ in the formula for the binomial distribution results in the following probabilities:

$$P(GG) = P(y = 2) = \binom{2}{2}(.90)^2(1 - .90)^0 \qquad = .81$$

$$P(GG) = (1)(.90)(.90) \qquad = .81$$

$$P(DD) = P(y = 0) = \binom{2}{0}(.90)^0(1 - .90)^2 \qquad = .01$$

$$P(DD) = (1)(.10)(.10) \qquad = .01$$

$$P(GD \text{ or } DG) = P(y = 1) = \binom{2}{1}(.90)^1(1 - .90)^1 = .18$$

$$P(GD \text{ or } DG) = P(y = 1) = 2 \ (.90)^1(.10)^1 \qquad = .18$$

In the last result, combinations count the following two possible ways of getting one G:

$$P(GD) = (.90)(.10) = .09$$
$$P(DG) = (.10)(.90) = .09$$

In order to relate this use of combinations to earlier examples, recall that

$$\binom{n}{y} = \text{the number of y length names from n letters}$$

where the order of the characters in y does not matter (distinguishing combinations from permutations). This formula yields two combinations for $y = 1$ and $n = 2$, as shown above. Therefore, in GD and DG, we are obtaining combinations, ways of choosing the first letter from the two available letters; once the first letter is chosen, the second is automatically determined. Thus, when $y = 1$ and $n = 2$, we focus on the first letter.

EXAMPLE 8

QUALITY CONTROL FOR BAD EGGS

A traditionally important aspect of quality control is the inspection of a manufactured product. Managers are not satisfied with finished product inspections only; they have moved inspection further up into the production line. When the source of a defect problem can be found, an effort is made to eliminate it, thereby reducing the need for inspection.

Finished products with unwanted attributes are deemed defective; such products are repaired, removed from shipment or sold as seconds. In this example, consider a carton of eggs. A bad egg might be nonconforming because of a cracked or dirty shell.

Problem Statement (a)   From historical data, suppose we know the defective rate, $p = .0833$, one bad egg of twelve. Assume that the supply of eggs is large enough that p is constant. From egg to egg, if p is constant and if the nonconformity of one egg does not depend on another, the binomial distribution tells us the probability of 0, 1, 2, . . . , or 12 bad egg(s), which are the possible values of y in a carton of twelve. Find each of these probabilities using MINITAB commands that are based on the following formula:

$$P(y) = \binom{n}{y} p^y (1 - p)^{(n-y)}$$

Problem Solution (a)   The binomial probabilities are listed below; the MINITAB commands are shown in Appendix 1.

```
          y    P(y)

ROW   C1   C2(PROBABILITIES)
  1    0    0.352149  (NO CRACKED EGGS)
  2    1    0.383995  (ONE CRACKED EGG)
  3    2    0.191914
  4    3    0.058130
  5    4    0.011885
  6    5    0.001728
  7    6    0.000183
  8    7    0.000014
  9    8    0.000001
 10    9    0.000001
 11   10    0.000001
 12   11    0.000001
 13   12    0.000001  (TWELVE CRACKED EGGS)
```

Problem Statement (b)   Show the graphical form of this binomial probability distribution; plot P(y) versus y.

Problem Solution (b)   C2 is P(y) and C1 is y.

In the binomial probability distribution below, the length of each spike represents the discrete probability, and its value can be read off the vertical axis. The horizontal axis displays the possible number of cracked eggs in a carton. This distribution is skewed to the right; few cartons have more than three bad eggs.

Problem Statement (c)   Show the graphical form of the cumulative binomial distribution (or cumulative distribution function, CDF).

Problem Solution (c)   Cumulative probabilities are in column C3 and y values are in C1.

When relating the cumulative distribution above to the probability distribution preceding it, the vertical axis appears compressed because it is scaled from 0 to 1. Nevertheless, notice that the step heights in the CDF are equal to the probabilities from the probability distribution. The very last top step goes up to a height of 1; at that point all probabilities have been accumulated.

Reading from the cumulative distribution, 75% of the time either 0 or 1 nonconforming eggs are in a carton. $(1 - .35) = 65\%$ (rounded) of the cartons have one or more bad eggs.

Example 8 Plot (a)

Probability (C2) of the Number of Cracked Eggs (C1)

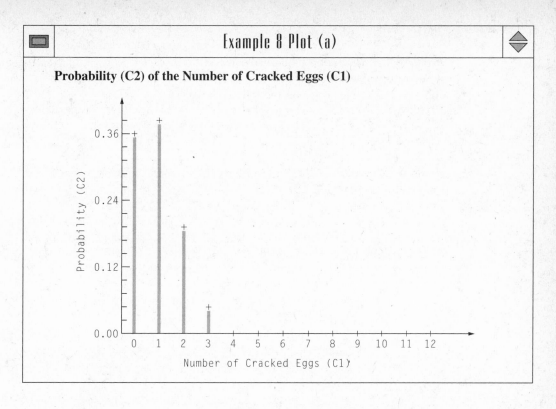

Example 8 Plot (b)

Cumulative Probability (C3) of the Number of Cracked Eggs (C1) or Fewer

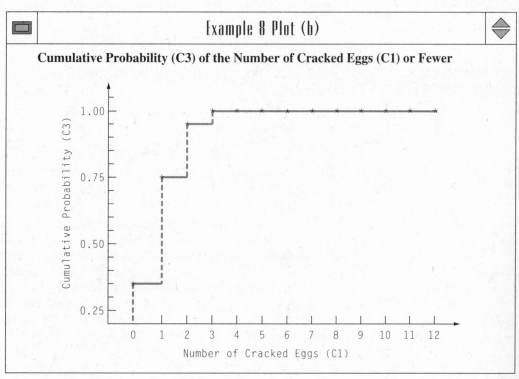

Problem Statement (d)   Find the mean and standard deviation of the binomial distribution as a way of characterizing it.

Problem Solution (d)   The mean is np = 12(.0833) = .9996. The variance is np(1 − p) = 12(.0833)(1 − .0833) = .9163 and the standard deviation is .9573, the square root of the variance.

Problem Discussion   The independence requirement and the constant probability (p) requirement should undergo a test of reasonableness for the specific, practical situation where the binomial is applied.

For example, in flipping a coin a number of times, the probability of a particular face coming up is constant from trial to trial and the flips are independent of one another. Cracks in eggs would not be independent from egg to egg if a carton had been mishandled during shipment; then cracks might not be independent from egg to egg in the damaged carton.

Navigating on the Cumulative Distribution Function in MINITAB

As you have seen, the cumulative distribution function (CDF) is a plot of cumulative probability; the CDF command in MINITAB makes it easy to obtain cumulative probabilities for the binomial and many other distributions.

The inverse cumulative distribution function, INVCDF in MINITAB, simply turns things inside-out. Given a probability or column of probabilities, INVCDF produces the corresponding values of the random variable.

COMMON CONTINUOUS DISTRIBUTIONS: NORMAL, STUDENT'S t, CHI-SQUARE, AND F DISTRIBUTIONS

This section provides a brief exposure to some continuous probability density functions common throughout this text. The purpose is to provide additional examples of continuous distributions and give you the opportunity to become familiar with the distributional shapes for identification purposes.

The Normal Approximation of the Binomial Distribution

Even with computers, discrete distributions can become cumbersome to work with under certain conditions. As a result, particular continuous distributions can be used to approximate discrete distributions. For example, the discrete binomial distribution can be approximated by the continuous normal distribution when n and p are large. Because the binomial probability formula contains p and (1 − p) and 0 ≤ p ≤ 1, p ≈ .5 is considered large.

When p is small, the normal approximation of the binomial distribution is not appropriate. As you have seen earlier, a binomial probability distribution with a small p is skewed and the bell-shaped normal does not fit.

EXAMPLE 9

A DISCRETE BINOMIAL APPROXIMATED
BY A CONTINUOUS NORMAL

Problem Statement (a)   In some electronic component manufacturing, defective rates are high with p = .5. If 200 components are produced, find the probability that there are 100 or fewer defective components, P(y ≤ 100). Use the binomial probability distribution.

Problem Solution (a)   In Appendix 1, MINITAB gave a message that the computation of the binomial probabilities was impossible.

Problem Statement (b)   Use a normal approximation of the binomial distribution with a mean np = 200(.5) and a standard deviation of 7.1 (the square root of npq = 200(.5)(.5)). Find the probability of 100 or fewer defective components, P(y ≤ 100).

Problem Solution (b)   The normal density function is shown below. C3 displays density (not probability values) and C1 is y = 0, 1, . . . , 200. Probability is the area under the density function. The same amount of area is on each side of the mean of the symmetrical normal distribution. For a mean of 100, 50% of the time there are 100 or fewer defective components.

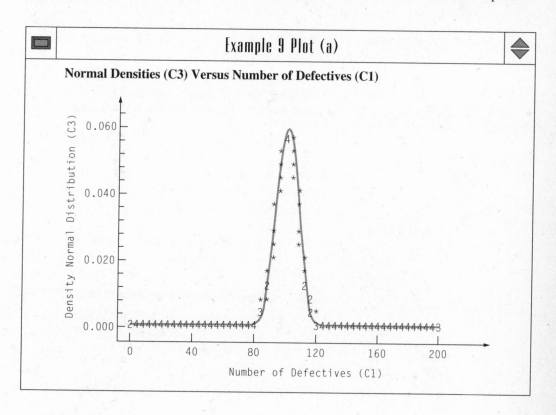

Example 9 Plot (a)

Normal Densities (C3) Versus Number of Defectives (C1)

Distributions Related to the Normal: Student's t, Chi-Square, and F Distributions

The **Student's t, chi-square,** and **F distributions** are related to the normal-distribution. These continuous distributions are used to perform statistical tests throughout this text. Using the commands in Appendix 1, you can view the shape of these density functions.

Keep in mind that these are continuous density functions and probability is the area under the curves.

Density Function for the Student's t Distribution

The Student's t distribution has a shape that depends on the degrees of freedom; therefore, this random variable has a subscript for the degrees of freedom (df), $t_{(df)}$. As the degrees of freedom increase, the distribution is less spread out and the tails are not as fat. When the degrees of freedom are over 30, a Student's t distribution is approximately normal (see Example 10 plot (b)).

EXAMPLE 10

STUDENT'S t DISTRIBUTION

Problem Statement   Graph the density function for the Student's t distribution for 1 degree of freedom and compare it to the density function for 30 degrees of freedom.

Problem Solution   In the plots below, the vertical axis (C2) shows density values (not probabilities) and the horizontal axis (C1) displays the Student's t values. In theory, the t values range from minus to plus infinity. Because this distribution is continuous, no probability spikes can be drawn on the plot; rather, a smooth curve should be drawn connecting all the plotting points.

Plot (a) shows a Student's t distribution for 1 degree of freedom.
Plot (b) shows a Student's t distribution for 30 degrees of freedom.

Problem Discussion   With 1 degree of freedom, plot (a) peaks at a lower density value and is slightly more spread out than plot (b). In plot (a) the density is about .05 at t = ±2; in plot (b) the density is about .04 at t = ±2. Thus, plot (a) has slightly fatter tails.

Density Function for the Chi-Square Distribution

The chi-square distribution has a shape that depends on the degrees of freedom; therefore, this random variable has a subscript for the degrees of freedom (df), $\chi^2_{(df)}$. As the degrees of freedom increase, the distribution is less peaked and less skewed.

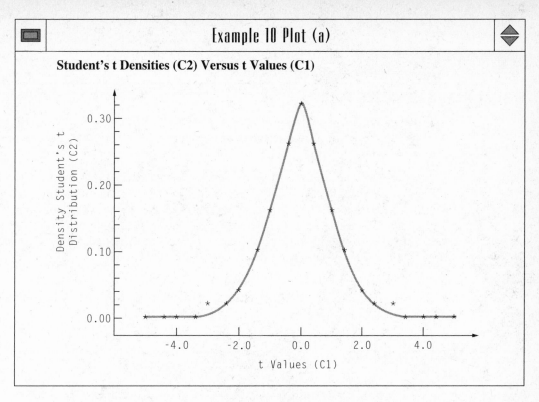

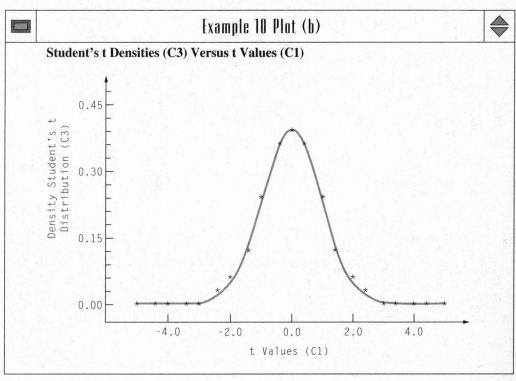

EXAMPLE 11

CHI-SQUARE DISTRIBUTION

Problem Statement   Graph the density function for the chi-square distribution for 5 degrees of freedom and compare it to the density function for 30 degrees of freedom.

Problem Solution   The vertical axis (C2) shows density values (not probabilities) and the horizontal axis (C1) displays χ^2 values. In theory, the χ^2 values range from zero to plus infinity. Because this distribution is continuous, no probability spikes can be drawn on the plot; rather, a smooth curve should be drawn connecting all the plotting points.
   Plot (a) shows chi-square distribution with 5 degrees of freedom.
   Plot (b) shows chi-square distribution with 30 degrees of freedom.

Problem Discussion   With 30 degrees of freedom, plot (b) is less peaked and less skewed than plot (a).

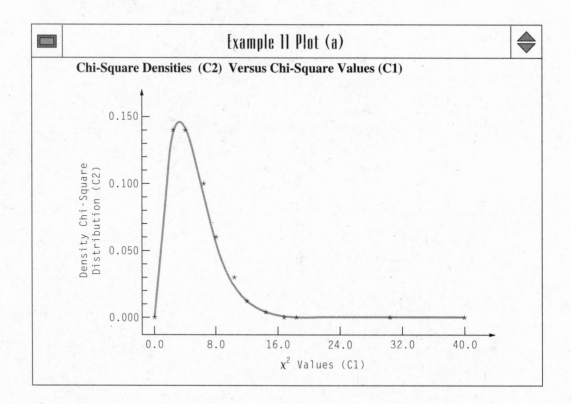

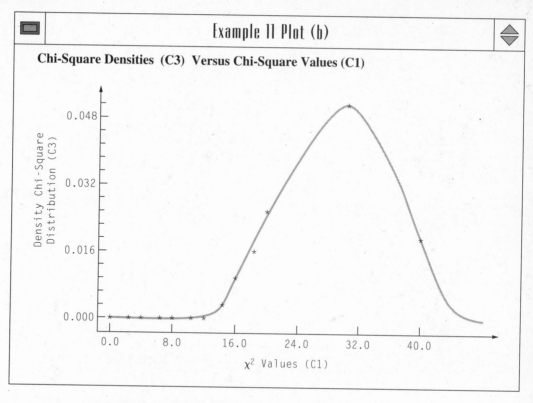

Density Function for the F Distribution

The F distribution has a shape that depends on numerator and denominator degrees of freedom of a ratio; therefore, this random variable has a subscript for each of the degrees of freedom (df), $F_{(df1, df2)}$. The peakedness and skewness are functions of the degrees of freedom.

EXAMPLE 12

THE F DISTRIBUTION (FISHER-SNEDECOR DISTRIBUTION)

Problem Statement   Graph the density function for the F distribution for degrees of freedom, (4, 1), and compare it to the density function for (25, 25) degrees of freedom.

Problem Solution   The vertical axis (C2) shows density values (not probabilities) and the horizontal axis (C1) displays F values. In theory, the F values range from zero to plus infinity. Because this distribution is continuous, no probability spikes can be drawn on the plot; rather, a smooth curve should be drawn connecting all the plotting points.

Plot (a): A density function for the F distribution with (4, 1) degrees of freedom.

Plot (b): A density function for the F distribution with (25, 25) degrees of freedom.

Problem Discussion   With (25, 25) degrees of freedom, plot (b) is more peaked and less skewed than plot (a).

Example 12 Plot (a)

F Distribution Densities (C2) Versus F Values (C1)

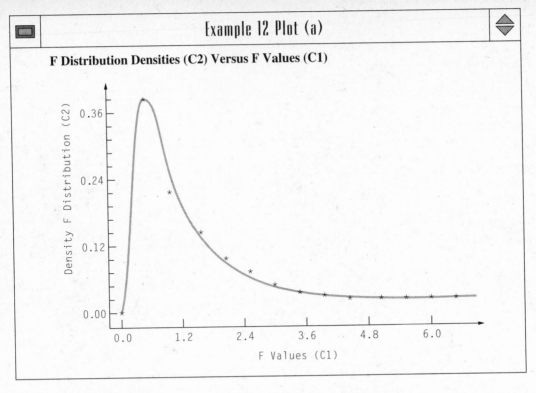

Example 12 Plot (b)

F Distribution Densities (C3) Versus F Values (C1)

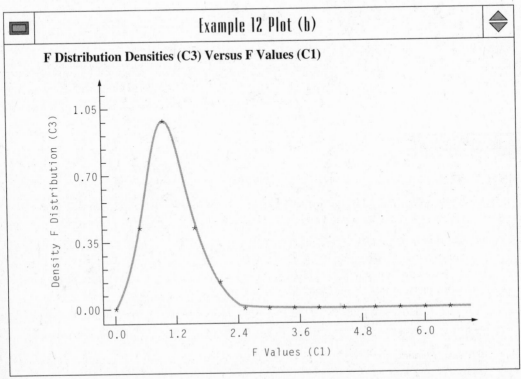

CHAPTER SUMMARY

To put our observations, analysis, and subsequent conclusions in the proper perspective, the concept of probability is critical to our thinking. The complete data analyst knows about the "machine" that generates the data and thinks about the multitude of conditions under which the data were produced. For example, when a manager contemplates a company's future financial picture in terms of profits or losses, chance is part of the assessment. Before this chapter, we said little about the chance mechanisms that play a role in generating the data a manager evaluates. With probability, we demarcate the slippery ground between ignorance and perfect knowledge.

We defined simple events that occur as outcomes of random experiments. Simple events may be grouped as collections to become unions or compound events. We established ground rules for working with unions and intersections of events. We introduced common ways of assigning probabilities to random events: relative frequency, classical (equally likely outcomes), and subjective methods.

Visual representations of the probabilities include Venn diagrams, probability trees, tables, and distributions. The distinction was made between discrete and continuous probability distributions. Cumulative distribution functions provide a convenient way to answer more than or less than types of probability questions. Probability distributions can be summarized neatly in terms of a few parameters such as, expected values, variances, and standard deviations. Usually the manager has to estimate these parameters from sample data.

We introduced a few important probability distributions, the discrete binomial and the continuous normal as an approximation of the binomial under certain conditions. The normal distribution will be discussed in more detail in Chapter 5. We looked briefly at several other continuous distributions because of their importance in statistical testing in upcoming chapters.

KEY TERMS

addition law, 158
and, 157
axioms, 162
Bayes' theorem, 161
binomial, 184
chi-square, 190
combination, 172
complement, 156
complete factorial, 170
compound events, 149
conditional probability, 159
continuous distributions, 173
covariance, 180
cumulative probability functions, 177
density, 173
dependent, 159
discrete distributions, 173
equally likely, 154
events, 149
exhaustive, 149
expected value procedure, 178

F distribution, 190
factorial product, 169
family, 163
impossible event, 150
incomplete factorial, 170
independent, 159
intersection, 157
joint probability tables, 163
law of large numbers, 153
marginal probabilities, 167
multiplication law, 159
mutually exclusive, 149
not, 156
null set, 162
odds, 157
or, 156
outcomes, 149
permutation, 170
posterior probability, 161
postulates, 163
prior probability, 161

probability, 150
probability axioms, 163
probability density functions, 173
probability distributions, 173
probability theory, 148
probability trees, 163
random events, 151
random experiments, 149
random variable, 151
range, 179
relative frequency, 152
sample points, 150
sample space, 150
set, 149
simple events, 149
Student's t, 190
unconditional probability, 159
unions, 149
Venn diagrams, 163

EXERCISES

1. Suppose the manager at the Harvest Moon Bakery decides to bake 7 loaves of a new bread every day.

(a) List the simple events for the possible number of loaves sold per day.

(b) List the outcomes.

(c) Are simple events and outcomes synonymous?

(d) Are simple events mutually exclusive?

(e) Are the simple events exhaustive?

(f) Write out the sample space.

(g) What are the sample points?

(h) If y is a random variable for this experiment that designates the number of loaves sold per day, is $y = 8$ a possible event?

(i) What is the probability $P(y = 8)$?

(j) Is it certain that at least one of the simple events will have occurred by the end of the day?

(k) What is the probability of a certain event?

(l) Suppose 20 days of sales were: 2 3 3 5 6, 6 1 2 2 4, 7 5 0 1 3, and 4 5 4 3 7. Assign probabilities to simple events using the relative frequency method and state the law of large numbers.

(m) Assign probabilities to simple events using the equally likely outcomes method. Is this an a priori approach?

(n) Name a third method of assigning probabilities to events.

(o) If the Harvest Moon Bakery makes a profit when more than 3 loaves are sold per day, what is the probability of *not* making a profit, which means selling (0 or 1 or 2 or 3) loaves? Use the probabilities established by the relative frequency method here and in the parts of this exercise that follow. Is (0 or 1 or 2 or 3) a compound event (a union) composed of four simple events?

(p) What is the complementary event to selling (0 or 1 or 2 or 3) loaves and what is its probability?

(q) What are the odds in favor of making a profit?

(r) If the Harvest Moon Bakery sells exactly 3 loaves per day of this bread, they break even. In terms of the simple events, write the compound event, CE_1, that they lose money or break even on this product? In terms of the simple events, write the compound event, CE_2, that they break even or profit on this product? What is the intersection and probability of CE_1 and CE_2?

(s) Use the addition law to find the probability of CE_1 or CE_2.

(t) If the number of loaves sold is independent from day to day, what is the probability on three consecutive days that 4, 6 and 5 loaves are sold? What law or rule did you use here?

(u) From the compound events in part (r), find the probability of CE_1 and CE_2. What is the prior probability of CE_2? What is the posterior probability of CE_2 given CE_1 has occurred? State Bayes' theorem.

(v) Draw a Venn diagram for the possible number of loaves sold that shows CE_1, CE_2, and the intersection.

(w) Suppose baked loaves are inspected and graded as grade A or grade B, where grade A is better. Sixty percent of the loaves are grade A; the remainder are grade B. Construct a probability tree for a sequence of three inspections.

2. Suppose a newspaper distributor delivers 21 copies of a newspaper to a newsstand each morning. Let the consumer demand be 20, 21, 22, or 23 newspapers on any given day, no more and no less.

(a) List the simple events for the possible number of newspapers demanded per day.

(b) List the outcomes for the possible number of newspapers demanded per day.

(c) Are simple events and outcomes synonymous?

(d) Are simple events mutually exclusive?

(e) Are the simple events exhaustive?

(f) Write out the sample space.

(g) What are the sample points?

(h) If y is a random variable for this experiment that designates the number of newspapers demanded per day, is $y = 25$ a possible event?

(i) What is the probability $P(y = 25)$?

(j) Is it certain that at least one of the simple events will have occurred by the end of the day?

(k) What is the probability of a certain event?

(l) Suppose 10 days of demand were: 20 21 23 21 22, 23 21 22 20 21. Assign probabilities to simple events using the relative frequency method and state the law of large numbers.

(m) Assign probabilities to simple events using the equally likely outcomes method. Is this an a priori approach?

(n) Name a third method of assigning probabilities to events.

(o) Let the newsstand cost be $1.50; this amount is not lost if a newspaper does not sell because unsold copies are returned to the distributor. This return policy for unsold copies motivates the newsstand to want to be overstocked. However, the distributor is motivated to minimize overstocking because unsold papers at one newsstand might be sold elsewhere. Let the sales price per newspaper be $2.00. Thus, there is a profit of $.50 on each newspaper sold. If total demand (20, 21, 22, or 23) exceeds the supply of newspapers (always 21), there is an opportunity loss of $.50 on each newspaper that could have been sold. Let the random variable, y, represent total profit less opportunity costs. What are the possible values for the random variable? Using the equally likely method of assigning probabilities to demand, find the values of P(y).

(p) What is the probability that y is $10 or less?

(q) What is the probability that y is $10 or more?

(r) What is the probability that y is less than $10?

(s) What is the probability that y is exactly $10?

(t) Let the random variable, s, represent number of newspapers sold per day. What are the possible values for this random variable?

(u) Using the equally likely method of assigning probabilities to demand, find the values of P(s).

(v) If the number of newspapers sold is independent from day to day, what is the probability on four consecutive days that 21, 21, 20, and 21 are sold?

(w) Suppose the newsstand owner refers to a good sales day, labeled (G), as one in which 21 or more newspapers were demanded; otherwise the day is bad, (B). Construct a probability tree for a sequence of three sales days.

3. After watching a movie in a mall parking lot on a cold night, suppose you try to start your car and the motor won't even make a sound. If the probability of a dead battery is $\frac{1}{1,000}$ and the probability of a dead starter motor is $\frac{1}{2,000}$.

(a) What is the probability that both the battery and the starter motor are dead?

(b) What is the probability that the battery alone or the starter motor alone or both are dead?

(c) If the probability of getting mugged in the parking lot is one in a million, what is the probability that the battery and the starter motor are dead and you get mugged?

(d) If the automobile manufacturer owns the mall and you have a slick lawyer friend who wins lawsuits with a probability of $\frac{1}{100}$ that involve car manufacturing flaws or the lack of adequate security in mall parking lots, what is the probability that the battery and the starter motor are dead and you get mugged and win the lawsuit that you file?

4. Once a year, company sales teams, A and B, run a playoff contest in CityOne and CityTwo. Potential buyers submit contract proposals to both teams. In CityOne, the teams are equally successful in winning contracts. In CityTwo, team A has twice as much chance as B of winning a contract. In the playoff, sales teams A and B bid on a series of proposals until one of them has won a total of four contracts, which ends the competition. The series begins in CityOne where two proposals are bid on. After the first two proposals from CityOne, at most, three proposals are bid on from CityTwo. After the fifth proposal, if the contest runs that long, the bidding is continued on proposals from CityOne.

(a) What is the probability that team A wins the first four bids?

(b) What is the probability that team B wins the first four bids?

(c) What is the probability that team A wins the first two bids, loses the third, and wins the last two?

5. An advertising target region for a new mail-order product is divided into four sectors whose populations reached by the advertising (as fractions of the target region's total population) are p_A, p_B, p_C, p_D. If three orders come in at random from within the target region, what is the probability that the first order is from sector A or C and the next two orders are from sector B or D?

6. A pack of cards, with the usual four suits, has 13 denominations within each suit. Two suits are red (hearts and diamonds) and two are black (clubs and spades). Four cards are dealt to four players.

(a) What is the probability that only one player receives a red card?

(b) What is the probability that each player receives an ace?

7. A population of N corporations is ranked according to their sizes, where the rank runs from 1 (the largest) to N (the smallest). For a market research survey, a random sample of size 3 is drawn from this population.

(a) What is the probability that the fifth largest corporation is not in this sample?

(b) What is the probability that the largest corporation is in this sample?

8. At random between 2:00 p.m. and 3:00 p.m., a consultant takes a 10-minute telephone call from an important client. At random during the same period, the consultant takes a 15-minute telephone call from a second, equally important client. If the consultant does not have to place either client on hold, what is the probability that the consultant is not on the telephone with either client?

9. An automobile manufacturer is to award a contract to one of three suppliers, A, B, or C, for an ignition system component. These three suppliers have no significant differences in average output quality. Thus, it was decided to award the contract to the winner of a five-day production comparison. At random, an inspector hired by the automobile manufacturer takes a sample of daily production in each supplier plant. These samples are then carefully compared to determine which plant produced the most reliable components on that day. The contract is awarded to the company whose components are found most reliable in five consecutive comparisons.

If company B has produced the most reliable component for the first two samples, what is the probability that company B ultimately wins the competition?

10. An accounting firm gives job applicants a 100-question multiple choice test. Each question has four choices with only one correct answer. One applicant was certain of the answers on half the questions but guessed on all of the remaining questions. In half of the guessed answers, two of the four choices were correctly eliminated as not possible. For the remaining guesses, all four choices were considered equally likely.

(a) What is the probability that this applicant guessed incorrectly on all questions that involved guessing?

(b) What is the probability that this applicant guessed incorrectly on all but one of the questions that involved guessing?

11. Two cases of a perishable product were produced in each of two production periods and delivered to a warehouse for storage. Due to packaging and shipping considerations, retailers order two cases at a time. After two orders from different retailers have accumulated at the warehouse, two cases are chosen at random and shipped to each retailer, where one randomly chosen case is put on display for sale and the other is kept in reserve. It is best if cases of the same age are on display simultaneously at the different retail sites. Find the probability that the two cases produced in the first production period are each on display.

12. A cookie machine turns out chocolate chip cookies of a standard size. The number of chocolate chips per cookie is a random variable, y, with values of 0, 1, 2, 3, or 4, each of which is equally likely.

(a) What is the probability that a cookie contains no less than two chocolate chips?

(b) What are the odds in favor of a cookie having zero or one chocolate chip?

13. Samples for road repair decisions are taken from randomly selected highway sections. The number of potholes per section is a random variable, y, whose values are 0, 1, 2, 3, 4, or 5, with probabilities of .37, .37, .18, .06, .01 and .01, respectively. If a segment of highway is composed of two such sections, what is the probability that the segment has exactly two potholes?

14. A certain car part is stocked by only 20 of every 100 outlets. If it takes three minutes for a person to call each outlet, and if the person's time is worth $60 an hour, what is the probability that it will cost an individual exactly $12 to contact an outlet that has the needed part?

15. The entrance to a bike trail is designed to block out motor vehicles; two small boulders are located on each side of the entrance, 8 feet apart, and a 5-inch diameter metal post bisects this span. The post (but not the boulders) is high enough to hit the handle bars of a bike not properly directed to the left or right of the post. Suppose a careless biker enters the trail and avoids the boulders; however, he or she is not paying attention and does not see the post. If random entry is made within the 8-foot entrance and the handle bars of the bike span 20-inches, what is the probability that the biker hits the post?

16. While students were on a trip to a manufacturing plant, 100 pickup trucks were observed rolling off the assembly line. Seventy pickups were painted all red and 20 pickups were painted all white. Each of the remaining pickups had red tops and white undersides. Consider these 100 trucks in all parts of the exercise that follow.

(a) Use a Venn diagram to classify the trucks by color.

(b) If a dealer gets one of the trucks at random for display purposes, what is the probability that it is all red?

(c) If a dealer gets one of the trucks at random for display purposes, what is the probability that it is all white?

(d) If a dealer gets one of the trucks at random for display purposes, what is the probability that it has a red top and a white underside?

(e) If a dealer gets one of the trucks at random for display purposes, what is the probability that it is all white or all red?

(f) If a dealer gets one of the trucks at random for display purposes, what is the probability that it is white, red, or includes both colors?

(g) If a dealer gets one of the trucks at random for display purposes, what is the probability that it is green? Show this probability on a Venn diagram.

(h) If a dealer gets one of the trucks at random for display purposes, what is the probability that it is red on top with white undersides or that it is all red?

(i) If a dealer gets one of the trucks at random for display purposes, what is the probability that it is red on top with white undersides or that it is all white?

(j) If a dealer gets one of the trucks at random for display purposes, what are the odds that it is red on top with white undersides?

(k) If two dealers each get one of the trucks at random for display purposes, what is the probability that the second dealer gets a red truck given the first dealer has been shipped a truck? Construct a decision tree for this sequence of shipments.

(l) Construct a probability table for the sequence of shipments in part (k).

17. Pizzas can be ordered with or without a particular topping.

(a) If there is only one topping, how many different kinds of pizzas can be ordered?

(b) If there are two toppings, how many different kinds of pizzas can be ordered?

(c) If there are three toppings, how many different kinds of pizzas can be ordered?

(d) If there are p toppings, where the letter p represents any number of toppings, how many different kinds of pizzas can be ordered?

18. A computer manufacturer will configure a personal computer for you with a choice of three monitors, two keyboards, two processors, four memory sizes, and three different disk capacities.

(a) How many different personal computers are possible?

(b) The company's cost accountant has suggested that too many consumer choices are provided and that this drives up inventory requirements and manufacturing costs. Do you think the cost accountant is blowing hot air or can this be true?

(c) Because of (b), suggest configuration limitations that cut the number in (a) in half.

19. If car license plates consist of three digits followed by three letters, how many distinct plates are possible?

20. If a telephone area code consists of any three digits and if a phone number consists of any seven digits, what is the total number of possible area code and phone number sequences?

21. In the design of a new fighter plane, there are four wing sizes and six tail sizes being debated in engineering. To settle the debate, engineering suggests to management that prototype planes be built. Because these prototypes are expensive to build, management wants to know how many prototype planes are possible.

(a) How many are possible?

(b) Because of the expense, management will probably suggest that engineering should rely on theory and computer simulation to drastically reduce the number of wing and tail sizes being considered. How do you think this will play out?

22. Section managers report product quality problems to a steering committee that in turn reports to a plant manager. The steering committee decides which of the pending quality problems get selected and designated as work projects. A group of work projects is called a portfolio.

(a) If there are eight quality problems and only enough resources to cope with four work projects, how many project portfolios are possible?

(b) If there are n quality problems and only enough resources to cope with y work projects, how many project portfolios are possible?

23. Starting with the total capital of $3 million, a company engages in a sequence of three speculations of $1 million each. The probability of losing the speculated $1 million is twice the probability of winning an additional $1 million.

(a) How many ways are there of winning $1 million and losing $2 million in three speculations?

(b) What is the probability of having $2 million of total capital at the end of the third speculation?

(c) What is the probability of having no dollars of total capital at the end of the third speculation?

(d) What is the probability of having $6 million of total capital at the end of the third speculation?

24. During production, hourly samples are taken of a mass-produced plastic part. If any defective parts are found in a sample of ten, the production process is stopped, examined, and, if necessary, corrective action taken. The process is operating at an acceptable quality level of only 2% defectives. What is the probability that the process is stopped.

25. Engineering has identified upper and lower specifications for piston ring diameters. Eighty-nine percent of production meets these specifications and are acceptable for use. What is the probability that fewer than two piston rings are unacceptable in every twelve produced?

26. A textile producer has a large number of similar knitting machines. A service crew repairs machines that break down. The repair time is a discrete random variable of 15, 30, or 45 minutes. The 30-minute repair time is twice as likely as the other times.

(a) Draw the discrete probability distribution.

(b) Draw the cumulative probability function.

(c) What is the probability that the repair time is 30 minutes or less?

(d) Find the mean (expected value) of repair time.

(e) Find the variance of repair time.

(f) Find the standard deviation of repair time.

27. A hospital surveys patients to get an indication of the quality of service. During one period, the satisfaction level was 90%. Find the probability that at most two of twelve of these patients were unsatisfied.

28. Willard's general store stocks maple syrup in pints, half gallons, and gallons. History suggests that half the customers want pints, three in ten customers want half gallons, and the rest want gallons. Prices are: pints, $8; half gallons, $20; and gallons, $35. The revenue generated from a future sale of one container of maple syrup is a discrete random variable.

(a) Draw the discrete probability distribution.

(b) Draw the cumulative probability function.

(c) What is the probability that the revenue is $20 or less?

(d) Find the mean (expected value) of revenue.

(e) Find the variance of revenue.

(f) Find the standard deviation of revenue.

29. A brother and sister hunt together with two dogs, Bark and Howl, on their farm. A pheasant will be dinner if the dogs flush the bird and the hunter hits the target when it is flushed. Bark and Howl have probabilities 0.90 and 0.80, respectively, of finding a certain pheasant. The sister and brother have probabilities 0.70 and 0.60, respectively, of slaying the pheasant when flushed. Either dog may pair up with either hunter. They hunt the same area independently. What is the probability of a pheasant dinner if the sister hunts with Bark?

30. A bakery has ten regular customers who come in early each morning and buy a single loaf of bread. The baker's records show that a loaf of rye bread is sold to 200 of every 1,000 such customers. On a particular morning, what is the probability of selling exactly y loaves (where y = 0, 1, 2, . . . , 10) of rye bread to the regular customers?

31. A filling machine tops off liquid storage containers in amounts ranging from 0 to 20 fluid ounces. The amount of fluid needed for filling, y, has a density function

$$f(y) = \frac{2}{20} - \frac{y}{200}$$

(a) What is the probability that less than 5 fluid ounces are needed for filling?

(b) What is the mean filling amount needed?

(c) What is the probability that the filling amount needed is less than the mean?

(d) What is the variance in the filling amount needed?

(e) What is the probability that the filling amount is within one standard deviation of the mean?

32. In a bottling plant, the weekly demand, y, for syrup (in hundreds of gallons) has a mean value of $\frac{11}{18}$ and a probability density function (where $0 < y < 1$):

$$f(y) = a + by$$

(a) Find an equation for the total area under the density function in terms of the constants, a and b.

(b) Find an equation for the mean in terms of the constants, a and b.

(c) Solve the two equations found above for the two unknown constants in the density function.

(d) Find the standard deviation of y.

(e) What is the probability that a weekly demand is within one standard deviation of its mean value?

33. A 5-inch diameter doughnut with a $1\frac{1}{2}$-inch hole diameter has only two blueberries in it. The blueberries are in the interior and can't be seen. However, the dough was mixed well enough so that the blueberries could be anywhere inside at random locations. Suppose you break off a piece of the doughnut for a friend that includes 2 inches of the outside circumference and the same proportion of the hole circumference.

(a) What is the probability (approximate if necessary) that your friend gets both blueberries?

(b) What is the probability (approximate if necessary) that you each get a blueberry?

34. A telephone survey indicated that 50 of 200 respondents who received free shampoo samples in the mail liked the product enough to switch brands. What is the probability that either 2 or 3 of 8 who received free shampoo switch brands?

35. Shoppers at a mall are intercepted and questioned to obtain marketing information. Twenty of 100 questioned in a preliminary sample said that they were between 15 and 25 years of age and that they were mouthwash users. If this preliminary sample is perfectly accurate, what is the probability that 2 or more of 12 shoppers in this age class are mouthwash users?

36. A large, nationally representative sample of households participate in mail questionnaires. The households are compensated for agreeing to respond. Corporations use such panels of consumers to gather marketing information. Of 150 responses to a product information questionnaire, 28% said that they were satisfied with their personal computer and that they were not intending to buy a new one during the next year. If a salesperson contacts five such households, what is the probability that three intend to buy a new personal computer based on these figures?

37. Magazine readers were questioned on a plan by the U.S. Fish and Wildlife Service to release wolves into the Yellowstone Park ecosystem.[3] The question was: Do you support the reintroduction of wolves in Yellowstone? Yes or No? The no's totaled 1,933 of 3,000 responses. In spite of this opposition, the U.S. Fish and Wildlife Service management insists that such a plan should be carried out. Of every dozen readers chosen at random, what is the probability that at least one supports such a plan?

38. Sport fishing is a multimillion dollar industry. Fishery management attempts to maintain a natural resource as well as satisfy anglers. Therefore, research on why people fish is important information. Two-hundred responses are available for the following question:

Q1. Do you fish to catch big fish?   Yes or No

(a) Based on these figures, if it is found that 19.5% of fishers fish to catch big fish, what is the probability that neither you nor your fishing friend fish to catch big fish?

(b) Of six fishers who you know, what is the probability that more than two fish to catch big fish?

39. In the manufacture of electronic components for personal computers, a supplier had a history of high defective rates with 1 in 10 components defective. As a result, the computer manufacturer devised a sampling plan as follows: (1) 5 sampled components are taken without replacement from lots of 20 components; (2) if any defectives are found in the sample, the whole lot is rejected and returned to the supplier. What is the probability of returning a lot to the supplier?

40. A manufacturing process produces good, nonrepairable and repairable subassemblies with historical rates of $p_1 = .85$, $p_2 = .05$, and $p_3 = .10$, respectively. Of six subassemblies, what is the probability that exactly three are good, one is nonrepairable, and the rest are repairable?

41. Certain risky stocks have a 30% chance of yielding a high return. For portfolios of five such stocks, y is the number of stocks yielding a high return; y = 0, 1, 2, 3, 4, or 5. Compute P(y) and the mean number of stocks yielding a high return.

42. In the following voter analysis, political ideology is classified as conservative, moderate, or liberal with probabilities of $\frac{399}{1083}$, $\frac{470}{1083}$, and $\frac{214}{1083}$, respectively. Party affiliation is classified as democratic, independent, or republican with probabilities of $\frac{368}{1083}$, $\frac{438}{1083}$, and $\frac{277}{1083}$, respectively. If political ideology is independent of party affiliation, what is the probability of not being a liberal democrat?

43. Consider four possible management decisions (D1, D2, D3, or D4) with probabilities of $\frac{94}{420}$, $\frac{107}{420}$, $\frac{110}{420}$, and $\frac{109}{420}$, respectively. The extent of the undesirable decision consequences are none, slight, or moderate (C1, C2, or C3) with probabilities of $\frac{242}{420}$, $\frac{124}{420}$, and $\frac{54}{420}$, respectively. If the decisions are independent of the consequences, what is the probability of decision D2 and slight C2 or moderate C3 undesirable consequences?

44. In the following analysis, rated performance of radio and TV networks is classified as poor, fair, or good with probabilities of $\frac{182}{1786}$, $\frac{780}{1786}$, and $\frac{824}{1786}$, respectively. The race of the raters is classified as white or black with probabilities of $\frac{1394}{1786}$ and $\frac{392}{1786}$, respectively. If the ratings are independent of race, what is the probability a fair or good rating is made by a black rater?

45. Women on a panel rate one of two advertisements as a success or a failure. The fraction of women who rate only the first advertisement is $\frac{120}{160}$. The fraction of successfully rated advertisements is $\frac{50}{160}$. What is the probability that a woman chosen at random from the panel rated the second advertisement as a failure?

46. Alpha Company has eight sequential weeks of production time available. A contract has been signed with Beta Company to construct three identical items of special-purpose electronic equipment. Each equipment item requires a complete week for construction, and only one item can be produced at a time. The contract specifies that Beta Company chooses the production weeks for the items prior to week one. Until Beta Company makes this choice, Alpha Company is completely in the dark as to which production weeks will be chosen. For production planning purposes, Alpha Company needs to know the probability that no more than one equipment item will have to be produced in the last four weeks. What is this probability?

47. Two identical automobile parts are selected for testing from each of three production lines. These six parts form a batch. From this batch, three inspectors each choose a part for inspection. What is the probability that all chosen items come from different production lines?

48. One-quarter of production is good enough to be classified as "grade A."

(a) If eight items are classified as they are produced, what is the probability that exactly four items in succession are grade A?

(b) If items are shipped in cartons of twelve packages and each package contains four items, what is the probability that a carton has exactly five packages with at least one grade A item in it?

49. A packaging machine's response pressure, y, ranges from zero to a maximum, m. The probability density function, $f(y)$, decreases constantly from k to zero at maximum pressure.

(a) Show that $km = 2$.
(b) Show that the mean pressure is $km^2/6$.
(c) Find the standard deviation of the pressure.
(d) What percentage of the time is the response pressure less than the mean?

50. Let y = 0, 1, 2, or 3 be the number of certain replacement parts needed in the life of a jet engine.

(a) If the probability, $P(y + 1)$, equals one-half of $P(y)$, what is $P(y = 0)$?

(b) What is the expected number of replacement parts needed in the life of the engine?

(c) What is the standard deviation of the number of replacement parts needed in the life of the engine?

(d) What is the probability that the number of replacement parts is less than the mean plus one standard deviation?

51. Two competing sales representatives alternately meet a prospect until a sale is made. The salesperson who makes the first contact has a probability of $\frac{1}{4}$ of making the sale, where i is the first salesperson's meeting number with the prospect, i = 1, 2, 3, or 4. The salesperson who makes the second contact has a probability of $\frac{1}{3}$ of making the sale, where i is the second salesperson's meeting number with the prospect, i = 1, 2, or 3. What is the probability that the salesperson who makes first contact with the prospect ultimately makes the sale?

52. An expert witness testified that bloodstains leading from a murder scene matched the blood characteristics of the accused murderer.[4] These characteristics are rare and found in 0.43 percent of the population. The defense lawyer argued that of the eight million people in Los Angeles, any one of about 40,000 people could have committed the murder. Based on this line of thinking, what is the probability that the accused did not commit the murder?

53. American companies provided the Ukraine with seeds and farm equipment that could be paid for in a year with the expected $70 million in crop revenues.[5] The deal soured because the Ukraine government valued the crop at less than one million dollars.

Of 200,000 bags of seed corn sold for $11 million, it was claimed that only 10% suited the growing season there. Also, a farmer claimed that only 30% of the seeds would germinate. American farmers seldom buy seeds with germination rates less than 92%. If ten seeds are sown, find for each germination rate the probability that none will germinate.

54. In manufacturing computer memory chips, yield is the number of good chips that can be produced from a single wafer of silicon. Foreign companies have achieved high yields and have driven lower-yield competitors out of business. Therefore, manufacturers strive for high yields. One veteran chip maker explained that the process of making a single chip might involve 300 steps. Even a 99% success rate for each step can result in a high probability of getting a bad chip. Explain.

55. Soft drinks are produced in packages of six cans. It is thought that there is a constant 10% chance of a can being overfilled or underfilled. Such cans are referred to as improperly filled. What is the probability of having no less than three improperly filled cans in a six pack?

56. The market shares for three companies, A, B, and C, are thought to be 60%, 25% and 15%, respectively. In a consumer panel of 15 consumers, what is the probability that the purchase preference mix is 10 for company A, 3 for company B, and 2 for company C?

57. In a recent production run, 5% of pizza sauce cans had weights in ounces that were beyond the specification limits. What is the probability that less than two of eight cans don't meet specifications?

58. The estimated probabilities for a person to have the following hair colors and eye colors are: (1) for black, brunette, red, and blond, $\frac{108}{592}$, $\frac{286}{592}$, $\frac{71}{592}$, and $\frac{127}{592}$, respectively; and (2) for brown, blue, hazel, and green, $\frac{220}{592}$, $\frac{215}{592}$, $\frac{93}{592}$, and $\frac{64}{592}$, respectively. Using these figures and assuming hair and eye color are independent, what is the probability that a person selected at random has blond hair with blue or green eyes or black hair with green eyes?

59. On a given day, suppose the probability it rains in Franklin Lakes, New Jersey, is .35 and that the probability it rains in Seattle, Washington, is .75. These cities are far enough away from one another that the events of rain can be assumed to be independent. What is the probability that

(a) It rains in Franklin Lakes and Seattle?
(b) It does not rain in either city?

(c) It does not rain in Franklin Lakes or it does not rain in Seattle?

60. The first batch of new cars manufactured at a certain factory were stored in a holding lot temporarily. These cars were given serial numbers from 000 to 131. If one of these cars is stolen at random from the holding lot, what is the probability it has a serial number with a last digit of four?

61. If the probability of catching a brook trout in the Swift River is .10 per hour, what is the probability of catching exactly two brookies in four hours?

62. Of 1,000 small retail stores with three employees each, how many would you expect to have (assuming it is equally likely that an employee is male or female)

(a) At least one male employee?
(b) Either one or two female employees?
(c) No female employees?

63. Two companies introduced an instant sports drink product at about the same time. The product names are Presto and Speed. Initially each company acquired half of a certain customer group. If during the first year Presto retains 60% of its customers and loses 40%, and Speed retains 80% of its customers and loses 20%,

(a) What percent of this customer group does each company expect to have at the end of the year?

(b) At the end of the year, if a customer is a Presto drinker selected at random, what is the probability that the customer is one who switched from Speed?

APPENDIX 1

Minitab Examples

(If you are using the WINDOWS version of MINITAB, you might issue the GSTD command first to use standard graphics in the session window. Also, if you want to save your output on a file, use the command OUTFILE 'A:CH4.LIS' to echo output to this file.)

EXAMPLE

DISCRETE BINOMIAL APPROXIMATED BY A CONTINUOUS NORMAL

```
MTB > SET C1
DATA> 0:200
DATA> END
MTB > PDF C1 C2;
SUBC> BINOMIAL N=200 P=.5.
#  * ERROR * Completion of computation impossible
#  Future MINITAB versions may approximate the solution.

MTB > PDF C1 C3;
SUBC> NORMAL MU=100 SIGMA=7.1.
MTB > PLOT C3 C1
```

EXAMPLE

BAD EGGS—QUALITY CONTROL (INSPECTION)

```
MTB > SET C1     # NUMBER OF BAD EGGS POSSIBLE
DATA> 0:12
DATA> END

MTB > PDF C1 C2;
SUBC> BINOMIAL N=12 P=.0833.

MTB > PRINT C1 C2
MTB > PLOT C2 C1     # I HAVE DRAWN SPIKES FOR THE
# PROBABILITIES, SPIKE HEIGHT IS THE DISCRETE PROBABILITY
```

```
MTB > CDF C1 C3;       # CUMULATIVE DISTRIBUTION FUNCTION
                              # IS VERY USEFUL IN PRACTICE
SUBC> BINOMIAL N=12 P=.0833.

MTB > PLOT C3 C1     # THE SPIKE HEIGHTS FORM THE DASHED
# STEP HEIGHTS IN THE CUMULATIVE DISTRIBUTION FUNCTION.
#  AFTER THE FOURTH STEP THE STEPS CONTINUE BUT THEY ARE
# SO SMALL THAT THEY CANNOT BE SEEN IN THIS PLOT
```

EXAMPLE

STUDENT'S t DISTRIBUTION

```
MTB > SET IN C1        # A RANGE OF STUDENT'S t VALUES
DATA> -5 -4.5 -4 -3.5 -3 -2.5 -2  -1.5  -1  -.5  0
DATA>.5 1 1.5 2 2.5 3 3.5 4 4.5 5
DATA> END

MTB > PDF FOR C1 PUT INTO C2;       # DENSITIES IN C2
SUBC> T    V=1.  # t DISTRIBUTION, ONE DEGREE OF FREEDOM;
# IN PRACTICE, WE ARE MOST INTERESTED IN THE DEGREES OF
# FREEDOM RANGING FROM 1-30.  AT 30, THE STUDENT'S t IS
# ALMOST NORMAL AS YOU WILL SEE.

MTB > PLOT C2 C1

MTB > PDF FOR C1 PUT INTO C3;
SUBC> T  V=30.  #  t DISTRIBUTION, 30 DEGREES OF FREEDOM

MTB > PLOT C3 C1  # NOTICE, AT 30 DEGREES OF FREEDOM THE
# t DISTRIBUTION IS NEARLY NORMAL.  BY TRYING OTHER
# VALUES BETWEEN 1 AND 30 DEGREES OF FREEDOM, YOU CAN
# SEE THE SHAPE CHANGE.

# TO MAGNIFY THE SHAPE CHANGES, SUBTRACT THE DENSITIES
# AND PLOT, FOR EXAMPLE, LET C4=C3-C2 AND PLOT C4 C1.
```

EXAMPLE

CHI-SQUARE DISTRIBUTION

```
MTB > SET INTO C1        # A RANGE OF CHISQUARE VALUES
DATA> 0 2 4 6 8 10 12 14 16 18 20 30 40
DATA> END

MTB > PDF FOR C1 PUT INTO C2;
SUBC> CHISQUARE V=5.  # THE MOST COMMON RANGE FOR THE
# DEGREES OF FREEDOM, IN PRACTICE, IS 1 THRU 30; FOR
# CONTRAST AND PLOTTING CLARITY, WE CHOOSE 5 DEGREES OF
# FREEDOM HERE AND 30 DEGREES OF FREEDOM AFTERWARDS.

MTB > PLOT C2 C1
```

```
MTB > PDF FOR C1 PUT INTO C3;
SUBC> CHISQUARE V=30.          # 30 DEGREES OF FREEDOM
MTB > PLOT C3 C1
```

EXAMPLE

THE F DISTRIBUTION (FISHER-SNEDECOR DISTRIBUTION)

```
MTB > SET INTO C1
DATA> 0 .5 1 1.5 2 2.5 3 3.5 4 4.5 5 5.5 6 6.5
DATA> END

MTB > PDF FOR C1 PUT INTO C2;
SUBC> F U=4 V=1.  #  THE F DISTRIBUTION REQUIRES TWO
# DEGREES OF FREEDOM, U FOR THE NUMERATOR AND V FOR THE
# DENOMINATOR, BECAUSE THE DISTRIBUTION ARISES FROM A
# RATIO OF TWO STATISTICS.  THE USUAL TABULATIONS OF F
# VALUES ARE FOR DEGREES OF FREEDOM FROM 1 TO 120 FOR
# EITHER U OR V.  FOR PLOTTING CLARITY, THE EXTREMES
# IN DEGREE OF FREEDOM CHOICE ARE AVOIDED HERE.

MTB > PLOT C2 C1

MTB > PDF FOR C1 PUT INTO C3;
SUBC> F U=25 V=25.
MTB > PLOT C3 C1
```

CHAPTER 5

The Normal Distribution

OBJECTIVES

◇ Recognize the normal distributional shape

◇ Distinguish between probability and density

◇ Use the normal density function to find probabilities

◇ Use the cumulative normal and its inverse

PRELUDE

The leaves on stem-and-leaf diagrams sometimes pile up in familiar patterns. One well-known pattern resembles the profile of a pile of sand on a beach or a pile of raked leaves. Technically, this distribution of leaves is said to be normal. So famous is the bell-shaped normal distribution that Carl Friedrich Gauss (1777–1855) is considered one of the founding fathers in statistics. In his honor, some statisticians refer to the normal as the Gaussian distribution.

Since Gauss's time, a large body of statistical theory that depends on the normal distribution has been developed. The normal density function is a workhorse for making probability statements about a random variable. When the mean and standard deviation are known for a normally distributed random variable, easy-to-use tabulations are available for finding cumulative probabilities and evaluating probability statements. ◇

INTRODUCTION

The **normal distribution** is a bell-shaped continuous distribution. It has roots that extend back in time to early developments in the field of statistics. Some refer to the normal as the Gaussian or Laplace-Gauss distribution. Pierre Simon de Laplace (1749–1827) exposed many of the mathematical properties of this distribution. Earlier, Abraham de Moivre (1667–1754) planted some seeds for getting things started.

The normal distribution forms a supporting pillar for much of the theory in probability and statistics. A plot of the density function, f(y), is bell-shaped. When stem-and-leaf diagrams, histograms, or dotplots have this shape, a rich body of statistical theory can be applied to practical problems. This distribution can be thought of as ideally suited for understanding the data. Achieving normality means that the data are prepared for the classical statistical analyses that might follow; and, from which probability statements can be easily made.

Nonnormal data distributions are often transformed in an attempt to attain normality. For example, logarithms or square roots of the original observations often produce normal distributions of the transformed data. Even when the normality objective is not achieved, symmetry alone can be helpful. Measures of central tendency and distributional spread are more meaningful when data distributions are symmetrical.

Although the normal distributional shape appeared in earlier chapters, in this chapter we examine the distribution more completely. After the mean and standard deviation of the normal distribution are known, you are equipped to specify the proportion of data values expected within regions of interest. This proportion is a probability that measures uncertainty in the value of the random variable, y.

APPROXIMATELY NORMAL DATA DISTRIBUTIONS

This chapter first reveals the normal shape as it emerges from a simple experiment. Later you will see how the normal distribution tells us about the proportions of the data values that are likely to fall in certain regions of the normal curve.

It is useful to relate stem-and-leaf diagrams and histograms to the normal distribution. To illustrate these relationships, consider the results of a coin-tossing experiment. Four coins are tossed 16 times. The resulting numbers of heads in each toss are displayed on a stem-and-leaf diagram in Exhibit 1.

Exhibit 1 shows the possible number of heads, 0, 1, 2, 3, and 4, from a total of 16 tosses of four coins. Their occurrence frequencies are 1, 4, 6, 4, and

EXHIBIT 1 Number of Heads in a Coin-Tossing Experiment

0	0	(no heads one time)
1	1, 1, 1, 1	(one head four times)
2	2, 2, 2, 2, 2, 2	(two heads six times)
3	3, 3, 3, 3	(three heads four times)
4	4	(four heads one time)

1, respectively. The relative frequencies are $\frac{1}{16}, \frac{4}{16}, \frac{6}{16}, \frac{4}{16}$, and $\frac{1}{16}$. This is the result of one experiment. If we were to toss four coins 16 times in a second experiment, we would likely get different results.

A histogram can also be constructed, as shown in Exhibit 2. Each bar has a width of one unit and a length equal to the relative frequency, $\frac{1}{16}, \frac{4}{16}, \frac{6}{16}, \frac{4}{16}$, and $\frac{1}{16}$.

The total area of all the bars of the histogram is equal to one.

$$\text{total area} = \frac{1}{16} + \frac{4}{16} + \frac{6}{16} + \frac{4}{16} + \frac{1}{16} = 1$$

S T A T I S T I C A L   H I G H L I G H T S

A histogram can be used to represent a stem-and-leaf diagram. If the bar width is one unit and the bar length is the relative frequency, bar length times bar width is bar area. The total area of all bars is one.

EXHIBIT 2 A Histogram

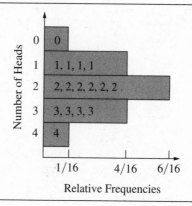

EXHIBIT 3 The Approximate Shape of the Normal Distribution

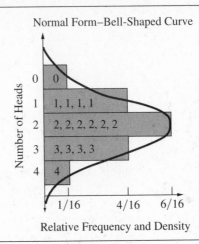

Normal Form–Bell-Shaped Curve

Number of Heads

0	0
1	1, 1, 1, 1
2	2, 2, 2, 2, 2, 2
3	3, 3, 3, 3
4	4

1/16   4/16   6/16

Relative Frequency and Density

A smooth curve can be drawn through the midpoints of the bar ends. The curve has approximately the same area under it as does the histogram as shown in Exhibit 3. The shape of this smooth curve is approximately that of the normal distribution, which is a symmetrical bell-shaped curve. This distribution is a good choice for an approximation of a histogram in a wide variety of situations.

The next example simulates coin-tossing experiments in MINITAB (see Appendix 1) and produces results similar to Exhibit 3. Repeated independent experiments with two possible outcomes and constant probabilities are called **Bernoulli trials.** Daniel Bernoulli (1700–1782) developed the theory that applies to coin-tossing experiments.

EXAMPLE 1

COIN-TOSSING SIMULATIONS

Problem Statement (a)   Simulate the tossing of four coins 16 times. Count the number of heads in each toss.

Problem Solution (a)   The result of tossing four coins appears as a row in the data set below; the 1s represent heads and the 0s represent tails. At the end of each row is a count of the number of heads (1s) in each toss. The head counts are listed in column C5. There are 16 tosses of four coins; this creates 16 rows.

```
COIN   1    2    3    4    ROW TOTAL (NUMBER OF HEADS)
TOSS   C1   C2   C3   C4      C5

  1    1    0    0    0        1
  2    1    1    1    1        4
  3    0    1    1    1        3
  4    1    0    1    0        2
  5    1    1    1    0        3
  6    1    1    0    0        2
  7    0    0    1    1        2
  8    1    1    1    0        3
  9    0    1    1    0        2
 10    1    1    1    1        4
 11    0    1    1    1        3
 12    1    1    0    1        3
 13    1    1    1    0        3
 14    0    1    1    0        2
 15    1    1    0    0        2
 16    1    0    0    0        1
```

Problem Statement (b)   From the count of the number of heads in each toss (C5), find the relative frequencies and express them as a percentage.

Problem Solution (b)

```
Number of Heads    Relative Frequency × 100
      1                    12.5
      2                    37.5
      3                    37.5
      4                    12.5
```

Problem Statement (c)   From the count of the number of heads in each toss (C5), construct a frequency histogram.

Problem Solution (c)

```
Number of Heads    Frequency Count    Histogram
      1                   2            **
      2                   6            ******
      3                   6            ******
      4                   2            **
```

Problem Statement (d)   Because larger experiments tend to produce better probability estimates, toss four coins 100 times. From the count of the number of heads in each toss (C5), find the relative frequencies and express them as a percentage.

Problem Solution (d)

Number of Heads	Relative Frequency × 100
0	5.0 (no heads 5% of the time)
1	21.0
2	41.0
3	20.0
4	13.0

Problem Statement (e) Repeat the larger experiment and notice the variation in the relative frequencies. Toss four coins 100 times. From the count of the number of heads in each toss (C5), find the relative frequencies.

Problem Solution (e) Notice that the relative frequencies are close but not exactly the same as in the previous experiment.

Number of Heads	Relative Frequency × 100
0	5.0
1	20.0
2	36.0
3	33.0
4	6.0

Problem Statement (f) If we were able to enlarge the experiment enough to include an infinite number of tosses, the relative frequencies would become theoretical probabilities. Find these binomial probabilities using MINITAB. Compare these probabilities to their relative frequency estimates made in the above simulations.

Problem Solution (f) In the simulations above, the relative frequency estimates are close to but not the same as the following probabilities.

Number of Heads	Binomial Probabilities × 100
0	6.25
1	25.00
2	37.50
3	25.00
4	6.25

A BINOMIAL PROBABILITY DISTRIBUTION APPROXIMATED BY A NORMAL DENSITY FUNCTION

The frequency histogram in part (c) of the previous example has a shape that resembles a normal distribution even though the distribution is binomial and the experiment is small. By enlarging the experiment, tossing 16 rather than 4 coins an infinite number of times, the normal density function becomes a better approximation of the binomial probability distribution.

Such an approximation is shown in Exhibit 4, which overlays binomial probabilities and normal densities. The orientation of Exhibit 4 is the same as Exhibits 2 and 3, which is similar to MINITAB's stem-and-leaf diagrams and histograms. This orientation will become useful. However, if you prefer the vertical axis to be the horizontal one, simply rotate the page counterclockwise.

Certain details of Exhibit 4 must be emphasized. First, the binomial probabilities are represented by 17 horizontal lines (spikes). The line lengths represent the probabilities of getting 0, 1, 2, . . . , or 16 heads. Second, a smooth normal density curve is drawn, which approximates the bell-shaped pattern of the horizontal line lengths. On this MINITAB plot, the plotting points have the following meanings: (1) A's mark the binomial probabilities; (2) B's mark the normal density values; and, (3) a "2" indicates that an A and B overlap and occupy the same location.

The distance to the normal curve from the axis of the random variable y is referred to as the density, f(y). The density depends on the number of heads, y = 0, 1, 2, . . . , 16. Notice that the density is greater, say, for 6 than for 2 heads. At y = 0, 1, 2, . . . , 16, the normal densities approximate the

EXHIBIT 4 Distribution of Heads, y, Tossing 16 Coins: Binomial Probabilities, P(y), and Normal Densities, f(y)

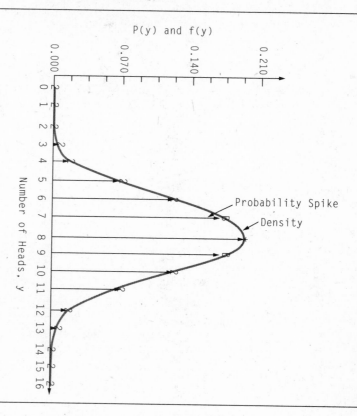

binomial probabilities, f(y) ≈ P(y). Nevertheless, probability and density are different but related concepts.

To understand the difference between probability and density, let's examine a particular number of heads, say 6. The binomial probability is P(y = 6) = .122; however, the probability of getting a noninteger number, say 6.2 heads, is 0. Yet, because the density, f(y), is a continuous function, there is a nonzero density value at both 6 and 6.2 and elsewhere. Therefore, density is not the same as probability. **Density** is the rate of probability accumulation as y changes.

Each binomial probability can be approximated by an average density. As an example, the probability of 6 heads, P(y = 6) = .122, is about equal to the average density from y = 5.5 to y = 6.5. A one-unit change in y from 5.5 to 6.5 times the approximate average density (1 × .122) is the area of one histogram bar in Exhibit 5; this area equals P(y = 6). Similarly, other bar areas can be found. In this way, the area under the normal density function approximates the binomial probabilities.

S T A T I S T I C A L   H I G H L I G H T S

Discrete distributions display probabilities at each value of the random variable. Continuous distributions display densities at each value of the random variable. Density is the rate of probability accumulation, and the area under the density function represents probability.

EXHIBIT 5 Histogram Bars for the Number of Heads, Tossing 16 Coins: Binomial Probabilities, P(y), and Normal Densities, F(y)

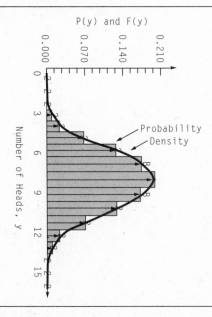

USING THE NORMAL DENSITY FUNCTION TO FIND PROBABILITIES

The area under the normal density function can approximate other data distributions in addition to the binomial. Because relative frequencies estimate probabilities, any relative frequency histogram with a normal shape and bar widths of one unit might be approximated as illustrated in the previous section. The one-unit bar width requirement is necessary for frequency histograms; density histograms simply need the normal bell shape.

When a data distribution can be approximated by the normal distribution, probabilities can be found easily. Working directly with the normal distribution avoids dealing with cumbersome histogram bars. If the mean and standard deviation of the normal distribution are known or estimated, probabilities can be found by referring to tabulations of areas under the normal density function.

The area under the normal density function represents a distribution of data. To make this association, think of the normal curve as a container that holds a certain percentage of the data values. Then, if you had a bucket filled with data values, you could pour a certain percentage of the data values into the container. Exhibit 6 shows the data bucket's contents being poured into the container so that it changes from empty to half-full and then to full.

At first the empty container has 0% of the data values in it. When half-full, the container has 50% of the data values in it. When full, the container includes 100% of the data values. Depending on the application, we could pour in different percentages such as .05%, .5%, 2.5%, 16%, 25%, and so on. Keep in mind that the data bucket pours the data values in an ordered fashion; such ordering is also found in stem-and-leaf diagrams.

Suppose we pour twice and ask what percentage of the data went into the container the first time and what percentage was poured the second time.

EXHIBIT 6 The Normal Distribution Shown As an Empty, Half-Full, and Full Container

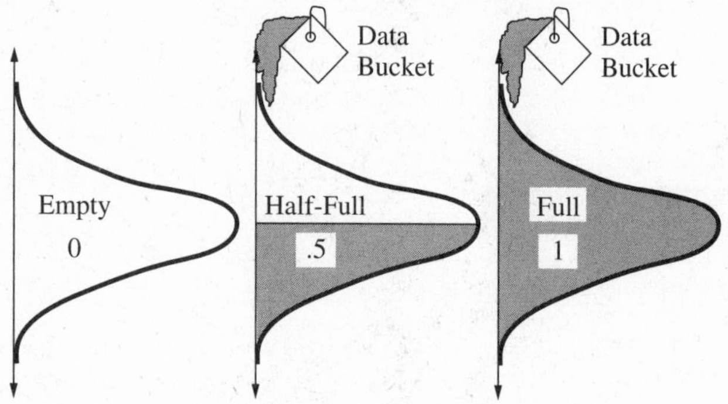

EXHIBIT 7 Percentage of Data Values on the First and Second Pourings

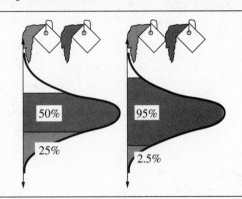

A lot of practical questions can be answered in these terms. For example, Exhibit 7 illustrates two such cases. In the left half of the exhibit, 25% is poured on the first pouring and 50% on the second pouring. In the right half of the exhibit, 2.5% is poured on the first pouring and 95% on the second pouring.

In the first case, notice that there is a 25% unfilled portion at the top of the distribution. In the second case, there is a 2.5% unfilled portion at the top. For each distribution, all the percentages add to 1, 25% + 50% + 25% = 1 and 2.5% + 95% + 2.5% = 1. These percentages are areas under the normal curve that are probabilities that the random variable y is in specific regions.

Because normal densities diminish as y moves away from the central body of the distribution, the 25% and 2.5% are sometimes called **tail areas.** If the sum of two tail areas is some arbitrary percentage, α, then, $\frac{\alpha}{2}$ is the area in each tail of a symmetrical distribution.

$$1\alpha = \frac{\alpha}{2} + \frac{\alpha}{2}$$

For example, when $\alpha = 50\%, \frac{\alpha}{2} = 25\%$; when $\alpha = 5\%, \frac{\alpha}{2} = 2.5\%$. Often we will use the decimal equivalents of the percentages, such as $\alpha = 50\% = .50$, $\frac{\alpha}{2} = 25\% = .25$, $\alpha = 5\% = .05, \frac{\alpha}{2} = 2.5\% = .025$.

EXAMPLE 2

UNIVERSITY ADMISSIONS

Problem Statement   Describe how a normal distribution of aptitude test scores might be used by a university's director of admissions in making admission decisions.

Problem Solution   As an example, the director of admissions at a major university only accepts students who score in the top 50% of the distribution of scores on a national aptitude test.

EXAMPLE 3

QUALITY CONTROL

Problem Statement   In automobile parts manufacturing, describe how a normal distribution of shaft diameter measurements might be used by a quality control manager to reject parts with diameters that are too large or too small.

Problem Solution   The quality control manager rejects shafts if their diameters fall outside the 95% control limits. This means that 2.5% of the diameters are too large and 2.5% are too small.

EXAMPLE 4

FINANCIAL MANAGEMENT

Problem Statement   In making collections on accounts receivable, describe how a normal distribution of collection period measurements might be used by a credit manager to evaluate credit management.

Problem Solution   If only a small percentage, say 25%, of the payments were made during the first 30 days during which the bills were outstanding, day-to-day credit management would be considered poor. But if a large percentage, say 80%, of the payments were made during the first 30 days during which the bills were outstanding, day-to-day credit management would be considered good.

The Normal Distribution As a Standard

Some nonnormal distributions have shapes that are more spread out than the normal distribution. Thus, their tail areas contain a larger percentage of the data values than those found in the tails of the normal distribution. Such distributions are referred to as **heavy-tailed** or **fat-tailed distributions** relative to the normal distribution. Thus, the normal distribution is a standard to which other distributions can be compared.

Compared to the normal distribution, heavy-tailed distributions tend to produce samples that contain a larger percentage of outlying data values. For classical estimators, such as the sample mean and standard deviation, outlier influence may be detrimental. Thus, exploratory summary values such as the median and the box length tend to be more reliable under these circumstances.

Filling a Normally Shaped Container Cumulatively

When viewing the normal distribution as a container, the shaded percentage of capacity depends on the level at which the container is filled. As the level rises, the percentage increases to a maximum of 100%, a full container. Exhibit 8(a) introduces the idea of partially filling the container. In addition,

EXHIBIT 8(a) A z Score and Corresponding Percent Full Reading

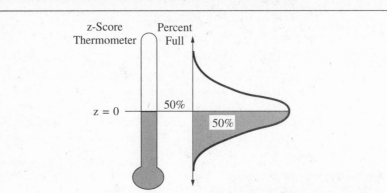

a thermometer appears as a useful prop to the left of the normal distribution. This thermometer doesn't measure temperature. Rather it measures in percentages the level to which the container is filled.

The thermometer has a **z score** or **z value** reading. The z is a normally distributed random variable with a mean of 0 and a standard deviation of 1. This is a **standard normal distribution.** The container in Exhibit 8(a) is a standard size and represents the standard normal distribution. Any normal random variable, say, y, can be transformed to **standard units,** z, by subtracting the mean, μ, and dividing by the standard deviation, σ,

$$z = \frac{y - \mu}{\sigma}$$

Instead of temperature, say in Fahrenheit degrees, F, this thermometer uses a z score scale. For a z score on the left side of the thermometer, there is a corresponding percent full reading on the right. For example, a z score of zero, z = 0, indicates that the container is half-full, 50%.

Traditional textbooks present Exhibit 8(a) as Exhibit 8(b), in which Exhibit 8(a) is flipped about a horizontal centerline and rotated 90° counterclockwise. The exhibits are identical in content and differ only in style. The Exhibit 8(a) style is consistent with stem-and-leaf displays, plots, and other computer-produced displays. It takes advantage of the container and thermometer props to build on a well-established context.

Adjusting the Props   The thermometer as used in Exhibit 8 is limited in its ability to represent the tails of the normal distribution that extend beyond the diagram. Therefore, conceptually the thermometer must be extended to plus and minus infinity. Because the tails of the distribution extend to infinity, the smooth curve never really touches the axis, so the container is not quite sealed at the bottom or top.

EXHIBIT 8(b) A z Score and Corresponding Percent Full Reading (Traditional View)

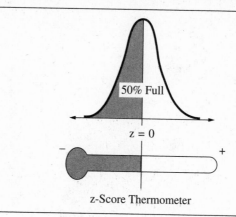

z-Score Thermometer

Although both the thermometer and container are shaded, the shading on the thermometer marks the z score. The container shading represents the percentage of capacity to which the container is filled. The container is presented as a two-dimensional object in which area supplants the concept of volume.

Finding Areas under the Normal Curve   To further illustrate the relation between a z score and the area under the normal curve, refer to Exhibit 9. A z score of −.675 leads to 25% of the distribution being shaded; this is the cumulative probability that z = −.675 or less.

Exhibit 10 shows another illustration. A z-score of +1.96 leads to 97.5% of the distribution being shaded; this is the cumulative probability that z = +1.96 or less.

EXHIBIT 9 A Negative z Score and Corresponding Cumulative Probability

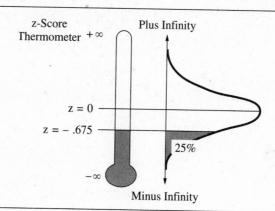

EXHIBIT 10 A Positive z Score and Corresponding Cumulative Probability

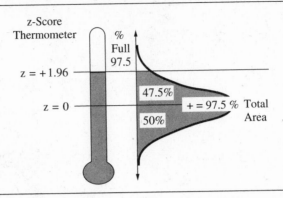

S T A T I S T I C A L   H I G H L I G H T S

When working with the normal distribution, we find z scores and use them to find the area under the curve, which is a probability. The z-scores are in standard units that enable us to take advantage of a standard normal distribution.

To avoid clutter, the shaded normal distribution in Exhibit 11 is implicit and not shown. Several z scores appear on the left side of the thermometer, and the related cumulative probabilities (from minus infinity to a specific z score) are shown on the right side.

Exhibit 11 simplifies finding the probability that a z score is between two particular values. For example, the probability a z score is between $z = +1$ and -1 is found by subtracting the corresponding cumulative percentages.

$$84.1 - 15.9 = 68.2\%$$

Similarly, in another example, the probability a z score is between $z = +3$ and -3 is found by subtracting the corresponding cumulative percentages.

$$99.9 - 00.1 = 99.8\%$$

For data distributions that are approximately normal, these results form the basis for asserting what percentage of the data values are within intervals of interest.

Cumulative Probabilities via MINITAB and Standard Tables   When a z score from the left side of Exhibit 11 is included in the MINITAB CDF command, the command produces the corresponding cumulative probability. For example, with z = 0, CDF 0 produces a cumulative probability of 50%.

EXHIBIT 11 z Scores and Corresponding Cumulative Probability

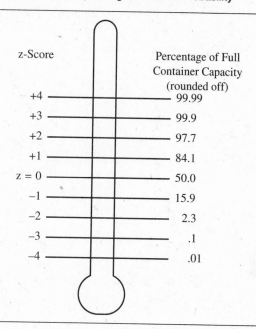

The inverse of this procedure can be accomplished. When given a cumulative probability, a z score can be found. For example, a cumulative probability of .50 in the command INVCDF .50 produces z = 0.

When the distribution is not specified by a subcommand, a standard normal distribution is used by default. The advantage of using the computer is that you are not restricted to the limited number of z scores in Exhibit 11.

Without using the computer, you can refer to Table 1 in Appendix A at the back of the book to find cumulative probabilities for the normal distribution. Table 1 is similar to Exhibit 11 in that z scores locate cumulative probabilities. However the table provides a wider range of z scores.

To find the cumulative probability in the body of the table, first break the z score into the sum of two parts. For example, if z = +2.12, then +2.12 = +2.1 + .02, where 2.1 includes one digit to the left and right of the decimal point and .02 is the second digit to the right of the decimal point. In Table 1 at the intersection of row +2.1 and column .02, read the cumulative probability of 0.9830.

The table-reading procedure can be reversed. Then a known cumulative probability, say, 0.9830, has row +2.1 and column .02 headings that sum to the z score, +2.1 + .02 = +2.12.

Transforming y to z   Any data value, y_i, can be transformed to standard units, z_i, by subtracting the mean, μ, and dividing by the standard deviation, σ,

$$z_i = \frac{y_i - \mu}{\sigma}$$

Thus, z_i is a **standardized data value,** which is a scaled deviation from the mean.

This transformation is necessary because the cumulative probabilities are tabulated for the z_i but not for y_i. Because y_i can have a variety of units such as dollars, inches, centimeters, miles, feet, and so on, standardization simplifies things by creating a standard unit. The next example illustrates the use of standardization in finding probabilities.

EXAMPLE 5

COMMON STOCK RETURNS

Regard yearly common stock returns as independent and normally distributed with a mean of 12% and a standard deviation of 21.2%.[1]

Problem Statement (a)   What is the probability that yearly common stock returns exceed 5.1%, which is an average annual return on corporate bonds?

Problem Solution (a)   To find $P(y_i > 5.1)$, standardize 5.1% by subtracting the mean of 12% and dividing by the standard deviation of 21.2%.

$$z_i = \frac{y_i - 12}{21.2} = \frac{5.1 - 12}{21.2} = -.3255$$

Round $-.3255$ to $-.33$ and from Table 1 in Appendix A find the probability of getting a z score *less than or equal to* $-.33$,

$$P(z \leq -.33) = 0.3707 \text{ or } 37\% \text{ (rounded)}$$

Because the complement of 37% is required, the probability of z exceeding $-.33$ is

$$P(z > -.33) = 1 - P(z \leq -.33) = 1 - 0.3707 = .6293 \text{ or } 63\%$$

If future common stock and corporate bond returns are like those in the past, there will be a 63% chance of common stock returns exceeding the average return on corporate bonds.

Problem Statement (b)   What is the probability that annual stock returns will exceed 15%?

Problem Solution (b)   To find $P(y_i > 15)$, standardize 15.

$$z_i = \frac{y_i - 12}{21.2} = \frac{15 - 12}{21.2} = +.14 \text{ (rounded)}$$

From Table 1, the probability of getting a z score *less than or equal to* .14 is

$$P(z \le .14) = 0.5557 \text{ or } 56\% \text{ (rounded)}$$

Because the complement of 56% is required, the probability of z exceeding .14, $P(z > .14)$, is

$$P(z > .14) = 1 - P(z \le .14) = 1 - 0.56 = .44 \text{ or } 44\%$$

Problem Statement (c)   What is the probability that annual stock returns will be between 5.1% and 15%?

Problem Solution (c)   To find $P(5.1 < y_i < 15)$, use probabilities from problem solution (a) of this example

$$P(y_i < 5.1) = P(z < -.33) = 0.37 \text{ or } 37\%$$

and from problem solution (b).

$$P(y_i > 15) = P(z > +.14) = .44 \text{ or } 44\%$$

The union, $(z < -.33) \cup (z > +.14)$, is the sum of these two probabilities.

$$P(z < -.33) \text{ or } P(z > .14) = (.37 + .44) = .81$$

The required probability is the complement of this figure,

$$P(-.33 < z < .14) = 1 - (.37 + .44) = .19 \text{ or } 19\%$$

Slightly less than one-fifth the time, 19%, common stock returns will be between 5.1% and 15%.

Data Value Intervals   The proportion of data values, y_i, expected within regions of practical interest will be referred to as **data value intervals.** Data value intervals improve the picture of the data distribution beyond that provided by the sample mean and the sample standard deviation.

The data value intervals described here depend on independent observations, y_i, with a mean, μ, a standard deviation, σ, and a normal distribution. A runs test can evaluate independence and indicate that a sequence of observations is random. A histogram and other graphical displays can confirm normality. Examples that follow demonstrate the runs test for randomness and various plots to confirm normality.

If the data values, y's, are transformed to z's, then the following data value intervals span from 68% to 99.9% of the data distribution:

68% of the z's between the limits ± 1
95% of the z's between the limits ± 2
99.7% of the z's between the limits ± 3
99.9% of the z's between the limits ± 4

Using the mean and standard deviation, these data value intervals can be expressed in terms of the y's to span from 68% to 99.9% of the data distribution.

68% of the y's between the limits $\mu \pm 1 \times \sigma$
95% of the y's between the limits $\mu \pm 2 \times \sigma$
99.7% of the y's between the limits $\mu \pm 3 \times \sigma$
99.9% of the y's between the limits $\mu \pm 4 \times \sigma$

EXAMPLE 6

FINDING THE PROPORTION OF OBSERVATIONS BETWEEN CERTAIN PRACTICAL LIMITS

Problem Statement (a)   For observations, y, from a normal distribution, find the probability that the standardized observations, z, are inside an interval of ± 1.

Problem Solution (a)   The result is obtained by subtracting cumulative proportions, $P(z < 1) - P(z < -1)$.

z	Proportion of observations yielding the given z score or a lessor one
1.0000	0.8413
-1.0000	0.1587 (subtract)
Proportion between ±1	0.6826

Problem Statement (b)   For observations, y, from a normal distribution, find the probability that the standardized observations, z, are inside an interval of ± 2.

Problem Solution (b)   The result is obtained by subtracting cumulative proportions, $P(z < 2) - P(z < -2)$.

z	Proportion of observations yielding the given z score or a lessor one
2.0000	0.9772
-2.0000	0.0228 (subtract)
Proportion between ±2	0.9544

Problem Statement (c)   For observations, y, from a normal distribution, find the probability that the standardized observations, z, are less than each of the following z scores:

$-4, -3, -2, -1, 0, +1, +2, +3, +4$

Problem Solution (c) The following results are the probabilities in Exhibit 11 to six decimal places.

C1 z	C2 Proportion of observations yielding the given z score or a lessor one
-4	0.000032
-3	0.001350
-2	0.022750
-1	0.158655
0	0.500000 (middle of the distribution)
1	0.841345
2	0.977250
3	0.998650
4	0.999968

Problem Statement (d) Plot the cumulative probabilities in problem solution (c) versus z. A smooth curve connecting these points would approximate a cumulative distribution function for the standard normal distribution.

Problem Solution (d) The z values versus the proportion of the observations less than or equal to particular z values is shown in Example 6 plot (a). You might connect the points, drawing a smooth curve. Notice the similarity this plot has to an ogive of cumulative relative frequencies.

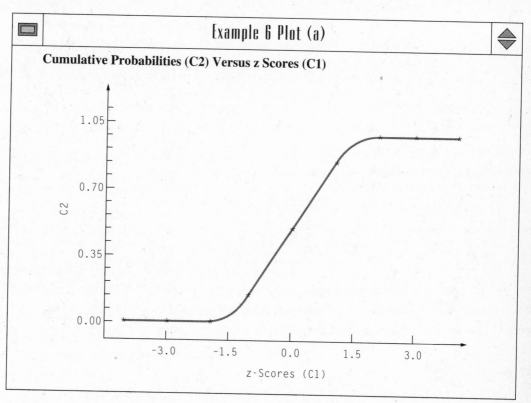

Example 6 Plot (a)

Cumulative Probabilities (C2) Versus z Scores (C1)

Problem Statement (e)   On the cumulative distribution function in problem solution (d), pick a z score on the horizontal axis, move vertically to a smooth curve connecting the plotted points, move horizontally (left) to the C2 axis, and read the proportion of observations less than or equal to the chosen z score. This proportion times 100 is referred to as a percentile. Also, the z score values can be transformed back to y values for those who prefer to view percentiles versus the original data values.

Problem Solution (e)   A z score of +1 on the horizontal axis results in a cumulative probability of 0.84 on the vertical axis. The reverse is also true. A cumulative probability, 0.84, on the vertical axis results in a z score on the horizontal axis of +1.

Atypical Data Values   Data values are regarded as **atypical** if standardized y values result in z scores beyond ±3. Such data values are suspected to be outliers. For example, a y value that transforms to $z = +5.23$ catches our attention as an atypical observation because it is beyond the limits of ±3 where only 0.27% of the observations are expected. On the other hand, a y value that transforms to $z = -1.22$ is not unusual because 95% of the observations are between the limits of ±2. Therefore, in scanning a list or examining a plot of standardizing data values, it is easy to spot unusual observations.

Bienayme-Chebyshev Rule

The data value intervals for a normal population with a known mean and standard deviation are intervals constructed under the *best* of conditions. In 1853, Jules Beinayme, a French statistician, discovered a rule for intervals under the *worst* conditions. The rule applies to any distribution that has a finite mean and standard deviation. Some 12 years later the Russian mathematician Chebyshev independently made the same discovery. Hence, the Bienayme-Chebyshev rule states that

For any distribution with a mean and a standard deviation, the percentage of observations within ±k standard deviations of the mean is at least $[1 - (\frac{1}{k^2})]$, *where k exceeds one.*

Substituting $k = 2, 3$, and 4 in the above expression results in the following data value intervals for any distribution with a finite standard deviation:

75% of the observations between the limits ±2 standard deviations
89% of the observations between the limits ±3 standard deviations
94% of the observations between the limits ±4 standard deviations.

Studentized Observations (Optional)

In many applications of statistical theory, μ and σ are unknown and must be estimated. When the sample mean and standard deviation replace the population mean, μ, and standard deviation, σ, in the standardization transformation, the result is a **studentized data value.**

$$t_i = \frac{y_i - \bar{y}}{s}.$$

This **t score** or **t value** follows a **Student's t distribution** rather than a normal distribution. For sample sizes over 30, $n > 30$ (large-sample conditions), the Student's t distribution is approximately normal. For smaller sample sizes, the Student's t distribution is a little more spread out than the normal with fatter tails.

Large-Sample Conditions   The following approximate data value intervals work best when the estimators are exactly on target, $\bar{y} = \mu$ and $s = \sigma$. When sample sizes exceed 30, roughly the data value intervals are

68%   of the t's between the limits ± 1
95%   of the t's between the limits ± 2
99.7% of the t's between the limits ± 3
99.9% of the t's between the limits ± 4

Using the sample mean and standard deviation, these data value intervals can be expressed in terms of the y's to span from 68% to 99.9% of the data distribution.

68%   of the y's between the limits $\bar{y} \pm 1s$
95%   of the y's between the limits $\bar{y} \pm 2s$
99.7% of the y's between the limits $\bar{y} \pm 3s$
99.9% of the y's between the limits $\bar{y} \pm 4s$

These limits are handy. It is convenient to think about the data distribution in terms of the estimators, $\bar{y}$ and s, which are some of the first quantities computed. These intervals help frame our thinking about the proportion of observations expected within certain regions. Even if the estimators miss their targets, we can get a rough picture of the distribution.

EXAMPLE 7

QUALITY CONTROL—A MANUFACTURING PROCESS IN A STATE OF STATISTICAL CONTROL

In a bottling operation, a machine filled bottles with a fruit drink. Six bottles were sampled from each of ten cases giving $(6 \times 10) = 60$ measurements of the contents (in ml) of each bottle. As a benchmark, these 60 measurements were taken while the machine was functioning properly. The contents of each bottle deviated from the mean randomly. Some variation in the amount of fruit drink in each bottle is unavoidable. The content figures shown below are in column, C1, and the studentized values of C1 are named STDOBS.

```
287  288  299  300  293  303  292  300  303  300  299
305  300  305  293  297  291  291  302  302  306  293
308  297  308  301  303  301  305  300  305  300  295
303  303  306  304  291  301  295  308  309  300  296
299  302  307  309  297  312  298  303  302  298  299
300  300  296  299  300
```

Problem Statement (a)   Obtain summary statistics for the bottle-content measurements.

Problem Solution (a)

	N	MEAN	MEDIAN	STDEV
C1	60	300.15	300.00	5.36

	MIN	MAX	Q1	Q3
C1	287.00	312.00	297.00	303.00

Problem Statement (b)   If the filling machine is functioning properly, nearly all the studentize bottle-content measurements will be between ± 3. List bottle contents and the corresponding studentized contents figures for the first 21 bottles. Are there any atypical content measurements?

Problem Solution (b)   By subtracting the sample mean of 300.15 and dividing by the sample standard deviation of 5.36, t values are obtained.

$$\text{STOBS} = t_i = \frac{y_i - 300.15}{5.36}$$

In the following list of bottle-content measurements and their studentized values, there are no atypical t values beyond ± 3.

ROW	C1	STDOBS
1	287	-2.45290
2	288	-2.26637
3	299	-0.21451
4	300	-0.02798
5	293	-1.33371
6	303	0.53162
7	292	-1.52024
8	300	-0.02798
9	303	0.53162
10	300	-0.02798
11	299	-0.21451
12	305	0.90468

```
ROW     C1     STDOBS
 13     300   -0.02798
 14     305    0.90468
 15     293   -1.33371
 16     297   -0.58758
 17     291   -1.70677
 18     291   -1.70677
 19     302    0.34508
 20     302    0.34508
 21     306    1.09121
```

Problem Statement (c)   Verify that studentizing results in a zero mean and a standard deviation of one for t values.

Problem Solution (c)   The following summary of the t-values results in a zero mean and a standard deviation of one.

```
              N      MEAN    MEDIAN    STDEV
STDOBS       60      0.000   -0.028    1.000

             MIN      MAX       Q1       Q3
STDOBS     -2.453    2.210    -0.588    0.532
```

Problem Statement (d)   The plant manager demands that bottle contents be monitored using a control chart that depends on the measurements distribution being approximately normal. Using a dotplot and a histogram, see if the distribution of studentized observations is roughly normal.

Problem Solution (d)   Roughly, the distribution looks normal in both of the following displays.

```
Histogram of STDOBS   N = 60

Midpoint   Count
   -2.5      2   **
   -2.0      0
   -1.5      7   *******
   -1.0      4   ****
   -0.5      5   *****
    0.0     18   ******************
    0.5     11   ***********
    1.0      6   ******
    1.5      6   ******
    2.0      1   *
```

Problem Statement (e)   In addition to the normality requirement for valid control chart construction, the bottle-content measurements must be random. Are they?

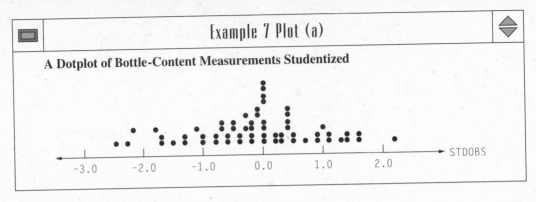

Problem Solution (e) Results from MINITAB's RUNS command are shown below that indicate these data are random.

```
C1 (a runs test for data in column, C1)
K (sample mean) = 300.15

The observed number of runs = 29.0
The expected number of runs = 30.7
27 observations K and 33 below
```

A nonrandom series of data values tends to produce a larger difference between the observed and expected number of runs than does a random series. In this example, a random series will produce an absolute difference of $(30.7 - 29)$ or more 65.48% of the time. Therefore, conclude that the observations are random.

MINITAB reports this information by determining that the runs test is significant at 0.6548. As a rule of thumb, when this figure, 65.48% in this example, is less than $\alpha = 5\%$, conclude that the series is nonrandom. MINITAB expresses the confidence in this conclusion as $(100\% - 5\%) = 95\%$.

Problem Statement (f) Construct a control chart on the studentized observations to monitor the bottle-filling process and to detect if content measurements go out of control beyond limit lines at ± 3.

Problem Solution (f) The ± 3 limits are designated as the upper control limit (UCL) with plotting symbol YYYYYY . . . YY, and the lower control limit (LCL) with plotting symbol, ZZZZZZ . . . ZZ. In addition, XXXXX . . . XX designates the centerline (CL). The plotting symbol "+" indicates a letter and number are overplotted. For a process in a state of statistical control, 99% of the observations will be within the control limits. None of the 60 observations are beyond these control limits.

Problem Statement (g) If control chart limit lines were set differently at ± 1, what percentage of the content measurements are expected within these limits? Construct such a control chart.

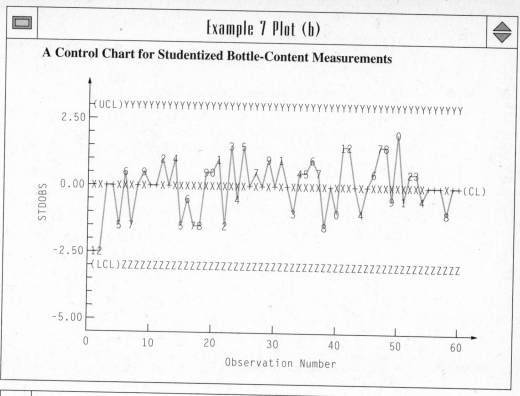

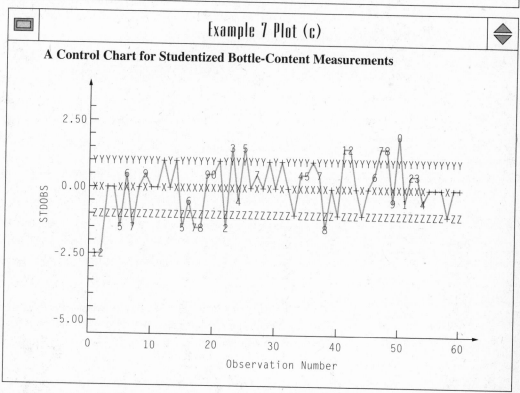

Problem Solution (g)   When control limits are placed at ± 1, expect them to include 68% of the observations because the data distribution approximates a standard normal distribution.

Process-Capability Analysis

In manufacturing, **process capability studies** compare a measure of product performance to design specifications. For example, 9-volt batteries are required by many home smoke detectors. In the safety-related uses of batteries, it is important that the actual battery voltage meets user design specifications. If the lower and upper voltage **specification limits** are 8.90(LSL) and 9.10(USL) volts and all voltage measurements of manufactured batteries fall within these limits, the specifications are met by the battery production process. Thus, the manufacturing process is capable of meeting specifications.

In many production processes, product performance measures tend to be normally distributed because they accumulate from many production operations, components, and raw materials. Suppose a production process in a state of statistical control produces batteries with voltages normally distributed with a mean of 9 volts and a standard deviation of .02 volts. Thus, $9 \pm 3(.02)$ or $9 \pm .06$ characterizes 99.73% of production. The $9 \pm .06$ produces lower and upper **natural tolerance limits** of 8.94(LNTL) and 9.06(UNTL) that characterize the capability of the manufacturing process.

Management must know how the manufacturing process is performing relative to the user design specifications. This is measured by the **process capability ratio (PCR),** which is

$$PCR = \frac{USL - LSL}{UNTL - LNTL}$$

$$PCR = \frac{9.10 - 8.90}{9.06 - 8.94} = 1.67$$

When the PCR *exceeds 1*, the design specifications are being met by a capable production process. A PCR *less than 1* indicates that the production process is not capable because the product design specifications are not being met. An incapable production process exhibits high variability (measured by the standard deviation of the product performance characteristic). For example, if voltages are normal with a mean of 9 volts and a standard deviation of .05 volts, then $9 \pm 3(.05)$, $9 \pm .15$, or 8.85 (LNTL) and 9.15 (UNTL). Thus,

$$PCR = \frac{9.10 - 8.90}{9.15 - 8.85} = .667$$

With this PCR, the design specifications relative to production characteristics are located at $9 \pm 2(.05)$, which means that 95.46% of the batteries meet specifications and $(1 - .9546) = .0546$ or 5.46% of the batteries fall out of the design specification limits. Product that falls outside of specifications might be scrapped, reworked, or sold as seconds. Thus, to reduce variability, management must take corrective action by changing the product's design, the manufacturing process, or the raw materials. The analysis of recent production data is required to determine that, say, the voltage measurements are normally distributed with a mean of 9 volts and a standard deviation of .05 volts.

EXAMPLE 8

BATTERY PRODUCTION VOLTAGE MEASUREMENTS

Problem Statement   To summarize recent production of 9-volt batteries, use the following figures to construct a histogram, approximate it by drawing the normal distribution, and display the design specifications of 8.90 (LSL) and 9.10 (USL) volts.

9.02	8.93	9.03	8.98	8.96	9.06	9.02	8.91	9.01	9.02	9.00	9.00	8.98
9.01	8.98	9.02	9.05	9.11	8.93	8.97	8.98	9.00	9.11	9.06	9.01	9.06
8.93	8.92	9.03	9.01	8.96	8.95	9.03	8.99	9.07	9.00	8.94	8.97	9.00
8.99	9.00	8.89	9.02	9.04	8.98	8.99	8.95	8.99	9.00	9.04	8.90	9.02
8.97	9.07	9.02	8.88	9.03	9.08	9.00	9.00	8.97	9.03	8.89	9.00	9.06
9.05	9.00	9.04	8.97	9.03	8.99	9.05	8.99	9.04	8.89	9.07	9.08	8.98
9.04	8.97	9.06	9.02	8.91	9.02	9.02	8.97	8.98				

Problem Solution   The production data with mean battery voltage of 9.0 and a standard deviation of .05 are plotted below.

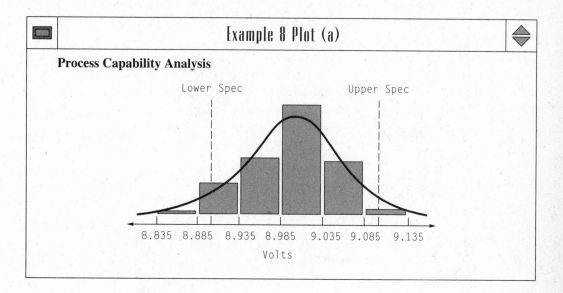

Example 8 Plot (a)

Process Capability Analysis

Lower Spec   Upper Spec

8.835 8.885 8.935 8.985 9.035 9.085 9.135

Volts

A More Thorough Check for Normality (Optional)

In the previous example and in many other practical situations, a simple visual examination of a dotplot or histogram is adequate to see if observations are roughly normal. But sometimes a more thorough examination is needed.

Usually a computer is required for these calculations. Consequently, results are shown from the MINITAB NSCORES command using the data from the previous example. The NSCORES command creates a column of theoretical standard normal values, C4. From problem solution (d) of the previous example, if the dotplot of STOBS looks just like the dotplot of C4 in Exhibit 12, then the bottle-content measurements are approximately normal. Thus, conclude that the measurements are approximately normal.

The bottle-content measurements, C1, studentized values, STDOBS, and theoretical standard normal values, C4, are listed below. Notice that the C4 values are relatively close to STDOBS in C2, confirming the impression that bottle content measurements are approximately normal.

ROW	C1	C2 STDOBS	C4 (theoretically, from a standard normal)
1	287	-2.45290	-2.31277
2	288	-2.26637	-1.93046
3	299	-0.21451	-0.40450
4	300	-0.02798	-0.08293
5	293	-1.33371	-1.14165
6	303	0.53162	0.56829
7	292	-1.52024	-1.32015
8	300	-0.02798	-0.08293
9	303	0.53162	0.56829
10	300	-0.02798	-0.08293
11	299	-0.21451	-0.40450
12	305	0.90468	0.89579
13	300	-0.02798	-0.08293
14	305	0.90468	0.89579
15	293	-1.33371	-1.14165
16	297	-0.58758	-0.69536
17	291	-1.70677	-1.55477
18	291	-1.70677	-1.55477
19	302	0.34508	0.33781
20	302	0.34508	0.33781
21	306	1.09121	1.10238

A Normal Probability Plot   A plot of the theoretical standard normal values, C4, versus the studentized data values, C2 (STDOBS), is a **normal probability plot.** A straight line results when C2 is approximately normal, as shown in Exhibit 13. Here the conclusion is that the studentized contents of each bottle of fruit drink follows a normal distribution. The evaluation of straightness is somewhat subjective. Therefore, practical experience with different data sets can be helpful.

EXHIBIT 12 A Dotplot of Theoretical Standard Normal Values

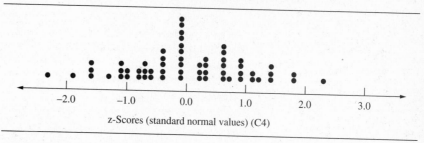

z-Scores (standard normal values) (C4)

Small-Sample Conditions for Studentized Observations (Optional)

These approximate data value intervals work best when the estimators are exactly on target, $\bar{y} = \mu$ and $s = \sigma$. When sample sizes are 30 or less (small-sample conditions), data value intervals are provided by the following formula:

$$\bar{y} \pm t_{(\alpha/2),(n-1)} \times s$$

EXHIBIT 13 Theoretical Standard Normal Values (C4) Versus the Studentized Data Values (STDOBS)

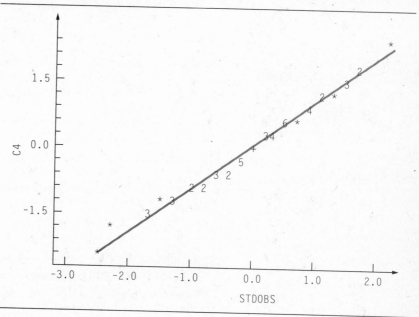

For studentized observations the interval is

$$\pm t_{(\alpha/2),\,(n-1)}$$

In general, these small-sample intervals are wider and more conservative than those for large-sample conditions. For example, consider a 95% interval under large-sample conditions; 95% of the y's are expected to be between the limits

$$\bar{y} \pm 2 \times s$$

In contrast, for a small sample, say, n = 13, the 95% interval limits are wider.

$$\bar{y} \times 2.179 \times s$$

The 2.179 is a Student's t value from Table 2 in Appendix A. The Student's t value depends on both the interval size and the sample size. Thus, two subscripts are needed to specify a unique t value. The first subscript on

$$t_{(.025),(13-1)}$$

is half of 1 minus the interval size; for example, $\frac{1-95}{2} = \frac{\alpha}{2} = .025$. The second subscript is the sample size minus 1, (13 − 1). Using the Student's t table, (Table 2 in Appendix A), you will find that

$$t_{(.025),(13-1)} = 2.179$$

Roughly, for a sample size of 13, studentized data values beyond the ±2.179 interval might be viewed as potential outliers because only 5% of the studentized t values are expected to be this far from the center (which is zero) of the Student's t distribution.

In MINITAB, the command INVCDF .975 with the subcommand T V = 12 produces this Student's t value, 2.179. For a particular interval, say, a 95% one; 5% of the distribution is outside the interval with $\frac{1-95\%}{2} = 2.5\%$ outside the interval on each side. As a result, cumulatively, at the left side of the interval 2.5% of the distribution is accumulated and at the right side of the interval 97.5% of the distribution is accumulated.

> ## S T A T I S T I C A L   H I G H L I G H T S
>
> For large samples the Student's t distribution is approximately normal. For small samples, it continues to resemble the normal distribution. However, the Student's t distribution is a little more spread out and has fatter distributional tails.

CHAPTER SUMMARY

This chapter discussed the normal distribution of data. As you gain experience across a variety of applications, you will see this distributional shape repeatedly. The bell-shape is so common that you may have a tendency to think that a data set is normal when it is not! Therefore, be aware that there are other distributions.

By way of the symmetrical normal distribution, we introduced universal concepts that apply to many other distributions. We introduced the probability density function and related it to relative frequencies and theoretical proba-

bilities. The density function was used to obtain probabilities.

We described the cumulative distribution function, displaying cumulative probabilities. In many practical situations, the cumulative distribution function is easier to work with than is the density function. The cumulative distribution function displays the probability of getting less than or equal to a particular data value. Its inverse identifies the z score or data value corresponding to the cumulative probability.

KEY TERMS

atypical data values, 226
Bernoulli trials, 210
data value intervals, 223
density, 214
fat-tailed distributions, 217
heavy-tailed distributions, 217
natural tolerance limits, 232
normal distribution, 208

normal probability plot, 234
process capability ratio, 232
process capability studies, 232
specification limits, 232
standard normal distribution, 218
standard units, 218
standardized data value, 222
Student's t distribution, 227

studentized data valve, 227
t score, 227
t value, 227
tail areas, 216
z score, 218
z value, 218

EXERCISES

General Exercises

1. Simulate or actually toss five coins 20 times. Summarize the results as done in the coin-tossing simulation in Example 1. In the example, four coins were tossed 16 times.

If you use MINITAB to do the simulation, be sure to be complete, and parallel the example by referring to Appendix 1 and by using such commands as RANDOM, BERNOULLI, PRINT, STEM, TALLY, HIST, PDF, BINOMIAL, MPLOT (if available), CDF, PLOT, and any other commands that you deem necessary.

2. In Example 6, a cumulative distribution function, CDF, is plotted for a standard normal distribution, using z scores of $+4, +3, +2, +1, 0, -1, -2, -3,$ and -4. The complement of the CDF is the probability of getting a particular z score or more. Find that complement for each of the z scores listed above.

For MINITAB users, the CDF command yields the probability of getting a particular z score or less. Using a LET command, you can define a new column that is [1 − (the less than or equal to probabilities)].

3. If the heights of individuals are approximately normal in distribution with a mean height of 69 in. and a standard deviation equal to 2.5 in.,

(a) What percentage of the individuals are over 72 in.?

(b) What percentage of the individuals have heights less than 64 in.?

(c) What percentage of the individuals are between 64 and 72 in.?

(d) Simulate the heights of 100 individuals, obtain a histogram, and use the histogram to empirically estimate the results in parts (a), (b), and (c).

4. If the number of John Wayne Biscuits (now known as Rambo/Terminator Rolls), sold per day at Little Mary's Bakery follows a normal distribution with a mean of 522 biscuits and a standard deviation of 30 biscuits,

(a) What proportion of the days are sales less than 490 biscuits?

(b) How many biscuits would Mary have to stock to satisfy 90% of the demand?

(c) Simulate daily sales for 100 days, obtain a histogram, and use the histogram to empirically estimate the results in parts (a) and (b).

5. Joe took a national examination used in college admission decisions. Scores on the examination are normally distributed with a median of 432 points and a standard deviation of 53.25 points.

(a) How many points would Joe have to score to be in the 85th percentile? That is, Joe would have to score above 85% of all other exam takers.

(b) Simulate scores for 100 students, obtain a histogram, and use the histogram to empirically estimate the results in part (a).

6. Successful sales representatives tend to concentrate their efforts on clients who are "big buyers" because such clients produce high commissions. Suppose only 10% of the clients are "big buyers." Given that the dollar amount of the clients' accounts is normally distributed with a mean of $30,000 and a standard deviation of $2,000, answer the following questions:

(a) Half of the accounts are larger than what dollar amount?

(b) How large must a client's account be for the client to be classified as a "big buyer"?

(c) What proportion of the accounts are between ±2 standard deviations?

7. Cola Cola machines drop paper cups with a maximum capacity of 8 oz into a filling position. The vendor sets the filling control mechanism at a mean number of ounces (usually less than 8) for these cups. If the amount of Cola Cola released into each cup is normally distributed with a standard deviation of 0.15 oz, what mean setting is necessary to limit the overflow condition to 5% of the cups?

8. Bars of soap produced by a molding machine have a mean weight of 100 g and a standard deviation of .33 g. The molding process is in a state of statistical control, the mean

and standard deviation are constant, weights are normally distributed, and the observations are independent.

Because the manufacturing process is automated, individual bars of soap are weighed and charted graphically. If a bar's weight falls outside ±3 standard deviations, the bar is said to fall out of the control limits. The process is barely capable, because the control limits and the specification limits coincide.

(a) What percentage of the bars fall out of control under the above conditions and don't meet specifications?

(b) What percentage will fall out of the control limits if the mean of the process shifts to 101 g and the standard deviation remains the same?

(c) What percentage will fall out of the control limits if the mean of the process stays at 100 g but the standard deviation increases to .45?

9. Managers frequently gamble when they make an investment. For example, suppose $100,000 is invested in a process that produces freeze-dried orange juice; all you have to do is place a couple spoons of powder in a glass of water and you get a robust orange juice that makes you the envy of all of Florida. The managers involved in this investment decision expect a net cash flow of $25,000 at the end of each year. Think of the net cash flow roughly as the sales revenues less any operating expenses that occur during a year. (Consult your finance or accounting books for more details.)

A net cash flow of $25,000 at the end of each year is not certain. In fact, the $25,000 could be viewed as management's best guess of the mean of a normal probability distribution. Suppose the standard deviation is $7,500. Often little or no data are available to fully justify these figures, but management is forced to take some gambles and use the normal distribution contemplatively.

(a) What net cash flow figure will be exceeded 25% of the time (the optimistic scenario)?

(b) What net cash flow figure will not be exceeded 15% of the time (the pessimistic scenario)?

(c) What percentage of the time will the net cash flows be between the two figures found in parts (a) and (b)?

(d) Would you expect the payback period to be normally distributed?

10. A profitability analysis found profits to be normal with a mean of $15,000. If 95% of the time profits are between $20,000 and $10,000, what is the standard deviation?

11. In an electronics firm, a job arrives at a workstation and waits in a queue until a machine is free. Then the job seizes control of the machine and maintains control for a period of time called a delay time. The delay time is normally distributed with a mean of 5 min and a standard deviation of 2 min. What percentage of the time does the delay exceed 8 min?

12. In a manual car wash, a person washes a car with a washing time that is normal with a mean of 20 min and a standard deviation of 5 min. What percentage of the people take less than 15 min to complete a wash?

13. At an airline ticket counter, service time for a regular customer is normal with a mean of 9 min and a standard

deviation of 3 min. Operational guidelines require that 90% of the regular customers, as opposed to frequent fliers, be serviced in less than 13 min. Are the operational guidelines being met?

14. Cities and towns usually fund public education, safety, and local highway maintenance with tax revenues. The revenue-raising capacity depends on property valuation per household, with some states limiting property taxes to $2\frac{1}{2}\%$ of property value. Suppose per household property value is normal with a mean of $90,000 and a standard deviation of $10,000, normal (90,000; 10,000). What percentage of the property values are between $80,000 and $110,000?

15. For simplicity, suppose a state is comprised of only two towns, each having the same population. The property values are (notationally, normal (mean; standard deviation)): TownOne, normal ($90,000; $10,000); and TownTwo, normal ($70,000; $10,000). Because of the disparity in mean property values, TownOne collects more tax revenues than TownTwo; therefore, TownOne has the capacity to finance better schools, roads, and so on.

The state government runs a lottery and distributes the proceeds to the towns in a way that lessens the impact of the property value disparity. A formula for distributing lottery proceeds is

$$\text{TownTwo share} = \frac{90,000}{70,000 + 90,000} \times \text{lottery proceeds}$$

TownOne receives the remaining share. If monthly lottery proceeds are normal ($10,000; 2,000), what percentage of the time does TownTwo get a share that exceeds $8,125?

16. Compute the sample mean and standard deviation of the following starting salaries of recent graduates (in thousands of dollars):

32, 41, 33, 31, 39, 37, 38, 38, 42, 33,
35, 38, 32, 32, 34, 40, 33, 30, 31, 35

Construct four intervals where you expect to see 68%, 95%, 99%, and 99.9% of the observations (approximately) assuming $\overline{y}$ is sufficiently close to μ and s to σ.

17. A college administrator is preparing to make a decision about an increase in charges to students for room and board. In thousands of dollars, a sample of anticipated room and board costs for accredited colleges and universities is[2]

4.8 9.0 4.6 5.0 8.0 4.4 7.0 5.4 6.2
5.8 3.6 4.0 3.2 6.4 5.0 6.0 6.0 7.4
6.8 4.2 8.4 7.0 6.0 3.4 4.8 7.2 4.4

(a) Check if these charges are approximately normal in distribution. If normal, studentize these figures and print charges and studentized charges side by side.

(b) Set the new room and board charges one sample standard deviation above the sample mean.

(c) Approximately what percentile does the setting in (b) place this college?

18. Part of an assembly operation is done by hand. The nominal time to assemble one unit is 10.5 min. A sample of observed times follows:

8.5 12.2 10.0 9.6 10.4 10.8 9.5 9.6 12.0 11.3
10.9 10.5 13.5 14.2 8.4 11.0 9.1 10.1 8.0 13.1

(a) Test these data for randomness and normality.

(b) Studentize the assembly times and print assembly times and studentized assembly times in two adjacent columns. Are any unusually large or small assembly times highlighted by the studentization?

19. A machine shop performs operations such as milling, cleaning, grinding, and facing. Direct labor costs (hours times wage rate) is computed for each of these operations by job number and type. For a specific job type, the direct labor costs in dollar amounts for grinding were

42.46 43.60 65.05 66.19 53.80 72.23 51.31 66.87 70.63
66.80 63.51 75.54 65.84 75.32 53.81 60.90 50.39 48.74
70.47 70.08 77.74 53.33 80.23 60.89 80.79 67.18 71.52
67.12 75.19 130.50 75.63 65.67 57.24 71.71 72.27 76.43
73.25 49.81 66.97 56.65 81.37 81.54 66.85 59.38 63.90
69.01 79.45 82.58 61.16 98.00 62.80 71.57 69.60

(a) Standardize these figures and plot them. Are there any data values beyond trial control limits located at ± 3 standard deviations beyond the standardized mean of zero?

(b) Test for randomness and normality before and after any trimming that might be necessary to compute revised limits.

20. For a large sample of milling operation jobs, the machine shop's direct labor costs are normally distributed with a mean of $44 and a standard deviation of $4. What percentage of the time are the costs between each of the following bounds: ± 1, ± 2, ± 3, and ± 4 standard deviations of the mean? Compute the boundaries of these intervals in dollar terms.

21. A company gives job applicants a standard aptitude test. The scores are normal with a mean score of 80 and a standard deviation of 5 for a large number of applicants.

(a) What percentage of the applicants score above 85, 90, and 95, respectively?

(b) What percentage of the applicants score below 75, 70, and 65, respectively?

22. Quality requirements on characteristics of a product are expressed in terms of tolerances (specification limits). Tolerances are often based on technical and economic considerations; however, statistical tolerances are sometimes used. For very large samples from a normal population (where the mean corresponds to the nominal diameter), an approximate tolerance interval is the mean ± 3 standard deviations.

(a) If the tolerance interval on the diameter of an automotive part is 3.450 to 3.475 cm, what is the mean (nominal) diameter and what is the standard deviation?

(b) What percentage of the parts fail to meet the specifications?

23. The consumer price index annual percentage changes over several years are:[3]

5.8 6.5 7.7 11.3 13.5 10.4 6.1 3.2 4.3 3.6 1.9 3.6 4.1 4.8 5.4
4.2 3.0 3.0

(a) Test for randomness and normality. If you see that these data are approximately normal but not random, the intervals, where you would expect to see the annual percentage change 68% and 95% of the time, are not as useful as with a random sequence. Nevertheless, some bounding helps frame the thinking.

(b) Even though this is not a random sample, assume normality and approximate the 68% and 95% intervals for the consumer price index annual percentage changes.

24. Cans of pizza sauce had weights in ounces that were normally distributed with a mean and standard deviation of 14.75 and 0.05, respectively. What proportion of cans contain at least 14.6 oz?

25. Burgers might be called half-pounders because the mean weight is a little over 9 oz. For a large number of normally distributed burger weights, the minimum weight is 8.47 oz and the maximum is 9.71 oz. Theory suggests that nearly all observations from a standard normal will fall between z scores of −3 and +3. Assume, that the mean is midway between the maximum and minimum. Obtain an estimate of the standard deviation from these figures.

APPENDIX 1

Minitab Examples

(If you are using the WINDOWS version of MINITAB, you might issue the GSTD command first to use standard graphics in the session window. If you want to save your output on a file, use the command OUTFILE 'A:CH5.LIS' to echo output to this file.)

COIN-TOSSING SIMULATIONS

```
# IF YOU TRY THESE SIMULATIONS, EXPECT DIFFERENT RESULTS
# EACH TIME BECAUSE OF SIMULATION'S RANDOM NATURE

MTB > RANDOM 16 OBSERVATIONS INTO C1 C2 C3 C4;
SUBC> BERNOULLI P =  .5.
MTB > LET C5 = C1+C2+C3+C4  # COUNTING HEADS
MTB > PRINT C1-C5
                           # C5 IS THE NUMBER OF HEADS

MTB > STEM C5

MTB > TALLY DATA IN C5;
SUBC> PERCENTS.             # THESE ARE RELATIVE FREQUENCIES
MTB > HIST C5               # ASTERISKS REPRESENT BARS

# INCREASING THE NUMBER OF TOSSES FROM 16 TO 100
MTB > RANDOM 100 OBS. INTO C1-C4;
SUBC> BERNOULLI P = .5.
MTB > LET C5 = C1+C2+C3+C4
MTB > TALLY DATA IN C5;
SUBC> PERCENTS.
```

Comment The Binomial rather than the Bernoulli command gets us directly to column C5 without having to deal with adding C1-C4. Due to the randomness, the relative frequencies change.

```
MTB > RANDOM 100 OBS. INTO C5;
SUBC> BINOMIAL N = 4  P = .5.
```

```
MTB > TALLY DATA IN C5;
SUBC> PERCENTS.
```

Comment   The PDF command computes probabilities for discrete outcomes in C1 and is sometimes called a discrete probability density function.

```
MTB > SET C1
DATA> 0:4
DATA> END

MTB > PDF C1 C6;   # COMPUTES THEORETICAL PROBABILITIES
                   # FOR OUTCOMES IN C1 AND PUTS THEM IN C6
SUBC> BINOMIAL N = 4 P = .5.

MTB > PRINT C1 C6

MTB > SET C1       # IN EFFECT, WE ARE GOING TO BE
                   # TOSSING SIXTEEN COINS AN INFINITE
                   # NUMBER OF TIMES
DATA> 0:16
DATA> END

MTB > PDF C1 C2;   # THEORETICAL PROBABILITIES FOR 0 THRU 16
                   # HEADS ARE COMPUTED AND PLACED IN C2
SUBC> BINOMIAL N = 16 P = .5.
```

Comment   When outcomes are continuous rather than discrete, as with the normal, PDF computes density values for this continuous probability density function.

```
MTB > PDF C1 C3;   # THE DENSITIES FOR THE NORMAL ARE
SUBC> NORMAL MU = 8 SIGMA = 2.   # COMPUTED AND PLACED IN C3
# THE MEAN OF THE NORMAL IS 16*.5 = 8 AND THE STANDARD
# DEVIATION IS (16*.5*.5).5 = 2.

MTB > MPLOT C2 C1 AND C3 C1 # THE A'S ARE FOR THE BINOMIAL
# PROBABILITIES (LENGTHS OF THE VERTICAL LINES); THE B'S
# ARE FOR THE NORMAL DENSITIES (SHOWN AS LINES CONNECTING
# THE POINTS (B'S), REPRESENTING A SMOOTH BELL-SHAPED CURVE).
# THE 2'S ON THE PLOT SHOWS THAT THE A'S AND B'S
# PRACTICALLY COINCIDE.
```

Comment   The normal distribution is not always a good approximation of the binomial. When both N and P are large, N (the number of coins tossed) and P (the probability of a success, heads here), the normal is a good approximation to the binomial. For N = 16 rather than four and P = .5, the theoretical binomial probabilities are generated below and compared to the normal densities. For the normal, we substitute the binomial mean, MU = N*P, and standard deviation, SIGMA = SQRT(N*P*(1 − P)). These are the well-known formulas for the mean and standard deviation of the binomial distribution.

```
MTB > CDF C1 C4;   # USING THE NORMAL APPROXIMATION TO THE
SUBC> NORMAL MU = 8 SIGMA = 2.   # BINOMIAL, C4
#                                   CONTAINS CUMULATIVE
```

```
# PROBABILITIES.  FOR ANY VALUE IN C1, SAY 6, C4 CONTAINS THE
# CUMULATIVE PROBABILITY (PERCENT OF THE TIME) YOU
# EXPECT 6 OR FEWER HEADS AMONG THE SIXTEEN COINS
# YOU TOSSED.

MTB > PLOT C4 C1 # THIS IS A CONTINUOUS CURVE BECAUSE THE
# NORMAL IS A CONTINUOUS APPROXIMATION OF THE DISCRETE BINOMIAL
```

EXAMPLE

FINDING THE PROPORTION OF OBSERVATIONS BETWEEN CERTAIN PRACTICAL LIMITS

```
MTB > INFO
MTB > ERASE C1-C6  # FROM THE PREVIOUS EXAMPLE, NOT NEEDED

MTB > SET Z-SCORES IN C1    # Z-SCORES
DATA> +1 -1
DATA> END

MTB > CDF C1;    # FINDS THE PROPORTION OF OBSERVATIONS
                 # YIELDING THE GIVEN Z-SCORE OR A LESSOR ONE

SUBC> NORMAL MU = 0 SIGMA = 1.

MTB > SET Z-SCORES IN C1  # FOR A 95% INTERVAL
DATA> +2 -2
DATA> END

MTB > CDF C1;
SUBC> NORMAL.    # DEFAULT MEAN = 0 STANDARD DEVIATION = 1
MTB > SET Z-SCORES IN C1
DATA> -4 -3 -2 -1 0 +1 +2 +3 +4
DATA> END

MTB > CDF C1 PUT IN C2; # FINDS THE PROPORTION
SUBC> NORMAL.           # OF OBSERVATIONS
                # YIELDING THE GIVEN Z-SCORE OR A LESSOR ONE
                # PUTS PROPORTIONS IN C2

MTB > PRINT C1 C2  # PROPORTIONS FOR THE APPROPRIATE
                   # INTERVALS
                   # CAN BE FOUND BY SUBTRACTION IN C2

MTB > PLOT C2 C1

# TRACE A CURVE THROUGH THE POINTS ON THE GRAPH; THEN,
# FOR A Z-SCORE ON THE HORIZONTAL AXIS (C1), MOVE VERTICALLY
# TO THE CURVE AND HORIZONTALLY (LEFT) TO THE C2 AXIS AND
# READ OFF THE C2 AXIS THE PROPORTION OF OBSERVATIONS
# YIELDING THE GIVEN Z-SCORE OR A LESSOR ONE. THIS IS
# A CUMULATIVE PLOT OF PROPORTIONS.

GO ON TO ANOTHER EXAMPLE, OR IF FINISHED MTB > STOP
```

EXAMPLE

QUALITY CONTROL—A MANUFACTURING PROCESS IN A STATE OF STATISTICAL CONTROL

(If you have the textbook's data diskette, **RETRIEVE 'B:FRUITDK'** and omit the data entry using SET.)

(If you are on a network and have my data stored in subdirectory DATA under the directory MTBWIN, **RETRIEVE 'FRUITDK';** otherwise, SET the data in columns.)

```
DON'T SET DATA IN C1 IF RETRIEVE WAS SUCCESSFUL
MTB > SET DATA IN C1  # FIGURES ARE ROUNDED OFF; YOU MAY
                      # SHORTEN THIS EXAMPLE USING HALF THE DATA

DATA>  287  288  299  300  293  303  292  300  303  300  299
DATA>  305  300  305  293  297  291  291  302  302  306  293
DATA>  308  297  308  301  303  301  305  300  305  300  295
DATA>  303  303  306  304  291  301  295  308  309  300  296
DATA>  299  302  307  309  297  312  298  303  302  298  299
DATA>  300  300  296  299  300
DATA> END

START HERE IF RETRIEVE SUCCESSFUL

MTB > AVERAGE C1
#   MEAN (SAMPLE) =   300.15

MTB > STANDARD DEVIATION C1
#   ST.DEV. (SAMPLE) = 5.3610

MTB > LET C2 = (C1 - 300.15) / 5.3610
# SUBTRACTING THE MEAN AND DIVIDING BY THE STANDARD DEVIATION IS
# CALLED STANDARDIZING; MORE SPECIFICALLY, STUDENTIZING WHEN
# USING THE SAMPLE MEAN AND SAMPLE STANDARD DEVIATION

MTB > NAME C2 'STDOBS'

# SKIP THIS COMMAND IF THE STUDENT VERSION OF MINITAB DOES NOT
# EXECUTE IT MTB > CENTER C1 C3  # AN ALTERNATIVE WAY TO
# STANDARDIZE, BOTH CENTERING AND SCALING IS DONE HERE!

MTB > DESCRIBE C1 C2

# OR, IF THE CENTER COMMAND WORKED
            MTB > DESCRIBE C1 C2 C3
# NOTICE FROM THIS OUTPUT THAT THE STANDARDIZATION
# PRODUCES A ZERO MEAN AND STANDARD
# DEVIATION EQUAL TO ONE

MTB > PRINT C1 C2    # NOTICE HOW EASY IT IS TO SEE, VIA
# THE STANDARDIZED OBSERVATIONS, WHICH ARE ABOVE OR
# BELOW THE MEAN AND HOW FAR FROM THE MEAN IN TERMS
# OF THE NUMBER OF STANDARD DEVIATIONS AWAY
```

```
MTB > DOTPLOT C2
MTB > HIST C2        # SAME AS DOTPLOT ON ITS SIDE
MTB > RUNS C1    # THIS IS A FORMAL TEST FOR RANDOMNESS
# RECALL THAT SUMMARY STATISTICS ARE MORE REPRESENTATIVE
# OF THE DATA WHEN THE OBSERVATIONS ARE RANDOM, I.E.
# INDEPENDENT OF ONE ANOTHER

CONTROL CHARTS FOR INDIVIDUAL, STANDARDIZED OBSERVATIONS
MTB > SET IN C6      # PREPARING A CONTROL CHART CENTER LINE
DATA> 60(0)          # NO BLANKS ALLOWED IN THIS LINE
DATA> END
MTB > SET IN C7
                     # AN UPPER CONTROL LIMIT AT PLUS 3 STD. DEV.
DATA> 60(3)          # NO BLANKS ALLOWED IN THIS LINE
DATA> END
MTB > SET IN C8
DATA> 60(-3)
DATA> END

# IF USING THE STUDENT VERSION OF MINITAB, YOU MAY HAVE TO
# SKIP THIS COMMAND AND SUBCOMMAND
            MTB > MTSPLOT C2 C6 C7 C8;
            SUBC> START -4.5.
```

Comment   Narrower control limits are used here; therefore, a higher proportion of observations will fall outside them. From what we know about the standard normal distribution, we expect about 33% of the observations to fall outside these limits.

```
MTB > SET IN C7  # TO SET UP NEW +1 AND -1 STD. DEV. LIMITS
DATA> 60(1)         # NO BLANKS ALLOWED IN THIS LINE
DATA> END
MTB > SET IN C8
DATA> 60(-1)
DATA> END

# THE STUDENT VERSION OF MINITAB MAY NOT EXECUTE THIS
# COMMAND AND YOU MAY HAVE TO SKIP IT
            MTB > MTSPLOT C2 C6 C7 C8;
            SUBC> START -4.5.

MTB > NSCORES C1 C4
MTB > DOTPLOT C4
MTB > PRINT C1 C2 C4 # NOTICE HOW CLOSE THE VALUES IN C2
# (STDOBS) ARE TO THE THEORETICAL ONES IN C4
MTB > PLOT C4 C1  # TO SEE IF THE DISTRIBUTION IS NORMAL
                    # IF SO, ROUGHLY, A STRAIGHT LINE RESULTS
                    # ON THIS PLOT

GO ON TO ANOTHER EXAMPLE OR, IF FINISHED  MTB > STOP
```

Comment   To obtain a better feel and develop a standard for what normal might look like on the above plot, you might simulate several sets of data (60 observations each) from a normal using the sample mean and standard deviation. Get NSCORES of each set and plot as done above. For example, the commands that you need are

```
MTB > RANDOM 60 OBSERVATIONS IN C10;
SUBC> NORMAL MU = 300.15 SIGMA = 5.3610.
MTB > NSCORES C10 PUT IN C13
MTB > PLOT C13 C10
```

EXAMPLE

FINDING T VALUES IN MINITAB

Student's t values in MINITAB can be obtained by using the INVerse CDF command. That is, you specify the proportion of observations less than a t value and MINITAB finds the t value for that proportion.

As an example, with a sample size less than 30, say, n = 13, the 95% interval limits are

$$\overline{y} \pm 2.179 \times s$$

This t value is found below in MINITAB.

```
MTB > INVCDF .025;    # 2.5% OF THE T'S LESS THAN -2.1788
SUBC> T V=12.         # T-DISTRIBUTION, (n-1) = 12
#   PROPORTION    T-VALUE
#     0.0250       -2.1788

MTB > INVCDF .975;    # 97.5% OF THE T'S LESS THAN +2.1789
SUBC> T V=12.
#   PROPORTION    T-VALUE
#     0.9750        2.1788
GO ON TO ANOTHER EXAMPLE OR, IF FINISHED MTB>STOP
```

EXAMPLE

BATTERY PRODUCTION VOLTAGE MEASUREMENTS

(If you have the textbook's data diskette, **RETRIEVE 'B:BAT'** and omit the data entry using SET.)

(If you are on a network and have my data stored in subdirectory DATA under the directory MTBWIN, **RETRIEVE 'BAT';** otherwise, SET the data in columns.)

Comment Version ten or more of MINITAB is required and the CAPA macro illustrated below is on drive C: with the given path. The user may have to choose a path appropriate for his or her computer installation.

```
MTB > GPRO  # FOR PROFESSIONAL GRAPHICS
# ALSO, YOU MIGHT TRY  %CAPA C1 1
MTB > %C:\MTBWIN\MACROS\CAPA C1 1;
SUBC> LSPEC 8.90;
SUBC> USPEC 9.10;
SUBC> TARGET 9.
```

CHAPTER 6

A Mix of Tools
for Business
and Economic Data

PRELUDE

Sounds of our country's economic engine echo in terms of variables such as interest rates, mortgage rates, home sales, housing construction, consumer spending, business investment, exports, imports, and so on. These play in the background while the executive listens in the foreground to sales, cost of goods sold, inventory, accounts receivable, assets, income, rate of return and so on. The tune of fortune or woe is played out over time. Time series data analysis helps managers chart a course for the corporate ship.

Some time series, such as the Dow Jones Industrial Index, are unpredictable. Other time series, such as the gross domestic product (GDP), have predictable and random components. Seldom will you find a totally predictable series such as a sum of money compounding at a fixed interest rate.

In this chapter, you will first encounter a totally predictable time series, a sum of money compounding at a fixed rate. Next, some random deposits and withdrawals are introduced, bringing a bit of reality into the process of accumulating money. In a similar way, the national economy has been accumulating for years. Corporate sales figures, particularly those of large, diversified companies, tend to grow like the national economy. For these series, you will learn to sort out what is predictable and what is not. Finally, you will see why series with small growth rates and high variability tend to be unpredictable. ⬥

RATES, RATIOS, AND PERCENTAGES

A **rate** is an amount of one thing (say, games won) in relation to a unit of another thing (games played). A **ratio** is a particular type of rate; for example, (games won)/(games played), also written as (games won):(games played). Sometimes rates are multiplied by 100 to obtain a rate per hundred, a **percentage.**

One rate compared to another is the basis for **relative comparisons.** The subtraction of two amounts is the basis for **absolute comparisons.**

Absolute and Relative Comparisons

Consider the following standings of teams in the Atlantic Division of the Eastern Conference of the National Basketball Association.[1]

	W	L	Pct.	GB
New York	29	16	.644	—
Philadelphia	29	16	.644	—
Boston	27	17	.614	$1\frac{1}{2}$
Washington	16	30	.348	$13\frac{1}{2}$
New Jersey	12	33	.267	17
Miami	10	36	.217	$19\frac{1}{2}$

The top team, New York, won 29 games, nearly twice as many games as Washington's 16. New York's "Pct." is .644 and Washington's is .348. What newspapers label "Pct." is the ratio (games won) to (games played). This compares teams on a relative basis. From row four of the team standings, Washington's winning "Pct." computation is

$$.348 = \frac{16}{16 + 30}$$

The ratio .348 is a particular type of a rate (a winning rate). And although newspapers use the "Pct." label, .348 is not a percentage until it is multiplied by 100.

The alternative absolute comparison depends on the number of games back (GB), which is a function of net wins. The net wins are computed and listed under the third heading of the following standings.

	W	L	Net Wins	GB
New York	29	16	29 − 16 = 13	—
Philadelphia	29	16	29 − 16 = 13	—
Boston	27	17	27 − 17 = 10	$1\frac{1}{2}$
Washington	16	30	16 − 30 = −14	$13\frac{1}{2}$
New Jersey	12	33	12 − 33 = −21	17
Miami	10	36	10 − 36 = −26	$19\frac{1}{2}$

From row five of the standings, New Jersey's 17 games back (of New York or Philadelphia) figure is a function of a difference in net wins. New York's net wins minus New Jersey's is

$$13 - (-21) = 34$$

Half of 34 is 17 games back. If New Jersey wins the next 17 games and New York loses the next 17 games, their records will be even, as shown below.

	W	L	Net Wins	GB
New York	29	16 + 17	29 − 33 = −4	—
New Jersey	12 + 17	33	29 − 33 = −4	$\frac{1}{2}(-4 - (-4)) = 0$

Percentage wins (relative comparison) and games back (absolute comparison) may result in different rankings for particular win and loss records when the teams play an unequal number of games.

The corporate world has managers and supporting organizations of players. In a sense, the corporations are like the basketball teams. When comparing one corporation to another or when comparing the financial performance over time (within an individual corporation), you will encounter both relative and absolute comparisons. In specifying a corporation's liquidity, for example, **net working capital** is defined as current assets minus current liabilities. Over time, net working capital (an absolute comparison figure) is used to determine a company's short-term financing needs. In contrast, when comparing the liquidity of different companies, each company's current assets are divided by current liabilities to yield the **current ratio** for relative comparisons.

ARITHMETIC AND GEOMETRIC PROGRESSIONS

A series that increases or decreases by a constant amount is called an **arithmetic progression.** A series that increases or decreases by a constant percentage (rather than by a constant amount) is called a **geometric progression.**

Arithmetic Progressions

As an example of an arithmetic progression, if you deposit $10 every week in a piggy bank, the sum of money increases arithmetically without interest.

$0 $10 $20 $30 $40 $50

Plotted against week numbers

0   1   2   3   4   5

a straight line results on arithmetically scaled graph paper. Although the amount of growth is constant at $10, this amount is a decreasing proportion of the total accumulation. Thus, in the example that follows, an arithmetic growth pattern for sales might warn management that sales are increasing by a decreasing proportion of each year's sales.

EXAMPLE 1

CUMMINS ENGINE—ARITHMETIC GROWTH IN SALES

Problem Statement   For Cummins Engine Company, plot yearly sales revenue figures over time to assess the growth pattern.[2]

Problem Solution   Although there is some variation from a straight line, the overall pattern is linear; therefore, revenues are increasing arithmetically.

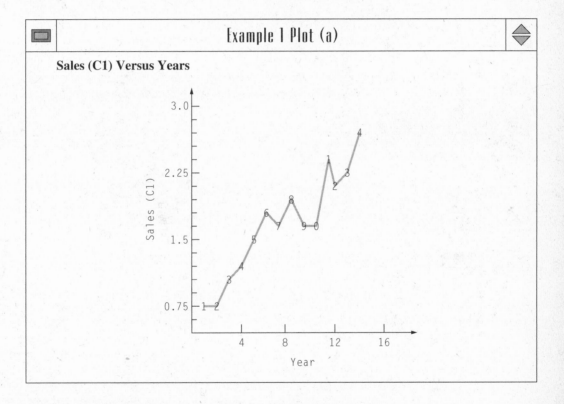

Problem Discussion   Although sales have been increasing by a nearly constant amount of a quarter of a billion dollars per year, this amount is a decreasing proportion of total sales. Perhaps you would not be surprised to learn that the latter part of this period was a bad time financially for Cummins. The management of Cummins should have foreseen problems, particularly if the economy softened, and attempted to improve the sales growth rate through mergers, acquisitions, new products, and so on.

Geometric Progressions

A geometric progression increases or decreases by a constant percentage rather than by a constant amount. As an example, suppose sales revenue of a hot new product increases by a constant percentage of 100% per year (doubling each year). If first-year sales revenue is $200,000, the geometric progression for five years is

$200,000 $400,000 $800,000 $1,600,000 $3,200,000

On arithmetically scaled graph paper, a plot of sales revenue versus years 1, 2, 3, 4, and 5 curves upward, reflecting the increasing amounts. A geometric series that decreases by a constant percentage curves downward. Example 2 illustrates this curvature.

TOTALLY PREDICTABLE GEOMETRIC GROWTH

A basic component of many economic data series is geometric growth. Seldom are these series totally predictable. However, to understand them, it is first necessary to focus on the predictable component.

EXAMPLE 2

GROWING MONEY

Problem Statement (a)   Suppose you are given $1,000 as a graduation gift. Instead of spending it immediately, you save it. Assume that the $1,000 grows at a fixed rate of 10% per year. Calculate future values of the $1,000 plus interest at the end of each year for 20 years, then plot these figures to confirm that the growth is geometric.

Problem Solution (a)   The future values of the $1,000 gift at the end of each year are found by multiplying each beginning year amount by (1 + .10). The results, which are in MINITAB column, C1, are listed and plotted below. The year-end dollar amounts are

```
1100.00   1210.00   1331.00   1464.10   1610.51   1771.56
1948.72 (seventh year, about double)   2143.59   2357.95
2593.74   2853.12   3138.43   3452.27   3797.50   4177.25
4594.97   5054.47   5559.92   6115.91   6727.50
```

Because this series grows geometrically, the plot of the future values curves upward.

Problem Statement (b)   Take the natural logarithms of each year-end dollar amount. Plot and list these figures.

Problem Solution (b)   Notice that the natural logarithms of a geometric series plots as a straight line. The slope of the line, 0.0953, is the approximate growth rate of the series.

Example 2 Plot (a)

Year-End Dollar Amounts Versus Year

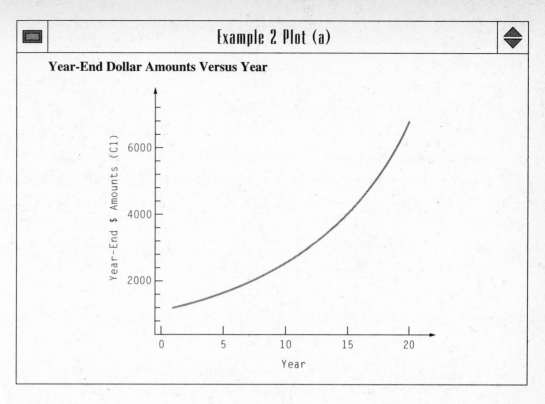

Example 2 Plot (b)

Logs of Year-End Dollar Amounts Versus Year

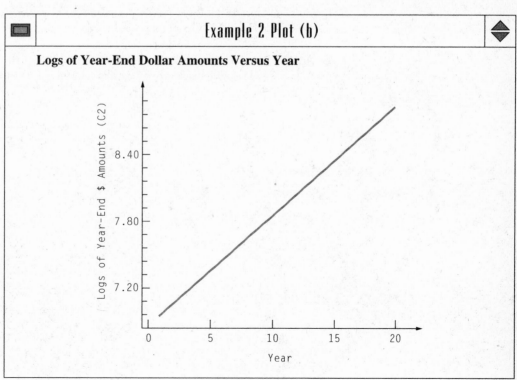

Logs of year-end amounts, C2, are

```
7.00307   7.09838   7.19369   7.28900   7.38431   7.47962
7.57493   7.67024   7.76555   7.86086   7.95617   8.05148
8.14679   8.24210   8.33741   8.43272   8.52803   8.62334
8.71865   8.81396
```

Problem Statement (c)   Subtract adjacent logarithm values to get differences, which is the slope of the above straight line and also the approximate compounding or growth rate.

Problem Solution (c)   These differences are constant, a 9.531% approximate growth rate. When these differences are not constant, the average of the differences approximates the growth rate.

Differences of logs of year-end amounts, C3, are

```
       *      0.0953102   0.0953102   0.0953102   0.0953102
0.0953102   0.0953102   0.0953102   0.0953102   0.0953102
0.0953102   0.0953102   0.0953102   0.0953102   0.0953102
0.0953102   0.0953102   0.0953102   0.0953102   0.0953102
```

Problem Discussion   In most practical applications of the ideas presented in this example, the differences of logs of a geometric series are not constant. Then the compounding rate varies; therefore, the average is used as a typical growth rate. Because the differences are constant in this example, the standard deviation is 0, which indicates no variability.

Rule of 72   For quick thinking about geometric growth, you might find the **rule of 72** useful. To illustrate, if you buy a house for $150,000 and housing prices grow at 7.2% per year (assuming that 7.2% is typical and variations are small), you can expect to sell your house for $300,000 in 10 years. At a 7.2% growth rate, you double your money in about 10 years. Years to double equals $\frac{72}{7.2} = 10$.

Therefore, the rule of 72 says that the approximate number of years (or periods) to double is obtained by dividing 72 by the growth rate. As another example, sales that grow at 10% per year double in $\frac{72}{10}$ or 7.2 years; they double again in another 7.2 years.

> ## S T A T I S T I C A L   H I G H L I G H T S
>
> When using the regular arithmetic scale on each axis of a plot, an arithmetic series plots as a straight line and a geometric series plots as a curved line.

COMPOUNDED GROWTH FLAVORED WITH A BIT OF RANDOM VARIATION

Geometric or compounded growth is rarely as pure as in the last example where the growth rate was a fixed constant. The reality is that growth rates vary about some mean.

EXAMPLE 3

CUMMINS ENGINE, A GEOMETRIC VIEW

Cummins Engine sales in billions of dollars are listed below for 14 years. A plot of these sales revenue figures (Example 1 plot (a)) looked arithmetic rather than geometric. When the average growth rate is small over a short time span, it is difficult to distinguish between arithmetic and geometric growth on a time series plot. Longer time spans give the curvature in a geometric series time to develop. Nevertheless, approximate compounding rates can be found and averaged as demonstrated here.

Sales in billions of dollars are

.8　.76　1.03　1.26　1.52　1.77　1.67　1.96　1.59　1.60　2.33
2.15　2.30　2.77

Problem Statement (a)　Take natural logarithms of Cummins Engine sales values and subtract adjacent values to get differences that approximate geometric growth rates. Plot these approximate growth rates in the observed sequence and examine.

Problem Solution (a)　Natural logarithms of these sales figures are taken and differences are found. These differences are the approximate yearly growth rates in column C3.

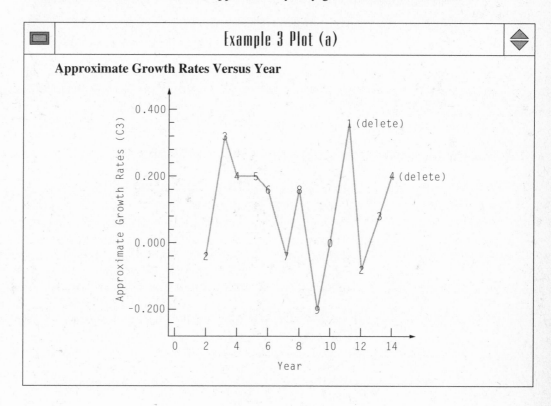

Example 3 Plot (a)

Approximate Growth Rates Versus Year

In the plot on page 255, if you delete two data points, the last and the fourth from the last, the remaining points will no longer look random because a pattern becomes evident. To see the pattern, cover those two points with your hand. Then notice that the growth rate pattern of the remaining points has a tendency to fall off with time. This is exactly what happens when a series is growing arithmetically. This explains why the original plot of sales over time looked linear.

Problem Statement (b)   From growth rate summary statistics, select a typical growth rate and a variability measure. Are these summary measures valid?

Problem Solution (b)   The plot of all approximate growth rates has no pattern and appears random; therefore, summary statistics will be valid. For a normal distribution, the average compounding rate of 9.55% would be thought of as typical. However, because the mean and median are so different, the normality assumption is doubted. Therefore, the median of 15.23% is preferred as a typical value under an optimistic financial planning scenario. A standard deviation of 16.71% is large relative to the mean and draws attention to the substantial year-to-year changes in sales.

	N	N*	MEAN	MEDIAN	STDEV
C3	13	1	0.0955	0.1523	0.1671

	MIN	MAX	Q1	Q3
C3	-0.2092	0.3759	-0.0547	0.1946

THE RANDOM, UNPREDICTABLE PART OF A TIME SERIES

You have seen two contrasting examples of geometric growth. First, perfectly predictable accumulations of principal and interest were found when compounding money at a 10% growth rate. From changes in logarithms of these accumulations, an approximate growth rate average was 9.531% with a standard deviation of 0 (no variability). In the second case, yearly sales for Cummins Engine were not perfectly predictable and yearly growth rates varied with an average of 9.55% and a standard deviation of 16.71%. Many real-life growth situations are more like Cummins Engine sales than the compounding money example. That is, the element of unpredictability or randomness is pervasive. We examine this random component of growth in more detail later in this section.

EXAMPLE 4

GROWING MONEY—RANDOM DEPOSITS AND WITHDRAWALS

Suppose you put the $1,000 graduation gift into a separate bank account. At the beginning of each year, you make a single deposit or withdrawal. As the years go by, assume that the transaction amounts tend to increase. Thus, the accumulation of money becomes more realistic.

Problem Statement (a)   Let the $1,000 collect interest and grow at 10% per year. Simulate the deposits and withdrawals from a normal distribution with a zero mean and an increasing standard deviation. Let the standard deviation begin at $100 and grow at a 10% per year rate. Plot the year-end accumulations of dollars. List these figures as well as deposits and withdrawals. Does the growth appear to be geometric?

Problem Solution (a)   The random deposits and withdrawals are small enough so that the geometric growth pattern dominates the plot below. Nevertheless, these deposits and withdrawals at the beginning of each year change the yearly growth rates, making each year's growth rate different from the 10%. The year-end dollar accumulations are in column C1.

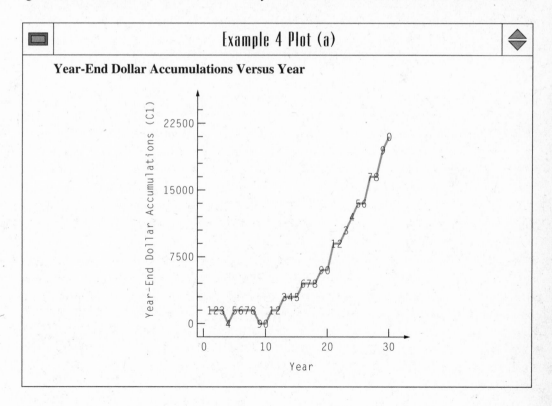

Example 4 Plot (a)

Year-End Dollar Accumulations Versus Year

The year-end dollar balances in the account are

841.0	913.6	842.6	711.7	857.5	899.2	985.9
823.1	537.4	707.0	1112.6	1663.3	2340.0	2783.7
3445.9	4233.1	4213.8	4983.8	5925.3	6583.2	8378.7
9285.4	10026.3	12353.6	13064.2	13988.7	15859.3	17124.3
18859.9	20478.6					

The deposits (+'s) and withdrawals (−'s) for the beginning of each year are

-235.42	-10.48	-147.60	-195.58	+67.82	-40.07
-2.92	-237.62	-334.54	+105.30	+304.50	+399.42
+464.03	+190.60	+348.95	+402.33	-402.38	+316.94
+402.83	+59.50	+1033.78	+62.55	-170.62	+1204.27
-477.07	-347.19	+428.93	-291.84	+21.11	-242.97

Problem Statement (b) Take natural logs (base e) of the year-end dollar accumulations in C1. Difference the logs to approximate yearly growth rates and plot. What does the plot show?

Problem Solution (b) The approximate yearly growth rates appear in column C3 and are plotted below.

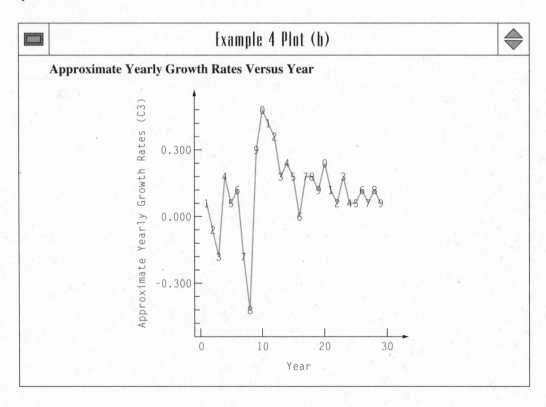

The growth rates show a decrease in variability over time as funds have accumulated to higher levels. This nonconstant variance phenomenon results in accumulations of money that are less sensitive to the pattern of deposits and withdrawals. As time progresses, the 10% compounding rate begins to dominate the accumulations.

Problem Statement (c)   Test for randomness of the approximate growth rates using a runs test. What implication does randomness have on growth rate summary statistics?

Problem Solution (c)   The results of the runs test below confirm that the growth rates are random even though the rates show some decrease in variability over time. Thus, summary statistics such as sample means and standard deviations are meaningful.

```
C3     RESULTS OF A RUNS TEST FOR RANDOMNESS
K =     0.1101
THE OBSERVED NO. OF RUNS =  13
THE EXPECTED NO. OF RUNS =  15.3448
13 OBSERVATIONS ABOVE K     16 BELOW
           THE TEST IS SIGNIFICANT AT 0.3701
           CANNOT REJECT AT ALPHA = 0.05
```

Problem Statement (d)   Summary statistics are even more meaningful if the distribution of approximate growth rates is normal. Use a histogram of growth rates to assess normality.

Problem Solution (d)   The distribution of growth rates is approximately normal.

```
Histogram of C3    N = 29

Midpoint   Count
   -0.4      1   *
   -0.3      0
   -0.2      2   **
   -0.1      1   *
    0.0      2   **
    0.1     11   ***********
    0.2      8   ********
    0.3      2   **
    0.4      1   *
    0.5      1   *
```

Problem Statement (e)   Summarize the approximate growth rates.

Problem Solution (e)   The average approximate growth rate is 11%, which is close to the known actual rate of 10%. The standard deviation of 17.53% characterizes the variability.

	N	MEAN	MEDIAN	STDEV
C3	29	0.1101	0.1027	0.1753

	MIN	MAX	Q1	Q3
C3	-0.4263	0.4535	0.0622	0.2072

EXAMPLE 5

ECONOMIC GROWTH—THE GROSS DOMESTIC PRODUCT (GDP)

National economic growth is geometric with varying rates. This growth is reflected in the gross domestic product (GDP), which measures the heartbeat of the national economy. Sales revenues of many corporations are related to GDP fluctuations. When the GDP goes up or down, sales tend to follow. Hence, corporate executives monitor GDP fluctuation.

The following 26 years of GDP figures are seasonally adjusted and in billions of dollars:[3]

533.8	574.6	606.9	649.8	705.1	772.0	816.4	892.7
963.9	1015.5	1102.7	1212.8	1359.3	1472.8	1598.4	1782.8
1990.5	2249.7	2508.2	2732.0	3052.6	3166.0	3405.7	3772.2
4010.3	4235.0						

Problem Statement (a)   Plot the GDP figures over time. Does the growth appear to be geometric?

Problem Solution (a)   The plot of GDP figures curves upward and appears to be growing geometrically.

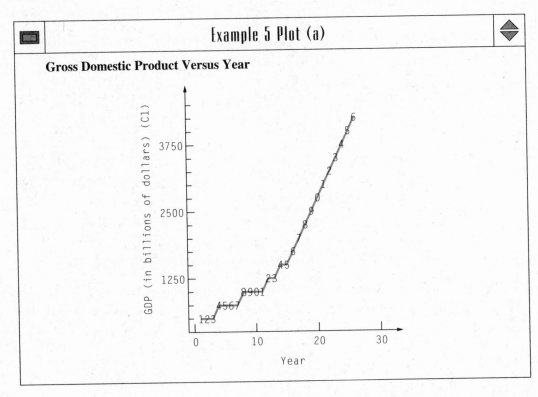

Problem Statement (b) Take natural logs (base e) of the GDP figures in C1. Difference the logs to approximate yearly growth rates and plot. What does the plot show?

Problem Solution (b) The approximate yearly growth rates appear in column C3 and are plotted below. Although there is a cluster of years with higher-than-average growth rates, they appear to be random.

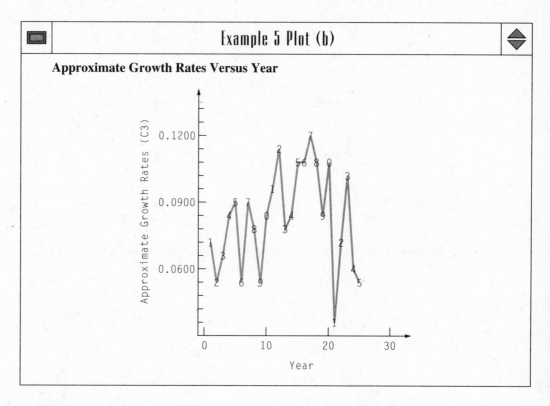

Problem Statement (c) Test for randomness of the approximate growth rates using a runs test. What implication does randomness have on growth rate summary statistics?

Problem Solution (c) The results of the runs test below confirm that the growth rates are random. Thus, summary statistics such as sample means and standard deviations are meaningful.

```
K =     0.0828
THE OBSERVED NO. OF RUNS =  11
THE EXPECTED NO. OF RUNS =  13.3200
11 OBSERVATIONS ABOVE K   14 BELOW
         THE TEST IS SIGNIFICANT AT  0.3361
         CANNOT REJECT AT ALPHA = 0.05
```

Problem Statement (d)   Summary statistics are even more meaningful if the distribution of approximate growth rates is normal. Use a histogram of growth rates to assess normality.

Problem Solution (d)   The distribution of growth rates is approximately normal.

```
Histogram of C3    N = 25

Midpoint    Count
   0.04        1    *
   0.05        3    ***
   0.06        2    **
   0.07        3    ***
   0.08        5    *****
   0.09        3    ***
   0.10        2    **
   0.11        5    *****
   0.12        1    *
```

Problem Statement (e)   Summarize the approximate growth rates.

Problem Solution (e)   The average approximate annual growth rate is 8.284% and the standard deviation of 2.273% characterizes the variability. The standard deviation is small relative to the mean. Therefore, the geometric growth dominates the initial GDP plot, making variations relatively hard to see.

```
              N     MEAN    MEDIAN    STDEV
C3           25  0.08284   0.08184  0.02273

            MIN      MAX        Q1       Q3
C3      0.03648  0.12241   0.06475  0.10549
```

STATISTICAL HIGHLIGHTS

Differences of the natural logs of a series can be used to approximate growth rates of a geometric series. The average difference approximates the average growth rate of the series. When the differences are random and normally distributed, 95% of the time the approximate growth rates are within ± 2 standard deviations of the mean.

EXAMPLE 6

HOUSE PRICES ON THE RISE

Examine the following median sales prices of new, privately owned, one-family houses in the United States over an 18 year period:[4]

23.4　25.2　27.6　32.5　35.9　39.3　44.2　48.8　55.7
62.9　64.6　68.9　69.3　75.3　79.9　84.3　92.0　104.5

Problem Statement (a)　Plot these prices and assess the growth pattern.

Problem Solution (a)　The plot of prices appears linear. Therefore, the growth is arithmetic and increases by a nearly constant amount.

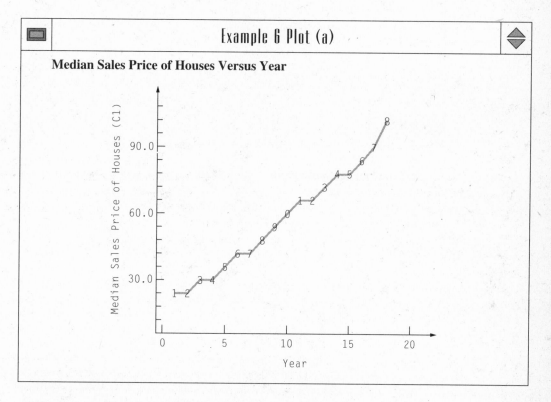

Example 6 Plot (a)

Median Sales Price of Houses Versus Year

Problem Statement (b)　Because this series is arithmetic, find changes in the median sales prices, plot, and check for randomness and normality.

Problem Solution (b)　Year-to-year price changes in C2 are plotted below. These differences in prices are examined to get a feel for price-change amounts. Price increases average about $5,000 per year, ignoring the last year's unusually large increase.

Example 6 Plot (b)

Changes in Median House Prices Versus Year

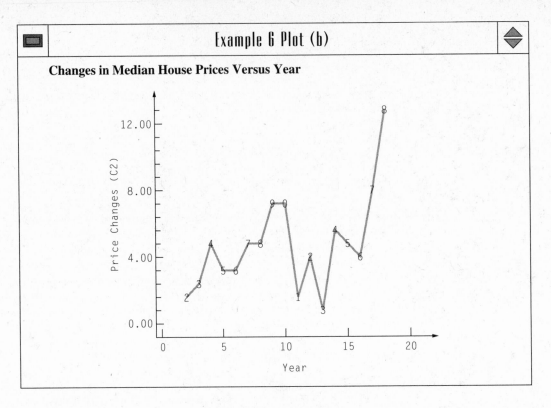

Except for one outlying point, these changes are roughly normal in distribution as shown by the histogram below.

```
Histogram of C2    N = 17    N* = 1

 Midpoint   Count
       0      1    *
       1      0
       2      3    ***
       3      2    **
       4      2    **
       5      4    ****
       6      1    *
       7      2    **
       8      1    *
       9      0
      10      0
      11      0
      12      0
      13      1    *
```

    Although the sample size is small, these changes are random as verified by the following runs test.

```
C2 (Runs Test)
K =      4.7706
THE OBSERVED NO. OF RUNS =  10
THE EXPECTED NO. OF RUNS =   9.2353
  7 OBSERVATIONS ABOVE K   10 BELOW
* N SMALL--FOLLOWING APPROX. MAY BE INVALID
           THE TEST IS SIGNIFICANT AT  0.6920
           CANNOT REJECT AT ALPHA = 0.05
```

Problem Statement (c)   Find summary statistics to sharpen the earlier visual impressions.

Problem Solution (c)   The average price change is \$4,771 per year. The standard deviation is much smaller than the mean; hence, the variability does not obscure the growth pattern.

	N	MEAN	MEDIAN	STDEV
C2	17	4.771	4.600	2.822

	MIN	MAX	Q1	Q3
C2	0.400	12.500	2.900	6.450

Problem Statement (d)   Proceed to examine this series as if it were geometric, using differences in logs of prices to approximate growth rates. Notice that the approximate growth rates tend to decrease with time and are not random, which makes the summary statistics less useful.

Problem Solution (d)   By taking the logs (base e) of sales prices in C1 and then the differences, approximate growth rates are obtained and plotted below. Except for the last year, the approximate growth rates tend to decrease over time as expected for arithmetic growth. Also, growth rates in the first 9 years tend to be higher than in the subsequent 6 years. Therefore, we suspect that the data are nonrandom.

    The impression of nonrandomness is confirmed by the runs test results shown below.

```
C3
K =      0.0880
THE OBSERVED NO. OF RUNS =   4
THE EXPECTED NO. OF RUNS =   9.4706
  9 OBSERVATIONS ABOVE K    8 BELOW
* N SMALL--FOLLOWING APPROX. MAY BE INVALID
  THE TEST IS SIGNIFICANT AT  0.0061
```

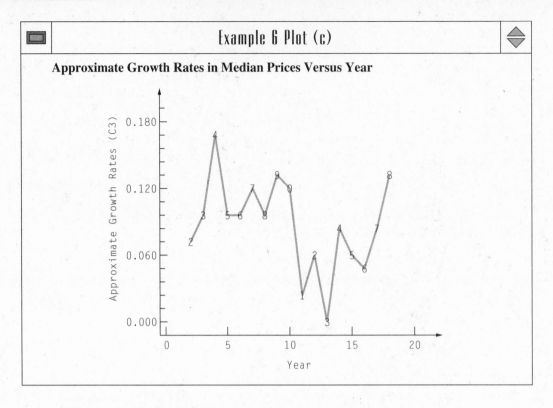

Example 6 Plot (c)

Approximate Growth Rates in Median Prices Versus Year

A histogram is used to check for normality.

```
Histogram of C3    N = 17

  Midpoint   Count
    0.00      1    *
    0.02      1    *
    0.04      0
    0.06      3    ***
    0.08      3    ***
    0.10      4    ****
    0.12      3    ***
    0.14      1    *
    0.16      1    *
```

Although the histogram indicates a normal distribution, the nonrandom behavior of the growth rates makes the summary statistics below misleading. You would not want to rely on the summary statistics alone without the qualifications that come from examining the plots.

	N	MEAN	MEDIAN	STDEV
C3	17	0.08803	0.09049	0.03934

	MIN	MAX	Q1	Q3
C3	0.00579	0.16342	0.06187	0.11953

HIGH VARIATION RELATIVE TO THE AVERAGE GROWTH RATE

So far, curvature has been the dominant feature on plots of geometric growth series such as the GDP. For arithmetic growth, straightness has been the dominant feature. These features stood out clearly because of the small standard deviation relative to the average growth rate. Many series have muted features and are less predictable. The next two examples illustrate unpredictable series, which are different from what you have seen so far. Stock market indices will be examined over time. You will find that the standard deviation of growth rates will be considerably larger than the mean, making growth patterns indefinite.

EXAMPLE 7

THE STOCK MARKET, YEARLY

The following Dow Jones average figures of 65 stock prices (30 industrial stocks, 20 transportation stocks, and 15 utility stocks) are examined over a 26-year period.[5]

232.44	221.07	253.67	294.23	318.50	308.70	314.79	322.19
301.35	243.92	298.12	319.36	286.73	237.33	247.25	303.91
301.70	283.63	293.46	328.23	364.61	345.40	472.24	463.10
541.56	702.50						

You will see that the growth rate variability is high relative to the average, which raises questions about the predictability of the Dow Jones average and indicates that there is some investment risk.

Problem Statement   Plot the Dow Jones average. Find and plot approximate growth rates. Test for randomness and summarize. Pay particular attention to how large the standard deviation is relative to the mean approximate growth rate. What do you conclude about the predictability of this series?

Problem Solution   In the last four years, notice that the Dow roared upward, increasing geometrically. However, the figures meandered more in prior years where the growth pattern was obscured by the variability.

By taking the logs (base e) of C1 and then the differences, approximate growth rates are obtained and placed in C3.

According to the results of a runs test shown below, the approximate growth rates in C3 are random; therefore, summary statistics are meaningful.

```
C3
K =      0.0442
THE OBSERVED NO. OF RUNS =  12
THE EXPECTED NO. OF RUNS =  13.3200
11 OBSERVATIONS ABOVE K   14 BELOW
          THE TEST IS SIGNIFICANT AT  0.5841
          CANNOT REJECT AT ALPHA = 0.05
```

Example 7 Plot (a)

Dow Jones Average Versus Year

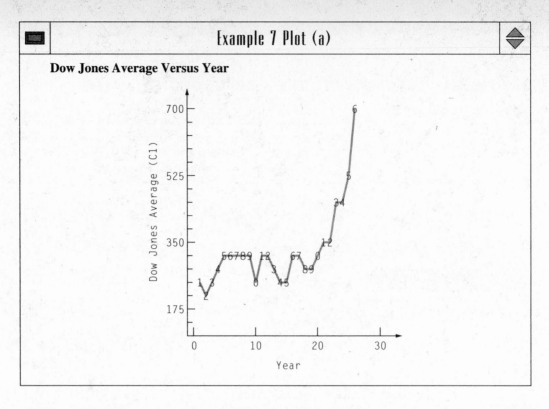

Example 7 Plot (b)

Approximate Growth Rates of the Dow Versus Year

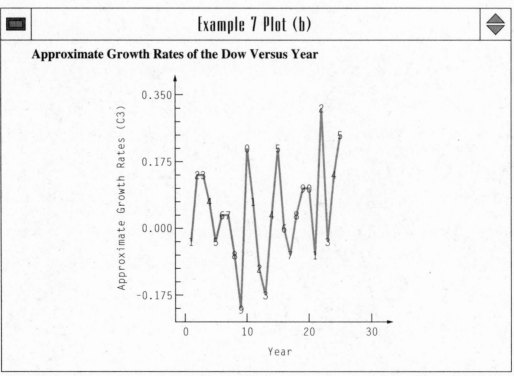

The following summary statistics confirm preliminary impressions. The mean of 4.42% indicates that the average approximate growth rate per year is small. The standard deviation of 13.08% is much larger than the mean. Therefore, the variability tends to swamp the growth pattern and makes the Dow Jones average unpredictable.

	N	MEAN	MEDIAN	STDEV
C3	25	0.0442	0.0341	0.1308

	MIN	MAX	Q1	Q3
C3	-0.2114	0.3128	-0.0521	0.1429

EXAMPLE 8

THE STOCK MARKET, MONTHLY

The following monthly Dow Jones average figures of 30 industrial stocks are examined over a four-year period.[6]

1064	1078	1129	1168	1212	1221	1213	1189	1237	1252	1250	1257
1258	1164	1161	1152	1143	1121	1113	1212	1213	1199	1211	1188
1238	1283	1268	1266	1279	1314	1343	1326	1317	1351	1432	1517
1534	1652	1757	1807	1801	1867	1809	1843	1813	1817	1883	1924

Compared to the 26 years of the previous example, this is a relatively short time span. You will find that the Dow's movement pattern is not clearly arithmetic or geometric; yet, considerable growth occurs. This four-year growth pattern falsely gives the impression of longer-term predictability; long-term predictability was cast into doubt in the previous example. This false sense of predictability keeps the chartists in business.

Problem Statement (a)   Plot the monthly Dow Jones average. Find and plot monthly changes. Test for randomness and normality and summarize. Pay particular attention to how large the standard deviation is relative to the mean changes. What do you conclude about the predictability of this series?

Problem Solution (a)   The monthly Dow Jones average of 30 stock prices is known to be a random walk. Here it meanders upward, giving the impression of predictability. Yet, as you see from this four-year period, you can be fooled into believing that there is something that can be gained by charting the Dow Jones average.

Month-to-month changes in the Dow are in C2 and plotted below to get a feel for the change amounts.

Monthly changes in the Dow are random, as indicated by the runs test results.

```
C2
K =    18.2979
THE OBSERVED NO. OF RUNS =  20
THE EXPECTED NO. OF RUNS =  23.6383
19 OBSERVATIONS ABOVE K   28 BELOW
         THE TEST IS SIGNIFICANT AT  0.2652
         CANNOT REJECT AT ALPHA = 0.05
```

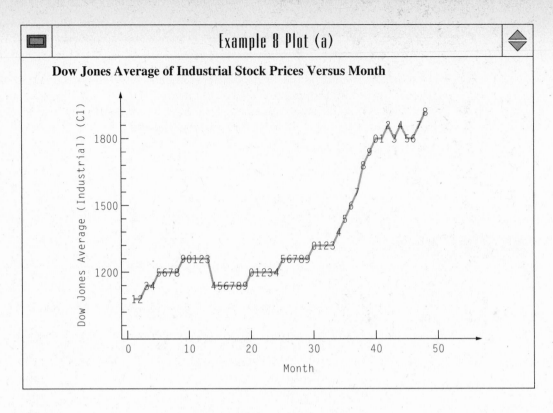

Dow Jones Average of Industrial Stock Prices Versus Month

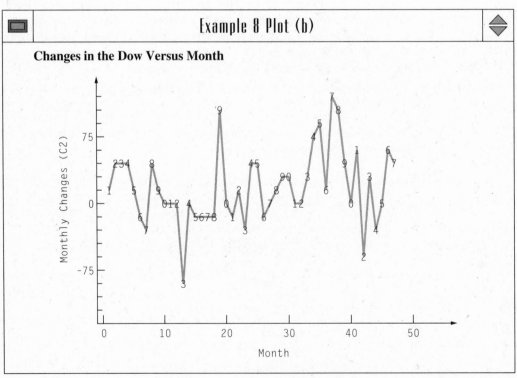

Changes in the Dow Versus Month

Monthly changes in the Dow are not quite normal. The distribution is skewed in the direction of positive changes.

```
Histogram of C2    N=47

  Midpoint   Count
     -100       1   *
      -80       0
      -60       1   *
      -40       0
      -20       7   *******
        0      14   **************
       20       6   ******
       40       8   ********
       60       5   *****
       80       2   **
      100       2   **
      120       1   *
```

During this period, the Dow stepped upward at an average of 18.30 points per month with a standard deviation of 41.69 points. Without the longer-term perspective of the previous example, you might be fooled into thinking the series is predictable.

```
             N     MEAN   MEDIAN    STDEV
C2          47    18.30    12.00    41.69

           MIN      MAX       Q1       Q3
C2      -94.00   118.00    -9.00    45.00
```

Problem Statement (b) Find and plot approximate growth rates. Test for randomness and normality and summarize. Pay particular attention to how large the standard deviation is relative to the mean approximate growth rate. What do you conclude about the predictability of this series?

Problem Solution (b) By taking the logs (base e) of C1 and then the differences, approximate growth rates are obtained and placed in C3. In the plot below, these rates appear random.

According to the results of a runs test shown below, the approximate growth rates in C3 are random.

```
C3
K =     0.0126
THE OBSERVED NO. OF RUNS =  19
THE EXPECTED NO. OF RUNS =  23.9787
20 OBSERVATIONS ABOVE K   27 BELOW
        THE TEST IS SIGNIFICANT AT  0.1333
(RANDOM) CANNOT REJECT AT ALPHA = 0.05
```

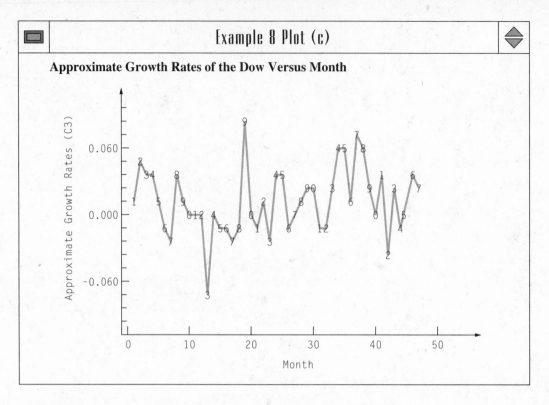

Example 8 Plot (c)

Approximate Growth Rates of the Dow Versus Month

The rates are not quite normal. However, the distribution is not badly skewed. As a result, the summary statistics will be meaningful.

```
Histogram of C3    N=47

Midpoint    Count
  -0.08        1    *
  -0.06        0
  -0.04        1    *
  -0.02        7    *******
   0.00       15    ***************
   0.02       10    **********
   0.04        8    ********
   0.06        3    ***
   0.08        2    **
```

From the summary statistics below, the monthly mean rate seems low at 1.26 %. However, 12 times 1.26% roughly approximates a substantial yearly compounding rate of over 15%.

```
          N      MEAN    MEDIAN    STDEV
C3       47   0.01260   0.00996  0.02982

          MIN      MAX        Q1       Q3
C3   -0.07766  0.08521  -0.00716  0.03568
```

Problem Discussion   This four-year view may lead you to believe that these high stock market returns may continue far into the future. Such continuation is doubtful because long-term stock market returns are historically lower. For example, the yearly growth rate in the previous example of 65 stocks was 4.42%.

S T A T I S T I C A L   H I G H L I G H T S

When the average approximate growth rate of a series is small relative to the standard deviation, and when this average ± 2 standard deviations includes zero in the interval, such series tend to be unpredictable.

COMPARING TWO SERIES

We will use an interesting data set on the earnings of men and women to further illustrate some principles we have learned. The data set is deliberately very small so that certain details of the analysis stand out. Scatterplots become very useful, particularly after various data transformations take place. Obviously, this examination is exploratory because it depends on a small data set. A more detailed, follow-up study would be expected.

E X A M P L E   9

COMPARING EARNINGS OF MEN AND WOMEN

The following median, yearly, full-time earnings of women and men summarize six 5-year intervals. The consumer price index (CPI) is included in column C3 for cost-of-living adjustment purposes. The CPI = 100 in the base year.[7]

C1	C2	C3	C4
WOMEN	MEN	CPI	TIME INTERVAL
3,257	5,368	88.7	1
3,828	6,388	94.5	2
5,323	8,966	116.3	3
7,504	12,758	161.2	4
11,197	18,612	246.8	5
15,624	24,195	322.2	6

Problem Statement (a)   Plot median earnings for men and women on the same plot, but code the plotting points differently.

Problem Solution (a)   The plotting symbols are "B" for men and "A" for women. Men consistently had higher earnings. In fact, the earnings gap appears to widen slightly over time.

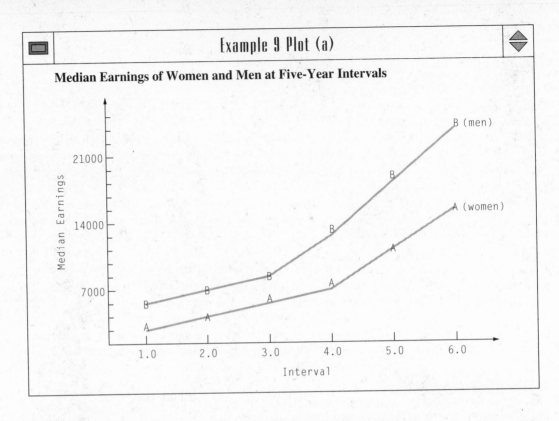

Example 9 Plot (a)

Median Earnings of Women and Men at Five-Year Intervals

Problem Statement (b)   Compute logs of earnings and plot again.

Problem Solution (b)   By taking the logs (base e) and plotting again, nearly parallel straight lines result, which indicate geometric growth. The slopes of the lines approximate the growth rates. A slightly steeper slope for women indicates that their earnings relative to men improved during the last two 5-year periods. This is in contrast to the impression obtained in problem solution (a).

Problem Statement (c)   To magnify the differences in the previous plot, subtract the logs of earnings for women from those of men. In other words, subtract the "A" values from the "B" values. Plot these differences.

Problem Solution (c)   The log earnings differences first increase and then decrease.

Problem Statement (d)   Plot the differences between actual earnings in absolute terms and current dollars to show how much women have lagged behind men in dollar terms.

Problem Solution (d)   The differences in earnings appear to increase arithmetically.

Example 9 Plot (b)

Logs of Earnings Versus Interval

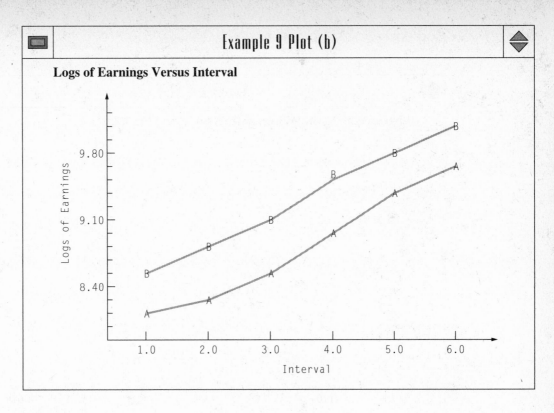

Example 9 Plot (c)

Differences in Logs of Earnings Versus Interval

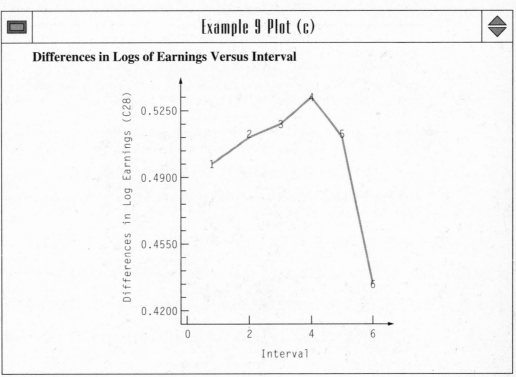

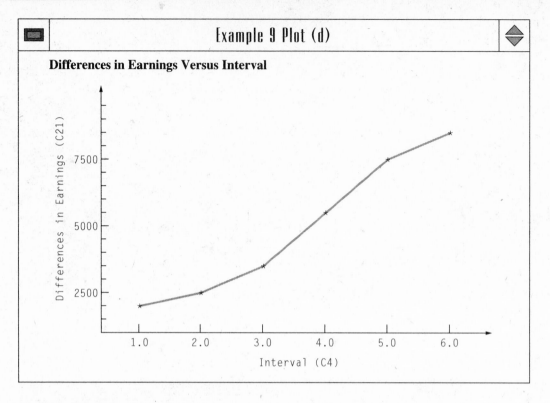

Example 9 Plot (d)

Differences in Earnings Versus Interval

Problem Statement (e)   Plot the ratio of earnings of men to women.

Problem Solution (e)   This plot reflects what was learned earlier, that the earnings ratio of men to women dropped during the last two five-year intervals.

Problem Statement (f)   Find the differences of the logs (base e) of women's earnings to approximate earnings growth rates for five-year periods. These approximate growth rates are in column C25.

Problem Solution (f)   For every five-year period, the average women's earnings are compounded by about 31.35%.

	N	MEAN	MEDIAN	STDEV
C25	5	0.3136	0.3332	0.0897

	MIN	MAX	Q1	Q3
C25	0.1615	0.4002	0.2456	0.3718

Problem Statement (g)   Find the differences of the logs (base e) of men's earnings to approximate earnings growth rates for five-year periods. These approximate growth rates are in column C26.

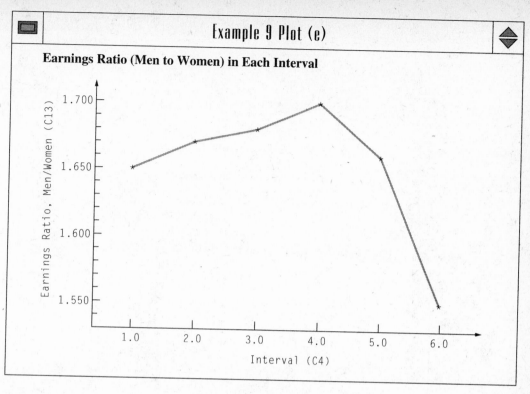

Example 9 Plot (e)

Earnings Ratio (Men to Women) in Each Interval

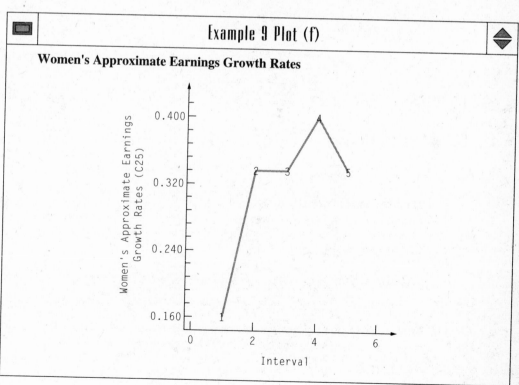

Example 9 Plot (f)

Women's Approximate Earnings Growth Rates

Problem Solution (g)   For every five-year period, the average men's earnings are compounded by about 30.11%.

	N	MEAN	MEDIAN	STDEV
C26	5	0.3011	0.3390	0.0831

	MIN	MAX	Q1	Q3
C26	0.1740	0.3776	0.2182	0.3652

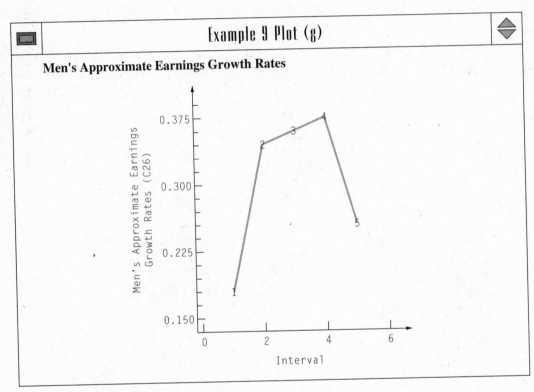

Example 9 Plot (g)

Men's Approximate Earnings Growth Rates

Problem Statement (h)   Recall that C21 = C2 − C1. This equation represents the earnings difference amount that women lag behind men in absolute dollar terms. C3 is the consumer price index. Find and plot $C27 = \frac{C21}{C3}$, which is the earnings difference deflated and expressed in CPI base-year dollars.

Problem Solution (h)   The deflated earnings differences are

2379.93   2708.99   3132.42   3259.31   3004.46   2660.15

In the plot below, these deflated earnings differences dropped in the last two 5-year periods, which is in contrast to the nondeflated figures in problem solution (d).

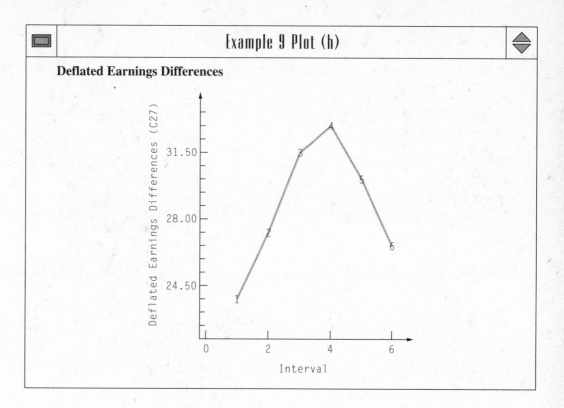

Example 9 Plot (h)

Deflated Earnings Differences

CHAPTER SUMMARY

We first illustrated absolute and relative comparisons by contrasting wins and losses of several professional basketball teams. In making these comparisons, we defined rates, ratios, and percentages.

Managers must deal with time series data such as sales revenues, profits, the gross domestic product, the Dow Jones average, economic indices, and rates of return. Some of these variables exhibit patterned growth. Two basic growth patterns are arithmetic (changes by constant amounts) and geometric (changes by constant percentages). The basic patterns often include some random variation. The random part is unpredictable; however, the amount of variability can be characterized by the standard deviation.

Some series are totally unpredictable (completely random), such as changes in the Dow Jones average. Because changes in the Dow can't be predicted, a plot of the Dow

Jones average (the original series and not the changes) tends to meander. Seldom do you find a totally predictable series like an amount of money compounding at a fixed rate of interest.

Managers frequently see time series data that are partially predictable and partially unpredictable (random). The predictable part can be characterized and explained; the unpredictable part remains unexplained except for some statement about the variability in terms of the standard deviation. The predictability of time series fluctuations is related to the ratio of the predictable to the unpredictable components of the mixture.

The analysis toolbox included plots, log transformations, differences, randomness and normality tests, means, standard deviations, and standard deviations relative to means.

KEY TERMS

absolute comparisons, 249	net working capital, 250	relative comparisons, 249
arithmetic progression, 250	percentage, 249	rule of 72, 254
current ratio, 250	rate, 249	
geometric progression, 250	ratio, 249	

EXERCISES

1. Prices of commodities, services, housing, and other consumer items are reflected in the Consumer Price Index (CPI). Eighteen yearly CPI figures are shown below.[8]

56.9	60.6	65.2	72.6	82.4	90.9	96.5	99.6	103.9	107.6
109.6	113.6	118.3	124.0	130.7	136.2	140.3	144.5		

Characterize the growth of the CPI. Is it arithmetic, geometric, or some other pattern? Is it predictable, unpredictable, or a mixture of the two?

2. Search data sources at a local library and find sales or other company financial data over time (one source might be *Moody's Industrial Manual*). For an individual company, collect data on several variables such as sales, cost of sales, and income.

Analyze these series individually and speculate about their relationships. In particular, determine the growth rates of sales, cost of sales, and income. When the cost of sales grows faster than sales, income usually suffers. Does the data support this proposition? In the analysis process, make liberal use of time series plots. Use ratios and transformations where necessary.

3. Display the geometric growth of $1,000 at different interest rates, say, 5%, 15%, and 25%.

4. One example in this chapter involved growing money at a fixed rate with random deposits and withdrawals. Conduct a similar exercise of your own; however, increase the size of the deposits and withdrawals by increasing the standard deviation of the normal distribution that generates them.

(a) What effect does this increase in variation have on the resulting series? Is it more or less predictable? Show the time series plot.

(b) Suppose you did not know how these figures were generated. Approximate the distribution of deposits and withdrawals. Find its mean and standard deviation.

5. The National Transportation Safety Board keeps statistics on airline safety. Given the yearly number of departures in millions and the number of fatal accidents shown below,[9] find and plot the number of fatal accidents per 100,000 departures. Is the latter series random? Does airline safety get better or worse over this period? If there is a pattern to the fatal accidents per 100,000 departures, is it arithmetic, geometric, or neither?

FATAL ACCIDENTS

2 3 5 4 0 4 4 4 1 4 2 4 3 11 6 4 4 1

DEPARTURES

4.8	4.9	5.0	5.4	5.4	5.2	5.0	5.0	5.4
5.8	6.4	6.6	6.7	6.6	6.9	6.8	7.1	7.2

6. A machine tool company's current assets and current liabilities in millions of dollars for 12 years are shown below.

CURRENT ASSETS

701   690   640   730   780   760   880   1000   1100   1200   1050   1060

CURRENT LIABILITIES

430   380   220   305   370   320   400   650   660   700   690   680

(a) Compute and plot the current ratio, which is current assets divided by current liabilities. The lower the current ratio, the greater the current liabilities relative to current assets. Characterize the behavior of this series.

(b) Plot the natural logarithms of current assets and current liabilities. Characterize the behavior of this series.

(c) Was the numerator or the denominator responsible for the drop in the current ratio over time? How did the components of the current ratio grow—arithmetically, geometrically, or otherwise? Are the growth rates the same?

7. Total U.S. population figures (in millions of persons), at the end of ten-year intervals starting in 1900 are[10]

76.2   92.2   106.0   123.2   132.2   151.3   179.3   203.3   226.5   248.7

Analyze the population growth pattern and predict the U.S. population at a point ten years into the future. Write a short summary of your analysis.

8. Divorce rates per thousand every five years starting in 1900 are[11]

0.7   0.8   0.9   1.0   1.6   1.5   1.6   1.7   2.0
5.5   2.6   2.3   2.2   2.5   3.5   4.8   5.2   5.0

Plot and analyze the data. Do these figures follow a random walk? In other words, do divorce rate changes behave randomly with a small mean and a relatively large standard deviation?

9. Analyze the growth patterns of the total number of births and the total number of deaths in the United States in millions, starting in 1955 in five-year intervals.[12]

BIRTHS

4.10   4.26   3.76   3.73   3.14   3.61   3.75   4.11

DEATHS

1.53   1.71   1.83   1.92   1.89   1.99   2.08   2.16

10. Find a time series that interests you. Analyze it. Build a MINITAB simulation of it. Provide the instructor with a word processing file (a WORD document is preferred on a 3.5-in.disk) of a written report of your work. Include in the witten report the MINITAB commands and output, your written text, and the data with appropriate references.

11. From a newspaper's sports section, find the current team standings for a sport in season. From the wins and losses listed, verify that the listed games won percentages and the games back figures are correct. Show how your calculations were made. Identify which measures are relative comparisons and which are absolute comparisons.

12. A machine tool company experienced the following sales (S) and accounts receivable (AR) figures in millions of dollars over 21 years:

SALES (S)

6.6   7.0   15.4   24.6   30.1   17.1   9.1   15.9
14.9   7.9   9.1   10.4   9.4   11.2   12.2   14.2
17.7   19.2   35.8   27.5   30.0

ACCOUNTS RECEIVABLE (AR)

.07   1.5   3.5   4.6   3.9   1.4   2.1   2.4   2.0
1.5   1.6   1.5   1.4   1.7   2.3   2.7   3.6   4.2
4.7   9.0   7.9

(a) Plot each series, separately, over time.

(b) Would you characterize the growth as geometric or arithmetic? Also characterize the growth numerically (how much per year).

(c) Characterize the random, unpredictable series components. Comment on the amount of random variation relative to the growth.

(d) Compute accounts receivable as a percentage of sales, AR/S $\times$ 100, and characterize its behavior over time.

13. Yearly total verbal and math SAT mean scores of college bound seniors over an eight-year period were[13]

VERBAL

430   428   427   424   422   423   424   423

MATH

476   476   476   476   474   476   478   479

(a) Plot these figures and write a summary statement concerning your findings.

14. In billions of dollars, the yearly interest paid on public debt in the United States over a 16-year period was[14]

48.7   59.6   74.9   95.6   117.4   128.8   153.8   178.9
190.2   195.4   214.1   240.9   264.8   285.4   292.3   292.5

(a) Characterize the growth of this series.

(b) If interest paid continues to grow like this, what do you think the consequences might be in terms of the financial health of this country?

15. The total world population in billions of inhabitants is listed by year below.[15]

1650   1750   1850   1900   1950   1980   1994
.550   .725   1.175   1.600   2.564   4.478   5.642

(a) Plot and characterize the growth of the world population. Note that the intervals between the time periods are not constant. Account for this on the plot and in the analysis.

16. Plot and characterize the following money winnings (in thousands of dollars) of professsional rodeo cowboy all-around champions over a 22-year period.[16]

61   64   67   50   88   77   104   96   106   106   123
153   123   130   166   144   122   135   214   244   226   298

17. Plot and characterize the yearly percentage of America's high-school seniors who have ever used marijuana.[17]

54.2   50.9   50.2   47.2   40.7   36.7   32.6   35.3

18. Plot and characterize the yearly totals of new AIDS cases in the United States in thousands of persons[18].

21   31   34   42   44   46   84

19. Yearly U.S. total personal income and personal taxes in billions of dollars is shown below.[19]

PERSONAL INCOME

2.165   2.429   2.584   2.838   3.108   3.325   3.526
3.776   4.070   4.384   4.679   4.828   5.058   5.375

PERSONAL TAXES

.336   .387   .404   .410   .440   .486   .512
.571   .591   .658   .621   .618   .627   .686

(a) Plot and summarize the growth of these series individually.

(b) Find total personal taxes as a percentage of total income. Plot and summarize these figures.

20. Part of a product's life cycle, in terms of units sold per quarter, can be seen in the following data set:

1012   16   20   26   34   38   40   38   54   60   70   87
99   102   113   90   140   150   159   130   164   165   169

When the product is new, demand is low. As consumers become aware of and interested in the product, the demand increases rapidly. Eventually the increases in demand begin to slow as the product reaches maturity. If left on the market long enough, demand for some products will die. Before a product's complete demise, replacement models are often introduced. Approximate the growth rate of these sales figures during the periods of rapid growth.

21. A history of year-end retained earnings figures (in millions of dollars) are used in long-range financial planning.

112 132 223 125 181 188 240 160 370 340
234 243 761 474 516 427 678 620 457 966

(a) Plot and characterize the growth of these retained earnings figures.

22. The president of Nuzzle Pet Food Company has been worried because quarterly sales in thousands of boxes of Old Blue dog food has been trending downward.

326 337 327 326 320 304 235 276
241 247 213 219 187 129 120 154

(a) Summarize the situation for the president by plotting the data and finding the average amount that sales drops per quarter.

(b) Explain to the president why a geometric drop in sales would be worse than the present situation.

23. Fortunately, the Nuzzle Pet Food Company has a diversified product line. Quarterly sales in thousands of boxes have been trending upward for its T-bone line of dog food.

532 555 557 578 531 583 624 592
589 659 611 666 660 669 717 702

(a) Summarize the situation for the company's president by plotting the data and finding the average amount that sales increases per quarter.

24. Quarterly unit sales figures (in thousands of dollars) are used to project revenues. These figures are for a rapidly growing new product.

118 138 153 121 217 200 82 263
446 285 332 420 323 334 475 642

(a) Plot these figures and approximate the overall growth rate of sales per quarter.

25. A company evaluates its market share position every six months. Eighteen market share estimates (in percent) are listed below. These figures begin when the company entered the market.

2 2 3 3 4 6 6 7 6 9 17 19 15 23 25 26 22 27 28 28

Although it has been quite successful with the product, management thinks that market share growth is beginning to decline. If so, management is contemplating the timing of new product introductions. What is your evaluation of the situation, and do the data support management's thinking?

26. Hourly earnings (in dollars) of production workers for 29 years were[20]

2.46 2.56 2.68 2.85 3.04 3.23 3.45 3.70 3.94 4.24
4.53 4.86 5.25 5.69 6.16 6.66 7.25 7.68 8.02 8.32
8.57 8.76 8.98 9.28 9.66 10.01 10.32 10.57 10.83

(a) Plot these figures over time. How are hourly earnings growing?

(b) Find the percentage changes in hourly earnings per year and plot over time.

(c) Is the series in part (a) random? Describe the pattern of the plot. Does it bode well for workers?

27. The following figures are median sales prices of new, privately owned, one-family houses in the United States over a 24-year period:[21]

23.4 25.2 27.6 32.5 35.9 39.3 44.2 48.8 55.7 62.9 64.6 68.9
69.3 75.3 79.9 84.3 92.0 104.5 112.5 120.0 122.9 120.0 121.5 126.5

(a) Plot these prices and assess the growth pattern.

(b) If this series is arithmetic, find changes in the median sales prices, plot, and check for randomness and normality.

(c) Find summary statistics to sharpen the earlier visual impressions.

(d) Proceed to examine this series as if it were geometric, using differences in logs of prices to approximate growth rates. Notice that the approximate growth rates tend to decrease with time and are not random, which makes the summary statistics less useful.

28. The following Dow Jones average figures of 65 stock prices (30 industrial stocks, 20 transportation stocks, and 15 utility stocks) are examined over a 33-year period.[22]

232.44 221.07 253.67 294.23 318.50 308.70 314.79 322.19   301.35   243.92   298.12
319.36 286.73 237.33 247.25 303.91 301.70 283.63 293.46   328.23   364.61   345.40
472.24 463.10 541.56 702.50 849.5   772.2   966.9   965.2   1048.3   1169.9   1381.0

Plot the Dow Jones average. Find and plot approximate growth rates. Test for randomness and summarize. Pay particular attention to how large the standard deviation is relative to the mean approximate growth rate. What would you conclude about the predictability of this series?

29. Yearly median income figures for men and women over an eight-year period were (in thousands of dollars)[23]

Men	14.9	15.2	16.1	17.0	17.9	17.9	18.1	17.8
Women	9.9	10.1	11.0	11.8	12.4	12.5	12.7	12.9

(a) Plot median incomes for men and women on the same plot, but code the plotting points differently.

(b) Plot the ratio of incomes of men to women.

(c) Does the gap between incomes of men and women seem to be getting better or worse for women?

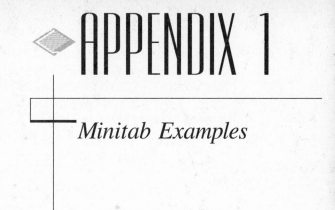

APPENDIX 1

Minitab Examples

(If you are using the WINDOWS version of MINITAB, you might issue the GSTD command first to use standard graphics in the session window. Also, if you want to save your output on a file, use the command OUTFILE 'A:CH6.LIS' to echo output to this file.)

CUMMINS ENGINE—ARITHMETIC GROWTH IN SALES

(If you have the data diskette, **RETRIEVE 'B:CUMMINS'** and omit the data entry using SET.)

(If you are on a network and have the data stored in subdirectory DATA under the directory **MTBWIN**, **RETRIEVE 'CUMMINS';** otherwise, SET the data in columns.)

```
DON'T SET DATA IN C1 IF RETRIEVE WAS SUCCESSFUL
MTB > SET DATA IN C1      #SALES IN BILLIONS OF DOLLARS
                         #CUMMINS ENGINE COMPANY
DATA> .8 .76 1.03 1.26 1.52 1.77 1.67
DATA> 1.96 1.59 1.60 2.33 2.15 2.30 2.77
DATA> END

START HERE IF RETRIEVE SUCCESSFUL
MTB > TSPLOT C1     # YEARLY SALES IN BILLIONS OF DOLLARS FOR
#  THE CUMMINS ENGINE COMPANY FOR FOURTEEN YEARS.
#  IF YOU RETRIEVED MTB  > ERASE C1-C5
```

GROWING MONEY

```
# WE GROW MONEY ($1000) GEOMETRICALLY FOR 20 YEARS
# AT A RATE OF 10 PERCENT PER YEAR

# C1 CONTAINS PRINCIPAL ($1000)` PLUS INTEREST AT THE
# END OF EACH YEAR
```

Comment The following macro, %B:GROW, requires release ten or higher of MINITAB. To examine the details of the macro, use a text editor or word processor to open the GROW.MAC file. Also, in MINITAB the command TYPE 'B:GROW.MAC' will list the macro. If you set OH = 24 in the session window, a "continue?" prompt will be issued by MINITAB which permits the user to view one screen of output at a time as the macro executes.

```
MTB > %B:GROW  # OR %A:GROW OR %GROW
              # OR %C:\MTBWIN\DATA\GROW
MTB > NAME C1 'DOLLARS' C2 'LOGDOL'
MTB > PRINT C1
MTB > TSPLOT C1    # NOTICE THE UPWARD CURVE OF GEOMETRIC
#  GROWTH ON AN ARITHMETICALLY SCALED PLOT

MTB > LET C2 = LOGE(C1)  # YOU WILL SEE THAT THE LOGARITHMS
# OF A GEOMETRIC SERIES PLOT AS A STRAIGHT LINE. WHEN
# USING NATURAL LOGARITHMS, BASE E, THE SLOPE OF THE LINE
# IS THE APPROXIMATE GROWTH RATE.

MTB > TSPLOT C2
MTB > PRINT C2

MTB > DIFF LAG 1 C2, PUT INTO C3  # THE CHANGES IN C2 FROM
# YEAR TO YEAR ARE CONSTANT HERE AND ARE APPROXIMATELY EQUAL
# TO THE GROWTH RATE.  AS WE WIDEN OUR APPLICATIONS ARENA, WE
# FIND THAT GEOMETRIC GROWTH RATES OFTEN VARY FROM YEAR TO
# YEAR.  WHEN SUCH RATES ARE RANDOM, OFTEN WE WORK WITH THE
# AVERAGE GROWTH RATE; ASIDE FROM THE RANDOMNESS, WE THINK
# OF SUCH A SERIES AS GROWING AT THE AVERAGE RATE.

MTB > PRINT C3     # STEP SIZES ON PREVIOUS PLOT
MTB > AVERAGE C3   # AVERAGING IS UNNECESSARY HERE BUT IS
# PRESENTED AS A REMINDER OF WHAT IS DONE WHEN GROWTH RATES
# CHANGE FROM YEAR TO YEAR.  HERE THE AVERAGE IS APPROXIMATELY
# EQUAL TO THE INTEREST (COMPOUNDING) RATE OF 10 percent
```

EXAMPLE

CUMMINS ENGINE VIEWED THROUGH A GEOMETRIC EYE

(If you have the data diskette, **RETRIEVE 'B:CUMMINS'** and omit the data entry using SET.)

(If you are on a network and have the data stored in subdirectory DATA under the directory MTBWIN, **RETRIEVE 'CUMMINS';** otherwise, SET the data in columns.)

```
DON'T SET DATA IN C1 IF RETRIEVE WAS SUCCESSFUL
MTB > SET DATA INTO C1  # SALES IN BILLIONS
DATA> .8 .76 1.03 1.26 1.52 1.77 1.67
DATA> 1.96 1.59 1.60 2.33 2.15 2.30 2.77
DATA> END
```

```
START HERE IF RETRIEVE WAS SUCCESSFUL
MTB > LET C2 = LOGE(C1)  # A STEP THAT LEADS TO THE GOAL
# OF OBTAINING CHANGES; REMEMBER THAT CHANGES IN LOGS
# APPROXIMATE COMPOUNDING RATES

MTB > DIFF LAG 1 C2, PUT C3     # GETTING THE CHANGES

MTB > TSPLOT C3  # THE COMPOUNDING RATE IS CLEARLY NOT
# CONSTANT LIKE IT WAS IN THE EARLIER EXAMPLE THAT
# COMPOUNDED MONEY IN THE BANK

MTB > DESCRIBE C3  # WITHOUT DELETING TWO DATA POINTS,
# THE MEAN COMPOUNDING RATE IS 9.55 percent; THESE
# STATISTICS MAKE SENSE IF THE DIFFERENCES IN LOGS ARE
# RANDOM;  WE WILL EXPLORE THE RANDOM, UNPREDICTABLE
# ASPECT OF TIME SERIES IN THE NEXT SECTION.

# IF YOU RETRIEVED, BE SURE TO DO THIS ERASE
# OTHERWISE, COLUMN NAMES AND DATA VALUES CARRY
# FORWARD TO THE NEXT EXAMPLE
#        MTB > ERASE C1-C5
```

EXAMPLE

GROWING MONEY, RANDOM DEPOSITS AND WITHDRAWALS

Comment The %B:GROWER macro grows money at a 10% rate and includes random deposits or withdraws.

```
MTB > %B:GROWER  # OR %A:GROWER OR %GROWER
                 # OR %C:\MTBWIN\DATA\GROWER

MTB > NAME C1 'DOLLARS'
MTB > TSPLOT C1     # THE RANDOM DEPOSITS AND WITHDRAWALS ARE
#  SMALL ENOUGH THAT THE GEOMETRIC GROWTH RATE IS THE MORE
#  DOMINANT FEATURE IN THE PLOT

MTB > PRINT C1     # IN CASE YOU WANT TO SEE HOW MUCH MONEY
# YOU HAVE AT THE END OF EACH YEAR

MTB > NAME C44 'DEPWITH'
MTB > PRINT C44     # IN CASE YOU WANT TO SEE THE DEPOSITS
#  AND WITHDRAWALS

MTB > LET C2 = LOGE(C1)  # WE KNOW THAT THE AVERAGE CHANGES
#  IN THE LOGS APPROXIMATES THE GROWTH RATE

MTB > DIFF LAG 1 C2, PUT INTO C3  # CHANGES
MTB > DELETE ROW 1 C3
MTB > NAME C3 'PCTCHG'
MTB > RUNS C3     # IF THESE TURN OUT TO BE RANDOM,
#                 SUMMARY STATISTICS WILL BE MORE USEFUL
```

```
MTB > TSPLOT C3  # DUE TO THE RANDOM DEPOSITS AND WITHDRAWALS,
#  WE SEE SOME VARIATION IN THE YEAR TO YEAR APPROXIMATE,
#  GROWTH RATES.  WE WILL AVERAGE THESE AND SEE THAT THE
#  AVERAGE GROWTH RATE IS NEAR THE 10 PERCENT COMPOUNDING RATE

MTB > HIST C3       # AS EXPECTED, THIS LOOKS NORMAL
MTB > DESCRIBE C3  #  THE APPROXIMATE MEAN GROWTH RATE
#  IS 11.01 PERCENT; BOTH THE STANDARD DEVIATION AND THE PLOT
#  HELP CHARACTERIZE THE VARIABILITY
```

EXAMPLE

ECONOMIC GROWTH, THE GROSS DOMESTIC PRODUCT (GDP)

(If you have the data diskette, **RETRIEVE 'B:GDP'** and omit the data entry using SET.)

(If you are on a network and have the data stored in subdirectory DATA under the directory **MTBWIN, RETRIEVE 'GDP';** otherwise, SET the data in columns.)

```
DON'T SET DATA IN C1 IF RETRIEVE WAS SUCCESSFUL
# TWENTY-SIX YEARS OF SEASONALLY ADJUSTED ANNUAL GDP
# FIGURES IN BILLIONS OF DOLLARS
       533.8    574.6    606.9    649.8    705.1    772.0    816.4   892.7
       963.9   1015.5   1102.7   1212.8   1359.3   1472.8   1598.4
      1782.8   1990.5   2249.7   2508.2   2732     3052.6   3166.0
      3405.7   3772.2   4010.3   4235

START HERE IF RETRIEVE WAS SUCCESSFUL
MTB > PRINT C1
MTB > TSPLOT C1

MTB > LET C2 = LOGE(C1)
MTB > DIFF LAG 1 C2 PUT INTO C3
MTB > DELETE ROW 1 C3

MTB > TSPLOT C3
MTB > RUNS C3

MTB > HIST C3  # ROUGHLY NORMAL

MTB > DESCRIBE C3  # NOTE THE MEAN GROWTH RATE IS 8.28
# PERCENT PER YEAR; ROUGHLY, 2 PERCENT PER QUARTER.
# THE STANDARD DEVIATION IS ABOUT ONE QUARTER THE MEAN
# SO THE GEOMETRIC GROWTH DOMINATES THE PLOT.
```

EXAMPLE

HOUSE PRICES ON THE RISE

(If you have the data diskette, **RETRIEVE 'B:NHOUSE'** and omit the data entry using SET.)

(If you are on a network and have the data stored in subdirectory DATA under the directory MTBWIN, **RETRIEVE 'NHOUSE';** otherwise, SET the data in columns.)

```
DON'T SET DATA IN C1 IF RETRIEVE WAS SUCCESSFUL
```

Median sales prices of new, privately owned, one-family houses in the United States for 18 years.

```
23.4   25.2   27.6   32.5   35.9   39.3   44.2   48.8   55.7
62.9   64.6   68.9   69.3   75.3   79.9   84.3   92.0   104.5
```

```
START HERE IF RETRIEVE WAS SUCCESSFUL
MTB > PRINT C1
MTB > TSPLOT C1

MTB > DIFF LAG 1 C1 PUT C2      # LOOKING AT PRICE CHANGES
MTB > TSPLOT C2                 # EXCEPT FOR THE LAST YEAR,
#  PRICE INCREASES SEEM TO AVERAGE ABOUT $5 THOUSAND A YEAR.

MTB > HIST C2                   # EXCEPT FOR ONE OBSERVATION,
#                                 THE DISTRIBUTION LOOKS NORMAL

MTB > DELETE ROW 1 OF C2
MTB > RUNS C2
MTB > DESCRIBE C2        # NOTE THAT THE MEAN IS NEARLY TWICE
#  THE STANDARD DEVIATION, INDICATING THAT THE GROWTH PATTERN
#  IS NOT OBSCURED BY THE VARIABILITY.

MTB > LET C2 = LOGE(C1)
MTB > DIFF LAG 1 C2 PUT IN C3    # APPROXIMATE GROWTH RATES

MTB > TSPLOT C3    # THIS PLOT LOOKS NONRANDOM, WITH PERCENT
#  GROWTH HIGHER IN THE FIRST NINE YEARS AND LOWER IN THE
#  LAST EIGHT YEARS.  ELIMINATING THE LAST POINT, YOU CAN
#  SEE THAT THE PERCENTAGE CHANGES ARE DECREASING AS YOU
#  WOULD EXPECT IN AN ARITHMETIC SERIES.

MTB > DELETE ROW 1 C3
MTB > RUNS C3

MTB > HIST C3    # NORMAL BUT NONRANDOM, MAKING THE SUMMARY
#            STATISTICS OF APPROXIMATE GROWTH RATES UNRELIABLE

MTB > DESCRIBE C3  # I WOULD RELY MORE ON THE PLOT OF C3;
#   NOTE THAT THE MEAN IS ABOUT TWICE THE STANDARD DEVIATION,
#   INDICATING THAT THE GROWTH PATTERN IS NOT OBSCURED BY THE
#   VARIABILITY.
```

EXAMPLE

THE STOCK MARKET, YEARLY

The yearly Dow Jones averages of 65 stock prices for 26 years are shown below.

(If you have the data diskette, **RETRIEVE 'B:DOW'** and omit the data entry using SET.)

(If you are on a network and have the data stored in subdirectory DATA under the directory MTBWIN, **RETRIEVE 'DOW'**; otherwise, SET the data in columns.)

```
DON'T SET DATA IN C1 IF RETRIEVE WAS SUCCESSFUL

   232.44   221.07   253.67   294.23   318.50   308.70   314.79   322.19
   301.35   243.92   298.12   319.36   286.73   237.33   247.25   303.91
   301.70   283.63   293.46   328.23   364.61   345.40   472.24   463.10
   541.56   702.50

START HERE IF RETRIEVE WAS SUCCESSFUL
MTB > PRINT C1
MTB > TSPLOT C1       # NOTICE THAT, IN THE LAST FOUR YEARS,
#   THE DOW ROARED UPWARD. THUS, TAKING ON A GEOMETRIC LOOK;
#   HOWEVER, PRIOR YEARS FIGURES MEANDER MORE AND THE GROWTH
#   PATTERN IS OBSCURED BY THE VARIABILITY

MTB > LET C2 = LOGE(C1)
MTB > DIFF LAG 1 C2 PUT INTO C3
MTB > DELETE ROW 1 C3

MTB > RUNS C3    # PERCENT CHANGES IN THE DOW APPEAR RANDOM
MTB > TSPLOT C3  # THE GROWTH RATES APPEAR RANDOM BUT THEY
#   BOUNCE AROUND CLOSE ENOUGH TO ZERO FOR YOU TO CONSIDER
#   BEING CAREFUL ABOUT YOUR MONEY IN THE MARKET, AT LEAST
#   BE AWARE OF THE RISKS!

MTB > DESCRIBE C3    # THE MEDIAN IS SMALL (INFLUENCED LITTLE
#   BY THE LAST FOUR YEARS) AND, RELATIVELY, THE STANDARD
#   DEVIATION LARGE (ABOUT FOUR TIMES THE MEAN).  THUS, WE CAN
#   SEE WITH THIS SMALL DATA SET THAT STOCK MARKET GROWTH
#   BEHAVIOR CAN BE OBSCURED BY THE VARIABILITY, GIVING IT
#   CONSIDERABLE UNPREDICTABILITY AND A RISKY PLACE FOR PUTTING
#   MONEY.  YOU MIGHT WISH TO COMPARE THE 4.42 PERCENT YEARLY,
#   COMPOUNDING RATE TO INFLATION FOR THE PERIOD.
```

EXAMPLE

THE STOCK MARKET, MONTHLY

(If you have the data diskette, **RETRIEVE 'B:DJ30'** and omit the data entry using SET.)

(If you are on a network and have the data stored in subdirectory DATA under the directory MTBWIN, **RETRIEVE 'DJ30'**; otherwise, SET the data in columns.)

```
DON'T SET DATA IN C1 IF RETRIEVE WAS SUCCESSFUL
# MONTHLY DOW JONES AVERAGES OF 30 INDUSTRIAL STOCKS
# FOR FORTY-EIGHT MONTHS

DATA> 1064 1078 1129 1168 1212 1221 1213 1189 1237 1252 1250 1257
DATA> 1258 1164 1161 1152 1143 1121 1113 1212 1213 1199 1211 1188
DATA> 1238 1283 1268 1266 1279 1314 1343 1326 1317 1351 1432 1517
DATA> 1534 1652 1757 1807 1801 1867 1809 1843 1813 1817 1883 1924
DATA> END

START HERE IF RETRIEVE WAS SUCCESSFUL
MTB > TSPLOT C1
MTB > DIFF LAG 1 FOR C1 PUT C2
MTB > DELETE ROW 1 C2
MTB > TSPLOT C2
MTB > RUNS C2
MTB > DESCRIBE C2    # DURING THIS TIME SPAN, THE AVERAGE
# MONTHLY, UPWARD STEP IN THE MARKET WAS 18.30 POINTS; THIS
# IS SUBSTANTIAL.  WERE THIS PATTERN (BULL MARKET) TO CONTINUE
# INDEFINITELY, THE MEAN CHANGE (+18.30) WOULD BE USEFUL FOR
# LONG TERM PREDICTIONS.

MTB > HIST C2
MTB > LET C2 = LOGE(C1)
MTB > DIFF LAG 1 C2 PUT C3
MTB > DELETE ROW 1 C3
MTB > RUNS C3

MTB > TSPLOT C3    # RANDOM, CAN'T PREDICT TODAY HOW THE DOW
#  WILL MOVE TOMORROW, PROVIDED YOU BELIEVE THE TRUE CENTER
#  LINE (LONG TERM MEAN) IS CLOSER TO ZERO THAN WHAT
#  YOU SEE BELOW.

MTB > DESCRIBE C3   # NOTE THAT THE MEAN GROWTH RATE IS SMALL
#  AND THE STANDARD DEVIATION IS LARGE, RELATIVELY; A RANDOM
#  WALK OF THIS NATURE IS UNPREDICTABLE.
MTB > HIST C3
```

EXAMPLE

COMPARING EARNINGS OF MEN AND WOMEN

(If you have the data diskette, **RETRIEVE 'B:EARNMW'** and omit the data entry using SET.)

(If you are on a network and have the data stored in subdirectory DATA under the directory MTBWIN, **RETRIEVE 'EARNMW';** otherwise, SET the data in columns.)

```
DON'T SET DATA IN C1 IF RETRIEVE WAS SUCCESSFUL
```

(If you SET the data in columns, you must repeat the SET command three times, SET DATA IN C1 (input a column of data), SET DATA IN C2 (input a column of data), and SET DATA IN C3.)

(An alternative is to use the READ command, READ C1 C2 C3, and enter the data row by row. Do not input the periods.)

```
SIX 5-YEAR        C1       C2       C3
PERIODS         WOMEN      MEN      CPI
   1            3257      5368     88.7
   2            3828      6388     94.5
   3            5323      8966    116.3
   4            7504     12758    161.2
   5           11197     18612    246.8
   6           15624     24195    322.2
```

START HERE IF RETRIEVE WAS SUCCESSFUL

Comment   Because of command similarities to previous examples, this example is presented as a macro, %B:E6-7-1.MAC. The macro requires version ten or more of MINITAB. To examine the details of the macro, use a text editor or a word processor to open the E6-7-1.MAC file. Also, in MINITAB, the command TYPE 'B:E6-7-1.MAC' lists the macro. If you set OH = 24 in the session window, a "continue?" prompt will be issued by MINITAB that permits the user to view one screen of output at a time as the macro executes.

```
MTB > %B:E6-7-1   # OR %A:E6-7-1 OR %E6-7-1
#                   OR %C:\MTBWIN\DATA\E6-7-1
```

CHAPTER 7

Sampling Distributions, Single Sample Confidence Intervals, and Hypothesis Tests

OBJECTIVES

- ◇ **Introduce the distribution of sample means**
- ◇ **Measure the variability of sample means with the standard error**
- ◇ **Build confidence intervals on the population mean and other values of interest**
- ◇ **Learn to test hypotheses**

PRELUDE

Imagine conducting the following experiment while sitting in a large room full of adults. Ask the person on your right, on your left, and in front of you to stand. Either measure all three of them or ask them their heights in inches. Find and record the mean height for the three individuals. You know that the mean height is an estimate of how tall a typical adult is.

Have someone else in the room repeat the same experiment for another group of three people. Chances are good that the mean heights of the two groups of three will differ. Repeat this experiment many times to see how much the sample mean varies. Medians, as well as means, will vary too.

Expect variability in estimators as you expect variability in individual measurements because estimators are computed from individual measurements. When using a sample mean as an estimator of what is typical, you will find that the sample mean varies from sample to sample.

The distribution of sample means tends to be normal. A stem-and-leaf display or histogram of sample means shows how sample means are distributed. The standard deviation of the distribution of sample means is inversely proportional to the square root of the sample size. Therefore, if the cost of collecting the sample information is constant, the larger the sample the better.

From a distribution of sample means, an interval can be constructed that tells us where the unknown population mean might be. Other similar intervals can be constructed; for example, bounds can be placed on single future observations.

Some intervals from sample data are useful in testing hypotheses about unknown population characteristics. For example, we might consider the hypothesis that the unknown, mean adult height is 5 ft 7 in. If 5 ft 7 in. falls outside an interval's bounds, we are likely to reject the hypothesis in favor of another. In this way, hypotheses are confirmed or denied. ◈

SAMPLING DISTRIBUTIONS

How deep is the water? is a question we might ask during a flood. The response could be that it covers the corn and soybeans but not the house. In the fields by the river the average depth is 8 ft. By the barn the average depth is 4 ft. On the front porch the average depth is 2 ft high and rising. Consequently, the average depth, or the sample mean, varies from one observation to another. In fact, it varies from sample to sample even when sampling from the same population. The study of this variation is key in this chapter.

The absolute value of the deviation of the sample mean from the population mean, $|\mu - \bar{y}|$, is a **sampling error.** It occurs when the sample mean misses the target population mean. If many samples were drawn of the same size from the same population, the average sampling error could be computed. The **standard error** is a measure of the average sampling error. It is defined as

$$\sigma_{\bar{y}} = \frac{\sigma}{n^{1/2}}$$

The standard error can also be described as the standard deviation of the distribution of sample means. Because of its inverse relationship with sample size, the average sampling error can be reduced by increasing the sample size. When the standard error of an estimator is small, the sample mean is desirably precise, and vice versa. **Nonsampling error** is not as easy to estimate or control. This error arises from flaws in the process of collecting, processing, and analyzing the data.

EXAMPLE 1

A DISTRIBUTION OF SAMPLE MEANS SIMULATED IN MINITAB

Problem Statement (a) Roll six dice 200 times. Summarize the numbers on the top face of one die. Find the mean, standard deviation, percentage occurrences of particular faces, and the distribution.

Problem Solution (a)   For each roll of six dice, the top faces appear as rows in columns C1, C2, C3, C4, C5, and C6. These columns are 200 rolls long. A summary is shown below of column C1, the results on the first die.

```
                N     MEAN   MEDIAN    STDEV
C1             200    3.345   3.000    1.724

                MIN    MAX      Q1       Q3
C1            1.000   6.000   2.000    5.000

        C1    PERCENT (ACTUAL % OCCURRENCES OF A PARTICULAR FACE IN 200 TOSSES)
        1      20.00
        2      16.00
        3      18.50
        4      16.00
        5      14.00
        6      15.50
```

The distribution of the numbers on the faces is nearly uniform, with almost $\frac{1}{6} \times 200 \approx 33$ observations in each histogram class.

```
Histogram of C1    n=200

Midpoint   Count
   1.000    40   ****************************************
   1.500     0
   2.000    32   ********************************
   2.500     0
   3.000    37   *************************************
   3.500     0
   4.000    32   ********************************
   4.500     0
   5.000    28   ****************************
   5.500     0
   6.000    31   *******************************
```

Problem Statement (b)   For each roll of six dice, compute the sample mean of the six faces across rows of C1, C2, C3, C4, C5, and C6. For all 200 such means, find the mean of the sample means and the standard deviation (an estimate of the standard error of the sample mean). What is the distribution of the sample means? Compare results in (a) and (b).

Problem Solution (b)   First, 200 row means are computed for each roll of six dice. These sample means are placed in column C7. In the summary below, notice that the mean of the sample means in C7 is close to the mean of C1. In contrast, the standard deviation (an estimate of the standard error) of the sample means in C7 is (.6822), which is much smaller than the standard deviation (1.724) of the 200 faces in C1.

```
                N     MEAN    MEDIAN    STDEV
C7             200   3.5150   3.5000   0.6822

                MIN     MAX      Q1       Q3
C7           2.0000  5.1667   3.0000   4.0000
```

Next, the sampling distribution of the sample means in C7 is examined using a histogram. The distribution is approximately normal with less variability (standard deviation = .6822) than the distribution of the 200 faces on a single die in C1 (standard deviation = 1.724). Sample means of measurements appear to have less variability than the individual measurements.

```
Histogram of C7, N=200; each * represents 2 observations.

Midpoint    Count
  1.000        0
  1.500        0
  2.000        6    ***
  2.500       19    **********
  3.000       48    ************************
  3.500       56    ****************************
  4.000       42    *********************
  4.500       21    ***********
  5.000        8    ****
```

Even though the sample means result from numbers generated from a uniform distribution, the distribution of sample means appears to be normal. The straightness of the probability plot below confirms that the distribution is normal. C8 contains the approximate, standard normal values that would result from these data values when a normal distribution is assumed. Thus, if what actually occurs in C7 lines up with the assumed distribution in C8, the data in C7 are normal.

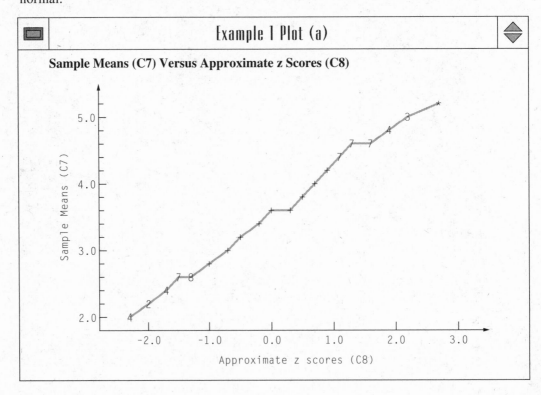

Example 1 Plot (a)

Sample Means (C7) Versus Approximate z Scores (C8)

A CLOSER LOOK AT THE STANDARD ERROR

If the sample means have variation like the individual data points do, this does not mean that the variation is the same. Nor does it mean that the distribution of sample means has the same standard deviation as the distribution of individual measurements.

There is one notable exception, however, and that is when the sample size is one. If we think of each observation as a sample of size one, then the sample mean of one observation is that observation. For a sample size of one, the sample means are spread exactly like the data values. Thus, these special-case sample means have the same standard deviation as the individual observations.

Usually, however, sample sizes are greater than one. In these cases, the spread of the distribution of sample means depends on the sample size and the standard deviation of the individual observations. As the sample size increases, the spread of the distribution of sample means decreases and the sample mean becomes a better estimator of the unknown population mean.

Estimating the Standard Error

In the simulation experiment of Example 1, each column displayed the results of rolling a single die 200 times. Summary statistics for column C1 indicate that the average of numbers on 200 faces was 3.345 and the sample standard deviation, s, was 1.724. The complete set of summary statistics is

	N	MEAN	MEDIAN	STDEV
C1	200	3.345	3.000	1.724

	MIN	MAX	Q1	Q3
C1	1.000	6.000	2.000	5.000

It is revealing to compare these summary statistics to those for a column of sample means, C7, which resulted from averaging rows across columns C1, C2, . . . , C6. Summary statistics for column C7 indicate that 200 sample means of six faces averaged 3.515 with a standard deviation of .6822. This standard deviation of a distribution of sample means estimates the standard error, and it was experimentally determined in a simulation experiment. Notationally, this estimate of the standard error is written as

$$s_{\bar{y}} = .6822 \text{ (experimentally determined)}$$

The complete set of summary statistics for the sample means in column C7 is

	N	MEAN	MEDIAN	STDEV
C7	200	3.5150	3.5000	0.6822

	MIN	MAX	Q1	Q3
C7	2.0000	5.1667	3.0000	4.0000

The experimentally determined estimate of the standard error, .6822, has a theoretical parallel. For a population of infinite size, it can be shown that an estimate of the standard error can be made from the results of a single sample and

$$s_{\bar{y}} = \frac{s}{n^{1/2}}$$

Thus, $s_{\bar{y}}$ can be computed from an estimate of the population standard deviation, s, and the sample size, n, which was used in calculating sample means. Thus, from any roll of n = 6 dice, s can be computed and used for finding $s_{\bar{y}}$.

However, from the simulation experiment, s = 1.724 is already available as an estimate of the population standard deviation. And each sample mean in C7 was based on the sample size n = 6. The square root of 6 is 2.4495. Therefore

$$s_{\bar{y}} = \frac{s}{n^{1/2}} = \frac{1.724}{2.4495} = .7038 \text{ (theoretically based)}$$

In practice this theory-based estimate of the standard error is commonly used. Sometimes this estimate will be referred to as the **sample standard error.**

It is important to recognize that the estimate of the standard error is inversely proportional to the sample size. Larger sample sizes tend to produce smaller standard error estimates and more precise estimators. Because sample size increases come at an additional cost of collecting data, the practitioner always has to decide if the precision improvements are worth the cost of a larger sample size.

Finite Population Adjustment of the Standard Error For finite populations of size N, $s_{\bar{y}}$ is multiplied by the **finite population correction factor,** which is

$$\left[\frac{N - n}{N - 1} \right]^{1/2}$$

This correction is negligible and not needed when n is less than 5% of N, as a rough rule of thumb.

EXAMPLE 2

ESTIMATED STANDARD ERROR FOR THE EGG SALES DATA

Problem Statement For the egg sales data set, it was found that s = 21.54 and n = 13. Estimate the standard error of the sample mean.

Problem Solution

$$s_{\bar{y}} = \frac{21.54}{13^{1/2}} = \frac{21.54}{3.61} = 5.97$$

Problem Discussion The finite population correction factor is not needed because the population of sales figures is very large. Thus large N and $(\frac{n}{N}) < .05$.

STATISTICAL HIGHLIGHTS

The sample standard error is the sample standard deviation divided by the square root of the sample size.

A CONFIDENCE INTERVAL ON THE POPULATION MEAN

Characterizing the variability of many sample means with the standard error can be put to further use in creating bounds on the location of an unknown population mean. Such bounds define the classical **confidence interval.** A confidence interval on the population mean establishes a region where the population mean presumably lies. Because the population mean is unknown, we cannot be certain that it falls within a confidence interval. Nevertheless, a **confidence level** can be specified to express the percentage of such intervals expected to contain the population mean. For example, considering repeated samples of the same size from the same population, a 95% confidence level specifies that 95 of 100 confidence intervals will contain the unknown population mean.

A confidence interval on the population mean, μ, is constructed by taking the sample mean plus and minus a number of standard errors. Because a variety of confidence intervals of other types are possible, a confidence interval on the population mean will be referred to as a **type (1) interval.**

A Type (1) Interval on the Unknown Population Mean

Consider independent random variables, y_i, with a mean μ and a standard deviation σ. The mean and standard deviation are estimated by $\bar{y}$ and s, respectively.

If we could observe an infinite number of y_i values under the same conditions, the population mean, μ, could be found. However, an infinite number of observations is not practical. Therefore, the sample mean, $\bar{y}$, estimates μ and anchors our thinking about the center of the distribution.

A single value, $\bar{y}$, as an estimator of μ, is a **point estimator.** In addition to this single point of reference, a confidence interval can be constructed by taking the sample mean plus and minus a number of estimated standard errors.

$$(\bar{y} \pm \text{ a number of estimated standard errors})$$

A confidence interval is an **interval estimator.** It places bounds on the unknown μ to improve our understanding about its possible location. The confidence level determines the particular number of standard errors needed in the interval computation. The higher the confidence level the wider the confidence interval for a fixed sample size.

Unfortunately, both component parts of this classical confidence interval, which are the sample mean and the estimated standard error, can be seriously distorted by the presence of outliers in the sample data. As a result, it is wise to compute a similar exploratory interval first.

An Exploratory Confidence Interval   An exploratory interval estimator is the **notched interval** on a boxplot. The notched interval bounds the population median and is a function of the sample median, the box length, and the sample size.

$$\text{sample median} \pm 1.82 \times \left(\frac{\text{box length}}{n^{1/2}}\right)$$

The constant, 1.82, is chosen to establish a 95% confidence interval on an unknown population median. The constant arises because $s \approx \left(\frac{3}{4}\right) \times$ box length and the standard error of the median is $\left(\frac{\pi}{2}\right)^{-1/2}$ larger than that of the sample mean.

$$1.82 \approx \left[1.96 \times \left(\frac{3}{4}\right)\right] \times \left(\frac{\pi}{2}\right)^{-1/2}$$

A boxplot with a notched interval on it is called a **notched boxplot.**

EXAMPLE 3

A NOTCHED BOXPLOT FOR EGG SALES

Problem Statement (a)   From the egg sales data, recall that the median = 33, the box length = 23, and the sample size is 13. Find a 95% interval estimate for the population median.

Problem Solution (a)

$$\left[33 \pm 1.82 \times \left(\frac{23}{13^{1/2}} \right) \right] = 21.4 \quad \text{and} \quad 44.6$$

Problem Statement (b)   Use MINITAB commands and subcommands to construct a boxplot with this notched interval on it.

Problem Solution (b)   A notched boxplot produced by MINITAB is shown below. On MINITAB output, the notch is represented by the region between the parentheses.

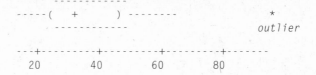

```
             ------------
      -----(     +     ) --------                     *
             ------------                          outlier

      ---+---------+---------+---------+-------
         20        40        60        80
```

Problem Discussion   If egg sales stay in a state of statistical control, we are confident that the population median will be included in 95 of 100 such notched intervals. Thus, our thinking goes beyond the initial sample median of 33 obtained from one set of observations.

    The narrower the interval spanned by the notch the more precise is the sample median and our understanding of what is typical. This interval can be made narrower by observing more than n = 13 days of sales, which makes the sample median more precise. Thus, in order to be more precise about typical sales, we need to see more than 13 days of sales.

    The next example illustrates that different samples from the same population produce different notched boxplots. Furthermore, larger sample sizes produce narrower notched intervals.

EXAMPLE 4

BOXPLOT INTERVALS ON HEIGHTS OF ADULTS

Problem Statement   Simulate samples from a normal distribution of adult heights with a known mean $\mu = 5$ ft 9 in. = 69 in. and standard deviation $\sigma = 2.5$ in. For five samples of size 10 and five more samples of size 40, construct ten notched boxplots. See if the first five boxplots have wider notches and more variation in location than the last five boxplots. What role does the sample size play?

Problem Solution   On the following boxplots, parentheses, ( ), mark the notched intervals. The printed characters do not always line up properly. Therefore, the notched intervals may not appear symmetrical about the median as they should be. The median is marked by a plus sign, +. The capital I's, I I, mark the box ends on the boxplot, unless both an I and a parenthesis coincide. Then a parenthesis left (, or right), will print instead of an I.

Larger sample sizes produce narrower and more stable notches. In this simulation, the population mean is known and we can see how the notched intervals perform relative to it. Usually we don't know the population mean, and we use these intervals to get an idea of where it might be. You may wish to duplicate this experiment changing sample sizes and using more columns and more boxplots to get a feel for how these intervals work.

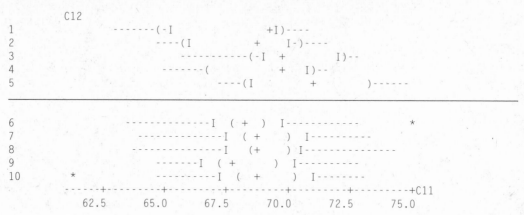

The Classical Analog of the Notched Interval

The Classical Analog of the Notched Interval   The classical analog of the exploratory notched interval is a 95% confidence interval on the unknown population mean.

$$(\text{sample mean} = \bar{y}) \pm 1.96 \times s_{\bar{y}}$$

Rounding 1.96 to 2 makes the formula easier to remember.

$$\bar{y} \pm 2 \times s_{\bar{y}}$$

The sample mean plus and minus two estimated standard errors (not standard deviations) is a commonly used interval. This interval is applicable when the sample size is greater than or equal to 30 and is known as a **large sample interval.**

A Type (1) Confidence Interval with μ and σ Unknown

Confidence interval width depends on multiples of standard errors. When μ and σ are unknown, the multiples depend on the Student's t distribution. Thus the MINITAB command for the computations is TINTERVAL with the prefix T. Although the Student's t distribution is approximately normal when $n > 30$, the TINTERVAL command is applicable for large or small samples.

EXAMPLE 5

CLASSICAL 95% CONFIDENCE INTERVALS ON HEIGHTS OF ADULTS (CONTINUED) σ ESTIMATED BY s, TINTERVALS

Problem Statement   Samples are simulated from a normal distribution of adult heights with a known mean μ = 5 ft 9 in. = 69 in. and standard deviation σ = 2.5 in. For five samples of size 10 and five more samples of size 40, construct ten 95% confidence intervals. Compute the sample means and standard deviations from the data as if the structure of the simulation were unknown. See if the first five intervals are wider and show more variation in location than the last intervals. What role does the sample size play?

Problem Solution   The two columns on the far right of the following table show lower and upper bounds for 95% confidence intervals. Notice that the sample size increases from 10 in the first five intervals to 40 in the last five intervals. Larger sample sizes result in smaller standard errors. As a result, the last five intervals are shorter than the first five.

	N	MEAN	STDEV	SE MEAN	95.0 PERCENT C.I.
C1	10	67.473	2.777	0.878	(65.487, 69.460)
C2	10	68.365	2.461	0.778	(66.604, 70.126)
C3	10	69.983	2.208	0.698	(68.403, 71.563)
C4	10	69.141	2.282	0.722	(67.508, 70.774)
C5	10	70.822	2.572	0.813	(68.982, 72.663)
C6	40	68.377	2.278	0.360	(67.648, 69.105)
C7	40	68.998	2.328	0.368	(68.253, 69.742)
C8	40	69.160	2.762	0.437	(68.277, 70.044)
C9	40	68.354	2.202	0.348	(67.649, 69.058)
C10	40	68.967	2.579	0.408	(68.142, 69.792)

The Computational Formula for a Confidence Interval on an Unknown Mean, σ Unknown   Although a 95% interval is common, other levels of confidence, such as 90%, 99%, 99.9%, and so on, may be needed. As the confidence level increases, the confidence intervals become wider. Thus, the confidence level choice involves a trade-off between interval width and the percentage of intervals containing the unknown population mean. This choice depends on what the investigator feels is appropriate for a particular application. In the MINITAB command, the desired confidence level is specified in the confidence interval command.

A 95% confidence interval indicates that 95 of 100 such intervals are expected to contain the population mean. Thus, if you were to randomly choose one of the 100 intervals, there would be a .95 chance that it would contain the unknown mean. Because $1 - .95 = .05$, there is a .05 chance that the interval does not include the population mean. By splitting .05 in half, $\frac{.05}{2} = .025$, we obtain the chances that the interval is to the left (or right) of the population mean.

To generalize, let α be the chance that the interval does not include the population mean, and $\frac{\alpha}{2}$ be the chance that the interval is to the left (or right) of the population mean. And α ranges between 0 and 1 but usually is less than .20.

The use of $\frac{\alpha}{2}$ enters into the discussion of the generic computational formula for confidence intervals on the population mean. For sample sizes $n \geq 30$, a 95% confidence interval has been constructed as follows:

$$(\text{sample mean} = \overline{y}) \pm 1.96 \times s_{\overline{y}}$$

The general form of a confidence interval is structurally similar to the above equation. The general form equation is

$$\bar{y} \pm t_{(\alpha/2),(n-1)} \times \frac{s}{n^{1/2}}$$

$$\bar{y} \pm t_{(\alpha/2),(n-1)} \times (s_{\bar{y}})$$

This confidence interval expression employs a subscripted Student's t value. The t is double subscripted, $t_{(\alpha/2),(n-1)}$. The first subscript represents the area (probability) to the right of the t-value on the Student's t distribution. The second subscript represents the degrees of freedom, $(n-1)$. The $(n-1)$ is a special case of $(n-p)$, which represents the sample size minus the number of parameters in a regression model. For the naive regression model, $p = 1$.

EXAMPLE 6

CONFIDENCE INTERVAL ON THE UNKNOWN MEAN LEVEL OF DAILY SALES

Problem Statement   For sales data in a state of statistical control, find the 95% confidence interval on μ, the unknown mean. Sample mean sales are 38.23 and the sample standard deviation is 21.54 for 13 days. The confidence interval expression is

$$\bar{y} \pm t_{(\alpha/2),(n-1)} \times \left(\frac{s}{n^{1/2}} \right)$$

Problem Solution   Substituting the given information into the above equation produces the following results:

$$38.23 \pm t_{.025,12} \times \left(\frac{21.54}{13^{1/2}} \right)$$

$$38.23 \pm (2.179) \times \left(\frac{21.54}{13^{1/2}} \right)$$

$$38.23 \pm (2.179) \times 5.97 = (25.22 \text{ and } 51.24)$$

A Graphical Display of the Classical Confidence Interval and a Notched Boxplot   This classical interval, rounded to 25 and 51, is shown in Exhibit 1 along with the exploratory notched boxplot. This particular interval is probably too wide to be of much practical use in managerial thinking about sales. However, it does point to the need for more observations.

Remember that the notched boxplot is a 95% confidence interval on the unknown population median. The classical parallel is a 95% confidence interval on the unknown population mean. Both the mean and the median are typical values. The notch is designed for exploratory work when there is little basis for the classical assumptions. Strictly speaking, the classical interval requires that the data values be independent and normal. Nonnormal fat-tailed distributions tend to draw the sample mean off center, inflate the sample standard deviation, and thereby degrade classical confidence intervals.

Usually exploratory analysis is done for a first look at the data. Later, if the evidence demonstrates that the data are normally distributed and independent, the classical interval can be constructed. Exhibit 1 shows both intervals for comparative purposes, using the same data values, which are not quite normal in distribution.

EXHIBIT 1 A Notched Boxplot and Its Classical Analog

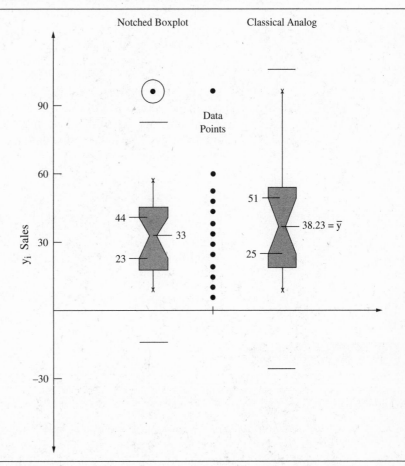

(For display purposes, the numerical values that mark the notches are rounded from 22.6 and 43.6 for the notched boxplot and from 25.22 and 51.24 for the classical analog.)

Also, because of one unusually large data value, $y_i = 95$, which might be considered an outlier, the classical interval is wider and shifted higher than the exploratory notch. Thus, you see the classical interval and what a minor aberration in the data can do to that interval.

Sample Size Effects on Confidence Intervals Because the estimated standard error is an inverse function of the sample size, $s_{\bar{y}} = s/n^{1/2}$, larger sample sizes make the confidence interval narrower.

A Type (1) Confidence Interval with μ Unknown and σ Known

Confidence interval width depends on multiples of standard errors. When σ is known, the multiples depend on the normal distribution. Thus, the MINITAB confidence interval command is ZINTERVAL, where the prefix Z refers to a standard normal variate.

Because the Student's t distribution is approximately normal when $n > 30$, both ZINTERVAL and TINTERVAL commands yield intervals that are approximately the same size under large sample conditions.

In the example that follows, σ is known. In a contrasting earlier example, σ was unknown and estimated by the standard deviation, s. When σ was unknown, the Student's t distribution came into play in the following confidence interval formula:

$$\bar{y} \pm t_{(\alpha/2),(n-1)} \times \left(\frac{s}{n^{1/2}}\right)$$

Seldom is σ known, but when it is, confidence intervals have less uncertainty because the need to estimate the standard error is eliminated. The resulting confidence interval is similar to the one shown above, except z replaces t and σ replaces s.

$$\bar{y} \pm z_{(\alpha/2)} \times \left(\frac{\sigma}{n^{1/2}}\right)$$

EXAMPLE 7

CLASSICAL CONFIDENCE INTERVALS, HEIGHTS OF ADULTS (CONTINUED) σ KNOWN, ZINTERVALS

Problem Statement Samples are simulated from a normal distribution of adult heights with a known mean $\mu = 5$ ft 9 in. = 69 in. and standard deviation $\sigma = 2.5$ in. For five samples of size 10 and five more samples of size 40, construct ten 95% confidence intervals. Compute the sample means from the data but assume σ is known. See if the first five intervals are wider and show more variation in location than the last intervals. What role does the sample size play?

Problem Solution   Using the MINITAB commands in Appendix 1 and the heights of adults data, these confidence intervals are demonstrated below. Five samples of size 10 and five more samples of size 40 are used in the computations. In the last two columns notice that the first five samples have wider intervals and the location of their midpoints varies more than the last five intervals, which involve larger sample sizes. Also, because σ is known, the standard error (SE MEAN in MINITAB's terminology) is a fixed constant for a particular sample size.

```
THE ASSUMED SIGMA =2.50

            N      MEAN    STDEV   SE MEAN    95.0 PERCENT C.I.
C1         10     67.473   2.777   0.791     (65.922,  69.025)
C2         10     68.365   2.461   0.791     (66.813,  69.917)
C3         10     69.983   2.208   0.791     (68.431,  71.534)
C4         10     69.141   2.282   0.791     (67.589,  70.693)
C5         10     70.822   2.572   0.791     (69.271,  72.374)
   ------------------------------------------------------------
C6         40     68.377   2.278   0.395     (67.601,  69.153)
C7         40     68.998   2.328   0.395     (68.222,  69.774)
C8         40     69.160   2.762   0.395     (68.384,  69.936)
C9         40     68.354   2.202   0.395     (67.578,  69.129)
C10        40     68.967   2.579   0.395     (68.191,  69.743)
```

Problem Discussion   If we had only one sample, say, the fifth, as a window for looking at the population, notice that this confidence interval, 69.271 to 72.374, would lead us to doubt a hypothesis that the mean height of adults is 69 in. because 69 is outside the interval.

Genesis of a Confidence Interval on an Unknown Population Mean   The basis of a confidence interval on an unknown mean is a probability statement about the following ratio:

$$\frac{\bar{y} - \mu}{\dfrac{\sigma}{n^{1/2}}} = z$$

This ratio is a standardized sample mean. The standardization of the sample mean is carried out by first **centering** ($\bar{y} - \mu$) and then by **scaling** (dividing by the standard error of the estimate, ($\sigma/n^{1/2}$)). When σ is known and sample means are normally distributed, the standardized variable, z, is normal. When σ is estimated by s, the standardized variable follows a Student's t distribution. Random samples of observations are needed to compute the sample mean and to satisfy the requirement that the observations are independent.

Normally Distributed Sample Means   The **Central Limit Theorem** states that: *If independent observations* y_i *are normal with mean* μ *and standard deviation* σ, *the distribution of the sample means,* $\bar{y}$*'s, is normal for samples of all sizes, with mean* μ *and standard deviation* $\sigma/n^{1/2}$. *Furthermore, if the* *distribution of independent observations y_i is not normal, has a finite standard deviation, σ, the distribution of the sample means is normal approximately, with mean μ and standard deviation $\sigma/n^{1/2}$, when the sample size is large.*

This theorem makes it realistic to assume that the sample means, $\bar{y}$'s, follow a normal distribution under the specified conditions.

A CONFIDENCE INTERVAL ON A SINGLE FUTURE OBSERVED VALUE

Once you understand the concept of a confidence interval on the population mean, you will be able to extend the idea to other distributional characteristics, such as single future observations or means of groups of future observations. A confidence interval on a single future observed value will be referred to as a **type (2) interval.**

A Type (2) Interval on a Single Future Observed Value

A confidence interval on a single future observed value, y_{if}, is wider than a confidence interval on an unknown mean μ because a single future observation is equal to the unknown mean plus an error (an individual deviation from that mean).

$$y_{if} = \mu + e_{if}$$

The combined uncertainty in estimating μ and e_{if} results in the following formula for a confidence interval on y_{if}:

$$\bar{y} \pm t_{(\alpha/2),(n-1)} \times s \times \left[\frac{1}{n} + 1\right]^{1/2}$$

Notice the subtle difference between this interval formula and that for the population mean. The only difference in the two formulas is one number, the $+1$, inside the brackets, $[\frac{1}{n} + 1]$, which is from the above equation. The $+1$ term accounts for the additional uncertainty in estimating the error associated with a single future value.

To understand a confidence interval on a single future value in practical terms, consider the egg sales data that we have been examining. Sales have been observed for 13 days and the data are random in a state of statistical control. This implies that there are no increasing or decreasing trends in sales, no systematic day-to-day patterns, and so on. The sample of 13 days sales is history. Therefore, when tomorrow, day 14, is considered, that is a single future value. Hence, a confidence interval can be placed on day 14's sales figure, y_{if}.

This confidence interval consists of two basic parts. The first part is the sample mean sales for the previous 13 days. This sample mean produces a reasonable prediction for sales on day 14 because the sample mean is typical and actual sales are expected to be above (or below) this figure half the time.

The second basic part of this confidence interval is concerned with the sources of variability. One source of variability is the sample mean; we are uncertain about the location of the true mean sales level. We are also uncertain about any single future observation because it varies about the true mean sales level. Thus, a confidence interval on a single future value is wider than a confidence interval on the unknown population mean.

EXAMPLE 8

A CONFIDENCE INTERVAL ON A SINGLE FUTURE VALUE OF SALES

Problem Statement   For the egg sales data, construct a 95% confidence interval for an individual sales figure on day 14.

Problem Solution   Substituting the given information into the above equation produces the following results:

$$38.23 \pm 2.179 \, (21.54) \left(\frac{1}{13} + 1 \right)^{1/2}$$

$$38.23 \pm 48.72 = -9.49 \quad \text{and} \quad 86.95 \text{ dozen}$$

Problem Discussion   Sales can't be negative, so the practical lower bound is 0 rather than −9.49.

Because these bounds are so wide, large forecasting errors are possible for the sales on day 14. This interval reflects the uncertainty in the unknown mean and in the individual deviation in sales from that mean. In contrast, the confidence interval on the population mean has narrower bounds that are 25.22 and 51.24.

A CONFIDENCE INTERVAL ON THE MEAN OF TWO OR MORE FUTURE OBSERVATIONS

Instead of a single future observation, sometimes the interest is in the average of two or more, q, future observations. This interval is wider than a confidence interval on the population mean but narrower than the interval on a single future observation.

A Type (3) Interval on the Mean of Two or More Future Observations

On inspecting the formula for this new interval, shown below, we can see that the number of future observations, q, plays a role in the width of the interval.

As q increases, the interval shrinks. If q = 1, this interval becomes the same as that for a single future observation.

$$\overline{y} \pm t_{(\alpha/2),(n-1)} \times s \times \left[\frac{1}{n} + \frac{1}{q}\right]^{1/2}$$

EXAMPLE 9

A CONFIDENCE INTERVAL ON THE MEAN OF q FUTURE OBSERVATIONS

Problem Statement Construct a 95% confidence interval on the mean of q = 2 future observations of egg sales.

Problem Solution Substituting the given information into the above equation produces the following results:

$$38.23 \pm (2.179)(21.54)\left(\frac{1}{13} + \frac{1}{2}\right)^{1/2}$$

2.58 and 73.88 dozen

Problem Discussion When q is small, this interval is quite wide, giving the user a feel for the risk in predicting the mean of a small number of future values.

A Visual Comparison Of Different Confidence Intervals See Exhibit 2 on the following page for a visual comparison of the different types of confidence intervals. The actual data points appear to the left of four shaded bars in the exhibit. The confidence limits are marked at the end of each shaded bar. These figures were found in the examples of each interval type.

The confidence intervals on the unknown population mean are shown for both n = 13 and n = 100 with s = 21.54. For n = 100, the confidence interval on the population mean becomes quite small and is the shortest shaded bar in the exhibit. The confidence interval on y_{if}, a single future value, produces the longest shaded bar in the exhibit, which spans all but one of the data values. The confidence interval on the average of two future observations is on the far right in the exhibit. It is a little shorter than that for a single future value.

THE NATURE OF HYPOTHESIS TESTING

Interval estimators provide likely location regions for the population mean, a single future observation, the mean of a number of future observations, and so on. Beyond that, interval estimators are useful in testing hypotheses. A **hypothesis** is a provisional conjecture that is possibly true. As an example from our analysis of egg sales data, we might state that the unknown mean

EXHIBIT 2 Confidence Intervals on the Population Mean, a Single Future Value, and the Mean of Two Future Values

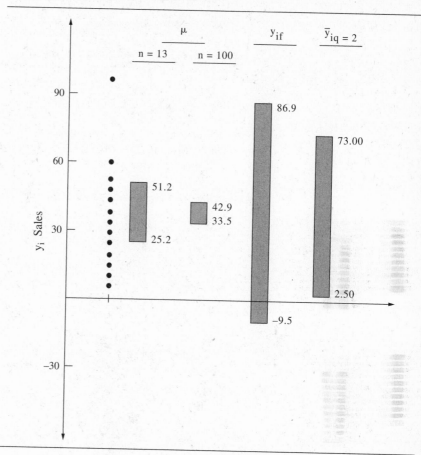

sales level is 30 dozen per day. The hypothesis that $\mu = 30$ can be subjected to a **hypothesis test** procedure that determines if sales data supports or refutes the conjecture. Thus, hypothesis testing is a simple extension of what you already know.

STATISTICAL HIGHLIGHTS

Confidence intervals can be found for single observations of a random variable as well as for any function of a random variable such as the population mean. Such intervals bound our thinking about unknown distributional characteristics that are estimated from the data.

HYPOTHESIS TESTS USING CONFIDENCE INTERVALS

We found that a 95% confidence interval on the population mean of egg sales extended from 25.22 to 51.24. Because $\mu = 30$ lies inside this interval, the data support this hypothesis and it is not rejected. The same can be said for any hypothesized value of μ between 25.22 and 51.24.

It is not certain that a confidence interval includes the population mean. Thus, the hypothesis testing procedure is not foolproof. Because the confidence interval is 95%, then $\alpha = (1 - .95) = .05$. The α is the **level of significance,** which is the proportion of the time that the null hypothesis is rejected when in fact it is true. The level of significance is also referred to as an **alpha-risk, alpha-error,** or **type I error.**

EXHIBIT 3 The Classical Equivalent of the Notch for Hypothesis Testing

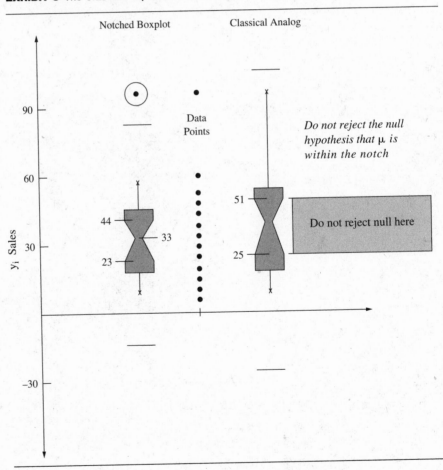

This confidence interval region forms the classical equivalent of a notch on a boxplot as shown in Exhibit 3. If the hypothesis is made so that the population mean is anywhere within this notched interval, then we cannot reject such a hypothesis.

The Null and Alternative Hypotheses   The hypothesis put forth as possibly true then tested for potential rejection is called the **null hypothesis.** It is denoted as H_n. Therefore, the null hypothesis that we have been examining is

$$\text{(null hypothesis) } H_n : \mu = 30$$

A rejection of the null hypothesis would suggest that the data support some other hypothesis. The second of two opposing hypotheses is the **alternative hypothesis.** It is denoted as H_a. For example, if the null hypothesis is $H_n : \mu = 30$, then an alternative is $H_a : \mu \neq 30$. Although a specific alternative hypothesis can be stated, such as $H_a : \mu = 39$, a more general statement such as $H_a : \mu \neq 30$ is usually made because it includes specific cases.

EXAMPLE 10

A HYPOTHESIS TEST ON THE MEAN SALES LEVEL

Problem Statement   For the egg sales data, test the null hypothesis, $H_n \mu = 30$ dozen per day, which is the proposed population mean sales level. Use a .05 level of significance.

Problem Solution   Because 30 falls within the 95% confidence interval

$$[25.22 \leq (\mu = 30) \leq 51.24]$$

do not reject the null hypothesis. See Exhibit 3 for a graphical illustration (note that the limits are rounded to 25 and 51 to make the display clear).

A Null Hypothesis That Is Rejected   In the previous example, if there had been some other null hypothesis, such as $\mu = 60$, it would have been rejected because 60 falls outside of the confidence interval. The same is true for some other null hypothesis, such as $\mu = 20$. The null hypothesis would be rejected because 20 falls outside the confidence interval.

The Two-Sided Nature of This Test   Because the null hypothesis is rejected when the value for μ in the null hypothesis is outside the confidence interval (drawn as a notch in Exhibit 3), rejection occurs when the μ value in the null hypothesis is above or below the notched interval. Thus, this form of a hypothesis test is said to be a **two-sided hypothesis test.**

HYPOTHESIS TESTS USING STUDENT'S t RATIO

An alternative to the confidence interval approach for testing hypotheses about the population mean is the **t test.** The two approaches are completely equivalent. In the t test, the relevant statistics are combined in the form of a ratio, which many investigators find easy to use. When the standard error of the sample mean is unknown and therefore estimated

$$s_{\bar{y}} = \frac{s}{n^{1/2}}$$

the t test is necessary. When the standard error of the sample mean is known

$$\sigma_{\bar{y}} = \frac{\sigma}{n^{1/2}}$$

a z test is used, which relies on the normal distribution.

t Test Procedure   The population mean in the null hypothesis, the sample mean, and the standard error form the following **t ratio** or **t test statistic:**

$$\left\{ \text{t test statistic} = \left| \frac{(\bar{y} - \mu)}{s_{\bar{y}}} \right| \right\}$$

The t test statistic measures the deviation between the sample and population means, $(\bar{y} - \mu)$, in terms of the number of standard errors. As this standardized deviation becomes larger, we begin to doubt the validity of the null hypothesis. To be definitive about when to reject the null hypothesis, the t test statistic is compared to a **critical t value** or **standard t value** at a specified level of significance. This comparison is shown below.

$$\underset{\left\{ \left| \frac{(\bar{y} - \mu)}{s_{\bar{y}}} \right| \right\}}{\text{t test statistic}} \quad > \quad \underset{t_{(\alpha/2),(n-1)}}{\text{critical t value}}$$

Testing Rule   If the t test statistic exceeds the critical t value, it is said to fall in the **critical region** and signals us to reject the null hypothesis that $H_n : \mu =$ (the particular μ value used in computing the t ratio). In a two-sided t test, rejection of the null hypothesis means that you favor the alternative $H_a : \mu \neq$ (the particular μ value used in computing the t ratio).

Given a significance level and the degrees of freedom, $(n - 1)$, the critical t value can be found in Table 2, Appendix A (in the back of the book) for the Student's t distribution or by using a MINITAB command. When the sample size exceeds 30, the Student's t distribution is approximately normal. Then, for example, with $\alpha = .05$, the critical t value is approximately equal to a z score of two.

Similarity to the Pseudo t Test This testing procedure is similar to the pseudo t test used in exploratory work. The exploratory analog is

pseudo t test statistic		**critical value**
$\left\lvert\dfrac{(\text{sample median} - \text{population median})}{\text{box length}^{1/2}}\right\rvert$	$>$	1.82

The postulated population median is rejected when the pseudo test statistic falls in the critical region and exceeds the critical value of 1.82 for a significance level of .05.

EXAMPLE 11

t RATIO FORM OF A HYPOTHESIS TEST

Problem Statement For the 13 egg sales figures, test the null hypothesis, $H_n : \mu = 30$, against the not equal alternative using a t test and a .05 level of significance. The sample mean is 38.23 and the estimated standard error of the sample mean is 5.97.

Problem Solution The t statistic is computed and compared to the critical t value. Notice that $\frac{\alpha}{2} = .025$ and the degrees of freedom are $(13 - 1) = 12$; both are needed to find the critical t value.

t test statistic		**critical t value**
$\left\lvert\dfrac{(38.23 - 30)}{5.97}\right\rvert$	compared to	$t_{(.025),(13-1)}$
$\left\lvert\dfrac{(38.23 - 30)}{5.97}\right\rvert$	compared to	2.179
$\lvert 1.38 \rvert$	does not exceed	2.179

The t test statistic does not exceed the critical value (is not in the critical region); therefore, do not reject the null hypothesis, $H_n : \mu = 30$.

z Test If the standard error of the sample mean is known, rather than estimated, the test statistic follows a normal rather than a Student's t distribution. Therefore, the test is referred to as a **z test.** For this test, the critical z value comes from the normal distribution to replace the critical t value. Otherwise the testing procedure is the same.

p Values For a two-sided test, a **p value** is the probability that the absolute difference, $\lvert \bar{y} - \mu \rvert$, is exceeded when the null hypothesis is true. A p value is also referred to as the **observed (attained) significance level.** This measures the chances of another sample mean from the same distribution being further away from μ than $\bar{y}$.

Like confidence intervals and ratio tests, p values can be used to test hypotheses. When p values are smaller than α, there is reason to reject the null hypothesis. In this case, it is possible that some alternative μ created a large difference between the sample mean and the null hypothesis mean.

Using MINITAB for Hypothesis Tests

MINITAB has two commands for ratio-type tests, ZTEST and TTEST. The first is used when the population standard deviation is known. The second is used when the population standard deviation is unknown. The fact that the population standard deviation is known implies that the standard error of the sample mean is known, and vice versa.

EXAMPLE 12

RATIO FORM OF HYPOTHESIS TESTS ON HEIGHTS OF ADULTS (CONTINUED) σ KNOWN (ZTEST) σ UNKNOWN (TTEST)

The following computer-generated samples let you see the sampling variability that occurs in test results from sample to sample.

Problem Statement (a)   At a .05 significance level, test the null hypothesis that the mean height of an adult is 69 in. against the not equal alternative. Do this for several samples, five with a sample size of 10 and five more with a sample size of 40. Assume σ is known.

Problem Solution (a)   The population standard deviation, σ, is known to be 2.50; therefore, a z test is appropriate. The first five samples are of size 10. The critical values for rejecting the null hypothesis are p values less than the specified significance level of .05 or z values exceeding 1.96 in absolute value.

	N	MEAN	STDEV	SE MEAN	Z	P VALUE
C1	10	67.473	2.777	0.791	-1.93	0.054
C2	10	68.365	2.461	0.791	-0.80	0.42
C3	10	69.983	2.208	0.791	1.24	0.21
C4	10	69.141	2.282	0.791	0.18	0.86
C5	10	70.822	2.572	0.791	2.31(reject)	0.021(reject)

Because the samples are simulated from a normal distribution with a known mean of 69 in., the fifth sample erroneously rejects the null hypothesis that the mean equals 69 in. This type of result is an example of an alpha error; due to sampling variability, the null hypothesis is rejected when it is true.

The sample size is increased to n = 40, which reduces the standard error (SE MEAN). No rejections of the null hypothesis occur.

	N	MEAN	STDEV	SE MEAN	Z	P VALUE
C6	40	68.377	2.278	0.395	-1.58	0.12
C7	40	68.998	2.328	0.395	-0.01	1.00
C8	40	69.160	2.762	0.395	0.41	0.69
C9	40	68.354	2.202	0.395	-1.64	0.10
C10	40	68.967	2.579	0.395	-0.08	0.93

Problem Statement (b)   At a .05 significance level, test the null hypothesis that the mean height of an adult is 69 in. against the not equal alternative. Do this for several samples, five with a sample size of 10 and five more with a sample size of 40. Assume σ is unknown.

Problem Solution (b)   The population standard deviation, σ, is unknown; therefore, a t test is appropriate. The fact that the standard error is estimated produces variation that gets reflected in both t and p values. This adds more uncertainty for decisions to reject or not reject. The additional uncertainty demands stronger evidence for a rejection. As a result, in sample five the null hypothesis is no longer rejected. Nevertheless, it is close to being rejected.

The first five samples are of size 10. The critical values for rejecting the null hypothesis are p values less than the specified significance level of .05 or t values exceeding 2.262 in absolute value. Because of the small sample size, the critical t value, $t_{.025,9} = 2.262$, is considerably different from the critical z value of 1.96 (used when σ was known).

	N	MEAN	STDEV	SE MEAN	T	P VALUE
C1	10	67.473	2.777	0.878	-1.74	0.12
C2	10	68.365	2.461	0.778	-0.82	0.44
C3	10	69.983	2.208	0.698	1.41	0.19
C4	10	69.141	2.282	0.722	0.20	0.85
C5	10	70.822	2.572	0.813	2.24	0.052

The sample size is increased to n = 40, which reduces the standard error (SE MEAN). The sample size increase results in a new critical t value, $t_{(.025),(39)}$, which is about 2.02. This t value is close to the z value of 1.96 because the sample size is over 30. No rejections of the null hypothesis occur.

	N	MEAN	STDEV	SE MEAN	T	P VALUE
C6	40	68.377	2.278	0.360	-1.73	0.091
C7	40	68.998	2.328	0.368	-0.01	1.00
C8	40	69.160	2.762	0.437	0.37	0.72
C9	40	68.354	2.202	0.348	-1.86	0.071
C10	40	68.967	2.579	0.408	-0.08	0.94

ONE-SIDED HYPOTHESIS TESTS

We have examined two opposing hypotheses: the null hypothesis, $H_n : \mu = 30$, versus the alternative hypothesis, $H_a : \mu \neq 30$. In the alternative hypothesis, because of the not equal sign, $\neq$, the possible alternatives to $\mu = 30$ include μ values that are greater or less than 30. As a result, this testing situation is referred to as two-sided. The alternative values for μ can be on either side of 30, above or below. As a result, the alpha error (the probability you erroneously reject the null hypothesis) was split in two, $\frac{\alpha}{2}$ on one side and $\frac{\alpha}{2}$ on the other.

Sometimes hypothesis tests are **one-sided** rather than two-sided. For example, suppose $H_n : \mu = 30$ versus the alternative hypothesis, $H_a : \mu < 30$. This one-sided alternative is in contrast to the two-sided alternative hypothesis, $H_a : \mu \neq 30$. For the two-sided case, a confidence interval was created for hypothesis testing using the following expression:

$$\bar{y} \pm t_{(\alpha/2),(n-1)} \, s_{\bar{y}}$$

For the two-sided test, the probability of a false rejection of the null hypothesis is α, with $\frac{\alpha}{2}$ of the probability in each tail of the Student's t distribution.

A One-Sided Test Using a Confidence Interval   The same confidence interval that is shown above can be used for one-sided hypothesis tests too. However, the type I error becomes $\frac{\alpha}{2}$ because the test is concerned with only one side of the Student's t distribution.

If you wish to maintain a type I error of α, a narrower confidence interval is needed for the one-sided test, which is

$$\bar{y} \pm t_{(\alpha),(n-1)} \, s_{\bar{y}}$$

Notice that this interval for a one-sided test uses a t value with a subscript of α rather than $\frac{\alpha}{2}$. Consequently, this interval is narrower than that for a two-sided test.

As an example of using a confidence for testing a *less than* alternative hypothesis, $H_a : \mu < 30$, reject the null hypothesis when the μ value in $H_n : \mu = 30$ falls above (to the right) of the confidence interval.

Similar reasoning applies to the *greater than* alternative hypothesis, $H_a : \mu > 30$. For this alternative hypothesis, $H_a : \mu > 30$, reject the null hypothesis when the μ value in $H_n : \mu = 30$ falls below (to the left) of the confidence interval.

A One-Sided t Test   This test is similar to the two-sided version in that a t test statistic is compared to a critical t value. The t test statistic computations are identical; however, do not take the absolute value of the test statistic. To maintain a type I error of α, the critical t value uses α instead of $\frac{\alpha}{2}$.

t test statistic		**critical t value**
$\left(\dfrac{\bar{y} - \mu}{s_{\bar{y}}} \right)$	compared to	$t_{(\alpha),(n-1)}$

Decision Rule for the Greater Than Alternative   If the t test statistic shown above exceeds the critical value, reject the null hypothesis that $H_n : \mu =$ (the particular μ value used in computing the t ratio) in favor of the *greater than* alternative, $H_a : \mu >$ (the particular μ value used in computing the t ratio).

Decision Rule for the Less Than Alternative The less than alternative is associated with the left side of the Student's t distribution; therefore, the critical value is negative.

t test statistic **critical t value**

$$\left(\frac{\overline{y} - \mu}{s_{\overline{y}}}\right) \quad \text{compared to} \quad -t_{(\alpha), (n-1)}$$

If the t test statistic is less than the critical t value, reject the null hypothesis that $H_n: \mu =$ (the particular μ value used in computing the t ratio) in favor of the *less than* alternative, $H_a: \mu <$ (the particular μ value used in computing the t ratio).

z Test If the standard error of the sample mean is known rather than estimated, the test statistic follows a normal rather than a Student's t distribution. For this test, the critical z value comes from the normal distribution to replace the critical t value. Otherwise the testing procedure is the same.

p Values For one-sided tests, decisions based on p values are the same as those for two-sided tests. When p values are smaller than α, reject the null hypothesis. However, in a one-sided test, the p value is in reference to one side of the distribution. Therefore, a p value is the probability that the difference, $(\overline{y} - \mu)$, is exceeded in one direction when the null hypothesis is true.

EXAMPLE 13

ONE-SIDED HYPOTHESIS TESTS ON TIRE LIFE

The marketing department for a tire and rubber company wants to claim that the average life of a tire the company recently developed exceeds the well-known average tire life of a competitive brand, which is known to be 32,000 miles.

Only 24 new tires were tested because the tests are destructive and take considerable time to complete. Six cars, all the same model and brand, were used to test the tires. Car model and brand were fixed so that car effects were the same from car to car. Although it was thought that tire life might be dependent rather than independent for the four tires on a particular car, the problem of dependence did not show up in the data. The tires were specially marked so that there was a clear visual cue at wear-out time. Tire life in miles was computed from changes in odometer readings. The tire life figures are

33978.5	32617.7	33052.1	32611.7	33418.9	32455.9
33463.1	32466.9	31624.3	33070.8	33127.0	33543.4
33224.5	30881.2	32597.3	31565.0	34036.7	34053.6
32584.5	31838.4	32290.4	32800.7	33844.9	34157.8

Problem Statement (a)   Summarize the tire life data.

Problem Solution (a)   Various descriptive statistics are

	N	MEAN	MEDIAN	STDEV	SEMEAN
C2	24	32888	32926	865	177

	MIN	MAX	Q1	Q3
C2	30881	34158	32459	33523

Problem Statement (b)   Test the null hypothesis, $H_n : \mu = 32{,}000$, versus the alternative hypothesis, $H_a : \mu > 32{,}000$. MINITAB refers to μ as MU.

Problem Solution (b)   The MINITAB TTEST command produces the following output:

	N	MEAN	STDEV	SE MEAN	T	P VALUE
C2	24	32888	865	177	5.03	0.0000

From this output, the t test statistic is compared to the critical t value as shown below.

t test statistic   **critical t value**

t statistic 5.03 compared to $t_{(\alpha),(n-1)} = t_{(.05),(23)} = 1.714$

Because the test statistic exceeds the critical value, reject the null hypothesis in favor of the alternative that the new tires have a life that exceeds 32,000 miles.

Problem Statement (c)   Use a confidence interval to test the same hypotheses.

Problem Solution (c)   The MINITAB TINTERVAL command produces the following output:

	N	MEAN	STDEV	SE MEAN	90.0 PERCENT C.I.	
C2	24	32888	865	177	(32585	33190)

The significance level is .05. Therefore, for a one-sided test, .05 is on each side of the Student's t distribution. Thus, a 90% interval is required. Because μ, in $H_n : \mu = 32{,}000$, falls to the left of the confidence interval, reject the null hypothesis in favor of the alternative that the new tires have a life that exceeds 32,000 miles.

STATISTICAL HIGHLIGHTS

By comparing test statistics to critical values, hypotheses can be tested.

ERRORS, TYPES I AND II, AND POWER

Hypothesis tests are not error-free. Therefore, it is important to know the kinds of errors that can occur and their chances of occurring.

Type I Error (α Error)

Hypothesis tests do not always lead to a correct decision to reject the null hypothesis. Inevitably some proportion of the time the null hypothesis is rejected when it should not be. This is a type I error that becomes evident from the nature of a confidence interval when used for hypothesis testing. For example, with a 95% confidence interval, we expect 95 of 100 such intervals to contain the unknown population mean. The complementary percentage, $(100 - 95)\% = 5\%$, is the fraction of intervals that don't contain the population mean. Furthermore, in hypothesis testing this 5% is the proportion of the time that the null hypothesis is rejected even though the null hypothesis is true. In this way, a $(1 - \alpha) \times 100\%$ confidence interval produces a type I error equal to $\alpha \times 100\%$. As a consequence, this type I error is referred to as an α error or alpha error.

Type II Error (β Error)

Hypothesis tests do not always lead to correct decisions to accept the null hypothesis. Inevitably, some proportion of times, the null hypothesis is accepted when it should not be because the alternative hypothesis is true. This is a **type II error, beta error,** or **β error.**

Type I and type II errors are companions in the sense that if you try to reduce the alpha error, you inadvertently increase the beta error, and vice versa. Usually, a compromise is necessary that balances these errors.

Often type II errors are computed for a wide range of specific alternatives to the null hypothesis. For example, suppose $H_n : \mu = 30$ and a type II error is computed for each of the following alternative hypotheses: $\mu = 26, 28, 32, 34,$ and 36. A plot of the type II errors versus the parameter values, $\mu = 26, 28, 32, 34,$ and 36, is called an **operating characteristic (OC) curve.** An operating characteristic curve is illustrated in Example 14.

The OC curve is important because it displays the type II error for any population mean in an alternative hypothesis. Thus, the probability of erroneously accepting the null hypothesis is known. When this probability is too high, it can be reduced by increasing the sample size.

Power

The complementary probability, one minus the type II error, is called the **power** of a hypothesis test. The power is the probability that the null hypothesis is rejected when it should be because it is not true.

A graphical display of the power versus different values of μ is called the **power curve.** The power curve is complementary to the OC curve and equals one minus the OC curve. When the power of a hypothesis test is too low, it can be increased by increasing the sample size. Some statistical testing procedures are more powerful than others. The power curve is useful in comparing different testing procedures and in judging the effectiveness of a particular procedure.

EXAMPLE 14

ALPHA ERROR, BETA ERROR, AND POWER FOR HYPOTHESES ABOUT THE MEAN HEIGHT OF THE ADULT POPULATION

Consider samples of size 10 from a normal population with a known mean of 69 in. and a standard deviation of 2.5 in. We are interested in how the samples perform in hypothesis tests where the null hypothesis is $H_n : \mu = 69$ and the two-sided alternative is $H_a : \mu \neq 69$. The standard error of the mean is $\frac{2.5}{(10)^{1/2}} = .7906$. Using an alpha error of .05 and the confidence interval

$$\overline{y} \pm t_{(\alpha/2),(n-1)} \times s_{\overline{y}}$$

the null hypothesis is rejected when the sample mean is less than $(69 - (2.262 \times .7906)) = 67.2117$ (the lower limit for rejection) or when the sample mean exceeds $(69 + (2.262 \times .7906)) = 70.7883$ (the upper limit for rejection). When $\mu = 69$, this decision rule leads to erroneous rejection of the null hypothesis 5% of the time.

Problem Statement (a) Except for $\mu = 69$, each of the following means are possible alternative hypotheses: $\mu = 64, 64.5, 65, 65.5, 66, 66.5, 67, 67.5, 68, 68.5, 69, 69.5, 70, 70.5, 71, 71.5, 72, 72.5,$ or 73 (these are placed in column C6). Use MINITAB to find the probability of getting sample means less than 67.2117 (the lower limit for rejection) assuming the population mean is located at each μ value listed above. Plot these probabilities versus the μ values.

Problem Solution (a) On the plot below, C3 is the probability that you will get sample means less than 67.2117 (the lower limit for rejection) for each μ value.

Problem Statement (b) Use MINITAB to find the probability of getting sample means greater than 70.7883 (the upper limit for rejection) assuming the population mean is located at each μ value listed above. Plot these probabilities versus the μ values.

Problem Solution (b) On the plot below, C5 is the probability that you will get sample means greater than 70.7883 (the upper limit for rejection) for each μ value.

Problem Statement (c) For each assumed value of μ, add the corresponding probabilities in the two previous plots, C3 + C5, and plot. What is this plot called?

Example 14 Plot (a)

Lower Limit Rejection Probabilities (C3) Versus Various Values for the Mean (C6)

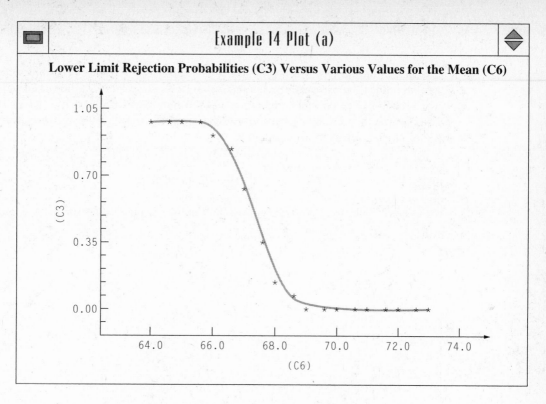

Example 14 Plot (b)

Upper Limit Rejection Probabilities (C5) Versus Various Values for the Mean (C6)

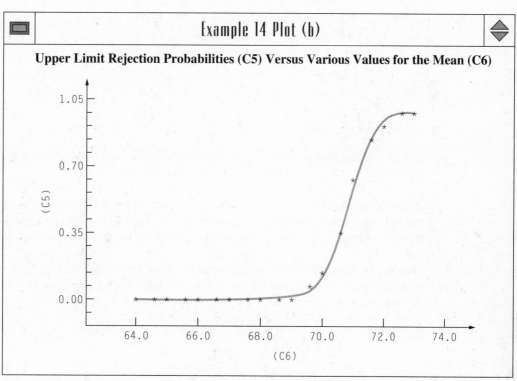

Problem Solution (c)   Each probability in C3 + C5 is the total probability of rejecting the null hypothesis at each assumed population mean. This plot is the power curve. The power is the probability of correctly rejecting the null hypothesis because it is false. The power increases in either direction as μ moves away from $H_n : \mu = 69$. The further away μ moves the more likely a rejection will occur.

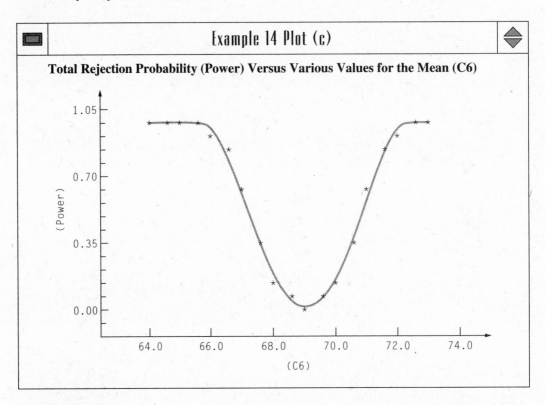

Problem Statement (d)   For each assumed value of μ, find the total probability of not rejecting the null hypothesis. What is this plot called?

Problem Solution (d)   This plot is the operating characteristic curve. It is complementary to the power curve and equals one minus the power. The OC curve is a plot of the type II or beta error.

Problem Discussion   If the beta error is too large for certain alternatives, it can be reduced by increasing the sample size. This concept of error reduction is useful in statistical quality control, where incoming parts are sampled and inspected. Decision rules alert management when there are too many defectives in the sample and when shipments of parts should be rejected.

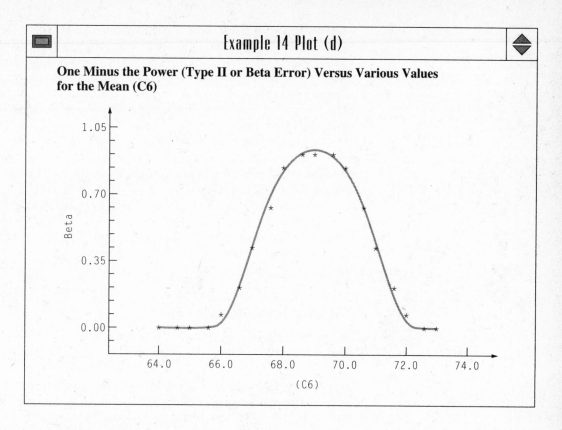

Example 14 Plot (d)

One Minus the Power (Type II or Beta Error) Versus Various Values for the Mean (C6)

NEOCLASSICAL METHODS (OPTIONAL)

The fact that statistics such as the sample mean vary from sample to sample lays the groundwork for confidence intervals and hypothesis tests. Even though confidence intervals and hypothesis tests are explained with statements such as "95 of 100 such intervals are expected to include the unknown population mean," the 100 such intervals are never computed in classical statistics. Usually a single sample is used to test a hypothesis or construct a confidence interval. However, computer-intensive methods are now available in which hundreds of confidence intervals can be computed. Thus, this newer methodology seems to come close to the explanation of what a confidence interval is.

Bootstrapping

Bootstrapping is simple random sampling with replacement from an existing sample. This **resampling** of the original (n) sample data values to generate new samples of size (n) is likely to result in new sample summary statistics. Resampling many times lets us see how much the summary statistics vary from sample to sample.

Bootstrapping is usually is done on a computer. However, it is instructive to carry out the operations by hand to learn how the procedure works. The following steps illustrate the technique: (1) write each data value on a separate piece of paper; (2) place all pieces of paper in a hat; (3) reach into the hat and draw a piece of paper at random, record the data value, and place the paper back in the hat; and (4) repeat the drawing with replacement until n observations are made.

For each resampled sample, obtain a sample median or any other summary statistic you wish to examine. By repeating this process many times, the variation and distribution of the summary statistic can be seen in a histogram, and the mean, standard deviation, and so on can be found.

Bootstrapping is tedious by hand, but computers can resample easily. For example, a computer can find hundreds of resampled sample medians quickly. Then a stem-and-leaf diagram or a histogram of, say, the 100 sample medians reveals the distribution, the central tendency, and the variation. The less the sample medians vary the more precise they are as estimators.

The Bootstrap Standard Error

The estimated standard error of the sample mean $\overline{y}$ resulted from a simple formula, $s_{\overline{y}} = \frac{s}{n^{1/2}}$, where $s^2 = \frac{\Sigma(y_i - \overline{y})^2}{n - 1}$. Unfortunately, the formula for $s_{\overline{y}}$ does not extend in any obvious way to estimators other than the sample mean. Such simple formulas for the variability of other estimators do not always exist. Yet there is a need to measure the precision of a wide variety of other estimators.

The bootstrap provides a general way to estimate the standard errors of a wide variety of estimators. The bootstrap approach makes use of the usual classical approach but applies it to resampled samples. As a result, the following numerical illustration reviews the standard computations for obtaining the estimated standard error of the sample mean.

The Usual Classical Approach   Suppose a small original sample consists of three observations, $y_1 = 3$, $y_2 = 4$, and $y_3 = 2$. The sample mean is $\overline{y} = \frac{9}{3}$. The sample standard deviation is the square root of

$$s^2 = \frac{((3 - 3)^2 + (4 - 3)^2 + (2 - 3)^2)}{(3 - 1)} = 1$$

Using the sample standard deviation, the estimated standard error of the sample mean is

$$s_{\overline{y}} = \frac{s}{n^{1/2}} = \frac{1}{3^{1/2}}$$

The Bootstrap Approach   The bootstrap analog of the procedure to find $s_{\bar{y}}$ can be found by carrying out the following steps:

Step (1):   Write each data value on a piece of paper and place the three pieces of paper in a hat.

Step (2):   Draw at random a piece of paper from the hat and record the value, say, $y_1^{*1} = 4$. (**Note:** In the superscript *1, the first character, *, indicates that this is a sample from a sample and not the original y_1. The second superscript character, 1, indicates that this is the first resampled sample of n = 3.)

Step (3):   Return the paper to the hat and draw again, repeating Step (2) until the number of recorded values equals the original sample size. For example, suppose $y_2^{*1} = 3$. Repeat and suppose $y_3^{*1} = 4$. Thus, in this sample of the original sample, the data values are 4, 3, and 4.

Discussion   Because the resampling was with replacement, each of the original data values had an equal chance of being selected on each draw. Data value 4 was selected twice, the 3 was selected once, and the 2 was not selected at all. These are the y_i^{*1} values for the first resample from the original sample.

If we repeat the resampling process again, the next resampled sample will have observations designated as y_i^{*2}, where the superscript 2 denotes the second sample of size three from the original set of data values. Suppose this resampling is done k times. Then the observations in the k-th resample would be designated as y_i^{*k}.

From each of the resamples, we can get an estimator, say, a sample mean. All these sample means are

$$\bar{y}^{*1}, \quad \bar{y}^{*2}, \quad \bar{y}^{*3}, \dots, \quad \bar{y}^{*k}$$

The bootstrap estimator of the standard error is

$$\text{(bootstrap) } s_{\bar{y}} = \left[\frac{\Sigma(\bar{y}^{*a} - \bar{y}^*)^2}{k - 1} \right]^{1/2}$$

where a = 1, 2, . . . , k and $\bar{y}^* = \dfrac{\Sigma \, \bar{y}^{*a}}{k}$.

The advantageous feature of the bootstrap is that the estimated standard errors can be obtained for any estimator. Therefore, in place of the sample mean we could measure the variability of the sample standard deviation, the range, and so on. Many estimators have no simple mathematical expression for their standard errors. Therefore, the bootstrap is a necessary approach where closed-form mathematical expressions are not available. Of course, the bootstrap is a computer intensive method.

EXAMPLE 15

THE BOOTSTRAP STANDARD ERROR FOR HEIGHTS OF ADULTS

Problem Statement   From the first sample of adult heights C1, resample ten times. Compute ten sample means, get a histogram, and summarize. From the summary statistics, find the bootstrap standard error.

Problem Solution   The MINITAB commands in Appendix 1 use the first sample, column C1, of adult heights for resampling. Because the sample size is 10, C13 contains 10 equal probabilities, .10, that give each observation in C1 an equal chance of being selected in the resampling process (this is like rolling a 10-sided die). Through resampling, ten samples (C20–C29) are generated; row means are computed and placed in C30. Although the sample size is small, the standard deviation of the column of means, C30, is a bootstrap estimate of the standard error.

```
Histogram of C30    n = 10

Midpoint    Count
    66.0      1    *
    66.5      2    **
    67.0      1    *
    67.5      2    **
    68.0      2    **
    68.5      1    *
    69.0      0
    69.5      1    *
```

```
             N      MEAN    MEDIAN   STDEV
C30         10     67.500   67.412   1.108 (bootstrap standard error)

           MIN     MAX       Q1       Q3
C30       65.866  69.692   66.599   68.192
```

Additional Notched Boxplot Examples

In the following examples, real-life situations are considered in which the data are random and in a state of statistical control. The notched boxplot is applied to commonly encountered business problems. Recall that the notched interval is an estimate of the region in which 95 of 100 resampled sample medians are expected to lie. It is computed as follows:

$$\text{median} \pm 1.82 \times \frac{\text{box length}}{n^{1/2}}$$

EXAMPLE 16

RETURNS ON A STOCK

Many investors watch stock prices. They want to buy when prices are low and sell when prices are high. To gauge how well investments are doing and to compare one investment to another, experienced investors examine stock returns. Investments and finance literature discusses investments in terms of returns. A monthly return on a stock is

$$\frac{\text{(price at month-end minus price at month beginning)}}{\text{(price at month beginning)}}$$

If capital gains (stock splits and dividends) and cash dividends occur during the month, they would be added to the numerator. A return is the rate of gain or loss (relative to a beginning period price) that would have occurred if you had purchased the stock at the beginning period price and sold it at the ending period price.

A return on a stock or any other investment facilitates the comparison of alternative investments. For example, you might wish to compare the return on a stock with the interest rate (return) offered by a bank. Stock returns vary over time, and that motivates us to examine returns over many periods and to use statistical tools to describe return behavior.

Returns are often random. Thus, common statistical summaries of returns are valid and convey useful information to the investor. As an example, you would like to put your money in stocks that yield high levels of return, which can be measured by the median return. Therefore, the median return can be computed for many different stocks (or other investments for that matter) and used to rank stocks from highest to lowest return.

In addition to the level of return, intelligent investors measure the variation in return because the greater the variability the greater will be the risk associated with the investment. For example, putting money in stocks is risky because returns vary, but a bank savings account offers relatively stable returns. The variation in the stock return can be seen in a stem-and-leaf diagram, histogram, or boxplot. The box length and standard deviation are convenient variability (risk) measures.

Problem Statement (a)   Using exploratory statistics, measure the level and variability of the following stock return percentages. Twenty-four monthly returns are listed. First plot the returns to see if they appear to be random.

−9.0	−8.5	1.2	1.7	−3.9	4.4	−5.0	2.0	3.7	2.0	0.5	5.9
1.5	5.8	−3.9	−0.7	−5.4	−6.2	3.6	3.4	6.9	−4.1	7.9	−0.7

Problem Solution (a)   The following statistical analysis sharpens our impressions of this investment opportunity and establishes a basis for comparison with other investments. First, a plot of returns appears random; therefore, the summary statistics will be valid.

The exploratory summary statistics on returns are

```
      DEPTH     LOWER     UPPER     SPREAD
N=     24
M      12.5              1.35  (median)
H       6.5     -4.00     3.65     7.65 (box length)
         1      -9.00     7.90    16.90
```

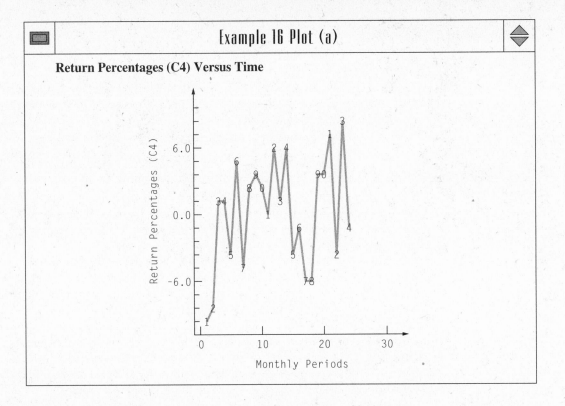

Example 16 Plot (a)

Return Percentages (C4) Versus Time

The median return level is 1.35% per month. For a year, the return is a little more than 12 times 1.35 because of compounding. The yearly return is 17.46 (1.0135 to the power 12 yields 1.1746). Note that 50% of the time the monthly return is between −4% and 3.65%, making this a risky stock.

Problem Statement (b) Construct and interpret a notched boxplot of the return percentages.

Problem Solution (b) The notches on the boxplot below provide a 95% interval estimate of the population median return.

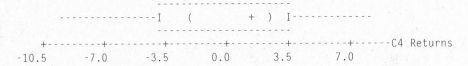

In the following example, because a bottle-filling machine does not always operate correctly, a sample of six bottles is taken periodically. The sample median contents for those six bottles acts as an alarm signal.

When the sample median is too high or too low, this signals an **out-of-control condition,** which indicates that the filling machine is not filling properly. Technically, this production monitoring is called **statistical process control (SPC).**

A notched interval establishes an **upper control limit (UCL)** and a **lower control limit (LCL)** on the sample median. A sample median that falls outside the notched interval is too high or too low. This indicates that the filling machine is not operating properly, which is an out-of-control condition. In addition to these control limits, a **centerline (CL)** marks the middle.

EXAMPLE 17

QUALITY CONTROL: A MANUFACTURING PROCESS IN A STATE OF STATISTICAL CONTROL

Six bottles were sampled from each of ten cases giving $(6 \times 10) = 60$ measurements of the contents of each bottle (in ml). As a benchmark, these 60 measurements were taken while the machine was functioning properly.

```
287  288  299  300  293  303  292  300  303  300  299
305  300  305  293  297  291  291  302  302  306  293
308  297  308  301  303  301  305  300  305  300  295
303  303  306  304  291  301  295  308  309  300  296
299  302  307  309  297  312  298  303  302  298  299
300  300  296  299  300
```

Problem Statement (a)   First, plot the content measurements to examine the variability and see if the measurements appear to be random.

Problem Solution (a)   A time series plot indicates that the contents of each bottle deviates randomly from the median. Some variation in the amount of fruit drink in each bottle seems to be unavoidable.

Problem Statement (b)   Find exploratory summary statistics for bottle content measurements. Are they valid?

Problem Solution (b)   The randomness of content measurements results in valid summary statistics of the 60 bottles.

```
       DEPTH    LOWER    UPPER    SPREAD
N=     60
M      30.5              300 (median)
H      15.5     297      303      6 (box length)
        1       287      312      25
```

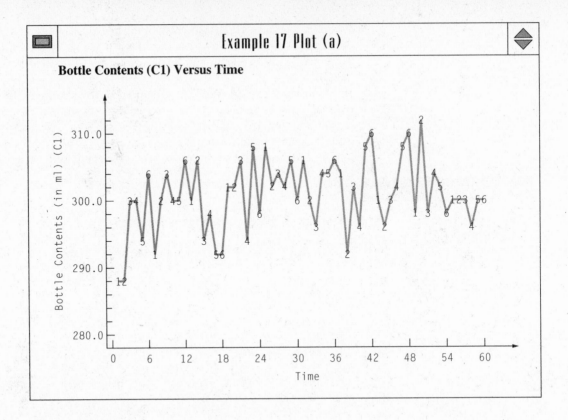

Example 17 Plot (a)

Bottle Contents (C1) Versus Time

Problem Statement (c)   Construct a control chart to monitor median contents of six bottles filled with a fruit drink. Overlay the control limits on a plot of the 60 content measurements.

Problem Solution (c)   The centerline is the median, (CL) = 300. The notched interval for the medians of six bottles forms the upper and lower control limits, which are 95% percent bounds for sample medians of six bottles.

$$\text{median} \pm 1.82 \times \frac{\text{box length}}{n^{1/2}}$$

$$(\text{upper control limit}) \; 304.5 = 300 + \left(1.82 \times \frac{6}{2.4495}\right)$$

$$(\text{lower control limit}) \; 295.5 = 300 - \left(1.82 \times \frac{6}{2.4495}\right)$$

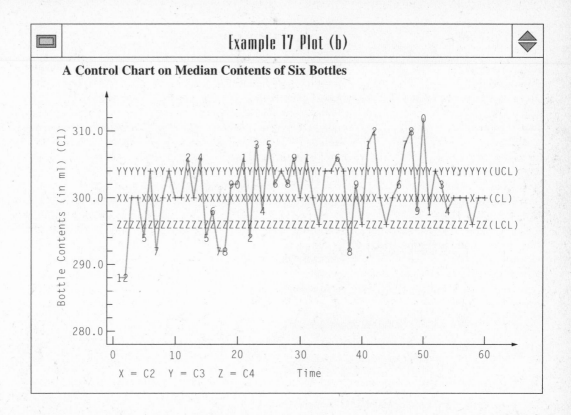

Example 17 Plot (b)

A Control Chart on Median Contents of Six Bottles

CHAPTER SUMMARY

Soon after becoming equipped with the sample mean, you became aware that different samples would likely result in different sample means. Thus, the problem of determining the variability of the sample mean became evident. The most common measure of the variability of the sample mean is the estimated standard error, $s_{\bar{y}} = \frac{s}{n^{1/2}}$, where s is the sample standard deviation.

In addition to being simply a variability measure, the standard error was used to create a confidence interval on the unknown mean, μ. Such an interval bounds our thinking about where the estimator might be. The classical interval estimator had its parallels in exploratory work in the form of the notched boxplot.

We built an awareness of different types of confidence intervals—intervals on single future observations and inter-vals on the mean of q future observations. Because all these intervals differed in width, the data analyst should be very careful in selecting and interpreting an appropriate interval type for a particular problem.

Interval estimation can be put to further use in hypothesis testing. The decision to reject one hypothesis in favor of another is not error-free. We described two types of decision errors—type I or alpha errors and type II or beta errors.

Finally, we introduced the bootstrap as a way to estimate the variability of estimators that don't have simple, mathematical formulae for computing a variability measure.

KEY TERMS

EXERCISES

1. Conduct the following simulation experiment:

(a) Roll four dice 100 times, compute 100 sample means of the numbers on the four faces, and print these results.

(b) Examine the sampling distribution of the sample means. Is the distribution of sample means normal? Do the sample means of the measurements have less variability than the individual measurements?

(c) Theoretically it is known that for a population of infinite size

$$\sigma_{\bar{y}} = \frac{\sigma}{n^{1/2}}$$

Each sample mean in your experiment was based on n = 4. Therefore, estimate the standard error of the sample means using the following formula:

$$s_{\bar{y}} = \frac{s}{n^{1/2}}$$

2. Suppose a normal distribution of adult heights has a known mean $\mu = 5$ ft 9 in. = 69 in. and a known standard deviation $\sigma = 2.5$ in.

(a) Simulate five samples of size 6 and five more samples of size 60. Then construct ten notched boxplots for these samples. The first five boxplots should have wider notches with midpoints that vary more than those for the last five boxplots that involve larger sample sizes. Therefore, larger sample sizes tend to produce narrower and more stable notches, which are more focused on the true mean. Usually we don't know the true mean and are using these intervals to get an idea of where it might be located.

(b) Construct and interpret the classical 95% confidence intervals on the population mean with these samples. First assume that σ is unknown and that you are simply presented with the simulation data. Next assume that σ is known and construct another set of confidence intervals. When σ is known, the uncertainty is reduced. This tends to produce narrower confidence intervals.

3. Managers who worry about the characteristics of their service facilities often sample queue lengths, recording the number of customers waiting to be served at different times.

(a) Construct a 95% confidence interval on μ, the unknown mean queue length for the population, based on the following sample of data:

Queue Lengths (# of Customers Waiting for Service)

4 7 3 8 2 2 5 6 12 9 7 6 6 9 13 11

(b) What null hypothesis values of μ, the mean number of customers waiting, would you reject as not being supported by the data?

(c) (Optional) Find exploratory summaries as well as a notched boxplot for queue lengths. Compare this information to the results in parts (a) and (b). Explain any unusually large differences by examining a histogram of the queue length figures. Which set of results do you think are more reliable in this situation?

(d) Astute managers realize that queue length is related to service time (the time it takes to service a customer) as well as the time between consecutive arrivals (the interarrival time). Queue lengths tend to increase (producing longer waiting lines) as the ratio of the typical service time to the typical interarrival time is increased. Therefore, in addition to queue lengths, service times and interarrival times are often sampled because they help provide a more complete view of the customer service situation.

Construct 95% confidence intervals on the unknown mean service time and on the unknown mean interarrival time for the corresponding populations based on the following samples:

SERVICE TIMES (MINUTES)
3.4 3.3 3.7 4.9 3.2 4.5 4.0 4.1 3.4 4.0 3.7 4.1

INTERARRIVAL TIMES (MINUTES)
7.6 5.7 8.8 3.2 4.1 3.2 4.3 3.4 7.6 3.7 1.9 6.4
5.3 3.6 5.4 4.8 4.4 6.5 2.1 2.5 1.4 7.5 3.3 4.5
7.2 5.6 4.4 6.7 4.2 7.7 3.3 2.4 7.8 6.2 5.0 4.2
5.1 6.0 8.9

(e) Find the ratio of the typical service time to the typical interarrival time. This is the fraction of time the server is busy. Do you think the server is busy enough?

4. The Consumer Price Index annual percentage changes over several years are[1]

5.8 6.5 7.7 11.3 13.5 10.4 6.1 3.2 4.3 3.6 1.9 3.6
4.1 4.8 5.4   4.2   3.0   3.0

(a) Is this sequence of observations random or nonrandom? Show how you tested for randomness.

(b) Construct a 95% confidence interval on μ, the mean percentage change (yearly) in the Consumer Price Index for a population of Consumer Price Index changes.

Note: Although the Central Limit Theorem eases the burden of the normality assumption for confidence intervals, it does not help you when it comes to the independence assumption. Clearly, you can work through the computational mechanics for confidence intervals, but a nonrandom series means that your interval may be misleading.

5. Accounts receivable amount balances in hundreds of dollars for a sample of GMO company debtors are

21 22 28 65 78 61 30 38 33 48 49 56 41 55 54
 9 12 23 40 45 49 54 37 35 30 51 33 37 42 49
41 50

(a) Construct a 90% confidence interval on μ, the unknown mean accounts receivable balance amount for the debtor population.

(b) What null hypothesis values of μ, the debtor mean accounts receivable balance, would you reject because they are not supported by the data?

6. A wholesale magazine distributor generates invoices for customers twice a week because there are two deliveries a week to each retail outlet. An invoice contains a listing of all books, magazines, and newspapers available for distribution to the retailer. Usually a particular retailer receives a subset of the items available.

In the wholesaler's warehouse, the invoices are the basis for packaging retailer deliveries. Because the packaging is manual and there are many items and retailers, some packaging errors are inevitable. Therefore, some retailers may receive more or less than stated invoice amounts of particular items. Usually a retailer requests a credit for shortages. The percentage of retailers receiving shortage credit is computed weekly as a control mechanism. When the shortage claims do not occur at random, retailers who make repeated claims are suspected of lying and their deliveries are double-checked at the warehouse.

(a) Using the following data, construct a 90% confidence interval on μ, the unknown mean percentage of retailers receiving shortage credit for the population.

WEEKLY PERCENTAGES OF RETAILERS RECEIVING SHORTAGE CREDIT

1.5	6.4	.5	5.5	2.5	3.5	4.5	3.0	12.2	9.0
4.5	2.5	3.5	.8	6.6	1.5	5.7	3.4	2.0	.5
6.0	3.0	2.0	2.2						

(b) Write a short description of your results in such a way that an employee without statistical training can use the results to monitor future percentages and to provide feedback (about packaging errors) to employees doing the packaging.

7. Broad-based statistics are available in the *Statistical Abstract of the United States.* Current ratios for nonfinancial corporations over an 11 year period are[2]

1.69   1.69   1.65   1.55   1.48   1.46   1.49   1.46   1.46   1.46   1.44

(a) Are these data random? If nonrandom, what is the effect on your interpretation of a confidence interval?

(b) Construct a 90% confidence interval on μ, the unknown mean current ratio for the population of nonfinancial corporations. What is it that management should worry about when the current ratio gets too low?

(c) For what null hypothesis values of the mean current ratio, μ, would you reject because they are not supported by the data?

8. Suppose you are interested in learning about starting salaries of students graduating from a large university from a sample of these figures.

(a) Based on the following random sample, construct a 99% confidence interval on μ, the unknown mean starting salary (in thousands of dollars) for the population of starting salaries.

32, 41, 33, 31, 39, 37, 38, 38, 42, 33, 35, 38, 32, 32, 34, 40, 33, 30, 31, 35

(b) What null hypothesis values of the mean starting salary, μ, would you reject because they are not supported by the data?

9. The following textile data was analyzed by Box and Cox in a classic paper on transformations.[3] The measurements which are on the cycles to failure of worsted yarn, are

674   370   292   338   266   210   170   118   90   1414   1198   634
1022   620   438   442   332   220   3636   3184   2000   1568   1070
566   1140   884   360

(a) Construct a 95% confidence interval on μ, the unknown mean number of cycles to failure for the population of worsted yarn.

(b) What null hypothesis values of the mean cycles to failure, μ, would you reject because they are not supported by the data?

10. A college administrator is preparing to make a decision about an increase in charges for room and board. In thousands of dollars, a sample of anticipated room and board costs for accredited colleges and universities is[4]

4.8   9.0   4.6   5.0   8.0   4.4   7.0   5.4   6.2
5.8   3.6   4.0   3.2   6.4   5.0   6.0   6.0   7.4
6.8   4.2   8.4   7.0   6.0   3.4   4.8   7.2   4.4

(a) Construct a 95% confidence interval on μ, the unknown mean charges for room and board for the population of accredited colleges and universities.

(b) What null hypothesis values of mean charges, μ, would you reject because they are not supported by the data?

(c) If you were on a committee making recommendations to administration, use the confidence interval to target the region where you think your charges should be (assuming that you do not wish to exceed the average of all universities).

11. Part of an assembly operation is done by hand. The nominal time to assemble one unit by hand is 10.5 min. A sample of observed times follows.

8.5   12.2   10.0   9.6   10.4   10.8   9.5   9.6   12.0   11.3
10.9   10.5   13.5   14.2   8.4   11.0   9.1   10.1   8.0   13.1

(a) Using a 95% level of confidence, create bounds called control limits on the sample mean for samples of 20 assembly times.

(b) What null hypothesis values of the mean assembly time, μ, would you reject because they are not supported by the data?

(c) When the interval created by control limits does not include the nominal time, the hand-assembly operation is said to be in conflict with the nominal specifications. For this sample, would you conclude that the hand-assembly operation is or is not in conflict with the specifications?

12. Total factory overhead costs (supervision, insurance, depreciation, utilities, and so on) are budgeted for each month of the year. Additionally, the factory produces a different number of units each month. A monthly overhead rate per unit produced is established by dividing budgeted overhead by the units produced during that month. Vastly different overhead rates are problematic because management loses touch with what is typical under normal production conditions.

(a) For the following monthly (January through December) overhead rates, find a 95% confidence interval on the typical overhead rate.

3.50   2.65   2.25   2.10   4.30   6.00
10.00   34.00   11.00   5.00   4.30   3.00

(b) Is the sequence of rates random? Discuss the implications of this result.

13. A machine shop performs operations such as milling, cleaning, grinding, and facing. Direct labor costs (hours times wage rate) is computed for each of these operations by job number and type. For a specific job type, the direct labor cost dollar amounts for grinding were

42.46	43.60	65.05	66.19	53.80	72.23	51.31
66.87	70.63	66.80	63.51	75.54	65.84	75.32
53.81	60.90	50.39	48.74	70.47	70.08	77.74
53.33	80.23	60.89	80.79	67.18	71.52	67.12
75.19	130.50	75.63	65.67	57.24	71.71	72.27
76.43	73.25	49.81	66.97	56.65	81.37	81.54
66.85	59.38	63.90	69.01	79.45	82.58	61.16
98.00	62.80	71.57	69.60			

(a) Construct a 95% confidence interval on μ, the unknown mean direct labor cost for the population of grinding cost figures for this job type.

(b) What null hypothesis values of the mean grinding cost, μ, would you reject because they are not supported by the data?

14. Compute and plot alpha errors, beta errors, and the power based on the behavior of samples from a normal population of adult heights with a known mean and standard deviation of 69 in. and 2.5 in., respectively. Use a sample size of n = 40, which results in a standard error of $\frac{2.5}{(40)^{1/2}} = .3953$.

When the null hypothesis is $H_n : \mu = 69$ and the two-sided alternative is $H_a : \mu \neq 69$, the alpha error is .05 and the null hypothesis is rejected for sample means less than $(69 - (1.96 \times .3953))$ or greater than $(69 + (1.96 \times .3953))$. When $\mu = 69$, this decision rule leads to rejection 5% of the time. When $\mu = 65, 65.5, 66,$ 66.5, 67, 67.5, 68, 68.5, 69, 69.5, or 70, the decision rule leads to rejection with other percentages called the power. If you use the MINITAB command sequence in Appendix 1, the power is in column C8. When $\mu = 65, 65.5, 66, 66.5,$ 67, 67.5, 68, 68.5, 69, 69.5, or 70, the decision rule leads to acceptance percentages that constitute the beta error. If you use the MINITAB command sequence in Appendix 1, the beta error is in column C7.

Use appropriate plots to show how the power and the beta error change as the population mean is changed. Compare your plots to those shown in Example 14. What effect did the sample size increase have?

15. You are given returns on a stock, which were computed from the i-th period price, P_i, and the price one period ahead. The return on a stock is $y_i = \frac{P_{i+1} - P_i}{P_i}$. Because we would like to see how the movement of a particular stock is related to the movement of the market as a whole, we use the Dow Jones (DJ) index or the Standard and Poor's Composite index as a price that represents the whole market. Hence, for example, the market return is $x_{1i} = \frac{DJ_{i+1} - DJ_i}{DJ_i}$. These returns have been computed for you, converted to a percentage, and rounded for simplicity. They are

PERIOD	1	2	3	4	5	6	7	8	9	10	11	12
$y_i =$	12	15	−4	1	3	−2	−8	−1	1	1	2	7
$x_{1i} =$	12	6	2	4	4	5	−6	−2	3	6	2	−1

(a) Construct a 90% confidence interval on the mean market return and on the mean return for the stock.

(b) If you were told that the mean market return typically exceeds 9%, do these data support that claim?

16. The approximate sample size needed to estimate the population mean with a maximum estimation error of $E = |(\bar{y} - \mu)|$ is given by

$$n = \frac{s^2 z_{\alpha/2}^2}{|E|^2}$$

In estimating the unknown typical height of adults, μ, such that the maximum estimation error equals 0.5 in. with a probability of $(1 - \alpha) = .99$, the resulting z score is $z_{.005} = 3$. The standard deviation is 2.5. Using these figures in the above formula yields the required sample size of

$$n = \frac{2.5^2 \times 3^2}{.05^2} = 225$$

Suppose different maximum estimation errors are contemplated. Obtain a plot of the approximate sample size versus maximum estimation error as the maximum estimation error takes on the following values: .1, .2, .3, .4, .5, .6, .7, .8, and .9. Use MINITAB (or some other statistical package) to make these sample size calculations and to construct the plot. For example, in MINITAB

```
SET INTO C1
.1 .2 .3 .4 .5 .6 .7 .8 .9
SET IN C2
9(2.5)
SET INTO C3
9(3)
LET C4 = ((C2**2)*(C3**2))/(C1**2)
PLOT C4 C1
```

17. An automobile manufacturer conducts quality control training programs in two of its supplier plants. The instructor gives the same exam in both plants to small samples of employees. The exam scores are

| Plant (Boston) | 90 | 73 | 78 | 82 | 66 | 69 | 85 | 86 | 76 | 89 | 70 |
| Plant (Atlanta) | 81 | 72 | 50 | 66 | 55 | 70 | 68 | 82 | 71 | | |

(a) Use the MINITAB DESCRIBE command (or a similar command in another statistical package) to find sample means, standard deviations, and standard errors. Then construct a 95% confidence interval on the unknown mean for the population of employees in each plant.

(b) Do these intervals suggest that the employees from one plant might have performed better than those in the second plant?

18. A manager who welcomes employee suggestions about reducing assembly time in a production operation decided to examine assembly times resulting from two assembly methods. The new assembly method was a result of a recent employee suggestion.

ASSEMBLY TIMES (OLD METHOD)							ASSEMBLY TIMES (NEW METHOD)						
21.6	21.7	23.9	24.0	22.7	24.6	22.5	23.5	23.5	22.0	21.3	21.7	22.3	23.3
24.0	24.4	24.0	23.7	24.9	23.9	24.9	23.6	21.5	24.1	21.6	22.5	22.3	21.6
22.7	23.4	22.4	22.2	24.4	24.4	25.1	21.7	22.0	22.0	21.1	21.8	21.9	24.3
22.7	25.3	23.4	25.4	24.1	24.5	24.1	22.9	20.1	21.8	20.6	21.7	22.3	21.5
24.9	23.9	24.9	23.9	23.1	24.5	24.6	22.9	21.5	22.2	21.4	21.9	21.1	22.8
25.0	24.7	22.3	24.0	23.0			21.8	21.5	23.4	22.6	20.6		

(a) Use the MINITAB DESCRIBE command (or a similar command in another statistical package) to find sample means, standard deviations, and standard errors. Then construct a 95% confidence interval on the unknown mean for the population of assembly times for each assembly method.

(b) Do these intervals suggest that the new assembly method might reduce the typical assembly time?

19. An investor collected monthly price data for the stocks of two companies in the same line of business. From prices, returns were computed. They are shown below.

COMPANY A RETURNS

0.112	0.115	0.158	0.160	0.135	0.172	0.130
0.161	0.169	0.161	0.155	0.179	0.159	0.178
0.135	0.149	0.128	0.125	0.168	0.168	0.183
0.134	0.187	0.149				

COMPANY B RETURNS

0.209	0.182	0.191	0.182	0.198	0.179	0.199
0.179	0.162	0.191	0.192	0.200	0.194	0.147
0.181	0.161	0.210	0.211	0.181	0.166	0.175
0.186	0.206	0.213				

(a) Use the MINITAB DESCRIBE command (or a similar command in another statistical package) to find sample means, standard deviations, and standard errors. Then construct a 95% confidence interval on the unknown mean for the population of returns for each company.

(b) Do these intervals suggest that these companies have different levels of typical returns?

20. (a) Find a 95% confidence interval on the population mean weight of burgers based on the following small systematic random sample of burgers (all 87 burger weights are available in file BURGER.MTW).

8.47	8.57	8.69	8.75	8.76	8.82	8.85	8.88	8.89	8.90	8.96
9.01	9.02	9.03	9.05	9.05	9.10	9.11	9.14	9.15	9.19	9.21
9.23	9.27	9.29	9.36	9.46	9.52	9.71				

(b) (Optional) If you have computer access to the BURGER.MTW file, try to determine how the systematic random sample was taken. Also construct a 95% confidence interval on the population mean weight using all the data in the file and compare this result to that in part (a).

21. Find a 90% confidence interval on the population mean time between arrivals of parts at an assembly operation (the figures are in minutes and are sorted).

0.03	0.49	0.78	1.45	2.46	3.12	4.54	4.98	7.08	7.90	8.81
9.92	11.28	12.49	14.71	16.24	17.73	23.69	27.26	32.38	60.68	

22. Manufacturing machinery is adjusted to control product quality characteristics. Certain engine head gaskets, for example, have thickness specifications of .040 ± .003 in., where .040 is the target for centering the process. Unfortunately, product measurements don't always meet the specifications, and adjustments in the process are needed.

(a) From the following product production data, construct a 95% confidence interval on the long-term center (population mean) of the gasket thickness measurements.

0.0395	0.0402	0.0400	0.0401	0.0403	0.0406	0.0400
0.0399	0.0397	0.0398	0.0395	0.0405	0.0400	0.0403
0.0400						

(b) If this interval includes the target, the process is considered to be centered on target. Is this process centered on target?

(c) The additional observations that follow were taken after a new batch of raw materials was used in the process. Construct a second 95% confidence interval on the long-term center of the process with the new data.

0.0409   0.0415   0.0412   0.0416   0.0413   0.0408   0.0399
0.0410   0.0411   0.0420   0.0410   0.0409   0.0418   0.0414
0.0410

(d) If this interval includes the target, the process is considered to be centered on target. Is this process centered on target now? If not, management will have to make adjustments to deal with the process or the raw materials.

23. (a) Find a 90% confidence interval on the population mean lost production time per day (in hours) from the following daily data:

3.0   2.9   3.0   3.3   3.1   3.0   3.2   3.0   3.0
3.1   3.2   3.0   3.1   2.9   3.2   2.5   2.8   2.6
3.0   3.1

(b) Management has been saying that the long-term average lost time per day is three hours. Does the interval in part (a) seem to confirm what management has been saying?

(c) Management corrected some of the causes for lost production time by dealing with the most frequent serious problems first. New figures on lost production time are

2.3   2.3   2.3   2.1   2.4   2.4   2.5   1.9   2.6   1.9

Test the one-sided alternative hypothesis that the average lost time has been reduced below the previous long-term average figure of three hours.

24. (a) Find a 99% confidence interval on the population mean weight in ounces of cans of pizza sauce (the figures comprise a systematic random sample sorted by weight).

14.63   14.67   14.69   14.70   14.72   14.73   14.73   14.74
14.75   14.76   14.77   14.78   14.78   14.80   14.81   14.82
14.82   14.86

(b) (Optional) If you have computer access to the PIZZA.MTW file, try to determine how the systematic random sample was taken. Also construct a 99% confidence interval on the population mean weight using all the data in the file and compare this result to that in part (a).

25. Hourly earnings (in dollars) of production workers for 29 years were[5]

2.46   2.56   2.68   2.85   3.04   3.23   3.45   3.70   3.94   4.24
4.53   4.86   5.25   5.69   6.16   6.66   7.25   7.68   8.02   8.32
8.57   8.76   8.98   9.28   9.66   10.01   10.32   10.57   10.83

(a) Find the percentage changes in hourly earnings per year and construct a 99% confidence interval on the long-term population mean.

(b) A time series plot of the figures in part (a) indicates that the percentage changes in income are nonrandom. Does this mean that the confidence intervals are not strictly valid and therefore have to be interpreted cautiously?

(c) Describe the pattern of the plot in part (b). Does it bode well for workers?

APPENDIX 1

Minitab Examples

(If you are using the WINDOWS version of MINITAB, you might issue the GSTD command first to use standard graphics in the session window. If you want to save your output on a file, use the command OUTFILE 'A:CH7.LIS' to echo output to this file.)

A DISTRIBUTION OF SAMPLE MEANS, SIMULATED IN MINITAB

```
MTB > RANDOM 200 C1-C6;      # SIX DICE ARE ROLLED 200 TIMES
SUBC> INTEGERS BETWEEN 1 AND 6.

MTB > DESCRIBE C1            # A COLUMN OF 200 FACES

MTB > TALLY C1;             # IN THEORY, THERE IS A 1/6 = 16.66%
#                             CHANCE OF GETTING A PARTICULAR FACE
SUBC> PERCENTS.

MTB > HISTOGRAM C1;         # DISTRIBUTION OF THE NUMBERS ON 200
#                            FACES (STANDARD DEVIATION = 1.724)
SUBC> INCREMENT OF .5;
SUBC> START WITH MIDPOINT OF 1.

MTB > RMEAN C1-C6 PUT IN C7  # C1-C6 FORMS AN ARRAY OF 200 ROWS;
#                              ROW MEANS ARE PLACED IN C7
MTB > DESCRIBE C7
MTB > HISTOGRAM C7;            # THIS IS THE DISTRIBUTION OF THE
# SAMPLE MEANS; EACH ROW IS A SAMPLE OF SIX. THE STANDARD
# DEVIATION IS .6822.
SUBC> INCREMENT OF .5;
SUBC> START WITH MIDPOINT OF 1.
MTB > NSCORES C7 PUT C8
MTB > PLOT C7 C8 # WHERE C8 FROM NSCORES C7 PUT C8

(OPTIONAL) SELECTED SUBSET OF ABOVE COMMANDS TO FOCUS ON THE
NOTION OF A STANDARD ERROR
```

```
MTB > RANDOM 200 C1-C6;        # SIX DICE ARE ROLLED 200 TIMES
SUBC> INTEGERS BETWEEN 1 AND 6.
MTB > DESCRIBE C1              # A COLUMN OF 200 FACES
MTB > RMEAN C1-C6 PUT IN C7 # C1-C6 FORMS AN ARRAY OF 200 ROWS;
#                             ROW MEANS ARE PLACED IN C7
MTB > DESCRIBE C7
```

EXAMPLE

A NOTCHED BOXPLOT FOR EGG SALES

(Assuming that you have the data diskette, **RETRIEVE 'B:EGGDATA'.** Otherwise SET the data in columns. The data are listed in the chapter.)

(If you are on a network and have the data stored in subdirectory DATA under the directory MTBWIN, **RETRIEVE 'EGGDATA'.** Otherwise, SET the data in columns. The data are listed in the chapter.)

MINITAB produces a notch on the boxplot when you specify the NOTCH subcommand. The notch is shown with parentheses ().

```
MTB > BOXPLOT 'SALES';        # ; SIGNALS A SUBCOMMAND
SUBC> NOTCHES.                # SUBCOMMANDS END WITH A .

GO ON TO ANOTHER EXAMPLE OR IF FINISHED, MTB > STOP
```

EXAMPLE

BOXPLOT INTERVALS ON HEIGHTS OF ADULTS

```
MTB > RANDOM 10 OBSERVATIONS INTO C1-C5;
SUBC> NORMAL MU = 69 SIGMA = 2.5.

MTB > RANDOM 40 OBSERVATIONS INTO C6-C10;
SUBC> NORMAL MU = 69 SIGMA = 2.5.

MTB > STACK C1-C10 PUT INTO C11

# BE CAREFUL TO GET THE FOLLOWING DATA SET CORRECT!
#*** THERE ARE NO EMBEDDED BLANKS ALLOWED IN
# SPECIFICATIONS SUCH AS 10(1),10(2), ETC.

MTB > SET C12 # IDENTIFYING SEPARATE SAMPLES
DATA> 10(1),10(2),10(3),10(4),10(5)
DATA> 40(6),40(7),40(8),40(9),40(10)
DATA> END

MTB > BOXPLOTS C11;
SUBC> BY C12;
SUBC> NOTCHES 95 PERCENT CONFIDENCE;
SUBC> LINES = 1.    # MAKES BOXPLOTS MORE COMPACT
```

EXAMPLE

CLASSICAL 95% CONFIDENCE INTERVALS ON HEIGHTS OF ADULTS (CONTINUED) σ ESTIMATED BY s, TINTERVALS

```
# THIS EXAMPLE IS TO BE RUN DURING THE SAME COMPUTER SESSION AS
# THE PREVIOUS EXAMPLE WHERE THE DATA WERE GENERATED--SIGMA
# UNKNOWN
MTB > TINTERVAL 95 PERCENT ON C1-C10
```

EXAMPLE

CLASSICAL CONFIDENCE INTERVALS, HEIGHTS OF ADULTS (CONTINUED) σ KNOWN, ZINTERVALS

```
# THIS EXAMPLE IS TO BE RUN DURING THE SAME COMPUTER SESSION
# AS THE PREVIOUS EXAMPLE USING THE DATA GENERATED EARLIER--
# SIGMA KNOWN
MTB > ZINTERVAL 95 PERCENT SIGMA = 2.5 ON C1-C10
# MINITAB VERSION TEN-XTRA HAS A MACRO %DESCRIBE C1
# FOR THE DATA DISTRIBUTION AND INTERVALS
```

EXAMPLE

RATIO FORM OF HYPOTHESIS TESTS ON HEIGHTS OF ADULTS (CONTINUED) σ KNOWN (ZTEST) σ UNKNOWN (TTEST)

```
# THIS EXAMPLE IS TO BE RUN DURING THE SAME COMPUTER SESSION
# AS THE PREVIOUS EXAMPLE USING THE DATA GENERATED EARLIER

# SIGMA KNOWN
MTB > ZTEST MU = 69 SIGMA = 2.5 ON C1-C10

# SIGMA UNKNOWN
MTB > TTEST MU = 69 ON C1-C10 # UNKNOWN STANDARD DEVIATION
```

EXAMPLE

ONE-SIDED HYPOTHESIS TESTS ON TIRE LIFE

```
# C2, TIRE LIFETIMES IN MILES FROM CHANGES IN ODOMETER READINGS
MTB > SET IN C2
DATA>  33978.5    32617.7    33052.1    32611.7    33418.9    32455.9
DATA>  33463.1    32466.9    31624.3    33070.8    33127.0    33543.4
DATA>  33224.5    30881.2    32597.3    31565.0    34036.7    34053.6
DATA>  32584.5    31838.4    32290.4    32800.7    33844.9    34157.8
DATA> END
MTB > DESCRIBE C2
```

```
MTB > TTEST MU = 32000 DATA IN C2; # ONE-SIDED TEST
SUBC> ALTERNATIVE = +1.  # Hₙ:  μ = 32,000
                         # Hₐ:  μ > 32,000
# THE SUBCOMMAND ALTERNATIVE = -1 FOR A LESS THAN (<)
# ALTERNATIVE HYPOTHESIS

# A CONFIDENCE INTERVAL APPROACH CAN BE USED, AS SHOWN
# BELOW, TO TEST THE SAME HYPOTHESIS
MTB > TINTERVAL 90 PERCENT FOR C2    # ALPHA = .05 BUT BECAUSE
#  THE TEST IS ONE-SIDED, A 90% INTERVAL GIVES 5% ON EACH SIDE
```

EXAMPLE

ALPHA ERROR, BETA ERROR AND POWER FOR HYPOTHESES ABOUT THE MEAN HEIGHT OF THE ADULT POPULATION (OPTIONAL, SOMEWHAT SOPHISTICATED)

Comment The following macro, %B:OCC, requires version ten or more of MINITAB. To examine the details of the macro, use a text editor or word processor to open the OCC.MAC file. Also, in MINITAB the command TYPE 'B:OCC.MAC' will list the macro. If you set OH = 24 in the session window, a "continue?" prompt will be issued by MINITAB that permits the user to view one screen of output at a time as the macro executes.

```
MTB > %B:OCC  # OR %A:OCC OR %OCC
             # OR %C:\MTBWIN\DATA\OCC
```

EXAMPLE

THE BOOTSTRAP STANDARD ERROR FOR HEIGHTS OF ADULTS

```
MTB > RANDOM 10 OBSERVATIONS IN C1;
SUBC> NORMAL MU = 69  SIGMA = 2.5.
MTB > SET IN C13
DATA> 10(.10)
DATA> END
MTB > RANDOM 10 C20-C29;
SUBC> DISCRETE C1 C13.
MTB > RMEAN C20-C29 PUT IN C30
MTB > HIST C30
MTB > DESCRIBE C30
```

EXAMPLE

RETURNS ON A STOCK

(If you have the data diskette, **RETRIEVE 'B:RETURNS'** and omit the data entry using SET.)

(If you are on a network and have the data stored in subdirectory DATA under the directory MTBWIN, **RETRIEVE 'RETURNS'.** Otherwise SET the data in columns.)

```
DON'T SET DATA IN C4 IF RETRIEVE WAS SUCCESSFUL
MTB > SET DATA IN C4  #24 MONTHLY RETURNS IN PERCENT
DATA>  -9.0  -8.5  1.2  1.7  -3.9  4.4  -5.0  2.0  3.7  2.0  0.5
DATA>   5.9   1.5  5.8 -3.9  -0.7 -5.4  -6.2  3.6  3.4  6.9 -4.1
DATA>   7.9  -0.7
DATA> END


START HERE IF RETRIEVE SUCCESSFUL
MTB > LVALS C4   #RETURN LEVEL (MEDIAN) AND RISK (SPREAD
#                OR BOX LENGTH) ARE IMPORTANT
MTB > BOXPLOT C4;
SUBC> NOTCHES.
MTB > TSPLOT C4 # CHECK FOR RANDOMNESS
GO ON TO ANOTHER EXAMPLE OR IF FINISHED, MTB > STOP
```

EXAMPLE

QUALITY CONTROL—A MANUFACTURING PROCESS IN A STATE OF STATISTICAL CONTROL

(If you have the data diskette, **RETRIEVE 'B:FRUITDK'** and omit the data entry using SET.)

(If you are on a network and have the data stored in subdirectory DATA under the directory MTBWIN, **RETRIEVE 'FRUITDK'.** Otherwise, SET the data in columns.)

```
DON'T SET DATA IN C1 IF RETRIEVE WAS SUCCESSFUL
MTB > SET DATA IN C1 # FIGURES ARE ROUNDED OFF

DATA>  287  288  299  300  293  303  292  300  303  300  299
DATA>  305  300  305  293  297  291  291  302  302  306  293
DATA>  308  297  308  301  303  301  305  300  305  300  295
DATA>  303  303  306  304  291  301  295  308  309  300  296
DATA>  299  302  307  309  297  312  298  303  302  298  299
DATA>  300  300  296  299  300

DATA> END


START HERE IF RETRIEVE SUCCESSFUL
MTB > TSPLOT PERIOD = 6 OF DATA IN C1  # LABELS POINTS 1-6
MTB > LVALS C1                         # OR DESCRIBE C1

MTB > LET K1 = 300 + (1.82*(6/2.4495)) # UCL
MTB > LET K2 = 300 - (1.82*(6/2.4495)) # LCL
MTB > PRINT K1 K2

# K1      304.5   UCL  (UPPER CONTROL LIMIT)
# K2      295.5   LCL  (LOWER CONTROL LIMIT)

MTB > SET C2  # 60 VALUES SET EQUAL TO 300, CENTER LINE
DATA> 60(300) # NO BLANK SPACE BETWEEN 60 AND (300)
DATA> END
```

```
MTB > SET IN C3   # 60 VALUES SET EQUAL TO 304.5, UCL
DATA> 60(304.5)   # NO BLANK SPACE IN THIS LINE
DATA> END

MTB > SET IN C4   # 60 VALUES EQUAL TO 295.5, LCL
DATA> 60(295.5)   # NO BLANK SPACE IN THIS LINE
DATA> END

# THE NEXT COMMAND, MTSPLOT, MAY NOT WORK ON THE STUDENT VERSION
# MINITAB; TO GET A FEEL FOR WHAT IT DOES, SUBSTITUTE TSPLOT C1
# AND TSPLOT C2.

MTB > MTSPLOT C1 C2 C3 C4;   # PLOTS ALL VALUES OVER TIME
                            # SHOWING CONTROL LIMITS AND CL
SUBC> START 280.            # STARTS VERTICAL SCALE

GO ON TO ANOTHER EXAMPLE OR IF FINISHED, MTB > STOP
```

CHAPTER 8

*Exploring
Relationships
Between Pairs
of Variables*

OBJECTIVES

- ◆ **Introduce methods to summarize relationships between pairs of variables**
- ◆ **Use variable x to partition y and then compare the two subsets of y**
- ◆ **Fit a straight line to relate x and y**
- ◆ **Examine residuals to determine if transformations are in order**

PRELUDE

What we have learned about the analysis of a single variable can easily be extended to two variables. Now we summarize the relationship between variables. We want to know if a change in one variable is associated with a change in another variable. For example, is diet related to the incidence of cancer? Is exercise related to heart disease? Does speed kill?

The analysis of a pair of variables can contribute to the process of establishing cause and effect. However, nothing in the methodology proves that a change in one variable causes a change in another. One variable might or might not cause a change in another variable. Cause requires a logical foundation beyond data analysis. Thus, the data analyst must understand the limitations of these methods. This chapter opens the door for thinking about situations characterized by many variables. ◆

Ms. President: Susan, I want you to know that your economic forecasts of the gross domestic product have been better than those provided by the chairman of the Federal Reserve Board and the chairman of the Council of Economic Advisors. Thank you very much.

Susan: You are welcome, Ms. President. I am pleased to be of some help. Have you told them how I make the forecasts?

Ms. President: No, but they are quite disturbed that I get better numbers from my assistant than from trained economists.

Susan: Could they be working with the wrong two variables?

Ms. President: Yes, they could be. The Federal Reserve Board seems to be watching how changes in the money supply are related to changes in the gross domestic product, a measure of economic activity.

Susan: What two variables interest the Council of Economic Advisors?

Ms. President: They are watching how changes in government expenditures are related to changes in the gross domestic product.

Susan: If we forecast better than they do for one more year, tell them the two variables we watch.

Ms. President: I'm sure they would rather watch what we watch—changes in gross domestic product and changes in dress length. Nevertheless, it might be difficult to convince them that dresses lengthen when the economy is bad and shorten when the economy is good. Certainly, some of them have been around long enough to notice such fashion changes.

COMPARISONS USING A SECOND VARIABLE, x, TO SEGREGATE DATA ON y INTO TWO CATEGORIES

In this section we introduce exploratory methods for examining the relationship between two variables. Some familiar methods for describing one variable can be used in the study of two variables. For example, two stem-and-leaf diagrams can be placed back-to-back to make comparisons. Similarly, boxplots can be placed side-by-side. In these types of situations, one variable, such as a pulse, is segregated into two groups by a second variable, such as gender (we might compare the pulses of a group of men to those of a group of women). Often the second variable (gender, for example) is categorical. However, the second variable may be a continuous measure, which is set at two levels.

Beginning to Explore Data Sets

We chose the presidential data set in Exhibit 1 because it is interesting and because some data problems occur that are common to many data sets[1]. The experienced data analyst learns to expect imperfections in the data and in the data collection process. Therefore, some particular problems with this data set are brought to your attention.

The presidential data set is not current. For example, Jimmy Carter is no longer president and his mother is no longer alive. Some data are missing, such as ages at death of Andrew Jackson's parents. At the time these data were published, age at death of Jimmy Carter's mother was not obtainable because she wasn't dead. This fact is indicated in the data set by the word *alive* in place of a number. The data are used as is so that you will be exposed to some of the problems that can occur when working with data sets. Most likely you will face these and other problems with your own data sets.

Notation and Terminology

We will explore the ages at death of the parents of presidents. These figures are in the last two columns of Exhibit 1. Ages of mothers or fathers are designated by the **response variable**, y_i. Response variables anticipate that y_i might respond to the behavior of other variables. Synonyms for response variable used in the statistical literature include **dependent variable, criterion variable,** and **endogenous variable.**

A **predictor variable**, x_{1i}, anticipates that x_{1i} might help to predict y_i. Synonyms for predictor variable used in the statistical literature include **independent variable, carrier variable,** and **exogenous variable.** In the presidential data set, the predictor variable, x_{1i}, segregates the ages, y_i, into two subsets, ages of mothers and ages of fathers. The x_{1i} is assigned a 0 value if y_i is a mother's age at death. The x_{1i} is assigned a value of 1 if y_i is a father's age at death. Thus, x_{1i} is a qualitative variable on the nominal scale. Therefore, the values 0 and 1 are identifiers and segregate ages into two categories.

EXPLORATORY COMPARISONS WITH STEM-AND-LEAF DIAGRAMS AND BOXPLOTS

Two stem-and-leaf diagrams can be placed back-to-back to make comparisons. Similarly, boxplots can be placed side by side. In the example below, the response variable, age at death, is segregated into two groups by a predictor variable coded 0 or 1 to identify a president's mother or father.

Comparisons, Back-to-Back Stem-and-Leaf Diagrams

For comparative purposes, back-to-back stem-and-leaf diagrams are shown in Exhibit 2 that display the ages of presidents' mothers and fathers at their time of death. Because the stem-and-leaf diagrams have a similar shape and

EXHIBIT 1 A Presidential Data Base—Longevity of Presidents of the United States

| President | FIRST INAUGURAL | | | AFTER FIRST INAUGURAL | | PARENTS' DEATH AGES | |
| | | | | YEARS LIVED | | | |
	Year	Age	Death Age	Expected	Actual	Father	Mother
George Washington	1789	57	67	17.1	10.5	49	81
John Adams	1797	61	90	14.4	29.3	70	98
Thomas Jefferson	1801	57	83	16.4	25.3	49	56
James Madison	1809	57	85	16.3	27.3	77	98
James Monroe	1817	58	73	15.6	14.3	22	??
John Q. Adams	1825	57	80	16.3	23.0	90	73
Andrew Jackson	1829	61	78	13.5	16.3	??	??
Martin Van Buren	1837	54	79	17.2	25.4	80	70
@William Harrison	1841	68	68	9.4	.1	65	62
John Tyler	1841	51	71	19.2	20.8	65	36
James Polk	1845	49	53	21.5	4.3	55	75
@Zachary Taylor	1849	64	65	12.8	1.3	84	61
Millard Fillmore	1850	50	74	20.7	23.7	91	51
Franklin Pierce	1853	48	64	22.0	16.6	81	70
James Buchanan	1857	65	77	11.9	11.3	60	66
#Abraham Lincoln	1861	52	56	19.8	4.1	73	34
Andrew Johnson	1865	56	66	17.2	10.3	33	72
Ulysses Grant	1869	46	63	22.8	16.4	79	84
Rutherford Hayes	1877	54	70	18.0	15.9	35	74
#James Garfield	1881	49	49	21.2	.5	33	86
Chester Arthur	1881	50	56	20.1	5.2	78	66
Grover Cleveland	1885	47	71	22.1	23.3	49	76
Benjamin Harrison	1889	55	67	17.2	12.0	73	40
#William McKinley	1897	54	58	18.2	4.5	85	88
Theodore Roosevelt	1901	42	60	26.1	17.3	46	49
William Taft	1909	51	72	20.2	21.0	80	80
Woodrow Wilson	1913	56	67	17.1	10.9	84	66
@Warren Harding	1921	55	57	18.0	2.4	80	61
Calvin Coolidge	1923	51	60	21.3	9.4	80	39
Herbert Hoover	1929	54	90	18.9	35.6	34	34
@Franklin Roosevelt	1933	51	63	21.7	12.1	72	86
Harry Truman	1945	60	88	15.0	27.7	78	82
Dwight Eisenhower	1953	62	78	14.4	16.2	79	84
#John Kennedy	1961	43	46	28.4	2.8	81	Alive
Lyndon Johnson	1963	55	64	19.2	9.2	60	77
Richard Nixon	1969	56	—	18.7	—	78	82
Gerald Ford	1974	61	—	15.3	—	59	75
Jimmy Carter	1977	52	—	21.4	—	59	Alive

Key: @ indicates died during tenure; # indicates was assassinated.
The expected years lived after the first inaugural is based on experience with the white male population in the United States. Calculations were made using white males who were born in the same years as the presidents.

EXHIBIT 2 Back-to-Back Stem-and-Leaf Diagrams—Death Ages of
Presidents' Parents

$x_{1i} = 0$ i-th Mother's Age		$x_{1i} = 1$ i-th Fathers's Age
8,8	9	0,1
8,6,6,4,4,2,2,1,0	8	0,0,0,0,1,4,4,5
7,6,5,5,4,3,2,0,0	7	0,2,3,3,7,8,8,8,9,9
6,6,6,2,1,1	6	0,0,5,5
6,1	5	5,9
9,0	4	6,9,9,9
9,6,4,4	3	3,3,4,5

about the same median and spread, the overall impression is that, as a group, the lifespans of presidents' mothers and fathers don't appear to differ substantially. In a sense, this result is a surprise because women in our society tend to outlive men.

We used only complete pairs of ages. That is, both the mothers' and fathers' ages were excluded for Presidents Monroe, Jackson, Kennedy, and Carter. Using complete pairs of data values is a matter of convenience because an average age at death could be substituted for the missing values.

Comparisons, Side-by-Side Boxplots

Boxplots are constructed and shown in Exhibit 3 as an additional means of comparison. Although side-by-side boxplots reveal a slight drop overall in longevity for fathers compared to mothers, the difference does not appear to be significant. Therefore, in this case a change in the predictor variable, x_{1i}, from 0 to 1 does not result in a significant longevity change in the response variable, y_i. Thus, the side-by-side boxplots confirm the initial impressions obtained from back-to-back stem-and-leaf diagrams.

What has been learned from stem-and-leaf diagrams and boxplots can be stated formally in a hypothesis that compares medians. The null hypothesis is that the median ages of presidents' mothers and fathers at death are the same. The alternative hypothesis is that the medians are not the same. Based

EXHIBIT 3 Side-by-Side Boxplots for Comparison
The Second Variable, x_{1i}, at Two Levels

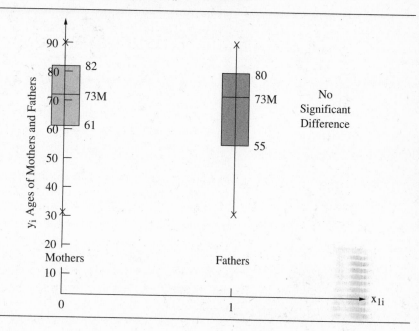

on the data that is known, it does not appear that the null hypothesis can be rejected. Furthermore, this also means that the predictor variable, x_{1i}, does not help in predicting lifespan. Thus, we have determined that age alone, y_i, can be summarized without regard to x_{1i}.

S T A T I S T I C A L   H I G H L I G H T S

A preliminary comparison of two samples can be made with side-by-side boxplots or stem-and-leaf diagrams.

A Closer Look at the Data

Think about the conditions that give rise to individual or groups of observations. Discernible groups of observations are called **clusters.** Notice that the boxplots and the stem-and-leaf diagrams show some asymmetry because some parents died at a young age. Closer examination of these data values reveals that mothers dying before the age of 50 included the mothers of Tyler, Lincoln, Harrison, Roosevelt, Coolidge, and Hoover. Most of these women were mothers of presidents whose first inaugural years were before 1901. Fathers dying before the age of 43 included Johnson, Hayes, Garfield, and Hoover, with several early parental deaths associated with presidents whose first inaugural years were in the late 1800s. Medical practice may have been rather primitive in those early years, which could have been a contributing factor to the early deaths. Thus a new variable, the element of time, comes into play. This additional element calls for a more formal analysis that should include plotting lifespans over time and checking for randomness.

Repeating the Analysis after Making Adjustments   Too often the inexperienced investigator thinks of an analysis as having a singular purpose. The experienced investigator realizes that the original question under study might be revised or changed completely. Therefore, the data analyst might continue an investigation beyond a preliminary conclusion, such as the typical president's mother living as long as the father. Often an initial disappointment in the analysis process leads to an important discovery later.

Investigative analysis should be thought of as a repetitive or iterative process in which you might interrogate the same witness (data source) several times if necessary. Expect to reexamine data after adjustments and modifications are made. For example, perhaps some data should be set aside and new stem-and-leaf diagrams and boxplots constructed from the remaining observations. For reasons explained earlier, we might set aside the ages of mothers who died before the age of 50 and the ages of fathers who died before the age of 43.

Another possible data adjustment consideration involves a few missing data values. In place of the missing data on President Monroe's mother, we could substitute the average of known mothers' ages, assuming Mrs. Monroe survived to an average age. The same replacement idea might apply to the ages of Andrew Jackson's mother and father; both parents' ages at death are missing. Sometimes a few missing data values are replaced with what the data analyst regards as reasonable substitutes.

At the time these data were compiled, John Kennedy's and Jimmy Carter's mothers were alive. Therefore, we knew their ages at that moment. Such information, called **censored observations,** could have replaced the ages in Exhibit 1 that are marked *alive*.

Such data set adjustments, along with the collection of additional information, might deserve further investigation. There are many interesting roads to follow when exploring most data sets.

Analyzing a Pair of Variables

The predictor variable, x_{1i}, is subscripted. The first subscript, 1, identifies a particular predictor variable among others. The second subscript, i, represents the i-th observed value. The first subscript could also be 2, 3, 4, and so on, identifying other possible predictor variables. It is important to recognize that a chosen predictor variable is one of many candidates.

Generally, we attempt to describe, control, or predict y_i based on predictor variable knowledge. Although a single predictor is considered in this chapter, complex problems often involve several variables. When a predictor variable helps the investigator's understanding of the response, y_i, it is kept. Otherwise it is set aside in search of a better candidate.

To understand the true relationship between y_i and x_{1i}, background variables need to be considered, as illustrated in Exhibit 4. The exhibit shows that the clearest view of the response variable, y_i, in relation to the predictor variable, x_{1i}, occurs in reference to other background variables, x_{2i}, x_{3i}, x_{4i}, and so on. It is desirable that background variables be held constant or that their average effect is zero. If these variables are not held constant or do not have an average effect of zero, then the view of the response and predictor pair of variables is likely to be distorted. Without considering other background variables, there is considerable danger that the data analysis will lead to the wrong conclusions.

Time as a Background Variable   The element of time can distort the relationship between two other variables of interest. For example, a scatterplot of sales revenue, y_i, versus advertising expenditure, x_{1i}, might not reveal the true relationship between these two variables because they are observed over time. Time is often an insidious nuisance variable. As a result, the astute manager would examine changes in sales revenue versus changes in advertising expenditure to purge the background variable, which is time.

EXHIBIT 4 The Response, Predictor, and Background Variables

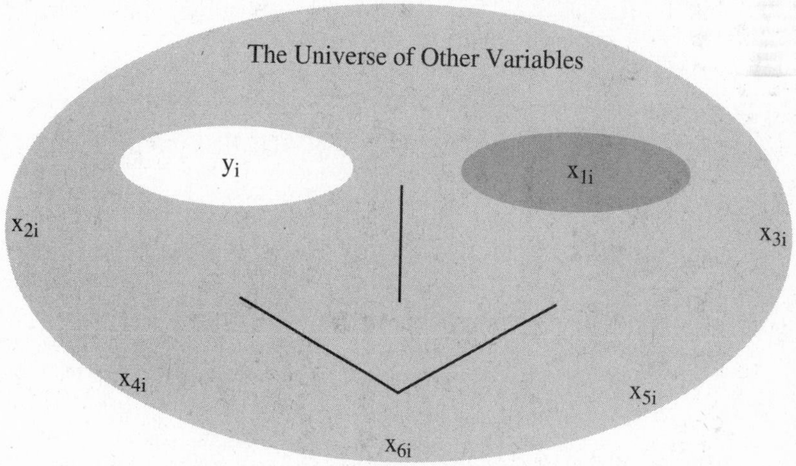

EXAMPLE 1

PURGING THE BACKGROUND VARIABLE OF TIME

Problem Statement (a)   Mathematically express sales revenue, y_i, and advertising expenditure, x_{1i}, as changes where the subscript i indicates the time period. What scatterplot do you recommend examining?

Problem Solution (a)   The changes or differences are $(y_{(i+1)} - y_i)$ and $(x_{1(i+1)} - x_{1i})$. It is likely that the differencing will remove period-to-period distortions imposed by time. Therefore, examine a scatterplot of these differences.

Problem Statement (b)   When economists relate gross domestic product and money supply figures, how do you think they deal with the fact that both variables are collected over time?

Problem Solution (b)   Trained economists are likely to examine changes in the gross domestic product versus changes in the money supply.

Problem Statement (c)   Investors are interested in the Dow-Jones Index (Average) in relation to stock price figures. The Dow-Jones Index (Average) represents the behavior of the market. Smart investors examine returns, relative price changes, rather than prices of stocks when relating a stock's movement relative to a market index, such as the Dow-Jones Index (Average). Mathematically express stock prices and the Dow-Jones Index (Average) as returns.

Problem Solution (c)   If y_i is the price of a stock in the i-th period, a return is computed by forming the ratio of a difference to a base period price, $\frac{y_{(i+1)} - y_i}{y_i}$. If x_{1i} is the Dow-Jones Average in the i-th period, the market return is $\frac{x_{1(i+1)} - x_{1i}}{x_{1i}}$. These returns can be related. They are adjusted for time in the background, which cannot be held constant.

FROM EXPLORATORY ANALYSIS TOWARD THE MORE FORMAL CLASSICAL ANALYSIS OF TWO VARIABLES, y AND x

Introducing a second variable, x_{1i}, in addition to y_i enables us to grapple with a richer variety of problems than previously possible. While this increase in sophistication may be a source of more information from the predictor variable, it is at the price of a slight increase in complexity and in the amount of data that must be collected and analyzed. The aim is to keep problems as simple as possible by using few variables. This is referred to as the **principle of parsimony.**

The potential gain in knowledge due to the introduction of a predictor variable must be assessed. If the additional variable does not contribute significantly, it is dropped. That takes us back to dealing with a single variable.

If the additional variable does contribute, then it can be used to predict the response variable. The hope is that the predictor variable carries enough information to improve understanding of the response variable.

Comparisons: The Predictor Variable at Two Levels

We compare ourselves to others. Others may be richer, taller, shorter, or more or less beautiful. We compare in order to relate one thing to another.

Case (1): The Predictor Variable **Does Not** *Carry a Significant Amount of Information*   In Exhibit 2, the back-to-back stem-and-leaf diagrams display values of the response variable (age) y_i; the left side shows ages of mothers and the right side shows ages of fathers. The left side and right side partitioning of the age data, y_i, is accomplished via the predictor variable, x_{1i} (at two coded levels, 0 or 1), which identifies ages of mothers and ages of fathers. Part of the data is assigned to one side of the diagram and part of the data is assigned to the other side. The predictor variable, x_{1i}, designates on which side of a stem-and-leaf diagram a data value goes. Thus, when making comparisons and when the predictor variable is at two coded levels, the data set is partitioned into two subsets (not necessarily equal in size). As a result, for comparison purposes stem-and-leaf diagrams can be placed back-to-back and the associated boxplots can be placed side by side.

Although x_{1i} is often categorical (nominal data such as mother or father), x_{1i} can be measured values on the interval or the ratio scale at two levels. Even if the values are not initially 1 or 0, it is simple to transform the values to 0 or 1. For example, if the x_{1i} values are initially 6 and 7, then subtract 6, $6 - 6 = 0$ and $7 - 6 = 1$. Or, if the x_{1i} values are 70 and 100, then subtract 70 and divide by the difference, $100 - 70 = 30$.

$$\frac{70 - 70}{30} = 0 \quad \text{and} \quad \frac{100 - 70}{30} = 1$$

If the predictor variable equals any two numbers, they can be transformed to the convenient 0 or 1 coding scheme that makes comparisons easy.

The purpose of the comparison is to see if the side-by-side boxplots or stem-and-leaf diagrams are roughly the same, implying they have about the same **level** (same means or medians) and about the same **spread** (same box lengths or standard deviations). If they are about the same, knowledge of the predictor variable does not really help us explain a difference in the two subsets of the response data because there is none. In such a case, we can say that the predictor variable does not carry a significant amount of information.

Another way of visualizing the sameness in level is to draw a line through the medians of the two boxplots, as shown in Exhibit 5. When this line is horizontal, or nearly so, the difference between the two subsets of the response data is not significant.

EXHIBIT 5 No Significant Difference in Median Ages

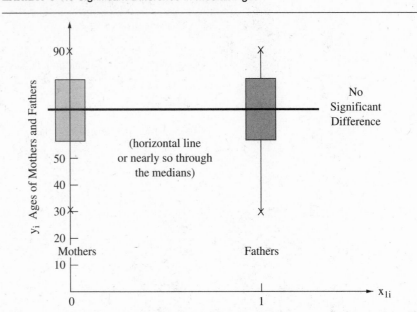

EXAMPLE 2

MINITAB ANALYSIS OF THE AGE DATA

Problem Statement (a)   Using descriptive statistics, verify that mothers of presidents live about as long as fathers do.

Problem Solution (a)   From the descriptive statistics, note that the means and medians are about the same. For variability, the standard deviations and box lengths, $(Q3 - Q1)$, are also about the same.

	N	MEAN	MEDIAN	TRMEAN	STDEV
C1(father's ages)	34	67.18	73.00	67.90	17.31
C2(mother's ages)	34	68.59	72.50	68.93	17.65

	MIN	MAX	Q1	Q3
C1	33.00	91.00	53.50	80.00
C2	34.00	98.00	59.75	82.00

Problem Statement (b)   Using dotplots, verify that mothers of presidents live about as long as fathers do.

Problem Solution (b)   Graphically, dotplots tell the same story as the descriptive statistics. You might mark the locations of the medians on the dotplots below as well as the mean plus or minus one standard deviation.

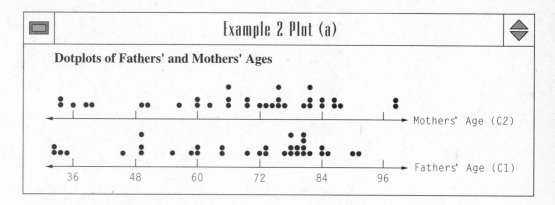

Example 2 Plot (a)

Dotplots of Fathers' and Mothers' Ages

Problem Statement (c)   Using a scatterplot of y versus x, verify that mothers of presidents live about as long as fathers do.

Problem Solution (c)   In order to plot the data, all ages were placed in column C3. The 0s or 1s were placed in column C4. This plot gives no indication that mothers of presidents live any longer than fathers do. However, this type of a plot can mislead you due to overplotting. For example, MINITAB prints a 3 when three data values plot in the same position. Yet the viewer sees one character in that position and must remember to give that observation the emphasis of three. Overplotting occurs because more than one data value falls at a plotting point location.

Problem Statement (d)   Using a scatterplot of y in observed order, verify that mothers of presidents live about as long as fathers do. Would you conclude that the variability of the two subsets of y is about the same, as reflected in the standard deviations, box lengths, and the disposition of points on the graphical displays?

Problem Solution (d)   The plot below improves on the plot above. This plot shows the age data in C3 versus the observation order, values 1, 2, 3, . . . , 34 of C5 for mothers and values 35, 36, . . . , 64 of C5 for fathers. A vertical line on the plot separates the two subsets of response data. What you should notice in the plot is that the average of the first 34 ages (a horizontal line at 68.6) appears to be about the same as the average of the second 34 points (a horizontal line at 67.2). Also, the variability appears to be about the same in both partitions, which is confirmed by the standard deviations and the box lengths.

Example 2 Plot (b)

Ages (C3) Versus a 0 or 1 for Mothers or Fathers (C4)

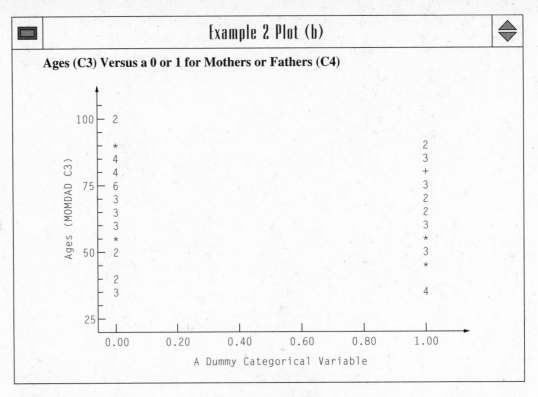

Example 2 Plot (c)

Ages Versus Observation Order (C5)

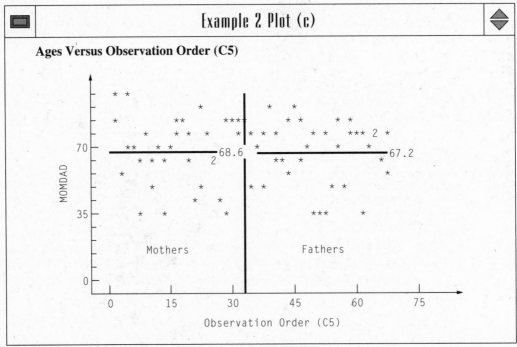

Case (2): The Predictor Variable Does Carry a Significant Amount of Information

Frequently a second variable, such as x_{1i}, helps explain the behavior of y_i. Under such circumstances, the use of this additional variable adds to the complexity, which results in the analysis of both y_i and x_{1i} rather than y_i alone. Even when more than two variables further increase the complexity, it is wise to start small, with one or two variables, and then consider additional variables one step at a time.

We will examine the effect of two different package designs on sales levels. The data are tabulated below. The table is called a **one-way table** because the predictor variable is concerned with a single factor—package design.

SALES DATA IN A ONE-WAY TABLE

Old package design	50	95	25	23	48	18	33	43	15	28
	26	34	59							
New package design	52	76	75	91	84	72	72	87	98	67
	92	86	61							

Exhibit 6 displays these sales data figures. Stem-and-leaf diagrams and box-plots are superimposed. The response variable, sales, is on the vertical axis, and the horizontal axis represents the two package designs. The predictor variable, x_{1i}, is coded 0 to identify sales of the product in the old package design. The predictor variable is coded 1 to identify sales of the product in the new package design. The problem is to determine if sales are influenced by

EXHIBIT 6 A Significant Difference in Sales for Different Package Designs

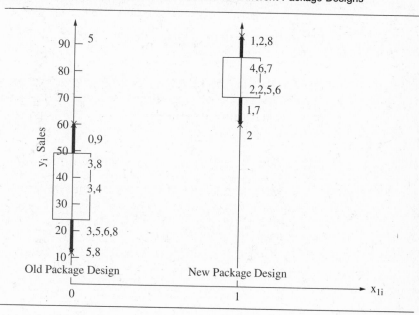

package design. Clearly, the new package design is associated with a higher sales level. There appears to be a significant difference in sales levels due to the knowledge about package design, which is captured by the predictor variable.

We could also say that the prima facie evidence leads us to reject the null hypothesis that sales levels are the same for both package designs. In fact, we would favor some alternative hypothesis that sales are *not* the same for the two different package designs.

EXAMPLE 3

MINITAB ANALYSIS OF THE PACKAGE DESIGN, SALES DATA

Problem Statement (a) Using descriptive statistics, verify that sales tend to be better when using the new package design.

Problem Solution (a) From the descriptive statistics, note that the means and medians are considerably different. Although the variability within the two groups is different, as reflected in the standard deviations and box lengths, this difference is not enough to lead us to doubt that the new package design improves sales.

	N	MEAN	MEDIAN	TRMEAN	STDEV
C1 (New Design)	13	77.92	76.00	78.45	13.28
C2 (Old Design)	13	38.23	33.00	35.18	21.54

	MIN	MAX	Q1	Q3
C1	52.00	98.00	69.50	89.00
C2	15.00	95.00	24.00	49.00

Problem Statement (b) Using dotplots, verify that sales tend to be better when using the new package design.

Problem Solution (b) Graphically the dotplots tell the same story as the descriptive statistics. You might mark the locations of the medians on the dotplots below as well as the mean plus or minus one standard deviation.

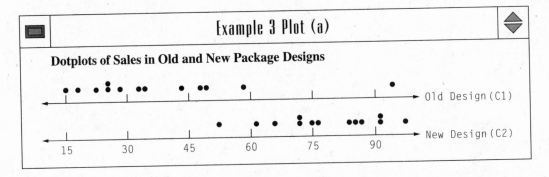

Example 3 Plot (a)

Dotplots of Sales in Old and New Package Designs

Problem Statement (c) Using a scatterplot of y versus x, verify that sales tend to be better when using the new package design.

Problem Solution (c) In order to plot the data, all sales figures were placed in column C3. The 0s and 1s were placed in column C4. This plot shows higher typical sales with the new package design. But these types of plots can be misleading due to overplotting. For example, MINITAB prints a 3 when three data values plot in the same position. Yet the viewer sees one character in that position and must remember to give that observation the emphasis of three.

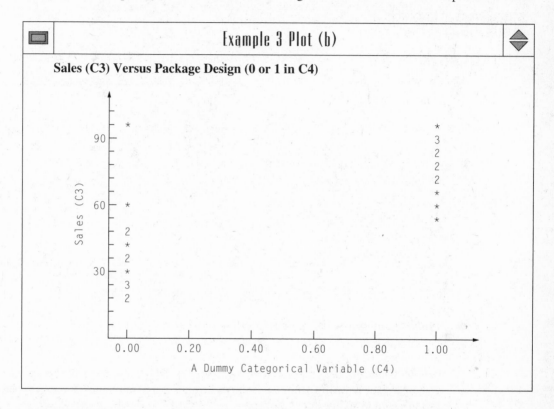

Problem Statement (d) Using a scatterplot of y in observed order, verify that sales tend to be better when using the new package design. Would you conclude that the variability of the two subsets of y is about the same, as reflected in the standard deviations, box lengths, and the disposition of points on the graphical displays?

Problem Solution (d) The plot below improves on the plot above. This plot shows the sales data in C3 versus the observation order, values 1, 2, 3, . . . , 13 of C5 for the old package design and values 14, 15, . . . , 26 of C5 for the new package design. A vertical line on the plot separates the two subsets of response data. What you should notice in the plot is that the average of the first 13 points (a horizontal line at 38.2) appears to be much different than the average of the second 13 points (a horizontal line at 77.9). Also, the variability appears to be about the same in both partitions, which is confirmed by the standard deviations and the box lengths.

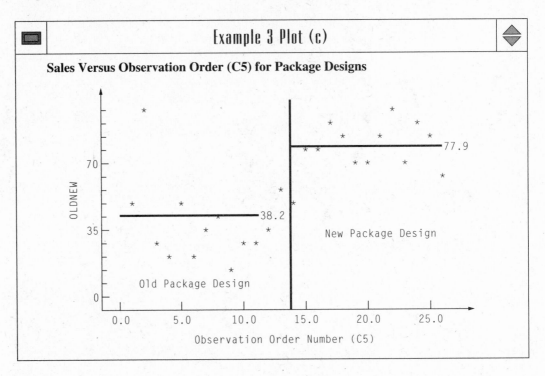

Example 3 Plot (c)

Sales Versus Observation Order (C5) for Package Designs

Problem Discussion   A word of caution about possible background variables is necessary. To be confident that the new package design actually improves sales, background variables must be constant or have an average effect of 0 during the experiment. If some variables can't be held constant, it may be possible to adjust for them if they are measured.

Examples of background variables to be held constant include store size, placement of the product within the store (so customer traffic patterns are about the same), shelf location, and geographic location. In other words, we want data that came from a carefully designed experiment. Additionally, if the data are normal in distribution and random, well-known classical statistical methods are applicable.

STATISTICAL HIGHLIGHTS

Descriptive statistics, dotplots, and scatterplots are helpful in comparing two samples of observations.

FITTING STRAIGHT LINES, RELATING y AND x

A single variable can be summarized by a median. The relationship between a pair of variables can be summarized by a straight line on a scatterplot. The mathematical expression for this straight line is a **prediction equation** or **fit.** An example of such an equation is

$$\hat{y}_i = 33 + 43\,x_{1i}$$

In exploratory work, this equation predicts the median response of y_i, which depends on the predictor variable, x_{1i}.

A Prediction Equation or Fit

In reference to the previous example, another way to see that there is a difference in sales because of package designs is to draw a straight line connecting the medians of the side-by-side boxplots. This is shown in Exhibit 7. This line, fitted through the medians, can be expressed as a prediction equation or fit.

Because the new package design increases sales significantly, the fitted line has a substantial tilt or **slope.** When the fitted line is not horizontal or not nearly horizontal, then there is a significant difference in sales due to the

EXHIBIT 7 A Prediction Equation Fitted Through the Medians

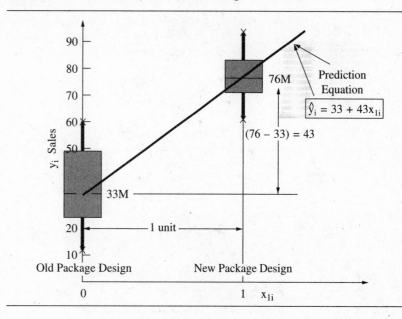

package designs. In other words, if the line has a substantial tilt upward to the right or downward to the right, then there is a significant difference in sales. The informal visual assessment of "substantial tilt" depends on the difference in medians and the spread of the data values about the medians. When the spread is small and the difference in medians is large as in Exhibit 7, we can clearly see the significant change in sales that results from different package designs.

A conclusion such as a significant difference in sales due to the package designs is preliminary because it is based on exploratory statistical methods. When the investigator finds it necessary, classical statistical hypothesis tests can follow to confirm or deny the exploratory conclusion.

Terminology, such as substantial tilt, is somewhat vague. But it is acceptable in an extreme situation such as that in Exhibit 7. As the tilt of the fitted line becomes less substantial, it becomes difficult to draw a conclusion from a simple visual assessment. Then more formal methods are needed.

The Prediction Equation in More Detail   The prediction equation or fit can be described in more detail as follows:

$$\hat{y}_i = \text{the predicted i-th data value of } y_i$$
$$y_{MO} = \text{Median sales for the } \underline{O}\text{ld package design}$$
$$y_{MN} = \text{Median sales for the } \underline{N}\text{ew package design}$$

Then, $(y_{MN} - y_{MO}) = (76 - 33) = 43$. This is the change in median sales as x_{1i} changes from 0 to 1. Thus, the ratio of these changes is the slope $\frac{43}{1}$, which measures the tilt of the prediction equation. This slope is evident in Exhibit 7. The prediction equation is

$$\hat{y}_i = y_{MO} + (y_{MN} - y_{MO})\, x_{1i}$$

After substituting the median values, one obtains

$$\hat{y}_i = 33 + (76 - 33)\, x_{1i} = 33 + 43\, x_{1i}$$

The prediction equation forms a straight line with an intercept of 33 and a slope of +43.

The substitution of a 1 or 0 for x_{1i} yields a median sales level prediction. For example, when the predictor variable is 0, the predicted median response is

$$33 + 43\,(0) = 33$$

This is simply the median sales for the old package design. When the predictor variable is 1, the predicted median response is

$$33 + 43\,(1) = 76$$

This is median sales for the new package design.

E X A M P L E 4

MINITAB, ROBUST FIT OF A STRAIGHT LINE, SALES DATA

Problem Statement   Use MINITAB to verify the correctness of the prediction equation in Exhibit 7.

Problem Solution   MINITAB produces the same slope and intercept shown in the exhibit.

$$\text{Slope} = 43.0 \qquad \text{Level} = 33.0 \text{ (intercept)}$$

Problem Discussion   Despite appearances that sales increased as a result of the new package design, this may not tell the whole story. Although the data may have come from a carefully designed experiment that was planned to expose the true relationship between sales and package design, the true cause may not have been observed. Package design may be a proxy for some other hidden variable. This unidentified variable may have caused the increase in sales, and the package design could be unappealing to the consumer. The investigator must interpret the data the best he or she can but realize the limitations inherent in analyzing data. Background variables may have more importance than we think. They have a potential distorting influence when examining a pair of variables.

The Slope of the Straight Line Fit   The slope is referred to as a **regression coefficient** or a **parameter estimate.** Both the sign and the magnitude of a regression coefficient are important. The sign indicates the direction of the change and the magnitude indicates the amount. In reference to the previous example, the slope's positive sign indicates that sales increases as the package design changes from old to new. The magnitude of the regression coefficient is large enough, relative to the box length, that we believe the new package design significantly increases sales.

If the slope were negative, the line in Exhibit 7 would slope downward to the right. A negative slope would have indicated that the new package design produced a drop in the sales level.

The overall effect of a predictor variable is reflected in the product of the regression coefficient and the predictor variable ($43 \times x_{1i}$). Sometimes this product is called a **component effect.**

TESTING THE STRENGTH OF THE RELATIONSHIP BETWEEN y AND x

The examples to this point have emphasized two obvious extremes: (1) there was no significant difference in typical lifespans of presidents' mothers and fathers, and (2) there was a significant difference in typical sales levels, based on a comparison of two different package designs. These determinations were made by visually inspecting stem-and-leaf diagrams and boxplot patterns.

Simple visual inspection of these diagrams has at least two key features. Both level (medians) and spread (box lengths) were key ingredients in the decisions. When medians are the same or nearly the same, this leads us to conclude that there is no significant difference in typical values. Otherwise there is a significant difference in typical values.

Although spread has received less attention in our decisions and examples, the decisions depend on spread as well as level. The reason why spread has played a subordinate role so far is because the examples have been selected so that (1) the spread has been about the same in the two batches of data being compared; and (2) the spread has been small enough, relative to the median, to make visual impressions easy and have them lead to correct decisions.

The Prediction Equation for Comparisons, Age Data

Our earlier exploratory comparison decisions are reviewed here in terms of a prediction equation. Suppose you were asked to predict the lifespan of a president's mother or father. The median lifespans are rounded to 73 years. The prediction equation for the age at death is

$$\hat{y}_i = 73 + (73 - 73)\, x_{1i}$$

The substitution of either a 1 or 0 value for x_{1i} yields a predicted lifespan of 73 years.

The slope is $b_1 = (73 - 73) = 0$ because the two side-by-side boxplots have the same median. Thus, the comparison decision is easy. A 0 slope means that the levels, reflected in the medians, are the same for the typical ages at death of presidents' mothers and fathers. Furthermore, the predictor variable x_{1i} does not help predict y_i.

The two box lengths are nearly the same (21 and 25), and they are small enough relative to the medians for a sound comparison conclusion.

EXAMPLE 5

MINITAB, ROBUST FIT OF A STRAIGHT LINE, AGE DATA

Problem Statement   Using MINITAB, find an exploratory robust fit of a line to the age data.

Problem Solution   The following prediction equation results:

$$\hat{y}_i = 72.50 + (73 - 72.50)\, x_{1i}$$

The 72.50 can be rounded to 73.

The Prediction Equation for Comparisons, Sales Data

A simple visual comparison of the sales data boxplots and stem-and-leaf displays in Exhibit 6 leads to the conclusion that the different package designs result in significantly different sales levels. The new package design has substantially higher median sales. It is assumed that no other factor, other than package design, influenced sales. Therefore, x_{1i} is the only predictor variable. In the prediction equation

$$\hat{y}_i = 33 + (76 - 33)\, x_{1i}$$

the predictor variable, x_{1i}, does help predict sales, and the regression coefficient, $b_1 = (76 - 33) = 43$, is not near 0.

Notched Boxplots for Comparisons

Although simple visual comparisons have worked for the extreme situations encountered so far, this approach is not adequate for many real-world problems. The inadequacy stems from the informal, intuitive assessment of level and spread. A formal rule is needed that combines levels (medians) and spreads (box lengths). The formality is important, especially in marginal situations where the comparison decisions are not obvious. Obvious differences in level occur when the side-by-side boxes do not overlap and the spreads are about equal, or small relative to the medians.

Exhibit 8 shows two types of comparison situations: (1) when it is hard to tell whether or not there is a significant difference in medians, and (2) when this comparison decision is easy. For the difficult comparison decisions, a formal rule is required because visual inspection is not reliable. A **decision**

EXHIBIT 8 Where It Is Easy and Where It Is Hard to Make Comparisons

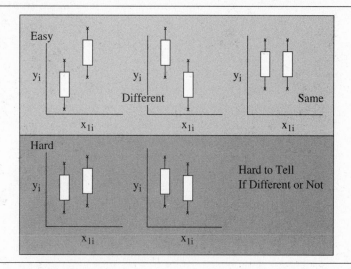

rule is a well-defined standard for making comparison decisions. This decision rule requires that side-by-side boxplots have notches, and, if the notches do not overlap, the medians are significantly different. Exhibit 9 shows some instances where notches overlap and where they do not. The notches are formulated to yield reliable decisions 95% of the time for samples from normal distributions.

Notch Construction   We can construct the notches on each boxplot as follows, where n is the number of data values summarized by the boxplot:

$$\text{median} \pm 1.58 \times \frac{\text{box length}}{n^{1/2}}$$

The constant term, 1.58, in this formula is different from the constant term, 1.82, used in an earlier chapter. The 1.82 was used for notches when working with a single variable. Velleman and Hoaglin provide an insightful discussion of the notch formula.[2]

EXHIBIT 9 Notches That Don't Overlap and Notches That Do Overlap

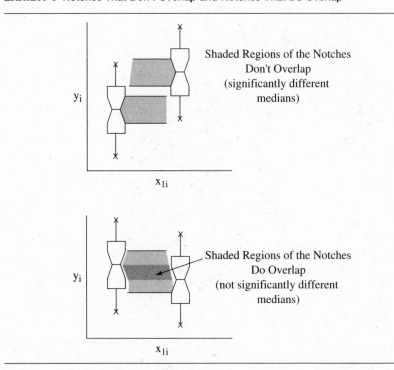

EXAMPLE 6

NOTCHED BOXPLOTS IN MINITAB

Problem Statement (a)   Construct notched boxplots in MINITAB for comparisons using the ages of presidents' parents. What do you conclude from these results?

Problem Solution (a)   In MINITAB, notches are marked by the parentheses. The first pair of notches overlap. Therefore, conclude that mothers of presidents do not tend to live longer or shorter than fathers do.

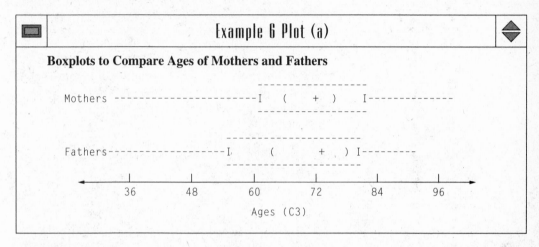

Problem Statement (b)   Construct notched boxplots in MINITAB for comparisons using the sales data for different package designs. What do you conclude from these results?

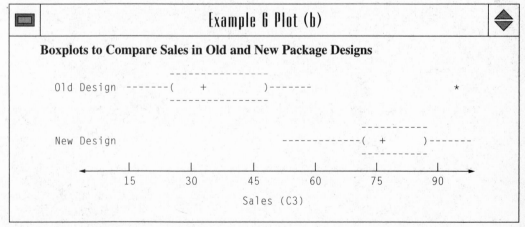

Problem Solution (b)   The notches don't overlap for the package design data, indicating that package design has a significant effect on sales.

Pseudo t Tests for Comparisons (Optional)

An alternative to the notched boxplot is a **pseudo t test.** The pseudo t test and notched boxplots lead to the same conclusions when making comparisons. There are two reasons for considering this alternative approach. First, the pseudo t test shows how the key elements of a visual comparison (level and spread) might be captured in a ratio, and the ratio statistic can be compared to a standard or critical value for making decisions. Second, the pseudo t test provides a conceptual link between exploratory and confirmatory work. In fact, the pseudo t test is linked to the powerful, confirmatory, Student's t test.

A pseudo t value is computed by dividing the difference in medians by a **pseudo standard error.** The pseudo standard error, s_p, is a function of box lengths and sample sizes.

$$s_p = \left[\frac{(\text{box length 1})^2}{n_1} + \frac{(\text{box length 2})^2}{n_2} \right]^{1/2}$$

Thus, the pseudo t statistic is

$$\text{pseudo t statistic} = \frac{y_{M2} - y_{M1}}{s_p}$$

where

$$y_{M1} = \text{the median of sample 1}$$
$$y_{M2} = \text{the median of sample 2}$$

Components of the pseudo t test appear in the prediction equation. The difference in medians is the slope or regression coefficient, $b_1 = (y_{M2} - y_{M1})$. The prediction equation is

$$\hat{y}_i = y_{M1} + (y_{M2} - y_{M1}) x_{1i}$$

Although both the pseudo t test and the notched boxplots are exploratory and therefore robust, ideal conditions include that box lengths do not differ greatly (the larger being no more than 1.5 times the smaller), and that the sum of the two sample sizes is greater than 30. It would be helpful if the samples were from a normal distribution.

Pseudo t Test Decision Rule If the absolute value of the pseudo t statistic exceeds the critical value of 1.58, reject the hypothesis that the two unknown population medians are equal, at a 95% level of significance.

Remember that this is a rough rule from an exploratory perspective. A more formal statistical test can be conducted if necessary.

RELATIONSHIPS SUMMARIZED BY A STRAIGHT LINE WHEN x IS NOT RESTRICTED TO TWO VALUES

So far the predictor variable has been restricted to two values, a 0 or 1. When the predictor variable is unrestricted and capable of taking on a wide range of values, the prediction equation becomes a more general summary of the relationship between two variables. No longer are we limited to simple comparisons, and any linear relationship is possible. As an example, sales revenue is a linear function of the number of units of a product sold. The number of units sold can span a wide range of values. Even if the relationship is nonlinear, the variables can often be transformed so that the relationship becomes linear.

A Prediction Equation When the Predictor Variable Is at More Than Two Levels

A prediction equation is a powerful way to summarize how two variables are related. This linear relationship is the main feature of concern on graphical displays of data values. Because the predictor variable is not restricted to two levels such as 0 and 1, the prediction equation should be thought of as a line connecting many medians. This is shown in Exhibit 10. For any value of x, this line provides a prediction of the median response.

In practice, the medians do not line up as well as those shown in Exhibit 10, and the data are not always observed at fixed intervals along the horizontal axis. Sometimes there are not enough data values to form all those boxplots. Nevertheless, Exhibit 10 provides a conceptually correct model for understanding that a prediction equation relates typical values of the response variable to predictor variable values.

EXHIBIT 10 A Summary of the Relationship Between Two Variables

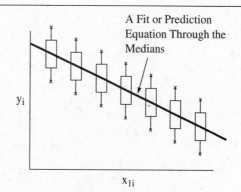

Fitting a Line on a Graphical Display of the Data To illustrate fitting a line to data, consider sales and assets of the 30 largest U.S. businesses in billions of dollars.[3]

	y_i	x_{1i}	
Row	Sales (C1)	Assets (C2)	Company Name
1	101.8	87.4	General Motors
2	76.4	74.0	Exxon
3	71.6	45.0	Ford Motor
4	54.2	63.7	International Business Machines
5	51.2	41.1	Mobil
6	39.3	38.9	General Electric
7	34.4	34.0	Texaco
8	33.6	38.4	AT&T
9	30.5	28.2	E.I. du Pont de Nemours
10	26.3	19.9	Chrysler
11	26.0	34.5	Chevron
12	22.3	19.1	Philip Morris
13	20.9	26.9	Shell Oil
14	20.2	24.8	Amoco
15	17.2	11.9	United Technologies
16	17.1	16.7	Occidental Petroleum
17	17.0	13.7	Procter and Gamble
18	16.3	22.7	Atlantic Richfield
19	15.9	16.9	RJR Nabisco
20	15.4	12.6	Boeing
21	15.1	18.5	Tenneco
22	14.6	23.3	BP America
23	14.0	19.6	USX
24	13.4	14.4	Dow Chemical
25	13.3	14.5	Eastman Kodak
26	13.1	8.5	McDonnell-Douglas
27	12.1	8.7	Rockwell International
28	11.6	10.2	Allied-Signal
29	11.5	9.0	Pepsico
30	11.4	6.3	Lockheed

Exhibit 11 is an **x-y plot** or **scatterplot** of sales versus assets. High sales levels tend to be associated with high asset levels.

Three rectangles are added to this scatterplot because they are to be used in the procedure for obtaining the prediction equation. Inside each rectangle there are two crossing lines for the same purpose. The three rectangles divide the data so that approximately one-third of the data points are in each rectangle.

Exhibit 12 shows a fit or prediction equation augmenting the scatterplot. The fit summarizes the linear relation between sales and assets, y_i and x_{1i}. The fit is more focused than the data point pattern that displays variability as well as the relationship between sales and assets.

EXHIBIT 11 A Scatterplot of Sales Versus Assets

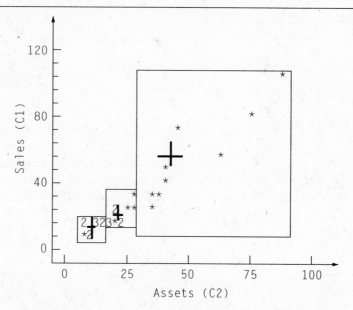

Note: On the plot, the symbol * indicates one plotting point representing one company, the number 2 indicates two overplotted points, the number 3 indicates three overplotted points, and so on.

EXHIBIT 12 A Robust Exploratory Straight Line Fit

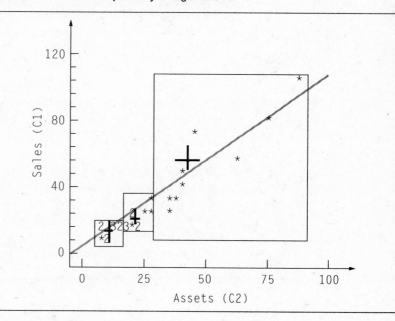

Because the fit is a general and powerful way of relating pairs of variables, there are many examples of interesting relationships, such as highway accidents and beer consumption, the incidence of lung cancer and packs of cigarettes smoked per day, and the number of cups of coffee and trips to the bathroom.

In many situations the background variables are not controlled (held constant). Therefore, what you see may be deceiving.

A Procedure for a Robust Fit   A robust exploratory fit of a straight line to data, as shown in Exhibit 12, is described here. This procedure positions a line without letting unusual data points have too much influence. In MINITAB, the RLINE command produces a similar fit.

The fitting procedure is based on the six steps that follow. Exhibit 12 serves as an illustration.

Step (1):   From the data set or from the scatterplot, count the number of data points, divide by three to find the number of data points in one-third (round off fractions to make counting easy).

Step (2):   On a scatterplot, position an imaginary vertical line or the edge of a sheet of paper just to the left of the left-most data point. Then move the imaginary vertical line (or sheet) to the right until it has moved past one-third of the data points.

Step (3):   Draw a rectangle that just encloses the data values you have passed over.

Step (4):   Repeating steps 2 and 3, move the imaginary vertical line past the second third of the data points and draw another rectangle. Do the same for the last third of the data points.

As shown in Exhibit 12, this step results in three rectangles. Depending on the disposition of the data values in other data sets, these rectangles may turn out to be tall and thin, tall and fat, short and fat, short and thin, and so on. In other words, not all scatterplots will look like Exhibit 12.

Step (5):   Within each rectangle, use imaginary vertical and horizontal lines to split the data values into two halves (vertically, half to the left and half to the right; horizontally, half above and half below). Draw a cross within each rectangle at the intersection of these imaginary vertical and horizontal lines.

Step (6):   Use the three crosses, rather than all the data points, to position a fitted line, by eye, equidistant from the crosses, as shown in Exhibit 12.

Finding Regression Coefficients for the Prediction Equation   The prediction equation is of the form

$$(\text{predicted sales}) = (\text{intercept}) + b_1 \times (\text{assets})$$
$$\hat{y}_i \qquad = \qquad b_0 \qquad + b_1 \qquad x_{1i}$$

Graphically estimate the intercept, b_0, and the slope, b_1. First determine where the fitted line crosses the vertical axis; b_0 is approximately 0 in Exhibit 12. The slope, b_1, is computed by picking two points on the fitted line and finding the change in sales divided by the change in assets. For example, as sales increase from 0 to 32, assets increase from 0 to 24, roughly; $\frac{32-0}{24-0} = \frac{4}{3} = 1.33$. A dollar change in assets generates a 1.33 dollar change in sales.

$$(\text{predicted sales}) = (\text{intercept}) + b_1 \quad \times (\text{assets})$$
$$\hat{y}_i \qquad = \qquad 0 \qquad + 1.33 \qquad x_{1i}$$

Be careful with graphical estimation. Many graphs are not scaled such that both variables have values of 0 at the origin. You may have to adjust for that fact.

S T A T I S T I C A L   H I G H L I G H T S

A fitted line summarizes a linear relationship between two variables.

EXAMPLE 7

MORE ON SALES VERSUS ASSETS IN MINITAB

Sales and assets of the 30 largest U.S. businesses in billions of dollars are explored in more detail using MINITAB. The analysis includes obtaining summary statistics, fitting a straight line, plotting the fit along with the data, and examining residuals briefly.

Problem Statement (a)   Compute the ratio of sales to assets and obtain summary statistics.

Problem Solution (a)   C3 contains the SALES to ASSETS ratio for the 30 largest U.S. businesses. Typically their SALES level is about the same as their ASSETS level with a mean ratio of 1.0817. Half of these ratios are between the quartiles .8422 and 1.2538.

	N	MEAN	MEDIAN	TRMEAN	STDEV
C3	30	1.0817	1.0282	1.0657	0.2884

	MIN	MAX	Q1	Q3
C3	0.6266	1.8095	0.8422	1.2538

Problem Statement (b)   Find a robust and resistant fit of a straight line relating sales and assets.

Problem Solution (b)   The MINITAB RLINE command produces a robust fit. The equation predicts the typical sales level needed to support a given asset base.

$$\text{slope} = 0.9236 \qquad \text{level} = 3.0930$$
$$(\text{predicted sales}) = (\text{intercept}) + b_1 \qquad \times (\text{assets})$$
$$\hat{y}_i \qquad = \qquad 3.093 \quad + .9236 \qquad x_{1i}$$

Problem Statement (c)   Simultaneously plot both the fitted line and the values of sales and assets.

Problem Solution (c)   The predicted sales figures are represented by the B's on the scatterplot shown below. Draw a straight line through the B's. Because this plot is constructed from printed characters, the straight line fit does not appear continuous unless you connect the B's to emphasize the fit. The A's are actual sales.

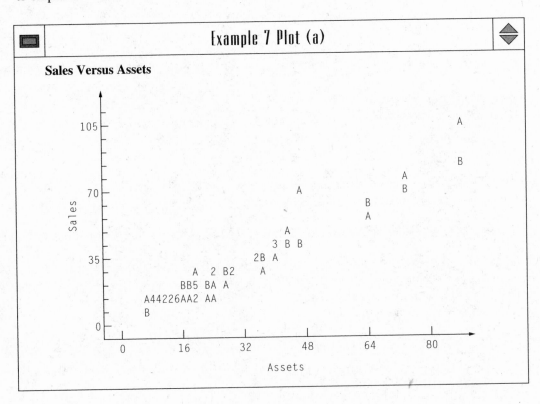

Example 7 Plot (a)

Problem Statement (d)   Because the scaling in problem solution (c) makes it difficult to see how a particular company deviates from the fitted line, plot the residuals (actual sales minus predicted sales) next. Residual plots magnify these deviations. Code residuals as well as the ratios of sales to assets and plot by company number, 1–30. Use the following codes: a 1 (A's on the plot) for an automobile company, a 2 (B's on the plot) for an oil company, and a 3 (C's on the plot) for all others. The MINITAB plotting command uses these codes.

Take a pencil and draw boundaries for any clusters of A's, B's, and C's that may exist. Some clusters of industries might differ from the norm. Any particularly unusual points should also be noted.

Problem Solution (d)   C4 is actual sales minus predicted sales or residuals (the A's minus the B's of the previous plot). The residuals are coded below by company type, A's for autos, B's for oils, and C's for others.

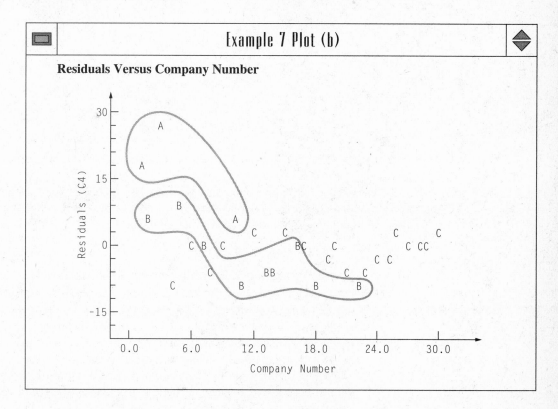

The variability of the residuals is greater for the larger companies (left side of the plot) than it is for the smaller companies (right side of the plot). This lack of uniformity in variability suggests that the data might need to be transformed (using logs or roots for example) and refitted.

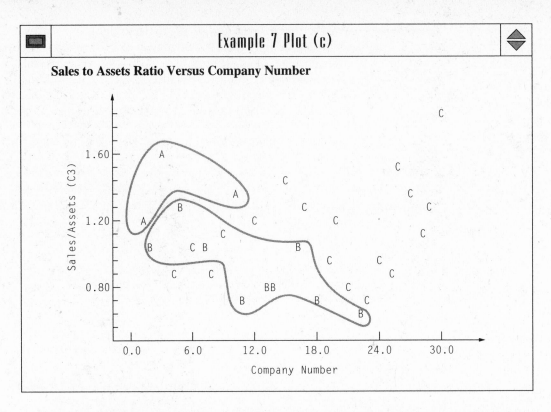

Example 7 Plot (c)

Sales to Assets Ratio Versus Company Number

Notice that the A's (automotive companies) and the B's (oil companies) cluster differently. Automotive companies tend to generate more sales dollars per asset dollar than do the oil companies. Oil companies tend to be more asset intensive.

The Emphasis on Graphing Pairs of Variables

Graphs, such as the scatterplots in the previous example, are an integral part of good statistical analysis. Therefore, the use of graphics must be emphasized. Modern statistical packages help simplify the problem of constructing graphical displays. They make a variety of graphs available. As a result, numerical calculations and mathematical formulas can be deemphasized. Moreover, the focus of the analysis can be directed toward learning about the data structure and solving a client's problems rather than making exact calculations.

Scatterplots vividly display relationships between pairs of variables. Not only do they illustrate the association between two variables, but they also expose unusual features. For example, outliers and clusters of points may be unveiled. During all phases of the analysis, scatterplots along with numerical calculations are used repeatedly. It is common, for example, to construct scatterplots with and without outliers or certain clusters of data points. In this way, the data gets viewed from different perspectives.

A thorough analysis involves a series of activities, such as making calculations, constructing scatterplots, and producing some assessments. These activities might be carried out repeatedly in a sequence of phases as the scientific learning process continues. Some phases may involve transforming data values or trimming unusual observations. In addition, residual plots are useful for validating certain assumptions. Finally, when the analysis is nearly complete, graphs are critical in presenting and reporting the results.

What to Look for on Scatterplots[4]   Identify the broad features in the data, stray values, clusters, and other relations. Key considerations include (1) linear relationships where the data points lie nearly on a straight line, (2) nonlinear relationships that data transformations may make linear, (3) the absence of a relationship where there is no pattern to the data points, and (4) perceptible relations along with some outliers and clusters of points that can be set aside while the analysis continues on what remains.

Scatterplots May Involve Transformed Variables   When a nonlinear pattern is discovered on a scatterplot, one or both variables may be transformed. Logarithms, square roots, reciprocals, and reciprocals of square roots are commonly used. Then, scatterplots of the transformed variables should be examined with the same intensity as the scatterplots of the original variables. The objective is to obtain a linear relationship because it is easier to work with than a nonlinear one. Also, scatterplots of transformed variables may be more revealing than those of the original variables.

CORRELATION

It is exciting for the researcher to discover and learn about interesting relations. It is equally important to communicate what has been found. If you have to tote a scatterplot around every time you need to show and tell what you have found, communication becomes slow and tedious. As a result, a summary statistic, r, called a sample **correlation coefficient,** is used to capture the essence of a scatterplot. A sample correlation coefficient estimates the unknown population correlation coefficient, ρ.

Correlation coefficient is a common term for communication in data analysis. We might say, for example, that bad breath is negatively correlated with the number of times you brush your teeth with a popular toothpaste. This means that the more often you brush, the less often bad breath occurs. More

EXHIBIT 13 Some Data Patterns and Correlation Coefficients

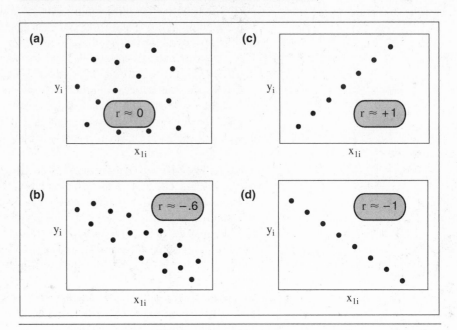

important relationships might be investigated, such as that between diet and heart disease. Again, a correlation coefficient becomes an important way to summarize experimental results, particularly in summarizing the relationships between the variables in a scatterplot. Exhibit 13 shows some contrasting data patterns and the corresponding sample correlation coefficients.

The Sign and Magnitude of a Correlation Coefficient

A correlation coefficient can have a negative sign, a positive sign, or no sign at all. A positive sign indicates that as y increases, x increases, and as y decreases, x decreases. In other words, high values of y are associated with high values of x, and low values of y are associated with low values of x. Thus, the two variables behave in the same way. See Exhibit 13(c).

When the sign is negative, the opposite is true. A negative sign indicates that as y increases, x decreases, and as y decreases, x increases. In other words, high values of y are associated with low values of x, and low values of y are associated with high values of x. Thus, the two variables behave in the opposite way. See Exhibit 13 (b) and (d).

No sign at all occurs when the magnitude of the sample correlation coefficient is 0. A 0 sample correlation coefficient leads us to believe that there is no relation between the two variables. See Exhibit 13 (a), where the data points are scattered with no particular pattern other than perhaps a circular cluster of points.

The magnitude of a correlation coefficient can range from -1 to $+1$. See Exhibit 13 for a selection of contrasting correlation coefficients. Exhibit 13 (c) and (d) illustrate the extremes of -1 and $+1$. These two magnitudes represent equally strong relationships and all the data points lie on a straight line. Exhibit 13 (a) illustrates a 0 sample correlation coefficient, which suggests that there is no relationship between the variables. Exhibit 13 (b) illustrates $r = -.6$, where the data point cloud has an oval-shaped or elliptical pattern.

Because the scatterplots depict samples of observations, each is summarized by a sample correlation coefficient, which estimates an unknown population correlation coefficient, ρ. Therefore, a sample result, say, $r = 0$, leads us to believe that $\rho = 0$ and that there is no relationship between the pair of variables.

Perfectly Correlated Variables   When $r = -1$ or $+1$, the variables are perfectly correlated. These extremes represent the strongest relationship possible.

In the presence of many variables, a perfect correlation between any pair is good news to the researcher because this means that the two variables behave predictably. Because either variable can represent the other, only one of the two may be needed. Therefore, fewer variables can characterize the complexity of a problem.

Between Perfect and No Correlation   A sample correlation coefficient of $r = 0$ suggests no relationship between a pair of variables, and $r = \pm 1$ suggests the strongest possible relationship. Often the strength of the relationship is between these extremes and the sample correlation coefficient falls between these values $-1 < r < 0$ or $0 < r < +1$. For sample correlation coefficients in these regions, the data point pattern tends to be elliptical in shape. As r approaches 0, the ellipse becomes circular. As r approaches plus or minus one, the ellipse becomes narrower and narrower until it collapses into a straight line when correlations are perfect.

An Exploratory Approximation of a Correlation Coefficient

An approximate sample correlation coefficient can be obtained graphically from a scatterplot. The following procedure refers to Exhibit 14. First draw an ellipse around the cloud of data values. On the ellipse, measure the maximum height, H, and middle height, h, as shown in the exhibit. Substitute H and h into the following formula:

$$r_{approx.} = \left(1 - \left(\frac{h}{H}\right)^2\right)^{1/2}$$

EXHIBIT 14 Approximating the Sample Correlation Coefficient

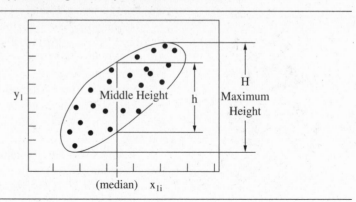

This approximation was presented in a paper by Chatillon.[5] It is valuable because it shows how the shape of the scatterplot is related to the approximate correlation coefficient. As h approaches H in size, their ratio approaches 1 and the correlation coefficient approaches 0. As h becomes very small, the ratio, $\frac{h}{H}$, approaches 0 and the correlation coefficient approaches 1.

This approximation is less accurate when (1) the sample plot scale makes the ellipse difficult to sketch, (2) there are too few data points, and (3) the points are not evenly distributed inside the ellipse.

Influence of Outliers on the Correlation Coefficient

As mentioned earlier, a correlation coefficient summarizes a scatterplot. However, you can be misled by it because a single outlier can radically alter a correlation coefficient's value. The scatterplot on the left of Exhibit 15 includes one stray data point. However, this data point is excluded from the right side of the exhibit. On the left side, all the data produce a deceptively high correlation coefficient of r = .95. On the right side, the trimmed data set produces a realistic low correlation coefficient of r = .002. As a result, trimming and recalculating correlation coefficients is recommended in exploratory work.

The Correlation Coefficient as a Goodness of Fit Measure

In addition to summarizing the linear relationship between x and y or transformed x and y, a correlation coefficient can be used to evaluate how well a fitted line summarizes the data. Then it becomes a **goodness of fit** measure.

EXHIBIT 15 The Correlation Coefficient, With and Without Influence
from a Stray Data Value

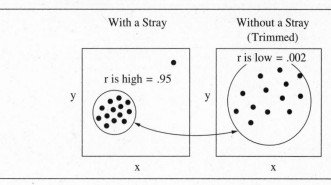

The correlation between the observed response, y_i, and the predicted response, $\hat{y}_i$, is a measure of how well the prediction equation predicts. In the
best predictive model, the y_i and $\hat{y}_i$ values are equal and their correlation
coefficient is 1. The worst possible fit produces a 0 correlation between y_i and
$\hat{y}_i$. Usually we find something in between.

Sometimes the correlation between y_i and $\hat{y}_i$ is squared and multiplied by
a hundred, which is the percentage of the variability in y_i that is explained by
$\hat{y}_i$. Because the predicted response depends on the predictor variable through
the equation, $\hat{y}_i = b_0 + b_1 x_{1i}$, the percentage of the variability in y_i that is
explained by $\hat{y}_i$ also depends on x_{1i}. Therefore, the correlation between y_i and
$\hat{y}_i$ equals the correlation between y_i and x_{1i}, when there is only one predictor
variable.

Sometimes the squared correlation between y_i and $\hat{y}_i$ is represented by
the symbol R^2, where R is the **multiple correlation coefficient.** $R^2 \times 100$ is
the percentage of the total variability that is explained by the predictor
variable(s).

EXAMPLE 8

CORRELATION USING MINITAB

Problem Statement   Plot sales versus assets of the 30 largest U.S. businesses in billions of
dollars. Then summarize the plot with a correlation coefficient.

Problem Solution   The correlation coefficient between sales and assets is 0.946. The fact that
it is near +1 reflects the strong relationship apparent in the plot.

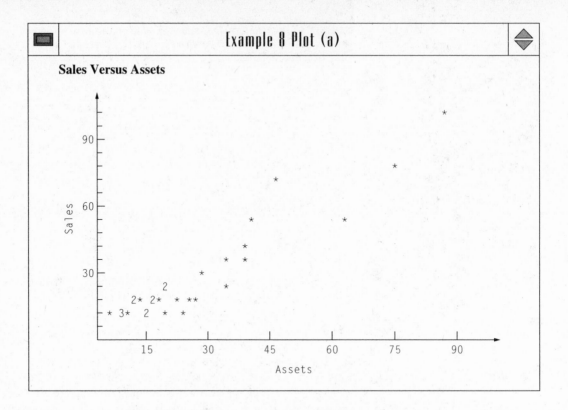

The Computational Formula for the Correlation Coefficient

All statistical packages will compute sample correlation coefficients for you. We include the computational formula for reference purposes. The formula makes use of the **sample covariance,** s_{yx}, which is defined as

$$s_{yx} = \sum_{1}^{n} \frac{\{(y_i - \bar{y}) \times (x_i - \bar{x})\}}{(n - 1)}$$

After the sample covariance is computed, it is divided by the product of the standard deviations of each variable to obtain the sample correlation coefficient.

$$\text{sample correlation coefficient} = r_{yx} = \frac{s_{yx}}{s_y s_x}$$

It is recommended that sample sizes exceed 20. Otherwise the sample correlation coefficient is imprecise.

There is no consensus about what magnitude of the correlation coefficient is necessary for it to be meaningful to the user. While some might regard a small correlation such as r = .20 as an important result, others may conclude that the same correlation reveals little. For discussion purposes, let's regard absolute values of r below .50 as small and absolute values of r above .80 as large.

EXAMINING RESIDUALS

Some of the greatest discoveries in science have resulted from the investigation of residual phenomena. To examine residual phenomena means to look at the remains after the main features have been removed (subtracted) and to discover why something unusual happened. Residuals highlight the unusual features in the data. Plots of residuals make unusual features stand out.

Computing Residuals

A residual is a deviation between an actual and predicted response. Therefore, when relating a pair of variables, a residual is defined as

$$\text{residual}_i = y_i - (b_0 + b_1 x_{1i}) = y_i - \hat{y}_i$$

Because $(b_0 + b_1 x_{1i})$ is subtracted from y_i, the component effect, $b_1 x_{1i}$, and a constant, b_0, have been removed from each response value. Therefore, the residual part that remains is purged of $(b_0 + b_1 x_{1i})$. This is reflected in the notation, where the i-th residual is y_i^{Rx1}. The superscript, Rx1, indicates that predictor x_{1i} has been removed and that y_i^{Rx1} should be viewed as adjusted response values. The notation conveys that residuals are modified response values that may be subjected to further analysis.

Finding Unusual Residuals from Summary Information

In order to analyze residuals further, a helpful beginning is to construct a stem-and-leaf diagram and a boxplot of the residuals. Ideally the median should be near 0 and the stem-and-leaf diagram should be normal in shape. Departures from these ideals deserve study and reflection to contemplate the causes. Departures from normality are often corrected by transforming the responses using logarithms, square roots, or reciprocals. Nevertheless, unusually large or small residuals may remain.

Spotting unusually large or small residuals is easier if each residual is divided by $\frac{3}{4}$ of the box length (or by the standard deviation). Such residuals, z_{yRx1}, are standardized.

$$z_{yRx1} = \frac{y_i^{Rx1}}{\frac{3}{4} \times \text{box length}} \quad \text{or} \quad \frac{y_i^{Rx1}}{s}$$

Most standard computer packages compute $\frac{y^{Rx1}}{s}$ for you. When z_{yRx1} is normally distributed, roughly 99.7% of the standardized residuals are expected to lie between -3 and $+3$. Therefore, an absolute value of a standardized residual that exceeds 3, $|z_{yRx1}| > 3$, is considered unusual.

A simple visual scan of a list of z_{yRx1} values (produced by the computer package) reveals the unusual data values where $|z_{yRx1}| > 3$. When the investigator sees z_{yRx1} values of 3.5, 4, -5, and the like, a detailed examination of those data points and the conditions surrounding their origin should ensue. Such unusual data values might be the seeds of discovery.

Residual Plots

Scatterplots of residuals signal either that the analysis is essentially finished or that it should be continued. In addition to looking for a few unusually large or small outlying residuals, various common residual scatterplot patterns are shown in Exhibit 16, where residuals are plotted against predictions, $\hat{y}_i$.

EXHIBIT 16 Residuals Versus Predictions: y_i^{Rx1} versus ($\hat{y}_i = b_0 + b_1 x_{1i}$)

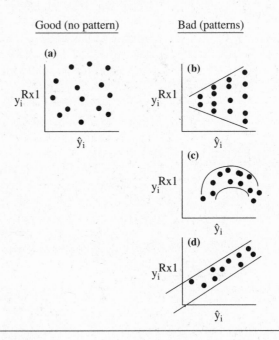

In Exhibit 16, residual plot (a) is marked "good" because the random dispersion of points does not reveal anything that requires more analysis. This signals that the investigator's data analysis work might be finishing.

In contrast, plots (b), (c), and (d) represent problematic residual plot patterns. These are marked "bad," which indicates to the investigator that additional analysis work is required.

In Exhibit 16, plot (b) is funnel-shaped, which indicates that the residual variability depends on the predicted response value. To stabilize this variability, the responses, y_i, should be transformed. Often after logarithms, square roots, or reciprocals of the responses are taken, the analysis is repeated and produces new residuals that no longer depend on the predicted response.

In plot (c) the systematic pattern is concave (it could also be convex). This suggests y_i or x_{1i} or both should be transformed to straighten the cloud of points. Then (1) fit a straight line to the transformed data and (2) plot the new residuals and have as a goal a random residual pattern like plot (a). An alternative to transformations, when using one predictor, is to introduce a second predictor that is a transformation of the first and build a prediction equation that includes both x_{1i} and x_{1i}^2.

If plot (d) occurs, suspect some sort of computational error in the analysis because the mechanics of the fitting procedure should remove x_{1i} from the residuals. Therefore, a plot of residuals versus the predictions, $(b_0 + b_1 x_{1i})$, should not display a linear relationship.

In the context of other potential predictor variables, such as x_{2i}, x_{3i}, x_{4i}, and so on, residuals can be plotted against them. These plots may display linear or curved patterns such as in plots (c) and (d). Then more complicated prediction equations must be considered that include the background variables, which are not constant or have an average effect of 0.

EXAMPLE 9

RESIDUAL ANALYSIS AND TRANSFORMATIONS OF SALES AND ASSETS

Problem Statement (a) For sales, C1, and assets, C2, of the 30 largest U.S. businesses in billions of dollars, an exploratory fit is:

$$\text{(predictions) C5} = 3.093 + (.9236) \times \text{C2}$$

Calculate the residuals, C4 = C1 − C5. Then plot residuals versus predictions. Note any unusual residuals or patterns.

Problem Solution (a)

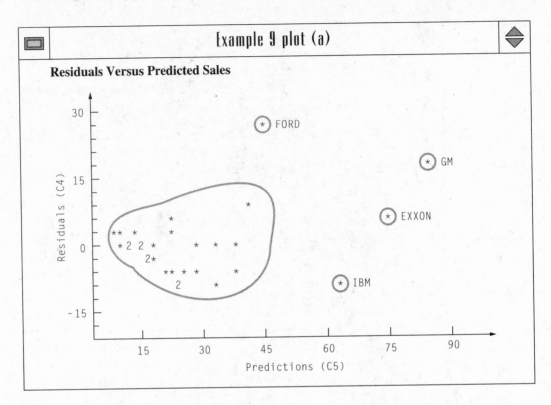

If you look back at Exhibits 11 or 12, you will notice that some data points are different from the rest. But in this residual plot these differences really stand out, as shown above. Because the residuals are not random as in Exhibit 16(a), the analysis should continue. The unusual residuals—Ford, EXXON, GM, and IBM—might be trimmed and the analysis repeated.

There is another vague pattern to notice in these residuals. As the predictions, C4, increase from small to large, the residuals tend to fan out in a funnel shape. This pattern resembles the one in Exhibit 16(b), in which the variability increases as the predicted response increases. Therefore, transformations to stabilize the variance are in order.

Problem Statement (b)   Take the natural logarithms of sales, letting C8 = LOGE (C1). Plot log sales versus assets, fit sales to assets, and draw the fitted line on the plot.

Problem Solution (b)

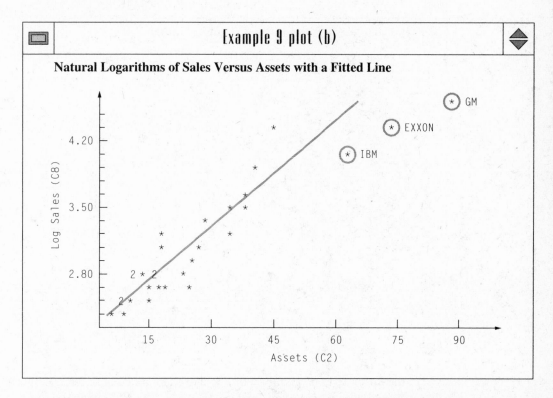

Example 9 plot (b)

Natural Logarithms of Sales Versus Assets with a Fitted Line

The fitted line is a good summary of the relationship between sales and assets for most of the companies. However, GM, EXXON, and IBM have less than expected sales for their asset levels, making them different from the remaining companies.

Is what we see a harbinger of future events for GM, EXXON, and IBM? Because these three big companies have an asset base that is larger than expected for their level of sales, they are either (1) poised for rapid expansion in sales or (2) poised for a fall. Four years after these data were collected and analyzed, IBM announced a workforce reduction of 20,000 employees in the midst of a recession. In a similar bombshell, GM announced that it would close 21 of its plants and eliminate 74,000 jobs over the next several years.

Problem Statement (c)   Trim GM, EXXON, and IBM and take another look.

Problem Solution (c)   The resulting fit is not influenced by the trimmed data values and is likely to yield a better relationship, representing the remaining companies. Trimming is a crude way to handle outliers, but it is acceptable in exploratory analysis.

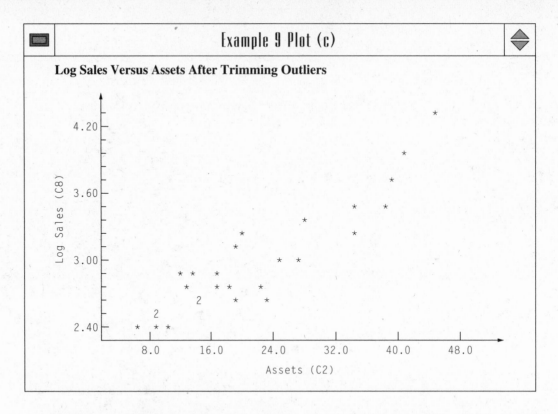

Example 9 Plot (c)

Log Sales Versus Assets After Trimming Outliers

In the upper-right-hand corner of the above plot, one data point exhibits slightly higher than expected sales. The trimming of GM, EXXON, and IBM unmasked this point. It does not fit the pattern. This point is Ford. Ford was able to generate more sales than expected from a given level of assets. Therefore, we trim Ford and plot again.

Problem Statement (d)   After trimming GM, EXXON, IBM and Ford from assets, C2, and LOGE (SALES), C8, obtain a new fit. Plot residuals from this fit.

Problem Solution (d)   Respectively, predicted values were obtained from C10 = 2.2109 + (.0337) C2. Then residuals were computed from C9 = C8 − C10.

Because of the trimming and transforming, residuals are random in Plot (e). This random pattern indicates that no systematic pattern remains in the residuals that needs to be accounted for in the analysis.

Problem Statement (e)   Based on the foregoing analysis, choose a prediction equation that adequately relates sales and assets for most of the companies in the data set.

Problem Solution (e)   Excluding GM, EXXON, IBM, and Ford, the prediction equation of choice relates LOGE (SALES) and ASSETS for the remaining companies. It is of the form

$$\hat{y}_i = b_0 + b_1 x_{1i}$$

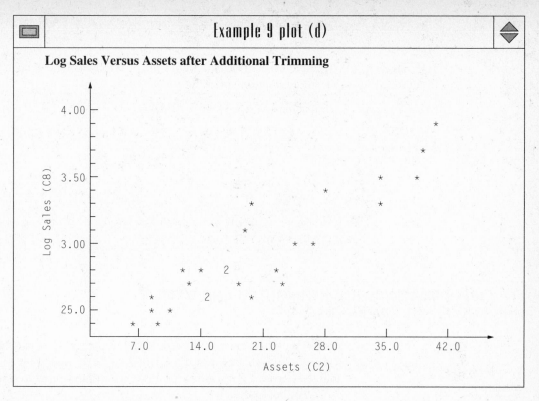

Log Sales Versus Assets after Additional Trimming

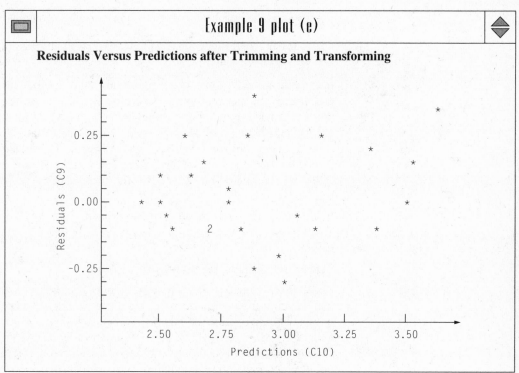

Residuals Versus Predictions after Trimming and Transforming

The intercept, 2.2109, and slope, .0337, are found with a MINITAB command. These are used to produce the following prediction equation:

$$\text{LOGE (SALES)} = 2.2109 + .0337 \text{ ASSETS}$$

If MINITAB is not available, the graphical fitting procedure described earlier in this chapter can be used.

S T A T I S T I C A L   H I G H L I G H T S

Consider the analysis of residuals as important as the analysis of the original observations.

TRANSFORMATIONS THAT STRAIGHTEN AND SIMPLIFY RELATIONSHIPS (OPTIONAL)

According to the laws of physics, a plot of energy, E, versus mass, m, forms a straight line. Different energies match different masses in a linear relationship. Perhaps the straightness of this relationship helped to clarify Einstein's thinking about physics.

> This was the equivalence of matter and energy, expressed in the epochal equation $E = mc^2$. Einstein hit upon it unintentionally, almost reluctantly, in the course of months of juggling with the symbols m, for mass, E for energy, c for the velocity of light.[6]

It is useful to relate Einstein's notation to that of a prediction equation; this emphasizes the fact that you are learning about tools of discovery. Furthermore, it provides motivation to straighten nonlinear relationships. Let the i-th energy level match with the i-th mass. Then suppose $\hat{y}_i = E_i$, $x_{1i} = m_i$, and $c^2 = b_1$, where c is the velocity of light. Einstein resolved a great paradox by asserting that the velocity of light is a fundamental constant. By looking at the following equations, you can see that they represent the same linear relationship.

$$E_i = c^2 m_i$$
$$\hat{y}_i = b_1 x_{1i}$$

Transformations to Straighten Lines

Recall that symmetry makes understanding easier because it reduces a problem's complexity. As an example, when one-half of a stem-and-leaf diagram or boxplot behaves like the other half, the displays are symmetrical and easy to understand. For a single variable, symmetry is about the median or another summary value. For a pair of variables on a scatterplot, symmetry of the data points is about the fitted line. In this sense, straightness is a form of symmetry that helps in understanding relationships.

EXAMPLE 10

GRAVITATIONAL FORCE

Problem Statement   After being struck on the head under an apple tree, it is said that Newton discovered the law of gravity.

$$\text{force} = \frac{\text{constant}}{\text{distance}^2}$$

A scatterplot would show a curved relationship between measurements of the force of gravity between the i-th pair of bodies, y_i, and the distance between the bodies, x_{1i}. What transformations result in a straight line relationship between these variables?

Problem Solution   Log(y_i) and log(x_{1i}) straightens this relationship as expressed in prediction equation form.

$$(\text{predicted}) \log(y_i) = b_0 - b_1 \log(x_{1i})$$

Antilogs of both sides of the linear prediction equation produce the nonlinear relationship between force, y_i, and distance, x_{1i}, with the regression coefficients as constants.

$$y_i = \frac{\text{antilog } b_0}{x_{1i}^{b_1}}$$

Logs of this equation yield the prediction equation.

Transformations for straightness are data analysis tools meant for discovery. Therefore, if b_1 from a fit of log(force) and log(distance) measurements is about 2, this would confirm Newton's law of gravity. In this way, transformations to straighten can help discover basic laws relating pairs of variables.

EXAMPLE 11

COMPOUNDING MONEY

Problem Statement   Consider compounding money at a fixed interest rate. A scatterplot would show a curved relationship between the future value, y_i, of an initial amount of money, P, compounded for b_1 periods at interest rate x_{1i}. Find a transformation that results in a straight line relationship.

Problem Solution   Log(y_i) and log($1 + x_{1i}$) straightens this relationship as expressed in prediction equation form.

$$(\text{predicted}) \log(y_i) = \log(P) + b_1 \log(1 + x_{1i})$$

Antilogs of both sides of the linear prediction equation produce the nonlinear relationship between the future value, y_i, and interest rate, x_{1i}, with the regression coefficients as constants.

$$y_i = (P)(1 + x_{1i})^{b_1}$$

In words, the future value is

$$\text{present value} \times (1 + \text{interest rate})^{\text{number of periods}}$$

The Similarity Between Single- and Two-Variable Transformations When relating a pair of variables, the idea of transforming to achieve straightness extends the idea of transforming a single variable to achieve symmetry. Such single variable transformations are shown in Exhibit 17. The "before" transformation boxplot has extending whiskers of vastly different lengths, and the median is not near the center of the box. The "after" transformation boxplot has whiskers that are more nearly equal, and the median is near the middle of the box (symmetry being achieved). When transformations make variables symmetrical as well as normal, many standard, well-known statistical tools are available to analyze the data.

The problem of choosing an appropriate transformation is simplified by using a collection of related transformations that are called **power transformations.** The term *power* means that y is taken to some power and then analyzed. These transformations are often tried on a trial-and-error basis from the following menu:

$$\frac{-1}{y^3}, \quad \frac{-1}{y^2}, \quad \frac{-1}{y}, \quad \frac{-1}{y^{1/2}}, \quad \log(y), \quad y^{1/2}, \quad y, \quad y^2, \quad y^3$$

Stem-and-leaf diagrams, boxplots, and histograms of transformed raw data are often more symmetrical, sometimes more normal, when the right transformation is selected. Logs, square roots, and reciprocals are the most successful items on the transformation menu.

For two variables, transformations are used to straighten a pattern of data points as shown in Exhibit 18. Symmetry is about a straight line. $T_p(y)$ denotes a transformation of the response variable, y. $T_p(x)$ denotes a transformation of the predictor variable, x.

EXHIBIT 17 Transforming a Single Variable to Improve Symmetry

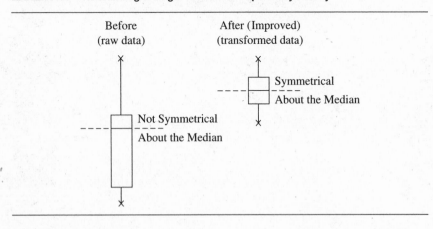

EXHIBIT 18 Transformations to Achieve Straightness

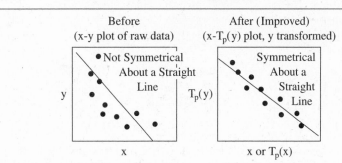

CHAPTER SUMMARY

This chapter discussed two-variable exploration. A response variable, y_i, responds (possibly) to the information carried by a predictor variable, x_{1i}. When other background predictor variables are held constant or their average effect is 0, there is a good chance of seeing how the response, y_i, is associated with the predictor variable, x_{1i}. However, this association does not necessarily imply cause and effect.

A simple case involves a predictor variable coded 0 or 1 to partition the response data into two subgroups. To compare these two subgroups, stem-and-leaf diagrams and boxplots may be placed side by side. If box lengths are about the same or made so through transformations, side-by-side boxplots can be compared visually to judge if the two medians are the same or not. At the extremes, the two subgroups of data have either about the same medians or the medians are much different. When the medians are nearly the same, a straight line through the two medians tends to have very little tilt. When the medians are vastly different, a straight line through the medians tends to have a substantial tilt upward or downward. In marginal situations where it is difficult to tell if the medians are or are not different,

notched boxplots or pseudo t tests can be used for the comparison decision.

A comparison can be extended to a more general relationship when the predictor variable is not limited to the values 0 or 1. When the predictor variable values range far and wide, a prediction equation or fit is used to highlight the main features of the linear relationship between the response and predictor variables.

Although the main features are of interest, so too are the unusual features. The x-y plots or scatterplots tell the complete story about the data points. Therefore, plots have become indispensible tools for the data analyst. It is recommended that plots be made with and without trimming unusual points or clusters. Plots of transformed variables might also be necessary. A complete analysis includes residual plots. Finally, plots that display curved relationships might be straightened with transformations.

The theme behind these exploratory methods is to understand the nature of the relationship between the two variables.

KEY TERMS

carrier variable, 350
censored observations, 354
clusters, 353
component effect, 367
correlation coefficient, 381

criterion variable, 350
decision rule, 369
dependent variable, 350
endogenous variable, 350
exogenous variable, 350

fit, 365
goodness of fit, 384
independent variable, 350
level, 357
multiple correlation coefficient, 385

one-way table, 361
parameter estimate, 367
power transformations, 396
prediction equation, 365
predictor variable, 350

principle of parsimony, 356
pseudo standard error, 372
pseudo t test, 372
regression coefficient, 367
response variable, 350

sample covariance, 386
scatterplot, 374
slope, 365
spread, 357
x-y plot, 375

EXERCISES

General Exercises

1. Use back-to-back stem-and-leaf diagrams and side-by-side boxplots to compare the batting averages of Buck Martinez and Gary Mathews. The yearly batting averages of each for much of their careers follow.[7]

BUCK MARTINEZ

.229 .111 .152 .250 .215 .226 .228 .225 .219 .270 .224 .227 .242
.253 .220 .162 .581

GARY MATHEWS

.290 .300 .287 .280 .279 .283 .285 .304 .278 .301 .281 .258 .291
.235 .259

(a) If all background factors were the same, who would be the better batter?

(b) What background factors might not be the same?

(c) Did you notice the batting average in the last year for Buck Martinez? He batted .581. Notice this figure had little impact on the boxplots and the comparison. Actually, the .581 was a data entry error. The figure should have been .181. In a traditional analysis, you might have to redo all of your work after trimming or correcting this data value. In the robust and resistant exploratory approach, you don't need to redo the analysis because such an error has little impact on the comparison mechanisms.

2. At a New England weather station, the 36-year average monthly temperatures in Fahrenheit are[8]

JAN.   **DEC.**

23.6 26.4 35.3 47.1 57.8 66.8 71.7 69.5 61.6 51.5 40.7 28.6

For the last year, the average monthly temperatures are

JAN.   **DEC.**

20.9 33.3 31.4 47.8 55.1 68.9 70.9 72.2 59.8 54.8 40.2 34.4

(a) Compare these using back-to-back stem-and-leaf diagrams.

(b) Subtract the 36-year average from last year's figures and construct a stem-and-leaf diagram for the differences. If there is no difference overall for 12 months, the median of the differences should be near zero.

(c) Plot the differences in part (b) by month.

(d) Plot the last year and the 36-year average figures both on a single plot with the numbers, 1, 2, . . . , 12, for months on the horizontal axis.

(e) Which of the above displays do you think does the best job in displaying the important information?

(f) Use the best approach from above on the precipitation data shown below.

36-Year Average Precipitation in Inches

JAN.   **DEC.**

3.17   3.02   3.49   3.83   3.68   3.74   3.68   3.78   3.45   3.39   3.77   3.87

The Last Year's Average Monthly Precipitation in Inches

JAN.   **DEC.**

1.75   6.42   3.68   4.30   11.95   1.69   4.64   1.34   1.02   3.13   3.97   2.84

(g) For the last year, are there any unusual months in temperature or precipitation? If so, which are they?

(h) Incidentally, in the last year, the growing season for plants sensitive to frost extended from May 3 through October 5, which is 156 days, or 2 days longer than usual. A May 28 through 31 storm raised the Connecticut River to its highest level since the prehurricane flood of 1938.

(i) What is the approximate correlation between the differences in temperature and the differences in precipitation?

3. You are given returns on a stock, that were computed from the i-th period price, P_i, and the price one period ahead. The return on a stock is $y_i = \dfrac{(P_{i+1} - P_i)}{P_i}$. Because we would like to see how the movement of a particular stock is related to the movement of the market as a whole, we use the Dow-Jones (DJ) Index or the Standard and Poor's Composite Index as a price that represents the whole market. Hence, for example, the market return is $x_{1i} = \dfrac{(DJ_{i+1} - DJ_i)}{DJ_i}$. These returns have been computed for you, converted to a percentage, and rounded for simplicity. They are

PERIOD	1	2	3	4	5	6	7	8	9	10	11	12
$y_i =$	12	15	−4	1	3	−2	−8	−1	1	1	2	7
$x_{1i} =$	12	6	2	4	4	5	−6	−2	3	6	2	−1

(a) Obtain a scatterplot of the returns on the stock versus the returns on the market.

(b) Compute the approximate correlation between the returns on the stock and the returns on the market.

(c) Obtain a robust and resistant fit of the form $b_0 + b_1 x_{1i}$.

(d) What does the regression coefficient for the slope, b_1, tell you about the change in the stock's return as the market return changes by one unit?

4. In the manufacture of a new missile component, it took 120 min to make the first unit, 92 min to make the second unit of the same component, 54 min to make the seventh unit, and 52 min to manufacture the eighth unit. The complete data set is shown below. It is clear that learning is taking place. As more units are produced, less time is needed to complete each unit. A plot of the time to manufacture each unit versus unit number is called a learning curve. The reduction in the completion time decreases as more units are produced.

UNIT

x_{1i}	1	2	3	4	5	6	7	8	9	10

TIME TO MANUFACTURE

y_i	120	92	80	70	61	59	54	52	51	49

(a) Plot the data.

(b) Is there curvature present?

(c) If there is curvature, try a log transformation of one variable to straighten the relationship.

(d) Obtain a robust and resistant straight line fit to the transformed data set.

(e) For the first eight units produced, obtain the predicted time to make each unit.

(f) To assess the goodness of the fit, obtain the approximate correlation between the predicted and the actual times.

(g) Obtain a robust and resistant straight line fit of the data before the transformations, compute the residuals, plot the residuals versus the predictions, and determine what it is about this plot that suggests that transformations were needed.

5. It is thought that certain standardized tests are useful in predicting the performance of students in college. One such test was taken by 30 students. Their scores on the mathematics (MATH) part of the test are shown below along with their grade point averages (GPA).

GPA

2.70   2.65   2.30   3.73   1.64   1.76   2.92   3.14   3.13   2.71
2.54   1.98   3.09   3.31   2.78   2.63   2.66   2.25   3.28   2.00
2.13   3.08   2.46   3.03   1.16   3.31   3.22   3.70   2.46   2.97

MATH

37   35   49   44   36   55   44 · 49   49   45   50   43   49   57   45
33   46   30   54   36   49   55   48   55   45   41   46   62   40   58

(a) Plot GPA versus MATH.

(b) Is the correlation between these two variables negative, positive, or zero?

(c) Obtain a robust and resistant fit to predict GPA from the MATH score.

(d) How good is this prediction equation?

(e) If you were an administrator in admissions at a university, how would you use these MATH scores along with other factors such as high school grades in making an admissions decision?

6. Using the presidential data base in Exhibit 1, examine life expectancy after the first inaugural and compare it to the actual years lived after the first inaugural.

(a) Make the comparison using side-by-side boxplots.

(b) Because these data do not arise from a carefully controlled study, generalizations from the results are weakly supported. Nevertheless, some preliminary exploratory work can lead to speculation and to the design and execution of better studies to be carried out at a later time. This data set has all the dangers associated with an observational study. If we make some simplifying assumptions and view these presidents as representative of future presidents, we may wish to notch the boxplots and say something about the proposition that the stress of this executive position has an adverse impact on lifespan. Do that. State your level of confidence in the conclusions.

(c) To look at part (b) in a different way, compute the pseudo t value and compare it to the standard of 1.58. Does the pseudo t test lead to the same or different conclusions than those reached using the notched boxplots?

7. To illustrate the use of boxplots for comparisons, conduct the following classroom experiment. Have students take their own resting pulse and record their gender. Next, have each student flip a coin, which is a randomization device. Have those getting tails stand and run in place or go out of the classroom for a brisk walk. Have those getting heads rest while the others exercise. Immediately afterwards take the pulse of all students and analyze to see if there is a pulse effect to mild exercise.

(a) Why might it be better to take your own pulse rather than have the person next to you take it? Could someone next to you cause your pulse to rise?

(b) Use boxplots to compare the pulse rates of those who exercised to those who did not.

(c) Using the initial data set (resting pulse for all students and gender), see if the male resting pulse is typically different from that of females.

8. In the United States, the northwest states generate about 80% of their electrical power from hydropower plants. During periods of low water runoff, high-cost thermoelectric plants must make up for reduced hydropower generation. The average annual flow in hundreds of cubic feet per second over 40 years was

1374	6234	1225	1679	1792	2275	1549	1639	1216	1787
1486	1490	1337	1665	1915	1376	1404	1835	1923	2242
1903	1860	2334	2069	1721	1927	1879	2497	2049	1813
1921	2054	1979	1646	1739	1740	2276	687	1857	1755

(a) As a manager you are thinking ahead because you know it takes 15 to 20 years to construct some thermoelectric plants. Borrowing power from other utility companies on large power grids is limited and expensive. Use any robust fit or RLINE in MINITAB to see if there is a trend in the runoff data over the 40 years. Note that you have to use the following commands to get the trend variable in column C2:

```
MTB> SET C2
DATA> 1:40
```

(b) Plot the average annual flow over time.

(c) Check to see if there are any potential outliers by examining residuals.

9. A twisting fall in skiing is dangerous because a spiral fracture can occur in the lower leg. Ski bindings are designed to release before the twist torque in foot-pounds gets to a critical level. The critical twist torque level depends on skier weight. The tabulated figures below are used to set binding twist torque levels (T) that depend on weight (W) in pounds.

T	16	20	24	28	32	36	40	44	48	50
W	55	75	95	115	135	155	175	195	215	235

(a) Obtain a robust and resistant summary of the relationship between (W) and (T) in which weight is used to predict torque.

(b) Use these results to predict the torque setting from your weight.

10. A random sample of professional golfers had the following one year official earnings (E) in thousands of dollars and scoring averages (A).[9] Using any robust fit or the RLINE command, examine the relationship between E and A, summarize your findings, and discuss.

EARNINGS (E)

71.6   55.8   147.8   117.4   112.3   82.7   22.8   58.8   60.5   55.4   43.6

SCORING AVERAGE (A)

71.5   72.75   71.34   71.27   70.95   71.65   72.49   71.46   71.95   71.61   72.39

11. A firm produces prefabricated houses by order only (a job-shop rather than an assembly line production facility) because a large number of styles and options are made available to the customer. For pricing purposes, the managers use budgeted costs because actual costs are not available until after the job is finished. A problem, however, became apparent in recent cost figures for part of the prefabrication work: the higher the actual cost (AC), the larger was the absolute deviation (DC) from budget. To assess the magnitude of the problem and to establish a benchmark from which improvements can be gauged, analyze and report on this relationship for the dollar figures below.

AC	35640	35730	35740	36000	37760	38700	39930	41210	43560
DC	500	610	615	854	1640	1100	1875	2044	1123

12. Some manufacturing companies refer to true physical production cost for a period as gross product. For financial planning in manufacturing, it is necessary to relate gross product to production factors such as payroll costs. Use any robust fit or the RLINE command in MINITAB to summarize the relationship between gross product (GP) and other factors such as payroll cost (PAY) for the actual production cost figures shown below (in thousands of dollars).

GP	69	210	156	166	120	100	112	125	175
PAY	66	143	115	122	117	90	95	110	135

13. A company maintains a fleet of automobiles. Management is interested in minimizing the total cost of ownership and operation. A portion of the total cost is for maintenance and operating costs (O&M dollars per mile). O&M costs tend to increase with vehicle age. Predict O&M costs using vehicle age (VA) in years.

O&M	.20	.28	.27	.32	.38	.42	.44	.49	.55	.56	.63	.66
VA	1	2	3	4	5	6	7	8	9	10	11	12

14. In establishing labor forecasts for a shipping center, it was necessary to predict man-hours (MH) from shipping units (SU in hundreds of units). Use any robust fit or the RLINE command to find the prediction equation and comment on the quality of the fit.

MH	3470	4650	5370	8320	5190	4180	3420	3890	3650
	5410	4110	3740						
SU	2178	3229	5530	6442	3767	2497	2229	3561	3791
	4184	3246	2813						

15. A manufacturing company found that the greater the capital investment (CI in hundreds of dollars) in automation, the fewer was the number of people employed (PE). For decision making purposes, quantify this relationship using a robust and resistant fit.

CI	985	715	585	500	412	198	190	146	56	14
PE	50	20	110	430	312	250	620	415	512	675

16. Flexible budgeting is needed in factories because production volume varies. Predicting cost behavior from past production experience is a supporting pillar of flexible budgeting. Although industrial engineering studies are used to determine how costs should vary with volume, statistical analysis is also used to summarize past cost-volume experience. Total mixed cost (TMC), a mixture of fixed and variable components, is often related to a production volume measure such as machine-hours (MH). Obtain an equation for predicting TMC (in hundreds of dollars) based on MH.

TMC	20	21	24	14	15	8	10	13	14	16	20
MH	22	27	23	19	18	14	13	10	12	20	26

17. An automobile manufacturer conducts quality control training programs in two of its supplier plants. The instructor gives the same exam in both plants. The exam scores are

Plant (Boston)	90	73	78	82	66	69	85	86	76	89	70
Plant (Atlanta)	81	72	50	66	55	70	68	82	71		

(a) Use notched boxplots to test (roughly) for a significant difference in sample medians. (A MINITAB Hint: Place all the exam scores in one column, say, C1. Use 1s and 0s in column C2 to identify Boston or Atlanta. Be sure to use the standard graphics mode (GSTD). Then use the BOXPLOT C1 command with subcommands BY C2 and NOTCHES.)

18. A production line worker suggested that a new assembly method might reduce assembly times. In response, the production manager decided to compare the new and old methods. Does there appear to be a significant difference in the median assembly times (in minutes)? (A MINITAB Hint: Place all the assembly times in one column, say, C1. Use 1s and 0s in column C2 to identify the old or new assembly method. Be sure to use the standard graphics mode (GSTD). Then use the BOXPLOT C1 command with subcommands BY C2 and NOTCHES.)

ASSEMBLY TIMES

OLD METHOD

21.6	21.7	23.9	24.0	22.7	24.6	22.5
24.0	24.4	24.0	23.7	24.9	23.9	24.9
22.7	23.4	22.4	22.2	24.4	24.4	25.1
22.7	25.3	23.4	25.4	24.1	24.5	24.1
24.9	23.9	24.9	23.9	23.1	24.5	24.6
25.0	24.7	22.3	24.0	23.0		

NEW METHOD

23.5	23.5	22.0	21.3	21.7	22.3	23.3
23.6	21.5	24.1	21.6	22.5	22.3	21.6
21.7	22.0	22.0	21.1	21.8	21.9	24.3
22.9	20.1	21.8	20.6	21.7	22.3	21.5
22.9	21.5	22.2	21.4	21.9	21.1	22.8
21.8	21.5	23.4	22.6	20.6		

19. An investor collected monthly price data for the stocks of two companies in the same line of business. From prices, returns were computed as shown below. Test to see if there is a significant difference in median returns using notched boxplots as well as pseudo t computations. (A MINITAB Hint: Place all the returns in one column, say, C1. Use 1s and 0s in column C2 to identify company A or B. Be sure to use the standard graphics mode (GSTD). Then use the

BOXPLOT C1 command with subcommands BY C2 and NOTCHES. Also, DESCRIBE or LVALS commands are needed to get the information for the pseudo t test.)

RETURNS COMPANY A

0.112	0.115	0.158	0.160	0.135	0.172	0.130
0.161	0.169	0.161	0.155	0.179	0.159	0.178
0.135	0.149	0.128	0.125	0.168	0.168	0.183
0.134	0.187	0.149				

RETURNS COMPANY B

0.209	0.182	0.191	0.182	0.198	0.179	0.199
0.179	0.162	0.191	0.192	0.200	0.194	0.147
0.181	0.161	0.210	0.211	0.181	0.166	0.175
0.186	0.206	0.213				

20. Some additional data sets for relating pairs of variables appear at the end of Chapter 11. All of those data sets may be examined first in an exploratory way, particularly as a first look, using the methods of this chapter. Therefore, if you wish to examine a wider variety of problems than those found here, jump ahead to the exercises in Chapter 11.

21. According to Robert Adair, former physicist for the National Baseball League, the distance (feet) a baseball travels is a function of the velocity (mph) of a pitched ball.[10] For the data below, assume that a 35-in., 32-oz bat is swung at 70 mph, waist-high, 10° upward from the horizontal plane, driving the ball at an angle of 35°. Using the data points below, which are approximations, fit a line to these points in which ball velocity predicts distance.

Distance	327	335	340	348	356	363	370	378	388
Velocity	20	30	40	50	60	70	80	90	100

Adair said that the fastest pitchers can throw a fastball about 100 mph; for example, Bob Feller (1946, 98.6 mph), Walter Johnson (1914, 99.7 mph), Nolan Ryan (100.7 mph), and Goose Gossage (about 100 mph). In contrast, a slow curve might have a velocity of 65 mph. Based on your fit, how far do you predict a slow curve will be hit?

22. A state department of transportation depends on computer processing for vehicle registrations and other transactions. A computer capacity management aid tracks central processor unit (CPU) hours used by month. Trends in CPU usage can be projected into the future to see when CPU capacity might be exceeded. As a result, early warning can be given of needed computer capacity enhancements, and budget requests for funding CPU enhancements can be sent to the legislature's Ways and Means Subcommittee for approval.

Fit a straight line to the monthly data shown below and determine when (how many months in the future) the CPU capacity of 300 hours will be exceeded.

CPU Usage	183	188	203	185	186	196	182	207	209	195
Month (Aug.)	1	2	3	4	5	6	7	8	9	10

CPU Usage	197	203	220	218	225	212	220	230	232	
Month	11	12	13	14	15	16	17	18	19	

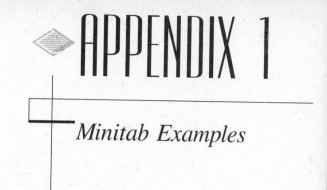

APPENDIX 1

Minitab Examples

(If you are using the WINDOWS version of MINITAB, you might issue the GSTD command first to use standard graphics in the session window. If you want to save your output on a file, use the command OUTFILE 'A:CH8.LIS' to echo output to this file.)

MINITAB ANALYSIS OF THE AGE DATA

```
DON'T TYPE THE NEXT BLOCK OF COMMANDS
SKIP AHEAD TO START....
```

It is instructive to see how to set up the data file that you retrieve below. We refer only to **complete rows** of the last two columns of Exhibit 1. The data can be entered row by row with MTB > READ C1 C2.

C2 (AGES OF MOTHERS) and C1 (AGES OF FATHERS) are in separate columns. We stack column C2 onto C1 to make C3, one long column containing both sets of ages.

```
MTB > STACK C2 ON C1 PUT IN C3  # AGES OF MOTHERS STACKED
#                                 ON TOP OF AGES OF FATHERS IN C3
MTB > DESCRIBE C1 C2
```

C4 will contain 0s or 1s and will be used to keep track of which part of C3 is ages of mothers or fathers.

```
MTB > SET IN C4  # A SECOND VARIABLE SET TO ZERO OR ONE TO
# SEGREGATE THE AGE DATA INTO TWO SUBSETS, AGES OF MOTHERS
# AND FATHERS
DATA> 34(0),34(1)  # NO SPACES BETWEEN CHARACTERS
DATA> END
MTB>  SAVE 'B:AGE'
```

(continued)

```
        START HERE TO RETRIEVE THE DATA SET
          (OR RETRIEVE 'AGE' whichever is appropriate.)
        MTB > RETRIEVE 'B:AGE'
        MTB > INFO

        MTB > PRINT C1-C4
        MTB > DESCRIBE C1 C2
        MTB > DOTPLOT C3;

        SUBC> BY C4;   # C4 USED TO SEGREGATE DATA SUBSETS
        SUBC> SAME.    # SAME SCALE FOR COMPARISON.  AS WITH BACK-TO-BACK
        # STEM-AND-LEAF DIAGRAMS, NO SUBSTANTIAL DIFFERENCE BETWEEN THE
        # SUBSETS

        MTB > RUNS C1   # RESULTS ARE NOT SHOWN
        MTB > RUNS C2   # BUT, CHECK FOR RANDOMNESS

        # IF THE MTSPLOT IS AVAILABLE ON YOUR VERSION OF MINITAB,
        # USE  MTB > MTSPLOT C1 C2 # VISUAL CHECK ON RANDOMNESS

        MTB > PLOT C3 C4 # BECAUSE OF OVERPLOTTING, YOU CAN'T SEE
        #                    MUCH HERE
        MTB > SET IN C5
        DATA > 1:68
        DATA > END
        MTB > PLOT C3 C5;
        SUBC> YSTART = 0.
```

EXAMPLE

MINITAB ANALYSIS OF THE PACKAGE DESIGN, SALES DATA

```
        DON'T TYPE THE NEXT BLOCK OF COMMANDS
        SKIP AHEAD TO START....
```

It is instructive to see how to set up the data file that you retrieve below. We refer to the data set below.

New package design: (C1) 52 76 75 91 84 72 72 87 98 67 92 86 61
Old package design: (C2) 50 95 25 23 48 18 33 43 15 28 26 34 59

```
            USE MTB > SET C1 and MTB > SET C2
        ---------------
        MTB > STACK C2 C1 PUT IN C3     # SALES WITH OLD DESIGN STACKED
        #                         ON TOP OF NEW DESIGN SALES, IN C3.
        MTB > DESCRIBE C1 C2

        MTB > SET IN C4         # A SECOND VARIABLE, SET TO ZERO OR ONE
        #                          TO IDENTIFY DIFFERENT DATA SUBSETS
        DATA> 13(0),13(1)  # NO SPACES BETWEEN CHARACTERS
        DATA> END
        MTB > SAVE 'B:SALES'
        ---------------
```

```
            START HERE TO RETRIEVE THE DATA SET
             (OR RETRIEVE 'SALES' whichever is appropriate.)
            MTB > RETRIEVE 'B:SALES'
            MTB > INFO

            MTB > PRINT C1-C4
            MTB > DESCRIBE C1 C2
            MTB > DOTPLOT C3;
            SUBC> BY C4;
            SUBC> SAME.    # SAME SCALE FOR COMPARISONS, SALES ARE
            #                   BETTER WITH THE NEW PACKAGE DESIGN

            MTB > RUNS C2  # RESULTS NOT SHOWN, BUT CHECK FOR RANDOMNESS
            MTB > RUNS C1
            MTB > PLOT C3 C4 # SALES ARE HIGHER WITH THE NEW PACKAGE DESIGN
            MTB > SET IN C5
            DATA > 1:26
            DATA > END
            MTB >  PLOT C3 C5;
            SUBC>  YSTART=0.
```

EXAMPLE

MINITAB, ROBUST FIT OF A STRAIGHT LINE, SALES DATA

(continuing from the above example)

```
            COMMAND NOT OPERATIVE IN STUDENT VERSION OF MINITAB
               MTB > RLINE C3 C4 # C3 = SALES; C4 = 0'S AND 1'S
```

EXAMPLE

MINITAB, ROBUST FIT OF A STRAIGHT LINE, AGE DATA

```
            COMMAND NOT OPERATIVE ON THE STUDENT VERSION
             (OR RETRIEVE 'AGE' whichever is appropriate.)
             MTB > RETRIEVE 'B:AGE'
             MTB > RLINE C3 C4  # C3 = AGES; C4= 0'S AND 1'S
```

EXAMPLE

NOTCHED BOXPLOTS IN MINITAB

```
             (OR RETRIEVE 'AGE' whichever is appropriate.)
            MTB > RETRIEVE 'B:AGE'
            MTB > BOXPLOT C3;  # LIFESPANS MOTHERS AND FATHERS
            SUBC> BY C4;  # OF PRESIDENTS C4=0 (MOTHERS); C4=1 (FATHERS)
            SUBC> NOTCHES.  # MARKED BY PARENTHESES, NOTCHES OVERLAP, THE
            #                   DATA SUBSETS ARE NEARLY THE SAME
```

(continued)

```
   (OR RETRIEVE 'SALES' whichever is appropriate.)
MTB > RETRIEVE 'B:SALES'
MTB > BOXPLOT C3;      # SALES OLD AND NEW PACKAGE DESIGNS
SUBC> BY C4;           # C4=0 (OLD DESIGN); C4=1 (NEW DESIGN)
SUBC> NOTCHES.         # NOTCHES DON'T OVERLAP, HIGHER LEVEL OF
#                        SALES WITH THE NEW PACKAGE DESIGN.
```

EXAMPLE

MORE ON SALES VERSUS ASSETS IN MINITAB

Comment   Here we use the data set that follows Exhibit 10. If the 'SALAS' file is not available to you, enter the data row by row with MTB > READ C1 C2 and then MTB > SAVE 'B:SALAS'.

Notice that the filename is 'SALAS' and is **not** 'SALES'.

```
START HERE TO RETRIEVE THE DATA SET
```

Notice that the filename is 'SALAS' and is **not** 'SALES'.

```
   (OR RETRIEVE 'SALAS' whichever is appropriate.)
MTB > RETRIEVE 'B:SALAS'

MTB > LET C3 = C1/C2 # RATIO, SALES TO ASSETS
MTB > DESCRIBE C3

(THE FOLLOWING COMMAND MAY BE UNAVAILABLE ON STUDENT VERSIONS OF MINITAB)
       MTB > RLINE C1 C2, PUT RESIDUALS C4, FITS C5

# NOTE THAT THE OUTPUT STATISTICS DIFFER SOMEWHAT
# FROM OUR ROUGH, GRAPHICALLY DETERMINED ONES

# IF RLINE IS UNAVAILABLE, COMPUTE C4 AND C5 AS FOLLOWS:
    LET C5 = 3.093 + (.9236 * C2)    # FITS
    LET C4 = C1 - C5                 # RESIDUALS

MTB > MPLOT C1 C2 C5 C2;
SUBC> YSTART AT 0;
SUBC> XSTART AT 0.  # ON THE PLOT THAT FOLLOWS, THE B'S ARE
# THE FITTED LINE VALUES, THE A'S ARE THE SALES AND
# ASSETS DATA POINTS.

# IN THIS PLOT, IT IS DIFFICULT TO SEE HOW MUCH A PARTICULAR
# COMPANY DIFFERS FROM THE FIT.  SO, RESIDUALS ARE PLOTTED TO
# FOCUS BETTER ON THE DEVIATIONS.

MTB > SET C6 # COMPANIES NUMBERED SEQUENTIALLY
DATA> 1:30
DATA> END

# COMPANY TYPES ARE CODED FOR AN LPLOT
MTB > SET C7  # CODES 1(AUTOS), 2(OIL), 3(OTHER)
DATA> 1 2 1 3 2 3 2 3 3 1 2 3 2 2 3 2 3 2 3 3 3
DATA> 2 3 3 3 3 3 3 3 3 # AT LEAST ONE SPACE BETWEEN NUMBERS
DATA> END
```

```
MTB > LPLOT C4 C6 USING LABELS C7
          # C4 = (ACTUAL - PREDICTED SALES) = RESIDUALS

MTB > LPLOT C3 C6 USING LABELS C7  # C3 IS THE RATIO OF SALES
# TO ASSETS.   THE AVERAGE OF THE RATIO IS ABOUT 1 AND THE
# STANDARD DEVIATION IS ABOUT .3; SO, A HORIZONTAL LINE AT 1
# AND BOUNDS AT 1±.9 MIGHT BE DRAWN ON THE PLOT BELOW.
```

EXAMPLE

CORRELATION USING MINITAB

Notice that the filename is 'SALAS' and is **not** 'SALES'.

```
  (OR RETRIEVE 'SALAS' whichever is appropriate.)
MTB > RETRIEVE 'B:SALAS'
MTB > PLOT C1 C2     # SALES VERSUS ASSETS OF THE 30 LARGEST
#                       U.S. COMPANIES

MTB > CORRELATE C1 C2  # USING THE SCATTERPLOT, ESTIMATE THE
# CORRELATION AND SEE HOW CLOSE YOU COME TO THE CORRELATION
# COMPUTED BY MINITAB BELOW
```

EXAMPLE

RESIDUAL ANALYSIS AND TRANSFORMATIONS OF SALES AND ASSETS

Notice that the filename is 'SALAS' and is **not** 'SALES'.

```
  (OR RETRIEVE 'SALAS' whichever is appropriate.)
MTB > RETRIEVE 'B:SALAS'
```

Comment   The following macro, %B:E8-8-1, requires version ten or more of MINITAB. To examine the details of the macro, use a text editor or word processor to open the E8-8-1.MAC file. Also, in MINITAB, the command TYPE 'B:E8-8-1.MAC' will list the macro. If you set OH = 24 in the session window, a "continue?" prompt will be issued by MINITAB which permits the user to view one screen of output at a time as the macro executes.

```
MTB > %B:E8-8-1   # OR %A:E8-8-1 OR %E8-8-1
               # OR %C:\MTBWIN\DATA\E8-8-1
```

CHAPTER 9

Classical Methods for Summarizing Relationships Between Pairs of Variables

OBJECTIVES

◇ Present the planning fundamentals for designed experiments

◇ Use variable x to partition y and then compare sample means in the two subsets of y

◇ Fit a straight line simple regression to relate x and y

◇ Evaluate the goodness of fit in simple regression

PRELUDE

During and after a baseball game, fans can tabulate the number of strikeouts, walks, and homers that occur during the game. At one time, statisticians were like these fans. Before R. A. Fisher's pioneering work, the statistician was an after-the-fact technical assistant. Now statisticians are more like managers or players. They are active collaborators in all stages of an investigation. In the client-statistician relationship, the statistician may be a helper, colleague, or leader. In these roles, the statistician charts the course of an investigation. This chapter looks at some critical aspects of planning the analysis or investigation. The concepts of control, randomization, replication, and bias are critical to our thinking.

Although the planning concepts are general and can be applied when studying many variables, this chapter focuses on the analysis of a pair of variables. The methods are classical and formalize the exploratory approaches for examining two variable relationships. Major topics include (1) planning simple experiments, (2) confirming or denying the hypotheses generated in the exploratory stage of an investigation, (3) making comparisons based on small sample inferences about differences in population means, and (4) fitting straight lines using regression. This chapter presents the classical version of Chapter 8, which explored relationships between pairs of variables. ◇

EXPLORATION FOLLOWED BY PLANNED CONFIRMATION

The research department of a large oil company reports to management that it might be possible to develop a gasoline additive that increases the octane number and automobile mileage. Seeing that increasing the octane number by as little as one unit is worth millions in revenue, management decides that the idea has potential because such an additive would likely boost sales.

Management responds by funding a research and development project. In effect, management tells researchers to take a look, explore the idea, experiment, test, and confirm or deny their hypotheses. In return for the funding, management expects timely reports on the progress and the results of the search for the additive. The reports should include recommendations and supporting facts, including numbers.

Data analysis plays an important role in establishing a rational basis for managerial decisions. For example, to justify using the gasoline additive, management must be assured that a new gasoline blend is better than the old, and that the product improvement is worth the cost.

Generally, two processes are essential in summarizing data (facts): exploration to generate ideas and confirmation to test ideas.

According to John Tukey, exploration increases the flow of new data that supplements the original data set.[1] Exploration generates questions and triggers theoretical insight. It also provides guidance on how a plan or design is progressing.

Unstructured exploration often leads to a more structured and focused series of activities. This so-called, **confirmatory pattern** of events is the refined part of the scientific learning process. It involves asking a question, designing an experiment, collecting data, analyzing the data, confirming or denying the hypothetical answer to the question, and reporting the conclusions. Tukey referred to this pattern of events as a **straight line paradigm** because the study proceeds step by step in a straight line, so to speak. This step-by-step pattern is shown in Exhibit 1.

Confirmatory work is routine and the analysis relies on classical statistical methods.

Traditionally, classical statistics has been the primary concern of most statistical textbooks. John Tukey, the father of exploratory data analysis, has suggested that a more thorough analysis results from using both the exploratory and confirmatory approaches as complements to one another.

Planning Experiments "As If the Chart Were Given"

I never saw a moor,
I never saw the sea;
Yet know I how the heather looks,
And what a wave must be.

I never spoke with God,
Nor visited in heaven;
Yet certain am I of the Spot
As if the chart were given.

Emily Dickinson

EXHIBIT 1 The Confirmation (Straight Line) Paradigm

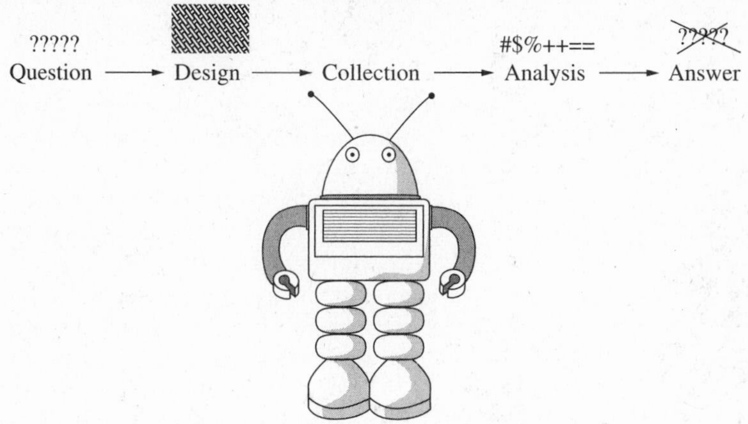

We know that data can arise from unplanned observational studies or carefully designed and planned experiments. In a planned experiment, the analyst has some control over the experimental setting. With control, the analyst tries to keep everything constant except the variables of interest. Therefore, when possible, plan your experiment. Follow the plan "as if the chart were given."

An example of a planned experiment is a corporate farmer who wants to study the effect of manure on crop yield. The farmer could treat one plot of land with manure and not treat another plot. The same crop could be planted in both plots, making the plots of land as nearly identical as possible except for the manure. If such control is possible on **nuisance variables** that are not of primary interest, such as fertility, sunlight, rainfall, and temperature, the planned experiment provides for a fair evaluation of the effect of manure on crop yield.

In many situations, control breaks down or does not exist. Yet, we attempt to learn from these observational studies in spite of the lack of control problem. The investigator must proceed very cautiously under these more difficult circumstances. The data analyst should be aware of the dangers in observational studies and realize that in some circumstances having no data may be better than having bad data.

Observation and trial and error are fundamental to learning. In planned experiments, trials are carefully thought out in the hope that the observations provide an accurate representation of what is being studied. In unplanned observational studies, accurate representation is much more elusive because of factors that might cloud or distort the picture. In both situations, we would like to proceed as if the chart were given, that is, given by the statistician who is responsible for the logic of the investigation.

The Research Question Framed As a Hypothesis

A theory that has aroused some interest is that deer won't eat where tigers tread. A corollary is that if tiger dung is under an apple tree, the deer won't eat the apples. Some California fruit growers got tiger manure from a local zoo and spread it about their orchards as a fertilizer to grow bigger and better fruits. The growers also thought that this manure spreading practice kept the wild deer away from the orchards, thereby decreasing the deer damage to the orchards.

Was it the tiger dung that decreased the deer damage to the orchards? This research question arose while the growers were exploring the effectiveness of the new fertilizer. Notice that the question is not too vague, nor would it require much time to study. We might frame the question as a hypothesis.

> The application of tiger dung has no effect on the average number of apple trees damaged by wild deer.

This "no effect hypothesis" is referred to as a **null hypothesis.** By designing an experiment, collecting data, and testing, the researcher can either reject or not reject the null hypothesis. If the null hypothesis is rejected, the evidence in the data might cause us to favor an **alternative hypothesis** such as

> The application of tiger dung has an effect on the average number of apple trees damaged by deer.

Sometimes experiments are conducted to test hypotheses as well as estimate effects. For example, if it is established that tiger dung has an effect on apple tree damage, it may be necessary to estimate how much change occurs in the amount of orchard damage due to a specific amount of tiger dung.

A team of people consisting of a variety of experts are typically involved in conducting experiments. Some experts know tigers, others know fruits, and a few know statistics.

When the experts gather to answer research questions, the statistician becomes a familiar face toward which others turn. As research problems evolve, different experts in specific application areas become involved. However, the statistician remains a constant, applying the same principles for the different research questions. Increasingly, prudent managers are turning to the statistician for help in framing the research question, planning, collecting data, performing the analysis, and drawing conclusions.

What do statisticians offer that make their role so vital? Statisticians help formulate goals, strategies, and tactics in conducting experiments. They clarify objectives. They assess how much control the researcher has over experimental elements such as nuisance variables. They design randomization schemes to mitigate the effect of nuisance variables. When successful, randomization reduces bias. Statisticians plan replications of the experiment. Finally, they make and report conclusions.

Goals, Strategies, and Tactics in Experiments

In discussing goals, strategies, and tactics for his company, a corporate president stated that the primary goal was for the company to grow to become one of the 500 largest corporations in the world. The strategy for achieving the growth goal was to sell products to other large companies whose growth would catapult the president's corporation in the right direction. Tactics were the detailed procedures needed to stay on course and carry out the strategy. An automobile manufacturer's rebate program for new car purchases is an example of a tactic.

Data analysts must also consider goals, strategies, and tactics when conducting experiments. Comprehensively, their goal is to understand, control, or predict some phenomenon. For example, a researcher may wish to understand how a gasoline additive increases an octane number. Experimental data may verify that certain theories about the chemistry work in practice. Furthermore, it may be necessary to predict how much of the additive is needed to obtain a desired octane number. In the refining process, the octane number of the gasoline product is controlled by regulating the amount of the additive used.

A research laboratory might experiment with different gasoline additive concentrations and measure the resulting octane numbers. These octane numbers may be much different from those for the gasoline that eventually reaches your car's gas tank. If the laboratory octane numbers resulted from a representative sample of observations, they should be similar in octane to the gasoline that reaches your car.

The purpose of the representative sample in the laboratory is to mirror the characteristics of the gasoline reaching the cars of consumers. The octane numbers of the gasoline purchased by consumers is the **target population.** The term *target population* is used because what is learned from the representative sample helps the company to understand, control, or predict the characteristics of the target population.

Usually the whole target population is elusive. As a result, the strategy is to analyze a representative sample of observations from the population and then make inferences about those characteristics of the population that are unknown. If the sample of observations is not representative of the population, then the inferences may be of little use.

Cervany et al. and Cervany, Benson, and Iyer also emphasized the importance of goals, strategies, and tactics in statistical analysis.[2] They characterize statistical reasoning as a three-stage process. Instead of using the terms *goals, strategies,* and *tactics,* they refer to the three stages of statistical reasoning as (1) comprehension, (2) planning and execution, and (3) evaluation and interpretation.

Stage 1   Cervany and his colleagues illustrate the nature of the comprehension stage by posing a management problem of understanding the difference between the daily output of assembly line A and assembly line B. Stage 1 involves the statistical formulation of the situational question. The statistical translation of the managerial question might be: Is there a difference in the mean daily output of the two assembly lines? Clearly, understanding and evaluating the difference between the two assembly lines is a goal.

Stage 2   The strategy is to obtain representative samples of assembly line outputs and to choose a particular statistical analysis procedure. The early period of strategy formulation must include interaction of the client and the statistician so that they can discuss the logical issues of the study, as pointed out by Bishop, Peterson, and Trayser.[3]

Stage 3   Evaluation and interpretation involves tactical considerations. First the plan from stage 2 is evaluated to determine if it is operationally feasible and appropriate. If not, stage 2 is repeated. If the plan from stage 2 is feasible and appropriate, the analysis that includes estimation and testing is performed. Finally, the results are interpreted and reported in the language of the original question, avoiding technical jargon when possible.

Clarifying Objectives

After research questions emerge based on the exploratory work, the statistician helps clarify and state objectives of the study. Usually the objective is to study what is believed to be the causal effects of certain predictor variables on a response variable. For example, does the application of tiger dung decrease deer damage in orchards? It is important to specify all influential variables. For each quantitative variable, the minimum and maximum values should be specified.

Assessing Control

Control refers to tactical activities designed to assure data efficacy. The statistician can assess the degree of control exercised in observational studies or planned experiments. In observational studies, control is difficult to impossible. In planned experiments, specific control devices are commonly used. By assessing control, the statistician exposes the dangers that might cloud the interpretation of the results.

Observational Studies   The investigator has little or no control over observational studies. Observations are taken that seem appropriate for answering the research questions. However, the investigator cannot control the assignment of treatments to subjects or experimental units. The nature of the problem preestablishes the treatment assigned to the subject. Therefore, this designation is not within the analyst's control. For example, in the study of the effect of cigarette smoking on health, researchers do not select one group of subjects and have them smoke and select another group of subjects and have them not smoke.[4] The smokers have already decided to use cigarettes, so the decision is beyond investigator control. The researcher simply observes (hence, the term observational study) the health of smokers and nonsmokers. In such observational studies, there is some risk of concluding that, say, smoking impairs health when some variable other than smoking is the real culprit.

Although planned experiments are preferred to observational studies, such experiments may not be possible. For example, controlled experiments cannot be conducted to study the national economy. Instead, economic activity is observed in an attempt to evaluate the benefits of government programs and policies. Such observational studies concern important problems worth investigating.

Planned Experiments   In contrast to unplanned observational studies, designed experiments are planned or controlled studies. Understanding control is easier, perhaps, if control devices are examined first. Cochran suggests three devices for control: (1) refinement of technique, (2) blocking and matching, and (3) control during the statistical analysis.[5]

Refinement of technique means to exercise great care in the conduct of an investigation. Measurements must be made with as little error as possible. If certain background variables are to be held constant, make certain that is accomplished. Refine all procedural elements of the investigation.

Cochran and Cox list four principal objectives of good technique.[6]

1. Secure uniformity in the application of treatments. For example, in cake mix experiments, certain amounts of baking powder are added to each batch of batter. Uniformity in treatment application means that the baking powder amounts are measured properly.
2. Exercise control over external influences.
3. Devise appropriate and unbiased measurements.
4. Prevent gross errors.

Blocking and matching groups observations in an attempt to hold variables of no interest constant within groups. Even in observational studies, when control is nearly impossible, investigators try to cluster observations into homogeneous groups. This grouping is referred to as **matching.** For example, consider the study of smoking and its relationship to the incidence of lung cancer. To hold background factors constant for smokers and nonsmokers, the individuals being studied would be considered a homogeneous group if they are all about the same age. Grouping by age keeps certain background factors relatively constant so they don't cloud the findings.

Planned experiments are easier to control because more uniform conditions prevail within each homogeneous group, which is called a **block.** Ideally, conditions are the same for the observations made within each block. As a result, repeated observations within a block vary due to randomness and the different treatments examined.

For example, blocks are often small plots of land in agricultural experiments. Uniform growing conditions (sun, rain, temperature, and so on) are expected within each block. Therefore, the effect of treatments (plant varieties) on the response (crop yield) is not clouded by nuisance variables in the background. Differences in crop yield would be attributed to the plant variety and not to the environmental conditions, which are controlled within each block.

Control during the statistical analysis involves computational adjustments to the observations. Here, the variables designated for control are identified and sometimes measured along with treatments and responses. The responses are then purged of these nuisance variables because other control devices cannot remove them. Following the argument of Cochran, let[7]

$$y_{ij} = \text{the observed response}$$

As an example, consider hog weight as a response to diet. Suppose this response is the final weight of the i-th hog where the hog is given diet $j = A$ or B. If there is no way to control for the initial weight, x_{1i}, of the hogs, it is regarded as a **covariate,** which can be measured and later purged from the responses. The final weight, y_{ij}, can be predicted by the initial weight, x_{1i}. The prediction equation is

$$\hat{y}_{ij} = b_0 + b_1 x_{1i}$$

The difference between the final weight and its prediction is a residual.

$$(y_{ij} - \hat{y}_{ij}) = (y_{ij} - (b_0 + b_1 x_{1i}))$$

Because the initial weight is included in the prediction

$$(b_0 + b_1 x_{1i})$$

these residuals approximate a weight gain. They can be viewed as adjusted response data and analyzed accordingly. More than one covariate can be accommodated.

Designing Randomization Schemes

As we have seen, the response, y, may be influenced by nuisance variables that are not of main interest. Such background variables can distort our perceptions about the variables of main interest. In both planned and unplanned experiments, we are concerned about the observations that might lead to faulty conclusions. How do we ensure that the results are not biased because of nuisance variables? Control is helpful, but it is not always possible to identify all factors that need to be controlled.

The idea of **randomization** is to make it difficult for any unidentified factor to systematically creep into and bias response measurements.

EXAMPLE 1

COMPARING METHODS OF INSTRUCTION[8]

Problem Statement   Management is trying to decide between two methods of instruction for a training program. In a planned experiment, trainees will be randomly assigned to two groups. One group will be taught by the lecture-recitation method. The second group will be taught by computer-aided instruction. The two methods of instruction are to be compared. Randomization is needed because the trainees differ considerably in uncontrollable variables such as basic intelligence, high-school backgrounds, culture, and so forth. Randomly assign trainees to the groups.

Problem Solution   By tossing a coin, trainees are randomly assigned to instruction-method groups. The occurrence of a tail assigns a trainee to group one; a head assigns a trainee to group two.

EXAMPLE 2

POWER REQUIREMENTS OF CERAMIC TOOLS[9]

Problem Statement   An experiment was conducted to study the effect of several factors on the power requirements for cutting metal with ceramic tools. Each of three factors—tool type, bevel angle, and cut type—were set at two different levels, which resulted in eight different sets of conditions. Four observations were taken at each of the eight sets of conditions. This resulted in a total of 32 measurements of the power requirement response. Randomization is needed because of the uncontrollable background variables such as machine operator, time of day, temperature, humidity, and so on. Run the experiment so that the sets of factor conditions are randomly assigned.

Problem Solution   Coins were tossed to randomize the conditions settings for power requirement measurements. A penny was used for tool type T, with heads for one type and tails for the other. A nickle was used for bevel angle B, which is 30° or 15°. A dime was used for cut type C, which is interrupted or continuous cut. If a toss of three coins resulted in tails, heads, and tails (THT), this would indicate that the machine, a lathe, should be set for tool type 1, bevel 2, and a continuous cut. Each distinct sequence, say, THT, is to be used four times. After that the sequence is ignored and the coins are tossed again.

As an alternative randomization scheme, each of the 32 sets of conditions could be written on a piece of paper, placed in a hat, and drawn at random to indicate the lathe setting for each experimental trial.

EXAMPLE 3

A WOMAN AND HER TEA[10]

Problem Statement   A woman declares that she can taste the difference in a cup of tea depending on whether the milk is added to the cup before or after the tea. Conduct an experiment to see if she can taste whether or not the milk was added first.

Problem Solution   Eight cups of tea were mixed for a taste test. Four cups had milk added first and four cups had milk added second. So that the order of tasting did not influence her judgment, the cups were presented to her in random order. She was asked to divide the eight cups into two sets of four. She judged one set as milk first and the other as milk second. The woman selected three right and one wrong in each set.

EXAMPLE 4

RANDOMIZATION IN A TAX EXPERIMENT[11]

Problem Statement   Establishing an empirical base to justify policy decisions, such as the use of a new income tax scheme, is difficult. Experiments for such social issues raise distinct problems that are not present in some other settings. Nevertheless, sound experimental design practices that include randomization should be used when possible. New Jersey considered a new taxation plan that guaranteed a minimum income to working poor families. The plan included an income tax incentive on additional earnings such that the more a family earned, the less it would be taxed. This is called a negative income tax. Describe an experiment for this policy decision and discuss the randomization issue.

Problem Solution   An experiment was conducted using three levels of taxation and different minimum income guarantees. Treatment groups were assigned a specific guarantee and tax rate. The control group did not receive the treatment. Assignments were made on a random basis without serious difficulty.

It was feared that the minimum income guarantees would create a large reduction in hours worked. The result, however, was that the reduction in the number of hours worked was small.

Problem Discussion   In spite of the careful design and execution of this social experiment, the results might not indicate what would happen beyond the experiment. The sample conditions may not be representative of the population of all low-income families who would be eligible for the taxation plan. The assumption in the experiment is that the response of a family receiving a treatment is independent of the fact that it is participating in an experiment and that its neighbors are not. Such independence is what randomization hopes to achieve but does not guarantee. The fact that participating families are special may influence experimental outcomes. When all families are eligible for such a program, their behavior might be different.

One-at-a-Time Experimental Plans[12]

Experiments dealing with social issues are not the only types of difficult experiments. Scientists who do their work in single steps use **one-at-a-time plans,** in which one factor at a time is varied. For example, a chemist might wish to investigate how the yield of a chemical process responds to changes in pressure and temperature. Using the one-at-a-time approach, the chemist might hold pressure constant and change temperature from one level to another. Then a response measurement is taken. Next, the chemist changes the temperature again from the preceding trial and takes another response measurement. Later, the chemist might execute the same procedure by changing pressure while holding temperature constant.

Those using a one-at-a-time plan hope to increase their knowledge incrementally from each experimental trial. The experiments are carried out sequentially over a short time. Because of their lack of randomization, one-at-a-time plans are seriously flawed. Other types of experiments are recommended for greater precision and validity.

Evaluating Bias

Many experimenters may not seek statistical advice or follow sound statistical principles. Some experimental situations may make control and randomization difficult. When the objectives of control and randomization are not met, predictions, on average, tend to miss their target. Such predictions are said to be **biased.**

For example, if $\hat{y}_i$ is the predicted octane number of a gasoline product, this prediction is based on the effects of several components of the gasoline and the refining process. If control or randomization is ineffective for some components, these variables may be missing from the prediction equation. Therefore, the prediction equation may be biased. Unfortunately, it is not difficult to conceive of circumstances where components are inadvertently missing from the fit. Complete and exhaustive identification and measurement of all components may be impractical or beyond present scientific knowledge. This makes bias a common problem.

Randomization attempts to obtain a zero net effect of unidentified components. Control attempts to hold identified component effects constant so they play no role in the prediction. However, control and randomization are far from foolproof. As a result, bias can be a serious problem. Sometimes we don't know how much bias exists. Too often the careless use of computerized statistical packages results in faulty analysis and conclusions.

Planning Replication

Replication refers to the number of measurements taken while a set of conditions is fixed in an experiment. For example, suppose we wish to compare sales of a product in a new and an old package design. To make the comparison, we measure sales of the product in the new package design in store 1 and sales of the product in the old package design in store 2. One measurement on sales is taken for the fixed condition—new package design in store 1. That is one replication under that set of conditions. Another measurement on sales is taken for the fixed condition—old package design in store 2. That is one replication under that set of conditions.

Another way to arrange these replications is as follows:

OLD PACKAGE DESIGN   **NEW PACKAGE DESIGN**

Store 1 sales, y_1 Store 2 sales, y_2

The y_1 and y_2 are sales measurements for two sets of conditions. Suppose the stores are nearly identical in every other way. One replication for each set of conditions is not enough because we do not have confidence in a comparison based on two observations. Furthermore, there is no precision measure for the variability of average sales because there are not enough replications.

Six replications for each set of conditions (a combined total of 12 observations) can be tabulated as follows:

OLD PACKAGE DESIGN   **NEW PACKAGE DESIGN**

Store 1	y_1	Store 2	y_2
Store 8	y_3	Store 10	y_4
Store 5	y_5	Store 11	y_6
Store 12	y_7	Store 3	y_8
Store 6	y_9	Store 4	y_{10}
Store 9	y_{11}	Store 7	y_{12}

Again, assume that the stores are nearly identical and that the stores were randomly assigned to the package designs. The store numbers shown above are for identification purposes only.

The difference in average sales can be used to compare package designs.

$$\overline{y}_{new} - \overline{y}_{old}$$

This difference can be written in terms of predicted sales.

$$\hat{y}_{new} - \hat{y}_{old}$$

The prediction equation is of the following form:

$$\hat{y}_i = b_0 + b_1 x_{1i}$$

where x_{1i} is coded 0 or 1 for the old and the new package designs, respectively. The regression coefficients are

$$b_1 = \overline{y}_{new} - \overline{y}_{old} \quad \text{and} \quad b_0 = \overline{y}_{old}$$

The tabulations on the following page list y and x. The x is coded with six 0s (six replications) and six 1s (six more replications). Replications repeat the response observations, y, at a fixed set of conditions specified by a set of predictor variables. This set includes only one predictor variable, x_{1i}.

y_i	x_{1i}
y_1	0
y_3	0
y_5	0
y_7	0
y_9	0
y_{11}	0
y_2	1
y_4	1
y_6	1
y_8	1
y_{10}	1
y_{12}	1

Experimental outcomes are sample results that should be representative of the target population. When experiments are repeated, the response measurements vary. As a consequence, differences in sample means have a distribution that is characterized by a mean and a standard deviation (referred to as a standard error). The smaller the standard error in relation to the difference in sample means, the easier it is to see a true difference in population means when one exists.

Increasing the number of replications in an experiment decreases the standard error. Although there is a price to be paid for more replications, the payoff is a reduced standard error. Therefore, the designer of an experiment has to make an intelligent decision about the number of replications needed to balance cost and payoff.

The relationship between the number of replications, g, and the standard error is well established. If the same number of replications, g, are chosen for the new and the old package designs, the standard error is proportional to $\frac{1}{g^{1/2}}$. Therefore, an increase in the number of replications decreases the standard error and increases the precision.

Cochran and Cox provide an excellent discussion concerning the determination of the number of replications necessary in an experiment to detect a significant difference in means with a specified probability.[13] Computer programs are available to evaluate precision and other design characteristics (see Meeker, Hahn, and Feder).[14] Clearly, the number of replications needed to obtain adequate precision is an important decision for the investigator.

Summary of Exploration and Planned Confirmation

We would like to sail the sea of an investigation as if a chart were given. Obviously, we can't always be on course, nor should we refrain from stopping along the way. Nevertheless, knowing enough to plan carefully helps us proceed directly (more or less) to the destination. Therefore, in the broadest terms, we need to know where we are going (goal), how we are going to get there (strategy) and what details (tactics) of the trip need to be completed.

Critical questions about the investigation include: (1) Is it possible to collect data? If data can be generated, the second question is (2) Is the nature of the study planned or unplanned (observational)? In observational studies, the lack of control can bias results and make comparison difficult.

When planned or designed experiments are required, we can take advantage of randomization, control, and replication to obtain a clearer view of the unknown through a representative sample from a target population.

COMPARISONS, SMALL SAMPLE INFERENCES ABOUT THE DIFFERENCE BETWEEN TWO POPULATION MEANS

When experiments are conducted to compare treatments, such as the effect of two different package designs on sales, the statistical methodology in this chapter relies on two independent random samples from two normal populations. If the sum of the two sample sizes is less than 32, $(n_1 + n_2) < 32$, they are considered **small samples.** If the sum is greater than 32, they are considered **large samples.** Sample means and standard deviations are used to form a test statistic for testing hypotheses about differences in population means. For example, we could test the null hypothesis that the means are the same

$$(\mu_1 - \mu_2) = 0$$

versus the alternative hypothesis that the means are not the same.

$$(\mu_1 - \mu_2) \neq 0$$

A test for no difference in population means is common, but any difference can be considered. The classical statistical methods in this chapter formally test hypotheses suggested by the exploratory methods described in Chapter 8.

The response measurements from both samples are designated as y_i, where $i = 1, 2, \ldots (n_1 + n_2)$. By coding a predictor variable, x_{1i}, 0 or 1, the two samples can be identified. These variables can be related in a **regression model** format that involves the population means and an error term.

$$y_i = \mu_2 + (\mu_1 - \mu_2) x_{1i} + e_i$$

Therefore, hypothesis tests about the difference in population means involves the relationship between the predictor and the response variables. This chapter describes both the standard test procedures as well as the regression approach for hypotheses about the differences in population means.

First we illustrate hypothesis testing procedures that apply when the population standard deviations are unknown and not assumed equal.

This situation is commonly encountered in practice. The hypothesis testing procedures use confidence intervals or t ratio tests that remain valid under small sample or large sample conditions. However, for large samples, the Student's t distribution is approximately normal. Therefore, test statistics and critical values can be based on the normal distribution.

When the standard deviations of different populations are known, they are used instead of the sample standard deviations. Known standard deviations, when substituted into small sample formulas for confidence intervals and t ratio tests, result in the Student's t distribution being replaced by the normal distribution.

We present two contrasting examples. The conclusion in the first example is that there is no difference in population means. The conclusion in the second example is that there is a difference in population means. In both cases, preliminary exploratory conclusions are confirmed and followed by the classical hypothesis testing procedures.

No Difference in Population Means

In Chapter 8, exploratory analysis led to the tentative conclusion that there is no significant difference in median lifespans of presidents' mothers and fathers. Exhibit 2 shows that the typical lifespans are about the same.

EXHIBIT 2 Exploratory Conclusion: No Significant Difference in Median Ages

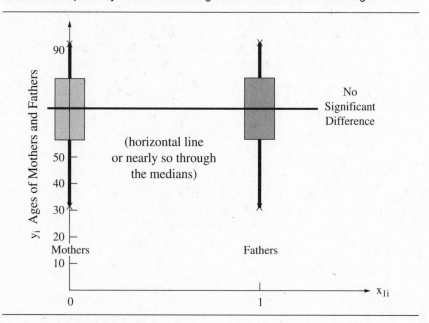

By comparing *sample means* in the following example, this exploratory conclusion is confirmed. The hypothesis, that there is no difference in population mean lifespans, is tested. Computer results are shown as well as the computational formulas. You can concentrate on the computer results and use the formulas for reference purposes. The two sample means and standard deviations are used to compute a t test statistic, which is compared to a critical t value. When the test statistic exceeds the critical value, the null hypothesis is rejected.

EXAMPLE 5

MINITAB ANALYSIS OF THE AGE DATA, THE CLASSICAL APPROACH

Problem Statement (a)   Test the null hypothesis that the population mean ages are the same, $(\mu_{fathers} - \mu_{mothers}) = 0$, against the not equal alternative at a .05 significance level. Use a confidence interval approach.

Problem Solution (a)   The MINITAB analysis produces sample means, standard deviations, standard errors, and a confidence interval on the difference between the unknown population means. The variable names, AGEF and AGEM, refer to ages of fathers and mothers.

```
TWOSAMPLE T FOR AGEF VS AGEM

        N     MEAN    STDEV   SE MEAN
AGEF   34     67.2    17.3    3.0
AGEM   34     68.6    17.7    3.0

95 PCT CI FOR (MU AGEF)-(MU AGEM): (-9.9, 7.1)
```

Newer versions of MINITAB print asterisks, *****, for one side of this interval, such as (*****, 7.1). This alerts you that the interval encloses zero; therefore, there is no significant difference in population means. Also, if MU AGEF is subtracted from MU AGEM, a sign reversal occurs to produce (−7.1, *****).

The 95% confidence interval, (−9.9, 7.1), is on the unknown difference between the population means. MINITAB refers to this difference as (MU AGEF) − (MU AGEM). This interval encloses zero; therefore, do not reject the hypothesis that the difference in population means is zero.

Fortunately, these computations have been done in MINITAB. In the background, the formula for making the interval computation is

$$(EST.MU\ AGEF - EST.MU\ AGEM) \pm t_{\alpha/2,DF}((SE\ AGEF)^2 + (SE\ AGEM)^2)^{0.5}$$

The figures shown above can be substituted into this formula.

$$(67.2 - 68.6) \pm 2(3^2 + 3^2)^{0.5}$$

MINITAB computes the degrees of freedom, DF = 65, from the following formula:

$$DF = ((SE\ AGEF)^2 + (SE\ AGEM)^2)^2 / (((SE\ AGEF)^4 / (N1-1)) + ((SE\ AGEM)^4 / (N2-1)))$$

Problem Statement (b)   Use a t ratio to test the null hypothesis that the population mean ages are the same against the not equal alternative.

Problem Solution (b)   An alternative to a confidence interval approach is a t ratio test. MINITAB produces both types of output information. For the t ratio approach, the output is

```
TTEST MU AGEF = MU AGEM (VS NE): T = -0.33  P = 0.74  DF = 65
```

The absolute value of the t test statistic for this comparison is 0.33. It does not exceed the critical value of 2, $t_{.05/2, 65}$, and there is not a significant difference in sample means. Accept the hypothesis that the two population means are equal.

When the sample means are significantly different at a 95% level and DF(degrees of freedom) > 30, the absolute value of the t statistic *exceeds* the critical t value of 2. In general, for a two-sided $(1 - \alpha)$ confidence level for small samples, the sample means are significantly different when the absolute value of the t test statistic is greater than the critical value of $t_{\alpha/2, DF}$.

The t test statistic of -0.33 is a studentized difference in sample means. The difference in sample means is divided by the standard error for the difference, which is

$$(3^2 + 3^2)^{0.5}$$

Both of the individual standard errors are equal to three. Using this information, you can verify that the t test statistic is

$$\text{t test statistic} = -0.33 = \frac{67.2 - 68.6}{(3^2 + 3^2)^{0.5}}$$

This t ratio approach leads to the same conclusion that the confidence interval did in part (a). There is no significant difference in sample means. Do not reject the null hypothesis that the population means are the same.

When the two populations have equal variances, more efficient formulas can be used for the hypothesis test. MINITAB has a POOLED subcommand that evokes these other formulas.

Problem Statement (c)   Use a p value to test the null hypothesis that the population mean ages are the same against the not equal alternative.

Problem Solution (c)   An alternative to either a confidence interval or a t ratio approach is to use a p value. When the null hypothesis is true, $(\mu_{fathers} - \mu_{mothers}) = 0$, the p value is high. In this example, the p value is .74. This is the probability of getting an absolute difference in sample means of $|(67.2 - 68.6)|$ or more when the null hypothesis is true. A high p value, greater than .10, means that it is likely the null hypothesis is true.

Problem Discussion   Although this example illustrates the nature of testing hypotheses concerning the difference in population means, a word of caution is necessary because this is an observational study.

The theory requires independent random samples from normal populations. This data set was collected in chronological order. However, preliminary examination of the data did not reveal a time-ordering, nonrandom pattern. Such potential problems must be contemplated because it is too easy to mistakenly accept computer results as valid simply because they come out of a computer.

A Difference in Population Means

In Chapter 8, exploratory analysis led to the tentative conclusion that there is a significant difference in median sales for the same product using two different package designs. This is illustrated in Exhibit 3, where stem-and-leaf diagrams and boxplots are superimposed. The response variable, sales, is on the vertical axis, and the horizontal axis represents the two package designs being examined. The predictor variable, x_{1i}, is coded 0 to identify sales of the product in the old package design and is coded 1 to identify sales of the product in the new package design.

The problem is to determine if sales are influenced by package design. If this is so, the population means are not equal.

$$(\mu_{new} - \mu_{old}) \neq 0$$

The new package design is clearly associated with a higher sales level. There appears to be a significant difference in typical sales levels due to package design.

More scientifically, we could say that the evidence leads to the rejection of the null hypothesis, $(\mu_{new} - \mu_{old}) = 0$. In fact, the alternative hypothesis, $(\mu_{new} - \mu_{old}) \neq 0$, is favored.

EXHIBIT 3 A Significant Difference in Median Sales for Different Package Designs

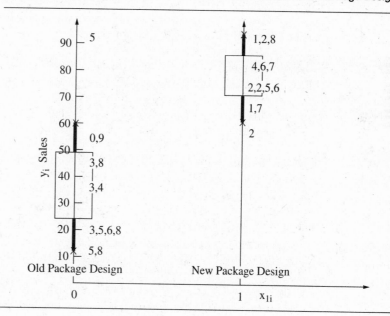

EXAMPLE 6

MINITAB ANALYSIS OF THE PACKAGE DESIGN SALES DATA, THE CLASSICAL APPROACH

Problem Statement (a)   For the old and new package designs, test the null hypothesis that there is no difference in population mean sales, $(\mu_{new} - \mu_{old}) = 0$. Use a .05 significance level and the alternative hypothesis that there is a difference in population mean sales, $(\mu_{new} - \mu_{old}) \neq 0$. Also make this test by using a confidence interval.

Problem Solution (a)   The MINITAB analysis produces sample means, standard deviations, standard errors, and a confidence interval on the difference between the unknown population means. The variable names, SNEW and SOLD, refer to dollar sales for new and old package designs.

```
TWOSAMPLE T FOR SNEW VS SOLD

          N      MEAN    STDEV   SE MEAN
SNEW     13      77.9    13.3      3.7
SOLD     13      38.2    21.5      6.0

95 PCT CI FOR (MU SNEW - MU SOLD): (25.0, 54.4)
```

The 95% confidence interval, (25.0, 54.4), is on the unknown difference between the population means. MINITAB refers to this difference as (MU SNEW) − (MU SOLD). This interval does not enclose zero; therefore, reject the hypothesis that the difference in population means is zero.

Problem Statement (b)   Use a t ratio to test the null hypothesis that the two population mean sales levels are the same against the not equal alternative.

Problem Solution (b)   An alternative to a confidence interval approach is a t ratio test. MINITAB produces both types of output information. For the t ratio approach, the output is

```
TTEST MU SNEW = MU SOLD (VS NE): T = 5.66 P = 0.0000 DF = 19
```

When the sample means are significantly different at a 95% level and DF(degrees of freedom) = 19, the absolute value of the t test statistic exceeds the critical t value of 2.1. Here the t statistic is 5.66, and it is greater than the critical value. Therefore, there is a significant difference in sample means.

In general, for a two-sided $(1 - \alpha)$ confidence level for small samples, the sample means are significantly different when the absolute value of the t test statistic is greater than the critical value of $t_{\alpha/2, DF}$.

This t test statistic of 5.66 is a studentized difference in sample means. The difference in sample means is divided by the standard error for the difference, which is

$$(3.7^2 + 6.0^2)^{0.5}$$

The individual standard errors are 3.7 and 6.0. Using this information, you can verify that the t test statistic is

$$\text{t test statistic} = 5.66 = \frac{77.9 - 38.2}{(3.7^2 + 6.0^2)^{0.5}}$$

If you verify these calculations by hand, you will find a small rounding error because these figures have been rounded. The t ratio test procedure leads to the same conclusion the confidence interval did. There is a significant difference in sample means. Reject the hypothesis that the population means are the same.

Problem Statement (c)   Use a p value to test the null hypothesis that the population means are the same against the not equal alternative.

Problem Solution (c)   An alternative to either a confidence interval or a t test approach is to use a p value. When the null hypothesis is true, ($\mu_{new} - \mu_{old}$) = 0, the p value is high. In this example, the p value of (0.000) is low, and the sample means are significantly different. The p value is the probability of getting an absolute difference in sample means of $|(77.9 - 38.2)|$ or more when the null hypothesis is true. A low p value, less than .10, means that it is unlikely the null hypothesis is true.

Problem Discussion   The theory requires independent random samples from normal populations. In this designed experiment, that is the case.

To be confident that the new package design *alone* resulted in a substantial increase in sales, the experiment had to be designed so that background variables were constant or had a zero average effect. This allows us to have a clear view of package design and sales as an isolated pair of variables. Remember that there are ways of adjusting for nonconstant background variables in the analysis if they can be measured.

Examples of background variables to hold constant include store size, placement of the product within the store (so customer traffic patterns are about the same), shelf location, and geographic location. In other words, carefully design the experiment.

The term *carefully designed experiment* implies that (1) background conditions were nearly the same for all variables except package design, which is the variable of interest; (2) the 13 replications for the old package design comprise the control group, while the 13 replications for the new package design comprise the treatment group; and (3) the 26 retail stores participating in the experiment were similar and randomly assigned to the control and treatment groups.

STATISTICAL HIGHLIGHTS

To test for a difference in population means, the difference in sample means is divided by the standard error for the difference. The resulting test statistic is compared to a critical value.

FITTING STRAIGHT LINES, RELATING y AND x: SIMPLE LINEAR REGRESSION AND CORRELATION

Testing hypotheses about the differences in population means can be accomplished in a regression model format. This approach is particularly important because it can be extended easily to complicated experiments. When the response and predictor variables are related in a regression model format, the difference in population means, $(\mu_1 - \mu_2)$, represents the slope of a straight line in the following model:

$$y_i = \mu_2 + (\mu_1 - \mu_2)\, x_{1i} + e_i$$

The predictor variable, x_{1i}, is coded 0 or 1. It is assumed that the population variances are the same.

Referring to Example 6, there is another way to see that there is a difference in package designs. Draw a line connecting the medians (or means) of the two boxplots, as shown in Exhibit 4.

An examination of Exhibit 4 leads to the exploratory conclusion that there is a significant difference in sales levels due to the different package designs because the fitted line has a substantial slope. This visual assessment depends on the difference in sample medians relative to the spread of the data values. In Exhibit 4, the difference in sample medians is large enough relative to the spread to conclude that there is substantial slope. The confidence

EXHIBIT 4 Fitting a Line to Side-by-Side Boxplots

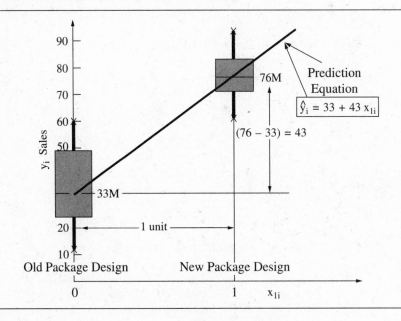

intervals and t ratio tests in Example 6 also confirm this. The fitted line or prediction equation can tilt upward or downward.

Using Sample Means to Determine the Prediction Equation

In classical statistics, the prediction equation can be written in terms of the two sample means and the predictor variable, x_{1i}. Let

$$\hat{y}_i = \text{the predicted i-th data value, } y_i$$
$$\overline{y}_{old} = \text{sample mean sales for the old package design}$$
$$\overline{y}_{new} = \text{sample mean sales for the new package design}$$

In these terms, the prediction equation is

$$\hat{y}_i = \overline{y}_{old} + (\overline{y}_{new} - \overline{y}_{old})\, x_{1i}$$

The sample means estimate population means in the regression model, which in this case is

$$y_i = \mu_{old} + (\mu_{new} - \mu_{old})\, x_{1i} + e_i$$

The change in sample mean sales as x_{1i} changes from 0 to 1 is

$$\overline{y}_{new} - \overline{y}_{old} = 77.92 - 38.23 = 39.69$$

This difference in sample means relative to the change in x_{1i} is $\frac{39.69}{1}$, which is the slope of the fitted line. In terms of the sample means, the fit is:

$$\hat{y}_i = (38.23 + (77.92 - 38.23)\, x_{1i}) = (38.23 + 39.69\, x_{1i})$$

When the predictor variable, x_{1i}, is 0, the predicted sales level is

$$\hat{y}_i = 38.23 + 39.69 \times (0) = 38.23$$

This is sample mean sales for the old package design. When the predictor variable, x_{1i}, is 1, the predicted sales level is

$$\hat{y}_i = 38.23 + 39.69 \times (1) = 77.92$$

This is sample mean sales for the new package design. Therefore, the prediction equation is in the form of a straight line with an intercept equal to 38.23 and with a slope equal to +39.69.

EXAMPLE 7

MINITAB, CLASSICAL FIT OF A STRAIGHT LINE, SALES DATA

Problem Statement   Fit a straight line to the sales data, y, for different package designs. The predictor variable, x, is coded 0 for old and 1 for new package designs.

Problem Solution   The classical version of a fit is referred to as a REGRESSION line in the MINITAB output shown below. Using the MINITAB variable names for the predictor and response variables, the regression equation is

$$\text{SALESON} = 38.2 + 39.7 \text{ DUMMY}$$

In the notation of this chapter, the equation can be written as

$$\hat{y}_i = 38.23 + (77.92 - 38.23)\, x_{1i}$$

TESTING THE STRENGTH OF THE RELATIONSHIP BETWEEN y AND x

In addition to the fitted line, auxiliary goodness of fit information is provided as standard output of computer procedures for this analysis. The process of examining the data, obtaining a straight fit, and evaluating the fit is referred to as **simple regression analysis.** Portions of this goodness of fit information will be described.

A Significant Difference in Sample Means

The information in the following table leads to the conclusion that the predictor variable, x_{1i}, carries a significant amount of information and helps in predicting the response. This also means that there is a significant difference in sample means. This conclusion is reached because the absolute value of the t test statistic of 5.66 *exceeds* the critical t value of 2.064. A significance level of α and $(n_1 + n_2 - 2)$ degrees of freedom specify the critical t value. For example,

$$t_{(\alpha/2),(n1+n2-2)} = t_{.025,24} = 2.064$$

In the computer output below, the t test statistic is referred to as the **t ratio.** The p value is also listed and leads to the same conclusion.

Predictor	Coef	Stdev	t ratio	p
Constant	38.231			
DUMMY	39.692	7.018	5.66	0.000

These regression results are practically identical to those shown earlier in the chapter for comparing two population means. Any differences are due to the fact that the regression approach assumes equal population variances. When comparing two population means in MINITAB, if the POOLED subcommand is used for the TWOSAMPLE and TWOT commands, the two sets of results will be identical.

In regression analysis, a practical way to validate the assumption of equal variances is to compare histograms of the residuals for the two samples to see if they have about the same spread.

The Slope of the Regression Line In both the text example and in Example 7, the slope of the regression line is +39.69. This slope's positive sign indicates a sales increase as the package design changes from old to new. This slope, referred to as a regression coefficient or a parameter estimate, estimates $(\mu_{new} - \mu_{old})$. Both the sign and the magnitude of a regression coefficient are important. Because the magnitude of the regression coefficient is large enough relative to the standard error, it was concluded that package design helps in predicting sales.

The overall effect of a predictor variable is reflected in the product of the regression coefficient and the predictor variable. This is called a **component effect.**

A Nonsignificant Difference in Sample Means

The information in Example 8 leads to the conclusion that the predictor variable, x_{1i}, does not carry a significant amount of information and does not help in predicting the response. This also implies that the sample means are not significantly different. This conclusion is reached because the absolute value of the t test statistic of -0.33 *does not exceed* the critical t value of 2.0.

EXAMPLE 8

MINITAB CLASSICAL FIT OF A STRAIGHT LINE, AGE DATA

Problem Statement (a) Fit a straight line to the age data, y, for mothers and fathers of presidents. The predictor variable, x, is coded 0 for mothers and 1 for fathers. Obtain a prediction equation and examine the slope.

Problem Solution (a) The mean age at death was 68.59 for mothers and 67.18 for fathers. Therefore, a prediction equation is

$$\hat{y}_i = 68.59 + (67.18 - 68.59)\, x_{1i}$$

Predicted lifespans are obtained by substituting a 1 or 0 value for x_{1i}. MINITAB prints this equation as

```
C3(AGEMF) = 68.6 - 1.41 C4(DUMMY)
```

The fitted line has a negative slope, which is

$$b_1 = (67.18 - 68.59) = -1.41$$

Although the difference in average ages of -1.41 is not 0, it is small enough relative to the standard error to conclude that there is no significant difference in the sample mean ages. The predictor variable, x_{1i}, then, does not help predict y_i.

Problem Statement (b) Evaluate the goodness of fit statistics.

Problem Solution (b)   We focus on the t ratio statistic in the following table:

```
Predictor        Coef      Stdev     t ratio       p
Constant       68.588
C4(DUMMY)      -1.412      4.240      -0.33      0.740
```

The absolute value of the t ratio for the slope, b_1, is 0.33. This is less than the critical t value of 2.0, where

$$t_{(\alpha/2),(n1+n2-2)} = t_{.025,66} = 2.0$$

Do not reject the null hypothesis that

$$(\mu_{fathers} - \mu_{mothers}) = \beta_1 = 0$$

where β_1 is the difference in the population mean ages of the two samples. The sample mean ages at death of mothers and fathers are not significantly different. The p value leads to the same conclusion.

Problem Discussion   These regression results are practically identical to those shown earlier in the chapter for comparing two population means. Any differences are due to the fact that the regression approach assumes equal population variances. When comparing two population means in MINITAB, if the POOLED subcommand is used for the TWOSAMPLE and TWOT commands, the two sets of results will be identical.

S T A T I S T I C A L   H I G H L I G H T S

Simple regression analysis relates two variables. A regression model can be formulated so that the slope represents the difference in two population means. Differences in sample means is the slope of a fitted line. If the slope is significantly different from 0, the population means are not the same.

FORMULAS FOR VARIOUS TESTS TO COMPARE SAMPLE MEANS

This section presents formulas for test statistics to test the hypothesis that two population means are equal against the not equal alternative hypothesis. Different formulas are used for the different situations described. Computer users will likely use these formulas for reference purposes only.

In this chapter, hypothesis tests have relied on a t test statistic, which is computed by dividing the difference in sample means by a sample standard error of the differences. The difference in sample means is also the slope in the following prediction equation, when the predictor variable is coded 0 or 1:

$$\hat{y}_i = \overline{y}_{M1} + (\overline{y}_{M2} - \overline{y}_{M1})\, x_{1i}$$

Recall that

$\hat{y}_i$ = the predicted or estimated value for the i-th observation

$\overline{y}_{M1}$ = the sample 1 mean

$\overline{y}_{M2}$ = the sample 2 mean

$\overline{y}_{Mi}$ = the predicted or estimated value for the i-th observation

Let

s_1 = the sample 1 standard deviation

s_2 = the sample 2 standard deviation

s_{2-1} = the sample standard error for the difference
in sample means

$$s_{2-1} = \left[\frac{s_1^2}{n_1} + \frac{s_2^2}{n_2}\right]^{1/2}$$

The validity of the test statistics that follow depends on independent random samples from normal distributions. However, the difference in sample means is approximately normal for very large samples when sampling from most distributions.

We provide formulas for three types of situations. Each situation is characterized by conditions concerning the population variances.

Situation 1: Variances Unknown and Not Assumed Equal, Small or Large Samples

Frequently the investigator must estimate the unknown variances of the two populations and cannot assume that these variances are equal. Then the following t test statistic is compared to a critical t value:

t TEST STATISTIC   **CRITICAL t VALUE**

$$\left|\frac{(\overline{y}_{M2} - \overline{y}_{M1})}{s_{2-1}}\right| \qquad\qquad t_{\alpha/2, DF}$$

If the test statistic exceeds the critical value, reject the hypothesis that the two unknown population means are equal at a $(1 - \alpha)$ level of confidence. The degrees of freedom, DF, are calculated as follows:

$$DF = \frac{\left(\dfrac{s_1^2}{n_1} + \dfrac{s_2^2}{n_2}\right)^2}{\dfrac{(s_1^2/n_1)^2}{(n_1 - 1)} + \dfrac{(s_2^2/n_2)^2}{(n_2 - 1)}}$$

This computational formula was used in Examples 5 and 6. The test statistic is valid for small or large samples; however, for large samples, $(n_1 + n_2) \geq 32$, its distribution is approximately normal. Then z's, representing a standard normal distribution, can be substituted for t's.

Situation 2: Variances Unknown and Assumed Equal, Small or Large Samples

When the population variances are equal, the s_{2-1} calculation is based on the following formula:

$$s_{2-1} = s_p \left[\frac{1}{n_1} + \frac{1}{n_2} \right]^{1/2}$$

In this formula, the standard deviation, s_p, is said to be **pooled.** It is computed from the individual sample standard deviations as follows:

$$s_p = \left[\frac{s_1^2(n_1 - 1) + s_2^2(n_2 - 1)}{(n_1 + n_2 - 2)} \right]^{1/2}$$

The assumption of equal population variances is tested informally in this chapter. Histograms of residuals from each sample mean are compared to see if the spread of the residual distributions are about the same.

To test the hypothesis that the two population means are equal, the following t test statistic is compared to a critical t value:

t TEST STATISTIC　　　**CRITICAL t VALUE**

$$\left| \frac{(\bar{y}_{M2} - \bar{y}_{M1})}{s_{2-1}} \right| \qquad\qquad t_{\alpha/2, DF}$$

If the test statistic exceeds the critical value, reject the hypothesis that the two unknown population means are equal at a $(1 - \alpha)$ level of confidence. In this situation, the DF(degrees of freedom) are $(n_1 + n_2 - 2)$.

The test statistic is valid for small or large samples; however, for large samples, $(n_1 + n_2) \geq 32$, its distribution is approximately normal. Then z's, representing a standard normal distribution, can be substituted for t's.

This pooled test produces the same results as regression analysis in Examples 7 and 8.

In MINITAB, when the two populations have the same variances, the computations are envoked by the POOLED subcommand. For example,

```
MTB > TWOSAMPLE T 95% 'SNEW' 'SOLD';
MTB > POOLED.
```

Situation 3: Variances Known, Small or Large Samples

This situation takes place less frequently than do the previous two situations. It occurs when there is a long history of observations under relatively stable conditions. Then the variances are treated as known. The formula structure is similar to that in the first situation, except that the sample standard deviations, s_1 and s_2, are replaced by the known population standard deviations, σ_1 and σ_2. Known variances produce test statistics that follow the normal distribution rather than the Student's t distribution. Thus t's are replaced by z's.

To test the hypothesis that the two population means are equal, the following z test statistic is compared to a critical z value:

z TEST STATISTIC	**CRITICAL z VALUE**
$\left\lvert \dfrac{(\overline{y}_{M2} - \overline{y}_{M1})}{\sigma_{2-1}} \right\rvert$	$z_{\alpha/2}$

where

$$\sigma_{2-1} = \left[\frac{\sigma_1^2}{n_1} + \frac{\sigma_2^2}{n_2} \right]^{1/2}$$

If the test statistic exceeds the critical value, reject the hypothesis that the two unknown population means are equal at a $(1 - \alpha)$ level of confidence.

Confidence Intervals on the Differences in Means

In each of the situations shown above, confidence intervals can be formed for the differences in population means. Use the standard errors appropriate for a particular situation. For situations 1 and 2, the $(1 - \alpha)$ confidence intervals are formed by

$$(\overline{y}_{M2} - \overline{y}_{M1}) \pm t_{\alpha/2,DF} s_{2-1}$$

For situation (3),

$$(\overline{y}_{M2} - \overline{y}_{M1}) \pm z_{\alpha/2} \sigma_{2-1}$$

RELATIONSHIPS SUMMARIZED BY A STRAIGHT LINE WHEN x IS AT MORE THAN TWO LEVELS

A prediction equation or fit summarizes how two variables are related. So far, this equation has been a function of two sample means and a predictor variable, x_{1i}, which has been coded 0 or 1.

$$\hat{y}_i = \overline{y}_{M1} + (\overline{y}_{M2} - \overline{y}_{M1}) x_{1i}$$

The sample means estimate population means.

If $b_0 = \overline{y}_{M1}$ and $b_1 = (\overline{y}_{M2} - \overline{y}_{M1})$, the prediction equation can be written as

$$\hat{y}_i = b_0 + b_1 x_{1i}$$

The intercept, b_0, and the slope, b_1 estimate the unknown parameters in the following model.

$$y_i = \beta_0 + \beta_1 x_{1i} + e_i$$

This section describes fits that no longer limit the predictor variable to two values. A robust way of obtaining such fits was described in Chapter 8.

This chapter describes simple regression fits that minimize the sum of the residuals squared. These fits are based on the least squares method, which makes them sensitive to outlying data points. However, when there are no outliers, these fits are better than robust fits.

EXAMPLE 9

MORE ON SALES VERSUS ASSETS IN MINITAB

This is an observational study of a data set described in Chapter 8. The prediction equation summarizes the relationship between sales and assets of the 30 largest U.S. businesses. Generalizing these results to other companies could be dangerous unless it is established that these businesses are representative of the other companies.

Because of the exploratory work done on this data set in Chapter 8, we can proceed to the classical summary of the relationship between sales and assets using simple regression analysis. To check assumptions, the residuals (actual sales minus predicted sales) are examined briefly since a more thorough examination was conducted in Chapter 8.

Problem Statement (a)   Fit a regression line to the following plot of sales versus assets. Evaluate the goodness of fit and examine residuals.

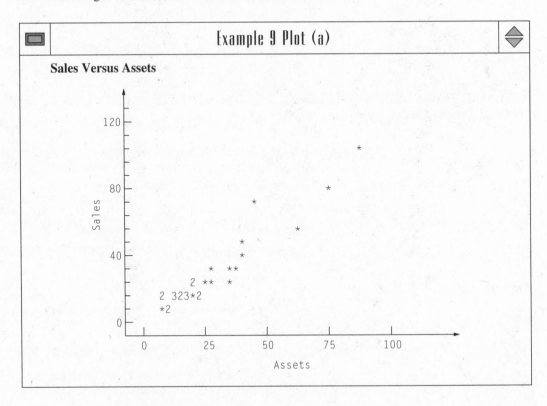

Problem Solution (a)   High sales levels tend to be associated with high asset levels.

The regression equation (fit) is

$$C1(SALES) = -0.70 + 1.07 \ C2(ASSETS)$$

For these large corporations, every dollar in sales is matched with about one dollar in assets as reflected in the slope of 1.07.

Predictor	Coef	Stdev	t ratio	p
Constant	-0.699	2.287	-0.31	0.762
C2(ASSETS)	1.069	0.069	15.44	0.000

The first t ratio of -0.31 is associated with the constant term or intercept, $b_0 = -0.699$. This t ratio of -0.31 is found by dividing the regression coefficient by the standard error, which is $-\frac{0.699}{2.287}$. Thus, the constant term is studentized to form a test statistic. Because the absolute value of -0.31 does not exceed the critical t value of 2, do not reject the hypothesis that $\beta_0 = 0$, where β_0 is the unknown intercept parameter.

Simply put, this means that when there are no assets, there are no sales. This result makes sense financially. However, there are no observations on assets in the sample that are near 0. Generally, a hypothesis such as $\beta_0 = 0$ is not of practical interest unless some observations on x_{1i} are in the region of $x_{1i} = 0$.

In the table above, the second t ratio of 15.44 is associated with the slope of the fitted line, $b_1 = 1.069$. This t ratio of 15.44 is found by dividing the regression coefficient by the standard error, which is $\frac{1.069}{0.069}$. Thus, the slope is studentized to form a test statistic. Because the absolute value of 15.44 exceeds the critical t value of 2, reject the hypothesis that $\beta_1 = 0$, where β_1 is the unknown slope parameter.

Other goodness of fit statistics include the following.

The standard deviation of the residuals, s = 7.336. This is a measure of the spread of the data points about the fitted line. The smaller this statistic is, the better. It is 0 when all the data points fall on the fitted line.

The squared correlation coefficient between the observed and predicted values of sales, R-sq = 89.5%. This statistic ranges from 0 to 1. The closer to 1, the better. It is one when all the data points fall on the fitted line.

The adjusted squared correlation coefficient between the observed and predicted values of sales, R-sq(adj) = 89.1%. The effect of this adjustment is small unless the number of parameters, β_0 and β_1 in this case, gets close to the number of observations. In such a situation, you have too few observations.

Unusual Observations

Obs.#	C2	C1	Fit	Stdev.Fit	Residual	St.Resid
1	87.4	101.80	92.71	4.41	9.09	1.55 X
2	74.0	76.40	78.39	3.53	-1.99	-0.31 X
3	45.0	71.60	47.40	1.84	24.20	3.41 R

In the last column above, the R denotes an observation with a large standardized residual. The X denotes an observation whose predictor variable value has a large influence in determining the fit. Observations 1 and 2 have small classical residuals because this least squares fit is drawn towards these data points. A robust exploratory fit would tend to produce larger residuals. This residual analysis suggests that these data points should be trimmed and the analysis continued.

The following graph displays the residuals, C5, versus the predictor variable, C2 (assets). Notice that the variability increases as assets increase. This suggests that a transformation of sales to log(sales) might be tried. Also, note the unusual nature of the residuals for the four largest asset figures. The companies producing these unusual residuals should be identified.

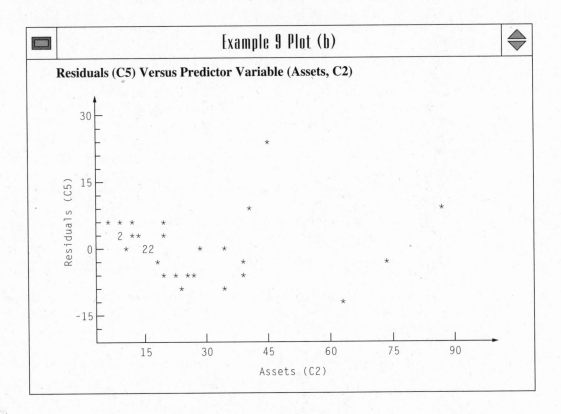

Example 9 Plot (b)

Residuals (C5) Versus Predictor Variable (Assets, C2)

Problem Statement (b)   As a result of the first phase of the analysis, the four largest companies are trimmed from the data set. Also, because the variability in sales increases as assets increase, logarithms of sales are used as the response variable. Fit a line to relate transformed sales to assets. Evaluate the fit and decide on which fit to use for relating sales and assets.

Problem Solution (b)   After deleting the four largest companies from the data set and transforming sales, the regression equation is.

```
C6(LOGE(SALES)) = 2.17 + 0.0371 C2(ASSETS)
```

Predictor	Coef	Stdev	t ratio	p
Constant	2.16927	0.07964	27.24	0.000
C2(ASSETS)	0.037078	0.003489	10.63	0.000

```
s = 0.1781    (the standard deviation of the residuals)
R-sq = 82.5% (the squared correlation between the observed and
predicted values of the response)
```

Unusual Observations These observations are not unusual enough to be of concern in this case.

Obs. #	C2	C6	Fit	Stdev.Fit	Residual	St.Resid
6	19.9	3.2696	2.9071	0.0350	0.3625	2.08R
18	23.3	2.6810	3.0332	0.0363	-0.3522	-2.02R

A correlation coefficient is used here to evaluate the goodness of fit. The correlation between y_i and $\hat{y}_i$, that is, the correlation between the observed and predicted values of the response (log(sales)), yields a measure of how well the prediction equation predicts. The closer to 1 the better.

In the best predictive model, y_i and $\hat{y}_i$ values are equal and their correlation is 1. Here a correlation coefficient of .908 indicates a good fit. The worst possible fit has a 0 correlation between y_i and $\hat{y}_i$. Usually something in between is found. A plot of y_i and $\hat{y}_i$ may be used in addition to the correlation coefficient because it would reveal any stray values that might inflate the correlation coefficient.

In the plot on the next page, C6 is LOGE (SALES) and C4 is predicted LOGE(SALES). The closer the data point pattern is to a straight line, the better the fit. This is a good fit!

In the next residual plot, residuals, C5, are plotted against assets, C2. There are no clusters, outliers, or other patterns in this plot. The residuals appear to be random, which means that by trimming some data points and transforming sales, all the systematic and extreme disturbances in the data have been included in the fit and don't show up in the residuals. Thus, the fit from this phase of the analysis will be the one used to relate sales and assets.

The final fit is

```
C6(LOGE(SALES)) = 2.17 + 0.0371 C2(ASSETS)
```

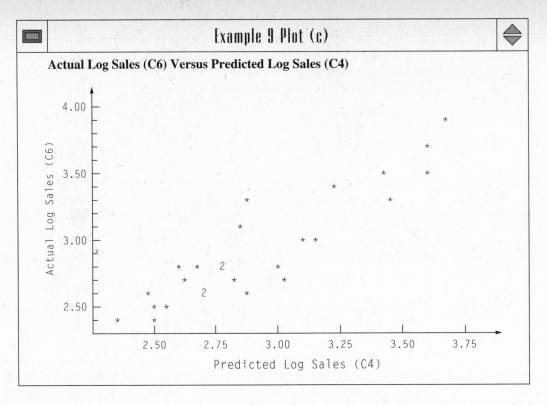

Example 9 Plot (c)

Actual Log Sales (C6) Versus Predicted Log Sales (C4)

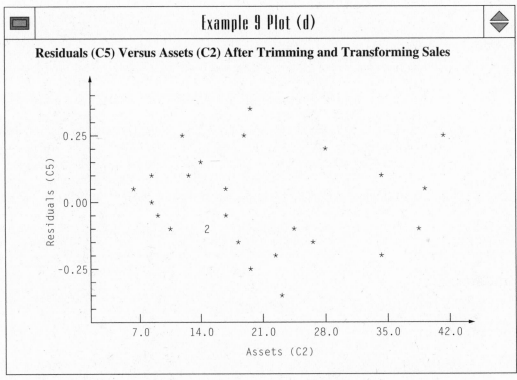

Example 9 Plot (d)

Residuals (C5) Versus Assets (C2) After Trimming and Transforming Sales

CHAPTER SUMMARY

After examining a pair of variables to see if they are related, it is often necessary to confirm tentative exploratory conclusions. Classical statistical methods have been designed for this task. Planned experiments are designed and conducted to test formal hypotheses about the relationship between pairs of variables.

This chapter discussed the analysis of such pairs of variables. Classical methods formalized the exploratory approaches for studying two variables. The major topics included (1) planning simple experiments; (2) confirming or denying hypotheses generated in the exploratory stage of an investigation; (3) making comparisons, small and large sample inferences about differences in population means; and (4) fitting straight lines to data using classical regression techniques.

When a response, y_i, is related to the information carried by a predictor variable, x_{1i}, often the relationship can be represented by a fitted line. If other background variables are held constant or their average effect is 0, there is a good chance to see how y_i is associated with x_{1i}. However, this association does not necessarily imply cause and effect.

In the first example of a fitted line, the predictor variable was coded 0 or 1 to partition the response variable into two groups. To compare the two groups, confidence intervals and hypothesis tests were used, which concerned the differences between the two population means. If the confidence interval on the difference in population means includes 0 within the interval, the null hypothesis of no difference in population means cannot be rejected. Other null hypotheses can be tested in a similar way. A ratio form of the same test can be used as an alternative to the confidence interval approach for testing hypotheses.

Population means can also be compared using regression analysis. When sample means are not significantly different, a regression line, fitted through the two sample means, has a slope that is not significantly different from 0. When the sample means are significantly different, the straight line through the means has a slope that is significantly different from 0. The tabular output from regression analysis computer programs includes t value computations for testing hypotheses about the slope of the straight line fit.

To conduct the regression analysis, the predictor variable must be coded 0 or 1. The reason for introducing the regression approach for comparisons is that regression is a more general way to relate a pair of variables in situations where the predictor variable is not limited to the values 0 or 1. Therefore, regression analysis builds on and extends the fundamental ideas of confidence intervals and hypothesis tests. When the value for the predictor variable ranges widely, a prediction equation or fit is used to highlight the main features of the relationship between the response and the predictor variable.

KEY TERMS

alternative hypothesis, 413
biased, 420
block, 417
component effect, 433
confirmatory pattern, 411
control, 415
covariate, 417

large samples, 423
matching, 416
nuisance variables, 412
null hypothesis, 413
one-at-a-time plans, 420
pooled, 432
randomization, 418

regression model, 423
replication, 420
simple regression analysis, 432
small samples, 423
straight line paradigm, 411
t ratio, 432
target population, 414

EXERCISES

1. Compare the batting averages of Buck Martinez and Gary Mathews.

BUCK MARTINEZ

.229   .111   .152   .250   .215   .226   .228   .225   .219   .270   .224   .227   .242
.253   .220   .162   .581

(continued)

GARY MATHEWS

.290   .300   .287   .280   .279   .283   .285   .304   .278   .301   .281   .258   .291
.235   .259

(a) Use TWOSAMPLE, TWOT, and REGRESSION commands in MINITAB (or, use similar commands in another statistical package or make the computations by hand) to make comparisons as if these data came from a carefully designed experiment. Summarize your findings.

(b) What aspect of this observational study could result in inaccurate conclusions if you attempt to rely exclusively on these classical results? Specifically address the question of independent (random) observations. Plot the data in the sequence observed.

(c) Did you notice that the last batting average figure for Buck Martinez is .581? Replace this erroneous figure of .581 with the correct value of .181. Examine how much this correct figure changes the computer output from the TWOSAMPLE, TWOT, and REGRESSION (or equivalent) commands.

2. At a New England weather station, the 36-year average monthly temperatures in Fahrenheit are[15]

JAN.   **DEC.**

23.6   26.4   35.3   47.1   57.8   66.8   71.7   69.5   61.6   51.5   40.7   28.6

For the last year, the average monthly temperatures are

JAN.   **DEC.**

20.9   33.3   31.4   47.8   55.1   68.9   70.9   72.2   59.8   54.8   40.2   34.4

(a) Use TWOSAMPLE, TWOT, and REGRESSION commands in MINITAB (or use similar commands in another statistical package or make the computations by hand) to make comparisons as if these data came from a carefully designed experiment. Summarize your findings.

(b) What aspect of this observational study could result in inaccurate conclusions if you attempt to rely exclusively on the classical results? Specifically address the question of independent (random) observations. Plot the data in the sequence observed.

(c) On the precipitation data shown below, use TWOSAMPLE, TWOT, and REGRESSION (or equivalent) commands to make comparisons as if these data came from a carefully designed experiment. Summarize your findings.

36-YEAR AVERAGE PRECIPITATION IN INCHES

JAN.   **DEC.**

3.17   3.02   3.49   3.83   3.68   3.74   3.68   3.78   3.45   3.39   3.77   3.87

THE LAST YEAR'S AVERAGE MONTHLY PRECIPITATION IN INCHES

JAN.   **DEC.**

1.75   6.42   3.68   4.30   11.95   1.69   4.64   1.34   1.02   3.13   3.97   2.84

3. You are given returns on a stock that were computed from the i-th period price, P_i, and the price one period ahead. The return on a stock is $Y_i = \frac{(P_{i+1} - P_i)}{P_i}$. Because we would like to see how the movement of a particular stock is related to the movement of the market as a whole, we use the Dow-Jones (DJ) Index or the Standard and Poor's Composite Index as a price that represents the whole market. Hence, for example, the market return is $x_{1i} = \frac{(DJ_{i+1} - DJ_i)}{DJ_i}$.

Converting prices to returns usually has the effect of purging the time variable, making y_i and x_{1i} random over time. Even though this is an observational study, working with returns often permits the valid use of classical methods. These returns have been computed for you, converted to a percentage, and rounded for simplicity. They are

PERIOD	1	2	3	4	5	6	7	8	9	10	11	12
y_i =	12	15	−4	1	3	−2	−8	−1	1	1	2	7
x_{1i} =	12	6	2	4	4	5	−6	−2	3	6	2	−1

(a) Obtain a scatterplot of the returns on the stock versus the returns on the market.

(b) Compute the correlation between the returns on the stock and the returns on the market.

(c) Obtain a classical straight line fit of the form $b_0 + b_1 x_{1i}$, using the REGRESSION command in MINITAB (or use similar commands in another statistical package or make the computations by hand). Evaluate the output.

(d) Can you reject the hypothesis that $\beta_1 = 0$? If so, what does the regression coefficient b_1 tell you about the change in the stock's return as the market return changes by one unit?

(e) What would be the purpose of computing residuals and analyzing them?

4. In the manufacture of a new missile component, it took 120 min to make the first unit, 92 min to make the second unit of the same component, 54 min to make the seventh unit and 52 min to manufacture the eighth unit. The complete data set is shown below. It is clear that learning is taking place. As more units are produced, less time is needed to complete each unit. The reduction in the completion time decreases as more units are produced.

UNIT

x_{1i}	1	2	3	4	5	6	7	8	9	10

TIME TO MANUFACTURE

Y_i	120	92	80	70	61	59	54	52	51	49

(a) Plot the data.

(b) Is there curvature present?

(c) If there is curvature, what transformation on the time to manufacture variable straightens the relationship?

(d) Obtain a classical straight line fit to the transformed data set using the REGRESSION command in MINITAB (or use similar command(s) in another statistical package or make the computations by hand). Be sure to obtain a column of predictions for part (f) below.

(e) For the first eight units produced, obtain the predicted time to make each unit.

(f) To assess the goodness of the fit, plot and obtain the correlation between the predicted and the actual times.

(g) Can you reject the hypothesis that $\beta_1 = 0$?

5. It is thought that certain standardized tests are useful in predicting grade performance of students in college. One such test was taken by 30 students. Their scores on the mathematics (MATH) part of the test are shown below along with their grade point averages (GPA).

GPA

2.70 2.65 2.30 3.73 1.64 1.76 2.92 3.14 3.13 2.71 2.54 1.98 3.09 3.31
2.78 2.63 2.66 2.25 3.28 2.00 2.13 3.08 2.46 3.03 1.16 3.31 3.22 3.70
2.46 2.97

(continued)

MATH

37 35 49 44 36 55 44 49 49 45 50 43 49 57 45 33 46 30 54
36 49 55 48 55 45 41 46 62 40 58

(a) Plot GPA versus MATH.

(b) Is the correlation between these two variables negative, positive, or zero?

(c) Obtain a classical straight line fit to predict GPA from the MATH score. Can you reject the hypothesis that $\beta_1 = 0$?

(d) How good is this prediction?

(e) If you were an admissions administrator at a university, how would you use these MATH scores along with other factors such as high school grades in making an admissions decision?

6. Using the presidential data base in Chapter 8 Exhibit 1, examine life expectancy after the first inaugural and compare it to the actual years lived after the first inaugural.

(a) Use TWOSAMPLE, TWOT, and REGRESSION commands in MINITAB (or use similar commands in another statistical package or make the computations by hand) to make comparisons as if these data came from a carefully designed experiment. Summarize your findings.

(b) Because these data do not arise from a carefully controlled study, are the conclusions weakly supported?

7. To illustrate a designed experiment and valid classical comparisons, conduct the following classroom experiment. Have students take their own resting pulse. Next, have each student flip a coin for randomization purposes. Those getting tails will be considered the treatment group. They stand and run in place or go out of the classroom for a brisk walk. Those getting heads will be considered the control group. They rest while the others exercise. Immediately afterwards record all the pulses again.

(a) Why might it be better to take your own pulse rather than have the person next to you take it? Could someone next to you cause your pulse to rise?

(b) Use TWOSAMPLE, TWOT, and REGRESSION commands in MINITAB (or use similar commands in another statistical package or make the computations by hand) to compare mean pulses and test for significant differences due to the treatment.

8. A major golf ball maker has been conducting research on a new golf ball designed to go farther than other premium golf balls. Management expects Long John, the code name for the new ball, to get more distance than competitive brands. Prototype Long Johns are available for testing.

(a) Frame the question "Do Long Johns get more, less, or the same distance than competitive balls?" as null and alternative hypotheses. Write the hypothesis statement(s).

(b) If Long John outshoots the competition, management plans to run advertisements that state how much more distance Long John produces for the average golfer. How would you handle this secondary problem of estimating how much more distance is expected from Long John?

(c) How might you define the "average" golfer in terms of handicap?

(d) What club or clubs might you use in distance testing? Explain your reasoning.

(e) If the company is not confident that the in-house statistical expertise is experienced enough to handle this project, discuss how you might use outside consultants. Be sure to comment on the project team composition.

(f) How would you randomize the assignment of Long John and "other" balls to the golfers doing the testing?

(g) How would you pick golfers for testing who are at about the same playing level (matched)?

(h) Do you think that distance measures should be omitted from the data set for "roller balls," "bloopers," "infield flies," or other exceptionally bad hits?

(i) In order to control for wind and temperature conditions, specify wind and temperature condition limits necessary for testing to proceed.

(j) Actual company advertising claims were that Long John beat other balls by about ten yards in average distance. As a golfer, do you think that you would buy Long Johns because of this distance effect?

(k) One golfer hit 12 drives with Long Johns and another 12 drives using a competitive brand. The balls were selected at random with the brand unknown to the golfer. Analyze the following distance data (in yards) and perform the necessary hypothesis tests.

LONG JOHNS

| 189 | 205 | 193 | 196 | 190 | 202 | 210 | 207 | 193 | 201 | 212 | 189 |

COMPETITIVE BRAND

| 187 | 172 | 179 | 191 | 170 | 189 | 196 | 186 | 189 | 181 | 173 | 172 |

9. Using MINITAB (or use similar commands in another statistical package or construct the simulation by hand), simulate ten drive distances with Long John golf balls (use a normal distribution with a mean of 190 yards and a standard deviation of 10 yards) and ten drive distances with "other" golf balls (use a normal distribution with a mean of 180 yards and a standard deviation of 10 yards).

(a) Make exploratory comparisons using notched boxplots.

(b) Through trial and error, increase your sample sizes until the exploratory tools seem to indicate a significant difference in mean drive distances.

(c) Using methods in this chapter, make a confirmatory comparison based on the data from the last simulated data set in part (b) of this exercise.

10. In the United States, the northwest states generate about 80% of their electrical power from hydropower plants. During periods of low water runoff, high-cost thermoelectric plants must make up for reduced hydropower generation. The average annual flow in hundreds of cubic feet per second for 40 years is

1374	1234	1225	1679	1792	2275	1549	1639	1216	1787
1486	1490	1337	1665	1915	1376	1404	1835	1923	2242
1903	1860	2334	2069	1721	1927	1879	2497	2049	1813
1921	2054	1979	1646	1739	1740	2276	1687	1857	1755

(a) As a manager you are thinking ahead because you know that it takes 15 to 20 years to construct some thermoelectric plants. Borrowing power on large power grids is limited and expensive. Fit a regression line and test the null hypothesis that β_1 is zero against the nonzero alternative hypothesis to see if there is a trend in the runoff data over these 40 years. When using MINITAB (or another statistical package or hand computations), you need a trend predictor variable. For example

```
MTB> SET C2
DATA> 1:40
```

(b) Check to see if residuals are random. If the residuals are nonrandom, a more sophisticated analysis may be necessary.

11. A particularly bad type of fall in skiing is one in which you twist your leg. This can result in a spiral fracture in the lower leg. Ski bindings are designed to release before the twist torque in foot-pounds gets to a critical level. The critical level of twist torque depends on skier weight.

The figures below are used to set twist torque (T) binding release levels that depend on weight (W) in pounds.

T	16	20	24	28	32	36	40	44	48	50
W	55	75	95	115	135	155	175	195	215	235

(a) Summarize the relationship between these variables with a regression equation, and evaluate the strength of the relationship between these two variables.

(b) Predict the twist torque setting needed for your weight.

12. A random sample of professional golfers had the following one-year official earnings (E) in thousands of dollars and scoring averages (A).[16] Use a fitted regression line and accoutrements to see if there is a strong relationship between these variables. Summarize your findings and discuss.

EARNINGS (E)

71.6	55.8	147.8	117.4	112.3	82.7	22.8	58.8	60.5	55.4	43.6

SCORING AVERAGES (A)

71.5	72.75	71.34	71.27	70.95	71.65	72.49	71.46	71.95	71.61	72.39

13. A firm produces prefabricated houses by order only (a job-shop rather than an assembly-line production facility) because a large number of styles and options are made available to the customer. For pricing purposes, the managers use budgeted costs because actual costs are not available until after the job is finished. A problem, however, became apparent in recent cost figures for part of the prefabrication work: the higher the actual cost (AC), the larger was the absolute deviation (DC) from budget. To assess the magnitude of the problem and to establish a benchmark from which improvements can be gauged, fit a regression line and analyze and report on this relationship for the dollar figures below:

AC	35640	35730	35740	36000	37760	38700	39930	41210	43560
DC	500	610	615	854	1640	1100	1875	2044	1123

14. Some manufacturing companies refer to true physical production cost for a period as gross product. For financial planning in manufacturing, it is necessary to relate gross product to production factors such as payroll costs. Use regression to summarize the relationship between gross product (GP) and other factors such as payroll cost (PAY) for the actual production cost figures shown below (in thousands of dollars).

GP	69	210	156	166	120	100	112	125	175
PAY	66	143	115	122	117	90	95	110	135

15. A company maintains a fleet of automobiles. Management is interested in minimizing the total cost of ownership and operation. A portion of the total cost is for maintenance and operating costs (O&M dollars per mile). O&M costs tend to increase with vehicle age. Find a regression equation to predict O&M costs using vehicle age (VA) in years.

O&M	.20	.28	.27	.316	.38	.42	.44	.49	.55	.56	.63	.66
VA	1	2	3	4	5	6	7	8	9	10	11	12

16. In establishing labor forecasts for a shipping center, it was necessary to predict man-hours (MH) from shipping units (SU in hundreds of units). Using regression, find the prediction equation and comment on the quality of the fit.

MH	3470	4650	5370	8320	5190	4180	3420	3890	3650	5410	4110	3740
SU	2178	3229	5530	6442	3767	2497	2229	3561	3791	4184	3246	2813

17. A manufacturing company found that the greater the capital investment (CI in hundreds of dollars) in automation, the fewer was the number of people employed (PE). For decision making purposes, quantify and evaluate this relationship using regression.

CI	985	715	585	500	412	198	190	146	56	14
PE	50	20	110	430	312	250	620	415	512	675

18. Flexible budgeting is needed in factories because production volume varies. Predicting cost behavior from past production experience is a supporting pillar of flexible budgeting. Although industrial engineering studies are used to determine how costs should vary with volume, regression analysis is also used to summarize past cost-volume experience. Total mixed cost (TMC), a mixture of fixed and variable components, is often related to a production volume measure such as machine-hours (MH). Obtain a regression equation for predicting TMC (in hundreds of dollars) based on MH. Is there a significant relationship between these variables?

TMC	20	21	24	14	15	8	10	13	14	16	20
MH	22	27	23	19	18	14	13	10	12	20	26

19. An automobile manufacturer conducts quality control training programs in two of its supplier plants. The instructor gives the same exam in both plants. The exam scores are

Plant (Boston)	90	73	78	82	66	69	85	86	76	89	70
Plant (Atlanta)	81	72	50	66	55	70	68	82	71		

(a) Use TWOT or TWOSAMPLE commands in MINITAB (or use similar commands in another statistical package or make the computations by hand) and use a 95% level of confidence to test for a significant difference in sample means.

(b) What are the null and alternative hypotheses being examined here?

20. A production line worker suggested that a new assembly method might reduce assembly times. In response, the production manager decided to compare the new and old methods. Is there a significant difference in the mean assembly times (in minutes)?

ASSEMBLY TIMES

Old Method

21.6	21.7	23.9	24.0	22.7	24.6	22.5
24.0	24.4	24.0	23.7	24.9	23.9	24.9
22.7	23.4	22.4	22.2	24.4	24.4	25.1
22.7	25.3	23.4	25.4	24.1	24.5	24.1
24.9	23.9	24.9	23.9	23.1	24.5	24.6
25.0	24.7	22.3	24.0	23.0		

New Method

23.5	23.5	22.0	21.3	21.7	22.3	23.3
23.6	21.5	24.1	21.6	22.5	22.3	21.6
21.7	22.0	22.0	21.1	21.8	21.9	24.3
22.9	20.1	21.8	20.6	21.7	22.3	21.5
22.9	21.5	22.2	21.4	21.9	21.1	22.8
21.8	21.5	23.4	22.6	20.6		

21. An investor collected monthly price data for the stocks of two companies in the same line of business. Based on those prices, returns were computed as shown below. Test to see if there is a significant difference in mean returns.

RETURNS COMPANY A

0.112	0.115	0.158	0.160	0.135	0.172	0.130
0.161	0.169	0.161	0.155	0.179	0.159	0.178
0.135	0.149	0.128	0.125	0.168	0.168	0.183
0.134	0.187	0.149				

RETURNS COMPANY B

0.209	0.182	0.191	0.182	0.198	0.179	0.199
0.179	0.162	0.191	0.192	0.200	0.194	0.147
0.181	0.161	0.210	0.211	0.181	0.166	0.175
0.186	0.206	0.213				

22. Try this simulation experiment (in MINITAB or in another statistical package) and test for significantly different means. Generate samples from normal distributions of starting salaries for two groups of business majors. Keep the standard deviations the same and initially keep means nearly the same. Later make step-by-step changes in the mean starting salary for one of the majors. With the sample size and standard deviation fixed, see how much of a mean shift is necessary for TWOSAMPLE to detect the shift. Use a text editor to create the following macro:

```
GMACRO  # BEGINS A MACRO
TWOGEN  # THE INITIALIZING THAT FOLLOWS CAN BE MOVED OUTSIDE
#         THE MACRO; THEN, DONE IN THE SESSION WINDOW
NOECHO
LET K1 =    20  # NUMBER OF OBSERVATIONS
LET K2 = 33000  # MEAN
LET K3 =  1000  # STANDARD DEVIATION
LET K4 =    20  # NUMBER OF OBSERVATIONS
LET K6 =  1000  # STANDARD DEVIATION
RANDOM K1 IN C1;  # ONE SET OF OBSERVATIONS
NORMAL MU=K2 SIGMA=K3.
RANDOM K4 IN C2;  # SECOND SET OF OBSERVATIONS
NORMAL MU=K5 SIGMA=K6.
PRINT C1
PRINT C2
ENDMACRO
```

Save the macro on drive B: as TWOGEN.MAC. Then start MINITAB and issue the following commands in the session window:

```
MTB > LET K5 = 32000  # MEAN
MTB > %B:TWOGEN
MTB > STACK C1 ON C2, PUT INTO C11  # I WANT TO LOOK
MTB > SET INTO C12  # AT THE DATA FIRST IN AN EXPLORATORY
DATA> 20(0), 20(1)  # WAY USING BOXPLOTS
DATA> END           # C12 IS USED IN A BOXPLOT SUBCOMMAND
```

```
MTB > BOXPLOT C11;   # MEDIANS DON'T LOOK SIGNIFICANTLY
SUBC> BY C12.        # DIFFERENT
C12
                     ---------------------------
0           -------------I                + I-------
                     ---------------------------
                     -------------------
1       -------------------I      +      I-------
                     -------------------
        --------+---------+---------+---------+---------+-------C11
           30800     31500     32200     32900     33600

MTB > TWOSAMPLE T C1 C2

TWOSAMPLE T FOR C1 VS C2

        N     MEAN    STDEV   SE MEAN
C1  20    32568     1038      232
C2  20    32225      891      199

95 PCT CI FOR MU C1 - MU C2: (-277, 963)

TTEST MU C1 = MU C2 (VS NE): T = 1.12  P=0.27  DF=  37

MTB > LET K5 = 35000   # A BIG SHIFT IN ONE MEAN
MTB > %B:TWOGEN
MTB > STACK C1 ON C2, PUT INTO C11
MTB > BOXPLOT C11;   # MEDIANS LOOK SIGNIFICANTLY DIFFERENT
SUBC> BY C12.
C12
                     -----------------
0           ---------I        +    I----
                     -----------------
                                      -------------
1                        -----------I    +    I----
                                      ------------
        +----------+---------+---------+---------+---------+------C11
           30000     31200     32400     33600     34800     36000

MTB > TWOSAMPLE T C1 C2

TWOSAMPLE T FOR C1 VS C2

        N     MEAN    STDEV   SE MEAN
C1  20    32568     1038      232
C2  20    35225      891      199

95 PCT CI FOR MU C1 - MU C2: (-3277, -2037)

TTEST MU C1 = MU C2 (VS NE): T= -8.69  P=0.0000  DF=  37
```

(a) For variations in this problem, you can repeatedly execute the macro after changing other initial values such as the sample size or the standard deviation. In separate simulations possibly done by separate teams of students, you might do the following: increase the standard deviation; decrease the standard deviation; increase the sample size; decrease the sample size; and, replace one or two of the simulated data values with known outliers to see the effect of outliers on the statistical comparisons.

23. Conduct some additional simulation studies similar to the previous exercise. Simulate from one or more of the following normal distributions where it is assumed that means and standard deviations are known:

(a) Compare price-earnings ratios of 50 merged and 50 nonmerged firms. For merged firms the mean is 8.5 and the standard deviation is 9.1. For nonmerged firms the mean is 12.2 and the standard deviation is 11.4.

(b) Compare service times for students waiting in two lines at the bursar's office for 15 students in line A and 18 students in line B. For line A the mean is 12.5 and the standard deviation is 13.2. For line B the mean is 15.2 and the standard deviation is 4.4.

(c) Compare workdays lost due to sickness (sickdays) in two similar plants. An autocratic management style is used in one plant and a democratic management style is used in the other plant. Simulate yearly records of 22 employees from each plant. For the autocratic management plant the mean is 10.3 sickdays and the standard deviation is 8. For the democratic management plant the mean is 14.7 sickdays and the standard deviation is 10.

(d) Simulate and compare mortgage loan sizes for 20 bank A loans and 20 bank B loans for single-family homes where the standard deviation is $15,000. In both cases, the mean bank A loan size is $195,000 and the mean bank B loan size is $185,000.

24. According to Robert Adair, former physicist for the National Baseball League, the distance (feet) a baseball travels is a function of the velocity (mph) of a pitched ball.[17] For the data below, assume that a 35-in., 32-oz bat is swung at 70 mph, waist-high, 10° upward from the horizontal plane, driving the ball at an angle of 35°. Using the data points below, which are approximations, fit a regression line to these points using ball velocity to predict distance. Would you reject the hypothesis that there is no relation between distance and velocity?

Distance	327	335	340	348	356	363	370	378	388
Velocity	20	30	40	50	60	70	80	90	100

Adair said that the fastest pitchers can throw a fastball about 100 mph; for example, Bob Feller (1946, 98.6 mph), Walter Johnson (1914, 99.7 mph), Nolan Ryan (100.7 mph), and Goose Gossage (about 100 mph). In contrast, a slow curve might have a velocity of 65 mph. Based on your fit, how far do you predict a slow curve will be hit?

25. A state department of transportation depends on computer processing for vehicle registrations and other transactions. A computer capacity management aid tracks central processor unit (CPU) hours used by month. Trends in CPU usage can be projected into the future to see when CPU capacity might be exceeded. As a result, early warning can be given of needed computer capacity enhancements, and budget requests for funding CPU enhancements can be sent to the legislature's Ways and Means Subcommittee for approval.

Obtain a regression equation for the monthly data shown below and determine when (how many months in the future) the CPU capacity of 300 hours will be exceeded. Evaluate the goodness of fit.

CPU Usage	183	188	203	185	186	196	182	207	209	195
Month (Aug.)	1	2	3	4	5	6	7	8	9	10

CPU Usage	197	203	220	218	225	212	220	230	232
Month	11	12	13	14	15	16	17	18	19

26. Chemical differences appear in brain tissue and platelets of patients suffering from clinically significant depression. For the treatment group (suicides) and the control group (other sudden death causes), the binding characteristics, B_{max}, of $[^3H]$ imipramine differ in each subject's frontal cortex.

In an ideal experiment, subjects would be assigned randomly to the treatment and control groups. Randomization obviously is not possible because all the subjects are dead. We can't assign which subjects are to be suicides and which are to die from other sudden causes. However, the control and treatment subjects can be matched in an attempt to simulate an ideal experiment. The matching was achieved by including control group subjects who were not significantly different from treatment group subjects in age, sex, and elapsed time between death and autopsy. For example, (the mean age) $\pm$ a *standard error* is 35.11 ± 5.40 for suicides and 34.15 ± 3.60 for controls.

Suicides were due to hanging (H), gunshot wound (GW) or jumping from height (JH). Control deaths were due to gunshot wound (GW, homicide), myocardial infarction (MI), or auto accident (AA). The B_{max} values are shown below.[18] Display side-by-side boxplots. Test for significant differences in mean B_{max} levels. State conclusions.

	H	**GW**	**H**	**GW**	**GW**	**H**	**H**	**JH**	**H**
Suicides	464	249	345	328	285	237	443	136	483

	GW	**GW**	**MI**	**GW**	**MI**	**AA**	**GW**	**MI**	**MI**
Controls	740	707	353	350	350	531	1017	695	544

APPENDIX 1

Minitab Examples

(If you are using the WINDOWS version of MINITAB, you might issue the GSTD command first to use standard graphics in the session window. If you want to save your output on a file, use the command OUTFILE 'A:CH9.LIS' to echo output to this file.)

MINITAB ANALYSIS OF THE AGE DATA, CLASSICAL APPROACH, ILLUSTRATING TWOSAMPLE AND TWOT COMMANDS

Comparison problems of this type can have the data arranged in different ways. MINITAB has two separate commands to handle the two most common data arrangements. These two commands make the same computations, but TWOSAMPLE expects the age data in two columns while TWOT expects the age data in one column with an additional column for a variable that identifies the two data subsets. The predictor variable does the identification and is coded 0 for mothers and 1 for fathers.

(If you have the data diskette, **RETRIEVE 'B:AGE'** and omit the data entry using SET.)

(If you are on a network and have the data stored in subdirectory DATA under the directory MTBWIN, **RETRIEVE 'AGE'.** Otherwise SET the data in columns.)

```
DON'T SET DATA IN C1 IF RETRIEVE WAS SUCCESSFUL
# EITHER SET FATHER'S AGES INTO C1 AND
# SET MOTHER'S AGES INTO C2
# (USE THE LAST TWO COLUMNS OF THE PRESIDENTIAL DATA SET
# SHOWN IN THE BEGINNING OF CHAPTER EIGHT-----
# BE SURE TO DELETE ALL DATA IN ROWS CORRESPONDING TO
# THE FOLLOWING PRESIDENTS:
# MONROE, JACKSON, KENNEDY AND CARTER)

START HERE IF RETRIEVE SUCCESSFUL
MTB > NAME C1 'AGEF'    # LONGEVITY FATHERS OF PRESIDENTS
MTB > NAME C2 'AGEM'    # LONGEVITY MOTHERS OF PRESIDENTS
```

454

```
MTB > STACK C2 ON C1 PUT IN C3
MTB > NAME C3 'AGEMF'
MTB > SET IN C4        # 0'S FOR MOTHERS 1'S FOR FATHERS
DATA> 34(0),34(1)      # NO SPACES BETWEEN CHARACTERS
DATA> END

MTB > NAME C4 'DUMMY'  # DUMMY, BINARY, CATEGORICAL AND
# INDICATOR ARE TERMS USED FOR THIS TYPE OF VARIABLE THAT
# IS USED TO IDENTIFY PARTICULAR SUBSETS OF DATA VALUES

# SKIP THIS SAVE IF YOU RETRIEVED MTB > SAVE 'B:AGE'

MTB > TWOSAMPLE T 95% 'AGEF' AND 'AGEM' # THIS THE FORMAL
# VERSION OF THE PSEUDO T TEST TO TEST IF THESE MEANS DIFFER
# SIGNIFICANTLY; THE COMMAND EXPECTS THE DATA IN TWO
# SEPARATE COLUMNS
```

Comment An alternative MINITAB command that performs the same test as TWOSAM-PLE T 95% 'AGEF' AND 'AGEM' is the TWOT command shown in this appendix. The reason for two commands to perform the same test is that the data can be arranged in two columns or stacked into one column. The TWOT command expects the ages of mothers and fathers in one column and a second column of data that identifies the subsets of mothers and fathers. The resulting output is identical to that shown above.

The TWOT test included an identifier (dummy) variable, which is called a predictor variable, x_{1i}. The predictor variable x_{1i} designates mothers or fathers through its 1 and 0 coding. The predictor variable was of little value in predicting the age at death. Knowing whether the age data was associated with a mother or a father was immaterial. The average age at death was not significantly different for the two groups of data.

```
MTB > TWOT 95% FOR 'AGEMF' GROUPED BY 'DUMMY'

# TWOT YIELDS THE SAME RESULTS AS AS TWOSAMPLE BUT TWOT IS
# DESIGNED FOR DATA IN A SINGLE COLUMN (AGEMF) SEPARATED INTO
# GROUPS BY DATA VALUES IN A SECOND COLUMN (DUMMY).  THE
# SIGN REVERSAL OCCURS BECAUSE MOTHER'S AGES ARE STACKED ON
# TOP OF FATHER'S AGES.

MTB > RUNS 'AGEF'         # RESULTS ARE NOT SHOWN
MTB > RUNS 'AGEM'         # BUT, CHECK FOR RANDOMNESS
MTB > MTSPLOT 'AGEF' 'AGEM'
```

EXAMPLE

MINITAB ANALYSIS OF THE PACKAGE DESIGN, SALES DATA, CLASSICAL APPROACH

(If you have the data diskette, RETRIEVE 'B:SALES2' and omit the data entry using SET.)

(If you are on a network and have the data stored in subdirectory DATA under the directory MTBWIN, RETRIEVE 'SALES2'. Otherwise SET the data in columns.)

```
DON'T SET DATA IN C1 IF RETRIEVE WAS SUCCESSFUL
# IF YOU DON'T HAVE ACCESS TO THE DATA FILES, SET
# NEW PACKAGE DESIGN SALES INTO C1 AND SET OLD
# PACKAGE DESIGN SALES INTO C2
# USE THE SALES DATA SET SHOWN IN THE BEGINNING
# OF CHAPTER EIGHT

START HERE IF RETRIEVE SUCCESSFUL
MTB > NAME C1 'SNEW'    # SALES NEW PACKAGE DESIGN
MTB > NAME C2 'SOLD'    # SALES OLD PACKAGE DESIGN
MTB > STACK 'SOLD' 'SNEW', PUT IN C3
MTB > NAME C3 'SALESON'

MTB > SET INTO C4
DATA> 13(0),13(1)       # NO SPACES BETWEEN CHARACTERS
DATA> END
MTB > NAME C4 'DUMMY'

MTB > RUNS 'SOLD'       # OUTPUT NOT SHOWN BUT RANDOM
MTB > RUNS 'SNEW'       # OUTPUT NOT SHOWN BUT RANDOM

MTB > TWOSAMPLE T 95% 'SNEW' 'SOLD'
```

Comment An alternative MINITAB command that performs the same test as TWOSAMPLE T 95% 'SNEW' AND 'SOLD' follows. The reason for two commands to perform the same test is that the data can be in two columns or stacked into one column. The TWOT command expects sales revenue of new and old package designs in one column and a second column of data that identifies the subsets of new and old package designs.

```
MTB > TWOT 95% 'SALESON' GROUPED BY 'DUMMY'
```

Comment In MINITAB, when the Gaussian distributions have the same standard deviations or variances, the computations are envoked by the POOLED subcommand. For example,

```
(OPTIONAL)
MTB > TWOSAMPLE T 95% 'SNEW' 'SOLD';
SUBC > POOLED.
```

As a reminder for one-sided hypothesis tests, the ALTERNATIVE = +1. or ALTERNATIVE = −1. subcommands are used (+1 for a greater than alternative and −1 for a less than alternative).

EXAMPLE

MINITAB, CLASSICAL FIT OF A STRAIGHT LINE, SALES DATA

The classical version of a fit, prediction equation, or a REGRESSION line can be obtained with the REGRESS command.

```
MTB > REGRESS 'SALESON' 1 PREDICTOR 'DUMMY'
```

(This chapter explains only part of the output from the REGRESS command. You should not be burdened now with items that will be explained in another chapter.)

E X A M P L E

MINITAB, CLASSICAL FIT OF A STRAIGHT LINE, AGE DATA

```
    (OR  RETRIEVE 'AGE' whichever is appropriate)
MTB > RETRIEVE 'B:AGE'
MTB > INFO
MTB > REGRESS C3 1 PRED C4
```

(For now, you are expected to understand only part of the output from the REGRESS command.)

E X A M P L E

MORE ON SALES VERSUS ASSETS IN MINITAB

Comment   The file name here is SALAS and not SALES.

```
    (OR  RETRIEVE 'SALAS' whichever is appropriate.)
MTB > RETRIEVE 'B:SALAS'

# OR IF THE DATA SET IS UNAVAILABLE, FROM CHAPTER EIGHT,
# SET DATA IN C1 # SALES
# AND SET IN C2 # ASSETS

MTB > PLOT C1 C2;
SUBC> YSTART AT 0 GO TO 120;
SUBC> XSTART AT 0 GO TO 120.

MTB > REGRESS C1 1 PRED IN C2, STD RES C3, FITS C4;
SUBC> RESIDUALS C5.

MTB > PLOT C5 C2  # RESIDUALS VERSUS ASSETS

MTB > DELETE ROWS 1,2,3,4 C1 C2     # BECAUSE OF INFLUENCE
                             # AND LARGE EXPLORATORY RESIDUALS

MTB > LET C6=LOGE(C1)       # BECAUSE THE SCATTER ON THE
# POINTS INCREASES AS ASSETS INCREASES, VIOLATING THE
# ASSUMPTION THAT THE SPREAD REMAINS RELATIVELY CONSTANT

MTB > REGRESS C6 1 PRED C2, ST RES C3, FITS C4;
SUBC> RESIDUALS C5.

MTB > CORRELATE C6 C4       # LOGE(SALES) AND PREDICTED
# LOGE(SALES); OVERALL, A GOOD FIT IS OBTAINED

MTB > PLOT C6 C4 # LOGE(SALES) VERSUS PREDICTED LOGE(SALES)

MTB > PLOT C5 C2 # RESIDUALS VERSUS ASSETS, HOPEFULLY,
# RANDOM-----NO PATTERNS BECAUSE WE HAVE CAPTURED THE
# SYSTEMATIC RELATIONSHIPS IN THE FIT AND SET ASIDE UNUSUAL
# CLUSTERS OF POINTS FOR SEPARATE CONSIDERATION
```

CHAPTER 10

The Analysis of Categorical (Qualitative) Variables and Tests of Goodness of Fit and Independence

OBJECTIVES

◇ Understand the analysis of categorical variables

◇ Conduct hypothesis tests on proportions for one or more categories

◇ Perform tests of independence of variables in contingency tables

◇ Evaluate goodness of fit

PRELUDE

An article was published in a campus newspaper to inform students that the college environment is particularly difficult for persons with eating disorders.[1] The article said that individuals with eating disorders will show some, but not necessarily all, of 16 symptoms, such as weight loss, lack of menstrual periods, distorted body image, dehydration, constipation, tooth decay, excessive exercise, insomnia, and low self-esteem. To encourage students to assess their own eating behavior, the article included 21 questions, such as Do you feel a desire to be thin? Do you feel societal pressures to be thin? Do you weigh yourself daily? Do you induce vomiting after eating?

The responses to these questions are categorical because the respondent chooses from two categories of answers. For example, in the question, Do you feel a desire to be thin? the answer choices are Yes or No. More than two response categories are possible, such as Yes, No, or Sometimes. After students respond to the 21 questions, they can measure their own eating behavior by adding numerical weights assigned to each Yes answer. Students with high measurement scores were recommended to make an appointment with a university health service nutritionist.

Both students and the university administration recommended publishing the eating disorders article in the school newspaper. They believed that eating disorders were prevalent enough to warrant this attention. *Prevalent enough* means that the proportion of students with at least x out of n symptoms is large enough to initiate action. It is useful to convert categorical responses to proportions, analyze them, and make decisions based on the proportions. This chapter describes such analysis of categorical variables.

The statistical aspects of the eating disorder problem are applicable to a wide variety of general management problems. Some examples include: What proportion of buyers prefer a particular brand? Are there differences in proportions by region of households that will purchase a product? In quality control, what proportion defective (nonconforming) alarms management and requires corrective action? What proportion of answers must an employee get correct to finish an in-house training program? This chapter provides the skills you need to deal with these and other management problems. ◇

WHAT IS A SURVEY AND HOW IS IT IMPLEMENTED?[2]

A **survey** is a method of gathering sample information to learn something about a population. The fact that a scientific sample is used differentiates a survey from a census. A census intends to examine the whole population. Surveys are classified in many ways, such as

1. *Method of data collection*—questionnaires, telephone surveys, and personal interview surveys.
2. *Size and type of sample*—total adult population, physicians, business leaders, the unemployed, and product users.
3. *Content*—opinion and attitude surveys.

Most surveys have specific administrative or commercial purposes. The U.S. Department of Agriculture might survey how poor people use food stamps. An economist might survey income and expenditure patterns. A market research firm might conduct a survey to determine consumers' intention to buy a company's new product. Organizations have information needs that must be satisfied, and surveys are one means of achieving them.

In this chapter you will learn about analysis techniques used in the latter stages of a survey. So many steps are required when conducting a survey that it is easy to underestimate the time and expense needed to complete all the activities. These activities include such tasks as preliminary planning, sample design, sample selection, questionnaire preparation, pretesting field procedures and the questionnaire, hiring and training interviewers, data collection, data processing, data reduction and analysis, and report preparation. The time to complete these activities can range from a month to more than a year.

Some obstacles to successfully completing a survey include (1) failure to use a proper sampling procedure—for example, using a convenience sample rather than a scientific probability design where each individual in the population has a known chance of being in the sample; (2) failure to pretest field procedures and questionnaires; (3) failure to follow up on nonrespondents, which might amount to over 50% of those surveyed; and (4) inadequate quality control at any stage of the study—for example, checks and verification are needed in sample selection, interviewing, editing and coding responses, and analysis methods.

THE CATEGORICAL NATURE OF QUESTIONNAIRE RESPONSES

We begin with the following question and move directly to the analysis of responses.

Q1. Do you feel a desire to be thin?   Yes or No

The response analysis lets you see immediately what and how you can learn about the larger population through survey question sampling. After you have obtained a feel for what can be accomplished with a single question, you can examine larger collections of questions as in questionnaires.

The above question was one of 21 questions used to assess eating behavior. Assessment results are useful in determining whether an individual might have an eating disorder. It is thought that the college environment is particularly difficult for persons with eating disorders.[3]

Because the measurement scale is nominal for categorical variables, the Yes or No responses to questions are assigned arbitrary numbers. Although any two numerical codes will do, a 1 for Yes and a 0 for No is useful because a count of the 1s is the total number of Yes answers. A count of the 0s is the total number of No answers. For our computer processing, a Yes answer has been coded 1 and a No answer has been coded 0.

There are a total of 200 responses to the question, Do you feel a desire to be thin? Only the first 15 and the last 15 responses are shown below for a variable named THIN. All responses can be found in the data file referenced in Appendix 1.

THIN
0 0 0 0 0 0 0 1 0 0 1 0 0 0 0
(first 15 responses)

0 0 0 0 0 0 0 1 0 0 0 0 0 0 0
(last 15 responses)

Of these 30 responses, the counts are 3 Yes's and 27 No's.

EXHIBIT 1 Q1. Responses in Counts and Percents

	THIN	COUNT	PERCENT
No's	0	171	85.50
Yes's	1	29	14.50
	n =	200	total responses

EXHIBIT 2 Q1. Responses in Cumulative Counts and Percents

	THIN	COUNT	PERCENT	CUMCNT	CUMPCT
No's	0	171	85.50	171	85.50
Yes's	1	29	14.50	200	100.00
	n =	200			

Tallying Categorical Data for a Single Variable in Terms of Counts, Percents, Cumulative Counts, and Cumulative Percents

Questionnaires often involve many questions and the survey of hundreds of individuals. As a result, computer analysis is commonplace. As an example, MINITAB results of the TALLY command (see Appendix 1) are shown in Exhibit 1. The column THIN lists the 0 and 1 codes. The column COUNT shows a count of the 1s and 0s of 200 responses. The PERCENT column shows that $\frac{171}{200} = 85.5\%$ answered No and $\frac{29}{200} = 14.5\%$ answered Yes to Do you feel a desire to be thin?

Also useful are cumulative counts and percents, which are shown in Exhibit 2.

Cumulative information becomes more important as the number of categories increase beyond two (for Yes and No responses). Cumulative percent provides a view across all categories whereas percent tends to focus attention on individual categories.

Examination of the TALLY results leads to a **summary statement** such as, "We found that 14.5% of the respondents answered Yes to Do you feel a desire to be thin?"

INFERENCES ABOUT A POPULATION PROPORTION

The **sample proportion**, 14.5% of the respondents, said Yes to Q1. This is an estimate of the unknown **population proportion** who would respond Yes. Both point and interval estimators are available for population proportions.

A Point Estimate, p̂, of the Population Proportion, p

The proportion in the sample of 200 who responded Yes to question Q1 is

$$\frac{29}{200} = .145 \ (14.5\%) = \hat{p}$$

The $\hat{p}$ is an estimate of the unknown population proportion, p.

If y is a count of the Yes responses, then

$$\hat{p} = \frac{y}{n}$$

Sample Size Determination   At the outset of an investigation, we don't know $\hat{p}$ or p, but we want to plan for enough responses, n, so that $\hat{p}$ is sufficiently close to p. For large samples, if $\hat{p}$ is standardized by subtracting p and dividing by the standard error

$$\sqrt{\frac{p(1 - p)}{n}}$$

the following ratio can be manipulated for sample size determination:

$$\left[\frac{\hat{p} - p}{\sqrt{\dfrac{p(1 - p)}{n}}} \right]^2 = [z_{(\alpha/2)}]^2$$

By squaring the terms on the left side of the equation, this result is easily solved for n.

$$\left[\frac{(\hat{p} - p)^2}{\dfrac{p(1 - p)}{n}} \right] = [z_{(\alpha/2)}]^2$$

The larger the sample size, the smaller is the standard error of $\hat{p}$. Then $\hat{p}$ tends to be closer to p, which reduces $(\hat{p} - p)^2$.

At the outset of an investigation, we want to solve the above equation for n, but neither p nor $\hat{p}$ are known. Consequently, a preliminary sample or experienced judgment is used to pick a **planning value** for p. Also, the **tolerable amount of error** squared, $(\hat{p} - p)^2$, can be specified by the investigator. The sample size is then determined by solving the above equation for n.

$$n = p(1 - p) \left[\frac{z_{(\alpha/2)}}{\hat{p} - p} \right]^2$$

A relatively small, scientifically selected sample can estimate total population characteristics with a very small margin of error. For example, national attitude and opinion surveys produce reliable estimates with sample sizes of about 2,000 individuals for populations of size, say, 250 million.

An Interval Estimate of the Population Proportion, p

Recall that y is a count of the Yes responses, and

$$\hat{p} = \frac{y}{n}$$

Because y has a binomial probability distribution (see Chapter 4, "The Binomial Distribution (Discrete)"), we know the mean is $E(y) = np$, and the variance is $V(y) = np(1 - p)$. Therefore, the expected value of the sample proportion is $E(\frac{y}{n}) = p$ and $V(\frac{y}{n}) = \frac{np(1-p)}{n^2} = \frac{p(1-p)}{n}$. Recall that the standard deviation is the square root of the variance, and the standard deviation of an estimator is referred to as a standard error.

Because p is unknown, the confidence interval on p is in terms of $\hat{p}$, n, and $z_{\alpha/2}$. The use of $z_{\alpha/2}$ is justified if $\hat{p}$ is normal in distribution, which is true, approximately, when *both* np *and* n(1 − p) *are greater than* 5 (*large sample conditions*).

Infinite Populations   For **infinite populations,** the large-sample confidence interval for p is

$$\hat{p} \pm z_{\alpha/2}\sqrt{\frac{\hat{p}(1 - \hat{p})}{n}}$$

This interval reflects **sampling error** that can be reduced by selecting larger sample sizes.

Nonsampling error is not as easy to estimate or control. Such an error arises from the process of conducting the survey, respondent misunderstanding or inadequacy, and processing errors.

EXAMPLE 1

CONFIDENCE INTERVAL ON THE POPULATION PROPORTION OF YES RESPONSES TO QUESTION Q1

Problem Statement   Construct a 95% confidence interval ($z_{.05/2} = 1.96$) for the population proportion, p, (population proportion of Yes responses to Do you feel a desire to be thin?).

Problem Solution   Recall that $\hat{p} = \frac{29}{200} = .145$, which is substituted in the following equation:

$$\hat{p} \pm z_{\alpha/2}\sqrt{\frac{\hat{p}(1 - \hat{p})}{n}}$$

$$.145 \pm 1.96\sqrt{\frac{.145(1 - .145)}{200}} = .1938 \text{ and } .0962$$

We are 95% confident that the true proportion p is in the interval 9.62% to 19.38%.

Finite Populations   For **finite populations** of size N, the standard error is multiplied by the finite population correction factor

$$\sqrt{\frac{N - n}{N - 1}}$$

producing the following interval:

$$\hat{p} \pm z_{\alpha/2} \sqrt{\frac{N - n}{N - 1}} \sqrt{\frac{\hat{p}(1 - \hat{p})}{n}}$$

S T A T I S T I C A L   H I G H L I G H T S

A sample proportion and the sample size can be used to find a confidence interval on the unknown population proportion.

HYPOTHESIS TESTS ABOUT A POPULATION PROPORTION

Confidence intervals, as well as ratio statistics, can be used to test hypotheses about population proportions.

A Two-Sided Test Using a Confidence Interval

In the previous section, a 95% confidence interval on p, the population proportion, p (Yes to Do you feel a desire to be thin?), extended from .0962 to .1938. Therefore, we *cannot reject* the hypothesis that p equals $\hat{p}$ = .145. The data would support the null hypothesis, p = .145.

Usually the null hypothesis is that p is a value other than $\hat{p}$. Then to use a confidence interval for hypothesis testing, you must recompute the confidence interval, using p under the square root sign in the standard error part of the following expression:

$$\hat{p} \pm z_{\alpha/2} \sqrt{\frac{p(1 - p)}{n}}$$

We refer to this interval as a **recomputed interval,** which is based on the value of p in the null hypothesis.

Rule for the Not Equal Alternative Hypothesis   If the value of p in the null hypothesis falls outside the recomputed interval, reject the null hypothesis in favor of the alternative.

In general, hypothesis testing enables us to evaluate alternative propositions as to what value the population proportion might equal. Such evaluations are conducted in a manner that minimizes the risk of being wrong.

EXAMPLE 2

HYPOTHESIS TEST ON THE POPULATION PROPORTION OF YES RESPONSES TO THE QUESTION Q1

Problem Statement   Test the null hypothesis, H_n, that the population proportion $p = .20$ for those who would respond Yes to question Q1. The alternative hypothesis is $H_a: p \neq .20$. The alpha error is .05.

Problem Solution   The recomputed interval, based on $p = .20$, is

$$.145 \pm 1.96 \sqrt{\frac{.20(1 - .20)}{200}} = .0896 \text{ and } .2004$$

Although we are very close to rejecting the null hypothesis, we cannot reject that $p = .20$ based on the data at hand. The value $p = .20$ falls within the region where we are confident that the unknown population proportion is located.

A Two-Sided Test Using a Ratio Test Statistic

An alternative way to test the null hypothesis is to form a test statistic and compare it to a critical value. The particular value of p specified in the null hypothesis is used in computing the test statistic.

$$\text{test statistic} \qquad \text{critical value}$$

$$\left| \frac{\hat{p} - p}{\sqrt{\frac{p(1 - p)}{n}}} \right| > z_{(\alpha/2)}$$

Rule for the Not Equal Alternative   If the test statistic exceeds the critical value, reject the null hypothesis. This rejection means that the data support the alternative hypothesis that p does not equal the value specified in the null hypothesis.

In the previous example, the null hypothesis was $H_n: p = .20$. The alternative hypothesis was $H_a: p \neq .20$. Because of the $\neq$ (not equal sign), possible alternatives to $p = .20$ include values of p that are greater than or less than .20. Therefore, this testing situation is said to be **two-sided.** In the two-sided case, the alternative values for p can be on either side of .20, above or below.

For the two-sided test, the probability of a false rejection of the null hypothesis is α, with $\frac{\alpha}{2}$ of the probability in each tail of the normal distribution.

One-Sided Hypothesis Tests

Sometimes hypothesis tests are **one-sided.** For example, suppose H_n: $p = .20$ versus the alternative hypothesis, H_a: $p < .20$. This one-sided alternative is in contrast to the two-sided alternative hypothesis, H_a: $p \neq .20$.

For the **one-sided test,** the probability of a false rejection of the null hypothesis is still α. However, because the alternative hypothesis refers to one side of the probability distribution, α and not $\frac{\alpha}{2}$ of the probability is in each tail of the normal distribution. As a consequence, the interval for a one-sided test uses a z value with a subscript α (not $\frac{\alpha}{2}$).

$$\hat{p} \pm z_\alpha \sqrt{\frac{p(1 - p)}{n}}$$

The interval for a one-sided test is narrower than that of a two-sided test. As an example, for the less than alternative hypothesis H_a: $p < .20$, *reject* the null hypothesis when the particular value of p in the null hypothesis is *to the right of* the interval. Similar reasoning applies for the alternative hypothesis H_a: $p > .20$. In this case, *reject* the null hypothesis when the particular value of p in the null hypothesis is *to the left of* the interval.

The ratio form of the test also applies to one-sided alternatives. As before, form the following test statistic, where the value of p is obtained from the null hypothesis and α replaces $\frac{\alpha}{2}$.

Rule for the Greater Than Alternative

test statistic	critical value
$\left(\left\| \dfrac{\hat{p} - p}{\sqrt{\dfrac{p(1 - p)}{n}}} \right\| \right)$ is compared to	$z_{(\alpha)}$

If the test statistic exceeds the critical value, reject the null hypothesis that H_n: $p = $ (the particular value in the test statistic computation) in favor of the alternative H_a: $p > $ (the particular value in the test statistic computation).

Rule for the Less Than Alternative

test statistic	critical value
$\left(\left\| \dfrac{\hat{p} - p}{\sqrt{\dfrac{p(1 - p)}{n}}} \right\| \right)$ is compared to	$-z_{(\alpha)}$

If the test statistic is less than the critical value, reject the null hypothesis that $H_n: p = $ (the particular value in the test statistic computation) in favor of the alternative $H_a: p < $ (the particular value in the test statistic computation).

> ## S T A T I S T I C A L   H I G H L I G H T S
>
> For large samples, the standardized difference between the sample proportion and the population proportion in the null hypotheses follows a normal distribution. Therefore, for testing hypotheses, ratio test statistics are compared to critical values from the normal distribution.

INFERENCES ABOUT DIFFERENCES IN POPULATION PROPORTIONS

We have been discussing a single survey of 200 responses to question Q1. Now we conduct this survey at a second location where 300 additional responses are obtained. For the two surveys, there are $n_1 = 200$ and $n_2 = 300$ responses. Suppose the n_1 responses were gathered in New York State and the n_2 responses were gathered in California. We want to compare the New York proportion of Yes responses with the California proportion. In this case, the proportions are from two *independent* samples. This is a requirement that must be satisfied for the following confidence interval and hypothesis test for differences in two population proportions:

$$(p_1 - p_2)$$

A large sample confidence interval for the differences in independent population proportions is

$$(\hat{p}_1 - \hat{p}_2) \pm z_{\alpha/2} \sqrt{\frac{\hat{p}_1(1 - \hat{p}_1)}{n_1} + \frac{\hat{p}_2(1 - \hat{p}_2)}{n_2}}$$

This interval formula is similar in structure to that for a single proportion except for modifications that account for differences in proportions.

The null hypothesis,

$$(p_1 - p_2) = 0$$

specifies that there is no difference in population proportions. The alternative hypothesis is that there is a non zero difference. The ratio form of the test compares the following test statistic and critical value:

test statistic	**critical value**
$\dfrac{(\hat{p}_1 - \hat{p}_2) - (p_1 - p_2 = 0)}{\sqrt{\dfrac{\hat{p}_1(1 - \hat{p}_1)}{n_1} + \dfrac{\hat{p}_2(1 - \hat{p}_2)}{n_2}}} \quad >$	$z_{(\alpha/2)}$

Reject the null hypothesis when the test statistic exceeds the critical value.

Comparing Two Proportions from the Same Questionnaire

The response proportions to different questions on the same questionnaire are often compared. This enables the investigator to examine related questions that provide more information about how the responder is thinking about different aspects of what is being studied. Unfortunately, the formulas shown above do not apply when comparing proportions within the same questionnaire when such proportions are *dependent*. Dependence exists because closely related questions tend to produce the same responses. For example, two closely related questions from the same survey are

Q1. Do you feel a desire to be thin?   Yes or No

Q2. Do you feel societal pressures to be thin?   Yes or No

Question Q2 attempts to identify the source of feelings whereas question Q1 simply queries the existence of a feeling. The response proportions would be dependent when a Yes answer to Q1 tends to produce a Yes answer to Q2.

When comparing the questions, it is easy to wrongly analyze the data by assuming that the proportions are independent and by using the standard formulas for comparing proportions. Dependent proportions complicate the analysis. Wild and Seber derived and illustrated confidence intervals for dependent proportions.[4] Based on 1,000 telephone poll responses of Yes or No answers, they examined the following closely related questions:

Q1. Should Iraq be forced to leave Kuwait?   Yes or No

Q2. Should Iraq's nuclear and chemical war capabilities
be destroyed?   Yes or No

A conservative interval on the difference in dependent proportions is

$$(\hat{p}_1 - \hat{p}_2) \pm z_{\alpha/2} \sqrt{\frac{\{\min(\hat{p}_1 + \hat{p}_2, \hat{q}_1 + \hat{q}_2) - (\hat{p}_1 - \hat{p}_2)^2\}}{n}}$$

where $\hat{p}_1 = .93$ (93% said Yes to Q1); $\hat{p}_2 = .90$ (90% said Yes to Q2); $(\hat{p}_1 - \hat{p}_2) = .03$; and the $\min(.93 + .90, .07 + .10)$ is $.17$. The resulting interval is $.03 \pm .0255$. The interval does not include 0. Therefore, the hypothesis that the proportions are equal is rejected.

S T A T I S T I C A L   H I G H L I G H T S

Well-known methods for inferences about the differences in population proportions depend on sample proportions from two independent samples. In contrast, closely related questions from the same survey are often dependent and require special and more complicated methods of analysis.

TALLYING CATEGORICAL DATA FOR SEVERAL VARIABLES IN TERMS OF COUNTS, PERCENTS, CUMULATIVE COUNTS, AND CUMULATIVE PERCENTS

So far we have examined one survey question, Q1, or two closely related questions. Now we address several survey questions. Let's consider the following four questions:

Q1. Do you feel a desire to be thin?   Yes or No

Q2. What is your sex?   Male or Female

Q3. How much television do you watch?   Little   Average   A Lot

Q4. What is your height in inches?   _____

Each question results in a column of responses under the variable names: THIN, SEX, TV, and HEIGHT. The numerical codes for responses to the first three questions are Yes (1), No (0); Male (1), Female (0); Little (1), Average (2), A Lot (3). The coding values are arbitrary, so some variety is shown. In Q4, height is a quantitative variable, which is measured on a ratio scale. There are 200 responses to each question from 200 individuals. Each individual's four responses form a row of coded response values. Only part of the data set is shown in Exhibit 3, which is for the first 10, middle 10, and last 10 individuals. Each row is a set of answers for one respondent.

Recall that when the variable THIN was first examined, the TALLY command was used to obtain counts and percents of Yes and No responses. Both categorical variables TV and SEX are also summarized this way. In Exhibit 4, the variable TV has three response categories.

The PERCENT figures are relative frequencies that can be plotted to approximate the probability distribution as shown in Exhibit 5. A plot of the cumulative relative frequencies, CUMPCT, approximate the distribution function. Vertical lines can be drawn to the plotted points. These lines are like the spikes on a discrete probability distribution.

For cumulative percents, the plotted points form a staircase that approximates the discrete distribution function as shown in Exhibit 6.

Similarly, the responses to Q2 are tabulated in Exhibit 7.

Finally, all categorical variables are TALLIED simultaneously and counts are displayed in Exhibit 8. Percents and cumulative percents are also available through various MINITAB subcommands.

EXHIBIT 3 Responses to Questions Q1, Q2, Q3, and Q4

Question (1)	(2)	(3)	(4)	
ROW THIN	SEX	TV	HEIGHT	
1 0	0	3	69	(first respondent)
2 0	0	2	63	(second respondent)
3 0	0	1	66	(etc.)
4 0	0	2	61	
5 0	0	1	69	
6 0	0	2	63	
7 0	0	2	62	
8 1	0	1	63	
9 0	0	3	66	
10 0	0	3	66	
96 0	0	2	67	
97 1	0	1	64	
98 0	0	3	67	
99 0	0	3	64	
100 0	0	1	67	
101 0	1	2	74	
102 0	1	2	72	
103 0	1	2	67	
104 0	1	1	73	
105 1	1	1	70	
191 0	1	3	73	
192 0	1	3	73	
193 1	1	1	76	
194 0	1	3	72	
195 0	1	3	69	
196 0	1	2	67	
197 0	1	1	71	
198 0	1	3	72	
199 0	1	2	69	
200 0	1	3	72	(last respondent)

EXHIBIT 4 Q3. Responses in Percents and Cumulative Percents for Categories

TV	PERCENT		CUMPCT
1	31.00	(watches a little television)	31.00
2	27.50	(average amount of watching)	58.50
3	41.50	(watches a lot of television)	100.00

EXHIBIT 5 Percents (Relative Frequencies) versus Response Categories

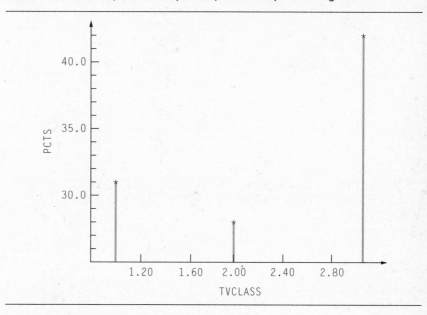

EXHIBIT 6 Cumulative Percents versus Response Categories

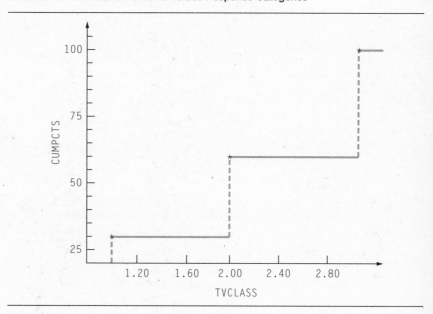

EXHIBIT 7 Q2. Responses in Counts and Percents

Sex	Count	Percent
0	100	50.00
1	100	50.00
n = 200		

EXHIBIT 8 Q1, Q2, and Q3 Responses in Counts

THIN	COUNT	SEX	COUNT	TV	COUNT
0	171	0	100	1	62
1	29	1	100	2	55
n = 200		n = 200		3	83
				n = 200	

PAIRS OF CATEGORICAL VARIABLES ORGANIZED IN TWO-WAY TABLES WITH COUNTS AND WITH ROW, COLUMN, AND CELL PERCENTS

After examining the responses to individual questions, pairs of questions can be examined jointly in two-way tables. Similarities or differences in responses to two questions within the same survey are exhibited in such displays. These two-way tables are called **contingency tables** when they contain counts. As an example, for the following pair of questions:

Q1. Do you feel a desire to be thin? Yes or No

Q2. What is your sex? Male or Female

the contingency table is shown in Exhibit 9.

Statistical packages make it easy to construct and analyze two-way tables. For the two questions above, the analysis determines if a desire to be thin is independent of gender.

The contingency table in Exhibit 9 displays table *cell counts:* 83 females responded No; 88 males responded No; 17 females and 12 males responded Yes. Marginal counts and totals are shown bordering the cells on the right and bottom.

In Exhibit 10, counts are converted to percents of various totals by using MINITAB subcommands. For example, $\frac{83}{171} = 48.54\%$ of all No's were

EXHIBIT 9 A Contingency Table of Response Counts for Q1 and Q2

	COLUMNS: THIN			
	NO	YES		
ROWS: SEX	0	1	ALL	
0	83	17	100	(females)
1	88	12	100	(males)
ALL	171	29	200	(total)

EXHIBIT 10 Contingency Table Counts Converted to Percents

```
      COLUMNS: THIN
ROWS: SEX  0         1      ALL
Females   NO       YES
   0   83.00    17.00  100.00  (count as percent of row total)
       48.54    58.62   50.00  (count as percent of column total)
       41.50     8.50   50.00  (count as percent of grand total)

Males     NO       YES
   1   88.00    12.00  100.00
       51.46    41.38   50.00
       44.00     6.00   50.00
```

females. These percents enable the data analyst to examine details of interest. In the Yes category, 58.62% of all Yes's were female. This could lead to the conclusion that females are more concerned about being thin than are men.

Chi-Square Test for Independence of Row and Column Variables

A **chi-square test** indicates whether or not the row and column variables in a contingency table are independent. In other words, it indicates whether the responses to two different questions on the same survey are unrelated (independent) or related (dependent). In this case, the preliminary analysis of table counts and various percentages lead to the investigative question, Is the desire to be thin independent of gender?

The TABLE 'SEX' 'THIN' command with a CHISQUARE subcommand in MINITAB produces a two-way contingency table with two values for each cell, **actual cell count** and **expected cell count.** This is shown in Exhibit 11.

EXHIBIT 11 Contingency Table Counts and Percents for Q1 and Q2

```
           COLUMNS: THIN
               0        1
ROWS: SEX     NO      YES
     0   83       17 (actual cell counts females)
        85.50    14.50 (expected cell counts females)

     1   88       12 (actual cell counts males)
        85.50    14.50 (expected cell counts males)
```

Independence of the row and column questions is assumed for the expected cell count computations. The expected cell count must be *five or more* to satisfy the large-sample size requirement.

For the chi-square test, MINITAB computes the following ratio for each cell, which is

$$\frac{(\text{actual cell count} - \text{expected cell count})^2}{\text{expected cell count}}$$

Then these ratios are summed over all cells.

Computational Details for Expected Cell Counts   The expected cell count is computed under the assumption that row and column variables are independent. In order to understand the computational details, let

$$y_{ij} = \text{actual cell count for row i and column j}$$
$$y_{i.row} = \text{actual count for row i, a row total}$$
$$y_{col.j} = \text{actual count for column j, a column total}$$
$$n = \text{total counts in all cells}$$
$$E_{ij} = \text{expected cell count for row i and column j}$$

Then the expected cell count is the following product:

$$E_{ij} = \left(\frac{y_{i.row}}{n}\right)\left(\frac{y_{col.j}}{n}\right)(n)$$

Under the independence assumption, the first two terms on the right, $(y_{i.row}/n)(y_{col.j}/n)$, estimate the probability that an observation falls in a row and column intersection (a cell). This probability estimate is multiplied by n to produce an expected value.

Chi-Square Statistic   The sum of

$$\frac{(\text{actual cell count} - \text{expected cell count})^2}{\text{expected cell count}}$$

over all cells is a **chi-square statistic.** In the contingency table for the variables THIN and SEX, the chi-square statistic is

$$\text{CHI-SQUARE} = 1.008 \text{ WITH D.F.} = 1$$

Critical Chi-Square Value   The **critical chi-square values** are found in Table 3 of Appendix A at the end of this book. The degrees of freedom specify a table row, the significance level specifies a table column, and the critical chi-square value is at the row and column intersection.

The degrees of freedom are based on the size of the contingency table and equal (the number of categories for the row variable minus one) $\times$ (the number of categories for the column variable minus one). In the contingency table for the variables SEX and THIN, there are two rows and two columns. Therefore, the degrees of freedom equal $(2 - 1) \times (2 - 1) = 1$. For one degree of freedom and a significance level of $\alpha = .05$, the critical chi-square value is $\chi^2_{\alpha=.05, df=1} = 3.84146$.

Comparing the Chi-Square Statistic and the Critical Value   The CHI-SQUARE statistic (calculated from the contingency table) is compared to the critical chi-square value to test for the independence of row and column variables in a contingency table. If the test statistic exceeds the critical value

test statistic   **critical value**

CHI-SQUARE (statistic from the two-way table) $>$ $\chi^2_{\alpha, df}$

reject the hypothesis that the row and column variables are independent.

For example, if the categorical variables SEX and THIN are independent, the CHI-SQUARE statistic will be less than the critical value $\chi^2_{\alpha, df}$.

EXAMPLE 3

TEST RESULT, DESIRE TO BE THIN INDEPENDENT OF GENDER

Problem Statement   Is the desire to be thin independent of gender?

Problem Solution   The chi-square statistic 1.008 *is not* $> \chi^2_{\alpha=.05, df=1} = 3.84146$. Conclude from these data that the desire to be thin is independent of gender.

EXAMPLE 4

ILLUSTRATION OF A CONTRASTING SITUATION WHERE DESIRE
TO BE THIN IS GENDER DEPENDENT

Problem Statement   Suppose the counts were different from those shown above with more of a difference between men and women. For example

Rows:	Sex	Columns: Thin		
		No	Yes	
		0	1	ALL
	0	80	20	100 (females)
	1	91	9	100 (males)
	ALL	171	29	200 (total)

Notice that the margins of the table have been kept the same, but the actual internal cell counts have changed (in a way that keeps the expected cell counts the same). Examine this two-way table of counts that leads to the opposite conclusion, which is that the desire to be thin is gender dependent.

Problem Solution   Now the results are different. The CHI-SQUARE (statistic from the two-way table) 4.88 *is* $> \chi^2_{\alpha=.05,\,df=1} = 3.84146$. Conclude from these data that the desire to be thin is gender dependent.

EXAMPLE 5

IS THE DESIRE TO BE THIN INDEPENDENT OF THE AMOUNT OF TELEVISION WATCHED?

Problem Statement   Consider another pair of questions in the following questionnaire:

Q1. Do you feel a desire to be thin?   Yes or No

Q3. How much television do you watch?   Little   Average   A Lot

Problem Solution   From the commands in Appendix 1, MINITAB produces the following CHI-SQUARE statistic:

```
ROWS: TV    COLUMNS: THIN
CHI-SQUARE = 1.098  WITH D.F. = 2
```

The degrees of freedom are equal to (the number of categories for the row variable, TV, minus one) $\times$ (the number of categories for the column variable, THIN, minus one). This is

$$(3 - 1) \times (2 - 1) = 2$$

The CHI-SQUARE (statistic from the two-way table) 1.098 *is not* $> \chi^2_{\alpha=.05,\,df=2} = 5.99147$. Conclude from these data that the desire to be thin is independent of the amount of television watched.

> ### STATISTICAL HIGHLIGHTS
> Use contingency tables and chi-square tests to relate response counts to two categorical variables.

TABLES FOR THREE CATEGORICAL VARIABLES

Although much can be learned from survey data by examining pairs of variables in two-way tables, sometimes the investigator wants to examine pairs of variables for each category of a third categorical variable. MINITAB refers to the third variable as a **control.** Using this approach, tables of response counts are produced for questions Q1 and Q2 while using Q3 as a control.

Q1. Do you feel a desire to be thin?   Yes or No

Q2. What is your sex?   Male or Female

Q3. How much television do you watch?   Little   Average   A Lot

The results of three-variable analysis is interesting and informative when the variables show considerable dependence. Then the two-way tables are considerably different from one another. In Exhibit 12, such dependence was not found in the responses.

A wide variety of subcommands are available in MINITAB for computing various percents and chi-square statistics associated with each of the tables shown above. Some of these are included in the commands shown in the Appendix 1.

EXHIBIT 12 Contingency Tables of Counts for Q1 and Q2 with Q3 As a Control

```
        CONTROL: TV =  1 (little television watched)

    ROWS: SEX      COLUMNS: THIN

               0        1       ALL

              NO       YES

     0        24        6      30 (females)
     1        27        5      32 (males)
    ALL       51       11      62 (total)

CONTROL: TV =  2 (average television watched)

    ROWS: SEX     COLUMNS: THIN

               0        1      ALL

              NO       YES

     0        22        4      26 (females)
     1        27        2      29 (males)
    ALL       49        6      55 (total)

CONTROL: TV =  3 (a lot of television watched)

    ROWS: SEX     COLUMNS: THIN

               0        1      ALL

              NO       YES

     0        37        7      44 (females)
     1        34        5      39 (males)
    ALL       71       12      83 (total)
```

AUGMENTING TABLES WITH SUMMARY STATISTICS ON OTHER BACKGROUND QUANTITATIVE VARIABLES

Questionnaires typically include quantitative as well as qualitative responses. Qualitative categorical responses have been examined for the first three questions below. Now we will look at question Q4, which has a quantitative response, and show how to augment the two-way table of the categorical variables SEX and THIN (questions Q1 and Q2) with information on the quantitative variable HEIGHT (question Q4).

Q1. Do you feel a desire to be thin?   Yes or No

Q2. What is your sex?   Male or Female

Q3. How much television do you watch?   Little   Average   A Lot

Q4. What is your height in inches?   _____

In Exhibit 13, the No and Yes responses are expressed as a percentage of all 200 responses. Directly below the percentages are the mean heights, which are computed from the quantitative responses to Q4. This is done separately for females and males because the row variable is associated with Q2.

In the Exhibit 13 table, counts of Yes and No responses are expressed as a percentage of all 200 responses. The percent calculations illustrate an option in the output computations, which is envoked by a MINITAB subcommand. In addition, mean heights were computed for males and females. It was found that females responding Yes to question Q1 tended to be about an inch shorter than females responding No. Males responding Yes to question Q1 tended to be about an inch taller than males responding No.

EXHIBIT 13 Tables of Percents for Q1 and Q2 Augmented by Mean Height from Q4

ROWS:	SEX	COLUMNS:	THIN	
	0	1	ALL	
	NO	YES		
0	41.50	8.50	50.00	(percent of all 200 responses)
	65.38	64.48		(mean height females)
	NO	YES		
1	44.00	6.00	50.00	(percent of all 200 responses)
	70.54	71.16		(mean height males)

GOODNESS OF FIT TESTS

An extension and alternative to hypothesis tests on proportions is the **goodness of fit test.** A goodness of fit test compares the distribution of sample data to a probability distribution thought to have generated the data. The goodness of fit test determines if the fit is good or not. For example, a binomial distribution with p $=$ .5 is thought to fit the sample distribution of heads and tails in flipping a fair coin. If the coin is loaded (not fair), a goodness of fit test can alert us that p $\neq$ .5.

Examples of goodness of fit tests are given for the binomial, multinomial, and normal distributions. The binomial and multinomial are discrete distributions and the normal is continuous.

Binomial Populations

The binomial distribution fits situations with two mutually exclusive outcomes where the probability of a specific outcome is constant from trial to trial and the trials are independent.

EXAMPLE 6

MOTOR PROTECTORS

Motor protectors shut off the current to motor coils to prevent overheating. Historically, a certain production facility has had an 8% defective rate on motor protectors. Recently, changes in management and suppliers have occurred. Of the last 100 protectors produced, 14 have been defective. Management is wondering if the population fraction defective rate has remained at p $=$ .08, or if this should be regarded as an alarm requiring immediate corrective action.

In other words, does a binomial distribution with p $=$ .08 still provide a good fit to the recently observed data?

Problem Statement (a)   First test the null hypothesis that p $=$ .08 against the not equal alternative. With an alpha error of .05, use the familiar ratio form of a hypothesis test on a single population proportion. In problem solution (b), the same conclusion results from a goodness of fit test.

Problem Solution (a)   In the following computation, the ratio test statistic exceeds the critical value and leads to the rejection of the null hypothesis.

$$\textbf{test statistic} \qquad\qquad \textbf{critical value}$$

$$\frac{\hat{p} - p}{\sqrt{\dfrac{p(1 - p)}{n}}} \qquad > \qquad z_{(\alpha/2)}$$

$$\left(\left| \frac{.14 - .08}{\sqrt{\dfrac{.08(1 - .08)}{100}}} \right| = 2.2116 \right) > \quad 1.96$$

Problem Statement (b)   Show that a chi-square goodness of fit test leads to the same conclusion as problem solution (a).

Problem Solution (b)   In order to compute the chi-square statistic, let

$y_1 = 14$, the actual count of defectives

$y_2 = 86$, the actual count of nondefectives

$E_1 = np = 100(.08) = 8$, the expected number of defectives

$E_2 = n(1 - p) = 100(1 - .08) = 92$, the expected number of nondefectives

These figures form a contingency table row with two columns.

Defective	Nondefective
14	86

For each row cell, the following ratio is computed:

$$\frac{(\text{actual count} - \text{expected count})^2}{\text{expected count}}$$

The sum of these ratios across all cells is the chi-square statistic for goodness of fit.

$$\frac{\Sigma\,(y_i - E_i)^2}{E_i}$$

By substituting actual and expected cell counts, the following chi-square statistic is found:

$$\frac{\Sigma\,(y_i - E_i)^2}{E_i} = \frac{(14 - 8)^2}{8} + \frac{(86 - 92)^2}{92} = 4.8913$$

The expected cell count must be five or more to satisfy the large-sample size requirement. The chi-square statistic exceeds the critical value.

$$\textbf{test statistic} \qquad \textbf{critical value}$$
$$4.8913 \quad > \chi^2_{\alpha=.05,df=1} = 3.84146$$

Therefore, conclude that a binomial distribution with $p = .08$ *does not* provide a good fit to the recently observed data. Management is alerted that the population fraction defective has not remained at $p = .08$. The sample fraction, $\frac{y}{n} = \frac{14}{100}$, should be regarded as an alarm, and corrective action needs to be taken.

Equivalent Tests on a Population Proportion (Optional)

Example 6 illustrated two equivalent hypothesis tests on a single population proportion. Here we show that these two tests are algebraically the same.

The equation for the ratio form of a hypothesis test on a single population proportion is shown below. Both sides of the equation are squared, which leads to the equivalent chi-square goodness of fit test. The z^2 is a chi-square variate indexed by one degree of freedom and α rather than $\frac{\alpha}{2}$. The squaring of both sides of the original equation makes any negative values become positive. Therefore, the alpha error is on one side of the chi-square distribution.

test statistic critical value

$$\left(\frac{\hat{p} - p}{\sqrt{\dfrac{p(1 - p)}{n}}}\right)^2 > z^2_{(\alpha/2)}$$

$$\frac{(\hat{p} - p)^2}{\dfrac{p(1 - p)}{n}} > z^2_{(\alpha/2)} = \chi^2_{\alpha}$$

$$\frac{(n\hat{p} - np)^2}{np(1 - p)} > z^2_{(\alpha/2)} = \chi^2_{\alpha}$$

In the numerator on the left side of the equation, notice that

$$(n\hat{p} - np)^2 = \left(n\left(\frac{y}{n}\right) - np\right)^2 = (y - np)^2$$

This result

$$(\text{actual count} - \text{expected count based on } p)^2$$

is a component in the numerator of a chi-square goodness of fit test. Dividing by $np(1 - p)$, produces

$$\frac{(y - np)^2}{np(1 - p)} = \left[\frac{(y - np)^2}{np}\right] + \left[\frac{((n - y) - n(1 - p))^2}{n(1 - p)}\right]$$

The two pieces on the right side of this equation are each cornerstones in chi-square statistic calculations for contingency tables and goodness of fit tests. Both pieces are of the form

$$\frac{(\text{actual count} - \text{expected count})^2}{\text{expected count}}$$

where actual count is y first then $(n - y)$ second, and expected count is based on p first and $(1 - p)$ second. In the next section, you will see that p is referred to as p_1 and $(1 - p)$ is referred to as p_2.

Multinomial Populations

For a binomial distribution, the random variable designates two categories. The **multinomial distribution** is an extension of the binomial distribution for many categories. Your familiarity with the binomial distribution eases the transition to the multinomial distribution. However, there are slight notational changes. For example, when producing n items, the binomial probability of getting exactly y defectives and $(n - y)$ nondefectives is written

$$P(y) = \binom{n}{y} p^y (1 - p)^{(n-y)}$$

By changing the notation slightly, this equation can be written to resemble the multinomial distribution. Let y_1 = the count of defectives; y_2 = the count of nondefectives; $p = p_1$; and $(1 - p) = p_2$. With this notation, the binomial distribution can be written as

$$P(y_1, y_2) = \frac{n!}{y_1! \, y_2!} p_1^{y_1} (p_2)^{y_2}$$

This is the probability of getting exactly y_1 defectives and y_2 nondefectives from n items. Equipped with this notational change, you can see that the multinomial distribution for three classes is a simple extension.

$$P(y_1, y_2, y_3) = \frac{n!}{y_1! \, y_2! \, y_3!} p_1^{y_1} p_2^{y_2} p_3^{y_3}$$

This is the probability of getting exactly y_1 items in category one, y_2 items in category two, and y_3 items in category three from n items. The extension to more classes is obvious.

The advantage of the chi-square goodness of fit test over hypothesis testing with proportions is that the goodness of fit approach, like the multinomial distribution, is more general. Thus, it can be applied to a wider variety of situations, as illustrated in the following examples.

EXAMPLE 7

FINISHED PRODUCTS

Problem Statement   In some manufacturing processes, finished products are classified as good (ready for sale), nonrepairable (scrapped), and repairable (reworked to make good). This example is a conceptual extension of Example 6. Instead of two classes (defective and nondefective), here we consider three classes (good, nonrepairable, and repairable).

Suppose a manufacturing process has historical rates of $p_1 = .85$ (good), $p_2 = .05$ (nonrepairable), and $p_3 = .10$ (repairable). Recent production of 200 products resulted in counts of $y_1 = 160$ (good), $y_2 = 10$ (nonrepairable), and $y_3 = 30$ (repairable). Considering the recent data, is a multinomial distribution with $p_1 = .85$, $p_2 = .05$, and $p_3 = .10$ a good fit (theoretical description) of the results of the manufacturing process? Test the null hypothesis that $p_1 = .85$, $p_2 = .05$, and $p_3 = .10$.

Problem Solution   A chi-square test is appropriate. Therefore

$$\text{CHI-SQUARE (statistic for goodness of fit)} = \frac{\Sigma \, (y_i - E_i)^2}{E_i}$$

Recall that $E_i = np_i$. Therefore, $E_1 = 200(.85)$, $E_2 = 200(.05)$, and $E_3 = 200(.10)$. Also, $y_1 = 160$, $y_2 = 10$, and $y_3 = 30$. By substituting these figures in the chi-square statistic formula shown above, the result is

$$\frac{(160 - 170)^2}{170} + \frac{(10 - 10)^2}{10} + \frac{(30 - 20)^2}{20} = 5.5882$$

The expected cell count must be five or more to satisfy the large-sample size requirement.
These calculations were made in MINITAB (commands are shown in Appendix 1). The critical chi-square value can be obtained from Table 3, in Appendix A or by using the MINITAB command below.

```
MTB > INVCDF .95;  # ALPHA = (1-.95)
SUBC> CHISQUARE V=2.  # TWO DEGREES OF FREEDOM

#  5.9915  CRITICAL CHI-SQUARE VALUE
```

The chi-square goodness of fit statistic is compared to the critical value.

chi-square statistic   **critical value**

5.5882   is not $> \chi^2_{\alpha=.05, \, df=2.} = 5.9915$

Because the test statistic is less than the critical value, conclude that a multinomial distribution with $p_1 = .85$, $p_2 = .05$, and $p_3 = .10$ *does* provide a good fit to the recently observed production data. Accept the null hypothesis that $p_1 = .85$, $p_2 = .05$, and $p_3 = .10$.

Another Binomial Population

A traditionally important aspect of quality control is the inspection of a manufactured product. Finished products with unwanted attributes are deemed defective (nonconforming or bad). These products are repaired, removed from shipment, or sold as seconds. A carton of eggs is considered in the following example. A bad egg might be nonconforming because of a cracked or dirty shell. Consumers prefer that these defective eggs be replaced.

From historical data, we can calculate the defective rate, p, the probability that an egg is bad over the long haul. Assume that the supply of eggs is large enough that p is constant. A bad egg is one that has at least one nonconforming attribute. From egg to egg, if p is constant and if the nonconformity of one egg does not depend on another (independence), the binomial distribution tells us the probability of 0, 1, 2, . . . , or 12 bad egg(s) in a carton of 12 eggs. With a chi-square goodness of fit test, we can see if the binomial distribution fits the actual distribution of data values.

EXAMPLE 8

BAD EGGS—QUALITY CONTROL (INSPECTION)

Problem Statement   In theory, the binomial distribution can be used to find the probability of an exact number of bad eggs in a dozen. In practice, suppose 1,000 dozens of eggs have been inspected with the following results:

Number of Bad Eggs	Number of Dozens
Zero	350
One	400
Two	200
Three	40
Four	8
Five	2

There are 12,000 eggs in 1,000 dozens. A total of

$$400 + 400 + 120 + 32 + 10 = 962$$

bad eggs have been found. This provides an estimate of p, which is $\frac{962}{12,000}$. Does a binomial distribution fit these data?

Problem Solution   The chi-square calculations were made in MINITAB. The commands are shown in Appendix 1. Results are shown below.

$$\text{CHI-SQUARE (statistic for goodness of fit)} = \frac{\Sigma (y_i - E_i)^2}{E_i}$$

Column C1 is the possible number of bad eggs in a dozen. C3 is E_i, which is the expected number of dozens (out of a 1,000) that have 0, 1, 2, . . . , or 12 bad eggs. For example, $E_1 = 1,000 \times (P(0))$, $E_2 = 1,000 \times (P(1))$, $E_3 = 1,000 \times (P(2))$, and so on.

```
ROW    C1    C3 = Eᵢ
  1     0    366.868
  2     1    383.686
  3     2    183.918
  4     3     53.430
  5     4     10.477
  6     5      1.461
  7     6      0.149
  8     7      0.011
  9     8      0.001
 10     9      0.000
 11    10      0.000
 12    11      0.000
 13    12      0.000
```

The expected cell count must be five or more to satisfy the large-sample size requirement. For large-sample conditions to apply, the expected number of bad eggs for any value of y in 1,000 dozen must be greater than or equal to 5, which is not the case in rows 6 thru 13 above. To abide by this rule, rows 6 thru 13 were lumped together with row 5, as you can see below.

C4 is y_i, the actual count, number of dozens (of 1,000), in which we found 0, 1, 2, . . . , or 12 bad eggs.

```
ROW   C1   C3 = Eᵢ    C4
 1    0    366.868    350
 2    1    383.686    400
 3    2    183.918    200
 4    3     53.430     40
 5    4     12.099     10
```

$$\text{CHI-SQUARE (for goodness of fit)} = \frac{\Sigma (y_i - E_i)^2}{E_i} = 6.6154$$

The chi-square goodness of fit statistic is compared to the critical value.

chi-square statistic   **critical value**

6.6154   is not $> \chi^2_{\alpha=.05, df=3} = 7.8147$

Because the test statistic does not exceed the critical value, conclude that a binomial distribution *does* provide a good fit to the actual data. The degrees of freedom are $5 - 1 - 1 = 3$, where the additional degree of freedom is lost because the proportion, p, had to be estimated from the data. The estimate of p is $\frac{962}{12,000}$.

Problem Discussion   These calculations were made in MINITAB (commands are shown in Appendix 1). The critical chi-square value can be obtained from Table 3 in Appendix A or by using the MINITAB command below.

```
MTB > INVCDF .95;
SUBC> CHISQUARE V=3.
# 7.8147  CRITICAL CHI-SQUARE VALUE
```

A Normal Population

The chi-square goodness of fit test can be applied to continuous distributions, such as the normal, as well as discrete distributions. A goodness of fit test for the normal distribution is shown in Example 9. For many data analysis situations, simple visual inspections of histograms, dotplots, or probability plots are informal tests for normality that many practitioners find adequate. Nevertheless, the more formal and traditional chi-square goodness of fit test is sometimes needed.

EXAMPLE 9

BURGER WEIGHTS

Problem Statement (a)   Perform a preliminary analysis of the weights of 87 burgers, C1, to see if a normal distribution might be a good fit.

Problem Solution (a)   Both the histogram and the dotplot below suggest that these data might be normally distributed.

```
Histogram of C1   N = 87

Midpoint   Count
   8.5        1   *
   8.6        4   ****
   8.7        4   ****
   8.8        9   *********
   8.9       13   *************
   9.0       12   ************
   9.1       13   *************
   9.2       14   **************
   9.3        7   *******
   9.4        3   ***
   9.5        5   *****
   9.6        0
   9.7        2   **
```

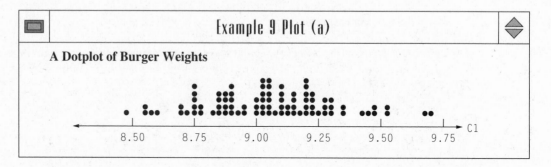

Example 9 Plot (a)

A Dotplot of Burger Weights

Descriptive statistics indicate that these burgers might be called half-pounders because the mean weight is a little over 9 oz. The minimum weight is 8.47 oz and the maximum is 9.71 oz. Theory suggests that nearly all observations from a standard normal will fall between z scores of −4 and +4.

	N	MEAN	MEDIAN	TRMEAN	STDEV	SEMEAN
C1	87	9.0495	9.0500	9.0471	0.2552	0.0274

	MIN	MAX	Q1	Q3
C1	8.4700	9.7100	8.8800	9.2100

Problem Statement (b)   Use a chi-square goodness of fit test to confirm the preliminary impressions.

Problem Solution (b)   To prepare for the calculation of a chi-square statistic, 10 intervals are created based on z scores from -4 to $+4$. The intervals are chosen so that each is expected to contain about 10% of the data values when the data are normally distributed. These intervals are shown below on the z score scale. Because $y = z\sigma + \mu$, these intervals can also be expressed on the scale of the data values. This is accomplished by the command MTB > LET C12 = 9.0495+C11*.2555, where 9.0495 is the mean burger weight and .2555 is the standard deviation. C11 is a column of z scores, and C23 is C11 with the first row deleted. C21 is the same as C12 with the first row deleted.

			Weight(ounces)	
	z_I to z_J		from	to
ROW	C11	C23	C12	C21
1	-4.00	-1.28	8.03	8.72
2	-1.28	-0.84	8.72	8.83
3	-0.84	-0.52	8.83	8.92
4	-0.52	-0.25	8.92	8.99
5	-0.25	0.00	8.99	9.05
6	0.00	0.25	9.05	9.11
7	0.25	0.52	9.11	9.18
8	0.52	0.84	9.18	9.26
9	0.84	1.28	9.26	9.38
10	1.28	4.00	9.38	10.07

From a standard normal distribution, a probability is found that represents the fraction of normally distributed data values expected within an interval. These probabilities are computed for each interval and appear in column C15, which is listed below. A total of 87 burger weights times C15 yields C22, which is the expected number of data values in each interval. C17 resulted from an actual count of the data values in each interval. This count was made from a sorted list of data values shown in the MINITAB appendix.

	Weight(ounces)		Normal	Data Values	
	from	to	Prob.	Expected	Actual
ROW	C12	C21	C15	C22	C17
1	8.03	8.72	0.098294	8.55162	7
2	8.72	8.83	0.096537	8.39871	9
3	8.83	8.92	0.111057	9.66196	13
4	8.92	8.99	0.101901	8.86535	3
5	8.99	9.05	0.092960	8.08751	11
6	9.05	9.11	0.092916	8.08368	9
7	9.11	9.18	0.101754	8.85264	7
8	9.18	9.26	0.099818	8.68416	11
9	9.26	9.38	0.107081	9.31604	9
10	9.38	10.07	0.097618	8.49274	8

The expected cell count must be five or more to satisfy the large sample size requirement.

Columns C22 and C17 were used to compute the following chi-square statistic:

$$\text{CHI-SQUARE (for goodness of fit)} = \frac{\Sigma \, (y_i - E_i)^2}{E_i} = 7.5557$$

The chi-square statistic is compared to the critical value.

chi-square statistic	critical value
7.5557	is not $> \chi^2_{\alpha = .05, df = 7.} = 14.0671$

Because the test statistic does not exceed the critical value, conclude that a normal distribution *does* provide a good fit to the burger weight data. This confirms our preliminary impressions. The degrees of freedom are $10 - 1 - 2 = 7$, where two additional degrees of freedom are lost because the population mean and standard deviation had to be estimated from the data.

STATISTICAL HIGHLIGHTS

A goodness of fit test compares the distribution of sample data to a probability distribution thought to have generated the data.

CHAPTER SUMMARY

This chapter emphasizes the analysis of qualitative categorical data. As an example, responses to questions are categorical. The question Do you feel a desire to be thin? has the answer choices of Yes or No. More than two choices are possible, such as Yes, No, or Sometimes.

Because the measurement scale is nominal for a categorical variable, numerical values for the Yes or No answers are arbitrary, and any two codes will do. However, a 1 for Yes and a 0 for No is often convenient. Tallying categorical responses results in counts that are converted to percents and cumulative percents.

We might compute a point estimate such as $\hat{p}$, the proportion of the sample who respond, say, Yes to a particular question. We discussed confidence intervals and hypothesis tests for proportions and differences in proportions.

After examining how to analyze the responses to single questions, we examined pairs of questions jointly in two-way

tables, which are also called contingency tables for counts. First we examined the following pair of questions:

Q1. Do you feel a desire to be thin?   Yes or No

Q2. What is your sex?   Male or Female

We wanted to know if a desire to be thin is independent of gender and we wanted to do this type of analysis for any pair of variables. A chi-square test for the independence of row and column variables was described.

The flexibility of the chi-square test enabled us to perform goodness of fit tests. We wanted to see if frequency distributions of observed data fit particular theoretical distributions such as the binomial, the multinomial, and the normal.

KEY TERMS

actual cell count, 473	control, 476	goodness of fit test, 479
chi-square statistic, 474	critical chi-square value, 474	infinite populations, 463
chi-square test, 473	expected cell count, 473	multinomial distribution, 482
contingency tables, 472	finite populations, 464	nonsampling error, 463

EXERCISES

1. A telephone survey indicated that 50 of 200 respondents who received free shampoo samples in the mail liked the product enough to seriously consider switching brands.

(a) Estimate the population proportion, p, who would like the shampoo enough to seriously consider switching brands.

(b) Is the sample size large enough to assume that $\hat{p}$ is normally distributed?

(c) Construct a 95% confidence interval on the population proportion, p.

2. At a mall, shoppers are intercepted and questioned to obtain marketing information. Twenty of 100 who were questioned in a preliminary sample said that they were between 15 and 25 years of age and that they were mouthwash users.

(a) Estimate the population proportion, p, of mouthwash users in that age class.

(b) If .20 is used as a planning value for p and the tolerable amount of error, $|(\hat{p} - p)|$, is .02, what sample size is needed for $\hat{p}$ to be sufficiently close to p?

(c) Is the preliminary sample, n = 100, large enough to assume that $\hat{p}$ is normally distributed?

(d) If p = .195, what is the probability that $\hat{p}$ is .20 or greater?

(e) From the preliminary sample, construct a 95% confidence interval on the population proportion, p.

(f) Would you reject the null hypothesis that p = .21 in favor of the alternative that p ≠ .21?

(g) Would you reject the null hypothesis that p = .30 in favor of the alternative that p ≠ .30?

3. A large, nationally representative sample of households participate in mail questionnaires. The households are compensated for agreeing to respond. Corporations use such panels of consumers to gather marketing information. Of 150 responses to a product information questionnaire, 28% said they were satisfied with their personal computer and were not intending to buy a new one during the next year.

(a) Estimate the population proportion, p, who were satisfied with their personal computer and were not intending to buy a new one during the next year.

(b) Is the sample size large enough to assume that $\hat{p}$ is normally distributed?

(c) Construct a 95% confidence interval on the population proportion, p.

4. Readers of *Outdoor Life* magazine were questioned about a plan by the U.S. Fish and Wildlife Service to release wolves into the Yellowstone National Park ecosystem.[5] The question was Do you support the reintroduction of wolves in Yellowstone? Yes or No? The No's totaled 1,933 of 3,000 responses. In spite of this opposition, the U.S. Fish and Wildlife Service management insists that such a plan should be carried out. What do you think?

(a) Estimate the population proportion against the plan.

(b) Construct a 99% confidence interval on the population proportion against the plan.

(c) Do you think that readers of this hunting and fishing magazine are representative of the country as a whole?

5. Shoppers are intercepted at two different malls and questioned to obtain marketing information. If $\hat{p}_1$ = .20, $\hat{p}_2$ = .25, n_1 = 100, and n_2 = 200, construct a 95% confidence interval on the difference in proportions, $(p_1 - p_2)$.

6. Free shampoo samples were mailed to consumers in two different towns. A sample of shampoo recipients were asked during a telephone survey if they liked the product enough to switch brands. The sample proportions of Yes responses were $\hat{p}_1$ = .25, $\hat{p}_2$ = .30, where n_1 = 100 and n_2 = 200. At α = .05, test the null hypothesis that $(p_1 - p_2)$ = 0 against the alternative hypothesis that $(p_1 - p_2) \neq 0$.

7. Sport fishing is a multimillion dollar industry. Fishery management attempts to maintain a natural resource as well as satisfy anglers. Therefore, research on why people fish is important information. Two-hundred responses are available for the following questions about why people fish:

Q1. Do you fish to catch big fish?   Yes or No

Q2. Do you fish to catch a lot of fish?   Yes or No

Q3. Do you fish to be outdoors?   Yes or No

Q4. Do you fish to be alone?   Yes or No

Q5. Do you fish to be with people?   Yes or No

Q6. What is your age?   _____

(a) Verify that the following counts of Yes (1s) or No (0s) responses result in the following percents for Q1:

BIG	Count	Percent
0	161	80.50
1	39	19.50
n = 200		

(b) Estimate the population proportion of anglers who fish to catch big fish.

(c) Construct a 95% confidence interval on the proportion of anglers who fish to catch big fish.

(d) Would you reject the null hypothesis that half of the anglers fish to catch big fish?

(e) If another 200 independent responses to Q1 are available and the sample proportion is .20 for Yes responses, construct a 95% confidence interval on the difference in population proportions.

(f) Is the difference in population proportions in part (e) significantly different from zero?

(g) Construct a 95% confidence interval on the difference in the dependent proportions responding Yes to Q1 and Q2, which are closely related questions on the same survey.

BIG	Count	Percent	LOT	Count	Percent
0	161	80.50	0	168	84.00
1	39	19.50	1	32	16.00
n = 200			n = 200		

(h) By hand, tabulate the following subset of the 200 responses to Q1–Q6. Obtain counts and average the age response.

Row	BIG	LOT	OUTDOORS	ALONE	WITHP	AGE
1	1	1	0	0	0	28
2	0	0	1	0	0	35
3	0	0	1	0	1	42
4	0	0	1	0	0	20
5	0	0	1	0	0	27
6	0	0	1	1	0	34
7	0	0	0	0	1	24

(continued)

Row	BIG	LOT	OUTDOORS	ALONE	WITHP	AGE
8	1	1	1	0	0	31
9	0	0	1	0	0	22
10	0	0	0	0	0	30
11	0	0	1	0	0	24
12	1	0	1	0	0	25
13	0	1	0	0	0	29
14	1	0	1	0	0	29
15	0	0	1	0	0	26
16	0	0	0	0	0	29
17	0	1	1	0	1	31
18	0	1	0	0	1	36
19	0	1	0	1	0	42
20	0	0	1	0	0	24

(i) Verify the following percents for counts of responses to Q3, Q4, and Q5.

OUTDOORS	Count	Percent
0	61	30.50
1	139	69.50
	n = 200	

ALONE	Count	Percent
0	157	78.50
1	43	21.50
	n = 200	

WITHP	Count	Percent
0	135	67.50
1	65	32.50
	n = 200	

(j) Verify that the following actual and expected counts for Q1 and Q2 produce a chi-square statistic of 18.19 with one degree of freedom. Compare this statistic to the critical value of 3.84 at a 5% significance level. Are the responses to Q1 and Q2 independent or dependent?

ROWS: BIG	COLUMNS: LOT		
	0	1	ALL
0	144	17	161 (actual counts)
	135.24	25.76	161.00 (expected counts)
1	24	15	39 (actual counts)
	32.76	6.24	39.00 (expected counts)
ALL	168	32	200

(k) Verify that the following actual and expected counts for Q4 and Q5 produce a chi-square statistic of 26.37 with one degree of freedom. Compare this statistic to the critical value of 3.84 at a 5% significance level. Are the responses to Q4 and Q5 independent or dependent?

ROWS: ALONE	COLUMNS: WITHP		
	0	1	ALL
0	92 105.97	65 51.03	157 157.00
1	43 29.02	0 13.98	43 43.00
ALL	135	65	200

(l) For questions Q4 and Q5, percents and average age (Q6) are tabulated below. It appears that those who answer yes to either question tend to be a few years older than those who answer no. Do you agree with this observation?

ROWS: ALONE	COLUMNS: WITHP		
	0	1	ALL
0	46.000 37.598	32.500 41.415	78.500 (percents) 39.178 (average age)
1	21.500 43.047	— —	21.500 (percents) 43.047 (average age)
ALL	67.500 39.333	32.500 41.415	100.000 (percents) 40.010 (average age)

8. In the manufacture of electronic components for personal computers, a manufacturer had a history of high defective rates with p = .20. Recently, the proportion defective in the production of 300 components was found to be .17.

(a) Test the null hypothesis that p = .20 against the not equal alternative. Use a ratio test approach.

(b) Show that a chi-square goodness of fit test leads to the same conclusion as the ratio test.

9. A manufacturing process produces good, nonrepairable, and repairable subassemblies with historical rates of p_1 = .85, p_2 = .05, and p_3 = .10, respectively. Recent production of 200 subassemblies yielded y_1 = 150 (good), y_2 = 15 (nonrepairable), and y_3 = 35 (repairable). Considering the recent production data, do the historical rates and a multinomial distribution provide a good theoretical description of the production process? Show the appropriate chi-square test results.

10. Suppose 1,000 dozens of eggs have been inspected. The number of dozens with zero bad eggs is 350, with one bad egg is 400, with two bad eggs is 200, with three bad eggs is 40, with four bad eggs is 8, and with five or more bad eggs is 2. Does a binomial distribution with p = .05 provide a good fit to the data? Perform a chi-square goodness of fit test.

11. Certain risky stocks have a 50% chance of yielding a high return. For portfolios of five such stocks, y is the number of stocks yielding a high return; y = 0, 1, 2, 3, 4, or 5.

Of 360 such portfolios, the count, c, falling into each class of y is

y =	0	1	2	3	4	5
c =	10	52	108	113	65	12

Does a binomial distribution with p = .5 fit this data distribution? Base your conclusions on the following analysis:

```
MTB > SET IN C1
DATA> 0 1 2 3 4 5
DATA> END
MTB > SET IN C2
DATA> 10 52 108 113 65 12
DATA> END
MTB > PDF C1 C3;
SUBC> BINOMIAL 5 .5.
MTB > LET C4 = 360*C3
MTB > LET K1 = SUM((C2 - C4)**2/C4)
MTB > CDF K1 K2;
SUBC> CHIS 5.
MTB > LET K3 = 1 - K2
MTB > PRINT C1 C2 C3 C4
```

Row	C1	C2	C3	C4
1	0	10	0.03125	11.25
2	1	52	0.15625	56.25
3	2	108	0.31250	112.50
4	3	113	0.31250	112.50
5	4	65	0.15625	56.25
6	5	12	0.03125	11.25

```
MTB > PRINT K1 K2 K3

K1     2.05333
K2     0.158353
K3     0.841647
```

12. In the following analysis, political ideology is classified as conservative, moderate, or liberal. Party affiliation is classified as democratic, independent, or republican. Of 1,083 voters, counts and expected counts are shown in the following table.[6] Expected counts are printed below observed counts.

Party	Political Ideology			Total
	C1	**C2**	**C3**	
1	100	156	143	399 (observed)
	135.58	161.37	102.05	(expected)
2	141	210	119	470 (observed)
	159.70	190.08	120.21	(expected)
3	127	72	15	214 (observed)
	72.72	86.55	54.73	(expected)
Total	368	438	277	1083

Use a chi-square test to test the hypothesis that political ideology is independent of party affiliation. Base your conclusions on the following analysis:

```
ChiSq =  9.337 +  0.179 + 16.430 +
         2.191 +  2.087 +  0.012 +
        40.523 +  2.446 + 28.846 = 102.049
df = 4, p = 0.000
```

(continued)

(continued)

```
MTB > SET IN C1
DATA> 100 141 127
MTB > SET IN C2
DATA> 156 210 72
DATA> SET IN C3
DATA> 143 119 15
DATA> END
MTB > CHISQUARE C1 C2 C3
MTB > INVCDF .95;
SUBC> CHIS 4.

Chisquare with 4 d.f.
  P( X <= x)            x

   0.9500      9.48773
```

13. Consider four possible management decisions and the extent of the undesirable consequences, which are none, slight, or moderate. Actual (observed) counts of responses to a questionnaire are tabulated in the following table along with expected counts. Expected counts are printed below the observed counts.

Decision	Consequences			Total
	C1	**C2**	**C3**	
1	60	27	7	94
	54.16	27.75	12.09	
2	71	22	14	107
	61.65	31.59	13.76	
3	57	38	15	110
	63.38	32.48	14.14	
4	54	37	18	109
	62.80	32.18	14.01	
Total	242	124	54	420

Are the consequences independent of the four decisions? Base your conclusion on the following analysis.

```
MTB > SET IN C1
DATA> 60 71 57 54
DATA> SET IN C2
DATA> 27 22 38 37
DATA> SET IN C3
DATA> 7 14 15 18
DATA> END
MTB > CHISQUARE C1 C2 C3
```

```
ChiSq =  0.629 +  0.020 +  2.140 +
         1.417 +  2.912 +  0.004 +
         0.642 +  0.940 +  0.052 +
         1.234 +  0.722 +  1.134 = 11.846
df = 6, p = 0.067

MTB > INVCDF .95;
SUBC> CHIS 6.

Chisquare with 6 d.f.

 P( X <= x)           x
    0.9500       12.5916
```

14. In the following analysis, rated performance of radio and TV networks is classified as poor, fair, or good. The race of the raters is classified as white or black. Counts and expected counts are shown in the following table.[7] Expected counts are printed below observed counts.

Race	Rated Performance			Total
	C1	**C2**	**C3**	**Total**
1	158	636	600	1394
	142.05	608.80	643.14	
2	24	144	224	392
	39.95	171.20	180.86	
Total	182	780	824	1786

Are the ratings independent of race? Base your conclusion on the following analysis:

```
MTB > SET IN C1
DATA> 158 24
DATA> SET IN C2
DATA> 636 144
DATA> SET IN C3
DATA> 600 224
DATA> CHISQUARE C1 C2 C3

ChiSq = 1.790 +  1.215 +  2.894 +
        6.366 +  4.321 + 10.292 = 26.878
df = 2, p = 0.000

MTB > CDF .95;
SUBC> CHIS 2.

Chisquare with 2 d.f.

        x      P( X <= x)
    0.9500       0.3781
```

15. Thirty people are asked if they prefer stock A or stock B. Twenty prefer stock B and the rest prefer stock A. Do these results support the hypothesis of equally likely preferences? Base your conclusions on the following analysis:

```
MTB > SET IN C1
DATA> 10 20
DATA> SET IN C2
DATA> 15 15
DATA> LET K1 = SUM((C1 - C2)**2/C2)
MTB > PRINT K1

Data Display

K1        3.33333
MTB > INVCDF .95;
SUBC> CHIS 1.

  P( X <= x)         x
    0.9500        3.8415
```

16. A panel of 160 women was asked to rate two advertisements as a success or failure. Counts and expected counts are shown in the following table. Expected counts are printed below observed counts.

Ad	Success C1	Failure C2	Total
1	40 37.50	80 82.50	120
2	10 12.50	30 27.50	40
Total	50	110	160

Are the advertisements equally effective? Base your conclusion on the following analysis:

```
MTB > SET IN C1
DATA> 40 10
DATA> SET IN C2
DATA> 80 30
DATA> CHISQUARE C1 C2

ChiSq = 0.167 +  0.076 +
        0.500 +  0.227 = 0.970
df = 1, p = 0.325

MTB > INVCDF .95;
SUBC> CHIS 1.

Chisquare with 1 d.f.

  P( X <= x)         x
    0.9500        3.8415
```

17. Two hundred consumers were asked to state their intention to buy two similar products as none, maybe, or for sure. Counts and expected counts are shown in the following table. Expected counts are printed below observed counts.

Product	None C1	Maybe C2	For Sure C3	Total
1	7 3.96	18 13.36	74 81.68	99
2	1 4.04	9 13.64	91 83.32	101
Total	8	27	165	200

Are buying intentions independent of the two products? Base your conclusion on the following analysis:

```
DATA> SET IN C1
DATA> 7 1
DATA> SET IN C2
DATA> 18 9
DATA> SET IN C3
DATA> 74 91
DATA> CHISQUARE C1 C2 C3

ChiSq =  2.334 +  1.607 +  0.721 +
         2.288 +  1.576 +  0.707 = 9.232
df = 2, p = 0.010
2 cells with expected counts less than 5.0

MTB > INVCDF .95;
SUBC> CHIS 2.

Chisquare with 2 d.f.

  P( X <= x)           x

    0.9500         5.9915
```

18. Soft drinks are produced in packages of six cans. It is thought that there is a constant 10% chance of a can being overfilled or underfilled. Such cans are referred to as improperly filled. In the following table, C1 is the possible number of improperly filled cans; C2 is the binomial probabilty corresponding to C1; C3 is C1 × C2, which is the expected number of improperly filled cans of 3,000 six packs; and C4 is the actual number of improperly filled cans of 3,000 six packs.

Row	C1	C2	C3	C4
1	0	0.531441	1594.32	1432
2	1	0.354294	1062.88	1210
3	2	0.098415	295.24	301
4	3	0.014580	43.74	27
5	4	0.001215	3.65	15
6	5	0.000054	0.16	10
7	6	0.000001	0.00	5

From the following analysis, are the actual observations in C4 significantly different from what is expected (C3), which is based on a binomial distribution with p = .10?

```
MTB > SET IN C1
DATA> 0:6
DATA> PDF C1 C2;
SUBC> BINOMIAL 6 .10.
MTB > LET C3 = 3000*C2
MTB > SET IN C4
DATA> 1432 1210 301 27 15 10 5
DATA> LET K1 = SUM ((C4-C3)**2/C3)
MTB > PRINT C1 C2 C3 C4 K1


K1        8999.56

MTB >  INVCDF .99;
SUBC> CHIS 6.

Chisquare with 6 d.f.

 P( X <= x)          x
   0.9900      16.8119
```

19. The market shares for three companies are thought to be 60%, 25%, and 15%, respectively. A panel of 300 consumers reported purchase preferences as 171, 78, and 51, respectively. Does the purchase preference data differ significantly from what is expected based on the assumed market shares? Base your conclusions on the following analysis.

```
MTB > SET IN C1
DATA> .60 .25 .15
DATA> LET C2 = 300*C1
MTB > SET IN C3
DATA> 171 78 51
MTB > LET K1 = SUM ((C3 - C2)**2/C2)
MTB > PRINT C1 C2 C3 K1

K1        1.37000

 Row     C1      C2      C3

   1    0.60     180     171
   2    0.25      75      78
   3    0.15      45      51

MTB > INVCDF .95;
SUBC> CHIS 2.

Chisquare with 2 d.f.

 P( X <= x)          x
   0.9500       5.9915
```

20. Cans of pizza sauce had the following weights in ounces (the data are sorted):

14.63	14.65	14.65	14.66	14.67	14.69	14.69	14.69
14.69	14.69	14.69	14.70	14.70	14.71	14.72	14.72
14.72	14.72	14.73	14.73	14.73	14.73	14.73	14.73
14.73	14.73	14.73	14.74	14.74	14.74	14.75	14.75
14.75	14.75	14.75	14.76	14.76	14.76	14.77	14.77
14.77	14.77	14.77	14.77	14.78	14.78	14.78	14.78
14.78	14.78	14.79	14.79	14.80	14.80	14.80	14.81
14.81	14.81	14.81	14.81	14.82	14.82	14.82	14.82
14.82	14.82	14.83	14.83	14.86			

These weights are available in file PIZZA.MTW. Summary statistics are

Variable	N	Mean	Median	TrMean	StDev	SEMean
C1 (weight)	69	14.753	14.750	14.754	0.051	0.006

Variable	Min	Max	Q1	Q3
C1 (weight)	14.630	14.860	14.720	14.795

The following tabulations are similar to those within the chapter for a chi-square goodness of fit test for the normal distribution. C22 consists of expected counts and C17 contains actual counts.

Row	C11	C23	C12	C21	C15	C22	C17
1	-4.00	-1.28	14.55	14.69	0.108324	7.4743	5
2	-1.28	-0.84	14.69	14.71	0.091216	6.2939	8
3	-0.84	-0.52	14.71	14.73	0.126422	8.7231	5
4	-0.52	-0.25	14.73	14.74	0.073399	5.0645	9
5	-0.25	0.00	14.74	14.75	0.077148	5.3232	3
6	0.00	0.25	14.75	14.77	0.154016	10.6271	8
7	0.25	0.52	14.77	14.78	0.071176	4.9112	6
8	0.52	0.84	14.78	14.80	0.119886	8.2722	8
9	0.84	1.28	14.80	14.82	0.083906	5.7895	8
10	1.28	4.00	14.82	14.96	0.094447	6.5168	9

Verify that the chi-square statistic is 9.6327. Compare it to the chi-square critical value of 14.067 with 7 d.f. and a significance level of .05. Does a normal distribution fit the data?

21. The time between arrivals of parts at an assembly operation had the following values in minutes (the data are sorted):

0.03	0.15	0.16	0.22	0.49	0.49	0.67	0.75
0.78	1.01	1.22	1.29	1.45	1.98	2.11	2.26
2.46	2.49	2.86	3.01	3.12	3.37	3.70	4.46
4.54	4.54	4.69	4.70	4.98	5.81	5.84	6.06
7.08	7.33	7.40	7.83	7.90	8.08	8.12	8.69
8.81	9.07	9.10	9.36	9.92	9.96	10.22	11.08
11.28	11.66	11.89	12.24	12.49	13.90	13.99	14.21
14.71	15.39	15.65	16.10	16.24	16.54	17.03	17.21
17.73	18.21	21.43	22.35	23.69	23.86	26.41	26.70
27.26	28.81	29.88	30.82	32.38	40.85	42.64	60.68

These times are available in file ARVT.MTW. Summary statistics are

```
Variable        N     Mean   Median   TrMean   StDev   SEMean
C1 (time)      80    11.57    8.75    10.40    11.26    1.26

Variable       Min     Max      Q1       Q3
C1 (time)     0.03   60.68    3.04    16.20
```

The following tabulations are similar to those within the chapter for a chi-square goodness of fit test for the normal distribution. C22 consists of expected counts and C17 contains actual counts.

```
Row    C11    C23     C12     C21      C15        C22     C17
  1  -4.00  -1.28  -33.47   -2.84   0.100285   8.02278     0
  2  -1.28  -0.84   -2.84    2.11   0.100098   8.00783    14
  3  -0.84  -0.52    2.11    5.71   0.100969   8.07752    15
  4  -0.52  -0.25    5.71    8.75   0.099739   7.97910    11
  5  -0.25   0.00    8.75   11.57   0.098878   7.91024     9
  6   0.00   0.25   11.57   14.39   0.098878   7.91024     7
  7   0.25   0.52   14.39   17.43   0.099739   7.97910     8
  8   0.52   0.84   17.43   21.03   0.100969   8.07752     2
  9   0.84   1.28   21.03   25.98   0.100098   8.00783     4
 10   1.28   4.00   25.98   56.61   0.100285   8.02278     9
```

Verify that the chi-square statistic is 26.536. Compare it to the chi-square critical value of 14.067 with 7 d.f. and a significance level of .05. Does a normal distribution fit the data?

22. Four brands of bathing suits were sold early, middle, or late in the sales period. The numbers of suits sold as well as the numbers expected are shown below.[8] Expected counts are printed below observed counts.

	Early	Middle	Late	Total
1	81	25	8	114
	60.74	34.57	18.69	
2	17	12	6	35
	18.65	10.61	5.74	
3	25	19	15	59
	31.43	17.89	9.67	
4	7	18	11	36
	19.18	10.92	5.90	
Total	130	74	40	244

```
ChiSq =  6.760 +  2.651 +  6.113 +
         0.146 +  0.181 +  0.012 +
         1.317 +  0.068 +  2.935 +
         7.735 +  4.594 +  4.404 = 36.916

df = 6,  p = 0.000
```

Verify the expected numbers and the chi-square statistic. Compare the chi-square statistic to a critical value to test the hypothesis that brand sales are independent of sales period.

23. Observed and expected counts of people with the following hair colors (columns) and eye colors (rows) are shown below. Expected counts are printed below observed counts.

	BLACK	BRUNETTE	RED	BLOND	Total
Brown	68 40.14	119 106.28	26 26.39	7 47.20	220
Blue	20 39.22	84 103.87	17 25.79	94 46.12	215
Hazel	15 16.97	54 44.93	14 11.15	10 19.95	93
Green	5 11.68	29 30.92	14 7.68	16 13.73	64
Total	108	286	71	127	592

```
ChiSq = 19.346 +  1.521 +  0.006 + 34.234 +
         9.421 +  3.800 +  2.993 + 49.697 +
         0.228 +  1.831 +  0.726 +  4.963 +
         3.817 +  0.119 +  5.211 +  0.375 = 138.290
df = 9, p = 0.000

MTB >  INVCDF .95;
SUBC> CHIS 9.
```

The critical chi-square with 9 d.f. is

```
P(X ≤ x)          x

0.9500     16.9190
```

Verify the chi-square statistic. Compare the chi-square statistic to a critical value to test the hypothesis that hair and eye color are independent.

APPENDIX 1

Minitab Examples

(If you are using the WINDOWS version of MINITAB, you might issue the GSTD command first to use standard graphics in the session window. If you want to save your output on a file, use the command OUTFILE 'A:CH10.LIS' to echo output to this file.)

EXAMPLE

ILLUSTRATIONS IN THE CHAPTER

```
      (OR RETRIEVE 'THIN'  whichever is appropriate.)
MTB > RETRIEVE 'B:THIN'  # THE FILE NAME IS THE SAME
MTB > INFO               # AS A VARIABLE NAME HERE
MTB > TALLY 'THIN';      # MINITAB KNOWS WHICH IS WHICH
SUBC> COUNTS;
SUBC> PERCENTS.

MTB > TALLY 'THIN';
SUBC> COUNTS;
SUBC> PERCENTS;
SUBC> CUMCOUNTS;
SUBC> CUMPERCENTS.

MTB > INFO
MTB > PRINT 'THIN' 'SEX' 'TV' 'HEIGHT'

MTB > TALLY 'TV';
SUBC> PERCENTS;
SUBC> CUMPERCENTS;
SUBC> STORE IN C7 C8 C9.
MTB > NAME C8 'PCTS'
MTB > NAME C9 'CUMPCTS'
MTB > NAME C7 'TVCLASS'
MTB > PLOT 'PCTS' 'TVCLASS'
MTB > PLOT 'CUMPCTS' 'TVCLASS'
```

```
MTB > TALLY 'SEX';
SUBC> COUNTS;
SUBC> PERCENTS.
MTB > TALLY 'THIN' 'SEX''TV'

MTB > TABLE 'SEX' 'THIN';
SUBC> COUNTS.

MTB > TABLE 'SEX' 'THIN';
SUBC> ROWPERCENTS;
SUBC> COLPERCENTS;
SUBC> TOTPERCENTS.

MTB > TABLE 'SEX' 'THIN';
SUBC> CHISQUARE K=2.

MTB > TABLE 'TV' 'THIN';
SUBC> CHISQUARE K=2.
```

I X H M P I I

ILLUSTRATION OF A CONTRASTING SITUATION WHERE DESIRE TO BE THIN IS GENDER DEPENDENT

```
MTB > READ C11 C12    # ENTERING MODIFIED COUNT DATA
DATA> 80 20           # IN SOME EMPTY COLUMNS
DATA> 91 9
DATA> END
MTB > CHISQUARE C11 C12

MTB > TABLE 'SEX' 'THIN' 'TV'
# SOME OPTIONAL SUBCOMMANDS ARE SHOWN HERE
          MTB > TABLE 'SEX' 'THIN' 'TV';
          SUBC> ROWPERCENTS;
          SUBC> COLPERCENTS;
          SUBC> TOTPERCENTS;
          SUBC> CHISQUARE K = 2.

MTB > TABLE 'SEX' 'THIN';
SUBC> TOTPERCENTS;
SUBC> MEANS 'HEIGHT'. # AUGMENTING THE TABLE WITH INFORMATION #
ON THE QUANTITATIVE VARIABLE, MEAN HEIGHT
```

EXAMPLE

FINISHED PRODUCTS

```
MTB > # SET COUNTS Y1 Y2 Y3 ETC. IN C1
MTB > SET C1
DATA> 160 10 30
DATA> END
MTB > # SET PROPORTIONS P1 P2 P3 ETC. IN C2
MTB > SET C2
DATA> .85 .05 .10
DATA> # SET TOTAL COUNTS N IN C3
DATA> SET IN C3
DATA> 3(200)  # NO SPACES (BLANKS) IN THIS LINE
DATA> LET C4 = ((C1-(C3*C2))**2)/(C3*C2)
MTB > SUM C4
#    SUM = 5.5882 CALCULATED CHI-SQUARE VALUE


MTB > INVCDF .95;
SUBC> CHISQUARE V=2.
#  5.9915  CRITICAL CHI-SQUARE VALUE
MTB > ERASE C1 C2 C3 C4
```

EXAMPLE

BAD EGGS—QUALITY CONTROL (INSPECTION)

```
MTB > # GOODNESS OF FIT FOR THE BINOMIAL
MTB > SET IN C1 # POSSIBLE BAD EGGS IN A DOZEN
DATA> 0:12
DATA> END
MTB > LET K1 = 962/12000 # ESTIMATE OF DEFECTIVE RATE
MTB > PRINT K1
#              K1       0.0801667
MTB > PDF C1 C2;    # OBTAINING ACTUAL PROBABILITIES IN C2
SUBC> BINOMIAL N=12 P=.0801667.


MTB > LET C3 = C2 * 1000 # EXPECTED COUNTS OUT OF 1000 DOZEN
MTB > PRINT C1 C3
# FOR LARGE SAMPLE CONDITIONS RULE WE NEED AT LEAST
# FIVE EXPECTED COUNTS IN A CATEGORY
# SEVERAL CATEGORIES ARE AGGREGATED HERE
MTB > LET C3(5)=C3(5)+C3(6)+C3(7)+C3(8)+C3(9)+C3(10)
MTB > LET C3(5)=C3(5)+C3(11)+C3(12)+C3(13)
MTB > DELETE ROWS 6:13 C1 C3 # DON'T NEED, AGGREGATED
MTB > PRINT C1 C3


MTB > SET IN C4 # ACTUAL COUNTS IN CATEGORIES
DATA> 350 400 200 40 10
DATA> PRINT C1 C3 C4
```

(continued)

```
MTB > LET C5 = ((C4-C3)**2)/C3 # ACTUAL-EXPECTED SQUARED
#                                DIVIDED BY EXPECTED
MTB > SUM C5      # CHI-SQUARE VALUE
#    SUM = 6.6154  CALCULATED CHI-SQUARE VALUE

MTB > INVCDF .95;
SUBC> CHISQUARE V=3.
# 7.8147  CRITICAL CHI-SQUARE VALUE
MTB > ERASE C1 C2 C3 C4 C5
```

EXAMPLE

BURGER WEIGHTS

```
         OR RETRIEVE 'BURGER' # whichever is appropriate.
MTB > RETRIEVE 'B:BURGER'
MTB > HIST C1
MTB > DOTPLOT C1  # PRELIMINARY IMPRESSION--NORMAL
MTB > DESCRIBE C1 # WE NEED MEAN AND STANDARD DEVIATION

MTB > SET IN C11  # Z-SCORES FOR 10 INTERVALS
DATA> -4 -1.28 -.84 -.52 -.25 0 .25 .52 .84 1.28 4
DATA> END

MTB > LET C12=9.0495+C11*.2555 # TRANSLATE Z'S TO DATA SCALE
MTB > LET C12=C12*100          # ROUNDING
MTB > ROUND C12 PUT C12
MTB > LET C12=C12/100

MTB > CDF C12  PUT C13; #  GETTING PROPORTION IN EACH INTERVAL
SUBC> NORMAL MU=9.0495 SIGMA=.2552.
MTB > LET C14=C13
MTB > DELETE ROW 1 C14
MTB > DELETE ROW 11 C13
MTB > LET C15 = C14-C13
MTB > PRINT C11 C12 C14 C13 C15

MTB > SORT C1 PUT C16 # NEED TO COUNT ACTUAL DATA EACH CLASS
MTB > PRINT C16
8.47    8.55    8.56    8.57    8.59    8.69    8.69    8.73    8.74
8.75    8.75    8.76    8.76    8.78    8.78    8.82    8.84    8.84
8.85    8.85    8.87    8.88    8.88    8.88    8.89    8.89    8.89
8.90    8.91    8.93    8.94    8.96    9.00    9.00    9.01    9.02
9.02    9.02    9.03    9.03    9.03    9.04    9.04    9.05    9.05
9.05    9.05    9.07    9.10    9.10    9.10    9.10    9.11    9.12
9.13    9.14    9.15    9.15    9.15    9.18    9.19    9.19    9.19
9.20    9.21    9.21    9.22    9.23    9.23    9.23    9.26    9.27
9.27    9.27    9.29    9.30    9.31    9.36    9.36    9.43    9.46
9.48    9.48    9.52    9.53    9.68    9.71

MTB > PRINT C12  # FROM TO CLASS INTERVALS FOR THE DATA ABOVE
   8.03    8.72    8.83    8.92    8.99    9.05    9.11    9.18
   9.26    9.38    10.07
```

(continued)

(continued)

```
MTB > SET IN C17  # ACTUAL COUNT OF DATA IN EACH CLASS
DATA> 7 9 13 3 11 9 7 11 9 8
DATA> END

MTB > LET C21=C12     # ADJUSTMENTS FOR PRINTING INTERVALS
MTB > DELETE ROW 1 C21
MTB > DELETE ROW 11 C12
MTB > LET C22 = C15*87
MTB > LET C23=C11
MTB > DELETE ROW 1 C23
MTB > DELETE ROW 11 C11
MTB > PRINT C11 C23 C12 C21 C15 C22 C17

MTB > LET C19=((C17-C22)**2)/C22  # CHI-SQUARE CALCULATION
MTB > SUM C19
#   SUM = 7.5557  CALCULATED CHI-SQUARE VALUE

MTB > INVCDF .95;
SUBC> CHISQUARE V=7.
#    14.0671 CRITICAL CHISQUARE VALUE
```

CHAPTER 11

Simple Regression Analysis and the Analysis of Variance

PRELUDE

Photographs, paintings, and drawings are all viewed in two-dimensional space. Similarly, a scatterplot provides an excellent display of observations on a pair of variables in two-dimensional space. On a scatterplot, a fitted line summarizes the essence of the relationship between a pair of variables. Large departures from the fit reveal unusual data points.

The classical approach for obtaining a fit and the related accoutrements are the subject of this chapter. This approach is more refined than the exploratory methods covered earlier, but the basic idea of relating a pair of variables is the same. Research questions involving pairs of variables are numerous. For example: Is diet related to the incidence of cancer? Is exercise related to heart disease? Does speed kill? ◇

INTRODUCTION TO SIMPLE REGRESSION ANALYSIS

Simple regression analysis relates a response variable, y, to a predictor variable, x, in a prediction equation or fit. Therefore, simple regression analysis produces fits like those you have learned about in exploratory work. These fits are more sensitive to outliers, but they tend to be more reliable when no outliers are present in the data set.

Recall that the initial exploratory fits involved two subsets of data that were compared by constructing side-by-side boxplots. An exploratory prediction equation was obtained by drawing a straight line through the sample medians of the two side-by-side boxplots. In the classical approach presented in this chapter, the straight line is drawn through the two sample means rather than the sample medians. A significant difference in sample means produces a fit with a slope that is significantly different from 0.

The notion of a fit extends beyond two subsets of data to a scatterplot of data points. This chapter introduces a fitting procedure based on the **ordinary least squares (OLS)** method. The resulting fit is referred to as a **regression line.**

As usual, residuals should be computed and carefully examined. However, the residuals from a regression line may not be quite as revealing as those from an exploratory fit. The regression line tends to be influenced by outlying data points and drawn towards them. Thus, unusually large residuals in exploratory fits may not be as noticeable in regression analysis.

Regression analysis works best when the response observations are random and normal in distribution. Residual examination can verify the presence of these conditions. Although the regression line does not depend on these assumptions, the related hypothesis tests and confidence intervals do. These hypothesis tests involve the slope and intercept regression coefficients. As a result, the standard errors of these estimators are found and described in this chapter.

A hypothesis test of main interest is whether or not the slope of a fitted line is significantly different from 0. The Student's t distribution and F distribution are used in this test. An **analysis of variance (ANOVA)** examines the components of the hypothesis test in more detail.

The next three sections of this chapter map out the basic theory. Then the emphasis is on applications and learning by example. Readers who prefer to deemphasize the theory can go directly to "Comparisons Using a Second Variable to Segregate Data into Two Categories" on page 527.

RELATING TWO VARIABLES, THE CLASSICAL APPROACH

The classical approach formalizes the exploratory methods described earlier. In addition to obtaining a fitted line, the exploratory methods generated hypotheses and influenced preliminary thinking about the data structure. The classical methods permit us to confirm or deny hypotheses and evaluate structural relationships. The **simple linear regression model** explains the behavior of an observation, y_i, in terms of a linear equation, $\beta_0 + \beta_1 x_{1i}$, plus an error term, e_i. The β's and e_i's are unknown and therefore estimated. The y's and x's are observed in pairs that plot as points on scatterplots.

A Simple Linear Regression Model

Observations, y_i, on a single response variable are considered where $i = 1$, $2, \ldots, n$, and where n is the sample size. One predictor variable, x_{1i}, is examined for its information-carrying potential. It is assumed that other predictor variables, x_{2i}, x_{3i}, and so on, have no systematic effect on what is observed.

The Full Model   A **full model** includes both an intercept and a slope parameter. Each individual observation, y_i, consists of three additive components that form a mathematical model or equation. The components are (1) an unknown intercept parameter, β_0; (2) an unknown slope parameter, β_1, times the predictor variable, x_{1i}, and (3) an unknown error term, e_i. The sum of these terms is the following **linear statistical model** or simple regression model:

$$y_i = \beta_0 + \beta_1 x_{1i} + e_i$$

The Reduced Model   If $\beta_1 x_{1i}$ is dropped from the full model, a **reduced model** results. In earlier chapters this more primitive model was referred to as a naive regression model. In the naive regression model, μ represents the population mean. Let $\mu = \beta_0^*$ because this notation is more common in regression analysis. The reduced model can then be written in either of the following ways:

$$y_i = \mu + e_i^*$$
$$y_i = \beta_0^* + e_i^*$$

Evaluating the Contribution of $\boldsymbol{\beta_1 x_{1i}}$ If the predictor variable, x_{1i}, contributes anything to explaining the variation in y_i, the standard deviation of e_i in the full model will be smaller than the standard deviation of e_i^* in the reduced model.

In other words, $\beta_1 x_{1i}$ was introduced because of its potential to decrease the standard deviation of the error, thereby explaining some of the variability in the response.

The Parameters and Their Estimators   Enlarging the naive model by including a **component effect,** $\beta_1 x_{1i}$, changes the meaning of certain parameters, making β_0^* represent something different from β_0. In the naive regression model, β_0^* is the population mean of the response y irrespective of the value of the predictor variable x. In the full model, β_0 is the population mean for the response only when x_{1i} is 0. Consequently, the estimators b_0 and b_0^* are likely to be quite different. The other regression coefficient, b_1, represents the slope or tilt of the straight line fit. It estimates the unknown slope β_1.

The Design Matrix (Optional)   Matrix methods provide a powerful way to describe the manipulations that go on behind the scenes in statistical packages. As a result, reading research papers about regression techniques requires knowledge of matrix methods. Because some MINITAB commands manipulate matrices and certain subcommands produce matrix results that sophisticated users find useful, we define a few matrices here.

The regression model can be written as $y_i = \beta_0 1 + \beta_1 x_{1i} + e_i$ to emphasize that β_0 is multiplied by 1 and β_1 by x_{1i}. The 1s form the first column of what is called a **design matrix.** MINITAB and other statistical packages automatically supply this column when performing regression analysis. The second column of the design matrix is composed of the values of the predictor variable x_{1i}. This is a data column the user supplies, say, to MINITAB.

Four responses can be expressed in regression model form as

$$y_1 = \beta_0 1 + \beta_1 x_{11} + e_1$$
$$y_2 = \beta_0 1 + \beta_1 x_{12} + e_2$$
$$y_3 = \beta_0 1 + \beta_1 x_{13} + e_3$$
$$y_4 = \beta_0 1 + \beta_1 x_{14} + e_4$$

From this set of equations, a simple design matrix can be constructed. The design matrix, **X,** is composed of two columns. The first column is all 1s. The second column contains the values of x_{1i}.

In addition to a design matrix, a **parameter matrix, B,** is defined. It has two rows. The first row contains β_0 and the second row contains β_1.

Once the values of x_{1i} are observed, these values can be included in the design matrix. Suppose for these four responses the first two observations were made when the predictor variable was 0, and for the second two observations when the predictor variable was equal to 1. The 0 and the 1 represent a low and a high level, respectively, of the predictor variable.

Substituting these data values in the above set of equations results in

$$26 = \beta_0 1 + \beta_1 0 + e_1$$
$$34 = \beta_0 1 + \beta_1 0 + e_2$$
$$98 = \beta_0 1 + \beta_1 1 + e_3$$
$$72 = \beta_0 1 + \beta_1 1 + e_4$$

Let a matrix with a prime, $'$, such as $\mathbf{B'}$, indicate a matrix transpose where columns become rows or rows become columns. Then, from the set of equations shown above, $\mathbf{Y'}$ is $[26 \quad 34 \quad 98 \quad 72]$, which are observations on the response variable. The first column of the design matrix, $\mathbf{X}$, is $[1 \quad 1 \quad 1 \quad 1]$ and the second column is $[0 \quad 0 \quad 1 \quad 1]$. The second column consists of observations on the predictor variable. Also, $\mathbf{B'}$ is $[\beta_0 \quad \beta_1]$.

In this example, the design matrix is structured so that β_1 is a difference in population means. In general, the design matrix can be structured to help us understand the results of very complex experiments.

A visual scan of the design matrix is worthwhile because gross data errors or other abnormalities might be spotted. One problem causing abnormality occurs when a predictor variable is always 0 or some other constant value. A column of 0s or constants (beyond the first column of 1s) in the design matrix results in the computer attempting to divide by 0. An attempt to divide by 0 is technically referred to as a **singularity problem.** When attempting to compute regression coefficients, the necessary matrix inversion can't be done in the usual sense.

A Graphical Display of a Simple Regression Model's Components   Exhibit 1 shows the genesis of the observed data based on a simple linear regression model. To construct the straight line, $\beta_0 + \beta_1 x_{1i}$, in the exhibit, the parameters were chosen as if they were known. In practice they are unknown and estimated. Therefore, the line, $\beta_0 + \beta_1 x_{1i}$, is drawn as a reminder that in theory such a line exists.

Data values (only four are shown to simplify the presentation) are generated from probability distributions whose means depend on the value of the predictor variable. Exhibit 2 depicts the probability distributions whose means are anchored at β_0 when x equals 0 and at $\beta_0 + \beta_1$ when x equals 1. This line passes through each population mean as x is changed. For example, when x is 0, $\beta_0 + \beta_1 x_{1i}$ becomes $\beta_0 + \beta_1 0 = \beta_0$. When x is 1, $\beta_0 + \beta_1 1$, the mean moves to a new location. $\beta_0 = \mu_1$ is the mean of the first population, and $\beta_1 = (\mu_2 - \mu_1)$ is the difference in population means. Notice that

$$\beta_0 + \beta_1 = \mu_1 + (\mu_2 - \mu_1) = \mu_2$$

Only the means of the distributions differ; the shape and standard deviations are identical. The distributions are offset to the right to avoid cluttering the exhibit.

EXHIBIT 1 The Genesis of Observed Data Based on a Simple Linear
Regression Model

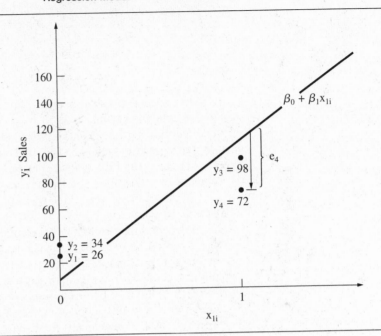

EXHIBIT 2 Observations from a Normal Distribution Where the Mean Depends on the
Predictor Variable

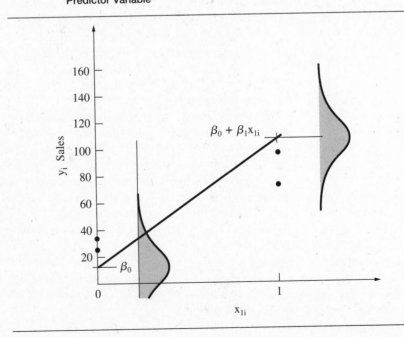

Estimating β_0 and β_1 with b_0 and b_1

Because β_0 and β_1 are unknown, in practical applications it is necessary to estimate these parameters using sample data. Formulas for the classical estimators b_0 and b_1 result from the ordinary least squares method. This method yields quality estimators that have minimum standard deviations and are unbiased.

The OLS method is outlined here. We start with the model

$$y_i = \beta_0 1 + \beta_1 x_{1i} + e_i$$

The "best" fit is found by minimizing the sum of the errors squared, which is the **least squares criterion.** This criterion measure is minimized by the preferred estimators b_0 and b_1. The mathematical function to be minimized is

$$Q = \Sigma\, (y_i - (\beta_0 1 + \beta_1 x_{1i}))^2 = \Sigma\, e_i^2$$

The summation is over all observations, $i = 1, 2, \ldots, n$. Q is minimized by taking a partial derivatives with respect to the unknown parameters and setting the results equal to 0. This results in two equations that are solved for two unknowns. The solutions produce formulas for computing b_0 and b_1. Behind the scenes in MINITAB, for example, the REGRESSION command relies on these formulas.

MINITAB Fit Results   The four data points in Exhibit 1 will be used as input data for the MINITAB REGRESSION command. Output from that command follows. Other statistical packages produce similar results.

A Prediction Equation   Column C3, [26   34   98   72], contains observations on the response variable, y. Column C4, [0   0   1   1], contains observations on the predictor variable, x. The resulting prediction equation or fit is

$$\hat{y}_i = 30.0 + 55.0 x_{1i}$$

Exhibit 3 shows this fit as well as the true theoretical relationship, $\beta_0 + \beta_1 x_{1i}$, where the parameters β_0 and β_1 are assumed to be known. In practice, these parameters are unknown and estimated from the data.

Notice that this fitted line passes through the two sample means. When $x = 0$, the response values of y are 26 and 34, and $b_0 = 30$, which is the sample mean of the first two observations, 26 and 34. When $x = 1$, the response values of y are 98 and 72, and $b_1 = (85 - 30) = 55$, which is the sample mean of the second two observations minus the sample mean of the first two observations. The difference in sample means, $b_1 = 55 = (85 - 30)$, is an estimate of $\beta_1 = (\mu_2 - \mu_1)$. This result is a special case that arises because of the 0 and 1 codes for the predictor variable. This coding created a classical fit that is analogous to the early exploratory fit through the medians of two boxplots.

This set of four observations is for illustration purposes only. Larger samples of 20 or more observations are needed in most applications.

EXHIBIT 3 The Prediction Equation and the Theoretical Relationship

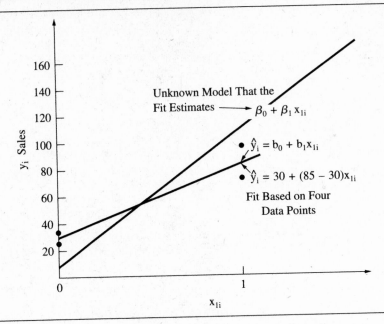

Regression Coefficients, Standard Errors, t Ratio, and p Values   In addition to the fit shown above, MINITAB's REGRESSION command produces the following table:

Predictor	Coef	Stdev	t Ratio	p Value
Constant	30.00	~~9.618~~	~~3.12~~	~~0.089~~
x_{1i} (C4)	55.00	13.60	4.04	0.056

The primary interest is in whether or not the sample means are significantly different ($b_1 = 55 = (85 - 30)$). Therefore, the struck-through values associated with b_0 are not of interest here.

The second t ratio of 4.04 can be used to test the null hypothesis that $\beta_1 = 0$, which is also ($\mu_2 - \mu_1$) $= 0$. Because the standard or critical value, $t_{.05,2} = 2.92$, is smaller than the computed t ratio $= 4.04$, the sample means are significantly different at a 90% level of confidence. Alternatively, the p value results in the same conclusion. Thus, reject the null hypothesis.

The same conclusion can be reached from the analysis of variance (ANOVA) table, which is standard output from regression analysis programs.

THE ANALYSIS OF VARIANCE

For simple linear regression, the analysis of variance that follows results in the same conclusions as the above t tests. Therefore, these two portions of output are somewhat redundant. The resulting F value in the ANOVA table is the same as the t ratio squared for the slope coefficient. Nevertheless, the analysis of variance (ANOVA) is presented in preparation for the more important role ANOVA will play later when several predictor variables are considered. Some goodness of fit information is also available in the ANOVA table.

Initially the analysis of variance (ANOVA) table will be used to evaluate the contribution of $\beta_1 x_{1i}$ to the regression model. If the contribution of $\beta_1 x_{1i}$ is insignificant, it should be dropped from the regression model in favor of a reduced model.

The Analysis of Variance (ANOVA) Table

```
SOURCE        DF      SS         MS              F value    p value

Regression    1     3025.0     3025.0             16.35       0.056
Error         2      370.0      185.0  = (s_y|x)²

Total         3     3395.0
```

Table Mechanics   The column headings in the table are SOURCE for source of variability, DF for degrees of freedom, SS for **sums of squares,** MS for **mean squares** ($\frac{SS}{DF}$), F for F value test statistic, and p for p value.

The degrees of freedom column displays the number of independent pieces of information used to compute the associated sum of squares.

To obtain the mean square (MS) column, the degrees of freedom (DF) are divided into the corresponding sum of squares (SS).

In the MS column, the regression component mean square is divided by the residual (or error) mean square to form an F ratio statistic ($\frac{3025.0}{185.0} = 16.35$), which is compared to a critical F value.

Evaluating the Contribution of $\beta_1 x_{1i}$ In general, the ANOVA table is particularly useful in dealing with the following situation. As a regression model is elaborated by an additional component, say, $\beta_1 x_{1i}$, we ask whether the explanatory gain is worth the increased model complexity. The analysis of variance helps answer the question.

In more formal statistical terms the question is, Does the additional component, $\beta_1 x_{1i}$, make a significant contribution in reducing the error sum of squares as we elaborate the fit? Therefore, we hope that the error sum of squares, displayed in the ANOVA table, is much smaller than the total sum of squares because the additional component, $\beta_1 x_{1i}$, explains away a portion of the total, resulting in small error variability.

If $\beta_1 x_{1i}$ makes no contribution, accept the null hypothesis that $\beta_1 = 0 = (\mu_2 - \mu_1)$. The regression line, in theory, has a 0 slope. The null hypothesis is tested by comparing the **F value test statistic** in the ANOVA table to a standard or critical F value.

Rule for Rejecting $\beta_1 = 0$ If

$$
\left\{ \text{F ratio statistic} = \frac{\left[\dfrac{\text{regression SS}}{1} \right]}{s_{y|x}^2} \right\} \geq F_{\alpha,(1,n-2)}
$$

F value test statistic   **critical F value**

reject the hypothesis that $\beta_1 = 0$.

For the example

F test statistic   critical F value
$$
16.35 \geq F_{.10,(1,2)} = 8.53
$$

Therefore, reject $\beta_1 = 0$. The sample means are significantly different.

The critical F value can be found in Table 4 of Appendix A in the back of the book or from a MINITAB command. To obtain a particular critical F value, the degrees of freedom $(1, n - 2)$ and the significance level α must be specified. For example, the following MINITAB commands produce $F_{.10,(1,2)} = 8.53$.

```
MTB> INVCDF FOR .90;
SUBC> F U = 1 V = 2.
```

Equivalence of **F** ***and*** t^2 ***in Simple Regression***   For simple linear regression, F value test statistic $= t^2$. The F test just described is equivalent to a t test in simple linear regression. For the calculated F and t^2 values, $16.35 = 4.04^2$. For the critical F_α and $t_{\alpha/2}^2$ values, $8.53 = 2.92^2$.

Later, when we evaluate several predictor variables, the F test can be different from a t test. Then the F test has an important advantage over a series of individual t tests.

Goodness of Fit

The following goodness of fit statistics result from figures in the ANOVA table.

Standard Deviation of the Residuals   The **standard deviation of the residuals** is a measure of the remaining variability after explaining as much as you can with the predictor variable, x. The smaller this standard deviation the better. For example, $s_{y|x} = 13.60 = (185.0)^{1/2} =$ the sample standard deviation of the residuals of y "given" x. Notice that the mean square error $185.0 = \frac{370.0}{2} = \frac{\text{error SS}}{(n-2)}$, where $(n - 2) = (4 - 2) = 2$. The $(n - 2)$ is used as a divisor because two degrees of freedom are consumed in estimating β_0 and β_1. Thus, the mean square error can be computed from the following formula:

$$s_{y|x}^2 = \sum \frac{(y_i - \hat{y}_i)^2}{n - 2}$$

R-*Squared* **R-squared** (R_{sq}) is a goodness of fit measure. The better the predictions, the closer R_{sq} is to 1. The worse the predictions, the closer R_{sq} is to 0. From the ANOVA table, the calculations are: $R_{sq} = 89.1\% = \frac{3025.0}{3395.0}(\times 100)$. $\frac{3025.0}{3395.0} = \frac{\text{regression SS}}{\text{total SS}}$. Of the total amount of variability, this is the proportion explained by the variable(s) in the regression equation. R_{sq} also equals the correlation coefficient squared $(\times 100)$ between actual y and predicted $\hat{y}$.

The R-squared value (89.1%) indicates a good fit here. However, you are not warned in the computer output that the sample size is too small, which artificially inflates the R-squared value.

R-*Squared Adjusted* In the example, $R_{sq(adj)} = 83.7\%$. A general expression for this statistic is

$$R_{sq(adj)} = 1 - (1 - R_{sq})\left(\frac{n - 1}{n - 2}\right)$$

The ratio $\frac{n - 1}{n - 2}$ consists of total degrees of freedom divided by error degrees of freedom. The effect of the adjustment is most noticeable when the number of parameters (two here because of β_0 and β_1) and the number of observations are nearly the same. Fits using completely different data sets can be compared on equal footing with this statistic.

Total *Sum of Squares* The **total sum of squares** in simple regression is the same quantity as the error sum of squares of the reduced model (without the component $\beta_1 x_{1i}$ in the model). To better understand the three rows of the ANOVA table and the sums of squares column, consider the most primitive, naive regression model without the component $\beta_1 x_{1i}$,

$$y_i = \beta_0^* + e_i^*$$

This model is compared to a simple linear regression model in which the component $\beta_1 x_{1i}$ is included.

$$y_i = \beta_0 + \beta_1 x_{1i} + e_i$$

For the naive regression model without the component, the estimated squared standard deviation of the error is

$$s^{2}* = \sum \frac{(y_i - \hat{y}_i)^2}{n - 1}$$

where $\hat{y}_i = \bar{y}$ for $y_i = \beta_0^* + e_i^*$.

Because of the component added to the more elaborate model, $y_i = \beta_0 + \beta_1 x_{1i} + e_i$, we know that there is the potential for a reduction in the estimated squared standard deviation of the error. Therefore, $s_{y|x}^2$ can be smaller than $s^{2}*$, where

$$s_{y|x}^{2} = \sum \frac{(y_i - \hat{y}_i)^2}{n - 2}$$

The $\hat{y}_i = b_0 + b_1 x_{1i}$. The subscript in $s_{y|x}^2$ reads y "given" x.

This view of the potential reduction in the estimated squared standard deviation is not completely clear because of the different divisors, $(n - 1)$ and $(n - 2)$. As a consequence, the numerators of these expressions, the sums of squares, are isolated and presented in an ANOVA table, as you can see below in the column SS.

The Analysis of Variance (ANOVA) Table

Source	DF	SS	MS	F value	p value
Regression	1	3025.0	3025.0	16.35	0.056
Error	2	370.0	185.0		
Total	3	3395.0			

The sum $\sum (y_i - \bar{y})^2 = 3395.0$ is the total sum of squares (TSS) and it is said to be adjusted for the mean. The total sum of squares is the sum of the deviations squared from a fit of the naive regression model (without the component $\beta_j x_{ji}$). These deviations are illustrated in Exhibit 4. Notice that the fit is the sample mean of all the responses, which is a horizontal straight line.

Error Sum of Squares   When the component $\beta_1 x_{1i}$ is included in the model, the error sum of squares depends on the fitted regression line, $\hat{y}_i = b_0 + b_1 x_{1i} = 30 + (85 - 30)x_{1i}$. This line passes through the sample means of each subgroup of data points (see Exhibit 5). Therefore, $\sum (y_i - \hat{y}_i)^2 = 370.0$, which is the **error sum of squares (ESS)** or the sum of the residuals squared. The deviations for these calculations are shown in Exhibit 5.

EXHIBIT 4 Deviations from a Naive Regression Model Fit

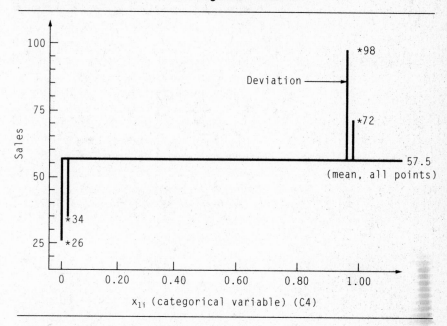

EXHIBIT 5 Deviations from the Fitted Regression Line

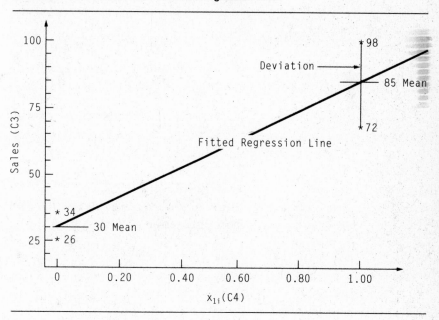

These sums of squares, TSS and ESS, appear in the numerators of expressions for the estimated squared standard deviations of different models, respectively, $s^{2*} = \Sigma \frac{(y_i - \bar{y})^2}{n-1}$ and $s_{y|x}^2 = \Sigma \frac{(y_i - \hat{y}_i)^2}{n-2}$.

Regression Sum of Squares   Any difference, TSS − ESS, is due to the difference between the naive regression model and a simple one-component regression model. Thus, the **regression sum of squares** is TSS − ESS = RSS. For a simple regression model, RSS is due to the single regression component $\beta_1 x_{1i}$. It can be shown that RSS = $\Sigma (\hat{y}_i - \bar{y})^2$. If the component $\beta_1 x_{1i}$ makes a significant contribution to reducing the error standard deviation, RSS should be large. The best fit occurs when RSS is as large as TSS and ESS is 0. The worst fit occurs when RSS is 0.

The General Formulation of the ANOVA Table   The figures in the previous ANOVA table can be verified using the following formulas:

Source	Degrees of Freedom	Sums of Squares	Mean Square	F ratio
Regression	1	RSS = $\Sigma (\hat{y}_i - \bar{y})^2$	$\frac{\text{RSS}}{1}$	$\left[\dfrac{\text{RSS}/1}{s_{y|x}^2} \right]$
Error	(n − 2)	ESS = $\Sigma (y_i - \hat{y}_i)^2$	$s_{y|x}^2 = \dfrac{\text{ESS}}{(n-2)}$	
Total	(n − 1)	TSS = $\Sigma (y_i - \bar{y})^2$		

The ANOVA table provides much information. $R_{sq} = \frac{\text{RSS}}{\text{TSS}} = R^2$ is the proportion of the total variability, TSS, explained by the additional component $\beta_1 x_{1i}$. In simple linear regression analysis, $R = r_{y\hat{y}}$, which is the simple correlation between the responses and the predictions. Also, $R = r_{yx}$ (correlation between x and y) for simple linear regression. In more complex models, R is referred to as the **multiple correlation coefficient.**

$1 - \left[\frac{\text{RSS}}{\text{TSS}} \right]$ is the proportion of variability that remains unexplained by the fit. Notice that TSS = RSS + ESS.

Estimating an Error, e_i, with a Residual, $\hat{e}_i$

The residuals are actual observations minus predictions. For example, the residuals shown in Exhibit 5 are

$$(26 - 30) = \;\; -4$$
$$(34 - 30) = \;\; +4$$

$$(98 - 85) = +13$$
$$(72 - 85) = -13$$

A residual is an estimator of an unknown error and is obtained as follows:

$$(y_i - \hat{y}_i) = \hat{e}_i$$

The usual assumptions about the error terms are that (1) the average value of the errors is 0; (2) the standard deviation of the errors is constant and equal to $\sigma_{y|x}$; (3) the errors are random; and (4) the errors follow a normal distribution. In order to validate these assumptions, residuals are examined. A large part of such an examination is informal and involves various residual plots.

The usual estimator of standard deviation of the errors, $\sigma_{y|x}$, is the standard deviation of the residuals, $s_{y|x}$. The subscript $y|x$ means y "given" x because this is an estimator of the standard deviation of the probability distributions that are anchored by their means, which in turn depend on the value of x (see Exhibit 2 where the means of the distributions are specified by the line $\beta_0 + \beta_1 x_{1i}$).

Variability Measure Under the Reduced Model   For the naive regression model, there is no predictor variable. Therefore, the residuals are based on deviations from the mean (see Exhibit 4), as in the formula for the squared standard deviation.

$$s_y^2 = \frac{\text{TSS}}{n-1} = \sum \frac{(y_i - \bar{y})^2}{n-1} = \sum \frac{\hat{e}_i^{*2}}{n-1}$$

The $\hat{e}_i^*$ is simply a residual, which is the actual data value minus the sample mean.

Variability Measure Under the Full Model   For a simple linear regression model, the residuals are deviations from a prediction equation that includes a predictor variable (see Exhibit 5). Because the prediction depends on x, the formula for the squared standard deviation becomes

$$s_{y|x}^2 = \frac{\text{ESS}}{n-2} = \sum \frac{(y_i - \hat{y}_i)^2}{n-2} = \sum \frac{\hat{e}_i^2}{n-2}$$

The square root of the above quantity, $s_{y|x}$, is often called the **standard error of the estimate.** But this term is awkward, if not confusing. $s_{y|x}$ is simply the estimated standard deviation of the errors. Because the response, y, includes an error term, $s_{y|x}$ is also the estimated standard deviation of the probability distribution of y. The mean of this distribution depends on the value of x.

In simple regression, $\hat{e}_i$ is simply a residual from a straight line fit. Because there are two parameters, β_0 and β_1, and each consumes a degree of freedom, $(n-2)$ is used as a divisor in place of $(n-1)$. In general, with p parameters the divisor is $(n-p)$.

[E X A M P L E 1]

THE STANDARD DEVIATION OF y "GIVEN" x (STANDARD DEVIATION OF THE RESIDUALS)

Problem Statement   Find $s_{y|x}^2$ for the residuals in Exhibit 5.

Problem Solution

$$s_{y|x}^2 = \frac{(-4)^2 + (+4)^2 + (+13)^2 + (-13)^2}{4 - 2} = \frac{370}{2} = 185$$

Standard Errors of b_0 and b_1

The regression coefficients b_0 and b_1 are point estimators. Good point estimators are precise and have distributions with small standard deviations. A standard deviation for the distribution of an estimator is a **standard error.** Notationally, the estimated standard errors of b_0 and b_1 are s_{b0} and s_{b1}. These estimated standard errors are included as standard output of regression analysis programs. For example, see the third column of the table below. This output is generated by MINITAB's REGRESSION command and the data in Exhibit 1.

Predictor	Coef	Stdev	t Ratio	p Value
Constant	30.00	9.618 = s_{b0}	~~3.12~~	~~0.089~~
C4	55.00	13.60 = s_{b1}	4.04	0.056

The Covariance Between Regression Coefficients   In simple regression analysis, b_0 and b_1 may depend on one another. A measure of this dependence is the **estimated covariance,** s_{b01}.

An important objective when designing experiments is to obtain a 0 covariance. This is desirable because the regression coefficients can then be interpreted singly. When the covariance is not 0, the regression coefficients covary. This makes them difficult to untangle and to understand individually.

For reference purposes, the formulas for the estimated standard errors squared and the covariance are given below.

$$s_{b0}^2 = s_{y|x}^2 \left\{ \frac{\sum x_{1i}^2}{n\sum (x_{1i} - \overline{x}_1)^2} \right\}$$

$$s_{b1}^2 = \frac{s_{y|x}^2}{\sum (x_{1i} - \overline{x}_1)^2}$$

$$s_{b01} = s_{y|x}^2 \left\{ \frac{-x_1}{\sum (x_{1i} - \overline{x}_1)^2} \right\}$$

Although computer calculations are usually made, knowledge of the formulas can be strategically useful when setting up an experiment. For example, for the slope estimator to be as precise as possible, make $s_{b_1}^2$ as small as possible. This can be accomplished by allocating half of the observations at the predictor variable extremes, which makes the term in the denominator, $\Sigma\,(x_{1i} - \overline{x}_1)^2$, as large as possible. This results in a very precise slope estimator.

Advanced Subcommand (Optional) MINITAB provides a subcommand, XPXINV PUT INTO M, for the REGRESS command that helps one assess the magnitude of covariances relative to the standard errors squared. You need to PRINT M and multiply each element of the matrix by $s_{y|x}^2$. The off-diagonal elements are the covariances and the diagonal elements are the standard errors squared.

S T A T I S T I C A L   H I G H L I G H T S

Goodness of fit refers to how well the fitted line summarizes the data. We depend on a variety of methods and statistics to evaluate the goodness of fit. They include standard errors of regression coefficients, t ratios, R-squared values, the analysis of variance, and the analysis of residuals.

HYPOTHESIS TESTS AND CONFIDENCE INTERVALS

The unknown parameters, the β's, in regression models have meaningful interpretations in practical applications. For example, β_1 can represent the difference between two population means. Consequently, it's not surprising that confidence intervals and hypothesis tests concerning these parameters are of interest.

Because a single random sample of data produces regression coefficients, the b_j's (where $j = 0$ or 1), the following question arises: If other random samples of the same size were taken, how much would the new b_j's be different from the initial ones? Would the new b_j's range widely or would they be close to the regression coefficient found in the first sample?

Theoretically, b_j follows a normal distribution that is centered on β_j with a standard error, σ_{b_j}, as a spread measure. Thus, it is not necessary to actually calculate new b_j's because upper and lower confidence limits can be found for β_j. These confidence intervals can be constructed from information in the initial sample.

Confidence intervals will be presented for an unknown parameter, β_j, where $j = 0$ or 1 in this chapter. Related hypothesis tests will also be described.

Hypothesis Tests on Unknown Parameters (Two-Sided)

The b_j can be studentized by subtracting β_j and dividing by the standard error.

$$\text{t ratio} = \frac{b_j - \beta_j}{s_{bj}}$$

For the null hypothesis, $\beta_j = 0$. This t ratio simplifies to

$$\text{t ratio} = \frac{b_j - 0}{s_{bj}}$$

MINITAB and other statistical packages perform this studentization for you, as you can see in the fourth column of the table below.

Predictor	Coef	Stdev	Computed t Ratio
Constant(b_0)	30.00	9.618 $= s_{b0}$	3.12 $= b_0/s_{b0}$
C4(x_{1i}) (b_1)	55.00	13.60 $= s_{b1}$	4.04 $= b_1/s_{b1}$

The absolute values (negative signs, if any, are ignored) of the computed t ratios are compared to a critical t value, $t_{(\alpha/2),(n-2)}$. In the example above, the critical $t_{.05,2} = 2.92$ is compared to both computed t values, which are: for b_0, t ratio = 3.12; and for b_1, t ratio = 4.04. Both 3.12 and 4.04 exceed the critical value of 2.92. Therefore, reject the null hypotheses that $\beta_0 = 0$ and that $\beta_1 = 0$. The degrees of freedom, 2, is associated with the error variability and found in the ANOVA table. In most applications, 18 or more degrees of freedom are needed. However, the degrees of freedom are a small number here to help illustrate the computational mechanics.

The null hypothesis that $\beta_1 = 0$ is of special interest because not rejecting this hypothesis means that the component, $\beta_1 x_{1i}$, is also 0. Therefore, it would make sense to drop this component from the full model and favor the reduced model. Also, as you will see, if a confidence interval on β_1 encloses 0, we cannot reject the null hypothesis that the parameter is 0, and we should seriously consider dropping the component from the model.

Rule for Rejecting the Hypothesis That β_j Equals Any Particular Value   In general, the null hypothesis can specify that β_j equals any particular value. Then the t ratio is computed using this value of β_j, which is specified in the null hypothesis.

$$\begin{array}{cc} \textbf{t ratio} & \textbf{critical t value} \\ \left|\dfrac{(b_j - \beta_j)}{s_{bj}}\right| & > \quad t_{(\alpha/2),(n-2)} \end{array}$$

If the left side of the above expression exceeds the right side, reject the null hypothesis.

Confidence Intervals on Unknown Parameters

The elements of the studentization and the hypothesis testing can be rearranged to form a $(1 - \alpha)$ confidence interval on the unknown parameter, β_j.

$$b_j \pm t_{(\alpha/2),(n-2)}(s_{bj})$$

Notice that smaller standard errors make the confidence interval narrower.

From the tabulations below, we can obtain the necessary regression coefficients and standard errors needed to construct confidence intervals on the unknown parameters.

```
Predictor          Coef        Stdev              t ratio

Constant(b₀)      30.00      9.618 = s_b0      3.12 = b₀/s_b0
C4(x₁ᵢ)  (b₁)     55.00     13.60  = s_b1      4.04 = b₁/s_b1
```

Figures from the above table and the critical t value are substituted in the following formula for a 90% confidence interval on β_0 and β_1:

$$b_j \pm t_{(\alpha/2),(n-2)}(s_{bj})$$

For β_0, the interval is $30 \pm 2.92 \times (9.618)$. For β_1, the interval is $55 \pm 2.92 \times (13.60)$.

One-Sided Hypothesis Tests on Unknown Parameters   Sometimes hypothesis tests are one-sided rather than two-sided, as shown above. For example, suppose $H_n: \beta_j = 30$ versus the alternative hypothesis $H_a: \beta_j < 30$. This is in contrast to the two-sided alternative hypothesis $H_a: \beta_j \neq 30$.

For the two-sided case, a confidence interval was created using the following expression:

$$b_j \pm t_{(\alpha/2),(n-2)} s_{bj}$$

For the two-sided test, the probability of a false rejection of the null hypothesis is α, with $\frac{\alpha}{2}$ of the probability in each tail of the Student's t distribution.

For the one-sided test, the probability of a false rejection of the null hypothesis is still α. However, because one side of the probability distribution is of no interest, α and not $\frac{\alpha}{2}$ of the probability is in each tail of the Student's t distribution. As a consequence, the confidence interval for a one-sided test is

$$b_j \pm t_{(\alpha),(n-2)} s_{bj}$$

Because $t_{(\alpha)}$ is always smaller than $t_{(\alpha/2)}$, a narrower interval results.

Rejection Rule   For the alternative hypothesis $H_a: \beta_j < 30$, reject the null hypothesis when the interval is to the left of 30.

For the alternative hypothesis $H_a: \beta_j > 30$, reject the null hypothesis when the interval is to the right of 30.

More Sophisticated Confidence Intervals (Optional)

Confidence intervals can be placed on the unknown regression line, individual future observations of the response, and the average of q future observations of the response.

Confidence Intervals on the Unknown Regression Line   The unknown regression line is a linear combination of component effects.

$$\beta_0 + \beta_1 x_{1i}$$

This equation represents the population mean, which changes as x changes. The fit, $\hat{y}_i = b_0 + b_1 x_{1i}$, is its estimator. Therefore, the confidence interval on the unknown regression line is

$$\hat{y}_i \pm t_{(\alpha/2),(n-2)} s(\hat{y})$$

The estimated standard deviation of the prediction is

$$s(\hat{y}) = [s_{b0}^2 + x_{1i}^{2*} s_{b1}^2 + 2x_{1i}^* s_{b01}]^{1/2}$$

An asterisk is used on x_{1i}^* to indicate that this interval computation can be for any value of x, which may include values not in the data set.

Confidence Intervals on a Single Future Observed Value of the Response
A single future observed value, y_{if}, deviates from its mean on the unknown regression line. Therefore, a confidence interval on a single future observed value is a confidence interval on $\beta_0 + \beta_1 x_{1i}$ plus an error.

$$y_{if} = \beta_0 + \beta_1 x_{1i} + e_{if}$$

The substitution of estimators for the unknowns on the right side of the above equation yields

$$\text{(estimated) } y_{if} = b_0 + b_1 x_{1i} + \hat{e}_{if}$$

The estimated standard deviation of the above equation is

$$[s(\hat{y})^2 + s_{y|x}^2]^{1/2}$$

Using this estimated standard deviation and the fact that the average error is 0, the confidence interval on a single future observed value is

$$(\hat{y}_i = b_0 + b_1 x_{1i}^*) \pm t_{(\alpha/2),(n-2)} [s(\hat{y})^2 + s_{y|x}^2]^{1/2}$$

Confidence Intervals on the Mean of q Future Observed Values of the Response   A confidence interval for the mean of q future observations is similar in structure to that for a single future observation. This confidence interval is

$$(\hat{y}_i = b_0 + b_1 x_{1i}^*) \pm t_{(\alpha/2),(n-2)} \left[s(\hat{y})^2 + \frac{s_{y|x}^2}{q} \right]^{1/2}$$

Notice that as q gets larger, the interval shrinks. When q is small, this interval is quite wide, giving the user a feel for the risk in predicting a single future value or the mean of a small number of future values.

S T A T I S T I C A L   H I G H L I G H T S

Confidence intervals and t tests can be used to test hypotheses about the parameters in regression models.

COMPARISONS USING A SECOND VARIABLE TO SEGREGATE DATA INTO TWO CATEGORIES

By coding the predictor variable x 0 or 1, the response variable y is segregated into two categories. The sample means of the y's in each category can be compared and inferences made about the unknown population means.

Comparisons, Small Sample Inferences About the Difference Between Two Population Means

We use two contrasting cases to illustrate the methodology. In Case 1 the data lead to the conclusion that there is no difference in population means, $\beta_1 = (\mu_2 - \mu_1) = 0$. In Case 2 the data lead to the conclusion that there is a difference in population means, $\beta_1 = (\mu_2 - \mu_1) \neq 0$.

Three distinct statistical methods support these conclusions and yield identical results: (1) simple linear regression, (2) **one-way analysis of variance,** and (3) the **pooled t test.** The traditional approach for comparing means is the pooled t test. However, the t test is limited to comparing two means. Both regression and one-way analysis of variance extend to more than two means.

Before computers were available for calculations, the pooled t test had the advantage of computational simplicity. That advantage has been lost, but the pooled t test continues to be taught. Because all three of these methods produce the same results, we present them collectively.

Case 1: No Difference in Population Means (the Predictor Variable *Does Not* Carry a Significant Amount of Information)

Exhibit 6 shows side-by-side boxplots for ages at death of presidents' mothers and fathers. From earlier exploratory work, we found no significant difference in median lifespans of mothers and to fathers. The typical lifespans are about the same.

EXHIBIT 6 Exploratory Conclusion—No Significant Difference in Medians

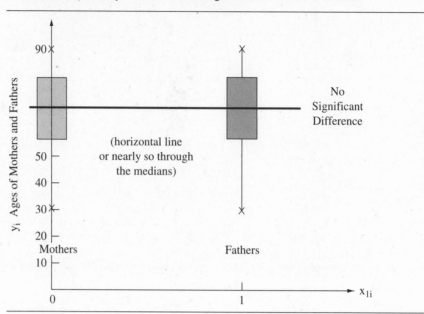

The data in Exhibit 6 come from an observational study. In this case it would be dangerous to generalize beyond our sample to mothers and fathers at large. Nevertheless, the statistical methods can be used to summarize this data set. The following example confirms the exploratory conclusion.

EXAMPLE 2

MINITAB AGE DATA ANALYSIS, ILLUSTRATING CLASSICAL REGRESSION, ONE-WAY ANALYSIS OF VARIANCE (ANOVA), AND THE POOLED T TEST APPROACHES

Problem Statement (a) Compare the sample mean ages of presidents' mothers and fathers. Illustrate the regression approach.

Problem Solution (a) The responses, y_i, consist of ages of presidents' mothers and fathers. The predictor variable, x_{1i}, is coded 0 or 1 to distinguish between mothers and fathers. Regression results are shown below. As usual, the MINITAB commands to produce these results are shown in Appendix 1.

The regression equation is

$$\text{(predicted death age) 'AGEMF'} = 68.6 - 1.41 \, C4$$
$$(C4 = 0, \text{ mothers}; \, C4 = 1, \text{ fathers})$$

Predictor	Coef	Stdev	t Ratio	p Value
Constant	68.588	2.998	22.88	0.000
C4	-1.412	4.240	-0.33	0.740

s = 17.48   R-sq = 0.2%   R-sq(adj) = 0.0%

Both R-sq values are near 0. This indicates that a large amount of variability is unexplained and the fit is poor.

Although a fit was obtained, the absolute value of the t ratio for b_1 equals 0.33, which is less than the critical t value of about 2. Do not reject $\beta_1 = 0$, where β_1 is the difference in the population mean ages of the two groups, mothers and fathers. The critical t value is $t_{(\alpha/2),(n-2)} = t_{.025, 66}$. The sample mean ages at death of mothers and fathers are not significantly different. The p value leads to the same conclusion.

The degrees of freedom, 66, for the critical t value come from the ANOVA table below in the DF column.

Analysis of Variance

SOURCE	DF	SS	MS	F	p
Regression	1	33.9	33.9	0.11	0.740
Error	66	20169.2	305.6		
Total	67	20203.1			

Notice that a very small proportion of the total sum of squares is explained by regression. The error SS is nearly the same as the total SS. The computed statistic F value is .11, which is less than the critical F value of 4, $F_{.05, 1, 66}$. This critical F value in simple regression equals the critical t value squared. Thus, both lead to the same conclusion—not to reject $\beta_1 = 0$.

Unusual Observations (Not enough to cause problems here.)

Obs.	C4	C3	Fit	Stdev.Fit	Residual	St.Resid
14	0.00	34.00	68.59	3.00	-34.59	-2.01R
28	0.00	34.00	68.59	3.00	-34.59	-2.01R

R denotes an observation with large standardized residuals.

Problem Statement (b)   Compare the sample mean ages of presidents' mothers and fathers. Illustrate the one-way analysis of variance approach.

Problem Solution (b)   A one-way analysis of variance gets directly to the same ANOVA table found in the regression approach. Thus, ANOVA is a special case of regression analysis. Before the widespread availability of computer packages, one-way analysis of variance was preferred to regression analysis because of its directness and simple computational formulas. Now practitioners can use either approach easily.

Both approaches produce identical results, as you can verify below. It is concluded that $\beta_1 = 0$, where β_1 is the difference in the population mean ages of the two groups, mothers and fathers. The confidence intervals shown below overlap, which provides a visual indication that sample means are not significantly different.

```
Analysis of Variance on C3

SOURCE      DF        SS        MS      F Value      p Value

C4(x₁ᵢ)      1        34        34       0.11        0.740
Error       66     20169       306
            ─────────────────────
Total       67     20203
```

```
                                    INDIVIDUAL 95 PCT CI'S FOR MEAN
                                         BASED ON POOLED STDEV

LEVEL      N      MEAN     STDEV   --------+---------+---------+--------
    0     34     68.59     17.65           (--------------*--------------)
    1     34     67.18     17.31   (--------------*--------------)
                                   --------+---------+---------+--------
POOLED STDEV =    17.48             64.0      68.0      72.0
```

Problem Statement (c)   Compare the sample mean ages of presidents' mothers and fathers. Illustrate the pooled t test approach.

Problem Solution (c)   The pooled t test approach is a special case of both regression and one-way analysis of variance. Whereas regression and one-way analysis of variance can be extended to compare 3, 4, 5, or more sample means, a pooled t test is limited to comparing two sample means. Its main historical advantages are its computational ease and conceptual directness. However, the availability of computer packages make any of the approaches computationally easy.

The formulas for the pooled t test were presented in Chapter 9. Therefore, only computer-produced results are shown below.

```
TWOSAMPLE T FOR AGEMF

DUMMY    N      MEAN     STDEV    SE MEAN
0       34      68.6      17.7      3.0
1       34      67.2      17.3      3.0

95 PCT CI FOR MU 0 - MU 1: (-7.1, 9.9)

TTEST MU 0 = MU 1 (VS NE): T = 0.33   P = 0.74   DF =  66

POOLED STDEV =        17.5
```

Note that the confidence interval on the difference in means encloses 0 and the computed statistic, a t ratio of 0.33, is less than the critical t value, $t_{.025, 66} = 2$. These facts lead us to accept the hypothesis that the population means are the same. The pooled t test produces the same results as simple regression and the one-way analysis of variance.

Validity Requirements for Simple Regression, One-Way Analysis of Variance, and the Pooled t Test

The validity of the results in the last example depends on the residuals being random and normal with standard deviations that are not significantly different. A runs test can be used to check the randomness assumption. Histograms or probability plots provide a visual assessment of the normality assumption. A squared ratio of the sample standard deviations is used to test for equal standard deviations.

A Visual Assessment   Roughly, the standardized residuals shown below are normal and have about the same spread.

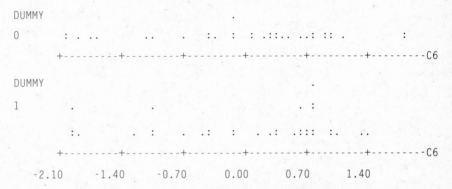

A Formal Test for Equal Standard Deviations   To test for equal standard deviations, form the ratio of standard deviations squared (larger on the top); for example, $\left[\frac{17.65}{17.31}\right]^2 = 1.04$. This ratio statistic is compared to a critical F value.

$$F_{\alpha, n1-1, n2-1} = F_{.05, 33, 33} \approx 1.84$$

Many F table tabulations don't show values for all combinations of degrees of freedom. Therefore, a conservative approximation uses fewer degrees of freedom, $F_{.05, 30, 30} = 1.84$. Because $1.04 < 1.84$, conclude that the standard deviations are not significantly different.

Case 2: A Significant Difference in Population Means (the Predictor Variable *Does* Carry a Significant Amount of Information)

Exhibit 7 displays side-by-side boxplots of sales data for the same product using two different package designs. A fitted line through the medians is also shown. The vertical axis represents the response variable, sales, and the horizontal axis represents the two package designs. The predictor variable, x_{1i}, is coded 0 to identify old package design sales and 1 to identify new package design sales.

EXHIBIT 7 Significantly Different Sales Levels Due to Package Designs

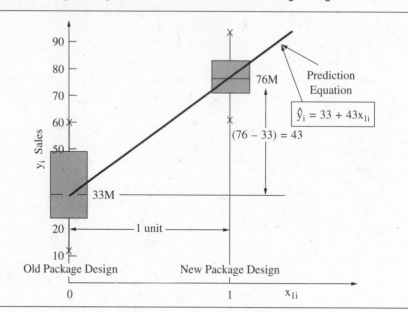

The problem is to investigate the effect of package design on sales. Clearly, the new package design has a higher sales level. There appears to be a significant difference in sales levels due to the different package designs. Thus, the predictor variable is useful in predicting sales.

In statistical terms, the evidence leads us to reject the null hypothesis that sales levels are the same for both package designs. An alternative hypothesis that sales are not the same for the two different package designs is favored. The analysis that follows summarizes these data and confirms that the null hypothesis should be rejected.

EXAMPLE 3

MINITAB SALES DATA ANALYSIS ILLUSTRATING CLASSICAL REGRESSION, ONE-WAY ANALYSIS OF VARIANCE (ANOVA), AND THE POOLED T TEST APPROACHES

Problem Statement (a)   Compare the sample mean sales for two package designs. Illustrate the simple regression approach.

Problem Solution (a)   To compare the sample mean sales for two package designs, recall that the responses, y_i, consist of sales figures for the two package designs. The predictor variable,

x_{1i}, is coded 0 or 1, to distinguish between the old and new package designs. Regression results are shown below.

The regression equation is

$$\text{SALESON} = 38.2 + 39.7 \text{ DUMMY}$$

(0 = old package design; 1 = new package design)

Predictor	Coef	Stdev	t Ratio	p Value
Constant	38.231	4.962	7.70	0.000
DUMMY	39.692	7.018	5.66	0.000

s = 17.89; R sq = 57.1%; R sq(adj) = 55.3%.

R-sq values are not near the extremes of 0 and 1. This indicates a mediocre fit.

The absolute value of the t ratio for b_1 of 5.66 is greater than the critical t-value of 2.064, $t_{(\alpha/2),(n-2)} = t_{.025,24}$. Therefore, reject the null hypothesis, $\beta_1 = 0$. The sample mean sales levels are significantly different for different package designs. The p value leads to the same conclusion.

The degrees of freedom, 24, for the critical t value comes from the ANOVA table below and is associated with the error variability.

Analysis of Variance

SOURCE	DF	SS	MS	F Value	P Value
Regression	1	10241	10241	31.99	0.000
Error	24	7683	320		
Total	25	17924			

Notice that a large proportion of the total sum of squares is explained by regression, and the error SS is much smaller than the total SS. The computed F value is 31.99, and it exceeds 4.26, the critical F value, $F_{.05,1,24} = 4.26$. This critical F value equals the squared critical t value in simple regression analysis.

Unusual Observations (Consider trimming this data value and reanalyzing)

Obs.	DUMMY	SALESON	Fit	Stdev.Fit	Residual	St.Resid
2	0.00	95.00	38.23	4.96	56.77	3.30R

R denotes an observation with a large standardized residual.

Problem Statement (b) Compare the sample mean sales for two package designs. Illustrate the one-way analysis of variance approach.

Problem Solution (b) A one-way analysis of variance gets directly to the ANOVA table. This approach is a special case of regression analysis. Therefore, these results are identical to those in problem solution (a). Conclude that $\beta_1 \neq 0$, where β_1 is the difference in the population mean levels of sales for the two package designs. Furthermore, the confidence intervals shown below do not overlap because the sample means are significantly different.

```
ANALYSIS OF VARIANCE ON SALESON

SOURCE      DF       SS        MS       F         p

DUMMY        1     10241     10241    31.99     0.000
ERROR       24      7683       320

TOTAL       25     17924
```

```
                                    INDIVIDUAL 95 PCT CI'S FOR MEAN
                                          BASED ON POOLED STDEV

LEVEL      N      MEAN     STDEV   -------+---------+---------+---------
    0     13     38.23     21.54   (----*----)
    1     13     77.92     13.28                        (----*----)
                                   -------+---------+---------+---------
POOLED STDEV =    17.89                  40        60        80
```

Problem Statement (c)   Compare the sample mean sales for two package designs. Illustrate the pooled t test approach.

Problem Solution (c)   The pooled t test approach is a special case of both regression and one-way analysis of variance. Whereas regression and one-way analysis of variance can be extended to compare 3, 4, 5, or more sample means, a pooled t test is limited to comparing two sample means. Its main historical advantages are its computational ease and conceptual directness. Modern computer packages make all three approaches computationally easy.

   MINITAB produced results are

```
TWOSAMPLE T FOR SALESON

DUMMY    N      MEAN     STDEV   SE MEAN
0       13      38.2     21.5      6.0
1       13      77.9     13.3      3.7

95 PCT CI FOR MU 0 - MU 1: (-54.2, -25.2)

TTEST MU 0 = MU 1 (VS NE): T = -5.66  P=0.0000  DF=   24

POOLED STDEV = 17.9
```

   Note that the confidence interval on the difference in means does not enclose 0 and the computed t value (T = 5.66 in absolute value terms) exceeds the critical t value, $t_{.025,24} =$ 2.064. This leads to the rejection of the null hypothesis that the population means are the same. The pooled t test results are the same as those from simple regression and the one-way analysis of variance.

Validity Requirements for Simple Regression, One-Way Analysis of Variance, and the Pooled t Test

The validity of the results in the last example depends on the residuals being random and normal with standard deviations that are not significantly different. A runs test can be used to check the randomness assumption. Histograms or probability plots provide a visual assessment of the normality assumption. A squared ratio of the sample standard deviations is used to test for equal standard deviations.

A Visual Assessment   Roughly, and except for one unusual observation that might be trimmed, the standardized residuals shown below appear to be normal with about the same standard deviation.

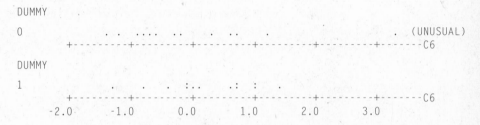

```
DUMMY

0                .  . ....  ..    .   ..     .                 . (UNUSUAL)
       +---------+---------+---------+---------+---------+------C6

DUMMY

1                .   .   . :..    .: :    .
       +---------+---------+---------+---------+---------+------C6
      -2.0     -1.0      0.0      1.0      2.0      3.0
```

A Formal Test for Equal Standard Deviations   To test for equal standard deviations, form the ratio of standard deviations squared (larger on the top), $\left[\frac{21.54}{13.28}\right]^2 = 2.63$. Compare this ratio to the critical value, $F_{\alpha, n1-1, n2-1} = F_{.05,12,12} = 2.69$. Because 2.63 is less than 2.69, conclude that the standard deviations are not significantly different.

Notice that one unusual data value inflated one standard deviation, which nearly led to the conclusion that the population standard deviations are not equal. When the unusual data value has a known cause such as a recording error, the usual procedure is to trim the unusual value and reanalyze.

For independent and normally distributed data values, when the hypothesis that the standard deviations are the same is accepted, the MINITAB commands TWOSAMPLE and TWOT (with POOLED subcommands), REGRESSION, and ONEWAY commands yield valid results.

The MINITAB commands REGRESSION and ONEWAY are designed for problems where two data subsets have or are adjusted to have (through transformations) standard deviations that are not significantly different. These commands can easily handle a larger number of data subsets—3, 4, 5, or more. The TWOSAMPLE and TWOT commands are limited to two data subsets but handle equal (POOLED subcommand) or unequal standard deviations.

> ## S T A T I S T I C A L   H I G H L I G H T S
>
> When comparing two samples, simple regression, one-way analysis of variance, and the pooled t test are alternative methods that yield the same results.

RELATIONSHIPS SUMMARIZED BY A STRAIGHT LINE

The idea of a prediction equation or fit is to summarize how two variables are related. This section considers a predictor variable that is not limited to two levels.

Prediction Equation (Fit) When the Predictor Variable Is at More Than Two Levels

This section provides a more complete and comprehensive view of the output from MINITAB's REGRESS command. In particular, the analysis of variance table is explained in more detail with emphasis on evaluating the goodness of fit. The following example is long, but it provides a complete set of analysis steps that may be necessary in a thorough analysis.

E X A M P L E 4

MORE ON SALES VERSUS ASSETS IN MINITAB

Examine sales versus assets for the 30 largest U.S. businesses in billions of dollars. These data were explored in an earlier chapter, and an exploratory fit was obtained. The exploratory results were revealing, but they did not complete the analysis. The analysis task is finished here.

Problem Statement (a)   Summarize sales and assets figures.

Problem Solution (a)   Descriptive statistics provide summary information about each variable. Note the typical values and the standard deviations. Figures from a few very large companies have inflated the means; therefore, we suspect that the distributions are a bit skewed. As a result, the median is the better indicator of central tendency.

	N	MEAN	MEDIAN	TRMEAN	STDEV	SEMEAN
C1(SALES)	30	27.92	17.15	24.48	22.23	4.06
C2(ASSETS)	30	26.78	19.75	24.12	19.68	3.59

	MIN	MAX	Q1	Q3
C1	11.40	101.80	13.85	33.80
C2	6.30	87.40	13.42	35.47

Problem Statement (b)   Correlate sales and assets and obtain a scatterplot.

Problem Solution (b)   Correlation of sales (C1) and assets (C2) = .946.

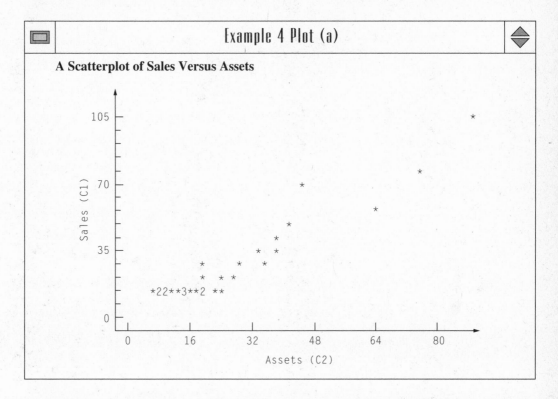

The absolute value of the correlation coefficient is near 1. Thus, we expect the scatterplot to show a strong linear association between sales and assets. However, recall that a few outliers can overstate the correlation coefficient. Therefore, scatterplots are examined as well for a complete picture.

Problem Statement (c)   Obtain a fitted regression line using assets to predict sales.

Problem Solution (c)   The MINITAB REGRESS command produces a least squares fit along with tables of statistics for hypothesis testing and goodness of fit assessment. The predictor variable, assets, makes a significant contribution in predicting the response, sales. This result is not a surprise because it was apparent in the scatterplot.

The MINITAB REGRESS command computes a column of standardized residuals (C3), a column of predictions (C4), and a column of raw residuals (C5). As you will see, C3, C4, and C5 are particularly useful for residual plots.

The regression (prediction) equation or fit is

$$\text{C1(SALES)} = -0.70 + 1.07\ \text{C2 (ASSETS)}   \text{(MINITAB's notation)}$$

$$\hat{y}_i\text{(SALES)} = -0.70 + 1.07\ x_{1i}\ \text{(ASSETS)}   \text{(textbook's notation)}$$

Problem Statement (d)   Find test statistics and goodness of fit information.

Problem Solution (d)

```
Predictor         Coef            Stdev    t ratio    p Value

Constant     b₀=-0.699      s_{b0}= 2.287      -0.31     0.762
C2(assets)   b₁=1.0688      s_{b1}= 0.06923    15.44     0.000

s_{y|x} = 7.336        R sq = 89.5%        R sq(adj) = 89.1%
```

The hypothesis that $\beta_0 = 0$ is not of interest here. Some regression analysis programs do not even compute its t ratio. The hypothesis that $\beta_1 = 0$ is of interest. The absolute value of the t ratio is 15.44, and it exceeds the critical $t_{.025,28} = 2.048$. Therefore, reject the null hypothesis that $\beta_1 = 0$. A zero change in sales as assets are changed is unlikely.

```
Analysis of Variance

SOURCE        DF          SS          MS        F value      p value

Regression     1        12826       12826       238.34       0.000
Error         28         1507          54

Total         29        14333
```

The error sum of squares is much smaller than the total, which indicates that a large proportion, R-sq = 89.5%, of the variability has been explained by the regression.

The computed F ratio is 238.34, and it exceeds the critical $F_{.05,1,28} = 4.20$. Therefore, reject the null hypothesis that $\beta_1 = 0$. This same conclusion was reached with the t test because for simple linear regression, $F_\alpha = t_{\alpha/2}^2$. Although the two tests are equivalent here, they will differ when many predictor variables are considered.

Sometimes it is useful to obtain a scatterplot and correlation of actual sales, C1, versus predicted sales, C4. A good fit results in high correlations for these variables.

Problem Statement (e)   List and comment on unusual observations revealed through large residuals. Plot residuals versus the predictor variable, assets, and predicted sales.

Problem Solution (e)

```
Unusual Observations

Obs.     C2        C1       Fit    Stdev.Fit    Residual    St.Resid

1 GM     87.4    101.80    92.71      4.41         9.09        1.55  X
2 EXXON  74.0     76.40    78.39      3.53        -1.99       -0.31  X
3 IBM    45.0     71.60    47.40      1.84        24.20        3.41  R

R denotes an observation with a large standardized residual.
X denotes an observation whose X value gives it large influence.
```

These unusual and influential observations along with residual plots lead us to consider trimming, transforming, and taking a second look at the resulting subset of these data.

In addition to the above tabulation, it is sometimes useful to PRINT C1(SALES) C4(PREDICTED SALES) C5(RESIDUALS = C1 − C4) C3(STANDARDIZED RESIDUALS).

As a reminder, residuals should be plotted at least to validate assumptions about the error terms. One of several possible plots is shown below, which is residuals versus assets, x_{1i}. Notice that the unusual and influential observations stand out.

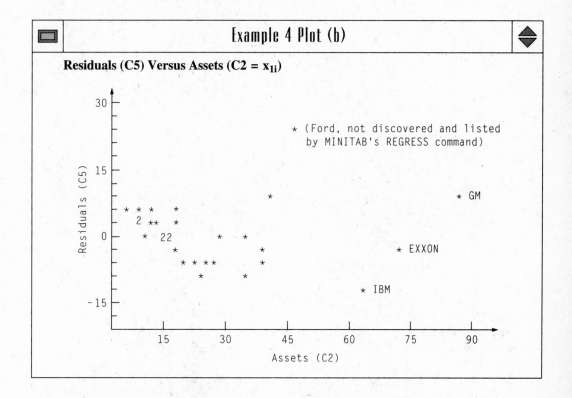

The next plot looks similar to the previous plot of residuals versus assets. At predicted sales of about $48 billion or more, Ford stands out while IBM, EXXON, and GM stand out as a cluster, which suggests that trimming be done. Notice too that because the point pattern tends to fan out, the spread increases as predicted sales increases. This suggests that transformations might be needed.

Problem Statement (f)   Check if the residuals are normally distributed and random.

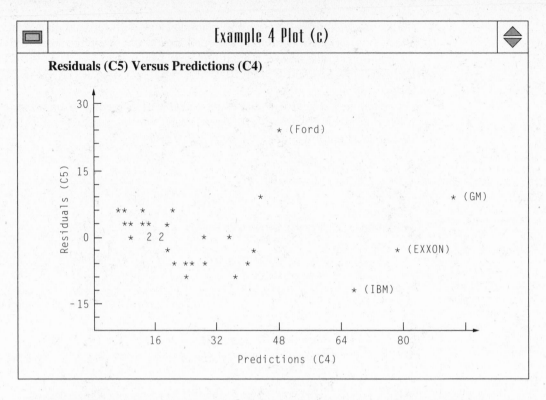

Problem Solution (f)   The MINITAB standardization is performed by dividing each residual by the square root of $[s^2_{y|x} - s^2(\hat{y})]$. The command HIST C3 is issued for a visual check on the normality of the standardized residuals.

```
Histogram of C3   N = 30

Midpoint    Count
   -2.0       1   *
   -1.5       2   **
   -1.0       5   *****
   -0.5       2   **
    0.0       8   ********
    0.5       7   *******
    1.0       3   ***
    1.5       1   *
    2.0       0
    2.5       0
    3.0       0
    3.5       1   * (Ford)
```

These standardized residuals look normal except for one unusual data point. Ford had a much higher level of sales than expected at Ford's assets level, which suggests that this point might be trimmed.

The results of a runs test show that the residuals are random, which is desirable.

```
C5
K =     -0.0000

THE OBSERVED NO. OF RUNS = 17
THE EXPECTED NO. OF RUNS = 15.9333
14 OBSERVATIONS ABOVE K   16 BELOW
        THE TEST IS SIGNIFICANT AT 0.6906
        CANNOT REJECT AT ALPHA = 0.05
```

Problem Statement (g)   As a result of the residual analysis, trim Ford, GM, IBM, and EXXON. Transform sales to the base (e) logarithm of sales. Then repeat the analysis cycle.

Problem Solution (g)   Begin another analysis cycle.

Problem Statement (h)   Obtain a fitted regression line using assets to predict log(sales).

Problem Solution (h)   The regression equation is

$$C6 \text{ (LOGESALES)} = 2.17 + 0.0371 \text{ C2(ASSETS)}$$

Problem Statement (i)   Find test statistics and goodness of fit information.

Problem Solution (i)

Predictor	Coef	Stdev	t Ratio	p value
Constant	2.16927	0.07964	27.24	0.000
C2	0.037078	0.003489	10.63	0.000

$s_{y|x} = 0.1781$ R-sq = 82.5%   R-sq(adj) = 81.7%

Analysis of Variance

SOURCE	DF	SS	MS	F value	p value
Regression	1	3.5834	3.5834	112.93	0.000
Error	24	0.7615	$0.0317 = s_{y|x}^2$		
Total	25	4.3450			

Although the computed t ratio, F ratio, and R-sq value have dropped some after trimming and transforming, they continue to indicate that the null hypothesis, $\beta_1 = 0$, is rejected. Before trimming and transforming, these statistics were all inflated artificially. Also note that the trimming changes the degrees of freedom in the analysis of variance table.

Evidence is accumulating that transforming and trimming have improved the fit. For example, the coefficient of variation, $\frac{s_{y|x}}{\bar{y}}$, has become smaller. Before trimming and transforming, this ratio was $\frac{7.336}{27.92} = .2628$; after trimming and transforming, it is $\frac{.1781}{2.9298} = .0608$.

The coefficient of variation is one of the few statistics designed to compare different models. The sample mean was obtained from the following descriptive statistics:

```
          N     MEAN   MEDIAN  TRMEAN   STDEV   SEMEAN
C6       26   2.9298   2.8122  2.9086  0.4169  0.0818

        MIN      MAX      Q1      Q3
C6    2.4336   3.9357  2.5934  3.2610
```

Problem Statement (j)   List and comment on unusual observations revealed through large residuals. Plot residuals versus the predictor variable, assets, and predicted log(sales).

Problem Solution (j)

```
Unusual Observations (But not too unusual now. Previously these
points were masked and not noticed at all.)

Obs.     C2        C6       Fit  Stdev.Fit  Residual  St.Resid
  6     19.9    3.2696    2.9071    0.0350    0.3625     2.08R
 18     23.3    2.6810    3.0332    0.0363   -0.3522    -2.02R

R denotes an observation with a large standardized residual.
```

The plot below is a good result. There are no particular patterns, no unusual observations or clusters, and no problems that require additional trimming or transforming.

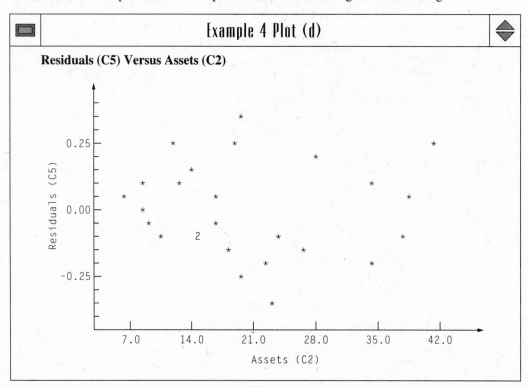

Example 4 Plot (d)

Residuals (C5) Versus Assets (C2)

Residuals plotted against predicted LOGESALES checks for constant spread (standard deviations) at different prediction levels. Again, the plot below is a good result. There are no particular patterns, no unusual observations or clusters, and no problems that require additional trimming or transforming.

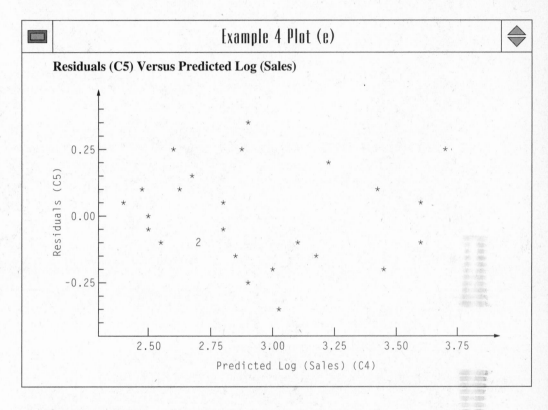

Problem Statement (k)   Check if the residuals are normally distributed and random.

Problem Solution (k)   A runs test for randomness indicates that the residuals are random, as we like to see.

```
C5
K =      -0.0000

THE OBSERVED NO. OF RUNS =  13
THE EXPECTED NO. OF RUNS =  14.0000
13 OBSERVATIONS ABOVE K    13 BELOW
        THE TEST IS SIGNIFICANT AT  0.6890
        CANNOT REJECT AT ALPHA = 0.05
```

The distribution of residuals is approximately normal, as shown in the following histogram.

```
Histogram of C3    N = 26

Midpoint   Count
  -2.0       1   *
  -1.5       2   **
  -1.0       2   **
  -0.5       7   ******* (Looks normal--improved from the
   0.0       3   ***              before trimming histogram)
   0.5       5   *****
   1.0       2   **
   1.5       3   ***
   2.0       1   *
```

Problem Statement (l) Which fit best represents the relationship between sales and assets?

Problem Solution (l) Because the residuals exhibit no patterns after trimming and transforming, this suggests that the preferred fit is:

$$C6 \text{ (LOGESALES)} = 2.17 + 0.0371 \text{ C2(ASSETS)}$$

This equation predicts log(sales). The antilogarithm of log(sales) can be taken to obtain sales.

Nevertheless, the choice of a fit is partly subjective. Therefore, some may prefer to use the original fit, although it is slightly inferior.

$$C1 \text{ (SALES)} = -0.70 + 1.07 \text{ C2 (ASSETS)}$$

In spite of the unusual and influential data points, this fit is reasonably good and simple to use.

CHAPTER SUMMARY

In this chapter, simple regression analysis summarized the relationship between two variables. Regression analysis was presented as a refinement of exploratory fitting, which initially involved side-by-side boxplots. The response variable, y, was on the vertical axis, and the predictor variable, x, assigned a value of 0 or 1, was on the horizontal axis. An exploratory straight line fit was obtained by drawing a line through the medians. Such a line with substantial tilt suggested that the medians of the two batches were significantly different. The classical analog in simple regression is a line through two sample means.

This simple concept of a fitted line through two sample means can be extended to situations where the predictor variable is not limited to two values. This more general fit is a powerful summary of the relationship between two variables. The classical fit of a straight line is called simple linear regression. In this approach, the linear model, $y_i = \beta_0 + \beta_1 x_{1i} + e_i$, is used to represent each data point. The model is theoretical in the sense that the β's and the errors are unknown. The classical approach to estimate the relationship, $\beta_0 + \beta_1 x_{1i}$, is based on the least squares method that minimizes the sum of the errors squared. The fit or prediction equation that results is of the form $\hat{y}_i = b_0 + b_1 x_{1i}$.

Once a fit is obtained, it is natural to be concerned about confidence intervals and hypothesis tests. Confidence intervals can be placed on the individual unknown parameters, the β's, linear combinations of the β's, and future predictions. Confidence intervals on individual parameters, t ratios or the F ratios, may be used for hypothesis testing. A hypothesis of particular interest is that the slope is 0, $\beta_1 = 0$. When this hypothesis cannot be rejected, the predictor variable does not appear to carry enough information to be significant.

The validity of these hypothesis tests and confidence intervals depends on the assumptions of random and normal error terms with a constant standard deviation. Residual analysis is used to check these assumptions.

The analysis of variance (ANOVA) table includes the F ratio as an alternative to the t ratio. However, either ratio leads to the same conclusion in simple regression. The analysis of variance table displays the variance partitioning, where the total sum of squares is partitioned into that which is explained (due to particular components in the regression model) and that which is unexplained (residual or error).

KEY TERMS

analysis of variance (ANOVA), 508
component effect, 510
critical F value, 516
design matrix, 510
error sum of squares (ESS), 518
estimated covariance, 522
full model, 509
F value test statistic, 516
least squares criterion, 513
linear statistical model, 509

mean squares, 515
multiple correlation coefficient, 520
one-way analysis of variance, 527
ordinary least squares (OLS), 508
parameter matrix, 510
pooled t test, 527
R-squared, 517
reduced model, 509
regression line, 508
regression sum of squares, 520

simple linear regression model, 509
simple regression analysis, 508
singularity problem, 511
standard deviation (residuals), 516
standard error, 522
standard error of the estimate, 521
sums of squares, 515
total sum of squares, 517

EXERCISES

The analysis presented in this chapter is a refinement of the preliminary exploratory work in Chapters 8 and 9. Therefore, several of the following exercises have been explored earlier. This chapter provides the opportunity to complete a more formal analysis of these exercises.

1. Compare the batting averages of Buck Martinez and Gary Mathews.

BUCK MARTINEZ

.229 .111 .152 .250 .215 .226 .228 .225 .219 .270
.224 .227 .242 .253 .220 .162 .181

GARY MATHEWS

.290 .300 .287 .280 .279 .283 .285 .304 .278 .301
.281 .258 .291 .235 .259

(a) Use a pooled t test, simple regression, and one-way analysis of variance to compare the two players as if the data came from a carefully designed experiment. Note that the results of each approach are the same. Summarize your findings. In particular, identify the hypotheses being tested and indicate how the tests are carried out.

(b) What is it about this observational study that makes it difficult to rely exclusively on the classical results?

2. At a New England weather station, the 36-year average monthly temperatures in Fahrenheit are

JAN.											DEC.
23.6	26.4	35.3	47.1	57.8	66.8	71.7	69.5	61.6	51.5	40.7	28.6

For the last year, the average monthly temperatures are:

JAN.											DEC.
20.9	33.3	31.4	47.8	55.1	68.9	70.9	72.2	59.8	54.8	40.2	34.4

(a) Use a pooled t test, simple regression, and the one-way analysis of variance to compare the two sets of temperatures as if the data came from a carefully designed experiment. Summarize your findings. In particular, identify the hypotheses being tested and indicate how the tests are carried out.

(b) What is it about this observational study that makes it difficult to rely on the classical results? Specifically address the question of independent (random) observations by plotting the data in the sequence observed.

3. You are given returns on a stock that were computed from the i-th period price, P_i, and the price one period ahead. The return on a stock is $y_i = \frac{(P_{i+1} - P_i)}{P_i}$. To study the movement of a particular stock, its return is related to the movement of the market as a whole by using the Dow-Jones (DJ) Index or the Standard and Poor's Composite Index as a price that represents the whole market. Therefore, the market return is $x_{1i} = \frac{(DJ_{i+1} - DJ_i)}{DJ_i}$.

Converting prices to returns usually has the effect of purging the time variable from returns, which makes y_i and x_{1i} random over time. Even though this is an observational study, working with returns often permits the valid use of classical methods. These returns have been computed for you. They are converted to a percent and rounded for simplicity. The returns are:

PERIOD	1	2	3	4	5	6	7	8	9	10	11	12
y_i =	12	15	−4	1	3	−2	−8	−1	1	1	2	7
x_{1i} =	12	6	2	4	4	5	−6	−2	3	6	2	−1

(a) Obtain a classical straight line fit of the form $b_0 + b_1 x_{1i}$ and predict the stock's return when the market return equals 6%. Write the theoretical model (in terms of the unknown parameters) that this fit estimates. What does the R-squared value tell you about the goodness of this fit?

(b) Test the hypothesis that the unknown regression coefficient, β_1, equals 0 versus the not equal alternative. Do the t test and F test result in the same conclusions?

(c) Find a 95% confidence interval on β_1.

(d) What would be the purpose of computing residuals and analyzing them?

4. In the manufacture of a new missile component, it took 120 min to make the first unit, 92 min to make the second unit of the same component, 54 min to make the seventh unit, and 52 min to manufacture the eighth unit. The complete data set is shown below. It is clear that learning is taking place. As more units are produced, less time is needed to complete each unit. The reduction in the completion time decreases as more units are produced.

UNIT										
x_{1i}	1	2	3	4	5	6	7	8	9	10

TIME TO MANUFACTURE

y_i 120   92   80   70   61   59   54   52   51   49

(a) Plot the data. Also plot the natural logarithm of y versus production unit number.

(b) Obtain a classical straight line fit to the transformed data set.

(c) For the first eight units produced, obtain the predicted time to make each unit.

(d) To assess the goodness of the fit, examine the analysis of variance table. Be sure to use the R-squared value and an F test.

5. It is thought that certain standardized tests are useful in predicting grade performance of college students. One such test was taken by 30 students. Their scores on the mathematics (MATH) part of the test are shown below along with their grade point averages (GPA).

GPA   2.70   2.65   2.30   3.73   1.64   1.76   2.92   3.14   3.13
2.71   2.54   1.98   3.09   3.31   2.78   2.63   2.66   2.25   3.28
2.00   2.13   3.08   2.46   3.03   1.16   3.31   3.22   3.70   2.46
2.97

MATH   37   35   49   44   36   55   44   49   49   45   50   43   49
57   45   33   46   30   54   36   49   55   48   55   45   41   46   62
40   58

(a) Plot GPA versus MATH.

(b) Find a prediction equation that predicts the GPA from the MATH score. Predict the GPA when the math score is 50.

(c) Assess the reliability of this prediction equation in predicting the GPA from the analysis of variance information.

(d) Use b_1 and its standard error to determine if the slope is significantly different from 0?

6. In the United States, the northwest states generate about 80% of their electrical power from hydropower plants. During periods of low water runoff, high-cost thermoelectric plants must make up for reduced hydropower generation. The average annual flow in hundreds of cubic feet per second for 40 years is:

1374   1234   1225   1679   1792   2275   1549   1639   1216   1787
1486   1490   1337   1665   1915   1376   1404   1835   1923   2242
1903   1860   2334   2069   1721   1927   1879   2497   2049   1813
1921   2054   1979   1646   1739   1740   2276   1687   1857   1755

(a) As a manager you are thinking ahead because it takes 15 to 20 years to construct some thermoelectric plants. Borrowing power on large power grids is limited and expensive. Use regression analysis to see if there is a trend in the runoff data over the 40 years. In MINITAB, the data for the trend variable is created in the following way:

```
MTB> SET C2
DATA> 1:40
```

(b) Use the analysis of variance table to test if the slope of the fitted line is significantly different from 0. How is the R-squared value obtained from information in this table?

7. A particularly bad type of fall in skiing is one in which you twist your leg. This can result in a spiral fracture in the lower leg. Ski bindings are designed to release before the twist torque in foot-pounds gets to a critical level. The critical level of twist torque depends on skier weight.

Tabulated figures are used to set twist torque (T) binding release levels based on weight (W) in pounds. Summarize the following tabulated figures in a regression equation.

T	16	20	24	28	32	36	40	44	48	50
W	55	75	95	115	135	155	175	195	215	235

(a) Does the analysis of variance table indicate that this is a good fit? What is it about the residual (error) sum of squares relative to the total sum of squares that supports your answer?

8. A random sample of professional golfers had the following one-year official earnings (E) in thousands of dollars and scoring averages (A).[1]

EARNINGS (E)

71.6   55.8   147.8   117.4   112.3   82.7   22.8   58.8   60.5   55.4   43.6

SCORING AVERAGES (A)

71.5   72.75   71.34   71.27   70.95   71.65   72.49   71.46   71.95   71.61   72.39

(a) Using regression analysis, see if there is a strong relationship between these two variables. Summarize your findings. In particular, identify the hypotheses being tested and indicate how the tests are carried out.

(b) Does the t value associated with the slope coefficient lead to the same conclusion as an F test from the analysis of variance table? Explain.

9. A firm produces prefabricated houses by order only because a large number of styles and options are made available to the customer. This is a job-shop rather than an assembly-line production facility. For pricing purposes, the managers use budgeted costs because actual costs are not available until after a job is finished. A problem became evident during the examination of recent cost figures. For a portion of the pre-fabrication work, as the actual cost (AC) increased, the absolute deviation (DC) from budget became larger. To assess the magnitude of the problem and to establish a benchmark for budgeting improvements, analyze and report on this relationship for the dollar figures below.

AC	35640	35730	35740	36000	37760	38700	39930	41210	43560
DC	500	610	615	854	1640	1100	1875	2044	1123

10. Some manufacturing companies refer to the true physical production cost for a period as the gross product. For financial planning in manufacturing, it is necessary to relate the gross product to production factors such as payroll costs. Regression provides a convenient way to summarize the relationship between gross product (GP) and other factors such as payroll cost (PAY). Summarize the relationship between gross product (GP) and payroll (PAY) for the actual production cost figures shown below (in thousands of dollars).

GP	69	210	156	166	120	100	112	125	175
PAY	66	143	115	122	117	90	95	110	135

11. A company maintains a fleet of automobiles. Management is interested in minimizing the total cost of ownership and operation. A portion of the total cost is for maintenance and operating costs (O&M dollars per mile). O&M costs tend to increase with vehicle age. Predict the fraction of O&M costs using vehicle age (VA) in years. Evaluate the quality of this fit.

O&M	.20	.28	.27	.316	.38	.42	.44	.49	.55	.56	.63	.66
VA	1	2	3	4	5	6	7	8	9	10	11	12

12. In establishing labor forecasts for a shipping center, it was necessary to predict man-hours (MH) from shipping units (SU in hundreds of units). Using regression, find the prediction equation and comment on the quality of the fit.

MH	3470	4650	5370	8320	5190	4180	3420	3890	3650	5410	4110	3740
SU	2178	3229	5530	6442	3767	2497	2229	3561	3791	4184	3246	2813

13. A manufacturing company found that the greater the capital investment (CI in hundreds of dollars) in automation, the fewer was the number of people employed (PE). For decision making purposes, quantify this relationship using simple regression analysis.

CI	985	715	585	500	412	198	190	146	56	14
PE	50	20	110	430	312	250	620	415	512	675

14. Flexible budgeting is needed in factories because production volume varies. Predicting cost behavior from past production experience is a supporting pillar of flexible budgeting. Although industrial engineering studies are used to determine how costs should vary with volume, regression analysis is also used to summarize past cost-volume experience. Total mixed cost (TMC), a mixture of fixed and variable components, is often related to a production volume measure such as machine-hours (MH). Obtain an equation for predicting TMC (in hundreds of dollars) based on MH.

TMC	20	21	24	14	15	8	10	13	14	16	20
MH	22	27	23	19	18	14	13	10	12	20	26

15. An automobile manufacturer conducts quality control training programs in two of its supplier plants. The instructor gives the same exam in both plants. The exam scores are

Plant (Boston)	90	73	78	82	66	69	85	86	76	89	70
Plant (Atlanta)	81	72	50	66	55	70	68	82	71		

(a) Use a pooled t-test, simple regression, and one-way analysis of variance to test the hypothesis that the average exam scores at the two different plants are the same at a 5% level of significance.

16. A manager who welcomes employee suggestions about reducing assembly time in a production operation decided to test a recent employee suggestion. Use information in the analysis of variance table to test for a significant difference in the mean assembly times (in minutes).

ASSEMBLY TIMES

OLD METHOD

21.6	21.7	23.9	24.0	22.7	24.6	22.5
24.0	24.4	24.0	23.7	24.9	23.9	24.9
22.7	23.4	22.4	22.2	24.4	24.4	25.1
22.7	25.3	23.4	25.4	24.1	24.5	24.1
24.9	23.9	24.9	23.9	23.1	24.5	24.6
25.0	24.7	22.3	24.0	23.0		

NEW METHOD

23.5	23.5	22.0	21.3	21.7	22.3	23.3
23.6	21.5	24.1	21.6	22.5	22.3	21.6
21.7	22.0	22.0	21.1	21.8	21.9	24.3
22.9	20.1	21.8	20.6	21.7	22.3	21.5
22.9	21.5	22.2	21.4	21.9	21.1	22.8
21.8	21.5	23.4	22.6	20.6		

17. An investor collected monthly price data for the stocks of two companies in the same line of business. Based on those prices, returns were computed as shown below. Test to see if there is a significant difference in mean returns using one-way analysis of variance.

RETURNS COMPANY A

```
0.112   0.115   0.158   0.160   0.135   0.172   0.130
0.161   0.169   0.161   0.155   0.179   0.159   0.178
0.135   0.149   0.128   0.125   0.168   0.168   0.183
0.134   0.187   0.149
```

RETURNS COMPANY B

```
0.209   0.182   0.191   0.182   0.198   0.179   0.199
0.179   0.162   0.191   0.192   0.200   0.194   0.147
0.181   0.161   0.210   0.211   0.181   0.166   0.175
0.186   0.206   0.213
```

18. According to Robert Adair, former physicist for the National Baseball League, the distance (feet) a baseball travels is a function of the velocity (mph) of a pitched ball.[2] For the data below, assume that a 35-in., 32-oz bat is swung at 70 mph, waist-high, 10° upward from the horizontal plane, driving the ball at an angle of 35°.

Distance	327	335	340	348	356	363	370	378	388
Velocity	20	30	40	50	60	70	80	90	100

(a) Use these figures to fit a line that summarizes the relationship between distance and velocity. Would you reject the hypothesis that there is no relationship between distance and velocity?

(b) Adair said that the fastest pitchers can throw a fast ball about 100 mph; for example, Bob Feller (1946, 98.6 mph), Walter Johnson (1914, 99.7 mph), Nolan Ryan (100.7 mph), and Goose Gossage (about 100 mph). In contrast, a slow curve might have a velocity of 65 mph. Based on your fit, how far will a slow curve be hit?

(c) What is it about the error sum of squares relative to the total sum of squares that makes the R-squared value close to 1 in this fit?

19. A state department of transportation depends on computer processing for vehicle registrations and other transactions. A computer capacity management aid tracks central processor unit (CPU) hours used by month. Trends in CPU usage can be projected into the future to see when CPU capacity might be exceeded. As a result, early warning can be given of needed computer capacity enhancements, and budget requests for funding CPU enhancements can be sent to the legislature's Ways and Means Sub-committee for approval.

Obtain a regression equation for the monthly data shown below and determine when (how many months in the future) the CPU capacity of 300 hours will be exceeded. Evaluate the goodness of fit.

CPU Usage	183	188	203	185	186	196	182	207	209	195
Month (Aug.)	1	2	3	4	5	6	7	8	9	10

CPU Usage	197	203	220	218	225	212	220	230	232
Month	11	12	13	14	15	16	17	18	19

20. An equipment list that was part of a bid document listed both rental cost (including maintenance) and purchase price. Use simple regression to relate rental cost to purchase price. Is there a relationship with a slope that is significantly different from 0? Do any of the residuals indicate an unusually large discrepancy between actual and expected rental cost?

Rent	1,292	1,798	180	43	290	64	188	421
Price	20,900	31,900	2,900	700	4,690	1,200	3,000	6,900

21. Determine if there is a strong relationship between the following average SAT scores and the midpoints of the parents' income classes.[3]

SAT AVERAGE

996 959 944 924 898 870 829 780

INCOME LEVEL (IN THOUSANDS OF DOLLARS)

80 65 55 45 35 25 15 5

22. For an old truck, summarize the relationship between miles per gallon (MPG) and the average speed it was driven (MPH). Evaluate the goodness of fit.

MPG	16.9	16.1	16.3	16.0	15.6	15.2	14.8	15.1	14.2
	13.7	13.9	13.5						

MPH	50	52	54	56	58	60	62	64	66	68	70	72

23. In the analysis of collegiate football scores, researchers were interested in the relationship between the winner's score as the loser's score increases.[4] Find an equation that predicts the winning score from the average losing score. As the average losing score increases, does the winning score increase or decrease in variability? Does this violate any of the assumptions about the error terms in a regression model?

WINNING SCORE

3	6	7	8	9	10	11	12	13	14	15	16	17	18	19	20	21	22
23	24	25	26	27	28	29	30	31	32	33	34	35	36	37	38	39	40

AVERAGE LOSING SCORE

.4	1.6	3.1	4.3	5.2	6.1	7.0	6.2	7.4	7.9	8.5	7.8
8.3	11.3	8.3	9.6	10.4	12.4	10.5	12.0	11.8	11.3	12.1	11.2
10.6	10.6	14.4	16.8	15.9	10.1	11.6	13.8	14.8	11.1	13.1	14.7

24. In attempting to reduce consumer complaints, airline management investigated the number of oversales related to the number of baggage problems. It was thought that oversales could be reduced. From the analysis of the following data, would you recommend reducing oversales?[5] Justify your conclusions.

BAGGAGE PROBLEMS

20 54 62 0 60 24 20 53 4 15 17 26 9 18 4 70 8

OVERSALES

13 19 26 0 17 34 14 12 1 53 42 25 6 8 2 36 4

25. In order to set delivery dates for spools of fabric, production time estimates were needed. Simple regression analysis was used to predict the number of hours needed to wind a spool of fabric. The winding time was related to the number of fabric bands sewn end-to-end. Obtain a prediction equation and evaluate the fit from the following data:

WINDING TIME

2.03　1.84　2.71　2.68　2.49　2.80　2.72　3.69　3.67　4.56
5.18　5.02　6.32　6.26　5.35　5.71　5.90　6.69　7.25　5.70

NUMBER OF BANDS

　1　　2　　3　　4　　5　　6　　7　　8　　9　　10　　11　　12　　13　　14　　15　　16　　17
18　　19　　20

26. Relate used-car price to mileage for a particular model. Plot price versus miles and write the car age next to each plotting point. Use residuals to spot underpriced vehicles.

AGE

8　　8　　7　　7　　7　　7　　7　　6　　6　　6　　5　　5　　5　　4

MILES

78000　66000　82000　51000　56000　66000　41000　39000
45000　61000　33000　27000　35000　25000

PRICE

3400　4000　3800　5800　5500　5000　6600　6200　7000　6100
7800　8100　7500　8300

APPENDIX 1

Minitab Examples

THE FIT IN EXHIBIT 1

```
MTB > SET INTO C3    # DATA FROM Exhibit 1
DATA> 26 34 98 72    # MATRIX Y TRANSPOSED
DATA> END

MTB > SET INTO C4
DATA> 0 0 1 1            # SECOND COLUMN OF MATRIX X
                        # MINITAB SUPPLIES THE FIRST COLUMN
DATA> END

MTB > REGRESS C3 1 PRED C4;    # OUTPUT FROM THIS COMMAND
SUBC> RESIDUALS C5.           # WILL BE DISCUSSED IN THE
                        # SECTIONS THAT DESCRIBE THESE RESULTS
```

MINITAB ANALYSIS OF THE AGE DATA, ILLUSTRATING CLASSICAL REGRESSION, ONE-WAY ANALYSIS OF VARIANCE (ANOVA), AND T TEST (POOLED) APPROACHES

```
      (OR RETRIEVE 'AGE' whichever is appropriate.)
MTB > RETRIEVE 'B:AGE'
MTB > NAME C1 'AGEF'  # LONGEVITY FATHERS OF PRESIDENTS
MTB > NAME C2 'AGEM'  # LONGEVITY MOTHERS OF PRESIDENTS

MTB > STACK C2 ON C1 PUT IN C3
MTB > NAME C3 'AGEMF'

MTB > SET IN C4       # 0'S FOR MOTHERS  1'S FOR FATHERS
DATA> 34(0),34(1)     # NO SPACES ALLOWED IN THIS LINE
DATA> END
```

```
MTB > NAME C4 'DUMMY'  # DUMMY, BINARY, CATEGORICAL AND
# INDICATOR ARE TERMS USED FOR THIS TYPE OF VARIABLE THAT
# IS USED TO IDENTIFY PARTICULAR SUBSETS OF DATA VALUES

MTB > REGRESS 'AGEMF' 1 PRED C4, STRES C6;
SUBC> RESIDUALS C5.
```

Comment Note that the output from ONEWAY is the same as part of the output from REGRESS.

```
MTB > ONEWAY C3 C4    # CAN COMPUTE RESIDUALS AND FITS TOO

MTB > DOTPLOT C6;      # STANDARDIZED RESIDUALS FROM REGRESSION
SUBC> BY C4;
SUBC> SAME.
```

Comment Note that the output from TWOT is the same as part of the output from REGRESS and ONEWAY.

```
MTB > TWOT 95% FOR 'AGEMF' BY 'DUMMY';
SUBC> POOLED.
```

EXAMPLE

MINITAB ANALYSIS OF THE SALES DATA ILLUSTRATING CLASSICAL REGRESSION, ONE-WAY ANALYSIS OF VARIANCE (ANOVA), AND T TEST (POOLED) APPROACHES

```
      (OR RETRIEVE 'SALES' whichever is appropriate.)
MTB > RETRIEVE 'B:SALES'
MTB > NAME C1 'SNEW'   # SALES NEW PACKAGE DESIGN
MTB > NAME C2 'SOLD'   # SALES OLD PACKAGE DESIGN
MTB > STACK 'SOLD' 'SNEW', PUT IN C3
MTB > NAME C3 'SALESON'

MTB > SET INTO C4
DATA> 13(0),13(1)        # NO SPACES ALLOWED IN THIS LINE
DATA> END
MTB > NAME C4 'DUMMY'

MTB > REGRESS 'SALESON' 1 PRED. 'DUMMY', STDRES C6;
SUBC> RESIDUALS C5.
```

Comment Note that the output from ONEWAY is the same as part of the output from REGRESS.

```
MTB > ONEWAY DATA IN 'SALESON', SUBSCRIPTS IN 'DUMMY'
MTB > DOTPLOT C6;   # STANDARDIZED RESIDUALS FROM REGRESSION
SUBC> BY C4;
SUBC> SAME.
```

Comment   Note that the output from TWOT is the same as part of the output from REGRESS and ONEWAY.

```
MTB > TWOT 95% 'SALESON' BY 'DUMMY';
SUBC> POOLED.
```

EXAMPLE

MORE ON SALES VERSUS ASSETS IN MINITAB

```
        THE FILE NAME IS SALAS AND NOT SALES.
   (OR RETRIEVE 'SALAS', whichever is appropriate.)
MTB > RETRIEVE 'B:SALAS'
MTB > DESCRIBE C1 C2

MTB > CORRELATE C1 C2   # SALES AND ASSETS

MTB > PLOT C1 C2;
SUBC> YSTART AT 0;
SUBC> XSTART AT 0.

MTB > REGRESS C1 1 PRED IN C2, STD RES C3, FITS C4;
SUBC> RESIDUALS C5.

MTB > PLOT C5 C2     # RESIDUALS VERSUS ASSETS
MTB > HIST C3        # STANDARDIZED RESIDUALS
MTB > PLOT C5 C4     # RESIDUALS VERSUS PREDICTIONS
MTB > RUNS C5        # GOOD- LOOKS RANDOM!

MTB > DELETE ROWS 1,2,3,4 C1 C2
MTB > LET C6=LOGE(C1)

MTB > REGRESS C6 1 PRED C2, ST RES C3, FITS C4;
SUBC> RESIDUALS C5.
MTB > DESCRIBE C6       # NEEDED TO GET ȳ

MTB > CORRELATE C6 C4  # LOGESALES VERSUS PREDICTED LOGESALES

MTB > PLOT C6 C4       # GOOD! PREDICTED CLOSE TO ACTUAL
MTB > HIST C3

MTB > PLOT C5 C2       # RESIDUALS VERSUS ASSETS
MTB > PLOT C5 C4     # RESIDUALS VERSUS PREDICTED SALES
MTB > RUNS C5        # GOOD RESULT, RANDOM RESIDUALS.
```

CHAPTER 12

Multiple Regression Analysis

PRELUDE

Like stars in the night sky, data points hang in space. Space as we know it in this chapter is beyond one dimension for a single variable and beyond two dimensions for a pair of variables. Now the data space dimensions are three and more.

As with the heavens, space humbles us quickly, reminding us of how little we know and how close to the limits of perception we are. Yet, under these more difficult circumstances, the data analyst's job is to spot and comprehend the patterned constellations of data points.

Those without statistical knowledge can barely visualize three-dimensional data clouds, and hopelessness descends on the untrained when problems involve four and more variables. Yet, we live in a complex world in which it is common to encounter situations characterized by many variables. This chapter is about navigating in such muddy waters.

In three-dimensional space, the data cloud is summarized by a plane; higher dimensional space is summarized by a hyperplane. The classical approach for obtaining such a summary fit and its related accoutrements falls under the heading of multiple linear regression analysis, a major research tool in nearly every discipline. ◆

Just as during the first weeks of life the object is confused with the sensory impressions connected with elementary action, so also at birth there is no concept of space except the perception of light and the accommodation inherent in that perception (pupillary reflex to light and palpebral reflex to dazzle). All the rest—perception of shapes, of sizes, distances, positions, etc.—is elaborated little by little at the same time as the objects themselves.

Space, therefore, is not at all perceived as a container but rather as that which it contains, that is, objects themselves; and, if space becomes in a sense a container, it is to the extent that the relationships which constitute the objectification of bodies succeed in becoming intercoordinated until they form a coherent whole. The concept of space is understood only as a function of the construction of objects, and it was necessary to start by describing the latter in order to understand the former; only the degree of objectification that the child attributes to things informs us of the degree of externality he accords to space.[1]

INTRODUCTION

Thus far, data points have been limited to one- or two-dimensional space. With a single variable, numbers were strung on a line from minus to plus infinity. As objects, numbers marked points on a line like the yardage markers on a football field that run the length of the field. When we encountered a more complicated situation involving two variables, the data were perceived as objects on a plane, like data points in a two-variable scatterplot. For an analogy in football, think of each player on the field as occupying a position on the x-y plane; the players on the field are like data points in a two-dimensional space.

One- or two-dimensional thinking does not adequately deal with more complex problems when working with three or more variables. Consider the problem of locating the position of a football at an instant after it has been punted high in the air above the field. The instantaneous position of the football is in an imaginary container of air at height y_i and positioned relative to the plane of the field in terms of x_{1i} (along the length of the field) and of x_{2i} (along the width of the field). Thus, the football is positioned in three-dimensional space. The best two-dimensional space can do is locate the football's shadow or projection on the playing field when the sun is directly overhead.

This chapter describes **multiple regression analysis,** which is a statistical tool for obtaining fits to data points in three-or-more-dimensional space. In three space, the data points are suspended, like many footballs punted simultaneously, and pictured at an instant in time, like raindrops suspended in a cloud.

Our statistical learning journey has come from simple situations characterized by one, two, or three variables to the boundaries of space that we can visualize. Although three-dimensional space is more difficult to visualize than two-dimensional space, constellations of data points can still be seen. What about four-dimensional space? How do we visualize data point patterns there?

Notation and Terminology

Coping with more complex problems requires extending the notation. Symbolically, the response variable is y_i and the predictor variables are x_{1i}, x_{2i}, x_{3i}, . . . , x_{ki}.

The use of more than one predictor variable results in a richer variety of prediction equations (or fits) than previously possible. With two predictor variables, for example, four fits are possible. These are listed below.

A superscript is used on each regression coefficient to indicate that different values for the coefficients can arise, depending on which variables are in or out of the equation. As a matter of convenience, the superscript is the equation number, (1), (2), (3), or (4). Its value has no significance except to identify different regression coefficients.

With two predictor variables, the four possible fits are

(1) $$\hat{y}_i = b_0^{(1)}$$

(2) $$\hat{y}_i = b_0^{(2)} + b_1^{(2)}x_{1i}$$

(3) $$\hat{y}_i = b_0^{(3)} + b_2^{(3)}x_{2i}$$

(4) $$\hat{y}_i = b_0^{(4)} + b_1^{(4)}x_{1i} + b_2^{(4)}x_{2i}$$

One objective of our analysis is to determine which prediction equation to use. Predictor variables are included in the fit when they make a significant contribution to explaining the response. Those that contribute little are dropped. Statistical tests help us decide whether a predictor variable is included or excluded from the prediction equation. In simple regression there is only one predictor variable. In multiple regression there are two or more predictor variables in the fit, such as in equation (4) above.

Four distinct fits are possible when there are two predictor variables because each variable may be in or out of the prediction equation. The predictor variables are like toppings for a pizza, where each variable can be on or off the pizza—two possible states. With only two toppings, think of x_{1i} as anchovies and x_{2i} as mushrooms. The possible pizzas are (a) a plain pizza, equation (1), no anchovies and no mushrooms; (b) a pizza with anchovies only, equation (2); (c) a pizza with mushrooms only, equation (3); or (d) a pizza with both anchovies and mushrooms as in equation (4). The number of possible equations is easy to compute. Take the number of states (on or off the pizza—two states) to a power equal to the number of predictor variables (toppings).

$$(\text{number of states})^{(\text{number of predictor variables})} = 2^2 = 4$$

For more predictor variables or toppings, say, 3, 4, or 5, then $2^3 = 8$, $2^4 = 16$, and $2^5 = 32$, respectively, are the numbers of potential prediction equations corresponding to 3, 4, or 5 variables.

As the number of predictor variables increases, the number of potential prediction equations becomes unmanageably large. It is understandable that people without proper training grope for solutions when confronted with multivariate problems.

EXAMPLE 1

PRODUCTION PLANT WATER USAGE COST

Analysis results are presented to emphasize that several prediction equations are possible. Furthermore, a choice has to be made as to which prediction equation to use. How regression coefficients are obtained is not of immediate concern. This topic will be covered later in the chapter.

Problem Statement In production plant operation, predict costly water usage considering two predictor variables, amount of production, and number of people on the monthly payroll. Show the possible prediction equations.

Problem Solution Draper and Smith analyzed production plant cost data.[2] A cost-control engineer examined the following variables: y, the monthly water usage (gallons); x_{1i}, the amount of production (millions of pounds), and x_{2i}, the number of people on the monthly plant payroll. Using Draper and Smith's results for these three variables, the prediction equations, $\hat{y}$, for water usage are

(1) $\qquad \hat{y}_i = b_0^{(1)} = 3304$

(2) $\qquad \hat{y}_i = b_0^{(2)} + b_1^{(2)}x_{1i} = 2273 + .08\,x_{1i}$

(3) $\qquad \hat{y}_i = b_0^{(3)} + b_2^{(3)}x_{2i} = 1778 + 8.39\,x_{2i}$

(4) $\qquad \hat{y}_i = b_0^{(4)} + b_1^{(4)}x_{1i} + b_2^{(4)}x_{2i} = 4601 + .2x_{1i} - 21.57\,x_{2i}$

Problem Discussion Multiple regression methods were used to estimate the regression coefficients, which are the b's that appear in the equations above. Draper and Smith found that either prediction equation (2) or (4) could be used, but equation (4) was a little better than (2).

Regarding the predictor variable contributions in explaining the response: x_{2i} alone is not significant; x_{1i} is significant; and x_{1i} and x_{2i} together are significant. Equation (4) includes both x_{1i}, the amount of production, and x_{2i}, the number of people on the monthly plant payroll. Notice that the regression coefficients do not remain the same in different equations because of correlated predictor variables.

When choosing which prediction equation to use, one objective is to select a fit that is no more elaborate than necessary. Therefore, if both of the following fits explain the response equally well, the first would be preferred

$$\hat{y}_i = 2273 + .08\,x_{1i}$$

in favor of the second, more complicated fit

$$\hat{y}_i = 4601 + .20\,x_{1i} - 21.57\,x_{2i}$$

If the additional variable, x_{2i}, substantially improves the predictive ability of the model, its inclusion might be worth the increase in complexity. Sometimes the knowledge gained by adding predictor variables to the prediction equation is worth the price of increased complexity. Such an evaluation has subjective as well as objective considerations that the statistician and the client should evaluate jointly.

Recall that in simple regression it was necessary to hold or assume that background variables were constant. Otherwise the true relationship between a pair of variables might not be found. In multiple regression, background variables, if known, can be incorporated into the fit.

THE MULTIPLE REGRESSION MODEL AND ACCOUTREMENTS BY EXAMPLE

Classical multiple regression analysis relates many predictor variables, x_{1i}, x_{2i}, x_{3i}, . . . , x_{ki}, to a single response variable, y_i. The analysis is generally carried out in the following three phases, which may be repeated if necessary.

First, the **identification phase** helps identify the potentially relevant variables and relationships, leading to postulated models of the phenomenon under study. Although correlations and scatterplots are useful in this phase, it might include any exploratory or descriptive work that helps the investigator understand the problem. The statistical impressions alone should not dominate the thinking; the science and lore associated with the application are equally important. Often the client must help provide this background to the investigator.

After postulated models are found, prediction equations and goodness of fit information are obtained in the **estimation phase.** This information is evaluated and residuals are calculated in preparation for examination in the **diagnostic phase.** Although classical fits are illustrated in the examples that follow, exploratory fits might also be carried out in the estimation phase.

Residuals are examined in the diagnostic phase. Residual plots suggest either that the analysis is completed or that the postulated models must be modified and the analysis process continued.

We present multiple regression analysis through a series of examples. A technical reference section on multiple regression analysis follows the examples and maps out the conceptual framework. You may prefer to concentrate on the examples and use the technical section as a reference.

EXAMPLE 2

BOX AND HUNTER'S POPCORN EXPERIMENT[3]

Relate the response variable, popcorn yield (cups), to the predictor variables brand (gourmet or ordinary) and amount ($\frac{1}{3}$ or $\frac{2}{3}$ cup of kernels). Brand is coded -1 for ordinary popcorn and $+1$ for gourmet. Amount is coded -1 for $\frac{1}{3}$ cup and $+1$ for $\frac{2}{3}$ cup of kernels. Eight experimental runs were conducted.

```
ROW   YIELD   BRAND   AMOUNT
 1     6.25    -1       -1
 2     8.00    +1       -1
 3     6.00    -1       -1
 4     9.50    +1       -1
 5     8.00    -1       +1
 6    15.00    +1       +1
 7     9.00    -1       +1
 8    17.00    +1       +1
```

For pedagogical purposes, illustrate that a sequence of simple regressions (some using residuals) produces a multiple regression fit. Also obtain the multiple regression fit directly, without simple regression.

It is recommended that a similar experiment be conducted by students who could analyze their own popcorn yield figures.

Problem Statement (a)   In an attempt to identify important relationships, correlate all pairs of variables and examine scatterplots.

Problem Solution (a)   A correlation matrix for all pairs of variables is

```
           YIELD    AMOUNT
AMOUNT     0.640
BRAND      0.673     0.000
```

This experiment was designed so brand and amount are uncorrelated, permitting multiple regression analysis to put its best foot forward. Unambiguously, we can clearly see the separate effects of brand and amount on yield.

In the following scatterplot (Plot (a)) of yield versus amount, yield increases as amount increases. When amount equals $+1$, ($\frac{2}{3}$ cup of kernels), there are two clusters of points. The two clusters are due to the third variable, brand.

In the next scatterplot of yield versus brand (Plot (b)), yield increases as brand increases. Also notice that when brand equals $+1$ (gourmet), there are two clusters of points. The two clusters are due to the third variable, amount. Although not as pronounced, there are two clusters at brand equals -1 too.

The next plot (Plot (c)) confirms that there is no correlation between brand and amount.

Problem Statement (b)   First, in the estimation phase, use amount of kernels alone to predict yield. Show how residuals are computed. Also find t value statistics and other goodness of fit information.

Problem Solution (b)   The fit is

$$\text{yield (predicted)} = 9.84 + 2.41 \text{ amount}$$

The residual, yield removing amount (YRA), is found as follows:

$$\text{YRA} = \text{yield(actual)} - \text{yield (predicted)}$$
$$\text{YRA} = \text{yield(actual)} - (9.84 + 2.41 \text{ amount})$$

As a result of the subtraction in the residual computation, amount is removed, in effect, from actual yield.

Example 2 Plot (a)

Popcorn Yield Versus Amount of Kernals

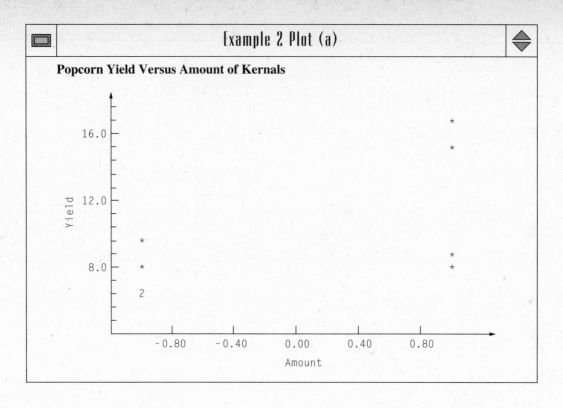

Example 2 Plot (b)

Popcorn Yield Versus Brand

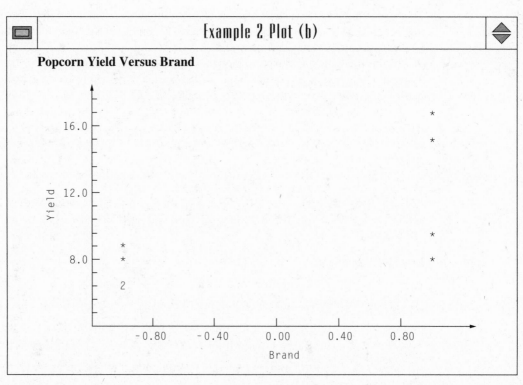

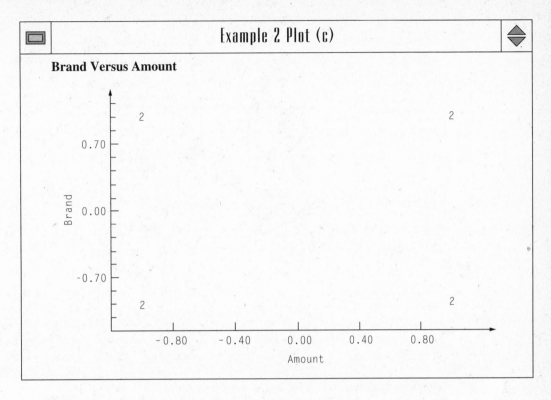

Before examining the tabulated statistics below, you might expect the effect of amount to be significantly different from 0, but it is not here (in simple regression) because of the small sample size and the inflated error sum of squares (inflated because the brand effect is in error and not yet in the regression equation).

Predictor	Coef	Stdev	t Ratio	p Value
Constant	9.844	1.180	8.34	0.000
AMOUNT	2.406	1.180	2.04	0.087

s = 3.337   R-sq = 40.9%   R-sq(adj) = 31.1%

Analysis of Variance

SOURCE	DF	SS	MS	F Value	p Value
Regression	1	46.32	46.32	4.16	0.087
Error	6	66.80	11.13		
Total	7	113.12			

Problem Statement (c)   Next, in the estimation phase, use brand alone to predict yield. Also find t value statistics and other goodness of fit information.

Problem Solution (c)   The fit is

$$\text{yield} = 9.84 + 2.53 \text{ brand}$$

Before examining the tabulated statistics below, you might expect the effect of brand to be significantly different from 0, but it is not here (in simple regression) because of the small sample size and the inflated error sum of squares (inflated now because the amount effect is in error and not in the regression equation).

Predictor	Coef	Stdev	t Ratio	p Value
Constant	9.844	1.135	8.67	0.000
BRAND	2.531	1.135	2.23	0.067

s = 3.21   R-sq = 45.3%   R-sq(adj) = 36.2%

Analysis of Variance

SOURCE	DF	SS	MS	F Value	p Value
Regression	1	51.26	51.26	4.97	0.067
Error	6	61.86	10.31		
Total	7	113.12			

Problem Statement (d)   Next, relate the two predictor variables, using amount of kernels to predict brand. This is done to demonstrate what happens when uncorrelated variables are regressed on one another. If we were able to predict brand based on amount, we would question the need for both variables; then it would seem that only one variable is needed. Show how residuals are computed. Also find t value statistics and other goodness of fit information.

Problem Solution (d)   The regression equation is

$$\text{brand (predicted)} = 0.000 + 0.000 \text{ amount}$$

The 0 values for the coefficients arise because brand and amount are uncorrelated.

It is unnecessary to compute residuals for brand regressed on amount because they are uncorrelated. Therefore, the residuals, BRA, shown below are identical to the data values in brand. Nevertheless, these residual equations are presented because, in many observational studies and in some designed experiments, nonzero correlations arise between the predictor variables. Then residual computations are needed and nonzero regression coefficients appear in the prediction equation. Such residuals remove the effect of one predictor variable from another.

$$\text{BRA} = \text{brand(actual)} - \text{brand (predicted)}$$
$$\text{BRA} = \text{brand(actual)} - (0.00 + 0.00 \text{ amount})$$

The reason for the subtraction in the computation is that amount is to be removed from the data values representing brand. Thus, a residual can be viewed as an original data column that has been adjusted. And this residual can be used as an artificially created new variable. If nonzero correlations had existed between the predictor variables, the predicted part of the residual, (0.00 + 0.00 amount), would have had nonzero coefficients.

It is instructive to examine the tabulated statistics below for the case of uncorrelated predictor and response variables.

Predictor	Coef	Stdev	t Ratio	p Value
Constant	0.0000	0.4082	0.00	1.000
AMOUNT	0.0000	0.4082	0.00	1.000

s = 1.155   R-sq = 0.0   %R-sq(adj) = 0.0%

Analysis of Variance

SOURCE	DF	SS	MS	F Value	p Value
Regression	1	0.000	0.000	0.00	1.000
Error	6	8.000	1.333		
Total	7	8.000			

Problem Statement (e)   Although many residual plots can be examined in this diagnostic phase, only yield removing amount, YRA, versus brand removing amount, BRA, is examined in this example. The reason is that this residual plot leads us to the objective of illustrating a multiple regression fit via a sequence of simple regressions, using residuals where needed.

Problem Solution (e)   This residual plot shows a strong relation between YRA and BRA.

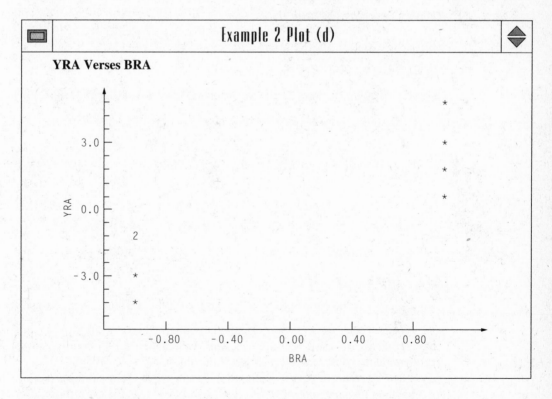

Example 2 Plot (d)

Problem Statement (f)   Next, fit residuals YRA to BRA. Obtain t values and other goodness of fit information.

Problem Solution (ƒ)   The fit is

$$YRA = -0.000 + 2.53 \ BRA$$

Both the tabulated F and t values show a significant effect here. By working with residuals, we have considered both brand and amount simultaneously, reducing the error sum of squares, which results in significant t and F values.

Predictor	Coef	Stdev	t Ratio	p Value
Constant	-0.0000	0.5690	-0.00	1.000
BRA	2.5313	0.5690	4.45	0.004

s = 1.609   R-sq = 76.7%   R-sq(adj) = 72.9%

Analysis of Variance

SOURCE	DF	SS	MS	F Value	p Value
Regression	1	51.258	51.258	19.79	0.004
Error	6	15.539	2.590		
Total	7	66.797			

Problem Statement (g)   In the fit relating residuals YRA to BRA, define these residuals in terms of the original variables, brand, amount, and yield. Arrange the resulting multiple regression equation so that brand and amount predict yield.

Problem Solution (g)   BRA and YRA in terms of the original variables are expressed in the following two fits that were found by simple regression earlier in this example:

$$BRA = brand - (0.00 + 0.00 \ amount)$$
$$YRA = yield - (9.84 + 2.41 \ amount)$$

These two equations are substituted in the prediction equation that relates BRA and YRA.

$$YRA = -0.000 + 2.53 \ BRA$$
$$yield - (9.84 + 2.41 \ amount) = -0.000 + 2.53 \ BRA$$
$$yield - 9.84 - 2.41 \ amount = +2.53 \ brand$$

Rearrangement of the above equation includes changing signs and moving the constant (9.84) and (2.41 times amount) to the right side. This produces a multiple regression equation fit.

$$yield \ (predicted) = +9.84 + 2.41 \ amount + 2.53 \ brand$$

Because the experiment was designed to have a 0 correlation between amount and brand, the coefficients in the multiple regression equation are the same as those in the simple regression equations, making interpretations clear.

When there are nonzero correlations (as in most observational studies), the regression coefficients in simple and multiple regression differ. This makes it more difficult, and sometimes impossible, to understand the relationship between three or more variables.

Because of the -1 and $+1$ coding of amount and brand, notice that

1. holding amount fixed, a brand change from (ordinary popcorn) to (gourmet) means a contribution to predicted yield change of (2.53 times -1) to (2.53 times $+1$). In other words, the gourmet brand gets you an additional $2.53 + 2.53 = 5.06$ cups of popcorn yield on the average.
2. holding brand fixed, an amount change from $\frac{1}{3}$ to $\frac{2}{3}$ cups of corn kernels means a contribution to predicted yield change from (-1 times 2.41) to ($+1$ times 2.41). In other words, a $\frac{1}{3}$ cup amount change gets you $(2.41 + 2.41) = 4.82$ cups of popcorn yield on the average.

If the two variables brand and amount had been correlated, we would not have been able to untangle them and see these separate effects so clearly. Thus, you see the value of intelligently designed experiments. Unfortunately, managers are often unable to design experiments for many situations they face so they have to make some decisions without them and their clear results.

Problem Statement (h) The multiple regression equation found above resulted from simple regression fits and the use of residuals. This approach is useful pedagogically. However, once understanding has been achieved, a multiple regression fit can be found directly, without simple regression. Illustrate that here.

Problem Solution (h) Using the MINITAB REGRESS command (see the Appendix 1), both amount and brand can be simultaneously included as predictors. The resulting multiple regression equation fit is

$$\text{yield} = 9.84 + 2.41 \text{ amount} + 2.53 \text{ brand}$$

Problem Statement (i) Find and evaluate goodness of fit information.

Problem Solution (i) From the tabulations below, you can see that both amount and brand effects are significantly different from zero (now that the error sum of squares has been reduced by including the relevant predictor variables in the regression). The process of searching the column of t ratios for significant variables is a rough procedure because a sequence of t tests loses power. Therefore, in multiple regression analysis the F test in the ANOVA table takes on a more important role than in simple regression.

Predictor	Coef	Stdev	t Ratio	p Value
Constant	9.8438	0.6233	15.79	0.000
AMOUNT	2.4062	0.6233	3.86	0.012
BRAND	2.5313	0.6233	4.06	0.010

s = 1.763   R-sq = 86.3%   R-sq(adj) = 80.8%

(continued)

(continued)
```
Analysis of Variance

SOURCE        DF        SS         MS       F Value      p Value

Regression    2      97.578     48.789      15.70        0.007
Error         5      15.539      3.108

Total         7     113.117

SOURCE        DF      SEQ SS (Partitioning the Regression SS)

AMOUNT        1      46.320 --- same as in simple regressions
BRAND         1      51.258
```

The F ratio statistic $= 15.70$ is greater than the critical F value $= F_{.05,2,5} = 5.79$. Therefore, reject the hypothesis that $\beta_1 = \beta_2 = 0$ in the model

$$y_i = \beta_0 1 + \beta_1 x_{1i} + \beta_2 x_{2i} + e_i$$

Problem Statement (j)   As a reminder that residuals should be examined for randomness and normality in the diagnostic phase of the analysis, construct a histogram and time series plot of residuals.

Problem Solution (j)   Residuals are examined to validate assumptions about the errors and spot outlying observations or clusters of observations. The diagnosis might lead us to stop the analysis when the residuals validate the assumptions, or continue the analysis and repeat the identification, estimation, and diagnostic phases after transformations and/or trimming. Previously unidentified variables or relationships might also surface in this phase.

A completely thorough residual analysis is not shown below for the sake of brevity and because more thorough residual analyses have been shown earlier in the text. The reality of this example is that there are too few data points to be confident in our assessment. Nevertheless, the histogram leads us to believe that the residuals are normal and the scatterplot suggests random errors.

```
Histogram of C8 (residuals from the multiple regression fit)
 N = 8

Midpoint   Count
    -2.0      1   *
    -1.5      1   *
    -1.0      0
    -0.5      2   **
     0.0      1   *
     0.5      0
     1.0      1   *
     1.5      1   *
     2.0      1   *
```

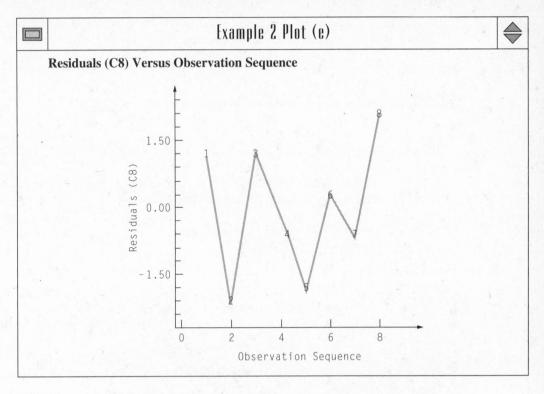

Example 2 Plot (e)

Residuals (C8) Versus Observation Sequence

The previous example dealt with a designed experiment (popcorn experiment) where the variables brand and amount were uncorrelated, permitting multiple regression analysis to put its best foot forward in predicting Yield. In the next example you will find that an experiment could not be designed and the predictor variables (sales and assets, for example) are highly correlated, which makes it difficult to tell exactly how they relate to profits. Furthermore, these multiple regression analysis results are ambiguous.

STATISTICAL HIGHLIGHTS

In multiple regression analysis, two or more predictor variables are included in the fit.

EXAMPLE 3

PROFITS, SALES, AND ASSETS, AN OBSERVATIONAL STUDY

Relate the response variable, profits (P), to the predictor variables, sales (S) and assets (A), for the 30 largest U.S. industrial corporations.[4] Some additional variables available for further analysis include stockholders' equity (E) and market value (M). Figures are in billions of dollars.

Again, for pedagogical purposes, illustrate that a sequence of simple regressions (some using residuals) produces a multiple regression fit. A multiple regression fit relates P to both S and A. Finally, obtain the multiple regression fit directly, without simple regression.

Problem Statement (a) List and visually inspect the data set.

Problem Solution (a) Although it seems trivial, a visual inspection of the data set is generally worthwhile. Among other things, look for missing data (the data value for market value (M) is missing for Shell Oil), obviously incorrect values, columns of constant values (sometimes zeros) or nearly constant values, clusters, and so on.

ROW	S	P	A	E	M	
1	126.97	4.22	173.30	34.98	27.79	GENERAL MOTORS
2	96.93	3.84	160.89	22.73	21.80	FORD MOTOR
3	86.66	3.51	83.22	30.24	57.97	EXXON
4	63.44	3.76	77.73	38.51	61.21	IBM
5	55.26	3.94	128.34	20.89	56.18	GENERAL ELECTRIC
6	50.98	1.81	39.08	16.27	25.12	MOBIL
7	39.07	2.95	38.53	9.57	34.61	PHILIP MORRIS
8	36.16	0.36	51.04	7.23	4.06	CHRYSLER
9	35.21	2.48	34.72	15.80	26.73	DU PONT
10	32.42	2.41	25.64	9.18	15.66	TEXACO
11	29.44	0.25	33.88	13.98	24.26	CHEVRON
12	24.21	1.61	30.43	13.68	27.75	AMOCO
13	21.70	1.41	27.60	16.05	*	SHELL OIL
14	21.70	1.21	16.35	6.22	21.02	PROCTER AND GAMBLE
15	20.28	0.97	13.28	6.13	15.62	BOEING
16	20.07	0.29	20.74	5.90	7.43	OCCIDENTAL PETROLEUM
17	19.77	0.70	14.60	4.74	6.60	UNITED TECHNOLOGIES
18	18.40	0.53	23.65	6.64	12.89	EASTMAN KODAK
19	17.76	0.96	17.50	5.74	9.20	USX
20	17.73	2.49	22.17	7.96	18.01	DOW CHEMICAL
21	17.64	0.70	30.09	5.04	5.04	XEROX
22	15.91	1.95	22.26	6.56	18.86	ATLANTIC RICHFIELD
23	15.42	0.90	15.13	3.89	15.46	PEPSICO
24	15.22	-1.15	36.41	1.24	*	RJR NABISCO
25	14.99	0.22	13.40	3.29	2.22	MCDONNELL DOUGLAS
26	14.44	0.58	17.38	3.28	8.52	TENNECO
27	12.87	1.07	10.67	8.04	9.34	DIGITAL EQUIPMENT
28	12.84	0.92	20.31	4.38	10.70	WESTINGHOUSE ELEC.
29	12.63	0.73	8.94	3.98	5.37	ROCKWELL INTER.
30	12.49	0.22	11.26	2.13	6.25	PHILIPS PETROLEUM

Problem Statement (b) Find summary statistics and a correlation matrix, and construct scatterplots for variables of interest.

Problem Solution (b) Summary values for each variable are

	N	N*	MEAN	MEDIAN	TRMEAN	STDEV	SEMEAN
S	30	0	32.62	20.17	28.06	27.91	5.10
P	30	0	1.528	1.020	1.485	1.351	0.247
A	30	0	40.62	24.64	33.26	42.67	7.79
E	30	0	11.14	6.93	9.90	9.68	1.77
M	28	2	19.85	15.64	18.93	16.07	3.04

	MIN	MAX	Q1	Q3
S	12.49	126.97	15.37	36.89
P	-1.150	4.220	0.567	2.482
A	8.94	173.30	16.04	38.67
E	1.24	38.51	4.65	15.86
M	2.22	61.21	7.70	26.33

The above summary information was obtained for each variable, singly. In order to begin the search for relations among variables, the correlation matrix is examined next.

	P	S
S	0.788	
A	0.745	0.928

Sales and assets are highly correlated with each other as well as with profits. Because of the high correlation between sales and assets, our results cannot be interpreted unambiguously. The correlations between profits and sales and between profits and assets are positive and nearly the same. This is reflected in Plots (a) and (b).

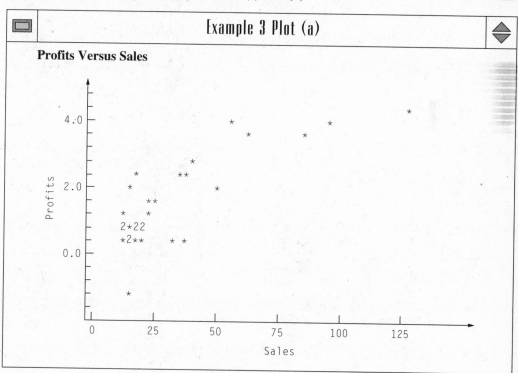

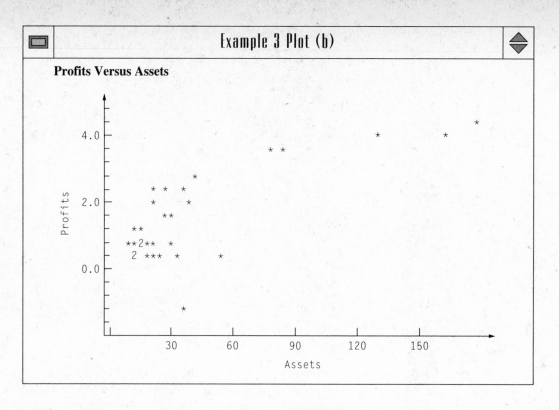

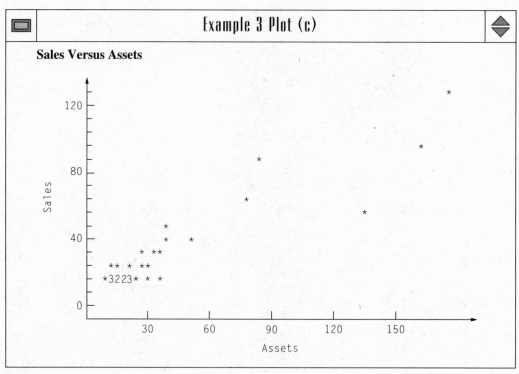

These plots confirm our impressions gained from the correlations. Additionally, we see the influential role the larger corporations have on our perception of the plot (the three largest firms are represented by the three right-most points on the plots). It might be interesting to get another view later, after trimming. Because this is an observational study and a nonrandom sample, we have sacrificed generalizability. Therefore, let's see what we can learn after trimming.

Problem Statement (c)   First, in the estimation phase, use sales alone to predict profits. Show how residuals are computed. Also find t value statistics and other goodness of fit information.

Problem Solution (c)   The simple regression of profits on sales is

$$P = 0.284 + 0.0381\ S$$

The residual, profits removing sales, PRS, for this fit is

$$PRS = P(actual) - P(predicted)$$
$$PRS = P(actual) - (.284 + .0381\ S)$$

As a result of the residual computation, sales, S, is in effect removed from actual profit.

From the tabulations below, you can see that the effect of sales, S, on profits, P, is significantly different from 0, even though the error sum of squares is somewhat inflated (inflated because the asset, A, effect is in error and not in the regression equation yet).

Predictor	Coef	Stdev	t Ratio	p Value
Constant	0.2839	0.2403	1.18	0.247
S	0.038142	0.005637	6.77	0.000

s = 0.8473   R-sq = 62.0%   R-sq(adj) = 60.7%

Analysis of Variance

SOURCE	DF	SS	MS	F Value	p Value
Regression	1	32.859	32.859	45.78	0.000
Error	28	20.100	0.718		
Total	29	52.959			

Problem Statement (d)   Find and list any unusually large residuals.

Problem Solution (d)   The following observations are unusual or influential in determining the fit.

Obs.	S	P	Fit	Stdev.Fit	Residual	St.Resid
1	127	4.220	5.127	0.554	-0.907	-1.41 X
2	97	3.840	3.981	0.394	-0.141	-0.19 X
24	15	-1.150	0.864	0.183	-2.014	-2.44R

R denotes an observation with a large standardized residual.
X denotes an observation whose X value gives it large influence.

Problem Statement (e)   Use assets alone to predict profits. Find t value statistics and other goodness of fit information. List unusual or influential observations.

Problem Solution (e)   The simple regression fit of profits on assets is

$$P = 0.570 + 0.0236A$$

From the tabulated statistics below, you can see that the effect of assets alone on profits is significantly different from 0, even though the error sum of squares is inflated (inflated now because the sales, S, effect is in error and not in the regression equation).

Predictor	Coef	Stdev	t Ratio	p Value
Constant	0.5695	0.2331	2.44	0.021
A	0.023601	0.003992	5.91	0.000

s = 0.9172   R-sq = 55.5%   R-sq(adj) = 53.9%

Analysis of Variance

SOURCE	DF	SS	MS	F value	p value
Regression	1	29.406	29.406	34.96	0.000
Error	28	23.553	0.841		
Total	29	52.959			

Unusual and influential observations are

Obs.	A	P	Fit	Stdev.Fit	Residual	St.Resid
1	173	4.220	4.660	0.555	-0.440	-0.60 X
2	161	3.840	4.367	0.508	-0.527	-0.69 X
24	36	-1.150	1.429	0.168	-2.579	-2.86R

R denotes an observation with a large standardized residual.
X denotes an observation whose X value gives it large influence.

Problem Statement (f)   Relate the two predictor variables, using sales to predict assets. Show how residuals are computed. Also find t value statistics and other goodness of fit information.

Problem Solution (f)   Relating two predictor variables, the simple regression of assets on sales is

$$A = -5.68 + 1.42 S$$

This result is much different from the result in the previous popcorn example, where 0 values resulted for the regression coefficients because brand and amount were uncorrelated. In this example, because sales and assets are highly correlated, the coefficients in the above fit are nonzero. In many observational studies and in some designed experiments, nonzero correlations arise between the predictor variables and can create interpretational problems.

The residuals that are obtained next remove the effect of one predictor variable from another. The residual, assets removing sales, ARS, for this fit is found as follows:

$$ARS = A(\text{actual}) - A(\text{predicted})$$
$$ARS = A(\text{actual}) - (-5.68 + 1.42 S)$$

Sales, S, is removed from the original asset data values. Thus, a residual can be viewed as adjusted data. Therefore, the residual can be used like an artificially created new variable.

From the tabulated statistics below, you can see that sales is a significant predictor of assets.

Predictor	Coef	Stdev	t Ratio	p value
Constant	-5.682	4.576	-1.24	0.225
S	1.4193	0.1074	13.22	0.000

s = 16.14   R-sq = 86.2%   R-sq(adj) = 85.7%

Analysis of Variance

SOURCE	DF	SS	MS	F Value	p Value
Regression	1	45503	45503	174.78	0.000
Error	28	7289	260		
Total	29	52792			

Unusual Observations

Obs.	S	A	Fit	Stdev.Fit	Residual	St.Resid
1	127	173.30	174.53	10.55	-1.23	-0.10 X
2	97	160.89	131.90	7.51	28.99	2.03RX
3	87	83.22	117.32	6.51	-34.10	-2.31R
5	55	128.34	72.75	3.82	55.59	3.55R

R denotes an observation with a large standardized residual.
X denotes an observation whose X value gives it large influence.

Problem Statement (g)   The next step toward the objective of obtaining a multiple regression equation is to relate the two residuals, profits removing sales, PRS, and assets removing sales, ARS.

Problem Solution (g)   The simple regression equation is

$$PRS = -0.000 + 0.00318 \; ARS$$

As you can see from the tabulations below, these residuals are unrelated. Both the F and t values show a nonsignificant effect. By working with residuals, we have considered both sales and assets simultaneously. They are unrelated because once you removed sales from assets, in effect nothing systematic remained in assets to relate to PRS. Both sales and assets, simultaneously, are not needed to predict profits.

Predictor	Coef	Stdev	t Ratio	p Value
Constant	-0.0000	0.1544	-0.00	1.000
ARS	0.003179	0.009905	0.32	0.751

s = 0.8457   R-sq = 0.4%   R-sq(adj) = 0.0%

(continued)

(*continued*)
```
Analysis of Variance

SOURCE       DF        SS         MS       F Value      p Value

Regression    1     0.0737     0.0737       0.10        0.751
Error        28    20.0259     0.7152

Total        29    20.0995

Unusual Observations

Obs.    ARS       PRS      Fit  Stdev.Fit  Residual    St.Resid
  5    55.6      1.548    0.177    0.572     1.372       2.20RX
 24    20.5     -2.014    0.065    0.255    -2.080      -2.58R

R denotes an observation with a large standardized residual.
X denotes an observation whose X value gives it large influence.
```

Problem Statement (h)   In the fit relating residuals PRS to ARS, define these residuals in terms of the original variables—sales, assets, and profit. Arrange the resulting multiple regression equation so that sales and assets predict profits.

Problem Solution (h)   PRS and ARS in terms of the original variables are expressed in the following two fits, which were found by simple regression earlier in this example:

$$\text{ARS} = \text{A(actual)} - (-5.68 + 1.42\ \text{S})$$
$$\text{PRS} = \text{P(actual)} - (.284 + .0381\ \text{S})$$

By substituting these equations for ARS and PRS in the following fit

$$\text{PRS} = -0.000 + 0.00318\ \text{ARS}$$

rearrangement of terms produces a multiple regression fit.

$$\text{P} = 0.302 + 0.0336\ \text{S} + 0.0032\ \text{A}$$

Because of the high correlation between sales, S, and assets, A, the coefficients in the multiple regression fit are different from those in the simple regression fits. This makes interpretations difficult and ambiguous. Unfortunately, these coefficients change when there are nonzero correlations between predictor variables. This is a common problem in most observational studies, making it difficult and sometimes impossible to understand how the variables are related.

In contrast, the previous example involved a designed experiment in which we were confident that gourmet popcorn gets us an additional 5.06 cups of popcorn yield on the average. Also, an amount change of $\frac{1}{3}$ cup of corn kernels gets us 4.82 cups of popcorn yield. Thus, you see the value of intelligently designed experiments, when they are possible. Unfortunately for managers, we are not able to design an experiment in this example.

Sales and assets are highly correlated and can't be untangled to clearly see the separate effects. A helpful approach is to monitor ratios of these variables, such as sales to assets, profits to sales, and profits to assets. If manufacturing plants are operating at capacity, more plants (assets) will be needed to get to higher sales and profit levels. Therefore, in broad terms some reasonable predictions are possible.

Problem Statement (i)   The multiple regression equation found above resulted from simple regression fits and the use of residuals. This approach is useful pedagogically. However, once understanding has been achieved, a multiple regression fit can be found directly, without simple regression. Illustrate that here.

Problem Solution (i)   In practice, multiple regression fits are obtained directly through computer commands such as MINITAB's

```
REGRESS 'P' 2 PRED 'S' 'A'
```

Results from this command are tabulated below. These tabulations are similar to those for simple regression except for the additional statistics due to two or more predictor variables.

The multiple regression fit is

$$P = 0.302 + 0.0336\ S + 0.0032\ A$$

In the tabulations below, notice that only the sales effect is significantly different from zero here in multiple regression. Yet, simple regressions showed the sales and assets effects separately and ambiguously significant. Therefore, either assets or sales alone are significant, but not both together. Intuitively this makes sense. When two variables are highly correlated, they are alike and you don't need both in the equation simultaneously.

The fact that sales and assets are highly correlated also inflates the standard errors, which deflates the t values.

Predictor	Coef	Stdev	t Ratio	p Value
Constant	0.3020	0.2509	1.20	0.239
S	0.03363	0.01542	2.18	0.038
A	0.00318	0.01009	0.32	0.755

s = 0.8612   R-sq = 62.2%   R-sq(adj) = 59.4%

Analysis of Variance

SOURCE	DF	SS	MS	F Value	p Value
Regression	2	32.933	16.467	22.20	0.000
Error	27	20.026	0.742		
Total	29	52.959			

SOURCE	DF	SEQ SS			
S	1	32.859	--- different from those found in simple regressions
A	1	0.074	

Problem Statement (j)   Examine the residuals to diagnose potential problems and to see if further analysis is necessary.

Problem Solution (j) Unusual and influential observations are

Obs.	S	P	Fit	Stdev.Fit	Residual	St.Resid
1	127	4.220	5.123	0.563	-0.903	-1.39 X
2	97	3.840	4.073	0.496	-0.233	-0.33 X
3	87	3.510	3.481	0.489	0.029	0.04 X
5	55	3.940	2.568	0.597	1.372	2.21RX
24	15	-1.150	0.930	0.278	-2.080	-2.55R

R denotes an observation with a large standarized residual.
X denotes an observation whose X value gives it large influence.

Selected data points that may have a detrimental influence on the fit are listed above automatically in MINITAB. Also, the REGRESS command has a subcommand that computes an influence statistic, h_{ii}, for all observations. These so-called HI VALUES, h_{ii}, are placed in column C14 and plotted below. In general, a HI VALUE is a leverage measure for the i-th data point's influence on the fit. High leverage points may draw the fit too much toward these points. Therefore, h_{ii} versus the observation number can be plotted to diagnose this problem.

When $h_{ii} > \frac{2p}{n}$, it is considered large, where p is the number of parameters (3 here) and n (30 here) is the sample size. For this example, $\frac{2p}{n} = 2 \times \frac{3}{30} = .20$. A horizontal line can be

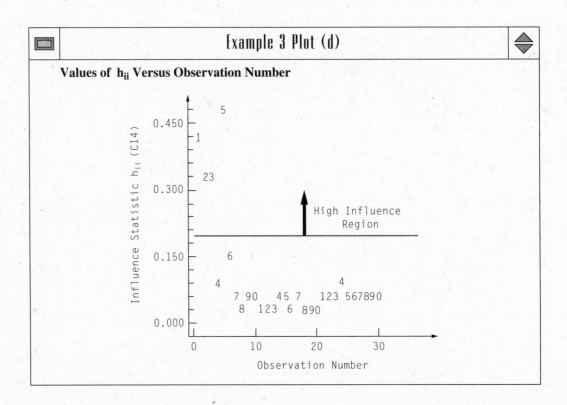

Values of h_{ii} Versus Observation Number

drawn on Plot (d) at this cutoff value of .20. Points above or near that line will be high in influence. At a glance, you can see that points 1, 2, 3, and 5 are influential.

The following plot of the residuals C10 versus the predictions C9 reveals the unusual points and some influential points. There is a difference between unusual and influential data points. For example, observations 1, 2, and 3 are on the far right of the plot below and are influential. Observation 24, the most negative residual, is unusual but it does not exert much influence on the fit.

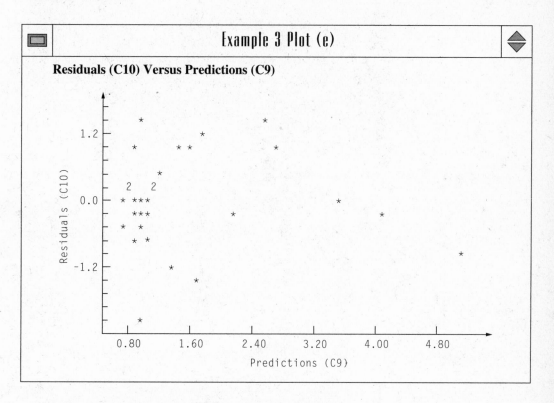

A histogram of the residuals looks normal in distribution.

```
Histogram of C8   N = 30
Midpoint    Count
    -2.5       1   *
    -2.0       0
    -1.5       3   ***
    -1.0       1   *
    -0.5       8   ********
     0.0       7   *******
     0.5       3   ***
     1.0       3   ***
     1.5       2   **
     2.0       2   **
```

Problem Statement (k) Does the theory and lore of financial management suggest any additional analysis?

Problem Solution (k) The analysis of financial ratios is an important financial management function. Of the many financial ratios, profits to assets (return on investment, ROI) is important. For the 30 top U.S. companies, ROI (C17) is computed and plotted below. This is an example of the type of auxiliary analysis that might accompany the more direct statistical analysis as a way to bridge the distance between the data analyst and the financial manager.

You might draw a horizontal line at the level of the upper quartile shown on the right; the same might be done at the mean level. Companies 7, 9, 10, 14, 15, 20, 22, 27, and 29 are in the upper quartile in ROI. Look back at the data list and find the names of those companies.

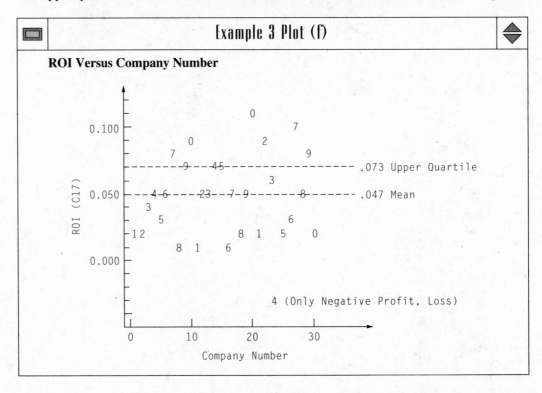

The mean and the upper quartile for the plot above were obtained from the descriptive statistics below.

	N	MEAN	MEDIAN	TRMEAN	STDEV	SEMEAN
C17	30	0.04702	0.04713	0.04702	0.03225	0.00589

	MIN	MAX	Q1	Q3
C17	-0.03158	0.11231	0.02305	0.07328

Problem Statement (l) Based on the residual analysis, decide if some unusual and influential data points should be trimmed from the data set and the analysis continued.

Problem Solution (l)   Because of the influence of several large companies, the first six companies were trimmed from the data set.

Problem Statement (m)   Examine the correlation matrix and discuss.

Problem Solution (m)   After trimming, another correlation matrix is computed. You might compare this matrix to the previous one and note the differences.

```
          P       S
S      0.485
A      0.110    0.749
```

To some extent, trimming has diminished the multicollinearity problem (high correlation between sales and assets). It has also reduced the correlations between profits and assets and profits and sales. This makes profits less predictable from sales and assets. Other unidentified predictor variables might exist that help determine profits.

Problem Statement (n)   Fit a multiple regression equation to the trimmed data set to predict profits. Examine goodness of fit information.

Problem Solution (n)   The multiple regression fit is

$$P = 0.000 + 0.107\ S - 0.0510\ A$$

High sales relative to assets seems to drive profits; both sales and assets are significant. Note that the regression coefficient of assets switched in sign from positive (earlier) to negative (here). When multicollinearity is present, the coefficients are unstable and sensitive to which variables are in or out of the fit. The estimated regression coefficients may be far from their unknown true values.

```
Predictor      Coef       Stdev      t Ratio      p Value
Constant      0.0003     0.4465       0.00        1.000
S             0.10655    0.03011      3.54        0.002
A            -0.05098    0.02288     -2.23        0.037

s = 0.7610      R-sq = 38.1%     R-sq(adj) = 32.2%
```

Analysis of Variance

SOURCE	DF	SS	MS	F Value	p Value
Regression	2	7.4890	3.7445	6.47	0.006
Error	21	12.1619	0.5791		
Total	23	19.6509			

SOURCE	DF	SEQ SS
S	1	4.6142
A	1	2.8749

(*continued*)

(*continued*)
```
Unusual Observations

Obs.       S        P      Fit   Stdev.Fit   Residual   St.Resid
 14     17.7    2.490    0.759      0.173      1.731      2.34R
 18     15.2   -1.150   -0.234      0.469     -0.916     -1.53 X
```

R denotes an observation with a large standardized residual.
X denotes an observation whose X value gives it large influence.

Trimming may unmask new influential observations. Note that observation number 18 here was number 24 before trimming six observations; this was the only company posting a loss.

S T A T I·S T I C A L   H I G H L I G H T S

> In observational studies, multiple regression analysis must be used with caution because the results may be dubious.

The following example is long and contains some optional, alternative solution sections. You may prefer to treat the whole example as optional and go on to the next example. In its entirety this example not only illustrates multiple regression analysis but uses it to approximate **autoregressive** time series models, where a response variable is related to lagged response variable values.

EXAMPLE 4

ARITHMETIC GROWTH OF QUARTERLY SALES, A FOURTH-QUARTER SALES JUMP, AND A RANDOM, UNPREDICTABLE COMPONENT

This example takes advantage of MINITAB's simulation capability. An instructor can simulate this sales pattern or modify it. Readers who are not using the computer can also benefit from this example.

Sales in dollars are simulated using the following known relationship:

$$\text{sales (C3)} = 10,000 + 250 \times \text{C1} + \text{random component}$$

C1 is a dummy trend variable that identifies the quarter numbers 1, 2, 3, . . . , 48 for four years. Sales are in thousands of dollars.

Problem Statement (a)   Pretend that the simulating equation is unknown. Fit and evaluate a regression equation to predict sales using quarter number as a trend predictor variable. Because the underlying simulation equation is known, we can see how close regression comes in estimating the underlying structure.

Problem Solution (a) An arithmetic time series is examined in which sales figures are trending upward. Although such time series are common, so are geometric series with increasing variability. Geometric series are often transformed by taking logarithms to produce an arithmetic series that can be analyzed, as shown below.

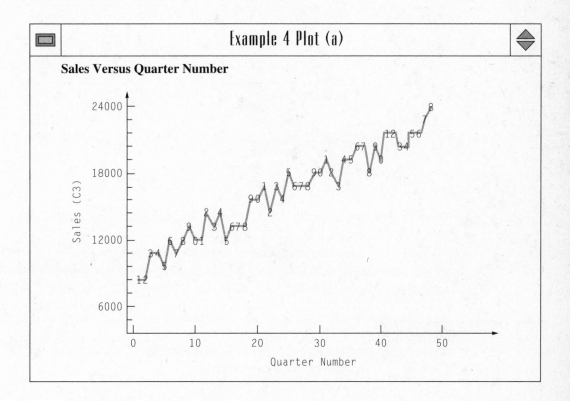

Example 4 Plot (a)

Sales Versus Quarter Number

Correlation of sales, C3, and C1 = 0.972, where C1 is a dummy trend variable, 1, 2, 3, . . . , 47, 48.

The simple regression fit follows. It is a good fit.

$$C3(\text{sales}) = 9{,}325 + 279\ C1\ (\text{trend variable})$$

Notice how well the fit estimates the first two terms of the equation used to simulate sales, which is (10,000 + 250 C1). The complete simulation is shown in Appendix 1.

For the random component, a normal distribution was chosen with a 0 mean and a standard deviation equal to 1,000. Its estimate is the standard error of the estimate s = 961.7, which is tabulated below. As an exercise in MINITAB, you might try different values for sigma, the standard deviation of the error, and observe the effect on the resulting plots and analyses.

Predictor	Coef	Stdev	t Ratio	p Value
Constant	9325.4	282.0	33.07	0.000
C1	278.77	10.02	27.82	0.000

s = 961.7   R-sq = 94.4%   R-sq(adj) = 94.3%

Analysis of Variance

SOURCE	DF	SS	MS	F Value	p Value
Regression	1	715895146	715895146	774.10	0.000
Error	46	42541192	924809		
Total	47	758436337			

Unusual Observations

Obs.	C1	C3	Fit	Stdev.Fit	Residual	St.Resid
38	38.0	17881	19919	194	-2038	-2.16R

R denotes an observation with a large standardized residual.

Although residual analysis is not shown, these residuals are random, independent, and normal, validating the goodness of this fit.

Alternative Solution (a) (Optional)   A few aspects of time series analysis are introduced here as an alternative way to model sales. Sales, C3, at time t is referred to as y_t. Sales lagged one period, C4, is y_{t-1}. Sales lagged two periods, C5, is y_{t-2}. Sales lagged three periods, C6, is y_{t-3}. And sales lagged four periods, C7, is y_{t-4}. To print the lagged data in MINITAB, issue the command PRINT C3 C4 C5 C6 C7.

From the correlation matrix in the identification phase, we see that sales, C3, and lagged sales, C4, C5, C6, C7, are highly correlated.

	C3	C4	C5	C6
C4	0.942			
C5	0.945	0.937		
C6	0.915	0.943	0.934	
C7	0.926	0.912	0.942	0.930

As you might expect, because of the arithmetic growth of sales, lagged sales figures are highly correlated with the original series. Data columns with different lags are highly correlated with one another, which reveals a multicollinearity problem. The first column of the correlation matrix represents sales correlated with lagged sales (lagged by 1, 2, 3, and 4 periods). Because sales is correlated with its lagged self, these correlations are called **auto-correlations.**

A single command in MINITAB, ACF, automatically lags all the way up to 16 rather than the four shown above. These lagged sales figures are also correlated in this command. Thus, in time series analysis the autocorrelation display replaces the correlation matrix.

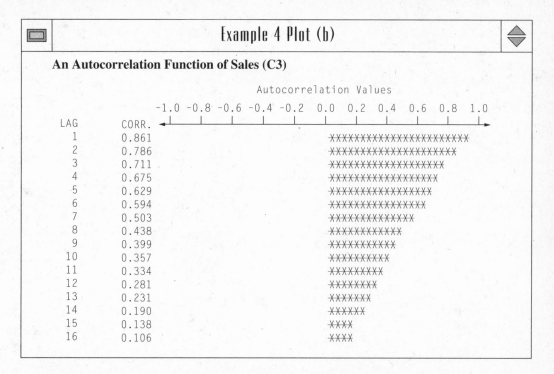

An Autocorrelation Function of Sales (C3)

```
                                    Autocorrelation Values

                -1.0 -0.8 -0.6 -0.4 -0.2  0.0  0.2  0.4  0.6  0.8  1.0
        LAG    CORR. +----+----+----+----+----+----+----+----+----+----+--->
         1     0.861                              XXXXXXXXXXXXXXXXXXXXXXX
         2     0.786                              XXXXXXXXXXXXXXXXXXXXXX
         3     0.711                              XXXXXXXXXXXXXXXXXXX
         4     0.675                              XXXXXXXXXXXXXXXXXX
         5     0.629                              XXXXXXXXXXXXXXXXX
         6     0.594                              XXXXXXXXXXXXXXXX
         7     0.503                              XXXXXXXXXXXXX
         8     0.438                              XXXXXXXXXXX
         9     0.399                              XXXXXXXXXX
        10     0.357                              XXXXXXXXX
        11     0.334                              XXXXXXXX
        12     0.281                              XXXXXXX
        13     0.231                              XXXXXX
        14     0.190                              XXXXX
        15     0.138                              XXXX
        16     0.106                              XXXX
```

The first four autocorrelations above show the same thing as the first column in the correlation matrix. The correlations between the lagged variables are not shown in the ACF display. Slight differences in the behind-the-scene formulas in the CORRELATE and ACF commands result in different but approximately the same correlation values. The formula differences are related to the way missing values are handled.

The autocorrelation pattern shows high correlations that slowly get smaller with increasing lags. When a series (sales in C3) has an autocorrelation pattern like this, it is said to be a **nonstationary series,** displaying a nonconstant mean over time (sales are trending upward here).

The **partial ACF,** or PACF, shown in Plot (c) helps to identify the more important lags in the sales variable. Lagging sales by 1, 2, 3, and 4 quarters produced the lagged variables in columns C4, C5, C6, and C7 that were highly intercorrelated, meaning that the columns all look alike. Since the columns all look alike, any one can be used to predict sales in C3 because of the high correlation with C3. The PACF partials out (adjusts for) the high intercorrelation between the lagged variables and identifies (see below) that the first lagged variable (C4, y_{t-1}) is most important in predicting sales.

Most time series analysis tools are designed for a **stationary series,** which may be achieved by differencing the original nonstationary series one or more times. When the pattern of an ACF of the differenced series drops off quickly with increasing lags (Plot (d)), the differences are stationary and you have differenced enough. First differences (C13 = $y_t - y_{t-1}$) are enough in this example.

The ACF of the differenced series (like the PACF) gives some clues about which time series model (which lags) might be appropriate.

Example 4 Plot (c)

A Partial Autocorrelation Function of Sales (C3)

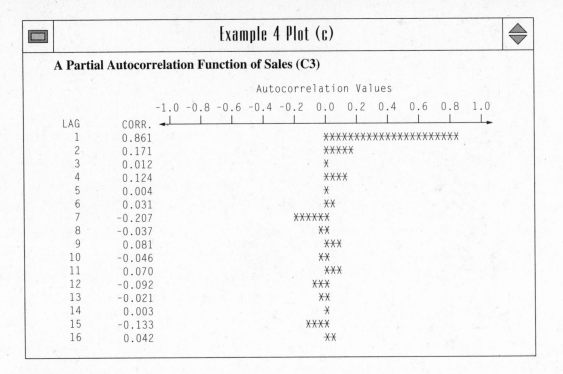

```
                              Autocorrelation Values
              -1.0 -0.8 -0.6 -0.4 -0.2  0.0  0.2  0.4  0.6  0.8  1.0
    LAG   CORR.  +----+----+----+----+----+----+----+----+----+----→
     1    0.861                           XXXXXXXXXXXXXXXXXXXXXXX
     2    0.171                           XXXXX
     3    0.012                           X
     4    0.124                           XXXX
     5    0.004                           X
     6    0.031                           XX
     7   -0.207                      XXXXX
     8   -0.037                         XX
     9    0.081                           XXX
    10   -0.046                         XX
    11    0.070                           XXX
    12   -0.092                        XXX
    13   -0.021                         XX
    14    0.003                          X
    15   -0.133                       XXXX
    16    0.042                          XX
```

Example 4 Plot (d)

An Autocorrelation Function of First Differences ($C13 = y_t - y_{t-1}$)

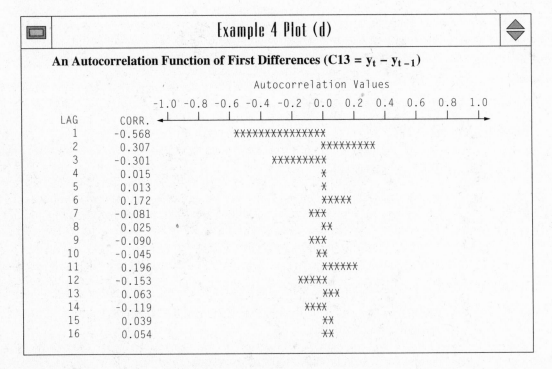

```
                              Autocorrelation Values
              -1.0 -0.8 -0.6 -0.4 -0.2  0.0  0.2  0.4  0.6  0.8  1.0
    LAG   CORR.  +----+----+----+----+----+----+----+----+----+----→
     1   -0.568            XXXXXXXXXXXXXXX
     2    0.307                           XXXXXXXX
     3   -0.301              XXXXXXXXX
     4    0.015                           X
     5    0.013                           X
     6    0.172                           XXXXX
     7   -0.081                         XXX
     8    0.025                          XX
     9   -0.090                        XXX
    10   -0.045                         XX
    11    0.196                           XXXXXX
    12   -0.153                       XXXXX
    13    0.063                           XXX
    14   -0.119                       XXXX
    15    0.039                          XX
    16    0.054                          XX
```

A correlation coefficient is studentized approximately by multiplying it by SQRT(n). In this example, SQRT(n) = $(48)^{1/2}$ = (almost) 7. For the first autocorrelation, the approximate t value is $7 \times (-.568) = -3.98$, which is significantly different from zero at the .05 alpha level. The next two autocorrelations are about 0.3, yielding a studentized value of 2.1, which is barely significant at the .05 alpha level.

The autocorrelation pattern shown in Plot (d) alternates in sign, drops off quickly with a significant autocorrelation at a lag of one, indicating that quarter $t - 1$ sales (produced in MINITAB by LAG 1 C3 C4) in C4 might be a good predictor of quarter t sales, C3. Therefore, a simple regression fit approximates this relation and this fit is shown below. This is called an **autoregression** of **order one, AR(1).** Had we used REGRESS C3 2 PRED C4 C5, we would have an AR(2), an autoregression of order two.

The following simple regression equation provides a good fit to the data:

$$\text{C3(predicted sales quarter t)} = 1397 + 0.934 \text{ C4(sales quarter } t - 1)$$

Of the 47 cases used, 1 case contains missing values.

Predictor	Coef	Stdev	t Ratio	p Value
Constant	1396.7	816.9	1.71	0.094
C4	0.93365	0.04965	18.81	0.000

s = 1314   R-sq = 88.7%   R-sq(adj) = 88.5%

Analysis of Variance

SOURCE	DF	SS	MS	F Value	p Value
Regression	1	611023035	611023035	353.68	0.000
Error	45	77742384	1727609		
Total	46	688765419			

Unusual Observations

Obs.	C4	C3	Fit	Stdev.Fit	Residual	St.Resid
41	19065	21787	19197	245	2590	2.01R

R denotes an observation with a large standardized residual.

An examination of these residuals shows that some autocorrelation remains in Plot (e); therefore, the residuals are not random. Thus, the independence assumption about the errors is violated. Although this time series model fits well, it needs to be refined. More sophisticated time series refinements are described in Chapter 16.

```
C9 (A RUNS test)
K =   -0.0000
THE OBSERVED NO. OF RUNS =  34
THE EXPECTED NO. OF RUNS =  24.4894
24 OBSERVATIONS ABOVE K   23 BELOW
        THE TEST IS SIGNIFICANT AT  0.0051 (non-random)
```

Example 4 Plot (e)

An Autocorrelation Function of Residuals (C9)

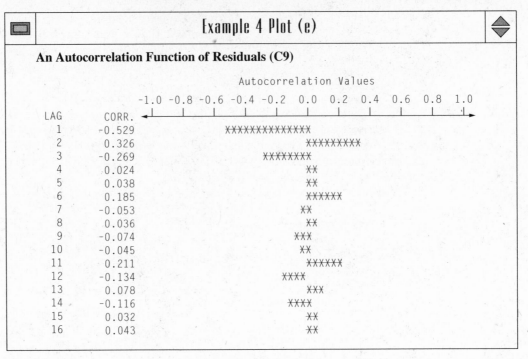

```
                                    Autocorrelation Values

                    -1.0 -0.8 -0.6 -0.4 -0.2  0.0  0.2  0.4  0.6  0.8  1.0
   LAG    CORR.   ◄─┼────┼────┼────┼────┼────┼────┼────┼────┼────┼────►
    1    -0.529                    XXXXXXXXXXXXX
    2     0.326                              XXXXXXXX
    3    -0.269                    XXXXXXX
    4     0.024                           XX
    5     0.038                           XX
    6     0.185                           XXXXXX
    7    -0.053                          XX
    8     0.036                           XX
    9    -0.074                          XXX
   10    -0.045                          XX
   11     0.211                           XXXXXX
   12    -0.134                        XXXX
   13     0.078                           XXX
   14    -0.116                        XXXX
   15     0.032                           XX
   16     0.043                           XX
```

Example 4 Plot (f)

Sales (C3) Versus Quarter Number

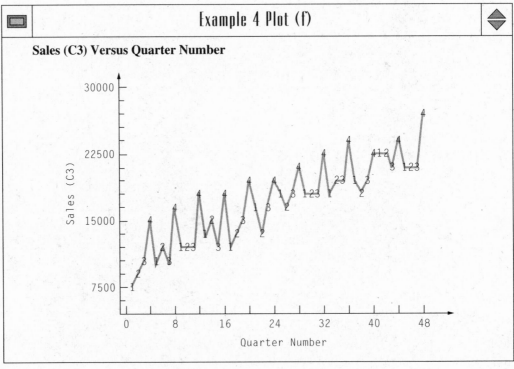

Problem Statement (b)   Modify simulated sales by adding a 4,000 increase to each fourth quarter. Fit and evaluate a multiple regression model for sales with quarter number and a fourth-quarter dummy variable as predictors.

Problem Solution (b)   In the simulation, 4,000 is added to sales in each fourth quarter. Thus, the company does 4,000 better (consistently) in the fourth quarter, say, due to the holiday season. Notice the higher fourth quarter in Plot (f).

Similar to what was done earlier, a simple trend line is fit. The regression equation is

$$C3 = 10{,}134 + 287\ C1$$

Notice that the slope of the fit has hardly changed. However, the constant term has increased from 9,325 to 10,134 in an attempt to accommodate the fourth-quarter jump in sales.

Notice below that s = 2,043, whereas it was 1,314 earlier, without the fourth-quarter jump in sales. Therefore, the variability has increased.

Predictor	Coef	Stdev	t Ratio	p Value
Constant	10133.9	599.1	16.92	0.000
C1	286.59	21.28	13.46	0.000

s = 2043   R-sq = 79.8%   R-sq (adj) = 79.3%

Analysis of Variance

SOURCE	DF	SS	MS	F Value	p Value
Regression	1	756600928	756600928	181.30	0.000
Error	46	191970466	4173271		
Total	47	948571394			

Unusual Observations

Obs.	C1	C3	Fit	Stdev.Fit	Residual	St.Resid
12	12.0	17954	13573	397	4381	2.19R

R denotes an observation with a large standardized residual.

The residuals (C9) are plotted over time (Plot (g)). Clearly they are not random. Systematically, a large fourth-quarter residual shows up. Therefore, our fit needs to be adjusted to accommodate this pattern and produce random residuals in the next go-around.

An exploratory approach called **smoothing** mimics the straight line fit produced above with a fit called a **smooth** and residuals called a **rough.** The MINITAB commands for this are shown in Appendix 1. The smooth is robust and more flexible than a regression-based straight line fit. The flexibility of a smooth fit is due to the fact that the smooth is not required to be a straight line. When curvature is present, the smooth will bend. Thus, the smooth fit produces residuals that mimic the true errors better than residuals from simple straight line regression.

The smooth fit is placed in C7 (Plot (h)), and residuals from the smooth are placed in C9 (Plot (i)). These residuals mimic the true errors better than residuals from a straight line fit; thus, the fourth- quarter effect is more pronounced.

You can see in Plot (j) that the smooth plus the rough (C7 + C9) reproduces the original data (C3).

Example 4 Plot (g)

Residuals (C9) Versus Quarter Number

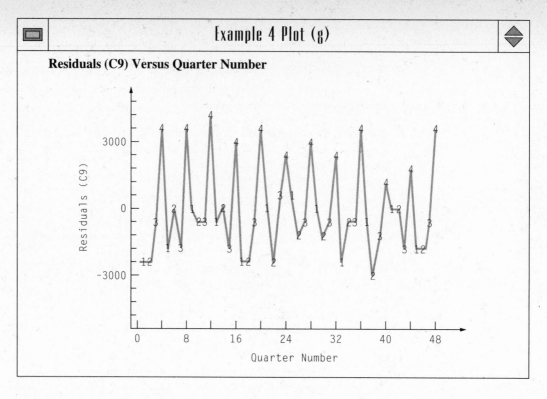

Example 4 Plot (h)

Smooth Fit of Sales by Quarter Number

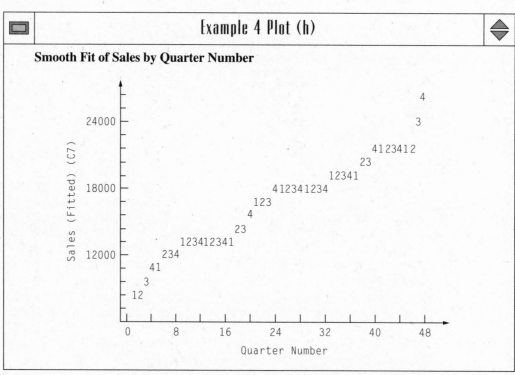

Example 4 Plot (i)

Residuals (or Rough (C9)) by Quarter Number

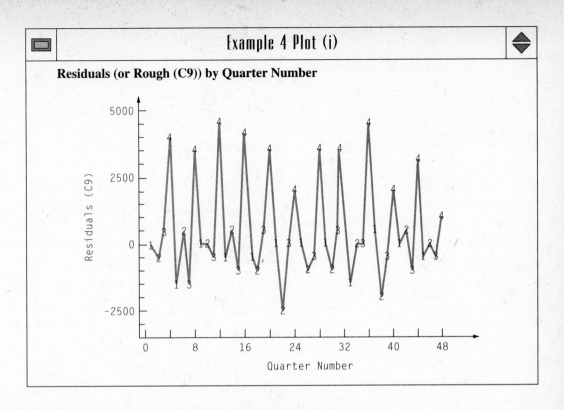

Example 4 Plot (j)

Sales (C7 + C9 = C3) by Quarter Number

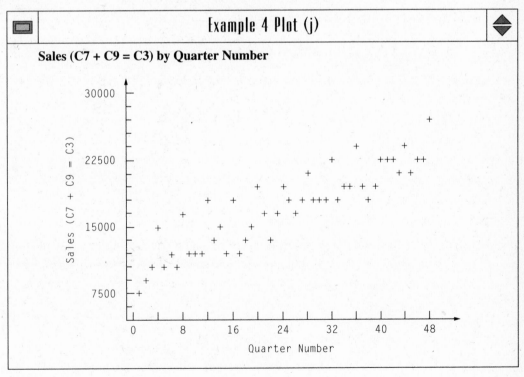

The fourth quarter jump in sales can be accommodated for in a multiple regression model by an additional dummy variable. Recall that C1 is a dummy trend variable taking on values 1, 2, 3, . . . , 48. A second dummy variable, C8, is introduced to adjust for the fourth-quarter jump in sales. C8 takes on values 0, 0, 0, 1; 0, 0, 0, 1; . . . ; 0, 0, 0, 1; where there is a 1 for each fourth quarter and otherwise there is a zero.

The multiple regression fit is

$$C3 = 9{,}309 + 279\ C1 + 4{,}084\ C8$$

Both the trend and fourth-quarter dummy variables are significant. Notice how the fit mirrors the simulation because the coefficient of C8 is 4084 and it estimates the 4000 fourth-quarter jump found in the simulation.

Predictor	Coef	Stdev	t Ratio	p Value
Constant	9308.5	292.4	31.84	0.000
C1	278.61	10.14	27.47	0.000
C8	4083.5	324.5	12.58	0.000

Again, SIGMA = 1,000 is estimated by the standard error below, s = 971.6. By entering C8 into the fit, we have reduced the standard error and now have a good estimate of it.

```
s = 971.6      R-sq = 95.5%    R-sq(adj) = 95.3%
```

Analysis of Variance

SOURCE	DF	SS	MS	F Value	p Value
Regression	2	906092781	453046390	479.94	0.000
Error	45	42478613	943969		
Total	47	948571394			

SOURCE	DF	SEQ SS
C1	1	756600928
C8	1	149491853

Unusual Observations

Obs.	C1	C3	Fit	Stdev.Fit	Residual	St.Resid
38	38.0	17881	19896	215	-2014	-2.13R

R denotes an observation with a large standardized residual.

The residuals of this fit (C10) are random and no longer display the fourth-quarter jump in sales because that jump has been explained away by the dummy variable, C8, in the fit.

```
C10  (Runs test, residuals are random)
K =    -0.0000
THE OBSERVED NO. OF RUNS =  22
THE EXPECTED NO. OF RUNS =  24.6250
27 OBSERVATIONS ABOVE K   21 BELOW
          THE TEST IS SIGNIFICANT AT  0.4365
          CANNOT REJECT AT ALPHA = 0.05
```

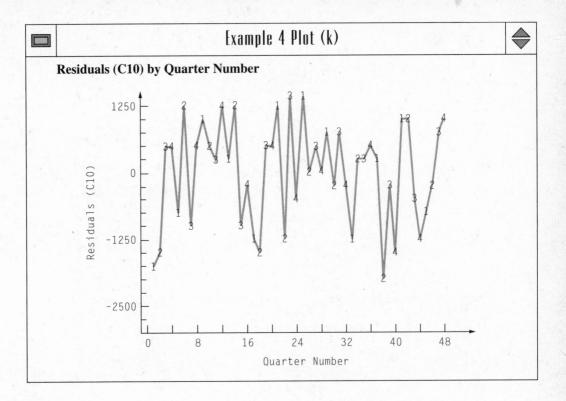

Example 4 Plot (k)

Residuals (C10) by Quarter Number

Alternative Solution (b) (Optional)   Although the multiple regression above using the trend (C1) and the fourth-quarter dummy C(8) produced a good fitting model, another fit is shown below as an alternative and as another illustration of the use of a lagged variable.

The autocorrelation pattern shows high correlations that slowly get smaller (Plot (l)). When a series (sales in C3) has an autocorrelation pattern like this, the sales series is said to be nonstationary. Mean sales is not constant. Here, the mean sales level is trending (drifting) upward over time. Most time series analysis tools are designed for a stationary series achieved by differencing. The pattern of an ACF of the differenced series gives some clues about which lagged variable might be used in a fit. A PACF is also used for this purpose (Plot (m)).

Examination of the PACF and the ACF reveals the following: the correlation coefficient is studentized approximately by multiplying it by SQRT (n) = $(48)^{1/2}$ = (almost) 7. Therefore, a lag of four (Plot (n)) yields the most significant correlation (as you would expect because of the fourth-quarter effect). This fact shows up in both the PACF and the ACF.

Sales (C3) is y_t; sales lagged by four quarters is C7 = y_{t-4}.

For technical reasons, multiple regression is an approximation, but it produces a reasonably good fit. The regression equation is

$$C3 = 3,716 + 69.0 \ C1 + 0.737 \ C7$$

Of the 44 cases used, 4 cases contain missing values due to the lags.

Example 4 Plot (l)

An Autocorrelation Function of Sales (C3)

```
                                    Autocorrelation Values
                     -1.0 -0.8 -0.6 -0.4 -0.2  0.0  0.2  0.4  0.6  0.8  1.0
       LAG   CORR.
        1    0.670                                XXXXXXXXXXXXXXXXX
        2    0.573                                XXXXXXXXXXXXXX
        3    0.536                                XXXXXXXXXXXXXX
        4    0.716                                XXXXXXXXXXXXXXXXXX
        5    0.482                                XXXXXXXXXXXX
        6    0.415                                XXXXXXXXXX
        7    0.376                                XXXXXXXXX
        8    0.513                                XXXXXXXXXXXXXX
        9    0.299                                XXXXXXX
       10    0.221                                XXXXXX
       11    0.236                                XXXXXX
       12    0.371                                XXXXXXXXXX
       13    0.166                                XXXX
       14    0.094                                XXX
       15    0.086                                XXX
       16    0.214                                XXXXX
```

Example 4 Plot (m)

A Partial Autocorrelation Function of Sales (C3)

```
                                    Autocorrelation Values
                     -1.0 -0.8 -0.6 -0.4 -0.2  0.0  0.2  0.4  0.6  0.8  1.0
       LAG   CORR.
        1    0.670                                XXXXXXXXXXXXXXXXX
        2    0.224                                XXXXXX
        3    0.168                                XXXXX
        4    0.524                                XXXXXXXXXXXXXX
        5   -0.374                     XXXXXXXXX
        6    0.018                                X
        7    0.029                                XX
        8    0.057                                XX
        9   -0.198                          XXXXXX
       10   -0.076                             XXX
       11    0.185                                XXXXXX
       12    0.031                                XX
       13   -0.184                          XXXXX
       14    0.026                                XX
       15   -0.060                             XX
       16    0.027                                XX
```

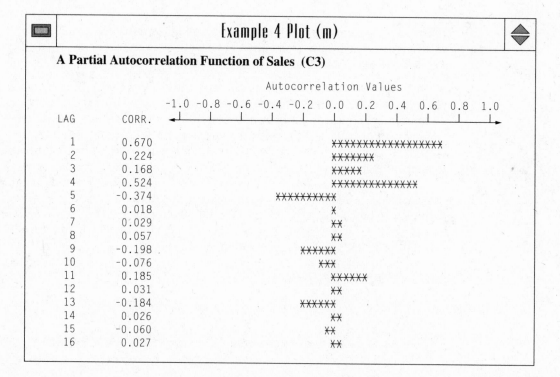

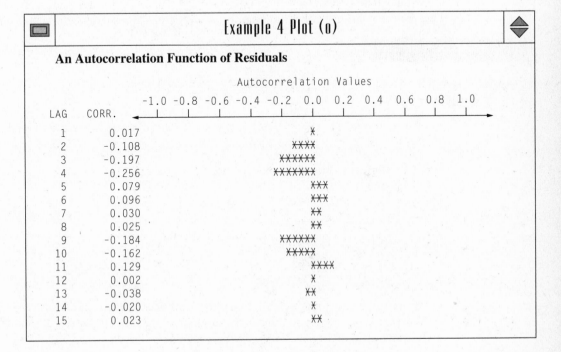

Example 4 Plot (n)

An Autocorrelation Function of First Differences of Sales (C13 = $(Y_t - Y_{t-1})$)

Autocorrelation Values

```
        -1.0 -0.8 -0.6 -0.4 -0.2  0.0  0.2  0.4  0.6  0.8  1.0
LAG   CORR.
 1    -0.416                XXXXXXXXXX
 2    -0.064                       XXX
 3    -0.381                XXXXXXXXXX
 4     0.724                          XXXXXXXXXXXXXXXXXX
 5    -0.254                   XXXXXX
 6    -0.146                     XXXX
 7    -0.271                   XXXXXXX
 8     0.670                          XXXXXXXXXXXXXXXXX
 9    -0.239                   XXXXXX
10    -0.171                     XXXX
11    -0.211                   XXXXXX
12     0.545                          XXXXXXXXXXXXXXX
13    -0.166                     XXXX
14    -0.192                    XXXXX
15    -0.159                     XXXX
16     0.480                         XXXXXXXXXXXXX
```

Example 4 Plot (o)

An Autocorrelation Function of Residuals

Autocorrelation Values

```
        -1.0 -0.8 -0.6 -0.4 -0.2  0.0  0.2  0.4  0.6  0.8  1.0
LAG   CORR.
 1     0.017                          X
 2    -0.108                       XXXX
 3    -0.197                      XXXXX
 4    -0.256                     XXXXXX
 5     0.079                          XXX
 6     0.096                          XXX
 7     0.030                          XX
 8     0.025                          XX
 9    -0.184                      XXXXX
10    -0.162                      XXXXX
11     0.129                          XXXX
12     0.002                          X
13    -0.038                         XX
14    -0.020                         X
15     0.023                          XX
```

Predictor	Coef	Stdev	t Ratio	p Value
Constant	3716	1024	3.63	0.001
C1	69.03	33.02	2.09	0.043
C7	0.7366	0.1014	7.26	0.000

s = 1327   R-sq = 90.0%   R-sq (adj) = 89.5%

Analysis of Variance

SOURCE	DF	SS	MS	F Value	p Value
Regression	2	648363556	324181778	184.06	0.000
Error	41	72213711	1761310		
Total	43	720577266			

SOURCE	DF	SEQ SS
C1	1	555440303
C7	1	92923253

Unusual Observations

Obs.	C1	C3	Fit	Stdev.Fit	Residual	St.Resid
18	18.0	12774	15589	242	-2815	-2.16R
48	48.0	27658	24958	426	2700	2.15R

R denotes an observation with a large standardized residual.

Notice that the quarterly effect no longer shows up as significant autocorrelations in Plot (o) because the quarterly effect has been removed from the residuals and included in the fit.

EXAMPLE 5

MARKET VALUE AND ITS RELATION TO SALES, PROFITS, ASSETS, AND EQUITY

For the 30 largest U.S. companies, relate market value (M) to the predictor variables, sales (S), profits (P), assets (A), and stockholders' equity (E).

Problem Statement (a)   Correlate all pairs of variables.

Problem Solution (a)   The correlation matrix is

	M	S	P	A
S	0.607			
P	0.795	0.788		
A	0.564	0.928	0.745	
E	0.823	0.869	0.821	0.782

From the first column—S, P, A, and E— all have at least moderately high correlations with market value (stock price times the number of shares). Of the four, E and P have higher correlations than do S and A with market value M.

The multicollinearity problem is severe, as all the predictor variables are highly correlated with one another. For the regression that follows, A is excluded simply because of its high correlation with S (one of the two must be excluded).

Problem Statement (b)   Obtain a multiple regression fit for the response variable M and predictor variables S, P, and E. Find and evaluate goodness of fit information.

Problem Solution (b)   The prediction equation is

$$M = 3.83 - 0.406S + 6.64P + 1.66E$$

Of the 28 cases used, 2 cases contain missing values.

The critical statistic is $t_{.025, 24} = 2.07$. Therefore, S, P, and E are all significant.

Predictor	Coef	Stdev	t Ratio	p Value
Constant	3.827	2.229	1.72	0.099
S	-0.4055	0.1069	-3.79	0.001
P	6.640	1.988	3.34	0.003
E	1.6647	0.3297	5.05	0.000

s = 7.165   R-sq = 82.3%   R-sq(adj) = 80.1%

Analysis of Variance

SOURCE	DF	SS	MS	F Value	p Value
Regression	3	5742.2	1914.1	37.29	0.000
Error	24	1232.0	51.3		
Total	27	6974.1			

SOURCE	DF	SEQ SS
S	1	2567.4
P	1	1865.8
E	1	1308.9

Problem Statement (c)   Examine the residuals.

Problem Solution (c)   See Plot (a) and Plot (b).

Unusual Observations

Obs.	S	M	Fit	Stdev.Fit	Residual	St.Resid
1	127	27.79	38.59	4.99	-10.80	-2.10RX
3	87	57.97	42.33	3.06	15.64	2.41R
4	63	61.21	67.18	5.80	-5.97	-1.42 X
5	55	56.18	42.36	3.24	13.82	2.16R

R denotes an observation with a large standardized residual.
X denotes an observation whose X value gives it large influence.

(continued)

(continued)
```
Histogram of C6   N = 28   N* = 2

Midpoint  Count  (Reasonably Normal)
    -2.0     1    *
    -1.5     3    ***
    -1.0     3    ***
    -0.5     6    ******
     0.0     5    *****
     0.5     4    ****
     1.0     3    ***
     1.5     1    *
     2.0     1    *
     2.5     1    *
```

The following statistics can be used to isolate companies that are highly over- or under-valued.

	N	N*	MEAN	MEDIAN	TRMEAN	STDEV	SEMEAN
C8	28	2	-0.00	-0.66	-0.19	6.75	1.28

	MIN	MAX	Q1	Q3
C8	-10.80	15.64	-5.40	3.24

C9 contains h_{ii} values that locate influential observations (Plot (c)). Observations 1, 2, 4, and 24 are influential. As a result, these observations are deleted and a new regression fit is obtained (Plot (c)).

Problem Statement (d)   After trimming companies 1, 2, 4, and 24 from the data set, fit the regression model again. Examine goodness of fit information and residuals.

Problem Solution (d)   The prediction equation is

$$M = -1.56 - 0.009S + 5.82P + 1.33E$$

Of the 25 cases used, 1 case contains missing values.

Predictor	Coef	Stdev	t Ratio	p Value	
Constant	-1.564	1.944	-0.80	0.430	
S	-0.0093	0.1614	-0.06	0.955	DROP !!
P	5.819	1.480	3.93	0.001	
E	1.3298	0.4506	2.95	0.008	

After trimming, it seems that M (market value) is largely determined by E (equity) and P (profits). Investors seem to value profitable firms that are high in equity (therefore, it is likely that there is lower debt).

Example 5 Plot (a)

Residuals (C8) Versus Predictions (C7)

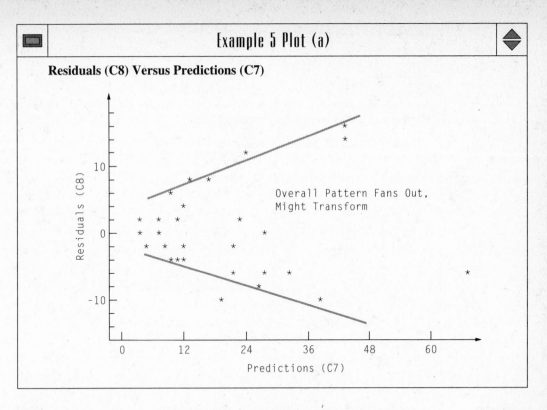

Example 5 Plot (b)

Residuals (C8) Versus Company Size Rank

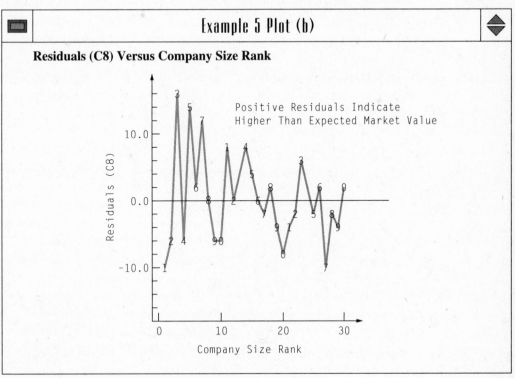

Example 5 Plot (c)

Values of h_{ii} Versus Observation Number

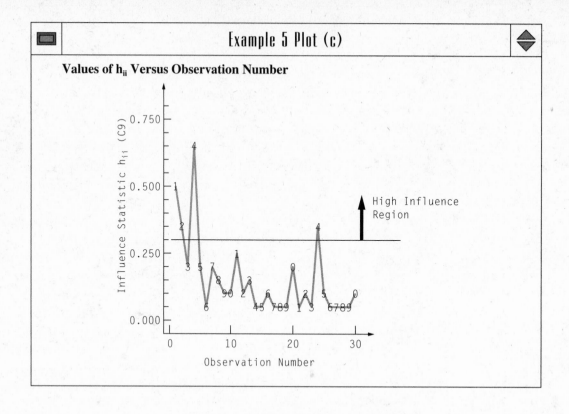

s = 5.184   R-sq = 88.9%   R-sq(adj) = 87.3%

Analysis of Variance

SOURCE	DF	SS	MS	F Value	p Value
Regression	3	4526.6	1508.9	56.14	0.000
Error	21	564.4	26.9		
Total	24	5091.0			

SOURCE	DF	SEQ SS
S	1	3584.1
P	1	708.4
E	1	234.1

Unusual Observations

Obs.	S	M	Fit	Stdev.Fit	Residual	St.Resid
1	86.7	57.97	58.27	3.94	-0.30	-0.09 X
10	21.7	*	27.78	4.00	*	* X

X denotes an observation whose X value gives it large influence.

Problem Statement (e)   Because of the insignificant t value for sales in the previous fit, drop it from the model and fit again.

Problem Solution (e)   With S (sales) dropped out of the regression, the new regression fit is

$$M = -1.60 + 5.81P + 1.31E$$

Of the 25 cases used, 1 case contains missing values.

```
Predictor      Coef      Stdev     t Ratio      p Value

Constant     -1.603      1.778      -0.90        0.377
P             5.811      1.440       4.04        0.001
E             1.3080     0.2373      5.51        0.000

s = 5.066      R-sq = 88.9%    R-sq (adj) = 87.9%
```

Analysis of Variance

```
SOURCE        DF         SS          MS       F Value      p Value

Regression     2       4526.5      2263.2      88.20        0.000
Error         22        564.5        25.7
Total         24       5091.0

SOURCE        DF       SEQ SS

P              1       3746.7
E              1        779.8
```

Problem Statement (f)   Examine residuals.

Problem Solution (f)

Unusual Observations

```
Obs.    P      M       Fit Stdev.Fit  Residual    St.Resid

 1    3.51   57.97    58.35     3.62     -0.38      -0.11 X
```

X denotes an observation whose X value gives it large influence.

Histogram of C6   N = 25   N* = 1

```
Midpoint  Count   (Roughly, Normal)
  -2.0      1     *
  -1.5      1     *
  -1.0      5     *****
  -0.5      4     ****
   0.0      3     ***
   0.5      5     *****
   1.0      1     *
   1.5      4     ****
   2.0      1     *
```

The following plot of residuals versus predictions no longer fans out. Therefore, transformations will not be needed.

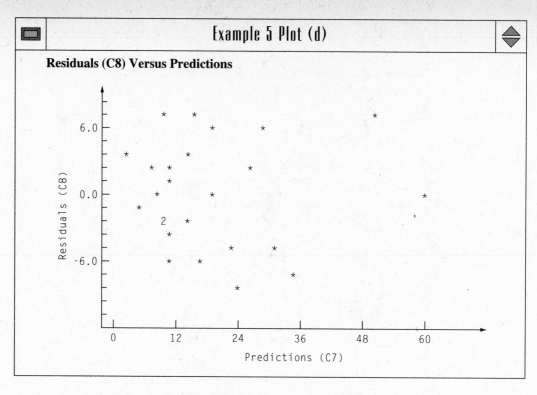

After trimming, the residuals versus company rank plot is

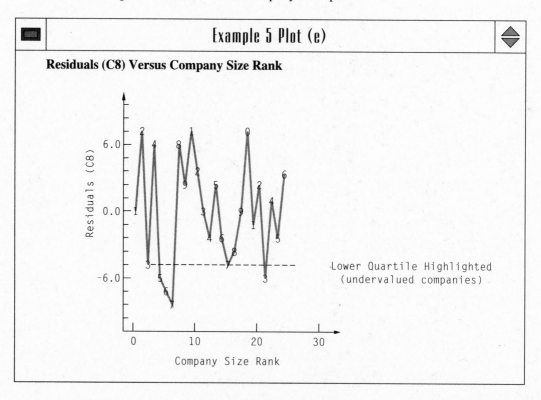

Look at the list of companies in Example 3. Trim observation rows 1, 2, 4, and 24 (GM, Ford, IBM, and RJR Nabisco). In the resulting trimmed list, the undervalued companies are in rows 3, 5, 6, 7, 17, and 23 (Mobil, Chrysler, Dupont, Texaco, Dow Chemical, and Digital Equipment). Mobil, Chrysler, and Digital had earnings drops from the previous year. Chrysler's drop was relatively severe. Dupont and Dow had modest earnings increases while Texaco had a substantial earnings increase the market seemed to ignore. Other factors may have led to the undervaluation. Perhaps at least one of these undervalued companies was a good stock buy.

Descriptive statistics on the residuals are

	N	N*	MEAN	MEDIAN	TRMEAN	STDEV	SEMEAN
C8	25	1	-0.000	-0.369	0.051	4.850	0.970

	MIN	MAX	Q1	Q3
C8	-8.748	7.564	-4.546	3.679

A new plot of h_{ii} values produces new influential points. However, further analysis is left to the reader.

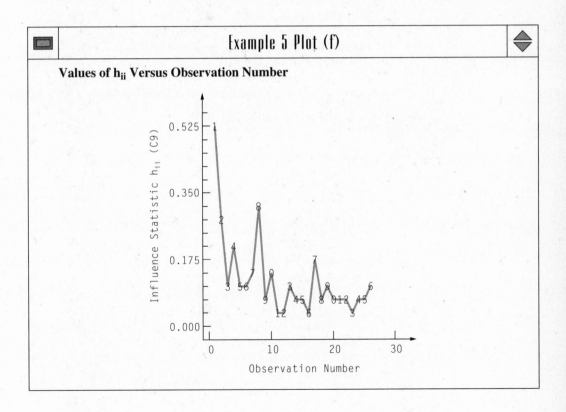

Example 5 Plot (f)

Values of h_{ii} Versus Observation Number

TECHNICAL REFERENCE SECTION FOR MULTIPLE REGRESSION

This section provides a general framework for the multiple regression model examples in the previous section. A response variable, y_i, is related to several predictor variables, $x_{1i}, x_{2i}, x_{3i}, \ldots, x_{ki}$. The predictor variables are evaluated to determine which ones are helpful in predicting the response. Recall that in simple regression only one predictor variable was considered, and the background variables were either fixed or their average effect was 0. In multiple regression analysis, the background variables can be incorporated into the regression model as long as they can be identified and measured.

A multiple regression model specifies that each observation, y_i, consists of $(k + 2)$ additive components. These components are (1) an unknown parameter, β_0; (2) the k unknown parameters, $\beta_1, \beta_2, \beta_3, \ldots, \beta_k$, times the predictor variables, $x_{1i}, x_{2i}, x_{3i}, \ldots, x_{ki}$; and (3) an unknown error term, e_i.

The sum of these terms is the following **general linear statistical model:**

$$y_i = \beta_0 1 + \beta_1 x_{1i} + \beta_2 x_{2i} + \cdots + \beta_k x_{ki} + e_i$$

By labeling the coefficient of β_0 as $x_{0i} = 1$, this model can be written more compactly as

$$y_i = \Sigma \beta_j x_{ji} + e_i$$

where $j = 0, 1, \ldots, k$.

The multiple regression model is an elaboration of the two following, more primitive models that were discussed earlier. Also recall that $\beta_0^* = \mu$, where an asterisk indicates that the parameters may differ in different models.

$$y_i = \beta_0^* 1 + e_i^* \quad \text{(naive regression model)}$$

and

$$y_i = \beta_0^{**} 1 + \beta_1^{**} x_{1i} + e_i^{**} \quad \text{(simple regression model)}$$

More sophisticated models build on the naive regression model by adding components $\beta_j x_{ji}$. When a newly introduced component or group of components contributes to explaining y_i, the standard deviation of e_i (in $y_i = \Sigma \beta_j x_{ji} + e_i$) is smaller than the standard deviation of e_i^*. In other words, $\beta_j x_{ji}$ is considered because of its potential to decrease the error standard deviation, which means that it helps explain the variation in the response variable. This can lead to sophisticated models that involve many terms, $\beta_2 x_{2i} + \cdots + \beta_k x_{ki}$.

The process of expanding or contracting regression models by changing the number of components results in parameters that may change in value and meaning. Thus, for example, β_0^*, β_0^{**}, and β_0 may differ. The same is true for the other β's, β^* and β^{**}. Consequently, estimators b_j, b_j^*, and b_j^{**} may be quite different. This can make the interpretation of the relationship between many variables difficult, particularly in observational studies. The b_j represents the slope or tilt of a fitted plane with respect to the axis of its corresponding predictor variable; b_j is an estimator of β_j.

Matrix Representation

Although the use of matrix methods is limited in this book, we define a few important matrices. Some can be useful in regard to MINITAB subcommands.

The 1 multiplied times β_0 becomes the first column in a design matrix. For the other columns, the values of the j-th (j > 0) predictor variable, x_{ji}, become the $j + 1$ column in a design matrix. To illustrate, suppose we have a sample of four data points that are represented by a linear model with two predictor variables.

$$y_1 = \beta_0 1 + \beta_1 x_{11} + \beta_2 x_{21} + e_1$$
$$y_2 = \beta_0 1 + \beta_1 x_{12} + \beta_2 x_{22} + e_2$$
$$y_3 = \beta_0 1 + \beta_1 x_{13} + \beta_2 x_{23} + e_3$$
$$y_4 = \beta_0 1 + \beta_1 x_{14} + \beta_2 x_{24} + e_4$$

The column structure of the design matrix, $\mathbf{X}$, is a first column of ones, a second column for x_{1i}, and a third column for x_{2i}.

In this situation, the parameter matrix $\mathbf{B}$ has three rows. Row one contains β_0, row two β_1 and row three β_2. Additional predictor variables would require additional columns in the $\mathbf{X}$ matrix and rows in the $\mathbf{B}$ matrix.

For the four observations in our illustration, suppose the first two observations of the response ($y_1 = 0$, $y_2 = 4$) were made when $x_{1i} = -1$. The second two observations ($y_3 = 6$, $y_4 = 6$) of the response were made when $x_{1i} = +1$. Similarly, $x_{2i} = +1, -1, +1, -1$, respectively, for the first through the fourth observation on the response. Let the -1 and the $+1$ represent, respectively, a low and a high level of a predictor variable.

Using these data values, the above set of equations becomes

$$0 = \beta_0 1 + \beta_1(-1) + \beta_2(+1) + e_1$$
$$4 = \beta_0 1 + \beta_1(-1) + \beta_2(-1) + e_2$$
$$6 = \beta_0 1 + \beta_1(+1) + \beta_2(+1) + e_3$$
$$6 = \beta_0 1 + \beta_1(+1) + \beta_2(-1) + e_4$$

Customarily, in matrix algebra, a matrix letter name followed by a prime, ', indicates a matrix transpose where columns become rows or rows become columns. For the set of equations shown above, $\mathbf{Y}'$ is $[0 \quad 4 \quad 6 \quad 6]$. The first column of $\mathbf{X}$ is $[1, 1, 1, 1]$, the second column is $[-1, -1, +1, +1]$, and the third is $[+1, -1, +1, -1]$. $\mathbf{B}'$ is $[\beta_0, \beta_1, \beta_2]$.

Estimating β_0, β_1, β_2, . . . , β_k with b_0, b_1, b_2, . . . , b_k

Because β_0, β_1, β_2, . . . , β_k are unknown, it is desirable to estimate these parameters using the sample data. Formulas for the estimators, b_0, b_1, b_2, . . . , b_k, result from the application of the ordinary least squares method. The objective in least squares is to minimize the sum of the errors squared, which is minimized by the best estimators. The quantity minimized is

$$\Sigma e_i^2$$

Σe_i^2 is a function of the unknown parameters. Partial derivatives of Σe_i^2 are taken with respect to the unknown parameters. This produces a set of equations that are set equal to zero and solved for the estimators, b_0, b_1, b_2, . . . , b_k. Behind the scenes in MINITAB, the REGRESSION command makes computations based on the least squares formulas.

In matrix terms, the formula for the regression coefficients is quite simple.

$$\mathbf{b} = (\mathbf{X'X})^{-1}\mathbf{X'Y}$$

where the -1 superscript indicates a matrix inverse. This matrix formulation is presented because some matrix results can be used by the data analyst. For example, the REGRESSION subcommand XPXINV computes $(\mathbf{X'X})^{-1}$.

As a reminder and a warning, a predictor variable cannot always be 0, constant, or dependent on another column in the design matrix. A column of zeros or dependent columns in the design matrix creates a **singularity problem** so that the matrix inversion in $(\mathbf{X'X})^{-1}$ can't be done in the usual sense.

Interpreting Coefficients and Determining What Influence the Observed Responses Have (Optional)

Johnson discussed the meaning of regression coefficients in certain experimental designs by focusing on two pieces of the matrix expression used to obtain them.[5] (Recall that the coefficients in Example 2 told us how popcorn yield was related to brand and amount.)

$$\mathbf{b} = (\mathbf{X'X})^{-1}\mathbf{X'Y}$$

The two parts of this expression are (1) $(\mathbf{X'X})^{-1}\mathbf{X'}$ and (2) $\mathbf{Y}$.

For the data in the illustration we have been using, these matrices are

$$\mathbf{Y'} = \begin{bmatrix} y_1 & y_2 & y_3 & y_4 \end{bmatrix}$$
$$\mathbf{Y'} = \begin{bmatrix} 0 & 4 & 6 & 6 \end{bmatrix}$$

$$\mathbf{K'} = (\mathbf{X'X})^{-1}\mathbf{X'} = \begin{bmatrix} \frac{1}{4} & \frac{1}{4} & \frac{1}{4} & \frac{1}{4} \\ -\frac{1}{4} & -\frac{1}{4} & \frac{1}{4} & \frac{1}{4} \\ \frac{1}{4} & \frac{1}{4} & \frac{1}{4} & -\frac{1}{4} \end{bmatrix}$$

The elements in the first row of $\mathbf{K}$ are multiplied by the corresponding elements in $\mathbf{Y'}$ and summed. The result is that each observation is weighted equally and b_0 equals the grand mean, $\Sigma\frac{y_i}{4}$. The elements in the second row of **K** are multiplied by corresponding elements in **Y**$'$ and summed. This weights the responses in such a way that $b_1 = \frac{1}{2}\left[\frac{(y_3 + y_4)}{2} - \frac{(y_1 + y_2)}{2}\right]$, which is one-half the differences in the means of the last two and first two observations. The last row of **K** produces results similar to the second but takes one-half the difference in the means of observations one and three and observations two and four.

Pairs of corresponding elements of **Y**$'$ and the elements in a row of **K** can be multiplied and plotted versus observation number to see the role each observation plays in determining the regression coefficient. We might want a separate plot for each row of **K**. In general, we would not like to see wild fluctuations in such a plot because that would indicate that some observations have too much weight relative to others. Johnson extended this discussion of **K** to design matrices for common experimental designs.

As you will see in the next example, the REGRESSION subcommand HI makes a computation using this matrix **K**. The HI subcommand finds the diagonal elements of the so-called **hat matrix,** which is $\mathbf{H} = \mathbf{XK}$. A general element of **H** is h_{ij}, where each element shows the potential effect of observation y_j on the prediction, $\hat{y}_i$.

Examining the hat matrix is an important aspect of regression diagnostics activities in which particular observations are found that might unduly influence the fit.

In general, the diagonal elements of h_{ij} are h_{ii}, the leverage of each data point on the fit. The h_{ii} versus the observation number can be examined in a scatterplot.

Rule for Finding Influential Data Points   Those $h_{ii} > 2\frac{p}{n}$ are considered large, where p is the number of parameters and n is the sample size.

Operationally, data points with high leverage might be set aside in order to obtain a fit that weights each observation almost equally.

The Prediction Equation

In multiple regression, the prediction equation forms a plane in space rather than a line. The general form of the prediction equation is

$$\hat{y}_i = b_0 1 + b_1 x_{1i} + b_2 x_{2i} + \cdots + b_k x_{ki}$$

It predicts the following average response

$$\beta_0 + \beta_1 x_{1i} + \beta_2 x_{2i} + \cdots + \beta_k x_{ki}$$

Recall that each observation can be written as

$$y_i = \beta_0 + \beta_1 x_{1i} + \beta_2 x_{2i} + \cdots + \beta_k x_{ki} + e_i$$

Therefore, when averaging the response, We average both sides of the above equation, and the average error is 0. Hence, the prediction equation estimates the average value of y_i at the location specified by the predictor variables. The unknown population mean depends on the values of the predictor variables.

Estimating an Error, e_i, with a Residual, $\hat{e}_i$

An actual observation minus the prediction is a residual. A residual is an estimator of an unknown error and may be obtained as follows, where $\hat{y}_i$ is a function of many variables in multiple regression:

$$(y_i - \hat{y}_i) = \hat{e}_i$$

The usual assumptions about the error terms are that (1) the average value of the errors is 0; (2) the standard deviation of the errors is constant and equal to σ; (3) the errors are uncorrelated with one another; and (4) the errors follow a normal distribution.

In order to validate these assumptions, residuals are examined. A large part of such an examination involves residual plots.

The usual estimator of σ is the standard deviation of the residuals, $s_{y|x1...xk}$. The subscript $y|x1 \ldots xk$ means y "given" $x1 \ldots xk$ are in the fit. The $s_{y|x1...xk}$ is an estimator of the standard deviation of probability distributions, which are located by the values of the predictor variables.

The No Predictor Variable Case   Without predictor variables, the squared sample standard deviation for the response is

$$s_y^2 = \frac{\Sigma(y_i - \hat{y}_i)^2}{n - 1} = \frac{\Sigma\hat{e}_i^{*2}}{n - 1}$$

The $\hat{e}_i^*$ is a residual, where $\hat{y}_i = \bar{y}$.

The Simple Regression Case   With one predictor variable the formula for the squared sample standard deviation changes slightly to

$$s_{y|x}^2 = \frac{\Sigma(y_i - \hat{y}_i)^2}{n - 2} = \frac{\Sigma\hat{e}_i^{**2}}{n - 2}$$

where $\hat{y}_i = b_0 + b_1 x_{1i}$ and $(n - 2)$ is the divisor because two parameters are estimated in the fit.

The Multiple Regression Case   When there are k predictor variables, there are $(k + 1) = p$ parameters and the squared sample standard deviation becomes

$$s_{y|x1...xk}^2 = \frac{\Sigma(y_i - \hat{y}_i)^2}{n - p} = \frac{\Sigma\hat{e}_i^2}{n - p}$$

where $\hat{y}_i = b_0 + b_1 x_{1i} + b_2 x_{2i} + \cdots + b_k x_{ki}$.

Because the subscripting is a bit cumbersome, we will simply use $s_{y|x}^2$, where x represents the predictor variables in the fit. You must be alert and remember which set of predictor variables are included in the fit. The square root of the above quantity, $s_{y|x}$, is often called the standard error of the estimate. The $s_{y|x}$ is simply the estimated standard deviation of the distribution of errors.

Standard Errors of b_0, b_1, b_2, . . . , b_k

The b_0, b_1, b_2, . . . , b_k are point estimators. Good point estimators are precise; therefore, small standard errors for these estimators are preferred. MINITAB has a REGRESSION subcommand, XPXINV, that produces the matrix $(\mathbf{X'X})^{-1}$. The $s_{y|x}^2$ times XPXINV produces squared sample standard errors of the regression coefficients on the diagonal and covariances off the diagonal.

$$s_{y|x}^2 (\mathbf{X'X})^{-1}$$

Because the formulas for these estimators are complicated, we rely on computers to make the calculations.

The sample standard errors of the estimators are the square roots of the diagonal elements. The notation used for them is s_{b0}, s_{b1}, s_{b2}, . . . , s_{bk}. The off-diagonal elements are the estimated covariances of the estimators, such as s_{b01}, s_{b12}, and s_{b2k}.

In some designed experiments, such as the popcorn experiment in Example 2, the covariances are zero because the regression coefficients are independent of one another. Independent regression coefficients are ideal because the coefficients can be interpreted singly and unambiguously. When the covariances are not 0, the estimators covary, which makes them difficult to untangle and to understand individually.

Confidence Intervals and Hypothesis Tests

Hypothesis tests and confidence intervals can be constructed for β_j, where $j = 0, 1, 2, . . . , k$.

The point estimator of an unknown parameter is b_j. Its computation is based on a single sample. If other samples of the same size were collected and new b_j's calculated, the new b_j's are likely to differ from the original ones. We prefer that the differences are small and that confidence intervals on β_j are narrow.

Theoretically, b_j follows a normal distribution, which is centered on β_j with a standard error, σ_{bj}, as a spread measure. Thus, it is not necessary to actually calculate new b_j's because upper and lower confidence limits can be found for β_j. These confidence intervals can be constructed from information in the initial sample.

Two-Sided Hypothesis Tests on Unknown Parameters A b_j can be student-ized by subtracting β_j and dividing by the estimated standard error.

$$\frac{b_j - \beta_j}{s_{bj}}$$

When testing for $\beta_j = 0$, this t ratio simplifies to

$$\frac{b_j - 0}{s_{bj}}$$

MINITAB and other statistical programs do this studentization for you.

The absolute values of the computed t ratios are compared to a standard or critical t value, $t_{(\alpha/2),(n-p)}$. When the absolute value of the computed t value exceeds the standard, reject the hypothesis that $\beta_j = 0$. Similarly, a confidence interval on β_j that encloses 0 indicates that the null hypothesis cannot be rejected. The degrees of freedom are $(n - p)$, which is the error degrees of freedom from the ANOVA table.

The null hypothesis that $\beta_j = 0$ is of special interest because not reject-ing it means that the component $\beta_j x_{ji}$ is also 0. Therefore, it makes sense to drop this component from the multiple regression model in favor of a smaller, more parsimonious fit.

Rule for Finding Regression Coefficients That Are Significantly Different from Zero In general, the null hypothesis can state that β_j is some value other than 0. Then, the following t ratio is compared to the critical value, where the value of β_j from the null hypothesis is used in computing the t ratio.

$$
\begin{array}{cc}
\textbf{t ratio} & \textbf{critical t value} \\[4pt]
\left| \dfrac{b_j - \beta_j}{s_{bj}} \right| \; > & \quad t_{(\alpha/2),(n-p)}
\end{array}
$$

If the left side of the above expression exceeds the right side, reject the null hypothesis.

In multiple regression analysis examples, a t value is computed for every component in the prediction equation to test the null hypothesis that each component parameter is 0. If the parameter is not significantly different from 0, it is likely that the component does not contribute significantly to the prediction. As a result, the component may be dropped from the prediction equation. In such decisions, an array of t ratios of the form

$$\left| \frac{b_j - \beta_j}{s_{bj}} \right|$$

is scanned by the investigator. This is referred to as a **t directed search** for significant predictor variables. A rough rule of thumb for large-sample sizes is that ratios exceeding two identify the predictor variables to be included in the prediction equation. Otherwise the predictor variables are removed from the fit. A word of caution is in order because a sequence of individual t tests loses power. Nevertheless, a t directed search for significant variables makes the t ratio an important tool for the investigator.

Confidence Intervals on Unknown Parameters   The elements of the studentization and the hypothesis testing can be rearranged to form a $(1 - \alpha)$ confidence interval on the unknown parameter, β_j.

$$b_j \pm t_{(\alpha/2),(n-p)}(s_{bj})$$

Notice that smaller standard errors make the confidence interval narrower.

One-Sided Hypothesis Tests on Unknown Parameters   Sometimes hypothesis tests are one-sided rather than two-sided as shown above. For example, suppose $H_n : \beta_j = 30$ versus the alternative hypothesis $H_a : \beta_j < 30$. This is in contrast to the two-sided alternative hypothesis $H_a : \beta_j \neq 30$.

For the two-sided case, an interval was created using the following expression:

$$b_j \pm t_{(\alpha/2),(n-p)}s_{bj}$$

For the two-sided test, the probability of a false rejection of the null hypothesis is α, with $\frac{\alpha}{2}$ of the probability in each tail of the Student's t distribution.

For the one-sided test, the probability of a false rejection of the null hypothesis is still α. However, because one side of the probability distribution is of no interest, α and not $\frac{\alpha}{2}$ of the probability is in each tail of the distribution. As a consequence, the interval for a one-sided test is

$$b_j \pm t_{(\alpha),(n-p)}s_{bj}$$

Because this interval uses $t_{(\alpha)}$ rather than $t_{(\alpha/2)}$, it produces a narrower interval. For the alternative hypothesis, say, $H_a : \beta_j < 30$, reject the null hypothesis as long as the confidence interval is to the left of 30. Similar reasoning applies for the alternative hypothesis $H_a : \beta_j > 30$. Reject the null hypothesis as long as the confidence interval is to the right of 30.

Confidence Intervals on the Unknown Regression Plane   Confidence intervals can be placed on any linear combination of component effects. For example, a confidence interval can be placed on the unknown regression plane, which is

$$\beta_0 + \beta_1 x_{1i} + \beta_2 x_{2i} + \cdots + \beta_k x_{ki}$$

The fit, $\hat{y}_i = b_0 + b_1 x_{1i} + b_2 x_{2i} + \cdots + b_k x_{ki}$, is an estimator of the unknown plane. Therefore, the confidence interval is of the form

$$\hat{y}_i \pm t_{(\alpha/2),(n-p)} s(\hat{y})$$

where

$$s(\hat{y}) = s_{y|x} \left[\mathbf{x}^{*\prime} (\mathbf{X}'\mathbf{X})^{-1} \mathbf{x}^* \right]^{1/2}$$

An asterisk is used on the matrix $\mathbf{x}^{*\prime} = [1, x_{1i}, x_{2i}, \ldots, x_{ki}]$ to indicate that this is a confidence interval at a set of x values that may or may not equal those used to obtain the fit. The matrix manipulations specified in the formulas can be done in statistical packages such as MINITAB through the use of subcommands.

Confidence Intervals on a Single Future Observed Value of the Response   Confidence intervals can also be placed on a single future observed value, y_{if}. A single future observed value is equal to $\beta_0 + \beta_1 x_{1i} + \beta_2 x_{2i} + \cdots + \beta_k x_k$ plus an error.

$$y_{if} = \beta_0 + \beta_1 x_{1i} + \beta_2 x_{2i} + \cdots + \beta_k x_k + e_{if}$$

The substitution of estimators for the unknowns yields

$$(\hat{y}_i = b_0 + b_1 x_{1i} + b_2 x_{2i} + \cdots + b_k x_{ki}) + \hat{e}_{if}$$

which has an estimated standard deviation of

$$[s(\hat{y})^2 + s_{y|x}^2]^{1/2}$$

As a result, a confidence interval on a single future observed value is constructed as follows:

$$(\hat{y}_i = \Sigma b_j x_{ji}^*) \pm t_{(\alpha/2),(n-p)} [s(\hat{y})^2 + s_{y|x}^2]^{1/2}$$

An asterisk on x_{ji}^* indicates that this is a confidence interval at a set of x values that may or may not equal those used to obtain the fit.

Confidence Intervals on the Mean of q Future Observed Values of the Response   Similar to the confidence interval for a single future observation, a confidence interval on the mean of q future observations is

$$(\hat{y}_i = \Sigma b_j x_{ji}^*) \pm t_{(\alpha/2),(n-p)} \left[s(\hat{y})^2 + \frac{s_{y|x}^2}{q} \right]^{1/2}$$

Notice as q gets larger, this interval shrinks. When q is small, this interval is quite wide, giving the user a feel for the risk in predicting a single future value or the mean of a small number of future values.

The Analysis of Variance

As a multiple regression model is expanded by adding one or more additional components, $\beta_j x_{ji}$, we question whether a larger, more complicated model is worth building. Do additional components make a significant contribution in reducing the error sum of squares? An analysis of variance (ANOVA) table is designed to help answer this question.

Statistical packages usually compute the ANOVA table cell values. Therefore, the formulas are shown below for reference purposes.

Source	Degrees of Freedom	Sums of Squares	Mean Square	F Ratio
Regression	$k = (p - 1)$	$RSS = \Sigma(\hat{y}_i - \overline{y})^2$	$\dfrac{RSS}{k}$	$\dfrac{\left[\dfrac{RSS}{k}\right]}{s_{y\mid x}^2}$
Error	$(n - p)$	$ESS = \Sigma(y_i - \hat{y}_i)^2$	$s_{y\mid x}^2 = \dfrac{ESS}{n - p}$	
Total	$(n - 1)$	$TSS = \Sigma(y_i - \overline{y})^2$		

To evaluate the worth of adding one or more additional components, $\beta_j x_{ji}$, the sums of squares column is used. First consider the naive regression model

$$y_i = \beta_0^* + e_i^*$$

compared to a full multiple regression model.

$$y_i = \beta_0 + \beta_1 x_{1i} + \beta_2 x_{2i} + \cdots + \beta_k x_k + e_i$$

A Reduced Model   Maximum response variability occurs when there are no predictor variables in the model. Thus, for the naive regression model, a measure of that variability is the estimated squared standard deviation

$$s^{2*} = \frac{\Sigma(y_i - \hat{y}_i)^2}{n - 1}$$

where $\hat{y}_i = \overline{y}$ for $y_i = \beta_0^* + e_i^*$. Notice that the numerator is the total sum of squares, $TSS = \Sigma(y_i - \hat{y}_i)^2$, from the ANOVA table.

A Full Model   For a full regression model with predictor variables, a measure of the remaining variability is another estimated squared standard deviation

$$s_{y\mid x}^2 = \frac{\Sigma(y_i - \hat{y}_i)^2}{n - p}$$

where $\hat{y}_i = b_0 + b_1 x_{1i} + b_2 x_{2i} + \cdots + b_k x_{ki}$. Notice that the numerator is the error sum of squares, ESS, from the ANOVA table.

The presence of significant predictor variables in a full model leads us to expect that $s_{y|x}^2$ will be smaller than s^{2*}, which should be reflected in the error sum of squares, ESS.

Any difference, TSS − ESS, is due to the difference between the naive regression (reduced) model and the full multiple regression model. TSS − ESS = RSS, where RSS is the regression sum of squares. RSS is due to the regression components $b_1 x_{1i} + b_2 x_{2i} + \cdots + b_k x_{ki}$.

If the components $b_1 x_{1i} + b_2 x_{2i} + \cdots + b_k x_{ki}$ make a significant contribution to reducing the error sum of squares, RSS should be large relative to ESS. In perfect fits, RSS is as large as TSS and ESS is 0.

Additional ANOVA Information   The ANOVA table makes other information available in a compact way, including.

1. $\frac{RSS}{TSS} = R^2$, which is the proportion of the total variability explained by the additional components in a full model compared to a naive model. R is the **multiple correlation coefficient,** which is the simple correlation between the actual and predicted responses.
2.   The proportion of unexplained variability is $1 - \left[\frac{RSS}{TSS}\right]$. Notice that TSS = RSS + ESS.
3.   The degrees of freedom column displays the number of independent pieces of information used to compute the associated sum of squares.
4.   The mean square column averages the sums of squares. The degrees of freedom are divided into their corresponding sum of squares.
5.   The regression mean square is divided by the residual mean square to form an F ratio statistic.

The F Test   The F ratio statistic is compared to a critical F value ($F_{\alpha,(k,n-p)}$) to test the null hypothesis that

$$\beta_1 = \beta_2 = \cdots = \beta_k = 0$$

If the F ratio statistic exceeds the critical F value

F ratio statistic		**critical F value**
$\dfrac{\frac{RSS}{k}}{s_{y|x}^2}$	$>$	$F_{\alpha(k,n-p)}$

reject the hypothesis that $\beta_1 = \beta_2 = \cdots = \beta_k = 0$. This F test simultaneously tests that all β's are 0. It has an important advantage over a series of individual t tests because the F test does not lose power.

Full and Reduced Models   When all k parameters are included in the multiple regression equation, the model is said to be full. Therefore, RSS is designated RSS(full), and a more explicit way to specify the F test is

F ratio statistic   **critical F value**

$$\frac{\dfrac{RSS(full)}{k}}{s_{y|x}^2} \quad > \quad F_{\alpha,(k,n-p)}$$

A full model of k predictor variables is often compared to a reduced model of g predictor variables, where $(g < k)$ and $(k - g)$ is the number of predictor variables dropped from the full model. If the dropped parameters are all 0

$$\beta_{g+1} = \beta_{g+2} = \cdots = \beta_k = 0$$

nothing is lost by omitting them from the model. The resulting reduced model is simpler.

Therefore, it is desirable to test the null hypothesis that

$$\beta_{g+1} = \beta_{g+2} = \cdots = \beta_k = 0$$

To implement this test, first compute the change in the sums of squares using RSS or ESS from full and reduced models.

$$RSS(full) - RSS(reduced) = ESS(reduced) - ESS(full)$$

Form the following F ratio statistic and compare it to the critical value.

F ratio statistic   **critical F value**

$$\frac{\dfrac{RSS(full) - RSS(reduced)}{(k - g)}}{s_{y|x(full)}^2} \quad > \quad F_{\alpha,(k-g,n-p)}$$

Reject the hypothesis that $\beta_{g+1} = \beta_{g+2} = \cdots = \beta_k = 0$ if the computed F ratio exceeds the critical F value.

ANOVA in Terms of R^2   The ANOVA table can be presented in terms of R^2, which is accomplished by dividing the items in the sum of squares column by the total sum of squares, TSS. The resulting table is

Source	Degrees of Freedom	Sum of Squares	Mean Square	F Ratio
Regression	$k = (p - 1)$	$RSS/TSS = R^2$	R^2/k	$\dfrac{R^2/k}{(1-R^2)/(n-p)}$
Error	$(n - p)$	$RSS/TSS = (1 - R^2)$	$(1 - R^2)/(n - p)$	
Total	$(n - 1)$	$TSS/TSS = 1$		

As R^2 approaches one, observe that the computed F ratio also gets large. Therefore, both statistics indicate a good fit. As a reminder, just as R^2 is subject to distortion by a few stray data values, the same is true for the F ratio. Therefore, it pays to plot the data and examine residuals.

Selecting the "Best" Fit

In selecting the "best" fit, one chooses a prediction equation with the highest predictive potential of all possible fits. The problem is most difficult when dealing with observational studies that involve a large number of highly correlated predictor variables. A large number of predictor variables produces a multitude of potential fits because each predictor variable can be in or out of the model. Furthermore, highly correlated predictor variables look alike. This makes it difficult to decide on which predictors should stay in the fits and which should be dropped. Although logical model selection strategies exist, they don't guarantee correct conclusions and models. Fortunately, well-designed experiments tend to lead to more trustworthy results. Nevertheless, many predictor variables still make the selection problem complex.

For k predictor variables, there are 2^k possible fits. For example, two predictor variables result in four possible prediction equations.

$$(\text{the number of states})^{(\text{number of predictor variables})} = 2^2 = 4$$

As the number of predictor variables increases, say, 3, 4, 5, or k, then the number of potential prediction equations to select from increases rapidly from $2^3 = 8$, $2^4 = 16$, $2^5 = 32$ to 2^k. The number of potential prediction equations can become unmanageably large.

The next example results in at least three competitive prediction equations. All three equations fit the data fairly well. Therefore, the final model choice depends on more than statistical assessments alone.

EXAMPLE 6

STACK LOSS DATA[6]

The response, stack loss, is related to three predictor variables that monitor plant operation: air flow, x_{1i}; cooling water inlet temperature, x_{2i}; and acid concentration, x_{3i}. Twenty-one observations were taken on four variables from the operation of a plant for the oxidation of ammonia to nitric acid.

These variables were observed over 21 consecutive days of plant operation. Therefore, this is an observational study rather than a designed experiment. In a designed experiment, randomization might be attempted in order to ensure against background variable problems such as a time trend in the data.

The stack loss data set is celebrated because it has received so much attention in the statistical literature. Draper and Smith use the stack loss problem as an exercise.[7] Daniel and Wood conduct a patient, thorough analysis of the data set.[8] They use transformations and set aside large residuals that include observations 1, 3, 4, and 21. Andrews illustrated a robust multiple regression method on this data set.[9] In one pass, the robust procedure produced a fit that gave less weight to observations 1, 3, 4, and 21. Overall, this example illustrates the difficulties in determining what might be considered the "best" fit.

Problem Statement (a) Preliminary examination of the data indicated that a trend variable, T, should be considered. List the data and highlight influential observations. Examine the correlation matrix.

Problem Solution (a) The variable names, Y, X1, X2, and X3, are for stack loss, air flow, cooling water temperature, and acid concentration, respectively. Additional variables named T and T2 (where T2 is time squared), have been added. To account for the possibility of a time trend, T was included because the data were collected over 21 consecutive days of plant operation. T2 was added after examining several plots, Y versus T and X1 versus T. The plots exhibited curvature.

Leverage values, h_{ii}, were computed and placed in column C7. These are the diagonal elements of the hat matrix that resulted from the full regression model using all the predictor variables. Recall that the h_{ii} values show the leverage of each row of predictor variables in determining the prediction of Y.

ROW	Y	X1	X2	X3	T	T2	C7	
1	42	80	27	89	1	1	**0.38**	Bold h_{ii} rows are leveraged enough to catch
2	37	80	27	88	2	4	**0.33**	our attention. Look for these points on
3	37	75	25	90	3	9	0.18	plots.
4	28	62	24	87	4	16	0.29	
5	18	62	22	87	5	25	0.22	
6	18	62	23	87	6	36	0.10	
7	19	62	24	93	7	49	0.26	
8	20	62	24	93	8	64	**0.36**	
9	15	58	23	87	9	81	**0.31**	
10	14	58	18	80	10	100	**0.34**	
11	14	58	18	89	11	121	0.20	
12	13	58	17	88	12	144	0.27	
13	11	58	18	82	13	169	0.27	
14	12	58	19	93	14	196	0.22	
15	8	50	18	89	15	225	0.26	
16	7	50	18	86	16	256	0.18	
17	8	50	19	72	17	289	**0.45**	
18	8	50	19	79	18	324	0.19	
19	9	50	20	80	19	361	0.28	
20	15	56	20	82	20	400	0.25	
21	15	70	20	91	21	441	**0.67**	

The correlation matrix is:

	Y	X1	X2	X3	
X1	.920	-------------------			most highly correlated with y
X2	.876	.782	-------------		high intercorrelated predictors
X3	.400	.500	.391		
T	-.811	-.696	-.767	-.426	negative sign-plot pattern has a downward tilt

High intercorrelation between predictor variables leads to a multicollinearity problem that, among other things, makes it difficult to tell which variable, X1 or X2, should be included in the fit.

Practical considerations and the physical theory associated with the application often helps us make the choice of variables to include in the fit and not the statistics. Additionally, there is an associated problem of inflated standard errors tending to deflate t values, which makes what might be significant variables look insignificant.

Although the plots are not shown here, you will find a slight curvilinear relationship between Y and T. T is a dummy time trend variable, taking on values 1, 2, 3, . . . , 21 (21 sequential days of plant operation). To adjust for the curve, T^2, a transformed variable, was introduced.

X1 also shows a time trend. Both X1 and Y display this trend, leading us to suspect time is in the background. As a result, considerable debate is possible as to which variables should be selected for inclusion in the fit. Additionally, after the variables are included, there is a problem in determining what they mean.

Problem Statement (b)   Fit a model that includes all prediction variables and evaluate the goodness of fit information.

Problem Solution (b)   For all predictor variables in the full model, the fit is

$$y_i = 10.21 + 0.38 \; X1 + 0.13 \; X2 - 0.005 \; X3 - 3.02 \; T + 0.097 \; T^2$$

VARIABLE	b_j REGRESSION COEFFICIENT	s_{bj} ST. ERROR OF COEF.	b_j/s_{bj} T RATIO = COEF/ST.ERROR	$H_0: \beta_j = 0$ Critical t $t_{.025,15} = 2.13$
	10.21	16.42	| 0.62|	
X1	0.38	0.15	| 2.54| > 2.13	Reject $\beta_1 = 0$
X2	0.13	0.43	| 0.30|	
X3	-0.005	0.14	|-0.04|	
T	-3.02	1.00	|-3.02| > 2.13	Reject $\beta_4 = 0$
T2	0.097	0.036	| 2.67| > 2.13	Reject $\beta_5 = 0$

A t directed search leads to the tentative conclusion that X1, T, and T2 are to be included in the model while X2 and X3 are to be excluded from the model (dropped). Confirmation of this tentative conclusion will be made using an F test on the hypothesis $\beta_2 = \beta_3 = 0$.

```
R-squared = 95.5% = 100 × (r_yŷ)²
   (appears to be a good fit)
```

ANALYSIS OF VARIANCE TABLE (full model)

SOURCE	SS	DF	MS = SS/DF	F RATIO	F CRITICAL
Regression	1976.33	5	395.27	63.86 (395.27/6.19)	> 2.9 = $F_{.05,(5,15)}$ Reject $\beta_1 = \beta_2 = \beta_3 = \beta_4 = \beta_5 = 0$
Error		92.91	15	6.19 = $s_{y\vert x}^2$	
Total		2069.24	20		

Problem Statement (c)   Fit and evaluate a reduced model in which X2 and X3 are dropped from the full model.

Problem Solution (c) Low t values for X2 and X3 led us to drop both variables from the fit. The reduced model fit is

$$\hat{y}_i = 13.8 + 0.38 \; X1 - 3.21 \; T + 0.10 \; T^2$$

```
                                          T RATIO =
VARIABLE COEFFICIENT  ST. ERROR OF COEF.  COEF/ST. ERROR

           13.83        10.07                 1.37
X1          0.38         0.12                 3.18
T          -3.21         0.61                -5.24   all three predictors
T2          0.10         0.023                4.44   are significant

R-squared = 95.5%

ANALYSIS OF VARIANCE TABLE  (reduced model)

 SOURCE          SS   DF   MS = SS/DF   F RATIO    F CRITICAL

Regression 1975.75   3      658.58     119.74 >  F.05.(3,17) = 3.2
Error        93.48  17        5.50     reject    β1 = β4 = β5 = 0

Total      2069.24  20
```

Problem Statement (d) Variables X2 and X3 were dropped from the fit because of low t values. Because a sequence of t tests loses power, confirm the decision to drop these variables with an F test.

Problem Solution (d) The model for the previous analysis of variance table was reduced because the predictors X2 and X3 were dropped from the fit. The first ANOVA table for the full model included five predictor variables. For the full model, the hypothesis is that $\beta_1 = \beta_2 = \beta_3 = \beta_4 = \beta_5 = 0$. For the reduced model, the hypothesis is that $\beta_1 = \beta_4 = \beta_5 = 0$.

To test the hypothesis associated with the dropped variables, that $\beta_2 = \beta_3 = 0$, an F test is preferred because a sequence of t tests to exclude X2 and X3 are not simultaneous tests. The F test makes use of the change in the regression sum of squares from the full and reduced models and divides it by the number of predictor variables excluded.

$$\frac{\text{RSS(full)} - \text{RSS (reduced)}}{\text{number of predictors excluded}}$$

Using regression sum of squares from the ANOVA tables, the expression above is evaluated for the numerator of an F ratio and is

$$\frac{1976.33 - 1975.75}{2}$$

The denominator of the F ratio is

$$s^2_{y|x} \; (\text{full}) = 6.19$$

The ratio of these two quantities is an F value statistic that equals $\frac{.58/2}{6.19} = .047$. The statistic .047 is less than the critical F value, $F_{.05,(2,15)} = 3.68$; hence, do not reject the hypothesis that $\beta_2 = \beta_3 = 0$. In this case, the t tests and the F test resulted in the same conclusion. When they conflict, the F test should be used because it is more powerful.

Problem Statement (e) Several diagnostic plots (not shown) were examined, such as plots of leverage versus observation number, probability plot of residuals, residuals versus predictions, rows of $(\mathbf{X}'\mathbf{X})^{-1}\mathbf{X}'$ versus observation number. From the examination of these plots, it was decided to set aside (trim) observations numbered 1, 2, 17, and 21. Repeat the analysis to see if any dramatic changes occur.

Problem Solution (e) A "T" has been appended to the variable names to remind the reader that some observations have been trimmed.

After trimming, the full fit is

$$\hat{y}T = -21 + 0.72 \, X1T + 0.05 \, X2T + 0.095 \, X3T - 2.7 \, TT + 0.10 \, TT^2$$

```
COLUMN   COEFFICIENT    ST. DEV. OF COEF.     T RATIO = COEF/S.D.

          -21.0            17.78                -1.18
X1T        0.72             0.18                 4.04**
X2T        0.05             0.39                 0.13 (similar to previous results)
X3T        0.095            0.16                 0.59
TT        -2.70             0.95                -2.85**
T2T        0.10             0.035                2.95**
```

Again, a reduced fit is obtained for the trimmed data set. It is likely to be used as the final fit. Although the same variables (X2 and X3) were dropped, notice that the trimming considerably changed the coefficients.

$$\hat{y}T = -13.5 + 0.76 \, X1T - 2.65 \, TT + 0.098 \, TT^2$$

```
R-Squared = 94.4%.
(all these included predictor variables are significant)

COLUMN   COEFFICIENT    ST. DEV. OF COEF.     T RATIO = COEF/S.D.

          -13.5            12.38                -1.09
X1T        0.76             0.16                 4.67
TT        -2.65             0.59                -4.46
T2T        0.098            0.02                 4.50
```

Diagnostic plots of the residuals (not shown) validated the assumptions.

Problem Statement (f) Decide the best fit to be used for predicting stack loss.

Problem Solution (f) Our choice for a final fit for the trimmed data set (omitting observations 1, 2, 17, 21) is

$$\hat{y}_i = -13.5 + 0.76 \, x_{1i} - 2.65 \, T_i + 0.098 \, T_i^2$$

Some alternative choices are available. Daniel and Wood set aside observations 1, 3, 4, and 21 and obtained the fit

$$\hat{y}_i = -15.4 - 0.07 \, x_{1i} + 0.53 \, x_{2i} + 0.0068 \, x_{1i}^2$$

Andrews showed the least squares fit after trimming observations 1, 2, 3, and 21 to be

$$\hat{y}_i = -37.6 + 0.80\, x_{1i} + 0.58\, x_{2i} - 0.7\, x_{3i}$$

The robust fit is nearly the same as Daniel and Wood's fit.

The final choice of a fit depends on a complicated mix of (1) the general characteristics, and theoretical and practical underpinnings of the application; (2) the statistical analysis; and (3) the judgment of the data analyst and the client. In multiple regression analysis, the final fit usually has some close competitor fits.

MINITAB'S Stepwise Variable Selection Procedure MINITAB provides the STEPWISE command for the stepwise addition (and deletion) of predictor variables to the fit. **Stepwise regression** refers to an automatic procedure for doing multiple regressions. In a stepwise fashion the procedure selects subsets of variables to be included in the fit.

Although potentially misleading because of its mechanical nature, which neglects the theory and lore associated with the application, the stepwise procedure has been popular because many users of multiple regression deal with observational studies and many predictor variables. So many predictor variables are often available that chaos results without an automatic procedure. Unfortunately, if used recklessly, the stepwise procedure can also result in chaos.

The stepwise procedure works in the following way:

1. First, with no predictor variables in the fit, all predictor variables are correlated with the response. The predictor variable that has the highest correlation with the response is entered into the fit if its F value, called a **partial F value,** exceeds a user-selected critical value called FENTER.

2. Given that one predictor variable is already in the fit, new partial F values are calculated for each remaining predictor variable. The second variable entered into the fit has the highest partial F value, which exceeds FENTER.

3. Next, each variable in the fit is reexamined as if it were to be removed and a new partial F value is computed. If the smallest new partial F value is less than a user-selected critical value called FREMOVE, the predictor variable is removed from the fit.

4. In a stepwise fashion, this procedure recycles, reexamining variables not in the fit for possible entry and variables in the fit for possible removal. The procedure stops cycling when no more variables can be entered or removed. The user-selected FENTER and FREMOVE values control the number of predictor variables in the fit. Lowering FENTER and FREMOVE tends to increase the number of variables in the fit. Raising FENTER and FREMOVE tends to decrease the number of variables in the fit.

The stepwise procedure steps forward in seeking a variable to enter and steps backward in seeking a variable to remove from the fit. Some users prefer to look at a full model with all the predictor variables in the fit initially and step backward only. This procedure is called **backward elimination.** Backward elimination can be achieved by setting FENTER = 100,000 (such a large value that variables never reenter) and FREMOVE at customary levels.

Conversely, some users prefer to step forward only. **Forward selection** is achieved by setting FREMOVE = 0 (such a small value prohibits removal) and FENTER set to customary levels.

Several STEPWISE subcommands mitigate the disadvantages associated with the procedure's automatic, unthinking nature. For example, REMOVE and ENTER subcommands allow user intervention, temporarily overriding the automatic entry and removal criterion until automatic selection is resumed. The FORCE subcommand forces certain variables into the fit. The BEST subcommand lists second-best, third-best, . . . , and K-best alternatives to a variable selected for entry into the fit.

Other Selection Procedures   Draper and Smith give a thorough discussion of a wide variety of selection procedures you may wish to examine.[10] In general, the intelligent use of these procedures is difficult and dangerous for the novice. A virtual smorgasbord of procedures are available that include: all possible regressions, best subset regression, backward elimination, stepwise, ridge regression, PRESS selection, principal component regression, latent root regression, stagewise regression and robust regression.

CHAPTER SUMMARY

This chapter examined multiple regression analysis that relates many variables. This was illustrated graphically for three variables. The response variable y was assigned to the vertical axis and the predictor variables x_{1i} and x_{2i}, formed two other axes. A plane, $\hat{y}_i = b_0 + b_1 x_{1i} + b_2 x_{2i}$, was fit and the regression coefficients, the b's, specified the tilt of the plane with respect to each axis. This is a powerful summary relating three variables. The notion of two predictors was extended to three, four, five, . . . , and k predictor variables.

The classical fit of a plane is referred to as multiple linear regression. In this approach, the general linear model $y_i = \Sigma \beta_j x_{ji} + e_i$ was used to represent each data point. The model is theoretical in the sense that the β's and the errors are unknown. The classical approach is to estimate the relationship $\Sigma \beta_j x_{ji}$ based on the least squares method that minimized the sum of the errors squared. The fit or prediction equation is of the form $\hat{y}_i = \Sigma b_j x_{ji}$. Matrix methods are often used to discuss least squares because of their efficiency and effectiveness.

Once a fit is obtained, it is natural to be concerned about confidence intervals and hypothesis tests. Confidence intervals can be placed on the individual unknown parameters, the β's, linear combinations of the β's, and future predictions. Confidence intervals on individual parameters, t tests, or F tests may be used for hypothesis testing.

A hypothesis of partictular interest is that $\beta_j = 0$. When this hypothesis cannot be rejected, the predictor variable does not appear to carry enough information to be included in the fit. The analysis of variance table produced the F test as an alternative to the t test; the two tests have a one-to-one correspondence for simple regression. The F test, however, is more powerful than the t test in the multiple predictor variable setting.

The analysis of variance table provided an elegant way to display the variance partitioning, where the total sum of squares is partitioned into that explained (due to particular components in the regression model) and that unexplained (residual or error).

KEY TERMS

EXERCISES

1. In Example 2, the popcorn experiment, suppose the brand and amount variables remain the same but yield is now

   6.5   9.4   5.0   9.8   10.0   18.0   12.2   19.5

Conduct an analysis similar to that shown in the example.

2. In Example 2, the popcorn experiment, suppose the brand and amount variables remain the same but yield is now

   12.1   14.0   13.2   16.0   5.2   8.1   5.0   8.5

Conduct an analysis similar to that shown in the example.

3. In Example 2, the popcorn experiment, suppose the brand and amount variables remain the same but yield is now

   9.8   9.4   8.2   9.8   10.0   9.5   11.0   9.2

Conduct an analysis similar to that shown in the example.

4. *(This exercise is quite long, but it is a valuable case study that includes some multiple regression at the end with considerable preliminary work.)*

The variables in this data set characterize 28 molds built for plastic-injection molding machines. The mold cavities are machined out of steel. Two blocks of steel (for example, each 20 in. long, 12 in. wide, and 5 in. thick) are machined so that, when the blocks are sandwiched together, a cavity (in the shape of a plastic part or parts) exists in the middle of the sandwich. Separate channels for molten plastic and coolant are also machined out. The variables are financial in nature.

To examine these data in MINITAB, RETRIEVE 'B:TOG1'. Then request information with INFO and PRINT C1–C9. The variable names are TNUM (a mold number for identification), PRICE (revenue, the bid price of the mold), BGTHRS (hours budgeted to make the mold), ACTHRS (actual hours to make the mold without corrective work on errors), CORHRS (corrective work hours), TOTHRS (= ACTHRS + CORHRS), ESTNP (estimated net profit), SUBCON (subcontracting cost), and REDGR (an artificial variable used to plot an R, called Reds, for molds the company lost a lot of money on, a G, called Greens, for molds the company made a lot of money on, and an A for all other molds).

REDGR was created because the data analyst knew that MINITAB has a command (LPLOT) to plot letters to identify certain data points and data clusters. REDGR was created after a preliminary analysis of the data revealed certain clustering that needed to be revealed on a number of plots.

You will be walked through a second analysis cycle below. The second analysis was quite similar to the preliminary one, except that the REDGR variable was not available in the preliminary analysis where PLOT replaced LPLOT.

The use of multiple regression appears only after considerable analysis that leads up to it. The multiple regression results summarize certain relationships; however, most of what we needed to know to help this company recognize its bidding/cost problems was learned along the way to multiple regression analysis through the careful analysis of several different plots.

The following sequence of MINITAB commands is used to examine this data set. Commentary is included to focus attention on important points. Your own analysis is not restricted to this command sequence.

RETRIEVE 'B:TOG1'
PRINT C1–C9   # You might label certain rows with R's and G's.
Note any unusual characteristics in the data columns.

DESCRIBE C2–C9   # C1 is a mold number. Descriptive statistics would be meaningless, so C2–C9. In particular, you should come away from these summary statistics with a feel for the typical bid price of a mold and the typical loss. The typical loss gives management a feel for how much costs need to be cut or bid prices increased to break even.

HIST 'PRICE'
HIST 'ESTNP'
HIST 'SUBCON'   # A few key variables were picked for closer examination. You might draw a box beside the histograms marking off the median and lower and upper quartiles. Also circle any unusual points such as molds with big losses in the tail of the distribution. Then return to the printed data to mark and examine data rows corresponding to these points.

LPLOT 'ESTNP' 'PRICE' USING 'REDGR'   # You might circle clusters of G's, R's, and A's. Draw a vertical line at the median price. Notice that molds priced above the median include the best and worst returns. These are higher-risk jobs than molds priced below the median.

As a result of this plot, management might consider the following actions:

(1) Some high-priced molds have to be bid higher, costs need to be lowered, or make no bid at all.

(2) Determine, if possible, the distinguishing characteristics of the clusters so you can better characterize the mold before the bid is made.

(3) Refine cost estimation procedures on molds priced above the median.

(4) Manage large jobs (molds) differently; for example, don't stop and restart these jobs.

LPLOT 'ESTNP' 'SUBCON' USING 'REDGR';
TITLE = 'ESTNP VERSUS SUBCON'.   # Although there are R and G clusters, they have no slope with respect to the SUBCON variable. Hence, subcontracting costs seem unrelated to ESTNP.

MPLOT 'PRICE' 'ACTHRS' 'PRICE' 'BGTHRS'   # Notice that this plot fans out because there is more uncertainty and risk on large jobs. Draw (fit by eye) two separate lines on this plot from the origin, one for the cluster of A's and one for the cluster of B's. Note that the larger the project, the greater is the difference between BGTHRS and ACTHRS. This means that complex, high-priced molds tend to be underestimated in terms of BGTHRS. It is no wonder that money is lost on these molds.

LPLOT 'PRICE' 'BGTHRS', USING 'REDGR'   # Fit by eye, separate lines through the G's and R's. Draw a vertical line at a fixed value of BGTHRS, say 480 hrs. Notice that the G's tend to be priced higher than the R's, given BGTHRS. At 480, the pricing difference is about $15,000.

Pricing a mold too low relative to its complexity and management pressure to get the job done in an incorrectly specified amount of time (BGTHRS) could generate unnecessary tension within the organization. This is the kind of connection a manager has to make, linking what is seen in the data to organizational problem solving.

LPLOT 'ACTHRS' 'PRICE' USING 'REDGR'   # At a given PRICE, the ACTHRS tend to be higher for R's than for G's. To be profitable, you have to raise the PRICE or lower the costs for the R's. Notice that the increased variability (risk) as PRICE increases boils down to distinguishing between Reds and Greens. This distinction must be made at bid time and related to the bid price and/or how the job is managed.

REGRESS 'ACTHRS' 1 PRED 'PRICE'   # If you obtain this fit after deleting the R rows from the data set, you obtain a benchmark (prediction) for what ACTHRS ought to be when a PRICE setting makes you money. If you do delete, RETRIEVE again to reinstate the original data file. Also, SAVE the pruned data set under a new filename.

REGRESS 'ACTHRS' 1 PRED 'BGTHRS'   # If the slope of this line is one, the BGTHRS are on target (ACTHRS). Unfortunately, the slope here is greater than one, meaning that, in bidding, the ACTHRS are consistently underestimated, costing the company money.

LPLOT 'ACTHRS' 'BGTHRS' USING 'REDGR'   # From this plot, it is clear that separate regressions might be fit to R's and G's. Also, for R's the slope of the fitted line would be steeper than the G's. At a given level of BGTHRS, ACTHRS will be higher and increase faster as the mold-building jobs are priced higher (more BGTHRS).

LPLOT 'CORHRS' 'BGTHRS' USING 'REDGR'   # The typical Red tends to be a much bigger job than the typical Green and has two to three times the CORHRS. You might circle the two major clusters on the plot.

LPLOT 'PRICE' 'SUBCON' USING 'REDGR'
REGRESS 'SUBCON' 1 PRED 'PRICE'   # Subcontracting is about 30% of the PRICE.

LPLOT 'BGTHRS' 'PRICE' USING 'REDGR'
REGRESS 'BGTHRS' 1 PRED 'PRICE'   # This is the historical relationship between BGTHRS and PRICE. Given BGTHRS, R's are underpriced.

LPLOT 'TOTHRS' 'PRICE' USING 'REDGR'
REGRESS 'TOTHRS' 1 PRED 'PRICE'   # Because TOTHRS = CORHRS + ACTHRS, this relationship is similar to that between ACTHRS and PRICE, except that the difference between R's and G's is more exaggerated because of CORHRS (more required for Reds).

MPLOT 'PRICE' 'TOTHRS' 'PRICE' 'BGTHRS'   # Note that BGTHRS underestimates TOTHRS at a given PRICE consistently. Knowing this, management could continue using the flawed budgeting procedure but adjust the BGTHRS according to its relationship with TOTHRS.

LPLOT 'TOTHRS' 'BGTHRS' USING 'REDGR'
REGRESS 'TOTHRS' 1 PRED 'BGTHRS'

CORRELATE C2–C8   # Rankings of variables in determining price are BGTHRS, SUBCON, ACTHRS, TOTHRS, and CORHRS. But BGTHRS tend to be consistently incorrect!

REGRESS 'PRICE' 5 PRED 'BGTHRS' 'ACTHRS' 'TOTHRS' 'CORHRS' 'SUBCON'   # Some variables can be dropped from the prediction equation because of low t values.

REGRESS 'PRICE' 2 PRED 'BGTHRS' 'SUBCON'   # This result is the essence of how bid price is set by management. Clearly, management must improve the accuracy in BGTHRS as a predictor of TOTHRS.

5. (*This exercise is quite long, but it is a valuable case study that includes some multiple regression at the end with considerable preliminary work.*)

In the woods, measurements are easily made on felled trees to provide a means of predicting the volume of timber in unfelled trees. Hence, a forest products company can predict the value of timber in an area of forest. A formula based on girth is the simplest, but perhaps both girth and height are needed to predict volume. RETRIEVE 'B:TREES' and ask for INFO to find that the observations are on 'DIAMETER', 'HEIGHT', and 'VOLUME'.

(a) Print the data set. Are the observations ordered in any way? If so, how? Note that variables not in the data set, such as time, location in the forest, or elevation (where cut), might lurk in the background and surreptitiously lead you to erroneous conclusions.

(b) Plot 'VOLUME' versus 'DIAMETER'.

(c) Plot 'VOLUME' versus 'HEIGHT'. Is this relationship as strong as the one in part (b)? Is there any evidence of heteroscedasticity, the spread of 'VOLUME' being dependent on the magnitude of 'DIAMETER' or 'HEIGHT'?

(d) Correlate 'VOLUME', 'DIAMETER', and 'HEIGHT'. Which of these correlations summarize parts (b) and (c)?

(e) NAME C4 'VRDI' C5 'VRHT'   # The names are for specific residuals, Volume Removing DIameter and Volume Removing HeighT.
REGRESS 'VOLUME' 1 PREDICTOR 'DIAMETER';
RESIDUALS 'VRDI'.
PLOT 'VRDI' VERSUS 'HEIGHT'   # Called a partial residual plot.
REGRESS 'VOLUME' 1 PREDICTOR 'HEIGHT';
RESIDUALS 'VRHT'.
PLOT 'VRHT' VERSUS 'DIAMETER'   # Another partial residual plot.

What do these plots reveal? When dealing with more than two variables, partial residual plots are thought to be better than the simple scatterplots in parts (b) and (c).

(f) NAME C6 'HTRDI' C7 'DIRHT'
REGRESS 'HEIGHT' 1 PREDICTOR 'DIAMETER';
RESIDUALS 'HTRDI'.
REGRESS 'DIAMETER' 1 PREDICTOR 'HEIGHT';
RESIDUALS 'DIRHT'.
PLOT 'VRHT' VERSUS 'DIRHT'
PLOT 'VRDI' VERSUS 'HTRDI'   # These plots are sometimes called added variable plots and are improvements over both partial residual plots and simple scatterplots.

(g) Why do you think the correlation between DIAMETER and HEIGHT is so high? Do you think that multicollinearity is present? If so, what potential problems result?

(h) NAME C8 'VRDIHT'
REGRESS 'VOLUME' 2 PREDICTORS 'DIAMETER' 'HEIGHT';
RESIDUALS 'VRDIHT'.   # Removing both diameter and height from volume.

PLOT 'VRDIHT' VERSUS 'DIAMETER'   # Curvature in the data point pattern means that a (DIAMETER)**2 variable should be added to the model or that some other transformations should be made, perhaps involving logarithms or powers of the original variables.

From basic geometry, we know that the volume of a cone with the top cut off (loglike in other words) is equal to

$$\text{volume} = \left(\frac{3.14*\text{height}}{3}\right) \text{ times } (r_b^2 + r_b r_t + r_t^2)$$

where r = radius at the top or bottom (subscript t or b). Recall that the radius is half the diameter. Clearly, volume is a nonlinear function of height and diameter. Thus, this background theory leads us to consider alternatives to our model in (8) that involve transformations.

(i) NAME C9 'LV' C10 'LDI' C11 'LHT'
LET 'LV' = LOGTEN ('VOLUME')
LET 'LDI' = LOGTEN ('DIAMETER')
LET 'LHT' = LOGTEN ('HEIGHT')

NAME C14 'LVRDIHT'
REGRESS 'LV' 2 PREDICTORS 'LDI' 'LHT';
RESIDUALS 'LVRDIHT'. # Examine these residuals.

NAME C12 'V13' C13 'V13RDIHT'
LET 'V13' = 'DIAMETER' ** (1/3)

REGRESS 'V13' 2 PREDICTORS 'DIAMETER' 'HEIGHT';
RESIDUALS 'LVRDINT'.   # Examine these residuals.

Both of these multiple regression fits are of high quality, supported by background theory, and useful in predicting tree volume. I prefer the last because the cube root of volume puts the dimension feet on the left side of the equation with the original variables on the right side in feet and inches. The dimensionality makes sense. Statistically, all residual patterns have been incorporated in the model.

6. Anthropologists have been interested in the effect of environmental change on physiological variables such as blood pressure. MINITAB has a data set (RETRIEVE 'PERU') that contains environmental as well as physiological variables. The data are from Peruvian Indians who migrated from a very primitive, rural, high-altitude environment to a modern, urban, low-altitude environment. It has been suggested that the migration might increase blood pressure.

Use INFO after RETRIEVE to obtain a list of the variables. The variables are AGE (C1), YEARS (C2), WEIGHT (C3), HEIGHT (C4), CHIN (C5), FOREARM (C6), CALF (C7), PULSE (C8), SYSTOL (C9), and DIASTOL (C10). Note that CHIN, FOREARM, and CALF refer to skinfold measurements (millimeters) of obesity that may be better predictors than WEIGHT because WEIGHT (kilograms) is likely to be influenced by HEIGHT (millimeters). However, these variables are obviously somewhat redundant. YEARS are years since migration. SYSTOL and DIASTOL are blood pressure measurements. SYSTOL is measured when the heart is contracting, and DIASTOL is measured when the heart is in dilation. PULSE (per minute) tends to increase as blood pressure increases.

For variables C1 through C10, obtain the following and answer related questions:

(a) A correlation matrix for the variables (CORRELATE C1–C10).

(b) What variable is most highly correlated with PULSE? Plot that variable versus PULSE.

(c) What variable is least correlated (nearest zero) with PULSE? Plot this variable and PULSE.

(d) How do the plots relate to the magnitudes of the correlations?

(e) Are the obesity variables correlated with one another and by how much?

(f) Use WEIGHT, AGE, and YEARS to predict SYSTOL. Use WEIGHT, AGE, and YEARS to predict PULSE. Comment on the goodness of these fits. Should the models be reduced to include fewer predictors, indicating how the decisions were made?

7. Determine if Scholastic Aptitude Test (SAT) scores, variables VERB and MATH are related to GPA, grade point average (0 to 4, with 4 the best grade). RETRIEVE 'B:GRADES'. Be sure to obtain summary statistics and a correlation matrix, plot variable pairs, use multiple regression, and examine residuals.

8. A mixture of orange juice, ginger ale, and Galliano produces a libation called a Harvey Ginger Ale. For a similar drink, Sahrmann, Piepel, and Cornell searched for the optimal-tasting Harvey recipe variation.[11] The component proportions range between certain limits, continuously, making for an infinite number of variations in the Harvey recipe. Mixture experiments are scientifically designed to search for the optimal taste with few observations. Cornell wrote a book on mixture experiments. Blending experiments and their analysis is of great interest to industry.

RETRIEVE 'B:HARVEY' and INFO accesses the results of the experiment. The variables are TASTE, OJ, RALE, and GALLI with two-way interactions created by multiplying appropriate column pairs to produce GR (GALLI*RALE, for example), GO, and RO.

Because the sum of the component proportions add to one, they are said to be linearly dependent. This causes a problem in fitting a model that MINITAB picks up on if you command REGRESS C1 6 PREDICTORS C2–C7. In mixture experiments, it is customary to omit the constant term and pure quadratic terms (OJ*OJ, for example) from the fit. In the HARVEY file, the pure quadratic terms were not created; REGRESS C1 6 PREDICTORS C2–C7; with the subcommand (NOCONSTANT.) circumvent the dependency problem.

Fit the models suggested above. Note that the small number (7) of blends in the experiment limits the value of many statistics used to evaluate goodness of fit (R^2, s^2 and t values, for example). Hence, the merit of the fitted model is in considerable doubt until more experimentation is done. Do you have any ideas about how to search for the best-tasting blend, using the results that were obtained from this preliminary analysis?

(Hint: An equilateral triangular plot of the three components can be constructed. Each corner of the triangle represents a single-component drink only, proportion = 1.0. The triangle side opposite a component corner represents a proportion = 0.0 of that component (resulting in a two-component-only drink). Next, order the seven taste scores from minimum to maximum. Beside each score draw a circle (to be used as a plotting point) whose area is proportional to the corresponding taste score magnitude. Using these circles as plotting points, locate them inside the triangle according to the known component proportions. For reference purposes, the best taste (largest circle) is at min RALE, max OJ, and low (but not min) GALLI. If we had them, more taste test results might lead to contours that show regions of different taste levels.)

9. This problem considers the proportions of light FCC, alkylate, butane, and reformate in the prediction of gasoline octane number.[12] The ability to select a blend that increases the octane number by as little as one point means millions in profits to oil companies. RETRIEVE 'B:GAS' and use INFO and PRINT C1–C5 to get started. Report on your analysis and recommend some blends, assuming the blends are on a par in cost.

10. The proportions of magnesium, sodium nitrate, strontium nitrate, and binder are used to predict flare illumination (in 1000 candles).[13] RETRIEVE 'B:FLARE' and use INFO and PRINT C1–C5 to get started. Report on your analysis and recommend some blends, assuming the blends are on a par in cost.

11. The following Scholastic Aptitude Test (SAT) score averages are listed by year and gender codes (RETRIEVE 'B:MFSAT'):[14]

Row	YEAR	SEX	MATH	VERBAL
1	1	1	514	463
2	1	0	467	468
3	2	1	512	464
4	2	0	470	466

Row	YEAR	SEX	MATH	VERBAL
5	3	1	513	459
6	3	0	470	466
7	4	1	509	459
8	4	0	465	461
9	5	1	507	454
10	5	0	466	457
11	6	1	505	454
12	6	0	461	452
13	7	1	502	446
14	7	0	460	443
15	8	1	501	447
16	8	0	459	442
17	9	1	495	437
18	9	0	449	431
19	10	1	497	433
20	10	0	446	430
21	11	1	497	431
22	11	0	445	427
23	12	1	494	433
24	12	0	444	425
25	13	1	493	431
26	13	0	443	423

(a) Use year and gender codes (1 designates males) to predict math scores. Is there a significant trend over time? Is the trend negative or positive? Is there a significant difference between average scores due to gender differences?

(b) Use year and gender codes (1 designates males) to predict verbal scores. Is there a significant trend over time? Is the trend negative or positive? Is there a significant difference between average scores due to gender differences?

(c) In both parts (a) and (b), assess the quality of the fit by examining the analysis of variance table.

12. Ski bindings can be set to release based on skier weight and ability. Recommended twist torque settings in foot-pounds are provided for weights of beginner (coded 0) or intermediate level skiers (RETRIEVE 'B:SKI').

Row	WEIGHT	BEG-INT	TWIST-T
1	105	0	26
2	105	1	34
3	115	0	28
4	115	1	36
5	125	0	30
6	125	1	38
7	135	0	32
8	135	1	40
9	145	0	34
10	145	1	42
11	155	0	36
12	155	1	46

Row	WEIGHT	BEG-INT	TWIST-T
13	165	0	38
14	165	1	48
15	175	0	40
16	175	1	50
17	185	0	42
18	185	1	52
19	195	0	44
20	195	1	54
21	205	0	46
22	205	1	56
23	215	0	48
24	215	1	58

Obtain a prediction equation for predicting twist torque based on skier weight and ability. Would you be willing to rely on this equation for setting the twist torque? Why or why not?

13. In the production of acetylene, the percentage conversion of a reactant to acetylene is thought to be related to reactor temperature (in hundreds of degrees Celsius), the hydrogen ratio, and contact time ($\times$ 100). Assess this relationship for the following data set (RETRIEVE 'B:ACET'):[15]

Row	TEMP	H2RATIO	TIME	ACET%
1	13	7.5	1.20	49.0
2	13	9.0	1.20	50.2
3	13	11.0	1.15	50.5
4	13	13.5	1.30	48.5
5	13	17.0	1.35	47.5
6	13	23.0	1.20	44.5
7	12	5.3	4.00	28.0
8	12	7.5	3.80	31.5
9	12	11.0	3.20	34.5
10	12	13.5	2.60	35.0
11	12	17.0	3.40	38.0
12	12	23.0	4.10	38.5
13	11	5.3	8.40	15.0
14	11	7.5	9.80	17.0
15	11	11.0	9.20	20.5
16	11	17.0	8.60	29.5

(a) What values of the predictor variables produced the maximum observed response?

14. Welding steel plates together is necessary in some metal fabrication operations. The strength of a welded joint is related to the shape of the weld puddle, which is formed by the welding gun as it moves along a joint and melts the steel. Thus, manufacturers are interested in welding process characteristics, such as current, voltage, velocity of movement,

(continued)

and plate thickness and their relationship to weld puddle size. From the following data set, predict puddle width based on welding process characteristics (RETRIEVE 'B:WELD').[16] Distinguish between significant and insignificant predictor variables at a .05 level of significance. If there are insignificant predictor variables, drop them from the full model and obtain a fit for the reduced model. Assess the quality of this fit.

Row	CUR	VOLT	VEL	PTH	WIDTH
1	100	13	3	0.25	0.197
2	100	13	9	0.25	0.160
3	100	13	15	0.25	0.143
4	100	15	9	0.25	0.176
5	100	15	15	0.25	0.142
6	100	17	9	0.25	0.184
7	100	17	15	0.25	0.159
8	200	13	9	0.25	0.286
9	200	13	15	0.25	0.206
10	200	15	9	0.25	0.296
11	200	15	15	0.25	0.222
12	200	17	9	0.25	0.318
13	200	17	15	0.25	0.257
14	300	13	9	0.25	0.413
15	300	13	15	0.25	0.313
16	300	15	9	0.25	0.423
17	300	15	15	0.25	0.354
18	300	17	15	0.25	0.418
19	100	13	3	0.50	0.184
20	100	13	9	0.50	0.150
21	100	13	15	0.50	0.127
22	100	15	3	0.50	0.219
23	100	15	9	0.50	0.167
24	100	15	15	0.50	0.150
25	100	17	3	0.50	0.241
26	100	17	9	0.50	0.181

15. A sample of professional golfers with low and high earnings is provided (RETRIEVE 'B:GOLF').[17] Use age, height, weight, experience (years on the tour), and average score to predict earnings. Distinguish between significant and insignificant predictor variables at a .05 level of significance. If there are insignificant predictor variables, drop them from the full model and obtain a fit for the reduced model. Assess the quality of this fit.

Row	AGE	HT	WT	EXP	AVESC	EARN
1	33	78	200	7	71.34	148
2	41	71	195	12	71.27	117
3	33	72	170	9	70.95	112
4	41	71	185	16	70.66	107
5	29	73	185	4	71.39	108
6	25	72	195	2	71.31	112

Row	AGE	HT	WT	EXP	AVESC	EARN
7	34	72	175	9	73.24	22
8	28	69	164	4	72.10	20
9	27	74	185	3	72.11	23
10	32	71	190	9	70.08	244
11	35	74	192	1	73.43	11
12	43	70	175	16	70.62	210
13	36	68	159	14	70.90	121
14	37	73	190	14	72.00	22
15	36	72	190	6	72.90	20
16	60	71	190	34	71.89	22
17	33	67	180	4	70.41	231
18	29	76	214	1	73.90	7
19	27	74	190	2	72.75	22
20	28	72	165	2	72.33	24

(a) Use age, height, weight, and experience (years on the tour) to predict average score. Distinguish between significant and insignificant predictor variables at a .05 level of significance. Repeat this analysis after deleting the oldest professional from the data set. Discuss.

16. Many home buyers look to buy in a subdivision of homes. Although the buying decision is related to the town and its school system, other factors are considered, such as the builder and the quality of construction. The following data set lists the number of lots being developed in various towns and the number of lots sold.[18] The middle of the lot price range is also given (RETRIEVE 'B:LOTS' for the complete data set). See if you can predict the number of lots sold based on the number of lots being developed and the typical price. Comment on the quality of this fit and the significance of each predictor variable.

Row	LOTS	LSOLD	PRICE
1	42	0	260
2	60	1	450
3	56	20	675
4	64	30	270
5	95	85	145
6	43	0	540
7	129	23	280
8	43	35	320
9	55	2	360
10	36	15	450
11	104	0	135
12	37	30	200
13	76	0	165
14	42	33	1000
15	56	48	265
16	172	101	265
17	46	31	210
18	200	180	290
19	70	50	290
20	63	5	275

(continued)

17. Without new construction, vacancy rates for apartments are down and rental rates are up. The following data set (RETRIEVE 'B:RENTS') includes average rents over four seasons by regions:[19]

Row	RENT	PERIOD	REGION	
1	748	1	1	Greater Boston
2	749	2	1	Greater Boston
3	761	3	1	Greater Boston
4	781	4	1	Greater Boston
5	813	1	2	Mid-Rt.128
6	845	2	2	Mid-Rt.128
7	851	3	2	Mid-Rt.128
8	872	4	2	Mid-Rt.128
9	571	1	3	Cape and Islands
10	577	2	3	Cape and Islands
11	583	3	3	Cape and Islands
12	582	4	3	Cape and Islands
13	567	1	4	Central Mass.
14	571	2	4	Central Mass.
15	578	3	4	Central Mass.
16	596	4	4	Central Mass.
17	691	1	5	Western Mass.
18	658	2	5	Western Mass.
19	640	3	5	Western Mass.
20	654	4	5	Western Mass.

(a) Predict rents by period and region. Use the time period as coded; however, introduce "dummy" variables for the five regions. Are there significant differences in rents due to period and region?

(b) By introducing "dummy" variables for periods and regions, the following results are obtained to determine if period and regional effects are significant:

```
Analysis of Variance for RENT

Source      DF      SS       MS
PERIOD       3     1112      371
REGION       4   218794    54698
Error       12     3367      281
Total       19   223273
```

```
                        Individual 95% CI
  PERIOD     Mean    ---------+---------+---------+---------+--
     1       678.0   (-----------*-----------)
     2       680.0   (-----------*-----------)
     3       682.6    (-----------*-----------)
     4       697.0           (-----------*-----------)
                     ---------+---------+---------+---------+--
                         675.0     690.0     705.0     720.0
```

```
                        Individual 95% CI
  REGION     Mean   -+---------+---------+---------+---------+
     1       759.8                        (-*-)
     2       845.3                             (--*-)
     3       578.3   (-*--)
     4       578.0   (-*--)
     5       660.8            (--*-)
                    -+---------+---------+---------+---------+
                   560.0     640.0     720.0     800.0     880.0
```

18. A total of 21 wards in England (comparable to a census tract in the United States) were examined in terms of four social condition variables and rates of incidence of three diseases (RETRIEVE 'B:MGOLD'). The social condition variables measured overcrowding, poor toilet facilities, no car, and the number of low-skilled workers. The first three variables are expressed as rates per thousand households; the fourth variable is the number per thousand involved in low-skilled work. The diseases were infectious jaundice, measles, and scabies in rates per hundred thousand people. Let the sum of the disease variables represent an overall health measure. Use multiple regression to relate overall health to the four social condition variables. Are any of the social condition variables significant? Plot the health measure versus the number of low-skilled workers and also the

number without a car. Both these predictors are measures of relative affluence; the smaller the predictor the more affluent is the ward. Although the multiple regression analysis was not particularly revealing, these plots tend to indicate slightly better health for the more affluent.

19. Vibration tests are performed on 20 guidance systems. The response, roll resonant frequency, is thought to be related to five predictor variables—roll transmissibility, pitch resonant frequency, pitch transmissibility, yaw resonant frequency, and yaw transmissibility (RETRIEVE 'B:GDANCE'). Obtain a correlation matrix for these variables. Because of the high correlations between some of the predictor variables, fit a model that does not include the pitch resonant frequency and pitch transmissibility. Does this fit appear to adequately predict the response?

20. In predicting solar radiation (btu/sqft) as a heat source, this response is thought to depend on average daily temperature (degrees F), average wind velocity (mi/hr), degree days, normal precipitation (in.) and cloudiness (mean number of days that are cloudy or partly cloudy). Monthly long-term averages for these variables are provided for a New England city and are (RETRIEVE 'B:SOLAR'):

Row	SR	TEMP	WINDV	DDAYS	NPRECP	CLOUD
1	480.00	23.7	9.8	1349	2.20	17
2	738.00	24.4	10.4	1162	2.11	15
3	1007.00	32.1	10.7	980	2.58	17
4	1247.00	44.9	10.5	543	2.70	16
5	1524.00	55.1	9.1	253	3.26	17
6	1653.00	65.7	8.2	39	3.00	14
7	1627.00	70.1	7.4	9	3.12	12
8	14.65	68.4	7.0	22	2.87	12
9	1103.00	61.5	7.3	135	3.12	12
10	804.00	51.5	8.0	422	2.63	14
11	472.00	39.8	8.9	762	2.84	19
12	384.00	29.3	9.2	1212	2.93	19

(a) Because of the wide variation in degree days, work with the square root of this variable. Then find a multiple regression fit to predict solar radiation amounts.

(b) Comment on the effect of having too few observations relative to the number of predictor variables. Does this artificially inflate goodness of fit measures such as R-squared?

21. A small university press lost $161,000 last year. Financial analysis revealed that fixed costs were $400,000 and variable costs were 43% of sales. Thus, net income can be predicted from gross sales, S, with the following equation:

$$\text{net income} = S - .43S - 400 \text{ (in thousands of dollars)}$$

Clearly, net income is sales driven. Sales arise from the sale of various titles of books. Management has 18 years of history on sales (in thousands of dollars) and the number of new titles published each year (RETRIEVE 'B:PRESS'):

Row	SALES	TITLES	YEAR
1	17	7	1
2	34	8	2
3	55	6	3
4	55	15	4
5	72	9	5
6	76	14	6
7	111	16	7
8	128	17	8
9	115	17	9
10	180	16	10
11	181	18	11
12	237	25	12
13	235	19	13
14	254	21	14
15	313	24	15
16	360	25	16
17	415	34	17
18	414	29	18

(a) After examining a plot of sales versus the number of titles, management thought that an increase in the number of titles over the next few years would drive sales up and eliminate the loss on the financial statement. An autocratic manager suggested that the existing employees simply must pump out more titles. A consultant agreed to produce a multiple regression equation to predict sales based on titles and a time variable. Obtain such an equation with your recommendation.

(b) A second consultant suggested that changes in sales versus changes in the number of titles showed no relationship, which you have to verify. Thus, management will not eliminate the losses by simply producing more titles. She suggested that the emphasis on the number of titles should be tempered somewhat and that additional emphasis should be on obtaining quality titles with high sales potential. This approach puts less pressure on production and adds some pressure in marketing, acquisitions and pricing. Which of these two consultants would you listen to?

APPENDIX 1

Minitab Examples

BOX AND HUNTER'S POPCORN EXPERIMENT

(If you have the data diskette, **RETRIEVE 'B:POP'** and omit the data entry using READ.)

(If you are on a network and have the data stored in subdirectory DATA under the directory MTBWIN, **RETRIEVE 'POP'.** Otherwise READ the data in columns.)

```
DON'T READ THE DATA IN IF RETRIEVE WAS SUCCESSFUL
# IF NECESSARY, ENTER THE DATA, A ROW AT A TIME, WHICH IS
# LISTED IN THE CHAPTER (YIELD, BRAND, AMOUNT)
#          WITH MTB > READ C1 C2 C3

START HERE IF RETRIEVE WAS SUCCESSFUL
MTB > NAME C1 'YIELD' C2 'BRAND' C3 'AMOUNT'
MTB > PRINT 'YIELD' 'BRAND' 'AMOUNT'

MTB > NAME C6 'YRA' C7 'BRA' # THESE ARE NAMES FOR COLUMNS
# OF RESIDUALS; 'YRA' STANDS FOR 'YIELD-REMOVING-AMOUNT' AND
# 'BRA' FOR 'BRAND-REMOVING-AMOUNT'.  THE RATIONALE FOR
# OBTAINING THESE RESIDUALS IS PRESENTED LATER.

IDENTIFICATION PHASE:
MTB > CORRELATE 'YIELD' 'AMOUNT' 'BRAND'

MTB > PLOT 'YIELD' 'AMOUNT'  # YIELD INCREASES WITH THE
# 'AMOUNT' OF KERNELS (1/3 OR 2/3 CUP).

MTB > PLOT 'YIELD' 'BRAND'   # THE GOURMET BRAND TENDS
#                            TO PRODUCE A HIGHER YIELD.

MTB > PLOT 'BRAND' 'AMOUNT' # NO RELATIONSHIP, UNCORRELATED
```

```
ESTIMATION PHASE:
MTB > REGRESS 'YIELD' 1 PRED 'AMOUNT';
SUBC> RESIDUALS 'YRA'.                    # SIMPLE REGRESSION

MTB > REGRESS 'YIELD' 1 PRED 'BRAND'

MTB > REGRESS 'BRAND' 1 PRED 'AMOUNT';
SUBC> RESIDUALS 'BRA'.

MTB > PLOT 'YRA' 'BRA' # THESE RESIDUALS ARE SIMPLY ADJUSTED,
# ORIGINAL DATA, THE EFFECT OF AMOUNT IS REMOVED FROM BOTH
# YIELD AND BRAND, GIVING A CLEARER VIEW.

MTB > REGRESS 'YRA' 1 PRED 'BRA';
SUBC> RESIDUALS C8. # SAME RESULTS AS THE MULTIPLE
                    # REGRESSION THAT FOLLOWS

MTB > REGRESS 'YIELD' 2 PRED 'AMOUNT' 'BRAND'

DIAGNOSTIC PHASE:
MTB > HIST C8
MTB > TSPLOT C8
```

EXAMPLE

PROFITS, SALES AND ASSETS OBSERVATIONAL STUDY

(If you have the data diskette, **RETRIEVE 'B:SPAEM'** and omit the data entry using READ.)

(If you are on a network and have the data stored in subdirectory DATA under the directory MTBWIN, **RETRIEVE 'SPAEM'.** Otherwise READ the data in columns.)

```
DON'T READ THE DATA IN IF RETRIEVE WAS SUCCESSFUL
#        MTB > READ C1 C2 C3 C4 C5, # ENTERING ROWS OF DATA
# SHOWN IN THIS EXAMPLE IN THE CHAPTER
         MTB > NAME C1 'S' C2 'P' C3 'A' C4 'E' C5 'M'
         MTB > SAVE 'B:SPAEM'

START HERE IF RETRIEVE WAS SUCCESSFUL
IDENTIFICATION PHASE:
MTB > PRINT 'S' 'P' 'A' 'E' 'M'
MTB > DESCRIBE C1-C5
MTB > CORRELATE 'P' 'S' 'A'   # THREE VARIABLES OF INTEREST
                             # IN THIS EXAMPLE
MTB > NAME C6 'PRS' C7 'ARS' # COLUMN NAMES FOR RESIDUALS
#     'PRS'-- PROFITS-REMOVING-SALES AND
#     'ARS'-- ASSETS-REMOVING-SALES
MTB > PLOT 'P' 'S'
MTB > PLOT 'P' 'A'
MTB > PLOT 'S' 'A'
```

```
ESTIMATION PHASE:
MTB > REGRESS 'P' 1 PRED 'S';      # SIMPLE REGRESSION
SUBC> RESIDUALS 'PRS'.
MTB > REGRESS 'P' 1 PRED 'A'
MTB > REGRESS 'A' 1 PRED 'S';
SUBC> RESIDUALS 'ARS'.

MTB > REGRESS 'PRS' 1 PRED 'ARS' # SIMPLE REGRESSION OF
# RESIDUALS, PRODUCING THE SAME RESULTS AS THE MULTIPLE
# REGRESSION THAT FOLLOWS

MTB > REGRESS 'P' 2 PRED 'S' 'A', STRES C8, FITS C9;
SUBC> RESIDUALS C10;
SUBC> HI PUT C14.         # STATISTICS USED TO IDENTIFY
#                           INFLUENTIAL OBSERVATIONS

DIAGNOSTIC PHASE:
MTB > TSPLOT C14    # CLEARLY, OBS. 1,2,3 AND 5 INFLUENTIAL
MTB > PLOT C10 C9 # RESIDUALS VERSUS PREDICTIONS,
#                     NOTE THE UNUSUAL/INFLUENTIAL POINTS
MTB > HIST C8       # STANDARDIZED RESIDUALS--NORMAL

SOME ADDITIONAL ANALYSIS SUGGESTED BY THE THEORY AND LORE OF
FINANCIAL MANAGEMENT:
MTB > LET C15 = 'P'/'S'     # PROFITS TO SALES
MTB > LET C16 = 'S'/'A'     # SALES TO ASSETS
MTB > LET C17 = C15*C16    # PROFITS TO ASSETS = RETURN ON
#                            INVESTMENT (ROI)

MTB > TSPLOT C17    # COMPANIES 7 9 10 14 15 20 22 27 29 ARE
# IN THE UPPER QUARTILE IN ROI;  LOOK BACK AT THE DATA LIST
# AND FIND THE NAMES OF THOSE COMPANIES

MTB > DESCRIBE C17
MTB > DELETE ROWS 1 2 3 4 5 6 C1-C5

IDENTIFICATION PHASE (REPEATED)
MTB > CORRELATE 'P' 'S' 'A'

ESTIMATION PHASE (REPEATED)
MTB > REGRESS 'P' 2 PRED 'S' 'A', STRES C8, FITS C9;
SUBC> RESIDUALS C10;
SUBC> HI PUT C14.

DIAGNOSTIC PHASE (REPEATED BUT NOT SHOWN)
```

EXAMPLE

ARITHMETIC GROWTH OF QUARTERLY SALES, PLUS A FOURTH QUARTER SALES JUMP, PLUS A RANDOM, UNPREDICTABLE COMPONENT

```
MTB > INFO
# THESE COLUMNS AND NAMES CARRY OVER FROM THE PREVIOUS
# EXAMPLES, YOU MUST ERASE C1 C2 ... AND SO FORTH.
# THIS ERASES BOTH COLUMNS AND NAMES.

MTB > SET INTO C1  # A PREDICTOR VARIABLE FOR A TREND EFFECT
                   # 1,2,3,....,48 (48 QUARTERS)
DATA> 1:48
DATA> END

MTB > RANDOM 48 OBS INTO C2;     # A RANDOM COMPONENT
SUBC> NORMAL MU = 0 SIGMA = 1000.

MTB > LET C3 = 10000 + (C1*250) + C2 # SIMULATED SALES IN
# THOUSANDS OF DOLLARS; STARTS AT 10 MILLION + .250 MILLION
# INCREASE PER QUARTER + PLUS A RANDOM COMPONENT

MTB > TSPLOT C3

MTB > CORRELATE C3 C1 # SALES AND THE DUMMY TREND VARIABLE

MTB > LAG 1 C3 C4     # CREATING LAGGED VARIABLES
MTB > LAG 2 C3 C5
MTB > LAG 3 C3 C6
MTB > LAG 4 C3 C7     # PRINT C3 C4 C5 C6 C7 #.TO SEE

MTB > CORRELATE C3-C7

MTB > ACF C3 # THE ACF COMMAND AUTOMATICALLY LAGS ALL THE
# WAY TO 16 LAGS RATHER THAN THE 4 WE DID ABOVE.

MTB > DIFF C3 C13  # IF ACF C13 DOES NOT QUICKLY DIE OUT
# WITH INCREASING LAGS, YOU WOULD DIFFERENCE AGAIN
# (DIFF C13 C14) AND GET ACF C14.

MTB > ACF C13

MTB > REGRESS C3 1 PRED C4, STRES C5, FITS, C6;
SUBC> RESIDUALS C9.

MTB > ACF C9
MTB > DELETE ROW 1 C9
MTB > RUNS C9
MTB > REGRESS C3 1 PRED C1 # FITTING A TREND LINE
```

```
PLUS A FOURTH QUARTER SALES JUMP
# TYPE THE FOLLOWING DATA EXACTLY AS LISTED, NO BLANKS
# WHERE THERE ARE NO BLANKS AND BLANKS WHERE THERE ARE BLANKS

MTB > SET INTO C8     # YOU MIGHT PRINT C8
DATA> 12(0 0 0 1)     # A COLUMN OF 0'S AND 1'S
DATA> END             # A 1 FOR EVERY 4TH QUARTER

MTB > LET C3 = C3 + (4000*C8)
MTB > TSPLOT 4 C3     # YOU CAN SEE THE 4TH QUARTER JUMP

MTB > REGRESS C3 1 PRED C1;   # SAME AS BEFORE
SUBC> RESIDUALS C9.           # RESIDUAL PLOT MAGNIFIES
                              # 4TH QUARTER EFFECT

MTB > TSPLOT 4 C9 # RESIDUALS OVER TIME, NOTICE FOURTH
#                   QUARTER SALES

SMOOTHING (optional)
# THIS IS A CONTINUATION OF THIS EXAMPLE
# THAT USES THE EXISTING DATA COLUMNS
```

Comment   The following macro, %B:SSMO, requires version ten or more of MINITAB. To examine the details of the macro, use a text editor or a word processor to open the SSMO.MAC file. Also, in MINITAB, the command TYPE 'B:SSMO.MAC' lists the macro. If you set OH = 24 in the session window, a "continue?" prompt will be issued by MINITAB that permits the user to view one screen of output at a time as the macro executes.

```
MTB > %B:SSMO  # OR %A:SSMO OR %SSMO
#                OR %C:\MTBWIN\DATA\SSMO
```

EXAMPLE

MARKET VALUE AND ITS RELATION TO SALES, PROFITS, ASSETS AND EQUITY

(If you have the data diskette, **RETRIEVE 'B:SPAEM'** and omit the data entry using READ.)

(If you are on a network and have the data stored in subdirectory DATA under the directory MTBWIN, **RETRIEVE 'SPAEM'.** Otherwise READ the data in columns.)

Comment   Because of command similarities to previous examples, this example is presented as a macro, %B:E12-2-4.MAC. The command TYPE 'B:E12-2-4.MAC' lists the macro. If you set OH = 24 in the session window, a "continue?" prompt will be issued by MINITAB that permits the user to view one screen of output at a time as the macro executes.

```
MTB > %B:E12-2-4  # OR %A:E12-2-4 OR %E12-2-4
#                   OR %C:\MTBWIN\DATA\E12-2-4
```

EXAMPLE

STACK LOSS DATA

(If you have the data diskette, **RETRIEVE 'B:STACK'** and omit the data entry using the READ command.)

(If you are on a network and have the data stored in subdirectory DATA under the directory MTBWIN, **RETRIEVE 'STACK'.** Otherwise READ the data in.)

Comment   Because of command similarities to previous examples, this example is presented as a macro, %B:E12-3-1.MAC. The command TYPE 'B:E12-3-1.MAC' lists the macro. If you set OH = 24 in the session window, a "continue?" prompt will be issued by MINITAB that permits the user to view one screen of output at a time as the macro executes.

```
MTB > %B:E12-3-1 ` # OR %A:E12-3-1 OR %E12-3-1
#               OR %C:\MTBWIN\DATA\E12-3-1
```

CHAPTER 13

Special Probability Distributions

◇ **Introduce additional discrete distributions—Poisson, hypergeometric, and discrete uniform**

◇ **Introduce additional continuous distributions—exponential, uniform, lognormal, and others**

◇ **Review the cumulative distribution function and its inverse**

◇ **Define measures of skewness and kurtosis**

PRELUDE

In practical problems, data distributions have many shapes. Some of those shapes—the normal, binomial, or Student's t distribution—you have already encountered in this text. This chapter introduces other special probability distributions.

The field of probability theory is rich in both discrete and continuous probability distributions. In addition to the familiar binomial distribution, some other useful discrete distributions are the Poisson, hypergeometric, and discrete uniform. In addition to the familiar normal distribution, some other useful continuous distributions are the exponential, uniform, lognormal, beta, gamma, and Weibull distributions.

To work with all these distributions, the cumulative distribution functions (CDFs) and their inverses (INVCDFs) are important. For example, CDFs make it easy to find the probability that a random variable is less than or equal to particular values of interest. Given a cumulative probability, the INVCDF produces the value of the random variable. The INVCDFs form the conceptual basis for generating random data from particular distributions.

In addition to the mean and standard deviation parameters, we introduce other parameters for describing distributional shape. ◇

THE DISCRETE POISSON DISTRIBUTION

In an earlier illustration of the discrete binomial distribution, eggs were packaged in cartons of n = 12 with the probability of a bad egg being small, p = .0833 (see Chapter 4, Example 8). Although egg carton sizes are relatively small, other products, such as resistors or transistors, are packaged in large numbers.

Historically, applications of the binomial distribution with large n and small p posed computational difficulties because of the nature of the mathematical formula for computing these probabilities. Today, many textbook tables for binomial probabilities don't go beyond n = 20. As a result, it is important that a convenient approximation of the binomial is known. Such an approximation can be made with the **Poisson distribution.**

In general for independent events, as the probability, p, of an event gets smaller, $p \leq .05$, and n gets larger, $n \geq 20$, and np remains constant, the binomial probability of an event, say, y bad eggs in a carton, is

$$P(y) = \binom{n}{y}p^y(1 - p)^{(n-y)}$$

This probability can be approximated by the Poisson distribution where

$$P(y) = \frac{(np)^y e^{-np}}{y!}$$

Although this formula looks computationally formidable, the probabilities are easy to find in MINITAB.

The mean and variance of the Poisson distribution is np.

EXAMPLE 1

THE POISSON APPROXIMATION OF THE BINOMIAL DISTRIBUTION

Although n = 12 is not large enough for the Poisson distribution to be a great approximation of the binomial distribution, the Poisson approximation is fairly good, as you will see. In some applications, better approximations are needed.

A link between the two distributions is n × p (12 × .0833 = .9996). The n × p is the mean of the binomial and it becomes the mean of the Poisson.

The variance of the binomial is np(1 − p), but, with p small and (1 − p) near one, the variance of the binomial approaches that of the Poisson, which is np. For the Poisson distribution, it can be shown that the mean equals the variance. Therefore, the standard deviation of the Poisson distribution is the square root of its mean.

Problem Statement (a) In a carton of 12 eggs, compute the probability of y bad eggs, where y = 0, 1, . . . , 12 and p = .0833. Find the binomial probabilities and Poisson approximations. Assume independence and that p is constant.

Problem Solution (a)

ROW	y C1	P(y) C2 POISSON	P(y) C3 BINOMIAL
1	0	0.368027	0.352149
2	1	0.367879	0.383995
3	2	0.183866	0.191914
4	3	0.061264	0.058130
5	4	0.015310	0.011885
6	5	0.003061	0.001728
7	6	0.000510	0.000183
8	7	0.000073	0.000014
9	8	0.000009	0.000001
10	9	0.000001	0.000001
11	10	0.000001	0.000001
12	11	0.000001	0.000001
13	12	0.000001	0.000001

Problem Statement (b)   Plot the Poisson probabilities versus y.

Problem Solution (b)   The Poisson probability distribution is shown below. Draw in the vertical probability spikes.

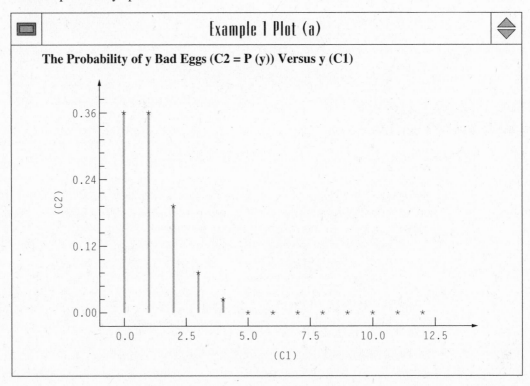

Example 1 Plot (a)

The Probability of y Bad Eggs (C2 = P (y)) Versus y (C1)

General Nature of the Poisson Distribution

Because the Poisson distribution is applicable when n is large and p is small, it may be thought of as a probability distribution for rare events. The Poisson distribution tells the manager the chances that a specific number of rare events will occur.

Usually we have some idea of the mean, which is the average number of rare events per unit length measure. An early application involved the chances of a certain number of deaths, y, by horse kicks. Other kinds of lights-out applications can be found: the number of lightning-caused power outages per month, the number of suicides at a university per year, the number of flawed shirts per bundle of shirts manufactured, the number of ships arriving at a port per hour, the number of customers arriving at a checkout counter per minute, and so forth.

E X A M P L E 2

A FLAW IN YOUR JEANS

Before denim is made into jeans, the cloth is inspected. The nature of the production process and the economics of the situation do not permit complete and continuous inspection. As a result, different blocks of fabric (in square meters) are inspected and the number of flaws are recorded. On the basis of flaw history, the average number of flaws per square meter can be used to compute the Poisson probabilities, the chances of getting a specific number of flaws.

According to management, the flaw history was compiled during different periods of time when the production process was well behaved and in a state of statistical control. Thus p, the probability of a flaw, was thought to be constant and the blocks of fabric were independent of one another because they were not from the same batch of raw materials.

The probabilities and cumulative probabilities for flaws provides management with a benchmark, a basis for knowing when the process is likely to be in control or when it is not. If the fabric quality deteriorates, management will be alerted to that fact by noticing when the observed number of flaws exceeds a control limit.

In this example, the Poisson distribution is not approximating a binomial, but rather, on its own, it is the appropriate distribution for this application. Take note of the Poisson distribution's characteristics: (1) y is a count of the number of flaws per hundred square meters; (2) p, the probability of a flaw, is constant per square meter; and (3) the number of flaws in different blocks of fabric are independent of one another. Then,

$$P(y) = \frac{(\mu)^y e^{-\mu}}{y!}$$

Problem Statement (a) In blocks of denim for your jeans (1,440 total square meters), 43 flaws were found. Per hundred square meters, the average flaw rate is $\mu = (\frac{43}{1,440}) \times 100 = 2.98611$. Find the Poisson probabilities, the chances that a specific number of flaws might occur. Also find cumulative probabilities.

Problem Solution (a)   The following probabilities were computed by the MINITAB commands in Appendix 1.

```
 y       P(y)       P(y ≤ a specific value)

 C3      C4          C5

FLAWS   PROB.       CUM.PROB.
 0     0.050483     0.05048
 1     0.150749     0.20123
 2     0.225077     0.42631
 3     0.224035     0.65034
 4     0.167248     0.81759
 5     0.099884     0.91748
 6     0.049711     0.96719
 7     0.021206     0.98839
```

Problem Statement (b)   From the cumulative probabilities, choose a control limit for warning management when the number of flaws might indicate denim quality problems.

Problem Solution (b)   Beyond 7 flaws, the probabilities are not listed. View 7 flaws per 100 square meters as an upper control limit; 98.839% of the time there will be 7 or fewer flaws per 100 square meters when the quality of the denim is in control. An occurrence of more than 7 flaws per 100 square meters is unlikely. Thus, an observation of 8 or more flaws per 100 square meters should trigger a warning alarm, a harbinger of the possible deterioration in quality accompanied by a shift in the mean (a higher average number of flaws per square meter).

S T A T I S T I C A L   H I G H L I G H T S

The Poisson distribution is a useful approximation of the binomial distribution when n is large. Both of these discrete distributions require that p, the probability of independent events, is constant.

THE DISCRETE HYPERGEOMETRIC DISTRIBUTION

Applications of the binomial and Poisson distributions require that p, the probability of independent events, is constant. The **hypergeometric distribution** fits situations in which p is not constant and events are dependent.

The binomial distribution would apply to coin flipping problems. From flip to flip, p stays the same and the flips are independent.

The binomial would also apply to card problems when the drawn cards are placed back in the deck. For example, if you draw a card from a well-shuffled deck of playing cards, the probability p of drawing an ace is $\frac{4}{52}$. After drawing a card, return it to the deck and shuffle the deck. This is **sampling with replacement.** The probability of getting an ace on the next draw is the same constant $\frac{4}{52}$ and independent of the previous draw.

The hypergeometric rather than the binomial distribution would apply to card problems when the cards drawn are not returned to the deck. This is **sampling without replacement.** For example, if you first draw an ace with a probability of $\frac{4}{52}$ without replacement, the probability of an ace on the second draw is $\frac{3}{51}$. This dependence and nonconstant probability rules out the use of the binomial or its Poisson approximation. The hypergeometric distribution is designed for dependent, nonconstant probability situations.
Let

N = number of items in a finite population

n = random sample size, items selected without replacement

p = initial proportion of type y items

y = the count of type y items in n

Accordingly, for the hypergeometric distribution, the probability P(y) is

$$P(y) = \frac{\binom{Np}{y}\binom{N-Np}{n-y}}{\binom{N}{n}}$$

EXAMPLE 3

DRAWING TWO ACES WITHOUT REPLACEMENT

Problem Statement (a) A_1 is the event you draw an ace from a deck of cards without replacement, and A_2 is the event you draw an ace from the remaining cards. What is the probability of drawing two aces? First use the multiplication law for dependent events.

Problem Solution (a) $P(A_1 \cap A_2) = (\frac{4}{52})(\frac{3}{51}) = \frac{12}{2,652}$

Problem Statement (b) What is the probability of drawing two aces? Show that the hypergeometric distribution yields the same result as problem solution (a).

Problem Solution (b) The following hypergeometric distribution was designed for these types of problems.
Let

N = 52, the full deck of cards

n = 2, the number of cards drawn without replacement

$p = \dfrac{4}{52}$, the initial proportion of aces

y = 0, 1, or 2 = the number of aces you can draw

Accordingly, the probability P(y) is

$$P(y) = \frac{\binom{Np}{y}\binom{N - Np}{n - y}}{\binom{N}{n}}$$

Making the proper substitutions produces the same answer as that in Problem Solution (a).

$$P(y = 2) = \frac{\binom{52(4/52)}{y = 2}\binom{52 - 4}{2 - 2}}{\binom{52}{2}} = \frac{\binom{4}{2}\binom{48}{0}}{\binom{52}{2}} = \frac{12}{2,652}$$

EXAMPLE 4

INSPECTING COMPONENTS

Problem Statement   In electronic component manufacturing, a process has a historical defective rate of p = .25. Small batches or lots are produced, and samples of size n = 5 are taken without replacement and inspected. For a lot size of N = 40, what is the probability that y = 2 defectives are found?

Problem Solution

$$P(y = 2) = \frac{\binom{40(.25)}{y = 2}\binom{40 - 10}{5 - 2}}{\binom{40}{5}} = \frac{\binom{10}{2}\binom{30}{3}}{\binom{40}{5}} = \frac{15,225}{54,834} = .2777$$

Binomial Approximation of the Hypergeometric   When the **sampling fraction** f = $\frac{n}{N}$ is small (less than .05), sampling without replacement probabilities are approximately the same as sampling with replacement probabilities. Therefore, the binomial distribution approximates the hypergeometric distribution.

STATISTICAL HIGHLIGHTS

For dependent events, constant probabilities are not expected and the hypergeometric distribution is used.

THE DISCRETE UNIFORM DISTRIBUTION

The **discrete uniform distribution** consists of equal probability spikes, which are all the same height. For a toss of a fair coin, there are two spikes of height $\frac{1}{2}$. For a roll of a fair die, there are six spikes of height $\frac{1}{6}$.

In general, for y = 1, 2, . . . , n faces, the probability function is

$$P(y) = \frac{1}{n}$$

EXAMPLE 5

ROLLING A DIE, DISCRETE UNIFORM PROBABILITIES

Problem Statement   Use MINITAB to generate the discrete probability function (C2) for a random variable y = 1, 2, 3, 4, 5, or 6 face numbers on a roll of a fair die (C1).

Problem Solution   The distribution is discrete. Draw the probability spikes by hand.

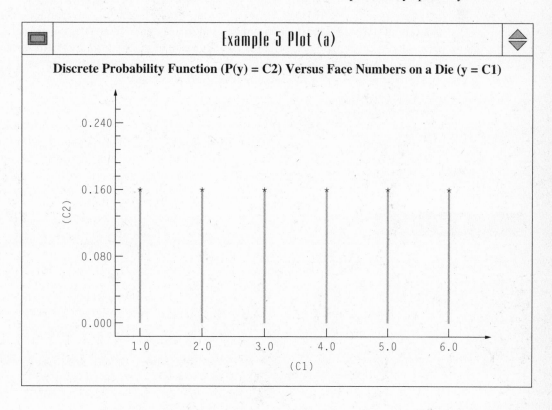

Example 5 Plot (a)

Discrete Probability Function (P(y) = C2) Versus Face Numbers on a Die (y = C1)

THE CONTINUOUS UNIFORM DISTRIBUTION

The **continuous uniform distribution** consists of equal probability density values, all the same height. In general for a ≤ y ≤ b, the uniform density function is

$$f(y) = \frac{1}{b - a} \text{ for a} \le y \le b$$

and

$$f(y) = 0 \text{ elsewhere}$$

EXAMPLE 6

THE MANAGER'S REGION OF IGNORANCE, THE UNIFORM DISTRIBUTION

Problem Statement   Suppose the potential revenue from a new product is estimated to be between $8,000 and $10,000 for the first quarter the product is on the market. Management is unable to be more specific about the possible revenue outcomes, admitting a lack of knowledge (a region of ignorance) about the future market conditions for the product. For any like-sized revenue intervals, say, 8 to 8.5 and 9.5 to 10, the probability of a revenue figure falling in one interval is the same as in the other interval.

Verify in MINITAB that the density function is the same height, uniformly, from 8 to 10 and the value (height) of the density is $\frac{1}{(10 - 8)}$.

Problem Solution   This distribution is continuous. Therefore, draw a step on the plot that follows. The step includes vertical lines from 8 and 10 to the density height .5, and a horizontal line from 8 to 10 at height .5.

EXAMPLE 7

PRODUCT SPECIFICATIONS USING THE UNIFORM DISTRIBUTION

Problem Statement (a)   An electronics company produces resistors with a nominal resistance of 1,000 ohms, and the company specifies that the actual resistance is uniformly distributed between 990 and 1,010 ohms, which leads to product specifications of 1,000 ±1% ohms. Use MINITAB to find and plot the probability density function for resistance.

Problem Solution (a)   See Example 7 Plot (a).

Problem Statement (b)   Find the proportion of the resistors between 1,000 ±6 ohms, which is the area under the density function between 994 and 1,006.

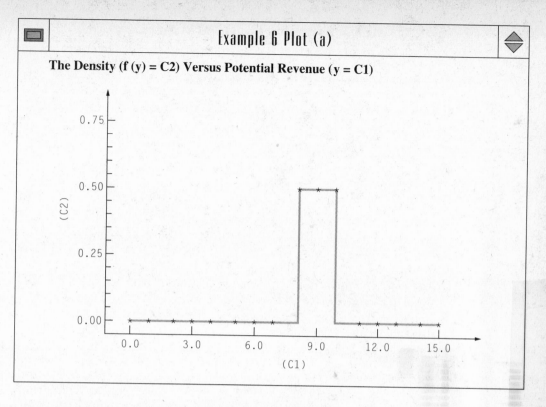

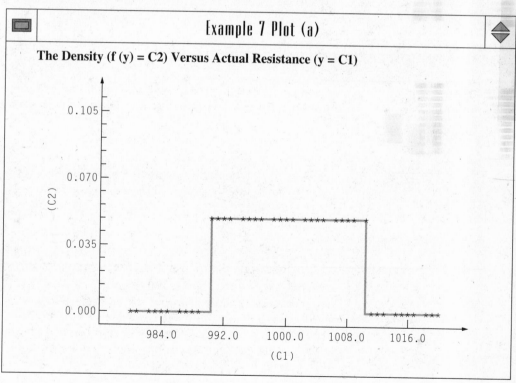

Problem Solution (b) The proportion of the resistors between 1,000 ±6 ohms is the area under the density function between 994 and 1006. This area is a rectangular region f(y) × (1006 − 994) = f(y) × (12). For this problem

$$f(y) = \frac{1}{b-a} \text{ for } a \le y \le b$$

becomes

$$f(y) = \frac{1}{1,010 - 990} = \frac{1}{20}$$

And the proportion of the resistors between 1,000 ±6 ohms is f(y) × (1,006 − 994) = $(\frac{1}{20})(12) = \frac{6}{10} = \frac{3}{5}$.

Alternative Solution (b) The same result can be obtained using cumulative probabilities, where the proportion of the resistors between 1,000 ±6 ohms is P(y ≤ 1006) − P(y ≤ 994) = $\frac{3}{5}$. As you can see in Appendix 1, the MINITAB CDF command was used to obtain these cumulative probabilities.

S T A T I S T I C A L   H I G H L I G H T S

The continuous uniform distribution has a flat top because the density is constant.

THE CONTINUOUS EXPONENTIAL DISTRIBUTION

A commonly encountered continuous distribution is the **exponential.** With a mean μ and variance μ^2, the exponential probability density function is

$$f(y) = \frac{e^{-y/\mu}}{\mu}$$

This distribution is widely used in product reliability studies. The mean μ is the **mean time to failure** (MTF) and $\frac{1}{\mu}$ is the **failure rate.** The area under the density function from 0 to a value of y is the probability the product fails in that time interval.

Relationship Between the Exponential and Poisson Distributions The exponential distribution can be derived from the following type of situation, which relates it to the Poisson distribution. Consider a single checkout counter at a convenience store. Suppose the number of customers that arrive in a small time slice, say, one minute, is a rare event for the time slice. Therefore, the probability of a specific number of customers arriving per minute follows a Poisson distribution. The probability of a specific number of customers being serviced in a time interval is also Poisson.

From the Poisson distribution of the number of customers serviced, the distribution of the time it takes to serve a customer (service time) can be derived. The service time distribution turns out to be exponential when the number of customers serviced is Poisson. In other situations, where many customers have short service times and few customers have long service times, the exponential is appropriate. Telephone call durations is another classic application of the exponential distribution.

EXAMPLE 8

SERVING CUSTOMERS

Because companies are in the business of serving customers, many managers are interested in characterizing customer arrival patterns and company service patterns. A classic thinking framework is the single-server model, such as a single checkout counter at a convenience store.

Managers want to know about service time. As you are about to see, the form of the exponential is such that most of the customers require little service time, but a few customers will require a very long time to serve.

You can verify the service time characteristics by collecting service time data for a single-server situation and constructing a stem-and-leaf diagram. Or, as you will see below, a service time distribution can be simulated in MINITAB.

Once managers recognize that some customers will require long service times, service systems can be redesigned or employees can be specially trained to deal with long service time situations when they arise. Therefore, the key is not only to recognize the characteristics of what you observe, but also to react as a manager and improve the system if possible.

Problem Statement (a)   Suppose the mean service time for customers is 4 min ($\mu = 4$) and the distribution is exponential, where the time to serve a customer is $y \geq 0$. Use MINITAB to find and plot values of the exponential density function.

Problem Solution (a)   In Plot (a) C2 on the vertical axis represents density values, $f(y)$, and C1 on the horizontal axis represents values of the random variable y, which is the time to serve a customer. You can draw a smooth curve connecting these points because the distribution is continuous.

Problem Statement (b)   Find and plot the cumulative probabilities.

Problem Solution (b)   In Plot (b) recall that the area under the density function of a continuous distribution is probability. As y is increased from 0, the cumulative distribution function shows cumulative probabilities, C3, for service times less than or equal to a specific value of y.

Problem Discussion   Smooth curves are drawn on the plots that connect the points because the exponential distribution is continuous and not discrete. Notice from the cumulative distribution function that, roughly, 80% of the customers are serviced in 7 min or less (rather quickly), yet 20% of the customers take more than 7 min to be serviced, with the tail of the distribution extending to infinity, theoretically.

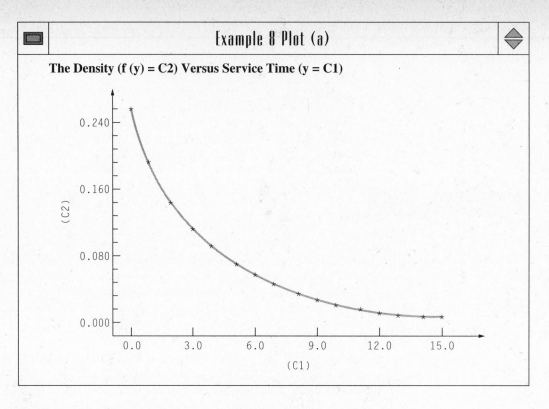

The Density (f (y) = C2) Versus Service Time (y = C1)

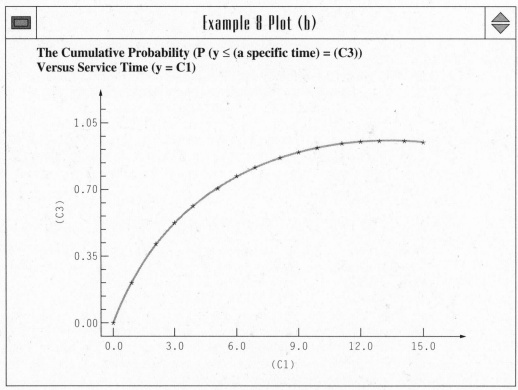

**The Cumulative Probability (P (y ≤ (a specific time) = (C3))
Versus Service Time (y = C1)**

THE CONTINUOUS LOGNORMAL DISTRIBUTION

The **lognormal** distribution is very useful in describing the sizes of things after undergoing geometric growth with a normal distribution of growth rates.

For example, those who make money in the stock market tend to buy a stock at a low price and sell it at a high price. The change in price divided by the initial price is called a return. Unfortunately, some returns are negative and the investor can lose money as well as gain it. Before the fact, returns are uncertain. If you buy a stock for $100 today, its worth one year from now is uncertain.

For the market as a whole, as gleaned from a market index like the Dow Jones Average, yearly returns are approximately normal. You can think of yearly returns as resulting from the sum of daily returns. In theory, the Central Limit Theorem tells us that yearly returns, a sum, tend to be normal regardless of the distribution of the independent daily returns. A stock bought today will be subject to geometric growth or contraction at varying daily growth rates. In this way, stock prices compound daily growth from some initial value of, say, $100 to some uncertain future value, P, at the end of a year.

It is interesting to note that this growth process applies to other economic and socioeconomic size variables such as population, incomes, wealth, real estate values, and so on. Even more fascinating is that although an aggregation of rates tends to be normal over long time periods, the size of what is growing, say, the final stock price, P, is lognormal in distribution. Therefore, the lognormal distribution becomes very useful in describing the sizes of things.

EXAMPLE 9

BUY LOW AND SELL HIGH, LOGNORMAL STOCK PRICES

Problem Statement   Find and plot the lognormal probability density function for the potential year-end price of a stock that was purchased for $100 at the beginning of the year. Assume yearly returns are normal with a mean of .1825 (18.25%) and a standard deviation of .2093.

Problem Solution   The lognormal probability density function is shown in Plot (a) for the potential year-end value of the stock.

Problem Discussion   Notice that the lognormal distribution is skewed to the right, indicating that prices are more likely to be on the high side rather than on the low side. Interestingly, this gives the impression (maybe a false one) that you are more likely to benefit from the high price than be hurt by the potential low ones. This is something for you to ponder.

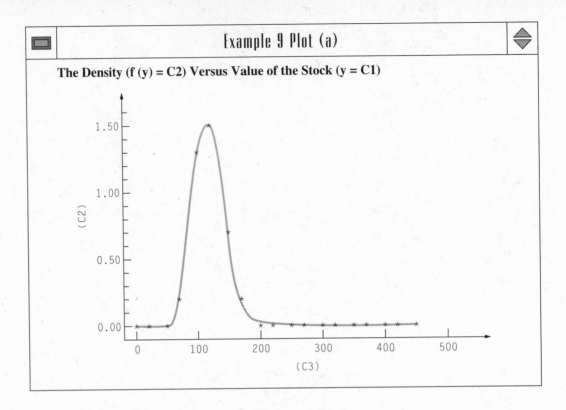

FLEXIBLE-SHAPED CONTINUOUS DISTRIBUTIONS

Sometimes data distributions have shapes that don't seem to fit any of the common distributions, and the need arises for flexible-shaped distributions. With the **beta, gamma,** and **Weibull distributions,** shape parameters can be set to vary the shape of the distribution.

EXAMPLE 10

ELAPSED TIME REQUIRED FOR AN ACTIVITY, THE BETA DISTRIBUTION

The successful management of large-scale projects such as building an airplane or a submarine depends on the planning, scheduling, and coordinating of many interrelated activities. The newer (a new submarine, for example) the large-scale project is, the more difficult it is to manage. Two prominent management techniques for dealing with new, large-scale projects have emerged. They are the Program Evaluation and Review Technique (PERT) and the Critical Path Method (CPM). Both these PERT-type techniques have, as a core, a network of interrelated activities.

In PERT, three time-to-complete-the-activity estimates are obtained for each activity in the network. The three time estimates to complete an activity are the optimistic, the most likely, and the pessimistic. Completion time is bounded from above (pessimistic time where everything goes wrong) and from below (optimistic time where everything goes right). It turns out that the beta distribution is bounded like this. Because of its flexibility in shape, the beta distribution has been useful for describing activity completion times. This flexibility is demonstrated in MINITAB below.

Problem Statement (a)   The beta distribution is useful for describing activity completion times of large-scale projects. The completion times are scaled to be between 0 and 1. Plot the beta distribution for the shape parameters A = 4 and B = 2.

Problem Solution (a)   C2 represents density values and C1 is scaled completion times for project activities.

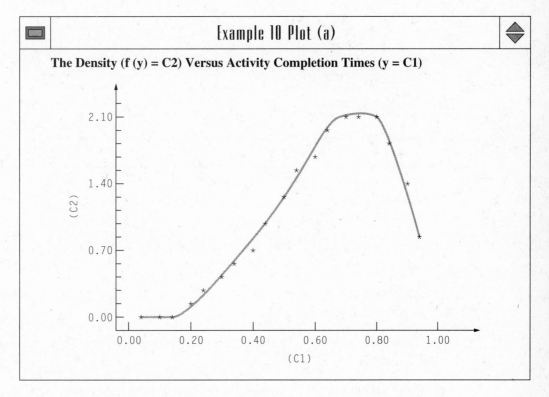

Problem Statement (b)   Plot the beta distribution with shape parameters A = 2 and B = 4.

Problem Solution (b) C2 represents density values and C1 is scaled completion times for project activities.

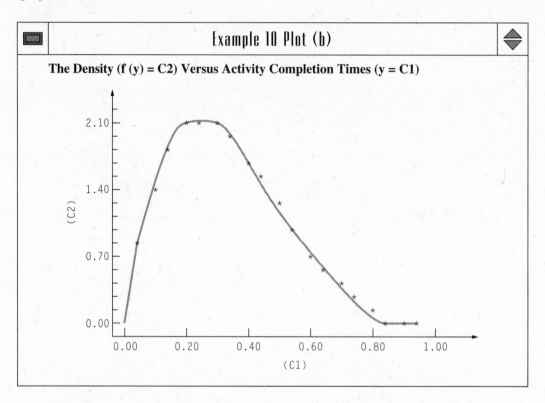

Problem Statement (c) Plot the beta distribution for the shape parameters A = 1 and B = 2.

Problem Solution (c) In Plot (c) C2 represents density values and C1 is scaled completion times for project activities.

Problem Statement (d) Plot the beta distribution for the shape parameters A = .5 and B = .5.

Problem Solution (d) In Plot (d) C2 represents density values and C1 is scaled completion times for project activities.

Problem Statement (e) Plot the beta distribution for the shape parameters, A = 1 and B = 1.

Problem Solution (e) In Plot (e) C2 represents density values and C1 is scaled completion times for project activities.

Example 10 Plot (c)

The Density (f (y) = C2) Versus Activity Completion Times (y = C1)

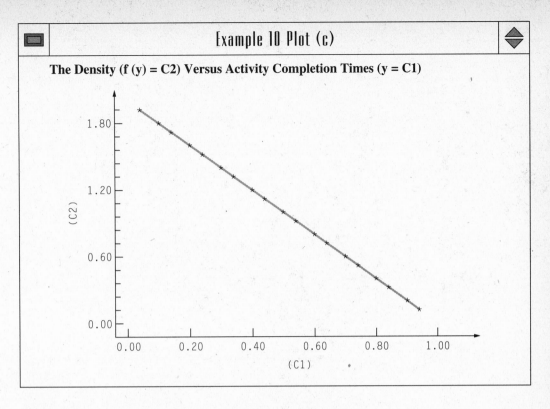

Example 10 Plot (d)

The Density (f (y) = C2) Versus Activity Completion Times (y = C1)

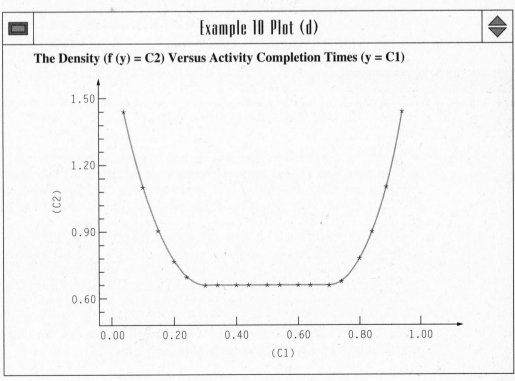

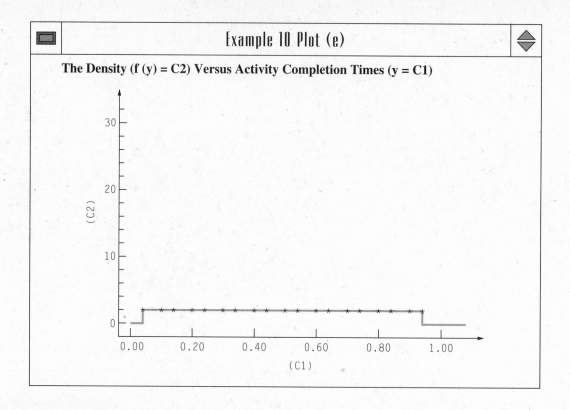

Example 10 Plot (e)

The Density (f (y) = C2) Versus Activity Completion Times (y = C1)

EXAMPLE 11

PRODUCT RELIABILITY, THE GAMMA AND WEIBULL DISTRIBUTIONS

An important area of quality control is concerned with product reliability. Product reliability is the probability a product will perform its required function for a stated period of time. Therefore, reliability theory deals with product lifetimes. For example, think of yourself as a product. The probability that you will live at least 65 years is an expression of reliability. In general, reliability is 1 − P [the product dies at time t or sooner].

The failure density function is the time rate of change of the probability, P[the product dies at time t or sooner]. As t gets larger (as you get older), the probability of failure, given that a certain age has been attained, is called a hazard density. When wear or deterioration with time is present, the product's hazard is increasing, as it is with human beings.

Both the failure density and the hazard density have many different shapes in practice, depending on the product. Therefore, many distributions are useful in reliability work, including the normal, lognormal, exponential, beta, binomial, gamma, and Weibull. The gamma and Weibull distributions are particularly flexible.

Problem Statement   Specify the MINITAB commands to plot the gamma and Weibull distributions in which different shape parameters are tried.

Problem Solution   No plots are shown here. However, commands and shape parameters are available in Appendix 1.

THE CAUCHY, LAPLACE, AND LOGISTIC DISTRIBUTIONS

At the time of this writing, MINITAB can generate densities for three other continuous density functions, the **Cauchy, Laplace,** and **logistic distributions.** These distributions are less common in management applications than many of the other distributions we have discussed. As a result, the MINITAB commands in Appendix 1 simply encourage experimentation and illustrate the shapes of these distributions.

EXAMPLE 12

THE CAUCHY, LAPLACE, AND LOGISTIC DISTRIBUTIONS

In sampling situations, the logistic distribution is difficult to distinguish from the normal distribution. This can be seen by comparing the density functions.

Although the Cauchy is not well known for its management applications, there are some interesting possibilities. Since the ratio of two independent, standardized normal variables have a Cauchy distribution, applications come to mind readily. For example, financial planners use financial ratios, such as return on investment ($ROI = \frac{income}{assets}$), which is the ratio of ($\frac{income}{sales}$) to ($\frac{assets}{sales}$). Under appropriate conditions, such ratios may follow a Cauchy distribution, which has fat tails, indicating that samples of ratios may display substantial variability (much more than you would expect under the normality assumption).

Like the Cauchy, the Laplace distribution also has fat tails.

Problem Statement   Specify the MINITAB commands to plot the Cauchy, Laplace, and logistic distributions.

Problem Solution   No plots are shown here. However, commands and parameters are available in Appendix 1.

STATISTICAL HIGHLIGHTS

A wide variety of continuous distributions exist because of the tremendous number of applications.

THE CUMULATIVE DISTRIBUTION FUNCTION (CDF) AND ITS INVERSE (INVCDF)

A **cumulative distribution function** is a plot of cumulative probability versus a random variable, cumulative P(y) versus y. Cumulative P(y) is the probability that a random variable, y, is less than or equal to some particular value, P(y ≤ some particular value) = F(y). Given a value of y on the horizontal axis, a corresponding F(y) is read off the vertical axis. With y as input, the MINITAB CDF command produces F(y) as output for distributions identified in subcommands.

Reading the CDF can be reversed. That is, given a value of F(y) on the vertical axis, a corresponding y is read off the horizontal axis. With F(y) as input, the MINITAB INVCDF command produces y as output, and INVCDF stands for the inverse cumulative distribution function.

The Cumulative Distribution Function

Once a density function is found that fits the data in a particular application, sweeping summary statements can be made in terms of the cumulative distribution function (CDF). In a variety of applications, many questions are posed in cumulative terms as in the following examples. What percentage of students score less than or equal to 500 on an entrance exam? What percentage of newly manufactured pistons have diameters less than or equal to 3.25 in.? What fraction of light bulbs fail in less than or equal to 600 hr? What percentage of time are there two or fewer cracked eggs in a dozen? What percentage of customers are served in 6 min or less? What percentage of accounts receivable are collected in 30 days or less?

Several examples of MINITAB's CDF and INVCDF commands are given in Appendix 1, and the results are shown below.

EXAMPLE 13

CDF AND INVCDF FOR THE NORMAL DISTRIBUTION

Problem Statement (a) For a normal (μ = 432, σ = 48) distribution of test scores, find the probability that a student scores less than or equal to 500.

Problem Solution (a) The CDF command produces P(y ≤ 500) = .92171.

Problem Statement (b) If the inverse of the above question were posed, P(y ≤ ?) = .92171, what test score is needed to reach the 92.171 percentile?

Problem Solution (b) The inverse function is $F^{-1}(.92171) = 500$. INVCDF simply turns things inside-out. Given a cumulative probability, INVCDF produces the corresponding values of the random variable.

Problem Statement (c)   For a normal ($\mu = 432$, $\sigma = 48$) distribution of test scores, plot the cumulative probabilities and find the probability that a student scores less than or equal to 500.

Problem Solution (c)   In the plot below, the cumulative probabilities C2 are plotted versus the random variable y, and the above results can be read directly from the plot. Move vertically from 500 to the curve, then horizontally to .92171. For the inverse, reverse the process.

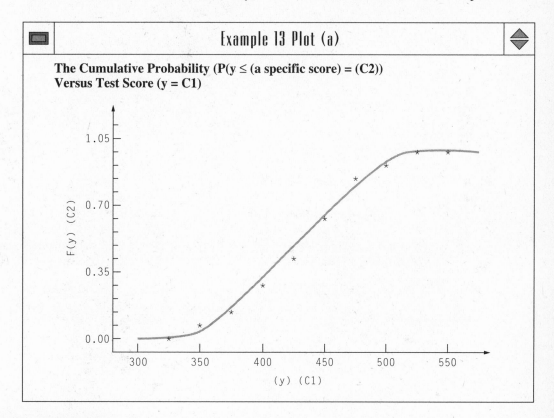

Example 13 Plot (a)

The Cumulative Probability (P(y ≤ (a specific score) = (C2))
Versus Test Score (y = C1)

E X A M P L E   1 4

CDF FOR THE STUDENT'S t DISTRIBUTION

Problem Statement   Using the cumulative distribution function (CDF) for the Student's t distribution, find the proportion of the distribution between t values of −2 and +2 for 30 degrees of freedom.

Problem Solution   MINITAB commands in Appendix 1 produced an answer of 0.945375 as the proportion of the distribution between t values of −2 and +2 for 30 degrees of freedom.

EXAMPLE 15

CDF AND INVCDF FOR THE EXPONENTIAL DISTRIBUTION

Problem Statement (a) For an exponential distribution of customer service times (the mean, $\mu = 4$), find the probability that a particular customer has a service time less than or equal to 6 minutes. Show how the result is found from a plot of the cumulative probabilities.

Problem Solution (a) The probability that the service time is less than or equal to 6 minutes is 0.77687, as read from the CDF below. From 6 on C1, go vertically to the curve and then horizontally to C2 to read the answer.

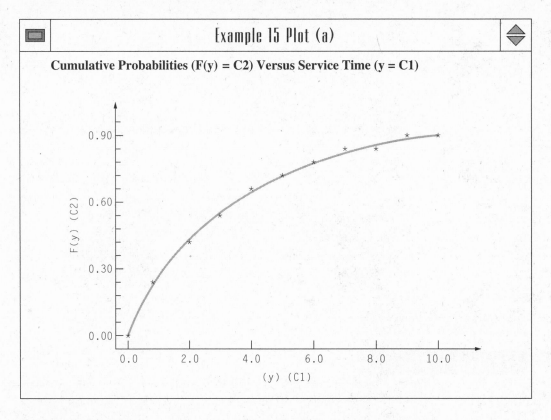

Problem Statement (b) Find the probability that a particular customer has a service time between 4 and 6 minutes.

Problem Solution (b) The probability that a particular customer has a service time between 4 and 6 minutes is found by subtracting the cumulative probabilities for 6 and 4 minutes, which is $0.144749 = F(6) - F(4)$.

```
ST A T I S T I C A L   H I G H L I G H T S
```

In practical problems, the cumulative distribution function is at least as useful as the probability density function.

GENERATING RANDOM DATA AND PROBABILITY PLOTTING

In **probability plotting,** actual observations are plotted versus corresponding values based on a theoretical distribution. When the actual observations follow the theoretical distribution, a probability plot produces a straight line. To demonstrate probability plotting, data are generated randomly from a known probability distribution. Then, as if the probability distribution were not known, various probability plots can be tried in an attempt to identify the correct theoretical distribution.

Generating Random Data

Random data can be generated from many distributions, such as the Bernoulli, binomial, Poisson, integer, normal, uniform, Student's t, F, Cauchy, Laplace, logistic, lognormal, chi-square, exponential, gamma, Weibull, and beta. In MINITAB, the distributional choice is made with a subcommand.

In addition, you can supply your own discrete values and probabilities. Then go on to generate data from this distribution, selecting the MINITAB subcommand DISCRETE.

Some examples appear below. As you have already seen, this simulation capability enables managers asking "what if" questions to carry out computational experiments on the computer before tampering with the real system.

```
E X A M P L E   1 6
```

EXPONENTIAL SERVICE TIMES

Problem Statement   What if 50 customers are served and the service times are exponential with a mean of 4 minutes? Obtain a dotplot of the service times.

Problem Solution   Service times are displayed in Plot (a).

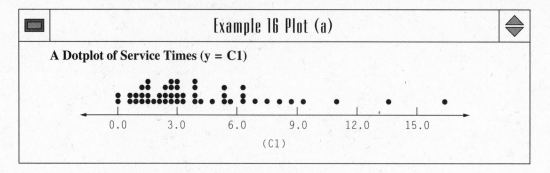

Example 16 Plot (a)

A Dotplot of Service Times (y = C1)

Probability Plotting

If we don't know what theoretical distribution corresponds to a data distribution, probability plotting can help to find the theoretical distribution that fits the data. This can be illustrated through probability plotting.

Consider the dotplot of service times shown in Example 16. Suppose by examining the dotplot it is not clear which theoretical distribution generated the data. First, let's guess that the service time dotplot is normal. The NSCORES command in MINITAB takes the actual service time data in C1 and computes corresponding values in C2 based on the theoretical standard normal. If the actual data, C1, are normal, a probability plot of C2 versus C1 should produce a straight line. This does not happen in Plot (b). Therefore, the service time data are not normal.

Because the normal does not fit the data, another distribution is tried. Rather than show a long trial-and-error process, let's move directly to the exponential distribution. MINITAB commands are shown in Appendix 1 that perform a similar function to the NSCORES command but for the exponential distribution (subcommand modification allows you to deal with any distribution).

MINITAB takes the actual service time data in C1 and computes corresponding values in C4 based on the theoretical exponential distribution. If the actual data C1 are exponential, a probability plot of C4 versus C1 should produce a straight line. The following probability plot (Plot (c)) shows a straight line pattern, which indicates that the data are exponential.

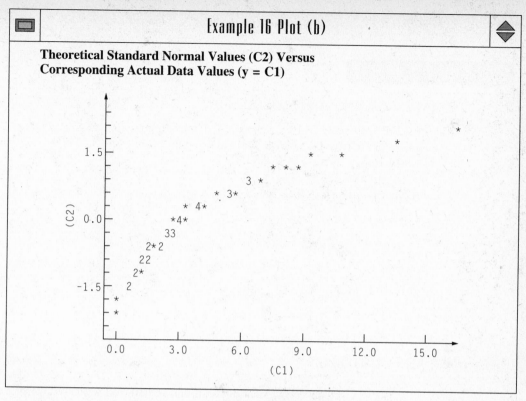

Example 16 Plot (b)

**Theoretical Standard Normal Values (C2) Versus
Corresponding Actual Data Values (y = C1)**

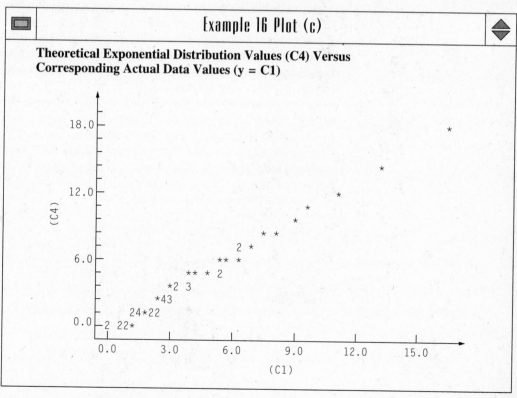

Example 16 Plot (c)

**Theoretical Exponential Distribution Values (C4) Versus
Corresponding Actual Data Values (y = C1)**

EXAMPLE 17

RANDOM DATA, ROLLING A LOADED DIE

Problem Statement Generate random data by rolling a loaded die 100 times. The faces 1, 2, 3, 4, 5, and 6, have the corresponding probabilities of .12, .17, .17, .17, .17, and .20. Summarize the results of these 100 rolls.

Problem Solution A TALLY of these results suggests that the die might be loaded.

```
        FACE   COUNT
           1     16
           2     11
           3     17
           4     20
           5     16
           6     20
     TOTAL =    100
```

SKEWNESS AND KURTOSIS

Nonsymmetrical distributions are **skewed** with one of the distribution's tails longer than the other. For example, the exponential distribution is asymmetrical, skewed positively to the right. The chi-square distribution is skewed to the right also. Contrasting examples include the symmetrical, normal, and Student's t distributions, which have no skew. A skewless distribution, such as the normal, provides a benchmark for measures of the amount and direction of skewness in other distributions.

Skewness is not just for statisticians. For example, the distribution of electricity usage tends to be skewed to the right. Electric utilities must design power generating and delivery systems to cope with this. The distribution of personal incomes is skewed to the right. Government taxation systems are designed with the nature of the income distribution taken into consideration. Some consumer product companies target the high end of the income distribution in product selection and pricing.

Two competing sample measures of skewness are defined below. Their MINITAB names are SKEW1 and SKEW2. C1 is a column of data values.

$$\text{LET 'SKEW1'} = 3 * \frac{\text{MEAN(C1)} - \text{MEDIAN(C1)}}{\text{STDEV(C1)}}$$

SKEW2 is a function of residuals from the mean, which are calculated first.

$$\text{LET 'RESIDS'} = \text{C1} - \text{MEAN(C1)}$$
$$\text{LET C3} = \text{'RESIDS'}**3$$
$$\text{LET 'SKEW2'} = \frac{\text{MEAN(C3)}}{(\text{STDEV(C1)})**3}$$

The formula for SKEW1 is due to statistical pioneer Karl Pearson. It is easy to compute by hand. The SKEW2 formula is based on the method of moments.

Like the standard deviation is a companion of the mean, **kurtosis,** a distribution's peakedness measure, is a companion of skewness. The normal distribution of intermediate peakedness is said to be **mesokurtic.** A distribution more sharply peaked than the normal is **leptokurtic.** A distribution more flat-topped than the normal distribution is **platykurtic.**

Like SKEW2, KURT is a function of residuals from the mean, which are calculated first.

$$\text{`RESIDS'} = C1 - \text{MEAN}(C1)$$

$$C4 = \text{`RESIDS'}**4$$

$$\text{`KURT'} = \frac{\text{MEAN}(C4)}{(\text{STDEV}(C1))**4}$$

In order to get a feel for the skewness and kurtosis of various distributions, generate random data from a variety of distributions. Then compute skewness and kurtosis measures. Compare these measures to those for the normal. MINITAB commands for computing skewness and kurtosis are shown in Appendix 1. MINITAB output for the normal is shown below. Sample measures of skewness and kurtosis are given for an exponential distribution as well. You might experiment with additional distributions on your own.

E X A M P L E 1 8

SKEWNESS FOR THE NORMAL DISTRIBUTION

Problem Statement   For 100 observations from a normal ($\mu = 12$, $\sigma = .5$), compute skewness measures.

Problem Solution

```
SKEW1 = 0.30395

SKEW2 = 0.207303
```

Problem Discussion   As the sample size increases, both skewness measures for the normal approach 0.

EXAMPLE 19

SKEWNESS FOR THE EXPONENTIAL DISTRIBUTION

Problem Statement For 100 observations from an exponential ($\mu = 4$), compute skewness measures.

Problem Solution

```
SKEW1 = 0.854536 (more positively skewed than the normal)

SKEW2 = 1.61062 (more positively skewed than the normal)
```

EXAMPLE 20

KURTOSIS FOR THE NORMAL DISTRIBUTION

Problem Statement For 100 observations from a normal ($\mu = 12$, $\sigma = .5$), compute kurtosis.

Problem Solution

```
KURT = 3.09519
```

Problem Discussion As the sample size increases, the kurtosis measure for the normal approaches three.

EXAMPLE 21

KURTOSIS FOR THE EXPONENTIAL DISTRIBUTION

Problem Statement For 100 observations from an exponential ($\mu = 4$) compute kurtosis.

Problem Solution

```
KURT = 6.31463     (more peaked than the normal)
```

CHAPTER SUMMARY

Many practical problems have data distributions that don't fit into the well-known patterns such as the normal or binomial distributions. In this unfamiliar distributional territory, you need some alternatives to fill the gap. This chapter added to your repertoire of discrete and continuous distributions. Additional discrete distributions include the Poisson, the hypergeometric, and the discrete uniform distributions. Continuous distributions include the exponential, uniform, lognormal, beta, gamma, and Weibull distributions.

We also discussed a few additional related concepts. First, cumulative distribution functions (CDFs) and their inverses (INVCDFs) proved useful for obtaining the probability that a random variable is less than or equal to particular values of interest. Second, we learned how to generate random data from particular distributions. Finally, we found that skewness and kurtosis parameters augment the mean and standard deviation in describing the shape and location of a distribution.

KEY TERMS

EXERCISES

1. A hospital is planning a facility for handling cancer patients. For facility size decisions, it needs to estimate the number of patients with rare cancers such as brain tumors. With seven years of history, its county experienced a rate of four brain tumor cases per 100,000 people per year.

(a) If the county population is 180,000 people, what is the probability of no cases of brain tumors in a given year?

(b) What is the probability that the number of tumor cases is less than three?

2. A manufacturing process produces electrical switches. On average, the process produces defective switches 4% of the time. The defectives occur at random and the defective rate is constant. A carton contains 100 switches.

(a) Use the Poisson distribution to find the probability of no defective switches in a carton?

(b) What is the probability of one or more defective switches?

(c) What is the probability of three or four defective switches?

3. For a refrigerator freezer door, 6 sq ft of sheet metal is formed and finished. Imperfections in the finish occur at random and are evenly distributed on the surface. If there is an average of one imperfection per door, what proportion of finished doors have four or more imperfections?

4. On average, there is one defect per 1,000 ft of pipe. The defects occur at random and are evenly distributed along the pipe. The pipe is shipped in 50-ft sections. What is the probability that a contractor who connects three sections finds no defects after inspection?

5. Weekly demand for flutes at a music store averages two flutes and follows a Poisson distribution.

(a) What is the probability that exactly four flutes are sold in a week?

(b) How many flutes would you stock in inventory to cover at least 80% of the demand?

6. If a surgeon makes one mistake on average out of 80 knee operations and the number of mistakes follows a Poisson distribution, what is the probability that no mistakes occur in the next 10 operations?

7. A recent college graduate is selling insurance by cold-calling potential buyers who are on a prospect list. On average, 2 prospects in 20 agree to meet with the salesperson for an assessment of insurance needs and for a description of insurance products. If 100 prospects are called and the Poisson distribution applies, what is the probability that the salesperson will meet with 5 or fewer prospects?

8. A company services its own fork lift trucks. A particular spare part is needed on average once every six months for each forklift truck. There are ten forklift trucks in the fleet. How many spare parts should be stocked to satisfy at least 90% of the demand for this spare part?

9. A milling machine produces ten parts. If eight parts are good and two are defective, what is the probability that an inspector, who samples four parts without replacement, finds exactly two defective parts in the sample?

10. Audit reports on five companies are in five folders on a manager's desk. The manager was informed that two companies had unfavorable audits; such audits tend to consume a lot of the manager's time. If the manager randomly selects three folders to work on, what is the probability that two of the three folders will consume a lot of the manager's time?

11. An executive randomly selects four steering committee members from a list of six male and four female managers. What is the probability that the committee will consist of four females?

12. The dean of a school randomly selects a 5-member student advisory committee from a list of 20 students. Eight of the students on the list are campus radicals. What is the probability that the committee includes 2 or fewer radicals?

13. A firm intends to hire two graduating seniors from the same school. Both accounting and finance majors have the necessary skills for good job performance. If eight students are interviewed, half are accountants, and the students do equally well in the interviews, what is the probability that two accountants are offered the jobs?

14. For a lot size of 15 parts, a random sample of 3 parts is selected and inspected. If a lot contains 10 good and 5 defective parts, what is the probability that fewer than 2 defective parts will be found in the sample?

15. The time between car arrivals at a parking lot follows an exponential distribution with a mean of five min. The parking lot has a capacity of 120 cars.

(a) What percentage of the interarrival times are between five an seven min?

(b) What percentage of the interarrival times are less than two min?

(c) What percentage of the interarrival times exceed 10 min?

(d) Use the computer to plot the probability density function and the cumulative distribution function.

16. A mail sorter receives mail pieces from a delivery mechanism. The mail pieces are grouped in batches with batch sizes from 1 to 50 pieces. The time between arrivals of batches is exponential in distribution with a mean of 10 min. What proportion of the batches have interarrival times that are less than 8 min?

17. A batch of mail pieces includes 10 pieces with city A zip codes, 6 pieces with city B zip codes, and 4 pieces with city C zip codes. If 6 mail pieces fall off a mail sorter at random, what is the probability that 2 pieces are from city A, 3 pieces are from city B, and 1 piece is from city C?

18. Customers arrive at an airline ticket counter with time between arrivals that follows an exponential distribution with a mean of three min.

(a) What percentage of the interarrival times are between one and six min?

(b) Use the computer to plot the probability density function and the cumulative distribution function.

(c) Use the cumulative distribution function in part (b) to verify the answer in part (a).

19. It is equally likely that a piece of mail has a zip code for one of seven cities.

(a) What is the probability that a mail sorter places a mail piece in either of the first two of seven bins?

(b) Draw the probability function and the cumulative probability function for a randomly chosen mail piece being sorted to a particular bin.

20. Forklift trucks must have their batteries charged daily during an eight-hour shift. Two-hour periods are required for charging. Therefore, charging can begin at any time from the beginning of hour one to the beginning of hour seven. If the need for charging is evenly distributed over this six-hour period, what is the probability that a forklift truck begins charging during hours two, three, or four?

21. Heated metal parts are processed on any one of three identical machines. Each machine has the same probability of being available.

(a) Draw the probability function for machine availability.

(b) What is the probability that the first and third machines are available but the second is not?

22. Several parts are put together at an assembly station and transported on a conveyor to a painting station. The time delay for the painting operation is uniformly distributed between 5 and 15 min.

(a) Draw the probability density function for the painting time.

(b) What is the probability that the painting will be done in less than 7 min?

(c) What is the probability that the painting operation will be completed in more than 13 min?

(d) Draw the cumulative distribution function for the painting time and show how the results in part (c) can be determined graphically.

23. Dump trucks refuel at a service terminal. The time to refuel is uniformly distributed from 4 to 11 min. What is the probability that it takes between 7.3 and 9.6 min to refuel a dump truck?

24. The duration of telephone calls made by Jane's friend Sara follows an exponential distribution with a mean of 10 min. What is the probability that Sara spends less than 12 min on the phone?

25. John had trouble getting a date one weekend. His brother said that the mean time to failure, the average duration of his phone calls, was 4 min and the distribution was exponential. What proportion of his calls lasted 3 min or less?

26. If the mean time to failure for a television set is 2,190 hr and the distribution is exponential,

(a) What is the probability of no failures in 4,380 hr?

(b) If the average family watches television for 12 hr a day 365 days a year, how many television set failures are expected in a year?

27. If the sales volume for boxed candy (in thousands of boxes) at a department store follows a gamma distribution with the scale parameter A = 3.2 and the shape parameter B = .8, what is the probability that at least 3,800 boxes of candy will be sold?

28. If electric power demand for a region (in millions of kilowatt-hours) has a gamma distribution with the scale parameter A = 2.5 and the shape parameter B = 2.5, what is the probability that the demand will exceed 7 million kilowatt-hours?

29. If the proportion of nondefectives has a beta distribution with two shape parameters, A = 15 and B = 3, what is the probability that the proportion of nondefectives is less than 0.90?

30. If a dollar invested in stocks has a year-end value that follows a lognormal distribution with a mean of .15 and a standard deviation of .20, what is the probability that the dollar will grow to more than $1.25 by year's end?

31. A contractor estimates that the construction time for a new home will range from a minimum of 100 days to a maximum of 180 days. Construction times, CTs, can be scaled by subtracting the minimum and dividing by the difference between the maximum and minimum. Therefore, CT(scaled) $= \frac{(CT - 100)}{80}$. Experience has shown that CT(scaled) follows a beta distribution with shape parameters A = 4 and B = 2. What is the probability that CT (scaled) is less than 0.75, which is a construction time of 160 days or less?

32. The Weibull distribution is useful for describing the time to failure when the failure rate increases or decreases with time. Find the probability that the time to failure is less than two time units for the following scale and shape parameters:

(a) A = 1 and B = .5.

(b) A = 1 and B = 3.

(c) A = 3 and B = 1.

33. Suppose standardized return on investment figures might be approximated by any of the following distributions: normal, Cauchy, logistic, or Laplace. If the location parameter for each distribution is 0 and the scale parameter is one, what is the probability that the standardized returns are between ±2 for each distribution?

34. A cookie machine turns out chocolate chip cookies of a standard size. The number of chocolate chips per cookie has a Poisson distribution with a mean of nine.

(a) What is the probability that a cookie contains no more than nine chocolate chips?

(b) What is the percentage of cookies produced in which the number of chocolate chips is within one standard deviation from its mean value?

APPENDIX 1

Minitab Examples

THE POISSON APPROXIMATION OF THE BINOMIAL DISTRIBUTION

```
MTB > SET DATA IN C1    # POSSIBLE VALUES OF y
DATA > 0:12
DATA > END

MTB > PDF C1 PUT IN C2;   # P(y) IN C2
SUBC > POISSON MU=.9996.  # MEAN IS np

MTB > PDF C1 PUT IN C3;
SUBC> BINOMIAL N=12 P=.0833.

MTB > PRINT C1 C2 C3  # C1 IS THE NUMBER OF BAD EGGS,
# C2 CONTAINS POISSON APPROXIMATIONS OF BINOMIAL
# PROBABILITIES (C3)---THEY ARE CLOSE

MTB > PLOT C2 C1  # THESE PROBABILITIES ARE FOR THE
# DISCRETE POISSON DISTRIBUTION, SO YOU SHOULD DRAW IN
# THE VERTICAL LINES FROM THE C1 AXIS TO THE ASTERISKS
```

A FLAW IN YOUR JEANS

```
MTB > SET DATA INTO C1  # HISTORICAL DATA TAKEN WHEN
# THE PROCESS WAS IN CONTROL, SQUARE METERS OF FABRIC
DATA> 90 120 180 320 100 80 275 70 120 85
DATA> END
```

```
MTB > SET DATA INTO C2  # MORE HISTORICAL DATA ON THE
# NUMBER OF FLAWS IN EACH BLOCK OF FABRIC IN C1 ABOVE
DATA>  6    3    5    10    2    4    8    1    2    2
DATA> END

MTB > SUM C1
#  SUM = 1440
MTB > SUM C2
#  SUM = 43

MTB > LET K1= 43/1440   # AVERAGE NUMBER OF FLAWS
#                             PER SQUARE METER
MTB > PRINT K1
# K1 = 0.0298611   MULTIPLYING BY 100 RESULTS IN AN
# AVERAGE OF 2.9861 FLAWS PER 100 SQUARE METERS

MTB > SET INTO C3
# RANGE OF INTEREST FOR THE NUMBER OF FLAWS
DATA> 0:15
DATA> END

MTB > PDF C3 PUT  IN C4;
SUBC> POISSON MU=2.98611. # AVERAGE PER 100 SQ. METERS

MTB > CDF C3 PUT IN C5;
# GETTING CUMULATIVE PROBABILITIES
SUBC> POISSON MU=2.98611.  # AVERAGE PER 100 SQ. METERS

MTB > PRINT C3 C4 C5
```

EXAMPLE

ROLLING A DIE, UNIFORM DISCRETE PROBABILITIES

```
MTB > SET DATA IN C1
DATA> 1:6  # FACE NUMBERS ON A DIE
DATA> END

MTB > PDF C1 PUT IN C2; # PROBABILITIES IN C2
SUBC> INTEGER A=1 B=6.

MTB > PLOT C2 C1; # C2 CONTAINS PROBABILITIES AND C1
# CONTAINS FACE NUMBERS ON A DIE
SUBC> YSTART AT 0 GO TO .25.
```

EXAMPLE

THE MANAGER'S REGION OF IGNORANCE, THE UNIFORM DISTRIBUTION

```
MTB > SET DATA IN C1
DATA> 0:15 # SETTING UP THE HORIZONTAL AXIS FOR A PLOT
DATA> END
```

```
MTB > PDF C1 PUT IN C2;   # DENSITY VALUES IN C2
SUBC> UNIFORM A=8 B=10.

MTB > PLOT C2 C1;   # C2 CONTAINS THE DENSITIES
# CORRESPONDING TO THE VALUES OF THE CONTINUOUS
# VARIABLE IN C1
SUBC> YSTART 0 GO TO .75.
```

E X A M P L E

PRODUCT SPECIFICATIONS USING THE UNIFORM DISTRIBUTION

```
MTB > SET DATA IN C1
DATA> 980:1020  # TO ESTABLISH THE HORIZONTAL AXIS
#                           ON A PLOT
DATA> END

MTB > PDF C1 PUT IN C2;   # DENSITY VALUES IN C2
SUBC> UNIFORM A=990 B=1010.

MTB > PLOT C2 C1; # C2 CONTAINS PROBABILITY DENSITIES AND
#  C1 CONTAINS SPECIFIC VALUES OF THE CONTINUOUS VARIABLE
# REPRESENTING THE RESISTANCE THE RESISTANCE
SUBC> YSTART 0 GO TO .10.

MTB > SET INTO C3
DATA> 1006 994 # FOR FINDING THE PROPORTION OF THE
#                  RESISTORS BETWEEN 1000 ± 6 OHMS
DATA> END

MTB > CDF C3 PUT C4;   # SEPARATE CUMULATIVE PROBABILITIES
# FOUND FOR THE VALUES IN C3 ARE PUT IN C4
SUBC> UNIFORM A=990 B=1010.

MTB > LET K1=C4(1)-C4(2)  # THE PROBABILITY OF A RESISTOR
# HAVING A RESISTANCE BETWEEN 994 AND 1006 IS 60%
MTB > PRINT K1
#   K1 = 0.60
```

E X A M P L E

SERVING CUSTOMERS

```
MTB > SET DATA IN C1
DATA> 0:15  # SOME VALUES ALONG THE HORIZONTAL AXIS
DATA> END

MTB > PDF C1 PUT IN C2;   # DENSITY VALUES IN C2
SUBC> EXPONENTIAL MU=4.
MTB > PLOT C2 C1          # PLOT OF DENSITY FUNCTION
```

```
MTB > CDF C1 PUT IN C3;   # CUMULATIVE PROBABILITIES IN C3
SUBC> EXPONENTIAL MU=4.
MTB > PLOT C3 C1          # PLOT OF THE CDF
```

EXAMPLE

BUY LOW AND SELL HIGH, LOGNORMAL STOCK PRICES

Comment   This example is presented as a macro, %B:E13-6-1.MAC. The macro requires version ten or more of MINITAB. To examine the details of the macro, use a text editor or a word processor to open the E13-6-1.MAC file. Also in MINITAB the command TYPE 'B:E13-6-1.MAC' lists the macro. If you set OH = 24 in the session window, a "continue?" prompt will be issued by MINITAB, which permits the user to view one screen of output at a time as the macro executes.

```
MTB > %B:E13-6-1  # OR %A:E13-6-1 OR %E13-6-1
#                 OR %C:\MTBWIN\DATA\E13-6-1
```

EXAMPLE

ELAPSED TIME REQUIRED FOR AN ACTIVITY, THE BETA DISTRIBUTION

Comment   This example is presented as a macro, %B:E13-7-1.MAC.

```
MTB > %B:E13-7-1  # OR %A:E13-7-1 OR %E13-7-1
#                 OR %C:\MTBWIN\DATA\E13-7-1
```

EXAMPLE

PRODUCT RELIABILITY, THE GAMMA AND WEIBULL DISTRIBUTIONS

Comment   This example is presented as a macro, %B:E13-7-2.MAC.

```
MTB > %B:E13-7-2  # OR %A:E13-7-2 OR %E13-7-2
#                 OR %C:\MTBWIN\DATA\E13-7-2
```

EXAMPLE

THE CAUCHY, LAPLACE, AND LOGISTIC DISTRIBUTIONS

Comment   This example is presented as a macro, %B:E13-8-1.MAC.

```
MTB > %B:E13-8-1  # OR %A:E13-8-1 OR %E13-8-1
#                 OR %C:\MTBWIN\DATA\E13-8-1
```

EXAMPLE

CDF AND INVCDF FOR DIFFERENT DISTRIBUTIONS

Comment   This example is presented as a macro, %B:E13-9.MAC.

```
MTB > %B:E13-9  # OR %A:E13-9 OR %E13-9
#                 OR %C:\MTBWIN\DATA\E13-9
```

EXAMPLE

EXPONENTIAL SERVICE TIMES

Comment   This example is presented as a macro, %B:E13-10-1.MAC.

```
MTB > %B:E13-10-1 # OR %A:E13-10-1 OR %E13-10-1
#                   OR %C:\MTBWIN\DATA\E13-10-1
```

EXAMPLE

RANDOM DATA, ROLLING A LOADED DIE

```
MTB > SET INTO C1  # NUMBERS ON THE FACE OF A DIE

DATA> 1 2 3 4 5 6
DATA> END
MTB > SET INTO C2  # PROBABILITIES OF GETTING A PARTICULAR
# FACE----THIS DIE IS LOADED!!!!
DATA> .12 .17 .17 .17 .17 .20
DATA> END
MTB > RANDOM 20 OBS. INTO C3;
SUBC> DISCRETE C1 C2.
MTB > PRINT C3  # FACES SHOWING ON 20 ROLLS
MTB > TALLY C3  # CAN'T TELL THAT IT IS LOADED HERE
MTB > RANDOM 100 OBS INTO C3;
SUBC> DISCRETE C1 C2.
MTB > TALLY C3  # SOME HINT THAT THE DIE MIGHT BE LOADED
```

EXAMPLE

SKEWNESS AND KURTOSIS FOR THE NORMAL AND EXPONENTIAL DISTRIBUTIONS

```
MTB > RANDOM 100 OBS INTO C1;
                        # COOKIE BOX WEIGHT, OUNCES
SUBC> NORMAL MU=12 SIGMA=.5.
MTB > NAME C10 'SKEW1'
MTB > NAME C11 'SKEW2'
MTB > NAME C12 'KURT'
MTB > NAME C2 'RESIDS'
MTB > LET 'SKEW1'=3*(MEAN(C1)-MEDIAN(C1))/STDEV(C1)
```

```
MTB > PRINT 'SKEW1'
# SKEW1 = 0.30395   NEAR ZERO FOR THE NORMAL
MTB > LET 'RESIDS' = C1-MEAN(C1)
MTB > LET C3='RESIDS'**3
MTB > LET C4='RESIDS'**4
MTB > LET 'SKEW2'=MEAN(C3)/((STDEV(C1))**3)
MTB > PRINT 'SKEW2'
# SKEW2 = 0.207303  AGAIN, NEAR ZERO FOR THE NORMAL
MTB > LET 'KURT'=MEAN(C4)/((STDEV(C1))**4)
MTB > PRINT 'KURT'
# KURT = 3.09519    NEAR THREE FOR THE NORMAL

MTB > RANDOM 100 OBS. INTO C1;
SUBC> EXPONENTIAL MU=4.
MTB > LET 'SKEW1'=3*(MEAN(C1)-MEDIAN(C1))/STDEV(C1)
MTB > PRINT 'SKEW1'
# SKEW1 = 0.854536  MORE SKEWED THAN THE NORMAL
MTB > LET 'RESIDS'=C1-MEAN(C1)
MTB > LET C3='RESIDS'**3
MTB > LET C4='RESIDS'**4
MTB > LET 'SKEW2'=MEAN(C3)/((STD(C1))**3)
MTB > PRINT 'SKEW2'
# SKEW2 = 1.61062 MORE SKEWED THAN THE NORMAL
MTB > LET 'KURT'=MEAN(C4)/((STDEV(C1))**4)
MTB > PRINT 'KURT'
# KURT = 6.31463  MORE PEAKED THAN THE NORMAL
```

CHAPTER 14

Some Statistical Aspects of Quality Control

OBJECTIVES

❖ Introduce control charts for statistical process control (SPC)

❖ Distinguish between qualitative attribute control charts and quantitative variables control charts

❖ Describe acceptance sampling

❖ Evaluate sampling plan performance with an operating characteristic curve

PRELUDE

The more competitive the marketplace, the more a product must satisfy the requirements of the consumer. Consumers demand that products are fit for use in function and in form. In the eyes of the consumer, for example, an automobile must not only function as "a good car should," but its form, look, and feel must satisfy the potential owner enough for a purchase to occur and for use to continue. Therefore, quality is fitness for use that meets the individual needs of the consumer.

Over time, the achievement of quality in a manufactured product or in a service requires excellence in product design, manufacture, and performance. Thus, an excellent system (people, concepts, and machines) must be in place to sustain the production of quality products. When something goes wrong in a process, it must be fixed. Because people fix and solve problems, quality is more of people doing things right and solving problems than a collection of techniques. As a result, quality is not statistics, even though statistical process control uses statistical tools and product design can be improved through the design of experiments.

Achieving quality requires in-depth, on-the-job experience with consumers, suppliers, and producers. Thorough knowledge is needed about what consumers want, what the product design parameters are, what the production process is like, how the people in the organization work together, and what statistical methods are useful.

Most of what you need to know to achieve quality comes from experience in the workplace. This puts the inexperienced in a difficult position; they have too many things to learn too fast. The purpose of this chapter is to ease on-the-job learning by presenting statistical tools proven helpful in quality improvement and taught worldwide. ◈

METHODS OF STATISTICAL PROCESS CONTROL

A product's quality characteristics must meet the customer's needs. Therefore, the quality characteristics must be on target with little variability. Then, because of relatively stable conditions, production processes can produce quality products repeatedly. Nevertheless, sporadic breakdowns in system stability occur. They must be identified and the problems must be corrected. Furthermore, efforts must be made to reduce variability. These accomplishments are aided by problem-solving tools used to carry out **statistical process control (SPC).** For example, a **control chart** is a well-known SPC tool.

An Introduction to Control Charts

If you have four new tires installed on your car, you expect small lead weights to be attached to the rims for balancing. The amount of lead needed is likely to differ from wheel to wheel. Therefore, even though the tires all look the same, apparently they are not the same. The manufacturer cannot produce tires that are perfect clones of one another. There will be variation from tire to tire in balance, weight, amount of rubber, diameter, tread width, tread depth, and so on.

Variation also exists in other car parts. From pistons to bolts, parts that look the same do not have identical measurements. Variability in quality characteristics is universal. It extends across the spectrum of products you buy, from the volume of soda in a bottle to the weight of corn chips or cereal boxes.

In many production processes variability can be reduced, which results in better products. Variability reductions are often expensive and require changing product design parameters, production systems, and raw materials. Even if we assume that a company has been successful in reducing variability, some residual amount usually remains and persists over time.

Control charts are magnificent tools for tracking quality measurements over time. They draw management's attention to things that go wrong, which are out-of-control production situations. When a process is running smoothly and in a state of statistical control, a predictably large percentage of the quality measurements will fall between the control chart's upper control limit (UCL) and lower control limit (LCL), causing no alarm. While the process is in a state of control, only a very small percentage of the time will a measurement stray beyond these limits and cause false alarms. The variability that is seen is expected. This **chance variability** is indigenous to the current state of product design, process operation, and raw material conditions.

The problem with real-life production processes is that things do go wrong. Processes do not stay in a state of statistical control forever. Randomly, processes tend to jump out of control, producing products that are flawed because of a **defective** or **nonconforming quality characteristic.** When a process goes out of control, unusual patterns in quality measures stand out on a control chart. Unusual patterns in quality measures might be due to a shift in the mean or an increase in the variability. Perhaps the out-of-control measurements (plotted as points on the control chart) are beyond the control limits, or perhaps sequences of points satisfy certain out-of-control rules that you will be introduced to.

In any case, control charts are likely to alert management that an out-of-control condition has occurred. Then, the variability in the quality characteristic being measured is no longer due to chance variability alone. The variability now reflects **assignable causes** as well, such as a maladjusted machine, an operator mistake, or bad raw materials. Once alerted, management must find the cause of the problem and get it fixed.

Usually, the fix is not simple, like sticking your thumb in a hole in a dam to stop the water flow. More likely the problem solution is not obvious, and the problem will take time to fix. A team of knowledgeable people has to be formed. They must meet and theorize as to the cause of the problem. They test the theories until they find the root cause of the problem. Other magnificent statistical tools can be useful at this stage, such as the histogram, data collection or **check sheets, Pareto charts, cause and effect diagrams, defect concentration diagrams,** and scatterplots. You have already learned about many of these statistical tools in previous chapters.

TYPES OF CONTROL CHARTS

Two broad classes of control charts are **Shewhart control charts** and **special control charts.**

Shewhart Control Charts

While working at AT&T Bell Laboratories, Dr. Walter Shewhart developed what has become the classical control chart. (See Chapter 1, page 15; Chapter 5, Example 7, page 231; and Chapter 7, Example 17, page 333 for earlier exposure to the control chart.) Depending on the nature of the data and the probability theory in the background, management picks a Shewhart chart that fits a production situation. For example, one might be working with the means (averages) of piston diameters, which follow a normal probability distribution. An appropriate control chart would be for average piston diameters, an *average chart* or $\bar{y}$ chart.

On the other hand, if one is working with the percent nonconforming glass bottles, which follows a binomial probability distribution, an appropriate control chart would be for percentages of nonconforming glass bottles, a **p chart.**

The p chart for percentages and the $\bar{y}$ chart for averages are members of two different categories of Shewhart control charts, which are categorized by variable types: (1) **qualitative attribute variables** (working with discrete-based measures such as percentages and counts) or (2) **quantitative variables** (working with continuous-based measures such as individual measurements, means, and ranges).

Each control chart category has several types of control charts as members. In production situations, different charts focus on particular aspects of the nonconformity data. When the nature of the nonconformity is a qualitative attribute variable (say, nonconforming glass bottles), you have a choice of four different control charts: (1) a p chart for percentages of nonconforming bottles produced; (2) an **np chart** for the number of bottles that have at least one nonconformity; (3) a **c chart** for the number of imperfections of various types on each bottle; or (4) a **u chart** for the number of imperfections per unit area of various types on each bottle, where the bottle size may vary.

In the second Shewhart control chart category, the nature of the nonconformity measure is a quantitative variable (say, piston diameters). Usually, two companion charts work together. One of the control charts monitors the process central tendency (such as the average of the diameter measurements). Thus, an off-center production process can be detected. The companion to this chart monitors the variability (such as the range of piston diameter measurements). Thus, production processes with too much variability can be identified.

For monitoring the central tendency of a process, some commonly used charts are (1) an **individual measurement chart** (also called **i chart, x chart,** or **y chart**); (2) an **average $\bar{y}$ chart** (also called **ybar** or **xbar** chart); and (3) a **moving average ma chart.**

For monitoring the variability of a process, some commonly used charts are (1) a **range r chart;** (2) a **standard deviation s chart;** and (3) a **moving range mr chart.**

The nature of the quantitative production data suggests which central tendency and variability charts should be used together. For example, an mr chart is the usual companion to an individual measurements chart. This is because a single production measurement per period does not provide enough observations to calculate the standard deviation, which would be needed for an s chart. If several production measurements per period are taken with sample sizes of ten or more, an s chart takes advantage of the standard deviation's efficiency at larger sample sizes. Then, an average $\bar{y}$ chart and an s chart would be used together. When the sample size is between two and ten, an r chart replaces the s chart because of the efficiency of the range statistic and its ease of calculation.

In practice, a variability chart is constructed first to see if the process variability is in a state of statistical control. Until it is, it makes no sense to chart central tendency because an *in-control* variability measure is needed to compute the control limits on a chart for central tendency. In spite of this practice, most textbooks present a chart for central tendency before a chart for variability. Probably, this is because an average in a $\overline{y}$ chart is easier for the beginner to understand than a range or standard deviation.

Special Control Charts

Special control charts tend to be more complex than Shewhart charts; therefore, examples will not be given here. For the price of the added complexity, these charts tend to alarm sooner. A notable special control chart is the **cumulative sum chart (CUSUM).** The cumulative sums can be computed for practically any statistic, such as percentages, means, ranges, and so on. Therefore, the CUSUM chart is very flexible and it alarms quickly.

Several examples of Shewhart-type control charts follow.

A p Chart for Percent Defective

When independent output items of a production process can be designated as defective or nondefective with a constant probability, the percentage of defective items can be monitored by constructing a p chart. Thus, the p chart relies on the same underlying conditions as the binomial probability distribution. The intent is for this chart to detect changes in the probability of a defective item as reflected in the sample percentage of defective items.

EXAMPLE 1

A DEMONSTRATION OF A PERCENTAGE, p CHART

Many people do not believe something unless they see a demonstration of it. To teach both the theory and the practice of control charting, classical demonstrations have been a part of quality control lectures and presentations since the inception of these methods. To display the variability in quality measurements and to illustrate the mechanics of control chart operations, boxes of colored beads (or marbles) have been employed. Bead colors, for example, can represent attributes such as defective or nondefective products. Thus, the known population proportion of defectives can be compared to sample proportions, which are obtained during a demonstration. After such basic concepts are understood, actual production examples and exercises become easier to follow.

Wadsworth, Stephens, and Godfrey used both beads and chips as demonstration props in two entire introductory chapters.[1] First they utilized a large box of colored beads—white, red, yellow, and black. For each color, the total bead count was known and used to compute the population proportions.

For 20 samples of 100 beads, the 20 sample proportions of red beads (representing defective, nonconforming product) were plotted on a p chart. The plotting points represented a manufacturing process that was running smoothly in a state of statistical control. The sample proportions were used to compute control limits for the chart.

Problem Solution (c)   The actual counts of defectives in samples 1–20, 21–30, and 31–40 are shown below in columns C1, C2, and C3.

ROW	C1	C2	C3
1	6	7	0
2	7	9	0
3	4	10	0
4	5	8	0
5	4	3	0
6	10	7	0
7	6	6	1
8	0	8	1
9	2	11	1
10	5	9	0
11	7		
12	7		
13	1		
14	2		
15	3		
16	4		
17	3		
18	2		
19	4		
20	2		

The means of the number of defectives are shown below. Clearly, the mean shifts up and then down as the defective rate changes.

	N	MEAN
C1	20	4.200
C2	10	7.800
C3	10	0.300

The dotplots below show location shifts as the defective rate changes. A variability decrease is evident in the last dotplot.

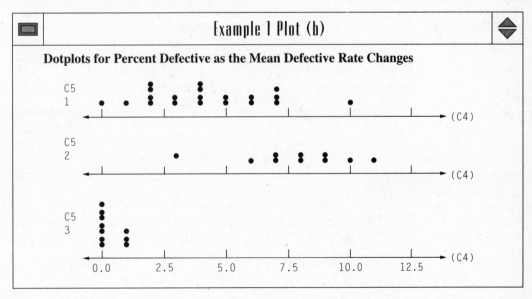

Example 1 Plot (b)

Dotplots for Percent Defective as the Mean Defective Rate Changes

p Chart Formulas When the defective rate, p, is known, the control limits on a p chart are established by the following formula:

$$p \pm 3\sqrt{\frac{p(1-p)}{n}}$$

When p is unknown, it is estimated by $\hat{p}$ from in-control samples. The control limits are

$$\hat{p} \pm 3\sqrt{\frac{\hat{p}(1-\hat{p})}{n}}$$

These control limits are based on confidence intervals on proportions.

np Chart Formulas An np chart is similar to a p chart because the counts of defectives in an np chart are simply converted to fractions in the p chart. Practically, the decision to choose one of these charts over the other depends on whether counts or percentages are more meaningful to the user. Also, it makes sense to keep the sample size constant in an np chart.

When p is known, the np chart formulation is

$$np \pm 3\sqrt{np(1-p)}$$

When p is unknown, it is estimated by $\hat{p}$ from in-control samples.

S T A T I S T I C A L   H I G H L I G H T S

The p charts and np charts are control charts for qualitative attribute variables.

Control Charts for Averages and Ranges

Another classical demonstration in quality control utilizes a bowl of numbered chips. The numbers on the chips represent measurements of a quantitative quality characteristic. Samples of chips represent product measurements that vary. A control chart for averages monitors the central tendency of the measurements while a control chart for ranges monitors the variability. As a result of the Central Limit Theorem, averages of quantitative measurements tend to be normally distributed. This is a tendency that the chart of averages relies on. The following demonstration illustrates how charts for ranges and averages work together.

E X A M P L E 2

A DEMONSTRATION OF AN AVERAGE $\bar{y}$ CHART
(ybar OR xbar CHART) AND AN r CHART FOR VARIABILITY

In a demonstration described by Wadsworth, Stephens, and Godfrey, each chip in a bowl is marked with one of the following numbers. $-5, -4, -3, -2, -1, 0, +1, +2, +3, +4,$ and $+5.$[2] These numbers represent deviations from nominal filling weight of jars of a medicated cream. The number of chips in the bowl is very large, and the distribution of these numbers is approximately normal. As a result, it is more likely that we will draw a chip marked, say, 0 or 1 than 4 or 5.

The demonstration progresses as follows: **1.** When a production process is in a state of statistical control, the chip markings have a mean of 0 and a standard deviation of 1.72. Then, control limits are established from samples of chips. **2.** Next, the mean is shifted to 2 and the standard deviation remains at 1.72. More samples are taken. The control chart for sample means alarms to detect this mean shift. **3.** Finally, the mean shifts back to 0, as it was when the process was in control. However, the standard deviation is increased to 3.47, which drives the variability out of control. An r chart detects this increase in variability.

In place of a physical demonstration of drawing chips from a bowl, a computer simulation is used here. Therefore, it is easy for you to experiment with simulations of your own.

Problem Statement (a)   Simulate 20 samples, each of five measurements (chip markings), from a normal distribution with a mean of 0 and a standard deviation of 1.72. Determine if the variability is in control with an r chart. If it is, construct a control chart for sample averages.

Problem Solution (a)   For the first 20 samples of size five, the ranges are plotted on the r chart below. Because there are no out-of-control points, the variability is in control.

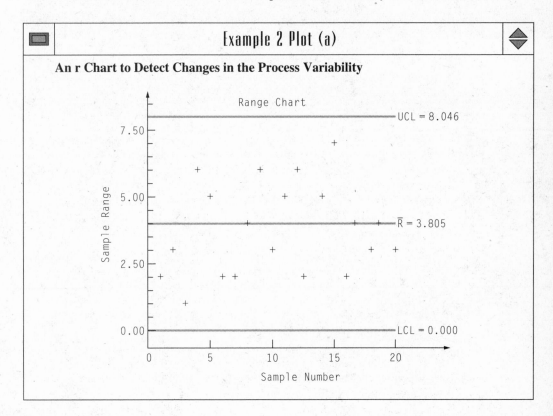

For the first 20 samples of size five, the sample means are plotted on the xbar chart below. The absence of out-of-control points indicates that the process is centered and in control.

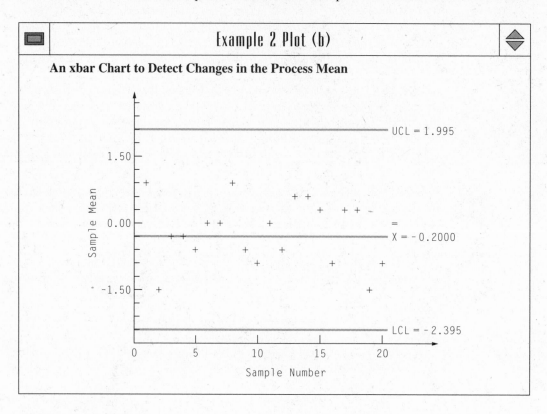

Problem Statement (b) Take 10 additional samples, each of five measurements (chip markings), from a normal distribution with a mean shifted to 2 and a standard deviation of 1.72. Determine if the variability is in control with an r chart. Include these results on the control chart for sample averages.

Problem Solution (b) Ten additional samples of size five are taken (in addition to the original 20 samples) and all 30 sample ranges are shown in Plot (c). The r chart indicates that the variability is in control because the standard deviation has remained at 1.72, even though the mean has been shifted upward to 2.

Recall that 10 additional samples of size five have been taken (in addition to the original 20 samples) and all 30 sample means are shown in Plot (d). The last 10 samples produce alarms on the xbar chart, indicating that the process is out of control, as expected, because the mean has been shifted upward to 2.

Several tests alarm simultaneously here. Any one test alarm is enough for us to take action to fix a production problem. Sometimes particular tests might provide clues as to the nature of difficult production problems. For example, six points in a row that are increasing or decreasing might indicate machine tool wear.

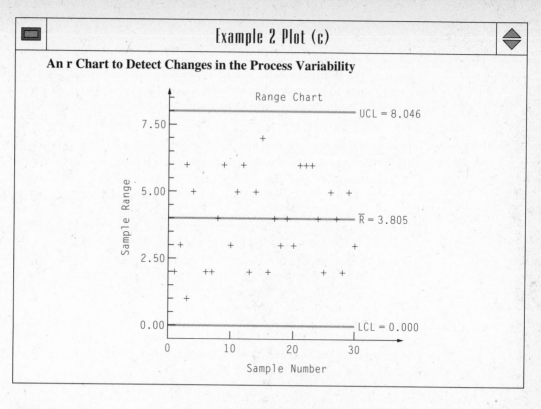

An r Chart to Detect Changes in the Process Variability

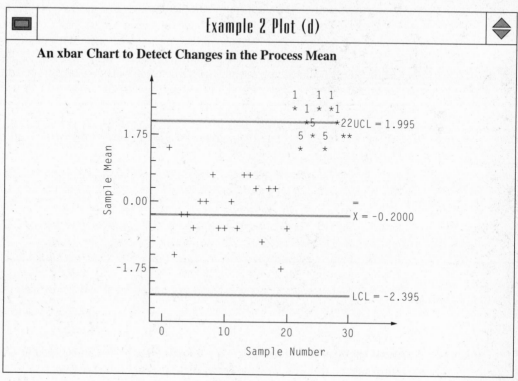

An xbar Chart to Detect Changes in the Process Mean

Because the distribution of sample means tends to be normal, four additional tests are applicable. These tests are numbered 5 through 8. Test 7 did not alarm and is not shown. Test 7 alarms if 15 points in a row are in zones C, above or below the centerline.

The alarms for each test are

Test 1. One point beyond zone A. The test failed at points 21, 23, 25, 27, and 28.

Test 2. Nine points in a row in zone C or beyond (on one side of CL). The test failed at points 29 and 30.

Test 5. Two of 3 points in a row in zone A or beyond (on one side of CL). The test failed at points 22, 23, 24, 25, 26, 27, 28, 29, and 30.

Test 6. Four of 5 points in a row in zone B or beyond (on one side of CL). The test failed at points 24, 25, 26, 27, 28, 29, and 30.

Test 8. Eight points in a row beyond zone C (above and below CL). The test failed at points 28, 29, and 30.

Problem Statement (c) Take 10 additional samples of measurements (chip markings) from a normal distribution with the mean shifted back to 0 and the standard deviation increased to 3.47. Determine if the variability is in control with an r chart. Include these results on the control chart for sample averages.

Problem Solution (c) Ten additional samples of size five are taken (in addition to the 30 samples accumulated so far) and all 40 sample ranges are shown in Plot (e). The last 10 sample ranges produce alarms on the r chart, indicating that the variability of the process is out of control, as we expected, because the standard deviation has more than doubled.

Recall that 10 additional samples of size five have been taken (in addition to the 30 samples accumulated so far) and all 40 sample means are shown in Plot (f). The last 10 samples produce alarms on the xbar chart, indicating that the process is out of control, as we might expect because the variability went out of control on the previous r chart. For the last 10 samples, the mean is 0 and the standard deviation shifted upward to 3.47.

The alarms are

Test 1. One point beyond zone A. The test failed at points 21, 23, 25, 27, 28, 33, and 39.

Test 2. Nine points in a row in zone C or beyond (on one side of CL). The test failed at points 29, 30, 31, and 32.

Test 5. Two of 3 points in a row in zone A or beyond (on one side of CL). The test failed at points 22, 23, 24, 25, 26, 27, 28, 29, and 30.

Test 6. Four of 5 points in a row in zone B or beyond (on one side of CL). The test failed at points 24, 25, 26, 27, 28, 29, 30, 31, 37, 38, and 39.

Test 8. Eight points in a row beyond zones C (above and below CL). The test failed at points 28, 29, 30, and 31.

Problem Statement (d) Find summary statistics for the 40 sample means. Construct dotplots of sample means from each of the three scenarios described above.

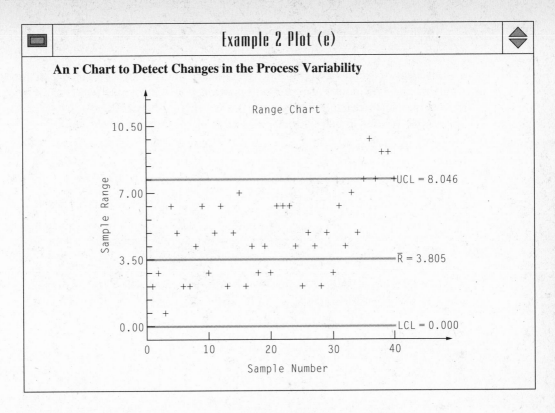

Example 2 Plot (e)

An r Chart to Detect Changes in the Process Variability

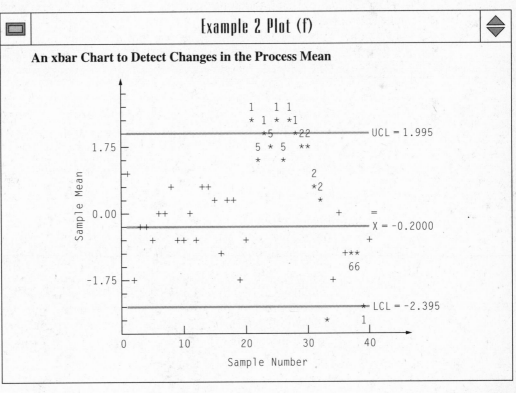

Example 2 Plot (f)

An xbar Chart to Detect Changes in the Process Mean

Problem Solution (d) Descriptive statistics and dotplots are shown for each of the three scenarios—20 points in control, 10 points out of control (due to a mean shift), and 10 points out of control (due to a variance shift). Column C7 is assigned values 1, 2, or 3 to partition the sample means C6 into the three classes to identify the three scenarios.

	C7	N	MEAN	STDEV	
C6	1	20	-0.200	0.734	
	2	10	1.940	0.443	mean increased
	3	10	-0.980	1.156	variance increased

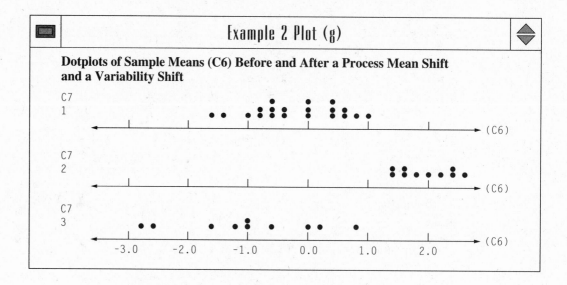

Example 2 Plot (g)

Dotplots of Sample Means (C6) Before and After a Process Mean Shift and a Variability Shift

Formulas for a Control Chart for Sample Means A formula for computing control limits for sample means is discussed here. If y is normally distributed with a mean μ and a standard deviation σ, then there is a $(1 - \alpha)$ probability that the sample mean, $\overline{y}$, will be in the following interval.

$$\mu \pm z_{(\alpha/2)}\left(\frac{\sigma}{n^{1/2}}\right)$$

Customarily, $z_{(\alpha/2=.0013)} = 3$ and the above interval forms the lower and upper control limits on a control chart. Unfortunately, μ and σ are generally unknown and have to be estimated from data. Therefore, the control limit formulas get slightly more complicated. The μ is estimated by the mean of $\overline{y}$'s from each of the samples, and σ is estimated from ranges or standard deviations. MINITAB makes these calculations with standard formulas available in the MINITAB reference manual.

EXAMPLE 3

AN AVERAGE ȳ-CHART (ybar OR xbar CHART) AND AN r CHART IN PRACTICE

Problem Statement (a)   In the packaging of a cornmeal product, samples of four packages are weighed periodically. Use 25 such samples of four to establish control charts for ranges and means. At first establish trial limits using all 25 samples.

Problem Solution (a)   Trial control limits are shown for ranges (variability) and for means (central tendency).

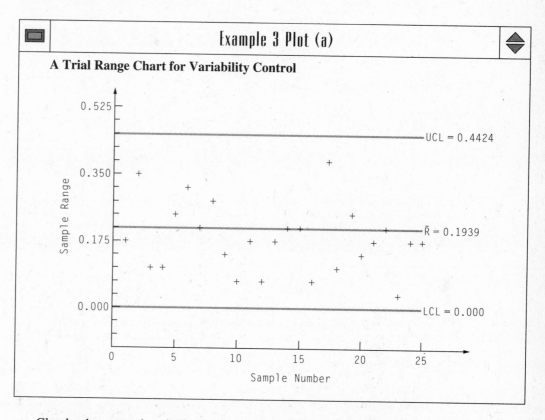

Example 3 Plot (a)

A Trial Range Chart for Variability Control

Clearly, the range chart indicates that the variability is in control. The xbar chart (Plot (b)) shows that three points are out of control, two above the UCL and one below the LCL.

Problem Statement (b)   Three out-of-control points have assignable causes. In two cases, there was overfilling due to filling-machine operator error. In a third case, there was underfilling due to partial clogging of a feeder chute. Calculate revised limits by deleting the

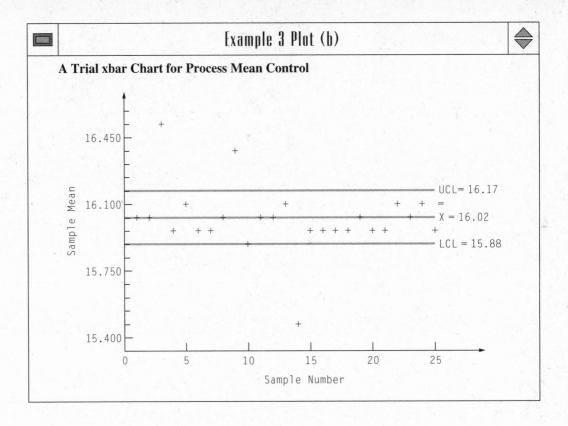

Example 3 Plot (b)

A Trial xbar Chart for Process Mean Control

out-of-control points from the control limit computations. Nevertheless, continue to show all the plotting points on the revised charts.

Problem Solution (b) Revised limits are shown for ranges (variability) and means (central tendency). In Appendix 1, the MINITAB subcommand ESTIMATE is used to delete the out-of-control points from the control limit calculations. Nevertheless, all points continue to be plotted.

Again, the variability is in control because no points are beyond the control limits (Plot (c)). Notice that the numerical values of the control limits have changed because of the recomputation for revised limits. These revised control limits will be used to monitor package weight variability as production continues.

Again, the MINITAB subcommand ESTIMATE is used to delete the out-of-control points from the control limit calculations. Nevertheless, all points continue to be plotted. Three sample means are out of control, as you can see in Plot (d). Notice that the numerical values of the control limits change because of the recomputation. These revised control limits will be used to monitor package weight central tendency as production continues.

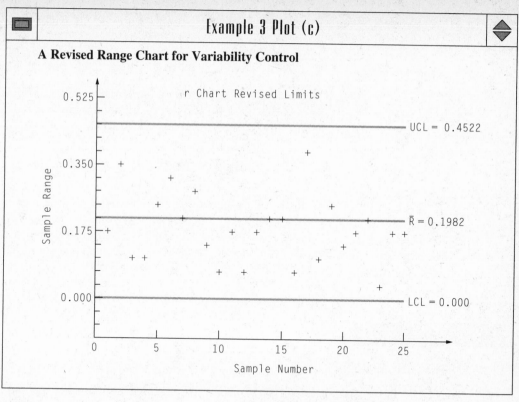

Example 3 Plot (c)

A Revised Range Chart for Variability Control

r Chart Revised Limits

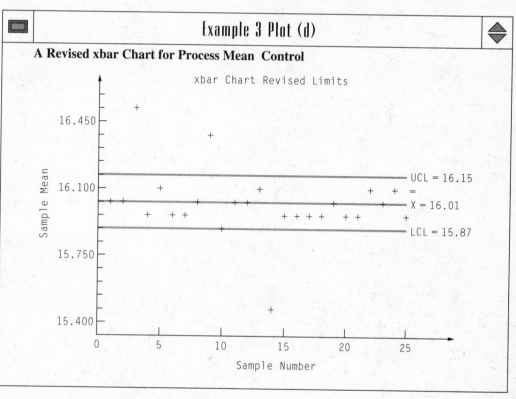

Example 3 Plot (d)

A Revised xbar Chart for Process Mean Control

xbar Chart Revised Limits

┌───┐
│ S T A T I S T I C A L   H I G H L I G H T S   │
│   │
│ The xbar and r charts are for quantitative variables. Typically, the r chart │
│ is used first to see if the variability is in control. If the variability is in │
│ control, it makes sense to use an xbar chart.   │
└───┘

A Control Chart for Counts of Nonconformities

When processes produce independent items of the same size (or group size), the count of the number of nonconformities on each item (or in each group) may be monitored by a c chart. The nonconformities can be of different types. However, each must have a small constant probability of occurrence and a very large number of opportunities to occur. Thus, the c chart depends on the conditions associated with the Poisson distribution. The intent is for this chart to detect changes in the probability of a nonconformity that is reflected in the mean number of nonconformities.

EXAMPLE 4

FLAWS IN YOUR JEANS

In the manufacture of denim jeans, the following are counts of the total number of flaws in each of 25 production runs of 100 jeans in each run. Each pair of jeans might have one or more flaws. The production process was in a state of statistical control.

23 15 16 20 18 17 16 15 12 13 21 12 24 19 16
17 20 12 20 20 23 21 16 21 16

Problem Statement (a) Summarize these figures.

Problem Solution (a)

```
Variable   N    Mean   Median   StDev    SEMean
PRFLAWS   25   17.72   17.00    3.542     0.71

Variable        Min     Max       Q1       Q3
PRFLAWS       12.00   24.00    15.50    20.50
```

Problem Statement (b) Determine if the next 10 production runs are in control. Use the above figures to establish a c chart for monitoring the flaw counts in the next 10 production runs, which are

20 24 22 25 22 16 18 32 18 31

Problem Solution (b) The following c chart shows that two points are out of control with 32 and 31 flaws.

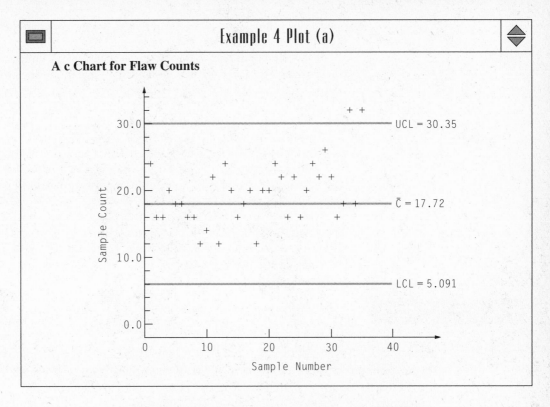

c Chart Formulas   When the mean count, c, is known, the control limits on a c chart are established by the following formula:

$$c \pm 3\sqrt{c}$$

When c is unknown, it is estimated by $\bar{c}$ from in-control samples. The control limits are

$$\bar{c} \pm 3\sqrt{\bar{c}}$$

For the Poisson distribution, the square root of the mean is the standard deviation, which appears in the above formulas.

ACCEPTANCE SAMPLING PLANS BASED ON ATTRIBUTES

Often it makes good business sense to inspect large batches (or **lots**) of mass-produced commodities. Sometimes these items are critical parts, and incoming defectives can't be tolerated by the buyer. Frequently, suppliers are under contract to guarantee high, outgoing quality levels.

When 100% inspection is not economical, **acceptance sampling plans** can be used. Simple acceptance sampling plans are defined by two numbers chosen by the user: (1) n, the sample size, and (2) c; the allowable number of defectives in the sample. The sampling plan is used to make accept or reject decisions on the whole lot of items.

If the actual number of defectives, d, in a random sample is less than or equal to the allowable number of defectives c, $d \leq c$, the whole lot is **accepted.** If $d > c$, the whole lot is **rejected.** When each accept/reject decision is based on a single sample, the plan is called a **single sampling plan.** The more complex *double* and *multiple sampling plans* will not be discussed here.

Customarily, if the inspection or testing is nondestructive, rejected lots are subjected to 100% inspection and all defectives are replaced by nondefectives. This procedure is referred to as **rectifying** the rejected lot. Rectification is fundamental to what are known as **Dodge-Romig sampling plans,** which submit all rejected lots to 100% inspection. The same is true for the widely used military standard, **MIL STD 105D,** and its civilian derivative, **ANSI/ASQC Z1.4.** These are **sampling systems** in which several simple plans can be used in concert for normal, tightened and reduced inspection. Switching between normal, tightened and reduced inspection adjusts the plan to the vendor's recent quality history.

EXAMPLE 5

AN ACCEPTANCE SAMPLING PLAN IN ACTION

The mechanics of a simple sampling plan, based on attributes, are developed in this example. The lots are large enough so that the defective rate p is approximately constant at 10%. Fifteen samples (rows) of size n = 10 (columns C1–C10) are shown below. The number 1 indicated a defective and 0 a nondefective. C11 is a count of the number of defectives in a row. There are no defectives in rows 1–4, 9, and 11. One defective is in rows 5–7, 10, and 12–13. Three defectives are in rows 14–15. Four defectives are in row 8.

Problem Statement (a)   Plan (1): n = 10 and c = 0. A sampling plan consists of two numbers chosen by the user. Suppose the sample size is n = 10, and the allowable number of defectives in the sample is c = 0. Which lots are accepted under this criterion, and what is the rejection rate?

Problem Solution (a)   Because no defectives are in the following rows, accept lots 1, 2, 3, 4, 9, and 11 (lot numbers are the same as row numbers). This sampling plan leads to a high lot rejection rate because 9 of 15 ($\frac{9}{15}$) lots are rejected.

ROW	C1	C2	C3	C4	C5	C6	C7	C8	C9	C10	C11
1	0	0	0	0	0	0	0	0	0	0	0
2	0	0	0	0	0	0	0	0	0	0	0
3	0	0	0	0	0	0	0	0	0	0	0
4	0	0	0	0	0	0	0	0	0	0	0
5	0	0	0	0	0	0	0	0	1	0	1
6	0	0	0	1	0	0	0	0	0	0	1
7	0	0	0	0	0	1	0	0	0	0	1

ROW	C1	C2	C3	C4	C5	C6	C7	C8	C9	C10	C11
8	0	1	0	1	0	1	0	0	0	1	4
9	0	0	0	0	0	0	0	0	0	0	0
10	0	0	0	0	0	0	0	1	0	0	1
11	0	0	0	0	0	0	0	0	0	0	0
12	0	0	0	0	0	0	0	1	0	0	1
13	0	1	0	0	0	0	0	0	0	0	1
14	1	0	1	0	0	0	1	0	0	0	3
15	0	0	1	1	0	0	0	0	1	0	3

Problem Statement (b)   Plan (2): $n = 10$ and $c = 1$. If the sample size is $n = 10$ and the allowable number of defectives in the sample is $c = 1$, which lots are accepted under this criterion, and what is the rejection rate?

Problem Solution (b)   Accept lots 1, 2, 3, 4, 9, and 11 because no defectives are in those rows. Also accept lots 5, 6, 7, 10, 12, and 13 because there is one defective in each of these rows, and one defective is allowable in this plan. This second sampling plan leads to a lower lot rejection rate because $\frac{3}{15}$ of the lots are rejected.

Probslem Statement (c)   List two other plans that arise by continuing to increase c while fixing n. Are these plans more or less discriminating? What would you expect with c fixed and n increasing?

Problem Solution (c)   Other plans that might be considered are Plan (3): $n = 10$ and $c = 2$, Plan (4): $n = 10$ and $c = 3$, and so on. As c increases while n is fixed, the plans become less and less discriminating. With c fixed and n increasing, the plans become more and more discriminating. You may wish to experiment with different sample sizes by modifying the MINITAB commands in Appendix 1.

Problem Statement (d)   Use MINITAB to summarize column C11, which is a count of the number of defectives in a row.

Problem Solution (d)   A TALLY command computes the number of lots that are accepted for a given choice of the allowable number of defectives. If $c = 0$, accept 6 lots. If $c = 1$, accept $6 + 6 = 12$ lots. If $c = 3$, accept $6 + 6 + 2 = 14$ lots. If $c = 4$, accept all 15 lots.

```
     C11  COUNT
       0     6
       1     6
       3     2
       4     1
Total Count = 15
```

Problem Statement (e)   To gauge the performance of potential sampling plans, conduct a larger experiment. Expanding beyond the 15 samples shown above, take 100 new samples under the same conditions. Summarize plan performance.

Problem Solution (e)   Percents and cumulative percents summarize plan performance. For example, if n = 10 and c = 1, 75% of the time lots are accepted. If n = 10 and c = 2, 96% of the lots are accepted. For further evaluation, a histogram and descriptive statistics of the defective counts in 100 samples are shown also.

```
      C11  COUNT PERCENT CUMPCT

        0    34    34.00  34.00
        1    41    41.00  75.00
        2    21    21.00  96.00
        3     4     4.00 100.00
```

```
Total Count = 100
Histogram of C11    N = 100

Midpoint   Count

   0       34  **********************************
   1       41  *****************************************
   2       21  *********************
   3        4  ****
```

```
           N    MEAN   MEDIAN  TRMEAN   STDEV   SEMEAN
C11      100  0.9500  1.0000  0.9000  0.8454  0.0845

                MIN     MAX      Q1      Q3
C11          0.0000  3.0000  0.0000  1.7500
```

OPERATING CHARACTERISTIC CURVE FOR A TYPICAL SAMPLING PLAN

As you learned in the last example, at a fixed population percent defective, a sampling plan's performance measure is the percentage of the time that lots are accepted. For example, if n = 10 and c = 1, 75% of the time lots are accepted. If n = 10 and c = 2, 96% of the lots are accepted.

For a fixed sampling plan in which n = 10 and c = 2, let the population percent defective change. In Exhibit 1, the population percent defective has the following values: 10, 30, 50, 70, and 90. Thus, from 10 to 90, lots get worse and worse. For a particular plan, say, n = 10 and c = 2, we are interested in the probability that a lot is accepted as the population percent defective gets worse.

In the plot in Exhibit 1, the probability that a lot is accepted, C14, drops off quickly as the percent defective, C20, is increased. In general, the probability of accepting drops off more quickly if the sample size is increased and c is decreased.

This plot is an **operating characteristic (OC) curve,** for the sampling plan. Each sampling plan has an operating characteristic curve that is used to evaluate the plan's performance as the population percent defective changes.

EXHIBIT 1 Approximate Operating Characteristic Curve

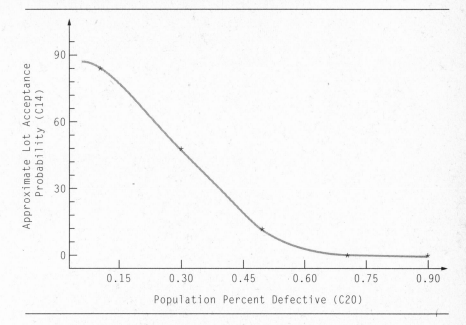

If the probability of accepting is too high for a specific plan at a specific population percent defective, the values of n and c can be changed appropriately to arrive at a new plan that gets the job done. Of course, since this plot is based on a simulation, it approximates the true operating characteristic curve that is based on probability theory.

Theoretical Operating Characteristic Curve

The approximate operating characteristic curve shown in Exhibit 1 was based on a simulation. The true operating characteristic curve can be obtained from probability theory. For a specific plan, once values of n and c are chosen, the probability of accepting is a function of p, the population proportion defective. For large lots, where p is approximately constant, a binomial probability distribution applies, and the probability of accepting a lot given p, n, and c is

$$P(\text{accept}|_{p,\,n,\,c}) = \sum_{y=0}^{c} \binom{n}{y} p^y (1 - p)^{(n-y)}$$

For n = 10, c = 2, and letting p = .05, .10, . . . , .95, the probabilities of accepting are found with the MINITAB commands in Appendix 1. The probability of accepting versus p is shown in the theoretical operating characteristic curve in Exhibit 2.

EXHIBIT 2 Theoretical Operating Characteristic Curve

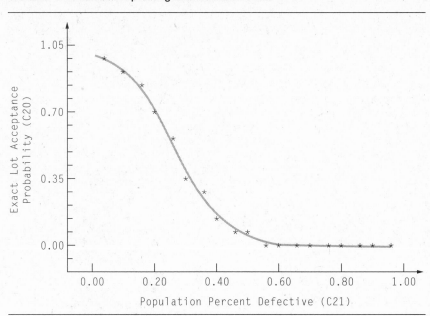

THE POISSON APPROXIMATION OF THE BINOMIAL

When p is very small and n is very large, the mean, np, is moderate and less than about 25. Under these circumstances, binomial probability calculations are burdensome even for the computer. As a result, a Poisson distribution is used to approximate the binomial. The following binomial accept probabilities are replaced by the Poisson probabilities for operating characteristic curves under the stated conditions.

$$\text{(binomial)} \quad P(\text{accept}\,|_{p,n,c}) = \sum_{y=0}^{c} \binom{n}{y} p^y (1 - p)^{(n-y)}$$

$$\text{(Poisson)} \quad P(\text{accept}\,|_{p,n,c}) = \sum_{y=0}^{c} \frac{(np)^y e^{-np}}{y!}$$

You can experiment with this approximation by modifying the MINITAB commands in Appendix 1. When c = 2 and n = 10, the accept probabilities can be calculated in MINITAB for the binomial distribution.

```
MTB > CDF 2 PUT C1;   # CALCULATING ACCEPT PROBABILITIES
SUBC> BINOMIAL N=10 P=.05.
```

To approximate the binomial distribution with the Poisson, use

```
MTB > CDF 2 PUT C1;   # CALCULATING ACCEPT PROBABILITIES
SUBC> POISSON MU=.5.
```

USING THE HYPERGEOMETRIC DISTRIBUTION
FOR SMALL LOT SIZES

When the lot size, N, is small (less than 50) and n items are sampled, the assumption that p is constant is no longer true. Therefore, neither the binomial nor the Poisson distribution is applicable. Under such circumstances the hypergeometric distribution must be used to determine the exact probabilities. Therefore

$$P(\text{accept}\,|_{p,n,c}) = \sum_{y=0}^{c} \frac{\binom{Np}{y}\binom{N-Np}{n-y}}{\binom{N}{n}}$$

Unfortunately, MINITAB does not have a subcommand for the hypergeometric distribution, and probabilities are not computed.

THE AVERAGE OUTGOING QUALITY (AOQ)

If incoming lots have a population proportion defective, p, then, as a result of replacing (rectifying) all defective units found in rejected lots, the outgoing quality on average should be better than p. Therefore, the **average outgoing quality (AOQ)** is smaller than p because a sampling plan is used. Accepted lots may contain defectives because they are not 100% inspected and rectified. The AOQ measures the outgoing quality. It is computed by weighting p by the probability of accepting a lot.

$$AOQ \approx p \times P(\text{accept}\,|_{p,n,c})$$

For small lots of N items, the AOQ is adjusted by multiplying it by $\frac{N-n}{N}$. The operating characteristic curve in Exhibit 3 shows the accept probabilities for the sampling plan, n = 10 and c = 2. The plotting symbol is A. Plotting symbol B is also on the plot to represent the AOQ. Each value of p along the horizontal axis is multiplied by the corresponding accept probability to compute the AOQ for each value of p.

Notice that the AOQ curve has a maximum at about p = .22. The maximum is called the **average outgoing quality limit (AOQL).** This is the worst the outgoing quality can get for any value of p when using the current sampling plan.

EXHIBIT 3 Accept Probabilities (A's) and AOQ (B's) Versus Population Proportion Defective (p)

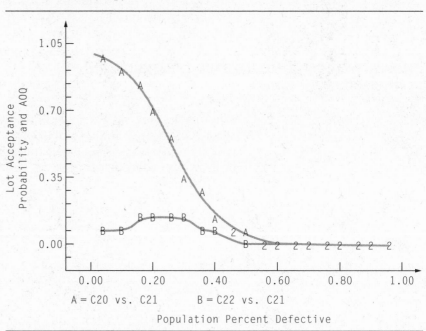

A = C20 vs. C21   B = C22 vs. C21

Population Percent Defective

PRODUCER'S AND CONSUMER'S RISKS

A sampling plan's AOQL protects a buyer of many lots against exceeding a certain fraction defective, provided that the lots are rectifiable.

When lots are not rectifiable, as in destructive testing, the AOQ and AOQL concepts are not applicable. Under these conditions the operating characteristic curve alone characterizes the protection that a sampling plan offers. This protection can be described in terms of the *producer's risk* and the *consumer's risk*.

Consumer's Risk

If the population proportion of defectives gets as bad as say, p_2, it is desirable to have a small probability of accepting a lot.

$$(\text{small}) \quad P(\text{accept}\,|_{p,n,c}) = \sum_{y=0}^{c} \binom{n}{y} p_2^y (1 - p_2)^{(n-y)}$$

Unfortunately, this small probability means that the consumer may accept some lots even though the proportion defective is as high as p_2. This accept probability is the **consumer's risk.**

Producer's Risk

If the population proportion of defectives is small enough to satisfy both the consumer and the producer, say p_1, it is desirable to have a large probability of accepting a lot.

$$\text{(large)} \quad P(\text{accept}|_{p,n,c}) = \sum_{y=0}^{c} \binom{n}{y} p_1^y (1 - p_1)^{(n-y)}$$

This large probability means that the consumer accepts a large proportion of the lots because the proportion defective is as low as p_1. The complement, $(1 - \text{the accept probability})$, is small and some good quality, p_1, lots are still rejected. The chances of getting rejected while doing a quality job is the **producer's risk,** which equals $(1 - \text{the accept probability})$.

The p_1 is called the **acceptable quality level (AQL).** The p_2 is called either the **limiting quality level (LQL),** or the **lot tolerance percent defective (LTPD).**

Initial reader exposure to this terminology, with AOQ, AOQL, AQL, LQL, and LTPD, is like looking into a bowl of alphabet soup. Yet, these terms are useful and very familiar to individuals who design and use sampling plans. Recall that a sampling plan consists of a value for the sample size, n, and the allowable number of defectives, c. The n and c are tabulated for different sampling systems and are simple to look up. For example, the military standard MIL STD 105D tables use the AQL to pick a column and the sample size, n, to pick a row. The allowable number of defectives, c, is found at the row-column intersection. Thus, the military standards MIL STD 105D are indexed by the AQL.

For another well-known set of sampling plans, the Dodge-Romig plans, a table is specified by the AOQL. The $p_{\text{process average}}$ is used to pick a column, and the lot size is used to pick a row. The allowable number of defectives, c, the sample size, n, and the LTPD are found at a row-column intersection.

CHAPTER SUMMARY

Quality is more a people thing—getting things right and solving problems—than a bunch of techniques. Quality is not statistics, even though statistical process control uses statistical tools such as control charts. Achieving quality requires in-depth, on-the-job experience with consumers, suppliers, and producers. Thorough knowledge is needed about what consumers want, what the product design parameters are, what the production process is, how the people in the organization work together, and what statistical methods are useful.

Most of what you need to know to produce quality products comes from experience in the workplace. This puts inexperienced people in a difficult position. They have too many things to learn too fast. This chapter helps simplify on-the-job-learning by presenting statistical tools that have proven helpful in quality improvement and are taught worldwide.

The control chart is a powerful process control tool designed to alert management that an out-of-control condition has occurred. Thus, the variability in the quality characteristic being measured is no longer due to chance variability alone but now reflects assignable causes as well, such as a maladjusted machine, an operator mistake, or bad raw materials. Once alerted, management must find the cause of the problem and get it fixed.

The two basic types of the classical Shewhart control chart are (1) those for qualitative attribute variables, working with percentages, counts, and so on, and (2) those for quantitative variables, working with individual measurements, means, ranges, and so on.

In this chapter we demonstrated a control chart for percent defective, a p chart. It is applicable to qualitative attribute variables, such as the proportion of nonconforming glass bottles that are produced. In contrast, when the nature of the nonconformity is a quantitative variable, such as piston diameters, two companion charts are used. For example, an xbar chart is used for central tendency, and an r chart is used for variability. We illustrated these companion charts as well as a c chart.

In addition to process control charts, acceptance sampling and inspection are useful tools in improving product quality. Often it makes good business sense to inspect large lots of mass-produced commodities. Sometimes these items are critical parts, and incoming defectives can't be tolerated by the buyer. Frequently, suppliers are under contract to guarantee high outgoing quality levels.

When 100% inspection is not economical, acceptance sampling plans can be used. Simple acceptance sampling plans require that two numbers be chosen by the user: (1) the sample size, n, and (2) the allowable number of defectives in the sample, c. A sampling plan is used to make accept or reject decisions on a complete lot of items. If the actual number of defectives, d, in a random sample is less than or equal to the allowable number of defectives, $d \leq c$, the whole lot is accepted. If $d > c$, the whole lot is rejected. Because each accept/reject decision is based on a single sample, such a plan is called a single sampling plan. Operating characteristic curves were found useful in evaluating a sampling plan's performance.

KEY TERMS

acceptable quality level (AQL), 705
acceptance sampling plans, 697
accepted, 698
ANSI/ASQC Z1.4, 698
assignable causes, 680
average chart, 681
average outgoing quality (AOQ), 703
average outgoing quality limit (AOQL), 703
c chart, 681
cause and effect diagrams, 680
chance variability, 679
check sheets, 680
consumer's risk, 704
control chart, 679
cumulative sum chart (CUSUM), 682
defect concentration diagrams, 680
defective quality characteristic, 680

Dodge-Romig sampling plans, 698
i chart, 681
individual measurement chart, 681
limiting quality level (LQL), 705
lot tolerance percent defective (LTPD), 705
lots, 697
MIL STD 105D, 698
moving average ma chart, 681
moving range mr chart, 681
nonconforming quality characteristic, 680
np chart, 681
operating characteristic (OC) curve, 700
p chart, 681
Pareto charts, 680
producer's risk, 705

qualitative attribute variables, 681
quantitative variables, 681
range r chart, 681
rectifying, 698
rejected, 698
sampling systems, 698
Shewhart control charts, 680
single sampling plan, 698
special control charts, 680
standard deviation s chart, 681
statistical process control (SPC), 679
u chart, 681
x chart, 681
xbar chart, 681
y chart, 681
ybar chart, 681

EXERCISES

1. Fiber pads used in clutches vary in thickness. Some of the variation is indigenous to the current state of product design, process operation, and raw materials.

(a) What is the term for this type of variation?

(b) If the variation in part (a) is the only source of variation and if the thickness measurements are in a state of statistical control, would you expect a control chart on thickness to alarm frequently or infrequently? Why?

(c) In addition to the variation specified in part (a), additional variation might be present due to assignable causes such as a maladjusted machine or shoddy raw materials. Does management expect control charts to detect this source of variability?

2. (a) Name a Shewhart control chart for a quantitative measurement such as piston diameter.

(b) Name a Shewhart control chart for a qualitative measurement such as the percentage of nonconforming glass bottles.

3. Several different Shewhart control charts are available for quantitative measurements. Usually two companion charts are used together. One chart monitors the central tendency of the measurement and its companion chart monitors the variation.

(a) Name two charts that might be used together.

(b) Until the variation is under control, does it make sense to construct a control chart for central tendency? Why?

4. In reference to control limits and the centerline on a control chart, what alarm condition rules would you provide a control chart user?

5. Construct a computer simulation like the bead demonstration described in the chapter. Use 20 samples of 100 beads with a defective rate of .06 (red beads represent defectives) to establish control limits on a p chart, assuming the

process is under control. Using these control chart limits, see if 10 more samples of 100 beads with a defective rate of .12 (red, black, and yellow beads represent defectives) result in an out-of-control condition. See if 10 more samples of 100 beads with a defective rate of .01 (black beads represent defectives) result in an out-of-control condition.

6. Simulate 20 samples of size five of deviations from nominal filling weights of jars of a medicated cream that follow a normal distribution with a mean of 0 and a standard deviation of 2.0.

(a) Determine if the variability is in control with an r chart. If the variability is in control, construct and evaluate a control chart for sample averages.

(b) Take 10 additional samples of size five from a normal distribution with a mean shifted to 2.5 and a standard deviation of 2.0. Using the control limits found when the process was in control in part (a), construct and evaluate an r chart and a control chart for sample averages.

(c) Take 10 additional samples of size five from a normal distribution with a mean shifted back to 0 and a standard deviation increased to 4.0. Using the control limits found in part (a), construct and evaluate an r chart and a control chart for sample averages.

(d) In reference to part (c), since the r chart includes out-of-control points, was the companion control chart for sample averages needed?

7. Cast iron parts used in truck assemblies are measured for tensile strength. Thirty samples of four castings were measured in thousands of pounds per square inch (RETRIEVE 'B:X14-7'):

61.20	60.18	61.19	61.42	63.01	61.03	60.38	62.38
59.43	61.51	62.50	61.36	59.79	61.22	59.76	60.38
61.87	61.88	60.41	61.62	61.64	61.53	60.08	61.37
61.98	62.01	60.79	62.25	59.43	62.06	61.56	60.45
60.24	61.26	60.89	61.23	58.44	58.63	59.06	57.14
61.21	60.89	61.54	62.12	61.42	60.85	61.39	60.62
61.55	61.81	60.65	62.09	59.90	60.12	62.85	60.99
62.31	61.56	61.07	61.43	60.66	62.86	61.77	61.53
61.51	61.13	62.34	60.39	61.88	60.88	61.19	60.39
61.62	60.30	61.22	61.92	60.65	61.53	60.31	60.26
56.70	57.81	58.02	57.55	60.37	60.89	61.69	62.07
60.82	61.64	60.99	60.82	61.02	59.61	60.54	60.62
61.21	60.58	59.03	61.85	60.43	60.57	61.02	61.52
61.60	60.11	60.86	62.72	61.78	61.34	61.14	62.40
60.92	60.69	60.15	61.51	61.04	59.98	61.59	59.46

(a) Obtain trial control limits for sample ranges and means of adjacent groups of four measurements. Are there any out-of-control observations on either control chart? Discuss.

(b) Two out-of-control sample means (sample 10 and 21) were due to assignable causes. Discussions with foundry workers revealed sporadic and consistency problems. As a result, obtain revised control limits for sample ranges and means after eliminating samples 10 and 21. These revised limits are to be used in monitoring the tensile strength of future castings.

8. Mass-produced springs are sampled in subgroups of five, and sample means and ranges of spring lengths (in inches) are computed from the following length measurements (RETRIEVE 'B:X14-8'):

```
2.82   2.98   2.57   2.38   2.44   1.82   1.91   1.78   1.83
1.77   2.37   2.56   2.44   2.57   2.02   1.98   1.96   1.96
1.96   2.10   2.00   1.98   2.03   2.03   2.02   1.97   1.98
1.94   2.04   1.98   2.01   2.03   2.00   1.98   1.94   1.97
2.02   2.03   1.96   1.92   2.03   1.92   1.96   1.93   1.97
1.95   2.02   1.99   1.95   2.05   2.07   1.92   1.94   2.03
2.05   2.05   2.02   1.99   2.09   2.03   1.90   2.02   1.98
1.99   2.07   1.97   1.98   2.00   1.99   2.01   2.00   1.98
2.03   2.01   1.99   2.00   2.12   2.04   2.04   1.90   2.02
2.03   2.04   1.96   1.96   2.04   2.10   2.14   1.91   2.09
1.92   2.05   1.93   1.99   2.04   1.91   2.00   1.99   2.00
2.03
```

(a) Obtain trial control limits for sample ranges and means. Discuss.

(b) Production management reported that the first three samples of five observations were unreliable because of mistakes made by an inexperienced new employee. Revise the control limits for ranges and sample means based on this information.

9. In the production of mercury-free 9-volt alkaline batteries, 25 samples of four batteries were taken every three hours (RETRIEVE 'B:X14-9'). Construct a control chart for sample ranges and averages. Does the production process seem to be in a state of statistical control?

```
8.99   9.06   8.97   8.94   9.00   9.05   8.96   8.99   9.08
9.00   9.03   9.01   8.99   9.04   9.00   8.92   9.03   8.87
8.98   9.03   9.03   8.99   9.06   9.05   8.98   9.02   9.02
8.88   9.08   8.99   9.01   8.94   9.05   9.09   8.92   8.98
9.00   8.94   8.96   8.97   9.04   8.94   8.96   8.98   9.03
8.94   9.14   9.06   9.03   9.00   8.94   8.97   9.03   9.01
8.96   9.01   9.01   8.97   9.02   8.95   9.02   9.04   9.03
8.94   8.99   9.10   8.97   9.03   8.94   9.02   9.03   8.99
9.04   8.95   9.00   9.02   9.00   9.03   8.94   8.93   9.00
8.97   9.04   9.01   8.95   9.06   8.96   9.05   9.04   8.91
8.97   8.95   8.92   9.02   8.99   8.98   9.02   8.93   9.08
8.98
```

10. In an acceptance sampling plan, the sample size is 10 ($n = 10$), and the allowable number of defectives is 1 ($c = 1$).

(a) If d is the actual number of defectives in a sample, what values of d would cause you to reject the lot of items being inspected?

(b) If c is increased to 2, is the sampling plan more or less discriminating? Why?

(c) What value of c leads to the highest rejection rate?

11. Assume that lots are large enough so that the defective rate, p, is approximately constant at 8%. Simulate 15 samples (rows) of size $n = 10$ (columns C1–C10) where the number 1 indicates a defective and the number 0 a nondefective. Count the number of defectives in a row.

(a) For these 15 samples, what is the lot rejection rate for a sampling plan in which n = 10 and c = 0?

(b) For these 15 samples, what is the lot rejection rate for a sampling plan in which n = 10 and c = 1?

(c) Simulate 100 new samples, count the number of lots accepted for various values of c, and obtain the percent and cumulative percent of the lots that are accepted for various values of c.

12. Using the computer to evaluate the binomial probabilities of accepting lots, find and plot the theoretical operating characteristic curves for the following sampling plans with p = .05, .10, .15, . . . , .95:

(a) n = 10 and c = 1
(b) n = 10 and c = 0
(c) n = 15 and c = 2
(d) n = 15 and c = 1
(e) n = 15 and c = 0

13. Use the Poisson distribution to approximate the binomial probabilities of accepting lots. Find and plot the operating characteristic curves for the following sampling plans:

(a) n = 200 and c = 2
(b) n = 200 and c = 1
(c) n = 200 and c = 0

14. For a lot size of N = 40, a sample of n = 10 is taken without replacement. If the number of defectives in the sample exceeds c = 0, the lot is rejected. What is the probability that the lot is rejected if the lot contains the following number of defectives?

(a) four
(b) eight
(c) fifteen

15. If packs of 30 hydraulic plugs have a population proportion defective of p = .10, what is the probability that a sample of eight plugs selected without replacement contains exactly one defective?

16. If incoming lots have a population proportion defective of p = .02 and if defectives are replaced with nondefectives in the whole lot when rejected, what is the average outgoing quality (AOQ) if the sampling plan's acceptance probability at p = .02 is .85?

17. If the average outgoing quality (AOQ) of a sampling plan is .019 and if the population proportion defective is p = .020, what is the probability that a lot is accepted under this sampling plan?

18. What term is used for the maximum of the average outgoing quality for all possible values of p, the population proportion of defectives?

19. What is the risk called in sampling plans that accept a small proportion of lots when the proportion of defectives is relatively high?

20. When the population proportion of defectives is small enough to satisfy both the consumer and producer, what term is used for the risk that a sampling plan rejects some lots?

21. Thin-skinned and therefore nonconforming sausage casings are monitored with a p chart. Samples of 80 casings are pressure-tested each day. The number of nonconforming casings found in 35 samples of 80 casings each are shown below. Use the first 25 sample proportions to establish control limits on a p chart. Extend these limits to monitor the following 10 samples. Are there any out-of-control points suggesting that management might encourage the casing supplier to improve quality?

```
2  5  3  3   2  4  3  3  3  3  3   5  4  0  2  5  1  4  3  3  1
3  2  5  4  12  3  4  3  5  4  1  14  6  1
```

22. Plastic tubes for shotgun shell construction are monitored with a p chart. Samples of 100 tubes are inspected and the number nonconforming are recorded below for 42 such samples. Use the first 30 samples proportions to establish control limits on a p chart. Extend these limits to monitor the following 12 samples. Are there any out-of-control points that require management action?

```
1  3  1  1  3  1  6  0  0  2  2  3  2  3  2  6  2  1  4  2  1  3
1  3  3  3  3  0  1  2  2  1  1  2  3  3  2  3  2  7  2  8
```

23. The count of imperfections on each of 28 galvanized steel sheets is

```
10   8  14  12  10   9  12  10  18   9   8   7   8  11  15   6   10
14  11  11  15  16  15  20  22  12  12  18
```

Construct a c chart based on the first 20 observations that were taken while the galvanizing process was in a state of statistical control. Are any of the last eight counts out of control?

Minitab Examples

A DEMONSTRATION OF A PERCENTAGE, p CHART

```
MTB > RANDOM 20 OBS IN C1;
SUBC> BINOMIAL N=100 P=.05. # STATE OF STATISTICAL CONTROL
MTB > # KNOWN FRACTION OF RED BEADS (DEFECTIVES)

MTB > RANDOM 10 OBS IN C2;  # OUT OF CONTROL JUMP IN PERCENT
SUBC> BINOMIAL N=100 P=.09. # DEFECTIVE
MTB > # KNOWN FRACTION DEFECTIVE (RED, BLACK AND YELLOW BEADS)

MTB > RANDOM 10 OBS IN C3;
SUBC> BINOMIAL N=100 P=.01. # OUT OF CONTROL WITH RESPECT TO
MTB > # THE LIMITS ESTABLISHED EARLIER
MTB > # A DROP TO A LOWER LEVEL OF DEFECTIVES
#      (BLACK BEADS ONLY)

MTB > STACK C2 ON C3, PUT C4
MTB > STACK C1 ON C4, PUT C4

MTB > PCHART C4, SAMPLE SIZE=100;
SUBC> P=.05;
SUBC> TEST 1 2 3 4;
SUBC> XLABEL 'SAMPLE NUMBER';
SUBC> YLABEL 'PROPORTION'.

MTB > PRINT C1 C2 C3

MTB > SET IN C5
DATA> 20(1),10(2), 10(3)
DATA> END
MTB > DOTPLOT C4;
SUBC> BY C5;
SUBC> SAME.

MTB > DESCRIBE C4;
SUBC> BY C5.
```

A DEMONSTRATION OF AN AVERAGE $\bar{y}$ CHART
(ybar OR xbar CHART) AND AN r CHART FOR VARIABILITY

```
MTB > RANDOM 100 C1;
SUBC> NORMAL MU=0 SIGMA=1.72. # IN CONTROL
MTB > ROUND C1 PUT C1         # CHIPS GET INTEGER NUMBERS
MTB > PRINT C1

MTB > RCHART C1 SUBGROUPS OF 5;
SUBC> TITLE 'RANGE CHART'. # SMALL CHANCE OF ALARMING

MTB > XBARCHART C1 SUBGROUPS OF 5;
SUBC> TEST 1:8;
SUBC> TITLE 'XBARCHART'.   # SMALL CHANCE OF ALARMING

MTB > RANDOM 50 C2;        # TEN ADDITIONAL SAMPLES SIZE 5
SUBC> NORMAL MU=2 SIGMA=1.72. # MEAN SHIFTS UPWARD
MTB > ROUND C2 PUT C2         # STD DEVIATION REMAINS UNCHANGED
MTB > STACK C1 ON C2 PUT C1
MTB > RCHART C1 SUBGROUPS OF 5;
SUBC> ESTIMATE 1:20;  # USES FIRST 20 SAMPLES FOR COMPUTATION
SUBC> TITLE 'RANGE CHART'. # SMALL CHANCE OF ALARMING

MTB > XBARCHART C1 SUBGROUPS OF 5;
SUBC> ESTIMATE 1:20;  # USES FIRST 20 SAMPLES FOR COMPUTATION
SUBC> TEST 1:8;
SUBC> TITLE 'XBARCHART'.   # EXPECT ALARM ON THE MEAN SHIFT

MTB > RANDOM 50 C3;         # TEN ADDITIONAL SAMPLES SIZE 5
SUBC> NORMAL MU=0 SIGMA=3.47. # MEAN IN CONTROL
MTB > ROUND C3 PUT C3         # STD DEVIATION INCREASES
MTB > STACK C1 ON C3 PUT C1
MTB > RCHART C1 SUBGROUPS 5;
SUBC> ESTIMATE 1:20;  # USES FIRST 20 SAMPLES FOR COMPUTATION
SUBC> TITLE 'RANGE CHART'. # EXPECT ALARM ON VARIABILITY CHANGE

MTB > XBARCHART C1 SUBGROUPS OF 5;
SUBC> ESTIMATE 1:20;  # USES FIRST 20 SAMPLES FOR COMPUTATION
SUBC> TEST 1:8;
SUBC> TITLE 'XBARCHART'.  # EXPECT ALARMS

MTB > SET IN C8  # A NUMBER 1 2 3 4 5 WITHIN EACH SAMPLE
DATA> 40(1:5)
DATA> END
MTB > UNSTACK C1 INTO C1-C5; # A SAMPLE IN EACH ROW
SUBC> SUBSCRIPTS IN C8.

MTB > RMEANS C1-C5 PUT C6    # SAMPLE MEANS IN C6
MTB > SET IN C7 # CONTROL, MEAN SHIFT AND VARIABILITY SHIFT
DATA> 20(1),10(2),10(3)  #                    INDICATORS
DATA> END
MTB > DESCRIBE C6;
SUBC> BY C7.
```

```
MTB > DOTPLOT C6;
SUBC> BY C7;
SUBC> SAME.
```

AN AVERAGE $\bar{y}$ CHART (ybar OR xbar CHART) AND AN r CHART IN PRACTICE

```
     OR  RETRIEVE 'CORN' (whichever is appropriate)
MTB > RETRIEVE 'B:CORN'

MTB > RCHART C1 SUBGROUPS 4;
SUBC> TITLE 'TRIAL RANGE CHART'.

MTB > XBARCHART C1 SUBGROUPS 4;
SUBC> TITLE 'TRIAL XBARCHART'.

# REVISED CHARTS ARE DEVELOPED BELOW
MTB > RCHART C1 SUBGROUPS 4; # OUT OF CONTROL POINTS DELETED
SUBC> ESTIMATE 1:2 4:8 10:13 15:25; # FROM COMPUTATIONS
SUBC> TITLE 'RCHART REVISED LIMITS'.

MTB > XBARCHART C1 SUBGROUPS 4;
SUBC> ESTIMATE 1:2 4:8 10:13 15:25;
SUBC> TITLE 'XBARCHART REVISED LIMITS'.
```

FLAWS IN YOUR JEANS

```
MTB > SET C1
DATA> 23  15  16  20  18  17  16  15  12  13  21  12  24
DATA> 19  16  17  20  12  20  20  23  21  16  21  16
DATA> END
MTB > NAME C1 'PRFLAWS'
MTB > DESCRIBE C1
MTB > SET C2
DATA> 20  24  22  25  22  16  18  32  18  31
DATA> END
MTB > STACK C1 ON C2 PUT C1
MTB > CCHART C1;
SUBC> ESTIMATE 1:25.
```

AN ACCEPTANCE SAMPLING PLAN IN ACTION

```
MTB > RANDOM 15 OBS C1-C10; # 15 SIZE 10 SAMPLES
SUBC> BERNOULLI P=.10.      # 10% DEFECTIVE RATE
MTB > RSUM C1-C10 PUT C11 # COUNT OF DEFECTIVE IN EACH SAMPLE
MTB > PRINT C1-C11
MTB > TALLY C11
```

```
# A SECOND SIMULATION 100 SIZE 10 SAMPLES
MTB > RANDOM 100 OBS IN C1-C10;
SUBC> BERNOULLI P=.10.
MTB > RSUM C1-C10 PUT C11

MTB > TALLY C11;
SUBC> COUNTS;
SUBC> PERCENTS;
SUBC> CUMPERCENTS.
MTB > HIST C11
MTB > DESCRIBE C11
```

EXAMPLE

OPERATING CHARACTERISTIC CURVE FOR A TYPICAL SAMPLING PLAN (OPTIONAL)

Comment The following macro, %B:E14-4, requires version ten or greater of MINITAB. To examine the details of the macro, use a text editor or a word processor and open the E14-4. MAC file. In MINITAB, the command TYPE 'B:E14-4.MAC' will list the macro. If you set OH = 24 in the session window, a "continue?" prompt will be issued by MINITAB that permits the user to view one screen of output at a time as the macro executes.

```
MTB > %B:E14-4  # OR %A:E14-4  OR %E14-4
#                 OR %C:\MTBWIN\DATA\E14-4
```

EXAMPLE

THEORETICAL OPERATING CHARACTERISTIC CURVE (OPTIONAL)

Comment The following macro, %B:TOCC, requires version ten or greater of MINITAB. To examine the details of the macro, use a text editor or a word processor and open the TOCC.MAC file. In MINITAB, the command TYPE 'B:TOCC.MAC' will list the macro. If you set OH = 24 in the session window, a "continue?" prompt will be issued by MINITAB that permits the user to view one screen of output at a time as the macro executes.

```
MTB > %B:TOCC    # OR %A:TOCC OR %TOCC
#                  OR %C:\MTBWIN\DATA\TOCC

MTB > LET C22 = C20 * C21    # AVERAGE OUTGOING QUALITY
MTB > PLOT C20 C21           # ACCEPT PROBABILITIES VERSUS P
MTB > MPLOT C20 C21 C22 C21 # AOQ AND OC CURVES
```

CHAPTER 15

Experimental Designs and the Analysis of Variance

OBJECTIVES

◈ **Compare more than two population means with independent samples, single-factor (one-way) experiments**

◈ **Analyze two-factor (two-way) experiments, a single factor of main interest and a nuisance factor forming blocks**

◈ **Examine many-factor (factorial) experiments, with or without nuisance factors**

PRELUDE

We have learned to estimate a single population mean with a sample mean, to form confidence intervals, and to make hypothesis tests. These ideas were extended to the difference of two population means for comparisons. Now we consider more complicated experiments in which more than two population means are compared.

For example, in making popcorn suppose yield in cups is the response to a single factor or variable, which is the amount of kernels. Then experiment with amount at three different levels, $\frac{1}{3}$, $\frac{2}{3}$, and $\frac{3}{3}$ cups. By replicating the experiment, several yield observations can be made at each level of amount. The sample mean yield can be computed at each level of amount. These three sample means can be compared in a one-way (factor) analysis of variance. Furthermore, the analysis extends to more than three levels of the single-factor.

It is easy to imagine how a second nuisance factor can come into play. Suppose as you begin to plan the popcorn experiment you realize that you have only two pots for popping, pot 1 and pot 2. You would like to know if this nuisance factor (pot) as well as amount influences yield. The yield at three levels of amount can be compared in a two-way (factor) analysis of variance, accounting for the pots. The analysis extends to more levels of each factor.

Suppose you find that pot has no significant influence on yield. Also suppose you begin to wonder if another factor, popcorn brand (gourmet or ordinary), as well as amount influences yield. Brand is not regarded as a nuisance factor but rather as another factor of main interest, like amount, that might influence yield. Although it is possible for each brand to run single-factor experiments with amount, factorial experiments require fewer runs and yield more information. In factorial experiments, these factors are investigated simultaneously. The analysis extends to more levels of each factor. ◈

SINGLE-FACTOR (ONE-WAY) EXPERIMENTS

A pharmaceutical company is comparing the effectiveness of two new drugs on subjects, which are referred to as **experimental units.** Half the subjects are treated with drug A, which is also referred to as **treatment** A, and the other half are treated with drug B, or treatment B. Other than specifying that half the subjects get each treatment, no restrictions are placed on the assignment of treatments to subjects. Prudently, the assignments are made at random and the experiment is a **completely randomized design.**

This is the simplest **single-factor experiment,** or **one-way experiment.** Measurements on drug effectiveness produce two columns of data because there are two treatments. The first column is a sample of observations from a population with a mean μ_1. The second column is a sample of observations from a population with a mean μ_2. The variances are assumed to be equal in the two populations.

In Chapter 9, you learned that a simple regression model

$$y_i = \beta_0 + \beta_1 x_{1i} + e_i$$

under special conditions (x coded 0 or 1) can be used to compare two means by testing the null hypothesis that $\beta_1 = (\mu_2 - \mu_1) = 0$. Recall that $b_1 = (\overline{y}_2 - \overline{y}_1)$ estimates β_1. If the null hypothesis is true, $\mu_2 = \mu_1$, and the two drugs are equally effective.

The null hypothesis can be tested by fitting a regression line and comparing the F statistic in the analysis of variance table to a critical F value (see Appendix A Table 4 in the back of the book). Hence, the term *analysis of variance* has become associated with testing hypotheses in experiments. A pooled t test and a one-way analysis of variance yield the same results as regression. The pooled t test is limited to the comparison of two means; regression and one-way analysis of variance can compare many means.

When more than two means are compared, multiple regression rather than simple regression is required. Some readers may prefer to go directly to Example 1 and later review the following section on multiple regression.

A Multiple Regression Model Representation of a Single-Factor Experiment

Multiple regression provides a well-known conceptual framework for understanding the analysis of variance in experiments. More sophisticated experiments are special cases of multiple regression. For example, to compare three means and test the null hypothesis that $\mu_1 = \mu_2 = \mu_3$, an appropriate model is

$$y_i = \beta_0 + \beta_1 x_{1i} + \beta_2 x_{2i} + e_i$$

with the following coding scheme:

	x_{1i}	x_{2i}
y_i data from a population with mean μ_1	0	0
y_i data from a population with mean μ_2	1	0
y_i data from a population with mean μ_3	0	1

Both x_{1i} and x_{2i} are 0 when y_i is a data value from a population with mean μ_1. The x_{1i} is 1 and x_{2i} is 0 when y_i is a data value from a population with mean μ_2. The x_{1i} is 0 and x_{2i} is 1 when y_i is a data value from a population with mean μ_3.

This multiple regression model describes a single factor (one-way) experiment for comparing three means. The null hypothesis that $\beta_1 = \beta_2 = 0$, where $\beta_1 = (\mu_2 - \mu_1)$ and $\beta_2 = (\mu_3 - \mu_1)$, is the same as $\mu_1 = \mu_2 = \mu_3$. This hypothesis can be tested by getting a multiple regression fit and comparing the F statistic in the analysis of variance table to a critical F value.

Similarly, any number of means can be compared.

Assumptions About the Errors   All the assumptions about the errors e_i in regression models apply to the analysis of variance. Generally, it is assumed that the errors have a mean of 0, a constant variance, are independent (random), and normal in distribution. As in regression, residual analysis is done to validate these assumptions.

Special ANOVA Computer Commands   Although designed experiments can be framed and analyzed through multiple regression, special formulas and computer commands have been developed for the analysis of variance in experiments. The MINITAB reference manual, for example, has separate sections for regression and the analysis of variance.

Many analysis of variance methods were developed before the widespread availability of computers and statistical packages. Furthermore, as experiments become more complex, the coding of the regression predictor variables can become messy with lots of 1s and 0s or other codes. As a result, the more convenient and specialized formulas for the analysis of variance are usually employed instead of regression. These formulas are implemented in the computer software. From the output of these programs, you can see that there is considerable focus on analysis of variance tables for hypothesis testing.

Two Contrasting Cases of Single-Factor (One-Way) Experiments

In Case 1 the null hypothesis that all means are equal is accepted. In Case 2 the null hypothesis that all means are equal is rejected. Pay particular attention to the resulting differences in the analysis of variance tables. For example, in Case 1 the error sum of squares is relatively large, and in Case 2 it is relatively small.

Case 1: Accept the Hypothesis That the Population Means Are All Equal,
$\mu_1 = \mu_2 = \mu_3$

GASOLINE BRANDS

Three brands of gasoline (treatments) were used in 15 identical sport utility vehicles (experimental units) to test the hypothesis that there is no difference in population mean mileage figures for brands. Under similar driving conditions, mileage data were recorded and the data set is

```
Row   BRAND1   BRAND2   BRAND3
 1     17.3     19.4     17.0
 2     18.8     17.9     17.2
 3     15.9     16.7     19.0
 4     17.8     17.3     19.8
 5     17.5     17.5     16.5
```

To help ensure independence of the errors, the treatments were randomly assigned to the experimental units. Three pieces of paper were marked 1, 2, and 3 for brands. This was done five times, and the 15 pieces of paper were placed in a hat and drawn without replacement to assign brands to vehicles.

Problem Statement (a)   Use side-by-side boxplots to arrive at a preliminary conclusion.

Problem Solution (a)   The boxplots on mileage figures (all in column C4 in MINITAB) for the three brands suggest that there is no significant difference. However, the middle 50% of the data values for brand 3 is more spread out than the others, drawing one's attention to the possibility that the variance may not be constant across brands.

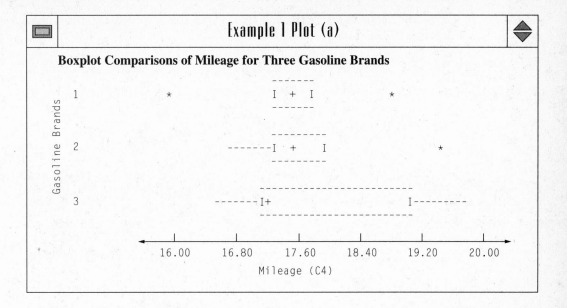

Problem Statement (b)   Follow this preliminary examination of the data with a one-way analysis of variance.

Problem Solution (b)   Do not reject the null hypothesis that $\mu_1 = \mu_2 = \mu_3$ because the confidence intervals shown below overlap, the F statistic is smaller than the critical F value of 3.88 for $\alpha = .05$ and 2,12 degrees of freedom (see Appendix A Table 4 in the back of the book), and the error sum of squares is nearly as large as the total sum of squares.

```
ANALYSIS OF VARIANCE

SOURCE      DF       SS       MS      F value      p value
FACTOR       2     0.51     0.25        0.18        0.835
ERROR       12    16.56     1.38

TOTAL       14    17.07

                                   INDIVIDUAL 95 PCT CI'S FOR MEAN
                                       BASED ON POOLED STDEV
LEVEL       N     MEAN    STDEV    -------+---------+---------+---------
BRAND1      5   17.460    1.045    (-------------*--------------)
BRAND2      5   17.760    1.014      (-------------*-------------)
BRAND3      5   17.900    1.421        (--------------*-------------)
                                   -------+---------+---------+---------
POOLED STDEV =    1.175              16.80    17.60    18.40
```

Problem Statement (c)   Briefly examine residuals.

Problem Solution (c)   Although the sample size is small, the errors appear random and normal in distribution.

```
    C6 (RESIDUALS)
    K =     0.0000
    THE OBSERVED NO. OF RUNS =    7
    THE EXPECTED NO. OF RUNS =    8.4667
       7 OBSERVATIONS ABOVE K     8 BELOW
  * N SMALL--FOLLOWING APPROX. MAY BE INVALID
               THE TEST IS SIGNIFICANT AT  0.4299
               CANNOT REJECT AT ALPHA = 0.05
```

```
Histogram of C6   N = 15

Midpoint    Count
    -1.5      2 **
    -1.0      2 **
    -0.5      3 ***
     0.0      3 ***
     0.5      1 *
     1.0      1 *
     1.5      2 **
     2.0      1 *
```

Case 2: Reject the Hypothesis That the Population Means Are All Equal

E X A M P L E 2

VEHICLE TYPES

Twenty-four vehicles (experimental units) of four types (treatments) were driven under similar conditions to estimate population mean mileage figures for vehicle types. The four vehicle types were (1) compact sport utility (CSU); (2) full-size sport utility (FSSU); (3) full-size cars (FSC); and (4) compact cars (CC). Under similar driving conditions, mileage data were recorded and the data set is

Row	CSU	FSSU	FSC	CC
1	22.7	19.3	21.5	23.2
2	22.0	17.6	23.3	26.0
3	23.4	17.6	22.2	26.0
4	20.5	18.5	20.6	19.8
5	22.1	18.0	17.9	23.7
6	22.6	18.9	22.6	25.3

Problem Statement (a)   Use side-by-side boxplots to summarize mileage for vehicle types.

Problem Solution (a)   The boxplots on mileage figures (all in column C5 in MINITAB) for vehicle types suggest that the population means are not all equal. Full-size sport utility (FSSU) have the worst mileage, and compact cars (CC) have the best mileage on average.

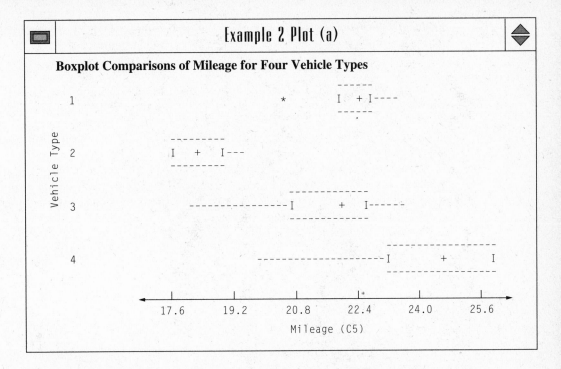

Problem Statement (b)   Test the null hypothesis that the population mean mileage is the same for all vehicle types, $\mu_1 = \mu_2 = \mu_3 = \mu_4$.

Problem Solution (b)   Reject the null hypothesis that $\mu_1 = \mu_2 = \mu_3 = \mu_4$. The confidence intervals below don't all overlap. The F statistic exceeds the critical F value of 3.0984 for $\alpha = .05$ and 3, 20 degrees of freedom (see Appendix A Table 4 in the back of the book). The error sum of squares is considerably smaller than the total sum of squares.

```
ANALYSIS OF VARIANCE ON C5

SOURCE      DF        SS        MS        F value      p value

C6           3     101.50     33.83        12.56        0.000
ERROR       20      53.89      2.69

TOTAL       23     155.39
```

```
                              INDIVIDUAL 95 PCT CI'S FOR MEAN
                              BASED ON POOLED STDEV

LEVEL      N      MEAN     STDEV    ---+---------+---------+---------+---
    1      6    22.217     0.979                    (-----*----)
    2      6    18.317     0.703       (----*-----)
    3      6    21.350     1.927                (----*-----)
    4      6    24.000     2.369                        (-----*-----)
                                      ---+---------+---------+---------+---
POOLED STDEV =      1.642             17.5      20.0      22.5      25.0
```

Problem Statement (c) (Optional)   Use the subcommand TUKEY to construct confidence intervals for all pairwise differences of vehicle type mean mileage.

Problem Solution (c)   For multiple comparisons, the subcommand TUKEY constructs confidence intervals for all pairwise differences of vehicle type mean mileage. For example, the interval on $(\mu_1 - \mu_2)$ is 1.25 to 6.55; it does not include 0. Therefore, mileage is significantly different (better) for compact sport utility (CSU) vehicles compared to full-size sport utility (FSSU) vehicles.

Similarly, intervals on $(\mu_2 - \mu_3)$ and $(\mu_2 - \mu_4)$ do not enclose 0. Full-size cars (FSC) and compact cars (CC) get significantly better mileage than full-size sport utility vehicles. Full-size sport utilities aside, remaining mileage comparisons are not significantly different. However, the differences may be important to buyers.

Intervals for (column level mean) $-$ (row level mean)

```
Vehicle Types     1          2          3
       2      1.25 (lower bound) interval on (μ₁ - μ₂)
              6.55 (upper bound)
--------------------------------------------------
       3     -1.79      -5.69
              3.52      -0.38
--------------------------------------------------
       4     -4.44      -8.34      -5.30
              0.87      -3.03       0.004
```

The individual error rate is the probability of falsely concluding that a pair means is significantly different. The family error rate is the probability of falsely concluding that one or more pairs of means are significantly different.

```
individual error rate = 0.0111 (individual comparison)
   family error rate = 0.0500 (overall comparisons)
```

Problem Statement (d)   Briefly examine residuals.

Problem Solution (d)   Although the sample size is small, the errors appear random and normal in distribution.

```
C7 (RESIDUALS)
K =    0.0000
THE OBSERVED NO. OF RUNS =  15
THE EXPECTED NO. OF RUNS =  12.9167
13 OBSERVATIONS ABOVE K   11 BELOW
        THE TEST IS SIGNIFICANT AT  0.3812
        CANNOT REJECT AT ALPHA = 0.05
```

```
Histogram of C7   N = 24
Midpoint   Count
   -4       1   *
   -3       1   *
   -2       1   *
   -1       4   ****
    0       8   ********
    1       6   ******
    2       3   ***
```

Problem Statement (e)   Display a table of fits (predicted mileage) produced by the analysis. Do the same for residuals.

Problem Solution (e)   Notice that the actual mileage shown on page 720 equals predicted plus residuals for cells in the two tables below.

Vehicle Type		Fits (Predicted Mileage)				
1	22.22	22.22	22.22	22.22	22.22	22.22
2	18.32	18.32	18.32	18.32	18.32	18.32
3	21.35	21.35	21.35	21.35	21.35	21.35
4	24.00	24.00	24.00	24.00	24.00	24.00

Vehicle Type				Residuals		
1	0.48	-0.22	1.18	-1.72	-0.12	0.38
2	0.98	-0.72	-0.72	0.18	-0.32	0.58
3	0.15	1.95	0.85	-0.75	-3.45	1.25
4	-0.80	2.00	2.00	-4.20	-0.30	1.30

S T A T I S T I C A L   H I G H L I G H T S

In single-factor or one-way experiments, experimental units are assigned randomly to two or more treatments. No other factors are considered to affect the response variable other than these treatments.

TWO-FACTOR (TWO-WAY) EXPERIMENTS, A SINGLE FACTOR OF MAIN INTEREST, AND A NUISANCE FACTOR FORMING BLOCKS

A **two-way** or **randomized complete-blocks design** groups experimental units into relatively homogeneous **blocks** with all the treatments appearing the same number of times in each block. Usually, this grouping diminishes the misleading effect that the nuisance variable, which is associated with the blocks, can have on the results. Typically, if a significant block effect were ignored, resulting in a one-way instead of a two-way experiment, the error sum of squares may be inflated enough to erroneously lead to the conclusion that all treatment means are equal when they are not.

In completely randomized one-way designs, the randomization of treatments to experimental units is unrestricted except for the number of times a treatment will be used. In contrast, for two-way designs the randomization is carried out within blocks and in that sense is restricted.

The previous one-way example is extended here. In that experiment, recall that four means were compared to test the null hypothesis that $\mu_1 = \mu_2 = \mu_3 = \mu_4$. For the one-way example, an appropriate regression model is

$$y_i = \beta_0 + \beta_1 x_{1i} + \beta_2 x_{2i} + \beta_3 x_{3i} + e_i$$

When the following coding scheme is employed, meaningful parameters result: $\beta_0 = \mu_1$; $\beta_1 = (\mu_2 - \mu_1)$; $\beta_2 = (\mu_3 - \mu_1)$; $\beta_3 = (\mu_4 - \mu_1)$.

The coding scheme is

	x_{1i}	x_{2i}	x_{3i}
y_i data from a population with mean μ_1	0	0	0
y_i data from a population with mean μ_2	1	0	0
y_i data from a population with mean μ_3	0	1	0
y_i data from a population with mean μ_4	0	0	1

The coding results are

1. The x_{1i}, x_{2i}, and x_{3i} are 0 when y_i is a data value from a population with mean μ_1.
2. The x_{1i} is 1 and x_{2i} and x_{3i} are 0 when y_i is a data value from a population with mean μ_2.
3. The x_{1i} is 0, x_{2i} is 1, and x_{3i} is 0 when y_i is a data value from a population with mean μ_3.
4. The x_{1i} and x_{2i} are 0 and x_{3i} is 1 when y_i is a data value from a population with mean μ_4.

Additional Predictor Variable(s) for Blocks Another predictor variable, x_{4i}, can be added to the regression model to account for the nuisance variable, which designates city (x_{4i} coded -1) or highway (x_{4i} coded $+1$) driving. By introducing and accounting for a second factor (a nuisance variable), we have designed a two-way experiment. This new and larger experiment is run in blocks as shown below, with one block for city driving and another for highway driving.

The drivers of the test vehicles had similar driving habits and lived either in the country or the city. For the duration of the experiment, their driving was restricted to one of the blocking classes, highway or city driving. For each row below, four drivers were randomly assigned to four vehicles.

Row	BLOCK	CSU	FSSU	FSC	CC
1	1	20.8	17.2	21.3	21.1
2	1	20.3	16.2	19.0	21.6
3	1	22.0	16.7	20.6	20.8
4	1	20.6	17.3	21.1	24.1
5	1	21.1	16.9	19.6	20.3
6	1	19.5	16.9	21.2	22.7
7	2	22.6	19.1	22.3	25.4
8	2	23.4	19.0	23.8	26.0
9	2	23.6	19.4	22.4	27.3
10	2	24.3	20.2	23.8	25.8
11	2	24.2	19.2	22.1	27.0
12	2	21.8	19.6	21.0	26.9

Because of the blocking, the regression model is enlarged to

$$y_i = \beta_0 + \beta_1 x_{1i} + \beta_2 x_{2i} + \beta_3 x_{3i} + \beta_4 x_{4i} + e_i$$

Recall that x_{4i} is coded -1 or $+1$ while the other x's are coded 0 or 1. Under this coding scheme, the first four parameters have the same meaning as before: $\beta_0 = \mu_1$; $\beta_1 = (\mu_2 - \mu_1)$; $\beta_2 = (\mu_3 - \mu_1)$; $\beta_3 = (\mu_4 - \mu_1)$. The last parameter is one-half the difference in mean mileages for blocks

$$\beta_4 = \frac{\mu_{highway} - \mu_{city}}{2}$$

The estimate of this parameter adjusts the predicted mileage up or down for each block.

Separate Hypothesis Tests for Groups of Parameters We are interested in hypothesis tests for separate groups of parameters in the regression model. Associated with treatments is the hypothesis that $\beta_1 = \beta_2 = \beta_3 = 0$. Associated with blocks is the hypothesis that $\beta_4 = 0$. In general, the model and the analysis extends to more treatments and more blocks.

EXAMPLE 3

VEHICLE TYPES AND DRIVING CONDITIONS

Forty-eight vehicles (experimental units) of four types (treatments) were driven under two distinct conditions, city and highway driving (blocks). The four vehicle types were: (1) compact sport utility (CSU); (2) full-size sport utility (FSSU); (3) full-size cars (FSC); and (4) compact cars (CC). The mileage data are shown above. The variable name for mileage is MAGE.

Problem Statement (a)   Use side-by-side boxplots to summarize mileage separately for vehicle types and for driving conditions.

Problem Solution (a)   The boxplots on mileage for vehicle types over all driving conditions suggest that the population means are not all equal. Full-size sport utility (FSSU) have the worst mileage and compact cars (CC) have the best mileage on average.

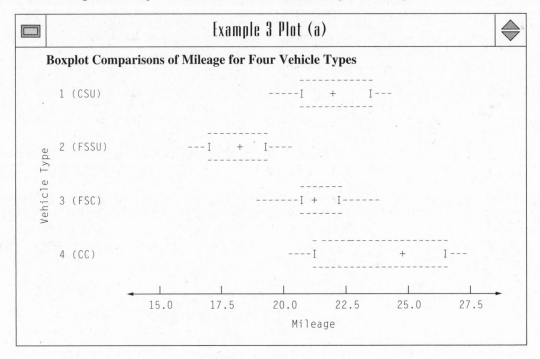

The boxplots on mileage for driving conditions across all vehicles suggest better highway mileage on average.

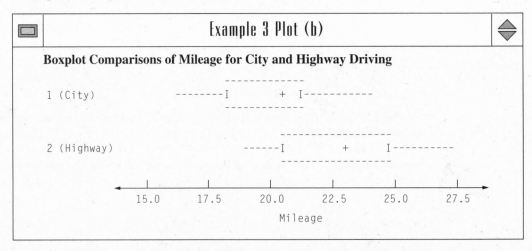

Problem Statement (b)   Test the null hypothesis that the population mean mileage is the same for all vehicle types, $\mu_1 = \mu_2 = \mu_3 = \mu_4$. Also, test the null hypothesis that the population mean mileage is the same for city and highway driving, $\mu_c = \mu_h$.

Problem Solution (b)   In the analysis of variance table, the treatment and block sums of squares are broken out separately for separate hypothesis tests.

Reject the null hypothesis that $\mu_1 = \mu_2 = \mu_3 = \mu_4$. This hypothesis is the same as $\beta_1 = \beta_2 = \beta_3 = 0$. The confidence intervals don't all overlap. The F statistic $\frac{72.82}{1.04}$ exceeds the critical F value of 2.8 (approximate) for $\alpha = .05$ and 3,43 degrees of freedom. The error sum of squares is considerably smaller than the total sum of squares.

Reject the null hypothesis that $\mu_c = \mu_h$, the population mean mileage is the same for city and highway driving. This hypothesis is the same as $\beta_4 = 0$. The confidence intervals don't overlap. The F statistic $\frac{105.91}{1.04}$ exceeds the critical F value of 4 (approximate) for $\alpha = .05$ and 1, 43 degrees of freedom. The error sum of squares is considerably smaller than the total sum of squares.

```
ANALYSIS OF VARIANCE MAGE

SOURCE      DF      SS        MS
TREATID      3    218.46     72.82
BLKID        1    105.91    105.91
ERROR       43     44.55      1.04

TOTAL       47    368.91
```

```
                     Individual 95% CI
TREATID     Mean    ---+---------+---------+---------+-------
   1        22.02                          (--*--)
   2        18.14        (--*--)
   3        21.52                    (--*--)
   4        24.08                              (--*--)
                    ---+---------+---------+---------+-------
                    18.00     20.00     22.00     24.00
```

```
                     Individual 95% CI
BLKID       Mean    -----+---------+---------+---------+------
   1        19.95    (----*---)
   2        22.92                            (---*---)
                    -----+---------+---------+---------+------
                    20.00     21.00     22.00     23.00
```

Problem Statement (c)   Briefly examine residuals. Plot residuals versus treatment number and block number.

Problem Solution (c)   The errors appear random; however, the distribution is not quite normal with no tail on the high end of the distribution. Nevertheless, this nonnormality is not too severe.

```
C7
K =    -0.0000
THE OBSERVED NO. OF RUNS = 27
THE EXPECTED NO. OF RUNS = 24.8333
26 OBSERVATIONS ABOVE K   22 BELOW
            THE TEST IS SIGNIFICANT AT  0.5244
            CANNOT REJECT AT ALPHA = 0.05
```

```
Histogram of C7    N = 48

Midpoint   Count
   -2.5      1   *
   -2.0      2   **
   -1.5      2   **
   -1.0      5   *****
   -0.5      7   *******
    0.0     12   ************
    0.5      8   ********
    1.0      5   *****
    1.5      6   ******
```

Except for full-size sport utility vehicles in Plot (c), the variance in mileage across vehicle types is about the same as required by our assumptions. Statistical tests are available to test the hypothesis that variances are equal across treatments or blocks. However, simple visual assessments will be used here. In the event that the variances are not equal, transformations in the response variable might be tried.

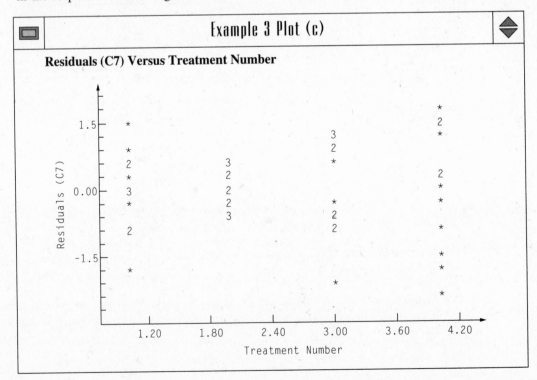

The variance in mileage across driving conditions in Plot (d) is about the same as required by our assumptions.

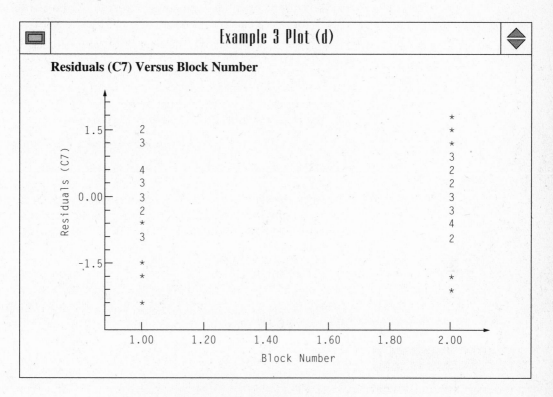

Example 3 Plot (d)

Residuals (C7) Versus Block Number

Standard Model Specification

A multiple regression model with specially coded predictor variables has been used to represent one-way and two-way experiments. As a result, it was easy to see that the analysis of variance is a special case of regression. It was emphasized that groups of parameters are associated with treatments and blocks. Also, in the analysis of variance, the parameters represent meaningful differences in means. In analysis of variance tables, the regression sum of squares is partitioned so that each resulting sum of squares is associated with a particular group of parameters so that separate hypotheses can be tested regarding treatments and blocks.

As experiments get larger and more complex, the regression model representation becomes cumbersome. The multiple regression equations become very long with a large number of predictor variables. The coding scheme gets more complicated. It's more difficult to code the predictors so that the parameters have the meanings you want.

As a result, a more compact notation is used in the standard model representation. This notation is similar to that found in the MINITAB manual on the analysis of variance.

One-Way Model Let y_{ij} represent the i-th response observation when the j-th treatment is used. Let the regression model's β's be replaced as follows: (1) β_0 is replaced with μ_g, the grand mean of all response observations; and (2) β's for treatments (factor A) are replaced by a_j for the j-th treatment (j-th level of factor A). The a_j represents treatment effects, $(\mu_j - \mu_g)$.

The regression model's predictors (x's) don't appear in the standard model because the subscript j switches the particular treatment effects in or out of the model. Finally, the error term is double subscripted, e_{ij}, like the response to associate it with a treatment.

The standard model for a one-way analysis is

$$y_{ij} = \mu_g + a_j + e_{ij}$$

The usual null hypothesis is that all treatment effects are 0.

Two-Way Model In the two-way model, block effects are added to the model and subscripts are added. The β's for blocks (factor B) are replaced by b_k for the k-th block (k-th level of factor B). The b_k represents block effects, $(\mu_k - \mu_g)$.

The standard model for a two-way analysis is

$$y_{ijk} = \mu_g + a_j + b_k + e_{ijk}$$

The usual separate null hypotheses are that (1) the treatment effects are all 0, and (2) the block effects are all 0.

EXAMPLE 4

JUDGING BREAKFAST CEREALS

Two new breakfast cereals, Boom and Bang, are compared by ten tasters and rated on a ten-point scale with ten being the highest possible score. The scores, mean scores for each taster, differences in scores, and cereal mean scores are

TASTER	BOOM	BANG	RMEANS	DIFF
1	6.1	7.1	6.60	-1.0
2	6.1	7.5	6.80	-1.4
3	6.6	7.5	7.05	-0.9
4	6.8	7.6	7.20	-0.8
5	6.9	7.7	7.30	-0.8
6	7.2	7.7	7.45	-0.5
7	7.2	7.8	7.50	-0.6
8	7.2	8.0	7.60	-0.8
9	7.4	8.0	7.70	-0.6
10	8.5	8.1	8.30	0.4

```
Column mean BOOM = 7.0  =  estimate of μ_boom
Column mean BANG = 7.7  =  estimate of μ_bang
Grand mean       = 7.35 =  estimate of μ_grand
```

Problem Statement (a)   Perform a two-way analysis with Boom and Bang as treatments and the tasters as blocks. Blocks are necessary because of each taster's scoring tendencies. For example, one taster might score a good taste as a seven while another taster might score a good taste as an eight.

Problem Solution (a)   The F statistics, 22.97 and 4.38, exceed their corresponding critical F values (5.1174 and 3.1789) for $\alpha = .05$ and (1,9 and 9,9) degrees of freedom. Bang is significantly different than Boom in taste. At least one block effect is significantly different from 0.

```
Analysis of Variance for B&B

Source     DF       SS        MS      F value    p value

B&BID       1     2.4500    2.4500     22.97      0.000
BLKID       9     4.2000    0.4667      4.38      0.019
Error       9     0.9600    0.1067

Total      19     7.6100
```

Problem Statement (b)   Show that the results in Problem Solution (a) are identical to those from a paired t test. A **paired t test** is a special case of two-way analysis of variance when there are only two treatments.

Problem Solution (b)   A paired t test is simply a t test on the cereal score differences across rows (blocks). The t statistic (-4.79) in absolute value exceeds the critical t (2.262) for $\alpha/2 = .025$ and 9 degrees of freedom (see Appendix A Table 2 in the back of the book). Bang is significantly different than Boom in taste. The critical t squared ($\alpha/2 = .025$) is the same as the first critical F value for treatments above ($\alpha = .05$).

```
TEST OF MU = 0.000 VS MU N.E. 0.000·

           N     MEAN    STDEV    SE MEAN       T    P VALUE

DIFF      10    -0.700   0.462     0.146     -4.79    0.0010
```

Problem Statement (c)   Estimate the treatment effect of Boom. Estimate the block effect of taster two. (In other words, in the model $y_{ijk} = \mu_g + a_j + b_k + e_{ijk}$, estimate a_1 and b_2.)

Problem Solution (c)   The $a_1 = (\mu_{boom} - \mu_g)$ is estimated by $(7.0 - 7.35)$. On average, Boom scores $-.35$ below the overall mean. The $b_2 = (\mu_{taster2} - \mu_g)$ is estimated by $(6.80 - 7.35)$. Taster two tends to score $-.55$ below the overall mean. The 6.80 is a block mean in the second row of scores.

S T A T I S T I C A L   H I G H L I G H T S

A two-way or randomized complete-blocks design groups experimental units into relatively homogeneous blocks with all the treatments appearing the same number of times in each block. Treatments are assigned at random within blocks to experimental units.

A SINGLE FACTOR OF MAIN INTEREST, VARIOUS EXTENSIONS (OPTIONAL)

The one- and two-way experiments you have seen above fit many practical situations. However, you should be aware that complications can occur in experiments that give rise to other design and analysis considerations. The purpose of this section is to outline some extensions of what you have learned so far and to give you a broader perspective.

Balanced Data

In two-or-more-way experiments, data tables are in two or more dimensions. For example, a two-way data table has a table cell for each row and column in two dimensions. A three-way data table has cells in three dimensions, in which cells can be thought of as small cubes that form a larger cube. If there are an equal number of observations in each cell, the data are said to be **balanced.** Otherwise the data are **unbalanced.**

The statistical methodology for balanced data may not apply to unbalanced data. For example, MINITAB'S TWO-WAY and ANOVA commands are for balanced data. The ANCOVA command can handle balanced data as well as certain types of unbalanced data. The GLM command is the most general and handles balanced and unbalanced data. However, the GLM command is slower and requires more memory space.

In one-way tables, the notion of balance is not required, and one-way tables may have unequal numbers of observations in treatment columns.

Accounting for Additional Nuisance Factors

Sometimes more than one nuisance factor arises and additional blocking is required. For example, in addition to the treatment effects of main interest a_j, consider two distinct blocking effects, b_k and c_l. As you can see, a standard model specification can be written to include the additional blocking variable,

$$y_{ijkl} = \mu_g + a_j + b_k + c_l + e_{ijkl}$$

In a similar way, the MINITAB ANOVA command is expanded for carrying out the analysis.

As more blocking variables come into play, the total number of experimental units can become large rapidly. This leads to expensive experiments. Special economical designs called **Latin squares** have been developed for two blocking variables. For three blocking variables there are **Graeco-Latin square** designs. Look for particular commands in statistical packages for these designs. In MINITAB, the ANCOVA command rather than the ANOVA command is used for such designs.

A Latin square is unbalanced in the sense that three factors are examined in a two-way data table. Thus, the cells in the third dimension are empty. Yet the design is arranged in such a way that, from a regression point of view, the predictor variables are orthogonal (uncorrelated). MINITAB's ANCOVA command was developed for such orthogonal designs.

Incomplete-Blocks Designs

Sometimes the number of experimental units fitting into a block is less than the number of treatments. The block is incomplete in the sense that it does not include all treatments. These **incomplete-blocks designs** may be balanced or unbalanced. Balance occurs when, for the subset of treatments fitting in the block, every treatment appears with every other treatment in the same block an equal number of times.

Again, special metholodgy is needed. Balanced incomplete-designs are orthogonal, and MINITAB's ANCOVA or GLM commands would be appropriate. However, the GLM command would be required for the unbalanced case.

Fixed Versus Random Effects Models

When an experiment's specific factor levels are the only levels of interest for drawing conclusions and all these levels are included in the experiment, the effects (for example, effect a_j) are said to be **fixed.** MINITAB assumes fixed effects unless told otherwise via a subcommand.

If the factor levels were chosen at random from a large number of possible levels and one is interested in drawing conclusions about the entire population of factor levels, the effects (for example, effect a_j) are **random.** MINITAB is informed of this via the subcommand RANDOM.

The standard model remains the same. For example

$$y_{ij} = \mu_g + a_j + e_{ij}$$

However, the interpretation of the parameters, the hypotheses tested, and the F statistic calculations all change.

For example, if each effect a_j has a variance σ_a^2, then the F statistic tests the hypothesis that this variance is 0. If accepted, then all factor levels are identical.

Some experiments have models that include a mix of fixed and random effects. These are called **mixed effects models.**

Interactions

If the effect, say a_j, of factor A is not constant and changes depending on the level of factor B, the factors are said to **interact.** Ideally, the blocks and treatments don't interact, but interaction is possible. The interaction, ab_{jk}, can be incorporated into the standard model. For example

$$y_{ijk} = \mu_g + a_j + b_k + ab_{jk} + e_{ijk}$$

The experiment must be replicated so each data cell contains a minimum of two observations that are used to estimate interaction effects. MINITAB commands such as ANOVA can be specified to include interaction and carry out the appropriate analysis. Separate F statistics are computed for interactions.

S T A T I S T I C A L   H I G H L I G H T S

Experimental designs are available for a single factor of main interest that is accompanied by several nuisance factors.

MANY-FACTOR (FACTORIAL) EXPERIMENTS (OPTIONAL)

So far you have seen experiments for a single factor of main interest. If other factors were present, they were of secondary interest as one or more nuisance factors. **Factorial experiments** simultaneously consider many factors of main interest; in addition, nuisance factors can be accommodated.

As an example of a **full factorial experiment,** consider two factors, factor A and factor B, each at two levels, low or high. All possible combinations of levels are

(1)	(low A, low B) or $(-, -)$
(a)	(high A, low B) or $(+, -)$
(b)	(low A, high B) or $(-, +)$
(ab)	(high A, high B) or $(+, +)$

In the rows above, the row identifiers, (1), (a), (b), and (ab), have two meanings. First, they identify four distinct **runs** of the experiment. Second, in computational formulas, they represent the total of the responses of all repetitions (replicates) of that run. In computations, the columns of $+$ and $-$ signs specify how to combine the response totals that are named (1), (a), (b), and (ab). This notation extends easily to more factors.

If all four runs are carried out, the experiment is a full factorial experiment. Anything less is a **fractional factorial experiment.**

Because each factor is at two levels, the total number of runs is $2 \times 2 = 4$. If each factor had three levels—low, medium, and high—the total number of runs would be $3 \times 3 = 9$. If the first factor had two levels and the second three levels, the total number of runs would be $2 \times 3 = 6$. For k factors each at two levels, the total number of runs would be 2^k. For 10 factors, $2^{10} = 1,024$ runs. As the number of factors and levels increase, the required number of runs for a full factorial increase even faster. When runs are expensive or time consuming, you can see how the need for fractional factorials arose.

Viewing Runs as Treatments

You can view each run, (1), (a), (b), and (ab), as a treatment, treatment 1, 2, 3, and 4. After replicating the experiment, it can be analyzed as a one-way experiment, or, if blocking is appropriate, as a two-or-more-way experiment. In such an analysis, recall that the treatment effects are found by subtracting the grand mean from treatment means. Unfortunately, with this approach each treatment effect would be the sum of factor A effect, factor B effect, and an interaction effect. Factorial analysis improves on this situation and gets at the individual rather than the aggregate effects.

Full Factorial Analysis

EXAMPLE 5

AIRPLANE DESIGN

A paper airplane can be made from two pieces of 8.5 by 11 in. writing paper. After a number of folds, one piece of paper forms the front third of the plane, called the "wing" here. From the other piece of paper, the rear two thirds of the plane, called the "tail" here, is constructed. Both the wing and tail are part fuselage. To assemble a plane, the tail slides into the wing and is held fast by folding down the nose.

The wing can be cut to have a slim or fat profile—two levels. The tail can be cut to have a slim or fat profile. Each factor, wing and tail, is at two levels. Therefore, there are four distinct plane designs.

Plane Design 1	(1)	(slim wing, slim tail)	or $(-, -)$
Plane Design 2	(a)	(fat wing, slim tail)	or $(+, -)$
Plane Design 3	(b)	(slim wing, fat tail)	or $(-, +)$
Plane Design 4	(ab)	(fat wing, fat tail)	or $(+, +)$

Examine flight distance for these planes and pick a winning design. For future design modification ideas, study the effects of each factor. Gentle and uniform launches were made from a sitting position. The data are listed below and are available in a computer file.

Problem Statement (a)   Exhibit the analysis methodology by analyzing one replication.

Problem Solution (a)   Full factorial summary information is first provided.

```
Factors:   2    Design:     2, 4
Runs:      4    Replicates:    1
```

Blocking, centerpoints, and aliasing are not considered in this example.

```
Blocks: none   Centerpoints:   0
All terms are free from aliasing
```

Under the headings A, B, and AB you find the same signs as those in the problem statement, except for the additional column AB for interactions. If the effect of factor A is not constant and changes depending on the level of factor B, the factors are said to interact. In factorial experiments, these signs are used to combine responses for estimating factor effects and for computing sums of squares.

```
                                              Run   A   B   AB
Plane Design 1  (1)  (slim wing, slim tail)    1    -   -   +
Plane Design 2  (a)  (fat wing,  slim tail)    2    +   -   -
Plane Design 3  (b)  (slim wing, fat tail)     3    -   +   -
Plane Design 4  (ab) (fat wing,  fat tail)     4    +   +   +
```

The signs from above are used below. The following table includes the response measures y (DIST) as well as the predictor variables x_{1i} (factor A WING), x_{2i} (factor B TAIL), $x_{1i} \times x_{2i}$ (interaction WING and TAIL).

```
       Row   DIST   WING   TAIL   WING×TAIL
(1)     1    111     -1     -1       +1
(a)     2     96      1     -1       -1
(b)     3     91     -1      1       -1
(ab)    4    105      1      1       +1
```

Estimated effects and the related regression coefficients are computed from the y's and x's as follows:

```
WING effect       = 1/2 [-111 + 96 - 91 + 105] = -.5
TAIL effect       = 1/2 [-111 - 96 + 91 + 105] = -5.5
WING×TAIL effect  = 1/2 [+111 - 96 - 91 + 105] = +14.5
```

In general, for a 2^2 design, effect = $1/2r$ [±(1) ±(a) ±(b) ±(ab)], where r is the number of replications (1 here) and (1), (a), (b), and (ab) are response totals.

Because each predictor x is at a low or high level and coded minus or plus one, from low to high spans two units. Therefore, a regression coefficient is half an effect. The constant is the grand average or half of what might be called a total effect.

$$\text{grand average} = \frac{1}{2} \times \frac{1}{2}[+111 \quad +96 \quad +91 \quad +105] = 100.75$$

$$\text{predicted } y_i = 100.75 - 0.25x_{1i} - 2.75x_{2i} + 7.25x_{1i}x_{2i}$$

```
Term          Effect    Coef
Constant                100.75
WING          -0.5      -0.25
TAIL          -5.5      -2.75
WING*TAIL     14.5       7.25
```

You can see in the analysis of variance table that sums of squares have been computed for the WING and TAIL main effects and the WING and TAIL interaction. However, no degrees of freedom are available to estimate the residual mean square error. As a result, we have effects but can't test their significance unless the experiment is replicated.

```
Analysis of Variance for DIST
```

Source	DF	Seq SS	Adj SS	Adj MS	F	P
Main Effects	2	30.50	30.50	15.25	**	
2-Way Interactions	1	210.25	210.25	210.25	**	
Residual Error	0	0.00	0.00	0.00		
Total	3	240.75				

Normal probability plots of effects help judge the significance of factors. If none of the effects are significantly different from zero, the estimated effects plot as a straight line because they are all from a normal population with a zero mean. Significant effects will stand out and deviate from the straight line through the zero effects plotting points. Although the plot is introduced here, it is more useful when many factors are investigated.

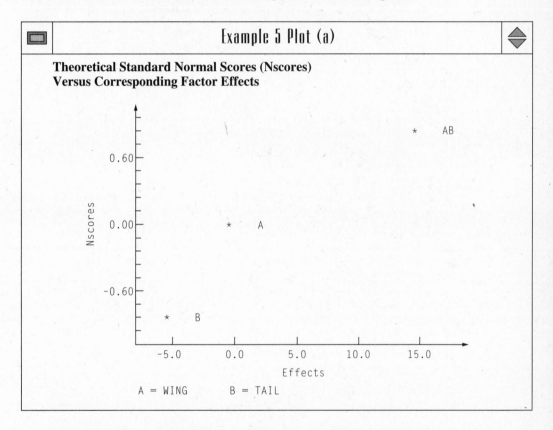

The subcommand CUBE WING*TAIL shows the flight distance response averages at all combinations of the variables WING and TAIL (Plot (b)).

In Plot (c), the flight distance decreases in variability for fat wings. Also, if lines are drawn connecting diagonally opposite points, one line represents fat tails and the other slim tails. Slim tails do best with a slim wing and fat tails do best with a fat wing. These lines cross, which identifies and is characteristic of the interaction effect.

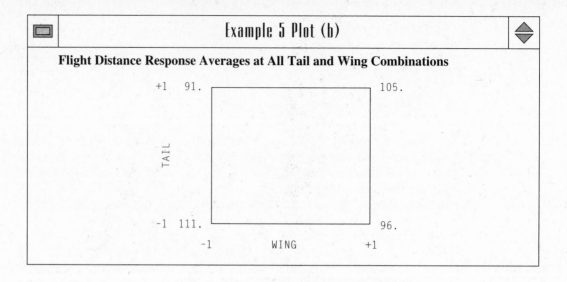

Example 5 Plot (b)

Flight Distance Response Averages at All Tail and Wing Combinations

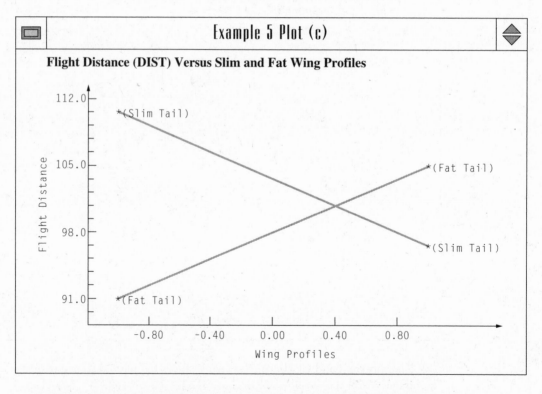

Example 5 Plot (c)

Flight Distance (DIST) Versus Slim and Fat Wing Profiles

In Plot (d), the flight distance has about the same variability for slim or fat tails. Also, if lines are drawn connecting diagonally opposite points, one line represents fat wings and the other slim wings. Slim wings do best with a slim tail and fat wings do best with a fat tail. These lines cross, which identifies and is characteristic of the interaction effect.

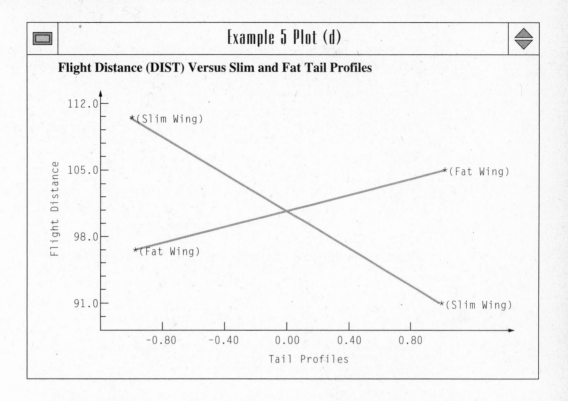

Example 5 Plot (d)

Flight Distance (DIST) Versus Slim and Fat Tail Profiles

Problem Statement (b)   Show the analysis of variance results for five replications of the experiment.

Problem Solution (b)   For the replicated experiment, enough degrees of freedom are available for significant tests. TAIL and the WING*TAIL interaction are significantly different from zero. Again, the plane design with slim wing and slim tail profiles seems to achieve the best flight distance.

```
Full Factorial Design

Factors:   2    Design:      2, 4
Runs:     20    Replicates:     5

Estimated Effects and Coefficients for DIST
```

Term	Effect	Coef	Std Coef	t value	p value
Constant		101.100	1.263	80.05	0.000
WING	-2.600	-1.300	1.263	-1.03	0.319
TAIL	-10.600	-5.300	1.263	-4.20	0.001
WING*TAIL	12.600	6.300	1.263	4.99	0.000

Analysis of Variance for DIST

For our purposes here, ignore the Seq. (sequential) and Adj. (adjusted) designations. For balanced experiments, these sums of squares are the same. These designations are used in unbalanced experiments and are beyond the scope of this presentation.

Source	DF	Seq SS	Adj SS	Adj MS	F	P
Main Effects	2	595.60	595.600	297.80	9.34	0.002
2-Way Interactions	1	793.80	793.800	793.80	24.88	0.000
Residual Error	16	510.40	510.400	31.90		
Total	19	1899.80				

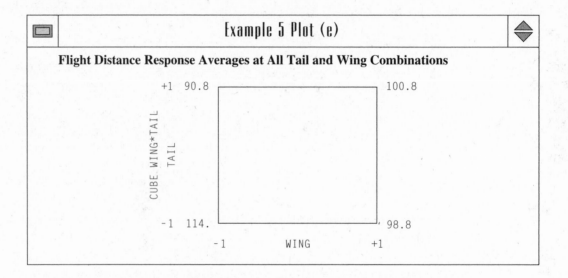

Example 5 Plot (e)

Flight Distance Response Averages at All Tail and Wing Combinations

> S T A T I S T I C A L   H I G H L I G H T S
>
> Factorial experiments simultaneously consider many factors of main interest. In addition, nuisance factors can be accommodated.

CHAPTER SUMMARY

This chapter extended the notion of comparing two population means to more population means. Many means can be compared in a one-way (single-factor) analysis of variance.

When a second nuisance factor comes into play, this factor is blocked and a two-way (factor) analysis of variance is needed. The analysis extends to many levels of each factor and can include additional blocking variables.

In factorial experiments, many factors are investigated simultaneously. Factorial designs allow for many levels of each factor. However, as the number of factors increase, it is economical to limit the factors to a small number of levels.

KEY TERMS

balanced data, 732
blocks, 723
completely randomized design, 716
experimental units, 716
factorial experiments, 734
fixed effects models, 733
fractional factorial experiment, 734
full factorial experiment, 734

Graeco-Latin square, 732
incomplete-blocks designs, 733
interactions, 733
Latin squares, 732
mixed effects models, 733
one-way experiment, 716
paired t test, 731
random effects models, 733

randomized complete-blocks design, 723
runs, 734
single-factor experiment, 716
treatment, 716
two-way design, 723
unbalanced data, 732

EXERCISES

1. Compare the utilization of three exact-change-only highway toll booths by performing a one-way analysis of variance and explain how you reached your conclusions. The figures were compiled during ten different periods of heavy traffic conditions. Maximum utilization is 100%. If the mean utilization is significantly different for the three booths (B1, B2, and B3), management is considering ways of directing the traffic flow to achieve a more balanced use of the three booths. (In MINITAB, RETRIEVE 'B:X15-1')

Row	B1	B2	B3
1	95	71	80
2	79	81	79
3	92	78	82
4	90	78	79
5	91	80	84
6	90	84	78
7	92	82	86
8	86	83	82
9	85	74	83
10	87	75	89

2. One bank teller serves drive-in customers and two tellers serve walk-in customers. The time in minutes to serve a dozen customers each is shown below. (In MINITAB, RETRIEVE 'B:X15-2')

Row	TEL1	TEL2	TEL3
1	2.8	2.9	3.1
2	2.6	3.9	3.2
3	2.6	2.6	3.5
4	2.9	3.1	3.3
5	2.9	3.9	3.5
6	2.8	2.6	2.8
7	2.3	3.3	2.8
8	2.4	3.0	3.1

Row	TEL1	TEL2	TEL3
9	2.0	3.5	2.8
10	2.5	3.1	3.4
11	2.4	3.2	2.9
12	2.0	2.4	2.8

(a) Does a one-way analysis of variance indicate a significant difference in teller mean service times? Explain how you reached your conclusion.

(b) The drive-in teller (TEL1) has requested a pay raise and claims to work faster than the other two tellers. Management asserts that this experiment does not prove the teller's point because drive-in customers may differ from walk-in customers and, therefore, require less service time. Furthermore, walk-in customers tend to talk more to tellers. What do you think should be done?

3. A job shop manufacturing facility has a number of different machines, including lathes, planers, drill presses, and shapers. Periodically, experiments are conducted to compare utilization rates for these machines. The following shaper utilization rates were compiled for three identical shapers. (In MINITAB, RETRIEVE 'B:X15-3')

Row	SH1	SH2	SH3
1	60	54	63
2	51	56	64
3	60	67	62
4	63	53	62
5	60	54	60
6	53	49	61
7	58	50	58
8	58	55	56
9	55	50	59
10		65	52
11		51	
12		49	

(a) Use a one-way analysis of variance to test the hypothesis that the mean utilization rates are the same for these three shapers.

4. Subassembly production rates (in units per hour) are examined for three machine operators (OP1, OP2, and OP3). Six observations are made at random times for each of the three operators. (In MINITAB, RETRIEVE 'B:X15-4')

Row	OP1	OP2	OP3
1	16	26	37
2	12	20	18
3	19	15	17
4	10	24	23
5	26	18	24
6	9	21	19

(a) Use one-way analysis of variance to test the hypothesis that the mean production rates are the same for all operators. If the hypothesis is rejected, management plans to further investigate the work methods of the operators to find out why some operators perform better than others. Thus, better work practices can be incorporated into training programs.

(b) A second experiment was conducted after streamlining work procedures to reduce the high variation in the production rates recorded earlier. Does the data from this experiment produce the same or different results? What evidence is there that the variation in production rates has been reduced? (In MINITAB, RETRIEVE 'B:X15-4b')

Row	OP1	OP2	OP3
1	9	20	26
2	11	22	24
3	14	23	27
4	11	20	22
5	14	20	27
6	13	20	32

5. Returns (in percent) for three different stocks (SK1, SK2, and SK3) are examined over 12 periods. An investment analyst suggested that these stocks have about the same level of risk. Evaluate the analyst's suggestion. In addition, test the hypothesis that the population mean returns the same. (In MINITAB, RETRIEVE 'B:X15-5')

Row	SK1	SK2	SK3
1	9.5	10.7	15.0
2	9.2	16.8	10.5
3	12.8	11.5	15.6
4	12.0	14.7	10.1

Row	SK1	SK2	SK3
5	13.8	14.2	12.3
6	8.7	14.0	10.8
7	10.9	17.0	10.0
8	13.0	11.2	12.5
9	10.3	11.6	11.3
10	15.0	11.2	14.0
11	15.9	10.6	14.6
12	12.5	7.7	16.1

6. Raw materials for a production operation arrive in batches from three suppliers (S1, S2, and S3). Each batch results in 250 units of a finished product. Management thinks that the number of defective finished units of each 250 units produced is attributable to the raw material supplier. Therefore, the number of defectives are recorded and associated with raw material suppliers as follows. (In MINITAB, RETRIEVE 'B:X15-6')

Row	S1	S2	S3
1	9	5	4
2	12	5	1
3	11	5	4
4	7	4	5
5	9	5	5
6	10	5	6
7	9	6	5
8		6	5
9		5	
10		6	
11		4	

(a) If management is considering reducing the number of suppliers and working more closely with suppliers to control raw material quality, which of the suppliers, if any, would seem to require less effort to improve raw material quality? Support your recommendations with data analysis.

7. When it comes to risk, not all mutual funds are alike. Return volatility relative to average annual return (SDRAR) is a risk measure. The higher a fund's SDRAR, the more the fund's price tends to fluctuate. For the following four funds (F1, F2, F3, and F4) over five periods, test the hypothesis that the mean SDRAR's are the same. (In MINITAB, RETRIEVE 'B:X15-7')

Row	F1	F2	F3	F4
1	1.0	1.8	7.3	7.1
2	1.3	2.6	7.6	7.2
3	1.0	1.6	7.2	6.9
4	1.4	2.9	8.1	7.7
5	1.2	2.8	9.0	6.1

8. To assess attitudes and perceptions about eating out, consumers were asked to react to reasons for eating out on a scale from (1) strongly disagree to (5) strongly agree. Perform a one-way analysis on 15 responses to the following reasons for eating out: R1, to enjoy restaurants; R2, for special occasions; R3, to enjoy different restaurants; and R4, to try different ethnic foods. What would you conclude from the analysis? (In MINITAB, RETRIEVE 'B:X15-8')

Row	R1	R2	R3	R4
1	4.8	2.3	3.7	3.0
2	3.0	2.4	4.5	3.1
3	3.4	2.6	3.5	2.1
4	4.2	2.1	2.6	2.5
5	3.6	2.7	2.3	2.6
6	4.4	2.6	3.9	2.4
7	3.4	2.2	3.6	2.6
8	3.4	3.1	3.7	3.1
9	3.8	2.7	2.3	2.0
10	3.7	2.5	3.9	2.6
11	3.6	3.0	3.2	2.0
12	3.2	2.7	2.8	2.1
13	3.6	2.1	3.7	2.7
14	3.6	3.2	4.2	2.5
15	3.6	2.1	3.4	2.9

9. Twenty-four consumers selected at random viewed one of three advertisements (AD1, AD2, and AD3) for a product. Other distractive advertisements were also shown. The following day these consumers were queried and the following recall scores were recorded (the higher the better). (In MINITAB, RETRIEVE 'B:X15-9')

Row	AD1	AD2	AD3
1	21.7	20.9	26.4
2	25.1	18.9	13.7
3	21.8	18.6	21.8
4	25.1	15.0	10.2
5	30.9	19.3	23.5
6	28.4	24.5	37.4
7	16.1	17.7	30.3
8	12.0	29.1	12.9

Test the hypothesis that the population mean recall scores are the same for all advertisements. Use a significance level of .05.

10. The durability of heavy machinery bearings was evaluated for four experimental lubricant types (L1, L2, L3, and L4). Twelve bearings were randomly assigned to each lubricant type to measure wear and tear. Wear and tear is ex-

pressed as a percentage relative to a known standard of 100. Evaluate these figures and pick a lubricant that you think is a clear winner. (In MINITAB, RETRIEVE 'B:X15-10')

Row	L1	L2	L3	L4
1	99	90	101	101
2	93	94	106	100
3	97	101	104	96
4	100	84	107	106
5	98	87	105	93
6	99	99	103	108
7	96	99	94	102
8	96	91	106	100
9	100	85	104	101
10	97	92	111	96
11	98	104	102	114
12	100	87	99	101

11. Machine output in units produced per hour is measured at five speed settings (coded as S = 1, 2, . . . , 5). These data were collected because experienced machine operators reported that output tended to fall at low- and high-speed settings. Few machine operational difficulties occurred at the low-speed settings. However, the output was less than desirable. On the other hand, operational difficulties were frequent at the high-speed settings. This tended to reduce output. Middle-range speed settings were thought to be a compromise. (In MINITAB, RETRIEVE 'B:X15-11')

Row	S=1	S=2	S=3	S=4	S=5
1	194	204	216	204	187
2	210	221	240	206	197
3	202	214	222	203	191
4	188	199	225	201	183

(a) Perform a one-way analysis of variance and test the hypothesis that the mean output is the same at all speed levels.

(b) Plot output versus the coded speed and pick the best speed setting.

(c) (Optional) If the null hypothesis in part (a) is rejected, fit a multiple regression model to predict output with two predictor variables, speed and speed squared. If speed is not restricted to integer values, what is the speed setting that maximizes output?

12. New car and truck long-term ownership cost ratings are provided by consumer magazines. Fuel, insurance, and repair costs are scored on a ten-point scale where a score of ten is the highest cost. These scores are averaged and rounded to obtain an overall average cost score for the following five vehicle class types: C1, subcompacts and compacts; C2, mid-size, full-size, and minivans; C3, luxury cars; C4, sports coupes; and C5, pickups and four-by-fours. Random samples of average cost scores for six vehicles in each class are listed in the right column. (In MINITAB, RETRIEVE 'B:X15-12')

Row	C1	C2	C3	C4	C5
1	4	5	5	7	5
2	3	6	6	4	5
3	4	4	6	6	7
4	3	6	8	5	7
5	2	4	7	8	6
6	2	5	5	8	6

(a) Perform a one-way analysis of variance on these cost figures and state your conclusions.

(b) Perform a separate analysis on the last four classes.

13. The week before professional football playoff games, newspapers are flooded with football statistics. These statistics are used to size up the teams and to help predict which team will win the upcoming game. The following statistics appeared in the *Boston Globe* prior to a playoff game between the Patriots and the Browns.[1] The table displays points scored per quarter (rows) for the year. The third, fourth, fifth, and sixth columns refer to the Patriots, the Patriots' opponents, the Browns, and the Browns' opponents, respectively. (In MINITAB, RETRIEVE 'B:X15-13')

Row	QTR	YRP	YRPO	YRB	YRBO
1	1	46	53	65	52
2	2	95	133	121	58
3	3	94	56	55	28
4	4	110	70	99	66

The following row means and confidence intervals show the tendency for more points to be scored in the second and fourth quarters than in other quarters.

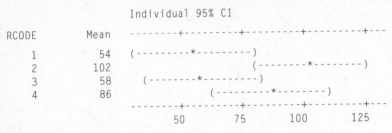

```
                    Individual 95% CI
RCODE      Mean   --------+---------+---------+---------+---
    1        54   (---------*---------)
    2       102                     (---------*---------)
    3        58     (--------*----------)
    4        86            (---------*--------)
                   --------+---------+---------+---------+---
                         50        75       100       125
```

The following column means and confidence intervals show the tendency for fewer points to be scored by the Browns' opponents.

```
                    Individual 95% CI
CCODE      Mean   --------+---------+---------+---------+----
    1        86                  (-----------*-----------)
    2        78                (-----------*-----------)
    3        85                 (----------*----------)
    4        51     (-------------*----------)
                   --------+---------+---------+---------+----
                         40        60        80       100
```

(a) Perform a two-way analysis on these data and state your conclusions. If column means are not significantly different, does this necessarily mean that observed differences (for example, points scored by the Browns' opponents) are not important? Incidentally, the Browns won the game by seven points and the defense played an important role.

(b) Perform a two-way analysis on the following data on the last eight games for each team and state your conclusions.

Row	QTR	S8P	S8PO	S8BO	S8BO
1	1	19	23	28	28
2	2	37	47	24	24
3	3	51	13	12	12
4	4	60	23	35	35

(c) Perform a two-way analysis on the following data on the first eight games for each team and state your conclusions.

Row	QTR	F8P	F8PO	F8B	F8BO
1	1	27	30	35	24
2	2	58	86	68	34
3	3	43	43	35	16
4	4	50	47	42	31

14. The following table lists, for the season, the total points scored against the top four teams in each division of the AFC and the NFC of the National Football League.[2] The weaker the defense, the more points were scored against them. (In MINITAB, RETRIEVE 'B:X15-14')

DIVRANK	AFCE	AFCC	AFCW	NFCE	NFCC	NFCW
1	327	234	306	248	314	296
2	312	203	298	305	287	407
3	320	406	327	267	342	385
4	356	352	396	308	307	365

(a) Perform a two-way analysis of variance on these data and state your conclusions about defensive play for the top four teams within and between divisions. If row means are not significantly different, does this necessarily mean that observed differences are not important to rankings within divisions?

(b) The following table lists, for the season, the total points scored for the top four teams in each division. The stronger the offense, the more points were scored. Perform the same analysis as in part (a).

DIVRANK	FAFCE	FAFCC	FAFCW	FNFCE	FNFCC	FNFCW
1	389	316	381	414	356	505
2	351	340	319	279	382	348
3	307	276	303	235	357	317
4	340	226	347	308	271	286

(c) The following table lists, for the season, the total points scored for minus the total points against the top four teams in each division. The stronger the combined offense and defense, the larger was the difference. Perform the same analysis as in part (a).

Row	DRANK	DAE	DAC	DAW	DNE	DNC	DNW
1	1	62	82	75	166	42	209
2	2	39	137	21	-26	95	-59
3	3	-13	-130	-24	-32	15	-68
4	4	-16	-126	-49	0	-36	-79

15. The number of defective pieces per thousand units produced is tabulated below for four workers (W1, W2, W3, and W4) during two-hour periods within a day. The periods are from eight to ten, ten to noon, one to three, and three to five. (In MINITAB, RETRIEVE 'B:X15-15')

Row	PERIOD	W1	W2	W3	W4
1	1	10	11	8	12
2	2	9	8	7	10
3	3	12	13	11	11
4	4	13	14	10	14

(a) Perform a one-way analysis that ignores the effects of the time period within each day. Is there a significant difference in the mean number of defectives for workers?

(b) Perform a two-way analysis that is preferred because it accounts for treatments (columns) and blocks (rows).

(c) Do different conclusions result in part (a) and part (b)? If so, what conclusions do you recommend?

(d) Is there any evidence that the time period within each day (which is included in a two-way analysis) reduces the error sum of squares in the analysis of variance table? If so, what effect does this have on the calculated F statistics?

(e) Management feels that fatigue sets in as the day progresses and therefore more defectives result. Would you agree?

16. The specific volume of a rubber-based product is thought to depend on pressure (P1, P2, P3) at four temperature settings. Management wants engineering to examine these data because product performance and durability are related to specific volume. Furthermore, if there are no significant differences in specific volume due to these levels of pressure and temperature, the manufacturing process can be simplified to reduce costs. (In MINITAB, RETRIEVE 'B:X15-16')

Row	TEMPLEVL	P1	P2	P3
1	1	182	213	258
2	2	240	279	320
3	3	296	348	387
4	4	325	367	420

(a) Perform a two-way analysis of variance and summarize the results.

(b) If the mean specific volume is significantly different at different termperature and pressure levels, plot specific volume versus temperature level for all pressure levels. Plot specific volume versus pressure level for all temperature levels. Are there any patterns apparent in these plots? If so, what are they?

(c) Fit simple regression lines to specific volume versus pressure level and to specific volume versus temperature level. The temperatures are 0, 10, 20, and 25° Celsius, and the pressures are 400, 300, and 200 kilograms per square centimeter, respectively.

17. Measuring consumer interest in a brand or product is the crux of many marketing research studies. As an example, a product that achieves the highest score (percentage of respondents) to the first of the following five queries is considered to have the strongest sales potential:

Definitely would buy.

Probably would buy.

Might buy.

Probably would not buy.

Definitely would not buy.

The "definitely would buy" percentage is referred to as a top box score.

Consider a two-way experiment to compare top box scores for a product packaged in three colors (C1, C2, and C3) and at three prices (P1, P2, and P3). For each of nine cells in a two-way table, 50 randomly chosen consumers provide top box scores after considering the package color and price in a cell. (In MINITAB, RETRIEVE 'B:X15-17')

COLORS	P1	P2	P3
1	37	40	36
2	34	56	42
3	35	38	39

(a) Perform a two-way analysis of variance to see if there is a significant difference in average scores due to different prices or different package colors.

(b) The research firm and their client decided to obtain additional data from two more replicates of this study because of the strong showing made by the package in the second color and price. Perform a two-way analysis on the combined data set shown below. (In MINITAB, RETRIEVE 'B:X15-17b')

Row	COLORS	P1	P2	P3
1	1	37	40	36
2	1	35	42	32
3	1	40	39	34
4	2	34	56	42
5	2	29	60	44
6	2	32	58	41
7	3	35	38	39
8	3	36	36	40
9	3	38	37	37

(c) (Optional) In MINITAB, for this data set use ANOVA C4 = C5 C6 C5*C6 for a two-way analysis that considers the interaction of the row and column variables.

18. The following average monthly rents are for four consecutive periods (P1, P2, P3, and P4) in five regions (R1, R2, . . . , R5). (In MINITAB, RETRIEVE 'B:RENTS')

Region	P1	P2	P3	P4
1	748	749	761	781
2	813	845	851	872
3	571	577	583	582
4	567	571	578	596
5	691	658	640	654

(a) Perform a two-way analysis of variance to test the hypothesis that average rents are the same in all periods and the hypothesis that average rents are the same in all regions.

19. Weld puddle size is important to the strength of metal fabrications. In the table below, weld puddle width is classified by weld gun current and voltage codes (In MINITAB, RETRIEVE 'B:WELD'). Because of an unequal number of observations in each cell, the data are unbalanced. This requires the use of MINITAB'S GLM command (GLM C5 = C7 C8). What do you conclude as a result of this two-way analysis?

ROWS (CURRENT CODES) COLUMNS (VOLTAGE CODES)

	1	2	3
1	0.197	0.176	0.184
	0.160	0.142	0.159
	0.143	0.219	0.241
	0.184	0.167	0.181
	0.150	0.150	
	0.127		
2	0.286	0.296	0.318
	0.206	0.222	0.257
3	0.413	0.423	0.418
	0.313	0.354	

20. The following average math SAT scores are classified by gender and year. Perform a two-way analysis with gender as treatments and time period as blocks. Also show that the results of the two-way analysis are identical to those from a paired t test. (In MINITAB, RETRIEVE 'B:MFSAT')

ROWS: YEAR COLUMNS: GENDER

	0	1
1	467	514
2	470	512
3	470	513
4	465	509
5	466	507
6	461	505
7	460	502
8	459	501
9	449	495
10	446	497
11	445	497
12	444	494
13	443	493

21. The following average verbal SAT scores are classified by gender and year. Perform a two-way analysis with gender as treatments and time period as blocks. Also show that the results of the two-way analysis are identical to those from a paired t test. (In MINITAB, RETRIEVE 'B:MFSAT')

ROWS: YEAR COLUMNS: GENDER

	0	1
1	468	463
2	466	464
3	466	459
4	461	459
5	457	454
6	452	454
7	443	446
8	442	447
9	431	437
10	430	433
11	427	431
12	425	433
13	423	431

22. The following data measure consumer reaction to three different promotional efforts based on coupons, discounts, or free samples. The three treatments were blocked according to five regions. For each block and treatment cell, 100 consumers selected at random were questioned. The highest score (percentage of respondents) to the first of the following five queries indicates the strongest reaction to the promotion:

Definitely would buy.

Probably would buy.

Might buy.

Probably would not buy.

Definitely would not buy.

The "definitely would buy" percentage is referred to as a top box score.

(a) Conduct a two-way analysis to compare top box scores for the three promotions (P1, P2, and P3) in five regions (R1, R2, . . . , R5). (In MINITAB, RETRIEVE 'B:X15-22')

Row	P1	P2	P3
1	38	62	35
2	42	60	39
3	40	64	40
4	44	58	38
5	39	61	41

(b) If the regions do not have significant effects, ignore them and perform a one-way analysis. Do these results lead to different conclusions from those in part (a)?

24. A financial analysis of a company's competitors (CP1, CP2, CP3, CP4) focused on operating expenses as a percentage of sales (OP/S) and research and development expenses as a percentage of sales (R&D/S). Comparative figures were compiled for four years. (In MINITAB, RETRIEVE 'B:X15-24' and 'B:X15-24b', respectively)

Operating Expenses as a Percentage of Sales

Row	YR1	YR2	YR3	YR4
CP1	32.1	28.7	31.2	32.8
CP2	39.7	38.6	38.3	37.6
CP3	32.6	34.1	37.8	39.3
CP4	22.5	25.2	26.1	24.6

Research and Development Expenses as a Percentage of Sales

Row	YR1	YR2	YR3	YR4
CP1	9.7	9.8	10.2	11.4
CP2	8.6	8.9	8.8	9.1
CP3	12.7	12.8	13.2	13.1
CP4	11.2	10.5	9.8	12.2

(a) Perform a two-way analysis on both of the data sets and report your conclusions.

25. Five years of average annual growth rates of exports are tabulated for the world, the United States, the European Economic Community, and Japan.[3] (In MINITAB, RETRIEVE 'B:X15-25')

Row	YR1	YR2	YR3	YR4	YR5
World	4.2	13.3	13.7	15.4	25.5
US	9.3	6.8	5.0	18.6	26.5
ECC	7.7	10.0	16.2	20.9	25.1
Japan	0.6	20.4	19.7	21.2	5.6

(a) Would you conclude that there are significant differences in row means? Would you conclude that there are significant differences in column means? Discuss.

23. Noise in decibels for four commuter aircraft (AP1, AP2, AP3, and AP4) is measured under conditions of take-off, sideline, and approach. (In MINITAB, RETRIEVE 'B:X15-23')

	AP1	AP2	AP3	AP4
Take-off	79	91	90	88
Sideline	88	101	102	93
Approach	89	97	98	96

(a) Perform a two-way analysis to test for equal mean noise levels for aircraft and conditions.

26. Boys and girls of ages three, five, and seven are each given ten pieces of candy.[4] The number of pieces they gave to friends is a measure of sharing. Perform a two-way analysis to see if sharing is related to age, gender, or both. (In MINITAB, RETRIEVE 'B:X15-26')

Row	BOYGRL	AGE3	AGE5	AGE7
1	1	1	3	7
2	1	1	3	5
3	1	0	4	3
4	1	2	5	6
5	2	1	4	9
6	2	0	6	8
7	2	2	5	6
8	2	1	3	7

27. Each of three groups of subjects (G1, G2, G3) were shown one of three videotapes of advertisements for a variety of products. The first tape focused on television advertisements (TA), the second focused on billboard advertisements (BA), and the third focused on newspaper advertisements (NA). Recall scores are listed below for one of the products featured in each advertising instrument. Is there a significant difference in mean recall scores? (In MINITAB, RETRIEVE 'B:X15-27')

	BA	TA	NA
Row	G1	G2	G3
1	7	12	12
2	9	13	4
3	11	11	4
4	13	14	6

28. Concept retention scores (a week after training occurred) are recorded below for morning and afternoon sessions (MAFT) of a company training program. Two groups of four employees received instruction by a lecture method (LECT). Another two groups of four employees received self-paced training (SP). Management believed that morning, self-paced training was best. Is there any statistical justification for this belief? (In MINITAB, RETRIEVE 'B:X15-28')

Row	MAFT	LECT	SP
1	1	11	12
2	1	9	13
3	1	7	11
4	1	13	14
5	2	2	12
6	2	1	7
7	2	0	8
8	2	5	9

29. In the early days of torpedo guidance systems, pigeons were trained to peck at torpedo directional buttons that were superimposed on a target screen. The pigeons were rewarded with food pellets of 20 or 45 milligrams in weight. Little did they know their final reward. Three hunger levels (in hours of food deprivation, 1, 4, or 12) were examined. Potential battleship target hit scores (the higher the better) were recorded with four pigeons in each cell, so to speak. (In MINITAB, RETRIEVE 'B:X15-29')

Row	PCODE	HD1	HD4	HD12
1	1	7	6	13
2	1	3	7	11
3	1	4	10	8
4	1	2	9	8
5	2	8	12	21
6	2	1	12	13
7	2	2	7	19
8	2	5	9	15

(a) Perform a two-way analysis (include interactions) and evaluate.

30. This exercise is similar to the airplane design example of a factorial experiment; however, the response measures differ in numerical value. The following table includes the response measure, y (DIST), as well as the predictor variables x_{1i} (factor A WING), x_{2i} (factor B TAIL), $x_{1i} \times x_{2i}$ (interaction WING and TAIL).

	Row	DIST	WING	TAIL	WING×TAIL
(1)	1	108	-1	-1	+1
(a)	2	92	1	-1	-1
(b)	3	88	-1	1	-1
(ab)	4	102	1	1	+1

(a) Compute the WING, TAIL, and WING × TAIL effects. Also find the grand average.

(b) Use the results in part (a) to find regression coefficients. Then write the prediction equation for predicting flight distance.

(c) Use the prediction equation in part (b) to predict flight distance for a paper plane with a fat wing and a fat tail.

(d) Construct an analysis of variance table and interpret.

31. This exercise is similar to the previous one except that there are two replications of the experiment rather than one. Therefore, there are two flight distance measures for each of the four plane designs. The following table includes the response measure, y (DIST), the total response for each design, as well as the predictor variables x_{1i} (factor A WING), x_{2i} (factor B TAIL), $x_{1i} \times x_{2i}$ (interaction WING and TAIL).

	ROW	DIST	DIST	TOTAL(DIST)	WING	TAIL	WING×TAIL
(1)	1	108	111	219	-1	-1	+1
(a)	2	92	96	188	1	-1	-1
(b)	3	88	91	179	-1	1	-1
(ab)	4	102	105	207	1	1	+1

(a) Compute the WING, TAIL, and WING × TAIL effects. Also find the grand average.

(b) Use the results in part (a) to find regression coefficients. Then write the prediction equation for predicting flight distance.

(c) Use the prediction equation in part (b) to predict flight distance for a paper plane with a fat wing and a fat tail.

(d) Construct an analysis of variance table and interpret.

32. This factorial experiment examines the effect of two factory noise levels (low and high) on the ability of experienced and inexperienced inspectors to detect defectives difficult to spot. The following table includes the response measure, y (percentage of defectives detected, DETPCT), as well as the predictor variables x_{1i} (factor A NOISE), x_{2i} (factor B EXPER), $x_{1i} \times x_{2i}$ (interaction NOISE and EXPER).

Row		DETPCT	NOISE	EXPER	NOISE×EXPER
(1)	1	60	-1	-1	+1
(a)	2	50	1	-1	-1
(b)	3	95	-1	1	-1
(ab)	4	75	1	1	+1

(a) Compute the NOISE, EXPER, and NOISE × EXPER effects. Also find the grand average.

(b) Use the results in part (a) to find regression coefficients. Then write the prediction equation for predicting percentage of defectives detected.

(c) Use the prediction equation in part (b) to predict percentage of defectives detected when inexperienced inspectors are in a high noise factory.

(d) Construct an analysis of variance table and interpret.

33. This exercise is similar to the previous one except that there are three replications of the experiment rather than one. Therefore, there are three response measures for each pair of noise and experience levels. Recall that this factorial experiment examines the effect of two factory noise levels (low and high) on the ability of experienced and inexperienced inspectors to detect defectives difficult to spot. The following table includes the response measure, y (percentage of defectives detected, DETPCT), as well as the predictor variables x_{1i} (factor A NOISE), x_{2i} (factor B EXPER), $x_{1i} \times x_{2i}$ (interaction NOISE and EXPER).

Row		DETPCT	NOISE	EXPER	NOISE×EXPER
(1)	1	60,55,58	-1	-1	+1
(a)	2	50,55,60	1	-1	-1
(b)	3	95,80,90	-1	1	-1
(ab)	4	75,60,70	1	1	+1

(a) Compute the NOISE, EXPER, and NOISE × EXPER effects. Also find the grand average.

(b) Use the results in part (a) to find regression coefficients. Then write the prediction equation for predicting percentage of defectives detected.

(c) Use the prediction equation in part (b) to predict percentage of defectives detected when inexperienced inspectors are in a high noise factory.

(d) Construct an analysis of variance table and interpret.

34. This factorial experiment examines the effect of advertising or no advertising on new product sales in thousands of dollars over a two-week period in cities of the same size. There are two cities (replicates) for each set of conditions. The two factors are television and newspaper advertising instruments. The following table includes the response measure, y (SALES), as well as the predictor variables x_{1i} (factor A TV), x_{2i} (factor B PAPER), $x_{1i} \times x_{2i}$ (interaction TV and PAPER).

Row		SALES	TV	PAPER	TV×PAPER
(1)	1	8.5,9.1	-1	-1	+1
(a)	2	15.2,14.5	1	-1	-1
(b)	3	14.6,12.7	-1	1	-1
(ab)	4	19.2,21.4	1	1	+1

(a) Compute the TV, PAPER, and TV $\times$ PAPER effects. Also find the grand average.

(b) Use the results in part (a) to find regression coefficients. Then write the prediction equation for predicting sales.

(c) Use the prediction equation in part (b) to predict sales when there is both television and newspaper advertising.

(d) Construct an analysis of variance table and interpret.

35. This factorial experiment examines the effect of advertising or no advertising on new product sales in thousands of dollars over a pair of two-week periods in cities of the same size. There are two cities (replicates) for each set of conditions. The two factors are television and newspaper advertising instruments. The following table includes the response measure, y (SALES), as well as the predictor variables x_{1i} (factor A TV), x_{2i} (factor B PAPER), $x_{1i} \times x_{2i}$ (interaction TV and PAPER); x_{3i} (PERIOD) identifies the first and second two-week period.

Row		SALES	TV	PAPER	TV×PAPER	PERIOD
(1)	1	8.5,9.1	-1	-1	+1	-1
(a)	2	15.2,14.5	1	-1	-1	-1
(b)	3	14.6,12.7	-1	1	-1	-1
(ab)	4	19.2,21.4	1	1	+1	-1
(1)	5	10.4,10.7	-1	-1	+1	+1
(a)	6	16.3,15.9	1	-1	-1	+1
(b)	7	15.7,14.2	-1	1	-1	+1
(ab)	8	22.4,24.1	1	1	+1	+1

(a) Compute the TV, PAPER, TV $\times$ PAPER, and PERIOD effects. Also find the grand average.

(b) Use the results in part (a) to find regression coefficients. Then, write the prediction equation for predicting sales.

(c) Use the prediction equation in part (b) to predict sales when there is both television and newspaper advertising during the second two-week period.

(d) Construct an analysis of variance table and interpret.

APPENDIX 1

MINITAB Examples

GASOLINE BRANDS

```
MTB > READ C1-C3
DATA >  17.3    19.4    17.0
DATA >  18.8    17.9    17.2
DATA >  15.9    16.7    19.0
DATA >  17.8    17.3    19.8
DATA >  17.5    17.5    16.5
MTB > NAME C1 'BRAND1' C2 'BRAND2' C3 'BRAND3'
MTB > STACK C1-C3 C4;
SUBC> SUBSCRIPTS C5.     # COLUMN NUMBERS IN C5 (BRANDS)
MTB > BOXPLOTS C4;
SUBC> BY C5.
MTB > AOVONEWAY C1-C3  # DATA IN THREE COLUMNS
MTB > ONEWAY C4 C5, PUT RESIDS C6
# ALTERNATIVE COMMAND, DATA ONE COLUMN C4
MTB > ANOVA C4=C5;        # ALTERNATIVE COMMAND, DATA ONE COLUMN
SUBC> RESIDUALS C6.      # C4=C5 SPECIFIES THE MODEL
MTB > RUNS C6            # $y_{ij} = \mu_g + a_j + e_{ij}.$

MTB > HIST C6
# FOR REGRESSION APPROACH
# SET IN C7
# 5(0),5(1),5(0)
# SET IN C8
# 5(0),5(0),5(1)
# REGRESS C4 2 PRED C7 C8
```

EXAMPLE

VEHICLE TYPES

```
        (OR RETRIEVE 'VEHM' whichever is appropriate.)
MTB > RETRIEVE 'B:VEHM'
MTB > INFO
MTB > PRINT C1-C4
MTB > STACK C1-C4 PUT C5;  # DATA FOR Y
SUBC> SUBSCRIPTS C6.        # TREATMENT INDICES
MTB > BOXPLOTS C5;
SUBC> BY C6.
MTB > ONEWAY C5 C6, RES C7, FITS C8;
SUBC> TUKEY.
MTB > RUNS C7
MTB > HIST C7
MTB > TABLE C6;
SUBC> DATA C8 C7.
# AN ALTERNATIVE GRAPHICAL ANALYSIS IS THE ANALYSIS
# OF MEANS(ANOM) WHICH PRODUCES A CONTROL CHART LIKE
# DISPLAY FOR IDENTIFYING SIGNIFICANTLY DIFFERENT MEANS.
# MTB > GPRO
# MTB > %ANOM C5 C6
```

EXAMPLE

VEHICLE TYPES AND DRIVING CONDITIONS

```
        (OR RETRIEVE 'BVEHM' whichever is appropriate.)
MTB > RETRIEVE 'B:BVEHM'
MTB > INFO
MTB > PRINT C11 C1 C2 C3 C4
MTB > BOXPLOT C5;
SUBC> BY C6.
MTB > BOXPLOT C5;
SUBC> BY C10.
MTB > TWOWAY C5 C6 C10, RESIDS C7, FITS C8;
SUBC> ADDITIVE;
SUBC> MEANS C6 C10.
# ALTERNATIVE COMMAND MTB > ANOVA C5 = C6 C10
```
FOR THE MODEL $y_{ijk} = \mu_g + a_j + b_k + e_{ijk}$
```
# WHERE Y IS C5, C6 TREATMENT INDICES, C10 BLOCK INDICES
MTB > RUNS C7
MTB > HIST C7
# OPTIONAL MTB > TABLE C6;
#          SUBC> DATA C8 C7.
MTB > PLOT C7 C6
MTB > PLOT C7 C10
# AN ALTERNATIVE GRAPHICAL ANALYSIS IS THE ANALYSIS
# OF MEANS(ANOM) WHICH PRODUCES A CONTROL CHART LIKE
# DISPLAY FOR IDENTIFYING SIGNIFICANTLY DIFFERENT MEANS.
# MTB > GPRO
# MTB > %ANOM C5 C6 C10
```

EXAMPLE

JUDGING BREAKFAST CEREALS

```
        (OR RETRIEVE 'CEREAL' whichever is appropriate.)
MTB > RETRIEVE 'B:CEREAL'
MTB > INFO
MTB > RMEAN C1 C2 PUT C7
MTB > MEAN C1
MTB > MEAN C2
MTB > NAME C7 'RMEANS'
MTB > PRINT C1 C2 C7 C6
MTB > ANOVA C3 = C4 C5
# FOR THE MODEL yijk = μg + aj + bk + eijk.
# WHERE Y IS C3, C4 TREATMENT INDICES, C5 BLOCK INDICES
MTB > TTEST C6
```

The commented line reads: FOR THE MODEL $y_{ijk} = \mu_g + a_j + b_k + e_{ijk}$.

EXAMPLE

AIRPLANE DESIGN

```
MTB > BRIEF 4  # LIMITS AMOUNT OF OUTPUT
MTB > NAME C1 'WING' C2 'TAIL' C3 'DIST'
MTB > SET C3
DATA> 111 96 91 105
DATA> END
MTB > FFDESIGN 2 4;  # TWO FACTORS AND FOUR RUNS
SUBC> TERMS C4;      # FOR MINITAB'S USE IN FFACTORIAL
SUBC> XMATRIX C1-C2. # DESIGN MATRIX FOR PREDICTORS
MTB > PRINT 'DIST' 'WING' 'TAIL'
MTB > FFACTORIAL 'DIST' = C4; # C4 FROM FDESIGN,
#                           SPECIFIES MODEL STRUCTURE
SUBC> CUBE WING*TAIL;  # PLOTS CELL MEANS
SUBC> EPLOT;  # NORMAL PROBABILITY VERSUS EFFECTS
SUBC> EFFECTS C10.
MTB > PLOT 'TAIL' 'WING'
MTB > PLOT 'DIST' 'WING'
MTB > PLOT 'DIST' 'TAIL'

        (OR RETRIEVE 'PLANE' whichever is appropriate.)
MTB > RETRIEVE 'B:PLANE'
MTB > INFO
MTB > BRIEF 4
MTB > NAME C1 'WING' C2 'TAIL' C3 'DIST'
MTB > FFDESIGN 2 4;
SUBC> REPLICATES = 5;
SUBC> TERMS C4;
SUBC> XMATRIX C1-C2.
MTB > PRINT 'DIST' 'WING' 'TAIL'
MTB > FFACTORIAL 'DIST'= WING TAIL WING*TAIL;
SUBC> CUBE WING*TAIL;
SUBC> EPLOT.
```

## CHAPTER 16

Classical Time Series Analysis and Forecasting

PRELUDE

Many economic variables that executives watch and need to forecast evolve over time, such as the gross domestic product (GDP), money supply, interest rates, home sales, housing construction, consumer spending, business investment, exports, imports, and so on. In response to anticipated movements of the economy, executives make business decisions that relate to a company's financial health in terms of sales, cost of goods sold, inventory, accounts receivable, assets, income, rate of return, and so on. The tune of fortune or woe is played out over time. Time series analysis and forecasting help managers chart a course for the corporate ship.

Seldom is a time series variable totally predictable. Usually there is a predictable part and an unpredictable part. Although the predictable portion may change over time, its historical pattern may provide clues to the future behavior of the series. Such historical patterns combined with qualitative assessments of current events can provide useful forecasts.

The analysis idea is to decompose the predictable part of a time series into elementary pieces that we try to understand and model. For example, the predictable part of monthly sales may include an overall trend portion and a seasonal portion. From a base figure, suppose sales trends upward, increasing at 100 units per month; however, seasonally, December sales tend to average 50 units above other months. Once such piecewise behavior is understood and summarized, it can be aggregated and used in forecasting. This chapter provides you with a variety of time series analysis and forecasting tools. ◈

INTRODUCTION TO TIME SERIES ANALYSIS

When you watch your money grow in a savings account by examining end-of-month balances, you are looking at **time series data.** Suppose your savings deposits consist of what's left after subtracting expenditures from your paycheck and other revenues. Deposits, expenditures, and revenues are all time series data. Your paycheck might depend on company sales, another time series. And company sales might be related to the gross domestic product. As the GDP moves, sales often follow. Such relationships among time series data can help managers describe, explain, and forecast sales.

Time series data are often contrasted to **cross-sectional data.** For example, your paycheck amounts, week after week, are time series data. But, for any specific week, your paycheck amount and the paycheck amounts for other employees that week are cross-sectional data. Cross-sectional data and time series data are different characters and require different methods of analysis because the data ordering over time is likely to reveal important facts. The purpose of the analysis often differs, too, because in time series analysis you want to know how observations are related in order to forecast what might happen next.

Frequently, cross-sectional data are random samples of unrelated (independent) observations, making histograms, means, standard deviations, and so on valid summaries. Different variables in cross-sectional data sets are often related by regression methods or analysis of variance techniques. Planned experiments are conducted usually at a point in time rather than extending over time because the analysis methodology is designed for such cross-sectional data.

Typically, time series data are not random and arise from observational studies. This complicates the analysis. For example, the month-end price of a stock P_i is not likely to be random. As a result, financial analysis is usually conducted on returns, $R_i = \frac{(P_i - P_{i-1})}{P_{i-1}}$, because returns tend to be random. The differencing in the return calculation tends to eliminate the time dependency in price data. Time series data are not always this easy to prepare for traditional analysis. Time series methods are designed to account for the dependency among data values.

Whereas most of the statistical methods you have encountered so far simply summarize variables or relationships, time series methods profess to summarize history and extend it into the future. This looking-ahead character of time series analysis makes it an important tool for managers who plan and develop strategies to improve an organization's future situation.

In forecasting, time series analysis identifies historical patterns and relationships and extends these patterns into the future. It does this well. Nevertheless, time series analysis is not a substitute for good subjective judgment and anticipation of future scenarios that might differ markedly from the past.

Discrete time series involve observations taken only at specific (often equally spaced) times. Sometimes variables such as the gross domestic product or the Dow-Jones Average are aggregated periodically and only available at specific times. In other cases, continuous variables are sampled at regular periods to form a discrete series. The methods in this chapter are concerned with the analysis of discrete time series data.

Time series methods range from simple to complex tools. Relatively simple methods include **moving averages, single exponential smoothing, trend analysis,** and **double exponential smoothing.** These simple methods model simplistic data patterns. For example, time series data with no trends and no seasonal patterns can be modeled with moving averages or single exponential smoothing. Such time series data tends to be short-term because there is not enough time for trends or seasonal patterns to develop. However, even long-term series without trends or seasonal patterns can be modeled adequately with these methods. When trends are present in the data without seasonal patterns, trend analysis and double exponential smoothing tend to work better than moving averages or single exponential smoothing.

Long-term time series, perhaps several years of data, tend to include trend, seasonal, and cyclical patterns; therefore, more sophisticated forecasting methods are needed. These methods can be classified broadly as **trend-seasonal analysis** and **Box-Jenkins time series analysis.** Trend-seasonal analysis uses a decomposition (or divide-and-conquer) approach. Time series components are isolated in terms of (1) a **long-term trend, T,** (2) a relatively short-term repeating **seasonal pattern, S,** (3) a medium-term **cyclical pattern** (ups and downs) **C,** and (4) an **irregular, I,** which is a random component like an error term in regression models. These components are isolated and their patterns are summarized. Once this is done, the component summaries can be assembled to make forecasts.

Box-Jenkins time series analysis is akin to multiple regression analysis in which some of the predictor variables are lagged response variables, lagged residuals from a fit of lagged response variables, or both lagged response variables and lagged residuals. Thus, Box-Jenkins analysis captures the trend, seasonal, cyclical, and irregular components of a series in its own special way. It is not as intuitive as trend-seasonal analysis. Forecasts and confidence intervals are made on the future behavior of the data series.

Goodness of Fit Measures

For a given time series, an important consideration in choosing a forecasting method is its goodness of fit. Goodness of fit or accuracy measures are a function of the difference between an actual observation, y_i, and a prediction or forecast of it, which is $\hat{y}_i$ at time periods $i = 1, 2, \ldots, n$. Commonly calculated goodness of fit measures in time series analysis include the **mean absolute percentage error (MAPE),** the **mean absolute deviation (MAD),** and the **mean squared deviation (MSD).** The smaller these measures the better. Calculations of these measures accompany examples of forecasting methods that follow. Their mathematical definitions are

$$\text{MAPE} = \frac{\sum \left| \dfrac{y_i - \hat{y}_i}{y_i} \right|}{n} \times 100$$

$$\text{MAD} = \frac{\sum |(y_i - \hat{y}_i)|}{n}$$

$$\text{MSD} = \frac{\sum (y_i - \hat{y}_i)^2}{n}$$

An Unpredictable Series

A random series of observations is unpredictable. There are no patterns, and the time series methodology is of no help in forecasting. A runs test can be used to test the randomness hypothesis.

A close relative of a random series that looks predictable but is not is a series exhibiting **random walk.** For example, the Dow-Jones Average looks predictable, but it is not because the changes (differences) in that series are random with a near 0 mean and a relatively high variance. A runs test on first differences can be used to test the randomness hypothesis of first differences.

A Predictable Series

A predictable series flunks the randomness tests mentioned above. The time series methods that follow are useful in predicting the behavior of nonrandom time series.

SIMPLE MOVING AVERAGE, TREND ANALYSIS, AND SMOOTHING

Short-term weekly sales of items such as bread, butter, milk, and eggs tend to meander about a fixed level without trends or seasonal patterns. Therefore, wholesalers or distributors who supply markets might use simple forecasting methods such as moving averages and single exponential smoothing for forecasting amounts of these items to deliver to each market. Furthermore, these distributors may supply hundreds of markets with thousands of different items. Over the course of a year millions of forecasts might be made. This computational burden is handled by specially designed computer software. Nevertheless, simple forecasting methods are often necessary because of the computational demands.

Moving Averages

Consider time series observations, y_1, y_2, . . . , y_n. A moving average of **length** two averages pairs of observations:

$$\frac{y_1 + y_2}{2}$$

$$\frac{y_2 + y_3}{2}$$

$$\frac{y_3 + y_4}{2}$$

and so on. To see which observations are averaged, draw a box around the first two observations in a list (column) of time series observations. Average those two observations. Then, push the box so that one observation drops out at the top and another enters at the bottom. Average the two observations in the box. Continue until the box includes the last two observations.

A moving average of length three averages three observations:

$$\frac{y_1 + y_2 + y_3}{3}$$

$$\frac{y_2 + y_3 + y_4}{3}$$

$$\frac{y_3 + y_4 + y_5}{3}$$

and so on. To see which observations are averaged, draw a box around the first three observations in a list of time series observations. Average those three observations. Then, push the box so that one observation drops out and another enters. Average the three observations in the box. Continue until the box includes the last three observations.

An increase in the length of a moving average decreases the influence of the entering and exiting observations. Therefore, long moving averages are slow to respond to a rapidly fluctuating time series. The preferred length of a moving average is one that produces the smallest of goodness of fit measures such as MAPE, MAD, or MSD.

EXAMPLE 1

FORECASTING WEEKLY MILK SALES

Problem Statement (a) For 24 weeks of milk sales (in half gallons) in a small market, obtain a time series plot.

Problem Solution (a)

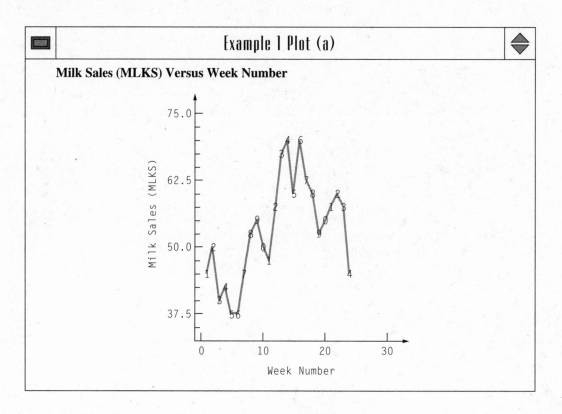

| | Example 1 Plot (a) | |

Milk Sales (MLKS) Versus Week Number

Problem Statement (b) Fit two-, three-, and six-week moving averages.

Problem Solution (b) The fit and forecast (MA2 below) at time, i, is based on observations at $(i - 1)$ and $(i - 2)$ of milk sales (MLKS). Similarly for MA3 and MA6, the previous three and six observations are used, respectively. Only the first 10 and last 4 rows are listed below.

Row	MLKS	MA2	MA3	MA6
1	45	*	*	*
2	51	*	*	*
3	40	48.0	*	*
4	43	45.5	45.3	*
5	38	41.5	44.7	*
6	37	40.5	40.3	*
7	45	37.5	39.3	42.3
8	52	41.0	40.0	42.3
9	56	48.5	44.7	42.5
10	51	54.0	51.0	45.2
21	57	54.5	56.0	60.3
22	59	56.5	55.3	59.8
23	57	58.0	57.3	57.8
24	45	58.0	57.7	56.8

Problem Statement (c)   Plot MA2 and MA6 to see that the longer length average responds more slowly.

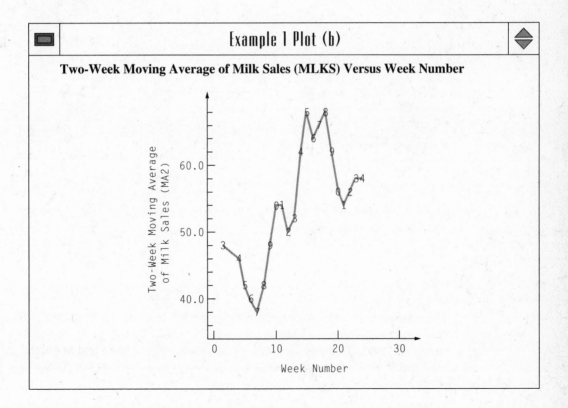

Example 1 Plot (b)

Two-Week Moving Average of Milk Sales (MLKS) Versus Week Number

Problem Solution (c)

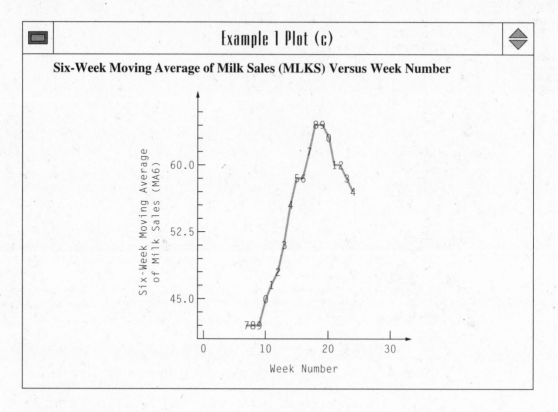

Problem Statement (d)   In terms of goodness of fit or accuracy, choose the best moving average length or fit.

Problem Solution (d)   The following accuracy measures are for moving averages of two, three and six, respectively.

```
        MA2     MA3     MA6
MAPE:  11.65   11.61   12.33
MAD:    6.14    6.24    7.07
MSD:   51.84   58.01   75.94
```

The lower MAPE, MAD, and MSD the better. Therefore, for this time series, MAD and MSD indicate that the shortest length moving average (MA2) is best. However, the MAPE indicates that an MA3 is best. Thus, either a length of two or three can be selected. When the goodness of fit measures conflict, other subjective factors, such as ease of calculation, may lead one to prefer a length of two over a length of three.

Problem Statement (e)   Using a moving average length of two, forecast 5 weeks into the future beyond the 24 weeks of data.

Problem Solution (e)   Forecasts are provided below with prediction limits.

| | | | Prediction Limits | |
Row	Period	Forecast	Lower	Upper
1	25	51	36.89	65.11
2	26	51	36.89	65.11
3	27	51	36.89	65.11
4	28	51	36.89	65.11
5	29	51	36.89	65.11

Single Exponential Smoothing

Like moving averages, single exponential smoothing is used to forecast data without trends or seasonal patterns. Such data tends to be short-term. In single exponential smoothing, a fit or prediction, $\hat{y}_i$, is made at time i, which is based on the previous prediction, $\hat{y}_{i-1}$, and its weighted difference from an observation at that time, $\alpha(y_{i-1} - \hat{y}_{i-1})$, where α is a **smoothing constant.** Therefore,

$$\hat{y}_i = \hat{y}_{i-1} + \alpha(y_{i-1} - \hat{y}_{i-1})$$

The smoothing constant, α, can range from 0 to 1. Smoothing constants at or near 1 result in predictions that are sensitive to recent data and that track rapid variations in the time series. Smoothing constants near 0 respond more slowly.

EXAMPLE 2

SMOOTHING WEEKLY MILK SALES

Problem Statement (a)   For 24 weeks of milk sales (in half gallons) in a small market, use single exponential smoothing to fit this series with three different smoothing constants, α equal to 0.1, 0.5, and 0.9.

Problem Solution (a)   The fits and forecasts at time, i, are listed below. The beginning fit in row one is the average of the first six sales values. Only the first 10 and last 4 rows are listed below. To understand what happens computationally, notice that

$$\hat{y}_i = \hat{y}_{i-1} + \alpha(y_{i-1} - \hat{y}_{i-1})$$

is for row two and a smoothing constant of 0.1.

$$\mathbf{42.6} = 42.3 + 0.1(45 - 42.3)$$

Row	MLKS	SES.1	SES.5	SES.9
1	45	42.3	42.3	42.3
2	51	42.6	43.7	44.7
3	40	43.4	47.3	50.4
4	43	43.1	43.7	41.0
5	38	43.1	43.3	42.8
6	37	42.6	40.7	38.5
7	45	42.0	38.8	37.1
8	52	42.3	41.9	44.2
9	56	43.3	47.0	51.2
10	51	44.6	51.5	55.5
21	57	54.9	56.7	55.8
22	59	55.1	56.9	56.9
23	57	55.5	57.9	58.8
24	45	55.6	57.5	57.2

Problem Statement (b)   Assess the goodness of fit or accuracy based on the smoothing constant choices.

Problem Solution (b)   The accuracy measure are MAPE, MAD, and MSD for the three smoothing constants.

Smoothing Constants

	SES.1	SES.5	SES.9
MAPE:	13.04	10.80	10.93
MAD:	7.32	5.69	5.72
MSD:	89.25	46.65	43.47

The lower MAPE, MAD, and MSD the better. Therefore, for this time series, smoothing constants of 0.5 or 0.9 do better than 0.1.

Problem Statement (c)   Using a smoothing constant of 0.9, forecast five weeks into the future beyond the 24 weeks of data.

Problem Solution (c)   Forecasts are provided below with prediction limits.

Prediction Limits

Row	Period	Forecast	Lower	Upper
1	25	46.22	32.21	60.22
2	26	46.22	32.21	60.22
3	27	46.22	32.21	60.22
4	28	46.22	32.21	60.22
5	29	46.22	32.21	60.22

Double Exponential Smoothing and Trend Analysis

Moving averages and single exponential smoothing perform poorly when time series data are trendy. As long as the time series does not contain seasonal patterns, trend analysis and double exponential smoothing can be used.

Trend analysis is nothing more than regression analysis where the predictor variable is some function of time. The same regression methods covered in earlier chapters can be used to fit linear trends, quadratic trends, exponential growth trends, and Pearl-Reed logistic trend models. These models are of the following form where the predictor variable is set equal to coded values of time, $t = 1, 2, 3, \ldots, n$:

$$\text{(linear trend)} \quad \hat{y}_i = b_0 + b_1 t$$

$$\text{(quadratic trend)} \quad \hat{y}_i = b_0 + b_1 t + b_2 t^2$$

$$\text{(growth trend)} \quad \hat{y}_i = b_0 b_1^t$$

$$\text{(logistic trend)} \quad \hat{y}_i = \frac{10^c}{b_0 + b_1 b_2^t}$$

where c is a constant.

Because trend analysis cannot deal with trend patterns that change, double exponential smoothing is available for both fixed and changing trend patterns. It extends single exponential smoothing of the trend pattern as well as data movements about the trend. However, the computational details of double exponential smoothing will not be presented here. Exercises are provided that use a MINITAB macro to perform double exponential smoothing for those who want to try it.

TREND-SEASONAL ANALYSIS (CLASSICAL DECOMPOSITION)

Certain time series are characterized by stable seasonal patterns, for example, quarterly gross domestic product figures or total U.S. retail sales. Executives and economists often look at such figures for long-range planning purposes with a two- to five-year planning horizon. From this view, they want to focus on trends and cyclical movements with seasonal effects removed. Time series that are aggregated across the whole economy tend to have stable seasonal patterns and tend to be used by planners this way.

Individual company sales tend to be less stable seasonally than aggregate retail sales. Nevertheless, in some industries, there is enough seasonal stability to take advantage of trend-seasonal analysis. In addition to the long-term planning view, company executives need short-term operational information that includes seasonal effects. From the short-term view, managers want to focus on seasonal effects with trend and cyclical movements removed. Trend-seasonal analysis provides views of data patterns to meet various executive needs.

The Multiplicative Time Series Model

Often in trend-seasonal analysis the deviation of the seasonal component from the trend is proportional to the magnitude of the data values. For example, as the data values increase in magnitude, the seasonal deviations from the trend increase. Then the time series y_i is described best by a **multiplicative time series model.**

$$y_i = T_i \times C_i \times S_i \times I_i$$

where $i = 1, 2, 3, \ldots, n$ (one is the first time period and n is the last); and T, C, S, and I represent trend, cyclical, seasonal, and irregular components. The I is regarded as a relative error term that averages out to one. Therefore, predicted y_i is a product of the estimates of T, C, and S.

$$\hat{y}_i = \hat{T}_i \times \hat{C}_i \times \hat{S}_i \times 1$$

When the deviation of the seasonal component from the trend is not proportional to the magnitude of the data values, an **additive time series model** is recommended. The multiplication signs in the above model are replaced by plus signs and the fitting procedure changes.

Model Manipulation   You can take advantage of this multiplicative form for shorter- or longer-term views of the data. Simply divide both sides of the model by whatever effect you want to remove and plot the result. For example, for a longer-term view, remove seasonal effects.

$$\frac{y_i}{S_i} = \frac{T_i \times C_i \times S_i \times I_i}{S_i} = T_i \times C_i \times I_i$$

For a shorter-term view, remove trend and cyclical effects.

$$\frac{y_i}{T_i \times C_i} = \frac{T_i \times C_i \times S_i \times I_i}{T_i \times C_i} = S_i \times I_i$$

Some Notational Alternatives (Optional)   The above notation has become traditional for the multiplicative time series model. It can be confusing for the student on two counts. First, in the regression analysis and analysis of variance from earlier chapters, additive rather than multiplicative models were more common. Second, T, C, and S replace the usual x's for predictors and I replaces e for errors. Although the traditional notation will be used in this chapter, the multiplicative time series model can be recast in more familiar terms to explain it more fully and to link it to the more familiar notation of this text.

(1) Traditional notation $y_i = T_i \times C_i \times S_i \times I_i$

(2) More familiar notation $y_i = (\beta_0 + \beta_1 x_{ti}) x_{ci} x_{si} e_i$

where $T_i = (\beta_0 + \beta_1 x_{ti})$, $C_i = x_{ci}$, $S_i = x_{si}$, and $I_i = e_i$.

Although the trend component is shown as a simple regression model, it can be more complicated, such as a quadratic form.

The trend component is expressed in the same units as y_i. The $C_i = x_{ci}$, $S_i = x_{si}$, and $I_i = e_i$ are all in relative terms. For example, a seasonal effect of $S_i = 1.25$ (a seasonal index of 125%) is 25% above the trend. A cyclical effect of $C_i = .90$ (a cyclical index of 90%) is 10% below the trend.

Now that the multiplicative time series model has been recast to look more like a regression model, why not use regression? Well, you can by introducing a number of dummy variables for cyclical and seasonal effects. However, the trend-seasonal analysis produces a more compact, economical model. Also, some might be inclined to take logarithms of the multiplicative model and transform it to an additive multiple regression model. Unfortunately, $C_i = x_{ci}$ and $S_i = x_{si}$ are not directly observable and have to be computed from observations on y_i. Thus, the traditional form of the multiplicative time series model is used.

Calculating the Seasonal Factors and Deseasonalizing a Time Series

Exhibit 1 is a partial listing of 48 quarters of sales that are deseasonalized. From the sales column on the left, the calculations produce deseasonalized sales in the right-most column, which is

$$\frac{y_i}{S_i} = \frac{T_i \times C_i \times S_i \times I_i}{S_i} = T_i \times C_i \times I_i$$

where S_i is estimated by $\frac{\text{SINDEX}}{100}$. SINDEX is in the next-to-last column. The columns in between are intermediate results of the **ratio-to-moving-average (centered) method,** which is described below.

EXHIBIT 1 Deseasonalizing a Time Series

Row	QSALES	MA4Q	MA2MA	SPCTMA	SINDX	DESES
1	10516.8	*	*	*	92.24	11401.0
2	11575.6	*	*	*	94.94	12192.3
3	10060.9	11922.1	12037.8	83.58	93.67	10740.3
4	15535.2	12153.6	12341.2	125.88	119.14	13039.4
5	11442.8	12528.8	12839.8	89.12	92.24	12404.8
6	13076.3	13150.9	13236.7	98.79	94.94	13773.0
7	12549.4	13322.6	13355.3	93.97	93.67	13396.8
8	16221.9	13388.1	13441.0	120.69	119.14	13615.8
9	11705.0	13493.9	13624.5	85.91	92.24	12689.1
10	13499.6	13755.1	13845.9	97.50	94.94	14218.9
11	13594.0	13936.7	14069.1	96.62	93.67	14511.9
12	16948.2	14201.5	14259.7	118.85	119.14	14225.5
	(rows 13–44 not shown)					
45	20185.8	21356.5	21593.4	93.48	92.24	21883.0
46	20144.8	21830.3	21993.3	91.60	94.94	21218.2
47	22416.9	22156.3	*	*	93.67	23930.7
48	25877.6	*	*	*	119.14	21720.4

The Ratio-to-Moving-Average Method   The details of the calculations for the quarterly data in Exhibit 1 are found in the MINITAB macros used in Appendix 1. Simply run TSANAL. An outline of the ratio-to-moving-average procedure follows:

Step (1):   In reference to Exhibit 1, draw a box around the first four values of QSALES and average them to get the first value of MA4Q.

```
Row    QSALES      MA4Q

 1    10516.8        *
 2    11575.6        *
 3    10060.9     11922.1
 4    15535.2
```

Imagine pushing the box down one row, covering the four values of QSALES in rows 2–5, and average them to get the second value of MA4Q. Continue in this way to compute all moving averages of four quarters in MA4Q.

Note that each MA4Q figure represents four QSALES figures. Hence, MA4Q, a moving average, does not vary as much as QSALES and would plot as a smoother series.

```
Row    QSALES      MA4Q

 1    10516.8        *
 2    11575.6        *
 3    10060.9     11922.1
 4    15535.2     12153.6
 5    11442.8
```

Step (2):   Average adjacent values in column MA4Q to get the values in MA2MA. This is a moving average of two figures in the MA4Q column. For example

```
Row    QSALES      MA4Q      MA2MA

 1    10516.8        *          *
 2    11575.6        *          *
 3    10060.9     11922.1    12037.8
 4    15535.2     12153.6
```

Because 11922.1 (in MA4Q) is an average of four, it actually falls between rows two and three and is off center. Therefore, MA2MA is computed to **center** the moving average.

Step (3):   (QSALES/MA2MA) $\times$ 100 = SPCTMA. This is QSALES as a percentage of a centered moving average.

Step (4):   Compute SINDX by sorting SPCTMA by quarter (Q1, Q2, Q3, Q4 below) averaging the quarter columns and adjusting the quarter averages.

Q1	Q2	Q3	Q4
*	*	83.58	125.88
89.12	98.79	93.97	120.69
85.91	97.50	96.62	118.85
88.48	95.83	97.83	115.82
95.63	87.90	92.52	127.63
88.76	92.83	93.54	120.59
95.38	95.04	89.60	121.41
90.00	94.98	97.41	116.54
96.59	87.62	100.23	110.86
95.06	101.96	88.19	115.64
94.59	98.57	95.22	114.42
93.48	91.60	*	*

QMEANS 92.091   94.783   93.518   118.941

For simplicity, all column values were used to calculate QMEANS; it is sometimes recommended that the largest and smallest column values be dropped before computing QMEANS.

The total of the quarterly means, TQMEANS = 399.333, is used for an adjustment. After adjusting, SINDX sums to 400 across four quarters. The adjustment factor ADJF = 1.00167 = 400/TQMEANS is multiplied times QMEANS to produce the four seasonal index values.

Q1	Q2	Q3	Q4
SINDX 92.24	94.94	93.67	119.14

Repeating themselves in blocks of four, these values of SINDX form the next to last column in Exhibit 1. SINDX/100 estimates S_i and is used to compute the last column of Exhibit 1 by dividing the first column, QSALES by SINDX/100.

$$\frac{y_i}{S_i} = \frac{T_i \times C_i \times S_i \times I_i}{S_i} = T_i \times C_i \times I_i$$

A Plot of Quarterly Sales and Deseasonalized Quarterly Sales In Exhibit 2 plot, the fourth quarter jump in sales is well above that for the other quarters. The other seasonal effects are present but not as exaggerated.

Deseasonalized sales is shown in Exhibit 3. The trend effect is dominant and no obvious cyclical pattern is present.

Once sales is deseasonalized, a linear trend remains that can be fit by simple regression. The fit is.

$$\text{DESES} = 11458 + 229 \times \text{TIME}$$

The predictor variable, TIME, is a MINITAB column, say C1, which is coded 1, 2, . . . , 48. R^2-sq = 93.8%, which indicates a good fit.

EXHIBIT 2 Quarterly Sales Versus Quarter Number

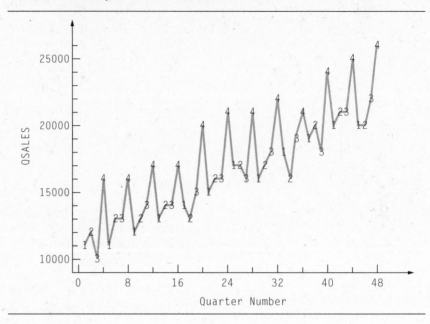

EXHIBIT 3 Deseasonalized Quarterly Sales Versus Quarter Number

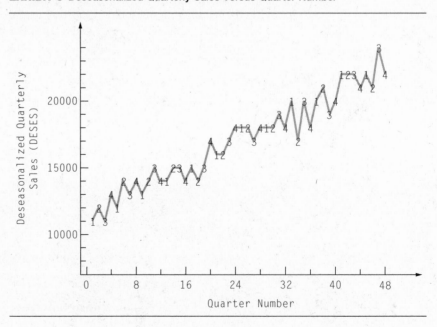

In trend-seasonal analysis, time series components are isolated in terms of (1) a long-term trend, T; (2) a short-term repeating seasonal pattern, S; (3) medium-term cyclical ups and downs, C; and (4) an irregular, I, random component like an error term in regression models. These components are isolated and the patterns summarized. Then the component summaries are assembled and forecasts are made.

Holt-Winters Seasonal Exponential Smoothing

An alternative to the traditional trend-seasonal analysis described above is **Holt-Winters seasonal exponential smoothing.** These models can be multiplicative or additive. Whereas moving averages are at the core of traditional trend-seasonal analysis, exponential smoothing is at the heart of Holt-Winters methods. The details of these procedures will not be described here; however, some chapter exercises provide MINITAB macros that you can try.

BOX-JENKINS TIME SERIES ANALYSIS

Box-Jenkins time series analysis is akin to multiple regression analysis in which some of the predictor variables are lagged response variables, lagged residuals from a fit of lagged response variables, or both lagged response variables and lagged residuals. Thus, Box-Jenkins analysis captures the trend, seasonal, cyclical, and irregular components of a series in its own special way. It is not as intuitive as trend-seasonal analysis, and it has complicated mathematical foundations. This approach also produces forecasts and confidence intervals on the future behavior of time series data.

The Random Walk Model (a Dow-Jones-Like Series)

First we examine a random walk (a Dow-Jones-like) time series. Month-ending values of the Dow-Jones Averages of 30 stock prices are used. This series has a nonconstant mean and is therefore **nonstationary.** This nonstationary series looks predictable because it meanders, but it is not predictable because the changes (or differences, $y_i - y_{i-1}$) are random with a small mean (near 0 over the long run) and a relatively large standard deviation.

On a time series plot, if the Dow-Jones Average, y_{i-1}, at time $(i - 1)$ is known, the change from there to the next future value, y_i, is unpredictable because the changes are random with a small long-term mean. Notationally, the subscripts are i for a particular time instance and $i - 1$ for the previous time instance. A data column of differences, $(y_i - y_{i-1})$, will be referred to as DY. This is a **backward difference** because we look back in time to get y_{i-1}.

To refresh your memory (see Chapter 6, Example 8), recall that month-ending Dow-Jones averages were SET into C1 and differences DY were computed and placed into C2 with the command DIFF LAG 1 FOR C1 PUT INTO C2. A TSPLOT of DY exhibited a constant mean, typifying a stationary series, and the series appeared to be random. If an original series is not stationary, it can be differenced once, DY, twice, DDY, three times, DDDY, or more until the resulting series is stationary. Then the differenced series is prepared for further analysis. A RUNS test confirmed that DY was random. The DESCRIBE command computed the short-term, bull-market sample mean and sample standard deviation of DY, 18.30 and 41.69, respectively. The histogram of DY was skewed a little, but roughly the shape was normal.

Through simulation, we can become more familiar with a Dow-Jones-like (random walk) type of series. Note that

$$DY_i = y_i - y_{i-1} = e_i$$

Recall that DY in Example 8 in Chapter 6 was approximately normal with a mean of 18.30 and a standard deviation of 41.69. During this time span, the Dow-Jones Average tended to drift upward so much that the monthly mean change of 18.30 was much higher than the long-run average. This short-term view can fool some investors. The e_i in a pure random walk has a mean of 0. The nonzero mean, in our example, creates a random walk model with drift. Therefore, the Dow-Jones Average is not a pure random walk; it drifts by a small amount, usually. In this bull market, there was more drift than usual. Perhaps a good time to get out of the market was near the end of this period.

From another earlier example (see Chapter 6, Example 7) a better long-run perspective on the mean change can be obtained. These yearly figures are for the Dow-Jones Average of 65 stock prices, whereas the monthly figures above are for 30 industrial stocks. These yearly figures are over a broader base. C2 contains yearly changes and the summary statistics are

	N	N*	MEAN	MEDIAN	TRMEAN	STDEV	SEMEAN
C2	25	1	18.8	9.8	15.9	50.1	10.0

	MIN	MAX	Q1	Q3
C2	-57.4	160.9	-14.7	38.5

Mean or median yearly changes can be divided by 12 for rough monthly approximations. Furthermore, the mean is inflated by a few observations; therefore, the median might be more representative. The 9.8 divided by 12 shows that over 26 years the monthly change increased less than one point a month. The standard deviation is so large relative to the median that the slow positive drift of the market is obscured because it is swamped by the variability. Hence, for all practical purposes the Dow-Jones Average is unpredictable, particularly in the short run.

Simulating the Dow　Since we know the sample mean and standard deviation of the changes in the monthly Dow-Jones Average, once a starting value, y_{i-1}, is selected, y_i can be simulated iteratively in a MINITAB macro, set up to make the following computation:

$$y_i = y_{i-1} + e_i = y_{i-1} + DY_i$$

DY_i is generated from a normal distribution with a mean of 18.30 and a standard deviation of 41.69, which is based on the sample period. The MINITAB commands for the simulation of the Dow-Jones Average are shown in Appendix 1; the results are shown and discussed below. What you get to see is the synthesis of a particular time series from its basic components.

Typically, in practice, we are confronted with a time series synthesized by Mother Nature. Thus, as a data analyst, our job is to desynthesize by **identifying** and **estimating** the basic components and their relationships. For the most part, identification and estimation can be done by combining experience and several familiar statistical tools.

The plan of this section is to use simulation to familiarize you with the characteristics of common types of time series. Thus, you gain experience through simulation to identify and estimate (fit) time series models.

EXAMPLE 3

SIMULATING THE MONTHLY DOW-JONES AVERAGE, THE SYNTHESIS OF A SERIES

Problem Statement (a)　Simulate and plot 47 monthly Dow-Jones Average figures for 30 industrial stocks based on a short history of performance. During this period, the actual differences, $DY_i = y_i - y_{i-1} = e_i$, had a mean of 18.30 and a standard deviation of 41.69. Use the MINITAB commands in Appendix 1 and a starting value of $y_{i-1} = 1064$ in the following model.

$$y_i = y_{i-1} + e_i$$

If you try MINITAB on a slow computer, excuse the computer's plodding ways. Be patient and say yes to the continue prompt. You might want to rerun the simulation, after setting the mean to one, $MU = 1$, to get a result closer to a pure random walk and the reality of the long-run Dow-Jones Average.

Problem Solution (a)　C2 is the simulated monthly Dow-Jones Average (Plot (a)).

Problem Statement (b)　Proceed with the desynthesis of the simulated Dow-Jones Average by finding the component parts of this simulated series. Thus, the time series data are approached as if we did not know that the series is a simulated one. Later we can compare parameter estimators with the actual parameters used to generate the series.

Examine the autocorrelation function for this series and perform a runs test for randomness.

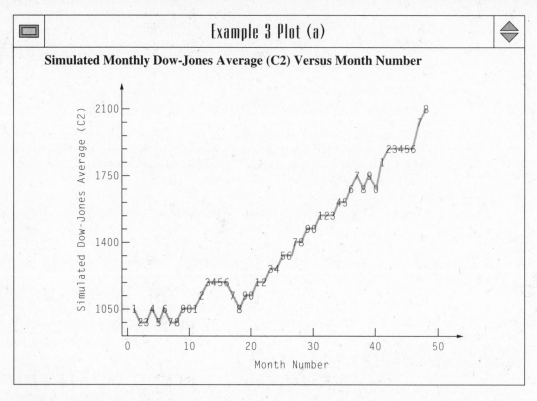

Example 3 Plot (a)

Simulated Monthly Dow-Jones Average (C2) Versus Month Number

Problem Solution (b) The simulated Dow-Jones Average figures in C2 are strongly autocorrelated (see Chapter 12, Example 4, alternative solution (a) and (b), for an introduction to the ACF display). The ACF is slow to decay, as is the case when a series is nonstationary. For good estimates of autocorrelations for lags up to the (series length)$/4$, you need 50 observations or more.

```
ACF of  C2

        -1.0 -0.8 -0.6 -0.4 -0.2  0.0  0.2  0.4  0.6  0.8  1.0
        +----+----+----+----+----+----+----+----+----+----+
   1   0.933                         XXXXXXXXXXXXXXXXXXXXXXXXX
   2   0.869                         XXXXXXXXXXXXXXXXXXXXXXXX
   3   0.809                         XXXXXXXXXXXXXXXXXXXXXXX
   4   0.754                         XXXXXXXXXXXXXXXXXXXXXX
   5   0.695                         XXXXXXXXXXXXXXXXXXXX
   6   0.632                         XXXXXXXXXXXXXXXXXX
   7   0.561                         XXXXXXXXXXXXXXXX
   8   0.500                         XXXXXXXXXXXXXX
   9   0.450                         XXXXXXXXXXXXX
  10   0.397                         XXXXXXXXXXX
  11   0.345                         XXXXXXXXXX
  12   0.283                         XXXXXXXX
  13   0.225                         XXXXXXX
  14   0.176                         XXXXX
  15   0.127                         XXXX
  16   0.080                         XXX
```

A runs test indicates that the series is nonrandom.

```
K =  1392.9610
THE OBSERVED NO. OF RUNS =   2
THE EXPECTED NO. OF RUNS =  24.8333
22 OBSERVATIONS ABOVE K   26 BELOW
         THE TEST IS SIGNIFICANT AT  0.0000
```

Problem Statement (c)   Because the simulated Dow-Jones Average is nonstationary, difference the series in an attempt to obtain stationary differences, which can be further analyzed. If the differences are stationary (random), summarize and compare these results to the actual Dow-Jones Averages during this period.

Problem Solution (c)   The following first differences in C3 appear to be random.

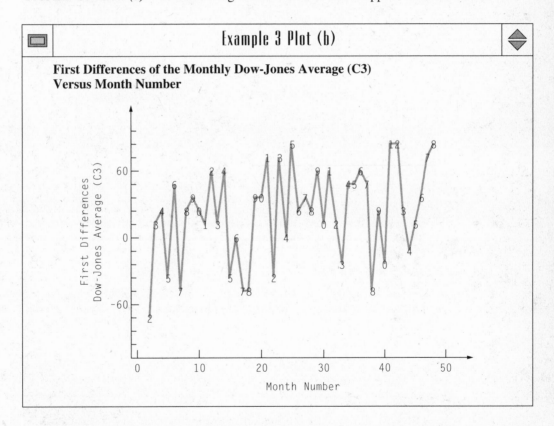

The following ACF of the differences in C3 shows no significant autocorrelations at any lag. Recall that an approximate studentized correlation coefficient is obtained by multiplying each correlation coefficient in the ACF times the square root of the sample size. These studentized coefficients can be compared to a standard or critical value of 2. For the ACF correlation values shown below, none is significantly different from 0. This confirms that changes in the simulated Dow-Jones Average are random.

```
       -1.0 -0.8 -0.6 -0.4 -0.2  0.0  0.2  0.4  0.6  0.8  1.0
       +----+----+----+----+----+----+----+----+----+----+
 1  -0.003                         X
 2   0.149                         XXXX
 3  -0.214                    XXXXXX
 4  -0.080                      XXX
 5   0.143                         XXXXX
 6   0.201                         XXXXX
 7  -0.027                        XX
 8  -0.090                       XXX
 9  -0.132                      XXXX
10  -0.065                       XXX
11   0.212                         XXXXXX
12  -0.006                         X
13   0.091                         XXX
14  -0.031                        XX
15   0.099                         XXX
16   0.149                         XXXXX
```

A runs test indicates that the differenced series is random.

```
        C3 (RUNS TEST)
        K =    21.6789
        THE OBSERVED NO. OF RUNS =  24
        THE EXPECTED NO. OF RUNS =  24.2340
        26 OBSERVATIONS ABOVE K   21 BELOW
                THE TEST IS SIGNIFICANT AT  0.9443
                CANNOT REJECT AT ALPHA = 0.05 (RANDOM)
```

A histogram indicates that the differenced series is not quite normal.

```
Histogram of C3   N = 47

Midpoint   Count

    -80      1   *
    -60      1   *
    -40      6   ******
    -20      2   **
      0      5   *****
     20     11   ***********
     40      9   *********
     60      6   ******
     80      6   ******
```

Because the changes are random, meaningful summary statistics can be computed.

	N	MEAN	MEDIAN	TRMEAN	STDEV	SEMEAN
C3	47	21.68	22.36	22.72	40.94	5.97

	MIN	MAX	Q1	Q3
C3	-75.07	87.41	-3.01	56.61

The descriptive statistics of the simulated changes, where

$$C3 = (y_i - y_{i-1}) = e_i$$

are relatively close to those for actual changes. The actual bull-market sample mean and sample standard deviation of the differences were 18.30 and 41.69, respectively. The differences, C3, arose from a normal distribution with this mean and standard deviation. A starting value of $y_{i-1} = 1,064$ was used.

Problem Discussion   The Dow-Jones Average is an unpredictable random walk type of time series. Its unpredictability is largely due to random changes with a small long-term mean and relatively large variability. The determination that the Dow-Jones Average is unpredictable has important consequences. As a result, it does not make sense to base stock buy-or-sell decisions today on how you think the Dow-Jones Average might chart a future course. This does not mean that you can't find stocks that are good buys or that you can't earn a good return in the stock market. Decisions about what constitutes a good buy are likely to depend on a firm's financial condition and economic factors rather than what you think the Dow Jones Average might do tomorrow.

Autoregressive Integrated Moving Average (ARIMA) Fits

In the acronym ARIMA, AR is for autoregressive, I is for integrated, and MA is for moving average. Examples that follow illustrate AR and MA models separately; then they are assembled or integrated to form ARIMA models. Both AR and MA are special cases of the more general ARIMA models.

Our short-term simulation of the Dow-Jones Average depended on the following model:

$$y_i = y_{i-1} + e_i$$

where e_i had a mean of 18.30 and a standard deviation of 41.69.

Another way to write this model is to include a constant term equal to the mean of 18.30, which results in a 0 mean of the errors, e_i.

$$y_i = 18.30 + 1y_{i-1} + e_i$$

This model is an **autoregressive model** of lag one, **AR(1),**

$$y_i = \beta_0 + \beta_1 y_{i-1} + e_i$$

Simple Regression as a Rough Approximation   Simple regression approximates an AR(1) fit roughly (via the REGRESSION command in MINITAB). Although the intercept is much different from 18.30, the slope is close to one.

$$\text{predicted } y_i = -12.8 + 1.02y_{i-1}$$

Because of nonlinearities (in the sum of the errors squared equation), least squares regression roughly approximates parameters in time series models.

ARIMA, a More Refined Fit   A more refined Box-Jenkins ARIMA fit shown below improves on the approximate regression fit. MINITAB's ARIMA command produces this improved fit.

$$\text{predicted } y_i = 18.298 + 1y_{i-1}$$

In a way that is different from linear regression, the ARIMA command estimates the slope and intercept parameters. Time series analysis theory requires that the parameters, such as β_1, be constrained to lie within certain bounds; otherwise reasonable estimators cannot be computed. Therefore, the ARIMA computational engine needs clean fuel, in the sense that the time series must be stationary. If the series is nonstationary, the series must be differenced enough that the differences become stationary, as evidenced by the ACF dying off quickly. As a result, you will see that the ARIMA command line has the provision for specifying the amount of differencing needed to achieve stationarity.

A first difference is referred to as

$$(y_i - y_{i-1}) = w_i$$

and a particular model structure, such as this one, can be specified in MINITAB's ARIMA command line. The fit below is made in terms of the differences w_i. The 18.298 figure is an estimator obtained in the example that follows.

$$\text{predicted } w_i = \text{predicted } (y_i - y_{i-1}) = 18.298$$

Therefore, after rearranging, the autoregressive form of this equation is

$$\text{predicted } (y_i) = 18.298 + 1y_{i-1}$$

Don't forget that this is a short-term look at the Dow-Jones Average, giving you the wrong impression that you can predict this series. Recall that long-term behavior is random walk with a smaller mean change than you see here.

EXAMPLE 4

DESYNTHESIS OF THE ACTUAL DOW-JONES AVERAGE

Various phases of Box-Jenkins time series analysis are illustrated on the actual Dow-Jones Averages in C1.

Problem Statement (a)   Obtain the ACF to see if the series is stationary. If nonstationary, obtain a partial ACF, PACF, to indicate the amount of differencing that might produce a stationary series. Confirm the stationarity of the differenced series with another ACF.

Problem Solution (a)   In this model identification phase, the ACF of C1 dies out slowly. Therefore, the series is nonstationary and must be differenced. The amount of differencing to achieve stationarity is later specified in MINITAB'S ARIMA command, which produces parameter estimates.

```
      -1.0 -0.8 -0.6 -0.4 -0.2  0.0  0.2  0.4  0.6  0.8  1.0
      +----+----+----+----+----+----+----+----+----+----+
 1   0.924                              XXXXXXXXXXXXXXXXXXXXXXXXX
 2   0.847                              XXXXXXXXXXXXXXXXXXXXXXX
 3   0.778                              XXXXXXXXXXXXXXXXXXXXX
 4   0.707                              XXXXXXXXXXXXXXXXXXX
 5   0.629                              XXXXXXXXXXXXXXXXX
 6   0.553                              XXXXXXXXXXXXXXX
 7   0.464                              XXXXXXXXXXXXX
 8   0.383                              XXXXXXXXXXX
 9   0.301                              XXXXXXXXX
10   0.224                              XXXXXX
11   0.159                              XXXXX
12   0.113                              XXXX
13   0.069                              XXX
14   0.028                              XX
15  -0.003                              X
16  -0.030                              XX
```

In the PACF that follows, there is a significant partial autocorrelation at lag 1. This indicates that lag 1 differencing might be appropriate.

```
      -1.0 -0.8 -0.6 -0.4 -0.2  0.0  0.2  0.4  0.6  0.8  1.0
      +----+----+----+----+----+----+----+----+----+----+
 1   0.924                              XXXXXXXXXXXXXXXXXXXXXXXXX
 2  -0.049                            XX
 3   0.019                              X
 4  -0.057                            XX
 5  -0.086                           XXX
 6  -0.035                            XX
 7  -0.150                          XXXXX
 8   0.005                              X
 9  -0.080                           XXX
10  -0.017                             X
11   0.029                              XX
12   0.068                              XXX
13  -0.005                             X
14  -0.035                            XX
15   0.033                              XX
16  -0.041                            XX
```

If β_1 is near 1 in an AR(1) model, it is equivalent to differencing, which can be shown by rearranging the following equation.

$$y_i = \beta_0 + \beta_1 y_{i-1} + e_i$$

The first differences in C3 produce a random stationary series with no significant autocorrelations. This suggests an ARIMA 0 1 0 fit, where differencing only is specified in the ARIMA argument 0 1 0. Other variations of the argument structure will be illustrated in other examples. The ARIMA command carries out a complicated nonlinear estimation procedure that produces better estimators than least squares regression. The numbers 0 1 and 0 in the ARIMA command line specify, respectively, a model that has 0 autoregressive terms, requiring differencing 1 (once) with 0 moving average terms.

```
ACF of C3

        -1.0 -0.8 -0.6 -0.4 -0.2 0.0  0.2  0.4  0.6  0.8  1.0
         +----+----+----+----+----+----+----+----+----+----+
 1   0.203                          XXXXXX
 2   0.123                          XXXX
 3   0.117                          XXXX
 4   0.084                          XXX
 5   0.032                          XX
 6  -0.041                        XX
 7  -0.165                     XXXXX
 8   0.032                          XX
 9   0.035                          XX
10   0.081                          XXX
11  -0.012                         X
12  -0.107                      XXXX
13   0.036                          XX
14  -0.010                         X
15  -0.015                         X
16   0.059                          XX
```

Problem Statement (b) Fit the model identified in part (a) using simple regression as a rough approximation.

Problem Solution (b) For an approximate AR(1) fit, the regression equation is

$$C1(y_i) = -12.8 + 1.02 \ C2(y_{i-1})$$

47 cases used 1 cases contain missing values

Predictor	Coef	Stdev	t ratio	p value
Constant	-12.82	33.64	-0.38	0.705
C2	1.02288	0.02433	42.05	0.000

s = 41.74   R-sq = 97.5%   R-sq(adj) = 97.5%

Analysis of Variance

SOURCE	DF	SS	MS	F value	p value
Regression	1	3080288	3080288	1767.78	0.000
Error	45	78411	1742		
Total	46	3158699			

Unusual Observations

Obs.	C2	C1	Fit	Stdev.Fit	Residual	St.Resid
14	1258	1164.00	1273.96	6.58	-109.96	-2.67R
20	1113	1212.00	1125.65	8.56	86.35	2.11R
38	1534	1652.00	1556.28	7.42	95.72	2.33R
43	1867	1809.00	1896.90	13.75	-87.90	-2.23R

R denotes an obs. with a large st. resid.

Problem Statement (c)   Fit the model identified in part (a) using a Box-Jenkins ARIMA model.

Problem Solution (c)   The ARIMA command carries out a complicated nonlinear estimation procedure that produces better estimators than least squares regression. The numbers 0 1 and 0 in the ARIMA command line specify, respectively, a model that has 0 autoregressive terms, requiring differencing 1 (once) with 0 moving average terms.

As you will see, differencing alone is a special case of autoregression. Differencing is required to produce a stationary series of differences. A more detailed discussion of moving average time series models is forthcoming.

The results are shown below from an older version of MINITAB's Box-Jenkin's command, ARIMA 0 1 0 data C1. ARIMA 0 1 0 is a special case fit, differencing only. Current MINITAB versions require that there be at least one autoregressive or moving average term. Therefore, the command ARIMA 0 1 0 data C1 won't execute unless you use an earlier version of MINITAB. Nevertheless, the output from the earlier version is quite instructive.

Each iteration of the estimation procedure produces parameter estimates that improve as the sum of the squared errors (SSE) gets smaller. For the model

$$w_i = (y_i - y_{i-1}) = \beta_0 + e_i$$

β_0 is estimated to be 18.298 in iteration two.

Iteration	SSE	Parameters
0	79952.3	18.398
1	79951.8	18.303
2	79951.8	18.298

Relative change in each estimate less than 0.0010; therefore, the estimation iterations are terminated.

Final Estimates of Parameters

Type	Estimate	St. Dev.	t ratio
Constant	18.298	6.081	3.01

The ARIMA 0 1 0 fit, differencing only, is a special case of autoregression as you can see after a little manipulation of the fitted equation. Using the DESCRIBE command, you can verify that changes in the Dow-Jones Average were approximately normal with a mean of 18.30 and a standard deviation of 41.69. From the final estimates of the parameters, listed above, we obtain the following fit:

$$\text{predicted } w_i = \text{predicted } (y_i - y_{i-1}) = 18.298$$

Therefore, this equation's autoregressive form is

$$\text{predicted } (y_i) = 18.298 + 1y_{i-1}$$

```
Differencing: 1 regular difference
No. of obs.:  Original series 48, after differencing 47
Residuals:    SSE = 79951.8 (back forecasts excluded)
              MS  = SSE/DF = 1738.1 where DF = 46.
```

The square root of 1738.1 = 41.69 and is the standard deviation of the changes in the Dow-Jones Averages.

In the table below, if the chi-square values are not substantially larger than the DF values beside them, the residuals have small autocorrelations as you like to see in a final fit, after all systematic components are included in the model. Alternatively, ACF C5, where C5 contains the residuals, would show no significant autocorrelations.

```
Modified Box-Pierce chi-square statistic

Lag                  12          24          36          48
Chi-square  6.9(DF=12)  19.4(DF=24)  28.3(DF=36)   * (DF= *)
```

The ARIMA command computes predictions. Therefore, the actual and predicted Dow-Jones Averages are simultaneously plotted below. The predictions, B's, are very close to the actual data, A's, and overplotting shows as a number.

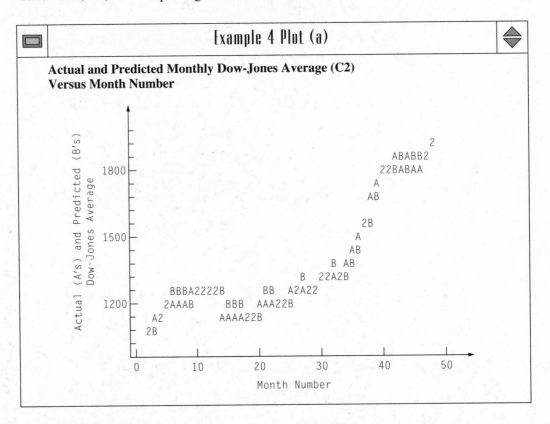

Example 4 Plot (a)

Actual and Predicted Monthly Dow-Jones Average (C2) Versus Month Number

Problem Statement (d) Fit an AR(1) model to first differences.

Problem Solution (d) We proceed to investigate the ARIMA command in more detail by going a step too far here. If the ACF of the differences (changes) in the Dow-Jones Average had a significant autocorrelation at lag 1, this would suggest that we try to fit an AR(1) model to the first differences, an ARIMA 1 1 0. Therefore, we intentionally overfit the Dow-Jones

Average by including both an AR(1) term and differencing. The AR(1) is not needed because there were no significant autocorrelations in the ACF of the differences. It is instructive to see that the AR(1) term is not significant; hence, it is dropped from the model.

The results of ARIMA 1 1 0 data C1 are shown below.

```
Estimates at each iteration

Iteration    SSE              Parameters
    0      77498.6        0.100    16.558
    1      76634.0        0.199    14.744
    2      76631.7        0.204    14.642
    3      76631.7        0.204    14.636
    4      76631.7        0.204    14.636
Relative change in each estimate less than   0.0010

Final Estimates of Parameters

Type      Estimate      St. Dev.   t ratio
AR 1       0.2045        0.1464       1.40   (not significant)
Constant   14.636        6.020        2.43
```

Because first differences

$$(y_i - y_{i-1}) = w_i$$

are specified in the ARIMA command, the fit is made in terms of these differences and is

$$\text{predicted } w_i = 14.636 + .2045w_{i-1}$$

Although the slope coefficient, .2045, is not significantly different from 0 and w_{i-1} is dropped eventually from the model in favor of an ARIMA 0 1 0 fit, it is instructive to substitute for w and to see the form of this model in terms of y.

$$\text{predicted } (y_i - y_{i-1}) = 14.636 + .2045(y_{i-1} - y_{i-2})$$

Adding (y_{i-1}) to both sides of the equation produces

$$\text{predicted } (y_i) = 14.636 + 1.2045y_{i-1} - .2045y_{i-2}$$

Thus, it appears that an AR(1) model of first differences, ARIMA 1 1 0, can be cast as an AR(2) model. However, the y_{i-2} term is not significant in this example.

Problem Statement (e)   Examine the residuals.

Problem Solution (e)   The following diagnostic phase information is produced by MINITAB's ARIMA 1 1 0 command. There is nothing in these diagnostic statistics that tells us that we have overfit the model. The lack of fit statistics are for advanced users.

```
Differencing: 1 regular difference
No. of obs.:  Original series 48, after differencing 47
Residuals:   SSE = 76630.9 (back forecasts excluded)
             MS =  1702.9  DF = 45
```

The square root of 1,702 is the standard deviation of the residuals.

In the table below, if the chi-square values are not substantially larger than the DF values beside them, the residuals have small autocorrelations as you like to see in a good fit. You might also see this result by computing ACF C5, C5 contains the residuals.

```
Modified Box-Pierce chi-square statistic
Lag                12          24          36          48
Chi-square  4.3(DF=11)  12.9(DF=23)  24.3(DF=35)   * (DF= *)
```

A Predictable Series That Exhibits Geometric Growth

In contrast to the unpredictability of the Dow-Jones Average, the GDP (gross domestic product) has a long-term, predictable systematic component. Annual GDP figures were SET into C1. Differences in the LOGE(GDP), called DLY, were computed and placed into C3. A TSPLOT C3, of DLY, exhibited a constant mean, typifying a stationary series, and the DLY series appeared to be random.

If an original series is not stationary, it is differenced once, DLY; twice, DDLY; three times, DDDLY; or more until the resulting series is stationary. Then the differenced series is prepared for further analysis. A RUNS test confirmed that DLY was random. The DESCRIBE command computed the sample mean of .08284 and sample standard deviation of .02273 for DLY. A practical interpretation of this result is that the GDP typically compounds at about 8.284% per year.

In contrast to the Dow-Jones Average, the GDP has a predictable systematic component. Specifically, for DLY (differences in the log of GDP), the standard deviation is about one-quarter of the mean. Whereas for DY (differences in the Dow-Jones Average), the standard deviation was a little more than twice the mean, letting the variability obscure things and make the Dow-Jones Average unpredictable.

EXAMPLE 5

DESYNTHESIS OF THE ACTUAL GROSS DOMESTIC PRODUCT

Seasonally adjusted, yearly GDP figures are examined to illustrate various phases of Box-Jenkins time series analysis.

Problem Statement (a)   Obtain the ACF to see if the series is stationary. If nonstationary, obtain a partial ACF, PACF, to indicate the amount of differencing that might produce a stationary series. Confirm the stationarity of the differenced series with another ACF.

Problem Solution (a)   In this identification phase, a plot of C1 increased geometrically. Therefore, a log transformation of C1, placed in column C2, is linear. Linear relationships are easier to model and to understand. Because changes in C1 tend to increase in variability over time, logs stabilize this increase in variability. Furthermore, the standard deviation of C1 relative to the mean of C1 is large, whereas the standard deviation of C2 (logs of C1) relative to the mean of C2 is substantially smaller than that for C1, which indicates that transformations are likely to be helpful.

The ACF of logs of GDP, C2, does not die out quickly. Therefore, the series is nonstationary and differences are needed.

```
        -1.0 -0.8 -0.6 -0.4 -0.2  0.0  0.2  0.4  0.6  0.8  1.0
         +----+----+----+----+----+----+----+----+----+----+
 1    0.896                        XXXXXXXXXXXXXXXXXXXXXXXX
 2    0.788                        XXXXXXXXXXXXXXXXXXXXXX
 3    0.676                        XXXXXXXXXXXXXXXXXXX
 4    0.566                        XXXXXXXXXXXXXXX
 5    0.457                        XXXXXXXXXXXX
 6    0.345                        XXXXXXXXXX
 7    0.237                        XXXXXXX
 8    0.133                        XXXX
 9    0.036                        XX
10   -0.056                      XX
11   -0.139                    XXXX
12   -0.212                  XXXXX
13   -0.274                 XXXXXXX
14   -0.329                XXXXXXXXX
15   -0.372               XXXXXXXXXX
```

The PACF of C2 indicates that there is a significant correlation at lag 1 and that lag 1 differences are needed.

```
        -1.0 -0.8 -0.6 -0.4 -0.2  0.0  0.2  0.4  0.6  0.8  1.0
         +----+----+----+----+----+----+----+----+----+----+
 1    0.896                        XXXXXXXXXXXXXXXXXXXXXXXX
 2   -0.072                      XXX
 3   -0.081                      XXX
 4   -0.059                       XX
 5   -0.067                      XXX
 6   -0.084                      XXX
 7   -0.067                      XXX
 8   -0.065                      XXX
 9   -0.061                      XXX
10   -0.064                      XXX
11   -0.055                       XX
12   -0.048                       XX
13   -0.049                       XX
14   -0.062                      XXX
15   -0.039                       XX
```

The ACF of differences of log GDP, C4, on the next page shows no significant autocorrelations of differences, suggesting an ARIMA 0 1 0 model for differencing only.

```
            -1.0 -0.8 -0.6 -0.4 -0.2  0.0  0.2  0.4  0.6  0.8  1.0
            +----+----+----+----+----+----+----+----+----+----+
 1   0.230                                XXXXXXX
 2   0.040                                XX
 3   0.249                                XXXXXXX
 4   0.072                                XXX
 5   0.026                                XX
 6  -0.090                             XXX
 7  -0.060                             XXX
 8  -0.105                            XXXX
 9  -0.388                  XXXXXXXXXXX
10  -0.253                        XXXXXXX
11  -0.097                            XXX
12   0.013                                X
13  -0.116                            XXXX
14  -0.285                       XXXXXXXX
15   0.018                                X
```

Problem Statement (b)   Fit the model identified in part (a) using simple regression as a rough approximation.

Problem Solution (b)   First in this estimation phase, simple regression approximates the fit. An approximate AR(1) fit is

$$C2 \ (\log \text{GDP}) = 0.0542 + 1.00 \ C3 \ (\text{lagged log GDP})$$

25 cases used 1 cases contain missing values

Predictor	Coef	Stdev	t ratio	p value
Constant	0.05422	0.05307	1.02	0.318
C3	1.00395	0.00729	137.71	0.000

s = 0.02307   R-sq = 99.9%   R-sq(adj) = 99.9%

Analysis of Variance

SOURCE	DF	SS	MS	F value	p value
Regression	1	10.095	10.095	18962.86	0.000
Error	23	0.012	0.001		
Total	24	10.108			

Unusual Observations

Obs.	C3	C2	Fit	Stdev.Fit	Residual	St.Resid
22	8.02	8.06022	8.10964	0.00728	-0.04942	-2.26R

R denotes an obs. with a large st. resid.

Problem Statement (c)   Fit the model identified in part (a) using a Box-Jenkins ARIMA model.

Problem Solution (c)   The ARIMA command carries out a complicated, nonlinear estimation procedure that produces better estimators than least squares regression. The numbers 0 1 and 0 in the ARIMA command line specify, respectively, a model that has 0 autoregressive terms, requiring differencing 1 (once) with 0 moving average terms. As you will see, differencing alone is a special case of autoregression. Differencing is required to produce a stationary series of differences. A more detailed discussion of moving average, time series models is forthcoming.

The results are shown below from an older version of MINITAB's Box-Jenkin's command, ARIMA 0 1 0 data C1. ARIMA 0 1 0 is a special case fit, differencing only. Current MINITAB versions require at least one autoregressive or moving average term. Therefore, the command ARIMA 0 1 0 data C1 won't execute unless you use an earlier version of MINITAB. Nevertheless, the output from the earlier version is quite instructive.

```
Estimates at each iteration

Iteration      SSE    Parameters
   0        0.262401    0.183
   1        0.013050    0.088
   2        0.012402    0.083
   3        0.012401    0.083
   4        0.012401    0.083
Relative change in each estimate less than 0.0010

Final Estimates of Parameters

Type       Estimate    St. Dev.   t ratio
Constant   0.082845    0.004546    18.22
```

The ARIMA 0 1 0 fit, differencing only, is a special case of autoregression, as you can see after a little manipulation of the equation. Using the DESCRIBE command, you can verify that changes in the log GDP were approximately normal with a mean of .08284 and a standard deviation of .02273. The Ly is short for the natural log of y, where y is the GDP. Also, this prediction is the average compounding rate for the GDP of 8.2845% per year.

$$\text{predicted } (Ly_i - Ly_{i-1}) = 0.082845$$

Rearranging the equation produces the autoregressive form, which is

$$\text{predicted } (Ly_i) = 0.082845 + 1Ly_{i-1}$$

The (square root of (MS = .0005167)) = .02273 and is the standard deviation of the changes in the log of the GDP. Because this variation is small relative to the mean, the GDP has a predictable, systematic growth rate.

```
Differencing: 1 regular difference
No. of obs.:  Original series 26, after differencing 25
Residuals:    SS = 0.0124007  (back forecasts excluded)
              MS = 0.0005167  DF = 24
```

```
Modified Box-Pierce chi-square statistic
Lag                 12          24          36          48
Chi-square    14.2(DF=12)  26.7(DF=24)  * (DF= *)   * (DF= *)
```

Descriptive statistics on the differences of the logs of the GDP are

	N	N*	MEAN	MEDIAN	TRMEAN	STDEV	SEMEAN
C4	25	1	0.08284	0.08184	0.08314	0.02273	0.00455

	MIN	MAX	Q1	Q3
C4	0.03648	0.12241	0.06475	0.10549

Problem Statement (d)   Examine diagnostic information.

Problem Solution (d)   The ARIMA command puts the predictions in C6. If we exponentiate C6, which is e^{C6}, and put the results into C8, C8 contains predictions on the same scale as actual GDP figures in C1. Both C1 and C8 are plotted simultaneously. Clearly, the fit is a good one.

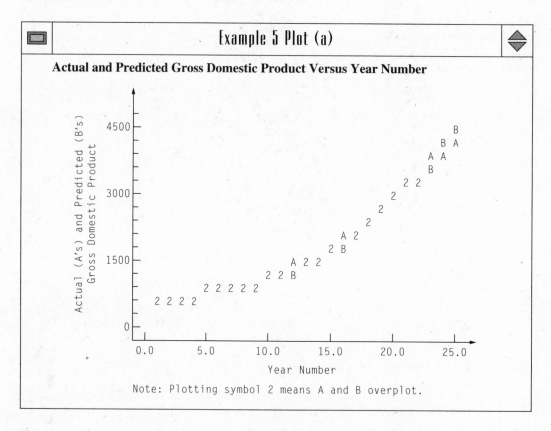

Example 5 Plot (a)

Actual and Predicted Gross Domestic Product Versus Year Number

Note: Plotting symbol 2 means A and B overplot.

Although residual analysis is not shown, it is expected that one would check residuals, C7, for normality and randomness. Typically, one might inspect a histogram, runs test, and an autocorrelation function.

More Sophisticated Time Series Models

Miller and Wichern have written three time series analysis chapters that are well worth reading.[1] One series they analyze is the percentage of U.S. unemployment rates. That series is simulated here, synthesizing it as if the parameters were known. In actuality, this series is generated by the U.S. economic engine. The synthesis done here illustrates the building blocks of an AR(2) time series.

After building the series, we take it apart. The parts form a fitted model. In this way, a time series model-building strategy is illustrated. Starting with an inadequate AR(1) fit, diagnostics suggest that an AR(2) fit might be better. A final AR(2) fit is made, which has parameter estimates that approximate the parameters used to simulate this series.

EXAMPLE 6

MODEL-BUILDING STRATEGY, MONTHLY UNEMPLOYMENT RATES

This simulation is based on the following autoregressive model. The parameters are known and e_i is random.

$$y_i = .5 + 1.5y_{i-1} - .6y_{i-2} + e_i$$

In general terms

$$y_i = \beta_0 + \beta_1 y_{i-1} + \beta_2 y_{i-2} + e_i$$

By picking different parameter values, you may experiment with a wide variety of AR(2) simulations as long as the parameter values are bounded, $(\beta_2 + \beta_1) < 1$, $(\beta_2 - \beta_1) < 1$, and $-1 < \beta_2 < 1$. For simulating an AR(1) series, drop the y_{i-2} term from the model and use the constraint, $-1 < \beta_1 < 1$.

Problem Statement (a)   Use a MINITAB macro in Appendix 1 to simulate monthly unemployment rates. Obtain the ACF to see if the series is stationary. If stationary, use the PACF to suggest the number of lagged autoregressive terms needed in the fit. If nonstationary, obtain a partial ACF (PACF) to indicate the amount of differencing that might produce a stationary series.

Problem Solution (a)   In this identification phase, C2 contains simulated monthly unemployment rates; 60 of the 61 values are shown in Plot (a).

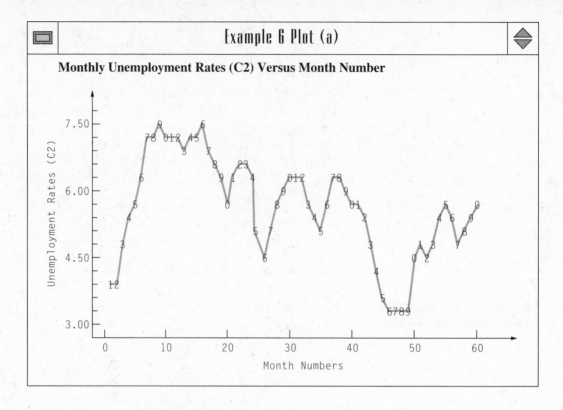

Example 6 Plot (a)

Monthly Unemployment Rates (C2) Versus Month Number

Descriptive statistics for C2 are

	N	MEAN	MEDIAN	TRMEAN	STDEV	SEMEAN
C2	61	5.635	5.730	5.671	1.133	0.145

	MIN	MAX	Q1	Q3
C2	3.191	7.369	4.914	6.411

The nonrandom nature of this series suggests that there is a predictable pattern present. Predictability will have the effect of reducing the uncertainty reflected in the standard deviation in the descriptive statistics above.

```
C2 (Runs test---nonrandom)
K =     5.6351
THE OBSERVED NO. OF RUNS =   10
THE EXPECTED NO. OF RUNS =   31.0984
34 OBSERVATIONS ABOVE K    27 BELOW
          THE TEST IS SIGNIFICANT AT   0.0000
```

The ACF of C2 follows. The ACF dies off rather quickly, indicating that differencing is not needed.

```
            -1.0 -0.8 -0.6 -0.4 -0.2  0.0  0.2  0.4  0.6  0.8  1.0
             +----+----+----+----+----+----+----+----+----+----+
   1   0.906                            XXXXXXXXXXXXXXXXXXXXXXXX
   2   0.746                            XXXXXXXXXXXXXXXXXXXX
   3   0.604                            XXXXXXXXXXXXXXX
   4   0.482                            XXXXXXXXXXXX
   5   0.379                            XXXXXXXXXX
   6   0.301                            XXXXXXXX
   7   0.246                            XXXXXX
   8   0.196                            XXXXX
   9   0.143                            XXXXX
  10   0.075                            XXX
  11   0.013                            X
  12  -0.021                           XX
  13  -0.040                           XX
  14  -0.049                           XX
  15  -0.059                           XX
  16  -0.067                          XXX
  17  -0.066                          XXX
```

In the PACF below, the first two partial autocorrelation coefficients are significantly different from 0, hinting that this series might be represented by an AR(2) model and using the ARIMA 2 0 0 command in MINITAB.

```
PACF of C2
            -1.0 -0.8 -0.6 -0.4 -0.2  0.0  0.2  0.4  0.6  0.8  1.0
             +----+----+----+----+----+----+----+----+----+----+
   1   0.906                            XXXXXXXXXXXXXXXXXXXXXXXX
   2  -0.417                 XXXXXXXXXXX
   3   0.163                            XXXXX
   4  -0.101                        XXXX
   5   0.028                            XX
   6   0.024                            XX
   7   0.022                            XX
   8  -0.074                          XXX
   9  -0.025                           XX
  10  -0.142                       XXXXX
  11   0.078                            XXX
  12   0.035                            XX
  13  -0.033                           XX
  14   0.036                            XX
  15  -0.090                          XXX
  16   0.040                            XX
  17   0.034                            XX
```

Problem Statement (b)   Fit and evaluate an AR(1) Box-Jenkins ARIMA model.

Problem Solution (b)   Although the identification phase indicated that an AR(2) fit is likely to be the fit of choice, for instructive purposes an AR(1) fit is made first. In particular, notice that the diagnostic examination of residuals leads to the conclusion that an AR(1) fit is inadequate. Therefore, proceed to try an AR(2) fit. The diagnostics from the AR(2) fit show that this fit is an adequate one.

For an AR(1) fit, the ARIMA 1 0 0 command in MINITAB is employed. The following fit information is obtained:

```
Estimates at each iteration

Iteration        SSE      Parameters
    0         64.2941    0.100    5.162
    1         47.1004    0.250    4.299
    2         33.2375    0.400    3.437
    3         22.7044    0.550    2.575
    4         15.5004    0.700    1.713
    5         11.6265    0.850    .0.852
    6         10.9577    0.918    0.459
    7         10.8905    0.934    0.359
    8         10.8782    0.941    0.318
    9         10.8758    0.944    0.298
   10         10.8753    0.946    0.288
   11         10.8753    0.947    0.283

Unable to reduce sum of squares any further

* WARNING * Back forecasts not dying out rapidly
```

In order to reduce approximation errors and to produce better parameter estimates, the ARIMA command **back forecasts.** It artificially extends the series into the past. Here the back forecasting procedure goes through several futile iterations, a harbinger of problems with the AR(1) fit.

```
Back forecasts (after differencing)
Lag  -98 -  -93    5.317  5.316  5.316  5.315  5.315  5.315
Lag  -92 -  -87    5.314  5.314  5.313  5.312  5.312  5.311
Lag  -86 -  -81    5.310  5.310  5.309  5.308  5.307  5.306
Lag  -80 -  -75    5.305  5.304  5.303  5.302  5.301  5.300

CONTINUE? (Say YES.  Lots of back forecasts are edited out.)

Final Estimates of Parameters

Type       Estimate    St. Dev.   t ratio
AR   1       0.9468      0.0475     19.92
Constant   0.28345      0.05604      5.06
Mean         5.323       1.052
```

This fit can be compared to the model simulating the data to see if the estimated parameters are approaching the known ones.

$$y_i = .5 + 1.5y_{i-1} - .6y_{i-2} + e_i \quad \text{(the known model)}$$
$$\hat{y}_i = .28345 + .9468y_{i-1} \quad \text{(the AR(1) fit)}$$

The parameter estimates are far from the true values at this stage.

The following diagnostic information is available.

```
Number of obs.:  61
Residuals:    SSE = 10.6597 (back forecasts excluded)
              MS =  0.1807 DF = 59

Modified Box-Pierce chi-square statistic

Lag                  12            24           36           48
Chi-square  20.0(DF=11)  28.5(DF=23)  38.6(DF=35)  60.8(DF=47)
```

The residuals, C5, look normal in the following histogram.

```
Histogram of C5   N = 61

Midpoint    Count
   -1.0       1   *
   -0.8       0
   -0.6       6   ******
   -0.4       6   ******
   -0.2      11   **********
    0.0      10   *********
    0.2      10   *********
    0.4       8   ********
    0.6       5   *****
    0.8       2   **
    1.0       2   **
```

　　The ACF of the residuals, C5, indicates that a significant autocorrelation remains at a lag of 1. Now the autocorrelations are smaller than those in the original series. This indicates that some progress has been made with the AR(1) model; however, the fit can be improved.

```
ACF C5
             -1.0 -0.8 -0.6 -0.4 -0.2  0.0  0.2  0.4  0.6  0.8  1.0
             +----+----+----+----+----+----+----+----+----+----+
  1   0.472                           XXXXXXXXXXXXX
  2   0.039                           XX
  3  -0.050                           XX
  4  -0.092                          XXX
  5  -0.055                           XX
  6  -0.029                           XX
  7   0.005                           X
  8   0.074                           XXX
  9   0.119                           XXXX
 10  -0.064                          XXX
 11  -0.167                        XXXXX
 12  -0.096                          XXX
 13  -0.018                           X
 14   0.047                           XX
 15   0.015                           X
 16  -0.121                         XXXX
 17  -0.148                        XXXXX
```

Problem Statement (c) Fit and evaluate an AR(2) model as the previous analysis suggests.

Problem Solution (c) The estimation phase is resumed here. The ACF of the AR(1) residuals suggested that this series might be represented by an AR(2) model. The ARIMA 2 0 0 command in MINITAB results in the following output.

```
Estimates at each iteration

Iteration       SSE      Parameters
     0       54.7994   0.100    0.100   4.588
     1       44.3185   0.250    0.035   4.099
     2       35.4766   0.400   -0.035   3.636
     3       28.0334   0.550   -0.107   3.191
     4       21.8614   0.700   -0.182   2.759
     5       16.8764   0.850   -0.259   2.337
     6       13.0154   1.000   -0.337   1.921
     7       10.2391   1.150   -0.415   1.509
     8        8.5138   1.300   -0.493   1.092
     9        7.8646   1.434   -0.557   0.693
    10        7.8391   1.441   -0.551   0.613
    11        7.8363   1.440   -0.546   0.589
    12        7.8360   1.439   -0.544   0.581
    13        7.8359   1.439   -0.543   0.578
    14        7.8359   1.439   -0.543   0.577

Relative change in each estimate less than  0.0010
CONTINUE? YES

Final Estimates of Parameters

Type       Estimate    St. Dev.   t ratio

AR    1      1.4392     0.1111     12.96
AR    2     -0.5432     0.1097     -4.95
Constant     0.5772     0.0464     12.44
Mean         5.5503     0.4462
```

The fit can be compared to the model simulating the data to see if the estimated parameters are approaching the known ones.

$$y_i = .5 + 1.5y_{i-1} - .6y_{i-2} + e_i \quad \text{(the known model)}$$
$$\hat{y}_i = .57723 + 1.4392y_{i-1} - .5432y_{i-2} \quad \text{(the AR(2) fit)}$$

The parameter estimates are relatively close to the known parameter values. The t ratios show that the estimators are significantly different from 0.

In general, the following diagnostics indicate that the residuals in C5 are normal and independent, confirming that the AR(2) fit is the fit of choice.

```
No. of obs.:  61
Residuals:    SS = 7.58249  (back forecasts excluded)
              MS = 0.13073  DF = 58
```

Modified Box-Pierce chi-square statistic

```
Lag                 12          24          36          48
Chi-square  8.4(DF=10)  15.1(DF=22)  24.4(DF=34)  34.9(DF=46)
```

Histogram of C5   N = 61

```
Midpoint   Count
    -1.0       1    *
    -0.8       0
    -0.6       2    **
    -0.4       7    *******
    -0.2      12    ************
     0.0      18    ******************
     0.2      11    ***********
     0.4       4    ****
     0.6       2    **
     0.8       4    ****
```

```
    C5 (RUNS TEST)
    K =      0.0225
    THE OBSERVED NO. OF RUNS =  29
    THE EXPECTED NO. OF RUNS =  31.0984
    27 OBSERVATIONS ABOVE K   34 BELOW
            THE TEST IS SIGNIFICANT AT  0.5830
            CANNOT REJECT AT ALPHA = 0.05
```

ACF of C5

```
          -1.0 -0.8 -0.6 -0.4 -0.2  0.0  0.2  0.4  0.6  0.8  1.0
          +----+----+----+----+----+----+----+----+----+----+
  1   0.040                            XX
  2  -0.186                         XXXXX
  3   0.027                            XX
  4  -0.012                            X
  5   0.059                            XX
  6   0.042                            XX
  7   0.014                            X
  8   0.066                            XXX
  9   0.222                            XXXXXXX
 10  -0.051                           XX
 11  -0.138                         XXXX
 12   0.002                            X
 13   0.022                            XX
 14   0.089                            XXX
 15   0.092                            XXX
 16  -0.098                          XXX
 17  -0.131                         XXXX
```

The original series C2 and the predictions C4 are plotted simultaneously in Plot (b). The AR(2) fit is a reasonably good one.

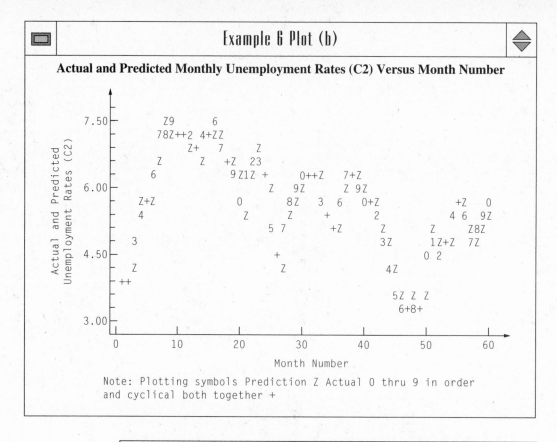

Example 6 Plot (b)

Actual and Predicted Monthly Unemployment Rates (C2) Versus Month Number

Note: Plotting symbols Prediction Z Actual 0 thru 9 in order and cyclical both together +

Box-Jenkins time series analysis is akin to multiple regression analysis in which some of the predictor variables are lagged response variables, lagged residuals from a fit of lagged response variables, or both lagged response variables and lagged residuals.

The General ARIMA (p, d, q) and Special Cases

In the foregoing discussion, the MINITAB ARIMA command was used to fit autoregressive, AR, models. ARIMA 1 0 0 specifies an AR(1) fit, predicting y_i with one lagged term, y_{i-1}. Similarly, ARIMA 2 0 0 specifies an AR(2) fit, predicting y_i with two lagged terms, y_{i-1} and y_{i-2}. In general, ARIMA p 0 0 specifies an autoregressive, AR(p), fit, predicting y_i with p lagged terms, y_{i-1}, $y_{i-2}, \ldots, y_{i-p}$. The decision on a value for p is based on partial autocorrelations and the diagnostic examination of residuals.

If a time series is nonstationary, the ACF does not die out quickly. Then the series should be differenced in an attempt to achieve stationarity. The amount of differencing is specified in the ARIMA command. An ARIMA 0 1 0 model has differencing only; the 1 in the command line specifies that the series is to be differenced once. Fortunately, the amount of differencing, d, needed in many practical applications, is 1 or 2.

Both differencing and autoregression can occur simultaneously in the same model. In general, an ARIMA p d 0 means that a series is differenced d times, and the differenced terms, w_i, are lagged p times. For example, ARIMA 1 1 0 fits the model

$$w_i = \beta_0 + \beta_1 w_{i-1} + e_i$$

where $w_i = y_i - y_{i-1}$. The I in ARIMA stands for integrated, which refers to differencing the original series to achieve stationarity.

The general ARIMA p d q model includes q moving average terms in addition to differencing and autoregressive terms. Moving averages alone are designated as MA(q), which is equivalent to ARIMA 0 0 q, where q refers to the number of moving average terms in the fit. For example, ARIMA 0 0 1 specifies an MA(1) model.

$$y_i = \beta_0 - \beta_{1m} e_{i-1} + e_i$$

where the subscript m on β_{1m} specifies a moving average parameter and distinguishes it from autoregressive parameters. ARIMA 0 0 2 specifies an MA(2) model

$$y_i = \beta_0 - \beta_{1m} e_{i-1} - \beta_{2m} e_{i-2} + e_i$$

where the parameters again have an extra subscript, m, which identifies moving average parameters.

Moving average and autoregressive parameters are distinguished from one another because some time series models are mixed, requiring both types of terms. Differencing might be necessary also. For example, an ARIMA 2 1 1 is expressed as

$$w_i = \beta_0 + \beta_1 w_{i-1} + \beta_2 w_{i-2} - \beta_{1m} e_{i-1} + e_i$$

The inclusion of both moving average and autoregressive model components results in parsimonious models with only a few terms. If there are many significant partial autocorrelations, an AR(p) representation will likely require many terms, in other words a large p. Alternatively, for this situation, an MA(q) with a small q might be a frugal substitute for AR(p) with a large p. Also, an MA(q) process that requires a large q can be replaced by an AR(p) model with a small p. Sometimes a mixture of the two types of components are needed for a parsimonious fit.

EXAMPLE 7

REFRIGERATOR SALES

Miller and Wichern predict refrigerator sales.[2] The sales series is differenced and an MA(1) model is fit to the differences. The model is

$$w_i = y_i - y_{i-1} = -\beta_{1m} e_{i-1} + e_i$$

Using a similar model, refrigerator sales are simulated here. The model is

$$w_i = y_i - y_{i-1} = -.75e_{i-1} + e_i$$

The model is rearranging so that sales alone appears on the left side of the equation.

$$SALES = C2 = y_i = y_{i-1} - .75e_{i-1} + e_i$$

The MINITAB macro in Appendix 1 uses this equation to simulate refrigerator sales and a moving average model is fitted. In this way, we can see if the parameter estimates come close to the known parameters.

Problem Statement (a) Observe the sales trend and therefore the nonstationary. Compute and plot differences in sales to see if they are stationary. Obtain the ACF and determine if a moving average model is appropriate.

Problem Solution (a) In this identification phase, refrigerator sales trend downward, which is indicative of a nonstationary series.

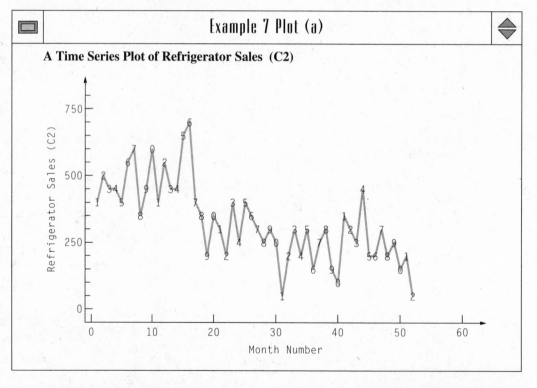

In Plot (b), C3 represents sales differences. Differences are clearly needed because the previous plot of sales is trending downward.

The plot of C3 has no obvious trend and is stationary.

The following ACF has a significant spike at a lag of 1. After that, the ACF has non-significant autocorrelations. This type of an ACF pattern suggests an MA(1) type model. In contrast for AR models, the ACF does not drop off as abruptly.

Example 7 Plot (b)

A Time Series Plot of Refrigerator Sales Differenced (C3)

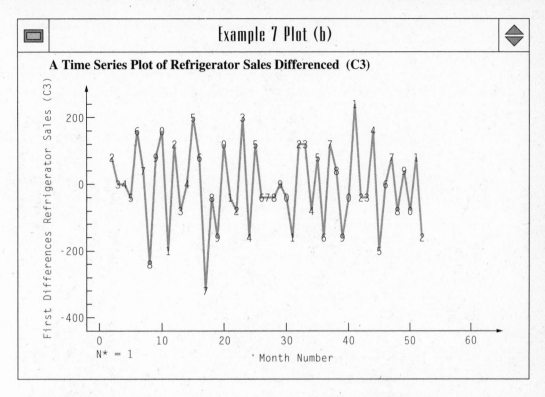

For your information, an MA(2) type model would have two significant autocorrelations followed by nonsignificant ones. An MA(3) would have three significant correlations and so on. In other words, an ACF of an MA(q) process tends to *cut off* after q lags. In contrast, recall that AR(p) processes tended to have ACF's that decay to 0 rather than cut off abruptly to 0.

```
ACF of C3:
            -1.0 -0.8 -0.6 -0.4 -0.2  0.0  0.2  0.4  0.6  0.8  1.0
             +----+----+----+----+----+----+----+----+----+----+
  1  -0.394                      XXXXXXXXXXX
  2  -0.161                      XXXXX
  3   0.217                           XXXXXX
  4  -0.144                      XXXXX
  5   0.034                         XX
  6   0.030                         XX
  7  -0.081                        XXX
  8  -0.074                        XXX
  9   0.163                         XXXXX
 10   0.029                         XX
 11  -0.090                        XXX
 12   0.001                         X
 13  -0.027                        XX
 14   0.146                         XXXXX
 15  -0.172                      XXXXX
 16  -0.045                        XX
 17   0.039                         XX
```

Problem Statement (b) Fit the model identified in part (a) using a Box-Jenkins ARIMA model. Examine diagnostic information.

Problem Solution (b) In this estimation phase, an ARIMA 0 1 1 command in MINITAB produces the following fit information and fit:

```
Estimates at each iteration

Iteration        SSE      Parameters
    0          720208      0.100
    1          652860      0.250
    2          603459      0.400
    3          572440      0.550
    4          564206      0.648
    5          564061      0.660
    6          564057      0.662
    7          564057      0.662
Relative change in each estimate less than 0.0010

Final Estimates of Parameters

Type      Estimate    St. Dev.   t ratio
MA   1      0.6620     0.1107     5.98
```

The ARIMA 0 1 1 fit is equivalent to an MA(1) fit to first differences. The known model used to simulate sales is

$$w_i = y_i - y_{i-1} = -.75e_{i-1} + e_i$$

The following fit approximates the known model quite well.

$$\text{predicted } w_i = \text{predicted } y_i - y_{i-1} = -0.6620e_{i-1}$$

Adding y_{i-1} to both sides produces predicted sales.

$$\text{predicted } y_i = y_{i-1} - 0.6620e_{i-1}$$

The following diagnostic statistics indicate that the fit is a reasonably good one.

```
Differencing: 1 regular difference
No. of obs.:  Original series 52, after differencing 51
Residuals:    SS =  561616  (back forecasts excluded)
              MS =   11232  DF = 50

Modified Box-Pierce chi-square statistic

Lag              12           24          36          48
Chi-square  6.5(DF=11)  15.7(DF=23)  33.5(DF=35)  36.4(DF=47)
```

The residuals (C5) shown below appear to be normal and independent (uncorrelated).

```
Histogram of C5    N = 51    N* = 1

Midpoint    Count
   -250       1    *
   -200       3    ***
   -150       3    ***
   -100       8    ********
    -50      11    ***********
      0       7    *******
     50       7    *******
    100       6    ******
    150       4    ****
    200       1    *
```

```
ACF of C5
            -1.0 -0.8 -0.6 -0.4 -0.2  0.0  0.2  0.4  0.6  0.8  1.0
             +----+----+----+----+----+----+----+----+----+----+
  1   0.011                            X
  2  -0.093                          XXX
  3   0.109                            XXXX
  4  -0.111                         XXXX
  5  -0.047                           XX
  6  -0.037                           XX
  7  -0.139                         XXXX
  8  -0.083                          XXX
  9   0.183                            XXXXXX
 10   0.074                            XXX
 11  -0.065                          XXX
 12  -0.016                            X
 13  -0.037                           XX
 14   0.013                            X
 15  -0.203                       XXXXXX
 16  -0.121                         XXXX
 17  -0.005                            X
```

Problem Statement (c)   Use the fitted model to forecast four periods ahead. Also find 95% confidence limits for forecasted sales.

Problem Solution (c)   Using an ARIMA subcommand, forecasts are made for four periods ahead. The 95% confidence limits are also computed and printed.

Forecasts from period 52

Period	Forecast	95% Limits	
		Lower	Upper
53	149.989	-57.779	357.756
54	149.989	-69.329	369.306
55	149.989	-80.299	380.277
56	149.989	-90.771	390.748

The plot below shows the predictions and forecasts (the B's), the upper confidence limit on the forecasts (C's), and the lower confidence interval on the forecasts (A's). The 2's simply show the 0 line.

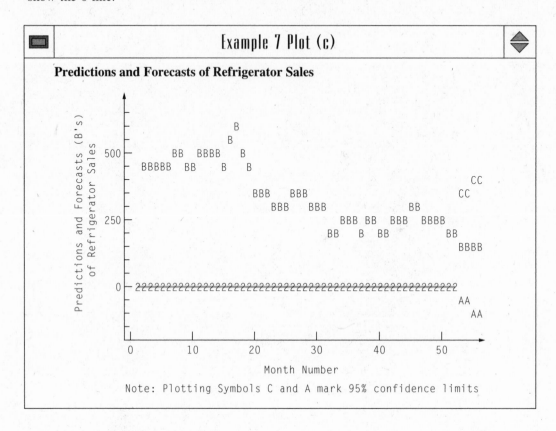

Seasonal ARIMA Models

The general ARIMA(p, d, q) specification for nonseasonal time series data is extended for seasonal data to become ARIMA(p, d, q) (P, D, Q)S. The new P, D, Q parts specify autoregressive, differencing, and moving average orders for the seasonal component of the series. The S indicates the seasonal lag. Again, the autocorrelation and partial autocorrelation functions are examined. Certain patterns suggest choices for P, D, Q, and S, as well as p, d, and q.

Typically, the ACF of y_i is examined first. As usual, if a sequence of significant autocorrelations are slow to decay, difference y_i (regular nonseasonal differences) to obtain an autocorrelation function that either decays quickly or initially decays quickly followed by clusters of spikes at seasonal lags of lengths S. The clusters appear when seasonality is present. As an example, clusters at seasonal lag lengths of S = 12 are likely when large

December retail sales occur. Such clusters of autocorrelations that don't decay quickly indicate seasonal differencing is needed.

As an example, suppose regular nonseasonal differences are needed which result in

$$w_i = y_i - y_{i-1}$$

Then, w_i is differenced seasonally (say a 12-month lag) to obtain

$$dw_i = w_i - w_{i-12}$$

This establishes d, D, and S as in ARIMA(p, 1, q)(P, 1, Q)12, and it gets us to the stage of determining p, q, P, and Q. As illustrated earlier, parts of the ACF and PFAC of dw_i (at less than seasonal lags) help you choose p and q. Similarly, clusters of autocorrelations (and partials) at seasonal lags help you choose P and Q.

CHAPTER SUMMARY

Moving averages, single exponential smoothing, trend analysis, double exponential smoothing, trend-seasonal analysis, Holt-Winters seasonal exponential smoothing, and Box-Jenkins time series analysis are widely used time series methodologies. The methods range from simple to complex. Generally, the longer the time series, the more likely it is that complex patterns will develop in the data, which require the complex methods for forecasting.

Trend-seasonal analysis is a decomposition, or divide-and-conquer approach. Time series components are isolated in terms of (1) a long-term trend, T; (2) a short-term repeating seasonal pattern, S; (3) a medium-term cyclical ups and downs C; and (4) an irregular, I, random component, which is like an error term in regression models. These components are isolated and the patterns summarized. Then the component summaries are assembled to make forecasts. Trend-seasonal analysis is intuitive and easy to understand. Holt-Winters methods can be used to model such time series, too.

An alternative to trend-seasonal analysis is Box-Jenkins time series analysis. Although this approach is quite powerful and often results in simple models, the methodology is complex in theory. However, modern statistical packages make it easy to apply.

Box-Jenkins time series analysis is akin to multiple regression analysis in which some of the predictor variables are lagged response variables (in autoregressive fits), lagged residuals (in moving average fits) from a fit of lagged response variables, or both lagged response variables and lagged residuals. Thus, Box-Jenkins analysis captures the trend, seasonal, cyclical, and irregular components of a series in its own special way. This method is not as intuitive as trend-seasonal analysis. Forecasts and confidence intervals are made on the future behavior of the data series.

KEY TERMS

EXERCISES

1. Cases of laundry detergent are shipped weekly from a warehouse to distributors. Fifty-two shipment totals are listed below. (In MINITAB, RETRIEVE 'B:X16-1')

```
292  300  300  303  302  292  286  284  278  282  282  287
283  285  295  287  287  280  280  273  275  273  279  268
272  277  265  274  282  290  291  295  290  291  291  281
285  291  294  304  301  307  314  315  317  314  313  312
302  307  295  289
```

(a) Over these 52 weeks, what minimum number of cases in inventory always meets distributor demand?

(b) Plot shipments versus time, and show where the answer to part (a) is on this plot.

(c) Overall, if there is no up-or-down trend and if you are assured that past years of shipments have not revealed regular seasonal patterns for this product, it is reasonable to use a moving average to model these data. Fit moving averages of lengths, 2, 4, and 8 to these data. For length two as an example.

```
%MA C1 2;    # A moving average at time, T, is used to
FITS IN C2.  # predict at T+1 and is a fitted value.
```

(d) Use accuracy measures to determine which moving average length provides the best fit to these data.

(e) Forecast shipments for weeks 53, 54, 55, 56, and 57. For example

```
%MA C1 4;
NOPLOT;      # May omit but use GPRO graphics.
FORECASTS 5; # Includes 95% prediction limits on forecasts.
ORIGIN 52.
```

2. In a region different from that in the previous exercise, cases of laundry detergent are shipped weekly from another warehouse to distributors. Fifty-two shipment totals are listed below. (In MINITAB, RETRIEVE 'B:X16-2')

```
351  351  348  361  360  354  352  355  364  369  354  358
349  350  365  357  353  355  345  353  359  352  361  351
351  348  362  355  354  355  360  360  368  366  375  374
367  356  371  367  354  355  359  367  365  350  355  358
355  367  365  367
```

(a) Over these 52 weeks, what minimum number of cases in inventory always meets distributor demand?

(b) Plot shipments versus time. If you did the previous exercise, compare plots. Do these shipments appear to be more or less volatile?

(c) Overall, if there is no up-or-down trend and if you are assured that past years of shipments have not revealed regular seasonal patterns for this product, it is reasonable to use a moving average to model these data. Fit moving averages of lengths 2, 4, and 8 to these data.

(d) Use accuracy measures to determine which moving average length provides the best fit to these data. Does the amount of volatility (see part (b)) seem to be related to the choice of average length?

(e) Forecast shipments for weeks 53, 54, and 55. For example

```
%MA C1 4;
NOPLOT;      # May omit but must use GPRO graphics.
FORECASTS 3; # Includes 95% prediction limits on forecasts.
ORIGIN 52.
```

3. A local retailer claims that the following weekly sales (in bags) of a new corn chip product are increasing rapidly. (In MINITAB, RETRIEVE 'B:X16-3')

```
25  27  26  27  28  26  25  27  27  29  29  30  31  32  33
33  33  34  35  35  36  35  36  38  39  39  38  38  38  36
```

(a) Plot sales to verify the retailer's claim.

(b) The retailer would like to spot product sales trends early. However, there are so many different products in the store that it is difficult to keep track of every product on an informal basis. As a result, new computer forecasting software is being evaluated. One inexpensive software package uses a four-week moving average to track sales. A second package is more expensive but has more sophisticated types of forecasting. Why might the retailer want to consider something more sophisticated than a moving average?

(c) Fit a four-week moving average to sales.

(d) Use simple regression to fit a trend line to sales where the independent variable is the week number 1, 2, 3, . . . , 29, 30. In MINITAB, you may use %TREND C1.

(e) Use accuracy measures to compare the moving average fit in part (c) to the regression fit in part (d). Does the moving average appear to be slower in responding to a trend than simple regression? If so, which method (and software package) would you choose?

4. Overstocking perishable products can be costly. However, sales opportunity costs occur when there is not enough stock. Thus, it is important to seek the optimal inventory level that considers both these costs. Many stocking rules for optimal inventory are derived for demand that is not trending upward or downward.

(a) Does the following market's weekly demand for eggs (in cartons) exhibit a trend? Plot demand. (In MINITAB, RETRIEVE 'B:X16-4')

```
69  65  67  62  66  69  64  60  65  68  58  61  65  63  67
66  68  68  63  64  61  58  59  59  60
```

(b) Fit a four-week moving average to sales.

(c) Use simple regression to fit a trend line to sales where the independent variable is the week number 1, 2, 3, . . . , 24, 25.

(d) Use accuracy measures to compare the moving average fit in part (b) to the regression fit in part (c). Does the moving average appear to be slower in responding to a trend than simple regression? If so, which method would you choose?

(e) Forecast shipments for weeks 26, 27, and 28. For example

```
%MA C1 4;      # %TREND C1; for the trend.
NOPLOT;        # May omit but use GPRO graphics.
FORECASTS 3;   # Includes 95% prediction limits on forecasts.
ORIGIN 25.
```

5. Because single exponential smoothing and moving averages work well in the same types of forecasting situations, use single exponential smoothing to fit the data in Exercise (1).

(a) Obtain fits using smoothing constants (weights) of 0.1, 0.4, and 0.9. For a weight of 0.9 as an example,

```
%SES C1;
NOPLOT;     # May omit but use GPRO graphics.
WEIGHT 0.90;
FITS C2.    # Use other columns for other weights.
```

(b) Which weight provides the best fit to these data according to accuracy measures?

(c) (Optional) Fit an ARIMA 0 1 1 model to this data set, which is equivalent to single exponential smoothing.

(d) Forecast shipments for weeks 53, 54, and 55. For example

```
%SES C1;
NOPLOT;        # May omit but use GPRO graphics.
FORECASTS 3;   # Includes 95% prediction limits on forecasts.
ORIGIN 52.
```

6. Because single exponential smoothing and moving averages work well in the same types of forecasting situations, use single exponential smoothing to fit the data in Exercise 2.

(a) Obtain fits using smoothing constants (weights) of 0.1, 0.4, and 0.9. Plot shipments versus time. If you did the previous exercise, compare plots. Do these shipments appear to be more or less volatile?

(b) Which weight provides the best fit to these data? Does the amount of volatility (see part (a)) seem to be related to the choice of smoothing constant (weight)?

(c) (Optional) Fit an ARIMA 0 1 1 model to this data set, which is equivalent to single exponential smoothing.

7. Because double exponential smoothing and trend analysis work well in the same types of forecasting situations (with no seasonal patterns and a constant trend), use double exponential smoothing to fit the data in Exercise 3.

(a) When obtaining fits for double exponential smoothing, there are two weights that can be defaulted and selected by MINITAB. As an example

```
%DES C1;
NOPLOT;    # May omit but use GPRO graphics.
FITS C2.
```

(b) Use double exponential smoothing to fit sales.

(c) Use single exponential smoothing to fit sales.

(d) Using accuracy measures, evaluate whether single or double exponential smoothing responds better to a trend.

(e) (Optional) Fit an ARIMA 0 2 2 model to this data set, which is equivalent to double exponential smoothing.

(f) Forecast shipments for weeks 31, 32, and 33. For example,

```
%DES C1;
NOPLOT;       # May omit but use GPRO graphics.
FORECASTS 3; # Includes 95% prediction limits on forecasts.
ORIGIN 30.
```

8. Continuous production processes, such as making chemicals, are monitored often by taking moving averages of certain chemical constituents. Find and plot a three-day moving average of the following percentages of calcium oxide. (In MINITAB, RETRIEVE 'B:X16-8')

```
0.28   0.21   0.25   0.21   0.18   0.26   0.23   0.19   0.24   0.23
0.17   0.22   0.20   0.20   0.20   0.19   0.24   0.20   0.21   0.30
0.29
```

9. For a continuous chemical production processes, find and plot a five-day moving average of the following percentages of carbon dioxide. (In MINITAB, RETRIEVE 'B:X16-9')

```
0.63   0.67   0.65   0.57   0.63   0.69   0.67   0.56   0.60   0.62
0.69   0.70   0.59   0.61   0.63   0.66   0.68   0.65   0.61   0.60
0.55   0.62   0.68   0.56   0.63   0.69   0.56   0.56   0.65   0.68
```

10. Hourly temperature in degrees Celsius is taken of a chemical soup in a manufacturing process. Find and plot an eight-hour moving average of the following temperatures. (In MINITAB, RETRIEVE 'B:X16-10')

```
404   397   396   397   399   400   403   404   404   410   418   417
414   415   413   408   410   408   398   399   400   399   400   398
395   399   404   410   412   412   413   411   407   403   404   408
410   414   413   414   411   411   408   406   405   406   406   410
```

11. Use single exponential smoothing to fit and forecast (four weeks beyond the last observation) weekly gasoline sales in thousands of gallons. (In MINITAB, RETRIEVE 'B:X16-11')

```
47   47   54   54   54   52   49   47   46   47   48   51   51   52   51
54   50   51   52   53   53   56   55   58
```

12. Use single exponential smoothing to fit and forecast (three months beyond the last observation) monthly production costs in thousands of dollars. (In MINITAB, RETRIEVE 'B:X16-12')

80 82 76 80 79 80 81 83 85 79 75 79 78 80 83
87 85 88

13. Use single exponential smoothing to fit and forecast (four months beyond the last observation) monthly cash requirements in thousands of dollars. (In MINITAB, RETRIEVE 'B:X16-13')

327 331 320 318 319 327 329 330 332 343 344 355
365 357 359 362 355 360 360 354 353 344 342 346

14. The Nuzzle Pet Food Company found that quarterly sales were trending upward for their T-bone line of dog food. Use double exponential smoothing to fit and forecast (four quarters beyond the last observation) quarterly sales in thousands of boxes. (In MINITAB, RETRIEVE 'B:X16-14')

532 555 557 578 531 583 624 592 589 659 611 666
660 669 717 702

15. The Nuzzle Pet Food Company used double exponential smoothing for any of their trendy dog food lines. Unfortunately, quarterly sales of Old Blue dog food were trending downward. Fit and forecast (four quarters beyond the last observation) quarterly sales in thousands of boxes. (In MINITAB, RETRIEVE 'B:X16-15')

326 337 327 326 320 304 235 276 241 247 213 219
187 129 120 154

16. A history of year-end retained earnings figures (in millions of dollars) are used in long-range financial planning. (In MINITAB, RETRIEVE 'B:X16-16')

112 132 223 125 181 188 240 160 370 340 234 243
761 474 516 427 678 620 457 966

(a) Fit a quadratic trend model to account for the curvature in retained earnings growth. Forecast the next five years of retained earnings figures. In MINITAB

```
%TREND C1;
QUADRATIC;   # Use GROWTH here for part (b).
FITS C2;
FORECASTS 5;
ORIGIN 20;
NOPLOT.
```

(b) Fit an exponential growth trend model as an alternative way to account for the curvature. Forecast the next five years of retained earnings figures.

(c) Is fit in part (a) better than in part (b) or are they about the same?

(d) (Optional) Use multiple regression analysis to find the fit in part (a). Code time as 1, 2, 3, . . . , 19, 20; use time and time squared as independent variables.

17. Quarterly unit sales figures (in thousands) are used to project revenues. These figures are for a rapidly growing new product. (In MINITAB, RETRIEVE 'B:X16-17')

118 138 153 121 217 200 82 263 446 285 332 420
323 334 475 642

(a) Fit a quadratic trend model to account for the curvature in sales growth. Forecast the next four quarters of sales.

(b) Fit an exponential growth trend model as an alternative way to account for the curvature. Forecast the next four years of sales.

(c) Is fit in part (a) better than in part (b), or are they about the same?

18. Part of a product's life cycle, in terms of units sold per quarter, can be seen in the following data set. (In MINITAB, RETRIEVE 'B:X16-18')

10	12	16	20	26	34	38	40	38	54	60	70
87	99	102	113	90	140	150	159	130	164	165	169

When the product is new, demand is low. As consumers become aware and interested in the product the demand increases rapidly. Eventually, the increases in demand begin to slow as the product reaches maturity. If left on the market long enough, demand for some products will die. Before a product's complete demise, replacement models are often introduced. They have their own life cycles. Companies usually have a portfolio of products in various life cycle stages. Management monitors sales data behavior in planning for the introduction of new products. Fit a Pearl-Reed logistic trend model (an S-shaped curve) to unit sales and forecast unit sales for the next four quarters.

```
%TREND C1;  # MINITAB macro.
SCURVE;
FITS C2;
FORECASTS 4;
ORIGIN 24;
NOPLOT.
```

19. A company evaluates its market share position every six months. Eighteen market share estimates (in percent) are listed below. These figures begin when the company entered the market. Although they have been quite successful with the product, management thinks that market share growth is beginning to decline. If so, management is contemplating the timing of new product introductions. Fit a Pearl-Reed logistic trend model (an S-shaped curve) to market share and forecast market share for the next four periods. (In MINITAB, RETRIEVE 'B:X16-19')

2	2	3	3	4	6	6	7	6	9	17	19	15	23
25	26	22	27	28	28								

20. The following are quarterly sales figures. (In MINITAB, RETRIEVE 'B:X16-20')

11331	9447	7498	16203	10438	9041	8768
13003	10584	10144	13740	16374	11168	12301
11057	15145	15166	11782	15022	17568	15900
16026	14116	20263	15014	12922	13628	21412
19866	16652	17156	23965	16742	19508	19861
24259	20092	19036	18079	25503	19840	20991
20108	24677	18227	21676	23614	27295	

(a) A plot of the data does not show an increase in seasonal variation with time (also see C2 below). Therefore, an additive trend-seasonal model is appropriate. Calculate the seasonal factors, detrend, deseasonalize, and forecast four quarters ahead. Plot the sales, fits, and other items of interest.

```
%DECOMP C1 4;      # A MINITAB macro.
ADDITIVE;          # MULTIPLICATIVE alternative.
FORECASTS 4;
ORIGIN 48;   # TSPLOT C2, C3, C4, and C5 is instructive.
DETREND C2;  # Only seasonal and error components in C2.
SEASONAL C3; # Seasonal indices.
DESEASONAL C4;
FITS C5;
NOPLOT.
```

(b) Fit a multiplicative model to these data and verify that the additive model performs a little better.

(c) (Optional) Fit a Holt-Winters seasonal exponential smoothing model to these data.

```
%WINTADD C1 4;      # A MINITAB macro.
FORECASTS 4;
ORIGIN 48;   # TSPLOT C2, C3, C4, and C5 is instructive.
SMOOTHED C2;
SEASONAL C3; # Seasonal indices.
FITS C5;
NOPLOT.
```

(d) (Optional) Show that moving average, single exponential smoothing, trend analysis, and double exponential smoothing models provide inferior fits to those in parts (a), (b), or (c).

21. The following are quarterly sales figures. (In MINITAB, RETRIEVE 'B:X16-21')

```
14959 14947 14815 13642 13321 13932 13607
13911 13161 11398 13089 13380 10677 11461
12611 13424 11568 10402 11158 11867 10915
10144  9965 10598 10256  8547  8936 10478
 9561  8222  8292 10249  8299  8348  7771
 8739  7516  5600  8554  8334  6441  6192
 6559  7594  5787  5221  4569  5975
```

(a) A plot of the data does not show an increase in seasonal variation with time (also see detrended data). Therefore, an additive trend-seasonal model is appropriate. Calculate the seasonal factors, detrend, deseasonalize, and forecast four quarters ahead. Plot the sales, fits, and other items of interest.

(b) Fit a multiplicative model to these data and verify that the additive model performs a little better.

(c) (Optional) Fit a Holt-Winters seasonal exponential smoothing model to these data.

(d) (Optional) Show that moving average, single exponential smoothing, trend analysis, and double exponential smoothing models provide inferior fits to those in parts (a), (b), or (c).

22. The following are quarterly sales figures. (In MINITAB, RETRIEVE 'B:X16-22')

5320	5840	5523	5855	8110	4647	6913
7693	3274	10402	2542	7483	6940	7775
9412	10764	12162	5332	11392	12308	10721
15573	14884	12097	5196	8950	10302	7548
14251	12631	14767	16732	16046	7746	4489
9852	14415	3798	12082	25511	9785	11552
19654	11322	9067	20706	12667	6162	

(a) A plot of the data suggests a proportional increase in seasonal variation with time (also see detrended data). Therefore, a multiplicative trend-seasonal model would be appropriate. Calculate the seasonal factors, detrend, deseasonalize, and forecast four quarters ahead. Plot the sales, fits, and other items of interest.

(b) Fit an additive model to these data and verify that the multiplicative model performs a little better.

(c) (Optional) Fit a Holt-Winters seasonal exponential smoothing model to these data.

```
%WINTMULT C1 4;     # A MINITAB macro.
FORECASTS 4;
ORIGIN 48;    # TSPLOT C2, C3, C4, and C5 is instructive.
SMOOTHED C2;
SEASONAL C3;  # Seasonal indices.
FITS C5;
NOPLOT.
```

(d) (Optional) Show that moving average, single exponential smoothing, trend analysis, and double exponential smoothing models provide inferior fits to those in parts (a), (b), or (c).

23. Monthly department store credit sales figures are listed below. (In MINITAB, RETRIEVE 'B:X16-23'):

20	22	26	19	21	25	20	27	25	33	37	55	23	29	25
27	29	27	26	35	33	33	41	49	31	28	28	31	34	30
31	35	30	37	36	53	29	39	40	30	35	41	33	53	42
47	44	52	36	45	35	36	34	32	37	40	44	58	50	65

(a) A plot of the data does not show an increase in seasonal variation with time (also see detrended data). Therefore, an additive trend-seasonal model is appropriate. Calculate the seasonal factors, detrend, deseasonalize, and forecast 12 months ahead. Plot the sales, fits, and other items of interest.

```
%DECOMP C1 12;     # A MINITAB macro.
ADDITIVE;          # MULTIPLICATIVE alternative.
FORECASTS 12;
ORIGIN 60;    # TSPLOT C2, C3, C4, and C5 is instructive.
DETREND C2;   # Only seasonal and error components in C2.
SEASONAL C3;  # Seasonal indices.
DESEASONAL C4;
FITS C5;
NOPLOT.
```

(b) Fit a multiplicative model to these data and verify that the additive model performs a little better.

(c) (Optional) Fit a Holt-Winters seasonal exponential smoothing model to these data.

```
%WINTADD C1 12;    # A MINITAB macro.
FORECASTS 12;
ORIGIN 60;   # TSPLOT C2, C3, C4, and C5 is instructive.
SMOOTHED C2;
SEASONAL C3; # Seasonal indices.
FITS C5;
NOPLOT.
```

(d) (Optional) Show that moving average, single exponential smoothing, trend analysis, and double exponential smoothing models provide inferior fits to those in parts (a), (b) or (c).

24. In a large new mall, monthly department store credit sales figures are listed below. (In MINITAB, RETRIEVE 'B:X16-24')

43	37	55	38	41	56	51	64	63	70	87	108	43	42	62
84	62	79	59	58	85	53	66	111	82	78	66	69	79	72
29	97	70	91	81	137	103	92	88	95	96	96	40	164	79
174	170	142	104	68	97	118	86	89	85	65	119	153	174	109

(a) A plot of the data suggests a proportional increase in seasonal variation with time (also see detrended data). Therefore, a multiplicative trend-seasonal model would be appropriate. Calculate the seasonal factors, detrend, deseasonalize, and forecast 12 months ahead. Plot the sales, fits, and other items of interest.

(b) Fit an additive model to these data and verify that the multiplicative model performs a little better.

(c) (Optional) Fit a Holt-Winters seasonal exponential smoothing model to these data.

```
%WINTMULT C1 12;    # A MINITAB macro.
FORECASTS 12;
ORIGIN 60;   # TSPLOT C2, C3, C4, and C5 is instructive.
SMOOTHED C2;
SEASONAL C3; # Seasonal indices.
FITS C5;
NOPLOT.
```

(d) (Optional) Show that moving average, single exponential smoothing, trend analysis, and double exponential smoothing models provide inferior fits to those in parts (a), (b), or (c).

25. Fit a Box-Jenkins time series model to the quarterly sales figures in Exercise 20. (In MINITAB, RETRIEVE 'B:X16-20')

(a) Verify that the autocorrelation function does not decay or cut off quickly, which suggests that differencing is needed.

(b) Verify that the partial autocorrelation function's first two spikes suggest regular first or second differences. Furthermore, spikes at lag four and beyond suggest that seasonal differences (quarterly) might be necessary.

(c) Verify that the autocorrelation function of first differences of sales begins to decay quickly but reveals spikes every four quarters that don't die out, which suggests that seasonal differencing might be needed.

(d) Difference the first differences in part (c) again using a seasonal lag of four. Obtain an autocorrelation and partial autocorrelation function of these differences. Verify that the autocorrelation function decays a little slower than we like; however, this decay is characteristic of autoregression. Verify that the partial autocorrelation function has a spike at the first lag and then cuts off, which suggests an AR(1) component in the regular model. Also, there are spikes at lags of four, six, and so on that decay, which suggests a MA(1) component in the seasonal model.

(e) Based on the analysis in (d), fit an ARIMA (p, d, q) (P, D, Q) S model. Evaluate and examine fits and residuals for a mixed autoregressive moving average seasonal model of the form ARIMA (1, 1, 0) (0, 1, 1) 4.

26. Proceed in a manner similar to that in the previous exercise and fit a Box-Jenkins time series model to the quarterly sales figures in Exercise 21. (In MINITAB, RETRIEVE 'B:X16-21')

27. Proceed in a manner similar to that in the previous exercise and fit a Box-Jenkins time series model to the quarterly sales figures in Exercise 22. (In MINITAB, RETRIEVE 'B:X16-22')

28. Proceed in a manner similar to that in the previous exercise and fit a Box-Jenkins time series model to the monthly sales figures in Exercise 23. (In MINITAB, RETRIEVE 'B:X16-23')

29. Proceed in a manner similar to that in the previous exercise and fit a Box-Jenkins time series model to the monthly sales figures in Exercise 24. (In MINITAB, RETRIEVE 'B:X16-24')

APPENDIX 1

Minitab Examples

Newer versions of MINITAB have several macros available for time series analysis that you may wish to try. These macros include: for trend analysis, %TREND; for trend-seasonal analysis, %DECOMP; for moving averages, %MA; for single exponential smoothing, %SES; for double exponential smoothing, %DES; for Holt-Winters seasonal exponential smoothing, %WINTMULT or %WINTADD. Because these macros can be used in chapter exercises, the commands are given there.

Additional macros appear in this appendix. They are specific to particular examples in the chapter and are used to illustrate certain methodology.

EXAMPLE

FORECASTING WEEKLY MILK SALES

```
      (OR RETRIEVE 'MLK16' whichever is appropriate.)
MTB > RETRIEVE 'B:MLK16'
MTB > TSPLOT C1
MTB > %MA C1 2;   # A MINITAB MACRO
SUBC> FITS C2;    # IN VERSION TEN OR BEYOND
SUBC> FORECASTS 5;
SUBC> ORIGIN 24;
SUBC> NOPLOT.
MTB > %MA C1 3;
SUBC> FITS C3;
SUBC> NOPLOT.
MTB > %MA C1 6;
SUBC> FITS C4;
SUBC> NOPLOT.
MTB > NAME C2 'MA2' C3 'MA3' C4 'MA6'
MTB > PRINT C1 C2 C3 C4
MTB > TSPLOT C2
MTB > TSPLOT C4
```

EXAMPLE

SMOOTHING WEEKLY MILK SALES

```
          (OR RETRIEVE 'MLK16' whichever is appropriate.)
     MTB > RETRIEVE 'B:MLK16'
     MTB > TSPLOT C1
     MTB > %SES C1;      # A MINITAB MACRO
     SUBC> WEIGHT 0.1;   # IN VERSION TEN OR BEYOND
     SUBC> FITS C2;
     SUBC> NOPLOT.
     MTB > %SES C1;
     SUBC> WEIGHT 0.5;
     SUBC> FITS C3;
     SUBC> NOPLOT.
     MTB > %SES C1;
     SUBC> WEIGHT 0.9;
     SUBC> FITS C4;
     SUBC> FORECASTS 5;
     SUBC> ORIGIN 24;
     SUBC> NOPLOT.
     MTB > NAME C2 'SES.1' C3 'SES.5' C4 'SES.9'
     MTB > PRINT C1-C4
```

TREND-SEASONAL ANALYSIS (QUARTERLY) MACRO

Comment　The following macro, %B:TSANAL, requires version 10 or more of MINITAB. It walks the user through the mechanics of the trend-seasonal analysis done in the chapter. To examine the details of the macro, use a text editor or a word processor to open the TSANAL.MAC file. Also, in MINITAB, the command TYPE 'B:TSANAL.MAC' will list the macro. If you set OH = 24 in the session window, a "continue?" prompt will be issued by MINITAB that permits the user to view one screen of output at a time as the macro executes.

```
     MTB > %B:TSANAL # OR %A:TSANAL OR %TSANAL
     #                 OR %C:\MTBWIN\DATA\TSANAL
```

THE RANDOM WALK MODEL (DOW-JONES-LIKE)

```
     # PRIOR TO THE NEXT SIMULATION EXAMPLE, WE TAKE A LOOK
     # AT THE ACTUAL DATA WHERE I GOT SUMMARY STATISTICS
     # FOR THE SIMULATION

       OR RETRIEVE 'DOW' whichever is appropriate.
     MTB > RETRIEVE 'B:DOW' # OR RE-ENTER IT
     MTB > TSPLOT C1
     MTB > DIFF LAG 1 C1 PUT INTO C2
     MTB > DESCRIBE C2
     MTB > TSPLOT C2
```

E X A M P L E

SIMULATING THE MONTHLY DOW-JONES AVERAGE, THE SYNTHESIS OF A TIME SERIES

```
MTB > INFO
# THESE COLUMNS AND NAMES CARRY OVER FROM THE PREVIOUS
# EXAMPLES; YOU MUST ERASE C1 C2 ... AND SO FORTH.
# THIS ERASES BOTH COLUMNS AND NAMES.
```

Comment The following macro, %B:SIMDOW, requires version 10 or more of MINITAB. To examine the details of the macro, use a text editor or a word processor to open the SIMDOW.MAC file. TYPE 'B:SIMDOW.MAC' will list the macro.

```
MTB > %B:SIMDOW # OR %A:SIMDOW OR %SIMDOW
#                OR %C:\MTBWIN\DATA\SIMDOW
MTB > TSPLOT C2 # THIS SIMULATED SERIES DRIFTS UPWARD HERE,
#                    THEREFORE, NONSTATIONARY!
```

DESYNTHESIS OF THE SIMULATED DOW-JONES AVERAGE

```
MTB > ACF C2  # STRONGLY AUTOCORRELATED; ACF IS SLOW TO
#                DECAY WHEN A SERIES IS NONSTATIONARY
MTB > RUNS C2 # NONRANDOM

MTB > DIFF C2 PUT INTO C3  # DIFFERENCE THE SERIES IN AN
# ATTEMPT TO PRODUCE A STATIONARY SERIES OF DIFFERENCES

MTB > TSPLOT C3 # DIFFERENCES LOOK RANDOM

MTB > ACF C3 # NO SIGNIFICANT AUTOCORRELATIONS AT ANY LAG
#            FOR CHANGES IN THE SIMULATED DOW JONES AVERAGE
MTB > DELETE ROW 1 C3
MTB > RUNS C3
MTB > HIST C3
MTB > DESCRIBE C3
```

E X A M P L E

DESYNTHESIS OF THE ACTUAL DOW-JONES AVERAGE

```
     OR RETRIEVE 'DOW' whichever is appropriate.
MTB > RETRIEVE 'B:DOW'  # OR RE-ENTER IT FROM CHAPTER SIX
```

IDENTIFICATION PHASE

```
MTB > ACF C1  # AUTOREGRESSIVE, AUTOCORRELATIONS DO NOT
#        DECREASE QUICKLY.  NONSTATIONARY SERIES THEREFORE
#        DIFFERENCING IS NEEDED
```

```
MTB > PACF C1  # A SIGNIFICANT PARTIAL AUTOCORRELATION AT
# LAG 1, INDICATING LAG 1 DIFFERENCING MIGHT BE APPROPRIATE

MTB > LAG 1 C1 PUT C2
MTB > DIFF LAG 1 C1 PUT C3

MTB > ACF C3  # FIRST DIFFERENCES PRODUCE A RANDOM, STATIONARY
# SERIES WITH NO SIGNIFICANT AUTOCORRELATIONS, SUGGESTING AN
# ARIMA 0 1 0 FIT, DIFFERENCING ONLY
```

ESTIMATION PHASE

```
MTB > REGRESS C1 1 PRED C2  # FOR PEDAGOGICAL PURPOSES,
# REGRESSION IS USED AS AN APPROXIMATION IN TIME SERIES
# ANALYSIS. YOU MAY WISH TO PLOT C1 C2 IN ORDER TO SEE THE
# ORIENTATION OF THE CLOUD OF DATA POINTS.
```

EXAMPLE

DESYNTHESIS OF THE ACTUAL GROSS DOMESTIC PRODUCT

(If you have the data diskette, **RETRIEVE 'B:GDP'** and omit the data entry using SET.)

(If you are on a network and have the data stored in subdirectory DATA under the directory MTBWIN, **RETRIEVE 'GDP';** otherwise, SET the data in columns.)

```
DON'T SET IN THE DATA IF RETRIEVE WAS SUCCESSFUL
# IF NECESSARY, ENTER THIS DATA WITH A   MTB > SET IN C1

START HERE IF RETRIEVE WAS SUCCESSFUL
```

IDENTIFICATION PHASE

```
MTB > INFO
MTB > LET C2 = LOGE(C1)
MTB > ACF C2   # DOES NOT DIE OUT QUICKLY, NONSTATIONARY,
#                DIFFERENCES NEEDED

MTB > PACF C2  # LAG 1 DIFFERENCES NEEDED
MTB > LAG 1 C2 PUT C3
MTB > DIFF LAG 1 C2 PUT C4

MTB > ACF C4   # NO SIGNIFICANT AUTOCORRELATIONS OF
#                DIFFERENCES, SUGGESTING ARIMA 0 1 0
```

ESTIMATION PHASE

```
MTB > REGRESS C2 1 PRED C3, STRES C5, FITS C6;
SUBC> RESIDUALS C7. # FOR PEDAGOGICAL PURPOSES, REGRESSION
                    # IS USED FOR AN APPROXIMATE FIT
```

EXAMPLE

MODEL-BUILDING STRATEGY, MONTHLY UNEMPLOYMENT RATES

```
MTB > INFO
# THESE COLUMNS AND NAMES CARRY OVER FROM PREVIOUS
# EXAMPLES, YOU MUST ERASE C1 C2 ... AND SO FORTH.
# THIS ERASES BOTH COLUMNS AND NAMES.
```

Comment   The following macro, %B:SIMEMP, requires version 10 or more of MINITAB. To examine the details of the macro, use a text editor or a word processor to open the SIMEMP.MAC file. TYPE 'B:SIMEMP.MAC' will list the macro.

```
MTB > %B:SIMEMP # OR %A:SIMEMP OR %SIMEMP
#               OR %C:\MTBWIN\DATA\SIMEMP
```

IDENTIFICATION PHASE

```
MTB > TSPLOT C2 # UNEMPLOYMENT RATE, SHOWING 60
#                   OF THE 61 MONTHLY FIGURES
MTB > DESCRIBE C2
MTB > RUNS C2 # THE NONRANDOM NATURE OF THIS
# SERIES SUGGESTS
# THAT THERE IS SOME PREDICTABLE PATTERN PRESENT.  THUS, WE
# CAN IMPROVE UPON THE DESCRIPTIVE STATISTICS LISTED ABOVE,
# IN PARTICULAR REDUCING THE UNCERTAINTY REFLECTED IN THE
# STANDARD DEVIATION.

MTB > ACF C2    # THE ACF DIES OFF RATHER QUICKLY,
# INDICATING THAT DIFFERENCING IS NOT NEEDED.

MTB > PACF C2  # AT LEAST THE FIRST TWO
# PARTIAL AUTOCORRELATION COEFFICIENTS ARE
# SIGNIFICANTLY DIFFERENT FROM ZERO, HINTING
# THAT THIS SERIES MIGHT BE REPRESENTED BY AN AR(2) MODEL,
# USING THE ARIMA 2 0 0 COMMAND.
```

ESTIMATION PHASE

```
MTB > ARIMA 1 0 0 DATA IN C2, RESIDUALS C5, FITS C4;
SUBC> CONSTANT.
```

DIAGNOSTIC/IDENTIFICATION PHASE

```
MTB > HIST C5
MTB > ACF C5 # A SIGNIFICANT (ALTHOUGH REDUCED FROM THE ONE
# IN THE ORIGINAL SERIES) AUTOCORRELATION IS PRESENT IN
# THE RESIDUALS AT LAG 1
MTB > PACF C5
```

ESTIMATION PHASE

```
MTB > ARIMA 2 0 0 DATA IN C2, RESIDUALS C5, FITS C4;
SUBC> CONSTANT.
```

DIAGNOSTIC PHASE

```
MTB > HIST C5
MTB > RUNS C5
MTB > ACF C5
MTB > MTSPLOT C2 C4   # SHOWING 60 OBSERVATIONS ONLY
```

EXAMPLE

REFRIGERATOR SALES

```
MTB > INFO
# THESE COLUMNS AND NAMES CARRY OVER FROM PREVIOUS
# EXAMPLES, YOU MUST ERASE C1 C2 ... AND SO FORTH.
# THIS ERASES BOTH COLUMNS AND NAMES.
```

Comment   The following macro, %B:SIMREF, requires version ten or more of MINITAB. To examine the details of the macro, use a text editor or a word processor to open the SIMREF.MAC file.

```
MTB > %B:SIMREF # OR %A:SIMDOW OR %SIMREF
#                OR %C:\MTBWIN\DATA\SIMREF

MTB > TSPLOT C2
MTB > DIFF LAG 1 C2 PUT C3
MTB > TSPLOT C3
MTB > ACF C3

MTB > ARIMA 0 1 1, DATA C2, RESIDUALS C5, FITS C4;
SUBC> NOCONSTANT;
SUBC> FORECAST ORIGIN = 52,AHEAD 4,STORE C7, LIMITS C6,C8.
MTB > HIST C5
MTB > ACF C5

MTB > STACK C4 ON C7 PUT C10

MTB > SET C9
DATA> 52(0)  # NO BLANKS IN THIS LINE
DATA> END
MTB > SET INTO C11
DATA> 52(0)  # NO BLANKS IN THIS LINE
DATA> END

MTB > SET C12
DATA> 1:56   # NO BLANKS IN THIS LINE
DATA> END

MTB > STACK C9 ON C6 PUT C9
MTB > STACK C11 ON C8 PUT C11
MTB > MPLOT C9 C12 C10 C12 C11 C12
```

CHAPTER 17

Index Numbers

PRELUDE

Millions of workers have wage contracts that contain escalator clauses for changing wage rates in relation to changes in the Consumer Price Index (CPI). Even those without such contractual arrangements are interested in measuring price changes. The CPI is a good measure of price changes in goods and services the consumer purchases. If wages are frozen while the CPI increases, the wage earner's *real* income is falling. If wages and the CPI increase at the same rate, real income is constant. Only if wages increase faster than the CPI is the wage earner making real gains and getting ahead of prices.

The concept of an index number is powerful enough to extend beyond prices of goods and services. The Dow-Jones Average is an example of an index of stock prices listed on the New York Stock Exchange. The Index of Industrial Production measures manufacturing production levels. In these and other areas of application, index numbers have become useful in summarizing the myriad of individual transactions in an aggregate way.

This chapter explains various ways to construct index numbers. Knowing how index numbers are structured will help you to understand and use them. ◈

PRICE RELATIVES

Let y_i be the price of an item (say, an orange) in period i, where i = 1, 2, 3, . . . , n, and where 1 is the first time period and n is the last. In understanding price movements it helps to express y_i relative to the period 1 price y_1 (or **base price**). Therefore, a **relative price,** ry_i, is defined as

$$\text{relative price} = ry_i = \left(\frac{y_i}{y_1}\right) \times 100$$

The ry_i is also referred to as a **price relative index,** I_i, expressed as a percentage of the base-period price.

$$I_i = \text{relative price index} = ry_i$$

When there are additional items, the notation is adjusted to identify particular items (say, apples, oranges, and so on). For item j, the relative price is

$$\text{relative price for item } j = ry_{ij} = I_{ij} = \left(\frac{y_{ij}}{y_{1j}}\right) \times 100$$

EXAMPLE 1

THE RELATIVE PRICE OF ONE-FAMILY HOUSES

Problem Statement   From 18 years of median sales prices of new, privately owned one-family houses, express these prices relative to the first-year price.[1] List prices and relative prices (RELP) and plot relative prices.

Problem Solution   Yearly median prices in thousands of dollars are:

23.4   25.2   27.6   32.5   35.9   39.3   44.2   48.8   55.7   62.9   64.6   68.9   69.3
75.3   79.9   84.3   92.0   104.5

Relative prices, RELP, are

100   108   118   139   153   168   189   209   238   269   276   294   296
322   341   360   393   447

A time series plot of relative prices is

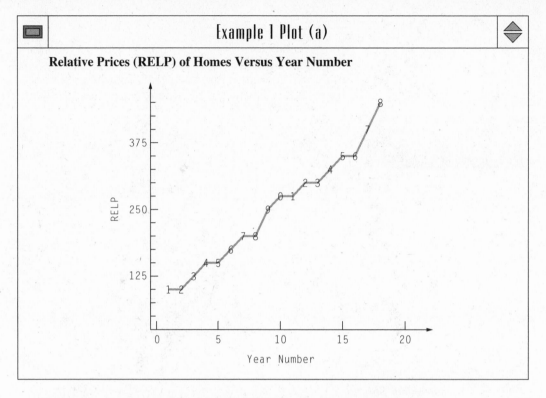

Example 1 Plot (a)

Relative Prices (RELP) of Homes Versus Year Number

Relative prices increased arithmetically over this 18-year period.

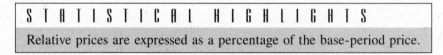

S T A T I S T I C A L   H I G H L I G H T S

Relative prices are expressed as a percentage of the base-period price.

AGGREGATE PRICE INDEXES

When shopping, we often purchase more than a single item. As a result, the need for a **group index** arises. A group of different items may be thought of as a basket of items. If we consider a particular basket of items consisting of one of each item (one orange, one apple, one banana, and so on), we can create a combined price-relative index called an **aggregate price index.**

When the group is comprised of single units of each item, the aggregate price index is *unweighted*. A *weighted* index is necessary when the quantities purchased differ from item to item.

Unweighted Aggregate Price Index   An **unweighted aggregate price index** is simply the ratio of the sum of the period i prices to the sum of the base-period prices for the group of j items.

$$\text{unweighted aggregate price index} = I_i = \left(\frac{\Sigma y_{ij}}{\Sigma y_{1j}}\right) \times 100$$

The summations are across all j items. Therefore, Σy_{1j} is the total base price of all items and Σy_{ij} is the total price of all items in period i. You can think of Σy_{ij} as the price of the whole basket in period i and Σy_{1j} as the price of the whole basket in period one.

EXAMPLE 2.

THE UNWEIGHTED AGGREGATE PRICE INDEX OF A BASKET OF DRUGSTORE ITEMS

Problem Statement   In each of five years, prices are given for toothpaste (9 oz), shampoo (7 oz), cough tablets (pkg. 100), and antiperspirant (2 oz). Create an unweighted aggregate price index for these items, assuming a basket of single units.

Row	TPST	SPOO	CTAB	APERS
1	2.39	2.99	1.29	1.69
2	2.59	3.25	1.35	1.79
3	2.69	3.49	1.39	1.89
4	2.99	3.79	1.50	1.90
5	3.10	3.99	1.69	1.99

Problem Solution   For each year (row), the four prices are summed to form row sums. The unweighted aggregate price index is formed by dividing each sum by the base-period sum (8.36). For example, the index in year 2 is $107 = \left(\frac{8.98}{8.36}\right) \times 100$.

Row	TPST	SPOO	CTAB	APERS	ROW SUMS	UWIDX
1	2.39	2.99	1.29	1.69	8.36	100
2	2.59	3.25	1.35	1.79	8.98	107
3	2.69	3.49	1.39	1.89	9.46	113
4	2.99	3.79	1.50	1.90	10.18	122
5	3.10	3.99	1.69	1.99	10.77	129

Weighted Aggregate Price Index   If the group (or basket) is no longer restricted to single units of each item (quantity $q_j = 1$), the aggregate price index must be weighted the quantities, q_j, purchased of each item. Thus, the weighted aggregate price index is

$$\text{(quantity weighted) } I_i = \frac{\Sigma y_{ij} \times q_j}{\Sigma y_{1j} \times q_j} \times 100$$

Laspeyres Index   In the weighted price index formula, when the fixed quantities are set to base-period values ($q_j = q_{1j}$) and don't change over time, the weighted aggregate price index is called the **Laspeyres index.** Base-period quantities are reflected in the following formula:

$$\text{(base period quantity weighted) } I_i = \left(\frac{\Sigma y_{ij} \times q_{1j}}{\Sigma y_{1j} \times q_{1j}} \right) \times 100$$

EXAMPLE 3

THE WEIGHTED AGGREGATE PRICE INDEX OF A BASKET OF DRUGSTORE ITEMS (QUANTITIES FIXED)

Problem Statement   In each of five years, prices are given for toothpaste (9 oz), shampoo (7 oz), cough tablets (pkg. 100), and antiperspirant (2 oz). In addition to prices, base-period quantities are shown in adjacent columns. These quantities are on a per-year basis. For example, six tubes of toothpaste are purchased per year. Create a weighted aggregate price index for these items, using the fixed quantities.

Row	TPST	QTP	SPOO	QSPOO	CTAB	QCTAB	APRES	QAPRES
1	2.39	6	2.99	4	1.29	2	1.69	3
2	2.59	6	3.25	4	1.35	2	1.79	3
3	2.69	6	3.49	4	1.39	2	1.89	3
4	2.99	6	3.79	4	1.50	2	1.90	3
5	3.10	6	3.99	4	1.69	2	1.99	3

Problem Solution   For each year (row), the four price × quantity figures are summed to form weighted row sums, WTSUM, as illustrated in the first row below. The weighted aggregate price index is formed by dividing each sum by the base-period sum (33.95). For example, the weighted index in year 2 is $108 = \left(\frac{36.61}{33.95}\right) \times 100$.

Row	TPST	Q	SPOO	Q	CTAB	Q	APRES	Q	WTSUM	INDX
1	2.39 × 6 +	2.99 × 4 +	1.29 × 2 +	1.69 × 3 =	33.95	100
2	2.59	6	3.25	4	1.35	2	1.79	3	36.61	108
3	2.69	6	3.49	4	1.39	2	1.89	3	38.55	114
4	2.99	6	3.79	4	1.50	2	1.90	3	41.80	123
5	3.10	6	3.99	4	1.69	2	1.99	3	43.91	129

Paasche Index   When the quantities of items purchased are not fixed, they vary from period to period, which is designated by the subscript i in q_{ij}. This weighted aggregate price index is called the **Paasche index.** Period i quantities are reflected in the following formula:

$$\text{(period i quantity weighted) } I_i = \left(\frac{\Sigma y_{ij} \times q_{ij}}{\Sigma y_{1j} \times q_{ij}} \right) \times 100.$$

EXAMPLE 4

THE WEIGHTED AGGREGATE PRICE INDEX OF A BASKET OF DRUGSTORE ITEMS (QUANTITIES VARYING WITH TIME)

Problem Statement   In each of five years, prices are given for toothpaste (9 oz), shampoo (7 oz), cough tablets (pkg. 100), and antiperspirant (2 oz). In addition to prices, time-varying quantities are shown in adjacent columns. These quantities are on a per-year basis. For example, six tubes of toothpaste are purchased in year 1, eight in year 2 and so on. Create a weighted aggregate price index for these items, using the varying quantities.

Row	TPST	QTP	SPOO	QSPOO	CTAB	QCTAB	APRES	QAPRES
1	2.39	6	2.99	4	1.29	1	1.69	3
2	2.59	8	3.25	3	1.35	2	1.79	5
3	2.69	7	3.49	6	1.39	4	1.89	5
4	2.99	5	3.79	6	1.50	4	1.90	4
5	3.10	9	3.99	5	1.69	3	1.99	4

Problem Solution For each year (row), the four price × quantity figures are summed to form weighted row sums, WTSUM. The next column, W1SUM, is formed by multiplying first row prices times i-th row quantities and summing across rows. Finally, the Paasche index is formed by dividing WTSUM by W1SUM.

Row	TPST	Q	SPOO	Q	CTAB	Q	APRES	Q	WTSUM	W1SUM	INDX
1	2.39	6	2.99	4	1.29	1	1.69	3	32.66	32.66	100
2	2.59	8	3.25	3	1.35	2	1.79	5	42.12	39.12	108
3	2.69	7	3.49	6	1.39	4	1.89	5	54.78	48.28	113
4	2.99	5	3.79	6	1.50	4	1.90	4	51.29	41.81	123
5	3.10	9	3.99	5	1.69	3	1.99	4	60.88	47.09	129

Commonly Encountered Aggregate Price Indexes Aggregate price indexes play an important role in describing business and economic conditions. Because many of these indexes represent broad components of the economic system, they are usually weighted. Several examples follow.

Price movements on the New York Stock Exchange are tracked by the **Dow-Jones Averages,** which are price indexes. Individual Dow-Jones Averages are available for subgroup classifications of stocks such as industrial, transportation, and utilities. The Dow-Jones Industrial Average began as the average of 12 stock prices and has expanded to the average of 30 stock prices. Because it is simply an average of prices, this index is so crude that it barely fits the definition of an unweighted aggregate price index.

To see this, let y_{ij} be the price of stock j in period i, and let y_{1j} be an assumed \$100 price of each stock in the base period. Then, the following formula reduces to an average of 30 stocks:

$$\text{unweighted aggregate price index} = I_i = \left(\frac{\Sigma y_{ij}}{\Sigma y_{1j}}\right) \times 100$$

$$\text{unweighted aggregate price index of 30 stocks} = I_i = \frac{\Sigma y_{ij}}{30}$$

To adjust for stock splits and different groups of companies included in the index during various periods, this index is divided by an adjustment constant published daily in the *Wall Street Journal*.

The popular Dow-Jones Industrial Average (DJIA) is criticized justly because it consists of a nonrandom sample of only 30 stocks and it reflects per-share prices instead of market values. As a result, many people prefer better indexes such as the **Standard and Poor's 500** and the **NYSE Composite,** which are market value based. Market value is computed by multiplying price per share times the number of shares. Thus, the q_j in the following formula is the number of shares of company j's stock: The y_{ij} are prices.

$$\text{(quantity weighted) } I_i = \left(\frac{\Sigma y_{ij} \times q_j}{\Sigma y_{1j} \times q_j}\right) \times 100$$

The widely reported **Consumer Price Index (CPI)** is used to measure general economic conditions. The CPI is a price index that represents market basket of items that include food, clothing, housing, medical expense transportation, and so on. The CPI reflects the cost of living. Eighteen year CPI figures are shown below.[2]

56.9	60.6	65.2	72.6	82.4	90.9	96.5	99.6	103
107.6	109.6	113.6	118.3	124.0	130.7	136.2	140.3	14

In the first year of this series, if your salary was \$56,900, then your s in the last year must be \$144,500 to keep abreast with the prices of wh buy.

The U.S. Bureau of Labor Statistics publishes the **Producer Price I (PPI),** formerly referred to as the Wholesale Price Index. The PPI refle prices in nonretail markets. Among other things, the PPI captures prices outputs in manufacturing, agriculture, forestry, mining, electricity, gas, pu lic utilities, and so on. Thus, the PPI tends to lead the CPI and is a harbinge of future retail prices.

STATISTICAL HIGHLIGHTS

When a particular basket or group of items is considered, a combined price-relative index is needed, which is an aggregate price index. Aggregate indexes can be weighted or unweighted.

USING PRICE INDEXES TO DEFLATE A SERIES

A series x_i is **deflated** by dividing it by an index I_i.

$$\text{deflated } x_i = \frac{x_i}{I_i}$$

For example, if x_i is an hourly wage and I_i is the Consumer Price Index, divide the hourly wage by the CPI to obtain a deflated hourly wage, which is the *real* wage with the price effect removed. The real wage is the purchasing power of each dollar earned. By removing the price effect, wages in different periods are on equal footing and can be compared.

Similarly, the gross domestic product (GDP) is deflated by a price index to properly reflect the real total value of all goods and services produced in a country.

EXAMPLE 5

DEFLATING THE PRICE OF TOOTHPASTE

Problem Statement   Use the index found in Example 4 to deflate the price of toothpa

Problem Solution   By dividing TPST by INDX, the deflated (or real) price of toothpaste computed and listed in the last column. DTPST is expressed in base-year dollars with the pric effect removed. The real price of toothpaste has remained nearly the same over the five-yea period.

Row	TPST	INDX	DTPST
1	2.39	100	2.39
2	2.59	108	2.40
3	2.69	113	2.38
4	2.99	123	2.43
5	3.10	129	2.40

QUANTITY INDEXES

A **quantity index** is similar to a price index except that y_i (which was price) is now quantity, q_i. For example, the Federal Reserve Board publishes the Index of Industrial Production, a quantity index. The Index of Industrial Production helps in understanding production quantity movements in manufacturing classifications, mining, and utilities.

Let q_i be the quantity of an item sold or produced in period i, where $i = 1, 2, 3, \ldots, n$ and where 1 is the first time period and n is the last. In understanding quantity movements it helps to express q_i relative to the period 1 quantity (or base quantity) q_1. Therefore, a **relative quantity,** rq_i, is defined as

$$\text{relative quantity} = rq_i = \left(\frac{q_i}{q_1}\right) \times 100$$

The rq_i is also referred to as a **quantity relative index,** I_i, which is expressed as a percentage of the base period quantity.

$$I_i = \text{relative quantity index} = rq_i$$

When a group of items is considered, the notation is adjusted to identify particular items. For item j

$$\text{relative quantity for item j} = rq_{ij} = I_{ij} = \left(\frac{q_{ij}}{q_{1j}}\right) \times 100$$

Aggregate Quantity Index For a group of different items, we can create a combined quantity-relative index called an **aggregate quantity index.**

If different items are of the same value, the aggregate quantity index is *unweighted*. A *weighted* index is necessary when the items have different values.

Unweighted Aggregate Quantity Index An **unweighted aggregate quantity index** is simply the ratio of the sum of the period i quantities to the sum of the base-period quantities for the group of j items.

$$\text{unweighted aggregate quantity index} = I_i = \left(\frac{\Sigma q_{ij}}{\Sigma q_{1j}}\right) \times 100$$

The summations are across all j items. Therefore, Σq_{1j} is the total base quantities of all items and Σq_{ij} is the total quantities of all items in period i.

Weighted Aggregate Quantity Index If the items are not of the same value, the aggregate quantity index must be weighted, where w_j is the weight or value of each item. Thus, the **weighted aggregate quantity index** is

$$\text{weighted aggregate quantity index} = I_i = \left(\frac{\Sigma q_{ij} \times w_j}{\Sigma q_{1j} \times w_j}\right) \times 100$$

Because prices reflect value, the weights are usually prices. In the weighted quantity index formula, the weights can be fixed and set to base-period prices, $w_j = p_{1j}$. These weights don't change over time. Base-period prices are weights in the following formula:

$$\text{(base-period price weighted) } I_i = \left(\frac{\Sigma q_{ij} \times p_{1j}}{\Sigma q_{1j} \times p_{1j}}\right) \times 100$$

When the prices of items purchased are not fixed, they vary from period to period, which is denoted by the subscript i in p_{ij}. Period i prices are weights in the following formula:

$$\text{(period i price weighted) } I_i = \left(\frac{\Sigma q_{ij} \times p_{ij}}{\Sigma q_{1j} \times p_{ij}}\right) \times 100$$

STATISTICAL HIGHLIGHTS

A quantity index is similar to a price index except that y_i (which was price) is now quantity, q_i.

CHAPTER SUMMARY

To better understand the price of an item over time, a relative price was defined as a percentage of a base-year price. A relative price can also be referred to as a price-relative index. The notion of an index was extended to a group or basket of items. Such an index is an aggregate price index, which can be unweighted or weighted by the quantities purchased. The Laspeyres index is weighted by fixed base-year quantities while the quantity weights vary for the Paasche index.

Indexes are useful in deflating prices by dividing the prices by the indexes. The deflation removes the price effect and expresses different period prices as an equivalent base-period price. Thus, you can compare different period prices on an equal basis without distortion.

Quantity indexes are like price indexes except that quantity and price exchange roles.

KEY TERMS

aggregate price index, 822
aggregate quantity index, 828
base price, 821
Consumer Price Index (CPI), 826
deflated, 826
Dow-Jones Averages, 825
group index, 822
Laspeyres index, 823

NYSE Composite, 826
Paasche index, 824
price relative index, 821
Producer Price Index (PPI), 826
quantity index, 827
quantity relative index, 827
relative price, 821
relative quantity, 827

Standard and Poor's 500, 826
unweighted aggregate price
   index, 822
unweighted aggregate quantity
index, 828
weighted aggregate price index, 823
weighted aggregate quantity
   index, 828

EXERCISES

1. Many .22-shooters are interested in the accuracy of ammunition from different manufacturers. For the following 21 brands of ammunition, accuracy is measured as average group size.[3] The group size is the center-to-center bullet hole distance between the two holes that are farthest apart in the group. Five groups of five shots were averaged for rounds that were fired at 50 yards. The figures are sorted from best to worst. (In MINITAB, RETRIEVE 'B:TTAMMO')

Row/Rank	.22 AMMO	GROUP SIZE
1	FCHI-R320	0.476
2	FCHI-P315	0.489
3	RUSS-OLY-R	0.489
4	FED-ULTRA	0.511
5	FCHI-P300	0.512
6	FCHI-R330	0.514
7	FCHI-P310	0.555
8	FED-MATCH	0.574
9	ELEY-BLUE	0.614
10	ELEY-RBOX	0.615
11	FCHI-R340S	0.622

Row/Rank	.22 AMMO	GROUP SIZE
12	FCHI-R340B	0.626
13	RWS-R50TOU	0.645
14	WIN-S-X HV	0.664
15	CCI-NEWGT	0.666
16	FED-GMTGT	0.683
17	WIN-T-22	0.717
18	WIN-SUP-SI	0.768
19	RWS-SMATCH	0.770
20	CCI-OLDGT	0.793
21	REM-TARGET	0.928

(a) Compute something like a price-relative index, which is the average group size as a percentage of the best, for this ammunition.

(b) Plot the index and identify arbitrary clusters of ammunition in similar performance groups.

2. Many .22-shooters are interested in the accuracy of rifles from different manufacturers. For the following 21 brands of rifles, accuracy is measured as average group size. The group size is the center-to-center bullet hole distance

21. The following are quarterly production figures (in units) for a computer product in a market that is becoming more and more competitive. The competition has introduced new models based on newer chips. (In MINITAB, RETRIEVE 'B:X17-21')

12038	10275	11966	12257	9554	10338	11488	12301
10445	9279	10035	10744	9792	9021	8842	9475
9133	7424	7813	9355	8438	7099	7169	9126
7176	7225	6648	7616	6393	4477	7431	7211
5318	5069	5436	6471	4664	4098	3446	4852

(a) Management wants you to compute and plot a quantity-relative index for these figures. This information will help them decide when to introduce their new models.

(b) In which year and quarter does production first dip below 50% of the base year?

22. In each of five months, production quantities (in hundreds of units) are given for a company's three main products. Create an unweighted aggregate quantity index to represent overall production.

Row	QP1	QP2	QP3
1	49	32	158
2	68	28	156
3	82	37	179
4	59	39	170
5	79	43	199

23. In each of five months, production quantities (in hundreds of units) are given for a company's three main products. In addition to quantities, base-period prices (in thousands of dollars) are shown in adjacent columns. Create a weighted aggregate quantity index for these products, using the fixed prices.

Row	QP1	P1	QP2	P2	QP3	P3
1	49	8	32	6.5	158	4
2	68	8	28	6.5	156	4
3	82	8	37	6.5	179	4
4	59	8	39	6.5	170	4
5	79	8	43	6.5	199	4

24. In each of five months, production quantities (in hundreds of units) are given for a company's three main products. In addition to quantities, time-varying prices (in thousands of dollars) are shown in adjacent columns. The company was experiencing intense price competition in the marketplace. Create a weighted aggregate quantity index for these products, using the varying prices.

Row	QP1	P1	QP2	P2	QP3	P3
1	49	8.0	32	6.5	158	4.0
2	68	7.9	28	6.4	156	3.8
3	82	7.9	37	6.3	179	3.5
4	59	7.8	39	6.3	170	3.2
5	79	7.8	43	6.2	199	3.1

25. Use the index found in the previous exercise to deflate the quantity of product three. Comment on the behavior of what might be called the *real* quantity of product three.

APPENDIX 1

Minitab Examples

EXAMPLE

THE RELATIVE PRICE OF ONE-FAMILY HOUSES

```
        (OR RETRIEVE 'NHOUSE'
MTB > RETRIEVE 'B:NHOUSE'
MTB > INFO
MTB > PRINT C1
MTB > LET C2 = (C1/23.4)*100
MTB > ROUND C2 PUT C2
MTB > PRINT C2
MTB > TSPLOT C2
```

EXAMPLE

THE UNWEIGHTED AGGREGATE PRICE INDEX OF A BASKET OF DRUGSTORE ITEMS

```
MTB > READ C1 C2 C3 C4
DATA> 2.39 2.99 1.29 1.69
DATA> 2.59 3.25 1.35 1.79
DATA> 2.69 3.49 1.39 1.89
DATA> 2.99 3.79 1.50 1.90
DATA> 3.10 3.99 1.69 1.99
DATA> END

MTB > NAME C1 'TPST' C2 'SPOO' C3 'CTAB' C4 'APERS'
MTB > NAME C6 'UWIDX'
MTB > RSUM C1-C4 PUT C5        # ROW SUMS
MTB > LET C6 = (C5/C5(1))*100  # INDEX COMPUTATION
MTB > ROUND C6 PUT C6
MTB > PRINT C1-C6
```

EXAMPLE

THE WEIGHTED AGGREGATE PRICE INDEX OF A BASKET OF DRUGSTORE ITEMS

```
        (OR RETRIEVE 'WI'
MTB > RETRIEVE 'B:WI'
MTB > INFO
MTB > PRINT C1 C11 C2 C12 C3 C13 C4 C14
MTB > NAME C15 'WTSUM'
MTB > LET C15 = (C1*C11)+(C2*C12)+(C3*C13)+(C4*C14)

MTB > NAME C16 'INDX'
MTB > LET C16 = (C15/C15(1))*100
MTB > ROUND C16 PUT C16
MTB > PRINT C1 C11 C2 C12 C3 C13 C4 C14 C15 C16
```

EXAMPLE

THE WEIGHTED AGGREGATE PRICE INDEX OF A BASKET OF DRUGSTORE ITEMS (QUANTITIES VARY WITH TIME)

```
        (OR RETRIEVE 'WIVAR'
MTB > RETRIEVE 'B:WIVAR'
MTB > NAME C15 'WTSUM' C17 'W1SUM' C16 'INDX'
MTB > LET C15 = (C1*C11)+(C2*C12)+(C3*C13)+(C4*C14)
MTB > LET C17 = (C1(1)*C11)+(C2(1)*C12)+(C3(1)*C13)+(C4(1)*C14)
MTB > LET C16 = (C15/C17)*100
MTB > ROUND C16 PUT C16
MTB > PRINT C1 C11 C2 C12 C3 C13 C4 C14 C15 C17 C16
```

EXAMPLE

DEFLATING THE PRICE OF TOOTHPASTE

```
MTB > NAME C1 'TPST' C2 'INDX' C3 'DTPST'
MTB > SET IN C1
DATA> 2.39 2.59 2.69 2.99 3.10
DATA> END
MTB > SET IN C2
DATA> 100 108 113 123 129
DATA> END

MTB > LET C3 = (C1/C2)*100
MTB > LET C3 = C3*100
MTB > ROUND C3 PUT C3
MTB > LET C3 = C3/100
MTB > PRINT C1 C2 C3
```

CHAPTER 18

Nonparametric Methods

PRELUDE

The statistical methods discussed in this chapter resemble exploratory methods because they are rough and ready in the sense that few restrictive assumptions are required beyond random samples. As a result, they are good for taking a first look at a data set. Additionally, you can rely on these methods when certain distribution-dependent assumptions fail to hold up. For example, in comparing two means, suppose the residuals are not normal in distribution as required. Furthermore, simple data transformations fail to produce normal residuals. Under such conditions, a comparison of two medians is a viable alternative to comparing two means. Additionally, methods are available for hypothesis testing and confidence intervals on single as well as pairs of medians. Moreover, there are alternatives to the distribution-dependent one-way and two-way analysis of variance. ◇

INTRODUCTION

As you have learned in earlier chapters, the validity of Student's t and z score-based confidence intervals and hypothesis tests depends on data from a normal distribution. Student's t tests, χ^2 and F tests all have the normality requirement. When the distribution is not normal but the sample size is large enough, the Central Limit Theorem tells us that the sample means tend to be normally distributed, which puts many methods back on solid ground. In other cases, the data can be transformed to be normal and then analyzed. Thus, the normal distribution has established an important place in statistical theory and in most methods you have learned so far.

Statistical methods that depend on specific distributional assumptions are referred to as **parametric methods.** Parametric methods are distribution-dependent, and many depend on the normal distribution. Parametric methods take advantage of all sample information to produce the most reliable results with the best precision when the assumptions hold. Parametric methods can be thought of as 100% efficient when the assumptions are satisfied. For a contrasting example, the nondistribution-dependent sample median requires 1.57 times the observations to perform as well as the sample mean. Generally, parametric methods lose efficiency and fall short when assumptions are violated. However, it should be noted that some parametric statistical methods continue to work well (are robust) even when the distributional assumptions are violated.

Statistical methods that do not depend on specific distributional assumptions are called **nonparametric methods.** Nonparametric methods are **distribution-free** for some of their characteristics. Neither term, nonparametric or distribution-free, is strictly correct terminology, but they have become accepted terms. A data analyst with no knowledge of the distributional form or of normalizing transformations can rely on nonparametric methods because they are designed to function well under weaker assumptions. Furthermore, weaker assumptions are imposed when the measurement scale is nominal or ordinal. Nonparametric methods are like four-wheel drive when the no snow assumption is violated and you find yourself in deep snow.

In addition to weaker assumptions, nonparametric methods are rough and ready and easy to compute. As a result, nonparametric methods are versatile and good for taking a first look at a data set. Therefore, they can be used in exploratory work. For example, the median is a good nonparametric estimator of the population mean as long as the distribution is symmetrical, without the normality requirement. For highly skewed distributions, the median is superior to the mean as a location measure. Nonparametric methods exist for hypothesis testing and confidence intervals on single as well as pairs of medians. Moreover, there are nonparametric alternatives to one-way and two-way analysis of variance where more than two medians are compared.

With the availability of easy-to-use statistical software, it is prudent to use both nonparametric and parametric methods to analyze statistical problems, particularly when sample sizes are relatively small and the normality assumption is tenuous.

ONE-SAMPLE HYPOTHESIS TESTS AND CONFIDENCE INTERVALS

Often, the nature of the question or problem at hand directs the researcher to a nonparametric method. For example, consider a marketing research question on consumer preferences where the distribution of responses is not expected to be normal. The nonparametric **sign test** has long been used for hypothesis tests concerning consumer preferences and other problems of similar structure. An important reason for choosing the sign-test procedures is that the population producing the data can have any shape and need not be symmetrical.

The **Wilcoxon signed-rank test** is an alternative to the sign test. It is a little more powerful but computationally more complex and assumes symmetrical populations.

Both approaches require random samples.

The Sign Test

After having tasted two types of coffee, a consumer might be asked, which gourmet coffee, chocolate almond or hazelnut, do you prefer?

The Sign Test for Small Samples, $n \leq 20$ This question might be asked of a random sample of n consumers. When $n \leq 20$, the binomial distribution is used to analyze the responses. In theory, the binomial distribution still applies for larger sample sizes. However, a normal approximation is recommended to simplify computations.

The responses of $n = 15$ consumers are shown in Exhibit 1. For analysis purposes, a preference for hazelnut is indicated by a plus ($+$) sign and for chocolate almond a minus ($-$) sign. Thus, the measurement scale is nominal.

Hypothesis Being Tested   The same population preferences for both coffees lead to the null hypothesis, $H_n : p = .50$. Then the population of preferences would consist of half plus signs and half minus signs. The alternative hypothesis is $H_a : p \neq .50$.

Informally, three plus signs in the sample is far from the $np = \frac{15}{2}$ expected under the null hypothesis. This leads us to doubt the null hypothesis from the start.

Formal Hypothesis Testing   We proceed to formally test the null hypothesis by examining the binomial probability for each possible number of plus signs.

EXHIBIT 1 Coffee Preferences Recorded by Signs

Consumer	Preference (in bold)	Sign
1	**chocolate almond** or hazelnut	−
2	chocolate almond or **hazelnut**	+
3	**chocolate almond** or hazelnut	−
4	**chocolate almond** or hazelnut	−
5	**chocolate almond** or hazelnut	−
6	**chocolate almond** or hazelnut	−
7	**chocolate almond** or hazelnut	−
8	**chocolate almond** or hazelnut	−
9	**chocolate almond** or hazelnut	−
10	**chocolate almond** or hazelnut	−
11	chocolate almond or **hazelnut**	+
12	**chocolate almond** or hazelnut	−
13	**chocolate almond** or hazelnut	−
14	chocolate almond or **hazelnut**	+
15	**chocolate almond** or hazelnut	−

The number of plus signs possible is any of the integers 0 through 15. Where $y = 0, 1, \ldots, 15$, the binomial probability of exactly y plus signs under the null hypothesis, $p = .50$, is expressed as

$$P(y) = \binom{n}{y} p^y (1 - p)^{(n-y)}$$

These probabilities are computed using the MINITAB commands in Appendix 1. The column names in Exhibit 2 are NPLUS for y, the number of plus signs; BPROB for $P(y)$; CUMDN for cumulative probabilities going down the column BPROB; and CUMUP for cumulative probabilities going up the column BPROB.

When the null hypothesis is true that $p = .50$, the probability of 3 or fewer plus signs or 12 or more plus signs in a sample of 15 responses is $.01758 + .01758 = .03516$ (see the cumulative probabilities in Exhibit 2).

At this significance level, $\alpha = .03516$, the decision rule is to reject the null hypothesis that $p = .50$ when there are 3 or fewer or 12 or more plus signs in the sample. Thus, the sample result of 3 plus signs causes us to reject the null hypothesis in favor of the not equal alternative hypothesis.

Similarly, the probability of 4 or fewer plus signs or 11 or more plus signs in a sample of 15 is $.05923 + .05923 = .11846$. At this significance level, $\alpha = .11846$, the decision rule is to reject the null hypothesis that $p = .50$ when there are 4 or fewer or 11 or more plus signs. Thus, the sample result of 3 plus signs causes us to reject the null hypothesis in favor of the alternative hypothesis.

In conducting a sign test, the procedure is to count the plus signs in the sample and compare the count to the bounds in the decision rule at the chosen significance level.

EXHIBIT 2 Binomial Probabilities and Cumulative Probabilities for the Number of Plus Signs, p = .50

Row	NPLUS	BPROB	CUMDN	CUMUP
1	0	0.000031	0.00003	1.00000
2	1	0.000458	0.00049	0.99997
3	2	0.003204	0.00369	0.99951
4	3	0.013885	0.01758	0.99631
5	4	0.041656	0.05923	0.98242
6	5	0.091644	0.15088	0.94077
7	6	0.152740	0.30362	0.84912
8	7	0.196381	0.50000	0.69638
9	8	0.196381	0.69638	0.50000
10	9	0.152740	0.84912	0.30362
11	10	0.091644	0.94077	0.15088
12	11	0.041656	0.98242	0.05923
13	12	0.013885	0.99631	0.01758
14	13	0.003204	0.99951	0.00369
15	14	0.000458	0.99997	0.00049
16	15	0.000031	1.00000	0.00003

A Sign Test for Continuous Measurements   Preference responses can be scored as a continuous measurement, say, from 0 to 10. As a result, the sign test is illustrated for continuous data. Continuous data arises frequently in many types of applications.

In Exhibit 3, you might notice that plus or minus signs are based on the continuous scores that are shown. A score greater than a hypothesized population median of 5 indicates a preference for hazelnut, a plus (+) sign. A

EXHIBIT 3 Coffee Preferences Recorded by Signs and Continuous Scores from 0 to 10

Consumer	Preference (in bold)	Sign	Score
1	**chocolate almond** or hazelnut	−	2.3
2	chocolate almond or **hazelnut**	+	6.0
3	**chocolate almond** or hazelnut	−	1.5
4	**chocolate almond** or hazelnut	−	.5
5	**chocolate almond** or hazelnut	−	4.2
6	**chocolate almond** or hazelnut	−	3.5
7	**chocolate almond** or hazelnut	−	2.5
8	**chocolate almond** or hazelnut	−	1.8
9	**chocolate almond** or hazelnut	−	4.5
10	**chocolate almond** or hazelnut	−	2.0
11	chocolate almond or **hazelnut**	+	6.5
12	**chocolate almond** or hazelnut	−	3.1
13	**chocolate almond** or hazelnut	−	2.2
14	chocolate almond or **hazelnut**	+	6.2
15	**chocolate almond** or hazelnut	−	1.0

score less than a hypothesized population median of 5 indicates a preference for chocolate almond, a minus $(-)$ sign. The same population preferences for both coffees leads to the null hypothesis, H_n: $p = .50$. This is equivalent to the hypothesis that the median is 5 when the score is continuous from 0 to 10. Therefore, the conceptual basis for the sign test can be used to test hypotheses and construct nonparametric confidence intervals on population medians.

First, the continuous score figures are tested for randomness using the familiar nonparametric runs test. Although the sample size is small enough to produce a warning, all indications are that the sample data are random.

```
SCORE
K =     3.1867
THE OBSERVED NO. OF RUNS =  11
THE EXPECTED NO. OF RUNS =   8.2000
  6 OBSERVATIONS ABOVE K    9 BELOW
* N SMALL--FOLLOWING APPROX. MAY BE INVALID
            THE TEST IS SIGNIFICANT AT  0.1172
            CANNOT REJECT AT ALPHA = 0.05
```

The MINITAB STEST command is issued to test the hypothesis that the median is 5 on the continuous scale from 0 to 10. This hypothesis is identical to $p = .50$ examined above. In the sample, the number of plus signs above the hypothesized median is 3. When the null hypothesis is true that $p = .50$, the probability of 3 or fewer plus signs or 12 or more plus signs in a sample of 15 is $.01758 + .01758 = .03516$ (see the cumulative probabilities in Exhibit 2).

At this significance level (MINITAB P VALUE), $\alpha = .03516$, the decision rule is to reject the null hypothesis that $p = .50$ when there are 3 or fewer or 12 or more plus signs in the sample. Thus, the sample result of 3 plus signs causes us to reject the null hypothesis in favor of the alternative hypothesis. MINITAB prints a count of data values above (plus) and below the median in the null hypothesis and the significance (P VALUE). MINITAB also finds the actual sample median of 2.5.

```
SIGN TEST OF MEDIAN = 5.000 VERSUS  N.E.  5.000

           N  BELOW  EQUAL  ABOVE  P VALUE   MEDIAN
SCORE     15    12      0      3   0.0352    2.500
```

A Sign-Based Confidence Interval Approach   An alternative way to test the null hypothesis that the median is 5 is to construct a confidence interval on the population median from the sample data. The hypothesized median of 5 falls outside the following intervals; therefore, the null hypothesis is rejected.

Confidence Level	Interval
.9648	1.8 to 4.5
.8815	2.0 to 4.2
.9500	1.875 to 4.388

Using the 95% interval, the alternative hypothesis, H_a: median $\neq$ 5, is supported at a 95% level of confidence. Alternatively, a one-sided, less-than-five alternative hypothesis, H_a: median $<$ 5, is also supported because the confidence interval lies to the left of 5. However, the confidence level is 97.5% because of the one-sided nature of the alternative hypothesis.

Because the distribution underlying the analysis is binomial and discrete, an exact confidence (say, 95%) may have to be approximated by nonlinear interpolation (which is denoted as NLI in the MINITAB output below). As a result, MINITAB prints the approximate interval as well as the two exact intervals used to get the approximation. For the 95% interval, MINITAB interpolates between these two adjacent, exact intervals.

```
SIGN CONFIDENCE INTERVAL FOR MEDIAN

                        ACHIEVED
            N  MEDIAN  CONFIDENCE   CONFIDENCE INTERVAL   POSITION
SCORE      15   2.500    0.8815     (2.000,    4.200)     exact 5
                         0.9500     (1.875,    4.388)         NLI
                         0.9648     (1.800,    4.500)     exact 4
```

Because the notch on the boxplot is a 95% interval on the median and is computed in the same way, a notched boxplot (see Chapter 7) is shown for comparison purposes.

```
                    -------------------
        -----------I(     +            )I------------------
                    -------------------
    --------+---------+---------+---------+---------+--------SCORE
        1.2       2.4       3.6       4.8       6.0
```

For comparison purposes, the parametric confidence interval on the population mean is shown below. Notice that this interval is narrower than the nonparametric ones on the median above, but its validity depends on the scores being random and normal.

```
          N    MEAN   STDEV  SE MEAN   95.0 PERCENT C.I.
SCORE    15   3.187   1.913   0.494    (2.127,   4.246)
```

To illustrate how specific sign-based confidence intervals are determined, consider the ordered scores from Exhibit 3.

0.5 1.0 1.5 **1.8** 2.0 2.2 2.3 2.5 3.1 3.5 4.2 **4.5** 6.0
6.2 6.5

The scores in the fourth position from each end form a .9648 confidence interval from 1.8 to 4.5. The confidence level .9648 = 1 − .03516, where .03516 is the probability of 3 or fewer plus signs or 12 or more plus signs in a sample of 15 (.01758 + .01758 = .03516, see the cumulative probabilities in Exhibit 2). It is possible for a median outside the interval (1.8, 4.5) to generate 3 or fewer plus signs or 12 or more plus signs.

The scores in the fifth position from each end form a .8815 confidence interval (2.0, 4.2). The confidence level .8815 = 1 − .1185, where .1185 is the probability of 4 or fewer plus signs or 11 or more plus signs in a sample of 15 is .05923 + .05923 = .11846 (see the cumulative probabilities in Exhibit 2). It is possible for a median outside the interval (2.0, 4.2) to generate 4 or fewer plus signs or 11 or more plus signs.

EXAMPLE 1

RETURNS ON A STOCK

Problem Statement (a)   From a sample of 24 monthly returns on a stock, construct a notched boxplot.

Problem Solution (a)   The notched boxplot on returns is

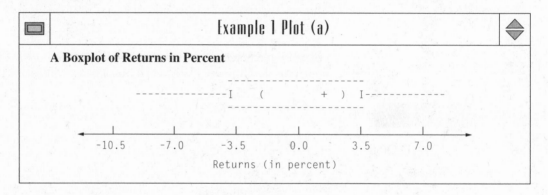

Problem Statement (b)   Construct a 95% sign confidence interval for the median.

Problem Solution (b)   Three sign confidence intervals for the median are found. The first and third intervals are used to compute the 95% interval through nonlinear interpolation.

	N	MEDIAN	ACHIEVED CONFIDENCE	CONFIDENCE INTERVAL		POSITION
PCTRETS	24	1.350	0.9361	(-3.900,	3.400)	8
			0.9500	(-3.900,	3.435)	NLI
			0.9773	(-3.900,	3.600)	7

Problem Statement (c)   Perform a sign test for the null hypothesis that the median return is 7% against the not equal alternative.

Problem Solution (c)   Reject the null hypothesis that the median is 7 because of the small P value and the median in the null hypothesis falls outside the above confidence intervals. There is only one data value above the median of 7; one plus sign in the sign test.

```
SIGN TEST OF MEDIAN = 7.000 VERSUS N.E. 7.000

              N  BELOW  EQUAL  ABOVE  P VALUE   MEDIAN
PCTRETS      24     23      0      1   0.0000    1.350
```

Problem Statement (d) For comparison purposes, find a parametric confidence interval (95% t interval) on the population mean (see Chapter 7).

Problem Solution (d) A parametric 95% confidence interval on the population mean is shown below.

```
              N    MEAN   STDEV  SE MEAN   95.0 PERCENT C.I.
PCTRETS      24   0.129   4.866    0.993  ( -1.926,   2.184)
```

The Sign Test for Large Samples, n > 20 Again, test the null hypothesis that p = .50. However, the normal approximation of the binomial distribution establishes bounds for an accept or reject decision. Recall that the mean of the binomial is np and the standard deviation is the square root of $np(1 - p)$. Therefore, when p = .50, a $(1 - \alpha)$ = .95 confidence interval on the number of plus signs in a sign test is (see Chapter 10)

$$np \pm z_{\alpha/2}\sqrt{np(1 - p)}$$

EXAMPLE 2

RETURNS ON A STOCK, LARGE SAMPLE COMPUTATION

Problem Statement From a sample of 24 monthly returns on a stock, compute a 95% confidence interval on the number of plus signs in a sign test. The null hypothesis is that the median return is 7% on this stock. If one data value exceeds the median (one plus sign), would you reject the null hypothesis?

Problem Solution The 95% interval for the number of plus signs is

$$np \pm z_{\alpha/2}\sqrt{np(1 - p)} = 24(.50) \pm 1.96\sqrt{24(.50)(.50)} = (7.2 \text{ and } 16.8)$$

Reject the null hypothesis that the median is 7 because there is only one plus sign outside the interval (7.2 and 16.8).

The Wilcoxon Signed-Rank Test and Confidence Intervals

The **Wilcoxon signed-rank test** is an alternative to the sign test. It is a little more powerful but computationally more complex and assumes symmetrical, continuous populations as well as random samples. For the sign-test procedures, the population producing the data can have any shape and need not be symmetrical.

EXHIBIT 4 Coffee Preferences Recorded by Signs, Continuous Scores, and Ranked Score Differences from the Hypothesized Median

Consumer	Preference (in bold)	Sign	Score	Diff.	Rank
1	**chocolate almond** or hazelnut	−	2.3	2.7	9
2	chocolate almond or **hazelnut**	+	6.0	1.0	3
3	**chocolate almond** or hazelnut	−	1.5	3.5	13
4	**chocolate almond** or hazelnut	−	.5	4.5	15
5	**chocolate almond** or hazelnut	−	4.2	0.8	2
6	**chocolate almond** or hazelnut	−	3.5	1.5	5.5
7	**chocolate almond** or hazelnut	−	2.5	2.5	8
8	**chocolate almond** or hazelnut	−	1.8	3.2	12
9	**chocolate almond** or hazelnut	−	4.5	0.5	1
10	**chocolate almond** or hazelnut	−	2.0	3.0	11
11	chocolate almond or **hazelnut**	+	6.5	1.5	5.5
12	**chocolate almond** or hazelnut	−	3.1	1.9	7
13	**chocolate almond** or hazelnut	−	2.2	2.8	10
14	chocolate almond or **hazelnut**	+	6.2	1.2	4
15	**chocolate almond** or hazelnut	−	1.0	4.0	14

Wilcoxon Signed-Rank Test   To illustrate the procedure for computing the **Wilcoxon signed-rank statistic, W,** the data in Exhibit 4 are used.

The median of 5 in the null hypothesis is subtracted from each score (zeros are discarded). The absolute values of these differences are ranked from small to large and given the signs from the sign column. Absolute differences that are the same (ties) are assigned the average rank. For example, the two differences that are the same (1.5 and 1.5) are assigned a rank of 5.5, which is the average of ranks 5 and 6.

The **positive signed ranks** are summed. This sum is the Wilcoxon statistic W (+3 + 5.5 + 4 = 12.5 = W). This calculation is shown on the MINITAB output below. Clearly, from the small P value, we reject the hypothesis that the population median equals 5.

```
TEST OF MEDIAN = 5.000 VERSUS MEDIAN N.E. 5.000

             N FOR  WILCOXON           ESTIMATED
         N   TEST   STATISTIC  P VALUE  MEDIAN
SCORE    15   15     12.5       0.008    3.100
```

For samples of $n \geq 20$, W is approximately normal with a

$$\text{mean } W = \frac{n(n + 1)}{4}$$

and a variance

$$\text{variance } W = \frac{n(n + 1)(2n + 1)}{24}$$

MINITAB uses this approximation, which degrades as the sample size gets smaller. Thus, the Wilcoxon statistic W can be standardized by subtracting the mean and dividing by the standard deviation. As a result, hypothesis tests and confidence intervals can be conducted as usual with critical values from the standard normal distribution.

For sample sizes less than 20, you can revert to the sign test shown earlier or consult special tables for the exact distribution of W found in books devoted to nonparametric methods.

A Wilcoxon-Based Confidence Interval Approach An alternative way to test the null hypothesis that the median is 5 is to construct a confidence interval on the population median from the sample data. The hypothesized median of 5 falls outside the intervals shown below. Therefore, the null hypothesis is rejected.

```
               ESTIMATED   ACHIEVED
           N    MEDIAN   CONFIDENCE   CONFIDENCE INTERVAL
SCORE     15     3.10      95.0        (2.00,    4.25)
```

Using the 95% interval, the alternative hypothesis, H_a: median $\neq$ 5, is supported at a 95% level of confidence. Alternatively, a one-sided, less-than-five alternative hypothesis, H_a: median $<$ 5, is also supported because the confidence interval lies to the left of 5. However, the confidence level is 97.5% because of the one-sided nature of the alternative hypothesis.

S T A T I S T I C A L   H I G H L I G H T S

For hypothesis tests and confidence intervals, both the sign and the Wilcoxon signed-rank approaches are effective nonparametric methods for single samples.

TWO-SAMPLE HYPOTHESIS TESTS AND CONFIDENCE INTERVALS

The first two-sample nonparametric class of problems involves two dependent sets of responses, paired (matched) samples. Typically, response differences are computed, which leads to one-sample analysis of differences using the familiar sign or Wilcoxon signed-rank approaches.

Other nonparametric methods are designed for two independent samples. These methods fall under the heading Mann-Whitney-Wilcoxon (**rank-sum** rather than a signed-rank) test.

Paired (Matched) Sample Tests, Dependent Responses

Suppose two new breakfast cereals, Boom and Bang, are compared by 10 tasters and rated on a 10-point scale, with 10 being the highest possible score

EXHIBIT 5 Cereal Taste Scores and Differences for 10 Tasters

TASTER	BOOM	BANG	DIFF
1	6.1	7.1	-1.0
2	6.1	7.5	-1.4
3	6.6	7.5	-0.9
4	6.8	7.6	-0.8
5	6.9	7.7	-0.8
6	7.2	7.7	-0.5
7	7.2	7.8	-0.6
8	7.2	8.0	-0.8
9	7.4	8.0	-0.6
10	8.5	8.1	0.4

(see Exhibit 5). Because each taster tends to score at his or her own level, the differences (DIFF) are usually analyzed because they remove taster effects.

Because each taster tastes both cereals, the responses are matched pairs and dependent on the taster. When the responses are normal in distribution, a paired t test is used, which is simply a t test on the cereal score differences for each taster. This problem is also a special case of two-way analysis of variance where the cereals are treatments and the tasters are blocks (see Chapter 15).

The parametric results depend on the normality assumption. The t statistic (-4.79) in absolute value exceeds the critical t (2.262) for $\alpha = .025$ and 9 degrees of freedom. Bang is significantly better than Boom in taste.

TEST OF MU = 0.000 VS MU N.E. 0.000

	N	MEAN	STDEV	SE MEAN	T	P VALUE
DIFF	10	-0.700	0.462	0.146	-4.79	0.0010

If the normality assumption is tenuous, the nonparametric sign and Wilcoxon tests and confidence intervals are worth examining.

EXAMPLE 3

JUDGING BREAKFAST CEREALS

Problem Statement Two new breakfast cereals, Boom and Bang, are compared by 10 tasters and rated on a 10-point scale, with 10 being the highest possible score. See Exhibit 5. Analyze differences using sign and Wilcoxon tests and intervals for the hypothesis that the median taste difference is 0 between Boom and Bang.

Problem Solution For a pictorial display, two notched boxplots of the taste scores are shown. The median scores appear to be significantly different for the two cereals. However, the taster effect has not been removed and there is one potential outlier.

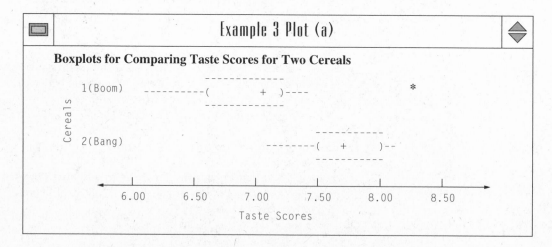

Example 3 Plot (a)

Boxplots for Comparing Taste Scores for Two Cereals

In the computer output that follows, the sign test (small P VALUE) and intervals (to the left of 0) indicate that we should reject the hypothesis that the cereals taste the same and have a 0 median taste score difference. The Wilcoxon test and interval lead to the same conclusion. However, the sample size is a little small for us to rely completely on the normal approximation used in the Wilcoxon test.

```
SIGN TEST OF MEDIAN = 0.00000 VERSUS  N.E.  0.00000

              N BELOW EQUAL ABOVE   P VALUE     MEDIAN
DIFF         10    9     0     1    0.0215     -0.8000

SIGN CONFIDENCE INTERVAL FOR MEDIAN

                         ACHIEVED
        N   MEDIAN     CONFIDENCE    CONFIDENCE INTERVAL  POSITION
DIFF   10  -0.8000       0.8906     ( -0.9000, -0.6000)         3
                         0.9500     ( -0.9342, -0.5658)       NLI
                         0.9785     ( -1.0000, -0.5000)         2

TEST OF MEDIAN = 0.000000 VERSUS MEDIAN N.E. 0.000000

            N FOR   WILCOXON          ESTIMATED
        N   TEST   STATISTIC  P VALUE  MEDIAN
DIFF   10    10      1.0       0.008   -0.7500

          ESTIMATED   ACHIEVED
        N   MEDIAN   CONFIDENCE  CONFIDENCE INTERVAL
DIFF   10   -0.750      94.7   ( -1.000, -0.300)
```

An Alternative Wilcoxon Normal Approximation for Paired (Matched) Samples   For n differences from matched samples from identical and symmetrical populations, $n \geq 10$, signed ranks are found as described earlier. Another Wilcoxon signed-rank statistic, W^*, is defined as the sum of *all* the signed ranks (rather than just the positive signed ranks). Under the null hypothesis of no difference in population medians, W^* is approximately normal with a mean,

$$\text{mean } W^* = 0$$

and a variance

$$\text{variance } W^* = \frac{n(n + 1)(2n + 1)}{6}$$

The Wilcoxon statistic W^* can be standardized by subtracting the mean and dividing by the standard deviation. As a result, hypothesis tests and confidence intervals can be conducted as usual with critical values from the standard normal distribution.

Mann-Whitney-Wilcoxon Rank-Sum Test for Two Independent Samples

This is a rank test on the difference in population medians based on two independent samples of observations. It is the nonparametric version of the pooled t test, which assumed normal populations with the same variance (see Chapter 9). The Mann-Whitney-Wilcoxon rank-sum test requires random samples from two continuous populations that have the same shape, which is not necessarily normal.

The procedure for this test is illustrated in Exhibit 6. Two independent samples of responses are in columns ATOLD and ATNEW and are stacked to form column OLDNEW. Column DUMMY identifies which observations are from which sample. OLDNEW is sorted in ascending order to form SORTC3. The sample identifiers in DUMMY continue to identify samples and are placed in SORTC4 and relate to SORTC3. In the RANK column, ranks are assigned to the SORTC3 values. Ranks in RANK associated with

EXHIBIT 6 Mann-Whitney-Wilcoxon Rank-Sum Test Procedure

Row	ATOLD	ATNEW	OLDNEW	DUMMY	SORTC3	SORTC4	RANK	RANKOLD
1	21.6	23.5	21.6	0	21.3	1	1.0	4.0
2	21.7	23.5	21.7	0	21.5	1	2.0	6.5
3	23.9	22.0	23.9	0	21.6	0	4.0	11.5
4	24.0	21.3	24.0	0	21.6	1	4.0	13.0
5	22.7	21.7	22.7	0	21.6	1	4.0	18.0
6	24.6	22.3	24.6	0	21.7	0	6.5	19.5
7	22.5	23.3	22.5	0	21.7	1	6.5	19.5
8	24.0	23.6	24.0	0	22.0	1	8.0	22.0
9	24.4	21.5	24.4	0	22.3	1	9.5	22.0
10	24.0	24.1	24.0	0	22.3	1	9.5	22.0
11	23.7	21.6	23.7	0	22.5	0	11.5	25.0
12	24.9	22.5	24.9	0	22.5	1	11.5	26.0
13	23.9	22.3	23.9	0	22.7	0	13.0	27.5
14	24.9	21.6	24.9	0	23.3	1	14.0	27.5
15			23.5	1	23.5	1	15.5	
16			23.5	1	23.5	1	15.5	
17			22.0	1	23.6	1	17.0	
18			21.3	1	23.7	0	18.0	
19			21.7	1	23.9	0	19.5	
20			22.3	1	23.9	0	19.5	
21			23.3	1	24.0	0	22.0	
22			23.6	1	24.0	0	22.0	
23			21.5	1	24.0	0	22.0	
24			24.1	1	24.1	1	24.0	
25			21.6	1	24.4	0	25.0	
26			22.5	1	24.6	0	26.0	
27			22.3	1	24.9	0	27.5	
28			21.6	1	24.9	0	27.5	
							SUM = 264.0	

the first sample values (identified by zeros in SORTC4) are placed in RANKOLD and summed. The sum, W**, is the Mann-Whitney-Wilcoxon rank sum statistic (W** = 264 in Exhibit 6). W** can be based on rank sums of either sample.

Under the null hypothesis of equal medians and when each sample size exceeds nine, W** is approximately normal with a

$$\text{mean } W^{**} = \frac{n_1(n_1 + n_2 + 1)}{2}$$

and a variance

$$\text{variance } W^{**} = \frac{n_1 n_2(n_1 + n_2 + 1)}{12}$$

The Mann-Whitney-Wilcoxon rank sum statistic W** can be standardized by subtracting the mean and dividing by the standard deviation. As a result, hypothesis tests and confidence intervals can be conducted as usual with critical values from the standard normal distribution.

EXAMPLE 4

COMPARING ASSEMBLY TIMES FOR TWO ASSEMBLY METHODS

Problem Statement A manager who welcomes employee suggestions about reducing assembly time in a production operation decided to compare a suggested new method with the old method. Two independent samples are taken of old and new assembly times and are shown in Exhibit 6. Use the nonparametric Mann-Whitney-Wilcoxon rank-sum statistic W** to test the null hypothesis that the population median assembly times are the same against the not equal alternative. For a rough visual comparison show two side-by-side notched box plots.

Problem Solution This is a close call. MINITAB provides several pieces of information that lead to the conclusion that the population median assembly times are not equal. A 95.4% confidence interval does not include 0. The significance level associated with the standardized rank-sum statistic is .0054. The less powerful notched boxplots have notches that overlap, which support the null hypothesis of no difference. However, the sample medians are far enough apart that the notches barely overlap. Management would be wise in this case to adopt the new assembly method for both statistical and nonstatistical reasons.

```
Mann-Whitney Confidence Interval and Test

ATOLD     N = 14    Median =      23.950
ATNEW     N = 14    Median =      22.300

Point estimate for ETA1-ETA2 is        1.300 (ETA refers to population median)

95.4 pct confidence interval for ETA1-ETA2 is (0.400,2.300)

W** = 264.0

Test of ETA1 = ETA2 vs. ETA1 n.e. ETA2 is significant at 0.0054;
the test is significant at 0.0053 when adjusted for ties.
```

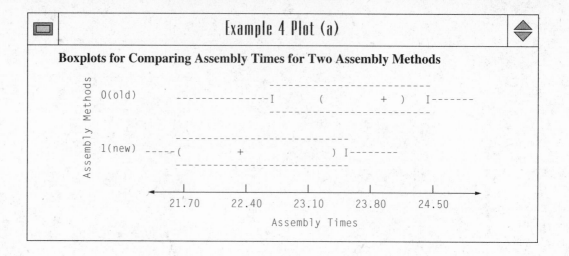

Boxplots for Comparing Assembly Times for Two Assembly Methods

---

S T A T I S T I C A L   H I G H L I G H T S

Two-sample comparison problems can involve dependent or independent samples. For dependent samples, response differences are treated as a single sample and analyzed by the sign or Wilcoxon signed-rank approaches. Independent samples are analyzed using the Mann-Whitney-Wilcoxon rank-sum approach.

NONPARAMETRIC ALTERNATIVE TO ONE-WAY ANALYSIS OF VARIANCE, COMPARING TWO OR MORE MEDIANS OF A SINGLE FACTOR

The Mann-Whitney-Wilcoxon rank-sum test compares population medians from two continuous populations that have the same shape. Two other nonparametric tests can make the same comparison for independent samples, the **Kruskal-Wallis test** and the **Mood test.** An added benefit is that both these tests can be extended to compare k medians from k continuous populations that have the same shape. The Kruskal-Wallis and Mood tests are the nonparametric versions of one-way analysis of variance (see Chapter 15), which assumed normal populations with the same variances. The Kruskal-Wallis and Mood tests require random samples from k continuous populations that have the same shape. The Mood test is particularly robust against outliers. Therefore, it is a good preliminary exploratory tool.

Kruskal-Wallis Test Statistic   The **Kruskal-Wallis test statistic H** is a function of summed ranks. As in the Mann-Whitney-Wilcoxon rank-sum test, the combined samples are ranked; however, k samples are now combined.

Let $\overline{R}_i$ be the average rank in sample i; $\overline{R}$ equal the average of all the ranks; n_i equal the size of sample i; and N equal the total combined sample size. Then, the test statistic is

$$H = \frac{12\Sigma n_i(\overline{R}_i - \overline{R})^2}{N(N + 1)}$$

Under the null hypothesis of equal population medians, H follows a chi-square distribution with $k - 1$ degrees of freedom, as long as each of the k samples has more than five observations. H is compared to critical values from this distribution to accept or reject hypotheses in the usual manner. Because some statisticians adjust this statistic for ties, MINITAB computes an adjusted H statistic also.

The Mood Test Statistic From a (2 by k) table of counts of observations less than or equal to the overall median and of observations greater than the overall median, a standard chi-square statistic is computed for independence of columns and rows is computed. Comparison is made to a critical value.

The Kruskal-Wallis and Mood Tests for Comparing Two Population Medians

The Kruskal-Wallis and Mood tests are demonstrated on the same assembly-time data used in the Mann-Whitney-Wilcoxon test where two assembly methods are compared.

EXAMPLE 5

COMPARING ASSEMBLY TIMES FOR TWO ASSEMBLY METHODS (KRUSKAL-WALLIS AND MOOD TESTS)

Problem Statement A manager who welcomes employee suggestions about reducing assembly time in a production operation decided to compare a suggested new method with the old method. Two independent samples are taken of old and new assembly times and are shown in Exhibit 6. Use the nonparametric Kruskal-Wallis and Mood tests to test the null hypothesis that the population median assembly times are the same against the not equal alternative.

Problem Solution Both methods lead to the conclusion that the population median assembly times are not equal. However, the output information is a little different for each test. As a result of the Kruskal-Wallis test, the significance level associated with the test statistic H is .005.

```
LEVEL     NOBS    MEDIAN   AVE. RANK    Z VALUE

   0        14     23.95      18.9        2.80
   1        14     22.30      10.1       -2.80
OVERALL     28                14.5

H = 7.86 (d.f. = 1  P VALUE = 0.005); the critical chi-square
value for alpha of .05 and one degree of freedom is 3.84.
H = 7.89  d.f. = 1  P VALUE = 0.005 (adj. for ties)
```

In the Mood test below, a significantly large chi-square value and a 95% confidence interval on the differences in medians that does not include 0 leads to the rejection of the hypothesis of equal medians. The chi-square value is based on the counts of the number of data values in each sample of the number of observations less than or equal to the overall median and the number of observations greater than the overall median. The confidence intervals on the individual sample medians are based on the sign-interval procedure.

```
Mood median test of OLDNEW

Chi-square statistic = 5.14 (df = 1   p = 0.024); the critical
chi-square value for alpha of .05 and one degree of freedom is
3.84.

A 95.0% C.I. for median(0) - median(1): (0.34,2.32)

                                      Individual 95.0% CI's
DUMMY  N<=   N>  Median   Q3-Q1  ----------+---------+---------+------
    0    4   10   23.95    1.80             (--------------+-----)
    1   10    4   22.30    1.90  (---------+--------------)
                                  ----------+---------+---------+------
                                      22.40     23.20     24.00

Overall median = 23.40
```

The Kruskal-Wallis and Mood Tests for Comparing k Population Medians

The Kruskal-Wallis and Mood tests are used to compare mileage figures for three gasoline brands. Next, these tests are used to compare mileage figures of four vehicle types.

EXAMPLE 6

GASOLINE BRANDS

Problem Statement   Three brands of gasoline (treatments) were used in 15 identical sport utility vehicles (experimental units) to test the hypothesis that there is no difference in population median mileage figures for brands. Under similar driving conditions, mileage data were recorded and the data set is

```
Row   BRAND1  BRAND2  BRAND3

 1    17.3    19.4    17.0
 2    18.8    17.9    17.2
 3    15.9    16.7    19.0
 4    17.8    17.3    19.8
 5    17.5    17.5    16.5
```

To help ensure independence of the errors, the treatments were randomly assigned to the experimental units. Three pieces of paper were marked 1, 2, and 3 for brands. This was done five times and the 15 pieces of paper were placed in a hat and drawn without replacement to assign brands to vehicles.

Perform both Kruskal-Wallis and Mood tests for the hypothesis that all three population medians are equal.

Problem Solution   Among other things, both the Kruskal-Wallis H statistic and the Mood chi-square statistic result in the acceptance of the null hypothesis that the population medians (miles per gallon) for the three brands are the same.

```
LEVEL    NOBS    MEDIAN  AVE. RANK    Z VALUE
   1        5     17.50     7.6        -0.24
   2        5     17.50     8.6         0.37
   3        5     17.20     7.8        -0.12
OVERALL   15                8.0

H = 0.14  d.f. = 2  p = 0.932
H = 0.14  d.f. = 2  p = 0.932 (adj. for ties)

Mood median test of MPG

Chi-square = 0.00  df = 2  p = 1.000

                                 Individual 95.0% CI's
BRAND  N<=   N>   Median   Q3-Q1  --------+---------+---------+--------
   1     3    2   17.50    1.70   (--------------+----------)
   2     3    2   17.50    1.65      (--------+------------)
   3     3    2   17.20    2.65     (-------+--------------------)
                                 --------+---------+---------+--------
                                      16.8      18.0      19.2

Overall median = 17.50
* NOTE * Levels with < 6 obs. have confidence < 95.0%
```

EXAMPLE 7

VEHICLE TYPES

Problem Statement   Twenty-four vehicles (experimental units) of four types (treatments) were driven under similar conditions to estimate population mean mileage figures for vehicle types. The four vehicle types were (1) compact sport utility (CSU); (2) full-size sport utility (FSSU); (3) full-size cars (FSC); and (4) compact cars (CC). Under similar driving conditions, mileage data were recorded and the data set is

```
Row   CSU    FSSU    FSC     CC

 1    22.7   19.3    21.5    23.2
 2    22.0   17.6    23.3    26.0
 3    23.4   17.6    22.2    26.0
 4    20.5   18.5    20.6    19.8
 5    22.1   18.0    17.9    23.7
 6    22.6   18.9    22.6    25.3
```

Test the null hypothesis that the population median mileage is the same for all vehicle types.

Problem Solution   Among other things, both the Kruskal-Wallis H statistic and the Mood chi-square value indicate that population median mileage is not the same across vehicle types.

Reject the null hypothesis. Confidence intervals on mileage for individual vehicle types indicate that the full-size sport utility vehicles get particularly low mileage.

```
LEVEL    NOBS    MEDIAN  AVE. RANK   Z VALUE

  1        6     22.35     14.4       0.77
  2        6     18.25      4.2      -3.33
  3        6     21.85     12.1      -0.17
  4        6     24.50     19.3       2.73
OVERALL   24                12.5

H = 14.40  d.f. = 3  p = 0.003
H = 14.42  d.f. = 3  p = 0.002  (adj. for ties)

Mood median test of MPG

Chi-square = 9.33   df = 3    p = 0.026

                                       Individual 95.0% CI's
VTYPES   N<=   N>   Median   Q3-Q1  ----------+---------+---------+------
  1       2    4    22.35    1.25                (----+---)
  2       6    0    18.25    1.40   (--+---)
  3       3    3    21.85    2.85        (-----------+----)
  4       1    5    24.50    3.65             (-------------+-----)
                                    ----------+---------+---------+------
                                         20.0      22.5      25.0

Overall median = 22.05
```

S T A T I S T I C A L   H I G H L I G H T S

The Kruskal-Wallis and Mood tests are the nonparametric versions of one-way analysis of variance, which assumed normal populations with the same variances. The Kruskal-Wallis and Mood tests require random samples from k continuous populations that have the same shape.

NONPARAMETRIC ALTERNATIVE TO TWO-WAY ANALYSIS OF VARIANCE, COMPARING TWO OR MORE MEDIANS OF A SINGLE FACTOR IN THE PRESENCE OF A BLOCKED NUISANCE FACTOR

The Wilcoxon signed-rank test compares population medians from two continuous populations that have the same shape; the data are paired (matched) and the samples are dependent. Each sample pair is a block. The **Friedman rank-sum test** can make the same comparison for dependent samples. An added benefit is that the Friedman test can be extended to compare k medians from k continuous populations that have the same shape; each of n blocks contains k treatments. The Friedman test is the nonparametric version of two-way analysis of variance (see Chapter 15), which assumed normal populations with the same variances. The Friedman test requires random samples from k continuous populations that have the same shape.

Friedman Test Statistic The **Friedman test statistic S** is a function of summed treatment ranks across blocks. The computational requirement is that there is one and only one observation in each block-treatment cell. Within each block, the k treatment observations are ranked from least to greatest. Let $\bar{R}_i$ be the average rank of treatment i across n blocks; $\bar{R}$ equal the average of all the ranks. Then, the test statistic is

$$s = \frac{12n\Sigma(\bar{R}_i - \bar{R})^2}{k(k + 1)}$$

Under the null hypothesis of equal population medians, S follows a chi-square distribution with $k - 1$ degrees of freedom. S is compared to critical values from this distribution to accept or reject hypotheses in the usual manner.

The Friedman Rank-Sum Test for Comparing Two Population Medians

The Friedman test is demonstrated on the same breakfast cereal data used in the Wilcoxon signed-rank test where two cereals are compared.

EXAMPLE 8

JUDGING BREAKFAST CEREALS (FRIEDMAN)

Problem Statement Two new breakfast cereals, Boom and Bang, are compared by 10 tasters and rated on a 10-point scale with 10 being the highest possible score. See Exhibit 5. Analyze differences using the Friedman test for the hypothesis that the median taste difference is 0 between Boom and Bang.

Problem Solution The median scores are significantly different for the two cereals at a significance level of .012. Also, the critical chi-square value is exceeded by the Friedman rank-sum statistic S.

```
Friedman test of B&B by B&BID blocked by BLKID

S = 6.40  (d.f. = 1  p = 0.012); the critical chi-square value
for alpha of .05 and one degree of freedom is 3.84.

                     Est.    Sum of
     B&BID      N   Median    RANKS

         1     10   6.9750     11.0
         2     10   7.7750     19.0

Grand median  =   7.3750
```

The Friedman Rank-Sum Test for Comparing k Population Medians

The Friedman test is demonstrated on mileage data for k = 4 vehicle types and n = 2 blocks for city and highway driving conditions.

EXAMPLE 9

VEHICLE TYPES AND DRIVING CONDITIONS

Problem Statement   Forty-eight vehicles (experimental units) of four types (treatments) were driven under two distinct conditions, city and highway driving (blocks). The four vehicle types were (1) compact sport utility (CSU); (2) full-size sport utility (FSSU); (3) full-size cars (FSC); and (4) compact cars (CC). The mileage data are shown earlier; the variable name for mileage is MAGE.

Test the null hypothesis that the population median mileage is the same for all vehicle types. Because there are six replicates in each block-treatment cell, use the median mileage of each cell in the Friedman test.

Problem Solution   Do not reject the null hypothesis that the population median mileage is the same for the four vehicle types. The Friedman rank-sum statistic S = 5.4 does not exceed the critical chi-square value.

```
Friedman test of BLOCK by C12 blocked by C13

S = 5.40  (d.f. = 3  p = 0.145); the critical chi-square value
for alpha of .05 and one degree of freedom is 7.81.

              Est.   Sum of
    C12    N  Median  RANKS

      1    2  22.100    5.0
      2    2  18.100    2.0
      3    2  21.600    5.0
      4    2  23.900    8.0

Grand median  =   21.425
```

S T A T I S T I C A L   H I G H L I G H T S

The Friedman test is the nonparametric version of two-way analysis of variance, which assumed normal populations with the same variances. The Friedman test requires random samples from k continuous populations that have the same shape.

Most statistical tests depend on random samples. Thus, the nonparametric tests for randomness are very important. Throughout this text, the MINITAB RUNS command has been used as a test for randomness to see if the data are random in observation order.

The Number-of-Runs Test

The **number-of-runs test** is based on a standardized count of the number of runs. A **run** is a string of one or more like (same category) observations in a sequence. If you toss two coins, consider the possible outcomes. Flip two tails TT. The number of runs is one, HH is one run, TH is two runs, and so is HT. For various numbers of tosses, the number-of-runs are

    HHHHHHHHH (one run)
    HHH TT (two runs)
    T HH TTT H TTTTT (five runs)

For a sequence of data values, subtract a location measure (median or mean for example) from each data value to obtain signed residuals. If you don't specify the constant, MINITAB subtracts the sample mean. To avoid residuals that are 0 and without a sign, a very small constant can be added to the location measure before subtraction; or, for large samples, 0 residuals can be ignored. The number of runs is found by counting strings of plus or minus signs. For various data sets the number of runs of plus and minus signs are

    +++ −− (two runs)
    − ++ −−− + −−−−−− (five runs)
    ++++ −− + −−−− (four runs)

When a sequence is random, there is no serial dependency. When a sequence is random, the mean and standard deviation of the number of runs is a function of sign counts. Let n_+ equal the total number of plus signs; n_- equal the total number of minus signs, and n equal the total number of signs. Then

$$\text{expected number of runs (mean)} = \left(\frac{2n_+ n_-}{n}\right) + 1$$

$$\text{variance of the number of runs} = \frac{2n_+ n_-(2n_+ n_- - n)}{n^2(n - 1)}$$

For large numbers of signs, the distribution of the number of runs tends toward normality. Thus, the count of the actual number of runs can be standardized by subtracting the mean and dividing by the standard deviation. As a result, hypothesis tests and confidence intervals can be conducted as usual with critical values from the standard normal distribution.

The Up-and-Down Runs Test (an Alternative Runs Test)

The **up-and-down runs test** is based on a standardized count of the number of up-and-down runs in a sequence of observations. An approximate up-and-down runs test was presented in Chapter 2 as a rough test for randomness. Up-and-down movements are designated in the following list of observations, where a **U** or **D** between two data values designates an **U**p or **D**own change (increase or decrease) in value.

$$50 \quad 95 \quad 25 \quad 23 \quad 48 \quad 18 \quad 33 \quad 43 \quad 15 \quad 28 \quad 26 \quad 34 \quad 59$$
$$\quad\; U \quad D \quad D \quad U \quad D \quad U \quad U \quad D \quad U \quad D \quad U \quad U$$

A sequence of U's or D's (one or more) is called a **run.** A count of the runs up or down is used for a randomness test. Here there are 9 runs.

$$\begin{array}{ccccccccc} U & DD & U & D & UU & D & U & D & UU \\ 1 & 2 & 3 & 4 & 5 & 6 & 7 & 8 & 9 \end{array}$$

When a sequence is random, there is no serial dependency. When a sequence is random, the mean and standard deviation of the number of up-and-down runs is a function of the series length n. Then

$$\text{expected number of runs (mean)} = \frac{2n - 1}{3}$$

$$\text{variance of the number of runs} = \frac{16n - 29}{90}$$

For large n, the distribution of the number of runs tends toward normality. Thus, the count of the actual number of runs can be standardized by subtracting the mean and dividing by the standard deviation. As a result, hypothesis tests and confidence intervals can be conducted as usual with critical values from the standard normal distribution.

Rank Correlation as a Measure of Linear Association Between Two Variables

When two variables x and y are measured on the interval or ratio scales, the strength of their association is expressed as the sample correlation coefficient (see Chapter 9). The sample correlation is also known as the **Pearson product moment correlation.** A nonparametric correlation coefficient is the **Spearman rank-correlation r_s.** The Spearman rank-correlation coefficient is based on rank-order (ordinal data).

Let x_i equal the rank of observation i for variable x; y_i equal the rank of observation i for variable y; and $d_i = (x_i - y_i)$ the difference in ranks. The Spearman rank-correlation coefficient can be computed from the following formula:

$$r_s = 1 - \frac{(6\Sigma d_i^2)}{n(n^2 - 1)}$$

For $n \geq 10$ and no association between x and y, the distribution of r_s tends toward normality with the following mean and variance.

$$\text{expected value of } r_s = 0$$

$$\text{variance of } r_s = \frac{1}{(n - 1)}$$

Thus, r_s can be standardized by subtracting the mean and dividing by the standard deviation. As a result, hypothesis tests and confidence intervals can be conducted as usual with critical values from the standard normal distribution.

CHAPTER SUMMARY

Classical parametric methods for the analysis of measurement data are dependent on the assumption of normality for the populations sampled. Nevertheless, it happens that some of these methods are relatively insensitive to the normality assumption. By design rather than happenstance, nonparametric methods avoid the normality assumption about the populations sampled. Interestingly, however, many of the statistics that result from manipulating nonnormal ranked data follow normal or the related chi-square distributions. By design, nonparametric methods have broader applicability and are easier to use than their parametric relatives.

The sign and Wilcoxon signed-rank tests and confidence intervals are used for population medians from single samples. For dependent two-sample problems, the differences of paired observations can be analyzed by sign or Wilcoxon signed-rank tests. For independent two-sample problems, the Mann-Whitney-Wilcoxon ranked-sum test compares population medians.

When comparing k population medians, either the Kruskal-Wallis test or the Mood test may be used. The Mood test is particularly insensitive to outliers and is good for exploratory work. Both of these approaches are the nonparametric versions of one-way analysis of variance. The Friedman test is the nonparametric version of two-way analysis of variance.

Finally, we concluded by presenting the runs tests for randomness and the Spearman rank-correlation coefficient for measuring the association of two variables.

KEY TERMS

distribution-free, 838
Friedman rank-sum test, 856
Friedman test statistic, S, 857
Kruskal-Wallis test, 852
Kruskal-Wallis test statistic, H, 852
Mood test, 852
nonparametric methods, 838

number-of-runs test, 859
parametric methods, 838
Pearson product moment correlation, 860
positive signed ranks, 846
rank-sum, 847
run, 859

sign test, 839
Spearman rank-correlation, 860
up-and-down runs test, 860
Wilcoxon signed-rank statistic, W, 846
Wilcoxon signed-rank test, 839, 845

EXERCISES

1. After having tasted two types of coffee, 15 consumers were asked which gourmet coffee, chocolate almond or hazelnut, they preferred. Coffee preferences are recorded below in bold and by the signs on the right.

Consumer	Preference (in bold)	Sign
1	**chocolate almond** or hazelnut	−
2	**chocolate almond** or hazelnut	−
3	chocolate almond or **hazelnut**	+
4	**chocolate almond** or hazelnut	−
5	**chocolate almond** or hazelnut	−
6	**chocolate almond** or hazelnut	−
7	**chocolate almond** or hazelnut	−
8	chocolate almond or **hazelnut**	+
9	**chocolate almond** or hazelnut	−
10	**chocolate almond** or hazelnut	−
11	**chocolate almond** or hazelnut	−
12	**chocolate almond** or hazelnut	−
13	**chocolate almond** or hazelnut	−
14	**chocolate almond** or hazelnut	−
15	**chocolate almond** or hazelnut	−

(a) Use a sign test to test the null hypothesis that the population preferences for both coffees are the same against the alternative hypothesis that the population preferences are not the same. State the level of significance used.

2. Each of 12 dogs were presented (downwind) with two bowls containing small portions of dog food. The brand, BowWow or T-Bone, that was consumed first was considered to be the preferred one. The preferences are recorded below in bold and by the signs on the right.

Dog	Preference (in bold)	Sign
1	BowWow or **T-Bone**	+
2	**BowWow** or T-Bone	−
3	BowWow or **T-Bone**	+
4	BowWow or **T-Bone**	+
5	**BowWow** or T-Bone	−
6	**BowWow** or T-Bone	−
7	**BowWow** or T-Bone	−
8	**BowWow** or T-Bone	−
9	BowWow or **T-Bone**	+
10	**BowWow** or T-Bone	−
11	BowWow or **T-Bone**	+
12	**BowWow** or T-Bone	−

(a) Use a sign test to test the null hypothesis that the population preferences for both brands of dog food are the same against the alternative hypothesis that the population preferences are not the same. State the level of significance used.

3. Many thought that the state senate race was a toss up. The two opposing candidates, Jack and Jill, were in the final stages of the campaign. The preferences of 14 randomly selected voters are recorded below in bold and by the signs on the right.

Voter	Preference (in bold)	Sign
1	Jack or **Jill**	+
2	Jack or **Jill**	+
3	Jack or **Jill**	+
4	Jack or **Jill**	+
5	Jack or **Jill**	+
6	Jack or **Jill**	+
7	**Jack** or Jill	−
8	Jack or **Jill**	+
9	Jack or **Jill**	+
10	**Jack** or Jill	−
11	Jack or **Jill**	+
12	Jack or **Jill**	+
13	Jack or **Jill**	+
14	Jack or **Jill**	+

(a) Use a sign test to test the null hypothesis that the population preferences for both candidates are the same against the alternative hypothesis that the population preferences are not the same. State the level of significance used.

4. After having munched on two different cookies, 13 cookie lovers were asked which cookie, Chunk or Hunk, they preferred. Cookie preferences are recorded on a continuous scale from 0 to 10 (from Chunk to Hunk).

Consumer	Preference (in bold)	Score
1	**Chunk** or Hunk	1.0
2	Chunk or **Hunk**	7.5
3	**Chunk** or Hunk	3.5
4	**Chunk** or Hunk	2.3
5	Chunk or **Hunk**	6.0
6	Chunk or **Hunk**	6.5
7	Chunk or **Hunk**	5.5
8	Chunk or **Hunk**	8.0
9	**Chunk** or Hunk	1.5
10	**Chunk** or Hunk	0.0
11	Chunk or **Hunk**	9.5
12	Chunk or **Hunk**	8.0
13	Chunk or **Hunk**	9.0

(a) Use a sign test to test the null hypothesis that the population preferences for both cookies are the same against the alternative hypothesis that the population preferences are not the same. State the level of significance used.

(b) Use a sign-based, 95% confidence interval approach to test the hypothesis that the preferences are the same (in other words, a median score of 5).

(c) For comparison purposes, construct a 95% confidence interval on the population mean score.

5. From the following sample of 24 monthly returns on a stock in percent:

23.7	19.2	20.4	20.5	17.4	23.5	12.5	21.5	24.7
13.1	14.1	25.9	18.6	20.5	21.6	19.8	19.8	16.3
18.9	21.4	21.3	19.3	23.8	18.9			

(a) Construct a notched boxplot.

(b) Construct a 95% sign confidence interval for the population median return. How does this compare to results in part (a)?

(c) Perform a sign test for the null hypothesis that the population median return is 17% against the not equal alternative.

(d) For comparison purposes, find a parametric 95% interval on the population mean return.

(e) Construct a 95% confidence interval on the number of plus signs in a sign test. If the null hypothesis is that the population median is 17%, do the number of plus signs cause you to reject this hypothesis in favor of the not equal alternative?

6. From the following sample of 24 monthly returns on a stock in percent:

0.8	−1.1	5.5	1.9	2.8	4.2	−4.0	−4.1	0.0
7.2	0.4	−0.8	0.2	−6.3	1.0	4.5	−7.3	−6.1
−3.3	8.1	9.2	4.6	0.8	1.7			

(a) Construct a notched boxplot.

(b) Construct a 95% sign confidence interval for the population median return. How does this compare with the results in part (a)?

(c) Perform a sign test for the null hypothesis that the population median return is 0 against the not equal alternative.

(d) For comparison purposes, find a parametric 95% t interval on the population mean return.

(e) Construct a 95% confidence interval on the number of plus signs in a sign test. If the null hypothesis is that the population median is 0, do the number of plus signs cause you to reject this hypothesis in favor of the not equal alternative?

7. Use the following student examination scores (in percent):

77 79 74 80 74 84 80 75 67 73 74 81 74 77 67 70
70 75 81 79

(a) Construct a notched boxplot.

(b) If these scores are representative of the percentage of the subject matter that has been mastered by the student, construct a 95% sign confidence interval for the population median percent.

(c) Perform a sign test for the null hypothesis that the population median percentage of the subject matter mastered is 80% against the not equal alternative.

8. Illustrate the use of the Wilcoxon signed-rank test and confidence interval approach in Exercise 4, parts (a) and (b).

9. Use the Wilcoxon signed-rank test and confidence interval approach in Exercise 5, parts (b) and (c).

10. Use the Wilcoxon signed-rank test and confidence interval approach in Exercise 6, parts (b) and (c).

11. Use the Wilcoxon signed-rank test and confidence interval approach in Exercise 7, parts (b) and (c).

12. The following average math SAT scores are classified by gender and year. (In MINITAB, RETRIEVE 'B:MFSAT')

ROWS: YEAR COLUMNS: GENDER

	0	1
1	467	514
2	470	512
3	470	513
4	465	509
5	466	507
6	461	505
7	460	502
8	459	501
9	449	495
10	446	497
11	445	497
12	444	494
13	443	493

(a) Analyze the yearly score differences using the sign and Wilcoxon tests and intervals for the hypothesis that the population median math scores are the same for men and women against the not equal alternative. Use a significance level of .05.

(b) Compare the results in part (a) with those from the Friedman rank-sum test.

13. The following average verbal SAT scores are classified by gender and year. (In MINITAB, RETRIEVE 'B:MFSAT')

ROWS: YEAR   COLUMNS: GENDER

	0	1
1	468	463
2	466	464
3	466	459
4	461	459
5	457	454
6	452	454
7	443	446

ROWS: YEAR   COLUMNS: GENDER

	0	1
8	442	447
9	431	437
10	430	433
11	427	431
12	425	433
13	423	431

(a) Analyze the yearly score differences using the sign and Wilcoxon tests and intervals for the hypothesis that the population median verbal scores are the same for men and women against the not equal alternative. Use a significance level of .05.

(b) Compare the results in part (a) with those from the Friedman rank-sum test.

14. The following data measure consumer reaction to two different promotional efforts based on coupons or discounts. The two treatments were blocked according to 10 regions.

Regions	P1	P2
1	38	62
2	42	60
3	40	64
4	44	58
5	39	61
6	45	56
7	41	57
8	38	62
9	37	58
10	43	53

For each block and treatment cell, 100 consumers selected at random were questioned. The highest score (percentage of respondents) to the first of the following five queries indicates the strongest reaction to the promotion:

Definitely would buy.

Probably would buy.

Might buy.

Probably would not buy.

Definitely would not buy.

The "definitely would buy" percentage is referred to as a top box score.

(a) Analyze the regional top box score differences using the sign and Wilcoxon tests and intervals for the hypothesis that the population median top box scores are the same for coupons and discounts against the not equal alternative. Use a significance level of .05.

(b) Compare the results in part (a) with those from the Friedman rank-sum test.

15. The durability of heavy machinery bearings was evaluated for two experimental lubricant types (L1 and L2). Twelve bearings were randomly assigned to each lubricant type to measure wear and tear. Wear and tear is expressed as a percentage, relative to a known standard of 100.

Row	L1	L2
1	99	90
2	93	94
3	97	101
4	100	84
5	98	87
6	99	99
7	96	99
8	96	91
9	100	85
10	97	92
11	98	104
12	100	87

(a) Analyze the wear-and-tear percentages using the Mann-Whitney-Wilcoxon rank-sum test for two independent samples. Test the hypothesis that the population medians are the same for the two lubricant types against the not equal alternative. Use a significance level of .05.

(b) Do the Kruskal-Wallis and Mood tests result in the same conclusions?

16. In order to assess attitudes and perceptions about eating out, consumers were asked to react to reasons for eating out on a scale from (1) strongly disagree to (5) strongly agree. Two reasons for eating out were compared: R1, to enjoy restaurants; and R2, for special occasions.

Row	R1	R2
1	4.8	2.3
2	3.0	2.4
3	3.4	2.6
4	4.2	2.1
5	3.6	2.7
6	4.4	2.6
7	3.4	2.2
8	3.4	3.1
9	3.8	2.7
10	3.7	2.5
11	3.6	3.0
12	3.2	2.7
13	3.6	2.1
14	3.6	3.2
15	3.6	2.1

(a) Analyze these figures using the Mann-Whitney-Wilcoxon rank-sum test for two independent samples. Test the hypothesis that the population medians are the same for the two reasons for eating out against the not equal alternative. Use a significance level of .05.

(b) Do the Kruskal-Wallis and Mood tests result in the same conclusions?

17. When it comes to risk, not all mutual funds are alike. Return volatility relative to average annual return (SDRAR) is a risk measure. The higher a fund's SDRAR, the more the fund's price tends to fluctuate. For the following four funds (F1, F2, F3, and F4) over five similar periods, use the Kruskal-Wallis and Mood tests to test the hypothesis that the population median SDRARs are the same. Use a significance level of .05.

Row	F1	F2	F3	F4
1	1.0	1.8	7.3	7.1
2	1.3	2.6	7.6	7.2
3	1.0	1.6	7.2	6.9
4	1.4	2.9	8.1	7.7
5	1.2	2.8	9.0	6.1

18. Raw materials for a production operation arrive in batches from three suppliers (S1, S2, and S3). Each batch results in 250 units of a finished product. Management thinks that the number of defective finished units of each 250 units produced is attributable to the raw material supplier. Therefore, the number of defectives are recorded and associated with raw material suppliers as follows:

Row	S1	S2	S3
1	9	5	4
2	12	5	1
3	11	5	4
4	7	4	5
5	9	5	5
6	10	5	6
7	9	6	5
8		6	5
9		5	
10		6	
11		4	

(a) If management is considering reducing the number of suppliers and working more closely with suppliers to control raw material quality, which of the suppliers, if any, would seem to require less effort to improve raw material quality? Support your recommendations by using the Kruskal-Wallis and Mood tests to test the hypothesis that the population medians are the same. Use a significance level of .05.

19. Each of three groups of subjects (G1, G2, and G3) were shown one of three videotapes of advertisements for a variety of products. The first tape focused on television advertisements (TA), the second focused on billboard advertisements (BA), and the third focused on newspaper advertisements (NA). Recall scores are listed below for one of the products featured in each advertising instrument. Use the Kruskal-Wallis and Mood tests to test the hypothesis that the population medians are the same. Use a significance level of .05.

	BA	TA	NA
Row	G1	G2	G3
1	7	12	12
2	9	13	4
3	11	11	4
4	13	14	6

20. New car and truck long-term ownership cost ratings are provided by consumer magazines. Fuel, insurance, and repair costs are scored on a 10-point scale where a score of 10 is the highest cost. These scores are averaged and rounded to obtain an overall average cost score for the following five vehicle class types: C1, subcompacts and compacts; C2, midsize, full size, and minivans; C3, luxury cars; C4, sports coupes; and C5, pickups and four-by-fours. Random samples of average cost scores for six vehicles in each class are listed below. Use the Kruskal-Wallis and Mood tests to test the hypothesis that the population medians are the same in all classes. Use a significance level of .05.

Row	C1	C2	C3	C4	C5
1	4	5	5	7	5
2	3	6	6	4	5
3	4	4	6	6	7
4	3	6	8	5	7
5	2	4	7	8	6
6	2	5	5	8	6

21. Machine output in units produced per hour is measured at five speed settings (coded as $S = 1, 2, \ldots, 5$). These data were collected because experienced machine operators reported that output tended to fall at low and high speed settings. Few machine operational difficulties occurred at the low speed settings; however, the output was less than desirable. On the other hand, operational difficulties were frequent at the high speed settings, and this tended to reduce output. Middle-range speed settings were thought to be a compromise.

Row	S=1	S=2	S=3	S=4	S=5
1	194	204	216	204	187
2	210	221	240	206	197
3	202	214	222	203	191
4	188	199	225	201	183

(a) Use the Kruskal-Wallis and Mood tests to test the hypothesis that the population median output is the same at all speed levels. Use a significance level of .05.
(b) Plot output versus the coded speed and pick the best speed setting.

22. Twenty-four consumers selected at random viewed one of three advertisements (AD1, AD2, and AD3) for a product. Other distractive advertisements were also shown. The following day these consumers were queried and the following recall scores were recorded (the higher the better):

Row	AD1	AD2	AD3
1	21.7	20.9	26.4
2	25.1	18.9	13.7
3	21.8	18.6	21.8
4	25.1	15.0	10.2
5	30.9	19.3	23.5
6	28.4	24.5	37.4
7	16.1	17.7	30.3
8	12.0	29.1	12.9

(a) Use the Kruskal-Wallis and Mood tests to test the hypothesis that the population median recall scores are the same for all advertisements. Use a significance level of .05.

23. Returns (in percent) for three different stocks (SK1, SK2, and SK3) are examined over 12 periods. An investment analyst suggested that these stocks have about the same level of risk. Evaluate the analyst's suggestion. In addition, test the hypothesis that the population median returns the same.

Row	SK1	SK2	SK3
1	9.5	10.7	15.0
2	9.2	16.8	10.5
3	12.8	11.5	15.6
4	12.0	14.7	10.1
5	13.8	14.2	12.3
6	8.7	14.0	10.8
7	10.9	17.0	10.0
8	13.0	11.2	12.5
9	10.3	11.6	11.3
10	15.0	11.2	14.0
11	15.9	10.6	14.6
12	12.5	7.7	16.1

24. Subassembly production rates (in units per hour) are examined for three machine operators (OP1, OP2, and OP3). Six observations are made at random times for each of the three operators.

Row	OP1	OP2	OP3
1	16	26	37
2	12	20	18
3	19	15	17
4	10	24	23
5	26	18	24
6	9	21	19

(a) Test the hypothesis that the median production rates are the same for all operators. If the hypothesis is rejected, management plans to further investigate the work methods of the operators in order to find out why some operators perform better than others. Thus, better work practices can be incorporated into training programs.

25. A jobshop manufacturing facility has a number of different machines, including lathes, planers, drill presses, and shapers. Periodically, experiments are conducted to compare utilization rates for these machines. The following shaper utilization rates were compiled for three identical shapers:

Row	SH1	SH2	SH3
1	60	54	63
2	51	56	64
3	60	67	62
4	63	53	62
5	60	54	60
6	53	49	61
7	58	50	58
8	58	55	56
9	55	50	59
10		65	52
11		51	
12		49	

(a) Test the hypothesis that the median utilization rates are the same for these three shapers.

26. One bank teller serves drive-in customers and two tellers serve walk-in customers. The time in minutes to serve a dozen customers each is shown below.

Row	TEL1	TEL2	TEL3
1	2.8	2.9	3.1
2	2.6	3.9	3.2
3	2.6	2.6	3.5
4	2.9	3.1	3.3
5	2.9	3.9	3.5

Row	TEL1	TEL2	TEL3
6	2.8	2.6	2.8
7	2.3	3.3	2.8
8	2.4	3.0	3.1
9	2.0	3.5	2.8
10	2.5	3.1	3.4
11	2.4	3.2	2.9
12	2.0	2.4	2.8

(a) Is there a significant difference in teller median service times? Explain how you reached your conclusion.

27. Compare the median utilization rates of three exact-change-only highway toll booths, and explain how you reached your conclusions. The figures below were compiled during ten different periods of heavy traffic conditions. Maximum utilization is 100%. If the median utilization is significantly different for the three booths (B1, B2, and B3), management is considering ways of directing the traffic flow to achieve a more balanced use of the three booths.

Row	B1	B2	B3
1	95	71	80
2	79	81	79
3	92	78	82
4	90	78	79
5	91	80	84
6	90	84	78
7	92	82	86
8	86	83	82
9	85	74	83
10	87	75	89

28. The number of defective pieces per thousand units produced is tabulated below for four workers (W1, W2, W3, and W4) during two-hour periods within a day. The periods are from eight to ten, ten to noon, one to three, and three to five.

Row	PERIOD	W1	W2	W3	W4
1	1	10	11	8	12
2	2	9	8	7	10
3	3	12	13	11	11
4	4	13	14	10	14

(a) Use the Kruskal-Wallis and Mood tests to test the hypothesis that the population median number of defectives is the same for all workers. Use a significance level of .05.

(b) Use the Friedman rank-sum test to perform a two-way analysis, which is preferred because it accounts for treatments (columns) and blocks (rows). Compare these results with those in part (a).

29. The specific volume of a rubber-based product is thought to depend on pressure (P1, P2, and P3) at four temperature settings. Management wants engineering to examine these data because product performance and durability are related to specific volume. Furthermore, if there are no significant differences in specific volume due to these levels of pressure and temperature, the manufacturing process can be simplified to reduce costs.

Row	TEMPLEVL	P1	P2	P3
1	1	182	213	258
2	2	240	279	320
3	3	296	348	387
4	4	325	367	420

(a) Use the Friedman rank-sum test to perform a two-way analysis and summarize the results.

(b) If the median-specific volume is significantly different at different temperature and pressure levels, plot specific volume versus temperature level for all pressure levels. Plot specific volume versus pressure level for all temperature levels. Are there any patterns apparent in these plots? If so, what are they?

(c) Fit simple regression lines to specific volume versus pressure level and to specific volume versus temperature level. The temperatures are 0, 10, 20, and 25° Celsius, and the pressures are 400, 300, and 200 kilograms per square centimeter, respectively.

30. The following average monthly rents are for four consecutive periods (P1, P2, P3, and P4) in five regions (R1, R2, . . . , R5). (In MINITAB, RETRIEVE 'B:RENTS')

Region	P1	P2	P3	P4
1	748	749	761	781
2	813	845	851	872
3	571	577	583	582
4	567	571	578	596
5	691	658	640	654

(a) Use the Friedman rank-sum test to perform a two-way analysis to test the hypothesis that median rents are the same in all periods and the hypothesis that median rents are the same in all regions.

31. Noise in decibels for four commuter aircraft (AP1, AP2, AP3, and AP4) is measured under conditions of takeoff, sideline, and approach.

	AP1	AP2	AP3	AP4
Takeoff	79	91	90	88
Sideline	88	101	102	93
Approach	89	97	98	96

(a) Perform a two-way analysis to test for equal median noise levels for aircraft and for conditions.

32. A financial analysis of a company's competitors (CP1, CP2, CP3, and CP4) focused on operating expenses as a percentage of sales (OP/S) and research and development expenses as a percentage of sales (R&D/S). Comparative figures were compiled for four years.

Operating Expenses as a Percentage of Sales

Row	YR1	YR2	YR3	YR4
CP1	32.1	28.7	31.2	32.8
CP2	39.7	38.6	38.3	37.6
CP3	32.6	34.1	37.8	39.3
CP4	22.5	25.2	26.1	24.6

Research and Development Expenses as a Percentage of Sales

Row	YR1	YR2	YR3	YR4
CP1	9.7	9.8	10.2	11.4
CP2	8.6	8.9	8.8	9.1
CP3	12.7	12.8	13.2	13.1
CP4	11.2	10.5	9.8	12.2

(a) Use the Friedman rank-sum test to perform a two-way analysis on both of the data sets and report your conclusions.

33. Boys and girls of ages three, five, and seven are each given 10 pieces of candy.[1] The number of pieces they gave to friends is a measure of sharing. Use the Friedman rank-sum test to perform a two-way analysis to see if sharing is related to age, gender, or both.

Row	BOYGRL	AGE3	AGE5	AGE7
1	1	1	3	7
2	1	1	3	5
3	1	0	4	3
4	1	2	5	6
5	2	1	4	9
6	2	0	6	8
7	2	2	5	6
8	2	1	3	7

34. At the end of a company training program, 11 machine operators were ranked by the instructor from best (rank 1) to worst (rank 11). A second ranking occurred on the job and was based on the number of defectives produced (the fewer the better). These rankings are

Instructor ranking	1	2	3	4	5	6	7	8	9	10	11
Second on-the-job ranking	4	3	1	2	6	7	5	9	11	8	10

Compute the Spearman rank-correlation coefficient as a measure of association between these rankings. Is the rank-correlation significantly different from 0?

APPENDIX 1

Minitab Examples

EARLY EXHIBITS, SIGN AND WILCOXON TESTS AND INTERVALS

```
MTB > SET IN C1    # NUMBERS OF PLUS SIGNS POSSIBLE
DATA> 0:15
DATA> END
MTB > SET IN C5    # NUMBERS REVERSE ORDER
DATA> 15:0
DATA> END
MTB > PDF C1 C2;
SUBC> BINOMIAL N=15 P=.50.
MTB > CDF C1 C3;
SUBC> BINOMIAL N=15 P=.50.
MTB > CDF C5 C4;
SUBC> BINOMIAL N=15 P=.50.
MTB > NAME C1 'NPLUS' C2 'BPROB' C3 'CUMDN' C4 'CUMUP'
MTB > PRINT C1-C4
MTB > # TO SEE THE DISTRIBUTION PLOT C2 C1
MTB > NAME C5 'SCORE'
MTB > SET IN C5
DATA> 2.3 6.0 1.5 .5 4.2 3.5 2.5 1.8 4.5
DATA> 2.0 6.5 3.1 2.2 6.2 1.0
DATA> END
MTB > ERASE C1-C4
MTB > RUNS C5
MTB > STEST MEDIAN = 5 ON C5
MTB > SINTERVAL CONFIDENCE = 95 ON C5
MTB > TINTERVAL 95 ON C5
MTB > BOXPLOT C5;
SUBC> NOTCHES.
MTB > WTEST MEDIAN = 5 ON C5
MTB > WINTERVAL CONFIDENCE = 95 ON C5
MTB > RETRIEVE 'RETURNS' # OR RETRIEVE 'B:RETURNS'
```

```
MTB > INFO
MTB > BOXPLOT C4;
SUBC> NOTCHES.
MTB > SINTERVAL CONFIDENCE = 95 ON C4
MTB > STEST MEDIAN = 7 ON C4
MTB > TINTERVAL 95 ON C4
```

EXAMPLE

JUDGING BREAKFAST CEREALS

```
      (OR RETRIEVE 'CEREAL'
MTB > RETRIEVE 'B:CEREAL'
MTB > INFO
MTB > PRINT C1 C2 C6
MTB > BOXPLOT C3;
SUBC> BY C4;
SUBC> NOTCHES.
MTB > STEST MEDIAN=0 ON 'DIFF'
MTB > SINTERVAL CONFIDENCE=95 ON 'DIFF'
MTB > WTEST MEDIAN = 0 ON 'DIFF'
MTB > WINTERVAL CONFIDENCE = 95 ON 'DIFF'
```

EXAMPLE

COMPARING ASSEMBLY TIMES FOR TWO ASSEMBLY METHODS

```
      (OR RETRIEVE 'MWW'
MTB > RETRIEVE 'B:MWW'
MTB > # THESE COMMANDS SHOW COLUMN CONSTRUCTION
MTB > # STACK C1 ON C2 PUT C3
MTB > # SET C4
MTB > # 14(0),14(1)
MTB > # SORT C3 C4 PUT C5 C6;
MTB > # BY C3.
MTB > # RANK C5 PUT C7
MTB > # COPY C7 C8;
MTB > # USE C6=0.
MTB > # SUM C8
MTB >  INFO

MTB > NAME C8 'RANKOLD'
MTB > COPY C7 C8;
SUBC> USE C6=0.
MTB > SUM C8
MTB > PRINT C1-C8
MTB > MANN-WHITNEY CONFIDENCE=95 C1 C2
MTB > BOXPLOT C3;
SUBC> BY C4;
SUBC> NOTCHES.
```

E X A M P L E

COMPARING ASSEMBLY TIMES FOR TWO ASSEMBLY METHODS (KRUSKAL-WALLIS AND MOOD TESTS)

```
        (OR RETRIEVE 'MWW'
MTB > RETRIEVE 'B:MWW'
MTB > INFO
MTB > KRUSKAL-WALLIS C3 C4
MTB > MOOD C3 C4
```

E X A M P L E

GASOLINE BRANDS

```
MTB > READ C1-C3
DATA> 17.3 19.4 17.0
DATA> 18.8 17.9 17.2
DATA> 15.9 16.7 19.0
DATA> 17.8 17.3 19.8
DATA> 17.5 17.5 16.5
DATA> END
MTB > STACK C1 C2 C3 PUT C4
MTB > NAME C4 'MPG'
MTB > SET IN C5
DATA> 5(1),5(2),5(3)
DATA> END
MTB > NAME C5 'BRAND'
MTB > KRUSKAL-WALLIS 'MPG' 'BRAND'
MTB > MOOD 'MPG' 'BRAND'
```

E X A M P L E

VEHICLE TYPES

```
        (OR RETRIEVE 'VEHM'
MTB > RETRIEVE 'B:VEHM'
MTB > STACK C1-C4 PUT C5
MTB > NAME C5 'MPG'
MTB > SET IN C6
DATA> 6(1),6(2),6(3),6(4)
DATA> END
MTB > NAME C6 'VTYPES'
MTB > KRUSKAL-WALLIS 'MPG' 'VTYPES'
MTB > MOOD 'MPG' 'VTYPES'
```

JUDGING BREAKFAST CEREALS (FRIEDMAN)

```
        (OR RETRIEVE 'CEREAL'
MTB > RETRIEVE 'B:CEREAL'
MTB > INFO
MTB > FRIEDMAN C3 C4 C5
```

VEHICLE TYPES AND DRIVING CONDITIONS (FRIEDMAN)

```
        # TO OBTAIN SINGLE TREATMENT AND BLOCK ENTRIES
        # USE THE MEDIANS FROM THE DESCRIBE COMMANDS AS
        # ILLUSTRATED BELOW
                # RETRIEVE 'B:BVEHM'
                # DELETE ROWS 7:12 C1-C4
                # DESCRIBE C1-C4
                # RETRIEVE 'B:BVEHM'
                # DELETE ROWS 1:6 C1-C4
                # DESCRIBE C1-C4
MTB > SET IN C11   # CELL MEDIANS FROM DESCRIBE RESULTS
                            # AND OTHER ABOVE COMMANDS
DATA> 20.7 16.9 20.85 21.35
DATA> 23.5 19.3 22.35 26.45
DATA> SET IN C12    # TREATMENT IDENTIFIER
DATA> 2(1 2 3 4)
DATA> END
MTB > SET IN C13   # BLOCK IDENTIFIER
DATA> 4(1),4(2)
DATA> END
MTB > FRIEDMAN C11 C12 C13   # REQUIRES ONE OBS. PER CELL
```

CHAPTER 19

Decision Theory

OBJECTIVES

◇ **Structure decision problems in two-way tables according to decision alternatives and states of nature**

◇ **Establish a payoff for each decision with each state of nature**

◇ **Specify decision criteria using payoffs**

◇ **Analyze payoff tables and decision trees to pick a winning decision**

PRELUDE

For a business to grow and prosper, management must see that products and services pay off in aggregate and make a profit. No organization can strike out too many times or lose too many ball games. Management makes decisions on what products to bring to market, who to hire and fire, how the organization is structured and financed, who reports to whom, and so on. The decisions are many and varied.

Nearly every decision situation has a number of decision alternatives. For example, there are alternative pricing decisions for products, alternative wage rates for workers, alternative advertising schemes, and alternative plant sizes. Clearly, alternative decisions make up a structural dimension of a decision-making situation. Usually the number of decision alternatives is limited to a manageable size.

Another dimension of decision making involves the future. Every manager has to think ahead and would love to have a crystal ball. Each decision alternative has different payoffs, depending on the future marketplace scenario. Rather than being confused by considering an infinite number of future scenarios, a small number of future states of nature are considered.

This chapter presents criteria that can be used to evaluate alternative decisions in payoff terms with respect to each state of nature. Given a decision criterion, you can pick the best decision. You will learn how to use probability information about the states of nature and what the value of the information is. ◇

THE ARCHITECTURE OF THE DECISION SITUATION

A local politician emphasized that the existing baseball park was one of the best places in the country to watch a baseball game. Nevertheless, he favored building a new baseball park instead of a football stadium as part of a proposed megaplex.[1]

The term *megaplex* implies a larger facility than simply a single sports arena. It might include a convention center as well as both a football stadium and a baseball park. The inclusion of a baseball park is particularly attractive because the large number of baseball games would help guarantee a high facility utilization rate. However, the football team owners are interested in moving out of their aging stadium and favor a dual baseball and football facility in spite of the increased cost of the structure. Some have worried that, if the facility is not built, the football team might eventually leave the state. What would we do, then, without a football team for entertainment?

As the megaplex fantasy has grown, many parties have become interested in the design and the pending decisions. Big real estate developers are licking their lips and have proposed various location sites. City officials, police, and residents are worried about traffic flow disruptions. Even worse, the possibility of some public financing has generated controversy because of the potential loss of taxpayer money if the project goes bottom up. As a result, there are heated discussions and intense lobbying in the state legislature. Surprisingly, one of the team owners has some land for a possible megaplex site and likes the public financing idea.

Alternative Decisions   Decision theory suggests that the alternative decisions be identified. Let d_i be the i-th **alternative decision.** For the problem at hand, we consider three.

$$d_1 = \text{don't build the megaplex}$$
$$d_2 = \text{build a baseball-only megaplex}$$
$$d_3 = \text{build a baseball and football megaplex}$$

Different decision makers will have different opinions as to which of these decisions is best or optimal. Only the first baseman on the baseball team knows the right decision. Unfortunately, he is out of town and unavailable for comment. Decision theory provides ways to select the decision alternative that is best with respect to an objective decision criterion.

States of Nature   The best decision depends on what happens in the future—the states or conditions that occur. Decision theory suggests that these **states of nature** be identified. Let s_j be the j-th state of nature. For the problem at hand, we consider two.

$$s_1 = \text{low fan acceptance}$$
$$s_2 = \text{high fan acceptance}$$

Nearly everyone agrees that low fan acceptance would turn a joint baseball and football megaplex into a costly disaster. On the other hand, high fan acceptance would make that decision a big profit winner. Each decision must be evaluated in a similar way with respect to the two states of nature. Each decision and state of nature payoff (profit or loss) can be nicely summarized in a **payoff table.**

The Payoff Table   Exhibit 1 shows six payoff cells (three decision alternatives by two states of nature) that contain present values of projected profits or losses at row and column intersections in millions of dollars.

The general notation for a payoff cell is $\$(d_i, s_j)$; therefore, $\$(d_1, s_1) = 600$, $\$(d_3, s_1) = -300$, and so on.

The Decision Tree Display of the Payoff Table

The payoff table can be presented in a **decision tree** format as shown in Exhibit 2. Each row of the table is represented by a **decision branch** emerging from the square root **decision node** on the left. Each decision branch ends at a round **state of nature node** from which two **state of nature branches** emerge. The payoffs are written beside the branch endings on the right. Thus, each of the six cells (payoffs) in the payoff table can be reached by traversing the branches from the root node on the left to the right-most branch ends. Any of the payoff tables in this chapter can be represented in a decision tree format for those who prefer that presentation style.

EXHIBIT 1 Payoff Table for the Megaplex Decision Alternatives and the States of Nature

	STATES OF NATURE	
ALTERNATIVE DECISIONS	Low Fan Acceptance (s_1)	High Fan Acceptance (s_2)
(d₁) **Don't Build the Megaplex**	600	1,000
(d₂) **Baseball-only Megaplex**	300	2,000
(d₃) **Baseball and Football Megaplex**	−300	3,000

EXHIBIT 2 The Megaplex Payoff Table in a Decision Tree Format

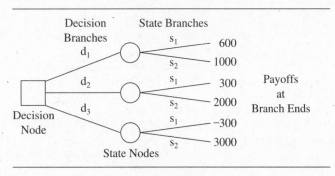

S T A T I S T I C A L   H I G H L I G H T S

Payoff tables display profit or loss for alternative decisions and states of nature. The analysis of a payoff table results in choosing the best decision alternative.

Decision Making Under Certainty or Uncertainty

The payoff table in Exhibit 1 depicts a **decision situation under uncertainty** because there is more than one state of nature and we don't know which course nature will take in the future. This kind of decision situation is often encountered. The remaining sections of this chapter describe how to evaluate and choose decisions under these challenging circumstances.

In contrast to an uncertain situation, certainty simplifies things considerably. For a **decision situation under certainty,** the payoff table has only one column, one known (certain) state of nature. Therefore, the best decision is the one that leads to the maximum payoff. Thus, the **decision criterion** or **decision choice rule** under certainty is to pick the decision with the maximum payoff.

For example, suppose there is only one state of nature, as shown in Exhibit 3. By not building the megaplex, you maximize the payoff. Thus, choose decision d_1 and don't build the megaplex.

EXHIBIT 3 Payoff Table for the Megaplex Decision Alternatives and One Certain State of Nature

	A CERTAIN STATE OF NATURE
ALTERNATIVE DECISIONS	**Low Fan Acceptance (certainty)** (s_1)
(d_1) **Don't Build the Megaplex**	**600** (certainty decision)
(d_2) **Baseball-only Megaplex**	300
(d_3) **Baseball and Football Megaplex**	−300

DECISION CRITERIA, UNCERTAIN STATES OF NATURE, WITHOUT USING PROBABILITIES

Under uncertainty, there are competing decision criteria for selecting a decision alternative. However, all these decision choice rules are based on the payoffs in a payoff table. The three most commonly used decision criteria are **maximin payoff, maximax payoff,** and **minimax regret.** Each of these criteria are illustrated in exhibits that follow.

Each decision criterion may lead to a different "best" decision. Although this fact is somewhat disconcerting, the personal preference of each decision maker can be accommodated. Thus, a conservative decision maker is likely to use a different criterion than a risk taker.

None of these criteria use probabilities. Although we will eventually employ probabilities as a measure of uncertainty, decision criteria are first presented for use without probabilities.

Maximin Payoff (Best Worst-Case Scenario)

In Exhibit 4, the payoff table for the megaplex decision alternatives and uncertain states of nature is augmented by adding a column of row minimums. In this case (but not always), the row minimums are all from the low fan acceptance column. These row minimums reflect the worst-case scenario for each decision alternative. The maximum of these row minimums is 600; thus, the so-called maximin criterion leads us to choose the best worst-case scenario, which is decision alternative d_1—don't build the megaplex.

EXHIBIT 4 A Payoff Table Augmented by Row Minimums for Illustrating the Maximin Decision Criterion

	UNCERTAIN STATES OF NATURE		
ALTERNATIVE DECISIONS	**Low Fan Acceptance** (s_1)	**High Fan Acceptance** (s_2)	**Row Minimums**
(d_1) Don't Build the Megaplex	600	1,000	**600**
(d_2) Baseball-only Megaplex	300	2,000	300
(d_3) Baseball and Football Megaplex	−300	3,000	−300

EXHIBIT 5 A Payoff Table Augmented by Row Maximums for Illustrating the Maximax Decision Criterion

	UNCERTAIN STATES OF NATURE		
ALTERNATIVE DECISION	Low Fan Acceptance (s_1)	High Fan Acceptance (s_2)	Row Maximums
(d$_1$) **Don't Build the Megaplex**	600	1,000	1,000
(d$_2$) **Baseball-only Megaplex**	300	2,000	2,000
(d$_3$) **Baseball and Football Megaplex**	−300	3,000	**3,000**

Maximax Payoff (Best Best-Case Scenario)

In Exhibit 5, the payoff table for the megaplex decision alternatives and uncertain states of nature is augmented by adding a column of row maximums. In this case (but not always), the row maximums are all from the high fan acceptance column. These row maximums reflect the best-case scenario for each decision alternative. The maximum of these row maximums is 3,000; thus, the so-called maximax criterion leads us to choose the best best-case scenario, which is decision alternative d_3—build the baseball and football megaplex.

The maximax decision criterion is not a conservative one and indicates the best decision when everything goes right. Notice that when things go wrong you have the most to lose with the third decision alternative selected by this criterion.

Minimax Regret or Opportunity Cost

The largest payoff in each column of a payoff table is the best you can do for each state of nature. For low fan acceptance, the best you can do is 600; for high fan acceptance, the best you can do is 3,000. By subtracting each column cell payoff from the best you can do in that column, you calculate the **regret** for each cell. These regret calculations are shown in Exhibit 6. A regret also can be referred to as an **opportunity cost** or **opportunity loss**.

EXHIBIT 6 Getting a Table of Regrets from a Payoff Table

	UNCERTAIN STATES OF NATURE	
ALTERNATIVE DECISIONS	Low Fan Acceptance (s_1)	High Fan Acceptance (s_2)
(d$_1$) **Don't Build the Megaplex**	(600 − 600)	(3,000 − 1,000)
(d$_2$) **Baseball-only Megaplex**	(600 − 300)	(3,000 − 2,000)
(d$_3$) **Baseball and Football Megaplex**	(600 − (−300))	(3,000 − 3,000)

EXHIBIT 7 A Regret Table Augmented with Row Maximums for Illustrating the Minimax Regret Decision Criterion

	UNCERTAIN STATES OF NATURE		
ALTERNATIVE DECISIONS	Low Fan Acceptance (s_1)	High Fan Acceptance (s_2)	Row Maximums
(d₁) Don't Build the Megaplex	0	2,000	2,000
(d₂) Baseball-only Megaplex	300	1,000	1,000
(d₃) Baseball and Football Megaplex	900	0	**900**

For example, in the low fan acceptance column the best you can do is 600. If you choose d_1, there is no regret because $(600 - 600) = 0$. If you choose d_2, you regret that you didn't choose d_1 by an amount $(600 - 300) = 300$. If you choose d_3, you regret that you didn't choose d_1 by an amount $(600 - (-300)) = 900$.

In Exhibit 7, the regret table for the megaplex decision alternatives and uncertain states of nature is augmented by adding a column of row maximums. These row maximums reflect the largest regret scenario for each decision alternative. The minimum of these row maximums is 900; thus, the so-called minimax regret criterion leads us to choose decision alternative d_3—build the baseball and football megaplex.

Although the minimax regret criterion led to the same decision as the maximax payoff decision, d_3, it is possible for each criterion to lead to a different decision. That is the nature of these decision criteria. They reflect individual decision-maker philosophies and preferences. None of these criteria takes advantage of the possibility of assigning probabilities to the states of nature.

S T A T I S T I C A L   H I G H L I G H T S

For uncertain states of nature without using probabilities, different decision criteria may lead to selecting different "best" decisions. Although this fact is somewhat disconcerting, the personal preference of each decision maker can be accommodated. Thus, a conservative decision maker is likely to use a different criterion than a risk taker.

DECISION CRITERIA, UNCERTAIN STATES OF NATURE, USING PROBABILITIES

When probabilities are assigned to the uncertain states of nature, they can be used to compute expected values, either expected payoffs or expected regrets. Thus, we can choose a decision based on the criteria of **maximum expected payoff** or **minimum expected regret.**

EXHIBIT 8 An Augmented Payoff Table with Prior Probabilities and Expected Values of the Payoffs for Each Decision Row

	UNCERTAIN STATES OF NATURE		
	Low Fan Acceptance (s_1)	High Fan Acceptance (s_2)	
Prior probabilities	$P(s_1) = .4$	$P(s_2) = .6$	
ALTERNATIVE DECISIONS			**Row Expected Values**
(d_1) Don't Build the Megaplex	600	1,000	840
(d_2) Baseball-only Megaplex	300	2,000	1,320
(d_3) Baseball and Football Megaplex	−300	3,000	**1,680**

Maximum Expected Payoff

The probabilities of each state of nature occurring are shown at the top of each column in Exhibit 8; $P(s_1) = .4$ and $P(s_2) = .6$. These are called **prior probabilities,** prior to any additional information gathering. The prior probabilities are multiplied times the corresponding payoffs in each decision row and summed across rows to obtain the expected payoff for each decision. For the first decision alternative, for example,

$$(600 \times .4) + (1000 \times .6) = 840$$

This computation is performed for each decision row, and the expected payoffs are listed in the right-most column. A general expression for this computation is

$$E(d_i \text{ payoffs}) = \Sigma P(s_j) \times (\text{payoff})_{ij}$$

The maximum expected payoff decision criterion leads us to choose decision d_3—build a baseball and football megaplex. Although this is the same decision reached via the minimax regret and maximax payoff criteria (without considering probabilities), these criteria can lead to different decision alternative choices.

Minimum Expected Regret

Again, the probabilities of each state of nature occurring are shown at the top of each column in Exhibit 9; $P(s_1) = .4$ and $P(s_2) = .6$. These probabilities are multiplied times the corresponding regrets in each decision row and summed across rows to obtain the expected regret for each decision. For the first decision alternative, for example

$$(0 \times .4) + (2,000 \times .6) = 1,200$$

EXHIBIT 9 An Augmented Payoff Table with Prior Probabilities and Expected Values of the Regrets for Each Decision Row

	UNCERTAIN STATES OF NATURE		
Prior probabilities	Low Fan Acceptance (s_1) $P(s_1) = .4$	High Fan Acceptance (s_2) $P(s_2) = .6$	
ALTERNATIVE DECISIONS			**Row Expected Values**
(d_1) Don't Built the Megaplex	0	2,000	1200
(d_2) Baseball-only Megaplex	300	1,000	720
(d_3) Baseball and Football Megaplex	900	0	**360**

This computation is performed for each decision row and the expected regrets are listed in the right-most column. A general expression for this computation is

$$E(d_i \text{ regrets}) = \Sigma P(s_j) \times (\text{regret})_{ij}$$

The minimum expected regret decision criterion leads us to choose decision d_3—build a baseball and football megaplex. Although this is the same decision reached by other decision criteria, sometimes these criteria lead to different decision choices.

S T A T I S T I C A L   H I G H L I G H T S

When probabilities are assigned to the uncertain states of nature, they can be used to compute expected values, either expected payoffs or expected regrets. Thus, we can choose a decision based on the criteria of maximum expected payoff or minimum expected regret.

EXPECTED VALUE OF INFORMATION

If we were God-like and all-knowing, we would have **perfect information** for decision making. We would not need state of nature probabilities. Even though we are mere mortals, there is enough information in a payoff or regret table for us to pretend or visualize what might happen if we had perfect information. As a consequence, we can evaluate the regret under such circumstances, which is a value benchmark of perfect information. The value of perfect information is the most we would want to pay for it.

Sample information is less than perfect and comes from expert opinion, consultant advice, survey results, market research, and so on. By definition, sample information cannot be as complete as perfect information; therefore, it should cost less. In this section, we show how to incorporate sample information in decision making. We compute the expected value of perfect as well as sample information.

Expected Value of Perfect Information

Earlier we found that each decision criterion—minimum expected regret and maximum expected payoff—led to the decision alternative d_3—build a baseball and football megaplex. From the regret table in Exhibit 10, we see that for decision d_3 there is no regret when s_2 occurs and a regret of 900 when s_1 occurs. Therefore, perfect information that s_1 will occur would be worth 900 because perfect information would allow us to avoid that regret and choose d_1 instead of d_3. Perfect information that s_2 will occur would be worthless because perfect information would lead us to choose what we already have, which is d_3 with regret 0.

After a probabilistic decision criterion (minimum expected regret or maximum expected payoff) has been used to pick a decision, the regret (or value) of perfect information for each state of nature can be computed (for example, 900 and 0 for d_3). These perfect information values can be multiplied by the state probabilities to obtain the **expected value of perfect information (EVPI).**

$$\text{EVPI} = E(d_3 \text{ regret}) = (900 \times .4) + (0 \times .6) = 360$$

The expected value of perfect information is shown to the right of the d_3 regrets in Exhibit 10. This is the expected regret of the best probability-based decision.

EXHIBIT 10 A Regret Table for Illustrating the Expected Value of Perfect Information

	STATES OF NATURE		
Prior probabilities	Low Fan Acceptance (s_1) $P(s_1) = .4$	High Fan Acceptance (s_2) $P(s_2) = .6$	
ALTERNATIVE DECISIONS			**Row Expected Value**
(d_1) Don't Build the Megaplex	0	2,000	
(d_2) Baseball-only Megaplex	300	1,000	
(d_3) Baseball and Football Megaplex	900	0	**360**

Expected Value of Sample Information

Sample information is less than perfect. Nevertheless, new information based on expert opinion, consultant advice, survey results, market research, and so on can be used to revise prior probabilities.

For example, consider the purchase of survey information. Typically, marketing research firms have the expertise to conduct such a survey. For the sports megaplex decision problem, surely questions about ticket prices would be asked to reveal the ticket-buying intentions of fans and the depth of their support.

Ticket price issues are complex yet critical to the payoff realization of any decision. The low fan acceptance state of nature s_1 translates to a die-hard core of the remaining loyal fans. These fans might have to pay somewhat higher ticket prices in order to cover costs and keep the enterprise afloat. Of course, the high fan acceptance state of nature s_2 is the one everyone would like to see. Large numbers of fans could be accommodated by the megaplex in the event it is built. In this situation, somewhat lower ticket prices might be possible because costs could be spread over more fans. On the other hand, if the megaplex is not built, the high demand for seats in old facilities might permit higher demand-driven ticket prices. In any case, management is very interested in fan responses to ticket price questions. Nevertheless, management is in a quandary and can't make up its mind whether to go ahead and fund a survey or not.

The marketing research firm would like to get the go-ahead on this project. Therefore, they present management with some results of intention to buy surveys done in other cities and relate these figures to the megaplex decision problem. They argue that known fans can be surveyed to get favorable or unfavorable indicators of ticket-buying intentions at proposed prices.

Favorable Response to Proposed Ticket Prices for Revising Probabilities Historical experience and a small pilot survey suggest that favorable survey results lead to an intention to buy of 10% given state s_1, low fan acceptance, and 70% given state s_2, high fan acceptance. The decimal equivalents of these percentages (.1 and .7) are listed as the intention-to-buy probabilities for each state in Exhibit 11. These conditional probabilities are

EXHIBIT 11 Revising Prior Probabilities When the Survey Result Is Favorable

	STATES OF NATURE	
	Low Fan Acceptance (s_1)	High Fan Acceptance (s_2)
Prior probabilities	$P(s_1) = .400$	$P(s_2) = .600$
P(intention to buy $\mid s_j$)	$= .100$	$= .700$
Revised probabilities	$= .087$	$= .913$

used to revise the prior probabilities (see Chapter 4 for conditional probabilities). The revised probabilities are called **posterior probabilities.**

The revised probabilities are state probabilities given the sample information—in other words, given the intention-to-buy probabilities. The revised probabilities are calculated as follows:

$$\frac{.4 \times .1}{(.4 \times .1 + .6 \times .7)} = .087 = P(s_1 | \text{intention to buy})$$

$$\frac{.6 \times .7}{(.4 \times .1 + .6 \times .7)} = .913 = P(s_2 | \text{intention to buy})$$

Let itb = intention to buy. Then the denominator in the above expressions is the unconditional intention-to-buy probability.

$$P(\text{unconditional itb}) = P(s_1)\, P(\text{itb} | s_1) + P(s_2)\, P(\text{itb} | s_2) = .46$$

And, for example, the first revised probability is

$$P(s_1 | \text{itb}) = \frac{P(s_1)\, P(\text{itb} | s_1)}{P(\text{unconditional itb})}$$

The second revised probability is

$$P(s_2 | \text{itb}) = \frac{P(s_2)\, P(\text{itb} | s_2)}{P(\text{unconditional itb})}$$

Maximum Expected Payoff with Revised Probabilities   In Exhibit 12, expected payoff calculations are made for each decision alternative (row). However, the revised or posterior probabilities are used now in the calculations.

Decision d_3 maximizes the expected payoff, 2,712.9, with the revised probabilities.

EXHIBIT 12 An Augmented Payoff Table with Posterior Probabilities and Expected Values of the Payoffs for Each Decision Row

	STATES OF NATURE		
	Low Fan Acceptance (s_1)	High Fan Acceptance (s_2)	
Revised probabilities	.087	.913	
ALTERNATIVE DECISIONS			**Row Expected Values**
(**d_1**) **Don't Build the Megaplex**	600	1,000	965.2
(**d_2**) **Baseball-only Megaplex**	300	2,000	1,852.1
(**d_3**) **Baseball and Football Megaplex**	−300	3,000	**2,712.9**

EXHIBIT 13 Revising Prior Probabilities When the Survey Result Is Unfavorable

	STATES OF NATURE	
	Low Fan Acceptance (s_1)	High Fan Acceptance (s_2)
Prior probabilities	$P(s_1) = .400$	$P(s_2) = .600$
P(intention not to buy $\mid s_j$)	$= .900$	$= .300$
Revised probabilities	$= .667$	$= .333$

Unfavorable Response to Proposed Ticket Prices for Revising Probabilities Historical experience and a small pilot survey suggest that unfavorable survey results lead to an intention not to buy of 90% given state s_1, low fan acceptance, and 30% given state s_2, high fan acceptance. The decimal equivalents of these percentages (.9 and .3) are listed as the intention-not-to-buy probabilities for each state in Exhibit 13. Following the same procedure as shown above, the prior probabilities are revised. The revised probabilities are called posterior probabilities.

The revised probabilities are state probabilities given the sample information—in other words, given the intention not-to-buy probabilities. The revised probabilities are calculated as follows:

$$\frac{.4 \times .9}{(.4 \times .9 + .6 \times .3)} = .667 = P(s_1 \mid \text{intention not to buy})$$

$$\frac{.6 \times .3}{(.4 \times .9 + .6 \times .3)} = .333 = P(s_2 \mid \text{intention not to buy})$$

Let intb = intention not to buy. Then the denominator in the above expressions is the unconditional intention-not-to-buy probability.

$$P(\text{unconditional intb}) = P(s_1) \, P(\text{intb} \mid s_1) + P(s_2) \, P(\text{intb} \mid s_1) = .54$$

And, for example, the first revised probability is

$$P(s_1 \mid \text{intb}) = \frac{P(s_1) \, P(\text{intb} \mid s_1)}{P(\text{unconditional intb})}$$

The second revised probability is

$$P(s_2 \mid \text{intb}) = \frac{P(s_2) \, P(\text{intb} \mid s_2)}{P(\text{unconditional intb})}$$

Maximum Expected Payoff with Revised Probabilities In Exhibit 14, expected payoff calculations are made for each decision alternative (row). However, the revised or posterior probabilities are used now in the calculations.

Decision d_2 maximizes the expected payoff, 866.1, with the revised probabilities.

EXHIBIT 14 An Augmented Payoff Table with Posterior Probabilities and Expected Values of the Payoffs for Each Decision Row

	STATES OF NATURE		
	Low Fan Acceptance (s_1)	High Fan Acceptance (s_2)	
Revised probabilities	.667	.333	
ALTERNATIVE DECISIONS			**Row Expected Values**
(d_1) Don't Build the Megaplex	600	1,000	733.2
(d_2) Baseball-only Megaplex	300	2,000	**866.1**
(d_3) Baseball and Football Megaplex	−300	3,000	798.9

The Expected Value of the Maximum Revised Expected Payoffs

When the survey result is favorable, the revised probabilities in Exhibit 12 lead to a maximum expected payoff of 2,712.9 and decision d_3. When the survey result is unfavorable, the revised probabilities in Exhibit 14 lead to a maximum expected payoff of 866.1 and decision d_2. Furthermore, P(unconditional intention to buy) = .46 and P(unconditional intention not to buy) = .54. The unconditional probabilities times the maximum revised expected payoffs result in the expected value of the maximum revised expected payoffs.

$$E(\text{maximum revised expected payoffs})$$
$$= .46 \times 2712.9 + .54 \times 866.1$$
$$E(\text{maximum revised expected payoffs})$$
$$= 1,247.93 + 467.69 = 1,715.62$$

In Exhibit 8, the prior probabilities led to a maximum expected payoff of 1,680. The difference, $(1,715.63 - 1,680) = 35.63$, is the **expected value of the sample information (EVSI)** in millions of dollars.

Thus, the marketing research firm argues that the value of the sample information far exceeds the price of their services. Therefore, the company should go ahead with a full-blown survey. If the survey result is favorable to the proposed ticket prices, choose decision d_3 and build a combined baseball and football megaplex. If the survey result is unfavorable to the proposed ticket prices, choose decision d_2 and build a baseball-only megaplex.

S T A T I S T I C A L   H I G H L I G H T S

Sample information is less than perfect. Nevertheless, new information based on expert opinion, consultant advice, survey results, market research, and so on can be used to revise prior probabilities. Then the "best" decision alternative can be selected based on revised expected payoffs.

CHAPTER SUMMARY

This chapter structured the decision situation in terms of alternative decisions, states of nature, and payoffs in a payoff table. A decision tree structure is an equivalent alternative to a payoff table.

Under certainty, there is only one state of nature, and the payoff table reduces to one column. The best decision is the one with the maximum payoff.

Under uncertainty, the payoff table has two or more columns, and picking the best decision becomes more complicated and even dependent on decision-maker characteristics such as how conservative they are. Without using probabilities, three commonly used criteria are maximin (best worst-case scenario), maximax (best best-case scenario),

and minimax regret (opportunity cost). These criteria can lead to different "best" decisions.

Under uncertainty and with probabilities, the maximum expected payoff and minimum expected regret criteria were introduced. After finding the best decision and by letting specific state probabilities go to 1, the value of perfect information can be found. Perfect information cannot be achieved; therefore, we settle for sample information. Sample information can be used to revise prior probabilities and calculate revised maximum expected payoffs. The value of sample information can also be found almost as a by-product of this analysis.

KEY TERMS

alternative decision, 875
decision branch, 876
decision choice rule, 877
decision criterion, 877
decision node, 876
decision tree, 876
decision under certainty, 877
decision under uncertainty, 877
expected value of perfect
   information (EVPI), 883

expected value of the sample
   information (EVSI), 887
maximax payoff, 878
maximin payoff, 878
maximum expected payoff, 880
minimax regret, 878
minimum expected regret, 880
opportunity cost, 879
opportunity loss, 879
payoff table, 876

perfect information, 882
posterior probabilities, 885
prior probabilities, 881
regret, 879
sample information, 883
state of nature branches, 876
state of nature node, 876
states of nature, 876

EXERCISES

1. This exercise is similar to the sports facility example in the chapter, except that the payoffs and the probabilities are different.

	STATES OF NATURE	
ALTERNATIVE DECISIONS	Low Fan Acceptance (s_1)	High Fan Acceptance (s_2)
(d_1) **Don't Build the Megaplex**	800	900
(d_2) **Baseball-only Megaplex**	−300	1,500
(d_3) **Baseball and Football Megaplex**	−2,000	3,500

(a) Using the general notation for a payoff cell, which is $\$(d_i, s_j)$, specify the payoffs for $\$(d_1, s_1) = \underline{\hspace{1cm}}$ and $\$(d_3, s_2) = \underline{\hspace{1cm}}$.

(b) Construct a decision tree for this payoff table.

(c) What would be the best decision alternative choice if the high fan acceptance state of nature were certain?

(d) Augment the table by adding a column of row minimums that reflect the worst-case scenario for each decision alternative. What is the maximin payoff, and what decision alternative choice does it lead to?

(e) Augment the table by adding a column of row maximums that reflect the best-case scenario for each decision alternative. What is the maximax payoff, and what decision alternative choice does it lead to?

(f) Construct a table of regrets or opportunity costs.

(g) What is the minimax regret, and what decision alternative choice does it lead to?

(h) Suppose the uncertain states of nature have prior probabilities, which are $P(s_1) = .7$ and $P(s_2) = .3$. Augment the payoff table by adding a column of expected payoffs. What is the maximum expected payoff, and what decision alternative choice does it lead to?

(i) Augment the regret table by adding a column of expected regrets. What is the minimum expected regret, and what decision alternative choice does it lead to?

(j) What is the expected value of perfect information (EVPI) in part (i)?

(k) Historical experience and a small pilot survey suggest that favorable survey results lead to the intention-to-buy probabilities shown below.

	STATES OF NATURE	
	Low Fan Acceptance (s_1)	**High Fan Acceptance** (s_2)
Prior probabilities	$P(s_1) = .7$	$P(s_2) = .3$
$P(\text{intention to buy} \mid s_j)$	$= .2$	$= .6$
Revised probabilities	____	____

Use the prior probabilities and the conditional intention-to-buy probabilities to calculate the revised or posterior probabilities.

(l) Augment the payoff table by adding a column of expected payoffs using the revised probabilities. What is the maximum revised expected payoff, and what decision alternative choice does it lead to?

(m) Historical experience and a small pilot survey suggest that unfavorable survey results lead to the intention-not-to-buy probabilities shown below.

	STATES OF NATURE	
	Low Fan Acceptance (s_1)	**High Fan Acceptance** (s_2)
Prior probabilities	$P(s_1) = .7$	$P(s_2) = .3$
$P(\text{intention not to buy} \mid s_j)$	$= .8$	$= .4$
Revised probabilities	____	____

Use the prior probabilities and the conditional intention-not-to-buy probabilities to calculate the revised or posterior probabilities.

(n) Augment the payoff table by adding a column of expected payoffs using the revised probabilities. What is the maximum revised expected payoff, and what decision alternative choice does it lead to?

(o) Find the unconditional intention-to-buy and not-to-buy probabilities, and calculate the expected value of the maximum revised expected payoffs.

(p) Use the results in parts (o) and (h) to calculate the expected value of sample information (EVSI).

2. Worldwide competition has forced many organizations to improve the quality of their products. To improve, organizations have had to change the way they operate. Such changes may result in low or high employee acceptance. Naturally, high employee acceptance is desirable. One type of change involves engaging in quality control activities to the extent that management finds it necessary. In the payoff table below (in millions of dollars), the company's investment in quality control activities can be small, medium, or large.

| | STATES OF NATURE | |
ALTERNATIVE DECISIONS	Low Acceptance (s_1)	High Acceptance (s_2)
(d_1) Small QC Investment	80	100
(d_2) Medium QC Investment	30	200
(d_3) Large QC Investment	−20	500

(a) Using the general notation for a payoff cell, which is $\$(d_i, s_j)$, specify the payoffs for $\$(d_1, s_2) =$ ____ and $\$(d_2, s_1) =$ ____ .

(b) Construct a decision tree for this payoff table.

(c) What would be the best decision alternative choice if the high employee acceptance state of nature were certain?

(d) Augment the table by adding a column of row minimums that reflect the worst-case scenario for each decision alternative. What is the maximin payoff, and what decision alternative choice does it lead to?

(e) Augment the table by adding a column of row maximums that reflect the best-case scenario for each decision alternative. What is the maximax payoff, and what decision alternative choice does it lead to?

(f) Construct a table of regrets or opportunity costs.

(g) What is the minimax regret, and what decision alternative choice does it lead to?

(h) Suppose the uncertain states of nature have prior probabilities, which are $P(s_1) = .5$ and $P(s_2) = .5$. Augment the payoff table by adding a column of expected payoffs. What is the maximum expected payoff, and what decision alternative choice does it lead to?

(i) Augment the regret table by adding a column of expected regrets. What is the minimum expected regret, and what decision alternative choice does it lead to?

(j) What is the expected value of perfect information (EVPI) in part (i)?

(k) Historical experience and a small pilot survey suggest that favorable survey results lead to the employee intention to buy into the quality control effort probabilities that follow.

	STATES OF NATURE	
	Low Acceptance (s_1)	High Acceptance (s_2)
Prior probabilities	$P(s_1) = .5$	$P(s_2) = .5$
$P(\text{intention to buy} \mid s_j)$	$= .1$	$= .6$
Revised probabilities	____	____

Use the prior probabilities and the conditional intention-to-buy probabilities to calculate the revised or posterior probabilities.

(l) Augment the payoff table by adding a column of expected payoffs using the revised probabilities. What is the maximum revised expected payoff, and what decision alternative choice does it lead to?

(m) Historical experience and a small pilot survey suggest that unfavorable survey results lead to the employee intention not to buy into the quality control effort probabilities shown below.

	STATES OF NATURE	
	Low Acceptance (s_1)	High Acceptance (s_2)
Prior probabilities	$P(s_1) = .5$	$P(s_2) = .5$
$P(\text{intention not to buy} \mid s_j)$	$= .9$	$= .4$
Revised probabilities	____	____

Use the prior probabilities and the conditional intention-not-to-buy probabilities to calculate the revised or posterior probabilities.

(n) Augment the payoff table by adding a column of expected payoffs using the revised probabilities. What is the maximum revised expected payoff, and what decision alternative choice does it lead to?

(o) Find the unconditional intention-to-buy and not-to-buy probabilities, and calculate the expected value of the maximum revised expected payoffs.

(p) Use the results in parts (o) and (h) to calculate the expected value of sample information (EVSI) in a survey of employee intentions.

3. A company's present machinery has the capacity to meet product demand. Management thinks that future demand has two possible states, a moderate demand or a large demand. Three decisions are considered regarding machine capacity investment possibilities: no change, moderate increase, and large increase. Estimated profit increases (in millions of dollars) are shown in the payoff table below.

	STATES OF NATURE	
ALTERNATIVE DECISIONS	**Moderate Demand (s_1)**	**Large Demand (s_2)**
(d_1) No Change in Machine Capacity	0	0
(d_2) Moderate Machine Capacity Increase	50	50
(d_3) Large Machine Capacity Increase	30	90

(a) Using the general notation for a payoff cell, which is $\$(d_i, s_j)$, specify the payoffs for $\$(d_2, s_2) = $ _____ and $\$(d_3, s_1) = $ _____ .

(b) Construct a decision tree for this payoff table.

(c) What would be the best decision alternative choice if the moderate demand state of nature were certain?

(d) Augment the table by adding a column of row minimums which reflect the worst case scenario for each decision alternative. What is the maximin payoff, and what decision alternative choice does it lead to?

(e) Augment the table by adding a column of row maximums that reflect the best-case scenario for each decision alternative. What is the maximax payoff, and what decision alternative choice does it lead to?

(f) Construct a table of regrets or opportunity costs.

(g) What is the minimax regret, and what decision alternative choice does it lead to?

(h) Suppose the uncertain states of nature have prior probabilities, which are $P(s_1) = .2$ and $P(s_2) = .8$. Augment the payoff table by adding a column of expected payoffs. What is the maximum expected payoff, and what decision alternative choice does it lead to?

(i) Augment the regret table by adding a column of expected regrets. What is the minimum expected regret, and what decision alternative choice does it lead to?

(j) What is the expected value of perfect information (EVPI) in part (i)?

(k) Historical experience suggests that a favorable economic forecast leads to the intention-to-buy probabilities for this product shown below.

	STATES OF NATURE	
	Moderate Demand (s_1)	**Large Demand** (s_2)
Prior probabilities	$P(s_1) = .2$	$P(s_2) = .8$
P(intention to buy $\mid s_j$)	$= .5$	$= .6$
Revised probabilities	_____	_____

Use the prior probabilities and the conditional intention-to-buy probabilities to calculate the revised or posterior probabilities.

(l) Augment the payoff table by adding a column of expected payoffs using the revised probabilities. What is the maximum revised expected payoff, and what decision alternative choice does it lead to?

(m) Historical experience suggests that an unfavorable economic forecast leads to the intention not-to-buy probabilities for this product shown below.

	STATES OF NATURE	
	Moderate Demand (s_1)	**Large Demand** (s_2)
Prior probabilities	$P(s_1) = .7$	$P(s_2) = .3$
P(intention not to buy $\mid s_j$)	$= .5$	$= .4$
Revised probabilities	_____	_____

Use the prior probabilities and the conditional intention-not-to-buy probabilities to calculate the revised or posterior probabilities.

(n) Augment the payoff table by adding a column of expected payoffs using the revised probabilities. What is the maximum revised expected payoff, and what decision alternative choice does it lead to?

(o) Find the unconditional intention to-buy and not-to-buy probabilities, and calculate the expected value of the maximum revised expected payoffs.

(p) Use the results in parts (o) and (h) to calculate the expected value of sample information (EVSI) in an economic forecast.

4. A corporate farmer thinks that the coming growing season has two possible states, relatively dry or wet. Three decisions are considered regarding crop-type planting possibilities: plant only a dry crop, plant half dry and half wet crops, or plant only a wet crop. Dollar profits per acre are shown in the payoff table below.

	STATES OF NATURE	
ALTERNATIVE DECISIONS	**Dry** (s_1)	**Wet** (s_2)
(d_1) Plant Dry Crop Only	120	25
(d_2) Plant Half Dry and Half Wet Crops	80	50
(d_3) Plant Wet Crop Only	30	100

(a) Using the general notation for a payoff cell, which is $\$(d_i, s_j)$, specify the payoffs for $\$(d_1, s_1) = $ _____ and $\$(d_3, s_1) = $ _____ .

(b) Construct a decision tree for this payoff table.

(c) What would be the best decision alternative choice if the wet growing season state of nature were certain?

(d) Augment the table by adding a column of row minimums that reflect the worst-case scenario for each decision alternative. What is the maximin payoff, and what decision alternative choice does it lead to?

(e) Augment the table by adding a column of row maximums that reflect the best-case scenario for each decision alternative. What is the maximax payoff, and what decision alternative choice does it lead to?

(f) Construct a table of regrets or opportunity costs.

(g) What is the minimax regret, and what decision alternative choice does it lead to?

(h) Suppose the uncertain states of nature have prior probabilities, which are $P(s_1) = .6$ and $P(s_2) = .4$. Augment the payoff table by adding a column of expected payoffs. What is the maximum expected payoff, and what decision alternative choice does it lead to?

(i) Augment the regret table by adding a column of expected regrets. What is the minimum expected regret, and what decision alternative choice does it lead to?

(j) What is the expected value of perfect information (EVPI) in part (i)?

(k) Historical experience suggests that a forecast of below normal or normal summer temperatures leads to the intention to plant wet crop (ipwc) probabilities shown below.

	STATES OF NATURE	
	Dry (s_1)	Wet (s_2)
Prior probabilities	$P(s_1) = .6$	$P(s_2) = .4$
$P(\text{ipwc} \mid s_j)$	$= .3$	$= .7$
Revised probabilities	_____	_____

Use the prior probabilities and the conditional probabilities to calculate the revised or posterior probabilities.

(l) Augment the payoff table by adding a column of expected payoffs using the revised probabilities. What is the maximum revised expected payoff, and what decision alternative choice does it lead to?

(m) Historical experience suggests that a forecast of above-normal summer temperatures leads to the intention not to plant wet crop (inpwc) probabilities shown below.

	STATES OF NATURE	
	Dry (s_1)	Wet (s_2)
Prior probabilities	$P(s_1) = .6$	$P(s_2) = .4$
$P(\text{inpwc} \mid s_j)$	$= .7$	$= .3$
Revised probabilities	_____	_____

Use the prior probabilities and the conditional probabilities to calculate the revised or posterior probabilities.

(n) Augment the payoff table by adding a column of expected payoffs using the revised probabilities. What is the maximum revised expected payoff, and what decision alternative choice does it lead to?

(o) Find the unconditional to plant a wet crop and not to plant a wet crop probabilities, and calculate the expected value of the maximum revised expected payoffs.

(p) Use the results in parts (o) and (h) to calculate the expected value of sample information (EVSI) in a summer temperature forecast.

5. Suppose a bakery manager has to decide each morning how many loaves of a specialty bread to make. Let the cost to make a loaf be $1. This amount is lost if a loaf does not sell. Let the sales price per loaf be $2. Thus, there is a profit of $1 on each loaf sold. If demand exceeds production, there is an opportunity loss of $1 on each loaf that could have been sold.

If the maximum baking capacity is two loaves, the decision alternatives are to bake 0, 1, or 2 loaves. Let the consumer-demand states of nature be 0, 1, or 2 loaves on any given day.

(a) Construct a payoff table.

(b) Construct a decision tree for this payoff table.

(c) What would be the best decision alternative choice if consumers demanded two loaves?

(d) Augment the payoff table by adding a column of row minimums that reflect the worst-case scenario for each decision alternative. What is the maximin payoff (best worst-case payoff), and what decision alternative choice does it lead to?

(e) Augment the payoff table by adding a column of row maximums that reflect the best-case scenario for each decision alternative. What is the maximax payoff (best best-case payoff), and what decision alternative choice does it lead to?

(f) Construct a table of regrets.

(g) What is the minimax regret, and what decision alternative choice does it lead to?

(h) Suppose the uncertain states of nature have prior probabilities, which are $P(s_1) = .2$, $P(s_2) = .4$, and $P(s_3) = .4$. Augment the payoff table by adding a column of expected payoffs. What is the maximum expected payoff, and what decision alternative choice does it lead to?

(i) Augment the regret table by adding a column of expected regrets. What is the minimum expected regret, and what decision alternative choice does it lead to?

6. Suppose a newspaper distributor must decide each morning how many copies of a newspaper to deliver to a newsstand. Let the newsstand cost be $1.50. This amount is not lost if a newspaper does not sell because unsold copies are returned to the distributor. This return policy for unsold copies motivates the newsstand to want to be overstocked. However, the distributor is motivated to minimize overstocking because unsold papers at one newsstand might be sold elsewhere. Let the sales price per newspaper be $2. Thus, there is a profit of $.50 on each newspaper sold. If demand exceeds inventory, there is an opportunity loss of $.50 on each newspaper that could have been sold.

Because of supply limitations, the distributor makes a decision to deliver 20, 21, 22, or 23 newspapers. Let the consumer-demand states of nature be 20, 21, 22, or 23 newspapers on any given day.

(a) Construct a payoff table based on newsstand profits less opportunity losses.

(b) Construct a decision tree for this payoff table.

(c) What would be the best decision alternative choice for the distributor if consumer demand were certain to be 22 newspapers?

(d) Augment the payoff table by adding a column of row minimums that reflect the worst-case scenario for each decision alternative. What is the maximin payoff (best worst-case payoff), and what decision alternative choice does it lead to?

(e) Augment the payoff table by adding a column of row maximums that reflect the best-case scenario for each decision alternative. What is the maximax payoff (best best-case payoff), and what decision alternative choice does it lead to?

(f) Construct a table of regrets.

(g) What is the minimax regret, and what decision alternative choice does it lead to?

(h) Suppose the uncertain states of nature have prior probabilities, which are $P(s_1) = .5$, $P(s_2) = .2$, $P(s_3) = .2$, and $P(s_4) = .1$. Augment the payoff table by adding a column of expected payoffs. What is the maximum expected payoff, and what decision alternative choice does it lead to?

(i) Augment the regret table by adding a column of expected regrets. What is the minimum expected regret, and what decision alternative choice does it lead to?

7. Management must decide on the size (small, medium, or large) of this year's advertising budget. History has shown that the budget size has payoffs that depend on the performance of the economy, which can be poor, average, or good. The payoff table is shown below in millions of dollars.

	STATES OF NATURE		
ALTERNATIVE DECISIONS	Poor (s_1)	Average (s_2)	Good (s_3)
(d_1) Small Advertising Budget	10	8	6
(d_2) Medium Advertising Budget	7	12	10
(d_3) Large Advertising Budget	3	10	15

(a) Construct a decision tree for this payoff table.

(b) Augment the payoff table by adding a column of row minimums that reflect the worst case scenario for each decision alternative. What is the maximin payoff (best worst-case payoff), and what decision alternative choice does it lead to?

(c) Augment the payoff table by adding a column of row maximums that reflect the best-case scenario for each decision alternative. What is the maximax payoff (best best-case payoff), and what decision alternative choice does it lead to?

(d) Construct a table of regrets.

(e) What is the minimax regret, and what decision alternative choice does it lead to?

(f) Suppose the uncertain states of nature have prior probabilities, which are $P(s_1) = .6$, $P(s_2) = .3$, and $P(s_3) = .1$. Augment the payoff table by adding a column of expected payoffs. What is the maximum expected payoff, and what decision alternative choice does it lead to?

(g) Augment the regret table by adding a column of expected regrets. What is the minimum expected regret, and what decision alternative choice does it lead to?

8. An investor has to choose one of three investment types, which have low, medium, or high risks. The investment payoffs depend on the performance of the national economy, which can be poor, average, or good. The payoff table is shown below in return percentages.

	STATES OF NATURE		
ALTERNATIVE DECISIONS	Poor (s_1)	Average (s_2)	Good (s_3)
(d_1) Low Risk Investment	7	7.5	8
(d_2) Medium Risk Investment	5	8	10
(d_3) High Risk Investment	-10	5	20

(a) Construct a decision tree for this payoff table.

(b) Augment the payoff table by adding a column of row minimums that reflect the worst-case scenario for each decision alternative. What is the maximin payoff (best worst-case payoff), and what decision alternative choice does it lead to?

(c) Augment the payoff table by adding a column of row maximums that reflect the best-case scenario for each decision alternative. What is the maximax payoff (best best-case payoff), and what decision alternative choice does it lead to?

(d) Construct a table of regrets.

(e) What is the minimax regret, and what decision alternative choice does it lead to?

(f) Suppose the uncertain states of nature have prior probabilities, which are $P(s_1) = .3$, $P(s_2) = .6$ and $P(s_3) = .1$. Augment the payoff table by adding a column of expected payoffs. What is the maximum expected payoff, and what decision alternative choice does it lead to?

(g) Augment the regret table by adding a column of expected regrets. What is the minimum expected regret, and what decision alternative choice does it lead to?

9. A manufacturing firm has over a hundred similar machines that are used to make a textile product. Factors such as the type of fabric, type of stitching, and machine speed can lead to machine breakdowns. Thus, standby repair crews are trained to fix broken machines quickly to keep machine utilization high. If few machines break down, large repair crews are underutilized. If many machines break down and the repair crew is small, the machines are not fixed quickly enough. Thus, a repair crew size decision is necessary. Three sizes are shown in the payoff table below. The machine breakdown states of nature are small, moderate, or large number of break-downs.

| | STATES OF NATURE | | |
ALTERNATIVE DECISIONS	Small (s_1)	Moderate (s_2)	Large (s_3)
(d_1) **12-Person Crew**	44	36	19
(d_2) **18-Person Crew**	28	51	30
(d_3) **24-Person Crew**	11	22	58

(a) Construct a decision tree for this payoff table.

(b) Augment the payoff table by adding a column of row minimums that reflect the worst-case scenario for each decision alternative. What is the maximin payoff (best worst-case payoff), and what decision alternative choice does it lead to?

(c) Augment the payoff table by adding a column of row maximums that reflect the best-case scenario for each decision alternative. What is the maximax payoff (best best-case payoff), and what decision alternative choice does it lead to?

(d) Construct a table of regrets.

(e) What is the minimax regret, and what decision alternative choice does it lead to?

(f) Suppose the uncertain states of nature have prior probabilities, which are $P(s_1) = .6$, $P(s_2) = .2$ and $P(s_3) = .2$. Augment the payoff table by adding a column of expected payoffs. What is the maximum expected payoff, and what decision alternative choice does it lead to?

(g) Augment the regret table by adding a column of expected regrets. What is the minimum expected regret, and what decision alternative choice does it lead to?

10. A gold mining company is trying to decide whether or not to mine at a site location. The site's predicted yield of gold is uncertain. There might be little, moderate, or large amounts of gold. If the company decides to open a mine, the risks are forcing it to decide between financing the operation alone or including a 50% partner. A partner would split the risks and the payoffs (in millions of dollars) as shown below.

| | STATES OF NATURE | | |
ALTERNATIVE DECISIONS	Little (s_1)	Moderate (s_2)	Large (s_3)
(d_1) **Don't Mine**	0	0	0
(d_2) **Mine It Alone**	-100	-20	850
(d_3) **Mine with a Partner**	-50	-10	450

(a) Construct a decision tree for this payoff table.

(b) Augment the payoff table by adding a column of row minimums that reflect the worst-case scenario for each decision alternative. What is the maximin payoff (best worst-case payoff), and what decision alternative choice does it lead to?

(c) Augment the payoff table by adding a column of row maximums that reflect the best-case scenario for each decision alternative. What is the maximax payoff (best best-case payoff), and what decision alternative choice does it lead to?

(d) Construct a table of regrets.

(e) What is the minimax regret, and what decision alternative choice does it lead to?

(f) Suppose the uncertain states of nature have prior probabilities, which are $P(s_1) = .3$, $P(s_2) = .4$, and $P(s_3) = .3$. Augment the payoff table by adding a column of expected payoffs. What is the maximum expected payoff, and what decision alternative choice does it lead to?

(g) Augment the regret table by adding a column of expected regrets. What is the minimum expected regret, and what decision alternative choice does it lead to?

APPENDIX A

Tables

These tables are computer-generated, and the figures are rounded. Sometimes figures in the textbook appear as they are generated before rounding; therefore, slight discrepancies may exist due to rounding.

TABLE 1 CUMULATIVE STANDARD NORMAL DISTRIBUTION

Negative z Values   Given a negative z value, the body of Table 1 contains the cumulative probability

$$P[z \leq \text{(a particular z value)}]$$

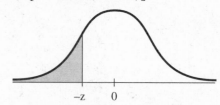

Row	z	−0.00	−0.01	−0.02	−0.03	−0.04
1	−3.9	0.0000	0.0000	0.0000	0.0000	0.0000
2	−3.8	0.0001	0.0001	0.0001	0.0001	0.0001
3	−3.7	0.0001	0.0001	0.0001	0.0001	0.0001
4	−3.6	0.0002	0.0002	0.0001	0.0001	0.0001
5	−3.5	0.0002	0.0002	0.0002	0.0002	0.0002
6	−3.4	0.0003	0.0003	0.0003	0.0003	0.0003
7	−3.3	0.0005	0.0005	0.0005	0.0004	0.0004
8	−3.2	0.0007	0.0007	0.0006	0.0006	0.0006
9	−3.1	0.0010	0.0009	0.0009	0.0009	0.0008
10	−3.0	0.0013	0.0013	0.0013	0.0012	0.0012
11	−2.9	0.0019	0.0018	0.0018	0.0017	0.0016
12	−2.8	0.0026	0.0025	0.0024	0.0023	0.0023
13	−2.7	0.0035	0.0034	0.0033	0.0032	0.0031
14	−2.6	0.0047	0.0045	0.0044	0.0043	0.0041
15	−2.5	0.0062	0.0060	0.0059	0.0057	0.0055
16	−2.4	0.0082	0.0080	0.0078	0.0075	0.0073
17	−2.3	0.0107	0.0104	0.0102	0.0099	0.0096
18	−2.2	0.0139	0.0136	0.0132	0.0129	0.0125
19	−2.1	0.0179	0.0174	0.0170	0.0166	0.0162
20	−2.0	0.0228	0.0222	0.0217	0.0212	0.0207
21	−1.9	0.0287	0.0281	0.0274	0.0268	0.0262
22	−1.8	0.0359	0.0351	0.0344	0.0336	0.0329
23	−1.7	0.0446	0.0436	0.0427	0.0418	0.0409
24	−1.6	0.0548	0.0537	0.0526	0.0516	0.0505
25	−1.5	0.0668	0.0655	0.0643	0.0630	0.0618
26	−1.4	0.0808	0.0793	0.0778	0.0764	0.0749
27	−1.3	0.0968	0.0951	0.0934	0.0918	0.0901
28	−1.2	0.1151	0.1131	0.1112	0.1093	0.1075
29	−1.1	0.1357	0.1335	0.1314	0.1292	0.1271
30	−1.0	0.1587	0.1562	0.1539	0.1515	0.1492
31	−0.9	0.1841	0.1814	0.1788	0.1762	0.1736
32	−0.8	0.2119	0.2090	0.2061	0.2033	0.2005
33	−0.7	0.2420	0.2389	0.2358	0.2327	0.2296
34	−0.6	0.2743	0.2709	0.2676	0.2643	0.2611
35	−0.5	0.3085	0.3050	0.3015	0.2981	0.2946
36	−0.4	0.3446	0.3409	0.3372	0.3336	0.3300
37	−0.3	0.3821	0.3783	0.3745	0.3707	0.3669
38	−0.2	0.4207	0.4168	0.4129	0.4090	0.4052
39	−0.1	0.4602	0.4562	0.4522	0.4483	0.4443
40	0.0	0.5000	0.4960	0.4920	0.4880	0.4840

EXAMPLE   GIVEN A z VALUE AND FINDING A PROBABILITY

For example, P $[z \le -2.12] = 0.0170$. The 0.0170 is found at the intersection of row 19 at z = −2.1 and column −0.02, where

$$\begin{array}{ccc}\textbf{Row} & \textbf{Column} & \textbf{Probability}\end{array}$$
$$P[z \le (-2.12 = \textbf{−2.10} − \textbf{0.02})] = 0.0170$$

EXAMPLE   GIVEN A PROBABILITY AND FINDING A z VALUE

When the probability is given, a corresponding z value can be determined by reversing the procedure. For example, the cumulative probability, 0.0170, in the body of the table is found at the intersection of row 19 at z = −2.10 and column −0.02. Therefore, z = −2.12.

Row	z	−0.05	−0.06	−0.07	−0.08	−0.09
1	−3.9	0.0000	0.0000	0.0000	0.0000	0.0000
2	−3.8	0.0001	0.0001	0.0001	0.0001	0.0001
3	−3.7	0.0001	0.0001	0.0001	0.0001	0.0001
4	−3.6	0.0001	0.0001	0.0001	0.0001	0.0001
5	−3.5	0.0002	0.0002	0.0002	0.0002	0.0002
6	−3.4	0.0003	0.0003	0.0003	0.0003	0.0002
7	−3.3	0.0004	0.0004	0.0004	0.0004	0.0003
8	−3.2	0.0006	0.0006	0.0005	0.0005	0.0005
9	−3.1	0.0008	0.0008	0.0008	0.0007	0.0007
10	−3.0	0.0011	0.0011	0.0011	0.0010	0.0010
11	−2.9	0.0016	0.0015	0.0015	0.0014	0.0014
12	−2.8	0.0022	0.0021	0.0021	0.0020	0.0019
13	−2.7	0.0030	0.0029	0.0028	0.0027	0.0026
14	−2.6	0.0040	0.0039	0.0038	0.0037	0.0036
15	−2.5	0.0054	0.0052	0.0051	0.0049	0.0048
16	−2.4	0.0071	0.0069	0.0068	0.0066	0.0064
17	−2.3	0.0094	0.0091	0.0089	0.0087	0.0084
18	−2.2	0.0122	0.0119	0.0116	0.0113	0.0110
19	−2.1	0.0158	0.0154	0.0150	0.0146	0.0143
20	−2.0	0.0202	0.0197	0.0192	0.0188	0.0183
21	−1.9	0.0256	0.0250	0.0244	0.0239	0.0233
22	−1.8	0.0322	0.0314	0.0307	0.0301	0.0294
23	−1.7	0.0401	0.0392	0.0384	0.0375	0.0367
24	−1.6	0.0495	0.0485	0.0475	0.0465	0.0455
25	−1.5	0.0606	0.0594	0.0582	0.0571	0.0559
26	−1.4	0.0735	0.0721	0.0708	0.0694	0.0681
27	−1.3	0.0885	0.0869	0.0853	0.0838	0.0823
28	−1.2	0.1056	0.1038	0.1020	0.1003	0.0985
29	−1.1	0.1251	0.1230	0.1210	0.1190	0.1170
30	−1.0	0.1469	0.1446	0.1423	0.1401	0.1379
31	−0.9	0.1711	0.1685	0.1660	0.1635	0.1611
32	−0.8	0.1977	0.1949	0.1922	0.1894	0.1867
33	−0.7	0.2266	0.2236	0.2206	0.2177	0.2148
34	−0.6	0.2578	0.2546	0.2514	0.2483	0.2451
35	−0.5	0.2912	0.2877	0.2843	0.2810	0.2776
36	−0.4	0.3264	0.3228	0.3192	0.3156	0.3121
37	−0.3	0.3632	0.3594	0.3557	0.3520	0.3483
38	−0.2	0.4013	0.3974	0.3936	0.3897	0.3859
39	−0.1	0.4404	0.4364	0.4325	0.4286	0.4247
40	0.0	0.4801	0.4761	0.4721	0.4681	0.4641

Positive z Values Given a positive z value, the body of Table 1 contains the cumulative probability, $P[z \leq$ (a particular z value)].

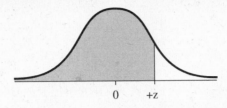

0   +z

GIVEN A z VALUE AND FINDING A PROBABILITY

For example, $P[z \leq +2.12] = 0.9830$. The 0.9830 is found at the intersection of row 22 at $z = +2.10$ and column $+0.02$, where

$$P[z \leq (+2.12 = \overset{\textbf{Row}}{\textbf{+2.10}} + \overset{\textbf{Column}}{\textbf{0.02}})] = \overset{\textbf{Probability}}{0.9830}$$

Row	z	+0.00	+0.01	+0.02	+0.03	+0.04
1	**0.0**	0.5000	0.5040	0.5080	0.5120	0.5160
2	**+0.1**	0.5398	0.5438	0.5478	0.5517	0.5557
3	**+0.2**	0.5793	0.5832	0.5871	0.5910	0.5948
4	**+0.3**	0.6179	0.6217	0.6255	0.6293	0.6331
5	**+0.4**	0.6554	0.6591	0.6628	0.6664	0.6700
6	**+0.5**	0.6915	0.6950	0.6985	0.7019	0.7054
7	**+0.6**	0.7257	0.7291	0.7324	0.7357	0.7389
8	**+0.7**	0.7580	0.7611	0.7642	0.7673	0.7704
9	**+0.8**	0.7881	0.7910	0.7939	0.7967	0.7995
10	**+0.9**	0.8159	0.8186	0.8212	0.8238	0.8264
11	**+1.0**	0.8413	0.8438	0.8461	0.8485	0.8508
12	**+1.1**	0.8643	0.8665	0.8686	0.8708	0.8729
13	**+1.2**	0.8849	0.8869	0.8888	0.8907	0.8925
14	**+1.3**	0.9032	0.9049	0.9066	0.9082	0.9099
15	**+1.4**	0.9192	0.9207	0.9222	0.9236	0.9251
16	**+1.5**	0.9332	0.9345	0.9357	0.9370	0.9382
17	**+1.6**	0.9452	0.9463	0.9474	0.9484	0.9495
18	**+1.7**	0.9554	0.9564	0.9573	0.9582	0.9591
19	**+1.8**	0.9641	0.9649	0.9656	0.9664	0.9671
20	**+1.9**	0.9713	0.9719	0.9726	0.9732	0.9738
21	**+2.0**	0.9772	0.9778	0.9783	0.9788	0.9793
22	**+2.1**	0.9821	0.9826	0.9830	0.9834	0.9838
23	**+2.2**	0.9861	0.9864	0.9868	0.9871	0.9875
24	**+2.3**	0.9893	0.9896	0.9898	0.9901	0.9904
25	**+2.4**	0.9918	0.9920	0.9922	0.9925	0.9927
26	**+2.5**	0.9938	0.9940	0.9941	0.9943	0.9945
27	**+2.6**	0.9953	0.9955	0.9956	0.9957	0.9959
28	**+2.7**	0.9965	0.9966	0.9967	0.9968	0.9969
29	**+2.8**	0.9974	0.9975	0.9976	0.9977	0.9977
30	**+2.9**	0.9981	0.9982	0.9982	0.9983	0.9984
31	**+3.0**	0.9987	0.9987	0.9987	0.9988	0.9988
32	**+3.1**	0.9990	0.9991	0.9991	0.9991	0.9992
33	**+3.2**	0.9993	0.9993	0.9994	0.9994	0.9994
34	**+3.3**	0.9995	0.9995	0.9995	0.9996	0.9996
35	**+3.4**	0.9997	0.9997	0.9997	0.9997	0.9997
36	**+3.5**	0.9998	0.9998	0.9998	0.9998	0.9998
37	**+3.6**	0.9998	0.9998	0.9999	0.9999	0.9999
38	**+3.7**	0.9999	0.9999	0.9999	0.9999	0.9999
39	**+3.8**	0.9999	0.9999	0.9999	0.9999	0.9999
40	**+3.9**	1.0000	1.0000	1.0000	1.0000	1.0000

EXAMPLE — GIVEN A PROBABILITY AND FINDING A z VALUE

When the probability is given, a corresponding z value can be determined by reversing the procedure. For example, the cumulative probability, 0.9830, in the body of the table is found at the intersection of row 22 at z = +2.10 and column +0.02. Therefore, z = +2.12.

Notation for Hypothesis Tests and Confidence Intervals In hypothesis testing and confidence interval construction, the notation, $z_{(\alpha \text{ or } \alpha/2)}$ is used. For example, let the area in the right tail of the standard normal distribution be designated as

$$\frac{\alpha}{2} = 1 - 0.9830 = 0.0170$$

Then, $z_{(\alpha/2 = 0.0170)} = +2.12$.

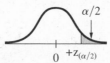

A commonly encountered z value is $z_{(\alpha/2 = 0.0250)} = +1.96$, where $0.0250 = 1 - 0.9750$.

Row	z	+0.05	+0.06	+0.07	+0.08	+0.09
1	+0.0	0.5199	0.5239	0.5279	0.5319	0.5359
2	+0.1	0.5596	0.5636	0.5675	0.5714	0.5753
3	+0.2	0.5987	0.6026	0.6064	0.6103	0.6141
4	+0.3	0.6368	0.6406	0.6443	0.6480	0.6517
5	+0.4	0.6736	0.6772	0.6808	0.6844	0.6879
6	+0.5	0.7088	0.7123	0.7157	0.7190	0.7224
7	+0.6	0.7422	0.7454	0.7486	0.7517	0.7549
8	+0.7	0.7734	0.7764	0.7794	0.7823	0.7852
9	+0.8	0.8023	0.8051	0.8078	0.8106	0.8133
10	+0.9	0.8289	0.8315	0.8340	0.8365	0.8389
11	+1.0	0.8531	0.8554	0.8577	0.8599	0.8621
12	+1.1	0.8749	0.8770	0.8790	0.8810	0.8830
13	+1.2	0.8944	0.8962	0.8980	0.8997	0.9015
14	+1.3	0.9115	0.9131	0.9147	0.9162	0.9177
15	+1.4	0.9265	0.9279	0.9292	0.9306	0.9319
16	+1.5	0.9394	0.9406	0.9418	0.9429	0.9441
17	+1.6	0.9505	0.9515	0.9525	0.9535	0.9545
18	+1.7	0.9599	0.9608	0.9616	0.9625	0.9633
19	+1.8	0.9678	0.9686	0.9693	0.9699	0.9706
20	+1.9	0.9744	0.9750	0.9756	0.9761	0.9767
21	+2.0	0.9798	0.9803	0.9808	0.9812	0.9817
22	+2.1	0.9842	0.9846	0.9850	0.9854	0.9857
23	+2.2	0.9878	0.9881	0.9884	0.9887	0.9890
24	+2.3	0.9906	0.9909	0.9911	0.9913	0.9916
25	+2.4	0.9929	0.9931	0.9932	0.9934	0.9936
26	+2.5	0.9946	0.9948	0.9949	0.9951	0.9952
27	+2.6	0.9960	0.9961	0.9962	0.9963	0.9964
28	+2.7	0.9970	0.9971	0.9972	0.9973	0.9974
29	+2.8	0.9978	0.9979	0.9979	0.9980	0.9981
30	+2.9	0.9984	0.9985	0.9985	0.9986	0.9986
31	+3.0	0.9989	0.9989	0.9989	0.9990	0.9990
32	+3.1	0.9992	0.9992	0.9992	0.9993	0.9993
33	+3.2	0.9994	0.9994	0.9995	0.9995	0.9995
34	+3.3	0.9996	0.9996	0.9996	0.9996	0.9997
35	+3.4	0.9997	0.9997	0.9997	0.9997	0.9998
36	+3.5	0.9998	0.9998	0.9998	0.9998	0.9998
37	+3.6	0.9999	0.9999	0.9999	0.9999	0.9999
38	+3.7	0.9999	0.9999	0.9999	0.9999	0.9999
39	+3.8	0.9999	0.9999	0.9999	0.9999	0.9999
40	+3.9	1.0000	1.0000	1.0000	1.0000	1.0000

TABLE 2   PERCENTILES OF THE STUDENT'S t DISTRIBUTION

Given a cumulative probability, $P[t \le$ (a particular t value)$]$, and the degrees of freedom (DF) in the *margins of the table,* the *body* of Table 2 contains the particular t value.

E X A M P L E   FINDING A PARTICULAR t VALUE

For example, if $P[t \le$ (a particular t value)$] = 0.800$ and DF = 2, the particular t value of $+1.061$ is found at the intersection of row DF = 2 and column 0.800, where

$$P[t \le +1.061] = 0.800$$

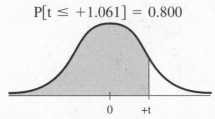

DF	.550	.600	.650	.700	.750	.800	.850
1	0.158	0.325	0.510	0.727	1.000	1.376	1.963
2	0.142	0.289	0.445	0.617	0.816	1.061	1.386
3	0.137	0.277	0.424	0.584	0.765	0.978	1.250
4	0.134	0.271	0.414	0.569	0.741	0.941	1.190
5	0.132	0.267	0.408	0.559	0.727	0.920	1.156
6	0.131	0.265	0.404	0.553	0.718	0.906	1.134
7	0.130	0.263	0.402	0.549	0.711	0.896	1.119
8	0.130	0.262	0.399	0.546	0.706	0.889	1.108
9	0.129	0.261	0.398	0.543	0.703	0.883	1.100
10	0.129	0.260	0.397	0.542	0.700	0.879	1.093
11	0.129	0.260	0.396	0.540	0.697	0.876	1.088
12	0.128	0.259	0.395	0.539	0.695	0.873	1.083
13	0.128	0.259	0.394	0.538	0.694	0.870	1.079
14	0.128	0.258	0.393	0.537	0.692	0.868	1.076
15	0.128	0.258	0.393	0.536	0.691	0.866	1.074
16	0.128	0.258	0.392	0.535	0.690	0.865	1.071
17	0.128	0.257	0.392	0.534	0.689	0.863	1.069
18	0.127	0.257	0.392	0.534	0.688	0.862	1.067
19	0.127	0.257	0.391	0.533	0.688	0.861	1.066
20	0.127	0.257	0.391	0.533	0.687	0.860	1.064
21	0.127	0.257	0.391	0.532	0.686	0.859	1.063
22	0.127	0.256	0.390	0.532	0.686	0.858	1.061
23	0.127	0.256	0.390	0.532	0.685	0.858	1.060
24	0.127	0.256	0.390	0.531	0.685	0.857	1.059
25	0.127	0.256	0.390	0.531	0.684	0.856	1.058
26	0.127	0.256	0.390	0.531	0.684	0.856	1.058
27	0.127	0.256	0.389	0.531	0.684	0.855	1.057
28	0.127	0.256	0.389	0.530	0.683	0.855	1.056
29	0.127	0.256	0.389	0.530	0.683	0.854	1.055
30	0.127	0.256	0.389	0.530	0.683	0.854	1.055
31	0.127	0.256	0.389	0.530	0.682	0.853	1.054
32	0.127	0.255	0.389	0.530	0.682	0.853	1.054
33	0.127	0.255	0.389	0.530	0.682	0.853	1.053
34	0.127	0.255	0.389	0.529	0.682	0.852	1.052
35	0.127	0.255	0.388	0.529	0.682	0.852	1.052
40	0.126	0.255	0.388	0.529	0.681	0.851	1.050
50	0.126	0.255	0.388	0.528	0.679	0.849	1.047
60	0.126	0.254	0.387	0.527	0.679	0.848	1.045
120	0.126	0.254	0.386	0.526	0.677	0.845	1.041
INF	0.126	0.253	0.385	0.524	0.674	0.842	1.036

Notation for Hypothesis Tests and Confidence Intervals In hypothesis testing and confidence interval construction, the notation, $t_{(\alpha \text{ or } \alpha/2),(DF)}$ is used. For example, with DF = 2, let the area in the right tail of the Student's t distribution be designated as

$$\frac{\alpha}{2} = 1 - 0.800 = 0.200$$

Then, $t_{(\alpha/2 = 0.200),(DF = 2)} = +1.061$.

As DF becomes infinitely large (row INF) and at

$$\frac{\alpha}{2} = 1 - 0.975 = 0.025$$

the t value, $t_{(\alpha/2 = 0.025),(DF = INF)} = +1.96$ is the same as a z value, $z_{(\alpha/2 = 0.025)} = +1.96$.

DF	.900	.950	.975	.990	.995	.997	.999
1	3.078	6.314	12.706	31.821	63.657	106.100	318.317
2	1.886	2.920	4.303	6.965	9.925	12.852	22.327
3	1.638	2.353	3.182	4.541	5.841	6.994	10.215
4	1.533	2.132	2.776	3.747	4.604	5.321	7.173
5	1.476	2.015	2.571	3.365	4.032	4.570	5.893
6	1.440	1.943	2.447	3.143	3.707	4.152	5.208
7	1.415	1.895	2.365	2.998	3.499	3.887	4.785
8	1.397	1.860	2.306	2.896	3.355	3.705	4.501
9	1.383	1.833	2.262	2.821	3.250	3.573	4.297
10	1.372	1.812	2.228	2.764	3.169	3.472	4.144
11	1.363	1.796	2.201	2.718	3.106	3.393	4.025
12	1.356	1.782	2.179	2.681	3.055	3.330	3.930
13	1.350	1.771	2.160	2.650	3.012	3.278	3.852
14	1.345	1.761	2.145	2.624	2.977	3.234	3.787
15	1.341	1.753	2.131	2.602	2.947	3.197	3.733
16	1.337	1.746	2.120	2.583	2.921	3.165	3.686
17	1.333	1.740	2.110	2.567	2.898	3.138	3.646
18	1.330	1.734	2.101	2.552	2.878	3.113	3.611
19	1.328	1.729	2.093	2.539	2.861	3.092	3.579
20	1.325	1.725	2.086	2.528	2.845	3.073	3.552
21	1.323	1.721	2.080	2.518	2.831	3.056	3.527
22	1.321	1.717	2.074	2.508	2.819	3.041	3.505
23	1.319	1.714	2.069	2.500	2.807	3.027	3.485
24	1.318	1.711	2.064	2.492	2.797	3.014	3.467
25	1.316	1.708	2.060	2.485	2.787	3.003	3.450
26	1.315	1.706	2.056	2.479	2.779	2.992	3.435
27	1.314	1.703	2.052	2.473	2.771	2.982	3.421
28	1.313	1.701	2.048	2.467	2.763	2.973	3.408
29	1.311	1.699	2.045	2.462	2.756	2.965	3.396
30	1.310	1.697	2.042	2.457	2.750	2.957	3.385
31	1.309	1.696	2.040	2.453	2.744	2.950	3.375
32	1.309	1.694	2.037	2.449	2.738	2.943	3.365
33	1.308	1.692	2.035	2.445	2.733	2.937	3.356
34	1.307	1.691	2.032	2.441	2.728	2.931	3.348
35	1.306	1.690	2.030	2.438	2.724	2.926	3.340
40	1.303	1.684	2.021	2.423	2.704	2.902	3.307
50	1.299	1.676	2.009	2.403	2.678	2.870	3.261
60	1.296	1.671	2.000	2.390	2.660	2.849	3.232
120	1.289	1.658	1.980	2.358	2.617	2.798	3.160
INF	1.282	1.645	1.960	2.326	2.576	2.748	3.090

TABLE 3   PERCENTILES OF THE CHI-SQUARE DISTRIBUTION

Given a cumulative probability, $P[\chi^2 \leq$ (a particular χ^2 value)], and the degrees of freedom (DF) in the *margins of the table,* the *body* of Table 3 contains the particular χ^2 value.

EXAMPLE   FINDING A PARTICULAR χ^2 VALUE

For example, if $P[\chi^2 \leq$ (a particular χ^2 value)] $= 0.500$ and DF $= 3$, the particular χ^2 value of $+2.366$ is found at the intersection of row DF $= 3$ and column 0.500, where

$$P[\chi^2 \leq +2.366] = 0.500$$

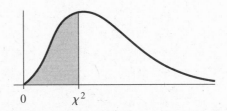

Notation for Hypothesis Tests and Confidence Intervals   In hypothesis testing and confidence interval construction, the notation, $\chi^2_{\alpha,\,DF}$ is used. For example, with DF $= 3$, let the area in the right tail of the chi-square distribution be designated as

$$\alpha = 1 - 0.500 = 0.500$$

Then, $\chi^2_{\alpha\,=\,0.500,DF\,=\,3} = +2.366$.

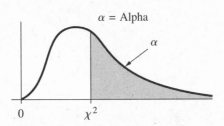

When DF $= 12$ and at a commonly used significance level

$$\alpha = 1 - 0.95 = 0.05$$

the $\chi^2_{\alpha\,=\,0.05,DF\,=\,12} = +21.026$.

DF	.010	.050	.100	.300	.500	.700	.900	.950	.990	.999
1	0.000	0.004	0.016	0.148	0.455	1.074	2.706	3.841	6.635	10.828
2	0.020	0.103	0.211	0.713	1.386	2.408	4.605	5.991	9.210	13.816
3	0.115	0.352	0.584	1.424	2.366	3.665	6.251	7.815	11.345	16.266
4	0.297	0.711	1.064	2.195	3.357	4.878	7.779	9.488	13.277	18.467
5	0.554	1.145	1.610	3.000	4.351	6.064	9.236	11.070	15.086	20.515
6	0.872	1.635	2.204	3.828	5.348	7.231	10.645	12.592	16.812	22.458
7	1.239	2.167	2.833	4.671	6.346	8.383	12.017	14.067	18.475	24.322
8	1.646	2.733	3.490	5.527	7.344	9.524	13.362	15.507	20.090	26.125
9	2.088	3.325	4.168	6.393	8.343	10.656	14.684	16.919	21.666	27.877
10	2.558	3.940	4.865	7.267	9.342	11.781	15.987	18.307	23.209	29.588
11	3.053	4.575	5.578	8.148	10.341	12.899	17.275	19.675	24.725	31.264
12	3.571	5.226	6.304	9.034	11.340	14.011	18.549	21.026	26.217	32.910
13	4.107	5.892	7.042	9.926	12.340	15.119	19.812	22.362	27.688	34.528
14	4.660	6.571	7.790	10.821	13.339	16.222	21.064	23.685	29.141	36.124
15	5.229	7.261	8.547	11.721	14.339	17.322	22.307	24.996	30.578	37.697
16	5.812	7.962	9.312	12.624	15.339	18.418	23.542	26.296	32.000	39.254
17	6.408	8.672	10.085	13.531	16.338	19.511	24.769	27.587	33.409	40.789
18	7.015	9.390	10.865	14.440	17.338	20.601	25.989	28.869	34.805	42.312
19	7.633	10.117	11.651	15.352	18.338	21.689	27.204	30.143	36.191	43.819
20	8.260	10.851	12.443	16.266	19.337	22.775	28.412	31.410	37.566	45.315
21	8.897	11.591	13.240	17.182	20.337	23.858	29.615	32.671	38.932	46.797
22	9.542	12.338	14.041	18.101	21.337	24.939	30.813	33.924	40.290	48.270
23	10.196	13.091	14.848	19.021	22.337	26.018	32.007	35.172	41.638	49.726
24	10.856	13.848	15.659	19.943	23.337	27.096	33.196	36.415	42.980	51.179
25	11.524	14.611	16.473	20.867	24.337	28.172	34.382	37.653	44.314	52.622
26	12.198	15.379	17.292	21.792	25.336	29.246	35.563	38.885	45.642	54.054
27	12.879	16.151	18.114	22.719	26.336	30.319	36.741	40.113	46.963	55.477
28	13.565	16.928	18.939	23.647	27.336	31.391	37.916	41.337	48.278	56.893
29	14.256	17.708	19.768	24.577	28.336	32.461	39.087	42.557	49.588	58.303
30	14.953	18.493	20.599	25.508	29.336	33.530	40.256	43.773	50.892	59.703

TABLE 4   PERCENTILES OF THE F DISTRIBUTION

Here a cumulative probability, $P[F \leq$ (a particular F value)] identifies the table subset. The numerator and denominator degrees of freedom are in the *margins of the table subset,* and the *body* of the Table 4 subset contains the particular F value. Two subsets of F values are provided: one subset (0.95) for

$$P[F \leq \text{(a particular F value)}] = 0.95$$

and, another subset (0.99) for

$$P[F \leq \text{(a particular F value)}] = 0.99$$

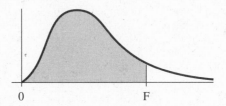

EXAMPLE   FINDING A PARTICULAR F VALUE

For example, if $P[F \leq$ (a particular F value)] = 0.95, the numerator (column) DF = 4 and the denominator (row) DF = 6, the particular F value of +4.53 is found at the intersection of column DF = 4 and row DF = 6 where

$$P[F \leq +4.53] = 0.95$$

Notation for Hypothesis Tests and Confidence Intervals   In hypothesis testing and confidence interval construction, the notation, $F_{\alpha, DFnum, DFdenom}$, is used. For example, with DFnum = 4 and DFdenom = 6, let the area in the right tail of the F distribution be designated as

$$\alpha = 1 - 0.95 = 0.05$$

Then, $F_{\alpha = 0.05, DFnum = 4, DFdenom = 6} = +4.53.$

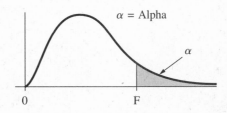

TABLE 4 SUBSET (0.95)

$P[F \leq$ (a particular F value)$] = 0.95$ for this table with numerator DF in columns and denominator DF in rows.

DF	1	2	3	4	5
1	161.45	199.50	215.71	224.58	230.16
2	18.51	19.00	19.16	19.25	19.30
3	10.13	9.55	9.28	9.12	9.01
4	7.71	6.94	6.59	6.39	6.26
5	6.61	5.79	5.41	5.19	5.05
6	5.99	5.14	4.76	4.53	4.39
7	5.59	4.74	4.35	4.12	3.97
8	5.32	4.46	4.07	3.84	3.69
9	5.12	4.26	3.86	3.63	3.48
10	4.96	4.10	3.71	3.48	3.33
11	4.84	3.98	3.59	3.36	3.20
12	4.75	3.89	3.49	3.26	3.11
13	4.67	3.81	3.41	3.18	3.03
14	4.60	3.74	3.34	3.11	2.96
15	4.54	3.68	3.29	3.06	2.90
16	4.49	3.63	3.24	3.01	2.85
17	4.45	3.59	3.20	2.96	2.81
18	4.41	3.55	3.16	2.93	2.77
19	4.38	3.52	3.13	2.90	2.74
20	4.35	3.49	3.10	2.87	2.71
21	4.32	3.47	3.07	2.84	2.68
22	4.30	3.44	3.05	2.82	2.66
23	4.28	3.42	3.03	2.80	2.64
24	4.26	3.40	3.01	2.78	2.62
25	4.24	3.39	2.99	2.76	2.60
26	4.23	3.37	2.98	2.74	2.59
27	4.21	3.35	2.96	2.73	2.57
28	4.20	3.34	2.95	2.71	2.56
29	4.18	3.33	2.93	2.70	2.55
30	4.17	3.32	2.92	2.69	2.53
40	4.08	3.23	2.84	2.61	2.45
50	4.03	3.18	2.79	2.56	2.40
60	4.00	3.15	2.76	2.53	2.37
120	3.92	3.07	2.68	2.45	2.29
INF	3.84	3.00	2.60	2.37	2.21

DF	6	7	8	9	10	11	12	13	14	15
1	233.99	236.77	238.88	240.54	241.88	242.98	243.90	244.69	245.36	245.95
2	19.33	19.35	19.37	19.38	19.40	19.40	19.41	19.42	19.42	19.43
3	8.94	8.89	8.85	8.81	8.79	8.76	8.74	8.73	8.71	8.70
4	6.16	6.09	6.04	6.00	5.96	5.94	5.91	5.89	5.87	5.86
5	4.95	4.88	4.82	4.77	4.74	4.70	4.68	4.66	4.64	4.62
6	4.28	4.21	4.15	4.10	4.06	4.03	4.00	3.98	3.96	3.94
7	3.87	3.79	3.73	3.68	3.64	3.60	3.57	3.55	3.53	3.51
8	3.58	3.50	3.44	3.39	3.35	3.31	3.28	3.26	3.24	3.22
9	3.37	3.29	3.23	3.18	3.14	3.10	3.07	3.05	3.03	3.01
10	3.22	3.14	3.07	3.02	2.98	2.94	2.91	2.89	2.86	2.85
11	3.09	3.01	2.95	2.90	2.85	2.82	2.79	2.76	2.74	2.72
12	3.00	2.91	2.85	2.80	2.75	2.72	2.69	2.66	2.64	2.62
13	2.92	2.83	2.77	2.71	2.67	2.63	2.60	2.58	2.55	2.53
14	2.85	2.76	2.70	2.65	2.60	2.57	2.53	2.51	2.48	2.46
15	2.79	2.71	2.64	2.59	2.54	2.51	2.48	2.45	2.42	2.40
16	2.74	2.66	2.59	2.54	2.49	2.46	2.42	2.40	2.37	2.35
17	2.70	2.61	2.55	2.49	2.45	2.41	2.38	2.35	2.33	2.31
18	2.66	2.58	2.51	2.46	2.41	2.37	2.34	2.31	2.29	2.27
19	2.63	2.54	2.48	2.42	2.38	2.34	2.31	2.28	2.26	2.23
20	2.60	2.51	2.45	2.39	2.35	2.31	2.28	2.25	2.22	2.20
21	2.57	2.49	2.42	2.37	2.32	2.28	2.25	2.22	2.20	2.18
22	2.55	2.46	2.40	2.34	2.30	2.26	2.23	2.20	2.17	2.15
23	2.53	2.44	2.37	2.32	2.27	2.24	2.20	2.18	2.15	2.13
24	2.51	2.42	2.36	2.30	2.25	2.22	2.18	2.15	2.13	2.11
25	2.49	2.40	2.34	2.28	2.24	2.20	2.16	2.14	2.11	2.09
26	2.47	2.39	2.32	2.27	2.22	2.18	2.15	2.12	2.09	2.07
27	2.46	2.37	2.31	2.25	2.20	2.17	2.13	2.10	2.08	2.06
28	2.45	2.36	2.29	2.24	2.19	2.15	2.12	2.09	2.06	2.04
29	2.43	2.35	2.28	2.22	2.18	2.14	2.10	2.08	2.05	2.03
30	2.42	2.33	2.27	2.21	2.16	2.13	2.09	2.06	2.04	2.01
40	2.34	2.25	2.18	2.12	2.08	2.04	2.00	1.97	1.95	1.92
50	2.29	2.20	2.13	2.07	2.03	1.99	1.95	1.92	1.89	1.87
60	2.25	2.17	2.10	2.04	1.99	1.95	1.92	1.89	1.86	1.84
120	2.18	2.09	2.02	1.96	1.91	1.87	1.83	1.80	1.78	1.75
INF	2.10	2.01	1.94	1.88	1.83	1.79	1.75	1.72	1.69	1.67

TABLE 4   SUBSET (0.99)

$P[F \leq$ (a particular F value)$] = 0.99$ for this table with numerator DF in columns and denominator DF in rows.

DF	1	2	3	4	5
1	4052.19	4999.50	5403.35	5624.57	5763.63
2	98.50	99.00	99.17	99.25	99.30
3	34.12	30.82	29.46	28.71	28.24
4	21.20	18.00	16.69	15.98	15.52
5	16.26	13.27	12.06	11.39	10.97
6	13.75	10.92	9.78	9.15	8.75
7	12.25	9.55	8.45	7.85	7.46
8	11.26	8.65	7.59	7.01	6.63
9	10.56	8.02	6.99	6.42	6.06
10	10.04	7.56	6.55	5.99	5.64
11	9.65	7.21	6.22	5.67	5.32
12	9.33	6.93	5.95	5.41	5.06
13	9.07	6.70	5.74	5.21	4.86
14	8.86	6.51	5.56	5.04	4.69
15	8.68	6.36	5.42	4.89	4.56
16	8.53	6.23	5.29	4.77	4.44
17	8.40	6.11	5.19	4.67	4.34
18	8.29	6.01	5.09	4.58	4.25
19	8.19	5.93	5.01	4.50	4.17
20	8.10	5.85	4.94	4.43	4.10
21	8.02	5.78	4.87	4.37	4.04
22	7.95	5.72	4.82	4.31	3.99
23	7.88	5.66	4.76	4.26	3.94
24	7.82	5.61	4.72	4.22	3.90
25	7.77	5.57	4.68	4.18	3.85
26	7.72	5.53	4.64	4.14	3.82
27	7.68	5.49	4.60	4.11	3.78
28	7.64	5.45	4.57	4.07	3.75
29	7.60	5.42	4.54	4.04	3.73
30	7.56	5.39	4.51	4.02	3.70
40	7.31	5.18	4.31	3.83	3.51
50	7.17	5.06	4.20	3.72	3.41
60	7.08	4.98	4.13	3.65	3.34
120	6.85	4.79	3.95	3.48	3.17
INF	6.63	4.61	3.78	3.32	3.02

EXAMPLE   FINDING A PARTICULAR F VALUE

$P[F \leq$ (a particular F value)$] = 0.99$, let the area in the right tail of the F distribution be designated as

$$\alpha = 1 - 0.99 = 0.01$$

Then, $F_{\alpha = 0.01, \text{DFnum} = 4, \text{DFdenom} = 6} = +9.15$.

DF	6	7	8	9	10	11	12	13	14	15
1	5858.97	5928.33	5981.05	6022.45	6055.82	6083.29	6106.29	6125.84	6142.64	6157.26
2	99.33	99.36	99.37	99.39	99.40	99.41	99.42	99.42	99.43	99.43
3	27.91	27.67	27.49	27.35	27.23	27.13	27.05	26.98	26.92	26.87
4	15.21	14.98	14.80	14.66	14.55	14.45	14.37	14.31	14.25	14.20
5	10.67	10.46	10.29	10.16	10.05	9.96	9.89	9.82	9.77	9.72
6	8.47	8.26	8.10	7.98	7.87	7.79	7.72	7.66	7.60	7.56
7	7.19	6.99	6.84	6.72	6.62	6.54	6.47	6.41	6.36	6.31
8	6.37	6.18	6.03	5.91	5.81	5.73	5.67	5.61	5.56	5.52
9	5.80	5.61	5.47	5.35	5.26	5.18	5.11	5.05	5.01	4.96
10	5.39	5.20	5.06	4.94	4.85	4.77	4.71	4.65	4.60	4.56
11	5.07	4.89	4.74	4.63	4.54	4.46	4.40	4.34	4.29	4.25
12	4.82	4.64	4.50	4.39	4.30	4.22	4.16	4.10	4.05	4.01
13	4.62	4.44	4.30	4.19	4.10	4.02	3.96	3.91	3.86	3.82
14	4.46	4.28	4.14	4.03	3.94	3.86	3.80	3.75	3.70	3.66
15	4.32	4.14	4.00	3.89	3.80	3.73	3.67	3.61	3.56	3.52
16	4.20	4.03	3.89	3.78	3.69	3.62	3.55	3.50	3.45	3.41
17	4.10	3.93	3.79	3.68	3.59	3.52	3.46	3.40	3.35	3.31
18	4.01	3.84	3.71	3.60	3.51	3.43	3.37	3.32	3.27	3.23
19	3.94	3.77	3.63	3.52	3.43	3.36	3.30	3.24	3.19	3.15
20	3.87	3.70	3.56	3.46	3.37	3.29	3.23	3.18	3.13	3.09
21	3.81	3.64	3.51	3.40	3.31	3.24	3.17	3.12	3.07	3.03
22	3.76	3.59	3.45	3.35	3.26	3.18	3.12	3.07	3.02	2.98
23	3.71	3.54	3.41	3.30	3.21	3.14	3.07	3.02	2.97	2.93
24	3.67	3.50	3.36	3.26	3.17	3.09	3.03	2.98	2.93	2.89
25	3.63	3.46	3.32	3.22	3.13	3.06	2.99	2.94	2.89	2.85
26	3.59	3.42	3.29	3.18	3.09	3.02	2.96	2.90	2.86	2.81
27	3.56	3.39	3.26	3.15	3.06	2.99	2.93	2.87	2.82	2.78
28	3.53	3.36	3.23	3.12	3.03	2.96	2.90	2.84	2.79	2.75
29	3.50	3.33	3.20	3.09	3.00	2.93	2.87	2.81	2.77	2.73
30	3.47	3.30	3.17	3.07	2.98	2.91	2.84	2.79	2.74	2.70
40	3.29	3.12	2.99	2.89	2.80	2.73	2.66	2.61	2.56	2.52
50	3.19	3.02	2.89	2.78	2.70	2.63	2.56	2.51	2.46	2.42
60	3.12	2.95	2.82	2.72	2.63	2.56	2.50	2.44	2.39	2.35
120	2.96	2.79	2.66	2.56	2.47	2.40	2.34	2.28	2.23	2.19
INF	2.80	2.64	2.51	2.41	2.32	2.24	2.18	2.13	2.07	2.04

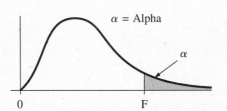

α = Alpha

α

0   F

REFERENCES

CHAPTER 1

[1]Joseph McCormack, "Why Are The Ducks Still on the Campus Pond?," *Collegian,* December 11, 1984, 4. [2]Peter Stoler, "Ali Fights a New Round," *Time,* October 1, 1984, 60. [3]Edward Tufte, *Data Analysis for Politics and Policy,* (Englewood Cliffs, NJ: Prentice-Hall, 1974), 1. [4]Roger Doyle, "On the Disease Trail," *Science 86,* (May, 1986), 16–17. [5]George Box, William Hunter, and Stuart Hunter, *Statistics for Experimenters* (New York: Wiley, 1978), 316. [6]Dave Anderson, "Ted Williams Surveys Darryl Strawberry," *The New York Times,* October 26, 1986, 1. [7]Tufte, *Data Analysis,* 5–30. [8]Nick Grabbe, "Gypsy Moths Buzzed Off This Year," *Amherst Bulletin,* July 7, 1982, 2. [9]Brian L. Joiner, "Lurking Variables: Some Examples," *The American Statistician* 35 (November 1981), 227–233. [10]G. E. P. Box, "Science and Statistics," *Journal of the American Statistical Association* 71, (1976), 791–799. [11]Tony Chamberlain, "Maine Lobster Outlook: Down," *The Boston Globe,* July 25, 1982, 16. [12]Judith Tanur, Frederick Mosteller, William Kruskal, Richard Link, Richard Pieters, Gerald Rising, Erich Lehmann, *Statistics: A Guide to the Unknown,* (San Francisco: Holden-Day, 1972), 368. [13]David Mehegan, "Does Detroit Have a Better Idea?," *The Boston Globe,* November 22, 1981, 10. [14]Richard Brautigan, "Tom Martin Creek," in Brian Murphy, *The Angler's Companion,* (New York: Paddington Press, 1978), 276. [15]S. S. Stevens, "On the Theory of Scales of Measurement," *Science,* 1946, 677–680. [16]Paul F. Velleman, and Leland Wilkinson, "Nominal, Ordinal, Interval and Ratio Typologies Are Misleading," *The American Statistician* 47 (February 1993), 65–72. [17]Frederick Mosteller, and John W. Tukey, *Data Analysis and Regression,* (Reading, MA: Addison-Wesley, 1977), [18]See Tanur, *Statistics,* Fairly and Mosteller, *Statistics and Public Policy* (Reading, MA: Addison-Wesley, 1977), and Tufte, *Data Analysis,* 5–30. [19]United Press International, "F Scale Measures Tornadoes," *The Sunday Republican,* April 6, 1986, B–5. [20]Adapted from Tanur, *Statistics,* 1–13. [21]Ibid., 14–22. [22]Ibid., 23–33. [23]Ibid., 34–39. [24]Ibid., 40–51. [25]Ibid., 52–65. [26]Ibid., 77–83. [27]Ben Brown, "Home Runs Are Out of Sight," *USA TODAY,* June 30, 1987, C-1. [28]Tanur, *Statistics,* 84–91. [29]Fairley and Mosteller, *Statistics,* 203.

CHAPTER 2

[1]Joseph Heller, *Catch-22* (New York, NY: Dell Books, 1961), 7. [2]David Quammen, "Deep Thoughts," *Outside,* November 1985, 23. [3]J. M. Juran, *Managerial Breakthrough* (New York: McGraw-Hill, 1964), and videotapes from the Juran Institute, Wilston, CN. [4]John, W. Tukey, *Exploratory Data Analysis* (Reading, MA: Addison-Wesley, 1977). [5]Harry Roberts, *Data Analysis for Managers* (San Francisco: The Scientific Press, 1991). [6]*Moody's Industrial Manual,* Moody's Investor's Service, 99 Church Street, New York, NY, 10007. [7]Ibid. [8]R. J. Beckman, and R. D. Cook, "Outlier . . . . s," *Technometrics* 25, (May 1983), 120. [9]V. Barnett, "The Study of Outliers: Purpose and Model," *Applied Statistics* 27 (1978), 242–250. [10]Tukey, *Exploratory Data Analysis.* [11]David Hoaglin, Frederick Mosteller, and John Tukey, *Understanding Robust and Exploratory Data Analysis* (New York: John Wiley and Sons, 1983). [12]*The Boston Globe,* 1982. [13]Bill James, and John Dewan, *The Great American Baseball Stat Book,* (New York: Ballantine Books, 1987), 13. [14]Ibid., 77. [15]*The World Almanac,* 1987, 773. (Accidental deaths by month and type. Their source: National Safety Council.) [16]*The World Almanac,* 1989, p. 880 and 1995, p. 879. [17]*The World Almanac,* 1995, 941. [18]Harry Roberts, *Data Analysis for Managers,* (San Francisco: The Scientific Press, 1988. [19]Caltech, USGS, and *Parade Magazine,* November 8, 1987, 20. [20]Transportation Research Board and the National Research Council in Washington D.C., Special report (#220), *A Look Ahead, Year 2020,* 1988. [21]American Iron and Steel Institute, 1989. [22]Barnett and Crandell, *Up from the Ashes,* The Brookings Institution, 1985. [23]*The World Almanac,* 1995, 109. (Consumer Price Index annual percentage change from 1976 through 1993. Their source: Bureau of Labor Statistics, U.S. Department of Labor.) [24]*USA TODAY,* June 14, 1989. [25]*Statistical Abstracts of the United States,* U.S. Department of Commerce Economics and Statistics Administration, Bureau of the Census, (1975–1985 figures). [26]*Moody's Industrial Manual,* (1982–1988 figures). [27]Department of Commerce, Bureau of Economic Analysis, 1994. (1973–1993 figures in current 1994 dollars.) [28]*The World Almanac,* 1995, 208. (Total U.S. sales, 1980–1993. Their source: Motor Vehicle Manufacturers Association.) [29]"Men Professionals at a Glance," *Golf Digest,* February 1972, 22. [30]Ronald D. Snee, "Techniques for the Analysis of Mixture Data," *Technometrics* 15, (August 1973), 519.

CHAPTER 3

[1]Feder, Barnaby J., "G. E.'s Costly Locomotive Gamble," *The New York Times,* January 25, 1987, 4. [2]Theodore, M. Smith, and Boris Iglewicz, "An Effective Classroom Technique for Comparison of Robust Estimators," *The American Statistician* 36, (August 1982), 163–168. [3]U.S. Department of Labor, Bureau of Labor Statistics, in

"Consumer Price Index Annual Percentage Change from 1976 Through 1993," *The World Almanac* (Mahwah, NJ: Funk and Wagnalls Corporation, 1995), 109. [4]Roger G. Ibbotson, and Rex A. Sinquefield, *Stocks, Bonds, Bills, and Inflation: The Past and the Future, 1926–1985* figures; R. L. Ibbotson, and C. L. Fall, "The United States Market Wealth Portfolio," *The Journal of Portfolio Management* (Fall 1979), 82–92; and Roger G. Ibbotson, and Rex, A. Sinquefield, "Stocks, Bonds, Bills, and Inflation: Year-by-Year Historical Returns," *The Journal of Business 49,* (January 1976), 40. [5]"Men Professionals at a Glance," *Golf Digest,* February, 1972, 22.

CHAPTER 4

[1]Clifford Konold, "Informal Conceptions of Probability," *Cognition and Instruction 6* (1989), 96. [2]Clifford Konold, "Understanding Students' Beliefs About Probability," *Radical Constructivism in Mathematics Education,* (Amsterdam, Netherlands: Kluwer Academic Publishers, 1991), 1. [3]Vin Sparano, "Is Anyone Listening," *Outdoor Life,* November 1994, 5. [4]Reuters, "Simpson Spends Birthday in Jail," *The Boston Globe,* July 10, 1994, 5. [5]Raymond Bonner, "A Bitter Harvest for Ukraine from American Seed Deal," *The New York Times,* June 19, 1994, 14.

CHAPTER 5

[1]Roger G. Ibbotson, and Rex A. Sinquefield, "Stocks, Bonds, Bills, and Inflation: Year-by-Year Historical Returns," *The Journal of Business 49,* (January 1976), 40. [2]*The Information Please Almanac,* 1989, 822. (Average annual room and board figures, doubled for inflation, from The Guidance Information System, Houghton Mifflin Company, Educational Software Division.) [3]*The World Almanac,* 1995, 109. (Consumer price index annual percentage change from 1976 through 1993 from U.S. Department of Labor, Bureau of Labor Statistics.)

CHAPTER 6

[1]"National Basketball, Eastern Conference Standings," *USA TODAY,* February 5, 1990, 4C. [2]*Moody's Industrial Manual,* New York: Moody's Investor's Service (1988), 1126. [3]U.S. Department of Commerce, Economics, and Statistics Administration, Bureau of the Census, *Statistical Abstract of the United States, 1987* (Washington, 1987), 416. [4]*Statistical Abstract, 707.* [5]Ibid., 494. [6]U.S. Department of Commerce, Economics and Statistics Administration, Bureau of Economic Analysis, *Business Statistics 1986,* (Washington, 1987), 75. [7]*Statistical Abstract, 441.* [8]*Statistical Abstract, 1994,* 493. [9]*The World Almanac,* (Mahwah, New Jersey: Funk and Wagnalls, 1995), 296. [10]Ibid., 377. [11]*World Almanac,* 1989, 808. [11]*World Almanac,* 1989, 807. [12]*World Almanac,* 1995, 957. [13]Ibid., 223. [14]Ibid., 109. [15]Ibid., 839. [16]Ibid., 937. [17]Ibid., 963. [18]Ibid., 971. [19]Ibid., 124. [20]Ibid., 150. [21]*Statistical Abstract 1994,* 729. [22]Ibid., 530. [23]Ibid., 477.

CHAPTER 7

[1]*The World Almanac,* (Mahwah, NJ: Funk and Wagnalls, 1995), 109. [2]U.S. Department of Labor, Bureau of Labor Statistics, *Statistical Abstract of the United States, 1985* (Washington, DC. 1985), 550. [3]G. E. P. Box, and D. R. Cox, "An Analysis of Transformations," *Journal of the Royal Statistical Society 26* (1964), 211. [4]*The Information Please Almanac,* (Boston, MA: Houghton Mifflin, 1989), 822. [5]*The World Almanac,* (Mahwah, NJ: Funk and Wagnalls, 1995), 150.

CHAPTER 8

[1]Charles Peterson, "U.S. Presidents . . . How Long Do They Live?" *Parade,* February 13, 1977, 7. [2]Paul F. Velleman and David C. Hoaglin, *ABC's of EDA* (Belmont, CA: Wadsworth 1981), 79. [3]"The Fortune 500," FORTUNE 500 and SERVICE 500, April, 1988 Time Inc., 1987 figures. All rights reserved. [4]Frank J. Anscombe, "Graphs in Statistical Analysis," *The American Statistician 27,* (February 1973), 17–21. [5]Guy Chatillon, "The Balloon Rules for a Rough Estimate of the Correlation Coefficient," *The American Statistician* (February, 1984) 38, 58–60. [6]Timothy Ferris, "Einstein's Wonderful Year," *Science84,* November 1984, 63. [7]Bill James, John De-

wan, *The Great American Baseball Stat Book,* (New York: Ballantine Books, 1987), 79–80. [8]Philip Ives, "1984 Was Warm and Wet," *Amherst Bulletin,* January 9, 1985, 13. [9]"Men Professionals at a Glance," *Golf Digest,* February 1972, 22. [10]Robert Adair, *The Physics of Baseball* (New York: Harper & Row, 1990), 66.

CHAPTER 9

[1]John W. Tukey, "We Need Both Exploratory and Confirmatory," *The American Statistician 34* (February 1980), 23–25. [2]Norman Cervany, et al., "A Framework for the Development of Measurement Instruments for Evaluating the Introductory Statistics Course," *The American Statistician 31* (1977), 17–23; and Norman L. Cervany, George B. Benson, and Raja K. Iyer, "The Planning Stage in Statistical Reasoning," *The American Statistician 34* (November 1980), 222–226. [3]Thomas Bishop, Bruce Peterson, and David Trayser, "Another Look at the Statistician's Role in Experimental Planning and Design," *The American Statistician 36* (November 1982), 387–389. [4]William G. Cochran, *Planning and Analysis of Observational Studies* (New York: John Wiley and Sons, 1983), 5. [5]Ibid., 9–10. [6]William G. Cochran, and Gertrude M. Cox, *Experimental Designs,* (New York: John Wiley and Sons, 1968), 7, 10, and 35. [7]Cochran, *Planning and Analysis,* 11. [8]Charles R. Hicks, *Fundamental Concepts in the Design of Experiments* (New York: Holt, Rinehart and Winston, 1973), 5. [9]Ibid., 7. [10]R. L. Anderson, and T. A. Bancroft, *Statistical Theory in Research,* (New York: McGraw-Hill Book Company, 1952), 17. [11]William B. Fairley, and Frederick Mosteller, *Statistics and Public Policy,* (Reading, MA: Addison-Wesley Publishing Company, 1977), 201, 245. [12]Cuthbert Daniel, "One-at-a-Time Plans," *Journal of the American Statistical Association 68* (June 1973), 353–360. [13]Cochran and Cox, *Experimental Designs,* 27. [14]William Q. Meeker, Jr., Gerald J. Hahn, and Paul I. Feder, "A Computer Program for Evaluating and Comparing Experimental Designs and Some Applications," *The American Statistician 29* (February

1975), 60–63. [15]Philip Ives, "1984 Was Warm and Wet," *Amherst Bulletin,* January 9, 1985, 13. [16]"Men Professionals at a Glance," *Golf Digest,* February 1972, 22. [17]Robert Adair, *The Physics of Baseball* (New York: Harper & Row, 1990), 66. [18]Michael Stanley, "Tritiated Binding Sites in Frontal Cortex of Suicides," *Science,* June 18, 1982, 1338.

CHAPTER 10

[1]"Why is the college environment particularly difficult for persons with eating disorders?" *Collegian,* September 30, 1987, 4. [2]Robert Ferber, Paul Sheatsley, Anthony Turner, and Joseph Waksberg, "What Is a Survey" (Washington, DC American Statistical Association, 1980). [3]"Why is the college environment particularly difficult for persons with eating disorders?" [4]C. T. Wild, and G. A. F. Seber, "Comparing Two Proportions from the Same Survey," *The American Statistician* 47 (August 1993), 178–181. [5]Vin Sparano, "Is Anyone Listening," *Outdoor Life* 23 (November 1994), 5. [6]Ronald Hedlund, "Cross-over Voting in a 1976 Open Presidential Primary," *Public Opinion Quarterly* 41 (1978), 498–514. [7]Otis Duncan, and James McRae, "Multiway Contingency Analysis with a Scaled Response of Factor," *Sociological Methodology* (San Francisco: Jossey-Bass, 1979). [8]Ronald Snee, "Graphical Display of Two-Way Contingency Tables," *The American Statistician* 28 (February 1974), 10. [9]Ibid., 11.

CHAPTER 11

[1]"Men Professionals at a Glance," *Golf Digest,* February, 1972, 22. [2]Robert Adair, *The Physics of Baseball* (New York: Harper & Row, 1990), 66. [3]Pat Ordovensky, "Minorities Gain but Gaps Remain", *USA TODAY,* September 12, 1989, 5D. [4]Frederick Mosteller, "Collegiate Football Scores, USA", *Journal of the American Statistical Association* 65 (March, 1970), 35–49. [5]Civil Aeronautics Board, 1984.

CHAPTER 12

[1]Jean Piaget, *The Construction of Reality in The Child,* (New York: Ballantine Books,

1954), 109–110. [2]N. R. Draper, and H. Smith, *Applied Regression Analysis,* (New York: John Wiley & Sons, 1981), 352. [3]George Box, William Hunter, and Stuart Hunter, *Statistics for Experimenters,* (New York: John Wiley & Sons, 1978), 316. [4]"The Fortune 500," *Fortune,* April 23, 1990, 360. [5]Arthur, F. Johnson, "Linear Combinations in Designing Experiments," *Technometrics* 13, (August 1971), 575–587. [6]K. A. Brownlee, *Statistical Theory and Methodology in Science and Engineering,* 2d ed. (New York: John Wiley & Sons, 1965), 454. [7]N. R. Draper, and H. Smith, *Applied Regression Analysis,* (New York: John Wiley & Sons, 1981), 361–373. [8]C. Daniel, and F. S. Wood, *Fitting Equations to Data,* (New York: John Wiley & Sons, 1971), 60–82. [9]D. F. Andrews, "A Robust Method for Multiple Linear Regression," *Technometrics* 16, (November 1974), 523–531. [10]Draper and Smith, *Applied Regression Analysis.* [11]Herman F. Sahrmann, Gregory F. Piepel, and John A. Cornell, "In Search of the Optimal Harvey Wallbanger Recipe," *The American Statistician* 41, (August 1987), 190–194. [12]Ronald D. Snee, "Techniques for the Analysis of Mixture Data," *Technometrics* 15 (August 1973), 519. [13]Ibid., 525. [14]UPI, *The Boston Globe,* September 9, 1979, 13. [15]D. E. Marquardt, and R. D. Snee, "Ridge Regression," *Proceedings: Kentucky Conference on Regression,* Lexington, Kentucky, 1973, 70. [16]Frank Zanner, "A Study of Weld Puddle Configuration," Ph.D. Dissertation, Rensselaer Polytechnic Institute, 1967, 112. [17]"Men Professionals at a Glance," *Golf Digest,* February 1972, 22. [18]Karen Curran, "Subdivision Decisions," *The Boston Globe,* Sunday, July 10, 1994, A1. [19]Tina Cassidy, "Apartments: The Giveaways Are Gone," *The Boston Globe,* Sunday, August 7, 1994, A63.

CHAPTER 14

[1]Harrison M. Wadsworth, Kenneth S. Stephens, and Blanton, A. Godfrey, *Modern Methods for Quality Control and Improvement,* (New York: John Wiley & Sons, 1986), 115–133. [2]Ibid. 142–162.

CHAPTER 15

[1]Kevin Dupont, "On a Roll," *The Boston Globe,* December 30, 1994, 86. [2]Jim McCabe, "They're Gearing Up to Make Their Playoff Run," *The Boston Globe,* December 30, 1994, 88. [3]*Handbook of International Trade and Development Statistics,* 1980, U.N. Conference on Trade and Development, Table 1.5, 14. [4]Michael James Royer, Professor of Psychology, University of Massachusetts, Amherst, MA.

CHAPTER 16

[1]Robert B. Miller, and Dean W. Wichern, *Intermediate Business Statistics: Analysis of Variance, Regression and Time Series* (New York: Holt, Rinehart and Winston, 1977), 330. [2]Ibid., 354.

CHAPTER 17

[1]U.S. Department of Commerce, Economics, and Statistics Administration, Bureau of the Census, *Statistical Abstract of the United States, 1987,* 707. [2]Ibid., 493. [3]Jim Carmichel, "Rimfire Revolution, Part II," *Outdoor Life,* February 1995, 23–27. [4]Ibid. [5]*Moody's Industrial Manual,* Moody's Investor's Service, 99 Church Street, New York, NY, 1988, 1126. [6]*Statistical Abstract of the United States,* 416. [7]Ibid., 494. [8]U.S. Department of Commerce, Economics and Statistics Administration, Bureau of Economic Analysis, *Business Statistics 1986,* 75.

CHAPTER 18

[1]Michael James Royer, Professor of Psychology, University of Massachusetts, Amherst, MA.

CHAPTER 19

[1]Nick Cafardo, "Menino Envisions Sox in Megaplex," *The Boston Globe,* March 2, 1994, 1.

INDEX